EXPLORING LITERATURE

Writing and Arguing About Fiction, Poetry, Drama, and the Essay

THIRD EDITION

FRANK MADDEN
SUNY Westchester Community College

PEARSON
Longman

New York   San Francisco   Boston
London   Toronto   Sydney   Tokyo   Singapore   Madrid
Mexico City   Munich   Paris   Cape Town   Hong Kong   Montreal

Managing Editor: Erika Berg
Director of Development: Mary Ellen Curley
Development Editor: Anne Brunell Ehrenworth
Executive Marketing Manager: Ann Stypuloski
Senior Supplements Editor: Donna Campion
Media Supplements Editor: Jenna Egan
Production Manager: Eric Jorgensen
Project Coordination, Text Design, Art, and Electronic Page Makeup: Elm Street
    Publishing Services, Inc.
Cover Designer/Manager: John Callahan
Cover Illustration: Artwork by David Hockney "Nichols Canyon" 1980, Acrylic on
    Canvas, 18" x 60"
Photo Researcher: Jody Potter
Senior Manufacturing Buyer: Alfred C. Dorsey
Printer and Binder: Quebecor World Taunton
Cover Printer: Phoenix Color Corporation

For permission to use copyrighted material, grateful acknowledgment is made to the
copyright holders on pp. 1357–1363, which are hereby made part of this copyright page.

Library of Congress Cataloging-in-Publication Data

Madden, Frank, 1946-
  Exploring literature : writing and arguing about fiction, poetry, drama and the essay /
Frank Madden.—3rd ed.
    p. cm.
  ISBN 0-321-36630-1
  1. Reader-response criticism. 2. Books and reading. 3. Literature—History and criticism—
Theory, etc. I. Title.
PN98.R38M27 2007
808—dc22
                                                                            2006016474

Copyright © 2007 by Pearson Education, Inc.

Please visit us at www.ablongman.com

ISBN 0-321-36630-1

1 2 3 4 5 6 7 8 9—QWT—09 08 07 06

In Memory of Jim Slevin (1945-2006)

BRIEF CONTENTS

DETAILED CONTENTS

CHAPTER 2
Communication: Writing a Response Essay   21

PART II   ANALYSIS, ARGUMENTATION, AND RESEARCH   53

CHAPTER 3
Exploration and Analysis: Genre and the Elements of Literature   55

102 √

102 √

Module I

CHAPTER 4
Argumentation: Writing a Critical Essay   148

CHAPTER 5
Research: Writing with Secondary Sources   174

CASE STUDY IN RESEARCH

PART III   A THEMATIC ANTHOLOGY   201

Family and Friends   202

CASE STUDY IN BIOGRAPHICAL CONTEXT
Lorraine Hansberry and A Raisin in the Sun *343*

Innocence and Experience 435

CASE STUDY IN HISTORICAL CONTEXT

Culture and Identity   939

Faith and Doubt   1152

CASE STUDY IN CONTEXTUAL CRITICISM

ALTERNATE CONTENTS BY GENRE

POETRY

DRAMA

ESSAYS

PAINTINGS

PREFACE TO
INSTRUCTORS

We can ask of every assignment or method or text, no matter what its short-term effectiveness: Does it get in the way of the live sense of literature? Does it make literature something to be regurgitated, analyzed, categorized, or is it a means toward making literature a more personally meaningful and self-disciplined activity?
— Louise Rosenblatt, *Literature as Exploration*

This third edition of *Exploring Literature* remains true to the belief that literature can have an important impact on students' lives, and that this impact will only be felt when students experience the "live sense of literature"—the joy, the sorrow, the comfort, and the wisdom that literature offers.

Many students have yet to discover why literature is important. By encouraging them to see their reading and writing in the light of their own experiences, *Exploring Literature* gives students a stake in the process—a reason to care about literature— and authorizes the "meaning-making" role they play when they write about literature. Students learn that the process of crafting a persuasive argument about a work of literature requires close reading and reflection, and that the quality of their writing will be measured by the strength of the evidence they bring to support it.

Exploring Literature is designed for instructors who believe that a successful reading and writing experience requires students' engagement as well as analysis not only as motivation to complete the requirements of a course but also as a prelude to a lifelong relationship with literature.

KEY FEATURES

Instructors have told us that one of the most important skills students should master is the ability to write an argumentative essay. The previous edition of *Exploring Literature* laid the groundwork for this often daunting task, and the new third edition further builds upon that foundation, providing even more coverage of argument in every facet of the text—from the apparatus in each chapter and in every theme, to the new subtitle—proof to our loyal adopters that we take their concerns seriously.

By exploring literature as an "experience" within a world of personal responses and contextual influences, the following features encourage students to invest their emotions, to build on their knowledge and experience, and to think more critically:

- *Making Connections.* The questions and exercises in Part I, "Making Connections," are designed to sensitize students to the impact of literature in their lives. Acknowledging, reviewing, and thinking critically about the personal responses students have while reading can provide them with valuable insight into literature and themselves. These early chapters present the process of personal response as a starting point in a recursive sequence leading from engagement and reflection to formal critical tasks and literary interpretation.

xxvii

- *Argumentation.* Whether reviewing their own judgments or citing evidence to support their views, students are encouraged to think critically about their responses throughout this book. Of special note is Chapter 4, "Argumentation: Writing a Critical Essay," which focuses directly on the process of critical thinking and argumentation. Students are guided through the process of choosing a topic for a critical essay and planning and supporting an argument. Issues of purpose, audience, and evidence are central to this discussion of argumentation, which culminates in writing a critical essay. The final section of this chapter exemplifies the process of critical thinking and argumentation by following a student's progress from initial journal entry to a final draft of a critical essay.

- *The Literary Selections.* The literature in this book, a broad selection of both classic and contemporary pieces, has been chosen for its quality, diversity, and appeal to students. Included in this edition are 45 pieces of fiction, 144 poems, 35 essays, and 11 plays. A complete list of literary selections can be found on pages xxi–xxvi.

- *Writing About Literature.* From informal journals to formal critical and research essays, *Exploring Literature* emphasizes writing as the means to learn about literature. Students who write about literature—and examine their own practices in reading and writing—become more self-aware, more independent, stronger readers and writers.

- *Samples of Student Writing.* There are nine student essays and many other samples of students' writing throughout the text. These models are included to assist students in formulating their ideas into coherent and cohesive writing.

- *The Case Studies.* A case study follows the literary selections in each thematic unit. These self-contained research projects offer a rich and provocative resource for students. The case study for Family and Friends, "**Lorraine Hansberry and *A Raisin in the Sun*,**" examines the life and work of Lorraine Hansberry—in her words and the words of others—and draws connections to her play, *A Raisin in the Sun.* The case study for Women and Men, "**Woman in Culture and History,**" highlights speeches and written artifacts from the eighteenth and nineteenth centuries and offers a glimpse into the cultural context of that period. Accompanying the selections from Innocence and Experience, "**Hamlet and Performance,**" is a case study that examines four different interpretations of a soliloquy from *Hamlet* and five new critical interpretations of *Hamlet* both on television and in the movies. Following this is a mini case study, "**Case Study in Aesthetic Context: Poetry and Painting,**" that includes pairings of eight famous paintings and nine poems written about them, as well as one student's response to a particular pairing and the process involved in formulating her critical essay. The case study for Culture and Identity, "**Writers of the Harlem Renaissance,**" highlights the literature of an especially creative era in American literature. Finally, a new case study for Faith and Doubt, "**The Poetry of Emily Dickinson,**" examines the life and work of this famous poet. All case studies conclude with a student essay relevant to the case study.

- *Voice.* The narrative "voice" of *Exploring Literature* is informal and conversational. This book is intended to be read by students—to be accessible, friendly, and informative.

FLEXIBLE ORGANIZATION

Exploring Literature can be used in many different ways. Its explanations, prompts, and literature are resources to be chosen by instructors and students as needed, in or out of sequence. Although the reading and writing activities in this book are organized in a sequence of increasing complexity, the recursive nature of both writing and responding to literature is emphasized throughout.

For instructors who want to explore personal response, have their students keep journals, or write response essays about literature, **Part I, "Making Connections,"** provides a rich source of material. Students are encouraged to think about the ways that their own backgrounds and personalities, their understanding of others, their knowledge of texts and contexts—their "meaning-making" processes—influence their responses to literature. Questions that accompany the literature help students clarify their responses and develop them into text-supportable hypotheses and critical essays. **Chapter 1, "Participation: Personal Response and Critical Thinking,"** helps students develop connections to literature through their own backgrounds and experiences. **Chapter 2, "Communication: Writing a Response Essay,"** introduces students to aspects of literary craft through its discussions of voice, description, and comparison, fostering the sensitivity to language necessary for a complete experience with literature. The chapter concludes with a discussion of the writing process, samples of drafts, and a final response essay.

Instructors who favor a more text-based approach may move directly to **Part II, "Analysis, Argumentation, and Research," Chapter 3, "Exploration and Analysis: Genre and the Elements of Literature,"** which emphasizes the importance of close reading and analysis. General introductions to fiction, poetry, drama, and the essay are followed by a comprehensive explanation of the elements that make each a distinct form. Carefully chosen literary selections illustrate and support these explanations. Wherever possible, explanations of the elements are illustrated with reference to students' experiences and are accompanied by specific examples from literature in the text.

Chapter 4, "Argumentation: Writing a Critical Essay," guides students through the process of critical thinking, reading, and writing. Based on the elements discussed in Chapter 3, students are provided with explanations, questions, prompts, and checklists that help them write a critical essay. A comprehensive discussion of argumentation helps students see the difference between response and critical essays and suggests specific questions to ask when constructing an effective argument. The chapter concludes with an examination of a student's process and product from journal entry to final draft of a critical essay.

Chapter 5, "Research: Writing with Secondary Sources," completes Part II with a discussion of writing using secondary sources. Explanations and exercises help students integrate secondary sources into their writing, explore popular areas of research, organize their research, gather information from the library (both print and online) and Internet, and avoid plagiarism. The chapter concludes with a case study that provides a glimpse of how literature, culture, and their own experiences may provide a rich context for research. A student writer describes his identification with the pull of family in James Joyce's "Eveline" and investigates conditions in

Ireland that prompted the vast migration of the Irish. A narrative of the student's process precedes a final essay.

Part III, "A Thematic Anthology," organizes the four genres of literature under five compelling themes: **"Family and Friends," "Innocence and Experience," "Women and Men," "Culture and Identity,"** and **"Faith and Doubt."** For those who prefer a genre approach, an alternative table of contents organizes the literature under the categories of fiction, poetry, drama, and essays. Each category includes the location of a comprehensive introduction to each of the genres. The literature in this book has been chosen for its quality, diversity, and appeal to students. These stories, poems, plays, and essays represent a broad selection of both classic and contemporary literature.

Each theme opens with a photograph and a series of short provocative quotations, a "Dialogue Across History," that provide a historical context for the literature that follows. An introductory statement about the theme and a brief statement about the literature included under that theme follow. In several thematic units, one work of literature is highlighted and is followed by two sample student essays written from different perspectives about the selected work. These essays illustrate diversity of opinion, exemplify ways in which the literature might be "read," and demonstrate how students' own experiences, behaviors, values, and opinions are tools for deepening their understanding and appreciation of literature. A case study follows the literature in each unit. These case studies are a resource for interpretation and biography; interpretation in cultural and historical context; interpretation and performance; interpretation—poetry and painting; culture, and research; and interpretation—poetry.

Appendix A, "Critical Approaches to Literature," is a succinct discussion of major critical theories for those who want to delve further into the study of interpreting literature. **Appendix B, "Writing About Film,"** provides guidelines to help students make the adjustment from writing about literary works to writing about films, another outlet in the development of critical thinking skills. **Appendix C, "Documentation,"** is a guide to the correct layout and citation for a research essay. The **Glossary of Literary Terms** provides a useful reference tool.

WHAT'S NEW IN THE THIRD EDITION?

To aid in the exploration and experience of literature, the following additions and enhancements have been made in this edition:

- **New selections in all genres** include 6 short stories, 22 poems, 2 plays, and 14 new essays, including works by bell hooks, Edgar Lee Masters, Edward Conlon, David Sedaris, Bessie Head, Essex Hemphill, Pablo Neruda, Thomas King, Dan Brown, John Millington Synge, and David Mamet.
- **Infusion of argument and critical thinking** throughout the text grounds students in forming strong, coherent arguments. *Exploring Literature* guides students through the process of writing a critical essay from the very beginning of the text, teaching the importance of establishing a connection with literature. Each chapter in Parts I and II builds on this idea and provides step-by-step guidance on thinking critically and constructing sound arguments. Part III provides numerous opportunities for students to create compelling and convincing arguments.

- **Chapter 4, "Argumentation: Writing a Critical Essay"** contains extensive guidelines for writing analytical, comparative, thematic, philosophical/ethical, and contextual essays. In addition, a detailed checklist ensures that students' essays are sound.
- **Making Connections** questions follow each selection to engage and challenge students, prompting them to develop their responses into critical essays.
- **Making an Argument** questions follow each selection and ask students to apply critical thinking skills and analyze themes within selections or across multiple works.
- **Connecting Through Comparison** sub-theme "clusters" provide related groupings of literature on which students can view similarities and differences and draw upon these works to form critical essays.
- **End-of-Theme** questions ask students to build on their critical thinking skills to formulate essays that combine literature across the five thematic units in the text.
- **Two new themes, Culture & Identity** and **Innocence & Experience** combine classic works from Alice Walker, e. e. cummings, and William Shakespeare with contemporary selections from Jamaica Kincaid, Martin Espada, and David Sedaris.
- **New and revised Case Studies** provide students with self-contained research units on interesting, timely subjects:
- **A new Case Study on Emily Dickinson** includes 16 poems, as well as letters and essays by the author and her peers, critical essays, and poetry by Linda Pastan and Billy Collins. This unique collection of sources provides students with a glimpse into the mind of a well known, yet very private poet, and further insight into her work through the words of her critics and fellow poets.
- **An expanded Case Study on Shakespeare's *Hamlet*** now contains a new section entitled "Hamlet On Screen," with additional critical commentary by Ernest Jones, Bernice Kliman, Claire Bloom, Stanley Kauffmann, and Russell Jackson. This Case Study, combined with Appendix B, "Writing About Film," provides a comprehensive, contained research model for students to connect what they read with what they view on screen and write convincing research papers.
- **A revised Case Study on Poetry and Painting** has been moved to the middle of the text for ease of use and contains a new pairing: Henri Matisse's "Dance" and Natalie Safir's "Matisse's Dancer."
- **Updated, comprehensive research and documentation information** is contained in **Chapter 5, "Research: Writing with Secondary Sources,"** providing students with strategies for using database and online resources. In addition, **Appendix C, "Documentation,"** includes complete coverage on citing database and online sources.

RESOURCES FOR STUDENTS AND INSTRUCTORS

The following resources are complimentary to adopters or can be value-packed at no additional cost or at a significant discount with Madden's *Exploring Literature,* Third Edition. Please see your local Longman representative for details.

Instructor's Manual (ISBN: 0-321-42468-9) An instructor's manual is available to adopters of this text. This manual includes topics, ideas, and prompts for generating student essays, frequent critical commentary about the works, useful teaching suggestions, sample syllabi, and Internet addresses for background sources and criticism for the literature and the case studies.

MyLiteratureLab (http://www.myliteraturelab.com) This password-protected Web site offers students a rich source of guidance in the key areas of reading, interpreting, writing, and research. Of special note are the distinctive Longman Lectures. These multimedia lectures, given by many of Longman's prestigious authors, including five lectures by Frank Madden, provide students with insights and support about reading and interpreting the most popular works of literature.

Included with MyLiteratureLab is *Research Navigator*™, a research tutorial tool that offers students tips on the writing process, online research, and finding and citing valid sources. Through Research Navigator™ students gain access to thousands of academic journals and periodicals, the NY Times Search by Subject Archive, Link Library, Library Guides, and more.

The Longman Test Bank for Literature (0-321-14312-4, CD: 0-321-14314-0) This test bank features various objective questions on the major works of fiction, short fiction, poetry, and drama. A versatile and handy resource, this easy-to-use test bank can be used for all quizzing and testing needs. Available in a print format or on CD. With the CD-ROM, instructors simply choose questions from the electronic test bank and then print out the complete test for distribution.

Glossary of Literary and Critical Terms (ISBN: 0-321-12691-2) The easy-to-use glossary includes definitions and examples for over 100 literary and critical terms that students commonly encounter in their readings or hear in class. Also included are terms and explanations related to literary history, criticism, and theory.

Literature Timeline (ISBN: 0-321-14315-9) This visually appealing timeline chronicles the major literary works written throughout history. Students gain historical and contextual insights into the impact historical events have had on writers and their works, and vice versa.

Responding to Literature: A Writer's Journal (ISBN: 0-321-09542-1) This journal provides students with their own personal space for writing. Helpful writing prompts for responding to fiction, poetry, and drama are included.

Merriam Webster's Reader's Handbook: Your Complete Guide to Literary Terms (0-321-10541-9) Includes nearly 2,000 entries including Greek and Latin terminology; descriptions for every major genre, style, and era of writing; and assured authority from the combined resources of Merriam-Webster and Encyclopedia Britannica.

Analyzing Literature, Second Edition (ISBN: 0-321-09338-0) The critical reading strategies, writing advice, and sample essays contained in this supplement help students interpret and write about literary works in a variety of genres. Also featured are suggestions for collaborative activities and online research as well as numerous exercises and writing assignments.

Penguin Discount Program Longman is proud to offer a large selection of Penguin paperbacks at a significant discount when packaged with any Longman title. Penguin titles offer additional opportunities to explore contemporary and classical fiction and drama. The complete list of titles and discounted prices are available at http://www.ablongman.com/penguin.

Video Program An impressive selection of videotapes is available to enrich students' experience of literature. Contact your sales representative to learn how to qualify.

Teaching Literature Online, Second Edition (ISBN: 0-321-10618-0) *Teaching Literature Online* provides instructors with strategies for incorporating electronic media into any literature classroom. Offering a range of information and examples, this manual provides ideas and activities for enhancing literature courses with the help of technology.

Acknowledgments

I am indebted to many people over the years who have had a direct and indirect influence on my teaching philosophy—and on the writing of this book. Most notable among these teacher-scholars was Louise Rosenblatt, my teacher at NYU thirty years ago. In addition, John Clifford, Alan Purves, Peter Elbow, Wayne Booth, Robert Scholes, Ann Berthoff, Toby Fulwiler, Robert Berlin, Carl Schmidt, Cindy Onore, John Mayher, Dawn Rodrigues, Jim Slevin Judith Stanford, Kathi Blake Yancey, and others have influenced and inspired my work. I am grateful to my generous colleagues at WCC: Bill Costanzo, who read the original manuscript with great care and contributed the Appendix, "Writing About Film;" Alan Devenish, Liz Gaffney, Linda Sledge, Mary Ellen LeClair, and Tahira Naqvi who contributed their own work; Joanne Falinski, Richard Courage, Mira Sakrajda, Maryanne Vent, Greta Cohan, Walter Kroczak, Jillian Quinn, Carolyn Cooper, Joe Zimbalatti, Richard Rodriguez and others who tried out the materials, contributed ideas, and/or submitted student samples. I am grateful to my students who have taught me so much about teaching and this book, especially those students who contributed their work to this volume: Janice Butwell, Dierdre Curran, Suzanne McCloskey, Michelle McAuliffe, Julie Fitzmaurice, Sara Roell, Marie Tymon, Barbara Pfister, Trisa Hayes, Alejandro Ramos, Debora VanCoughnett, Charles Chiang, William Winters, Kevin Chamberlain, and others. I am indebted to President Joseph Hankin for fostering an atmosphere at WCC that made this work possible. And I am especially grateful to my brother John, who early in my life gave me a reason to care about literature, and to my wife, Sharon, my most discerning reader and loving supporter.

For their thoughtful and insightful comments to many drafts of manuscript, I am very grateful to the reviewers of the first and second editions, and to the following reviewers of the third edition: Shanan Ballam, *Utah State University;* Kathryn B. Benzel, *University of Nebraska—Kearney;* Mary Anne Bernal, *Alamo Community College District;* Michael S. Bodek, *Bergen Community College;* Jacqueline Bradley, *Southern Methodist University;* Lauren Brosnihan, *University of Florida;* Diane Burton, *The University of Tulsa;* Thad Cockrill, *Southwest Tennessee Community College—Memphis;* Michael Franco, *Oklahoma City Community College;* Dawn A. Gallo-Pasquale, *Montclair State University;* Simone Gers, *Pima Community College;* Katherine Gordon, *St. Louis Community College at Florissant Valley;* Susan Hudson Grimland, *Collin County Community College;* Debra G. Harroun, *Baker College—Clinton Township;* Jessica Hausmann, *Drew University;* Elizabeth Howells, *Armstrong Atlantic State University;* Kaushalya G. Jagasia, *Illinois Valley Community College;*

Alan G. Johnson, *Idaho State University;* Zhanshu Liu, *Nassau Community College;* Kelley L. Logan, *Southwestern Oklahoma State University;* Donna Mayes, *Blue Ridge Community College;* Neal E. Migan, *Baker College—Flint Campus;* Kimme Nuckles, *Baker Collge—Auburn Hills;* David B. Raymond, *Northern Maine Community College;* David Rollinson, *College of Marin;* Jane E. Rosencrans, *J. Sargeant Reynolds Community College;* Kathy Sanchez, *Tomball College;* Paige Smitten, *Utah State University;* Pamela Stinson, *Northern Oklahoma Community College;* Regina L. St. John, *Ball State University;* Angell Stone, *Marshall University;* Joe Wilferth, *University of Tennessee at Chattanooga.* And of course, Lauren Puccio.

At Longman, I am especially grateful to Anne Brunell Ehrenworth, whose skill, patience, and advice were much appreciated through the process, and to Erika Berg and Joe Terry, whose vision and support made this third edition possible. I also wish to thank Ann Stypuloski for getting the word out about this book so effectively, and Eric Jorgensen and Brandi Nelson for their dedication, fine work, and patience while turning a manuscript into a book.

Frank Madden
SUNY Westchester Community College

◆ ABOUT THE AUTHOR ◆

Frank Madden is SUNY Distinguished Professor and Chair of the English Department at SUNY Westchester Community College where he also holds the Carol Russett Endowed Chair for English. He has a Ph.D. from NYU, has taught in graduate programs at CCNY, Iona College, and the New School for Social Research, and in 1998 was Chair of the NCTE College Section Institute on the Teaching of Literature. He is a recipient of the SUNY Chancellor's Award for Excellence in Teaching, the SUNY Chancellor's Award for Excellence in Scholarship, the Foundation for Westchester  Community College Award for Excellence in Scholarship, and the Phi Delta Kappan Educator of the Year Award from Iona College. He was awarded the 2003 Nell Ann Pickett Service Award, granted by the NCTE to an outstanding teacher whose vision and voice have had a major impact on two-year college professionalism and whose teaching exemplifies such outstanding personal qualities as creativity, sensitivity, and leadership. He has been Chair of the College Section of the NCTE; Chair of TYCA; and served on the Executive Committees of the NCTE, the CCCC, the MLA Association of Departments of English, the SUNY Council on Writing, as Chair of the MLA ad hoc Committee on Teaching, and as NCTE delegate to the American Council of Learned Societies. His articles, chapters, and commentary about the teaching of literature have appeared in a variety of books and journals, including *College English, PMLA, College Literature, English Journal, Computers and Composition, Computers and the Humanities,* and the *ADE Bulletin.*

PART I

MAKING
CONNECTIONS

Chapter 1

Participation
Personal Response and Critical Thinking

We begin our exploration of literature with you, the reader. Your engagement creates the literary experience. By itself, the literature in this book, as brilliantly crafted or as famous or critically acclaimed as it may be, is just words on a page. It is your reading of these words through the lenses of your own experiences and beliefs that brings them to life and gives them meaning, a meaning ultimately as unique as you are.

Literature reveals a possible world to us. Our engagement and involvement are the keys to enter this world and to imagine its possibilities. Our backgrounds and personalities, our understanding of others, our prior experience with literature, our knowledge of the world—our sources for making meaning—are important factors in this process. And unlike our busy lives, which sometimes race forward with little time for reflection, literature awaits our examination. We can participate in it as we experience it, and analyze it as we step back and observe it.

Investing your emotions and connecting your knowledge and experience with what you read is an important first step toward our ultimate goal—an appreciation of literature and the ability to think and to write critically about it. In subsequent chapters, we will build on these connections and analyze the craft with which literature is created. That analysis will require rereading and reflection, writing and revising, gathering evidence, and constructing a solid argument to support your responses.

THE PERSONAL DIMENSION OF READING LITERATURE

Most literature does not intend to convey a moral or lesson. At its best, it reveals as life reveals. But like life, our *reading* of literature evokes our emotion and judgment. Narrators and literary characters express their beliefs in what they say or do, and as we read, we respond to their words and actions through our own beliefs—comparing their choices with our own, and approving or disapproving as they meet or fail to meet our expectations. While most good literature does not teach or preach, it does explore and reveal what it means to be human and provides us with a substantial opportunity for learning and self-understanding.

Later on in this chapter, and throughout the book, you are asked to consider how your own experiences and beliefs influence your responses to literature. Acknowledging, reviewing, and thinking critically about the judgments you make as you read may provide you with valuable insights into literature and yourself.

PERSONAL RESPONSE AND CRITICAL THINKING

Thinking critically about literature is an outgrowth of our personal responses. It is natural for us to want to comprehend what moves us or has meaning to us. As children, we may have tried to make sense of what we read by making connections with our experiences or other stories we read. We knew which books we liked, and even if we didn't analyze our reading systematically, we may have wondered what made those stories appealing to us.

When we think critically about literature, we build on our personal responses—recording them, reviewing them, discussing them, and supporting them. Being engaged is a crucial initial component of a complete literary experience. But once we experience this engagement and believe that literature has something to offer us, it follows that we want to know more about it, to see how it triggers our responses and judgments, to understand the skill with which it was created, and to articulate what it means to us.

Critical thinking does not mean searching for one right answer. There may be as many answers as there are readers. *Your best answers are those that analyze and articulate your responses in light of supporting evidence.* This is critical thinking, a process that can make your opinions about literature well-informed ones.

WRITING TO LEARN

Writing is an excellent way to learn about literature. Whether you are jotting down notes, writing in a journal, or constructing a formal essay, you're learning. You're learning when you struggle to choose the right words to describe your impressions, and when you revise those words because they are not quite what you mean. And you are learning when you "get it just right" and see your words match what you want to say. In short, writing your responses down helps you learn and articulate what you think and feel more clearly—an essential step in the critical thinking process.

Your First Response

When you read a work of literature for the first time, relax and give yourself enough time to experience it. Don't try too hard to figure it out. Get impressions. Notice words and phrases. Read them out loud. Listen to the rhythms. Follow the personal associations that come up. Let yourself feel the emotions connected to them. Don't be discouraged if you have difficulty understanding every word or line your first time through. Have a dictionary handy and look up unfamiliar words. Let your unanswered questions stick with you. Write them down if you think you won't remember them later. Capture your response while it's fresh. If you wait until later, you may forget. In fact, you may come away from your reading with more questions than answers. So a second or third reading with these questions in mind may clarify much that was confusing the first time through.

☑ CHECKLIST: YOUR FIRST RESPONSE

❏ Write down your first impressions and questions that come to mind during and after your reading.

❏ What confuses you? What do you want to know more about? How can you find out?

❏ What words or phrases affect you most?

❏ Do any of the characters remind you of yourself or people you know? Do any of the events remind you of ones in your own life?

❏ Do these associations help or interfere with your response? If so, how?

❏ Is there anything that you don't like about the work? If so, what and why?

❏ What do you find most interesting or compelling about the work? Do any of the characters especially appeal to you or bother you? Do you find any of the events especially pleasing or disturbing? Explain.

Keeping a Journal or Reading Log

One of the best tools for exploring and thinking about your experiences in writing is a journal or reading log. Journals and reading logs can help you view and review your ideas. Writing and reading your words on paper may help you articulate, clarify, and expand your ideas. Use your journal to identify and express your reactions, what moves or bothers you, or what seems intriguing or confusing. Write in your most natural voice and don't worry about sounding wise. Take chances and try out ideas.

Your responses, along with subsequent reading and the comments of classmates, can help you develop ideas as you write the essays required by your instructor. If you are conscientious about keeping your log, your entries will evolve naturally into a statement of the meaning you've constructed from the work. In the long run, the most important ingredient in your essays will not be the position you take, but the support you derive from the literature and your experience with it. Recording these observations now may provide you with some of this support later.

What you write in your journal or log is your choice. You may or may not like what you read. You may find it engaging or filled with meaning. You may find it confusing or boring. Whatever your response, you'll benefit most from keeping a journal or log if your entries honestly reflect your experience.

An electronic variation of the journal or response log is a designated space in an online **discussion forum** like **WebCT** or **Blackboard.** Like a journal response, each posting accounts for your first impressions during and after your reading. Both your instructor and other members of your class may read and respond to your postings and use them to initiate class discussion—online or in the classroom.

There is no one correct way of keeping a journal or log. The brief excerpts from student journals that follow are all different, but each is a start and might be built upon to develop a more formal essay. ("Araby" appears on p. 463 and "There's a Certain Slant of Light" on p. 1308.) Even if you are not familiar with these pieces, these samples reflect the kinds of issues that might be addressed in response to any work of literature.

From confusion:

I found the story of "Araby" to be a little confusing. I couldn't really fathom what the actual point of the story was. There is a boy whose name is not mentioned, and he apparently has some sort of infatuation with a nun. He spies on her, peering through a tiny crack in his shades. He ends up talking to her and telling her that if he goes to Araby, the bazaar, he will buy her a present because she cannot go.

The last line of the story intrigued me. "Gazing up into the darkness I saw myself as a creature driven and derided by vanity; and my eyes burned with anguish and anger." I guess he said this because he did not buy her anything at Araby. I don't exactly know why.

To an appreciation of the author's artistry:

The beginning of "Araby" was written with a lot of descriptive words. As soon as I began to read sentence by sentence, the words formed pictures in my mind. I got the feeling of a painting being painted stroke by stroke. The description of the street being blind and quiet except when the school set the boys free gave me a feeling of quiet and then sudden noise, as the boys came rushing through the streets. Describing the air as cold, the space of the sky as ever-changing violet allowed me to feel the cold and see the colors.

From identification:

The first time I read the lines "There's a certain slant of light, / Winter Afternoons-- / That oppresses, like the Heft / of Cathedral Tunes--" I had an immediate picture of grayish-white skies and cold, bare ground. It was almost frightening. The first stanza expresses a feeling I've had for a lifetime of hideous, anxiety-filled, depressing Sunday winter afternoons. From childhood, with homework unfinished and school rearing its terrifying Monday-morning head, through adulthood and its end-of-the-weekend, back to work dread, I've experienced that "Seal Despair--."

To complete frustration:

I've read this poem over and over, repeatedly, nonstop, until I finally collapsed from total exhaustion. WHAT DOES IT MEAN!? What light? The winter afternoon light? As heavy as cathedral tunes? Find a scar from what? Internal difference? Meanings? Aggggh!

Help. Could the author be talking about the sun? All I have are questions when it comes to this poem. I do like the choice of words, though. They sounded grand, royal, imperial, and made me feel like there was something to grab from them. But I couldn't make sense of it.

Double-Entry Journals and Logs

Because you may be asked to read and write comments about your journal or log entries from time to time, an especially effective format is the double-entry journal. By writing on only the front side of each page (or on the right half of each page), you will leave the back of the previous page (or the left half of each page) free for subsequent commentary (new ideas, revisions, summation, etc.) while rereading and reflecting. Leaving this space, you may go back later, read through your comments, circle and make notes about entries you've made, or add additional comments based on subsequent readings or class discussion.

(Original Response)

I could relate what Joyce was saying to nowadays. I myself have felt that way. All your

(Subsequent Comment)

She's not a nun. I found out in class that parochial schools were sometimes called convent schools back then. You didn't have to be a nun to go there. That part of the story makes much more sense to me now.

words and feelings are jumbled around one person. A crush. It's very stressful and exhilarating at the same time. I do have one question, though. Was the object of Joyce's desire and affection a nun? I didn't feel that aspect was presented too clearly. Maybe I'm misreading.

The Social Nature of Learning: Collaboration

Writing ideas down is one effective way to learn, but so much of what we learn is also learned through conversation. Sharing our responses with others, and listening to their feedback and ideas, help us build and clarify our own ideas. By articulating what you think you know and what you need to know through conversation, you may develop a clearer understanding of the literature.

Interpretive Communities   Stanley Fish, a professor and literary critic, has suggested that groups of readers who value the same approach to responding to literature belong to "an interpretive community." Although our interpretations are influenced by whatever collaborative group or class we are in at present, we also carry and apply our own individual values and those of the many other communities (family, friends, religion) to which we belong. In this respect, we are members of many interpretive communities, and we are continually refiguring and revising our interpretations and evaluations in the light of our personal beliefs and group discussions. Throughout this text you'll be encouraged to share and exchange your ideas and collaborate with your classmates in pairs and small groups. You may find it worthwhile and productive to keep track of this complex mix of personal response and group discussion as you write about the literature you read and discuss.

Personal, Not Private

Many of the questions that follow in this chapter prompt you to write about personal issues. These questions are not an attempt to invade your privacy or encourage you to write about aspects of your life or experience that may embarrass you or make you feel uncomfortable. What is personal or private is very different for each of us. You may choose to write some responses for your eyes only, some to share, or some not at all. That choice is always yours.

OURSELVES AS READERS

Our early experiences with books may have a significant influence on how we feel about reading. For many of us who enjoy reading, this joy was discovered outside the classroom. We felt free to experience the books we read without fear of having our responses judged as right or wrong. For many who do not like to read, however, reading was often a painful chore, usually an assignment for the classroom with all the accompanying pressures of being evaluated. How often we read now and whether we see ourselves as good readers may have much to do with these earlier experiences.

You might find it worthwhile to write about some of these reading experiences in your journal or share them with others. It may be illuminating to see how much you have in common as a reader with other members of the class.

> *The process of reading often raises more questions than it answers. Some of the most important questions to address are the ones you have raised yourself. So before you answer the questions that follow each selection in this chapter, you may want to write down your first impressions and any questions that came to mind during and after your reading.*

Different Kinds of Reading

Unfortunately, for many of us, the different types of reading we were given in school were often treated the same way. Reading assignments that primarily dealt with content or factual information were often not distinguished from imaginative literature.

We know, however, that different types of reading material require very different kinds of involvement. Reading a science text, for example, requires that we focus on acquiring information for future use, whereas a poem, play, or work of fiction, while requiring our understanding of the facts, seeks to involve us personally in the moment—to have us share an experience, to evoke our feelings.

Read the following paragraph.

CAUTION—NOT FOR PERSONAL USE—If splashed on skin or in eyes, rinse immediately. If accidentally taken internally give large amounts of milk or water. Call a physician. Point mouth of container away from you when removing cap. AVOID TRANSFER TO FOOD OR BEVERAGE CON-TAINERS—KEEP CONTAINER UPRIGHT IN A COOL PLACE TIGHTLY CAPPED.

FIRST RESPONSES

1. What is your response to the advice in this paragraph?
2. To what extent is this warning label subject to personal interpretation?
3. Did you find yourself more engaged with the emotion or with the information in this paragraph? Explain.

Read the following poem.

PETER MEINKE [B. 1932]

ADVICE TO MY SON   [1981]

—for Tim

The trick is, to live your days
as if each one may be your last
(for they go fast, and young men lose their lives
in strange and unimaginable ways)
but at the same time, plan long range   5
(for they go slow: if you survive
the shattered windshield and the bursting shell
you will arrive
at our approximation here below
of heaven or hell).   10

To be specific, between the peony and the rose
plant squash and spinach, turnips and tomatoes;
beauty is nectar
and nectar, in a desert, saves—
but the stomach craves stronger sustenance   15
than the honied vine.
Therefore, marry a pretty girl

after seeing her mother;
speak truth to one man,
work with another;   20
and always serve bread with your wine.

But, son,
always serve wine.

FIRST RESPONSES

1. What is your response to the advice in this poem?
2. To what extent is the poem subject to personal interpretation?
3. Did you find yourself more engaged with the emotion or the information in this poem? Explain.

MAKING CONNECTIONS

Compare your response to the warning label paragraph with your response to the poem "Advice to My Son."

1. Both the poem and the warning label give advice. In what way was your reading experience with each different?
2. Did the physical appearance of each influence *how* you read it? If the warning label were written in verse form, would you have read it with different expectations?
3. To what extent can you connect the advice given in the poem to your own background or experience? To what extent can you connect the advice given in the warning label?
4. Did you learn anything from the poem? From the warning label? If so, did the *nature* of what you learned differ in each case? Explain.

MAKING CONNECTIONS WITH LITERATURE

Among the many factors that influence our response to literature is identification with characters, circumstances, and issues. Our personalities, backgrounds, and experiences can have a strong impact on these connections. Being aware of these influences can help us think critically about our responses to literature—and the works themselves.

We may identify with characters because we see aspects of our own personalities in them or admire aspects of their personalities and wish we had them ourselves. We might respond negatively to characters because aspects of their personalities are different from ours or similar to ones we don't like in ourselves. We may agree or disagree with what the characters say or do, or ask ourselves if we would have behaved the same way.

Conversely, by showing us a view of life that is different from our own, literature might influence our beliefs and behavior. We may learn from literature as we learn from life itself.

Images of Ourselves

How we view ourselves in relation to the world around us is very complex. We probably have an image of who we are that we carry within ourselves most of the time, but we are likely to project a different personality according to the situations (home, work, school, etc.) in which we find ourselves. Depending on our relationships with them, the people we know are also likely to describe us very differently. Our families, friends, casual acquaintances, employers, and teachers may experience who we are in very different ways.

CONNECTING THROUGH EXPERIENCE

The self-images we carry with us into adulthood may be formed during childhood. Try to remember how you felt about yourself as a child and compare that self-image with how you see yourself now.

PAUL ZIMMER [B. 1934]

ZIMMER IN GRADE SCHOOL   [1983]

In grade school I wondered
Why I had been born
To wrestle in the ashy puddles,
With my square nose
Streaming mucus and blood.   5
My knuckles puffed from combat
And the old nun's ruler,
I feared everything: God,
Learning and my schoolmates.
I could not count, spell or read.   10
My report card proclaimed
These scarlet failures.
My parents wrang their loving hands.
My guardian angel wept constantly.

But I could never hide anything.   15
If I peed my pants in class
The puddle was always quickly evident.
My worst mistakes were at
The blackboard for Jesus and all
The saints to see.   20
     Even now
When I hide behind an elaborate mask
It is always known that I am Zimmer,
The one who does the messy papers
And fractures all his crayons,   25
Who spits upon the radiators
And sits all day in shame
Outside the office of the principal.

CONNECTING THROUGH EXPERIENCE

Many of us have had the experience of being told by people that once they got to know us, they discovered we differed greatly from their earlier impression of us. Can you recall an experience like that in your own life? If so, try to remember how it made you feel to hear that.

STEVIE SMITH   [1902–1971]

NOT WAVING BUT DROWNING   [1957]

Nobody heard him, the dead man,
But still he lay moaning:
I was much further out than you thought
And not waving but drowning.

Poor chap, he always loved larking   5
And now he's dead
It must have been too cold for him his heart gave way,
They said.

Oh, no no no, it was too cold always
(Still the dead one lay moaning)   10
I was much too far out all my life
And not waving but drowning.

MAKING CONNECTIONS

1. What did you wonder about yourself in grade school? To what extent do you still wonder the same things?
2. In "Zimmer in Grade School" what does the speaker mean by "When I hide behind an elaborate mask / It is always known that I am Zimmer"? Who is Zimmer?
3. What do you think is happening in "Not Waving but Drowning"? Who is drowning?
4. There is more than one speaker in this poem. Who are these speakers?
5. To what extent is your response to these poems affected by your own experience?

Culture, Experience, and Values

Who we are and how we respond to literature is also influenced by many other factors. Family, religion, race, gender, friends, other influential people in our lives, and our experiences shape our views in significant ways. Once again, an awareness of these factors can help us think critically about our responses to literature—and the works themselves.

We may come from a family that is strongly connected to its ethnic roots, religious or not religious at all, closely knit or disconnected, warm and welcoming, suffocating, or cold and impersonal. Or we may not have a family at all. Our friends, too, may affect who we are, what we believe, and how we act.

We may be strongly influenced by our race, ethnic background, or gender. If we have never experienced or witnessed discrimination, we might not be able to understand its significance. If we have witnessed prejudice or had it directed against us, we know how devastating it can be. Our gender may affect the expectations others have for us, the encouragement we receive for education and career goals, marriage and family, even our involvement in sports. And it certainly influences our view of the opposite sex.

If we are deeply religious, it might be at the heart of everything we value. If we are not, our religious backgrounds may still exert a strong influence on our lives. What we do for a living, how old we are, our sexual orientation, our disabilities, or other factors may also affect how we see the world—and the literature we read.

CONNECTING THROUGH EXPERIENCE

Most of us can probably identify a person who was "always there" for us and who seemed to do the things that really mattered without being asked and who may often have been taken for granted.

Before you read the following poem, try to recall someone like that in your own life.

ROBERT HAYDEN   [1913–1980]

THOSE WINTER SUNDAYS   [1962]

Sundays too my father got up early
and put his clothes on in the blueblack cold,
then with cracked hands that ached
from labor in the weekday weather made
banked fires blaze. No one ever thanked him.   5

I'd wake and hear the cold splintering, breaking.
When the rooms were warm, he'd call,
and slowly I would rise and dress,
fearing the chronic angers of that house,

Speaking indifferently to him,   10
who had driven out the cold
and polished my good shoes as well.
What did I know, what did I know
of love's austere and lonely offices?

MAKING CONNECTIONS

1. Describe the situation in the poem. Who is the speaker?
2. How does the speaker feel? Have you ever had similar feelings?
3. If you could identify a person who was "always there" for you, how does this remembrance influence your understanding of the poem?
4. What does the speaker mean by "love's austere and lonely offices"?
5. What other words, phrases, or parts of the poem had an impact on you? How so?
6. Compare this poem to Theodore Roethke's "My Papa's Waltz" (p. 281) or "Advice to My Son" on page 9.

CONNECTING THROUGH EXPERIENCE

In a world that bombards us with images from television, films, and magazines, many of us feel great pressure to look or behave in particular ways. Sometimes this pressure may even make us value our own individual strengths less favorably than what is simply more popular. See if you can recall a time when you felt pressured this way and how you reacted to that pressure.

MARGE PIERCY   [B. 1936]

BARBIE DOLL   [1969]

This girlchild was born as usual
and presented dolls that did pee-pee
and miniature GE stoves and irons
and wee lipsticks the color of cherry candy.
Then in the magic of puberty, a classmate said: 5
You have a great big nose and fat legs.

She was healthy, tested intelligent,
possessed strong arms and back,
abundant sexual drive and manual dexterity.
She went to and fro apologizing.   10
Everyone saw a fat nose on thick legs.

She was advised to play coy,
exhorted to come on hearty,
exercise, diet, smile and wheedle.
Her good nature wore out   15
Like a fan belt.

So she cut off her nose and her legs
and offered them up.
In the casket displayed on satin she lay
with the undertaker's cosmetics painted on,   20
a turned-up putty nose,
dressed in a pink and white nightie.
Doesn't she look pretty? everyone said.

Consummation at last.
To every woman a happy ending.   25

 ## MAKING CONNECTIONS

1. To what extent is your response influenced by your own experience? Could you identify with the feelings of the "girlchild" in this poem?
2. The media bombards all of us with images that pressure us to act or look in a certain way. How does your experience with advertisements, television, movies, magazines, or newspapers influence your response to the poem?
3. Do you think a female reader is likely to respond differently to this poem than a male reader? Explain.
4. Do you think the "girlchild" is literally dead at the end of the poem? Explain.
5. What do you think "Consummation at last. / To every woman a happy ending." means?
6. What other words, phrases, or parts of the poem affected you? How so?
7. Compare this poem with "Advice to My Son" (p. 9). If Meinke's poem were called "Advice to My Daughter," do you think the advice would be the same?

BEING IN THE MOMENT

We can't get at the heart of our experience with literature by summarizing it. We might account for all that matters on the "Caution" label on the bleach bottle (p. 9) by saying, "This is a very caustic liquid and you could hurt yourself by coming in contact with it." But we couldn't get at our experience of the poem "Those Winter Sundays" (p. 13) by saying, "The poet learned to appreciate how his father expressed love for him." We read the warning label for the information we take away with us; the label seeks to inform us. Literature seeks to involve us.

A newspaper article, for example, might relate the "who, what, when, where, and why" of an event, but literature must do much more than that. It may even move us to question events in our own lives and influence us as we make our own decisions. The following newspaper account appeared in the *New York Times* the day after the racially motivated bombing of a church in Birmingham, Alabama, in 1963.

Birmingham Bomb Kills
4 Negro Girls in Church;
Riots Flare; 2 Boys Slain

GUARD SUMMONED

Wallace Acts on City Plea
for Help as 20 Are Injured

By CLAUDE SITTON
Special to *The New York Times*
BIRMINGHAM, Ala., Sept. 15—[1963]

A bomb severely damaged a Negro church today during Sunday school services, killing four Negro girls and setting off racial rioting and other rioting in which two Negro boys were shot to death. Fourteen Negroes were injured in the explosion. One Negro and five whites were hurt in the disorders that followed.

Some 500 National Guardsman in battle dress stood by at armories here tonight on orders of Gov. George C. Wallace. And 300 state troopers joined the Birmingham police, Jefferson County sheriff's deputies and other law-enforcement units in efforts to restore peace.

Governor Wallace sent the guardsmen and the troopers in response to requests from local authorities.

Sporadic gunfire sounded in Negro neighborhoods tonight, and small bands of residents roamed the streets. Aside from the patrols that cruised the city armed with riot guns, carbines and shotguns, few whites were seen.

Fire Bomb Hurled

At one point, three fires burned simultaneously in Negro sections, one at a broom and mop factory, one at a roofing company and a third in another building. An incendiary bomb was tossed into a supermarket, but the flames were extinguished swiftly. Fire marshals investigated blazes at two vacant houses to see if arson was involved.

The explosion at the 16th Street Baptist Church this morning brought hundreds of angry Negroes pouring into the streets. Some attacked the police with stones. The police dispersed them by firing shotguns over their heads. Johnny Robinson, a 16 year old Negro, was shot in the back by a policeman with a shotgun this afternoon. Officers said the victim was among a group that hurled stones at white youths driving through the area in cars flying Confederate battle flags.

When the police arrived, the youths fled, and one policeman said he had fired low but that some of the shot had struck the Robinson youth in the back.

Virgil Wade, a 13-year old Negro, was shot and killed just outside Birmingham while riding a bicycle. The Jefferson County sheriff's office said "there apparently was no reason at all" for the killing, but indicated that it was related to the general racial disorders.

Wallace Offers Reward

Governor Wallace, at the request of city officials, offered a $5,000 reward for the arrest and conviction of the bombers.

None of the 50 bombings of Negro property here since World War II have been solved.

The four girls killed in the blast had just heard Mrs. Ellis C. Demand, their teacher, complete the Sunday School lesson for the day. The subject was "The Love That Forgives."

The blast occurred at about 10:25 A.M. (12:25 P.M. New York time).

Church members said they found the girls huddled together beneath a pile of masonry debris.

Parents of 3 Are Teachers

Both parents of each of the victims teach in the city's schools. The dead were identified by University Hospital officials as:

Cynthia Wesley, 14, the only child of Claude A. Wesley, principal of the Lewis Elementary School, and Mrs. Wesley, a teacher there.

Denise McNair, 11, also an only child, whose parents are teachers.

Carol Robertson, 14, whose parents are teachers and whose grandmother, Mrs. Sallie Anderson, is one of the Negro members of a biracial committee established by Mayor Boutwell to deal with racial problems.

Adie Mae Collins, 14, about whom no information was immediately available.

The blast blew gaping holes through walls in the church basement. Floors of offices in the rear of the sanctuary appeared near collapse. Stairways were blocked by splintered window frames, glass, and timbers.

Chief Police Inspector W. J. Haley said the impact of the blast indicated that at least 15 sticks of dynamite might have caused it. He said the police had talked to two witnesses who reported having seen a car drive by the church, slow down and then speed away before the blast.

❧ FIRST RESPONSES

1. What is your response to this newspaper article?
2. Did you find yourself more engaged with the emotion or the information in this article? Explain.

Read the following poem about the same event.

DUDLEY RANDALL [B. 1914]

BALLAD OF BIRMINGHAM [1964]

"Mother dear, may I go downtown
Instead of out to play,
And march the streets of Birmingham
In a Freedom March today?"

"No, baby, no, you may not go,   5
For the dogs are fierce and wild,
And clubs and hoses, guns and jails
Aren't good for a little child."

"But, mother, I won't be alone
Other children will go with me,   10
And march the streets of Birmingham
To make our country free."

"No, baby, no, you may not go,
For I fear those guns will fire.
But you may go to church instead   15
And sing in the children's choir."

She has combed and brushed her night-dark hair,
And bathed rose petal sweet,
And drawn white gloves on her small brown hands,
And white shoes on her feet.   20

The mother smiled to know her child
Was in that sacred place,
But that smile was the last smile
To come upon her face.

For when she heard the explosion,   25
Her eyes grew wet and wild.
She raced through the streets of Birmingham
Calling for her child.

She clawed through bits of glass and brick,
Then lifted out a shoe.   30
"O, here's the shoe my baby wore,
But, baby, where are you?"

FIRST RESPONSES

1. What is your response to this poem?
2. Did you find yourself more engaged with the emotion or the information in this article? Explain.
3. In what way did your reading experience of the poem differ from your reading of the article?

MAKING CONNECTIONS

1. Both the newspaper article and the poem recount the bombing. What makes the poem different from the newspaper account?
2. What did you learn from the newspaper account? What did you learn from the poem? How was the *nature* of what you learned different?

3. To what extent is your response to "Ballad of Birmingham" influenced by your own experience?
4. How does the rhyme scheme affect your response to the poem's content? The second and fourth lines of each stanza rhyme. How does this rhyme scheme and the rhythm of the poem affect you? How might it change your response if the first and third lines rhymed instead—or as well?

PARTICIPATING, NOT SOLVING

It's essential that we are *active* participants when we read or listen to imaginative literature. But if we look for the parts of a poem before we have experienced the whole, we may shut down the emotions we need to experience it—and miss the *life* of the poem. Placing ourselves *emotionally* inside the poem, rather than examining it *rationally* from the outside, enables us to feel and sense the words and images and lets these impressions wash over us. Poetry sometimes involves an imagining that is like our dreams and reveals things to us that are not always understood in rational ways.

However, like much of the "academic" reading we do, reading poetry occurs most often in school. And school, with its right and wrong answers, has a way of making us tense and rigid (and very rational). If you had heard (studied) some of your favorite songs and music for the first time in school, you might never have loosened up enough to like them at all. Poems are not math problems—they don't have one "correct" answer. They might not even "add up." The right answer is the one that makes the most sense to you, a "sense" supported by your own imagination and the text of the poem itself. Being confused and making mistakes along the way is part of the process of finding your own right answer.

USING OUR IMAGINATIONS

When we read, the strength of our emotional involvement is based on our ability to experience scenes as if we were there. If we "surrender" ourselves, we not only imagine the details provided, we create ones that are not. We may occasionally say, or hear people say, "I liked the book better than the movie" or "I can't believe so and so was cast in that role." We probably mean, "I liked the movie of the book in my mind better than the movie on the screen" or "That actor is nothing like the character I created in my mind." Unless we complete the picture in our minds by filling in the details, we won't have a satisfying experience with literature.

Where do we get these details? Some of what we imagine is shared and comes from our cultural backgrounds. And some of what we imagine is personal and familiar and is fueled by our own experiences—the people, places, or events in our own lives. For example, it doesn't have to be summer for us to imagine the sun and heat on the beach—or winter for us to imagine snow. Through our "sense" memories, we can "recall" now what we felt and saw then. What we see in our "mind's eye" may also derive from music, television, film, other forms of media, and other things we have read.

CONNECTING THROUGH COLLABORATION

In this exercise, you may find it illuminating to share your work with a partner or a small group.

1. Take a look back through your responses and select some of your strongest reactions or impressions. For example, how did you picture the house in Robert Hayden's poem "Those Winter Sundays"? What did the mother and the little girl look like in "Ballad of Birmingham"? Think about the pictures in your mind from other poems or stories you have read.
2. Where do your pictures come from? How much of what you picture in each of these scenes comes from detail that the author provided and how much completely from your imagination?
3. Compare the pictures you've created with those of your partner or other classmates in your group. What is similar and what is different about their responses? How can you account for your differences?
4. If you wrote down details to support your own response, do those details adequately convey it? Do those details include specific references to the text?
5. Are there places where you might have clarified your response through a comparison (with other characters, people you know, other students' responses)?
6. If you did not write down supporting details or if you did not cite the text for support, go back to the poem(s) and see if you can.

THE WHOLE AND ITS PARTS

You've probably come across the statement "The whole is equal to the sum of its parts." Seems to make sense, doesn't it? Well, in some areas of study it does, but it cannot account for our response to literature. In literature and other artistic expressions, there is a whole that is greater than the sum of its parts, a whole that blossoms as the parts come together in our imaginations.

We don't like our favorite music because we identify the parts and add them up to a whole experience; we like it because we experience the sound of the instruments, the rhythms, the voices, the lyrics, all together and all at once. For all of us that means more than the sum of the notes or words we hear, and to each of us that means something different.

Like music, literature cannot be reduced to its parts to account for its meaning. But like music, there are parts, and as we become more experienced listeners or readers—and believe that literature has something to offer us—we want to know how those parts work together. In subsequent chapters, we will try to comprehend the craft with which the parts are assembled.

Chapter 2

Communication
Writing a Response Essay

The goal in this chapter is to develop your initial responses into an essay about literature. We begin by emphasizing the response essay, but the habits of thinking and writing stressed in this chapter apply equally well to the critical essay explored in later chapters:

- Finding our writing voices;
- Developing a clear thesis statement;
- Showing what we mean through detail, illustration, and comparison;
- Citing evidence from the text.

These are core principles for writing an essay about literature. Our emphasis on analysis, argumentation, and research in Chapters 3, 4, and 5 will complement and build on our discussion in this chapter.

THE RESPONSE ESSAY

The purpose of a response essay is to share our experience with literature. Why would we want to share our experience with literature? Perhaps the most compelling reason is the same one we have for communicating any other important event. Why do we discuss our experiences of movies, games, concerts, exhibits, or parties? Why do we chat about dates, meaningful events in our lives, or interesting people we have met? Many of us share because we have a need to "review" or "reexperience" with others, to have them say, "I see what you mean" or "I understand why you were affected that way." We don't want advice; we want caring listeners. This kind of sharing has a give-and-take to it. We give a rendering of our experience, and we receive other people's understanding, affirmation, and appreciation—their participation. It's not "scoring points" or *proving* we are right; it's an experience in itself.

If the voice in our writing, the reader's sense of who we are, is that of a "sharer," not a "prosecuting attorney" in a courtroom, the essay will feel like a welcome invitation, not a summons. Readers are better able to see when we *show what we tell.*

21

The strength of their involvement is based on how much they care about what we share. Our voice in presenting that experience strongly influences their level of interest. For readers who accept our invitation, "I see what you mean" takes on a literal dimension. The clarity and thoughtfulness with which we write will determine how glad they are that they came.

☑ CHECKLIST: THE BASICS OF A RESPONSE ESSAY

❑ Write down your impressions and whatever questions came to mind during and after your reading.

❑ What confuses you? What do you want to know more about? How can you find out?

❑ Is there anything that you don't like about the work? If so, what and why?

❑ What do you find most interesting or compelling about the work? Do any of the characters especially appeal to you or bother you? Do you find any of the events especially pleasing or disturbing? Why?

❑ Do any of the characters or events remind you of ones in your own life? Do these reminders help or interfere with your response? If so, how?

❑ Can you compare or contrast this work or its elements with another work you've read? If so, how?

❑ Stay anchored and "show" what made this literature so compelling for you.

❑ What details or passages in the work or works illustrate or support your response?

Voice and Writing

We know that the tone of voice we use when speaking is likely to make an impression—that *how* we say the words out loud can convey as much meaning as the words themselves. But speech and writing are different. We can think about and revise most writing, but speech is usually spontaneous, and we don't revise what we say in normal conversation. Spontaneous speech contains lots of stops and false starts and sound fillers that would look silly in writing. Unless we say something especially memorable or inflammatory, we're confident these words won't be heard (or read) over and over again. So, what does voice have to do with writing?

Virtually all of us learned to speak before we learned to read. Throughout our lives, we've been conditioned to hear the words we read. As children, many of us said the words out loud as we read to ourselves. Even if we don't move our lips or say the words out loud now, it's difficult to read them without triggering the nerves that activate speech and help us to "subvocalize" and hear the words voiced in our minds.

So, too, readers of our writing want to hear our voices—to get a sense of who we are. As writers we are conscious of this. For example, when writing an e-mail message or a letter, our voices may change according to whom we send it, what we want, and how we want to be perceived. In a personal note to an old friend we are probably free "to be ourselves." Our friends know us, and usually we're not anxious about the impression we will make. We are confident they will recognize our voices in the words. However, when writing a letter "To the Editor," flirting with a new romantic interest, or applying for a job, our voices are likely to be quite different. We may want to convey a sense of responsibility, wisdom, wit, or whatever else we can demonstrate to make a positive impression.

What we write about may also have a strong influence on how we are heard. As you might imagine, we write with more feeling and a clearer, stronger voice about issues that move us. Here too, we write with more confidence when we are sure of our audience. Those entries that are private (and for our eyes only) are likely to be different from those we know will be read by others. Those entries written for our friends or agreeable classmates will probably be different from those written for an unknown audience.

Voice and Response to Literature

Staying Anchored in the Literature   When sharing personal responses, it can be very easy to see the work simply as a prompt to tell our own stories. Seeing and sharing the parallels between our own experiences and those in a work may strengthen our voices and clarify our responses, but the work on the page must remain prominent in the presentation. To write an effective response essay, it is essential to stay "anchored" in the work and to balance references to personal experience with references to the literature itself.

Showing and Telling   Most of us are best convinced when we see for ourselves. It would certainly seem risky to buy a car "sight unseen." We would probably insist on seeing it, trying it out, getting the "feel" of it before we decided to buy. When we talk with friends about a concert, game, or party, we probably would not settle for "It was great." Again, we would like to get the "feel" of it, to hear the details, to imagine ourselves there, to share the experience.

As readers, we have a similar need. We are not likely to settle for being told an issue is compelling or trivial; an event exciting, suspenseful, or sad; a character fascinating, dull, or manipulative. We want to be moved by the issue, to be present at the event, to know the character for ourselves. Writers' voices are believable when we experience characters and events with them—when the conclusions ("exciting," "sad," "dull") are ours—when we are shown, not simply told.

CONNECTING THROUGH EXPERIENCE

If you have ever been called a derogatory name because of your race, ethnic background, gender, or other factor, you know how disturbing that experience can be. If you have ever been in this position or witnessed it happening to someone else, try to recall your reaction. If you've never been in this position, try to imagine how it might make someone feel.

COUNTEE CULLEN [1903–1946]

INCIDENT   [1925]

Once riding in old Baltimore,
  Heart-filled, head-filled with glee,
I saw a Baltimorean
  Keep looking straight at me.

Now I was eight and very small,   5
  And he was no whit bigger,
And so I smiled, but he poked out
  His tongue, and called me, "Nigger."

I saw the whole of Baltimore
  From May until December: 10
Of all the things that happened there
  That's all that I remember.

MAKING CONNECTIONS

1. Can you describe an event in your life that made such a lasting impression
   on you?
2. If you have experienced or observed an event like the one described in
   "Incident," how does this influence your response? If you have not experienced or observed an event like this, how does this affect your response to
   the poem?
3. If the speaker were describing a racist incident he experienced as an adult,
   how do you think the poem would be different? Why does the speaker say,
   "That's all that I remember"?
4. In what way does the title of the poem fit the poem's content?
5. How does the rhyme scheme of the poem affect your response to the
   poem's content?

  The entry that follows was written in response to Countee Cullen's "Incident."
If you haven't read the poem and written your own response, you might want to do
that before you read the entry below.

Janice's Response:
  I have not had any experiences as powerful as what that child

experienced. I do remember being picked on by a bully when my friends and

I were walking to school and hearing him say gross things about Catholics

(we were in uniforms!), but I remember thinking he was the idiot not us. I

thought this was a powerful little poem. I didn't see the 'n' word coming. It

begins so simply with an upbeat tone, "Heart-filled, head-filled with glee," and

the sing-song quality of it remains even when the poem turns so serious. I think the rhythmic quality it has helps to remind us that this is happening to a small child. The line "That's all that I remember" I think refers more to that being all that was really memorable about the Baltimore experience, or even that that is the strongest memory. The title is perfect because that's basically what Baltimore is boiled down to in this child's eyes, "the incident" and not much more.

MAKING CONNECTIONS

1. How was Janice's response influenced by her experience?
2. Consider your response to the poem. How does it compare to hers?
3. To what extent has she stayed anchored in the poem?
4. To what extent has she "shown" what she's told?
5. How would you describe the voice in Countee Cullen's poem "Incident"? What factors make it effective?
6. In what way is "showing" a factor in both the poem and the response to it? What scenes, details, words, or phrases had the biggest impact on you?

WRITING TO DESCRIBE

You are likely to write with more feeling and a clearer, stronger voice about issues that move you, so your strongest response or impression may provide the best topic to write about; but selecting relevant details to support that response is equally important. You are not only describing how you felt, but what prompted you to feel this way.

An effective description is much more than a summary. A summary has no voice. An engaging description has our voice, impressions, and feelings, as well as relevant details. When someone asks us to describe a person we know very well (a friend, lover, spouse, parent) or a place with which we are very familiar (our home, bedroom, car, or a favorite hangout), we're not likely to respond with factual information alone. A summary of facts (dimensions, features, or colors) will not adequately convey what we feel is most important. Those details support our impression but do not replace it. Important details, however, do help the reader picture what we are describing and clarify *why* we feel the way we do.

Choosing Details

Which details we choose when describing and supporting our responses can make a big difference. Writing, "Tanya makes me feel very comfortable" by itself will not be as clear as combining it with examples or details of what she does that show it is true: "She's very soft-spoken, smiles a lot, and is a good listener." We would not include every detail ("She's wants to graduate next year") unless it's relevant ("so she knows the kind of pressure I'm feeling"). Including details not important to our impression will not support, and may even dilute, the impact of ones that are.

Choosing Details from Literature

So, too, the details we choose to clarify and support our responses to literature have an important impact on readers. For example, to describe the young man's disillusionment in "Incident" and not make reference to the name he's called omits a crucial detail in this painful memory. Those details, those parts, capture the whole of a work in miniature.

CONNECTING THROUGH EXPERIENCE

From our perspectives as adults, many of the problems of childhood may seem relatively unimportant. However, what may seem unimportant to us now may have affected us very differently when we were growing up.

Can you remember what it was like to be an eleven-year-old? See if you can recall an event that you found especially humiliating or embarrassing at that age. Try to remember what you were feeling and what you found especially difficult about the experience.

SANDRA CISNEROS [B. 1954]

ELEVEN   [1983]

What they don't understand about birthdays and what they never tell you is that when you're eleven, you're also ten, and nine, and eight, and seven, and six, and five, and four, and three, and two, and one. And when you wake up on your eleventh birthday you expect to feel eleven, but you don't. You open your eyes and everything's just like yesterday, only it's today. And you don't feel eleven at all. You feel like you're still ten. And you are—underneath the year that makes you eleven.

Like some days you might say something stupid, and that's the part of you that's still ten. Or maybe some days you might need to sit on your mama's lap because you're scared, and that's the part of you that's five. And maybe one day when you're all grown up maybe you will need to cry like if you're three, and that's okay. That's what I tell Mama when she's sad and needs to cry. Maybe she's feeling three.

Because the way you grow old is kind of like an onion or like the rings inside a tree trunk or like my little wooden dolls that fit one inside the other, each year inside the next one. That's how being eleven years old is.

You don't feel eleven. Not right away. It takes a few days, weeks even, sometimes even months before you say Eleven when they ask you. And you don't feel smart eleven, not until you're almost twelve. That's the way it is.

5   Only today I wish I didn't have only eleven years rattling inside me like pennies in a tin Band-Aid box. Today I wish I was one hundred and two instead of eleven because if I was one hundred and two I'd have known what to say when Mrs. Price put the red sweater on my desk. I would've known how to tell her it wasn't mine instead of just sitting there with that look on my face and nothing coming out of my mouth.

"Whose is this?" Mrs. Price says, and she holds the red sweater up in the air for all the class to see. "Whose? It's been sitting in the coatroom for a month."

"Not mine," says everybody. "Not me."

"It has to belong to somebody," Mrs. Price keeps saying, but nobody can remember. It's an ugly sweater with red plastic buttons and a collar and sleeves all stretched out like you could use them for a jump rope. It's maybe a thousand years old and even if it belonged to me I wouldn't say so.

Maybe because I'm skinny, maybe because she doesn't like me, that stupid Sylvia Saldivar says, "I think it belongs to Rachel." An ugly sweater like that, all raggedy and old, but Mrs. Price believes her; Mrs. Price takes the sweater and puts it right on my desk, but when I open my mouth nothing comes out.

10　"That's not, I don't, you're not . . . Not mine," I finally say in a little voice that was maybe me when I was four.

"Of course it's yours," Mrs. Price says. "I remember you wearing it once." Because she's older and the teacher, she's right and I'm not.

Not mine, not mine, not mine, but Mrs. Price is already turning to page thirty-two and math problem number four. I don't know why but all of a sudden I'm feeling sick inside, like the part of me that's three wants to come out of my eyes, only I squeeze them shut tight and bite down on my teeth real hard and try to remember today I am eleven, eleven.

Mama is making a cake for me for tonight, and when Papa comes home everybody will sing Happy birthday, happy birthday to you.

But when the sick feeling goes away and I open my eyes, the red sweater's still sitting there like a big red mountain. I move the red sweater to the corner of my desk with my ruler. I move my pencil and books and eraser as far from it as possible. I even move my chair a little to the right. Not mine, not mine, not mine.

15　In my head I'm thinking how long till lunchtime, how long till I can take the red sweater and throw it over the schoolyard fence, or leave it hanging on a parking meter, or bunch it up into a little ball and toss it in the alley. Except when math period ends Mrs. Price says loud and in front of everybody, "Now, Rachel, that's enough," because she sees I've shoved the red sweater to the tippy-tip corner of my desk and it's hanging all over the edge like a waterfall, but I don't care.

"Rachel," Mrs. Price says. She says it like she's getting mad. "You put that sweater on right now and no more nonsense."

"But it's not—"

"Now!" Mrs. Price says.

This is when I wish I wasn't eleven, because all the years inside of me—ten, nine, eight, seven, six, five, four, three, two, and one—are pushing at the back of my eyes when I put one arm through one sleeve of the sweater that smells like cottage cheese, and then the other arm through the other and stand there with my arms apart like if the sweater hurts me and it does, all itchy and full of germs that aren't even mine.

20　That's when everything I've been holding in since this morning, since when Mrs. Price put the sweater on my desk, finally lets go, and all of a sudden I'm crying in front of everybody. I wish I was invisible but I'm not. I'm eleven and it's my birthday today and I'm crying like I'm three in front of everybody. I put my head down on the desk and bury my face in my stupid clown-sweater arms. My face all hot and spit coming out of my mouth because I can't stop the little animal noises from coming out of me, until there aren't any more tears left in my eyes, and it's just my body shaking like when you have the hiccups, and my whole head hurts like when you drink milk too fast.

But the worst part is right before the bell rings for lunch. That stupid Phyllis Lopez, who is even dumber than Sylvia Saldivar, says she remembers the red sweater is hers! I take it off right away and give it to her, only Mrs. Price pretends like everything's okay.

Today I'm eleven. There's a cake Mama's making for tonight, and when Papa comes home from work we'll eat it. There'll be candles and presents and everybody will sing Happy birthday, happy birthday to you, Rachel, only it's too late.

I'm eleven today. I'm eleven, ten, nine, eight, seven, six, five, four, three, two, and one, but I wish I was one hundred and two. I wish I was anything but eleven, because I want today to be far away already, far away like a runaway balloon, like a tiny *o* in the sky, so tiny-tiny you have to close your eyes to see it.

 MAKING CONNECTIONS

1. If you could recall a childhood event that you found humiliating or embarrassing, how did that memory influence your response to this story?
2. How does the voice of the narrator affect your response?
3. What descriptions and what details in the story had an impact on you? How so?
4. If you find the voice of the story convincing, what features of the writing seem to make it effective? To what extent does the story "show" what is told?

 CONNECTING THROUGH COLLABORATION

In this exercise, you may find it illuminating to share your work with a partner or a small group.

1. How do you respond when someone asks you to describe a work of literature that you've read? To what extent does a summary convey what you've experienced—what you feel is most important? To what extent does it seem inadequate? The following exercise may provide some insight:
   a. Summarize Sandra Cisneros's "Eleven."
   b. Write down your strongest impressions of the work. Write down the details—from your experience and the literature—that support or clarify those impressions.
   c. What is the difference between the summary and your details and impressions?
   d. Rewrite your summary with your details and impressions.
   e. Compare your summary of the work with that of your partner or others in your group.

WRITING TO COMPARE

How many times are we asked to describe something, and our first reaction is "Well, it's like . . . " or "It reminds me of . . . "? In fact it seems hard to describe anything without resorting to comparison somewhere along the way. When we think about our friends, we may compare and contrast them consciously and unconsciously with each other. When we take part in important events, we may compare them to similar events in our past: "This reminds me of the wedding I went to last year" or "My brother's graduation was done very differently."

Comparing and contrasting are also natural ways to describe our responses to literature. We might compare ourselves or others with literary characters, or our own experiences with those in a work of literature. We may compare the choices made by various characters with the choices we would make. We might even be reminded of previous reading experiences and compare the work—or elements of the work—we are reading with one we've read before. We might even compare a work of literature with a work from another form of art, like painting. A good example of both process and product is the student sample of Barbara Pfister (see p. 701), who compares van Gogh's *Starry Night* with Anne Sexton's poem about the painting.

√ ## Comparing and Contrasting Using a Venn Diagram *2 Characters for oce.* *2 Texts*

Sometimes it's easier to generate and organize ideas when we can see them and their relationships to one another side by side in a whole picture. One effective technique for generating and organizing ideas when writing to compare is to create a Venn diagram (Figure 2.1). This technique works equally well when comparing personal experience with the work (Figure 2.2) or comparing works or characters with one another (Figure 2.3). The three poems used as examples, "Those Winter Sundays," "Not Waving but Drowning, " and "Barbie Doll," are in Chapter 1.

1. Draw two interconnecting circles. Identify each circle.

2. In the common, interconnecting area, write down what the subjects have in common.

3. In the separate sections, write down what is different.

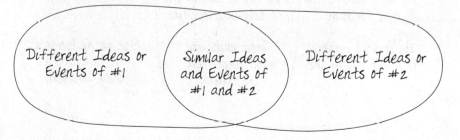

Different Ideas or Events of #1

Similar Ideas and Events of #1 and #2

Different Ideas or Events of #2

Figure 2.1 *Venn Diagram*

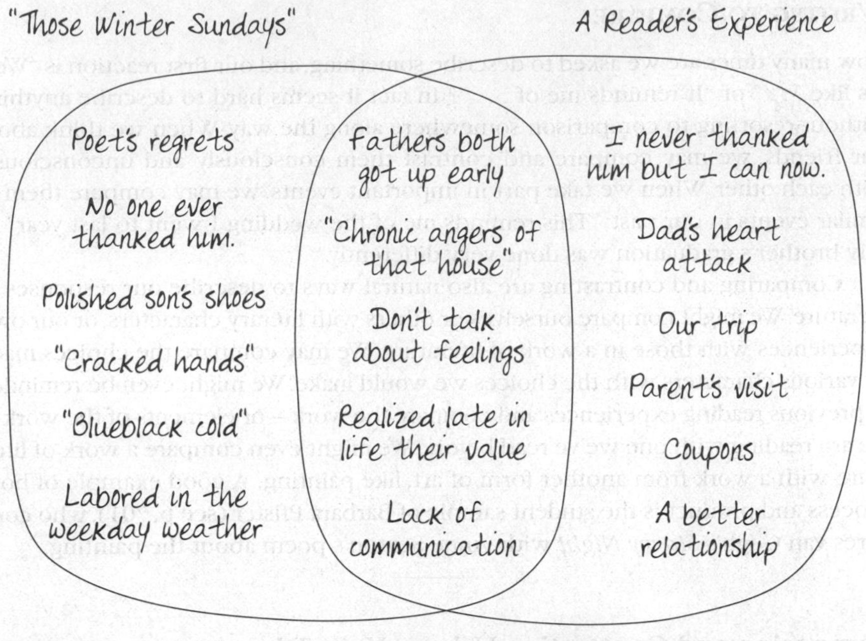

"Those Winter Sundays"   A Reader's Experience

Poet's regrets

No one ever thanked him.

Polished son's shoes

"Cracked hands"

"Blueblack cold"

Labored in the weekday weather

Fathers both got up early

"Chronic angers of that house"

Don't talk about feelings

Realized late in life their value

Lack of communication

I never thanked him but I can now.

Dad's heart attack

Our trip

Parent's visit

Coupons

A better relationship

Figure 2.2 *Comparing Experience with Literature*

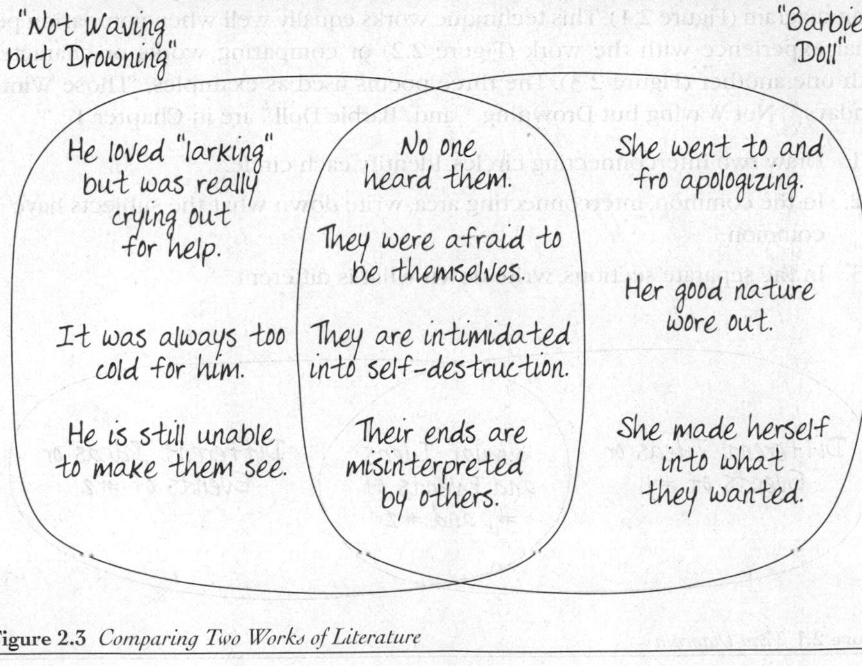

"Not Waving but Drowning"   "Barbie Doll"

He loved "larking" but was really crying out for help.

It was always too cold for him.

He is still unable to make them see.

No one heard them.

They were afraid to be themselves.

They are intimidated into self-destruction.

Their ends are misinterpreted by others.

She went to and fro apologizing.

Her good nature wore out.

She made herself into what they wanted.

Figure 2.3 *Comparing Two Works of Literature*

CONNECTING THROUGH EXPERIENCE

We would all probably like some things in our lives to be different. Before you read the essay that follows, see if you can think of something in your life that you wish was different. If that "something" were different, how might it change your life? Would everything be better? Might anything be worse?

ANNA QUINDLEN [B. 1953]

MOTHERS   [1988]

The two women are sitting at a corner table in the restaurant, their shopping bags wedged between their chairs and the wall: Lord & Taylor, Bloomingdale's, something from Ann Taylor for the younger one. She is wearing a bright silk shirt, some good gold jewelry; her hair is on the long side, her makeup faint. The older woman is wearing a suit, a string of pearls, a diamond solitaire, and a narrow band. They lean across the table. I imagine the conversation: Will the new blazer go with the old skirt? Is the dress really right for an afternoon wedding? How is Daddy? How is his ulcer? Won't he slow down just a little bit?

It seems that I see mothers and daughters everywhere, gliding through what I think of as the adult rituals of parent and child. My mother died when I was nineteen. For a long time, it was all you needed to know about me, a kind of vestpocket description of my emotional complexion: "Meet you in the lobby in ten minutes—I have long-brown hair, am on the short side, have on a red coat, and my mother died when I was nineteen."

That's not true anymore. When I see a mother and a daughter having lunch in a restaurant, shopping at Saks, talking together on the crosstown bus, I no longer want to murder them. I just stare a little more than is polite, hoping that I can combine my observations with a half-remembered conversation, some anecdotes, a few old dresses, a photograph or two, and re-create, like an archaeologist of the soul, a relationship that will never exist. Of course, the question is whether it would have ever existed at all. One day at lunch I told two of my closest friends that what I minded most about not having a mother was the absence of that grown-up woman-to-woman relationship that was impossible as a child or adolescent, and that my friends were having with their mothers now. They both looked at me as though my teeth had turned purple. I didn't need to ask why; I've heard so many times about the futility of such relationships, about women with business suits and briefcases reduced to whining children by their mothers' offhand comment about a man, or a dress, or a homemade dinner.

I accept the fact that mothers and daughters probably always see each other across a chasm of rivalries. But I forget all those things when one of my friends is down with the flu and her mother arrives with an overnight bag to manage her household and feed her soup.

5   So now, at the center of my heart there is a fantasy, and a mystery. The fantasy is small, and silly: a shopping trip, perhaps a pair of shoes, a walk, a talk, lunch in a good restaurant, which my mother assumes is the kind of place I eat at all the time. I pick up the check. We take a cab to the train. She reminds me of somebody's birthday. I

invite her and my father to dinner. The mystery is whether the fantasy has within it a nugget of fact. Would I really have wanted her to take care of the wedding arrangements, or come and stay for a week after the children were born? Would we have talked on the telephone about this and that? Would she have saved my clippings in a scrapbook? Or would she have meddled in my affairs, volunteering opinions I didn't want to hear about things that were none of her business, criticizing my clothes and my children? Worse still, would we have been strangers with nothing to say to each other? Is all the good I remember about us simply wishful thinking? Is all the bad self-protection? Perhaps it is at best difficult, at worst impossible for children and parents to be adults together. But I would love to be able to know that.

Sometimes I feel like one of those people searching, searching for the mother who gave them up for adoption. I have some small questions for her and I want the answers: How did she get her children to sleep through the night? What was her first labor like? Was there olive oil in her tomato sauce? Was she happy? If she had it to do over again, would she? When we pulled her wedding dress out of the box the other day to see if my sister might wear it, we were shocked to find how tiny it was. "My God," I said, "did you starve yourself to get into this thing?" But there was no one there. And if she had been there, perhaps I would not have asked in the first place. I suspect that we would have been friends, but I don't really know. I was simply a little too young at nineteen to understand the woman inside the mother.

I occasionally pass by one of those restaurant tables and I hear the bickering about nothing: You did so, I did not, don't tell me what you did or didn't do, oh, leave me alone. And I think that my fantasies are better than any reality could be. Then again, maybe not.

CONNECTING THROUGH EXPERIENCE

The desire for approval can be a very strong incentive when making important decisions. Making a decision that meets with the disapproval of our parents or others we respect can be difficult and emotionally painful—even if we believe that we've made the right choice. We may even have strong ethical reasons for taking a position, yet feel reluctant to disappoint those with whom we have emotional ties.

Try to recall an event in your life when the pressure of approval was a major factor in an important decision. Try to remember what you were feeling at the time.

LANGSTON HUGHES [1902–1967]

SALVATION

[1940]

I was saved from sin when I was going on thirteen. But not really saved. It happened like this. There was a big revival at my Auntie Reed's church. Every night for weeks there had been much preaching, singing, praying, and shouting, and some very hardened sinners had been brought to Christ, and the membership of the church had grown by leaps and bounds. Then just before the revival ended, they held a special meeting for children, "to bring the young lambs to the fold." My aunt spoke of it for days ahead. That night I was escorted to the front row and placed on the mourners' bench with all the other young sinners, who had not yet been brought to Jesus.

My aunt told me that when you were saved you saw a light, and something happened to you inside! And Jesus came into your life! And God was with you from then on! She said you could see and hear and feel Jesus in your soul. I believed her. I had heard a great many old people say the same thing and it seemed to me they ought to know. So I sat there calmly in the hot, crowded church, waiting for Jesus to come to me.

The preacher preached a wonderful rhythmical sermon, all moans and shouts and lonely cries and dire pictures of hell, and then he sang a song about the ninety and nine safe in the fold, but one little lamb was left out in the cold. Then he said: "Won't you come? Won't you come to Jesus? Young lambs, won't you come?" And he held out his arms to all us young sinners there on the mourners' bench. And the little girls cried. And some of them jumped up and went to Jesus right away. But most of us just sat there.

A great many old people came and knelt around us and prayed, old women with jet-black faces and braided hair, old men with work-gnarled hands. And the church sang a song about the lower lights are burning, some poor sinners to be saved. And the whole building rocked with prayer and song.

5   Still I kept waiting to *see* Jesus.

Finally all the young people had gone to the altar and were saved, but one boy and me. He was a rounder's son named Westley. Westley and I were surrounded by sisters and deacons praying. It was very hot in the church, and getting late now. Finally Westley said to me in a whisper: "God damn! I'm tired o' sitting here. Let's get up and be saved." So he got up and was saved.

Then I was left all alone on the mourners' bench. My aunt came and knelt at my knees and cried while prayers and song swirled all around me in the little church. The whole congregation prayed for me alone, in a mighty wail of moans and voices. And I kept waiting serenely for Jesus, waiting, waiting—but he didn't come. I wanted to see him, but nothing happened to me. Nothing! I wanted something to happen to me, but nothing happened.

I heard the songs and the minister saying: "Why don't you come? My dear child, why don't you come to Jesus? Jesus is waiting for you. He wants you. Why don't you come? Sister Reed, what is this child's name?"

"Langston," my aunt sobbed.

10   "Langston, why don't you come? Why don't you come and be saved? Oh, Lamb of God! Why don't you come?"

Now it was really getting late. I began to be ashamed of myself, holding everything up so long. I began to wonder what God thought about Westley, who certainly hadn't seen Jesus either, but who was now sitting proudly on the platform, swinging his knickerbockered legs and grinning down at me, surrounded by deacons and old women on their knees praying. God had not struck Westley dead for taking his name in vain or for lying in the temple. So I decided that maybe to save further trouble, I'd better lie, too, and say that Jesus had come, and get up and be saved.

So I got up.

Suddenly the whole room broke into a sea of shouting, as they saw me rise. Waves of rejoicing swept the place. Women leaped in the air. My aunt threw her arms around me. The minister took me by the hand and led me to the platform.

When things quieted down, in a hushed silence, punctuated by a few ecstatic "Amens," all the new young lambs were blessed in the name of God. Then joyous singing filled the room.

15   That night, for the last time in my life but one—for I was a big boy twelve years old—I cried. I cried, in bed alone, and couldn't stop. I buried my head under the quilts, but my aunt heard me. She woke up and told my uncle I was crying because the Holy Ghost had come into my life, and because I had seen Jesus. But I was really crying because I couldn't bear to tell her that I had lied, that I had deceived everybody in the church, that I hadn't seen Jesus and that now I didn't believe there was a Jesus any more, since he didn't come to help me.

MAKING CONNECTIONS

1. To what extent is your response to "Mothers" or "Salvation" influenced by your own experience?
2. In "Mothers" what does Quindlen mean when she says, "My mother died when I was nineteen. For a long time, it was all you needed to know about me"? How are you affected by the description of her imagined relationship?
3. In "Salvation" how are you affected by the description of the pressure on young Langston as the only unsaved "lamb"? Do you think young Langston made the right decision? Why?
4. How does the voice of the narrator in each essay affect your response? In what way do the narrators "show" what they tell?
5. What other passages in these essays affect you the most? What details help to make them effective?
6. Can you compare your experience with that in "Mothers" or "Salvation"? Can you compare "Incident," "Eleven," "Mothers," or "Salvation" with each other? For example, "Eleven" and "Salvation" both describe a child in an embarrassing situation. How are they alike and how different?

CONNECTING THROUGH COLLABORATION

In this exercise, you may find it illuminating to share your work with a partner or a small group.

1. If you are jotting down responses to your reading, take a look back through your entries. How many times did a work remind you of someone or something in your own life? If none did at the time you wrote your response, are there entries that bring a comparison to mind now?
2. In a group or with a partner, choose two works from this chapter ("Incident," "Eleven," "Mothers," or "Salvation") and construct a Venn diagram to compare them. How are they alike? How different?
3. Compare your diagrams with those of other groups or partners.

Possible Worlds

The frequent comments and questions about "identifying with characters" or "connecting your experience" in the first two chapters of this text are not suggesting that it is necessary to have had similar experiences or to identify with characters to have a fulfilling experience with literature. In fact, connecting the characters and events in a work too closely with our own lives—so closely that we can't distinguish one from the other—can interfere with our ability to understand and appreciate the work.

When taking us where we have never been, literature has the power to increase the breadth and depth of our vision—to help us learn and grow in the way that all new experiences can. It is not necessary for us to have been embarrassed in school as an eleven-year-old, to have lost our mothers, or to have feigned being "saved" at a church service to be moved by "Eleven," "Mothers," or "Salvation."

The journal responses of Christine Leibowitz below to "Salvation" and "Mothers" illustrate this point. Here is Christine's response to Langston Hughes's "Salvation":

> The essay "Salvation" is wonderful! I remember being saved in ninth grade. There was this boy who went to my church and I thought that he parted the seas, so to speak. One day he invited me to go to Sunday Youth Group with him. I figured that if Shawn went then it couldn't be that bad. And, well, as my parents said, "He was such a nice boy!" So I went.
>
> This essay reminded me of that period of my life. It was funny, as was my own mission. When Langston was kneeling at the altar and everyone was waiting for him to be saved, I thought about how we used to close our eyes in church and the pastor would ask us to raise our hands if we sought salvation and were ready to give our lives to Christ. (Should I raise my hand and get it over with?) It was always a dilemma.
>
> I think Jesus forgave Langston. In fact, I believe that his true salvation was achieved when he lay in bed that night crying for not being honest. He was probably the only lamb of lambs that was truly saved on that blessed day.

Obviously, Christine's ability to identify with young Langston brought this scene vividly to life for her and intensified her reading experience, but this does not mean that she wouldn't have appreciated the essay otherwise.

Here is Christine's response to Anna Quindlen's "Mothers":

> I cannot identify with the speaker of this essay because my mother is alive and well. We share all of the things that the speaker fantasizes about. We laugh together, shop together, share stories and ideas, and give each other advice and criticism. I have a wonderful and warm relationship with my mother. She is the first person I call when something good happens in my life and when I need a shoulder to cry on.
>
> The speaker of the essay lost her mother at age nineteen. She dreams about sharing things with her mother that I would normally take for granted. She speaks of meeting someone in the lobby and describes herself

as "on the short side, have on a red coat, and my mother died when I was nineteen." That is how I think I would describe myself if I had outlived my mother. It is as if she is somehow not a complete person. She calls it "a vest-pocket description of [her] emotional complexion." And for a while "all you needed to know about [her]."

The speaker tries to rationalize that "mothers and daughters probably always see each other across a chasm of rivalries," but I think that she may be trying to compensate for her loss. I am enriched and blessed by my relationship with my mother and what happens in our lives, the love that we share transcends all.

I am so thankful to be able to read this essay knowing that my mother is just a phone call away and waiting to share with me a little bit of everything or a whole bunch of nothing.

In this response, unlike her response to "Salvation," Christine cannot identify with the plight of the speaker in "Mothers" because her own mother is still alive. However, rather than interfering with her response, her different circumstances make Quindlen's essay rich in meaning for her. The essay has taken her to a possible world. Ultimately, it is our intelligence and sensitivity to the human condition, not simply a shared experience, that help us imagine the possibilities and become engaged with the work.

CONNECTING THROUGH COLLABORATION

In this exercise, you may find it illuminating to share your work with a partner or a small group.

1. Take a look back through your responses and select some of your strongest reactions or impressions.
2. If you wrote down details to support your response, do those details adequately convey it? Do those details include specific references to the text?
3. Are there places where you might have clarified your response through a comparison (with other works, characters, people you know, other students' responses)?
4. If you did not write down supporting details or if you did not cite the text for support, go back to the work and see if you can.
5. Exchange your response with a partner or someone else in your group. Discuss the details and comparisons in these responses and their effectiveness.

FROM FIRST RESPONSE TO FINAL DRAFT

In the section that follows, we look at Dierdre Curran's response to Robert Hayden's "Those Winter Sundays" and follow its progress through to the final draft of her essay. Though her goal is to write a response essay, the strategies she illustrates work equally well when planning and generating ideas for a critical essay.

The purpose of the strategies that follow is not to move you step-by-step through a rigid sequence. Whether you are composing a response or a critical essay, writing is a continuous process of moving forward and returning and moving forward again. The best way to organize an essay may occur to you early or late in the process. You may get some of your best new ideas just when you thought you were almost finished. Try to let your ideas flow freely throughout the process. Don't close out ideas by imposing a structure that will keep you from expressing what you would really like to say.

Reading literature encourages a variety of responses—and perhaps more questions than answers. Generate and explore as many of your questions and ideas as possible before you decide on one direction. Free your ideas and follow them where they go. You may be surprised by what you find on your journey.

The Importance of Revision

It may seem odd to bring up revising before you generate ideas for your essay, but if you know in advance that your writing process will include revision and more than one draft, you may be more creative and explore options that you might not otherwise consider. Everything you write is temporary—until you are satisfied that you've "got it right."

Revision is much more than proofreading. It is "re-visioning," rethinking, and rewriting. It means looking at a draft of your essay and determining how the parts you have already constructed work together to form a coherent, convincing whole. It may involve changing the structure of the essay—adding, deleting, combining, or changing the order of paragraphs and sentences. It may mean eliminating redundancies and digressions or adding details and textual support. *Most professional writers think of this part of the writing process as most important.* Many students, however, mistake revision for sentence-level editing or proofreading (e.g., correcting punctuation, sentence structure, spelling, confused words, formatting)—a process that should occur after your revision and rewriting is complete.

Using First or Third Person in Formal Essays

There is much disagreement in the academic world about the use of the first-person pronoun ("I") in formal essay writing. The student sample that follows is written in the first person. Given the nature of the response essay and the personal connection the student makes with the poem, first person is a natural fit. On the other hand, the student samples of the critical essay in Chapter 4 and the research essay in Chapter 5 are written in the third person—a form that works especially well with argumentation and research.

Many instructors, however, require that all essays be written in the third person. It is essential, therefore, that you find out the individual requirements of your instructor and your course before you submit your essay.

STEP 1: *USING YOUR FIRST RESPONSE*

If you've been keeping a journal or writing other initial responses to your reading, chances are you have already generated some good ideas for writing an essay. After you read your entries and add any comments based on rereading and class discussion, go back and underline or circle what you believe are your strongest impressions.

Let's look at Dierdre Curran's initial response to "Those Winter Sundays" (p. 13) as an example:

> I love this poem because I am totally able to relate. <u>It brought so many things back to me about my relationship with my father--some painful, some happy</u>. I grew up in a similar situation, and although there was no love verbally communicated by my gruff father, he always did little things, like getting up early to turn up the heat, digging my car out of the snow and warming it up while I dressed. The day we read this poem in class I got home to find an envelope from my still gruff, uncommunicative father (age has softened him a little). There was no card or letter, just a bunch of coupons, mostly for stuff for my cat, which is his way of sending love. Coupons. It was very nice, and I zipped off a letter of appreciation. I'm glad I still have the opportunity.

STEP 2: *CHOOSING A TOPIC*

When making a choice or choices about which idea(s) to pursue, you may want to answer two essential questions:

1. Do I care enough about this idea to pursue it further?
    You will write with your strongest voice about issues that have the most meaning to you and about which you believe you want to say something that is important for both you and your readers.

2. Is it "do-able"?
    Can you write an essay about this? No matter how compelling your idea is, you won't be able to write an essay about it unless you have enough to say, or you can support it from both your experience and the work (of literature). Remember, if the point you are trying to make is obvious, abstract, or very general, it may be impossible to develop it into an appealing essay in a reasonable amount of time.

STEP 3: *BRAINSTORMING*

Extending Your Ideas

Dierdre chose the second sentence (underlined) from the entry above as the core of her response. It's obvious that she cares about this idea very much. And she feels confident that there are many lines in the poem that she can use to support the comparison between her relationship and that in the poem. But a look at her journal entry tells us that she has not identified many of them yet. Still, her essay seems very "do-able," and her journal entry has given her a start.

Dierdre has already followed her core idea with some specific support from her own experience, but she has not provided much specific support from the text of the poem itself. So if she wants to generate more ideas or extend or expand her support, there are a few other techniques she might use.

Directed Freewriting   If you don't have a journal entry or other initial response, or if you want to generate more ideas, directed freewriting can be a useful technique. The best time to do this exercise is immediately after you finish reading, while your thoughts and impressions are still fresh. The intention of this exercise is to release what you know without blocking it with pauses for reflection, punctuation, or editing.

1. Write down the name of the topic, phrase, or sentence you want to focus on.
2. Write down (nonstop) everything that comes into your mind for five or ten minutes. If punctuation or capitalization gets in the way, don't even use it.
3. Read what you have written and choose (circle or underline) your strongest responses. Here is Dierdre Curran's directed freewriting response to Robert Hayden's "Those Winter Sundays" in response to the sentence from her journal entry: <u>It brought so many things back to me about my relationship with my father—some painful, some happy</u>.

> My father does not express his love for us by telling us. He does things instead. Growing up was really hard I wanted him to tell me he loved me. It has taken me years to believe that he really does even though he never says it. Did the poet ever get to tell his own father about these things. I'll bet not. He sounds as if he regrets not understanding that his father was really expressing love in the things he did. I really like Robert Hayden's descriptions of how the house felt. My house felt the same way. Why did he have to be so cold? But not everything was as bleak as it seems now. There were good times but it just feels not. My father is old now and had a heart attack and only now are we beginning to say what I wish we had said before. I love him so much. I only hope I will have the chance to express before he's gone.

Dierdre's freewriting adds more detail to her earlier statement, and she was able to generate some very compelling ideas about her relationship with her father and her connections to the poem itself. By asking questions about and listing details of the selected statements, she may uncover even more specific material.

Asking Questions   Having already narrowed her choice to a particular idea, she might ask as many questions (and subquestions) as she can about some aspect of that idea. Of course, it's useful to ask only questions that will provide new information (and cannot be answered yes or no).

1. Choose an important word, phrase, or sentence from your journal entry and write down as many related questions as you can.
2. Choose and answer the questions that will add to or clarify your support.

> My father does not express his love for us by telling us.
>
> How often do we talk?
>
> What do we talk about?
>
> How does he express his love?
>
> Where is the similarity in the poem?
>
> I'm glad I still have the opportunity to express appreciation.
>
> Did the speaker in the poem ever get to tell his father what he felt?
>
> How do I/will I express my appreciation?
>
> I really like Robert Hayden's description of the house.
>
> What language does he use?
>
> Why is it effective?

3. Follow up with detailed answers to these questions, and you will provide additional specific support for the original core idea.

Listing   By choosing key words or sentences from your response, and then listing as many related details and examples as you can below them, you can build the specific support you will need to justify your understanding of the literature.

1. Choose key words or sentences from your response (the name of a character, an event, an element of literature, etc.).
2. List as many related details under each as you can. By choosing some key phrases that apply to her identification with the speaker in the poem, Dierdre is able to uncover other specific details.

> My father does things for me instead.
>
> He got up early and turned up the heat.
>
> Dug my car out of the snow and warmed it up.
>
> Sent me envelopes with coupons.
>
> He comforted me when my dog died.
>
> He sometimes laughed and joked around with me and my sister.
>
> He recently sent me the first letter I have ever received from him.
>
> I really like Robert Hayden's description of the house in the poem.
>
> I could feel the pain of the "blueblack cold."
>
> I could feel and hear the cold "splintering, breaking."

Remembering getting dressed quickly in the cold.

Imagining the rooms getting warm.

The house was like their relationship.

Semantic Mapping, or Clustering

For some of us, it is easier to follow directions by looking at a map than following directions in a printed sequence. Sometimes we need to see the whole picture. When writing in response to literature, too, sometimes we can understand, see relationships, and generate and extend ideas better spatially than linearly. A technique called **semantic mapping** or **clustering** makes it possible to see ideas and relationships this way (Figure 2.4). This is how it works:

1. Write down a question or statement in the center of a blank page in your journal or on another piece of paper. Put a circle around it.

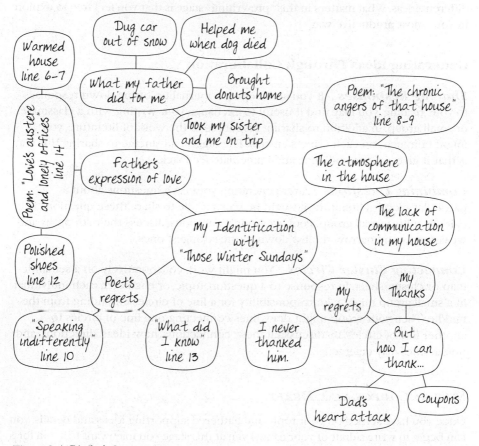

Figure 2.4 *Dierdre's Semantic Map*

2. Draw lines out from the circle and write a statement or idea related to that central idea.

3. Continue to draw lines out from the central circle and the subcircles. Those from the central circle are subsets of ideas; each circle farther along each line is a level of greater specificity.

Mix and Match

The strategies above are not an end in themselves, but simply the means to generate and extend ideas, ask questions, and make choices. They should be used in whatever way they work for you. There is no one "right" way to ask questions or list ideas. If a particular method is working, keep using it. If it is not, try something else. For example, you may find that only the first few circles in a mapping exercise are useful. In order to generate details quickly, you may prefer to list them instead of putting circles around them. So you might want to start with a map, get a few ideas, and then make a list to get at the details. Along with keeping a journal, you may want to freewrite as well. Different ways, combinations, and paces of writing may bring different ideas. What matters in this "prewriting" stage is that you feel free to explore in your most productive way.

Generating Ideas Through Collaboration

Sharing Responses   If you are keeping a journal or jotting down responses to your reading, you may find it useful to exchange your writing with a classmate or small group. In addition to sharing responses to the work of literature, you might comment on each other's entries. The biggest advantage to sharing this way is that it gives you an audience and immediate feedback.

Combining Questions   After generating your own questions about a particular piece of literature, it might be worthwhile to share these questions in pairs or with a small group. Pool everyone's questions, discuss their strengths and weaknesses, and narrow the list down to the strongest ones.

Connecting Cluster Circles   You might work collaboratively on a semantic map or cluster sheet. In response to a question, topic, or character, each individual in a small group might take responsibility for a line of circles extending from the middle. Then your group might draw lines connecting one line of circles to another line of circles. By discussing these connections, new ideas, directions, and possibilities may emerge.

STEP 4: COMPOSING A DRAFT

Once you have settled on your topic and gathered supporting ideas and details, you can begin to write a draft of your essay. Even at this stage you may want to avoid forcing your writing into an inflexible outline. There may be possibilities you haven't thought of, so avoid putting walls around your work just yet.

As in earlier stages of the process, what works best for each of us may be different. Some students may work best by writing this first draft as quickly as possible without stopping and then going back to review and revise when finished. Many students (and probably most experienced writers) find that writing more reflectively at this stage works best for them. And if you have already narrowed your focus to a particular idea and generated lots of details to support it, you may want to proceed with more reflection and review what you have written while you write. You may want to read it out loud to hear how the wording sounds and if the ideas are complete and clear. Evaluating your writing may give you valuable insight into where you need to go.

Once you have narrowed your focus to a particular idea and generated lots of details in support of the idea, you are ready to create a thesis statement. Your thesis statement should incorporate all the evidence that you have, but also be specific enough for you to support. Your thesis statement should also reveal what you intend to show in your essay.

Dierdre's Draft

Earlier in this section, we saw Dierdre Curran's journal entry, freewriting, listing, asking questions, and her semantic map in response to Robert Hayden's "Those Winter Sundays." Let's follow up by looking at a draft of her response essay.

Twice on Sunday

The relationship between parent and child is often a significant one in literature. In his poem "Those Winter Sundays," Robert Hayden illustrates the starkness of one such relationship. The author of this poem is left, as an adult, feeling guilt and regret over never being able to communicate understanding and appreciation of the father's limited demonstrative abilities. I found myself being able to fully relate to the emotions of this poem, as I have a strong personal connection with the situation that is detailed.

The author tells of "fearing the chronic angers of that house." The house I grew up in always seemed filled with anger to me, too. The only communication that ever went on between my parents, myself, and all of my brothers and sisters involved displays of anger; we never had conversations, we had arguments and disagreements. It was a home filled with much bitterness and stress. There was nothing to ever balance it out, no tangible expressions of love from my parents . . . or so I thought until I got a little older and came to understand more.

The author tells of how the father got up early "in the blueblack cold," and then with "cracked hands that ached from labor in the weekday weather made banked fires blaze. No one ever thanked him." My Dad has always been a painfully early riser; he would get up hours before the rest of us had to. In the wintertime, he always made sure that he was up and had turned on the heat so that when the rest of us awoke it was to a warm house. In the winters of my late teens, when I needed his car to get to work, he would always go outside to start it and warm it up. Often he dug it out of a night's snowfall for me, too. I was still reeling from the trauma of my teenage years, so, seething with bitterness, I actually resented him doing me a favor. I never once thanked him for it--I was annoyed by it! My obnoxious, sullen, and ungrateful attitude led me to believe that he was only doing something he was expected to do. My behavior is well described when the author tells how he spoke "indifferently to him, who had driven out the cold."

The poem's author realizes, later in life, that although his father never outwardly expressed his love in so many words, it was expressed through a variety of gestures. Something as simple as shining his son's shoes can be interpreted as an open display of affection. When I think back on my childhood, I realize that although he is a very gruff and restrained man, my father also showed his love in the only ways he knew how.

In retrospect, I realize that my Dad has done many things over the years to convey his affection. When we were very little, I shared a room with my sister Lucy. Sometimes at night if he was in a good mood, right before we went to bed, my Dad would pretend that he was Frankenstein. He would close his eyes and stretch out his arms in front of him, walking like a fictional monster. He would chase us to our beds, approaching slowly, while we shrieked in terrified laughter, running from him. When he finally caught us, we got tickled to the point of hysteria, and then it was time for bed.

The worst day of my life was when I had to put my fifteen-year-old diabetic dog, Freebie, to sleep. The guilt has never left me. No one in my family would go with me to the vet. When my best friend, John, came to the house that morning to drive me and the dog, my mother wouldn't even come downstairs, but at least my father said goodbye to her. He was the only one that was as upset as I was, and I was crushed, only he never showed it. The day I brought her ashes back to throw around the yard, he found me in the house crying hysterically; I was totally heartbroken. The day I brought Freebie back home for the last time and fell apart in the backyard, my father's only way of acknowledging my grief was to come outside and yell at me. He just stood there and kept yelling, and I just sat there and kept crying.

Finally he got quiet and told me that he missed the dog as much as me, and hadn't gone with me because he didn't have the guts to do what I had done. Then he helped me up and walked me up the driveway, hugging me for the very first time in memory.

My parents moved to Indiana. A few weeks ago, my oldest sister called to tell me that my father had suffered a heart attack. I was basically floored, and promptly drank a bottle and a half of Merlot. While I was sucking that down, I was crying hysterically. Two very long days later, I was on a plane to see him, even though he tried to tell me it was not necessary because he was doing so well. I had to see for myself. The plane trip was hellacious. It took twelve hours to get there, and the delays were torture. I made it to the hospital ten minutes before visiting hours ended on my birthday. As I rushed down the hall frantically toward his room, I heard him call out my name in excited surprise and saw him slowly hurrying toward me, pale, be-tubed and in his hospital gown. I could not believe how happy he was to see me; it made the whole trip worth it. He repeatedly held my hand and offered me his cheek for a kiss, every couple of minutes. When he asked me "what in the hell" I was doing out there, my reply was that I had the day off anyway and decided to come see him for my birthday. He had a good laugh at that one. He was a much less gruff man than the last time I had seen him.

Never in my life has my father verbally expressed his love. In younger years I was blind to the fact that he just doesn't know how, but that he shows it in other ways. That used to make me so mad and frustrated. But he has mellowed with the coming of grandchildren and his own older age, and I have opened my eyes and learned to appreciate the gestures and to interpret their meaning. In "Those Winter Sundays," the author tells of the guilt of his own ignorance of "love's austere and lonely offices." While I can't imagine the day either one of us is ever able to actually say "I love you" to the other one, I am secure in the knowledge that it is mutually understood. We still don't talk about personal feelings, although now that his health has dealt him a major wake-up call I see that changing a little. This past month has marked the first letter he ever wrote to me--three pages about the weather, constantly interjected with <u>SO THERE</u>! in large, capital underlined letters. I also received my very first birthday card, which not only did he sign himself, he signed it with "Love." Of course, it doesn't say "Love, Dad," it says "Love,

J.C."--his initials. I laughed when I read it, and I was thrilled that he has been able to make so much progress.

The author of this poem conveys some universal feelings of guilty realization that I think all children reach as they become adults. I am just thankful that I have been given the time and opportunity in life to establish a bond with my father that I am not sure any of his other children have the privilege of sharing. I love him very much, and I have a relationship with him that may seem comparatively odd to other people, but that I treasure. Luckily I also have the sense of humor that is necessary to appreciate it.

STEP 5: *REVISION*

Rethinking, "re-visioning," and rewriting are just as important for a response essay about literature as they are for any other kind of writing. Having discovered what you want to say, you can now focus on how well you have said it. How well is your draft organized? Does it have unnecessary or redundant information? Are there gaps that need to be filled in? Are there enough details? Is there enough support from the work of literature? Have you expressed yourself as clearly as possible?

✓ **CHECKLIST: REVISION**

Organization and Unity

❏ Do all the paragraphs relate to the central thesis?

❏ Is the organization of those paragraphs within the essay clear?

❏ Do each of the sentences within the paragraphs relate to the central idea of the paragraph?

Support

❏ Are there enough details to support or clarify your assertions? Have you "shown" what you've told?

❏ Are there enough quotes from the work of literature to support your assertions?

❏ Are the paragraphs fully developed?

❏ Is the essay fully developed? Have you accounted for all aspects of your thesis statement?

Clarity

❏ Is the central thesis of the essay clearly stated?

❏ Does the title of your essay account for your thesis?

❑ Is the language clear?

❑ Are there redundancies, digressions, or meaningless phrases that could be cut?

❑ Is the essay written in the format required by your instructor? Have you documented your references to the text and included a list of works cited?

Voice

❑ Does it sound like you? When you read it out loud, can you hear your voice and emotion?

Revising Dierdre's Draft

Organization and Unity   One of the most effective ways of checking the organization of a draft is by doing an **after-draft outline.** Go back to each paragraph and find the controlling idea. List the main ideas they represent, one after the other. This should give you an outline of your draft.

Let's look at an outline of Dierdre's draft:

> Paragraph #1. Introduction and Thesis Statement--I found myself being able to fully relate to the emotions of this poem.
>
> Paragraph #2. The house I grew up in always seemed filled with anger too.
>
> Paragraphs #3 and #4. Both my father and the poet's father expressed their love in the same way.
>
> Paragraph #5. My father has done things to express his love.
>
> Paragraph #6. The worst day of my life is also my fondest memory of my father.
>
> Paragraph #7. My parents moved to Indiana, and two weeks ago, my father had a heart attack.
>
> Paragraph #8. I didn't understand when I was younger--now I know.
>
> Paragraph #9. We still don't talk about personal feelings, but our relationship is better.
>
> Paragraph #10. Conclusion--I'm glad I've had the chance the poet missed.

When Dierdre looked at her list, she was concerned that she might have too many paragraphs. For the most part, the organization of her essay followed the pattern of the poem itself. She compared her relationship with her father to that of the poet's with his father. She took lines from the poem and then commented on how each matched her experience. *This pattern made sense to her, but it appeared that several of these paragraphs were too long and unwieldy.*

Showing Support   The support Dierdre used in this essay came from two sources: the poem and her personal experience. She supported her references to the text by quoting the poem. She supported references to her experience by giving examples. *She believed she had enough support in both cases and that her examples firmly established the connection.*

Clarity   Dierdre realized that she would have to tighten up her language by deleting unnecessary words, expressions, and sentences. After cutting and combining, she could decide if some of the paragraphs should be combined as well. *She also realized that her choice of words did not always express what she meant. In paragraphs 4 and 5 in particular, she decided that cutting, combining, and reordering some of the examples would strengthen the pace and organization of the essay.*

Her most difficult decision was what to cut. She wanted her essay to be clearly expressed and tightly organized, but she didn't want to sacrifice the concrete details and scenes that gave it a strong voice.

Voice   She believed that one of the strengths of this piece was its voice, a voice which "showed" through quotes and examples. Her biggest task was to maintain a strong voice throughout the essay while tightening up her prose overall.

FORMATTING AND DOCUMENTING YOUR ESSAY

Before you submit the final draft of your essay, check with your instructor for the format you are required to follow when you submit your essay. *For more detail, see the directory of MLA Formatting and Documentation in Appendix C (p. 1345). The student essay that follows on page 50 provides examples for many of the basics listed below.*

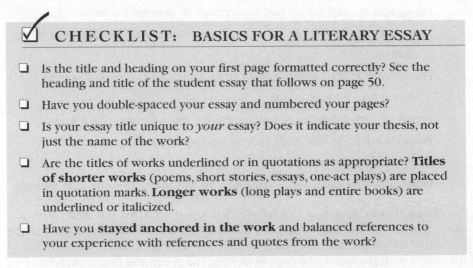

☑ CHECKLIST: BASICS FOR A LITERARY ESSAY

❏ Is the title and heading on your first page formatted correctly? See the heading and title of the student essay that follows on page 50.

❏ Have you double-spaced your essay and numbered your pages?

❏ Is your essay title unique to *your* essay? Does it indicate your thesis, not just the name of the work?

❏ Are the titles of works underlined or in quotations as appropriate? **Titles of shorter works** (poems, short stories, essays, one-act plays) are placed in quotation marks. **Longer works** (long plays and entire books) are underlined or italicized.

❏ Have you **stayed anchored in the work** and balanced references to your experience with references and quotes from the work?

❏ Have you **introduced quotes** with your own language—integrating them smoothly into your own writing? Use ellipses (three spaced periods) to indicate omitted material within a quotation (see p. 184). Use brackets to indicate that you have added your own language (see p. 184).

❏ Have you avoided **unnecessary plot summary?**

❏ Have you **referred to authors by their full or last names**—not their first names? Have you used **present-tense verbs** to describe the characters and events in the work?

❏ Have you acknowledged all your sources? When quoting **poetry,** have you cited line numbers (1–5)? When quoting **fiction and nonfiction prose** or **modern drama,** have you indicated page numbers (26)? When quoting **verse drama,** have you indicated act, scene, and line numbers (3.1. 15–20)?

❏ Have you placed *periods and commas* **inside quotation marks?** Have you placed other punctuation outside quotation marks when appropriate?

❏ Have you cited your sources correctly in the text of your essay? Have you followed your essay with a **Work(s) Cited** to indicate the work or works you have cited in your essay? Is it in the correct format? See Appendix C.

Editing or proofreading is a crucial final step in the process of producing an essay. In addition to making any changes that did not occur to you earlier and fine-tuning your writing, it's essential to check your essay for correct grammar, spelling, punctuation, and typos.

☑ CHECKLIST: EDITING AND PROOFREADING

❏ Are all of your sentences complete sentences?

❏ Are all of your sentences punctuated appropriately?

❏ Are the words spelled correctly? Have you checked for easily confused words (then/than, your/you're, its/it's, etc.)?

❏ Are you sure of the meaning of all the words you've used?

❏ Are there particular errors you have a tendency to make? Have you looked for those in this essay?

Remember, computer spell checkers do not make choices about word usage. Confused words (than/then, there/their/they're, etc.) will not be flagged by a spell checker. You will have to use your own eyes and judgment to correct those errors.

STEP 6: *DIERDRE'S REVISED ESSAY*

After rewriting her introduction to make it clearer, Dierdre cut many words and phrases, combined many sentences, and shifted some of her examples. After reading this clearer, shorter version, she decided to stay with the same number of paragraphs. She could have combined several of them but decided not to. The resulting paragraphs would have been too long and much more difficult for the reader to absorb.

Dierdre Curran

Prof. Madden

English 102

Fall 200X

Twice on Sunday

In his poem "Those Winter Sundays," Robert Hayden illustrates the starkness of his relationship with his father. As a child, he was never able to understand or appreciate what his father did for him. As an adult, he feels guilt and regret because it is too late to communicate his appreciation. I have experienced a similar relationship, and I can relate strongly to the emotions expressed in this poem.

The poet tells of "fearing the chronic angers of that house" (9). The house I grew up in always seemed filled with anger to me, too. We never had conversations; we had arguments and disagreements. There was nothing to ever balance it out, no tangible expressions of love from my parents . . . or so I thought until I got a little older and came to understand more.

He begins the poem by writing:

> Sundays too my father got up early
>
> and put his clothes on in the blueblack cold,
>
> then with cracked hands that ached
>
> from labor in the weekday weather made
>
> banked fires blaze. No one ever thanked him. (1-5)

In the wintertime, my dad was always up before the rest of us and had turned on the heat so that we awoke to a warm house. When I was older and needed his car to get to work, he would always go outside to start and warm it up. Often he dug it out of a night's snowfall. Reeling from the trauma of my teenage years and seething with bitterness, I actually resented his doing me a favor. I never once thanked him for it. I was annoyed and believed that he was only doing something he was expected to do. My behavior is well described when Hayden tells how he spoke "indifferently to him / who had driven out the cold" (10-11).

Later in life, the poet realizes that while his father never expressed his love in words, he expressed it through a variety of gestures, like shining his son's shoes. When I recall my childhood, I realize that my father also showed his love in the only ways he knew how. When we were very little, I shared a room with my sister Lucy. Sometimes at night if he was in a good mood, right before we went to bed, my Dad would pretend that he was Frankenstein. He would close his eyes and stretch out his arms in front of him, walking like the fictional monster, approaching slowly, while we shrieked in terrified laughter, running from him. When he finally caught us, we got tickled to the point of hysteria.

The worst day of my life is also my fondest memory of my father. It was the day I had to put my fifteen-year-old, diabetic dog Freebie to sleep. The guilt has never left me. No one in my family would go with me to the vet. At least my father said goodbye to her. He was the only one who was as upset as I was, and I was crushed. He never showed it. When I brought her ashes back to throw around the yard, he found me in the house crying hysterically. I was totally heartbroken. No one hugged me, no one said, "I'm sorry." My father's only way of acknowledging my grief was to come outside and yell at me. He just stood there and kept yelling, and I just sat there and kept crying. Finally, he got quiet and told me that he missed the dog as much as I did, and hadn't gone with me because he didn't have the guts to do what I had done. Then he helped me up and walked me up the driveway, hugging me for the first time I can remember.

After I graduated from high school, my parents moved to Indiana. A few weeks ago, my oldest sister called to tell me that my father had suffered a heart attack. I was floored. Two very long days later, I was on a plane to see him. The plane trip was horrible. It took twelve hours to get there, and the delays were torture. I didn't care about the inclement weather or the size of the plane. I didn't care about anything but getting to South Bend as soon as I could. I made it to the hospital on my birthday, ten minutes before visiting hours ended. As I rushed down the hall looking frantically for his room, I heard him call out my name in excited surprise and saw him slowly hurrying toward me, pale, be-tubed and in his hospital gown. I could not believe how happy he was to see me. It made the whole trip worth it. He repeatedly held my hand and offered me his cheek for a kiss every couple of minutes. When he asked me "what in the hell" I was doing out there, I replied that I had the day off anyway, and decided to come see him for my birthday. He had a good laugh at that one. He seemed much less gruff than the last time I had seen him.

Never in my life has my father verbally expressed his love. In younger years I was blind to the fact that he just didn't know how, but that he showed it in other ways. That used to make me so mad and frustrated. But he has mellowed with the coming of age and grandchildren, and I have opened my eyes and learned to appreciate his gestures, and to interpret their meaning. In "Those Winter Sundays," the poet tells of the guilt of his own ignorance "of love's austere and lonely offices" (14). While I can't imagine the day when we will ever be able to actually say "I love you" to each other, I am secure in the knowledge that it is mutually understood.

We still don't talk about personal feelings, but now that his health has dealt him a major wake-up call, I see that changing a little. This past month has marked the first letter he ever wrote to me--three pages about the weather, constantly interjected with <u>SO THERE</u>! in large, capital underlined letters. I also received my very first birthday card. Not only did he sign it himself, but he signed it with love. Of course, it doesn't say "Love, Dad," it says "Love, J.C."--his initials. I laughed when I read it, and I was thrilled that he has been able to make so much progress.

In "Those Winter Sundays," Robert Hayden conveys feelings of guilt that I think most children experience as they become adults. I am just thankful that I have been given the time and the opportunity in life to establish a bond with my father. I love him very much, and I have a relationship with him that may seem comparatively odd to other people, but it's one that I treasure. Luckily, I also have the sense of humor that is necessary to appreciate it.

[New Page]

Work Cited

Hayden, Robert. "Those Winter Sundays." <u>Exploring Literature</u>. Ed. Frank
  Madden. 3rd ed. New York: Longman, 2007. 13.

PART II

ANALYSIS, ARGUMENTATION, AND RESEARCH

Chapter 3

Exploration and Analysis
Genre and the Elements of Literature

To analyze anything is to look closely at how it works—to examine its parts. Our intention in this chapter, however, is not to reduce literature to parts. *Our goal is to provide you with tools to articulate and develop your responses into effective critical essays.*

We know that the parts of a literary work alone cannot account for its meaning, a meaning that fully blossoms only as the parts work together. Once you've experienced the whole of the work, however, reading it carefully and analyzing its parts can tell you a great deal about it—and how it triggered your response. Analysis is an important step in interpreting or evaluating literature, and it is through this process that you may gather the support to make your opinion an informed one.

CLOSE READING

Analysis requires close reading. In a way the term *close reading* means the opposite of what it sounds like. When we read closely, we step back. We move from being inside the work to looking at it from the outside, from participating to observing. This process requires a careful reading and a conscious examination of the elements of the work and how they contribute to its overall meaning. *A close reading is not a first reading, it is a rereading.* When you return to read the literature or your notes again after discussion in class, you are doing a close reading. You have already stepped back from your own views to hear the responses of others. You are reading your notes and the work informed by what you have learned from those discussions.

ANNOTATING THE TEXT

An effective way to do a close reading of fiction, poetry, drama, or essays is to mark up the text by underlining, circling, highlighting, or making notes in the margins. You may even find it useful to make these annotations in more than one stage. In the first stage you might want to concentrate on your understanding of the text by summarizing, noting words or passages you don't understand, and asking questions—exploring the text. Later on, as you narrow your focus, you may want to identify elements of the text, patterns, evidence, or quotations to support your thesis—analyzing the text. If you don't want to mark up the pages of your book, make a copy of the work and do your annotations on this copy. Or write your annotations on Post-it notes and attach them in the margins of the work.

The following example illustrates a two-stage process of annotating a poem.

First Annotation: Exploration

PERCY BYSSHE SHELLEY [1792-1822]

OZYMANDIAS   [1818]

I met a traveler from an antique land   *What does he mean "trunkless legs"?*
Who said: "Two vast and trunkless legs of stone
Stand in the desert . . . Near them on the sand,   *Look up visage.*
Half-sunk, a shattered visage lies, whose frown   *"cold command"—a ruler?*
And wrinkled lip, and sneer of cold command,   5
Tell that its sculptor well those passions read   *A sculptor—a statue?*
Which yet survive, stamped on these lifeless things,
The <u>hand that mocked</u> them, and the <u>heart that fed</u>   *Hand that mocked & heart that fed—How does "hand" differ from "heart"?*
And on the pedestal these words appear
'My name is Ozymandias, king of kings.   *Summary—He met someone*   10
Look on my works, ye Mighty, and despair!'   *from a faraway country who*
Nothing beside remains. Round the decay   *saw an ancient, large, broken*
Of that colossal wreck, boundless and bare   *statue with an arrogant*
The lone and level sands stretch far away."   *statement on it.*

This first annotation is an exploration of your first reading. You may clarify what you understand and ask questions about what you don't understand, or indicate what you need to know more about. You might make guesses, note impressions, summarize, and, in general, give yourself something to think about when you begin a second reading.

Second Annotation: Analysis

PERCY BYSSHE SHELLEY [1792–1822]

OZYMANDIAS   [1818]

I met a traveler from an antique land
Who said: "Two vast and trunkless legs of stone
Stand in the desert . . . Near them on the sand,
Half-sunk, a shattered visage lies, whose frown
And wrinkled lip, and sneer of cold command,   5
Tell that its sculptor well those passions read
Which yet survive, stamped on these lifeless things,
The <u>hand</u> that mocked them, and the <u>heart</u> that <u>fed</u>
And on the pedestal these words appear
'My name is Ozymandias, king of kings.   10
Look on my works, ye Mighty, and despair!'
Nothing beside remains. Round the decay
Of that colossal wreck, boundless and bare
The lone and level sands stretch far away."

Handwritten annotations:

How does this compare with other Shelley poems I've read? What was going on in England at this time? Who was the king?

Why "antique" and not just "old" or "ancient"?

The rhyme scheme: abab—"land and sand" / "stone" and "frown"?

Not just grand, but arrogant as well.

"read" and "fed" rhyme, but not "command" and "things." The hand of the sculptor/the heart of the king?

A powerful image—decayed and worn-out grandeur and arrogance in a desert.

Rhymes: despair/bare—decay/away
What a powerful ironic contrast!

The second annotation is a closer reading and more analytical. Here you might look for some of the elements of literature we discuss in this chapter, try to find patterns, seek evidence to support your early conclusions, or even place the work within a larger historical, social, or biographical context.

LITERATURE IN ITS MANY CONTEXTS

Our focus on textual analysis in this chapter—on genres and their elements—is not an attempt to limit the scope of your writing to types of literature or parts of the work alone. Those parts and those works exist in a larger world—a context framed by personal, cultural, historical, biographical, and other influences. Seeing beyond the work to the contexts that influenced its writing—and your reading—may enliven and enrich your experience of the work and help you produce a more interesting essay.

Your Critical Approach

What you value most about literature, your critical stance, can be an important factor in determining what you analyze and write about when interpreting and evaluating literature. Critical approaches are broadly classified as reader based (emphasizing the reader's response and the text), text based (emphasizing the text), context based (emphasizing the background of the work), and author based (emphasizing connections to the author's life or intentions). Whatever approach you take may determine the strategy and terms you use in your writing. For a more comprehensive explanation of these approaches see Appendix A (p. 1331). Keep in mind that critical approaches may easily overlap, and critics often combine them in their analyses. The difference between one critical stance and another may be more a matter of emphasis than kind, and drawing upon several approaches can yield a rich interpretation.

READING AND ANALYZING FICTION

Telling stories and listening to stories seem to be a natural part of our lives. When we meet with friends to hear about an experience, "just the facts" won't do. We want to hear the stories that give meaning to those facts. Why do we read and listen to stories? What kind of experience do we expect to have when we sit down to read a short story or "curl up with a good book"? Many of us might say that we want to "escape" from the stress of everyday life. But in this highly complex world there are many other ways to escape. What is it about the experience of reading a good story that makes it unique and draws us to it?

Beyond an escape, reading a story brings us to a place in our imaginations where we can live through the experience of others. Prompted by the author's words, we imagine the scenes, characters, and conflicts. We take the chances, feel the emotions, and share the insights—but without suffering the risks or consequences that living through them ourselves might bring.

Stories and storytelling have been an important part of every culture since people first roamed the earth. Before there was written language to record them, people shared stories orally and passed them down to their descendants. Even today, these stories convey the "truths" of many cultures and religions and give meaning to the lives of millions of people.

Fiction and Truth   In many ways, the designation "fiction" is misleading. Most fiction tells a story that is "made up"—or at least the specific details of the story probably did not occur in exactly the way described, in this place, at this time, to characters with these names. The most important quality of good fiction, though, is the truth or truths it tells—about being human and struggling to make sense of a complex world. The truth of fiction transcends fact. In it we see a model of our own struggle, a model not limited by the daily news of specific time and place and fact.

NARRATION

The narrator is the storyteller, the intermediary who shapes and flavors the story for us. Try to distinguish between the author of the story and the narrator, or speaker. The narrator has been created by the author with a particular effect in mind. As you can imagine, *who* tells the story and *how* it is told can make a big difference. The same story told from a different point of view or with a different voice affects everything we experience as we read.

Point of View

Think about the last time you watched a concert or sports event on television. Can you recall how many different camera shots you were shown? When the camera gave you a distant shot, you could see a large part of the arena and most of the performers. You could see what no one performer could see. But you could not experience what it was like to be in the middle of the action. Only a close-up camera shot could help you feel the physical energy, the emotion, and give you the perspective of an individual performer. But, of course, by isolating your view to one performer, you lost the larger view of the entire event. Directors, camera operators, and announcers make choices about which perspectives work best at given times. From any of these distances and angles the event we witness is the same, but the point of view we have makes our experience of it quite different.

In similar fashion, our reading of fiction is strongly influenced by the narrator's point of view. *Point of view is the perspective from which the narrator tells the story.* Generally, the pronoun that dominates the narration signals which point of view is represented. The terms most commonly used to identify point of view are first person; third-person limited, omniscient, or objective; and shifting.

Authors, like directors or camera operators, make choices about which point of view will convey the story most effectively. In Sandra Cisneros's short story "Eleven," (p. 26) for example, we experience the humiliation of the young girl from her perspective—so "close up" that we share what she thinks and feels. The author might have chosen to describe the event through a narrator who was looking on or from the viewpoint of the teacher or another student in her class. But because we see the event through the girl's eyes, we experience her pain as if it is happening to us. From any of these perspectives the event remains the same, but in each case our experience of it is quite different.

First person uses the pronoun *I* and places the narrator in the story. We see through the view of that character (as an announcer and camera might isolate what we see to the view of one performer). The narrator sees through that character's eyes (as a camera sees through a performer's eyes). We see what he or she sees. As readers, we will only know what this one person experiences. The short story "A&P" (p. 490) is a good example of first-person point of view. The action and the characters in this story are described solely through the eyes and mind of one character, Sammy. Because of its very limited perspective, however, we rely completely on the credibility of the narrator, so the **reliability** of that narrator is a crucial factor. Are there discrepancies between what we are being told and your own judgment of the same events or characters in the story? For example, our response to a story like "The Yellow Wallpaper" (p. 725) is very dependent on our judgment of the narrator's stability.

Third person uses the pronouns *he* or *she,* but usually limits us to one character's view. The narrator does not see through the character's eyes but focuses on the character and what he or she sees and thinks. Specifically, this is called **third-person**

limited point of view. The narrative perspective of Liliana Heker's story "The Stolen Party" (p. 459) is third-person limited. The narrator describes the action and the characters from the distance of third person, but limits us to the thoughts of one character, Rosaura. **Third-person omniscient point of view** also uses the pronouns *he, she,* and *they,* but the narrator is "all knowing" and able to move in and out of the mind of more than one character, choosing what and when to share. Kate Chopin's "Désirée's Baby" (p. 951) is an example of third-person omniscient. **Third-person objective point of view** minimizes the intervention of the narrator. The setting and the action are described, and we "listen in" on the dialogue, but the narrator does not interpret for us. We must do that ourselves. Hemingway's "Hills Like White Elephants" (p. 745) is written in objective point of view. The narrator describes the setting, the characters, and the action from a distance while we seem to overhear their conversation from a neighboring table. Stories with **shifting point of view** may shift from the narrowly focused first person or third-person limited to the broad spectrum of omniscient narration.

Voice refers to the narrator's persona, the personality that seems to come alive in the words. It is quite possible to have the same point of view but very different voices. The short stories "A&P" and "The Yellow Wallpaper" both have a first-person point of view, but the voice of the brash nineteen-year-old Sammy in "A&P" is very different from that of the troubled narrator in "The Yellow Wallpaper."

For a concise checklist of questions for Narration, see page 66.

SETTING

In literature, **setting** *is the location and the atmosphere of the story.* It has a direct and indirect impact on character and conflict; it supports and emphasizes the story's meaning. Its most important function is to make us feel present in the world that the characters inhabit. The more we can visualize, the more we participate, the more satisfying the experience.

In our own lives, the places and company we seek have much to do with how we want to feel. When we want to relax, we go somewhere informal and familiar. When hungry but with little time to eat, we may go to a bare and efficient place where they serve fast food. On a dinner date, however, we are more likely to seek a restaurant with a sophisticated, romantic atmosphere.

If you were asked to describe the setting you are in right now, what factors would go into your description? Would you include more than its physical features? Setting is more than just physical surroundings. It includes the atmosphere, and atmosphere changes regularly. The weather, lighting, and time of day or night may change it. The people present may change it. Who are they? What is our relationship to them? Are we or they happy or sad? Can you "cut the tension with a knife"? Permanent factors, like physical qualities, are a "shell" for this atmosphere, but those factors that vary (people, time, weather, task) strongly influence a setting too.

Location tells us where and when the story is taking place. John Updike's "A&P" (p. 490), set in the 1960s in suburban Massachusetts, has a very different feel to it than James Joyce's "Araby" (p. 463), set in Dublin in the 1890s, or John

Steinbeck's "The Chrysanthemums" (p. 1208), set in rural California in the 1930s. Both the *where* and the *when* will strongly influence the values and behavior of the characters and color the rest of the story.

Atmosphere in a story arises from the mix of location and variable circumstances, such as the personalities present, the conflict, time of day, season, and even the weather. An effectively rendered atmosphere helps us see and experience concrete details of the setting as if we were present. It supports and complements the conflict and characters and helps to convey the story's meaning.

For a concise checklist of questions for Setting, see page 66.

CONFLICT

In literature, **conflict** *is the struggle of opposing external or internal forces.* Conflict is at the heart of every story. In fact, without it we don't have a story—at least not one most of us would want to hear or read. The impediments and complications of conflict keep us reading. The more important, challenging, believable, and coherent the conflict is, the more we are engaged by the story and want to follow it to its conclusion.

In our own lives, we spend a good portion of every day resolving conflicts. Most of them are so small we don't even think of them as conflicts. We solve them easily without much effort or anxiety. We get up in the morning when we don't feel like it. We wait patiently for the traffic light to change before we go forward. The solutions and consequences are clear. If we stay in bed, we'll lose pay or miss important information in class. If we go through the red light, we might kill someone. There is not much internal strife here. And these dilemmas are not likely to make compelling stories.

As the conflicts become more complex, however, our anxiety increases and the choices seem more difficult: "What classes will I take next semester?" "How will I get to school tomorrow?" "Should I ask that person for a date?" Increase the complexity to another level and we get: "Should I stay in school next semester?" "Will I have to buy a car?" "Should I get married?" As the stakes are raised, our internal conflict increases. As you might imagine, the internal nature of conflict also has a lot to do with the personalities of the people involved. For people who are sensitive and shy, asking for a date may be a major conflict. The possibility of being rejected may cause great anxiety. For someone very depressed, even getting out of bed may seem like a major accomplishment.

External conflict may be physical (characters against nature) or social (characters against each other or against society). **Internal conflict** is a struggle of opposing forces within a character. The best stories contain elements of both types of conflict, but the emphasis is usually on internal conflict.

Internal conflict has much to do with the makeup of the characters in the story. Consider the personality of each character. What provokes an internal conflict in one person may go unnoticed by another. A character who is insecure and self-conscious is likely to react very differently to some situations than a character who is confident and self-absorbed.

PLOT

Plot is the structure of the story. It is the pattern of twists and turns the story takes. Most plots spring from conflict. To have a discernible plot, we must have impediments and complications for the work to take the twists and turns necessary to keep us reading.

When we share our own stories we structure them not only to convey the facts but also to have maximum impact. We might withhold information until later for the effect it will have on our listeners. We don't jump to answer the plea: So what happened!? We might say, "Hold on, I'm getting there, but you have to hear this part first to get a good sense of what happened later." We are naturally sensitive to the way that the arrangement of the details adds suspense or helps the listener "to be there" and feel the experience.

One traditional arrangement of plot in a short story follows a pattern of exposition, rising action, crisis (sometimes called climax), falling action, and resolution (sometimes called denouement or untying).

The diagram of this structure in Figure 3.1 is a bit misleading. Even stories that contain these elements in their plots are generally not balanced so evenly. The crisis, for example, rarely falls right in the middle of the story. The bulk of most stories is spent building (exposition and rising action) to the crisis. Once the crisis is reached, the story usually winds down (falling action and resolution) quickly.

Many television shows and crime stories are classic examples of this formula. In the early days of TV, Erle Stanley Gardner's *Perry Mason* mysteries were turned into a television series. As seen in the following excerpt, each episode fit this pattern especially well—so well it was easy to work in commercial breaks between stages of the plot as if they were part of the show.

> *Exposition:* A desperate client appears at the office of famous defense attorney Perry Mason, reveals that a hideous crime has been committed (usually murder), indicates that he or she is a suspect, and proclaims innocence. Perry confers with his secretary and confidant, Della Street, and calls in private detective Paul Burke. In the course of these deliberations, we (the viewers or readers) find out about the circumstances, characters, and conflict of the story. (*Commercial break*)

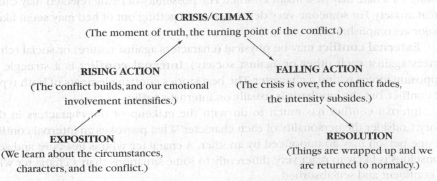

CRISIS/CLIMAX
(The moment of truth, the turning point of the conflict.)

RISING ACTION
(The conflict builds, and our emotional involvement intensifies.)

FALLING ACTION
(The crisis is over, the conflict fades, the intensity subsides.)

EXPOSITION
(We learn about the circumstances, characters, and the conflict.)

RESOLUTION
(Things are wrapped up and we are returned to normalcy.)

Figure 3.1 *Plot Structure*

Rising Action: The client is arrested and charged with the hideous crime. The conflict builds as a motive is established and overwhelming circumstantial evidence mounts. Meanwhile, Paul desperately seeks information and other suspects and the setting shifts to the courtroom. The conflict intensifies: the suspense increases. (*Commercial break*)

Crisis or Climax: In the courtroom, the district attorney continues to build an ironclad case against the defendant. Occasionally private eye Paul enters the courtroom and passes notes to Perry. Perry occasionally sends Della on an errand. The crucial moment occurs when Perry calls the real killer (or an accomplice) to the stand and he or she breaks down under his scrutiny and the weight of the newly discovered evidence (gathered by the relentless Paul) and confesses to the crime. (*Commercial break*)

Falling Action: The murderer reveals motive and method. (*Commercial break*)

Resolution: Perry reveals how the good guys found out the truth and shares a joke with Della, Paul, and the grateful, relieved former defendant. Justice is done, and all return to normalcy. (*End of show*)

Consider some of your favorite television shows. Do they have predictable plot structures? Can you describe them? How well do they work?

A major impediment to finding a traditional plot structure is that it doesn't fit some of the best fiction. In many works of fiction, the crisis or climax occurs at the end of the story. Things are not wrapped up for us. There is no intention to provide us with a resolution. Life doesn't come in episodes that resolve conflict so neatly. Stories that intend to capture life as it is don't "wrap up" so neatly either. Joyce's "Araby" (p. 463), Steinbeck's "The Chrysanthemums" (p. 1208), Updike's "A&P" (p. 490), Bobbie Ann Mason's "Shiloh" (p. 762), and many other stories don't fit this pattern. Most of these stories reach their crisis or climax and end when the protagonist or central character sees beyond a comforting illusion and confronts painful reality. After this climax there is no resolution—nor would we want one.

For a concise checklist of questions for Conflict and Plot, see page 66.

CHARACTER

Do you remember the first day of class? Surrounded by unfamiliar faces, you may have wondered, Who are these people? Even the instructor may have been unfamiliar to you. By the end of that class, though, you had probably formed many impressions. You had some sense of what your classmates were like, perhaps even which ones you might like to know better. Some of those impressions may have come from *what* your classmates said about themselves and *how* they said it. But it's unlikely, even if they described themselves, that they told you what to think or feel about them. That was your decision. You probably decided what to think of them on the basis of their appearances, what they did, what they said, how they said it, and what others said about them. You wouldn't have settled for being told what to think; you wanted to see for yourself.

***Characterization** is the development of characters in a story.* At its best, the author brings characters to life and lets us "get to know them" as we know people in our own lives. While the narrator may tell us some things directly about the characters, we find out much of what we know indirectly through action and dialogue. We are not told what to think or feel about them. We observe the characters thinking, speaking, and doing. We hear what others say about them. They seem believable and motivated. And like our responses to people in our own lives, our reactions and judgments are based on our own observations.

The main character in a story is called the **protagonist.** When we find a character or characters who seem to be a major force in opposition to the protagonist, that character or characters is called the **antagonist** or **antagonists.** For example, the protagonist in Sandra Cisneros's short story "Eleven" (p. 26) is the young girl who narrates the story. The antagonist is Mrs. Price, who humiliates her in front of her classmates. In Ralph Ellison's "Battle Royal" (p. 448), the protagonist is the young man who narrates the story. The antagonists are "the town's leading white citizens," who degrade him at their brutally racist ceremony.

When characters lack the development that seems to bring them to life, lack the complexity that lets us know them as we know people in our own lives, and seem to represent "types" more than real personalities, they are called **flat** or **stock characters.** When they seem fully developed, with all the complexities of real people, they are described as **round characters.**

For a concise checklist of questions for Characterization, see page 66.

LANGUAGE AND STYLE

It's not possible to separate language and style from other elements. Language is the vehicle that carries narration, setting, conflict, plot, characterization, and theme to you. The formal or informal style of the language is an integral part of narration. The evocative nature of the language used to describe setting has so much to do with our visualization and response to it. The style of the language used by the characters tells us a great deal about who they are. And the symbolic nature of the language may complement and support the story's theme or meaning.

Diction

The type of language narrators and characters use, their **diction,** tells us a lot about them and establishes their voices. Their use of formal or informal vocabulary or non-standard words or phrases may tell us about their education or place in society. The frequency of images and figurative language in the narration may also have an effect on our reading and response to a story.

Symbol

A **symbol** is something that represents more than itself. Just about anything in a story might be symbolic. In fiction, symbols are most likely to be objects, names, or places, but they might be actions, sounds, or colors as well.

Irony

Irony is a contrast between appearance/expectation and reality. The two most popular forms of irony in fiction are verbal irony and situational irony. Verbal irony results from the contrast between what is said by the narrator or a character and what is meant. Irony of situation results from the contrast between what is expected and what actually happens.

For a concise checklist of questions for Language and Style, see page 66.

THEME

Theme is the central idea expressed by the story. It is a generalization, an insight about life derived from the work as a whole. Identifying and articulating this meaning is not easy. Although our experience of the theme may be holistic or impressionistic, the analysis and support required for its articulation demand a close look at the parts—the language, events, characters, and outcome of the story.

Theme or Moral?   When writing about literature, a temptation is to reduce what it means to a moral or lesson. Good literature reveals a complex world. A statement such as "Honesty is the best policy" may seem to reverberate with truth until we examine it closely. Is honesty always the best policy? Is it always the most ethical policy? Is it "moral" to tell people things that will hurt them? Didactic stories intend to deliver a moral. A moral preaches; it teaches a lesson or a code of conduct. A theme reveals; it gives us insight into human nature.

Consider the difference between revealing and preaching. If we read a story in which John loves Mary and Mary falls in love with Bill, we might state the simplified theme of the story as: People don't necessarily fall in love with those who are in love with them. To identify this theme, we examine the particulars of the story, come to a conclusion about them, and then expand this conclusion into a generalization about life itself.

A moral, however, is a simple lesson or rule of conduct. If we tried to find a moral in the previous John-Mary-Bill example, we might write, "Fall in love only with people who love you." But we know from our experience of the world that such a statement is much too simple to account for the complex nature of this situation. It would also seem silly to reduce John Steinbeck's story "The Chrysanthemums" to the moral "Don't trust strangers." It's clear that Eliza's unfulfilled desire for appreciation and love reveals a much more complex situation than such a moral could encompass. Similarly, the frustration and humiliation of the protagonists in "Eleven" and "Battle Royal," or the intense emotional and ethical dilemma of the couple in "Hills Like White Elephants," cannot be reduced to clear lessons or morals. They reveal, as life reveals, complexity intact. In most modern literature, theme is not usually expressed as a moral, and it will probably take more than a few words to state the theme of a complex work

For a concise checklist of questions for Theme, see page 67.

☑ CHECKLIST: ANALYZING FICTION

Narration

❑ What is the point of view? Who is the narrator?

❑ How would you describe the narrator's voice? What is the narrator's relationship to the story? Is the narrator reliable?

❑ To what extent does the narration (point of view and voice) effectively convey the story's meaning?

Setting

❑ What physical location is this? What does it look like? What details help us visualize the setting? How is the lighting? What are the dominant colors? What is the weather like? How would you describe the atmosphere?

❑ When does the story take place? What difference does it make to the story?

❑ How are the people behaving? How are they dressed?

Conflict and Plot

❑ What is the primary external conflict? The primary internal conflict?

❑ Are there other conflicts? If so, what are they?

❑ How would you support your identification of conflict by what is in the text?

❑ To what extent do the traits of the characters lead to conflict?

❑ Can you identify the plot? Does it conform to the traditional structure? If so, how so? If not, what is the structure?

Character

❑ What is your impression of the characters? What do the characters do that makes you feel this way? What do they say? What is said about them?

❑ To what extent are the characters motivated and consistent? Believable? Flat or stock characters?

❑ Who is the protagonist? One or more antagonists?

❑ What evidence from the text of the story supports your responses?

Language and Style

❑ Is the language formal or informal? In what way does the language tell you about the narrator or characters?

For a concise checklist of questions for Theme, see page 67.

❏ Are there many instances of figurative language (imagery, simile, metaphor)? Is there a dominant symbol? Are there any other symbols? Explain.

❏ Are there instances of verbal or situational irony? Explain.

Theme

❏ What are the major details (characters, conflicts, outcome) of the story?

❏ What conclusion about the story did you draw from these details?

❏ To what extent does this conclusion lead to a generalization about life? What is the central idea or theme of the story?

❏ Is the story didactic? Does it reveal or does it preach? Explain.

GETTING IDEAS FOR WRITING ABOUT FICTION

The purpose of the story, the prompts, and the questions in this section is to show how the elements we've discussed earlier might be applied to a work of fiction. Following "The Story of an Hour," many of the questions from the summary checklist above are applied to the story, and we consider some of the ways the elements on this list might be used to prompt ideas for a critical essay.

KATE CHOPIN [1851–1904]

THE STORY OF AN HOUR [1891]

Knowing that Mrs. Mallard was afflicted with a heart trouble, great care was taken to break to her as gently as possible the news of her husband's death.

It was her sister Josephine who told her, in broken sentences, veiled hints that revealed in half concealing. Her husband's friend Richards was there, too, near her. It was he who had been in the newspaper office when intelligence of the railroad disaster was received, with Brently Mallard's name leading the list of "killed." He had only taken the time to assure himself of its truth by a second telegram, and had hastened to forestall any less careful, less tender friend in bearing the sad message.

She did not hear the story as many women have heard the same, with a paralyzed inability to accept its significance. She wept at once, with sudden, wild abandonment, in her sister's arms. When the storm of grief had spent itself she went away to her room alone. She would have no one follow her.

There stood, facing the open window, a comfortable, roomy armchair. Into this she sank, pressed down by a physical exhaustion that haunted her body and seemed to reach into her soul.

5   She could see in the open square before her house the tops of trees that were all aquiver with the new spring life. The delicious breath of rain was in the air. In the street below a peddler was crying his wares. The notes of a distant song which some one was singing reached her faintly, and countless sparrows were twittering in the eaves.

There were patches of blue sky showing here and there through the clouds that had met and piled above the other in the west facing her window.

She sat with her head thrown back upon the cushion of the chair quite motionless, except when a sob came up into her throat and shook her, as a child who has cried itself to sleep continues to sob in its dreams.

She was young, with a fair, calm face, whose lines bespoke repression and even a certain strength. But now there was a dull stare in her eyes, whose gaze was fixed away off yonder on one of those patches of blue sky. It was not a glance of reflection, but rather indicated a suspension of intelligent thought.

There was something coming to her and she was waiting for it, fearfully. What was it? She did not know; it was too subtle and elusive to name. But she felt it, creeping out of the sky, reaching toward her through the sounds, the scents, the color that filled the air.

10   Now her bosom rose and fell tumultuously. She was beginning to recognize this thing that was approaching to possess her, and she was striving to beat it back with her will—as powerless as her two white slender hands would have been.

When she abandoned herself a little whispered word escaped her slightly parted lips. She said it over and over under her breath: "Free, free, free!" The vacant stare and the look of terror that had followed it went from her eyes. They stayed keen and bright. Her pulses beat fast, and the coursing blood warmed and relaxed every inch of her body.

She did not stop to ask if it were not a monstrous joy that held her. A clear and exalted perception enabled her to dismiss the suggestion as trivial.

She knew that she would weep again when she saw the kind, tender hands folded in death; the face that had never looked save with love upon her, fixed and gray and dead. But she saw beyond that bitter moment a long procession of years to come that would belong to her absolutely. And she opened and spread her arms out to them in welcome.

There would be no one to live for her during those coming years; she would live for herself. There would be no powerful will bending her in that blind persistence with which men and women believe they have a right to impose a private will upon a fellow creature. A kind intention or a cruel intention made the act seem no less a crime as she looked upon it in that brief moment of illumination.

15   And yet she had loved him—sometimes. Often she had not. What did it matter! What could love, the unsolved mystery, count for in face of this possession of self-assertion which she suddenly recognized as the strongest impulse of her being.

"Free! Body and soul free!" she kept whispering.

Josephine was kneeling before the closed door with her lips to the keyhole, imploring for admission. "Louise, open the door! I beg; open the door—you will make yourself ill. What are you doing, Louise? For heaven's sake open the door."

"Go away. I am not making myself ill." No; she was drinking in a very elixir of life through that open window.

Her fancy was running riot along those days ahead of her. Spring days, and summer days, and all sorts of days that would be her own. She breathed a quick prayer that life might be long. It was only yesterday she had thought with a shudder that life might be long.

20   She arose at length and opened the door to her sister's importunities. There was a feverish triumph in her eyes, and she carried herself unwittingly like a goddess of

Victory. She clasped her sister's waist, and together they descended the stairs. Richards stood waiting for them at the bottom.

Some one was opening the front door with a latchkey. It was Brently Mallard who entered, a little travel-stained, composedly carrying his grip-sack and umbrella. He had been far from the scene of accident, and did not even know there had been one. He stood amazed at Josephine's piercing cry; at Richards' quick motion to screen him from the view of his wife.

But Richards was too late.

When the doctors came they said she had died of heart disease—of joy that kills.

 ## CONNECTING THROUGH WRITING

One of the best ways to get ideas for an essay is to ask and answer your own most compelling questions.

- Write down whatever questions come to mind during and after your reading. See if your answers to these questions provide topics for writing.

- Choose a compelling idea from a journal entry.

- Draw a Venn diagram to compare elements, characters, or stories (pp. 29–30), use directed freewriting (p. 39), ask questions (p. 39), list (p. 40), or draw a cluster or semantic map (pp. 41–42) to loosen up ideas.

Listed below is a much more structured approach based on the elements of fiction discussed earlier in this section. Applying these questions to "The Story of an Hour" may demonstrate how the elements might be applied to any work of short fiction.

FIRST RESPONSES

1. What questions came to mind as you read "The Story of an Hour"?

2. To what extent can you connect "The Story of an Hour" to your own background or experience?

3. What do you find most compelling or provocative about the story?

NARRATION

1. Unlike the first-person narrative of Sandra Cisneros's "Eleven" in Chapter 2, this story is told from the third-person point of view. How does this narrative perspective affect your experience of the story?

2. What is the tone of the narration? What is the attitude of the narrator toward Mrs. Mallard? To what extent is the narrator reliable?

3. If the story were told in the first person by Mrs. Mallard herself, how would it change the way you experience it? Would you know any more than you do now? If so, what?

4. If the story were told by her sister, Josephine; Brently Mallard; or the doctors, how would it change the way you experience the story?

SETTING

1. Describe the setting of "The Story of an Hour." In what location does the story take place? When does it occur?

2. What effect does the setting have on your response to the story?

3. The weather is described as: ". . . patches of blue sky showing here and there through the clouds that had met and piled above the other in the west facing her window." In what way does the weather agree with or contrast the action in the story?

4. What other details in Kate Chopin's writing were most effective in conveying the setting? Quote them from the text.

5. This story was originally published in 1891. If the story were written and published recently, would you have responded differently? Explain.

CONFLICT AND PLOT

1. What event in "The Story of an Hour" leads to the conflict?

2. How would you describe the conflict? Which elements of the conflict are external? Which ones are internal?

3. To what extent does the conflict derive from Mrs. Mallard and her beliefs?

4. What is the climax of this story? What is the resolution? To what extent are you satisfied with the resolution?

CHARACTER

1. Describe Mrs. Mallard. How does what she says and does show you who she is? Do you learn about her directly or indirectly? Explain.

2. How would you describe Mrs. Mallard's sister, Josephine? Richards? The doctors? Brently Mallard? What do they do or say that supports your description? Are they round or flat characters? Why?

3. What quotes from the text support your description of Mrs. Mallard?

4. To what extent does Mrs. Mallard change or develop in the story?

5. If Mrs. Mallard is the protagonist, who is the antagonist?

LANGUAGE AND STYLE

1. Is the language of "The Story of an Hour" formal or informal?

2. What does the nature of the language Mrs. Mallard uses tell you about her? The language of other characters? Cite examples.

3. How does the language of the narration affect you? For example, the description: "She sat with her head thrown back upon the cushion of the chair quite motionless, except when a sob came up into her throat and shook her, as a child who has cried itself to sleep continues to sob in its dreams" paints an especially touching picture. What other descriptions or images appeal to you and why?

4. Do you see any symbols in "The Story of an Hour"? If so, explain.

5. To what extent do you find the story ironic?

THEME

1. What conclusion do you draw from "The Story of an Hour"?
2. What details and events lead to this conclusion?
3. What is the point of the story? What is the theme?

TOPICS FOR WRITING

The following list is not exhaustive, but simply illustrative of the kinds of questions that might emerge from more specific analytical questions (and combinations of questions) like those above. Your responses to these questions might provide worthwhile topics for writing.

1. What is the effect of third-person narration on the characterization of Mrs. Mallard?
2. What would this story be like if told by Mrs. Mallard?
3. In what way is the setting a factor in the "The Story of an Hour"?
4. In what way is the cultural context a factor in the outcome?
5. What were relationships or marriages between men and women like in 1891?
6. How does "The Story of an Hour" fit within the time period and culture in which it was written? To what extent would this story be told differently today?

READING AND ANALYZING POETRY

We are not likely to say of any event, "You can't write a poem about that." Birth, death, youth, old age, love, jealousy, ambition, loyalty, laughter, triumph, defeat—if we can experience it, we can write poetry about it. The more an experience moves us, the more important it seems to record the emotion, sensation, or memory with a poem. *Reading* poetry is a personal as well as a social experience. It is personal in the way it offers us a reflection of our own interior lives, our thoughts and emotions expressed in the words of others; and it is social in the way it offers us a glimpse of other people's interior lives, the shared expression of their hearts and minds.

If we reduce our reading to analysis alone, we may "figure out" the poem's structure, its rhyme scheme and rhythm, or how it might be classified, but we may miss the experience of the poem itself. That experience relies on our ability to imagine—the ability to take the "sleeping" poem from the print on the page and "wake it up" through our senses and emotions. This is not the kind of reading we might be used to doing in an academic environment, where we often read for information alone. And it may not be the style of reading we are used to in our everyday lives—in a world that bombards us with the exaggerated language of advertising, TV commercials, and talk shows, or reduces everything to sound bites. Given the lack of meaning in so much of that language, we may speed through it or ignore it altogether.

Poetry invites your engagement and comprehension. To be engaged by a poem, you need the time to read slowly and participate fully with your mind and senses. Once engaged, you have reason to analyze the poem's language, its structure, its rhymes or rhythms—to comprehend *how* it has prompted your response. Reading a poem this way involves your mind, senses, and emotions—and it has the power to change you the way that all meaningful experiences can.

LANGUAGE AND STYLE

Denotation and Connotation

Faced with an unfamiliar word—dictionary in hand—you might look up its definition and be reasonably satisfied with what you find. But if you are already familiar with that word, a dictionary definition is not likely to account for everything the word means to you. While you might not disagree with the dictionary definition, or **denotation,** of the word, you probably won't be entirely satisfied with it, either. Your own definitions, or **connotations,** for familiar words are flavored with personal associations. Dictionary definitions alone cannot account for this complex response to language.

The compressed nature of language and meaning in poetry makes word choice crucial. Poets are very conscious of the effect that connotations, or suggested meanings, have on readers. Synonyms for the word *thin,* for example, include *slim, slender, lean, skinny,* and *trim*—words that mean almost the same thing. But each of these words has a different connotation and slightly different meaning for each of us—and a different effect on us when we read it. Being conscious of word choices and patterns of language may tell us a great deal about what makes a poem effective and how it triggers our responses.

Voice

Be sure to differentiate between the poet and the speaker in a poem. In some poems the poet and the speaker are virtually the same, and we can assume the thoughts of the speaker are those of the poet as well. In Robert Hayden's poem "Those Winter Sundays" (p. 13), the speaker's remembrance seems to be that of the poet himself. On the other hand, the speaker (the "voice") in a poem may use vocabulary and express attitudes that are not characteristic of the poet. The speaker in Robert Browning's "Porphyria's Lover" (p. 784), a demented, homicidal lover, is clearly not the poet himself. Being able to identify the speaker, the speaker's attitude toward the poem's content, and the speaker's intended audience helps us read the poem more effectively.

Tone

The key to **tone** is voice. When we see or hear a poet speaking, the words, intonations, physical gestures, and facial expressions tell us the attitude of the speaker toward the subject. When we "hear" voice in our reading, we can also sense the intonations. Cues in a printed poem are not always obvious, however, and to sense the tone we must often rely on the pattern and types of words the poet chooses. Sometimes the contradictory nature of the language can give us a strong sense of that tone. For example, the repeated phrase in the Stephen Crane poem below is "War is kind," yet every detail he uses to describe war is anything but "kind" and indicates what he really means.

Irony

Irony is the contrast between appearance/expectation and reality. As in fiction, the two most popular forms of irony in poetry are verbal irony and situational irony. Verbal irony results from the contrast between what is said by a speaker and what is meant. Irony of situation results from the contrast between what is expected and what actually happens.

The following poem relies on an ironic tone to convey its meaning.

STEPHEN CRANE [1871–1900]

WAR IS KIND [1899]

Do not weep, maiden, for war is kind.
Because your lover threw wild hands toward the sky
And the affrighted steed ran on alone,
Do not weep.
War is kind.   5

    Hoarse, booming drums of the regiment,
    Little souls who thirst for fight,
    These men were born to drill and die.
    The unexplained glory flies above them,
    Great is the battle god, great, and his kingdom   10
    A field where a thousand corpses lie.

Do not weep, babe, for war is kind.
Because your father tumbled in the yellow trenches,
Raged at his breast, gulped and died,
Do not weep.   15
War is kind.

    Swift blazing flag of the regiment,
    Eagle with crest of red and gold,
    These men were born to drill and die.
    Point for them the virtue of slaughter,   20
    Make plain for them the excellence of killing
    And a field where a thousand corpses lie.

Mother whose heart hung humble as a button
On the bright splendid shroud of your son,
Do not weep.   25
War is kind.

MAKING CONNECTIONS

1. How do your feelings about war influence your response?
2. What do you think about the choice of words Crane uses to describe war?
3. With many poems, being sensitive to the voice of the speaker is crucial to our response. The tone expressed by that voice may change the meaning. How are you affected by the tone in this poem?
4. What indications of irony are there in the text of the poem? Is there a contradiction between the title "War Is Kind" and the details that Crane uses to support it?
5. How does the poet's tone and use of irony affect the meaning of "War Is Kind"?

Imagery

An **image** is a mental picture prompted by words. Images result from concrete language that appeals to our senses. "Nice image," we've heard people say about particularly striking words or phrases. But images do not exist in words on a page. They exist in our minds. The words on the page may prompt the images in our minds, but it is our own senses and memories that evoke the pictures. Experiments have shown that we use the same parts of our brains when we see or hear the word for an object as we do when encountering the object itself. It is our sense memories that bring a poet's words to life to form an image. We can see (hear, taste, touch, or smell) them in our mind's eye (ear, tongue, hand, or nose).

These sense memories are evoked by the following poems.

HELEN CHASIN [B. 1938]

THE WORD PLUM   [1986]

The word *plum* is delicious

pout and push, luxury of
self-love, and savoring murmur

full in the mouth and falling
like fruit   5

taut skin
pierced, bitten, provoked into
juice, and tart flesh
question
and reply, lip and tongue   10
of pleasure.

ROBERT BROWNING [1812–1889]

MEETING AT NIGHT   [1845]

The gray sea and the long black land:
And the yellow half-moon large and low;
And the startled little waves that leap
In fiery ringlets from their sleep,
As I gain the cove with pushing prow,   5
And quench its speed in the slushy sand.

Then a mile of warm sea-scented beach;
Three fields to cross till a farm appears;
A tap at the pane, the quick sharp scratch
And blue spurt of a lighted match,   10
And a voice less loud, through its joys and fears,
Than the two hearts beating each to each!

PARTING AT MORNING   [1845]

Round the cape of a sudden came the sea,
And the sun looked over the mountain's rim:
And straight was a path of gold for him,°
And the need of a world of men for me.

3 the sun

MAKING CONNECTIONS

1. Not all poetry intends to make a serious statement. Some poems simply
    intend to engage us in an aesthetic or sensory experience. Does "The Word
    Plum" have a different effect on you than "Meeting at Night," "Parting at
    Morning," or "War Is Kind"? Explain.
2. To what extent can you connect "The Word *Plum*" and Browning's poems
    to your own experience? How does that connection affect your response to
    the imagery?
3. In "The Word *Plum*," the senses of taste and touch are primarily the senses
    we rely on to experience the images in the poem. How many senses do you
    use to experience the images in "Meeting at Night" and "Parting at
    Morning"?
4. How do these images add to the overall effect of the poems for you?

Figurative Language: Everyday Poetry

There is nothing unusual about figurative language. In fact, we would have a hard
time communicating with each other without it. Comparison is at the core of

"figures of speech," or figurative language. We use what is already familiar to describe something new, or we describe something familiar in a new way. Used in tandem with concrete language, similes and metaphors can lead to very striking images.

A **simile** is an announced comparison. We announce or introduce this comparison by using the words *like* or *as*. For example, "He's as quiet as a church mouse" or "She swims like a fish." Those things compared usually have only one characteristic in common. Some of the most evocative descriptions in literature are similes. James Joyce's description of a young boy's infatuation, "But my body was like a harp and her words and gestures were like fingers running upon the wires" (see "Araby," p. 463) and Marge Piercy's words, "Her good nature wore out like a fan belt" (see "Barbie Doll," p. 14) are vivid examples of how simile can evoke lasting images in our minds.

Simile is the dominant poetic effect in the two poems that follow.

LANGSTON HUGHES [1902–1967]

A DREAM DEFERRED   [1951]

What happens to a dream deferred?

Does it dry up
like a raisin in the sun?
Or fester like a sore—
And then run?
Does it stink like rotten meat?   5
Or crust and sugar over—
like a syrupy sweet?
Maybe it just sags
like a heavy load.   10

Or does it explode?

N. SCOTT MOMADAY [B. 1934]

SIMILE   [1974]

What did we say to each other
that now we are as the deer
who walk in single file
with heads high
with ears forward   5
with eyes watchful
with hooves always placed on firm ground
in whose limbs there is latent flight

MAKING CONNECTIONS

1. Each of these poems relies on comparison to make its point. To what extent do these comparisons bring personal experiences to mind?
2. There are five announced comparisons (similes) and one implied comparison (metaphor) in "A Dream Deferred." What are they? What images do they prompt in you? What senses do you use to experience them?
3. As its title suggests, there is one announced comparison in "Simile." What is it? What image does it prompt in you?
4. To what extent are you affected differently by the many brief similes of "A Dream Deferred" in comparison to the one extended simile in "Simile"?
5. What is the point of each poem? In each case, how do the similes present it effectively?
6. To what extent is "A Dream Deferred" similar to Hughes's short story "One Friday Morning" (p. 1121)?

A **metaphor** is a more direct and more complete comparison than a simile. A metaphor does not announce itself; it states that something *is* something else (My love is a red rose) or implies it (My love has red petals and sharp thorns). Our everyday language is filled with metaphors. We call attractive-looking people hunks and foxes. Businesses use implied metaphors to name their products. We buy an antiperspirant named Arrid, soap named Irish Spring, laptop computers named Thinkpads, and cars named Jaguars. Sometimes, however, people get carried away and mix metaphors, with confusing rather than clarifying results. A baseball manager once remarked about a suspended player that "The ball was in his court now [tennis], so he better not step out of bounds [basketball], or he'd be down for the count [boxing]."

Note the metaphor in the following poem.

CARL SANDBURG [1878–1967]

FOG

[1916]

The fog comes
on little cat feet.
It sits looking
over harbor and city
on silent haunches
and then moves on.

Personification is a frequently used form of metaphor. To personify is to give human characteristics or qualities to something not human. Consider how often you personify objects in your everyday use of language. The following poem illustrates personification.

JAMES STEPHENS [1882–1950]

THE WIND [1915]

The wind stood up and gave a shout.
He whistled on his fingers and

Kicked the withered leaves about
And thumped the branches with his hand

And said he'd kill and kill and kill,   5
And so he will and so he will.

MAKING CONNECTIONS

1. To what extent is your response to "Fog" or "The Wind" influenced by your own experience? Support your explanation with reference to the poems.
2. What are the metaphors in each poem?
3. What images do they prompt in you?
4. What senses do you use to experience them?
5. How do these images add to the overall effect of the poems?

Symbol

A **symbol** is something that represents more than itself. Every word we speak is a symbol. Government flags, religious objects, and logos on college sweatshirts are all symbols. We have personal symbols (meaningful objects, special songs), public symbols (flags), and conventional symbols (a road as the journey of life, seasons to represent the stages of our lives). Symbols are subject to personal interpretation. A nation's flag may symbolize truth and justice to one person, but deceit and oppression to another. Note the symbol in the following poem.

ROBERT FROST [1874–1963]

THE ROAD NOT TAKEN [1915]

Two roads diverged in a yellow wood
And sorry I could not travel both
And be one traveler, long I stood
And looked down one as far as I could
To where it bent in the undergrowth;   5

Then took the other, as just as fair,
And having perhaps the better claim,
Because it was grassy and wanted wear,
Though as for that the passing there
Had worn them really about the same.   10

And both that morning equally lay
In leaves no step had trodden black.
Oh, I kept the first for another day!
Yet knowing how way leads on to way,
I doubted if I should ever come back.   15

I shall be telling this with a sigh
somewhere ages and ages hence:
Two roads diverged in a wood, and I—
I took the one less traveled by,
And that has made all the difference.   20

MAKING CONNECTIONS

1. To what extent is your response to "The Road Not Taken" influenced by your own experience?
2. What is the symbol in "The Road Not Taken"?
3. What images does the poem prompt in you?
4. What senses do you use to experience these images?
5. How does the symbolism add to the overall effect of the poem for you?

For a concise checklist of questions for Language and Style, see page 85.

SOUND AND STRUCTURE

Long before we had the ability to speak, we enjoyed making and listening to sounds. As newcomers to the world, we were probably soothed or frightened by the sound of the adult voices around us. The sounds we made helped us develop our vocal chords, but there was much more to it than that. We listened to the sounds we made and adjusted them until we got them just right. We made the leap from gurgles and hisses to new sounds with real syllables like ba-ba, ma-ma, da-da.

The amazing thing is that all of this happened before we could speak and understand words or sentences from the adult language that surrounded us. Those sounds were a universal language we shared with children all over the world. And those sounds, like music, seemed to have an appeal in and of themselves—an appeal we haven't forgotten. Sometimes we listen to songs and sing along or sing the songs to ourselves—even when we don't know all the words. And sometimes we like the sounds of the words and the rhymes and rhythms of poems just as much as their meanings.

Alliteration, Assonance, and Rhyme

As kids in school, we may have used rhymes to memorize the number of days in each month or the names of the states or presidents. The most obvious rhymes come at ends of lines when final vowel and consonant sounds in a word at the end of one line match vowel and consonant sounds at the end of another (l*and* and s*and*, th*ings* and k*ings*, b*are* and desp*air*).

Less obvious are repeated initial consonant sounds ("*d*o or *d*ie," "*s*ink or *s*wim," "*s*uffering *s*uccotash"), which is called **alliteration.**

Less obvious still are **assonance,** or repeated vowel sounds (t*i*me l*i*ne, fr*ee* and *ea*sy), and **consonance,** or repeated consonant sounds (sho*rt* and sma*rt*, st*ruts* and f*rets*).

When we listen to music, we are moved along (in spirit and time) and can anticipate structure by patterns and combinations of repeated tones. If we listen sensitively to rhyme and rhythm in poetry, we are likely to have a similar experience.

Look at the following quatrains (units of four lines) from two different William Blake poems. This quatrain has an *ab, ab* rhyme scheme:

From "London"

In every cry of every Man, (*a*)
In every Infant's cry of fear, (*b*)
In every voice, in every ban, (*a*)
The mind-forg'd manacles I hear. (*b*)

This quatrain has an *aa, bb* rhyme scheme:

From "The Tyger"

In what distant deeps or skies (*a*)
Burnt the fire of thine eyes? (*a*)
On what wings dare he aspire? (*b*)
What the hand dare seize the fire? (*b*)

Recite each quatrain out loud several times. How does the ordering of rhyme affect your pace? How does it affect the content of the lines and the units of thought you remember?

Examine other poems in this section. For example, Robert Browning's "Meeting at Night" and Robert Frost's "The Road Not Taken" have very different rhyme schemes. Read them out loud and see how the rhyme scheme affects how you hear and organize the content of the poems.

Rhyme and Rhythm: Limericks

A light, usually humorous, form of poetry that is helpful for getting the feel of rhyme and rhythm is the **limerick.** Limericks are very common and almost always anonymous (usually for good reason), and we're just as likely to see them scrawled on a wall as on paper.

There was a young maid who said, "Why   (*a*)
Can't I look in my ear with my eye?   (*a*)
   If I put my mind to it,   (*b*)
   I'm sure I can do it.   (*b*)
You never can tell till you try."   (*a*)

Read it out loud several times. Listen to the rhythm. Look at the rhyme pattern or scheme. Which lines rhyme? What is the rhythm like? Can you describe the pattern of a limerick? If you need to, read it out loud again.

Limericks have five lines. The first, second, and fifth lines rhyme (*aaa,* above) and so do the third and fourth (*bb,* above). The first, second, and fifth have approximately the same verbal rhythm (**meter**) and length, and so do the third and fourth.

Meter

Some rhythm in poetry is described by the word *meter.* Meter refers to the pattern of stressed (/) and unstressed (ˇ) syllables in a line. The group of syllables making up one metrical unit is called a foot. The metrical feet most commonly used are iambic (unstressed, stressed), trochaic (stressed, unstressed), anapestic (two unstressed, one stressed), and dactylic (one stressed, two unstressed).

The number of feet in each line is described as **monometer** (one foot), **dimeter** (two feet), **trimeter** (three feet), **tetrameter** (four feet), **pentameter** (five feet), **hexameter** (six feet), **heptameter** (seven feet), and **octameter** (eight feet).

The most common form of meter in poetry written in English is **iambic** (unstressed, stressed) **pentameter** (five feet).

The pair of lines from two sonnets written over three hundred years apart are examples of iambic pentameter (five feet of iambic per line):

Děsír\iňg thís\ măn's árt \aňd thát\ măn's scópe
Wǐth whát\ Ǐ móst\ ěnjóy\ cŏntént\ěd leást;
—William Shakespeare [1609]

Nŏr yét\ă flóat\iňg spár\ tŏ mén\ thǎt sínk
Aňd ríse\ aňd sínk\ aňd ríse\ aňd sínk\ aǧaín;
—Edna St.Vincent Millay [1931]

Formal Verse: The Sonnet

One of the most popular and enduring formal verse structures is the sonnet. Sonnets are fourteen lines long and are usually written in iambic pentameter. Rhyme schemes will vary according to type. The oldest form of the sonnet is the Italian, or Petrarchan, sonnet (named for its greatest practitioner, Petrarch). Its rhyme scheme is usually an octave (eight lines) and a sestet (six lines). The octave usually follows a pattern of *abbaabba.* The concluding sestet may be *cdecde* or *cdcdcd* or *cdedce.*

In English, the most popular form is the English, or Shakespearean, sonnet (named for its greatest practitioner, Shakespeare, who wrote 154 of them), so we use it here to illustrate formal verse. The Shakespearean sonnet is a fourteen-line poem of three quatrains (four-line units) and a final couplet (a two-line unit) in the rhyme scheme *abab cdcd efef gg.* It is a structure that presents the content of the poem in predictable ways. The first two quatrains often present a problem. The third quatrain is often pivotal and begins a reversal. The final couplet most often suggests a solution.

WILLIAM SHAKESPEARE [1564–1616]

SONNET NO. 29   [1609]

When, in disgrace with Fortune and men's eyes, (*a*)
I all alone beweep my outcast state, (*b*)
And trouble deaf heaven with my bootless° cries, (*a*)
And look upon myself, and curse my fate, (*b*)
Wishing me like to one more rich in hope, (*c*)   5
Featured like him, like him with friends possessed, (*d*)
Desiring this man's art and that man's scope, (*c*)
With what I most enjoy contented least; (*d*)
Yet in these thoughts myself almost despising, (*e*)
Haply I think on thee—and then my state, (*f*)   10
Like to the lark at break of day arising (*e*)
From sullen earth, sings hymns at heaven's gate; (*f*)
For thy sweet love remembered such wealth brings (*g*)
That then I scorn to change my state with kings. (*g*)

3 bootless useless

MAKING CONNECTIONS

1. Describe the emotions of the speaker in this poem.
2. Does his situation bring to mind any of your own experiences? Would you describe love in these terms? How does that affect your response?
3. In what way does the sonnet structure affect your response? To what extent do the first two quatrains present a problem that is resolved by the remaining quatrain and final couplet?

Blank Verse

Another popular form is **blank verse.** Blank verse is unrhymed but follows a regular verse form, usually iambic pentameter. Some of the greatest epic poems and plays (including Milton's *Paradise Lost* and Shakespeare's plays) have been written in blank verse, and it is still a very popular form today.

Here are the first four lines from Robert Frost's "Mending Wall." The entire poem is forty-five lines long (see p. 269).

Something there is that doesn't love a wall
That sends the frozen ground swell under it
And spills the upper boulders in the sun,
And makes gaps even two can pass abreast.

While it does not rhyme, the iambic pentameter still moves us from line to line in a regular, predictable rhythm and influences our "hearing" of the poem. Read it out loud several times and see if you can hear and feel the regular beat.

Iambic pentameter is the dominant pattern in blank verse, but every word and every line may not conform to this pattern. For example, "Something," the first word of Frost's poem above, with its emphasis on the first syllable, is trochaic (stressed, unstressed), not iambic (unstressed, stressed). So, too, while the dominant pattern of Shakespeare's sonnets and plays is blank verse, not every foot is iambic, nor every line pentameter. You will find a number of exceptions to this pattern in the sonnets and *Hamlet* (p. 537) in this text.

Free or Open Form Verse

As its name implies, this is verse that is not constrained by an imposed form. **Free or open form verse** does not have a rhyme scheme or regular rhythm. It is not form-less, however, but relies on its own words and content to determine its best form. The poem that follows was written by Walt Whitman, a celebrated pioneer of free-verse writing.

WALT WHITMAN [1819–1892]

WHEN I HEARD THE LEARN'D ASTRONOMER   [1865]

When I heard the learn'd astronomer,
When the proofs, the figures, were ranged in columns before me,
When I was shown the charts and diagrams, to add, divide, and measure them,
When I sitting heard the astronomer where he lectured with applause in the
    lecture-room,
How soon unaccountable I became tired and sick,   5
Till rising and gliding out I wander'd off by myself,
In the mystical moist night-air, and from time to time,
Look'd up in perfect silence at the stars.

MAKING CONNECTIONS

1. Have you ever been in a situation where the explanation of the experience paled in comparison to the experience itself? Explain.
2. What does the speaker mean when he says, "How soon unaccountable I became tired and sick"?
3. How does the free verse affect your response to the poem?

For a concise checklist of questions for Sound and Structure, see page 85.

Interpretation: What Does the Poem Mean?

Theme is the meaning we construct from the poem. It is an insight about life that we derive from the poem as a whole. Identifying and articulating this meaning is not an easy task. While our experience of the poem may be holistic or impressionistic, the analysis and support required for its articulation demand a close look at the parts—the language, events, and outcome of the poem.

As with fiction, be wary of reducing what the poem means to a moral or lesson. Good literature reveals a complex world. A moral preaches; it teaches us a lesson or a code of conduct. A theme reveals; it gives us insight into human nature.

Explication

An **explication** involves a line-by-line analysis of a text. Since works of fiction or drama are usually long, an explication would take quite a bit of time and space and would probably be better left to a lengthy term paper. Most poems, however, are relatively brief and by their nature "packed with meaning." So they present a good opportunity for a very close reading and examination—an opportunity to look closely at sounds, words, images, lines, and how they all work together to deliver the poem's meaning. An explication is not just a summary or translation of the poet's language into your own; it is a detailed interpretation of *how* and *what* you believe the poem means.

Like other forms of literature, poems are not problems to be solved. They don't have one correct answer or interpretation. Remember, what makes an interpretation convincing or defensible is your ability to support it.

For a concise checklist of questions for Interpretation and Theme, see page 85.

TYPES OF POETRY

For the sake of clarification and simplification, poetry may be classified into two types: lyric and narrative. As with other forms of literature, classifications of this kind are not exclusive. There is overlap between the designations lyric and narrative. Poems in each of these categories may have elements characteristic of the other. And both lyric and narrative poetry have dramatic qualities.

Lyric Poetry

Lyric poetry is the most popular form of poetry written today. Lyric poems are characterized by the expression of the speaker's innermost feelings, thoughts, and imagination. The word *lyric* is taken from a stringed musical instrument called the lyre, which was used in classical and medieval times to accompany a singer. In addition to the very subjective stance of the speaker, lyric poems are melodic—a melody not derived from a lyre but from words and their arrangement. It's not mere coincidence that the words that accompany the melody in a song are called lyrics. Most of the poetry in this text can be classified as lyric poetry, and a specific example of this type is Edna St. Vincent Millay's "Love Is Not All" (p. 791).

One kind of lyric poetry that deserves special mention is the **dramatic monologue.** In a dramatic monologue, the poet, like an actor in a play, assumes a different persona and speaks to us through the voice and personality of another person. Robert Browning's "Porphyria's Lover" (p. 784) is an example of a dramatic monologue.

Narrative Poetry

A narrative poem tells a story. The poet takes on a role similar to that of a narrator in a work of fiction. The oldest stories were recorded in poetry and recited by "bards" who used the rhythms of the verse to help them memorize their lines. One difference between the narratives of short stories and those of narrative poems is length. With the exception of epic poems—book-length narrative poems with lots of room for development of conflict and character—the length of most narrative poems limits the development of conflict and character. The brevity of the poems allows little space for exposition, and the poem usually moves quickly to the "chase," or crisis, beginning virtually in the middle of the story (or *in medias res*). Dudley Randall's "Ballad of Birmingham" (p. 17) and Seamus Heaney's "Mid-Term Break" (p. 507) are examples of narrative poems.

For a concise checklist of questions for Types of Poetry, see page 86.

✓ CHECKLIST: ANALYZING POETRY

Language and Style

❑ How are you affected by the speaker's voice?

❑ Is there anything ironic in the poem? How so?

❑ What images do you experience? Are there similes or metaphors? Is there symbolism? If so, identify them in the poem.

❑ How do voice, irony, imagery, figurative language, and/or symbolism affect your response?

Sound and Structure

❑ Is there a rhyme scheme in the poem? If so, what is its pattern? How does the rhyme scheme add to the overall effect of the poem?

❑ Are there other sound devices (alliteration, assonance, consonance)? If so, identify them and indicate how they affect your response.

❑ Is there a regular pattern to the verse? If so, describe it. How does it add to the effect of the poem? If there is no regular pattern, how does the unique form of the poem match the content? How did it affect your response?

Interpretation and Theme

❑ What are the major details (images, symbols, rhymes, rhythms, etc.) of the poem?

❑ What conclusion can you draw from these details?

(continued)

❏   To what extent does this conclusion lead to a generalization about life?
     What is the central idea expressed by the poem?

Types of Poetry

❏   Is the poem an expression of the poet's thoughts and feelings, or is it
     telling a story? Is it a narrative or lyric poem?

GETTING IDEAS FOR WRITING ABOUT POETRY

The purpose of the poem, the prompts, and the questions in this section is to show
how the elements we've discussed earlier might be applied to poetry. Following
"Pigeon Woman," many of the questions from the summary checklist above are
applied to the poem, and we consider some of the ways the elements discussed in
this section might be used to prompt ideas for an essay.

MAY SWENSON [1919–1989]

PIGEON WOMAN   [1958]

Slate, or dirty-marbled-colored,
or rusty-iron-colored, the pigeons
on the flagstones in front of the
Public Library make a sharp lake

into which the pigeon woman wades   5
at exactly 1:30. She wears a
plastic pink raincoat with a round
collar (looking like a little

girl, so gay) and flat gym shoes,
her hair square-cut, orange.   10
Wide-apart feet carefully enter
the spinning, crooning waves

(as if she'd just learned how
to walk, each step conscious,
an accomplishment); blue knots in the   15
calves of her bare legs (uglied marble),

age in angled cords of jaw
and neck, her pimento-colored hair,
hanging in thin tassels, is gray
around a balding crown.   20

The day-old bread drops down
from her veined hand dipping out
of a paper sack. Choppy, shadowy ripples,
the pigeons strike around her legs.

Sack empty, she squats and seems to rinse   25
her hands in them—the rainy greens and
oily purples of their necks. Almost
they let her wet thirsty fingertips—

but drain away in an untouchable tide.
A make-believe trade   30
she has come to, in her lostness
of illness or age—to treat the motley

city pigeons at 1:30 every day, in all
weathers. It is for them she colors her own
feathers. Ruddy-footed   35
on the lime stained paving,

purling to meet her when she comes,
they are a lake of love. Retreating
from her hands as soon as empty
they are the flints of love.   40

CONNECTING THROUGH WRITING

One of the best ways to get ideas for an essay is to ask and answer your own most
compelling questions.

- Write down whatever questions come to mind during and after your reading. See if your answers to these questions provide topics for writing.

- Choose a compelling idea from a journal entry.

- Draw a Venn diagram to compare elements, characters, or stories (pp. 29–30),
  use directed freewriting (p. 39), ask questions (p. 39), list (p. 40), or draw a
  cluster or semantic map (pp. 41–42) to loosen up ideas.

Listed below is a more structured approach based on the elements of poetry discussed earlier in this section. Applying these questions to "Pigeon Woman" may
demonstrate how the elements might be applied to any poem.

FIRST RESPONSES

1. What questions came to mind as you read "Pigeon Woman"?

2. What words or expressions are not clear to you?

3. To what extent can you connect "Pigeon Woman" to your own background
   or experience?

4. What do you find most compelling or provocative about the poem?

LANGUAGE AND STYLE

1. Who is the speaker in "Pigeon Woman"? What kind of voice does she have?
   What is the speaker's tone? What is the speaker's attitude toward the
   woman being described?

2. One image in the poem describes the pigeons as making "a sharp lake into which the pigeon woman wades." Where else in the poem is that image supported?

3. What other images in the poem have an effect on you? To what senses do the images appeal?

4. What similes or metaphors do you find in the poem? How do they contribute to the imagery?

5. How does the figurative language in "Pigeon Woman" help to convey its meaning?

6. Is there symbolism in the poem? Explain.

SOUNDS AND STRUCTURE

1. This poem does not have an obvious rhyme scheme. How does that affect your response?

2. What instances of alliteration or assonance can you identifiy?

3. To what extent does "Pigeon Woman" have a rhythm or a regular pattern to the verse? How does that influence your reading?

4. How does the form of "Pigeon Woman" match its content? To what extent does it help to convey its meaning?

INTERPRETATION AND THEME

1. What does the last line, "they are the flints of love," mean?

2. What are the major details of the poem?

3. What conclusion can you draw from the details? What is the poem about?

4. To what extent does this conclusion lead to a generalization about life?

5. What is the theme of "Pigeon Woman"?

TYPES OF POETRY

1. Is "Pigeon Woman" expressing the poet's innermost thoughts and feelings, or is it telling a story? Is it a narrative or lyric poem? Explain.

TOPICS FOR WRITING

The following list is not exchaustive, but simply illustrative of the kinds of questions that might emerge from the more specific analytical questions (and combinations of questions) like those above. Your responses to these questions might provide worthwhile topics for writing.

1. To what extent is "Pigeon Woman" a love story?

2. Some poems paint pictures; some make statements. In what way does this poem do both?

3. How do the structure, images, and sounds of the poem convey the meaning of "Pigeon Woman"?

4. To what extent is this poem a comment about human relationships?

5. It is not unusual to see lonely old people looking for companionship. In what way does "Pigeon Woman" enable us to "be there" and experience what that means?

6. Many people rely on the company of "nature's creatures" for companionship. To what extent is this a poem about this kind of mutual dependency?

7. How necessary was it to understand the social circumstances of the woman to make sense of the poem?

8. Can you compare this poem or the woman in it to another work or character in that work? Explain.

9. This poem was written in 1958. Does it still make sense today? How so?

10. Are you familiar with other poems of May Swenson? If so, how does this poem compare with them?

READING AND ANALYZING DRAMA

Since earliest times, people have had the need to act out and witness stories. Telling them and hearing them was important too, but witnessing the drama of the story as it happened was a different kind of experience. Ancient hunters wore masks of the animals they hunted because they believed that by mimicking their behavior they would come to know, understand, and honor them—and, of course, hunt them more effectively. From the time of the ancient Greeks to the present, however, we have shared a somewhat more idealistic goal. We've believed that by acting out and witnessing the struggle of other human beings, we are enlightened about the nature of our own lives.

To look at the history of drama, to see its development, is to learn a great deal about who people were and what they valued at different times in history. Whatever technological, social, or political developments have changed us over the last several thousand years, it is clear that there are important ties at the core of human experience that still bind us with our ancient ancestors.

Although we have seen dramatists' definitions of a hero or protagonist change over the years, from Aristotle's "characters of a higher type" to Arthur Miller's "common man [and woman]," the focus of drama remains the struggle of characters to face life with a sense of purpose and dignity. From the Greeks to the present, characters struggle with the gods, themselves, each other, and society. They rise to heroic heights or fall from them. Of noble birth, they may fail to be humble, and fall. Of humble birth, they may struggle to be noble, and triumph.

As we witness drama at its best from any period, we see ourselves and recollect the struggle of our own lives. And most of all, we are reminded of the human drama outside the theater, where joy and suffering, courage and cowardice, have been acted out for no audience in particular for thousands of years.

Reading a Play

Drama is meant to be seen and heard, so attending a good performance of a play is almost always preferable to reading it. In addition to what you see and hear onstage, the sense of community you share with the audience can be an integral part of your experience. If you are reading a play, though, there are a few strategies that may enhance your experience.

To read a play effectively, try to create the stage in your mind. Imagine you are sitting in a theater watching a performance. If there are stage directions, read them carefully. Try to imagine the set, props, and action, and hear the voices. Be conscious of what the characters say and how their words can help you picture the scene. If you are not sure who a character is, you may need to go back from time to time to read the list of characters or reread the dialogue.

Point of View

A play does not usually have a narrator to interpret the action for us. Most often we see the play through our own eyes. We observe the actions of the characters, hear what they say and what is said about them, and make our own judgments.

✓   In Greek drama, however, it is the function of the chorus and *Choragos* (the leader of the chorus) to address the audience from time to time to remind us about the cultural and historical context of the play and the significance of the action and dialogue. In Shakespearean drama, the characters themselves will sometimes speak
✓ directly to us in asides or soliloquies. In the play *Hamlet,* for example, the character Hamlet shares his thoughts directly with us at important times throughout the play. And occasionally in a modern play a character acts as narrator and comments on the action at timely intervals. Such is the role that Tom plays in Tennessee Williams's *The Glass Menagerie* (p. 284). But generally, whether attending a performance or reading a play, we are on our own.

For a concise checklist of questions for Point of View, see page 102.

Set and Setting

In drama, the immediate setting is the set itself. When attending a play, it's often the first part of the drama we experience. It draws us into another world. We know it's not real, but we are prepared to forget that once the action starts. As we look at the set and wonder what the action will be like, we are already beginning to experience the play.

As in fiction, setting is more than the place and time period of the play. It has a direct and indirect impact on character and conflict. It supports and emphasizes the play's meaning. *Its most important function is to make us feel present in the world that the characters inhabit.*

✓   In the history of theater, sets and settings have varied widely. Greek and Shakespearean plays were originally performed on a bare set, and the setting was sometimes described by the characters themselves or by a narrator, but always imagined by the audience. Over the years, both Greek and Shakespearean drama have often been performed with elaborate sets (particularly in videos and films). In most modern plays, the nature of the setting is spelled out in detail in the script. For example, the printed texts in this volume of the Greek plays *Antigonê* (p. 104) and *Oedipus Rex* (p. 1018), and the Shakespearean play *Hamlet* (p. 537) contain little indication of the nature of the setting beyond a broad reference to location. On the other hand, the texts of modern plays like *A Doll's House* (p. 856), *The Glass Menagerie* (p. 284), and *A Raisin in the Sun* (p. 344) contain very specific details about the nature of the set and setting.

Location tells us where and when the story is taking place. Both the *where* and the *when* will strongly influence the values and behavior of the characters and color the rest of the play. **Atmosphere** is the mix of location and more changeable circumstances, such as conflict, the characters present, the time of day, the season, and the weather. Its overall effect supports and complements conflict and character and helps to convey the play's meaning.

For a concise checklist of questions for Set and Setting, see page 102.

Conflict

Conflict is at the heart of every play. The impediments and complications the characters must overcome keep us watching or reading. The more important, challenging, believable, and coherent a conflict is, the more we are engaged by the action and dialogue, and the greater our desire to follow it to its conclusion.

Internal and External Conflict

External conflict may be physical (characters against nature) or social (characters against each other or against society). **Internal conflict** is a struggle of opposing forces within a character. The best drama contains elements of both types of conflict, but the emphasis is usually on the internal elements.

Conflict and Characterization

As in fiction, who the characters are, how they feel about themselves, and how they behave are at the core of both external and internal conflict.

Plot

Plot is the structure of the play. It is the pattern of twists and turns that the play takes. Most plots spring from conflict. To have a discernible plot, we must have impediments, complications, and opposition.

The traditional arrangement of plot in drama is virtually the same as it is in fiction. It follows a pattern of exposition, rising action, crisis (sometimes called climax), falling action, and resolution (sometimes called denouement or untying).

The fundamental difference between plot in fiction and drama is how we experience the plot. Without the benefit of a narrator, we are limited to action and dialogue, so the plot must develop entirely through what we see and hear onstage.

Exposition: We learn what we need to know about the circumstances, characters, and the potential conflict through dialogue and action.

Rising Action: An event occurs that builds the conflict, and our emotional involvement intensifies.

Crisis, or Climax: The main character is in the moment of truth. The turning point of the conflict (sometimes called a reversal) begins.

Falling Action: The conflict is beyond the crisis, the intensity subsides, and the outcome seems inevitable.

Resolution: The details are wrapped up and we are returned to normalcy.

Applying this pattern to drama can be problematic. Modern playwrights in particular do not limit their work to conform to a pattern that wraps the conflict up so neatly. The structure of many modern plays emerges naturally from the content of the play and bears little resemblance to this classical pattern.

The Poetics

The Poetics of Aristotle is the earliest surviving work of literary criticism in the Western world. Written from 335 to 322 B.C., more than one hundred years after the works of Aeschylus, Sophocles, and Euripides were first produced, it was modeled on plays that Aristotle liked best. It is our earliest written set of standards for dramatic art, and it continues to be influential today. The plays of Sophocles were particularly favored by Aristotle, so both of Sophocles' plays in this text are good models of these standards.

Tragedy

The Poetics defines tragedy as the imitation of an action that is serious and of sufficient magnitude, that is expressed in artistic language, that is performed through drama instead of narration, and that accomplishes catharsis through the arousal of pity and fear. Aristotle emphasizes the nature of the **tragic hero** and the importance of plot in tragedy. He defines his tragic hero as a character of noble stature who is admired by society but flawed. The flaw (often excessive pride, or hubris) leads directly to a reversal of good fortune (catastrophe). But the punishment usually exceeds the crime, and the character deserves our pity. The tragic fall is not a complete loss, as the character gains in wisdom and self-knowledge. Finally, there is a recognition of the causes and consequences of this reversal, and a resolution returns things to normal. The audience, enlightened by the play, experiences **catharsis** (emotional purging or cleansing).

Comedy

Aristotle does not have as much to say about comedy, which he considers a lower form of drama. The traditional plot of comedy is the reverse of tragedy. The protagonist, usually an ordinary person, faces a dilemma. The plot of the play is an extrication from this dilemma and an improvement of circumstances. The reversal of fortune, therefore, is from bad to good; the falling action becomes a rising action with a happy ending. Aristotle suggests that "characters of a higher type" are fit subjects for tragedy, but "persons inferior" are appropriate for comedy.

Although these classifications of tragedy and comedy have been in place since the age of Greek drama, most plays since that time have not strictly conformed to these requirements. Modern plays in particular often contain elements of both tragedy and comedy, a classification called tragicomedy, which is discussed later in the chapter.

For a concise checklist of questions for Conflict and Plot, see page 102.

Characterization

As in fiction, **characterization** *in drama is the development of characters.* But unlike fiction, where some characterization is done through description, characterization in most drama is limited to action and dialogue. We find out about the characters indirectly. We are not told what to think or feel about them. We observe them speaking and doing. We hear what other characters have to say about them. If they are well developed, they seem believable and motivated. Like our response to people in our lives, our response to them and our judgments about them are based on our own observations.

The same terms in both drama and fiction are used to describe characters. The main character in a drama is called the *protagonist.* A character who seems to be a major force in opposition to the protagonist is called an *antagonist.* When characters are not fully developed but seem to represent "types" more than real personalities, we call them *flat,* or *stock, characters.* When they seem fully developed with the complexities of real people, they are described as *round characters.*

For a concise checklist of questions for Characterization, see page 102.

LANGUAGE AND STYLE

Language is the vehicle that carries the characters to you. The style of language used by the characters tells us a lot about them. And the symbolic nature of the language may complement and support the story's theme or meaning.

Greek and Shakespearean plays are written in verse. This very formal style has a very different effect on the audience than the informal vernacular used in modern drama.

Diction

An important element in establishing characters is the kind of language they use to express themselves. This is especially important in drama, because what we know is usually limited to dialogue and action. Characters are often defined as much by *how* they say something as *what* they say. Diction is particularly important in the naturalistic speech of modern drama, where it tells us a great deal about class and cultural distinctions.

Symbol

A **symbol** is something that represents more than itself. In drama, the set, costumes, and props are often used symbolically. The set (the furniture, the size of the room, the light, and color, etc.) often reflects the content of the play itself. The props (the objects onstage and those used by the characters) often reflect the conflict, characters, and theme of the play. The costumes tell us a great deal about the characters themselves.

Irony

Irony is the contrast between appearance/expectation and reality. As in fiction and poetry, the two most popular forms of irony in drama are verbal irony and situational irony. Verbal irony results from the contrast between what is said by characters and what is meant. Irony of situation results from the contrast between what is expected and what actually happens.

For a concise checklist of questions for Language and Style, see page 103.

THEME

As in fiction and poetry, *theme is the central idea expressed by the play.* It is a generalization, an insight about life, that we derive from the play as a whole. Identifying and articulating this meaning is not an easy task. While our experience of the theme may be holistic or impressionistic, the analysis and support required for its articulation demand a close look at the parts—the language, events, characters, and outcome of the play.

Like fiction and poetry, plays do not have one correct answer or interpretation. What makes an interpretation convincing or defensible is your ability to support it. Your belief about what the play means may change as you move back and forth through the stages of your reading or viewing experience. The first time you experience a play, you may feel one way, but writing down your reflections, rereading the play, and discussing it with others may lead to a different, better-informed understanding and interpretation.

Theme or Moral? A temptation when writing about literature is to reduce what it means to a moral or lesson. Good literature reveals a complex world. A moral preaches; it teaches us a lesson or a code of conduct. A theme reveals; it gives us an insight into human nature.

One of the functions of classical drama is to illuminate the audience spiritually, so it's almost certain that we will be left with a clear message by the end of a play. In this respect, Greek plays tend to be **didactic,** or lesson-giving, in a way that most drama since the time of Shakespeare does not.

For a concise checklist of questions for Theme, see page 103.

PERIODS OF DRAMA: A BRIEF BACKGROUND

Greek Drama

Ancient Greece was a remarkable place. It was a democratic society flourishing in the midst of totalitarian regimes and foreign wars. It was also a place where achievements in art, literature, and philosophy were so great that they are still revered as models today, thousands of years after their creation.

Greek drama emerged from religious rituals of the time, but Greek religion bore little resemblance to the dominant religions of the modern Western world. Modern Western religions acknowledge a single, just, and benevolent God, whereas Greek religion was polytheistic and recognized many gods—deities who were just as likely to be arbitrary and nasty as to be just and benevolent. For the ancient Greeks, their world was a microcosm, or smaller version, of the divine world. And since the deities themselves were capable of both good and evil, the existence of evil in their world did not contradict these beliefs.

The Greeks believed that they had little control of their fate but had much control of and responsibility for how they faced up to it. This view, which espoused dignity and humility in the face of adversity, is at the core of most Greek drama. The Greeks saw life as a series of struggles to be faced with courage and humility.

During the fifth century B.C., dramatic or religious festivals were held each spring to celebrate Dionysus, the god of wine and fertility. These festivals are thought to be the origin of Greek tragedy. Playwrights from all over Greece competed for prizes awarded by wealthy citizens, with each competing playwright presenting a trilogy of tragic plays. Though we know the names of more than 150 of these ancient writers, we have only a small sample of their work. Of the almost three hundred plays from the three most prominent playwrights of this period, Euripides, Aeschylus, and Sophocles, only thirty-two remain. Given the quality of these plays, it is sad to imagine the treasures that have been lost.

Staging and Acting   The word *theater* is taken from the Greek *theatron* or "seeing-place," a term used to describe the huge open-air amphitheater that seated the audience during performances. Despite their huge dimensions, these theaters had excellent acoustics that were aided by small megaphones in the actors' masks and a style of acting more in keeping with religious ritual than real life. The number of actors with individual roles onstage at once was limited to two or three. The set was bare and the actors were stationary. All the roles were played by males who wore ornate costumes and large masks to reflect the mood of the play and represent types as much as individuals. Though the dialogue itself and the choral odes contained references to and descriptions of violent actions, no violence was actually shown.

The Chorus   The chorus entered during the **parodos** (the choral ode) and remained onstage throughout the play. The role of the chorus came directly from drama as religious ritual, and dates to a time when there were no individual actors. What the chorus said about the action reflected the traditional values of an Athenian audience. When a passage of dialogue was finished, the characters left the stage and the chorus came forward to comment on it. They chanted their lines together and moved as a unit in one direction, then the other. The chorus explained the action, built anticipation for the upcoming scene, and reminded the audience about the significance of the action or dialogue and the cultural or historical context of the play.

The **choragos** was the leader of the chorus. He acted and spoke as the group's representative, and he was free to speak with both the chorus and the other characters onstage.

Audience Participation   An ancient Greek audience would have already known the myths that inspired the plays. They would have been more curious, then, about the play's dramatization (the acting out of the dramatic moments) than the story line. Suspense was based on the tension of the crises, not on the outcome of the plot. According to Aristotle, the tragic nature of a play should not leave its audience depressed or disheartened. Instead, the audience should be enlightened and inspired by what they had witnessed.

The Language of the Script   Because the text is a translation into modern English, you should not have too much trouble reading it. The verse form was a convention of the time and a requirement. It is not written as people of this time would have spoken to one another. The diction is formal and represents the exalted speech of nobility.

Shakespearean Drama

It is difficult in the twenty-first century to see the world in the light (or darkness) of Elizabethan England. Central to the worldview of this period was the idea of a vertical hierarchy (God superior to the king, the king superior to nobles, the nobles superior to peasants, etc.). People's places in this hierarchy directly affected their quality of life and the kind of rights they had. The king or queen ruled by "divine right," not as elected leaders "through the consent of the governed." Although we regularly make claims for equal opportunity as guaranteed by law today, the idea of peasants in the sixteenth century claiming equal rights with people above their rank would have seemed outrageous. People were not free to worship as they chose. They were not even free to dress as they chose. Though the "sumptuary laws" were not always enforced, they prohibited peasants from dressing in other than coarse fabrics and dull colors, with fine fabrics and bright colors reserved for the nobility. What we call science was nonexistent; very little was known about the cause or spread of disease, and very little could be done for those who became ill. For much of the population, the sole means of transportation was on foot, and life was difficult and short.

And yet, life had never been better. England was emerging as a world power. Trade had opened up with the Continent, providing an exchange of goods, culture, language, and literature never seen before. The printing press was mass-producing pamphlets and books, and literacy among the general public was improving dramatically.

It is into this atmosphere that Shakespeare was born in 1564, the year the great Renaissance artist Michelangelo died. It is fitting that Shakespeare was born near the end of the Renaissance. The Renaissance was a "rebirth"—a revival of a golden age—a triumph of classical creation. Shakespeare's art is distinguished by a looking forward.

Like the explorers of his time, his is a genius of discovery. He explores what is most essential to individual human experience. Rather than types, he discovers highly individualized characters who struggle with each other and themselves, not with fate, the gods, or heredity. But most of all, he discovers language to express these characters and their struggles in verse unparalleled for the quality of its poetry and insight.

Staging and Acting   Before the late sixteenth century, acting companies traveled from town to town and rented space in yards of local inns. Plays were produced on a platform at one end of the yard and the audience gathered around the platform. Wealthier members of the audience viewed the action from the balconies of the surrounding rooms of the inn. The major advantages of this arrangement were its informal, festive atmosphere; the attendance of all classes; and the intimate actor-audience relationship that it encouraged. The close proximity of actor and audience allowed for direct eye contact, an ideal situation for the many soliloquies and asides that playwrights of this period included in their plays.

The Globe Theatre, where most of Shakespeare's plays were performed, was built in 1599 and reflected the kind of space that actors were used to—a space that maintained the intimate atmosphere of the innyards. The Globe was typical of theaters of its kind: a tight, enclosed structure with galleries around the periphery, a projecting platform (about as deep as it was wide) with two upstage entrances, and at least one balcony. The stage itself was almost bare, with only a few simple props or a table, chair, or throne when appropriate. It was a very versatile acting area; there were two exit and entrance doors in the rear of the platform; a curtained alcove between them; a second-story balcony above the stage; a third-story balcony for musicians; a ceiling or heavens extending over the platform, supported by two pillars on the stage; and a trapdoor in the stage platform from which ghosts or devils might emerge.

Although the costumes were elaborate, they reflected current fashion and were not designed to convey the actual clothing of the different countries or times in history depicted in the plays. As in ancient Greece, all parts were played by males. Violence was depicted onstage and quite realistically. Public executions and an abundance of brutal entertainment gave Elizabethans particular expectations. Actors did their best to meet them.

Audience Participation   Audience members who paid the highest admission prices sat in the three stories of covered galleries that enclosed the theater. Here they were protected from the often inclement English weather. Those who paid the least stood in the open area below and around the stage and were called groundlings, a term meant to disparage their social standing as much as to describe their location in the theater.

Throughout his plays, Shakespeare created opportunities for characters to speak directly with the audience. Delivered by a character alone onstage, these **soliloquies** are a "thinking out loud"; true to the speaker, they range from philosophical to diabolical in nature. And they are often the highlights of Shakespeare's plays. Sometimes characters address the audience while not alone onstage. These brief comments, usually in the midst of ongoing dialogue, are called **asides.** The close proximity of actor and audience in an Elizabethan theater made both types of "confidences" particularly effective.

Tips on Reading the Language of Shakespeare

Most of the verse in Shakespeare's plays is written in unrhymed iambic pentameter or blank verse (see p. 82 for a detailed description). This pattern of rhythm (alternating unstressed and stressed syllables) is the natural way English is spoken. The predictability of the pattern made it easier for actors of this period to memorize their lines.

Shakespeare wrote in modern English, but it was a relatively early form of modern English. Some of the words he used have disappeared from the language, some have different meanings now than they did then, and some sentences have a syntax, or word order, we no longer recognize.

Look at the following passage from Shakespeare's play *Othello* (Act III, scene 4).

OTHELLO: That's a fault.

That handkerchief
Did an Egyptian to my mother give;
She was a charmer, and could almost read
The thoughts of people: she told her, while she kept it,   5
'Twould make her amiable and subdue my father
Entirely to her love, but if she lost it
Or made a gift of it, my father's eye
Should hold her loathed and his spirits should hunt
After new fancies: she, dying, gave it me;   10
And bid me, when my fate would have me wive,
To give it her.

Although the plays are written in blank verse, don't let the capital letters at the beginning of each line affect your reading. Don't stop at the end of each verse line unless it has punctuation. Use the punctuation to create pauses or stops as you would with language in prose. Let's look at one of the sentences above in prose form, with the capitals removed:

She told her, while she kept it, 'twould make her amiable and subdue my father entirely to her love, but if she lost it or made a gift of it, my father's eye should hold her loathed and his spirits should hunt after new fancies.

Even in prose, this is a long sentence and requires patience and concentration to understand. But by reading it as prose, you can focus on the punctuation. Some of the phrases might still seem a bit elusive, but read it a few times and see if it is easier to understand.

Reading Out Loud

Good actors help the audience understand the language by the tone and pacing of their voices. But when you are reading from the text of the play, you won't have the benefit of hearing an actor's voice. Reading the lines aloud may help. When you read silently, you subvocalize and hear the words in your brain. But the sound and sense of these words will be clearer if you say and hear the word combinations out loud.

Read the verse passage from *Othello* above aloud and see what you learn about its meaning (and your understanding) in the process.

Word Order

Getting used to the language of Shakespeare means adjusting our expectations for word order in a sentence. In today's English, we generally express ourselves in a subject-verb-object pattern. For example: "A girl hit that ball to her brother." But earlier forms of English sometimes used a word order with the verb at the end. In this earlier form our sentence would read: "That ball did a girl to her brother hit." Takes a little longer to figure out, doesn't it? We need to read the whole sentence to get to the verb. And it is only after we get to the verb that we understand what is being said.

If you look at the first sentence of the quote from *Othello* (above), "That handkerchief / Did an Egyptian to my mother give," you'll see the same pattern. If those words were written in the subject-verb-object pattern we are used to, they would read: "An Egyptian gave that handkerchief to my mother." Made sense much faster, didn't it? You've seen this older verb pattern before in language carried down through the ages for meaningful rituals, like the marriage ceremony (e.g., "With this ring I thee wed" and "Til death do us part").

Most often, the key to reading unusual word order is patience. The meaning may not be clear until you reach the last word of the sentence—and even then you may have to pause to unravel it.

Words, Words, Words

While many other modern languages still have them, English dropped the second-person "familiar" pronoun form some time ago, and uses the "you" form exclusively. When Shakespeare wrote his plays, however, *thou, thee, thy,* and *thine* were the second-person singular "familiar" versions of *you, your,* and *yours.* In general, they indicated a caring relationship with the person addressed—a lover, family member, servant. Dropped as well are verb endings like *st* that agreed with these familiar pronouns (thou dost, thou shalt, thou goest). Other third-person verb endings like *th* ("It *hath* made me ill"; "It *doth* give me heartburn") have simply become obsolete.

It is not unusual to see letters replaced with apostrophes occasionally. ("Whether *'tis* nobler"; "*'twould* make her amiable"; "*overstep* not the modesty of nature"). By leaving a letter out, Shakespeare often managed to eliminate a beat and keep the blank verse intact. In these cases, the context of the statement will usually tell you that *'tis* means "it is," *'twould* means "it would," and *overstep* means "overstep."

In other cases, entire words seem to be left out ("Let's [?] to bed knight"; "My father had a daughter [?] loved a man"). Again in these cases the context of the sentence should tell you that *go* and *who* are the words assumed to be understood.

Shakespeare was a master of making up words too (*assassinate, dislocate, obscene, reliance, submerged,* and hundreds of others we still use), and changing words from one part of speech to another, for example, in the above quote from *Othello,* the use of *wive* instead of *marry:* "And bid me, when my fate would have me wive, / To give it her." So don't be surprised when you come across a verb that you're used to as a noun. The meaning is likely to be what you think it is.

You may notice that when a king speaks, he often uses the pronouns *our, us,* and *we* to refer to himself. In the first line of his opening speech in Act I, scene 2 of *Hamlet,* Claudius refers to himself this way: "Though yet of Hamlet *our* dear brother's death / The memory be green." This use of the "royal plural," or "imperial we," was common among royalty, who saw themselves as personifying the kingdom and everyone in it.

Finally, it is very helpful to read the notes that accompany the text. You'll need help with words no longer in use and words that had a different meaning than they do now. It will take a little longer to read the text, but remember that patience is a key to having a successful experience with Shakespeare's work.

Modern Drama

Modern drama, like so much else "modern," was born in the nineteenth century. Its emergence was a natural outgrowth and reflection of the profound social, political, and technological changes taking place around it. Like so many other modern movements, it arose as a reaction—to the content, staging, and acting of the neoclassical drama and romantic melodrama so popular in the era that preceded it. As this reaction ran its course, virtually every aspect of theater changed.

The preceding seventeenth and eighteenth centuries were dominated early by neoclassicism (or new classicism), which was notable for its rigid adherence to the forms of classical drama. While there were a number of highly successful comedies, the power and passion of ancient tragedy was missing in an age that seemed to prefer form over substance. Later in this period, melodramas with elaborate but oversimplified plots, flat characters, excessive sentiment, and happy endings were most popular. The physical layout of the theater changed during this period, too, and theaters moved indoors. The stage was recessed behind and framed by a **proscenium arch** at the end of a long room or hall. The audience was seated directly in front of the stage and in the surrounding galleries. This layout is the one we still see today in most school auditoriums and many theaters. Settings for each play were painted on canvas backdrops behind the acting area. A scene could be changed simply by changing the backdrop. Both the audience and the actors behaved with great flamboyance. The audience came to the theater as much to be seen as to see the action onstage. Consequently, both audience and actors spent much money on elaborate costumes. And as the size of theaters increased, so did the volume of the actors' voices and the exaggeration of their gestures.

A transformation to what we recognize as modern drama came slowly, and it took much of the nineteenth century to make real progress. But that change and that movement toward **realism** in both content and technique would affect every aspect of drama. Writers depicted the reality of struggling, ordinary people. Set designers produced authentic settings onstage. Actors spoke and behaved like real people.

But even as realism was becoming established, it was generating reactions to its own form and objective view of reality. In the twentieth century, **symbolism** would seek its truth in symbols, myths, and dreams; **expressionism** in the subjectivity of perception; and **surrealism** in the irrationality of the unconscious mind.

Modern drama is a synthesis of many forms and philosophies. More than a single approach, it is characterized by variety and diversity—diversity of content, perspective, and staging. The traditional categories of tragedy and comedy are inadequate to classify most modern drama. Tragic, comic, and absurd views of life often mix together in the same script, side by side, back-to-back. This diverse combination of views and styles is described as **tragicomedy.**

Staging and Acting In general, theaters built today have better acoustical, visual, and spatial arrangements than ever before. Interiors with rising tiers of seats give audiences clear sight lines and encourage a more naturalistic style of acting. In many ways the era of modern drama began with the development of the **box set**—a set composed of **flats,** or connected walls enclosing three sides of the stage, with an invisible "fourth wall" open to the audience. Through this invisible fourth wall the audience sees the action and eavesdrops on the conversations of characters, who occupy a room with authentic furniture, rugs, hanging fixtures, and other realistic props.

Today, there are many types of stages. Several variations of the proscenium stage with enclosed box set have evolved. And since the 1940s, thrust stages—a throwback to the Elizabethan platform that extends into the audience—and the arena stage, or theater in the round—a circular acting area surrounded by the audience—have been designed to bring audiences closer to the actors.

Artificial light and sound create realistic stage settings. Lighting can project times, places, and moods, and can even divide the stage into different acting areas. Computerized light boards control hundreds of lights and lighting combinations. Electronic amplification and portable microphones make it easier for actors to speak in their natural voices. Authentic costumes complement the set, support historical authenticity, and enrich characterization.

As the twentieth century approached and the demands for realism increased, the training of actors changed too. The work of Constantine Stanislavski epitomized this movement. Stanislavski's *method* required that actors express the interior lives of the characters they played—to live the role by finding the character's emotions and motivation in themselves. More than a century after he developed his method, it is still the most popular approach used by actors to prepare their roles.

Audience Participation While realistic staging and lighting highlight a real setting peopled by real characters, they put the audience literally in the dark. Though the box set encourages actors to move more deeply into "character," its fourth wall maintains a distance from the audience. The actors move on a lighted stage very visible to the audience, but the audience often sits in the dark invisible to the actors.

The Language and Style of the Script Characters in modern drama almost always speak in colloquial language, not verse. What they say sounds like everyday speech. Following the lead of fiction writers in the late nineteenth century, dramatists began to write dialogue in the regional speech of the characters. Having "an ear" for dialogue, for realistic speech and how it sounds, is a crucial skill for any dramatist today.

Stage directions in the text of modern plays are more detailed than ever before. Descriptions of the set, props, movements of the actors, and the lighting are often specified in the script and integrated with action and characterization.

☑ CHECKLIST: ANALYZING DRAMA

Point of View

❑ Does the play have a narrator? If so, who is it and what effect does this narration have on your response?

Set and Setting

❑ When is the play set? What role does the setting have? What physical location is this? The country? The city? What does the set look like? What props are present?

❑ Can you describe the atmosphere? What time of day is this? What is the lighting? What are the dominant colors? What is the weather like? Who is present? How are they dressed?

❑ Does the setting support and emphasize the story's meaning?

Conflict and Plot

❑ What is the primary external conflict in the play? The primary internal conflict? Are there other conflicts? If so, what are they?

❑ Support your identification of conflict by citing action and dialogue in the text.

❑ In what way do the personality traits of the characters lead to conflict?

❑ Can you identify the plot? Does it conform to the traditional structure? If so, how? If not, what is the structure?

❑ Is it a tragedy or a comedy? Explain.

Characterization

❑ How do you feel about the characters? What do the characters do to make you feel this way? What do the characters say to make you feel this way? What is said about the characters to make you feel this way?

❑ Are the characters motivated and consistent? Are they believable? Are there flat, or stock, characters in the play? Explain.

❑ Who is the protagonist? The antagonist(s)?

❑ Support your responses to the characters by citing action and dialogue in the play.

Language and Style

❑   Is the language used in the play formal or informal? What does the nature of their language use tell you about the characters?

❑   Are there any symbols? Is the set symbolic? Are the props or the costumes symbolic? If so, how do they connect to or support the story?

❑   Are there instances of verbal or situational irony? Explain.

Theme

❑   What are the major details (characters, conflicts, outcome) of the play?

❑   What conclusion about the play did you draw from these details? What generalization about life does this conclusion lead to?

❑   What is the central idea expressed by the play? What is its theme? Does the play reveal or does it preach? Explain.

GETTING IDEAS FOR WRITING ABOUT DRAMA

The purpose of the play, the prompts, and the questions in this section is to show how the elements we've discussed earlier might be applied to drama. Following *Antigonê*, many of the questions from the summary checklist above are applied to the play, and we consider some of the ways the elements discussed in this section might be used to prompt ideas for an essay.

Tips on Reading *Antigonê*

To prepare for reading *Antigonê*, be sure to read the background section on Greek Drama (pp. 95–96). Since this is an ancient full-length play and some of its conventions may seem unusual to you, give yourself enough time to read (and reread). The translation that follows is in modern English, so you should have no trouble understanding the language. But you may be a bit confused by the verse form and the choral odes, so here are two suggestions to make your reading easier:

1.   *Read the verse lines as if they are prose.* Instead of stopping at the end of each verse line, read right through the caps at the beginning of the next line and stop or pause at the punctuation. Each verse line does not contain a complete thought, but the sentences do.

2.   *The first time you read the play, skip the Choral Odes.* They are not intended to advance the action but to comment upon it. After your first reading, go back and read the choral odes informed by your understanding of what has happened in the play.

SOPHOCLES [496?–406 B.C.]

ANTIGONÊ [CA. 441 B.C.]

AN ENGLISH VERSION BY DUDLEY FITTS AND ROBERT FITZGERALD

CHARACTERS

ANTIGONÊ
ISMENÊ
EURYDICÊ
CREON
HAIMON
TEIRESIAS
A SENTRY
A MESSENGER
CHORUS

SCENE: *Before the palace of* CREON *King of Thebes. A central double door, and two lateral doors. A platform extends the length of the facade, and from this platform three steps lead down into the orchestra, or chorus-ground.*

TIME: *Dawn of the day after the repulse of the Argive army from the assault on Thebes.*

PROLOGUE

ANTIGONÊ *and* ISMENÊ *enter from the central door of the palace.*

ANTIGONÊ: Ismenê, dear sister,
    You would think that we had already suffered enough
    For the curse on Oedipus:°
    I cannot imagine any grief
    That you and I have not gone through. And now—   5
    Have they told you of the new decree of our King Creon?

ISMENÊ: I have heard nothing: I know
    That two sisters lost two brothers, a double death
    In a single hour; and I know that the Argive army
    Fled in the night; but beyond this, nothing.   10

---

3 Oedipus the father of Antigonê, Ismenê, and their brothers Polyneicês and Eteoclês, and former king of Thebes. Oedipus unknowingly killed his father, Laios, and married his mother, Iocastê. When he discovered the truth, he blinded himself and left Thebes. After Oedipus abdicated the throne, the two brothers ruled. But they quarreled. Polyneicês was defeated but returned to attack Thebes. Both brothers were killed in battle. Creon, who became king, ordered that Polyneicês remain unburied.

ANTIGONÊ: I thought so. And that is why I wanted you
　　　To come out here with me. There is something we must do.
ISMENÊ: Why do you speak so strangely?
ANTIGONÊ: Listen, Ismenê:
　　　Creon buried our brother Eteoclês   15
　　　With military honors, gave him a soldier's funeral,
　　　And it was right that he should; but Polyneicês,
　　　Who fought as bravely and died as miserably,—
　　　They say that Creon has sworn
　　　No one shall bury him, no one mourn for him,   20
　　　But his body must lie in the fields, a sweet treasure
　　　For carrion birds to find as they search for food.
　　　That is what they say, and our good Creon is coming here
　　　To announce it publicly; and the penalty—
　　　Stoning to death in the public square!   25
　　　　　　　　　　　　　　　　　There it is,
　　　And now you can prove what you are:
　　　A true sister, or a traitor to your family.
ISMENÊ: Antigonê, you are mad! What could I possibly do?
ANTIGONÊ: You must decide whether you will help me or not.
ISMENÊ: I do not understand you. Help you in what?   30
ANTIGONÊ: Ismenê, I am going to bury him. Will you come?
ISMENÊ: Bury him! You have just said the new law forbids it.
ANTIGONÊ: He is my brother. And he is your brother, too.
ISMENÊ: But think of the danger! Think what Creon will do!
ANTIGONÊ: Creon is not strong enough to stand in my way.   35
ISMENÊ: Ah sister!
　　　Oedipus died, everyone hating him
　　　For what his own search brought to light, his eyes
　　　Ripped out by his own hand; and Iocastê died,
　　　His mother and wife at once: she twisted the cords   40
　　　That strangled her life; and our two brothers died,
　　　Each killed by the other's sword. And we are left:
　　　But oh, Antigonê,
　　　Think how much more terrible than these
　　　Our own death would be if we should go against Creon   45
　　　And do what he has forbidden! We are only women,
　　　We cannot fight with men, Antigonê!
　　　The law is strong, we must give in to the law
　　　In this thing, and in worse. I beg the Dead
　　　To forgive me, but I am helpless: I must yield   50

To those in authority. And I think it is dangerous business
To be always meddling.

ANTIGONÊ: If that is what you think,
    I should not want you, even if you asked to come.
    You have made your choice, you can be what you want to be.
    But I will bury him; and if I must die,   55
    I say that this crime is holy: I shall lie down
    With him in death, and I shall be as dear
    To him as he to me.
              It is the dead,
    Not the living, who make the longest demands:
    We die for ever . . .
              You may do as you like,   60
    Since apparently the laws of the gods mean nothing to you.

ISMENÊ: They mean a great deal to me; but I have no strength
    To break laws that were made for the public good.

ANTIGONÊ: That must be your excuse, I suppose. But as for me,
    I will bury the brother I love.

ISMENÊ: Antigonê,   65
    I am so afraid for you!

ANTIGONÊ: You need not be:
    You have yourself to consider, after all.

ISMENÊ: But no one must hear of this, you must tell no one!
    I will keep it a secret, I promise!

ANTIGONÊ: O tell it! Tell everyone!   70
    Think how they'll hate you when it all comes out
    If they learn that you knew about it all the time!

ISMENÊ: So fiery! You should be cold with fear.

ANTIGONÊ: Perhaps. But I am doing only what I must.

ISMENÊ: But you can do it? I say that you cannot.   75

ANTIGONÊ: Very well: when my strength gives out,
    I shall do no more.

ISMENÊ: Impossible things should not be tried at all.

ANTIGONÊ: Go away, Ismenê:
    I shall be hating you soon, and the dead will too,   80
    For your words are hateful. Leave me my foolish plan:
    I am not afraid of the danger; if it means death,
    It will not be the worst of deaths—death without honor.

ISMENÊ: Go then, if you feel that you must.
    You are unwise,   85
    But a loyal friend indeed to those who love you.

      Exit into the palace. ANTIGONÊ *goes off, left. Enter the Chorus.*

PARODOS°

Strophe 1°

CHORUS: Now the long blade of the sun, lying
    Level east to west, touches with glory
    Thebes of the Seven Gates. Open, unlidded
    Eye of golden day! O marching light
    Across the eddy and rush of Dircê's stream°   5
    Striking the white shields of the enemy
    Thrown headlong backward from the blaze of morning!
CHORAGOS°:   Polyneicês their commander
    Roused them with windy phrases,
    He the wild eagle screaming   10
    Insults above our land,
    His wings their shields of snow,
    His crest their marshalled helms.

Antistrophe 1°

CHORUS: Against our seven gates in a yawning ring
    The famished spears came onward in the night;   15
    But before his jaws were sated with our blood,
    Or pinefire took the garland of our towers,
    He was thrown back; and as he turned, great Thebes—
    No tender victim for his noisy power—
    Rose like a dragon behind him, shouting war.   20
CHORAGOS: For God hates utterly
    The bray of bragging tongues;
    And when he beheld their smiling,
    Their swagger of golden helms,
    The frown of his thunder blasted   25
    Their first man from our walls.

Strophe 2

CHORUS: We heard his shout of triumph high in the air
    Turn to a scream; far out in a flaming arc
    He fell with his windy torch, and the earth struck him.
    And others storming in fury no less than his   30
    Found shock of death in the dusty joy of battle.

Parodos the entrance song of the chorus   **Strophe** sung as the chorus moves from stage
right to stage left   **5 Dircê's stream** a river near Thebes   **8 Choragos** the leader of the
chorus   **Antistrophe** sung as the chorus moves from stage left to stage right

CHORAGOS: Seven captains at seven gates
            Yielded their clanging arms to the god
            That bends the battle-line and breaks it.
            These two only, brothers in blood,   35
            Face to face in matchless rage,
            Mirroring each the other's death,
            Clashed in long combat.

Antistrophe 2

CHORUS: But now in the beautiful morning of victory
            Let Thebes of the many chariots sing for joy!   40
            With hearts for dancing we'll take leave of war:
            Our temples shall be sweet with hymns of praise,
            And the long night shall echo with our chorus.

SCENE I

CHORAGOS: But now at last our new King is coming:
            Creon of Thebes, Menoikeus' son.
            In this auspicious dawn of his reign
            What are the new complexities
            That shifting Fate has woven for him?   5
            What is his counsel? Why has he summoned
            The old men to hear him?

        Enter CREON *from the palace, center. He addresses the Chorus
                    from the top step.*

CREON: Gentlemen: I have the honor to inform you that our Ship of State,
            which recent storms have threatened to destroy, has come safely to harbor   10
            at last, guided by the merciful wisdom of Heaven. I have summoned you
            here this morning because I know that I can depend upon you: your
            devotion to King Laïos was absolute; you never hesitated in your duty to
            our late ruler Oedipus; and when Oedipus died, your loyalty was trans-
            ferred to his children. Unfortunately, as you know, his two sons, the princes   15
            Eteoclês and Polyneicês, have killed each other in battle; and I, as the next
            in blood, have succeeded to the full power of the throne.
                I am aware, of course, that no Ruler can expect complete loyalty from
            his subjects until he has been tested in office. Nevertheless, I say to you at
            the very outset that I have nothing but contempt for the kind of Governor   20
            who is afraid, for whatever reason, to follow the course that he knows is
            best for the State; and as for the man who sets private friendship above the
            public welfare,—I have no use for him, either. I call God to witness that if
            I saw my country headed for ruin, I should not be afraid to speak out
            plainly; and I need hardly remind you that I would never have any dealings   25

with an enemy of the people. No one values friendship more highly than I; but we must remember that friends made at the risk of wrecking our Ship are not real friends at all.

These are my principles, at any rate, and that is why I have made the following decision concerning the sons of Oedipus: Eteoclês, who died as   30
a man should die, fighting for his country, is to be buried with full military honors, with all the ceremony that is usual when the greatest heroes die; but his brother Polyneicês who broke his exile to come back with fire and sword against his native city and the shrines of his fathers' gods, whose   35
one idea was to spill the blood of his blood and sell his own people into slavery—Polyneicês, I say, is to have no burial: no man is to touch him or say the least prayer for him; he shall lie on the plain, unburied; and the birds and the scavenging dogs can do with him whatever they like.

This is my command, and you can see the wisdom behind it. As long as   40
I am King, no traitor is going to be honored with the loyal man. But who-ever shows by word and deed that he is on the side of the State,—he shall have my respect while he is living, and my reverence when he is dead.

CHORAGOS: If that is your will, Creon son of Menoikeus,
You have the right to enforce it: we are yours.

CREON: That is my will. Take care that you do your part.

CHORAGOS: We are old men: let the younger ones carry it out.   45

CREON: I do not mean that: the sentries have been appointed.

CHORAGOS: Then what is it that you would have us do?

CREON: You will give no support to whoever breaks this law.

CHORAGOS: Only a crazy man is in love with death!

CREON: And death it is, yet money talks, and the wisest   50
Have sometimes been known to count a few coins too many.

Enter SENTRY *from left.*

Sentry: I'll not say that I'm out of breath from running, King, because every time I stopped to think about what I have to tell you, I felt like going back. And all the time a voice kept saying, "You fool, don't you know you're walking straight into trouble?"; and then another voice: "Yes, but   55
if you let somebody else get the news to Creon first, it will be even worse than that for you!" But good sense won out, at least I hope it was good sense, and here I am with a story that makes no sense at all; but I'll tell it anyhow, because, as they say, what's going to happen's going to happen and—

CREON: Come to the point. What have you to say?   60

SENTRY: I did not do it. I did not see who did it. You must not punish me for what someone else has done.

CREON: A comprehensive defense! More effective, perhaps,
If I knew its purpose. Come: what is it?

SENTRY: A dreadful thing . . . I don't know how to put it—   65

CREON: Out with it!

SENTRY: Well, then;

    The dead man—

                    Polyneicês—

                        Pause. The SENTRY *is overcome, fumbles for words.*
                        CREON *waits impassively.*

                        out there—   70
                                        someone,—

    New dust on the slimy flesh!

                        Pause. No sign from CREON.

    Someone has given it burial that way, and

    Gone . . .

            Long pause. CREON *finally speaks with deadly control.*

        CREON: And the man who dared do this?   75

SENTRY: I swear I

    Do not know! You must believe me!

                            Listen:

    The ground was dry, not a sign of digging, no,

    Not a wheeltrack in the dust, no trace of anyone.   80

    It was when they relieved us this morning: and one of them,

    The corporal, pointed to it.

                        There it was,

    The strangest—

                Look: 85

    The body, just mounded over with light dust: you see?

    Not buried really, but as if they'd covered it

    Just enough for the ghost's peace. And no sign

    Of dogs or any wild animal that had been there.

    And then what a scene there was! Every man of us   90

    Accusing the other: we all proved the other man did it,

    We all had proof that we could not have done it.

    We were ready to take hot iron in our hands,

    Walk through fire, swear by all the gods,

    It was not I!   95

    I do not know who it was, but it was not I!

CREON'S *rage has been mounting steadily, but the* SENTRY *is too intent upon his
                        story to notice it.*

    And then, when this came to nothing, someone said

    A thing that silenced us and made us stare

    Down at the ground: you had to be told the news,

    And one of us had to do it! We threw the dice,   100

    And the bad luck fell to me. So here I am,

No happier to be here than you are to have me:
Nobody likes the man who brings bad news.

CHORAGOS: I have been wondering, King: can it be that the gods have done this?

CREON [*furiously*]:   Stop!   105
Must you doddering wrecks
Go out of your heads entirely? "The gods"!
Intolerable!
The gods favor this corpse? Why? How had he served them?
Tried to loot their temples, burn their images,   110
Yes, and the whole State, and its laws with it!
Is it your senile opinion that the gods love to honor bad men?
A pious thought!—

No, from the very beginning
There have been those who have whispered together,
Stiff-necked anarchists, putting their heads together,   115
Scheming against me in alleys. These are the men,
And they have bribed my own guard to do this thing.
[*Sententiously.*] Money!
There's nothing in the world so demoralizing as money.
Down go your cities,   120
Homes gone, men gone, honest hearts corrupted,
Crookedness of all kinds, and all for money!

To SENTRY.

But you—!
I swear by God and by the throne of God,
The man who has done this thing shall pay for it!
Find that man, bring him here to me, or your death   125
Will be the least of your problems: I'll string you up
Alive, and there will be certain ways to make you
Discover your employer before you die;
And the process may teach you a lesson you seem to have missed:
The dearest profit is sometimes all too dear: 130
That depends on the source. Do you understand me?
A fortune won is often misfortune.

SENTRY: King, may I speak?

CREON: Your very voice distresses me.

SENTRY: Are you sure that it is my voice, and not your conscience?

CREON: By God, he wants to analyze me now!   135

SENTRY: It is not what I say, but what has been done, that hurts you.

CREON: You talk too much.

SENTRY: Maybe; but I've done nothing.

CREON: Sold your soul for some silver: that's all you've done.

SENTRY: How dreadful it is when the right judge judges wrong!

CREON: Your figures of speech   140
          May entertain you now; but unless you bring me the man,
          You will get little profit from them in the end.

                          Exit CREON *into the palace.*

SENTRY: "Bring me the man"—!
           I'd like nothing better than bringing him the man!
           But bring him or not, you have seen the last of me here.   145
           At any rate, I am safe!

                          Exit Sentry.

ODE I

Strophe 1

CHORUS: Numberless are the world's wonders, but none
           More wonderful than man; the stormgray sea
           Yields to his prows, the huge crests bear him high;
           Earth, holy and inexhaustible, is graven
           With shining furrows where his plows have gone   5
           Year after year, the timeless labor of stallions.

Antistrophe 1

           The lightboned birds and beasts that cling to cover,
           The lithe fish lighting their reaches of dim water,
           All are taken, tamed in the net of his mind;
           The lion on the hill, the wild horse windy-maned,   10
           Resign to him; and his blunt yoke has broken
           The sultry shoulders of the mountain bull.

Strophe 2

           Words also, and thought as rapid as air,
           He fashions to his good use; statecraft is his,
           And his the skill that deflects the arrows of snow,   15
           The spears of winter rain: from every wind
           He has made himself secure—from all but one:
           In the late wind of death he cannot stand.

Antistrophe 2

           O clear intelligence, force beyond all measure!
           O fate of man, working both good and evil!   20
           When the laws are kept, how proudly his city stands!
           When the laws are broken, what of his city then?
           Never may the anárchic man find rest at my hearth,
           Never be it said that my thoughts are his thoughts.

SCENE II

Reenter SENTRY *leading* ANTIGONÊ.

CHORAGOS: What does this mean? Surely this captive woman
    Is the Princess, Antigonê. Why should she be taken?
SENTRY: Here is the one who did it! We caught her
    In the very act of burying him—Where is Creon?
CHORAGOS: Just coming from the house.

Enter CREON, *center.*

CREON: What has happened?   5
    Why have you come back so soon?
SENTRY [*expansively*]:   O King,
    A man should never be too sure of anything:
    I would have sworn
    That you'd not see me here again: your anger
    Frightened me so, and the things you threatened me with;   10
    But how could I tell then
    That I'd be able to solve the case so soon?
    No dice-throwing this time: I was only too glad to come!
    Here is this woman. She is the guilty one:
    We found her trying to bury him.   15
    Take her, then; question her; judge her as you will.
    I am through with the whole thing now, and glad of it.
CREON: But this is Antigonê! Why have you brought her here?
SENTRY: She was burying him, I tell you!
CREON [*severely*]:   Is this the truth?
SENTRY: I saw her with my own eyes. Can I say more?   20
CREON: The details: come, tell me quickly!
SENTRY: It was like this:
    After those terrible threats of yours, King,
    We went back and brushed the dust away from the body.
    The flesh was soft by now, and stinking,
    So we sat on a hill to windward and kept guard.   25
    No napping this time! We kept each other awake.
    But nothing happened until the white round sun
    Whirled in the center of the round sky over us:
    Then, suddenly,
    A storm of dust roared up from the earth, and the sky   30
    Went out, the plain vanished with all its trees
    In the stinging dark. We closed our eyes and endured it.
    The whirlwind lasted a long time, but it passed;
    And then we looked, and there was Antigonê!
    I have seen   35

A mother bird come back to a stripped nest, heard
Her crying bitterly a broken note or two
For the young ones stolen. Just so, when this girl
Found the bare corpse, and all her love's work wasted,
She wept, and cried on heaven to damn the hands   40
That had done this thing.
                         And then she brought more dust
And sprinkled wine three times for her brother's ghost.
We ran and took her at once. She was not afraid,
Not even when we charged her with what she had done.
She denied nothing.
                         And this was a comfort to me,   45
And some uneasiness: for it is a good thing
To escape from death, but it is no great pleasure
To bring death to a friend.
                         Yet I always say
There is nothing so comfortable as your own safe skin!
CREON [*slowly, dangerously*]:   And you, Antigonê,   50
        You with your head hanging,—do you confess this thing?
ANTIGONÊ: I do. I deny nothing.
CREON [*to Sentry*]:   You may go.

                    Exit SENTRY.

[*to* ANTIGONÊ] Tell me, tell me briefly:
        Had you heard my proclamation touching this matter?
ANTIGONÊ: It was public. Could I help hearing it?   55
CREON: And yet you dared defy the law.
ANTIGONÊ: I dared.
        It was not God's proclamation. That final Justice
        That rules the world below makes no such laws.

        Your edict, King, was strong,
        But all your strength is weakness itself against   60
        The immortal unrecorded laws of God.
        They are not merely now: they were, and shall be,
        Operative for ever, beyond man utterly.

        I knew I must die, even without your decree:
        I am only mortal. And if I must die   65
        Now, before it is my time to die,
        Surely this is no hardship: can anyone
        Living, as I live, with evil all about me,
        Think Death less than a friend? This death of mine
        Is of no importance; but if I had left my brother   70
        Lying in death unburied, I should have suffered.

Now I do not.
　　　　　You smile at me. Ah Creon,
Think me a fool, if you like; but it may well be
That a fool convicts me of folly.
CHORAGOS:　　Like father, like daughter: both headstrong, deaf to reason!　　75
She has never learned to yield.
CREON:　　　　　　　　　　　　　She has much to learn.
The inflexible heart breaks first, the toughest iron
Cracks first, and the wildest horses bend their necks
At the pull of the smallest curb.
　　　　　　　　　　Pride? In a slave?
This girl is guilty of a double insolence,　　　　　　　　80
Breaking the given laws and boasting of it.
Who is the man here,
She or I, if this crime goes unpunished?
Sister's child, or more than sister's child,
Or closer yet in blood—she and her sister　　　　　　85
Win bitter death for this!

　　　　　　[*to* SERVANTS]

　　　　　Go, some of you,
Arrest Ismenê. I accuse her equally.
Bring her: you will find her sniffling in the house there.

Her mind's a traitor: crimes kept in the dark
Cry for light, and the guardian brain shudders;　　　　90
But how much worse than this
Is brazen boasting of barefaced anarchy!
ANTIGONÊ:　　Creon, what more do you want than my death?
CREON:　　　　　　　　　　　　　　　　　Nothing.
That gives me everything.
ANTIGONÊ:　　　　　　　Then I beg you: kill me.
This talking is a great weariness: your words　　　　95
Are distasteful to me, and I am sure that mine
Seem so to you. And yet they should not seem so:
I should have praise and honor for what I have done.
All these men here would praise me
Were their lips not frozen shut with fear of you.　　　100
[*Bitterly.*] Ah the good fortune of kings,
Licensed to say and do whatever they please!
CREON:　　You are alone here in that opinion.
ANTIGONÊ:　　No, they are with me. But they keep their tongues in leash.
CREON:　　Maybe. But you are guilty, and they are not.　　　105
ANTIGONÊ:　　There is no guilt in reverence for the dead.

CREON: But Eteoclês—was he not your brother too?

ANTIGONÊ: My brother too.

CREON: And you insult his memory?

ANTIGONÊ [*softly*]:   The dead man would not say that I insult it.

CREON: He would: for you honor a traitor as much as him.   110

ANTIGONÊ: His own brother, traitor or not, and equal in blood.

CREON: He made war on his country. Eteoclês defended it.

ANTIGONÊ: Nevertheless, there are honors due all the dead.

CREON: But not the same for the wicked as for the just.

ANTIGONÊ: Ah Creon, Creon,   115

    Which of us can say what the gods hold wicked?

CREON: An enemy is an enemy, even dead.

ANTIGONÊ: It is my nature to join in love, not hate.

CREON [*finally losing patience*]:   Go join them, then; if you must have your love,

    Find it in hell!   120

CHORAGOS: But see, Ismenê comes:

Enter ISMENÊ, *guarded.*

    Those tears are sisterly, the cloud

    That shadows her eyes rains down gentle sorrow.

CREON: You too, Ismenê,

    Snake in my ordered house, sucking my blood   125

    Stealthily—and all the time I never knew

    That these two sisters were aiming at my throne!

                                    Ismenê,

    Do you confess your share in this crime, or deny it?

    Answer me.

ISMENÊ: Yes, if she will let me say so. I am guilty.   130

ANTIGONÊ [*coldly*]:   No, Ismenê. You have no right to say so.

    You would not help me, and I will not have you help me.

ISMENÊ: But now I know what you meant; and I am here

    To join you, to take my share of punishment.

ANTIGONÊ: The dead man and the gods who rule the dead   135

    Know whose act this was. Words are not friends.

ISMENÊ: Do you refuse me, Antigonê? I want to die with you:

    I too have a duty that I must discharge to the dead.

ANTIGONÊ: You shall not lessen my death by sharing it.

ISMENÊ: What do I care for life when you are dead?   140

ANTIGONÊ: Ask Creon. You're always hanging on his opinions.

ISMENÊ: You are laughing at me. Why, Antigonê?

ANTIGONÊ: It's a joyless laughter, Ismenê.

ISMENÊ: But can I do nothing?

ANTIGONÊ: Yes. Save yourself. I shall not envy you.   145

    There are those who will praise you; I shall have honor, too.

ISMENÊ: But we are equally guilty!

ANTIGONÊ: No more, Ismenê.

> You are alive, but I belong to Death.

CREON [*to the Chorus*]:   Gentlemen, I beg you to observe these girls: 150

> One has just now lost her mind; the other,
> It seems, has never had a mind at all.

ISMENÊ: Grief teaches the steadiest minds to waver, King.

CREON: Yours certainly did, when you assumed guilt with the guilty!

ISMENÊ: But how could I go on living without her?   155

CREON: You are.

> She is already dead.

ISMENÊ: But your own son's bride!

CREON: There are places enough for him to push his plow.

> I want no wicked women for my sons!   160

ISMENÊ: O dearest Haimon, how your father wrongs you!

CREON: I've had enough of your childish talk of marriage!

CHORAGOS: Do you really intend to steal this girl from your son?

CREON: No; Death will do that for me.

CHORAGOS: Then she must die?   165

CREON [*ironically*]:   You dazzle me.

>   —But enough of this talk!

> [*to* GUARDS] You, there, take them away and guard them well:
> For they are but women, and even brave men run
> When they see Death coming.   170

> *Exeunt* ISMENÊ, ANTIGONÊ, *and* GUARDS.

ODE II

Strophe 1

CHORUS: Fortunate is the man who has never tasted God's vengeance!

> Where once the anger of heaven has struck, that house is shaken
> For ever: damnation rises behind each child
> Like a wave cresting out of the black northeast,
> When the long darkness under sea roars up   5
> And bursts drumming death upon the windwhipped sand.

Antistrophe 1

> I have seen this gathering sorrow from time long past
> Loom upon Oedipus' children: generation from generation
> Takes the compulsive rage of the enemy god.
> So lately this last flower of Oedipus' line   10
> Drank the sunlight! but now a passionate word
> And a handful of dust have closed up all its beauty.

Strophe 2

> What mortal arrogance
> Transcends the wrath of Zeus?
> Sleep cannot lull him nor the effortless long months   15
> Of the timeless gods: but he is young for ever,
> And his house is the shining day of high Olympos.
>> All that is and shall be,
>> And all the past, is his.
> No pride on earth is free of the curse of heaven.   20

Antistrophe 2

> The straying dreams of men
>> May bring them ghosts of joy:
> But as they drowse, the waking embers burn them;
> Or they walk with fixed eyes, as blind men walk.
> But the ancient wisdom speaks for our own time: 25
>> *Fate works most for woe*
>> *With Folly's fairest show.*
> Man's little pleasure is the spring of sorrow.

SCENE III

CHRAGOS: But here is Haimon, King, the last of all your sons.
> Is it grief for Antigonê that brings him here,
> And bitterness at being robbed of his bride?

> *Enter* HAIMON.

CREN: We shall soon see, and no need of diviners.
>   —Son,
> You have heard my final judgment on that girl: 5
> Have you come here hating me, or have you come
> With deference and with love, whatever I do?
HAIMON: I am your son, father. You are my guide.
> You make things clear for me, and I obey you.
> No marriage means more to me than your continuing wisdom.   10
CREON: Good. That is the way to behave: subordinate
> Everything else, my son, to your father's will.
> This is what a man prays for, that he may get
> Sons attentive and dutiful in his house,
> Each one hating his father's enemies,   15
> Honoring his father's friends. But if his sons
> Fail him, if they turn out unprofitably,
> What has he fathered but trouble for himself
> And amusement for the malicious?

                          So you are right
Not to lose your head over this woman.   20
Your pleasure with her would soon grow cold, Haimon,
And then you'd have a hellcat in bed and elsewhere.
Let her find her husband in Hell!
Of all the people in this city, only she
Has had contempt for my law and broken it.   25

Do you want me to show myself weak before the people?
Or to break my sworn word? No, and I will not.
The woman dies.
I suppose she'll plead "family ties." Well, let her.
If I permit my own family to rebel,   30
How shall I earn the world's obedience?
Show me the man who keeps his house in hand,
He's fit for public authority.
                          I'll have no dealings
With law-breakers, critics of the government:
Whoever is chosen to govern should be obeyed—   35
Must be obeyed, in all things, great and small,
Just and unjust! O Haimon,
The man who knows how to obey, and that man only,
Knows how to give commands when the time comes.
You can depend on him, no matter how fast   40
The spears come: he's a good soldier, he'll stick it out.

Anarchy, anarchy! Show me a greater evil!
This is why cities tumble and the great houses rain down,
This is what scatters armies!
No, no: good lives are made so by discipline.   45
We keep the laws then, and the lawmakers,
And no woman shall seduce us. If we must lose,
Let's lose to a man, at least! Is a woman stronger than we?
CHORAGOS: Unless time has rusted my wits,
        What you say, King, is said with point and dignity.   50
HAIMON [*boyishly earnest*]:   Father:
        Reason is God's crowning gift to man, and you are right
        To warn me against losing mine. I cannot say—
        I hope that I shall never want to say!—that you
        Have reasoned badly. Yet there are other men   55
        Who can reason, too; and their opinions might be helpful.
        You are not in a position to know everything
        That people say or do, or what they feel:
        Your temper terrifies them—everyone

Will tell you only what you like to hear.   60
But I, at any rate, can listen; and I have heard them
Muttering and whispering in the dark about this girl.
They say no woman has ever, so unreasonably,
Died so shameful a death for a generous act:
"She covered her brother's body. Is this indecent?   65
She kept him from dogs and vultures. Is this a crime?
Death?—She should have all the honor that we can give her!"

This is the way they talk out there in the city.

You must believe me:
Nothing is closer to me than your happiness.   70
What could be closer? Must not any son
Value his father's fortune as his father does his?
I beg you, do not be unchangeable:
Do not believe that you alone can be right.
The man who thinks that,   75
The man who maintains that only he has the power
To reason correctly, the gift to speak, the soul—
A man like that, when you know him, turns out empty.

It is not reason never to yield to reason!

In flood time you can see how some trees bend,   80
And because they bend, even their twigs are safe,
While stubborn trees are torn up, roots and all.
And the same thing happens in sailing:
Make your sheet fast, never slacken,—and over you go,
Head over heels and under: and there's your voyage.   85
Forget you are angry! Let yourself be moved!
I know I am young; but please let me say this:
The ideal condition
Would be, I admit, that men should be right by instinct;
But since we are all too likely to go astray,   90
The reasonable thing is to learn from those who can teach.
CHORAGOS: You will do well to listen to him, King,
    If what he says is sensible. And you, Haimon,
    Must listen to your father.—Both speak well.
CREON: You consider it right for a man of my years and experience   95
    To go to school to a boy?
HAIMON: It is not right,
    If I am wrong. But if I am young, and right,
    What does my age matter?
CREON: You think it right to stand up for an anarchist?
HAIMON: Not at all. I pay no respect to criminals.   100

CREON: Then she is not a criminal?

HAIMON: The City would deny it, to a man.

CREON: And the City proposes to teach me how to rule?

HAIMON: Ah. Who is it that's talking like a boy now?

CREON: My voice is the one voice giving orders in this City!   105

HAIMON: It is no City if it takes orders from one voice.

CREON: The State is the King!

HAIMON: Yes, if the State is a desert.

Pause.

CREON: This boy, it seems, has sold out to a woman.

HAIMON: If you are a woman: my concern is only for you.

CREON: So? Your "concern"! In a public brawl with your father!   110

HAIMON: How about you, in a public brawl with justice?

CREON: With justice, when all that I do is within my rights?

HAIMON: You have no right to trample on God's right.

CREON [*completely out of control*]:   Fool, adolescent fool! Taken in by a woman!

HAIMON: You'll never see me taken in by anything vile.   115

CREON: Every word you say is for her!

HAIMON [*quietly, darkly*]:   And for you.

And for me. And for the gods under the earth.

CREON: You'll never marry her while she lives.

HAIMON: Then she must die.—But her death will cause another.

CREON: Another?   120

Have you lost your senses? Is this an open threat?

HAIMON: There is no threat in speaking to emptiness.

CREON: I swear you'll regret this superior tone of yours!

You are the empty one!

HAIMON: If you were not my father,

I'd say you were perverse.   125

CREON: You girlstruck fool, don't play at words with me!

HAIMON: I am sorry. You prefer silence.

CREON: Now, by God—!

I swear, by all the gods in heaven above us,

You'll watch it, I swear you shall!

[*To the* SERVANTS.]

Bring her out!

Bring the woman out! Let her die before his eyes!   130

Here, this instant, with her bridegroom beside her!

HAIMON: Not here, no; she will not die here, King.

And you will never see my face again.

Go on raving as long as you've a friend to endure you.

Exit HAIMON.

CHORAGOS: Gone, gone.   135
    Creon, a young man in a rage is dangerous!
CREON: Let him do, or dream to do, more than a man can.
    He shall not save these girls from death.
CHORAGOS: These girls?
    You have sentenced them both?
CREON: No, you are right.
    I will not kill the one whose hands are clean.   140
CHORAGOS: But Antigonê?
CREON [*somberly*]:   I will carry her far away
    Out there in the wilderness, and lock her
    Living in a vault of stone. She shall have food,
    As the custom is, to absolve the State of her death.
    And there let her pray to the gods of hell: 145
    They are her only gods:
    Perhaps they will show her an escape from death,
    Or she may learn,
                though late,
    That piety shown the dead is pity in vain.

                        Exit CREON.

ODE III

Strophe

CHORUS: Love, unconquerable
    Waster of rich men, keeper
    Of warm lights and all-night vigil
    In the soft face of a girl:
    Sea-wanderer, forest-visitor!   5
    Even the pure Immortals cannot escape you,
    And mortal man, in his one day's dusk,
    Trembles before your glory.

Antistrophe

    Surely you swerve upon ruin
    The just man's consenting heart,   10
    As here you have made bright anger
    Strike between father and son—
    And none has conquered but Love!
    A girl's glance working the will of heaven:

Pleasure to her alone who mocks us,   15
Merciless Aphroditê.°

SCENE IV

CHORAGOS [*as* Antigonê *enters guarded*]:   But I can no longer stand in
    awe of this,
    Nor, seeing what I see, keep back my tears.
    Here is Antigonê, passing to that chamber
    Where all find sleep at last.

Strophe 1

ANTIGONÊ: Look upon me, friends, and pity me   5
    Turning back at the night's edge to say
    Good-by to the sun that shines for me no longer;
    Now sleepy Death
    Summons me down to Acheron,° that cold shore:
    There is no bridesong there, nor any music.   10

CHORUS: Yet not unpraised, not without a kind of honor,
    You walk at last into the underworld;
    Untouched by sickness, broken by no sword.
    What woman has ever found your way to death?

Antistrophe 1

ANTIGONÊ: How often I have heard the story of Niobê,   15
    Tantalos's wretched daughter, how the stone
    Clung fast about her, ivy-close: and they say
    The rain falls endlessly
    And sifting soft snow; her tears are never done.
    I feel the loneliness of her death in mine.   20

CHORUS: But she was born of heaven, and you
    Are woman, woman-born. If her death is yours,
    A mortal woman's, is this not for you
    Glory in our world and in the world beyond?

Strophe 2

ANTIGONÊ: You laugh at me. Ah, friends, friends,   25
    Can you not wait until I am dead? O Thebes,
    O men many-charioted, in love with Fortune,

16 Aphroditê the goddess of love   **9 Acheron** a river of the underworld where death reigns

Dear springs of Dircê, sacred Theban grove,
Be witnesses for me, denied all pity,
Unjustly judged! and think a word of love 30
For her whose path turns
Under dark earth, where there are no more tears.

CHORUS: You have passed beyond human daring and come at last
Into a place of stone where Justice sits.
I cannot tell 35
What shape of your father's guilt appears in this.

Antistrophe 2

ANTIGONÊ: You have touched it at last: that bridal bed
Unspeakable, horror of son and mother mingling:
Their crime, infection of all our family!
O Oedipus, father and brother! 40
Your marriage strikes from the grave to murder mine.
I have been a stranger here in my own land:
All my life
The blasphemy of my birth has followed me.

CHORUS: Reverence is a virtue, but strength 45
Lives in established law: that must prevail.
You have made your choice,
Your death is the doing of your conscious hand.

Epode

ANTIGONÊ: Then let me go, since all your words are bitter,
And the very light of the sun is cold to me. 50
Lead me to my vigil, where I must have
Neither love nor lamentation; no song, but silence.

CREON *interrupts impatiently.*

CREON: If dirges and planned lamentations could put off death,
Men would be singing for ever.

[*to the* SERVANTS]

Take her, go!

You know your orders: take her to the vault 55
And leave her alone there. And if she lives or dies,
That's her affair, not ours: our hands are clean.

ANTIGONÊ: O tomb, vaulted bride bed in eternal rock,
Soon I shall be with my own again
Where Persephonê° welcomes the thin ghosts underground: 60

60 Persephonê the queen of the underworld

And I shall see my father again, and you, mother,
And dearest Polyneicês—
                              dearest indeed
To me, since it was my hand
That washed him clean and poured the ritual wine:
And my reward is death before my time!   65

And yet, as men's hearts know, I have done no wrong,
I have not sinned before God. Or if I have,
I shall know the truth in death. But if the guilt
Lies upon Creon who judged me, then, I pray,
May his punishment equal my own.

CHORAGOS: O passionate heart,   70
    Unyielding, tormented still by the same winds!
CREON: Her guards shall have good cause to regret their delaying.
ANTIGONÊ: Ah! That voice is like the voice of death!
CREON: I can give you no reason to think you are mistaken.
ANTIGONÊ: Thebes, and you my fathers' gods,   75
    And rulers of Thebes, you see me now, the last
    Unhappy daughter of a line of kings,
    Your kings, led away to death. You will remember
    What things I suffer, and at what men's hands,
    Because I would not transgress the laws of heaven.   80
    [*To the* GUARDS, *simply.*] Come: let us wait no longer.

                Exit ANTIGONÊ, *left, guarded.*

ODE IV

Strophe 1

CHORUS: All Danaê's beauty was locked away
    In a brazen cell where the sunlight could not come:
    A small room still as any grave, enclosed her.
    Yet she was a princess too,
    And Zeus in a rain of gold poured love upon her.   5
    O child, child,
    No power in wealth or war
    Or tough sea-blackened ships
    Can prevail against untiring Destiny!

Antistrophe 1

    And Dryas' son° also, that furious king,   10

10 Dryas' son Lycurgus, king of Thrace

Bore the god's prisoning anger for his pride:
Sealed up by Dionysos in deaf stone,
His madness died among echoes.
So at the last he learned what dreadful power
His tongue had mocked: 15
For he had profaned the revels,
And fired the wrath of the nine
Implacable Sisters° that love the sound of the flute.

Strophe 2

And old men tell a half-remembered tale
Of horror where a dark ledge splits the sea   20
And a double surf beats on the gray shores:
How a king's new woman,° sick
With hatred for the queen he had imprisoned,
Ripped out his two sons' eyes with her bloody hands
While grinning Arês° watched the shuttle plunge   25
Four times: four blind wounds crying for revenge,

Antistrophe 2

Crying, tears and blood mingled.—Piteously born,
Those sons whose mother was of heavenly birth!
Her father was the god of the North Wind
And she was cradled by gales,   30
She raced with young colts on the glittering hills
And walked untrammeled in the open light:
But in her marriage deathless Fate found means
To build a tomb like yours for all her joy.

SCENE V

Enter blind TEIRESIAS, *led by a boy. The opening speeches of* TEIRESIAS *should be in singsong contrast to the realistic lines of* CREON.

TEIRESIAS: This is the way the blind man comes, Princes, Princes,
        Lockstep, two heads lit by the eyes of one.
CREON: What new thing have you to tell us, old Teiresias?
TEIRESIAS: I have much to tell you: listen to the prophet, Creon.

---

18 Implacable Sisters the Muses of poetry and music, arts and sciences   **22 king's new woman** Eidothea, second wife of King Phineas, blinded her stepsons after the king had imprisoned their mother in a cave   **25 Arês** the god of war who loves bloodshed

CREON: I am not aware that I have ever failed to listen.   5
TEIRESIAS: Then you have done wisely, King, and ruled well.
CREON: I admit my debt to you. But what have you to say?
TEIRESIAS: This, Creon: you stand once more on the edge of fate.
CREON: What do you mean? Your words are a kind of dread.
TEIRESIAS: Listen Creon: 10
    I was sitting in my chair of augury, at the place
    Where the birds gather about me. They were all a-chatter,
    As is their habit, when suddenly I heard
    A strange note in their jangling, a scream, a
    Whirring fury; I knew that they were fighting,   15
    Tearing each other, dying
    In a whirlwind of wings clashing. And I was afraid.
    I began the rites of burnt-offering at the altar,
    But Hephaistos° failed me: instead of bright flame,
    There was only the sputtering slime of the fat thigh-flesh   20
    Melting: the entrails dissolved in gray smoke,
    The bare bone burst from the welter. And no blaze!

    This was a sign from heaven. My boy described it,
    Seeing for me as I see for others.

    I tell you, Creon, you yourself have brought   25
    This new calamity upon us. Our hearths and altars
    Are stained with the corruption of dogs and carrion birds
    That glut themselves on the corpse of Oedipus' son.
    The gods are deaf when we pray to them, their fire
    Recoils from our offering, their birds of omen   30
    Have no cry of comfort, for they are gorged
    With the thick blood of the dead.
                     O my son,
These are no trifles! Think: all men make mistakes,
But a good man yields when he knows his course is wrong,
And repairs the evil. The only crime is pride.   35

    Give in to the dead man, then: do not fight with a corpse—
    What glory is it to kill a man who is dead?
    Think, I beg you:
    It is for your own good that I speak as I do.
    You should be able to yield for your own good.   40
CREON: It seems that prophets have made me their especial province.

19 Hephaistos the god of fire

All my life long
I have been a kind of butt for the dull arrows
Of doddering fortune-tellers!

                   No, Teiresias:

If your birds—if the great eagles of God himself   45
Should carry him stinking bit by bit to heaven,
I would not yield. I am not afraid of pollution:
No man can defile the gods.

                      Do what you will,

Go into business, make money, speculate
In India gold or that synthetic gold from Sardis,   50
Get rich otherwise than by my consent to bury him.
Teiresias, it is a sorry thing when a wise man
Sells his wisdom, lets out his words for hire!

TEIRESIAS: Ah Creon! Is there no man left in the world—
CREON: To do what?—Come, let's have the aphorism!   55
TEIRESIAS: No man who knows that wisdom outweighs any wealth?
CREON: As surely as bribes are baser than any baseness.
TEIRESIAS: You are sick, Creon! You are deathly sick!
CREON: As you say: it is not my place to challenge a prophet.
TEIRESIAS: Yet you have said my prophecy is for sale.   60
CREON: The generation of prophets has always loved gold.
TEIRESIAS: The generation of kings has always loved brass.
CREON: You forget yourself! You are speaking to your King.
TEIRESIAS: I know it. You are a king because of me.
CREON: You have a certain skill; but you have sold out.   65
TEIRESIAS: King, you will drive me to words that—
CREON: Say them, say them!

     Only remember: I will not pay you for them.

TEIRESIAS: No, you will find them too costly.
CREON: No doubt. Speak:

     Whatever you say, you will not change my will.

TEIRESIAS: Then take this, and take it to heart!   70
The time is not far off when you shall pay back
Corpse for corpse, flesh of your own flesh.
You have thrust the child of this world into living night,
You have kept from the gods below the child that is theirs:
The one in a grave before her death, the other,   75
Dead, denied the grave. This is your crime:
And the Furies and the dark gods of Hell

Are swift with terrible punishment for you.

Do you want to buy me now, Creon?

                                        Not many days,

And your house will be full of men and women weeping,   80

And curses will be hurled at you from far

Cities grieving for sons unburied, left to rot

Before the walls of Thebes.

These are my arrows, Creon: they are all for you.

[*To boy.*] But come, child: lead me home.   85

Let him waste his fine anger upon younger men.

Maybe he will learn at last

To control a wiser tongue in a better head.

                        Exit TEIRESIAS.

CHORAGOS: The old man has gone, King, but his words

    Remain to plague us. I am old, too,   90

    But I cannot remember that he was ever false.

CREON: That is true.... It troubles me.

    Oh it is hard to give in! but it is worse

    To risk everything for stubborn pride.

CHORAGOS: Creon: take my advice.

CREON: What shall I do?   95

CHORAGOS: Go quickly: free Antigonê from her vault

    And build a tomb for the body of Polyneicês.

CREON: You would have me do this!

CHORAGOS: Creon, yes!

    And it must be done at once: God moves

    Swiftly to cancel the folly of stubborn men.   100

CREON: It is hard to deny the heart! But I

    Will do it: I will not fight with destiny.

CHORAGOS: You must go yourself, you cannot leave it to others.

CREON: I will go.

                —Bring axes, servants:

    Come with me to the tomb. I buried her,   105

    Will set her free.

                    Oh quickly!

My mind misgives—

The laws of the gods are mighty, and a man must serve them

To the last day of his life!

                        Exit CREON.

PAEAN°

Strophe 1

CHORAGOS: God of many names

CHORUS: O Iacchos°

                                                            son

            of Kadmeian Sémelê°

                            O born of the Thunder!

            Guardian of the West

                                    Regent

            of Eleusis' plain

                            O Prince of maenad Thebes

            and the Dragon Field by rippling Ismenos.°   5

Antistrophe 1

CHORAGOS: God of many names

CHORUS: the flame of torches

            flares on our hills

                            the nymphs of Iacchos

            dance at the spring of Castalia.°

            from the vine-close mountain

                            come ah come in ivy:

            Evohé evohé! sings through the streets of Thebes   10

Strophe 2

CHORAGOS: God of many names

CHORUS: Iacchos of Thebes

            heavenly Child

                            of Sémelê bride of the Thunderer!

            The shadow of plague is upon us:

                                    come

            with clement feet

                            oh come from Parnasos

            down the long slopes

                            across the lamenting water   15

Antistrophe 2

CHORAGOS: Iô Fire! Chorister of the throbbing stars!

            O purest among the voices of the night!

            Thou son of God, blaze for us!

Paean a triumphant song   **1 Iacchos** also called Bacchos or Dionysos, god of wine and revelry   **2 Sémelê** mother of Iacchos, consort of Zeus   **5 Ismenos** a river near Thebes where, legend has it, the ancestors of Thebes sprang from a dragon's teeth   **7 Castalia** a spring on Mount Parnassus

CHORUS: Come with choric rapture of circling Maenads°
    Who cry *Iô Iacche!*

God of many names!   20

EXODOS

Enter MESSENGER *from left.*

MESSENGER: Men of the line of Kadmos,° you who live
    Near Amphion's citadel,°

I cannot say
Of any condition of human life "This is fixed,
This is clearly good, or bad." Fate raises up,
And Fate casts down the happy and unhappy alike: 5
No man can foretell his Fate.

    Take the case of Creon:
Creon was happy once, as I count happiness:
Victorious in battle, sole governor of the land,
Fortunate father of children nobly born.
And now it has all gone from him! Who can say   10
That a man is still alive when his life's joy fails?
He is a walking dead man. Grant him rich,
Let him live like a king in his great house:
If his pleasure is gone, I would not give
So much as the shadow of smoke for all he owns.   15

CHORAGOS: Your words hint at sorrow: what is your news for us?

MESSENGER: They are dead. The living are guilty of their death.

CHORAGOS: Who is guilty? Who is dead? Speak!

MESSENGER: Haimon.
    Haimon is dead; and the hand that killed him
    Is his own hand.

CHORAGOS: His father's? or his own?   20

MESSENGER: His own, driven mad by the murder his father had done.

CHORAGOS: Teiresias, Teiresias, how clearly you saw it all!

MESSENGER: This is my news: you must draw what conclusions you can from it.

CHORAGOS: But look. Eurydicê, our Queen:
    Has she overheard us?   25

Enter EURYDICÊ *from the palace, center.*

---

18 Maenad female worshipper, attendant of Iacchos   **1 Kadmos** sowed the dragon's teeth
and founded Thebes   **2 Amphion's citadel** Amphion's lyre playing was so beautiful that he
charmed stones to form a wall around Thebes

EURYDICÊ: I have heard something, friends:
As I was unlocking the gate of Pallas'° shrine,
For I needed her help today, I heard a voice
Telling of some new sorrow. And I fainted
There at the temple with all my maidens about me.   30
But speak again: whatever it is, I can bear it:
Grief and I are no strangers.

MESSENGER: Dearest Lady,
I will tell you plainly all that I have seen.
I shall not try to comfort you: what is the use,
Since comfort could lie only in what is not true?   35
The truth is always best.

                        I went with Creon
To the outer plain where Polyneicês was lying,
No friend to pity him, his body shredded by dogs.

We made our prayers in that place to Hecatê°
And Pluto,° that they would be merciful. And we bathed   40
The corpse with holy water, and we brought
Fresh-broken branches to burn what was left of it,
And upon the urn we heaped up a towering barrow
Of the earth of his own land.

                        When we were done, we ran
To the vault where Antigonê lay on her couch of stone.   45
One of the servants had gone ahead,
And while he was yet far off he heard a voice
Grieving within the chamber, and he came back
And told Creon. And as the King went closer,
The air was full of wailing, the words lost,   50
And he begged us to make all haste. "Am I a prophet?"
He said, weeping, "And must I walk this road,
The saddest of all that I have gone before?
My son's voice calls me on. Oh quickly, quickly!
Look through the crevice there, and tell me   55
If it is Haimon, or some deception of the gods!"

We obeyed; and in the cavern's farthest corner
We saw her lying:
She had made a noose of her fine linen veil
And hanged herself. Haimon lay beside her,   60

---

27 **Pallas** Athena, the goddess of wisdom   39 **Hecatê** the goddess of witchcraft   **40 Pluto**
king of the underworld

His arms about her waist, lamenting her,
His love lost under ground, crying out
That his father had stolen her away from him.

When Creon saw him the tears rushed to his eyes
And he called to him: "What have you done, child? Speak to me.   65
What are you thinking that makes your eyes so strange?
O my son, my son, I come to you on my knees!"
But Haimon spat in his face. He said not a word,
Staring—
    And suddenly drew his sword
And lunged. Creon shrank back, the blade missed; and the boy,   70
Desperate against himself, drove it half its length
Into his own side, and fell. And as he died
He gathered Antigonê close in his arms again,
Choking, his blood bright red on her white cheek.
And now he lies dead with the dead, and she is his   75
At last, his bride in the houses of the dead.

     Exit EURYDICÊ *into the palace.*

CHORAGOS: She has left us without a word. What can this mean?
MESSENGER: It troubles me, too; yet she knows what is best,
 Her grief is too great for public lamentation,
 And doubtless she has gone to her chamber to weep   80
 For her dead son, leading her maidens in his dirge.

     Pause.

CHORAGOS: It may be so: but I fear this deep silence.
MESSENGER: I will see what she is doing. I will go in.

    Exit MESSENGER *into the palace.*

  Enter CREON *with attendants, bearing* HAIMON'S *body.*

CHORAGOS: But here is the king himself: oh look at him,
 Bearing his own damnation in his arms.   85
CREON: Nothing you say can touch me any more.
 My own blind heart has brought me
 From darkness to final darkness. Here you see
 The father murdering, the murdered son—
 And all my civic wisdom!   90

 Haimon my son, so young, so young to die,
 I was the fool, not you; and you died for me.
CHORAGOS: That is the truth; but you were late in learning it.
CREON: This truth is hard to bear. Surely a god
 Has crushed me beneath the hugest weight of heaven,   95

And driven me headlong a barbaric way
To trample out the thing I held most dear.

The pains that men will take to come to pain!

Enter MESSENGER *from the palace.*

MESSENGER: The burden you carry in your hands is heavy,
But it is not all: you will find more in your house.   100
CREON: What burden worse than this shall I find there?
MESSENGER: The Queen is dead.
CREON: O port of death, deaf world,
Is there no pity for me? And you, Angel of evil,
I was dead, and your words are death again.   105
Is it true, boy? Can it be true?
Is my wife dead? Has death bred death?
MESSENGER: You can see for yourself.

The doors are opened and the body of EURYDICÊ *is disclosed within.*

CREON: Oh pity!
All true, all true, and more than I can bear!   110
O my wife, my son!
MESSENGER: She stood before the altar, and her heart
Welcomed the knife her own hand guided,
And a great cry burst from her lips for Megareus° dead,
And for Haimon dead, her sons; and her last breath   115
Was a curse for their father, the murderer of her sons.
And she fell, and the dark flowed in through her closing eyes.
CREON: O God, I am sick with fear.
Are there no swords here? Has no one a blow for me?
MESSENGER: Her curse is upon you for the deaths of both.   120
CREON: It is right that it should be. I alone am guilty.
I know it, and I say it. Lead me in,
Quickly, friends.
I have neither life nor substance. Lead me in.
CHORAGOS: You are right, if there can be right in so much wrong.   125
The briefest way is best in a world of sorrow.
CREON: Let it come,
Let death come quickly, and be kind to me.
I would not ever see the sun again.

114 Megareus the other son of Eurydice and Creon who had sacrificed himself to Arês to
save Thebes from the seven who attacked it

CHORAGOS: All that will come when it will; but we, meanwhile,   130
        Have much to do. Leave the future to itself.
CREON: All my heart was in that prayer!
CHORAGOS: Then do not pray any more: the sky is deaf.
CREON: Lead me away. I have been rash and foolish.
        I have killed my son and my wife.   135
        I look for comfort; my comfort lies here dead.
        Whatever my hands have touched has come to nothing.
        Fate has brought all my pride to a thought of dust.

As CREON *is being led into the house, the* CHORAGOS *advances and speaks directly
to the audience.*

CHORAGOS: There is no happiness where there is no wisdom;
        No wisdom but in submission to the gods.   140
        Big words are always punished,
        And proud men in old age learn to be wise.

CONNECTING THROUGH WRITING

One of the best ways to get ideas for an essay is to ask and answer your own most
compelling questions.

- Write down whatever questions come to mind during and after your reading. See if your answers to these questions provide topics for writing.
- Choose a compelling idea from a journal entry.
- Draw a Venn diagram to compare elements, characters, or stories (pp. 29–30),
  use directed freewriting (p. 39), ask questions (p. 39), list (p. 40), or draw a
  cluster or semantic map (pp. 41–42) to loosen up ideas.

Listed below is a more structured approach based on the elements of drama discussed earlier in this section. Applying these questions to *Antigonê* may demonstrate how the elements might be applied to any work of drama.

FIRST RESPONSES

1. To what extent is your response to *Antigonê* influenced by your own experience?
2. If you were placed in their positions, would you behave the same way as
   Antigonê? Creon? Haimon? Ismenê? Explain.
3. Do you think loyalty to your family, religion, or country is more important?
   Explain.

LANGUAGE AND STYLE

1. How does the formal language and verse form of the play affect you?
2. What does Creon's use of language tell you about him?
3. Is there symbolism in this play? Explain.

NARRATION

1. How are you affected by the comments of Choragos and the chorus?

2. How does the nature of what they say differ from what the individual characters say?

3. How does the role of Choragos differ from that of the other characters?

SETTING

1. When and where is *Antigonê* set?

2. What is the atmosphere in this play?

3. How does the setting influence the conflict between Antigonê and Creon?

4. To what extent does the setting support and emphasize the play's meaning?

5. There are very few stage directions in *Antigonê*. To what extent did that affect your reading of the play?

CONFLICT AND PLOT

1. What is the main conflict in the play? Is it external or internal? Explain.

2. How many other conflicts are there?

3. In what way are they related to the main conflict?

4. To what extent does the plot follow a traditional structure?

CHARACTER

1. How does what Antigonê, Ismenê, Creon, and Haimon say tell you about them?

2. How does what they do tell you about them?

3. What is the function of Teiresias in this play?

4. To what extent is conflict in *Antigonê* connected to characterization?

5. Who is the protagonist and who is the antagonist in this play?

THEME

1. What is the theme of *Antigonê*?

2. How do setting, conflict, and character contribute to this theme?

3. To what extent does the play preach as well as reveal?

TOPICS FOR WRITING

The following list is not exhaustive, but simply illustrative of the kinds of questions that might emerge from the more specific analytical questions (and combinations of questions) like those above. Your responses might provide worthwhile topics for writing.

1. Compare the characterizations of Antigonê and Creon. To what extent are they alike or different?

2. To what extent was it possible for Antigonê to achieve the burial of her brother through different means?

3. Is Creon powerless to respond differently to her behavior? Explain.

4. What is the role of Ismenê? To what extent can you justify her behavior?

5. What is the impact of power on the characters in *Antigonê?*

6. What is the impact of pride on the characters in this play?

7. How important is it that a woman broke the law? What does the play tell us about the place of women in that society?

8. What is the connection between the choral odes and the play's meaning?

9. To what extent is *Antigonê* typical of the work of Sophocles? How does this play compare with *Oedipus Rex?*

10. How does it compare to the work of other Greek dramatists of this period?

11. How well does *Antigonê* fulfill Aristotle's requirements for tragedy?

12. In what way is this play a reflection of the cultural beliefs of ancient Greece?

13. In what way does the conflict in *Antigonê* transcend that period and speak to us now?

READING AND ANALYZING ESSAYS

Of all forms of literature, you are probably most familiar with the essay. You have read them in newspapers and magazines most of your life. And you have had lots of practice writing them. If reading and writing essays has been a good experience, you already know why they are important. They let us express who we are and what we think—our personal stories, impressions, feelings, ideas, and opinions. They let us know who other people are and what they think. They spring from a basic human need to communicate.

In late-sixteenth-century France, Michel de Montaigne, the first modern essay writer, introduced his book *Essais* by writing, "I am myself the subject of my book." Whatever form the essay has taken since then, Montaigne's statement is still at the heart of effective essay writing. Both of the earliest popular essay writers, Montaigne and his English counterpart Francis Bacon, were personal and informal. They wrote about whatever intrigued them, usually in a light, speculative way. They didn't write about the strange or unusual; they wrote about everyday topics— conversation, education, friendship, gardening. But they wrote about these topics in such an entertaining and insightful way that their voices, as if in conversation with us, come back to life when we read them three hundred years later. Since that time some of our most prominent writers have expanded the scope of the essay to moral, social, and political criticism, and its tone from bawdy humor and biting satire to great solemnity.

Most of our favorite essay writers today write in newspapers and magazines. We may call them columnists, op-ed writers, or sports writers, but they are in fact essay writers. They don't tell us the news; they tell us what they think of the news. They are emotional, outspoken, and opinionated in predictable ways—and very much the inheritors of Montaigne's "I." They have strong "voices," and we have gotten to know them. Whether we agree or disagree with them, we usually look forward to reading what they have to say.

When you're reading an essay for the first time, imagine you're in a conversation, that the writer is talking to you. Relax and listen. And talk back from time to time by writing down your responses.

TYPES OF ESSAYS

There is no easy or entirely accurate way to classify essays. Instead of giving a clear picture of how each category is different, the discussion of types below blurs distinctions. After all, narrative and expository essays may be argumentative: exposition and argumentation may use narrative to make or to prove their points. Basically, the intention of all essays is to be persuasive, to have readers respond by thinking, "I see what you mean" or "Yes, you're right."

It may be helpful to think of the designations "narrative," "expository," and "argumentative" as degrees of emphasis rather than discrete or exclusive types.

Narrative

Narrative essays tell a story. Most essays of this type spring from an event or experience in the writer's life. Beyond sharing an aspect of the writer's life, however, their intention is to make a point, present an idea, or make an argument. They not only recount what's happened, they emphasize the importance of the occurrence. This narration is often "seasoned" with personal comment, reflection, and opinion.

Voice is crucial to this kind of essay. All of the personal narratives in this text rely heavily on the narrator as a participant who feels frustration, pain, or joy; who experiences insight and earns the right to tell the story.

Among the narrative essays in this text are "Salvation" (p. 32) and "The Midnight Tour" (p. 521).

Expository

Expository essays share, explain, suggest, or explore information, emotion, and ideas. You might ask, "What else is there?" This is the broadest category. Many of these essays may seem to be narrative or argumentative; they may use stories as examples or may imply an argument or position. The key to exposition is the emphasis on showing and sharing insight—not primarily on telling a story or making an argument.

A few examples of exposition in this text are "Mothers" (p. 31), Bettelheim's "Cinderella" (p. 807), and "Why I Write" (p. 1076).

Argumentative

The intention of a formal argumentative essay is to prove a point by supporting it with evidence. Note that proving and persuading are not the same thing. Proving may persuade or convince us if we are open-minded and have not formed a contrary opinion. If we feel differently about an issue, the amount of logical evidence might not matter. People are often persuaded by advertisements that offer little or no evidence but appeal almost exclusively to their emotions or sense of style.

The most effective argumentative essays do not rely on evidence alone to convince us. While facts and statistics may lie at the foundation of a strong persuasive argument, examples and personal anecdotes often do the real convincing. We think with our heads, but we pay attention with our hearts. When we look at some of the essays in this book that make convincing arguments, we see that they appeal to both head and heart.

Two wide-ranging examples of argumentative essays in this text are "A Modest Proposal" (p. 1093), and "I Have a Dream" (p. 1085).

For a concise checklist of questions for Types of Essays, see page 141.

LANGUAGE, STYLE, AND STRUCTURE

Formal or Informal

Formal essays are usually about a serious topic; they have a fairly tight, clear structure and strategy. Their narrative perspective emphasizes objectivity, and the writer's voice is often impersonal and detached. This type of essay is more likely to gather its support from facts, data, or statistics, and to use formal language, not everyday words or phrases.

Though many formal essays have a complex structure, the classic structure of a formal essay has an introduction that involves the reader and states the thesis; a middle that gives details and examples; and a conclusion that restates support for the thesis and (if successful) leaves the reader enlightened and convinced.

Informal essays deal with both lighthearted and serious topics. They generally rely on detail, emotion, narrative, and personal examples for support. The choice of words and sentence structure is more likely to be conversational and informal, with everyday phrases, dialogue, narration, imagery, and figurative language. The overall structure of an informal essay is likely to emerge from the subject matter rather than adhere to a predetermined structure.

Voice

Voice refers to the individual personality that comes alive in the words. It is the key to **tone,** and tone is not always easy to pick up. When we see or hear a person speaking words, their intonations, physical gestures, and facial expressions tell us the attitude of the speaker toward the subject. When we hear "voice" in our reading too, we can also sense the intonations. Cues in a printed text are not always obvious, however, and we must often rely on the pattern and types of words the writer chooses to sense the tone.

Irony

Irony is the contrast between appearance/expectation and reality. As in other forms of literature, the two most popular forms of irony in essays are verbal irony and situational irony. Verbal irony results from the contrast between what is said by the writer and what is meant. Irony of situation results from the contrast between what is expected and what actually happens. Jonathan Swift's "A Modest Proposal" (p. 1093) is a classic example of an essay that relies on verbal irony to make its point.

Word Choice and Style

Choice of language is an important element in creating voice in an essay. Figurative language brings the writing to life. Concrete details and evocative images pull us into the text. Formal vocabulary evokes a different response from us than informal or nonstandard words. So, too, the frequency of images and figurative language has an effect on our reading and response. Using what you already know about language in fiction, poetry, and drama tells you much about imagery, figurative language, syntax, rhythm, and sound in essays as well.

For a concise checklist of questions for Language, Style, and Structure, see page 141.

Theme: What's the Point?

The theme of an essay is the insight the writer shares; or the point the writer wants to teach, prove, or convince us of. Because they often have a tight structure and direct writing style, it may be easier to identify and to articulate the theme in a formal essay than in a narrative or informal one.

The Aims of an Essay: Inform, Preach, or Reveal

Many formal, expository essays intend to inform or teach us. Likewise, it's the intention of many formal, argumentative essays to teach a lesson or convince us of a particular moral view. Essays of this type are often written in response to a perceived political or social problem. In this respect they have a moral, or message.

At the beginning of the essay, formal-essay writers often announce what they intend to prove or to explain and then remind us again at the end. The predictability of the structure itself is designed to make it clear. Like other forms of literature, however, most good narrative and informal essays share or reveal something insightful about human nature. Our experience of the theme, however, may be holistic or impressionistic—and a bit more elusive.

Regardless of the type of essay, what makes your interpretation convincing or defensible is your ability to support it. Your belief about what the essay means may change as you move back and forth through the stages of your reading experience. The first time you read an essay, you may feel one way. Writing down your reflections, rereading the essay, and discussing it with others may lead to a different, better-informed understanding and interpretation.

For a concise checklist of questions for Theme, see below.

✓ CHECKLIST: ANALYZING ESSAYS

Types of Essays

❏ Would you classify the essay as narrative, expository, or argumentative? Explain. Is the classification clear? If not, why?

Language, Style, and Structure

❏ In general, is the essay formal or informal? How so?

❏ How would you describe the writer's voice? Do you find the author believable? Why?

❏ Was the voice of the author effective in conveying the essay's meaning? Why?

❏ Is the language formal or informal? What does the nature of the language tell you about the essay?

❏ Are there many instances of imagery and figurative language (simile, metaphor)? If so, how do they connect to or support the essay?

Theme

❏ What is the intention of the essay? Is it trying to inform us of something? To prove or convince us of something? To share an insight?

❏ What is its theme?

GETTING IDEAS FOR WRITING ABOUT THE ESSAY

The purpose of the essay, the prompts, and the questions in this section is to show how the elements we've discussed earlier might be applied to an essay. Following "Mother Tongue," many of the questions from the summary checklist above are applied to the essay, and we consider some of the ways the elements discussed in this section might be used to prompt ideas for your own critical essay.

AMY TAN [B. 1952]

MOTHER TONGUE   [1990]

I am not a scholar of English or literature. I cannot give you much more than personal opinions on the English language and its variations in this country or others. I am a writer. And by that definition, I am someone who has always loved language. I am fascinated by language in daily life. I spend a great deal of my time thinking about the power of language—the way it can evoke an emotion, a visual image, a complex idea, or a simple truth. Language is the tool of my trade. And I use them all—all the Englishes I grew up with.

Recently, I was made keenly aware of the different Englishes I do use. I was giving a talk to a large group of people, the same talk I had already given to half a dozen other groups. The nature of the talk was about my writing, my life, and my book, *The Joy Luck Club*. The talk was going along well enough, until I remembered one major difference that made the whole talk sound wrong. My mother was in the room. And it was perhaps the first time she had heard me give a lengthy speech, using the kind of English I have never used with her. I was saying things like, "The intersection of memory upon imagination" and "There is an aspect of my fiction that relates to thus-and-thus"—a speech filled with carefully wrought grammatical phrases, burdened, it suddenly seemed to me, with nominalized forms, past perfect tenses, conditional phrases, all the forms of standard English that I had learned in school and through books, the forms of English I did not use at home with my mother.

Just last week, I was walking down the street with my mother, and I again found myself conscious of the English I was using, the English I do use with her. We were talking about the price of new and used furniture and I heard myself saying this: "Not waste money that way." My husband was with us as well, and he didn't notice any switch in my English. And then I realized why. It's because over the twenty years we've been together I've often used that same kind of English with him, and sometimes he even uses it with me. It has become our language of intimacy, a different sort of English that relates to family talk, the language I grew up with.

So you'll have some idea of what this family talk I heard sounds like, I'll quote what my mother said during a recent conversation which I videotaped and then transcribed. During this conversation, my mother was talking about a political gangster in Shanghai who had the same last name as her family's, Du, and how the gangster in his early years wanted to be adopted by her family, which was rich by comparison. Later, the gangster became more powerful, far richer than my mother's family, and one day showed up at my mother's wedding to pay his respects. Here's what she said in part:

5   Du-Yusong having business like fruit stand. Like off the street kind. He is Du like Du Zong-but not Tsung-ming Island people. The local people call putong, the river east side, he belong to that side local people. That man want to ask Du Zong father take him in like become own family. Du Zong father wasn't look down on him, but didn't take seriously, until that man big like become a mafia. Now important person, very hard to inviting him. Chinese way, came only to show respect, don't stay for dinner. Respect for making big celebration, he shows up. Mean gives lots of

respect. Chinese custom. Chinese social life that way. If too important won't have to stay too long. He come to my wedding. I didn't see, I heard it. I gone to boy's side, they have YMCA dinner. Chinese age I was nineteen.

You should know that my mother's expressive command of English belies' how much she actually understands. She reads the *Forbes* report, listens to *Wall Street Week,* converses daily with her stockbroker, reads all of Shirley MacLaine's books with ease—all kinds of things I can't begin to understand. Yet some of my friends tell me they understand 50 percent of what my mother says. Some say they understand 80 to 90 percent. Some say they understand none of it, as if she were speaking pure Chinese. But to me, my mother's English is perfectly clear, perfectly natural. It's my mother tongue. Her language, as I hear it, is vivid, direct, full of observation and imagery. That was the language that helped shape the way I saw things, expressed things, made sense of the world.

Lately, I've been giving more thought to the kind of English my mother speaks. Like others, I have described it to people as "broken" or "fractured" English. But I wince when I say that. It has always bothered me that I can think of no way to describe it other than "broken," as if it were damaged and needed to be fixed, as if it lacked a certain wholeness and soundness. I've heard other terms used, "limited English," for example. But they seem just as bad, as if everything is limited, including people's perceptions of the limited English speaker.

I know this for a fact, because when I was growing up, my mother's "limited" English limited my perception of her. I was ashamed of her English. I believed that her English reflected the quality of what she had to say. That is, because she expressed them imperfectly her thoughts were imperfect. And I had plenty of empirical evidence to support me: the fact that people in department stores, at banks, and at restaurants did not take her seriously, did not give her good service, pretended not to understand her, or even acted as if they did not hear her.

My mother had long realized the limitations of her English as well. When I was fifteen, she used to have me call people on the phone to pretend I was she. In this guise, I was forced to ask for information or even to complain and yell at people who had been rude to her. One time it was a call to her stockbroker in New York. She had cashed out her small portfolio and it just so happened we were going to go to New York the next week, our very first trip outside California. I had to get on the phone and say in an adolescent voice that was not very convincing, "This is Mrs. Tan."

10   And my mother was standing in the back whispering loudly, "Why he don't send me check, already two weeks late. So mad he lie to me, losing me money."

And then I said in perfect English, "Yes, I'm getting rather concerned. You had agreed to send the check two weeks ago, but it hasn't arrived."

Then she began to talk more loudly. "What he want, I come to New York tell him front of his boss, you cheating me?" And I was trying to calm her down, make her be quiet, while telling the stockbroker, "I can't tolerate any more excuses. If I don't receive the check immediately, I am going to have to speak to your manager when I'm in New York next week." And sure enough, the following week there we were in front of this astonished stockbroker, and I was sitting there red-faced and quiet, and my mother, the real Mrs. Tan, was shouting at his boss in her impeccable broken English.

We used a similar routine just five days ago, for a situation that was far less humorous. My mother had gone to the hospital for an appointment, to find out about a benign brain tumor a CAT scan had revealed a month ago. She said she had spoken very good English, her best English, no mistakes. Still, she said, the hospital did not apologize when they said they had lost the CAT scan and she had come for nothing. She said they did not seem to have any sympathy when she told them she was anxious to know the exact diagnosis, since her husband and son had both died of brain tumors. She said they would not give her any more information until the next time and she would have to make another appointment for that. So she said she would not leave until the doctor called her daughter. She wouldn't budge. And when the doctor finally called her daughter, me, who spoke in perfect English—lo and behold—we had assurances the CAT scan would be found, promises that a conference call on Monday would be held, and apologies for any suffering my mother had gone through for a most regrettable mistake.

I think my mother's English almost had an effect on limiting my possibilities in life as well. Sociologists and linguists probably will tell you that a person developing language skills is more influenced by peers. But I do think that the language spoken in the family, especially in immigrant families which are more insular, plays a large role in shaping the language of the child. And I believe that it affected my results on achievement tests, IQ tests, and the SAT. While my English skills were never judged as poor, compared to math, English could not be considered my strong suit. In grade school I did moderately well, getting perhaps B's, sometimes B-pluses, in English and scoring perhaps in the sixtieth or seventieth percentile on achievement tests. But those scores were not good enough to override the opinion that my true abilities lay in math and science, because in those areas I achieved A's and scored in the nineti-eth percentile or higher.

15   This was understandable. Math is precise; there is only one correct answer. Whereas, for me at least, the answers on English tests were always a judgment call, a matter of opinion and personal experience. Those tests were constructed around items like fill-in-the-blank sentence completion, such as, "Even though Tom was—, Mary thought he was—" And the correct answer always seemed to be the most bland combinations of thoughts, for example, "Even though Tom was shy, Mary thought he was charming," with the grammatical structure "even though" limiting the correct answer to some sort of semantic opposites, so you wouldn't get answers like, "Even though Tom was foolish, Mary thought he was ridiculous." Well, according to my mother, there were very few limitations as to what Tom could have been and what Mary might have thought of him. So I never did well on tests like that.

The same was true with word analogies, pairs of words in which you were supposed to find some sort of logical, semantic relationship—for example, "*Sunset* is to *nightfall* as— is to —." And here you would be presented with a list of four possible pairs, one of which showed the same kind of relationship: *red* is to *stoplight, bus* is to *arrival, chills* is to *fever, yawn* is to *boring*. Well, I could never think that way. I knew what the tests were asking, but I could not block out of my mind the images already created by the first pair, "*sunset* is to *nightfall*"—and I would see a burst of colors against a darkening sky, the moon rising, the lowering of a curtain of stars. And all the other pairs of words—red, bus, stoplight, boring—just threw up a mass of confusing images, making it impossible for me to sort out something as logical as saying: "A sunset precedes nightfall" is the same as "a chill precedes a fever." The only way I would have gotten that answer right would have been to imagine an associative situation, for example, my being disobedient and staying out past sunset, catching a chill at night, which turns into feverish pneumonia as punishment, which indeed did happen to me.

I have been thinking about all this lately, about my mother's English, about achievement tests. Because lately I've been asked, as a writer, why there are not more Asian Americans represented in American literature. Why are there few Asian Americans enrolled in creative writing programs? Why do so many Chinese students go into engineering? Well, these are broad sociological questions I can't begin to answer. But I have noticed in surveys—in fact, just last week—that Asian students, as a whole, always do significantly better on math achievement tests than in English. And this makes me think that there are other Asian-American students whose English spoken in the home might also be described as "broken" or "limited." And perhaps they also have teachers who are steering them away from writing and into math and science, which is what happened to me.

Fortunately, I happen to be rebellious in nature and enjoy the challenge of disproving assumptions made about me. I became an English major my first year in college, after being enrolled as pre-med. I started writing nonfiction as a freelancer the week after I was told by my former boss that writing was my worst skill and I should hone my talents toward account management.

But it wasn't until 1985 that I finally began to write fiction. And at first I wrote using what I thought to be wittily crafted sentences, sentences that would finally prove I had mastery over the English language. Here's an example from the first draft of a story that later made its way into *The Joy Luck Club,* but without this line: "That was my mental quandary in its nascent state." A terrible line, which I can barely pronounce.

20   Fortunately, for reasons I won't get into today, I later decided I should envision a reader for the stories I would write. And the reader I decided upon was my mother, because these were stories about mothers. So with this reader in mind—and in fact she did read my early drafts—I began to write stories using all the Englishes I grew up with: the English I spoke to my mother, which for lack of a better term might be described as "simple"; the English she used with me, which for lack of a better term might be described as "broken"; my translation of her Chinese, which could certainly be described as "watered down"; and what I imagined to be her translation of her Chinese if she could speak in perfect English, her internal language, and for that I sought to preserve the essence, but neither an English nor a Chinese structure. I wanted to capture what language ability tests can never reveal: her intent, her passion, her imagery, the rhythms of her speech and the nature of her thoughts.

Apart from what any critic had to say about my writing, I knew I had succeeded where it counted when my mother finished reading my book and gave me her verdict: "So easy to read."

CONNECTING THROUGH WRITING

One of the best ways to get ideas for an essay is to ask and answer your own most compelling questions.

- Write down whatever questions come to mind during and after your reading. See if your answers to these questions provide topics for writing.

- Choose a compelling idea from a journal entry.

- Draw a Venn diagram to compare elements, characters, or stories (pp. 29–30), use directed freewriting (p. 39), ask questions (p. 39), list (p. 40), or draw a cluster or semantic map (pp. 41–42) to loosen up ideas.

Listed below is a more structured approach based on the elements discussed earlier in this section. Applying these questions to "Mother Tongue" may demonstrate how the elements might be applied to any essay.

FIRST RESPONSES

1. To what extent is your response to "Mother Tongue" influenced by your own background or experience?

2. What questions came to mind as you read the essay?

3. What do you find most provocative or compelling about the essay?

TYPE OF ESSAY

1. How does the voice of the writer influence your response?

2. Amy Tan opens her essay by writing "I am not a scholar of English or literature." How does that influence your response to her?

3. Would you classify this as a narrative, expository, or argumentative essay? Why? To what extent is the classification clear?

LANGUAGE, STYLE, AND STRUCTURE

1. In general, is "Mother Tongue" formal or informal? How so?

2. Is Amy Tan's use of language formal or informal?

3. Are there many instances of imagery and figurative language (simile, metaphor)? If so, how do they connect to or support the essay?

4. How would you describe Amy Tan's voice? Do you find her believable? Why?

5. Was she effective in conveying the essay's meaning? How so?

THEME

1. Do you gain any insights about yourself or your writing from this essay? If so, explain.

2. What is the intention of the essay? Is it trying to inform us of something? To prove or convince us of something? To share an insight?

3. What do you think the author is trying to say? What is the essay's theme?

TOPICS FOR WRITING

The following list is not exhaustive, but simply illustrative of the kinds of questions that might emerge from the more specific analytical questions (and combinations of questions) like those above. Your responses to these questions might provide worthwhile topics for writing.

1. How does the way people use language influence other people's opinion of them?

2. Amy Tan writes, "the language spoken in the family, especially in immigrant families which are more insular, plays a large role in shaping the language of the child." Do you think this is true? Explain.

3. In what way is it possible for someone to be articulate and not have a formal command of the language?

4. To what extent is there an advantage to using "different Englishes" for different occasions?

5. Do you think many people have a "mother tongue"? Do you? Explain.

6. Do you think everyone should learn to use standard English correctly? Why?

Chapter 4

Argumentation
Writing a Critical Essay

The goal in this chapter is to develop your writing and analysis into a critical essay. Writing a critical essay is a natural extension of your earlier work. At their best, your essays should continue to express, in your strongest voice, what you believe is important. There is no need for you to become completely formal or use complicated terminology. But writing a critical essay will require

- Reading and rereading a text carefully;
- Gathering textual evidence;
- Building observations into an interpretation or evaluation;
- Articulating a sound argument.

Convincing others requires clear thinking and writing. We may write with a stronger voice when we feel passionate about an issue, but it is our ability to *explain why with evidence,* not just our passion, that gives clarity and credibility to our arguments.

THE CRITICAL ESSAY

The difference between a response essay and a critical essay is a matter of emphasis rather than kind. A response essay describes our experience with literature—how we are personally affected by the work. The primary intention of a response essay is to share our personal experience, not to argue for a position.

A **critical essay,** while motivated by our experience with literature, *shifts the emphasis toward the work itself and builds an argument for what the work or some aspect of it means (an interpretation), or its worth (an evaluation), or both.* In addition to analyzing or explicating the text of a work, or making comparisons, a critical essay may evaluate philosophically or ethically, or view a work or its elements within a variety of historical, cultural, biographical, or other contexts (see Appendix A on p. 1331 for an explanation of these approaches).

Writing a critical essay builds on your earlier work. Beyond this work, you must be prepared to offer arguments in support of your views and state them clearly and persuasively. The following response may give you an insight into the difference between a personal and a critical response.

Suzanne's Response to *Antigonê:*

> The central focus throughout the play seems to be public policy vs. individual conscience. I found it very interesting that even though <u>Antigone</u> was written so long ago it dealt with civil disobedience, which remains a major social issue to this day. I liked the way Antigone stood up for what she felt was right instead of letting Creon force her to live with something she felt was morally wrong. Creon's sexist attitude became his downfall. At first I thought Haimon would side with his father, so I was pretty surprised when they found him dead in Antigone's cave. Everyone tried to reason with Creon, and he had plenty of chances to change his mind, so I thought he got what he deserved. I really liked this play, and I thought it was very well written.

Suzanne comments about how the play affected her, but she has taken her comments a step further. When she writes, "The central focus throughout the play seems to be public policy vs. individual conscience," she is stating what she believes the play is about—the subject (or issue) of the play. By going one step further and stating what she believes the play is saying about this subject, she may have a strong proposition, or thesis statement, for a critical essay.

When she writes, "I thought it was very well written," she is making an evaluative statement about the quality of writing in the play. Again, if she defines what she means by well written, and indicates how *Antigonê* fulfills that description, she may have a good proposition, or thesis statement, for a critical essay.

In each case, her support for these propositions (not the propositions themselves) is the crucial factor in building either of these statements into a clear thesis statement and effective critical essay. In both cases, she would have to build an argument by gathering support from the text. To support her interpretation of what *Antigonê* is saying about "public policy vs. individual conscience," she would have to define what she meant by these terms, cite evidence, and identify connecting patterns of this theme in the text of the play. To support her evaluation that "it was very well written," she would have to define her standards for well written and show with reference to the text—how the play matched them.

INTERPRETATION AND EVALUATION

Like many other classifications in literature, *interpretation* and *evaluation* are not separate and distinct. In our reading, both often occur at the same time. When we write about our reading, however, we can make choices about which to emphasize. Do we want to interpret what the work, or an aspect of it, means or its worth? While each is a different emphasis, it may be difficult to separate them, and many critical essays are a combination of both.

Interpretation: What Does It Mean?

The idea of coming up with an interpretation may seem a bit overwhelming, but in our everyday lives we hear and respond to this request regularly. "What do you make of that?", "What was that all about?", and "What's your read on that?" are among the many ways we might be asked for an interpretation. At the core of all these questions is a basic request for an explanation of "meaning." When we construct and articulate that meaning, we are giving our interpretation.

What goes into our explanation of meaning, of course, has a lot to do with who we are. Our interpretations are influenced by many personal factors, but *what makes an interpretation convincing or credible is our ability to explain why—a why not based on unsupported personal opinion but on support with evidence.*

An interpretation of literature may involve almost any aspect of a work, from the meaning of a single word, image, character, or place to a statement of its overall meaning. It may even involve more than one work, so don't feel that you must limit yourself to choosing from the possibilities discussed here. The first time you read a work you may feel one way, but writing down your reflections, rereading the text, and discussing it with others—doing a close reading—may lead to a different, better-informed understanding and interpretation.

Evaluation: How Well Does It Work?

You've been evaluating literature since you first started reading. You like it or don't like it, believe it's good or bad. How specific you are about "why" may depend on your experience as a reader. Those of us who read often have probably given some thought to why we like to read some things more than others. Experienced readers are likely to respond to "why" by pointing to particular qualities that are present or absent. Those of us who don't read very much might simply say, "I couldn't get into it" or "It was boring" and leave it at that.

We live in the world that literature reveals. Our standards, the principles by which we evaluate literature, tend to be developed through experience and over time. We make judgments about the nature of that world—people's biases, our surroundings, difficult circumstances, and the authenticity of people we meet. In this way we have already experienced and developed standards about point of view, setting, conflict, character, and other aspects of the literary experience.

The standards we have for evaluating literature are also affected by our expectations. Is the primary purpose of this literature to thrill or entertain? To make a social comment? To reveal something essential about the human condition? All of these? Some of these? It would be unfair to apply the same standards to a mystery thriller that we would to "Araby." On the other hand, applying our "thrill and entertain" standards to a story that intends to give insight into the human condition seems equally unfair.

CONNECTING THROUGH COLLABORATION

You may even find it interesting to share your responses to the prompts that follow with other members of the class in pairs or small groups.

1. Choose a topic you know a lot about (music, dance, sports, cars, computers, etc.). How did you learn about it? By yourself? Did someone show you or teach you? Why do you think you know a lot about it?
2. What are your standards or criteria for evaluating the topic you chose in question 1? See if you can make a list and explain the importance of each standard.
3. Think back to a large purchase you made recently (clothes, car, computer, stereo, etc.). What were your standards or criteria for evaluation? Make a list and explain the importance of each of these standards.
4. Do you feel as if you know a lot about literature? How do you feel when someone asks you to evaluate a poem, story, play, or essay? Explain.
5. What are your standards for evaluating literature? See if you can make a list and explain the importance of each one.
6. If you had trouble coming up with a list or explanations, read the Options for a Critical Essay below for help.

OPTIONS FOR A CRITICAL ESSAY: PROCESS AND PRODUCT

The following checklist is an outline of five types of critical essays: analytical, comparative, thematic, philosophical or ethical evaluation, and contextual. Most of the terms in the checklist have been explained in Chapter 3 and should already be familiar to you. Brief explanations of each with examples follow the checklist.

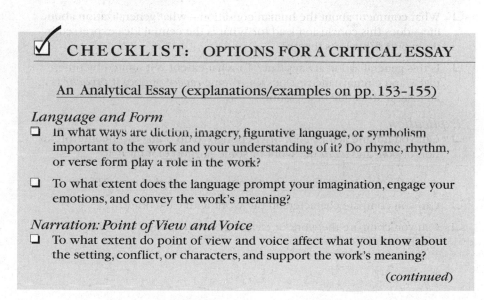

☑ CHECKLIST: OPTIONS FOR A CRITICAL ESSAY

An Analytical Essay (explanations/examples on pp. 153–155)

Language and Form

❑ In what ways are diction, imagery, figurative language, or symbolism important to the work and your understanding of it? Do rhyme, rhythm, or verse form play a role in the work?

❑ To what extent does the language prompt your imagination, engage your emotions, and convey the work's meaning?

Narration: Point of View and Voice

❑ To what extent do point of view and voice affect what you know about the setting, conflict, or characters, and support the work's meaning?

(continued)

Setting
❏ How effective is the setting in presenting concrete details and enabling you to feel like you're present?

❏ To what extent does the setting complement conflict and character and support the work's meaning?

Conflict
❏ How important is the conflict? How believable are the internal and external conflicts? How challenging is the struggle?

❏ How unified is the conflict? How well do the minor conflicts complement each other and support the major conflict?

❏ In what ways do setting and characterization support the conflict?

Plot
❏ What is the plot structure? To what extent does the plot structure convey the conflict and the work's meaning?

Characterization
❏ How effectively are the characters developed? To what extent are you shown, not told, who they are? How believable are the characters? How complex? How motivated and consistent? Does their behavior make sense?

❏ To what extent do narration, setting, or conflict influence characterization?

❏ In what ways does characterization affect the work's meaning?

Theme
❏ What conclusion can you draw from what happens in the work?

❏ What comment about the human condition—what generalization about life—does this conclusion lead to? What is the central idea expressed by the work? What is its theme?

❏ Is this generalization always true? To what extent is it limited by time, place, and circumstances? Does this theme *reveal* or does it *preach?* Is it an insight about life or a lesson?

Explication
❏ Can you do, and is this work brief enough to do, a line-by-line interpretation of *how* and *what* the work or some portion of it means?

A Comparative Essay (explanation/examples on p. 155)

❏ Can you compare characters in the work with each other?

❏ Can you compare the work or characters or elements in it with those in another work?

A Thematic Essay (explanation/example on pp. 155–156)

❑   Is there a theme or topic common to two or more works that you can
    write about?

A Philosophical or Ethical Evaluation (explanation/examples on p. 156)

❑   What beliefs are expressed by the narrator or characters in the work and
    how does what they say or do exemplify these beliefs or actions?

❑   Can you write about whether you agree or disagree with these beliefs or
    actions?

A Contextual Essay (explanation/examples on p. 156)

❑   How much do you know about the contextual background of the work?
    What do you need to know? How will you find out more?

❑   How is the work influenced by historical, cultural, biographical, or other
    contextual factors? Can you write about the work in the light of these
    contextual factors?

An Analytical Essay

To analyze a work of literature is to look closely at how it works—to examine its
parts or elements as they contribute to the work's meaning. Our brief discussion of
these elements below is a carryover from a more comprehensive explanation of
these terms in Chapter 3. *If you have unanswered questions about these elements,
you may find it helpful to refer to that discussion beginning on page 139.*

   Language and **form** are the vehicles that carry literature to us. The diction of
the narrator or characters, concrete images, similes, metaphors, and symbols may all
contribute in crucial ways to the meaning of a work. The sounds and structures of
rhyme, rhythm, and verse may play a vital role in conveying a work's meaning.
When language is used effectively, it prompts our imaginations and provides us
with clear images, rhythm, and insight. Form complements content and effectively
conveys meaning to us.

   For example, you might write about the powerful, concrete imagery in Robert
Hayden's "Those Winter Sundays" (p. 13) or Marge Piercy's "Barbie Doll" (p. 14). You
could address the impact of Sammy's slang and concrete descriptions in John Updike's
"A&P" (p. 490). You could write about the rhymes, rhythms, and verse form in Countee
Cullen's "Incident" (p. 24) or Dudley Randall's "Ballad of Birmingham" (p. 17)—or in
other pieces you've read.

   Narration includes *point of view,* the perspective from which the narrator
speaks to us, and *voice,* the personality behind the words. This narrative "lens" controls what we see and know about the setting, the characters, or the conflict in a
work. When point of view and voice are used effectively, we see the characters,

setting, and events from a perspective and with a flavor that help us experience the overall meaning of a work.

Here, you might write about point of view by addressing Mama's up close, first-person narration and its influence on your interpretation of Alice Walker's "Everyday Use" (p. 983). Or you might write about the impact of the distanced, third-person narration on Ernest Hemingway's "Hills Like White Elephants" (p. 745).

Setting includes location, time, atmosphere, and mood and has a direct and indirect impact on character and conflict. It supports and emphasizes the story's meaning. An effective setting will help us see and experience the concrete details of a work's environment. We "sense" the sights, sounds, and emotions of the atmosphere as if we were really there.

As an example, you might write about the dreary, dark atmosphere in James Joyce's "Araby" (p. 490) and how it contrasts with the warmth of the boy's feelings for Mangan's sister.

Conflict is the struggle of opposing external or internal forces. Most good literature contains both types of conflict, but places greater emphasis on the internal component. In many cases, it is our ability to identify with the *internal nature* (the anxiety, frustration, and disappointment) of the conflict that gives us a feel for it. We may never have faced this kind of external dilemma, but other experiences we have had may give us an idea of what the dilemma feels like inside. We won't care about the conflict if it's not important to the characters and to us. As we know from our own lives, a conflict doesn't need to be a life-and-death struggle to have an impact on us. Well-developed conflict, like a game between two evenly matched teams or players, keeps us involved until the outcome is decided.

To write about conflict, you might address the extraordinary external and internal conflicts in the brutal, racist humiliation experienced by the young man in Ralph Ellison's "Battle Royal" (p. 448), or write about the ordinary but painful internal conflict that results from the young girl's humiliation in Sandra Cisneros's "Eleven" (p. 26).

Plot is the structure of the story. Think about the plots of stories you've read. How and how well does the structure of each work convey the setting, the conflict, the characters, and ultimately the story's meaning?

Characterization is the creation and development of characters in a work. In our own lives, we react to people on the basis of how they look and what they say and do. In most good literature, we're able to observe characters thinking, speaking, and doing—and judge who they are for ourselves. Effective characters seem lifelike. Like real people, they are not simple, but have depth and complexity. We "see" and experience them through their words and actions and what others have to say about them.

To write about characterization, you might address how much you learn about the characters Antigonê and Ismenê solely from their conversation in the Prologue of Sophocles's *Antigonê* (p. 104), or write about the description, actions, and reactions of Eliza as her character gradually emerges in John Steinbeck's "The Chrysanthemums" (p. 1208). The narration, conversations, settings, and conflicts all provide opportunities for us to witness these characters thinking, saying, and doing.

Theme is the central idea expressed by a work. What conclusion can you draw from what happens in the work? Can you expand your conclusion into a generalization or idea that addresses the human condition? When literature preaches or teaches a lesson, it doesn't usually account for the complexities of the real world. An effective theme transcends the time and place of its setting. It has universal qualities that make it applicable to human nature in any time or place.

For example, the final draft of Suzanne McCloskey's sample essay at the end of this chapter (p. 171) argues for what she believes is the theme of *Antigonê:* "The arrogance of political power cannot defeat moral justice, for conscience and the will of the gods will always triumph."

Explication is a detailed analysis, a line-by-line interpretation of *how* and *what* a short work (or brief section of a larger work) means. Because they are longer pieces, works of fiction, drama, and essays usually don't lend themselves to such close reading. Most poems, however, are relatively brief, and by their nature packed with meaning. Poetry presents a good opportunity for a very close reading and an examination of sounds, words, images, and lines, and how they all work together to deliver the work's meaning. An explication is not just a summary or translation of the author's language into your own; it is a detailed explanation of *how* the work conveys meaning.

There is a good example on page 665, where Charles Chiang explicates the text of the "To be or not to be" soliloquy from Shakespeare's *Hamlet* by closely examining each line of the speech and building it into an interpretation of Hamlet's character and Shakespeare's intended effect on the audience.

A Comparative Essay

To what extent is the work or some aspect of it comparable to other works or aspects of them? In what way are characters or other aspects of this work comparable to each other? The objective of a comparison is not just to list similarities and differences but to reveal something important about whatever is being compared. Which details you choose as the basis of this comparison can make a difference. To give yourself a clear direction, and an overview of what you have, it may be helpful to make separate lists of similarities and differences before you start to write. Ask yourself what's worth comparing and what's not—and how this comparison might yield an effective essay. One useful method of lining up similarities and differences is the Venn diagram, described in Chapter 2 on pages 29-30.

William Winters exemplifies this approach in his essay on page 1145, where he compares Langston Hughes's "Theme for English B" with Countee Cullen's "Incident" and concludes that both poems reflect Hughes's views as expressed in "The Negro Artist and Racial Mountain." And on page 704, Barbara Pfister compares two different types of art—a van Gogh painting, *Starry Night,* and an Anne Sexton poem written in response to it.

A Thematic Essay

A variation of both the comparative essay and the contextual essay (below) is a thematic essay. **A thematic essay** compares several works that treat the same theme or topic (such as "family and friends," "innocence and experience," or "faith and doubt"), and may include works from different genres (poems, stories, plays). In addition to writing about the literature, it is essential that you explore the theme or topic and state why—and in what ways—the literature exemplifies the topic so well.

For example, you might address the theme of sibling relationships in Sophocles's *Antigonê* (p. 104), Louise Erdrich's "The Red Convertible" (p. 236), and Tennessee Williams's *The Glass Menagerie* (p. 284).

A Philosophical or Ethical Evaluation

Narrators and literary characters often express their beliefs in what they say or do, and it's natural for us to judge their words and actions through our own values. Based on your own clearly stated criteria, you might interpret the wisdom or virtue of their actions and beliefs or build an argument for or against them. Before you evaluate the beliefs or actions of the narrator or characters, be clear about what they are and be clear about your own standards for judging them. Only when you have clarified both will you be able to take a position and build an argument.

Here, you might write about the beliefs or actions (or potential actions) expressed by the man or the woman in Ernest Hemingway's "Hills Like White Elephants" (p. 745). Or you could address the beliefs expressed by the narrator/protagonist in Langston Hughes's "Salvation" (p. 32). The student essays of Michelle McAuliffe (p. 496) and Julie Fitzmaurice (p. 498) about John Updike's "A&P" illustrate this type of response. Both students comment on the protagonist's decision to quit his job, but they disagree about the wisdom of his decision. Michelle criticizes his decision and believes that he will regret it because of the consequences it will have for him and his family. Julie, however, sees his action as an inspiring statement that he will refuse to sell out and live his life like the store manager in the story.

A Contextual Essay

To write about literature in context is to consider the work within a framework of cultural, historical, biographical, or other factors, and articulate the influence that context has on the work or an element of the work. If you're not very knowledgeable about this background, it may be necessary to do additional reading and research before you write your essay.

For example, in her sample essay on page 931, Trisa Hayes critiques Ibsen's *A Doll's House* and Kate Chopin's "The Story of an Hour" within the historical and social framework of the nineteenth century. And Kevin Chamberlain's essay about James Joyce's "Eveline" on page 196 examines the cultural imperatives of late-nineteenth-century Ireland as they seem to determine the fate of the story's protagonist.

For a more comprehensive explanation of these approaches (including historical, gender, political-economic, psychoanalytic, archetypal, and biographical criticism), see Appendix A: Critical Approaches to Literature, on page 1331.

Argumentation: Writing a Critical Essay

There are many different ways to plan and structure a critical essay. The suggestions that follow represent one approach. The purpose of this discussion is not to move you step-by-step through a rigid sequence. Constructing an argument is a continuous process of moving forward and returning and moving forward again. The strongest thesis, the most convincing evidence, the most effective structure may occur to you early or late. Let your ideas flow freely throughout the process. Some of your best ideas may come to you when you think you're almost finished.

For those more comfortable with the classic rhetorical terms "issue," "claim," "reason," and "assumption or warrant," those terms are indicated in parentheses below their equivalents.

The Shape of an Argument

The subject

(The issue)

The proposition about the subject (thesis)

(The claim)

The evidence that supports the proposition about the subject

(The reasons)

The explanation that connects the evidence to the proposition about the subject

(The warrant or assumption)

 CHECKLIST: WRITING A CRITICAL ESSAY
(For detailed explanations see pages 159–165)

Planning Your Argument

Determine Its Feasibility
❏ Can you write a critical essay about this?

❏ Do you have enough to say, and can you find enough evidence to support your case?

Consider Your Motivation
❏ Will this topic sustain your interest long enough for you to do a good job?

Clarify Your Thesis (The Claim)
❏ Do you have a clear understanding of the thesis you want to argue? Can you articulate it in a thesis statement?

Know Your Readers
❏ What assumptions can you make about your readers? Are they likely to agree or disagree with your thesis?

(continued)

<u>Supporting Your Argument</u>

Arrange Your Support Effectively

❑   Is the support for your thesis arranged in the most effective way? Is it more effective to develop your argument by stating your thesis first and then supporting it with evidence, or by allowing the evidence to build into your thesis?

Support Your Thesis with Facts from the Text (The Reasons)

❑   Is your support based on facts or opinions? Have you supported your opinions with facts and quotes from the text?

Account for All the Evidence (The Reasons)

❑   Have you accounted for *all* the evidence in the text? Have you accounted for evidence that may not support your thesis?

Explain the Connections (The Warrant or Assumption)

❑   Have you explained *how* the evidence you've chosen supports your thesis?

<u>Opening, Closing, and Revising</u>

Write or Rewrite Your Introduction After Your First Draft

❑   Is your introduction clear, informative, and interesting?

❑   If appropriate, does it map out the journey for the reader?

Close Your Argument Reasonably

❑   Have you explained the connections between the thesis and your support?

❑   Have you claimed anything for which you haven't delivered evidence?

Revise with a Fresh View

❑   Have you reread and reviewed your essay?

❑   How well is your draft organized? Does the sequence make sense? Are there gaps that need to be filled? Is there enough support?

❑   Have you explained the connections between your support and your thesis?

❑   Have you expressed those connections as clearly as possible?

❑   Have you maintained a consistent "voice" throughout the essay?

Review Your Intentions and Organization

❑   Is the central thesis of the essay clearly stated? Does the title account for your thesis?

❑   Is the essay fully developed? Have you accounted for all aspects of your thesis statement? Are there enough details to support or clarify your thesis? Have you *shown* what you've told?

❑   Are there enough quotes from the work to support your thesis? Do all the paragraphs relate to your thesis? Is the essay fully developed? Is the organization of the paragraphs within the essay clear? Are the paragraphs fully developed? Do each of the sentences within the paragraphs relate to the paragraph's central idea?

❏ Is the language clear? Are there redundancies, digressions, or meaningless phrases that could be cut?

Proofread Carefully
❏ Are all your sentences complete sentences? Are all your sentences punctuated appropriately?

❏ Have you checked for easily confused words (then/than, your/you're, its/it's, etc.)? Are you sure of the meaning of all the words you've used?

❏ Are the titles of works underlined or in quotations, as appropriate?

❏ Are there particular errors that you have a tendency to make? Have you looked for those in this essay?

❏ Is the essay written in the format required by your instructor? Have you documented your references to the text and included a list of works cited?

Planning Your Argument

Determine the Argument's Feasibility (The Issue)   Can you write a critical essay about this? No matter how compelling your proposition, you cannot write an essay about it unless you have enough to say and can find enough evidence to support your argument. If the point you want to make is obvious, abstract, or very general, it may be impossible to come up with a solid argument and develop it into a convincing essay in a reasonable amount of time.

Consider Your Own Motivation   How much do you care about the subject? Will it sustain your enthusiasm long enough for you to complete the essay? Can you identify strongly with the situation in the work? Do you approve or disapprove of a character's action? Do you believe the work has helped you to understand yourself or inspired you to act in a particular way? Have you learned something about your own life through your experience of the work? Finally, do you feel strongly about your ability to convince an audience of your argument?

You will work with more enthusiasm and write with a stronger voice when you care about the subject.

Clarify Your Proposition: Write a Thesis Statement (The Claim)   Do you have a clear understanding of the proposition you are trying to prove? If you don't, you won't be able to express it in a form your readers will understand. Try to put your proposition into the form of a complete sentence that connects it to the subject. This thesis statement will sit at the core of your argument. Everything in your argument must relate back to and support this thesis statement. If you've put it in a form that you and your readers clearly understand, you will know if the evidence you've gathered adequately supports it.

If your thesis is an interpretation, define what you mean by the terms of the proposition or thesis. In her journal entry at the beginning of this chapter, Suzanne has identified the subject of *Antigonê* as "public policy vs. individual conscience." Her proposition about this subject, her thesis statement (what she believes the play is saying about public policy and individual conscience), will not be clear unless she spells out what she means by those terms. What "public policy" and "individual conscience" mean to her may be different from what they mean to other readers.

If your thesis is an evaluation, define your standards. If (like Suzanne) you believe *Antigonê* is well written, what are your standards for a well-written play? If you believe the characters are well developed, what are your standards for effective characterization?

Be careful to distinguish between the *subject* (or issue) of your essay and your *proposition* or claim about the subject—your thesis statement. Suzanne's subject is "public policy vs. individual conscience." What she believes the play, *Antigonê*, is saying about this subject—her thesis statement—(as reflected in the final draft of her essay) is "The arrogance of political power cannot defeat moral justice, for conscience and the will of the gods will always triumph."

As you consider the evidence you have and gather new evidence, you may discover that your thesis statement must be adjusted to accommodate this new information. Be flexible. Match the statement to the evidence, and the evidence to the statement. Until you submit your final draft, it's never too late to make adjustments to strengthen your thesis.

Know Your Readers   What can you assume about your readers? If you're writing this essay to be read by those in your class, you may already have some idea what your classmates and instructor think about your opinion. If so, does your thesis statement agree with the majority of responses you've heard? If not, it's important to "speak to" these contrary views when you present your own view.

No matter how convincing your evidence may be, if you don't address their contrary position, your readers will always wonder, "Yes, but what about. . . .?" This doesn't mean you must change their minds, but it does mean that you must account for all the evidence, especially the evidence that may seem (to some) to go against your thesis statement. If you cannot account for it, it may be time to reexamine your original proposition.

Remember, a number of interpretations may be acceptable. The strength of your thesis is in its support, not the thesis itself. So don't offend your readers by being inflexible and suggesting that anyone holding a different view is ignorant. Feeling strongly about what you want to prove gives you a stronger voice, but insulting or overpowering your readers is not likely to be persuasive.

Supporting Your Argument: Induction and Substantiation

Have you ever watched a toddler discover the world? The child crawls through the grass, stops to examine it blade by blade, picks it up, feels it, shakes it, tastes it. The child explores the surroundings and tests them piece by piece, and after several tries, probably comes to a conclusion: Grass is good for crawling but not so great for eating. When someone offers you a type of food you've never eaten before, how do you respond? How do you discover if you like it or not? Well, you probably ask for a taste. If you like the taste, you might ask for more. If you don't like the taste, you may or may not try more. This kind of examining, testing, making tentative observations, retesting, and concluding is a fairly common process in our lives. It is called **inductive reasoning.**

When you think or write inductively, you move from specific observations to conclusions. If you try a new food and like it, the next time it's offered you can respond with more certainty. You've tested it and can come to a tentative conclusion. Each subsequent tasting gives you more information and solidifies your conclusion: I like sushi; it tastes good.

Once you arrive at your conclusion, you are ready to make a generalization: Sushi tastes good or not. The process of supporting this generalization is called **substantiation.** When we substantiate, we support our conclusion with specific observations. This brings the process full circle. We discover how much we like or don't like sushi through specific tastings. We explain why sushi is good with support from those tastings: This sushi sits lightly on my tongue; it's soft and moist with a full seafood flavor and pleasant smell. We arrive at our conclusion inductively; we support, defend, and explain it through substantiation.

In many ways, writing about literature follows a similar induction and substantiation pattern. As we initially read, respond, discuss, and write about our experience with literature, we build on our specific observations of the text and arrive at our conclusions inductively. With those conclusions in hand, we substantiate them with reference to our specific observations of the text.

Arrange Your Support Effectively   You substantiate your argument when you place the thesis statement or proposition at the beginning of the essay and lay out evidence in the rest of the essay to support it. You begin with a generalization and support it with specific examples as evidence. You immediately make it clear to your readers what you intend to prove. Your thesis remains in their minds as they encounter each piece of subsequent evidence. In fact, if what you propose at the outset is interesting enough, your thesis statement may act as a "hook" for your readers and pull them into the essay.

Substantiation

$(a = b + b + b + b + b + b)$

(Your thesis equals the sum of the evidence.)

This approach may not work well if you are trying to convince skeptical readers, that is, readers who have already made up their minds and hold a contrary view. Encountering a proposition they disagree with at the beginning may interfere with their response through the rest of the essay. Once they know what you want to prove, they may not give you an open-minded reading. They may be predisposed to disagree with you no matter how compelling your evidence.

Inductive argumentation moves from specific examples to a generalization or conclusion. It mimics the process you probably went through when you came up with your proposition to begin with. As the specifics of the work built up in your mind, they moved you toward a conclusion and a proposition. A more effective strategy to convince a skeptical reader may be to withhold your proposition until the end. By first providing support before readers know what your position is, they may withhold judgment and be more likely to accept your thesis when it comes as the natural conclusion of strong evidence.

Induction

$(b + b + b + b + b + b = a)$

(The sum of the evidence equals your thesis.)

And, of course, there are variations of these strategies. For example, if you're stating your thesis up front, you may want to provide background information to "educate" the reader before you present your thesis, and then follow with supporting evidence. If you are using an inductive approach, you may want to build your support to a natural conclusion, and then discuss why this conclusion makes sense. In any case, you should consider your audience and your intentions before you decide which strategy will work best.

Support Your Thesis with Facts from the Text (The Reasons)   All of us have probably been criticized at some time for not being objective or for allowing our personal feelings to influence our judgment. It's not possible, of course, to be entirely objective—to separate the facts from who we are and how we see them. In the course of our daily lives, we're not usually required to justify our feelings or our opinions. But writing an effective critical essay requires a rationale for our judgments—reasons derived not only from our feelings and values but also from ingredients in the work of literature that prompt those judgments. Although there is no guarantee that everyone will agree with our conclusions, we can make sure that our evidence is recognized and respected as valid.

Facts are verifiable. You can cite them in the text. They should be the core of the evidence that supports your argument. For example, it is a fact that in John Updike's poem "Ex-Basketball Player" (p. 1010), Flick Webb was a high school basketball star. You can verify this fact by citing the text of the poem:

Once Flick played for the high-school team, the Wizards.
He was good: in fact, the best. In '46
He bucketed three hundred ninety points,
A county record still. The ball loved Flick.

And you can verify the fact of his current employment by citing the text:

He never learned a trade, he just sells gas,
Checks oil, and changes flats.

But if (based on these few facts) you say that Flick is an "unhappy loser," you are expressing an opinion, not a fact. You may hold this opinion for any number of personal reasons, prompted by a few facts in the poem. But if you want to build an argument to support this opinion, you will need to connect most or all the facts in the poem in a convincing way, and logically demonstrate how they lead to this conclusion. A good critical essay requires reasons for your judgments, factual support derived not only from your feelings and values but also from ingredients in the text that logically combine to prompt them. There is no guarantee, of course, that every-one will agree with your conclusions, but you should make sure that your evidence is recognized and respected as valid.

Account for All the Evidence (The Reasons)   A strong thesis is

constructed from all the evidence, not just the parts that agree with your conclusion. A discerning reader sees contrary evidence whether you point it out or not. For example, it is a fact that the speaker in Robert Frost's "The Road Not Taken" (p. 78) has taken the road less traveled, as suggested in the first two lines of this stanza:

Then took the other, as just as fair,
And having perhaps the better claim,
Because it was grassy and wanted wear:
Though as for that the passing there
Had worn them really about the same.

To suggest that one road was very different from the other, though, is to ignore the last two lines. It is a fact that he says his choice will make a difference in his life:

I shall be telling this with a sigh
Somewhere ages and ages hence:
Two roads diverged in a wood, and I—
I took the one less traveled by,
And that has made all the difference.

But suggesting that the speaker knows that this choice was the best one and has made him happiest is to ignore other lines in this last stanza that seem to indicate uncertainty. Do we know that "all the difference" means a positive difference? How would you support that from the text?

So too, in Alice Walker's "Everyday Use" (p. 983), if you ignore the fact that the story is told by Dee's mother, you fail to account for the subjectivity of her descriptions. By addressing her subjectivity, however, and demonstrating that she is a reliable narrator by matching her descriptions to Dee's actions in the story, you may establish credibility for her narration and what she tells you.

None of this is to say that the personal meaning you derive from the work is not the most important meaning for you—a meaning that is often based on many factors beyond the text. But for the purposes of a critical essay, you must rely heavily on the text and its factual support to make a convincing case for your reader.

Explain the Connections (The Warrant or Assumption)   Sometimes

what seems self-evident to us is not so evident to our readers. In addition to highlighting the facts to support your argument, explain the connections. Explicitly show your readers *how* the chosen evidence supports your conclusion. For example, if your proposition about the play *Antigonê* is that "Ismenê is not as courageous as Antigonê," and your evidence is that Ismenê says, ". . . I have no strength / To break laws that were made for the public good," it is still necessary to explain the connection between the evidence (what Ismenê has said) and the proposition (that Ismenê is not as courageous as Antigonê).

Consider the explanation: "While Antigonê is willing to accept the consequences of her action and suffer death if necessary, Ismenê indicates that she is afraid of Creon's directive and will not join her sister in the burial." This explanation shows the connection between the proposition and the quoted evidence and makes your logic clear to the reader.

Opening, Closing, and Revising Your Argument

Write Your Introduction After You Know Your Argument   It may seem strange to wait until you're almost finished with the first draft of an essay before writing its introduction. However, introducing an essay is a bit like introducing a person. In both cases, you can make a more effective introduction when you know who or what you are introducing. This does not mean you have to mention everything you know. It means that you know your subject well enough to say the essential things.

Make your introduction interesting. You want the reader to continue reading beyond the first paragraph. Remember what seemed so interesting to you about the work, and try to pass that interest on to the reader. Make sure that what you say flows smoothly and maintains the same voice used in the rest of the essay. If you're developing your argument through substantiation, this is the place to state your thesis as clearly as possible.

Close Your Argument Reasonably   Although there is no need to summarize your essay in the conclusion, it may be helpful to remind the reader of the logic of your argument and explain the basic connections between your support and your thesis. Avoid being too ambitious. Only make claims or take credit for connections you've actually established.

If you've developed your argument inductively, this is the place where you want to state your thesis. Remember not to overstate your case. If you've proved your point, the evidence will carry it.

Revise with a Fresh View   If you really want to "re-vision" your essay, to see it again from a fresh perspective, it's best to let some time pass. Try to place yourself in the position of the reader who is reading your essay for the first time.

As with any other essay, it can be very useful to do an after-draft outline. Go back and identify the point of each paragraph. List those points. This should give you a pretty good overview of your essay. How well is your draft organized? Does the sequence make sense? Are there gaps that need to be filled? Is there enough support?

Within the body of the essay, have you explained the connections between your support and your thesis? Have you expressed those connections as clearly as possible? Have you maintained a consistent voice throughout the essay?

Check Against Your Intentions and Organization   State your thesis clearly. Support and clarify your thesis with enough details and examples from the work of literature. *Show* what you have stated. Give the essay a title based on your thesis. If you're having trouble thinking of a title, it may be an indication that the thesis itself is not clear. Make sure that your essay is fully developed. Account for all aspects of your thesis statement.

All your paragraphs must relate to that central thesis, and the organization of those paragraphs within the essay should be clear. Each paragraph should be fully developed too; each of the sentences within your paragraphs should relate to the central idea of that paragraph. All your statements should add something to the essay. Are there redundancies, digressions, or meaningless phrases that could be cut?

Proofread Carefully Proofreading is a crucial final step in the process of producing an essay. In addition to making any changes that did not occur to you earlier and fine-tuning your writing, check your essay for correct grammar, spelling, punctuation, and typos. Make sure all your sentences are complete and punctuated appropriately. Check to see that all of your words are spelled correctly. Check for easily confused words (then/than, your/you're, its/it's, etc.), which computerized spell checkers do not pick up. Check on the meaning of any words you are not sure of. Make sure the titles of works are underlined or in quotations, as appropriate.

If there are types of errors you personally have a tendency to make, look carefully for them. Finally, make sure you've followed the *MLA Handbook for Writers of Research Papers* or another documentation format recommended by your instructor. Have you cited and documented your sources correctly? Do you have a "Work(s) Cited" section at the end of your essay?

FROM FIRST RESPONSE TO CRITICAL ESSAY

The same processes that are so useful in generating ideas for a response essay are just as valuable for giving you ideas and narrowing your topic for a critical essay. Reading literature encourages a variety of responses—and perhaps raises more questions than answers. It is a good idea to generate and explore as many of your questions and ideas as possible before you decide on a topic. Below is a quick review of strategies to get started. For a detailed explanation of these techniques, with examples, see Chapter 2, pages 36–43.

- *Using directed freewriting* can generate ideas. The best time to do this exercise is immediately after you finish reading, while your thoughts and impressions are still fresh. The intention of this exercise is to release what you know without blocking it with pauses for reflection, punctuation, or editing.

- *Asking questions about a general topic* is likely to provide you with new information. Responding with detailed answers to these questions may provide you with ideas for a narrowed thesis and specific support for that thesis.

- By *choosing a few key words or phrases* that apply to your topic and then *listing* as many related details under each as you can, you should be able to generate many concrete details and much specific support for your ideas.

- *Clustering your ideas* or drawing a semantic map may help you discover and understand relationships, and generate and extend ideas better by seeing them spatially rather than linearly.

THE DEVELOPMENT OF A CRITICAL ESSAY

Earlier in this chapter, we looked at Suzanne's journal response to Sophocles's *Antigonê* in Chapter 3. Let's follow up as she develops this response into a critical essay.

Step 1: Planning an Argument

Suzanne's Proposition (The Issue? Or the Claim?)   Suzanne's proposition in her first draft was that the focus of *Antigonê* is public policy versus individual conscience. In addition, she wanted to address Creon's sexism as a feature of that policy.

Feasibility   During her own reading and in class discussion, she saw much support for this thesis. Several statements in the play immediately came to mind that would support this idea, and she felt confident that this evidence would provide her with a strong argument.

Motivation   Suzanne had strong motivation to write about this issue. She liked the play and felt strongly about its issues, especially individual conscience and women's equality.

Clarity of the Thesis Statement (The Claim)   Her thesis statement, "The theme of *Antigonê* is public policy versus individual conscience" seems clear. But, as we will see when she revises, this statement identifies the subject of the play, not what the play is saying about this subject.

Audience   Based on general class discussion and the response of her small group, she was confident about her position. Occasionally, someone would sympathize with Creon's position, but in general her classmates were supportive of her views.

Step 2: Supporting the Argument

Arranging Support (The Reasons)   In class discussion, Suzanne had already received a generally sympathetic response. She was not trying to convince a hostile audience, so she believed that it would be most effective to state her position at the beginning and substantiate that position with support from the text.

Her plan was to introduce her thesis as clearly as possible, state and connect her beliefs about Creon and Antigonê with support from the play, and conclude by reaffirming her belief and how the text supported it.

Deriving Factual Support from the Text (The Reasons)   She derived her support from two basic sources: first, her description and interpretation of the actions of Creon and Antigonê; second, what Creon, Antigonê, and Haimon said that confirmed her judgments and her thesis statement.

Accounting for All the Evidence   In addition to the evidence that favored her views, she considered views that were more sympathetic to Creon's position. The most common argument sympathetic to Creon was that Antigonê put him in an impossible position through her aggressive stance, that had she approached him in a more reasonable way, he might have listened. She intended to use Haimon's experience with Creon to counter this argument.

Explaining the Connections (The Warrant or Assumption)   Suzanne knew that she would have to explain the connections between her support (the quotes from the text and the actions of the characters) and her proposition, which was that Creon and Antigonê were representative of "public policy" and "individual conscience," respectively.

Suzanne's Draft

Based on her journal entry and notes, Suzanne wrote the following draft:

Might Against Right

Antigone is a tragic story that deals with the struggles between public policy and individual conscience, and on a lesser level, a woman's conflict with a man. Sophocles broaches the issues of might against right and civil disobedience in this shockingly tragic play.

In this play, Creon stands for public policy and Antigone symbolizes the individual conscience. The major conflict lies between these two headstrong figures. Creon has just been made king of Thebes because his nephews have killed each other in battle. Creon decreed that Eteocles, who died defending Thebes in battle, should be buried with full military honors. Polyneices was to be left to rot in the fields because Creon believed him to be a traitor who didn't deserve to be honored. Creon's law was clear: whoever disobeyed him and buried Polyneices was sentenced to be stoned to death in the public square. Creon is more concerned with forcing everyone to obey his decree than whether or not he has done the right thing. He seems to be an extremely headstrong and stubborn man who has a very hard time admitting that he's wrong. It is these very qualities that cause the chain reaction that dictates the downfall of Creon and all whom he loves.

Antigone is the sister of Eteocles and Polyneices, and she decides that she cannot abide by Creon's law. Polyneices was her brother just as much as Eteocles was, and to leave him to rot in the fields was wrong according to her conscience and God's law. She felt that Creon had no right to try to overstep God's boundaries; kings shouldn't presume to dictate who is privileged enough for a burial. Burial is supposed to be a universal right given to all of mankind. When Creon is informed that it is Antigone who has defied his law, he explodes. Not only has Antigone blatantly disregarded his wishes, she is both smug and righteous about the whole situation: "It was not God's proclamation. That final Justice that rules the world below makes no such laws." This shows the strength of Antigone's convictions. She knows that she will die for what she has done, but she stands firmly behind her decision and just wants it to be over with.

Creon is doubly enraged; Antigone has deliberately defied him and she is a woman. Women are supposed to be timid, weak, and docile creatures who need to be guided by men and their laws. Creon might have considered revoking his decree if it had been anyone else, but a woman has defied him and he can't let a mere woman get the better of him. This has now become, to a smaller degree, a battle of the sexes: "This girl is guilty of a double insolence, breaking the given laws and boasting of it. Who is the man here, she or I, if this crime goes unpunished?" This quote illustrates the lengths to which Creon would go to triumph over Antigone. Antigone defied a man's law and now a man is going to teach her a lesson. Creon's sense was being affected by his discriminatory and condescending attitude toward women. His irrationality is further proven when his son, Haimon, tries to reason with him. Haimon points out the validity of Antigone's actions and the fear that prevents any of the other citizens to voice their support of her: "I have heard them muttering and whispering in the dark about this girl. They say no woman has ever, so unreasonably, died so shameful a death for a generous act: 'She covered her brother's body. Is this indecent? She kept him from dogs and vultures. Is this a crime? Death?--She should have all the honor that we can give her!'"

The citizens of Thebes are starting to discreetly voice their disapproval of Creon's condemnation of Antigone's act of mercy. Creon interprets Haimon's speech as a sign that Haimon has chosen Antigone over him and forces Haimon to denounce his own father. This further alienates Creon from his subjects, and the play's atmosphere begins to change. Creon is not in complete control anymore. A woman has managed to disrupt his reign and turn his most precious son against him. Creon is going to force Antigone to regret her actions against him by sentencing her to a slow, painful death in a sealed cave with no food or water. A quick death would be too easy. Creon wants her to suffer. From this point on, the atmosphere of the play continues to spiral into a whirlwind of chaos and tragedy.

Teiresias, the old prophet who's never wrong, comes to warn Creon that the wrath of the gods will be upon him if he doesn't right his wrongs: "The time is not far off when you shall pay back corpse for corpse, flesh of your own flesh." But by then it's too late. By the time he sees the error of his ways, Creon's course of destruction is already set and the damage has already been done.

Creon's foolish superiority complex led to the downfall of everyone he cared about and his credibility as a king. He let his attitude toward women and his thirst for absolute power cloud his judgment and drove his family into the arms of death and tragedy. Antigone's fight against the unjust decree of the king could be characterized as the beginnings of civil disobedience. She is driven by her firm belief in God's laws and her own views on right and wrong. Antigone believed that a law is not right just because it's a law and that God's law outweighs public policy every time.

Step 3: Revising the Essay

Introduction   While Suzanne's introductory paragraph was adequate to keep her focused throughout the draft, it would have to be revised to integrate Creon's sexism. In addition, she has not defined what she means by "public policy" and "individual conscience." This would be an appropriate place to define her terms.

Finally, she realizes that her "public policy versus individual conscience" statement is only identifying the subject (the issue) of the play, not *what the play is saying* about that subject or issue. She must come up with a thesis statement that more clearly represents the theme of the play. She changes her thesis statement (her claim) to

> "Sophocles' message is clear: the arrogance of political power cannot defeat moral justice, for conscience and the will of the gods will always triumph."

Closing   Her closing could be more inclusive of her whole argument. Her statement about the "beginnings of civil disobedience" is a nice touch and will leave readers with a sense of its relevance to today.

After-Draft Outline   When Suzanne examined the structure of her draft by creating an after-draft outline from her paragraphs, it took the following form:

> Paragraph #1—Introduction (a brief statement of the thesis and comment about Creon's sexism). A statement about the subject (public policy vs. individual conscience) but not what the play was saying about that subject (a thesis statement).
>
> Paragraph #2—Creon's stance as public policy and summary of the major conflict
>
> Paragraph #3—Antigonê's position
>
> Paragraph #4—Creon's sexism
>
> Paragraph #5—Haimon's reasonable approach, Creon's response, and Teiresias' prophecy
>
> Paragraph #6—Conclusion (a brief statement summarizing the conflict, Antigonê's motivation, and its significance then and now)

For the most part, her draft contained the information and support she needed, but the thesis statement could be clearer, some of the paragraphs more tightly structured, and the essay's organization more coherent. By combining her first two paragraphs into a more substantial introduction concluding in a thesis statement, and combining and reorganizing subsequent paragraphs, she came up with the following revised outline:

> Paragraph #1—Introduction (explains the basic conflict, defines the terms, and states the thesis). That thesis now reads: "Sophocles' message is clear: the arrogance of political power cannot defeat moral justice, for conscience and the will of the gods will always triumph."
>
> Paragraph #2—Fleshes out the conflict
>
> Paragraph #3—Antigonê's position
>
> Paragraph #4—Creon's response and its motivation (to include sexism)
>
> Paragraph #5—Haimon's reasoned approach
>
> Paragraph #6—Creon's response
>
> Paragraph #7—The warning and prophecy of Teiresias
>
> Paragraph #8—Conclusion (a more inclusive summary and reminder of the play's thesis)

Checking Against Intentions   Suzanne's intentions were to explain and support her now clearer thesis that the play's theme is "The arrogance of political power cannot defeat moral justice, for conscience and the will of the gods will always triumph," and that part of Creon's motivation for condemning Antigonê was sexist. She believed that this reorganization and integration would accomplish her goal.

Proofreading   In addition to correcting a few minor problems, she would have to cite the line sources of her textual support, format it correctly, and add a "Work Cited" section at the end of her essay.

Step 4: Suzanne's Revised Essay

Suzanne McCloskey

Dr. Madden

English 102

November 3, 200X

Might Against Right

Sophocles' tragic play, <u>Antigone</u>, is a powerful example of the struggle between public policy and individual conscience. Throughout history, rulers have imposed and enforced laws for what they claim is the best interest of the public. At times, courageous individuals have refused to obey these laws, despite the consequences, because these policies interfered with their own consciences. Creon stands for public policy in this play, and Antigone represents individual conscience, loyalty to the gods, and civil disobedience. Sophocles' message is clear: the arrogance of political power cannot defeat moral justice, for conscience and the will of the gods will always triumph.

The major conflict in this play is between Creon and Antigone. Creon has just been made king of Thebes because his nephews have killed each other in battle. He decrees that Eteocles, who died defending Thebes, will be buried with full military honors. The body of Polyneices, however, will be left to rot in the fields. Creon believed that Polyneices was a traitor who didn't deserve to be honored. His law was clear: whoever disobeyed him and buried Polyneices was to be stoned to death in the public square. Creon, however, seems more concerned with forcing everyone to obey his decree than whether or not he has done the right thing. He is an extremely headstrong and stubborn man who has a very hard time admitting that he is wrong. It is these personal weaknesses that begin the chain reaction that destroys Creon and those he loves.

Antigone is the sister of Eteocles and Polyneices, and she decides that she cannot abide by Creon's law. Polyneices was her brother, just as much as Eteocles was. According to her conscience and the laws of the gods, leaving his body to rot in the fields was wrong. She felt that Creon had no right to overstep the boundaries of what the gods decreed. Kings shouldn't presume to dictate who is privileged enough for a burial. Burial is a universal right given to all humanity. When Creon is informed that it is Antigone who has defied his law, he explodes in anger. Not only has Antigone blatantly disregarded his wishes, she is smug and righteous about it. She says, "It was not God's proclamation. That final Justice / That rules the world below makes no such laws" (II, 58-59). Her statement shows the strength of her convictions. She knows that she will die for what she has done, but she stands firmly behind her decision.

Creon is doubly enraged; Antigone has deliberately defied him, and she is a woman. In Creon's view, women are supposed to be timid, weak, and docile creatures who need to be guided by men and their laws. He can't let a mere woman get the better of him. He says, "This girl is guilty of a double insolence, / Breaking the given laws and boasting of it. / Who is the man here, / She or I, if this crime goes unpunished?" (II, 80-83). Creon's statement illustrates the lengths to which he will go to triumph over Antigone. Antigone defied a man's law, and now a man is going to teach her a lesson. His judgment is clearly affected by his discriminatory and condescending attitude toward women.

Creon's blind stubbornness is demonstrated further when his son, Haimon, tries to reason with him. Haimon points out the validity of Antigone's actions and the fear that prevents any of the other citizens from voicing their support of her:

HAIMON. I have heard them
Muttering and whispering in the dark about this girl.
They say no woman has ever, so unreasonably,
Died so shameful a death for a generous act:
"She covered her brother's body. Is this indecent?
She kept him from dogs and vultures. Is this a crime?
Death?--She should have all the honor that we can give her!" (III, 61-67)

The citizens of Thebes are discreetly voicing their disapproval of Creon's condemnation of Antigone's act of mercy. Creon interprets Haimon's speech as a sign that Haimon has chosen Antigone over him and forces his own son to denounce him. This further alienates Creon from his subjects, and the play's atmosphere begins to change. Creon is not in complete control anymore. A woman has managed to disrupt his reign and even turn his son against him. He tries to make Antigone regret her actions by sentencing her to a slow, painful death in a sealed cave with no food or water. A quick death would be too easy. Creon wants her to suffer.

From this point on, the atmosphere of the play continues to spiral into a whirlwind of chaos and tragedy. Teiresias, the old prophet who is never wrong, comes to warn Creon that the wrath of the gods will be upon him if he doesn't right his wrongs: "The time is not far off when you shall pay back / Corpse for corpse, flesh of your own flesh" (V, 71-72). But by then it's too late. By the time Creon sees the error of his ways, his course of destruction is already set and the damage has already been done.

Creon's "public policy" destroys his credibility as a king and everyone he cares about. He lets his thirst for absolute power and his condescending attitude toward women cloud his judgment and drives his family into the arms of death and tragedy. Antigone's fight against the unjust decree of the king is an act of civil disobedience. She is driven by her firm belief in her religion and her own views on right and wrong. Antigone believes that a law is not right just because it is a law. Individual conscience and the laws of the gods must always outweigh public policy.

[New page]

Work Cited

Sophocles. <u>Antigone</u>. Trans. Dudley Fitts and Robert Fitzgerald. <u>Exploring Literature</u>. Ed. Frank Madden. 3rd ed. New York: Longman, 2007. 104-135.

Chapter 5

Research
Writing with Secondary Sources

O
ur goal in this chapter is to build on the work you've done in previous chapters and to develop your ideas and your writing into a research essay. Making connections, analyzing the work and its influences, gathering evidence, and constructing an argument are also essential components of writing a research essay. In the pages that follow, however, we will expand our focus to include

- Choosing your research topic;
- Conducting your search;
- Evaluating your sources;
- Integrating secondary source research into your writing;
- Documenting your sources and avoiding plagiarism.

THE RESEARCH ESSAY

When you hear the word *research*, you may groan and think of piles of impenetrable books and late nights at the library. But research is probably a commonplace event in your life. When you call a friend to seek advice about hooking up your computer or stereo, you are doing research. When you look up the spelling or meaning of a word, you are doing research. When you ask the opinion of a classmate about a poem, you are doing research. So despite the ominous connotations the word might have for you in an academic setting, it's an activity you already know a lot about.

For the most part, writing a research essay about literature is not a new activity for you either. You are doing research whenever you go to the text of the work itself, the **primary source,** to support your opinions and interpretations. But a *research essay expands the range of your research to include **secondary sources**— sources beyond the text of the work and your classroom—sources that may help to clarify, enrich, or add clout to your interpretation.* By going to secondary sources, you can also expand the scope of your writing. You might, for example, consult articles, books, or online sites that were written about the work or its author. You might consult sources that were written about the cultural or historical period in which the work was written. Or you might explore any number of other possibilities. The choices are only limited by your time and imagination.

CREATING, EXPANDING, AND JOINING INTERPRETIVE COMMUNITIES

Previously, we discussed how your classmates and collaborative groups become "interpretive communities," groups of readers who help to shape your views about how and what literature means. Your initial responses to literature are based on many factors. And through the social and intellectual exchanges of your small and large groups, you confirm, supplement, or change these responses. Of course, the people and what they value about literature are different in each of those groups. In this respect, you already belong to many different interpretive communities. By using secondary sources, however, you join new communities and share the views of many other readers and writers across hundreds of years and around the world.

IT IS YOUR INTERPRETATION

Regardless of how much research you do, this essay should be *your* interpretation in *your* own voice. Remember, what makes an interpretation convincing or defensible is your ability to support it. Doing research continues this process and adds to your support. In the same way that writing down your reflections, rereading the text, and discussing it with others informs your response, seeking information and ideas from secondary sources may lead you to a different, better-informed understanding and interpretation. Integrating these sources into your own writing style, however, is not always easy and may take some practice.

CONNECTING THROUGH COLLABORATION

1. Look back through your writing and pick out a work of literature that you discussed in class.
2. Try to remember what others in your class said about it.
   a. Did any of their comments help you to see the work in a different way?
   b. Did you disagree with any of their comments?
3. Write a response that includes their comments and your reactions to them.
4. Read your response.
   a. Does it accurately reflect your experience of the group's discussion?
   b. Were you able to integrate others' comments comfortably into your own writing?
   c. If not, what problems did you encounter?

GETTING STARTED

Choosing a Topic

If you are choosing your own topic, you might begin by asking yourself the same questions you would ask about any other kind of essay. If you are keeping a journal or other notes, you've probably jotted down some potential topics for your research. Look back at your entries. Make sure you feel confident about the details and your understanding of the work. What did you find most interesting about the work? What would you like to know more about?

Remember, you are seeking information from other sources. You are not limited to what you already know. So be flexible. You don't have to decide on your final topic right away. Share your early ideas with other students. They may give you ideas you haven't considered. In the process of putting your ideas into words and getting feedback, try out and develop the language and strategies you will use later in the essay itself.

Some Popular Areas of Literary Research

A Particular Work, Features of a Work, or Different Critical Views of a Work   A research essay on a single work is similar to the critical essays you have been writing, but by going to secondary sources you can tap the views of critics who may give you insights you haven't considered. For example, Sophocles's *Antigonê* contains several complex external and internal conflicts; the attitudes and behavior of Nora and Mrs. Linde in Ibsen's *A Doll's House* raise compelling questions about the role of women; the strong narrator in Alice Walker's "Everyday Use" might provide an interesting study of the effect of point of view.

A Particular Author or the Relationship Between the Author's Life and Work   Is there something about the work that makes you curious about the person who wrote it? Or about the connection of that person's life to the work? For example, Robert Hayden's "Those Winter Sundays" (p. 13), James Joyce's "Araby" (p. 463), and Liliana Heker's "The Stolen Party" (p. 459) are personal pieces about growing up. When you read them you may wonder how closely they are tied to the authors' own experiences. It might be interesting to explore the authors' lives in search of these connections.

The Social, Historical, or Cultural Background of a Work   When was the work written? Under what circumstances was it written? What impact did this background have on the work and its reception by the public? For example, when you read or see Ibsen's *A Doll's House,* it may make you curious about the marriage customs that existed when the play was written. You may wonder how audiences of 1879 responded to the play. Lorraine Hansberry's *A Raisin in the Sun* or Dudley Randall's "Ballad of Birmingham" may arouse your interest in race relations in America in the 1950's and 60's.

Political, Philosophical, and Artistic Influences on the Author's Work   What political, philosophical, and artistic sources influenced the work or its author? In what way was the author influenced? How did the work of this author influence other authors? For example, how did the philosophical or political atmosphere of the time influence W. H. Auden's "The Unknown Citizen"? How did Sophocles's plays influence Aristotle's writing of *The Poetics?*

A Theme or Characters Compared Across Two or More Works   Is there a common theme that is shared by two or more works? Are there characters in different works who share similar traits? How do they compare? How are they alike? How are they different? How do secondary sources describe this theme or these characters? For example, you might address the theme of sibling relationships in Tennessee Williams's *The Glass Menagerie,* Louise Erdrich's "The Red Convertible," and Sophocles's *Antigonê.* To fully account for the complexity of these relationships, you could do research about the very different times, places, and cultures from which these pieces and their characters spring.

YOUR SEARCH

People

Sometimes the best sources to start with are people. If you are struggling to find a topic, share your struggle with your friends, classmates, and teachers. If you have chosen a topic, try it out. Explain why you think it's interesting. See what they think. They may be able to give you ideas you hadn't considered, and spot problems. Use them for support, and cite them in your essay.

The Library

Again, your best initial source here may be people themselves, the librarians. Librarians are specially educated to know about the library's resources. They not only want to help you find what you need for this project, they want to help you learn how to use the library for future projects. Go to the library's information desk. Most libraries have one just inside the front door. Ask if there is a library map or information guide. Learn the location of the reference desk. The reference librarian can help you find the resources you need and show you how to use them.

Once you have some idea about what you're looking for, go to the library's online catalog. Most academic libraries list their resources in an online public access catalog. Here you can look for information under the author's name, the title of the book or other resource, its subject, or key words in its title. Most library systems are computerized and share resources with other libraries, so you not only have access to the listings in your library, but other libraries as well. You can find most college and university libraries on the Internet and tap into their online public access catalogs. If you find the sources you are looking for, you can request them through interlibrary loan. Many libraries also have their own Web pages that will show you how to access their reference works or useful databases through your computer.

Reference Works

A particularly valuable source in your search for literary criticism is the *MLA International Bibliography*. It lists scholarly books and articles published each year, and it's organized by period and author. Most academic libraries have both the CD-ROM and hard copies of this *Bibliography*. An especially useful computerized database for literary research is the Gale Group's *Literature Resource Center,* which has an enormous collection of critical, biographical, and historical information. Reference works like *The Oxford Companion to English Literature, The Oxford Companion to American Literature,* or *The Reader's Encyclopedia* can also be good places to start. The *New York Times* index may be very useful for book and play reviews. Even the *Reader's Guide to Periodical Literature* may contain some useful reviews located in popular magazines like the *Atlantic Monthly, Time, Newsweek,* and the *New Yorker.*

Some Other Encyclopedias and Indexes Useful for Literary Research

> *Biographical Dictionary of Irish Writers*
>
> *Black Writers*
>
> *Cassell's Encyclopedia of World Literature*
>
> *Columbia Dictionary of Modern European Literature*
>
> *Contemporary Authors*
>
> *Contemporary Dramatists*
>
> *Contemporary Novelists*
>
> *Contemporary Poets*
>
> *Dictionary of British Folk-Tales in the English Language*
>
> *Dictionary of Celtic Myth and Legend*
>
> *Dictionary of Celtic Mythology*
>
> *Dictionary of Concepts in Literary Criticism and Theory*
>
> *Dictionary of Literary Biography*
>
> *Dictionary of Mythology, Folklore, and Symbols*
>
> *Dictionary of Native American Mythology*
>
> *Encyclopedia of Contemporary Literary Theory*
>
> *Encyclopedia of Continental Women Writers*
>
> *Encyclopedia of Literature and Criticism*
>
> *Encyclopedia of World Literature in the Twentieth Century*
>
> *Encyclopedia of World Theater*
>
> *Funk and Wagnall's Standard Dictionary of Folklore, Mythology and Legend*
>
> *Handbook to Literature*
>
> *Larousse Encyclopedia of Mythology*

Larousse World Mythology
Literary History of England
Literary History of the United States
Masterplots
McGraw-Hill Encyclopedia of World Drama
Mythology of All Races
New Princeton Encyclopedia of Poetry and Poetics
New York Times Theater Reviews, 1920–1970
Oxford Companion to American Literature
Oxford Companion to American Theatre
Oxford Companion to Canadian Literature
Oxford Companion to Children's Literature
Oxford Companion to Classical Literature
Oxford Companion to the Theatre
Oxford Guide to British Women Writers
The Reader's Encyclopedia
Reader's Encyclopedia of World Drama
Theater Dictionary
Twentieth-Century Authors

Some Bibliographies, Indexes, and Abstracts Useful for Literary Research

Abstracts of English Studies
American Literature Abstracts
Annual Bibliography of English Language and Literature
Centennial Index
Contemporary Literary Criticism
Cumulated Dramatic Index 1909–1949
Language and Literature
MLA International Bibliography
New Cambridge Bibliography of English Literature
Play Index
Short Story Index
Year's Work in English Studies

Most of these reference works now come in CD-ROM form or are available online. Most libraries have periodical databases on CD-ROM that are updated frequently. For example, *Humanities Index* is a database that is very useful for literary research. CD-ROMs are also available that contain the complete texts of literary works along with critical commentary, historical and biographical information, and dramatic readings by the authors. Check with your librarian to see what electronic resources are available.

Finding Sources on the Internet

The Internet can be an excellent source of information for your research. But while most indexes and sources of information about books and periodicals are organized in alphabetical or chronological order, the Internet is not organized in such an easily accessible way. The World Wide Web is a hypertext system that moves you from one source to another. It finds the connections you request between pieces of information and helps to generate new ones. By typing in key words or phrases, you request the combinations. Instead of choosing an item on a menu, you use your mouse to click on a highlighted term or topic on a Web "page."

Web Browsers and Search Engines   Most Internet systems provide access to Web browsers, like Microsoft Explorer or Netscape Navigator. Web browsers give you access to search engines and make it easy for you to save or print the information you uncover. Search Engines such as Google, Yahoo!, Alta Vista, Excite, HotBot, Infoseek, or Lycos act as directories and create indexes of key words that help you to find the information you seek. They provide a long, horizontal box in which you type a key word or words that describe your subject. In order to work as efficiently as possible, it is essential to narrow the field of your search. Here are some useful suggestions:

Add plus or minus signs to key words to narrow your search. If you add plus signs before each word (+Shakespeare +The Tempest +Prospero), a search engine like Google will only come up with sites that include all three key words. If you wish to look at sites that exclude one of these elements, use a minus sign in front of a key word you wish to exclude (+Shakespeare +The Tempest – Prospero), and only Web sites without Prospero's name will come up.

Use quotation marks to keep key words together and narrow your search. If you place quotation marks around the information you seek (e.g., "William Shakespeare The Tempest"), the search engine will only come up with instances of that exact combination. If you don't use quotation marks, it will yield every instance of related and unrelated material bearing those terms (e.g., The tempest over Frank Shakespeare was explained by William Smith).

Type in more key words to narrow your field; otherwise your search will come up with many more sources than you will have time to examine.

Type in fewer or different key words to broaden your field. If your search comes up with very few items, it may be necessary to cut down on the number of key terms or try different ones with a similar meaning.

Discussion Groups/Listservs and Newsgroups   Two resources for direct online communication with other people who have similar interests are discussion groups or listservs and newsgroups. You can join a discussion, or chat, group by subscribing to a mailing list and receiving messages via e-mail. Newsgroups are like bulletin boards—everyone in the group reads the same messages. They provide information similar to discussion groups but don't send individual messages. Users can post and read messages without subscribing to a list. Newsgroups are joined through a newsreader or a World Wide Web browser.

Some Internet Sources Useful for Literary Research

Literary Resources on the Net: <http:dept.english.upenn.edu/~jlynch/Lit>

American Literature: <http://www.academicinfo.net/amlit.html>

English Literature: <http://www.academicinfo.net/englit.html>

Carnegie Mellon English Server: <http://english-server.hss.cmu.edu>

Resources in English Language and Literature:
<www.lib.cmich.edu/bibliographer/billmiles/english.htm>

The Voice of the Shuttle: <vos.ucsb.edu>

Theater Links Page: <www.theatre-link.com>

Shakespeare and the Internet: <http://shakespeare.palomar.edu/>

Electronic Shakespeare: <http://www.wfu.edu/%7Etedforrl/shakespeare>

Evaluating Internet Sources

Prior to publication, books and articles in scholarly journals are usually reviewed and carefully edited by those with expertise in the field. So, too, editors at reputable newspapers and magazines usually ask writers to verify the accuracy of their sources before they will publish their work. But anyone can put information on the Internet.

Always check the source of any information you take from the Internet. This information is not always screened for accuracy. Look for biographical or other data that might tell you something about the author or the author's academic or scholarly affiliation. If the author provides additional links or other sources, check them out to verify the accuracy of the information. Look for publication or revision dates. As with any source, make sure the assertions made are supported with evidence and that you give credit to the author, and correctly cite the information when you quote or paraphrase from a Web site.

Remember, you are ultimately responsible for the accuracy of your support information, not an unknown and potentially unreliable source on the Internet.

 CHECKLIST: EVALUATING INTERNET SOURCES

❑   Make sure that the author of the document or the person or group responsible for the Web site is identified. Is this person or group a credible source? How is this verifiable? Is there a phone number or postal address?

(continued)

❏   Is the page well written? Is it well organized? If not, it may have been constructed by a child or an unreliable source.

❏   Is there a link to a page describing the purpose of the sponsoring organization? Is this information provided as a public service? Might there be any reasons for bias or prejudice? How will that affect the accuracy of the information?

❏   What kind of Web site is indicated? Addresses that end in ".edu" are educational institutions; ".gov" is a government site; ".mil" is military; ".com" and ".net" are commercial sites; and ".org" is a nonprofit organization. Being aware of this may tell you about the potential biases of these sources.

❏   Check to see that the work's sources are indicated. Is there a list of works cited? Does the list seem sufficient?

❏   Are there "links" to other sources indicated? Do they seem reliable?

❏   Check the dates of the sources. Are they current? Is there a different date for an earlier print source? Have the sources been revised?

TAKING NOTES

Whether you use slips of paper, note cards, or a computer, you should be able to rearrange your information according to your needs. Cards are easier to move around and rearrange, so you may find it convenient to use 3" x 5" or 4" x 6" file or note cards to record documentation information and notes, usually with a separate source on each card.

Using a computer to take notes and record bibliographic information will save you time later. You can open a separate file for bibliographic entries and copy and paste this information directly into your essay later. You can organize your notes into separate files—placing quotation marks around direct quotes and noting their sources—then copy and paste as you write and revise.

Be selective when you go through your sources. Keep the focus of your essay in mind as you take notes. Some material is irrelevant and should be ignored. Those sources that are particularly valuable may provide you with much information and point you to additional sources as well. As you read, be sure to jot down your own ideas as they occur to you. If you wait until later, you may forget them.

Don't forget to copy all the information you will need for documentation later, including page numbers. In fact, whether you are using note cards or a computer, it is a good idea to record the bibliographic information of your print or electronic resources in the form you will be using on the Works Cited page of your essay. You can simply rearrange them in alphabetical order so that you will have the appropriate format ready when listing your works cited.

Integrating Sources into Your Writing

When you listen to the views of others in your class, you can still claim your final interpretation as your own. You might refer to someone else's view to support your opinion—or comment on others' views as a point of disagreement. But your interpretation and the support behind it are still your own. Ultimately, this is your essay, not simply the views of other students and the instructor strung together. An essay that uses secondary sources for support should be no different. But it's not always easy to integrate secondary sources into our writing without being too artificial or making the essay look like a list of other people's statements pasted together.

Be selective about using direct quotes from secondary sources. Sometimes a summary or paraphrase (see below) will be more effective and fit seamlessly into your own writing style. When you quote, make sure that you have introduced the quote adequately so that its relevance to your argument is clear. You may be able to integrate the quote smoothly into your own writing style by only quoting those words that are relevant and by using ellipses (see below) to indicate omitted material or brackets (see below) to indicate you have included your own word(s) for clarification.

What Must Be Documented

- Information that is not common knowledge—knowledge that you or most others would not have without reference to this or a similar source.

- Information or ideas from another source (text or interview) that you have paraphrased (rephrased in your own words) or summarized (reduced to its essential points).

- Direct quotations from another source (text or interview).

Where and How

- In the text of the essay itself, you must indicate the author and page number(s) of borrowed information or quotations.
- On a separate page at the end of the essay, you must include an alphabetized list of all the sources you have used in the text.

Paraphrasing and Summarizing

Most of your notes should paraphrase or summarize rather than quote directly (record the author's exact words). In addition to helping you comprehend what you are reading, putting the material into your own words (in your own writing style and in your own voice) will clarify your ideas and help you build the language you will need later when you write your essay.

Paraphrasing *To paraphrase you must thoroughly understand what the author has written and then rewrite that material in your own words and sentences.* If you use any of the author's language, you must enclose it in quotation marks. (See example on p. 185.)

Summarizing   *To summarize you must understand what the author has written and then condense the source material to its main points.* If you use any of the author's language, you must enclose it in quotation marks. (See example on p. 185.)

Quoting

Remember, this is *your* essay. It is *your* argument or point you want to express. It is not other people's points pasted together. Bring in secondary sources only when you need them. Use direct quotes only when the language in your source makes an impact that your own wording would not. Be sure to surround any quotes you use with sufficient support. Give them an adequate introduction, and explain how they work as evidence. Work quotes smoothly into your writing style. Combine what you paraphrase and summarize with brief quotations.

When you are quoting most (but not all) of a sentence, or you are leaving out unnecessary parts of a long sentence, an **ellipsis** signals to the reader that the quoted material has been taken out of the context of its original sentence. For example, if you wanted to describe some of the physical characteristics of Maggie in Alice Walker's "Everyday Use," wanted to indicate a larger context, but did not want to quote an entire sentence, you might choose to write: In contrast to her attractive and confident sister Dee, Maggie is described as ". . . homely and ashamed of the burn scars down her arms and legs . . . " (983).

When you add your own word or words to the quote for integration and clarification, **brackets** [ ] tell the reader that this is your language, not that of the source material: "It is hard to tell what Dee thought when she looked at 'the burn scars down [Maggie's] arms and legs. . . ' " (983).

Avoiding Plagiarism

Plagiarism is taking someone else's ideas or words and passing them off as your own. The most basic rule of all documentation is that direct quotations and summarized or paraphrased information or ideas from another source must be appropriately credited. This includes information that is not common knowledge (information that you would not have without reference to this or a similar source), information or ideas from another source that you have paraphrased or summarized, and direct quotations from another source.

In the text of the essay itself, you must indicate the author and page number(s) of borrowed information or quotations. On a separate page at the end of the essay, you must include an alphabetized list (Works Cited) of all the sources you have used in the text.

You must always make it clear which words and ideas are yours and which ones come from other sources. Before you submit your essay, check your paraphrases and summaries against the original sources. Make sure that the words and sentences are your own and that they accurately reflect the meaning of the source material. *To use other people's words and ideas and not give them credit is a serious academic offense.*

Examples of Paraphrasing, Summarizing, Quoting, and Plagiarizing

The Original Source
(From Shulevitz, Judith. "The Hall of Fame." Rev. of <u>Genius</u>, by Harold Bloom. <u>New York Times Book Review</u> 27 Oct. 2002.)

Bloom is not so easily dismissed, however. His style may be disheveled and his book shockingly attuned to the demands of the marketplace, but both have a virtue that trumps those flaws. Bloom's focus on genius is not just commercial opportunism, the usual blather about the moral import of cultural literacy or part of the national obsession with success, though critics will find all three if they go looking for them.

Summarizing
Shulevitz says Bloom's book is stylistically "disheveled" and market driven, but these may be greater strengths than weaknesses. She believes critics will reduce it to these weaknesses if they want to, but the book has greater value than that (11).

Paraphrasing
Shulevitz says Bloom's work remains important even though it seems a bit "disheveled" in style and market driven. She asserts that these features of his writing are actually greater strengths than weaknesses, and that this work is not just an attempt to make money by taking advantage of the public's desire for books about cultural literacy or success. But she believes that critics will be able to reduce the book to these weaknesses if they want to, and ignore its qualities (11).

Quoting
Shulevitz says Bloom's work remains important and adds, "His style may be disheveled and his book shockingly attuned to the demands of the marketplace, but both have a virtue that trumps those flaws" (11).

Plagiarizing
Shulevitz insists that Bloom is not so easily dismissed. He may have a disheveled style and his book is shockingly attuned to the marketplace, but both of these things have a virtue that trumps those flaws.

See Appendix C (p. 1345) for a Directory of MLA Formatting and Documentation.

FROM FIRST RESPONSE TO RESEARCH ESSAY

The same processes that are so useful in generating ideas for personal or critical essays may be just as valuable for giving you ideas and narrowing your topic for a research essay. Reading literature encourages a variety of responses and perhaps raises more questions than it answers. It is a good idea to generate and explore as many of your questions and ideas as possible before you decide on one direction. Here is a quick review of strategies to get started. For a detailed explanation of these techniques, with examples, see Chapter 2, pages 36–43.

- Employing directed freewriting can be a useful technique for loosening up ideas. The best time to do this exercise is immediately after you finish reading, while your thoughts and impressions are still fresh. The intention of directed freewriting is to release what you know without blocking it with pauses for reflection, punctuation, or editing.

- Asking questions about a general topic is likely to provide you with new information. Responding with detailed answers to these questions may provide you with ideas for a narrowed thesis and specific support for that thesis.

- Choosing a few key words or phrases that apply to your topic and then listing as many related details under each as you can should help you generate many concrete details and much specific support for your ideas.

- Clustering your ideas or drawing a semantic map may help you understand, see relationships, and generate and extend ideas better by looking at them spatially rather than linearly.

☑ CHECKLIST: WRITING A RESEARCH ESSAY

Planning Your Essay

Consider Your Motivation
❏ Will this topic sustain your interest long enough for you to do a good job?

Determine Its Feasibility
❏ Can you write a research essay about this subject? Do you have enough to say and can you find enough evidence to support your case?

Secondary Sources
❏ Can you find appropriate secondary sources? Where will you get them? Are you sure of their reliability?

Taking Notes
❏ Do you have an effective system to organize your notes? What is it? Can you use a computer to save time later?

❑   Have you copied down all the information you will need to document your sources?

❑   Have you decided which sources to summarize, paraphrase, and quote?

Clarify Your Thesis
❑   Do you have a clear understanding of the thesis you want to argue? Can you articulate it in a thesis statement?

Know Your Readers
❑   What assumptions can you make about your readers? Are they likely to agree or disagree with your thesis?

Supporting Your Argument

Arrange Your Support Effectively
❑   Is the support for your thesis arranged in the most effective way? Is it more effective to develop your argument by stating your thesis first and then supporting it with evidence or by allowing the evidence to build into your thesis?

Integrating Secondary Sources
❑   How can you effectively and smoothly integrate your secondary sources into your own writing style? What should be paraphrased? What should be quoted? Why?

Support Your Thesis with Facts from the Text and Secondary Sources
❑   Is your support based on facts or opinions? Have you supported your opinions with facts and quotes from the text?

❑   Do your secondary sources support your view? How?

Account for All the Evidence
❑   Have you accounted for *all* the evidence in the text? Have you accounted for evidence that may not support your thesis? Have you accounted for secondary source material that may not support your thesis?

Explain the Connections
❑   Have you explained *how* the evidence you have chosen supports your thesis?

❑   Are the connections between your secondary sources and your thesis clear?

Opening, Closing, and Revising

Write or Rewrite Your Introduction After Your First Draft
❑   Is your introduction clear, informative, and interesting?

❑   If appropriate, does it map out the journey for the reader?

(continued)

Close Your Argument Reasonably
❑ Have you explained the connections between the thesis and your primary and secondary source support? Have you only claimed what you have really delivered?

Revise with a Fresh View
❑ Have you reread and reviewed your essay?

❑ How well is your draft organized? Does the sequence make sense?

❑ Are there gaps that need to be filled? Is there enough support? Have you explained the connections between your support and your thesis? Have you expressed those connections as clearly as possible?

❑ Have you maintained a consistent "voice" throughout the essay?

Review Your Intentions and Organization
❑ Is the central thesis of the essay clearly stated? Does the title of your essay account for your thesis?

❑ Is the essay fully developed? Have you accounted for all aspects of your thesis statement?

❑ Do all the paragraphs relate to your thesis? Is the organization of those paragraphs within the essay clear? Are the paragraphs fully developed? Do each of the sentences within the paragraphs relate to the central idea of the paragraph?

❑ Are there enough details to support or clarify your proposition? Have you "shown" what you've "told"? Are there enough quotes from both primary and secondary sources to support your thesis?

❑ Are there redundancies, digressions, or meaningless phrases that could be cut?

Proofread Carefully
❑ Are all of your sentences complete sentences? Are all of your sentences punctuated appropriately?

❑ Are all the words spelled correctly? Have you checked for easily confused words (then/than, your/you're, its/it's, etc.)?

❑ Are you sure of the meaning of all the words you've used?

❑ Are the titles of works underlined or in quotations as appropriate?

❑ Are there particular errors you have a tendency to make? Have you looked for those in this essay?

❑ Is the essay written in the format required by your instructor? Have you documented your references to the text and included a list of works cited?

CASE STUDY
IN RESEARCH

James Joyce and "Eveline"

The purpose of the Case Study that follows is to provide a model of one student's process as he moved from an initial idea to a research essay. In many ways, what kept this student's interest alive—and gave him the energy to pursue his goal to the finish—was the personally compelling nature of his topic. Having such a topic will not guarantee a successful research experience, but it's a good place to start.

As we have emphasized throughout this book, writing an effective essay is not always a straightforward process. Many factors may influence the choices we make along the way. This is particularly true when using secondary source research in our writing. One possible topic, and a rich source for research, may be the connection we find between our own backgrounds or culture and that presented in the work. The best research springs from our need to know more—to fill in the gaps in our knowledge. This research is not imposed on our writing but evolves naturally from it.

Below is James Joyce's short story "Eveline," and questions to prompt your own response. Following the story and questions is the commentary of Prof. Alan Devenish, and the research essay of his student Kevin Chamberlain. Dr. Devenish recalls their conferences and the process Kevin experienced while writing his research essay. He explains that Kevin did not set out to do research. While reading James Joyce's short story "Eveline," Kevin found similarities between himself and the protagonist. He started to write a response essay, but his interest in the protagonist inspired him to want to know more. He sought information about the conditions of her background. This, in turn, led him to do research about the author and to read more of Joyce's work. What began as a personal response developed naturally into an informative and personally meaningful research essay.

All readers may not have such a strong personal identification with the work or, like Kevin, follow up their reading of one work by reading other works by the same author. But the process Kevin followed is a strong model for anyone doing secondary source research. He did not begin by gathering all the information he could and refashioning it into an essay. He began by writing a draft of his own response. In the process, he identified the issues he wanted to explore and generated the questions he needed to answer to make this exploration successful. The objective of his search was not to gather the most information, but to gather answers to his questions. His search was motivated by his "need to know," and it was only through his early writing and reflection that *what* he needed to know became clear to him.

JAMES JOYCE [1882–1941]

James Joyce was one of ten children born into a middle-
class family of declining fortunes in a suburb of Dublin,
Ireland. In spite of an unhappy childhood dominated by a
drunken father, Joyce managed to receive a thorough clas-
sical education, first in Jesuit schools and then at
University College, Dublin. Though he spent most of his
adult life living outside of Ireland, Dublin is the backdrop
for nearly all of his work. His three innovative novels,
Portrait of the Artist as a Young Man *(1916),* Ulysses *(1922), and* Finnegans Wake
(1939), established him as one of the greatest writers of modern times. "Eveline"
(below) and "Araby" (p. 463) are taken from his collection of short stories,
Dubliners, *which appeared in 1914 after an eight-year battle with publishers*
who feared it would offend important residents of the city.

EVELINE   [1914]

She sat at the window watching the evening invade the avenue. Her head was
leaned against the window curtains and in her nostrils was the odour of dusty cretonne. She was tired.

Few people passed. The man out of the last house passed on his way home; she
heard his footsteps clacking along the concrete pavement and afterwards crunching
on the cinder path before the new red houses. One time there used to be a field
there in which they used to play every evening with other people's children. Then
a man from Belfast bought the field and built houses in it—not like their little brown
houses but bright brick houses with shining roofs. The children of the avenue used
to play together in that field—the Devines, the Waters, the Dunns, little Keogh the
cripple, she and her brothers and sisters. Ernest, however, never played: he was too
grown up. Her father used often to hunt them in out of the field with his blackthorn
stick; but usually little Keogh used to keep *nix* and call out when he saw her father
coming. Still they seemed to have been rather happy then. Her father was not so bad
then; and besides, her mother was alive. That was a long time ago; she and her
brothers and sisters were all grown up; her mother was dead. Tizzie Dunn was
dead, too, and the Waters had gone back to England. Everything changes. Now she
was going to go away like the others, to leave her home.

Home! She looked around the room, reviewing all its familiar objects which she
had dusted once a week for so many years, wondering where on earth all the dust came
from. Perhaps she would never see again those familiar objects from which she had
never dreamed of being divided. And yet during all those years she had never found out
the name of the priest whose yellowing photograph hung on the wall above the
broken harmonium beside the coloured print of the promises made to Blessed
Margaret Mary Alacoque. He had been a school friend of her father. Whenever he
showed the photograph to a visitor her father used to pass it with a casual word:

—He is in Melbourne now.

5   She had consented to go away, to leave her home. Was that wise? She tried to
weigh each side of the question. In her home anyway she had shelter and food; she

had those whom she had known all her life about her. Of course she had to work hard both in the house and at business. What would they say of her in the Stores when they found out that she had run away with a fellow? Say she was a fool, perhaps; and her place would be filled up by advertisement. Miss Gavan would be glad. She had always had an edge on her, especially whenever there were people listening.

—Miss Hill, don't you see these ladies are waiting?

—Look lively, Miss Hill, please.

She would not cry many tears at leaving the Stores.

But in her new home, in a distant unknown country, it would not be like that. Then she would be married—she, Eveline. People would treat her with respect then. She would not be treated as her mother had been. Even now, though she was over nineteen, she sometimes felt herself in danger of her father's violence. She knew it was that that had given her the palpitations. When they were growing up he had never gone for her, like he used to go for Harry and Ernest, because she was a girl; but latterly he had begun to threaten her and say what he would do to her only for her dead mother's sake. And now she had nobody to protect her. Ernest was dead and Harry, who was in the church decorating business, was nearly always down somewhere in the country. Besides, the invariable squabble for money on Saturday nights had begun to weary her unspeakably. She always gave her entire wages—seven shillings—and Harry always sent up what he could but the trouble was to get any money from her father. He said she used to squander the money, that she had no head, that he wasn't going to give her his hard-earned money to throw about the streets, and much more, for he was usually fairly bad of a Saturday night. In the end he would give her the money and ask her had she any intention of buying Sunday's dinner. Then she had to rush out as quickly as she could and do her marketing, holding her black leather purse tightly in her hand as she elbowed her way through the crowds and returning home late under her load of provisions. She had hard work to keep the house together and to see that the two young children who had been left to her charge went to school regularly and got their meals regularly. It was hard work—a hard life—but now that she was about to leave it she did not find it a wholly undesirable life.

10   She was about to explore another life with Frank. Frank was very kind, manly, open-hearted. She was to go away with him by the night-boat to be his wife and to live with him in Buenos Ayres where he had a home waiting for her. How well she remembered the first time she had seen him; he was lodging in a house on the main road where she used to visit. It seemed a few weeks ago. He was standing at the gate, his peaked cap pushed back on his head and his hair tumbled forward over a face of bronze. Then they had come to know each other. He used to meet her outside the Stores every evening and see her home. He took her to see *The Bohemian Girl* and she felt elated as she sat in an unaccustomed part of the theatre with him. He was awfully fond of music and sang a little. People knew that they were courting and, when he sang about the lass that loves a sailor, she always felt pleasantly confused. He used to call her Poppens out of fun. First of all it had been an excitement for her to have a fellow and then she had begun to like him. He had tales of distant countries. He had started as a deck boy at a pound a month on a ship of the Allan Line going out to Canada. He told her the names of the ships he had been on and the names of the different services. He had sailed through the Straits of Magellan and he

told her stories of the terrible Patagonians. He had fallen on his feet in Buenos Ayres, he said, and had come over to the old country just for a holiday. Of course, her father had found out the affair and had forbidden her to have anything to say to him.

—I know these sailor chaps, he said.

One day he had quarreled with Frank and after that she had to meet her lover secretly.

The evening deepened in the avenue. The white of two letters in her lap grew indistinct. One was to Harry; the other was to her father. Ernest had been her favourite but she liked Harry too. Her father was becoming old lately, she noticed; he would miss her. Sometimes he could be very nice. Not long before, when she had been laid up for a day, he had read her out a ghost story and made toast for her at the fire. Another day, when their mother was alive, they had all gone for a picnic to the Hill of Howth. She remembered her father putting on her mother's bonnet to make the children laugh.

Her time was running out but she continued to sit by the window, leaning her head against the window curtain, inhaling the odour of dusty cretonne. Down far in the avenue she could hear a street organ playing. She knew the air. Strange that it should come that very night to remind her of the promise to her mother, her promise to keep the home together as long as she could. She remembered the last night of her mother's illness; she was again in the close dark room at the other side of the hall and outside she heard a melancholy air of Italy. The organ-player had been ordered to go away and given sixpence. She remembered her father strutting back into the sickroom saying:

15   —Damned Italians! Coming over here!

As she mused the pitiful vision of her mother's life laid its spell on the very quick of her being—that life of commonplace sacrifices closing in final craziness. She trembled as she heard again her mother's voice saying constantly with foolish insistence:

—Derevaun Seraun! Derevaun Seraun!°

She stood up in a sudden impulse of terror. Escape! She must escape! Frank would save her. He would give her life, perhaps love, too. But she wanted to live. Why should she be unhappy? She had a right to happiness. Frank would take her in his arms, fold her in his arms. He would save her.

She stood among the swaying crowd in the station at the North Wall. He held her hand and she knew that he was speaking to her, saying something about the passage over and over again. The station was full of soldiers with brown baggages. Through the wide doors of the sheds she caught a glimpse of the black mass of the boat, lying in beside the quay wall, with illumined portholes. She answered nothing. She felt her cheek pale and cold and, out of a maze of distress, she prayed to God to direct her, to show her what was her duty. The boat blew a long mournful whistle into the mist. If she went, to-morrow she would be on the sea with Frank, steaming towards Buenos Ayres. Their passage had been booked. Could she still draw back

(Gaelic) "The end of pleasure is pain."

after all he had done for her? Her distress awoke a nausea in her body and she kept moving her lips in silent fervent prayer.

20   A bell clanged upon her heart. She felt him seize her hand:

—Come!

All the seas of the world tumbled about her heart. He was drawing her into them: he would drown her. She gripped with both hands at the iron railing.

—Come!

No! No! No! It was impossible. Her hands clutched the iron in frenzy. Amid the seas she sent a cry of anguish!

25   —Eveline! Evvy!

He rushed beyond the barrier and called to her to follow. He was shouted at to go on but he still called to her. She set her white face to him, passive, like a helpless animal. Her eyes gave him no sign of love or farewell or recognition.

MAKING CONNECTIONS

1. To what extent is your response to this story influenced by your own background or experience?
2. Were you hoping that Eveline would leave or stay? Why?
3. Describe Frank. What does he represent to Eveline?
4. To what extent is Eveline a prisoner of her setting? Of her own culture?
5. Do you think Eveline really has a choice at the end of the story? Explain.

MAKING AN ARGUMENT

1. At the end of the story, Eveline decides to stay with her father. Citing the text of the story and/or other pertinent sources for support, write an essay that argues for or against her decision.

Professor Devenish's Commentary

Before beginning my commentary on his essay "Leaving Home," I met with Kevin Chamberlain to discuss his paper. In preparation for our informal interview I asked him to write a short "process reflection" describing the researching, writing, and revising of his essay. I am tempted to delete this last phrase—"researching, writing, and revising"—because Kevin's actual process did not follow this neat, if unnatural, progression of discrete steps or stages. His process was rich in recursions and excursions, in rethinkings that led to new inquiries, which in turn led to further thinking and writing. The finished essay is not the one Kevin thought he was going to write when he started out.

So, how *did* he start out? Why did he choose to write on James Joyce's "Eveline," a story about a young woman's unsuccessful struggle to leave home, when he had any number of literary works and authors from which to select?

Kevin's Motivation and Process

"I was drawn to this story because I, too, am attached to my home and family," Kevin writes in his process reflection. "I have lived in the same house all of my life and I often dread the thought of leaving." Kevin adds similarly: "I was able to empathize with Eveline because I am at a similar point in my life—too long in the nest." Kevin's impetus for this paper was at heart a personal one. He responded emotionally to the title character's fears and desires, to the terrible conflict between home and self. Kevin also notes that he had read other works by Joyce and enjoyed his "writing style." Clearly, however, "Eveline" struck a special chord.

In our conversation, Kevin spoke of his initial impatience with the character Eveline, how he felt "anxious to push this person out of her home—to do what I would do." On further reading and research, however, he tempered this impulse, as he looked more closely at the conditions and culture that gave rise to Eveline's quandary. Reading Joyce's *Portrait of the Artist as a Young Man* and *Dubliners,* along with relevant critical research on the author and Ireland itself, brought Kevin to a more complex and empathetic understanding of the character. No doubt, too, rereading the story reminded Kevin of his own unresolved tensions between loyalties to home and family on one hand, and change and "beginning my own life" on the other.

Along with Kevin's intimate connection with the story's protagonist must be added another: culture. Eveline is not only a person struggling with fierce inner conflicts, she is a person living in a particular place and time, Ireland of the early twentieth century. Again, in his process, Kevin writes of "being part Irish" and how this cultural heritage leads him to share similar values with Eveline in regard to family, religion, and change. At the same time, he realized that he needed to know more of the particular Ireland of Joyce's "Eveline" and how the author "intertwines political, social, religious, and economic themes into his writing . . . That is where the research began."

Cultural relevance, then, became a starting point for inquiry into the important complexities that form the backdrop of Joyce's story. Interestingly, Kevin did not presume that his own Irish heritage gave him a satisfactory understanding of the character or story. Being part Irish did, however, stir his interest in the Ireland that gave rise to Eveline, and indeed to Joyce himself. In our interview, Kevin made the surprising assertion that in Joyce the characters are "the least important things in the story. The characters show one whole side of life, are representative of a whole class of people." What Kevin meant by this, I believe, is that "Eveline," far from being the idiosyncratic story of a particularly troubled young woman, is the story of many an Irish woman of Joyce's day, these Evelines holding fast to the dock railing as their figurative or real ships left for distant ports. In his essay, Kevin makes amply clear the enormous historical, economic, religious, and familial forces that converged into a sort of paralysis in Eveline and so many like her, and how these selfsame forces acted more centrifugally on Joyce and others like him who broke from home, and "the old sow" of Ireland "that eats her farrow," as Kevin quotes Joyce's biting indictment. Most notable in this analysis is that Kevin undertook his research from a need to know more of the very culture whose personal relevance first connected him to the story.

Here I would like to quote Kevin's description of how his initial intent to write an interpretive essay relying solely on his reading of "Eveline" evolved rather organically into a more complex inquiry:

My first step was to respond to the story, writing an essay that examined the primary source [the story "Eveline"] without any outside influences such as literary criticism. Once the draft was completed I made a list of things in the story that I did not understand but felt were important to understanding the work as a whole. . . . By making a list of things I did not understand, I had something to look for in the outside sources. . . . Once I felt I had enough information to revise my first draft, I added in the research to my already existing essay . . . without letting my research write the paper for me. I simply used the research to support my already existing thesis.

Clearly, Kevin did not start out with either the requirement or the intention of writing a research paper. His method was not to get books out of the library and then figure out a way to incorporate all the research into a readable—or writable—essay. Rather, as his process reflection here and his finished essay demonstrate, he *grew* into the research, beginning with that important personal connection, that moment of recognition between himself and the text. He saw something of himself in Eveline, as he did in the Ireland that lived in her. From this recognition he wrote his first draft, a draft that led him to other questions. These questions, in turn, led him to further reading and writing, thereby strengthening the original connection between himself and the story. He repeated this process through several revisions, each time returning to the library when he felt "there were things that were still not strong enough," until he had satisfied the questions raised by his reading and writing. What started, then, as a response to a short story related to his own life grew to a larger inquiry into cultural contexts, literary criticism, and the author's work. That initial personal response, however, was not simply a starting point for the "real" work of research and writing. From Kevin's process reflections, as from his completed essay, I am convinced that his ongoing—indeed deepened—connection with the character and culture of this story sustained his research, writing, and revision throughout.

By citing Kevin's approach to writing about a literary work I am not claiming that students need to share a cultural identity with an author or text, or find exact parallels with the circumstances of their own lives. What I do believe Kevin's example illustrates is the importance of a personal connection with the work. Clearly, Kevin did not need a male protagonist in a familiar, contemporary setting in order to "relate." He did, however, feel a need to find in the work something that touched him. As it happened, he found this through cultural and psychological perspectives. More important, he then broadened these perspectives, questioning what he read and wrote, adding to it, seeing what was previously unseen. In the process, he learned about women in Joyce's Ireland; he read other works by the author; he saw historical and political patterns in Eveline's painful stasis; he deciphered religious references as significant symbols; he studied the human heart through the particulars of one fictive but very human creation. As important, I think, is that Kevin came to experience this story and his response to it as integral to his own life.

A Student Research Essay

Kevin Chamberlain

Dr. Devenish

English 102

March 20, 200X

Leaving Home

James Joyce's short story "Eveline" is the story of a girl who turns down a marriage proposal because of her attachment to her home and family. This story still has relevance today. Many young adults live in the homes they grew up in and often dread the thought of leaving. These adult children and their parents depend on each other emotionally and financially and moving out would alter their lives significantly. Eveline, the main character in Joyce's story, is faced with a similar dilemma. Should she abandon her father and begin her own life? Or should she stay home and take care of her father, but give up her own future in the process?

Eveline's devotion to her father stems from a promise to her deceased mother to keep her home together. Even after the home falls apart, Eveline feels that she must stay. On the surface, it is Eveline's tale of how and why she cannot leave. Beneath the surface, the story is a metaphor for women's conditions in turn-of-the-century Ireland. There are many factors that influence Eveline's decision, but the most compelling are religion, family, and fear of change.

There is not much to the story on the surface. It appears to be nothing more than the story of a girl who makes a bad decision, but Joyce has neatly interwoven a metaphor for what keeps Irish people in an idle state. He is using his story to point out how Irish people, especially women, let themselves be trapped. He does not entirely blame the individual, because conditions gave people a poor foundation to build on. Finally, when there is some certainty, they cling to it and are reluctant to change. This is the plight of Eveline.

In the 1890s, when this story was set, Ireland was still suffering the effects of the potato famine of the 1840s. Around this time, the country had lost millions of its people to starvation and emigration. The people left behind suffered many effects. "For a full century after 1845, poverty was widespread, jobs few and precarious, salaries meager, and opportunities for advancement rare" (Walzl 33). This was especially true for women, who were relegated to more traditional roles.

Lack of financial resources led people to put off marriage. Postponing marriages kept women with their families longer, causing them to become dependent on that lifestyle. As one becomes more devoted to family, the option of marriage becomes less likely. Eveline's chance to marry Frank, her fiancé, is important because it may be her only chance to marry and leave the country. By deciding not to marry Frank, she identifies herself as one woman who will not leave her homeland. In this sense, Eveline is representative of many of her fellow citizens. "Even when emigration had become established as an almost automatic part of rural life, it conflicted sharply with the high value that Irish country people put upon communalism, kinship and a sense of place. To leave here meant a psychic disruption" (Foster 351).

The story opens with Eveline sitting motionless, contemplating leaving the home she has known. After her mother's death, Eveline takes over her duties in the home and tends to her abusive father: ". . . growing up he had never gone for her, . . . but latterly he had begun to threaten her" (Joyce, "Eveline" 191). Usually, his rage is about money and the idea that she squanders it. The truth is that after working at her job all week, she gives her wages to him, ultimately to support his drinking habits. A family that has a minimal income should treat alcohol as a luxury, yet "he was usually fairly bad of a Saturday night" (191).

This kind of life should create a fear of remaining at home, yet Eveline feels that the unknown is much more frightening. It is clear that her social paralysis is self-inflicted and reinforced by her beliefs. Perhaps it is the thought that her father cannot survive without her that keeps her from leaving. She expends herself and her earnings just to support him. In a way she is acting more like a wife or mother than like a daughter: ". . . she had to work hard both in the house and at business" (191), but her marriage to Frank would change all that. He offers to take her to Buenos Aires, where she could live a comfortable life, but she finally chooses not to go with him because of her attachment to the life she has known. She is paralyzed by her fear of change and her devotion to her family.

During the scene that depicts her mother's final moments, when the promise to keep the home together is made, Eveline muses that her mother's life is a "life of commonplace sacrifices closing in final craziness" (192). This describes Eveline's life as well. Her own commonplace sacrifice is staying in her home and tending to her father. To her, it is a necessary sacrifice for her family's sake not to take interest in her own future. Her final craziness happens when she tries to escape. In the final scene at the station, she "clutched the iron [railing] in frenzy" trying to hold on to the life she has known (193). Her decision could mark the end of her social existence. She will probably never have this kind of opportunity again. Even if the opportunity again were to arise, she would most likely act the same way.

It is obvious that religion plays a role in Eveline's decision as well. In his description of her home, Joyce includes a "coloured print of the promises made to Blessed Margaret Mary Alacoque" (190). This is a symbol of devotion to home and family in the Catholic Church. The promises that are made by Jesus himself include, "I will establish peace in their homes. / I will comfort them in all their afflictions. / I will be their secure refuge during life, and above all in death" (Gifford 49). Joyce refers to this in his narration because Eveline's promise to her mother parallels these promises. He does this to show how religion only increases the guilt felt by someone who leaves home to make a life for herself. Since Eveline's promise was to keep her family together, it becomes impossible for her to leave. In the final scene, she stands at the station, unable to board the boat: "she prayed to God to direct her, to show her what was her duty" (Joyce, "Eveline" 192). It is clear that she feels it is her duty to stay at home and give up her only chance at starting a life of her own.

There is great emphasis on the promise that Eveline made to her mother, "to keep the home together as long as she could" (192). This might be seen, metaphorically, as the people of Ireland promising to stay together as long as possible because their own country has been taken from them. Weakened by the famine and exploited by the British, the country was in shambles. Although Ireland did not have control of its own government, the people maintained collective unity.

During this time, one of the country's worst periods, people depended on each other to survive. Afterward, the people had trouble getting back on their feet and relied mostly on religion to guide them. Joyce reacted against this. He felt that people should get out of Ireland and writes that "Ireland is the old sow that eats her farrow" (Joyce, <u>Portrait</u> 220). He makes his feelings very clear in this story by drawing on Eveline's promise to her mother.

Throughout the story, Eveline is tormented by the thought of leaving her home, and it ultimately consumes her. Her home life is not at all desirable, yet she stays. It is a condition often depicted by Joyce in his stories: "[Joyce] expresses the fragmentation experienced by individuals unable to rely on old certainties, whether religious, economic, or political" (Werner 27). It is these certainties that Eveline and many others were unable to part with. Her faith and bond to her family helped instill a fear of change that, for her, is too great to overcome.

One of the main reasons that many young adults still live at home is that they are dependent on the security and simplicity of being where they have always been. By living with their families, they know that they will never go hungry or worry about where they will sleep. They are secure in their surroundings. There may be the proud fear that their families cannot survive without them, and the belittling fear that they can't survive without their families. Perhaps it is one or both of these fears that influence Eveline's actions and ultimately control them.

[New Page]

Works Cited

Foster, Roy F. <u>Modern Ireland 1600–1972</u>. London: Penguin, 1988.

Gifford, Don. <u>Joyce Annotated</u>. Berkeley: U of California P, 1982. 48-52.

Joyce, James. "Eveline." <u>Exploring Literature</u>. Ed. Frank Madden. 3rd ed.
    New York: Longman, 2007. 190-193.

———. <u>Portrait of the Artist as a Young Man</u>. New York: Penguin, 1987.

Walzl, Florence L. "Dubliners: Women in Irish Society." <u>Women in Joyce</u>. Ed.
    Suzette Hanke and Elaine Unkless. Champaign-Urbana: U of Illinois P,
    1982. 31-54.

Werner, Craig Hanson. <u>Dubliners. A Student's Companion to the Stories.</u>
    <u>Robert Lecker</u>. Boston: Twayne Publishers, 1988.

PART III

A THEMATIC
ANTHOLOGY

Family & Friends

Family & Friends
A DIALOGUE ACROSS HISTORY

Friends have all things in common.
— Plato, *Dialogues,* 428–348 B.C.

He who has a thousand friends has not a / Friend to spare. / And he who has one enemy will meet him / Everywhere.
— Ali ibn-Abi-Talib, c. 602–661

In the misfortune of our best friends we often find something that is not displeasing.
— La Rochefouchaud, *Maxims,* 1665

It is impossible to please all the world and one's father.
— Jean de la Fontaine, 1668

I lay it down as fact that if all men knew what others say of them, there would not be four friends in the world.
— Blaise Pascal, *Pensees,* 1670

Fate chooses our relatives, we choose our friends.
— Jacques Delille, *Malheur et Pitie,* 1803

The only way to have a friend is to be one.
— Ralph Waldo Emerson, *Friendship,* 1841

A friend is a person with whom I may be sincere. Before him, I may think aloud.
— Ralph Waldo Emerson, *Friendship,* 1841

Give a little love to a child, and you get a great deal back.
— John Ruskin, *The Crown of Wild Olive,* 1866

Happy families are all alike; every unhappy family is unhappy in its own way.
— Leo Tolstoy, *Anna Karenina,* 1877

So long as we serve; so long as we are loved by others, I would almost say that we are indispensable; and no man is useless while he has a friend.
—Robert Louis Stevenson, *Across the Plains*, 1892

The little world of childhood with its familiar surroundings is a model of the greater world. The more intensely the family has stamped its character upon the child, the more it will tend to feel and see its earlier miniature world again in the bigger world of adult life.
—Carl Jung, *The Theory of Psychoanalysis*, 1913

Home is the place where, when you have to / go there, / They have to take you in.
—Robert Frost, *The Death of the Hired Man*, 1914

Each friend represents a world in us, a world possibly not born until they arrive, and it is only by this meeting that a new world is born.
—Anaïs Nin, 1937

The more people have studied different methods of bringing up children the more they have come to the conclusion that what good mothers and fathers instinctively feel like doing for their babies is the best after all.
—Benjamin Spock, *The Common Sense Book of Baby and Child Care*, 1946

If we were to see the family as a wealthy source of traditions, stories, characters and values, we might not feel so alone and abandoned to a life that has to be manufactured every day.
—Thomas Moore, *Soul Mates*, 1994

Every parent knows that raising children requires bicycle pumps, Beanie babies, notebook paper, prayers, skill, and plain dumb luck. But what many of us don't ever come to grips with is this: we must take responsibility for the world our children inhabit. We make the world for them. We give it to them. And if we fail them, they will break our hearts ten different ways.
—Amy Dickinson, *Time*, 1999

FAMILY AND FRIENDS: EXPLORING YOUR OWN VALUES AND BELIEFS

A look at depictions of family life over the last fifty years shows us how much the public image of family has changed. It is a long journey from the stable, wise, supportive families of television shows of fifty years ago to the chaotic, unstable families depicted in current shows like *The Simpsons* or *The Sopranos*. We live in an age that bombards us with traditional "family values" while urging our recovery from "dysfunctional family" experiences. Our families may be large and extend to distant relations or be as small as a single parent and child. Until we have the opportunity to form our own families, we don't have much choice about family membership. "Home," as Robert Frost writes, may be "the place where, when you have to / go there, / They have to take you in." And this same sense of responsibility may also compel us to love our brothers or sisters even when we don't like them very much.

For many of us, friends are a chosen family. We rely on friends to provide the kind of stability, wisdom, and support that make us think of them as "family" in the most favorable sense of the word. We confide in our friends or ask for their help when we're in trouble, and we selflessly rush to help and comfort them when they are most in need.

Our families and friends can have a powerful effect on our lives. They influence and shape our values, our behavior, our aspirations. We may be happy in their company and so attached to them that we have difficulty pulling away. We may be unhappy and disconnected from them and yearn for the warmth we believe we're missing. How important have family and/or friends been in the formation of your beliefs and values? As we experience the issues of family and friends that we encounter in literature, we will naturally compare them to similar circumstances in our own lives.

READING AND WRITING ABOUT FAMILY AND FRIENDS

Exploring your beliefs and values and connecting your experience with what you read is an important first step toward our ultimate goal—an appreciation of literature and the ability to think and write critically about it. Critical analysis will require rereading and reflection, writing and revising, gathering evidence, and constructing a solid argument to support your responses.

At least one aspect of the many stories, poems, plays, and essays in this section is about the impact that family and/or friends have on characters: the heartbreaking father-son conflict over tradition and values in Chinua Achebe's short story "Marriage Is a Private Affair"; the realization and application of a gift handed down from his father in Li-Young Lee's poem "The Gift"; the vulnerability of a young woman and her protective family in Tennessee Williams's play *The Glass Menagerie;* and the life-long lessons learned by bell hooks in her essay "Inspired Eccentricity." The brief quotes that open this section also give you some idea of the number of compelling views that are connected to family and friends. Issues of parent-child tension, mutual support, loneliness, loyalty, comfort, personal growth, and parental responsibility head a long list of concerns. Any of these or other related issues might provide a fine topic for building an argument and writing an essay.

◆ FICTION ◆

CHINUA ACHEBE [B. 1930]

The son of a mission schoolteacher, Chinua Achebe was born and raised in eastern Nigeria, a British colony that later became the Republic of Nigeria after gaining independence in 1963. Educated both in Africa and England, he first burst into prominence with his 1958 novel Things Fall Apart, *a moving portrayal of the conflicts between traditional tribal customs and European culture in colonial Africa. He has since become one of the most influential African voices of his generation. Much of his later work, including the novels* Man of the People *(1966) and* Anthills of the Savannah *(1988), explores the corruption and conflicts of contemporary Nigeria. His most recent works are* Home and Exile *(2000) and* Collected Poems *(2004). He is currently Charles P. Stevenson Professor of Languages and Literature at Bard College.*

MARRIAGE IS A PRIVATE AFFAIR   [1972]

"Have you written to your dad yet?" asked Nene one afternoon as she sat with Nnaemeka in her room at 16 Kasanga Street, Lagos.

"No. I've been thinking about it. I think it's better to tell him when I get home on leave!"

"But why? Your leave is such a long way off yet—six whole weeks. He should be let into our happiness now."

Nnaemeka was silent for a while, and then began very slowly as if he groped for his words: "I wish I were sure it would be happiness to him."

5   "Of course it must," replied Nene, a little surprised. "Why shouldn't it?"

"You have lived in Lagos all your life, and you know very little about people in remote parts of the country."

"That's what you always say. But I don't believe anybody will be so unlike other people that they will be unhappy when their sons are engaged to marry."

"Yes. They are most unhappy if the engagement is not arranged by them. In our case it's worse—you are not even an Ibo."

This was said so seriously and so bluntly that Nene could not find speech immediately. In the cosmopolitan atmosphere of the city it had always seemed to her something of a joke that a person's tribe could determine whom he married.

10   At last she said, "You don't really mean that he will object to your marrying me simply on that account? I had always thought you Ibos were kindly disposed to other people."

"So we are. But when it comes to marriage, well, it's not quite so simple. And this," he added, "is not peculiar to the Ibos. If your father were alive and lived in the heart of Ibibio-land he would be exactly like my father."

"I don't know. But anyway, as your father is so fond of you, I'm sure he will forgive you soon enough. Come on then, be a good boy and send him a nice lovely letter . . . "

"It would not be wise to break the news to him by writing. A letter will bring it upon him with a shock. I'm quite sure about that."

"All right, honey, suit yourself. You know your father."

15   As Nnaemeka walked home that evening he turned over in his mind the different ways of overcoming his father's opposition, especially now that he had gone and found a girl for him. He had thought of showing his letter to Nene but decided on second thought not to, at least for the moment. He read it again when he got home and couldn't help smiling to himself. He remembered Ugoye quite well, an Amazon of a girl who used to beat up all the boys, himself included, on the way to the stream, a complete dunce at school.

I have found a girl who will suit you admirably—Ugoye Nweke, the eldest daughter of our neighbor, Jacob Nweke. She has a proper Christian upbringing. When she stopped schooling some years ago her father (a man of sound judgment) sent her to live in the house of a pastor where she has received all the training a wife could need. Her Sunday School teacher has told me that she reads her Bible very fluently. I hope we shall begin negotiations when you come home in December.

On the second evening of his return from Lagos Nnaemeka sat with his father under a cassia tree. This was the old man's retreat where he went to read his Bible when the parching December sun had set and a fresh, reviving wind blew on the leaves.

"Father," began Nnaemeka suddenly, "I have come to ask forgiveness."

"Forgiveness? For what, my son?" he asked in amazement.

20   "It's about this marriage question!"

"Which marriage question?"

"I can't—we must—I mean it is impossible for me to marry Nweke's daughter."

"Impossible? Why?" asked his father.

"I don't love her."

25   "Nobody said you did. Why should you?" he asked.

"Marriage today is different . . . "

"Look here, my son," interrupted his father, "nothing is different. What one looks for in a wife are a good character and a Christian background."

Nnaemeka saw there was no hope along the present line of argument.

"Moreover," he said, "I am engaged to marry another girl who has all of Ugoye's good qualities, and who . . . "

30   His father did not believe his ears. "What did you say?" he asked slowly and disconcertingly.

"She is a good Christian," his son went on, "and a teacher in a girls' school in Lagos."

"Teacher, did you say? If you consider that a qualification for a good wife I should like to point out to you, Emeka, that no Christian woman should teach. St. Paul in his letter to the Corinthians says that women should keep silence." He rose slowly from his seat and paced forwards and backwards. This was his pet subject, and he condemned vehemently those church leaders who encouraged women to teach in their schools. After he had spent his emotion on a long homily, he at last came back to his son's engagement, in a seemingly milder tone.

"Whose daughter is she, anyway?"

"She is Nene Atang."

35   "What!" All the mildness was gone again. "Did you say Neneatang? What does that mean?"

"Nene Atang from Calabar. She is the only girl I can marry." This was a very rash reply and Nnaemeka expected the storm to burst. But it did not. His father merely walked away into his room. This was most unexpected and perplexed Nnaemeka. His father's silence was infinitely more menacing than a flood of threatening speech. That night the old man did not eat.

When he sent for Nnaemeka a day later he applied all possible ways of dissuasion. But the young man's heart was hardened, and his father eventually gave him up as lost.

"I owe it to you, my son, as a duty to show you what is right and what is wrong. Whoever put this idea into your head might as well have cut your throat. It is Satan's work." He waved his son away.

"You will change your mind, Father, when you know Nene."

40   "I shall never see her," was the reply. From that night the father scarcely spoke to his son. He did not, however, cease hoping that he would realize how serious was the danger he was heading for. Day and night he put him in his prayers.

Nnaemeka, for his own part, was very deeply affected by his father's grief. But he kept hoping that it would pass away. If it had occurred to him that never in the history of his people had a man married a woman who spoke a different tongue, he might have been less optimistic. "It has never been heard," was the verdict of an old man speaking a few weeks later. In that short sentence he spoke for all of his people. This man had come with others to commiserate with Okeke when news went round about his son's behavior. By that time the son had gone back to Lagos.

"It has never been heard," said the old man again with a sad shake of his head.

"What did Our Lord say?" asked another gentleman. "Sons shall rise against their Fathers; it is there in the Holy Book."

"It is the beginning of the end," said another.

45   The discussion thus tending to become theological, Madubogwu, a highly practical man, brought it down once more to the ordinary level.

"Have you thought of consulting a native doctor about your son?" he asked Nnaemeka's father.

"He isn't sick," was the reply.

"What is he then? The boy's mind is diseased and only a good herbalist can bring him back to his right senses. The medicine he requires is *Amalile,* the same that women apply with success to recapture their husbands' straying affection."

"Madubogwu is right," said another gentleman. "This thing calls for medicine."

50   "I shall not call in a native doctor." Nnaemeka's father was known to be obstinately ahead of his more superstitious neighbors in these matters. "I will not be another Mrs. Ochuba. If my son wants to kill himself let him do it with his own hands. It is not for me to help him."

"But it was her fault," said Madubogwu. "She ought to have gone to an honest herbalist. She was a clever woman, nevertheless."

"She was a wicked murderess," said Jonathan who rarely argued with his neighbors because, he often said, they were incapable of reasoning. "The medicine was prepared for her husband, it was his name they called in its preparation and I am sure it would have been perfectly beneficial to him. It was wicked to put it into the herbalist's food, and say you were only trying it out."

Six months later, Nnaemeka was showing his young wife a short letter from his father:

> It amazes me that you could be so unfeeling as to send me your wedding picture. I would have sent it back. But on further thought I decided just to cut off your wife and sent it back to you because I have nothing to do with her. How I wish that I had nothing to do with you either.

55   When Nene read through this letter and looked at the mutilated picture her eyes filled with tears, and she began to sob.

"Don't cry, my darling," said her husband. "He is essentially good natured and will one day look more kindly on our marriage." But years passed and that one day did not come.

For eight years, Okeke would have nothing to do with his son, Nnaemeka. Only three times (when Nnaemeka asked to come home and spend his leave) did he write to him.

"I can't have you in my house," he replied on one occasion. "It can be of no interest to me where or how you spend your leave—or your life, for that matter."

The prejudice against Nnaemeka's marriage was not confined to his little village. In Lagos, especially among his people who worked there, it showed itself in a different way. Their women, when they met at their village meeting were not hostile to Nene. Rather, they paid her such excessive deference as to make her feel she was not one of them. But as time went on, Nene gradually broke through some of this prejudice and even began to make friends among them. Slowly and grudgingly they began to admit that she kept her home much better than most of them.

60   The story eventually got to the little village in the heart of the Ibo country that Nnaemeka and his young wife were a most happy couple. But his father was one of the few people who knew nothing about this. He always displayed so much temper whenever his son's name was mentioned that everyone avoided it in his presence. By a tremendous effort of will he had succeeded in pushing his son to the back of his mind. The strain had nearly killed him but he had persevered, and won.

Then one day he received a letter from Nene, and in spite of himself he began to glance through it perfunctorily until all of a sudden the expression on his face changed and he began to read more carefully.

> . . . Our two sons, from the day they learnt that they have a grandfather, have insisted on being taken to him. I find it impossible to tell them that you will not see them. I implore you to allow Nnaemeka to bring them home for a short time during his leave next month. I shall remain here in Lagos . . .

The old man at once felt the resolution he had built up over so many years falling in. He was telling himself that he must not give in. He tried to steel his heart against all emotional appeals. It was a reenactment of that other struggle. He leaned against a window and looked out. The sky was overcast with heavy black clouds and a high wind began to blow filling the air with dust and dry leaves. It was one of those rare occasions when even Nature takes a hand in a human fight. Very soon it began to rain, the first rain in the year. It came down in large sharp drops and was accompanied by the lightning and thunder which mark a change of season. Okeke was trying hard not to think of his two grandsons. But he knew he was now fighting a losing battle. He tried to hum a favorite hymn but the pattering of large rain drops on the roof broke up the tune. His mind immediately returned to the children. How could he shut his door against them? By a curious mental process he imagined them standing, sad and forsaken, under the harsh angry weather—shut out from his house.

That night he hardly slept, from remorse—and a vague fear that he might die without making it up to them.

MAKING CONNECTIONS

1. At the start of the story Nnaemeka has a letter from his father that he doesn't share with Nene. Why does he conceal its contents? Is he justified in not sharing such information with his fiancée?
2. Nnaemeka's father objects to his marriage to Nene because she is not an Ibo. Are there any groups whose members it would be difficult for you to marry? Explain.
3. It is commonly assumed that marriages are based upon love, but even in our society people marry for reasons other than love. Is marriage for a motive other than love justifiable? Might it even be preferable? Explain.
4. What do you think of the way that Okeke treats his son and daughter-in-law? Is it ever appropriate to disown a child? Explain.
5. Do you think the rain near the end of the story is symbolic? Explain.
6. Throughout the story, Nnaemeka seems optimistic that his father will come to accept his marriage. To what extent do Okeke's reactions to Nene's letter at the end of the story validate his son's optimism? Why?
7. To what extent does this story exemplify the Jean de la Fontaine adage "It is impossible to please all the world and one's father"?

MAKING AN ARGUMENT

1. Write about the characterization of father and son and its relationship to the conflict in this story. What are the cultural values of father and son in this story? Despite their differences over the marriage, in what ways are they alike? To what extent does their conflict result from who they are as individuals as much as what they believe in? Cite evidence from the text of the story for support.

JAMES BALDWIN [1924–1987]

*James Baldwin grew up in poverty in Harlem with his
mother, eight half-brothers and -sisters, and a stepfather
whom he hated. He became a preacher at the age of fourteen, but after graduating from high school he left the
ministry disillusioned. Turning to writing, he struggled for
over ten years to complete his first novel, the autobiographical* Go Tell It on the Mountain *(1953), a publication
that instantly made Baldwin one of the most important
American writers of his time. In his subsequent work, which included numerous
novels, plays, and essays, Baldwin continually explored issues of racial and
sexual identity, and the civil rights movement, often writing of his own experiences of his family and Harlem. Unhappy with racial conditions in the United
States, Baldwin spent most of his adult life in Paris, returning to the United
States only occasionally.*

SONNY'S BLUES

[1957]

I read about it in the paper, in the subway, on my way to work. I read it, and I couldn't
believe it, and I read it again. Then perhaps I just stared at it, at the newsprint spelling
out his name, spelling out the story. I stared at it in the swinging lights of the subway car,
and in the faces and bodies of the people, and in my own face, trapped in the darkness
which roared outside.

It was not to be believed and I kept telling myself that, as I walked from the
subway station to the high school. And at the same time I couldn't doubt it. I was
scared, scared for Sonny. He became real to me again. A great block of ice got settled
in my belly and kept melting there slowly all day long, while I taught my classes algebra. It was a special kind of ice. It kept melting, sending trickles of ice water all up
and down my veins, but it never got less. Sometimes it hardened and seemed to
expand until I felt my guts were going to come spilling out or that I was going to
choke or scream. This would always be at a moment when I was remembering some
specific thing Sonny had once said or done.

When he was about as old as the boys in my classes his face had been bright and
open, there was a lot of copper in it; and he'd had wonderfully direct brown eyes,
and great gentleness and privacy. I wondered what he looked like now. He had
been picked up, the evening before, in a raid on an apartment downtown, for ped-
dling and using heroin.

I couldn't believe it: but what I mean by that is that I couldn't find any room for it
anywhere inside me. I had kept it outside me for a long time. I hadn't wanted to know.
I had had suspicions, but I didn't name them, I kept putting them away. I told myself that
Sonny was wild, but he wasn't crazy. And he'd always been a good boy, he hadn't ever
turned hard or evil or disrespectful, the way kids can, so quick, so quick, especially in
Harlem. I didn't want to believe that I'd ever see my brother going down, coming to
nothing, all that light in his face gone out, in the condition I'd already seen so many
others. Yet it had happened and here I was, talking about algebra to a lot of boys who
might, every one of them for all I knew, be popping off needles every time they went
to the head. Maybe it did more for them than algebra could.

5   I was sure that the first time Sonny had ever had horse,[1] he couldn't have been much older than these boys were now. These boys, now, were living as we'd been living then, they were growing up with a rush and their heads bumped abruptly against the low ceiling of their actual possibilities. They were filled with rage. All they really knew were two darknesses, the darkness of their lives, which was now closing in on them, and the darkness of the movies, which had blinded them to that other darkness, and in which they now, vindictively, dreamed, at once more together than they were at any other time, and more alone.

When the last bell rang, the last class ended, I let out my breath. It seemed I'd been holding it for all that time. My clothes were wet—I may have looked as though I'd been sitting in a steam bath, all dressed up, all afternoon. I sat alone in the classroom a long time. I listened to the boys outside, downstairs, shouting and cursing and laughing. Their laughter struck me for perhaps the first time. It was not the joyous laughter which—God knows why—one associates with children. It was mocking and insular, its intent was to denigrate. It was disenchanted, and in this, also, lay the authority of their curses. Perhaps I was listening to them because I was thinking about my brother and in them I heard my brother. And myself.

One boy was whistling a tune, at once very complicated and very simple, it seemed to be pouring out of him as though he were a bird, and it sounded very cool and moving through all that harsh, bright air, only just holding its own through all those other sounds.

I stood up and walked over to the window and looked down into the courtyard. It was the beginning of the spring and the sap was rising in the boys. A teacher passed through them every now and again, quickly, as though he or she couldn't wait to get out of that courtyard, to get those boys out of their sight and off their minds. I started collecting my stuff. I thought I'd better get home and talk to Isabel.

The courtyard was almost deserted by the time I got downstairs. I saw this boy standing in the shadow of a doorway, looking just like Sonny. I almost called his name. Then I saw that it wasn't Sonny, but somebody we used to know, a boy from around our block. He'd been Sonny's friend. He'd never been mine, having been too young for me, and, anyway, I'd never liked him. And now, even though he was a grown-up man, he still hung around that block, still spent hours on the street corners, was always high and raggy. I used to run into him from time to time and he'd often work around to asking me for a quarter or fifty cents. He always had some real good excuse, too, and I always gave it to him, I don't know why.

10   But now, abruptly, I hated him. I couldn't stand the way he looked at me, partly like a dog, partly like a cunning child. I wanted to ask him what the hell he was doing in the school courtyard.

He sort of shuffled over to me, and he said, "I see you got the papers. So you already know about it."

"You mean about Sonny? Yes, I already know about it. How come they didn't get you?"

He grinned. It made him repulsive and it also brought to mind what he'd looked like as a kid. "I wasn't there. I stay away from them people."

[1]**horse** heroin

"Good for you." I offered him a cigarette and I watched him through the smoke. "You come all the way down here just to tell me about Sonny?"

15   "That's right." He was sort of shaking his head and his eyes looked strange, as though they were about to cross. The bright sun deadened his damp dark brown skin and it made his eyes look yellow and showed up the dirt in his kinked hair. He smelled funky. I moved a little away from him and I said, "Well, thanks. But I already know about it and I got to get home."

"I'll walk you a little ways," he said. We started walking. There were a couple of kids still loitering in the courtyard and one of them said goodnight to me and looked strangely at the boy beside me.

"What're you going to do?" he asked me. "I mean, about Sonny?"

"Look. I haven't seen Sonny for over a year, I'm not sure I'm going to do anything. Anyway, what the hell *can* I do?"

"That's right," he said quickly, "ain't nothing you can do. Can't much help old Sonny no more, I guess."

20   It was what I was thinking and so it seemed to me he had no right to say it.

"I'm surprised at Sonny, though," he went on—he had a funny way of talking, he looked straight ahead as though he were talking to himself—"I thought Sonny was a smart boy, I thought he was too smart to get hung."

"I guess he thought so too," I said sharply, "and that's how he got hung. And how about you? You're pretty goddamn smart, I bet."

Then he looked directly at me, just for a minute. "I ain't smart," he said. "If I was smart, I'd have reached for a pistol a long time ago."

"Look. Don't tell *me* your sad story, if it was up to me, I'd give you one." Then I felt guilty—guilty, probably, for never having supposed that the poor bastard *had* a story of his own, much less a sad one, and I asked, quickly, "What's going to happen to him now?"

25   He didn't answer this. He was off by himself some place. "Funny thing," he said, and from his tone we might have been discussing the quickest way to get to Brooklyn, "when I saw the papers this morning, the first thing I asked myself was if I had anything to do with it. I felt sort of responsible."

I began to listen more carefully. The subway station was on the corner, just before us, and I stopped. He stopped, too. We were in front of a bar and he ducked slightly, peering in, but whoever he was looking for didn't seem to be there. The juke box was blasting away with something black and bouncy and I half watched the barmaid as she danced her way from the juke box to her place behind the bar. And I watched her face as she laughingly responded to something someone said to her, still keeping time to the music. When she smiled one saw the little girl, one sensed the doomed, still-struggling woman beneath the battered face of the semiwhore.

"I never *give* Sonny nothing," the boy said finally, "but a long time ago I come to school high and Sonny asked me how it felt." He paused, I couldn't bear to watch him, I watched the barmaid, and I listened to the music which seemed to be causing the pavement to shake. "I told him it felt great." The music stopped, the barmaid paused and watched the juke box until the music began again. "It did."

All this was carrying me some place I didn't want to go. I certainly didn't want to know how it felt. It filled everything, the people, the houses, the music, the dark, quicksilver barmaid, with menace; and this menace was their reality.

"What's going to happen to him now?" I asked again.

30   "They'll send him away some place and they'll try to cure him." He shook his head. "Maybe he'll even think he's kicked the habit. Then they'll let him loose"—he gestured, throwing his cigarette into the gutter. "That's all."

"What do you mean, that's *all?*"

But I knew what he meant.

"I *mean,* that's *all.*" He turned his head and looked at me, pulling down the corners of his mouth. "Don't you know what I mean?" he asked, softly.

"How the hell *would* I know what you mean?" I almost whispered it, I don't know why.

35   "That's right," he said to the air, "how would *he* know what I mean?" He turned toward me again, patient and calm, and yet I somehow felt him shaking, shaking as though he were going to fall apart. I felt that ice in my guts again, the dread I'd felt all afternoon; and again I watched the barmaid, moving about the bar, washing glasses, and singing. "Listen. They'll let him out and then it'll just start all over again. That's what I mean."

"You mean—they'll let him out. And then he'll just start working his way back in again. You mean he'll never kick the habit. Is that what you mean?"

"That's right," he said, cheerfully. "*You* see what I mean."

"Tell me," I said at last, "why does he want to die? He must want to die, he's killing himself, why does he want to die?"

He looked at me in surprise. He licked his lips. "He don't want to die. He wants to live. Don't nobody want to die, ever."

40   Then I wanted to ask him—too many things. He could not have answered, or if he had, I could not have borne the answers. I started walking. "Well, I guess it's none of my business."

"It's going to be rough on old Sonny," he said. We reached the subway station. "This is your station?" he asked. I nodded. I took one step down. "Damn!" he said, suddenly. I looked up at him. He grinned again. "Damn it if I didn't leave all my money home. You ain't got a dollar on you, have you? Just for a couple of days, is all."

All at once something inside gave and threatened to come pouring out of me. I didn't hate him any more. I felt that in another moment I'd start crying like a child.

"Sure," I said. "Don't sweat." I looked in my wallet and didn't have a dollar, I only had a five. "Here," I said. "That hold you?"

He didn't look at it—he didn't want to look at it. A terrible closed look came over his face, as though he were keeping the number on the bill a secret from him and me. "Thanks," he said, and now he was dying to see me go. "Don't worry about Sonny. Maybe I'll write him or something."

45   "Sure," I said. "You do that. So long."

"Be seeing you," he said. I went on down the steps.

And I didn't write Sonny or send him anything for a long time. When I finally did, it was just after my little girl died, he wrote me back a letter which made me feel like a bastard.

Here's what he said:

Dear brother,

50   You don't know how much I needed to hear from you. I wanted to write you many a time but I dug how much I must have hurt you and so I didn't write. But now I feel like a man who's been trying to climb up out of some deep, real deep and funky hole and just saw the sun up there, outside. I got to get outside.

I can't tell you much about how I got here. I mean I don't know how to tell you. I guess I was afraid of something or I was trying to escape from something and you know I have never been very strong in the head (smile). I'm glad Mama and Daddy are dead and can't see what's happened to their son and I swear if I'd known what I was doing I would never have hurt you so, you and a lot of other fine people who were nice to me and who believed in me.

I don't want you to think it had anything to do with me being a musician. It's more than that. Or maybe less than that. I can't get anything straight in my head down here and I try not to think about what's going to happen to me when I get outside again. Sometime I think I'm going to flip and *never* get outside and sometime I think I'll come straight back. I tell you one thing, though, I'd rather blow my brains out than go through this again. But that's what they all say, so they tell me. If I tell you when I'm coming to New York and if you could meet me, I sure would appreciate it. Give my love to Isabel and the kids and I was sure sorry to hear about little Gracie. I wish I could be like Mama and say the Lord's will be done, but I don't know it seems to me that trouble is the one thing that never does get stopped and I don't know what good it does to blame it on the Lord. But maybe it does some good if you believe it.

Your brother,
Sonny

55   Then I kept in constant touch with him and I sent him whatever I could and I went to meet him when he came back to New York. When I saw him many things I thought I had forgotten came flooding back to me. This was because I had begun, finally, to wonder about Sonny, about the life that Sonny lived inside. This life, whatever it was, had made him older and thinner and it had deepened the distant stillness in which he had always moved. He looked very unlike my baby brother. Yet, when he smiled, when we shook hands, the baby brother I'd never known looked out from the depths of his private life, like an animal waiting to be coaxed into the light.

"How you been keeping?" he asked me.

"All right. And you?"

"Just fine." He was smiling all over his face. "It's good to see you again."

"It's good to see you."

60   The seven years' difference in our ages lay between us like a chasm: I wondered if these years would ever operate between us as a bridge. I was remembering, and it made it hard to catch my breath, that I had been there when he was born; and I had heard the first words he had ever spoken. When he started to walk, he walked from our mother straight to me. I caught him just before he fell when he took the first steps he ever took in this world.

"How's Isabel?"

"Just fine. She's dying to see you."

"And the boys?"

"They're fine, too. They're anxious to see their uncle."

65   "Oh, come on. You know they don't remember me."

"Are you kidding? Of course they remember you."

He grinned again. We got into a taxi. We had a lot to say to each other, far too much to know how to begin.

As the taxi began to move, I asked, "You still want to go to India?"

He laughed. "You still remember that. Hell, no. This place is Indian enough for me."

70   "It used to belong to them," I said.

And he laughed again. "They damn sure knew what they were doing when they got rid of it."

Years ago, when he was around fourteen, he'd been all hipped on the idea of going to India. He read books about people sitting on rocks, naked, in all kinds of weather, but mostly bad, naturally, and walking barefoot through hot coals and arriving at wisdom. I used to say that it sounded to me as though they were getting away from wisdom as fast as they could. I think he sort of looked down on me for that.

"Do you mind," he asked, "if we have the driver drive alongside the park? On the west side—I haven't seen the city in so long."

"Of course not," I said. I was afraid that I might sound as though I were humoring him, but I hoped he wouldn't take it that way.

75   So we drove along, between the green of the park and the stony, lifeless elegance of hotels and apartment buildings, toward the vivid, killing streets of our childhood. These streets hadn't changed, though housing projects jutted up out of them now like rocks in the middle of a boiling sea. Most of the houses in which we had grown up had vanished, as had the stores from which we had stolen, the basements in which we had first tried sex, the rooftops from which we had hurled tin cans and bricks. But houses exactly like the houses of our past yet dominated the landscape, boys exactly like the boys we once had been found themselves smothering in these houses, came down into the streets for light and air and found themselves encircled by disaster. Some escaped the trap, most didn't. Those who got out always left something of themselves behind, as some animals amputate a leg and leave it in the trap. It might be said, perhaps, that I had escaped, after all, I was a school teacher; or that Sonny had, he hadn't lived in Harlem for years. Yet, as the cab moved uptown through streets which seemed, with a rush, to darken with dark people, and as I covertly studied Sonny's face, it came to me that what we both were seeking through our separate cab windows was that part of ourselves which had been left behind. It's always at the hour of trouble and confrontation that the missing member aches.

We hit 110th Street and started rolling up Lenox Avenue. And I'd known this avenue all my life, but it seemed to me again, as it had seemed on the day I'd first heard about Sonny's trouble, filled with a hidden menace which was its very breath of life.

"We almost there," said Sonny.

"Almost." We were both too nervous to say anything more.

We live in a housing project. It hasn't been up long. A few days after it was up it seemed uninhabitably new, now, of course, it's already rundown. It looks like a parody of the good, clean, faceless life—God knows the people who live in it do their best to make it a parody. The beat-looking grass lying around isn't enough to make their lives green, the hedges will never hold out the streets, and they know it. The big windows fool no one, they aren't big enough to make space out of no space. They don't bother with the windows, they watch the TV screen instead. The playground is most popular with the children who don't play at jacks, or skip rope, or roller skate, or swing, and they can be found in it after dark. We moved in partly because it's not too far from where I teach, and partly for the kids; but it's really just like the houses in which Sonny and I grew up. The same things happen, they'll have the same things to remember. The moment Sonny and I started into the house I had the feeling that I was simply bringing him back into the danger he had almost died trying to escape.

80   Sonny has never been talkative. So I don't know why I was sure he'd be dying to talk to me when supper was over the first night. Everything went fine, the oldest boy remembered him, and the youngest boy liked him, and Sonny had remembered to bring something for each of them; and Isabel, who is really much nicer than I am, more open and giving, had gone to a lot of trouble about dinner and was genuinely glad to see him. And she's always been able to tease Sonny in a way that I haven't. It was nice to see her face so vivid again and to hear her laugh and watch her make Sonny laugh. She wasn't, or, anyway, she didn't seem to be, at all uneasy or embarrassed. She chatted as though there were no subject which had to be avoided and she got Sonny past his first, faint stiffness. And thank God she was there, for I was filled with that icy dread again. Everything I did seemed awkward to me, and everything I said sounded freighted with hidden meaning. I was trying to remember everything I'd heard about dope addiction and I couldn't help watching Sonny for signs. I wasn't doing it out of malice. I was trying to find out something about my brother. I was dying to hear him tell me he was safe.

"Safe!" my father grunted, whenever Mama suggested trying to move to a neighborhood which might be safer for children. "Safe, hell! Ain't no place safe for kids, nor nobody."

He always went on like this, but he wasn't, ever, really as bad as he sounded, not even on weekends, when he got drunk. As a matter of fact, he was always on the lookout for "something a little better," but he died before he found it. He died suddenly, during a drunken weekend in the middle of the war, when Sonny was fifteen. He and Sonny hadn't ever got on too well. And this was partly because Sonny was the apple of his father's eye. It was because he loved Sonny so much and was frightened for him, that he was always fighting with him. It doesn't do any good to fight with Sonny. Sonny just moves back, inside himself, where he can't be reached. But the principal reason that they never hit it off is that they were so much alike. Daddy was big and rough and loud-talking, just the opposite of Sonny, but they both had—that same privacy.

Mama tried to tell me something about this, just after Daddy died. I was home on leave from the army.

This was the last time I ever saw my mother alive. Just the same, this picture gets all mixed up in my mind with pictures I had of her when she was younger. The way I always see her is the way she used to be on a Sunday afternoon, say, when the old folks were talking after the big Sunday dinner. I always see her wearing pale blue. She'd be sitting on the sofa. And my father would be sitting in the easy chair, not far from her. And the living room would be full of church folks and relatives. There they sit, in chairs all around the living room, and the night is creeping up outside, but nobody knows it yet. You can see the darkness growing against the windowpanes and you hear the street noises every now and again, or maybe the jangling beat of a tambourine from one of the churches close by, but it's real quiet in the room. For a moment nobody's talking, but every face looks darkening, like the sky outside. And my mother rocks a little from the waist, and my father's eyes are closed. Everyone is looking at something a child can't see. For a minute they've forgotten the children. Maybe a kid is lying on the rug, half asleep. Maybe somebody's got a kid in his lap and is absentmindedly stroking the kid's head. Maybe there's a kid, quiet and big-eyed, curled up in a big chair in the corner. The silence, the darkness coming, and the darkness in the faces frightens the child obscurely. He hopes that the hand which strokes his forehead will never stop—will never die. He hopes that there will never come a time when the old folks won't be sitting around the living room, talking about where they've come from, and what they've seen, and what's happened to them and their kinfolk.

85   But something deep and watchful in the child knows that this is bound to end, is already ending. In a moment someone will get up and turn on the light. Then the old folks will remember the children and they won't talk any more that day. And when light fills the room, the child is filled with darkness. He knows that every time this happens he's moved just a little closer to that darkness outside. The darkness outside is what the old folks have been talking about. It's what they've come from. It's what they endure. The child knows that they won't talk any more because if he knows too much about what's happened to *them,* he'll know too much too soon, about what's going to happen to *him.*

The last time I talked to my mother, I remember I was restless. I wanted to get out and see Isabel. We weren't married then and we had a lot to straighten out between us.

There Mama sat, in black, by the window. She was humming an old church song, *Lord, you brought me from a long ways off.* Sonny was out somewhere. Mama kept watching the streets.

"I don't know," she said, "if I'll ever see you again, after you go off from here. But I hope you'll remember the things I tried to teach you."

"Don't talk like that," I said, and smiled. "You'll be here a long time yet."

90   She smiled, too, but she said nothing. She was quiet for a long time. And I said, "Mama, don't you worry about nothing. I'll be writing all the time, and you be getting the checks. . . . "

"I want to talk to you about your brother," she said, suddenly. "If anything happens to me he ain't going to have nobody to look out for him."

"Mama," I said, "ain't nothing going to happen to you or Sonny. Sonny's all right. He's a good boy and he's got good sense."

"It ain't a question of his being a good boy," Mama said, "nor of his having good sense. It ain't only the bad ones, nor yet the dumb ones that gets sucked under." She stopped, looking at me. "Your Daddy once had a brother," she said, and she smiled in a way that made me feel she was in pain. "You didn't never know that, did you?"

"No," I said, "I never knew that," and I watched her face.

95   "Oh, yes," she said, "your Daddy had a brother." She looked out of the window again. "I know you never saw your Daddy cry. But I did—many a time, through all these years."

I asked her, "What happened to his brother? How come nobody's ever talked about him?"

This was the first time I ever saw my mother look old.

"His brother got killed," she said, "when he was just a little younger than you are now. I knew him. He was a fine boy. He was maybe a little full of the devil, but he didn't mean nobody no harm."

Then she stopped and the room was silent, exactly as it had sometimes been on those Sunday afternoons. Mama kept looking out into the streets.

100   "He used to have a job in the mill," she said, "and, like all young folks, he just liked to perform on Saturday nights. Saturday nights, him and your father would drift around to different places, go to dances and things like that, or just sit around with people they knew, and your father's brother would sing, he had a fine voice, and play along with himself on his guitar. Well, this particular Saturday night, him and your father was coming home from some place, and they were both a little drunk and there was a moon that night, it was bright like day. Your father's brother was feeling kind of good, and he was whistling to himself, and he had his guitar slung over his shoulder. They was coming down a hill and beneath them was a road that turned off from the highway. Well, your father's brother, being always kind of frisky, decided to run down this hill, and he did, with that guitar banging and clanging behind him, and he ran across the road, and he was making water behind a tree. And your father was sort of amused at him and he was still coming down the hill, kind of slow. Then he heard a car motor and that same minute his brother stepped from behind the tree, into the road, in the moonlight. And he started to cross the road. And your father started to run down the hill, he says he don't know why. This car was full of white men. They was all drunk, and when they seen your father's brother they let out a great whoop and holler and they aimed the car straight at him. They was having fun, they just wanted to scare him, the way they do sometimes, you know. But they was drunk. And I guess the boy, being drunk, too, and scared, kind of lost his head. By the time he jumped it was too late. Your father says he heard his brother scream when the car rolled over him, and he heard the wood of that guitar when it give, and he heard them strings go flying, and he heard them white men shouting, and the car kept on a-going and it ain't stopped till this day. And, time your father got down the hill, his brother weren't nothing but blood and pulp."

Tears were gleaming on my mother's face. There wasn't anything I could say.

"He never mentioned it," she said, "because I never let him mention it before you children. Your Daddy was like a crazy man that night and for many a night thereafter. He says he never in his life seen anything as dark as that road after the lights of that car had gone away. Weren't nothing, weren't nobody on that road, just your Daddy and his brother and that busted guitar. Oh, yes. Your Daddy never did really get right again. Till the day he died he weren't sure but that every white man he saw was the man that killed his brother."

She stopped and took out her handkerchief and dried her eyes and looked at me.

"I ain't telling you all this," she said, "to make you scared or bitter or to make you hate nobody. I'm telling you this because you got a brother. And the world ain't changed."

105   I guess I didn't want to believe this. I guess she saw this in my face. She turned away from me, toward the window again, searching those streets.

"But I praise my Redeemer," she said at last, "that He called your Daddy home before me. I ain't saying it to throw no flowers at myself, but, I declare, it keeps me from feeling too cast down to know I helped your father get safely through this world. Your father always acted like he was the roughest, strongest man on earth. And everybody took him to be like that. But if he hadn't had *me* there—to see his tears!"

She was crying again. Still, I couldn't move. I said, "Lord, Lord, Mama, I didn't know it was like that."

"Oh, honey," she said, "there's a lot that you don't know. But you are going to find it out." She stood up from the window and came over to me. "You got to hold on to your brother," she said, "and don't let him fall, no matter what it looks like is happening to him and no matter how evil you gets with him. You going to be evil with him many a time. But don't you forget what I told you, you hear?"

"I won't forget," I said. "Don't you worry, I won't forget. I won't let nothing happen to Sonny."

110   My mother smiled as though she were amused at something she saw in my face. Then, "You may not be able to stop nothing from happening. But you got to let him know you's *there.*"

Two days later I was married, and then I was gone. And I had a lot of things on my mind and I pretty well forgot my promise to Mama until I got shipped home on a special furlough for her funeral.

And, after the funeral, with just Sonny and me alone in the empty kitchen, I tried to find out something about him.

"What do you want to do?" I asked him.

"I'm going to be a musician," he said.

115   For he had graduated, in the time I had been away, from dancing to the juke box to finding out who was playing what, and what they were doing with it, and he had bought himself a set of drums.

"You mean, you want to be a drummer?" I somehow had the feeling that being a drummer might be all right for other people but not for my brother Sonny.

"I don't think," he said, looking at me very gravely, "that I'll ever be a good drummer. But I think I can play a piano."

I frowned. I'd never played the role of the older brother quite so seriously before, had scarcely ever, in fact, *asked* Sonny a damn thing. I sensed myself in the presence of something I didn't really know how to handle, didn't understand. So I made my frown a little deeper as I asked: "What kind of musician do you want to be?"

He grinned. "How many kinds do you think there are?"

120   "Be *serious,*" I said.

He laughed, throwing his head back, and then looked at me. "I *am* serious."

"Well, then, for Christ's sake, stop kidding around and answer a serious question. I mean, do you want to be a concert pianist, you want to play classical music and all that, or—or what?" Long before I finished he was laughing again. "For Christ's *sake,* Sonny!"

He sobered, but with difficulty. "I'm sorry. But you sound so—*scared!*" and he was off again.

"Well, you may think it's funny now, baby, but it's not going to be so funny when you have to make your living at it, let me tell you *that.*" I was furious because I knew he was laughing at me and I didn't know why.

125   No," he said, very sober now, and afraid, perhaps, that he'd hurt me, "I don't want to be a classical pianist. That isn't what interests me. I mean—" he paused, looking hard at me, as though his eyes would help me to understand, and then gestured helplessly, as though perhaps his hand would help—"I mean, I'll have a lot of studying to do, and I'll have to study *everything,* but, I mean, I want to play *with*—jazz musicians." He stopped. "I want to play jazz," he said.

Well, the word had never before sounded as heavy, as real, as it sounded that afternoon in Sonny's mouth. I just looked at him and I was probably frowning a real frown by this time. I simply couldn't see why on earth he'd want to spend his time hanging around nightclubs, clowning around on bandstands, while people pushed each other around a dance floor. It seemed—beneath him, somehow. I had never thought about it before, had never been forced to, but I suppose I had always put jazz musicians in a class with what Daddy called "good-time people."

"Are you *serious?*"

"Hell, *yes,* I'm serious."

He looked more helpless than ever, and annoyed, and deeply hurt.

130   I suggested, helpfully: "You mean—like Louis Armstrong?"

His face closed as though I'd struck him. "No. I'm not talking about none of that old-time, down home crap."

"Well, look, Sonny, I'm sorry, don't get mad. I just don't altogether get it, that's all. Name somebody—you know, a jazz musician you admire."

"Bird."

"Who?"

135   "Bird! Charlie Parker! Don't they teach you nothing in the goddamn army?"

I lit a cigarette. I was surprised and then a little amused to discover that I was trembling. "I've been out of touch," I said. "You'll have to be patient with me. Now. Who's this Parker character?"

"He's just one of the greatest jazz musicians alive," said Sonny, sullenly, his hands in his pockets, his back to me. "Maybe *the* greatest," he added, bitterly, "that's probably why you never heard of him."

"All right," I said, "I'm ignorant. I'm sorry. I'll go out and buy all the cat's records right away, all right?"

"It don't," said Sonny, with dignity, "make any difference to me. I don't care what you listen to. Don't do me no favors."

140   I was beginning to realize that I'd never seen him so upset before. With another part of my mind I was thinking that this would probably turn out to be one of those things kids go through and that I shouldn't make it seem important by pushing it too hard. Still, I didn't think it would do any harm to ask: "Doesn't all this take a lot of time? Can you make a living at it?"

He turned back to me and half leaned, half sat, on the kitchen table. "Everything takes time," he said, "and—well, yes, sure, I can make a living at it. But what I don't seem to be able to make you understand is that it's the only thing I want to do."

"Well, Sonny," I said, gently, "you know people can't always do exactly what they *want* to do—"

"*No,* I don't know that," said Sonny, surprising me. "I think people *ought* to do what they want to do, what else are they alive for?"

"You getting to be a big boy," I said desperately, "it's time you started thinking about your future."

145   "I'm thinking about my future," said Sonny, grimly. "I think about it all the time."

I gave up. I decided, if he didn't change his mind, that we could always talk about it later. "In the meantime," I said, "you got to finish school." We had already decided that he'd have to move in with Isabel and her folks. I knew this wasn't the ideal arrangement because Isabel's folks are inclined to be dicty and they hadn't especially wanted Isabel to marry me. But I didn't know what else to do. "And we have to get you fixed up at Isabel's."

There was a long silence. He moved from the kitchen table to the window. "That's a terrible idea. You know it yourself."

"Do you have a *better* idea?"

He just walked up and down the kitchen for a minute. He was as tall as I was. He had started to shave. I suddenly had the feeling that I didn't know him at all.

150   He stopped at the kitchen table and picked up my cigarettes. Looking at me with a kind of mocking, amused defiance, he put one between his lips. "You mind?"

"You smoking already?"

He lit the cigarette and nodded, watching me through the smoke. "I just wanted to see if I'd have the courage to smoke in front of you." He grinned and blew a great cloud of smoke to the ceiling. "It was easy." He looked at my face. "Come on, now. I bet you was smoking at my age, tell the truth."

I didn't say anything but the truth was on my face, and he laughed. But now there was something very strained in his laugh. "Sure. And I bet that ain't all you was doing."

He was frightening me a little. "Cut the crap," I said. "We already decided that you was going to go and live at Isabel's. Now what's got into you all of a sudden?"

155   "*You* decided it," he pointed out. "*I* didn't decide nothing." He stopped in front of me, leaning against the stove, arms loosely folded. "Look, brother. I don't want to stay in Harlem no more, I really don't." He was very earnest. He looked at me, then over toward the kitchen window. There was something in his eyes I'd never seen before, some thoughtfulness, some worry all his own. He rubbed the muscle of one arm. "It's time I was getting out of here."

"Where do you want to go, Sonny?"

"I want to join the army. Or the navy, I don't care. If I say I'm old enough, they'll believe me."

Then I got mad. It was because I was so scared. "You must be crazy. You god-damn fool, what the hell do you want to go and join the *army* for?"

"I just told you. To get out of Harlem."

160   "Sonny, you haven't even finished *school.* And if you really want to be a musi-cian, how do you expect to study if you're in the *army?*"

He looked at me, trapped, and in anguish. "There's ways. I might be able to work out some kind of deal. Anyway, I'll have the G.I. Bill when I come out."

"*If* you come out." We stared at each other. "Sonny, please. Be reasonable. I know the setup is far from perfect. But we got to do the best we can."

"I ain't learning nothing in school," he said. "Even when I go." He turned away from me and opened the window and threw his cigarette out into the narrow alley. I watched his back. "At least, I ain't learning nothing you'd want me to learn." He slammed the window so hard I thought the glass would fly out, and turned back to me. "And I'm sick of the stink of these garbage cans!"

"Sonny," I said, "I know how you feel. But if you don't finish school now, you're going to be sorry later that you didn't." I grabbed him by the shoulders. "And you only got another year. It ain't so bad. And I'll come back and I swear I'll help you do *whatever* you want to do. Just try to put up with it till I come back. Will you please do that? For me?"

165   He didn't answer and he wouldn't look at me.

"Sonny. You hear me?"

He pulled away. "I hear you. But you never hear anything I say."

I didn't know what to say to that. He looked out of the window and then back at me. "OK," he said, and sighed. "I'll try."

Then I said, trying to cheer him up a little, "They got a piano at Isabel's. You can practice on it."

170   And as a matter of fact, it did cheer him up for a minute. "That's right," he said to himself. "I forgot that." His face relaxed a little. But the worry, the thoughtfulness, played on it still, the way shadows play on a face which is staring into the fire.

But I thought I'd never hear the end of that piano. At first, Isabel would write me, saying how nice it was that Sonny was so serious about his music and how, as soon as he came in from school, or wherever he had been when he was supposed to be at school, he went straight to that piano and stayed there until suppertime. And, after supper, he went back to that piano and stayed there until everybody went to bed. He was at the piano all day Saturday and all day Sunday. Then he bought a record player and started playing records. He'd play one record over and over again, all day long sometimes, and he'd improvise along with it on the piano. Or he'd play one section of the record, one chord, one change, one progression, then he'd do it on the piano. Then back to the record. Then back to the piano.

Well, I really don't know how they stood it. Isabel finally confessed that it wasn't like living with a person at all, it was like living with sound. And the sound didn't make any sense to her, didn't make any sense to any of them—naturally. They began, in a way, to be afflicted by this presence that was living in their home. It was as though Sonny were some sort of god, or monster. He moved in an atmosphere which wasn't like theirs at all. They fed him and he ate, he washed himself, he walked in and out of their door; he certainly wasn't nasty or unpleasant or rude, Sonny isn't any of those things; but it was as though he were all wrapped up in some cloud, some fire, some vision all his own; and there wasn't any way to reach him.

At the same time, he wasn't really a man yet, he was still a child, and they had to watch out for him in all kinds of ways. They certainly couldn't throw him out. Neither did they dare to make a great scene about that piano because even they dimly sensed, as I sensed, from so many thousands of miles away, that Sonny was at that piano playing for his life.

But he hadn't been going to school. One day a letter came from the school board and Isabel's mother got it—there had, apparently, been other letters but Sonny had torn them up. This day, when Sonny came in, Isabel's mother showed him the letter and asked where he'd been spending his time. And she finally got it out of him that he'd been down in Greenwich Village, with musicians and other characters, in a white girl's apartment. And this scared her and she started to scream at him and what came up, once she began—though she denies it to this day—was what sacrifices they were making to give Sonny a decent home and how little he appreciated it.

175   Sonny didn't play the piano that day. By evening, Isabel's mother had calmed down but then there was the old man to deal with, and Isabel herself. Isabel says she did her best to be calm but she broke down and started crying. She says she just watched Sonny's face. She could tell, by watching him, what was happening with him. And what was happening was that they penetrated his cloud, they had reached him. Even if their fingers had been a thousand times more gentle than human fingers ever are, he could hardly help feeling that they had stripped him naked and were spitting on that nakedness. For he also had to see that his presence, that music, which was life or death to him, had been torture for them and that they had endured it, not at all for his sake, but only for mine. And Sonny couldn't take that. He can take it a little better today than he could then but he's still not very good at it and, frankly, I don't know anybody who is.

The silence of the next few days must have been louder than the sound of all the music ever played since time began. One morning, before she went to work, Isabel was in his room for something and she suddenly realized that all of his records were gone. And she knew for certain that he was gone. And he was. He went as far as the navy would carry him. He finally sent me a postcard from some place in Greece and that was the first I knew that Sonny was still alive. I didn't see him any more until we were both back in New York and the war had long been over.

He was a man by then, of course, but I wasn't willing to see it. He came by the house from time to time, but we fought almost every time we met. I didn't like the way he carried himself, loose and dreamlike all the time, and I didn't like his friends, and his music seemed to be merely an excuse for the life he led. It sounded just that weird and disordered.

Then we had a fight, a pretty awful fight, and I didn't see him for months. By and by I looked him up, where he was living, in a furnished room in the Village, and I tried to make it up. But there were lots of people in the room and Sonny just lay on his bed, and he wouldn't come downstairs with me, and he treated these other people as though they were his family and I weren't. So I got mad and then he got mad, and then I told him that he might just as well be dead as live the way he was living. Then he stood up and he told me not to worry about him any more in life, that he *was* dead as far as I was concerned. Then he pushed me to the door and the other people looked on as though nothing were happening, and he slammed the door behind me. I stood in the hallway, staring at the door. I heard somebody laugh in the room and then the tears came to my eyes. I started down the steps, whistling to keep from crying, I kept whistling to myself, *You going to need me, baby, one of these cold, rainy days.*

I read about Sonny's trouble in the spring. Little Grace died in the fall. She was a beautiful little girl. But she only lived a little over two years. She died of polio and she suffered. She had a slight fever for a couple of days, but it didn't seem like anything and we just kept her in bed. And we would certainly have called the doctor, but the fever dropped, she seemed to be all right. So we thought it had just been a cold. Then, one day, she was up, playing, Isabel was in the kitchen fixing lunch for the two boys when they'd come in from school, and she heard Grace fall down in the living room. When you have a lot of children you don't always start running when one of them falls, unless they start screaming or something. And, this time, Grace was quiet. Yet, Isabel says that when she heard that *thump* and then that silence, something happened in her to make her afraid. And she ran to the living room and there was little Grace on the floor, all twisted up, and the reason she hadn't screamed was that she couldn't get her breath. And when she did scream, it was the worst sound, Isabel says, that she'd ever heard in all her life, and she still hears it sometimes in her dreams. Isabel will sometimes wake me up with a low, moaning, strangled sound and I have to be quick to awaken her and hold her to me and where Isabel is weeping against me seems a mortal wound.

180   I think I may have written Sonny the very day that little Grace was buried. I was sitting in the living room in the dark, by myself, and I suddenly thought of Sonny. My trouble made his real.

One Saturday afternoon, when Sonny had been living with us, or, anyway, been in our house, for nearly two weeks, I found myself wandering aimlessly about the living room, drinking from a can of beer, and trying to work up the courage to search Sonny's room. He was out, he was usually out whenever I was home, and Isabel had taken the children to see their grandparents. Suddenly I was standing still in front of the living room window, watching Seventh Avenue. The idea of searching Sonny's room made me still. I scarcely dared to admit to myself what I'd be searching for. I didn't know what I'd do if I found it. Or if I didn't.

On the sidewalk across from me, near the entrance to a barbecue joint, some people were holding an old-fashioned revival meeting. The barbecue cook, wearing a dirty white apron, his conked hair reddish and metallic in the pale sun, and a cigarette between his lips, stood in the doorway, watching them. Kids and older people paused in their errands and stood there, along with some older men and a couple of very tough-looking women who watched everything that happened on the avenue, as though they owned it, or were maybe owned by it. Well, they were watching this, too. The revival was being carried on by three sisters in black, and a brother. All they had were their voices and their Bibles and a tambourine. The brother was testifying and while he testified two of the sisters stood together, seeming to say, amen, and the third sister walked around with the tambourine outstretched and a couple of people dropped coins into it. Then the brother's testimony ended and the sister who had been taking up the collection dumped the coins into her palm and transferred them to the pocket of her long black robe. Then she raised both hands, striking the tambourine against the air, and then against one hand, and she started to sing. And the two other sisters and the brother joined in.

It was strange, suddenly, to watch, though I had been seeing these street meetings all my life. So, of course, had everybody else down there. Yet, they paused and watched and listened and I stood still at the window. "*'Tis the old ship of Zion,*" they sang, and the sister with the tambourine kept a steady, jangling beat, "*it has rescued many a thousand!*" Not a soul under the sound of their voices was hearing this song for the first time, not one of them had been rescued. Nor had they seen much in the way of rescue work being done around them. Neither did they especially believe in the holiness of the three sisters and the brother, they knew too much about them, knew where they lived, and how. The woman with the tambourine, whose voice dominated the air, whose face was bright with joy, was divided by very little from the woman who stood watching her, a cigarette between her heavy, chapped lips, her hair a cuckoo's nest, her face scarred and swollen from many beatings, and her black eyes glittering like coal. Perhaps they both knew this, which was why, when, as rarely, they addressed each other, they addressed each other as Sister. As the singing filled the air the watching, listening faces underwent a change, the eyes focusing on something within; the music seemed to soothe a poison out of them; and time seemed, nearly, to fall away from the sullen, belligerent, battered faces, as though they were fleeing back to their first condition, while dreaming of their last. The barbecue cook half shook his head and smiled, and dropped his cigarette and disappeared into his joint. A man fumbled in his pockets for change and stood holding it in his hand impatiently, as though he had just remembered a pressing appointment further up the avenue. He looked furious. Then I saw Sonny, standing on the edge of the crowd. He was carrying a wide, flat notebook with a green cover, and it made him look, from where I was standing, almost like a schoolboy. The coppery sun brought out the copper in his skin, he was very faintly smiling, standing very still. Then the singing stopped, the tambourine turned into a collection plate again. The furious man dropped in his coins and vanished, so did a couple of the women, and Sonny dropped some change in the plate, looking directly at the woman with a little smile. He started across the avenue, toward the house. He has a slow, loping walk, something like the way Harlem hipsters walk, only he's imposed on this his own half-beat. I had never really noticed it before.

I stayed at the window, both relieved and apprehensive. As Sonny disappeared from my sight, they began singing again. And they were still singing when his key turned in the lock.

185   "Hey," he said.

"Hey, yourself. You want some beer?"

"No. Well, maybe." But he came up to the window and stood beside me, looking out. "What a warm voice," he said.

They were singing *If I could only hear my mother pray again!*

"Yes," I said, "and she can sure beat that tambourine."

190   "But what a terrible song," he said, and laughed. He dropped his notebook on the sofa and disappeared into the kitchen. "Where's Isabel and the kids?"

"I think they went to see their grandparents. You hungry?"

"No." He came back into the living room with his can of beer. "You want to come some place with me tonight?"

I sensed, I don't know how, that I couldn't possibly say no. "Sure. Where?"

He sat down on the sofa and picked up his notebook and started leafing through it. "I'm going to sit in with some fellows in a joint in the Village."

195   "You mean, you're going to play, tonight?"

"That's right." He took a swallow of his beer and moved back to the window. He gave me a sidelong look. "If you can stand it."

"I'll try," I said.

He smiled to himself and we both watched as the meeting across the way broke up. The three sisters and the brother, heads bowed, were singing *God be with you till we meet again.* The faces around them were very quiet. Then the song ended. The small crowd dispersed. We watched the three women and the lone man walk slowly up the avenue.

"When she was singing before," said Sonny, abruptly, "her voice reminded me for a minute of what heroin feels like sometimes—when it's in your veins. It makes you feel sort of warm and cool at the same time. And distant. And—and sure." He sipped his beer, very deliberately not looking at me. I watched his face. "It makes you feel— in control. Sometimes you've got to have that feeling."

200   "Do you?" I sat down slowly in the easy chair.

"Sometimes." He went to the sofa and picked up his notebook again. "Some people do."

"In order," I asked, "to play?" And my voice was very ugly, full of contempt and anger.

"Well"—he looked at me with great, troubled eyes, as though, in fact, he hoped his eyes would tell me things he could never otherwise say—"they *think* so. And *if* they think so—!"

"And what do *you* think?" I asked.

205   He sat on the sofa and put his can of beer on the floor. "I don't know," he said, and I couldn't be sure if he were answering my question or pursuing his thoughts. His face didn't tell me. "It's not so much to *play.* It's to *stand* it, to be able to make it at all. On any level." He frowned and smiled: "In order to keep from shaking to pieces."

"But these friends of yours," I said, "they seem to shake themselves to pieces pretty goddamn fast."

"Maybe." He played with the notebook. And something told me that I should curb my tongue, that Sonny was doing his best to talk, that I should listen. "But of course you only know the ones that've gone to pieces. Some don't—or at least they haven't *yet* and that's just about all *any* of us can say." He paused. "And then there are some who just live, really, in hell, and they know it and they see what's happening and they go right on. I don't know." He sighed, dropped the notebook, folded his arms. "Some guys, you can tell from the way they play, they on something *all* the time. And you can see that, well, it makes something real for them. But of course," he picked up his beer from the floor and sipped it and put the can down again, "they *want* to, too, you've got to see that. Even some of them that say they don't—*some, not all.*"

"And what about you?" I asked—I couldn't help it. "What about you? Do *you* want to?"

He stood up and walked to the window and remained silent for a long time. Then he sighed. "Me," he said. Then: "While I was downstairs before, on my way here, listening to that woman sing, it struck me all of a sudden how much suffering she must have had to go through—to sing like that. It's *repulsive* to think you have to suffer that much."

210   I said: "But there's no way not to suffer—is there, Sonny?"

"I believe not," he said and smiled, "but that's never stopped anyone from trying." He looked at me. "Has it?" I realized, with this mocking look, that there stood between us, forever, beyond the power of time or forgiveness, the fact that I had held silence—so long!—when he had needed human speech to help him. He turned back to the window. "No, there's no way not to suffer. But you try all kinds of ways to keep from drowning in it, to keep on top of it, and to make it seem—well, like *you*. Like you did something, all right, and now you're suffering for it. You know?" I said nothing. "Well you know," he said, impatiently, "Why *do* people suffer? Maybe it's better to do something to give it a reason, *any* reason."

"But we just agreed," I said, "that there's no way not to suffer. Isn't it better, then, just to—take it?"

"But nobody just takes it," Sonny cried, "that's what I'm telling you! *Everybody* tries not to. You're just hung up on the *way* some people try—it's not *your* way!"

The hair on my face began to itch, my face felt wet. "That's not true," I said, "that's not true. I don't give a damn what other people do, I don't even care how they suffer. I just care how *you* suffer." And he looked at me. "Please believe me," I said, "I don't want to see you—die—trying not to suffer."

215   "I won't," he said, flatly, "die trying not to suffer. At least, not any faster than anybody else."

"But there's no need," I said, trying to laugh, "is there? in killing yourself."

I wanted to say more, but I couldn't. I wanted to talk about will power and how life could be—well, beautiful. I wanted to say that it was all within; but was it? or, rather, wasn't that exactly the trouble? And I wanted to promise that I would never fail him again. But it would all have sounded—empty words and lies.

So I made the promise to myself and prayed that I would keep it.

"It's terrible sometimes, inside," he said, "that's what's the trouble. You walk these streets, black and funky and cold, and there's not really a living ass to talk to, and there's nothing shaking, and there's no way of getting it out—that storm inside. You can't talk it and you can't make love with it, and when you finally try to get with it and play it, you realize *nobody's* listening. So *you've* got to listen. You got to find a way to listen."

220   And then he walked away from the window and sat on the sofa again, as though all the wind had suddenly been knocked out of him. "Sometimes you'll do *anything* to play, even cut your mother's throat." He laughed and looked at me. "Or your brother's." Then he sobered. "Or your own." Then: "Don't worry. I'm all right now and I think I'll *be* all right. But I can't forget where I've been. I don't mean just the physical place I've been, I mean where I've *been*. And *what* I've been."

"What have you been, Sonny?" I asked.

He smiled—but sat sideways on the sofa, his elbow resting on the back, his fingers playing with his mouth and chin, not looking at me. "I've been something I didn't recognize, didn't know I could be. Didn't know anybody could be." He stopped, looking inward, looking helplessly young, looking old. "I'm not talking about it now because I feel *guilty* or anything like that—maybe it would be better if I did, I don't know. Anyway, I can't really talk about it. Not to you, not to anybody," and now he turned and faced me. "Sometimes, you know, and it was actually when I was most *out* of the world, I felt that I was in it, that I was *with* it, really, and I could play or I didn't really have to *play*, it just came out of me, it was there. And I don't know how I played, thinking about it now, but I know I did awful things, those times, sometimes, to people. Or it wasn't that I *did* anything to them—it was that they weren't real." He picked up the beer can; it was empty; he rolled it between his palms: "And other times—well, I needed a fix, I needed to find a place to lean, I needed to clear a space to *listen*—and I couldn't find it, and I—went crazy, I did terrible things to *me,* I was terrible *for* me." He began pressing the beer can between his hands, I watched the metal begin to give. It glittered, as he played with it, like a knife, and I was afraid he would cut himself, but I said nothing. "Oh well. I can never tell you. I was all by myself at the bottom of something, stinking and sweating and crying and shaking, and I smelled it, you know? *my* stink, and I thought I'd die if I couldn't get away from it and yet, all the same, I knew that everything I was doing was just locking me in with it. And I didn't know," he paused, still flattening the beer can, "I didn't know, I still *don't* know, something kept telling me that maybe it was good to smell your own stink, but I didn't think that *that* was what I'd been trying to do—and—who can stand it?" and he abruptly dropped the ruined beer can, looking at me with a small, still smile, and then rose, walking to the window as though it were the lodestone rock. I watched his face, he watched the avenue. "I couldn't tell you when Mama died—but the reason I wanted to leave Harlem so bad was to get away from drugs. And then, when I ran away, that's what I was running from—really. When I came back, nothing had changed, I hadn't changed, I was just—older." And he stopped, drumming with his fingers on the windowpane. The sun had vanished, soon darkness would fall. I watched his face. "It can come again," he said, almost as though speaking to himself. Then he turned to me. "It can come again," he repeated. "I just want you to know that."

"All right," I said, at last. "So it can come again. All right."

He smiled, but the smile was sorrowful. "I had to try to tell you," he said.

225   "Yes," I said. "I understand that."

"You're my brother," he said, looking straight at me, and not smiling at all.

"Yes," I repeated, "yes. I understand that."

He turned back to the window, looking out. "All that hatred down there," he said, "all that hatred and misery and love. It's a wonder it doesn't blow the avenue apart."

We went to the only nightclub on a short, dark street, downtown. We squeezed through the narrow, chattering, jam-packed bar to the entrance of the big room, where the bandstand was. And we stood there for a moment, for the lights were very dim in this room and we couldn't see. Then, "Hello, boy," said a voice and an enormous black man, much older than Sonny or myself, erupted out of all that atmospheric lighting and put an arm around Sonny's shoulder. "I been sitting right here," he said, "waiting for you."

230   He had a big voice, too, and heads in the darkness turned toward us.

Sonny grinned and pulled a little away, and said, "Creole, this is my brother. I told you about him."

Creole shook my hand. "I'm glad to meet you, son," he said, and it was clear that he was glad to meet me *there,* for Sonny's sake. And he smiled, "You got a real musician in *your* family," and he took his arm from Sonny's shoulder and slapped him, lightly, affectionately, with the back of his hand.

"Well. Now I've heard it all," said a voice behind us. This was another musician, and a friend of Sonny's, a coal-black, cheerful-looking man, built close to the ground. He immediately began confiding to me, at the top of his lungs, the most terrible things about Sonny, his teeth gleaming like a lighthouse and his laugh coming up out of him like the beginning of an earthquake. And it turned out that everyone at the bar knew Sonny, or almost everyone; some were musicians, working there, or nearby, or not working, some were simply hangers-on, and some were there to hear Sonny play. I was introduced to all of them and they were all very polite to me. Yet, it was clear that, for them, I was only Sonny's brother. Here, I was in Sonny's world. Or, rather: his kingdom. Here, it was not even a question that his veins bore royal blood.

They were going to play soon and Creole installed me, by myself, at a table in a dark corner. Then I watched them, Creole, and the little black man, and Sonny, and the others, while they horsed around, standing just below the bandstand. The light from the bandstand spilled just a little short of them and, watching them laughing and gesturing and moving about, I had the feeling that they, nevertheless, were being most careful not to step into that circle of light too suddenly: that if they moved into the light too suddenly, without thinking, they would perish in flame. Then, while I watched, one of them, the small, black man, moved into the light and crossed the bandstand and started fooling around with his drums. Then—being funny and being, also, extremely ceremonious—Creole took Sonny by the arm and led him to the piano. A woman's voice called Sonny's name and a few hands started clapping. And Sonny, also being funny and being ceremonious, and so touched, I think, that he could have cried, but neither hiding it nor showing it, riding it like a man, grinned, and put both hands to his heart and bowed from the waist.

235   Creole then went to the bass fiddle and a lean, very bright-skinned brown man jumped up on the bandstand and picked up his horn. So there they were, and the atmosphere on the bandstand and in the room began to change and tighten. Someone stepped up to the microphone and announced them. Then there were all kinds of murmurs. Some people at the bar shushed others. The waitress ran around, frantically getting in the last orders, guys and chicks got closer to each other, and the lights on the bandstand, on the quartet, turned to a kind of indigo. Then they all looked different there. Creole looked about him for the last time, as though he were making certain that all his chickens were in the coop, and then he—jumped and struck the fiddle. And there they were.

All I know about music is that not many people ever really hear it. And even then, on the rare occasions when something opens within, and the music enters, what we mainly hear, or hear corroborated, are personal, private, vanishing evocations. But the man who creates the music is hearing something else, is dealing with the roar rising from the void and imposing order on it as it hits the air. What is evoked in him, then, is of another order, more terrible because it has no words, and triumphant, too, for that same reason. And his triumph, when he triumphs, is ours. I just watched Sonny's face. His face was troubled, he was working hard, but he wasn't with it. And I had the feeling that, in a way, everyone on the bandstand was waiting for him, both waiting for him and pushing him along. But as I began to watch Creole, I realized that it was Creole who held them all back. He had them on a short rein. Up there, keeping the beat with his whole body, wailing on the fiddle, with his eyes half closed, he was listening to everything, but he was listening to Sonny. He was having a dialogue with Sonny. He wanted Sonny to leave the shoreline and strike out for the deep water. He was Sonny's witness that deep water and drowning were not the same thing—he had been there, and he knew. And he wanted Sonny to know. He was waiting for Sonny to do the things on the keys which would let Creole know that Sonny was in the water.

And, while Creole listened, Sonny moved, deep within, exactly like someone in torment. I had never before thought of how awful the relationship must be between the musician and his instrument. He has to fill it, this instrument, with the breath of life, his own. He has to make it do what he wants it to do. And a piano is just a piano. It's made out of so much wood and wires and little hammers and big ones, and ivory. While there's only so much you can do with it, the only way to find this out is to try; to try and make it do everything.

And Sonny hadn't been near a piano for over a year. And he wasn't on much better terms with his life, not the life that stretched before him now. He and the piano stammered, started one way, got scared, stopped; started another way, panicked, marked time, started again; then seemed to have found a direction, panicked again, got stuck. And the face I saw on Sonny I'd never seen before. Everything had been burned out of it, and, at the same time, things usually hidden were being burned in, by the fire and fury of the battle which was occurring in him up there.

Yet, watching Creole's face as they neared the end of the first set, I had the feeling that something had happened, something I hadn't heard. Then they finished, there was scattered applause, and then, without an instant's warning, Creole started into something else, it was almost sardonic, it was *Am I Blue.* And, as though he commanded, Sonny began to play. Something began to happen. And Creole let out the reins. The dry, low, black man said something awful on the drums, Creole answered, and the drums talked back. Then the horn insisted, sweet and high, slightly detached perhaps, and Creole listened, commenting now and then, dry, and driving, beautiful and calm and old. Then they all came together again, and Sonny was part of the family again. I could tell this from his face. He seemed to have found, right there beneath his fingers, a damn brand-new piano. It seemed that he couldn't get over it. Then, for awhile, just being happy with Sonny, they seemed to be agreeing with him that brand-new pianos certainly were a gas.

240   Then Creole stepped forward to remind them that what they were playing was the blues. He hit something in all of them, he hit something in me, myself, and the music tightened and deepened, apprehension began to beat the air. Creole began to tell us what the blues were all about. They were not about anything very new. He and his boys up there were keeping it new, at the risk of ruin, destruction, madness, and death, in order to find new ways to make us listen. For, while the tale of how we suffer, and how we are delighted, and how we may triumph is never new, it always must be heard. There isn't any other tale to tell, it's the only light we've got in all this darkness.

And this tale, according to that face, that body, those strong hands on those strings, has another aspect in every country, and a new depth in every generation. Listen, Creole seemed to be saying, listen. Now these are Sonny's blues. He made the little black man on the drums know it, and the bright, brown man on the horn. Creole wasn't trying any longer to get Sonny in the water. He was wishing him Godspeed. Then he stepped back, very slowly, filling the air with the immense suggestion that Sonny speak for himself.

Then they all gathered around Sonny and Sonny played. Every now and again one of them seemed to say, amen. Sonny's fingers filled the air with life, his life. But that life contained so many others. And Sonny went all the way back, he really began with the spare, flat statement of the opening phrase of the song. Then he began to make it his. It was very beautiful because it wasn't hurried and it was no longer a lament. I seemed to hear with what burning he had made it his, with what burning we had yet to make it ours, how we could cease lamenting. Freedom lurked around us and I understood, at last, that he could help us to be free if we would listen, that he would never be free until we did. Yet, there was no battle in his face now. I heard what he had gone through, and would continue to go through until he came to rest in earth. He had made it his: that long line, of which we knew only Mama and Daddy. And he was giving it back, as everything must be given back, so that, passing through death, it can live forever. I saw my mother's face again, and felt, for the first time, how the stones of the road she had walked on must have bruised her feet. I saw the moonlit road where my father's brother died. And it brought something else back to me, and carried me past it. I saw my little girl again and felt Isabel's tears again, and I felt my own tears begin to rise. And I was yet aware that this was only a moment, that the world waited outside, as hungry as a tiger, and that trouble stretched above us, longer than the sky.

Then it was over. Creole and Sonny let out their breath, both soaking wet, and grinning. There was a lot of applause and some of it was real. In the dark, the girl came by and I asked her to take drinks to the bandstand. There was a long pause, while they talked up there in the indigo light and after awhile I saw the girl put a Scotch and milk on top of the piano for Sonny. He didn't seem to notice it, but just before they started playing again, he sipped from it and looked toward me, and nodded. Then he put it back on top of the piano. For me, then, as they began to play again, it glowed and shook above my brother's head like the very cup of trembling.

 ## MAKING CONNECTIONS

1. Who is the narrator? What kind of relationship does he have with Sonny?
2. How does the tale of the narrator's father and his father's brother shed light on this story?
3. Why do you think the narrator writes to Sonny after his daughter, Grace, dies? What does he mean by "My trouble made his real"?
4. Describe the relationship between Sonny and his music. Why does it mean so much to him?
5. The relationship between Sonny and his brother changes. What helps the narrator to understand Sonny better? Find passages in the story to indicate that.
6. In what way do you think "Sonny's Blues" is an appropriate title for this story?

 ## MAKING AN ARGUMENT

1. To what extent is darkness symbolic throughout the story? Interpret and write about the statement "All they knew were two darknesses, the darkness of their lives, which was now closing in on them, and the darkness of the movies, which had blinded them to that other darkness." Cite the text and quote other passages in the story for support.

2. Write an essay comparing the narration and the relationship of the brothers in "Sonny's Blues" with that in "The Red Convertible" (p. 236). In "Sonny's Blues" it is the older brother who narrates, but in the "Red Convertible" it is the younger brother. What difference does relative age make to each relationship and to the voice and tone of the narration? Cite the text of each story for support.

JOHN CHEEVER [1912–1982]

John Cheever was born in Quincy, Massachusetts, and published his first story, "Expelled," in the New Republic *shortly after he was expelled from prep school at the age of eighteen. Instead of attending college, Cheever moved to New York City and devoted himself to writing. His stories, which often appeared in the* New Yorker, *gradually earned him a reputation as a master short-story writer, and, as they were usually set among upper-middle-class subur-banites, led one critic to dub Cheever the "Chekhov of the Suburbs." Though his reputation rests mainly on his short stories, Cheever published a number of well-received novels, most notably* The Wapshot Scandal *(1965), which won the National Book Award. His best-selling* Stories of John Cheever *was awarded the Pulitzer Prize in 1978.*

REUNION   [1962]

The last time I saw my father was in Grand Central Station. I was going from my grandmother's in the Adirondacks to a cottage on the Cape that my mother had rented,—and I wrote my father that I would be in New York between trains for an hour and a half, and asked if we could have lunch together. His secretary wrote to say that he would meet me at the information booth at noon, and at twelve o'clock sharp I saw him coming through the crowd. He was a stranger to me—my mother divorced him three years ago and I hadn't been with him since—but as soon as I saw him I felt that he was my father, my flesh and blood, my future and my doom. I knew that when I was grown I would be something like him; I would have to plan my campaigns within his limitations. He was a big, good-looking man, and I was terribly happy to see him again. He struck me on the back and shook my hand. "Hi, Charlie," he said. "Hi, boy. I'd like to take you up to my club, but it's in the Sixties, and if you have to catch an early train I guess we'd better get something to eat around here." He put his arm around me, and I smelled my father the way my mother sniffs a rose. It was a rich compound of whiskey, after-shave lotion, shoe polish, woolens, and the rankness of a mature male. I hoped that someone would see us together. I wished that we could be photographed. I wanted some record of our having been together.

We went out of the station and up a side street to a restaurant. It was still early, and the place was empty. The bartender was quarreling with a delivery boy, and there was one very old waiter in a red coat down by the kitchen door. We sat down, and my father hailed the waiter in a loud voice. "*Kellner!*" he shouted. "*Garçon!*

Cameriere! You!" His boisterousness in the empty restaurant seemed out of place. "Could we have a little service here!" he shouted. "Chop-chop." Then he clapped his hands. This caught the waiter's attention, and he shuffled over to our table.

"Were you clapping your hands at me?" he asked.

"Calm down, calm down, *sommelier,*" my father said. "If it isn't too much to ask of you—if it wouldn't be too much above and beyond the call of duty, we would like a couple of Beefeater Gibsons."

5   "I don't like to be clapped at," the waiter said.

"I should have brought my whistle," my father said. "I have a whistle that is audible only to the ears of old waiters. Now, take out your little pad and your little pencil and see if you can get this straight: two Beefeater Gibsons. Repeat after me: two Beefeater Gibsons."

"I think you'd better go somewhere else," the waiter said quietly.

"That," said my father, "is one of the most brilliant suggestions I have ever heard. Come on, Charlie, let's get the hell out of here."

I followed my father out of that restaurant into another. He was not so boisterous this time. Our drinks came, and he cross-questioned me about the baseball season. He then struck the edge of his empty glass with his knife and began shouting again. "Garcon! Kellner! Cameriere! *You!* Could we trouble you to bring us two more of the same."

10   "How old is the boy?" the waiter asked.

"That," my father said, "is none of your God-damned business."

"I'm sorry, sir," the waiter said, "but I won't serve the boy another drink."

"Well, I have some news for you," my father said. "I have some very interesting news for you. This doesn't happen to be the only restaurant in New York. They've opened another on the corner. Come on, Charlie."

He paid the bill, and I followed him out of that restaurant into another. Here the waiters wore pink jackets like hunting coats and there was a lot of horse tack on the walls. We sat down, and my father began to shout again. "Master of the hounds! Tallyhoo and all that sort of thing. We'd like a little something in the way of a stirrup cup. Namely, two Bibson Geefeaters."

15   "Two Bibson Geefeaters?" the waiter asked, smiling.

"You know damned well what I want," my father said angrily. "I want two Beefeater Gibsons, and make it snappy. Things have changed in jolly old England. So my friend the duke tells me. Let's see what England can produce in the way of a cocktail."

"This isn't England," the waiter said.

"Don't argue with me," my father said. "Just do as you're told."

"I just thought you might like to know where you are," the waiter said.

20   "If there is one thing I cannot tolerate," my father said, "it is an impudent domestic. Come on, Charlie."

The fourth place we went to was Italian. *"Buon giorno,"* my father said. *"Per favore, possiamo avere due cocktail americani, forti, forti. Molto gin, poco vermut."*

"I don't understand Italian," the waiter said.

"Oh, come off it," my father said. "You understand Italian, and you know damned well you do. *Vogliamo due cocktail americani. Subito.*

The waiter left us and spoke with the captain, who came over to our table and said, "I'm sorry, sir, but this table is reserved."

25   "All right," my father said. "Get us another table."

"All the tables are reserved," the captain said.

"I get it," my father said, "You don't desire our patronage. Is that it? Well, the hell with you. *Vada all'inferno.* Let's go, Charlie."

"I have to get my train," I said.

"I'm sorry, sonny," my father said. "I'm terribly sorry." He put his arm around me and pressed me against him. "I'll walk you back to the station. If there had only been time to go up to my club."

30   "That's all right, Daddy," I said.

"I'll get you a paper," he said. "I'll get you a paper to read on the train."

Then he went up to a newsstand and said, "Kind sir, will you be good enough to favor me with one of your God-damned, no-good, ten-cent afternoon papers?" The clerk turned away from him and stared at a magazine cover. "Is it asking too much, kind sir," my father said, "is it asking too much for you to sell me one of your disgusting specimens of yellow journalism?"

"I have to go, Daddy," I said. "It's late."

"Now, just wait a second, sonny," he said. "Just wait a second. I want to get a rise out of this chap."

35   "Goodbye, Daddy," I said, and I went down the stairs and got my train, and that was the last time I saw my father.

MAKING CONNECTIONS

1. Characterize the father and his behavior. What do you think is motivating him to behave as he does? Do you think the son should have said something to him about his behavior? Explain.

2. Were you surprised by the last line of the story? Do you think that he will ever want to see his father again? Would you in this situation?

MAKING AN ARGUMENT

1. Narrated by the son in the past tense, "Reunion" begins with a brief descriptive paragraph, but most of what follows is heated dialogue in a series of quick encounters with waiters—and a quick good-bye. To what extent does this style adequately convey the characterization of the father and the son—their relationship—and the conflict in the story? What is not said by the narrator? Do you think more should have been said? Write about the effectiveness of the writing style in this story. Cite the text of the story for support.

LOUISE ERDRICH [B. 1954]

The daughter of a Chippewa Indian mother and a German-American father, Louise Erdrich was raised in Wahpeton, North Dakota, near the Turtle Mountain Reservation. Her parents both worked in the Bureau of Indian Affairs boarding school. From an early age, she was encouraged to write stories (she says: "My father used to give me a nickel for every story I wrote"). Following graduation from Dartmouth College in 1976, she earned an M.A. from Johns Hopkins University in 1979. Her works include Love Medicine *(1984, and an expanded edition in 1993);* The Beet Queen *(1986);* Tracks *(1988);* The Crown of Columbus *(1991), which she coauthored with her late husband, Michael Dorris;* The Bingo Palace *(1994);* The Antelope Wife *(1998); and* The Master Butchers Singing Club *(2003). Her most recent novel,* The Painted Drum, *was published in 2005.*

THE RED CONVERTIBLE   [1984]

Lyman Lamartine

I was the first one to drive a convertible on my reservation. And of course it was red, a red Olds. I owned that car along with my brother Henry Junior. We owned it together until his boots filled with water on a windy night and he bought out my share. Now Henry owns the whole car, and his youngest brother Lyman (that's myself), Lyman walks everywhere he goes.

How did I earn enough money to buy my share in the first place? My own talent was I could always make money. I had a touch for it, unusual in a Chippewa. From the first I was different that way, and everyone recognized it. I was the only kid they let in the American Legion Hall to shine shoes, for example, and one Christmas I sold spiritual bouquets for the mission door to door. The nuns let me keep a percentage. Once I started, it seemed the more money I made the easier the money came. Everyone encouraged it. When I was fifteen I got a job washing dishes at the Joliet Café, and that was where my first big break happened.

It wasn't long before I was promoted to busing tables, and then the order-order cook quit and I was hired to take her place. No sooner than you know it I was managing the Joliet. The rest is history. I went on managing. I soon became part owner, and of course there was no stopping me then. It wasn't long before the whole thing was mine.

After I'd owned the Joliet for one year, it blew over in the worst tornado ever seen around here. The whole operation was smashed to bits. A total loss. The fryalator was up in a tree, the grill torn in half like it was paper. I was only sixteen. I had it all in my mother's name, and I lost it quick, but before I lost it I had every one of my relatives, and their relatives, to dinner, and I also bought that red Olds I mentioned, along with Henry.

5   The first time we saw it! I'll tell you when we first saw it. We had gotten a ride up to Winnipeg, and both of us had money. Don't ask me why, because we never mentioned a car or anything, we just had all our money. Mine was cash, a big bankroll

from the Joliet's insurance. Henry had two checks—a week's extra pay for being laid off, and his regular check from the Jewel Bearing Plant.

We were walking down Portage anyway, seeing the sights, when we saw it. There it was, parked, large as life. Really as *if* it was alive. I thought of the word *repose,* because the car wasn't simply stopped, parked, or whatever. That car reposed, calm and gleaming, a FOR SALE sign in its left front window. Then, before we had thought it over at all, the car belonged to us and our pockets were empty. We had just enough money for gas back home.

We went places in that car, me and Henry. We took off driving all one whole summer. We started off toward the Little Knife River and Mandaree in Fort Berthold and then we found ourselves down in Wakpala somehow, and then suddenly we were over in Montana on the Rocky Boy, and yet the summer was not even half over. Some people hang on to details when they travel, but we didn't let them bother us and just lived our everyday lives here to there.

I do remember this one place with willows. I remember I laid under those trees and it was comfortable. So comfortable. The branches bent down all around me like a tent or a stable. And quiet, it was quiet, even though there was a powwow close enough so I could see it going on. The air was not too still, not too windy either. When the dust rises up and hangs in the air around the dancers like that, I feel good. Henry was asleep with his arms thrown wide. Later on, he woke up and we started driving again. We were somewhere in Montana, or maybe on the Blood Reserve—it could have been anywhere. Anyway it was where we met the girl.

All her hair was in buns around her ears, that's the first thing I noticed about her. She was posed alongside the road with her arm out, so we stopped. That girl was short, so short her lumber shirt looked comical on her, like a nightgown. She had jeans on and fancy moccasins and she carried a little suitcase.

10   "Hop on in," says Henry. So she climbs in between us.

"We'll take you home," I says. "Where do you live?"

"Chicken," she says.

"Where the hell's that?" I ask her.

"Alaska."

15   "Okay," says Henry, and we drive.

We got up there and never wanted to leave. The sun doesn't truly set there in summer, and the night is more of soft dusk. You might doze off, sometimes, but before you know it you're up again, like an animal in nature. You never feel like you have to sleep hard or put away the world. And things would grow up there. One day just dirt or moss, the next day flowers and long grass. The girl's name was Susy. Her family really took to us. They fed us and put us up. We had our own tent to live in by their house, and the kids would be in and out of there all day and night. They couldn't get over me and Henry being brothers, we looked so different. We told them we know we had the same mother, anyway.

One night Susy came in to visit us. We sat around in the tent talking of this and that. The season was changing. It was getting darker by that time, and the cold was even getting just a little mean. I told her it was time for us to go. She stood up on a chair.

"You never seen my hair," Susy said.

That was true. She was standing on a chair, but still, when she unclipped her buns the hair reached all the way to the ground. Our eyes opened. You couldn't tell how much hair she had when it was rolled up so neatly. Then my brother Henry did something funny. He went up to the chair and said, "Jump on my shoulders." So she did that, and her hair reached down past his waist, and he started twirling, this way and that, so her hair was flung out from side to side.

20   "I always wondered what it was like to have long pretty hair," Henry says. Well we laughed. It was a funny sight, the way he did it. The next morning we got up and took leave of those people.

On to greener pastures, as they say. It was down through Spokane and across Idaho then Montana and very soon we were racing the weather right along under the Canadian border through Columbus, Des Lacs, and then we were in Bottineau County and soon home. We'd made most of the trip, that summer, without putting up the car hood at all. We got home just in time, it turned out, for the army to remember Henry had signed up to join it.

I don't wonder that the army was so glad to get my brother that they turned him into a Marine. He was built like a brick outhouse anyway. We liked to tease him that they really wanted him for his Indian nose. He had a nose big and sharp as a hatchet, like the nose on Red Tomahawk, the Indian who killed Sitting Bull, whose profile is on signs all along the North Dakota highways. Henry went off to training camp, came home once during Christmas, then the next thing you know we got an overseas letter from him. It was 1970, and he said he was stationed up in the northern hill country. Whereabouts I did not know. He wasn't such a hot letter writer, and only got off two before the enemy caught him. I could never keep it straight, which direction those good Vietnam soldiers were from.

I wrote him back several times, even though I didn't know if those letters would get through. I kept him informed all about the car. Most of the time I had it up on blocks in the yard or half taken apart, because that long trip did a hard job on it under the hood.

I always had good luck with numbers, and never worried about the draft myself. I never even had to think about what my number was. But Henry was never lucky in the same way as me. It was at least three years before Henry came home. By then I guess the whole war was solved in the government's mind, but for him it would keep on going. In those years I'd put his car into almost perfect shape. I always thought of it as his car while he was gone, even though when he left he said, "Now it's yours," and threw me his key.

25   "Thanks for the extra key," I'd said. "I'll put it up in your drawer just in case I need it." He laughed.

When he came home, though, Henry was very different, and I'll say this: the change was no good. You could hardly expect him to change for the better, I know. But he was quiet, so quiet, and never comfortable sitting still anywhere but always up and moving around. I thought back to times we'd sat still for whole afternoons, never moving a muscle, just shifting our weight along the ground, talking to whoever sat with us, watching things. He'd always had a joke, then, too, and now you couldn't get him to laugh, or when he did it was more the sound of a man choking, a sound that stopped up the throats of other people around him. They got to leaving him alone most of the time, and I didn't blame them. It was a fact: Henry was jumpy and mean.

I'd bought a color TV set for my mom and the rest of us while Henry was away. Money still came very easy. I was sorry I'd ever bought it though, because of Henry. I was also sorry I'd bought color, because with black-and-white pictures seem older and farther away. But what are you going to do? He sat in front of it, watching it, and that was the only time he was completely still. But it was the kind of stillness that you see in a rabbit when it freezes and before it will bolt. He was not easy. He sat in his chair gripping the armrests with all his might, as if the chair itself was moving at a high speed and if he let go at all he would rocket forward and maybe crash right through the set.

Once I was in the room watching TV with Henry and I heard his teeth click at something. I looked over, and he'd bitten through his lip. Blood was going down his chin. I tell you right then I wanted to smash that tube to pieces. I went over to it but Henry must have known what I was up to. He rushed from his chair and shoved me out of the way, against the wall. I told myself he didn't know what he was doing.

My mom came in, turned the set off real quiet, and told us she had made something for supper. So we went and sat down. There was still blood going down Henry's chin, but he didn't notice it and no one said anything, even though every time he took a bite of his bread his blood fell onto it until he was eating his own blood mixed in with the food.

30   While Henry was not around we talked about what was going to happen to him. There were no Indian doctors on the reservation, and my mom couldn't come around to trusting the old man, Moses Pillager, because he courted her long ago and was jealous of her husbands. He might take revenge through her son. We were afraid that if we brought Henry to a regular hospital they would keep him.

"They don't fix them in those places," Mom said; "they just give them drugs."

"We wouldn't get him there in the first place," I agree, "so let's just forget about it." Then I thought about the car.

Henry had not even looked at the car since he'd gotten home, though like I said, it was in tip-top condition and ready to drive. I thought the car might bring the old Henry back somehow. So I bided my time and waited for my chance to interest him in the vehicle.

35   One night Henry was off somewhere. I took myself a hammer. I went out to that car and I did a number on its underside. Whacked it up. Bent the tail pipe double. Ripped the muffler loose. By the time I was done with the car it looked worse than any typical Indian car that has been driven all its life on reservation roads, which they always say are like government promises—full of holes. It just about hurt me, I'll tell you that! I threw dirt in the carburetor and I ripped all the electric tape off the seats. I made it look just as beat up as I could. Then I sat back and waited for Henry to find it.

Still, it took him over a month. That was all right, because it was just getting warm enough, not melting, but warm enough to work outside.

"Lyman," he says, walking in one day, "that red car looks like shit."

"Well it's old," I says. "You got to expect that."

"No way!" says Henry. "That car's a classic! But you went and ran the piss right out of it, Lyman, and you know it don't deserve that. I kept that car in A-one shape. You don't remember. You're too young. But when I left, that car was running like a watch. Now I don't even know if I can get it to start again, let alone get it anywhere near its old condition."

40   "Well you try," I said, like I was getting mad, "but I say it's a piece of junk."

Then I walked out before he could realize I knew he'd strung together more than six words at once.

After that I thought he'd freeze himself to death working on that car. He was out there all day, and at night he rigged up a little lamp, ran a cord out the window, and had himself some light to see by while he worked. He was better than he had been before, but that's still not saying much. It was easier for him to do the things the rest of us did. He ate more slowly and didn't jump up and down during the meal to get this or that or look out the window. I put my hand in the back of the TV set, I admit, and fiddled around with it good, so that it was almost impossible now to get a clear picture. He didn't look at it very often anyway. He was always out with that car or going off to get parts for it. By the time it was really melting outside, he had it fixed.

I had been feeling down in the dumps about Henry around this time. We had always been together before. Henry and Lyman. But he was such a loner now that I didn't know how to take it. So I jumped at the chance one day when Henry seemed friendly. It's not that he smiled or anything. He just said, "Let's take that old shitbox for a spin." Just the way he said it made me think he could be coming around.

We went out to the car. It was spring. The sun was shining very bright. My only sister, Bonita, who was just eleven years old, came out and made us stand together for a picture. Henry leaned his elbow on the red car's windshield, and he took his other arm and put it over my shoulder, very carefully, as though it was heavy for him to lift and he didn't want to bring the weight down all at once.

45   "Smile," Bonita said, and he did.

That picture. I never look at it anymore. A few months ago, I don't know why, I got his picture out and tacked it on the wall. I felt good about Henry at the time, close to him. I felt good having his picture on the wall, until one night when I was looking at television. I was a little drunk and stoned. I looked up at the wall and Henry was staring at me. I don't know what it was, but his smile had changed, or maybe it was gone. All I know is I couldn't stay in the same room with that picture. I was shaking. I got up, closed the door, and went into the kitchen. A little later my friend Ray came over and we both went back into that room. We put the picture in a brown bag, folded the bag over and over tightly, then put it way back in a closet.

I still see that picture now, as if it tugs at me, whenever I pass that closet door. The picture is very clear in my mind. It was so sunny that day Henry had to squint against the glare. Or maybe the camera Bonita held flashed like a mirror, blinding him, before she snapped the picture. My face is right out in the sun, big and round. But he might have drawn back, because the shadows on his face are deep as holes. There are two shadows curved like little hooks around the ends of his smile, as if to frame it and try to keep it there—that one, first smile that looked like it might have hurt his face. He has his field jacket on and the worn-in clothes he'd come back in and kept wearing ever since. After Bonita took the picture, she went into the house and we got into the car. There was a full cooler in the trunk. We started off, east, toward Pembina and the Red River because Henry said he wanted to see the high water.

The trip over there was beautiful. When everything starts changing, drying up, clearing off, you feel like your whole life is starting. Henry felt it, too. The top was down and the car hummed like a top. He'd really put it back in shape, even the tape on the seats was very carefully put down and glued back in layers. It's not that he smiled again or even joked, but his face looked to me as if it was clear, more peaceful. It looked as though he wasn't thinking of anything in particular except the bare fields and windbreaks and houses we were passing.

The river was high and full of winter trash when we got there. The sun was still out, but it was colder by the river. There were still little clumps of dirty snow here and there on the banks. The water hadn't gone over the banks yet, but it would, you could tell. It was just at its limit, hard swollen, glossy like an old gray scar. We made ourselves a fire, and we sat down and watched the current go. As I watched it I felt something squeezing inside me and tightening and trying to let go all at the same time. I knew I was not just feeling it myself; I knew I was feeling what Henry was going through at that moment. Except that I couldn't stand it, the closing and opening. I jumped to my feet. I took Henry by the shoulders and I started shaking him. "Wake up," I says, "wake up, wake up, wake up!" I didn't know what had come over me. I sat down beside him again.

50   His face was totally white and hard. Then it broke, like stones break all of a sudden when water boils up inside them.

"I know it," he says. "I know it. I can't help it. It's no use."

We start talking. He said he knew what I'd done with the car. It was obvious it had been whacked out of shape and not just neglected. He said he wanted to give the car to me for good now, it was no use. He said he'd fixed it just to give it back and I should take it.

"No way," I says. "I don't want it."

"That's okay," he says, "you take it."

55   "I don't want it, though," I says back to him, and then to emphasize, just to emphasize, you understand, I touch his shoulder. He slaps my hand off.

"Take that car," he says.

"No," I say. "Make me," I say, and then he grabs my jacket and rips the arm loose. That jacket is a class act, suede with tags and zippers. I push Henry backwards, off the log. He jumps up and bowls me over. We go down in a clinch and come up swinging hard, for all we're worth, with our fists. He socks my jaw so hard I feel like it swings loose. Then I'm at his rib cage and land a good one under his chin so his head snaps back. He's dazzled. He looks at me and I look at him and then his eyes are full of tears and blood and at first I think he's crying. But no, he's laughing. "Ha! Ha!" he says. "Ha! Ha! Take good care of it."

"Okay," I says. "Okay, no problem. Ha! Ha!"

I can't help it, and I start laughing, too. My face feels fat and strange, and after a while I get a beer from the cooler in the trunk, and when I hand it to Henry he takes his shirt and wipes my germs off. "Hoof and mouth disease," he says. For some reason this cracks me up, and so we're really laughing for a while, and then we drink all the rest of the beers one by one and throw them in the river and see how far, how fast, the current takes them before they fill up and sink.

60   "You want to go on back?" I ask after a while. "Maybe we could snag a couple nice Kashpaw girls."

He says nothing. But I can tell his mood is turning again.

"They're all crazy, the girls up here, every damn one of them."

"You're crazy too," I say, to jolly him up. "Crazy Lamartine boys!"

He looks as though he will take this wrong at first. His face twists, then clears. And he jumps up on his feet. "That's right!" he says. "Crazier 'n hell. Crazy Indians!"

65   I think it's the old Henry again. He throws off his jacket and starts springing his legs up from the knees like a fancy dancer. He's doing something between a grass dance a bunny hop, no kind of dance I ever saw before, but neither has anyone else on all this green growing earth. He's wild. He wants to pitch whoopee! He's up and at me and all over. All this time I'm laughing so hard, so hard my belly is getting tied up in a knot.

"Got to cool me off!" he shouts all of a sudden. Then he runs over to the river and jumps in.

There's boards and other things in the current. It's so high. No sound comes from the river after the splash he makes, so I run right over. I look around. It's getting dark. I see he's halfway across the water already, and I know he didn't swim there but the current took him. It's far. I hear his voice, though, very clearly across it.

"My boots are filling," he says.

He says this in a normal voice, like he just noticed and he doesn't know what to think of it. Then he's gone. A branch comes by. Another branch. And I go in.

70   By the time I get out of the river, off the snag I pulled myself onto, the sun is down. I walk back to the car, turn on the high beams, and drive it up the bank. I put it in first gear and then I take my foot off the clutch. I get out, close the door, and watch it plow softly into the water. The headlights reach in as they go down, searching, still lighted even after the water swirls over the back end. I wait. The wires short out. It is all finally dark. And then there is only the water, the sound of it going and running and going and running and running.

❦ MAKING CONNECTIONS

1. In the first paragraph the narrator, Lyman, says of the red convertible: "We owned it together until his boots filled with water." Were you puzzled by this comment? In what way does it make sense at the end of the story, literally and metaphorically?
2. Why do you suppose Lyman refers to himself in the third person at the end of the first paragraph?
3. What do you think happened to Henry in Vietnam that changed him?
4. Why does Lyman push the car into the water after Henry?

❦ MAKING AN ARGUMENT

1. To what extent is the red Oldsmobile a central symbol in the story? In what way do the changes the car goes through seem to reflect the changes in Lyman and Henry and their relationship? Write about symbolism in this story. Cite the text of the story to support your view.

2. Identify a common thread and write about sibling relationships as exemplified by this story and other works in the text [e.g., "Sonny's Blues" (p. 211), "How to Watch Your Brother Die" (p. 273), or *The Glass Menagerie* (p. 284)]. Consider narration, setting, characterization, and conflict as elements to be addressed. Cite the text of each work for support.

LINDA CHING SLEDGE [B. 1944]

Born in Hawaii, Linda Ching Sledge holds a B.A. from the University of California at Berkeley and a Ph.D. in English Literature from the City University of New York. She has written two award-winning historical novels, Empire of Heaven *(Bantam, 1990) and* A Map of Paradise *(Bantam, 1997) as well as* Shivering Babe, Victorious Lord *(Eerdmans, 1981), a literary history. She is currently Professor of English at SUNY Westchester Community College.*

The story below is taken from A Map of Paradise, *a historical novel set in nineteenth-century Hawaii, which depicts the struggle of emigrants from south China as they lay claim to their new island home. In this episode, a Chinese father clashes with his son over the boy's desperate longing to abandon the family's lucrative construction business to enter an all-white mission school. The domestic crisis unfolds against the background of a rapidly changing Hawaii torn by forces of Hawaiian court politics, American sugar interests, Chinese labor, and rival immigrant clans.*

THE ROAD

[1997]

The hurricane proved a boon for Pao An. His was not the kind of inventory that could be spoiled by wind or rain, and now everyone needed hammers and wire nails, lumber and coral stone to rebuild. Roads, dikes, dams, fishponds also needed repairing, thus prompting the king to auction off contracts for a massive public works scheme across Oahu. The grass shacks and wooden tenements built in Queen Emma's reign[1] were proving woefully inadequate to house the foreigners flocking to Hawaii's shores; and King Kalakaua, having already depleted his treasury in the building of his brick and iron frame palace, intended to do still more to reshape Honolulu into the commercial center of the islands. His next plan was to construct a road encircling the island so that a man might go from Waianae Beach to Honolulu in less than half a day. With the cost of construction soaring and pitting him against

---

[1]**Queen Emma (reigned 1856–1863) and King David Kalakaua (1874–1891)** two popular native rulers of the Kingdom of Hawaii. Kalakaua was the second-to-the-last monarch of Hawaii before its annexation by the United States in 1898.

a reluctant legislature, Kalakaua had turned to Claus Spreckels[2] to bail him out of his gambling debts.

By skillfully underbidding his rivals, Pao An was granted a lucrative contract for the building of a section of the road and promptly hired a crew of Chinamen and *kanakas*[3] to dig the windward end. With his adopted son Lincoln as surveyor and a road crew led by three Tang men[4] who had blasted tunnels through the Sierras for the railroad, Pao An began by reducing the lava cliffs to rubble, then leveling the roadbed with drag sledges pulled by oxen. On the bluffs, the soil was porous and ashy, the residue of a long-dormant volcano called Kaimana-hila, or Diamond Hill, for the false hopes sparked decades before by crystalline fragments that occasionally winked in the rock. The grading was as tedious as dredging the heavy, waterlogged peat of the deltas of China or California by hand. Although Pao An fell easily into the familiar task of moving earth, he could no longer discount the changes that age and toil had wrought on the powerful body that had once been his pride; his broad back was beginning to bend, and after a day of hauling rock his ribs, knees, and shoulders had pains that sleep could not cure.

Yet despite the cost to his body, moving rock was finally earning Pao An the prosperity for which he had labored so long. Squinting into the harsh light from under the brim of his conical straw hat, he saw the distant shape of Maui across the channel; behind him rose Kaimana-hila blanketed by clouds. Generations of Chens in On Ting[5] village had spent their lives tilling their few square miles of Delta earth before laying their bones there. Yet he, an outcast son of the village, had walked from the southern tip of the empire to the very outskirts of Peking. He, the poorest boy in On Ting, was now turning the red earth of a land his kin knew only in talk story, the place they called *Fusan,* the Blessed Isles. Given a chance, Pao An thought proudly, even he, the humblest of Tang men, might accomplish feats worthy of an emperor. In its own way, the building of this road was as grandiose a project as the wall the first Chin emperor had made to safeguard his empire from northern invaders.

One day, his vendors would travel this road from his lumberyards to small fishing villages on the coast to bring tools and lumber to any man who wanted a store or restaurant or cottage of his own. By then, roads would crisscross the island and buildings made from the Chens' stone and lumber would dot the horizon. He envisioned an Oahu furnished with dwellings to suit every purpose: one-story plantation cottages stuck side by side on stilts so that workers need not sleep like animals penned in a barn but live decently with wives and children and a vegetable garden of their own, dwellings made from clapboard or adobe and thatch like those he had seen along the levees in California, stately edifices of lava stone where bankers and merchants came to trade.

[2]**Claus Spreckels** California sugar magnate who controlled sugar manufacturing in the islands and had the ear of King Kalakaua.   [3]**kanaka** native term for people of Hawaiian ancestry.
[4]**Tang men** Chinese immigrants from southern China (Guangdong Province) call themselves "people of Tang" after the Tang dynasty (A.D. 618–907) in which the South achieved particular distinction.   [5]**On Ting village** a village in the Pearl River Delta in Guangdong Province, the region where nineteenth-century immigrants to Hawaii and California came from.

5   "Some day," he told Lincoln, gesturing at imaginary roads and canals and dwellings as if he were presenting the boy a kingdom, "this business will be yours. Something for you and your sons."

In truth, Lincoln didn't want what his father proffered. At least, not this way. He revered the man who had taken him in, but he hated reducing himself to a mindless thing of sinew and bone. He hated the mud and the sweat and the agony of pitting himself against the relentless drift of earth and sea. The summer before, he had steeped himself in the writings of Emerson, Wordsworth, and Rousseau and come away convinced that by meditation, one could cross over at will from the real world into a veritable paradise of the mind. Escape from the drudgery of each day came as easily as thought. He had discovered that any rhythmical activity performed for prolonged periods—the swinging of a pickax, the steady contemplation of the swell of the waves—would create answering interior rhythms that would send his mind soaring above his aching body. In those moments of "transcendings," Lincoln neither heard the cacophony of animals and men nor felt the soreness in his muscles nor remembered his despair.

The Widow had won a contract too, a lucrative franchise to supply the workers' canteen, a natural extension of her fish and vegetable markets. Because her provisions were abundant and cheap, she was soon supplying food to road gangs all over the island. For an extra fee, a laborer might buy a packet of opium, which the Widow's vendors, all brothers of the *tong*,[6] hid inside covered baskets of rice. Pao An had forbidden opium on the job; even so, the Widow managed to do a thriving clandestine business in the drug. The day was coming, she foresaw, when the bankrupt kingdom would reissue the lucrative opium license and assess taxes on the smoking of dirt as other kings had done before. Having heard that the king's advisers were pressing Kalakaua to reintroduce the opium license, the Widow was spending a fortune on bribes. When the license was issued, she would be ready for trade.

A week after the crew broke ground, the Widow ordered her driver to take her in an ancient rig to various construction sites to oversee the midday distribution of food. She came dressed in a shiny coat of embroidered black satin and a black Buddhist headband encrusted with seed pearls, making a great show of scolding her workers for not being liberal enough with portions of food.

Pao An saw her coming from the hillock where he was helping Lincoln mark off the section of land for the next day's blasting. His immediate response was to throw her off the site. Yet one glimpse of the Widow fanning herself in the rig while her menservants scurried like puppies to do her bidding brought back a disturbing recollection. He remembered her at their first meeting, a girl of fourteen borne aloft on her wedding palanquin and he a stone-stupid youth teasing the bride on her way along the levee road. When she had peeked fearfully out of her covered palanquin and raised her veil to look at him, he had been struck dumb by her beauty and felt for the first time the meanness of his estate. He was a paddy boy too poor and dirty

---

[6]**tong** a club or society of immigrants whose activities ranged from financing illegal operations such as gambling or opium to charitable operations for indigents.

to touch the hem of her garment and as much an ox as the one he drove through the mud. The realization that he was still mucking about in mud made him ashamed. Rather than face her, he grabbed up his pickax and shovel and headed up the road toward the sea.

10   The Widow, however, had come to waylay someone else. For some time, she had been gathering reports on Lincoln who inspected the food baskets and calculated the invoices from her cooks and suppliers. Her overseers had been grumbling about the scrupulousness of his tallying. Now she watched the tall, rawboned youth oversee the apportioning of food; he had not yet lost the clumsiness of boyhood and was covered with red dirt as dry as powder.

"You, boy," the Widow called. "Come here."

Lincoln sauntered over, preparing himself for a fight. The Widow had her driver pull into the shade of a *hala* tree, the only one in that barren section of rocky ground. "You like crawling through the dirt like a gecko in this heat?" the Widow asked, fanning herself as she reclined under the canopy of her buggy. "Give me a stool in a Chinatown shop any day." She was rewarded by Lincoln's rueful smile. "This work is fit only for *gu li,* " she said vehemently. "You are not a 'rough man.' Why do you stay?"

"My father needs me," Lincoln replied with what courtesy he could muster. He wondered why others thought this small woman with her pretentious city accent so formidable. Still, the Widow was sensible enough to divine his dislike of dirt and stone and his unease among the rough, crude men. For he did indeed miss the order of the shop, the clean floors and polished wooden countertops, the logic of commerce and inventory and the smooth abacus beads under his fingers.

"How is your father going to pay you?" She prodded, "In Kalakaua dollars?"[7] She laughed at her own joke. The newly minted coins stamped with the king's head were considered worthless by the Chinese, who would not accept wages or trade goods in them. Claus Spreckels had beguiled the king into creating the new coinage as a means of skimming money off the treasury.

15   "My father's coins are as good as his word," Lincoln replied.

The Widow went on reprovingly, "Not your father by blood! You're more filial to this stranger than his own daughter!" Suddenly the Widow leaned over and said in a conspiratorial tone, "Quit this job and come to me! I could use a bookkeeper who speaks English and Hawaiian as well as you. And I pay in American money!"

"There are twenty Tang boys at the Fort Street Mission who can figure as well as I," Lincoln replied.

"Perhaps, but you are shrewd and my men fear you. So if you decide to do something better than smash stone for a living, come see me."

"I am already learning a trade."

20   "Pah! Crushing rock is not a trade for an educated man. And any apprenticeship can be bought off," the Widow retorted. "You're old enough to make your own way. How will you get a wife if you have no decent livelihood? And do not tell me

---

[7]**Kalakaua dollars** Hawaiian silver coinage minted in Kalakaua's reign, the source of much scandal and economic havoc.

you intend to muck about in mud, for you are not built along your father's lines. You would surely fail at his business!"

Lincoln shifted his feet self-consciously and looked down at the ground. The Widow was nosy and impertinent, yet she was putting into words the same doubts that had plagued him for months.

"I will pay you five hundred Yankee dollars a year to keep my company's books and oversee the food concessions." When his eyes widened at the princely sum, she continued with a smile, "Tell your father about my offer. See if he puts your interests above his own!"

"My place is with him," Lincoln affirmed.

Anger blazed up in her eyes. "*Aiya, I* see you are the consummate businessman," she snapped, "one who intends to set the pace of the bargaining. Well, every man has his price, and I mean to discover yours."

25   Lincoln left feeling soiled and guilty. The Widow had a way of reaching into the recesses of his mind and dragging out his secret fears.

"The Chens have no breeding, no appreciation for the scholarly mind. I tell you, they are wasting that boy's gifts," the Widow told the *tong* council, which was meeting that morning on one of their charitable schemes to impress the government. This time, they were selecting the most worthy youth for further study at a private high school. The training would be at their expense, for any youth who lifted himself up did the same for all Tang people in the islands. It was a shrewd investment too, for if the boy were a brother bound by oath to the *tong,* he would eventually be in a position to pay them back handsomely in the form of favors. "Even the *kanaka* teacher at the common school says Lin Kong should not be apprenticed. A scholar should use his brains, not his back."

The council brother with the smoothest tongue was delegated to convey the news to Pao An that Lincoln had been selected as that year's scholar. But the man had uttered no more than a few sentences before Pao An drove him out of his shop for interfering in matters that were not the *tong*'s concern.

In bed that night, Pao An raged at his wife. The man was undoubtedly sent by the Widow who was trying to entice the boy into her employ, for the *tong* emissary had implied that Pao An treated Lincoln too harshly. No man had done more for the boy than he! Didn't these fools know, moreover, that they were sowing the seeds of their own destruction by sending Tang boys to school with the *bak kuei?*[8] The day was coming when there would be no more brave Tang men laboring in earthworks or plantations or fishing boats up and down the coast of California or in the port cities of the Hawaiian kingdom. The builders and the dreamers would be gone. Soon they would all be talking in the strangled accents of the deceivers!

Back at the digging, Pao An saw that Lincoln had pushed the road ahead another mile along the mountain. Yet Pao An was short-tempered and rude to the boy, unable to praise. To mollify his father, Lincoln talked about the prospects the road

---

[8]**bak kuei** "white devil"; Chinese term for a Caucasian.

presented for cross-island trade, but Pao An snapped at him, saying that the road would never be completed if he could not stop chattering long enough to lift a spade. When the cook boys came with buckets of hot rice and tea, Pao An saw Lincoln take his bowl to eat rice with the men. The boy was angry with him. And angry at himself too, Pao An concluded ruefully, for pretending an enthusiasm for the work he did not feel. Had never felt.

30   They worked side by side in edgy silence. Lincoln's anger had burned itself off in the heat of the afternoon. Now memories of his father's past kindnesses returned to haunt him: he remembered drinking from his father's cup when they worked together on the farm in Antioch. Another time, his father had fed him from his own bowl during one lean season on the levees. The memories were as painful as a magistrate's bamboo on the frail flesh of an unfilial son.

"Where have you hidden the book?" Pao An asked Lincoln that night. He had returned to their tent after visiting the privy to find the coal oil lamp relit, the flame turned down low.

Lincoln's face fell, embarrassed for having been caught yet again. "Here," Lincoln said, holding out a well-thumbed copy of Edward Everett's orations from beneath his blanket as if it were an excrescence.

Outside the tent, the men were playing a noisy game of *fan-tan* around the fire. Pao An turned the small volume over in his big leathery hand. "What is in this book?"

"Grand phrases, big ideas," Lincoln muttered. "I don't always know what they mean but I like the sound."

35   "You would rather read than sleep, wouldn't you?" Pao An asked.

"I don't read while I am working," Lincoln said defensively.

"I know you don't," Pao An growled. "You work hard. You are the best man of all my crew."

Lincoln inclined his head. His father's praise was rare and therefore precious.

"You prefer books to anything, especially this . . . the rock, mud, noise, oxen . . . the *fan-tan* game. The road." The words were more statement than accusation

40   The lamp threw Pao An's craggy features into cruel relief—the corners of eyes and mouth dragged down by disappointment, the cheeks sagging from exhaustion and care. Seated on his cot, Lincoln raised a hand in mute resignation. He was convinced that his father was seething at having raised a boy to manhood only to have him scorn the legacy of sweat and tears constructed on his behalf.

"So, boy," Pao An said gruffly, throwing the book down upon the cot, "I am taking you off the job."

"Why?" Lincoln wailed, a frightened child again. "How have I failed you, father?"

"You have not failed me. I am the one to blame. I have taken away the thing you love."

"No!"

45   "Tomorrow you leave me. I will get another boy to take your apprenticeship. Go to Bethel Mission or Fort Street Mission or Mills Institute or wherever clever Tang boys go these days to turn themselves into scholars. But be forewarned. Take what you wish from them but believe nothing the *bak kuei* say."

"But you need me!" the boy insisted.

"No. Not now, not anymore." With a gesture of finality, Pao An reached over and turned the little metal knob that stopped the flow of coal oil. The flame instantly shrank and died.

The next day, after Lincoln had departed, Pao An composed a poem, the first he had made in Hawaii, for the urge to make poems had vanished with his domestic responsibilities. Now faced with the dissolution of his house, he felt words welling up like tears.

The son I have is not my own
Only a shadow, myself in miniature,
Hiding, always hiding.

50   I offer him the earth,
But he refuses, longing instead for the sky.
I ask nothing of him.

We went together, he and I,
Two warriors to tame a mountain.
Side by side, we thrust shovel and pike into the red rock.

I cannot begin to tell you
What it was that
Made him lay a trail toward the west.
I want a sword
To carve out the mountain before him.

An arrow to mark the distance
He must travel
Away from me.

MAKING CONNECTIONS

1. Discuss Pao An's poem at the end of the story. What does it mean? What do you think he is saying about the future of his relationship with his son?
2. Why does Pao An change his mind at the end of this story? Do you think it is natural for fathers to want sons to follow in their footsteps? Explain.
3. Compare this story with "For My Father" on page 278. If Lincoln were writing a poem about his relationship with his father, what might he write about?

MAKING AN ARGUMENT

1. There are a number of works in this text that address father-son relationships, but the narration in poems like "Those Winter Sundays" (p. 13), "My Papa's Waltz" (p. 281), and "Digging" (p. 270), and the story "Reunion" (p. 233) is from the son's view. The third-person narration of "The Road" shows us more of the father's view than these other pieces. Write about the impact of this shift in narrative perspective as it affects characterization and conflict in this story. Cite the texts of "The Road" and other works for support.

AMY TAN [B. 1952]

Amy Tan was born in Oakland, California, several years after her mother and father emigrated from China. Upon the deaths of her brother and father in 1967 and 1968, the family began a haphazard journey through Europe, before settling in Switzerland. For the next seven years, Tan attended five schools before graduating with honors from San Jose State University, where she later earned an M.A. in Linguistics. In 1989, The Joy Luck Club *(from which "Two Kinds" is taken) was published and, through word-of-mouth endorsements by independent booksellers, became a surprise best seller. Though Tan wrote the book as a collection of linked short stories, reviewers enthusiastically and erroneously referred to the book as an intricately woven "novel." It was nominated for the National Book Award and the National Book Critics Award and was adapted into a film for Hollywood Pictures in 1994 with Tan as a co-screenwriter.* The Kitchen God's Wife *was published in 1991, followed by* The Hundred Secret Senses *in 1995, and* The Bonesetter's Daughter *in 2001. Her short stories and essays have appeared in* The Atlantic, Harper's, *The* New Yorker, *and other publications. Her essay "Mother Tongue" (in this text on p. 142) was chosen for best American Essays 1991, and she was the guest editor for the 1999* Best American Short Stories. *Her latest book,* The Opposite of Fate: A Book of Musings, *was published in 2003.*

TWO KINDS [1989]

My mother believed you could be anything you wanted to be in America. You could open a restaurant. You could work for the government and get good retirement. You could buy a house with almost no money down. You could become rich. You could become instantly famous.

"Of course you can be prodigy, too," my mother told me when I was nine. "You can be best anything. What does Auntie Lindo know? Her daughter, she is only best tricky."

America was where all my mother's hopes lay. She had come here in 1949 after losing everything in China: her mother and father, her family home, her first husband, and two daughters, twin baby girls. But she never looked back with regret. There were so many ways for things to get better.

We didn't immediately pick the right kind of prodigy. At first my mother thought I could be a Chinese Shirley Temple. We'd watch Shirley's old movies on TV as though they were training films. My mother would poke my arm and say, "*Ni kan.*"—You watch. And I would see Shirley tapping her feet, or singing a sailor song, or pursing her lips into a very round O while saying "Oh, my goodness."

"*Ni kan,*" said my mother as Shirley's eyes flooded with tears. "You already know how. Don't need talent for crying!"

Soon after my mother got this idea about Shirley Temple, she took me to a beauty training school in the Mission district and put me in the hands of a student who could barely hold the scissors without shaking. Instead of getting big fat curls, I emerged with an uneven mass of crinkly black fuzz. My mother dragged me off to the bathroom and tried to wet down my hair.

"You look like Negro Chinese," she lamented, as if I had done this on purpose.

The instructor of the beauty training school had to lop off these soggy clumps to make my hair even again. "Peter Pan is very popular these days," the instructor assured my mother. I now had hair the length of a boy's, with straight-across bangs that hung at a slant two inches above my eyebrows. I liked the haircut and it made me actually look forward to my future fame.

In fact, in the beginning, I was just as excited as my mother, maybe even more so. I pictured this prodigy part of me as many different images, trying each one on for size. I was a dainty ballerina girl standing by the curtains, waiting to hear the music that would send me floating on my tiptoes. I was like the Christ child lifted out of the straw manger, crying with holy indignity. I was Cinderella stepping from her pumpkin carriage with sparkly cartoon music filling the air.

10   In all of my imaginings, I was filled with a sense that I would soon become *perfect.* My mother and father would adore me. I would be beyond reproach. I would never feel the need to sulk for anything.

But sometimes the prodigy in me became impatient. "If you don't hurry up and get me out of here, I'm disappearing for good," it warned. "And then you'll always be nothing."

Every night after dinner, my mother and I would sit at the Formica kitchen table. She would present new tests, taking her examples from stories of amazing children she had read in *Ripley's Believe It or Not,* or *Good Housekeeping, Reader's Digest,* and a dozen other magazines she kept in a pile in our bathroom. My mother got these magazines from people whose houses she cleaned. And since she cleaned many houses each week, we had a great assortment. She would look through them all, searching for stories about remarkable children.

The first night she brought out a story about a three-year-old boy who knew the capitals of all the states and even most of the European countries. A teacher was quoted as saying the little boy could also pronounce the names of the foreign cities correctly.

"What's the capital of Finland?" my mother asked me, looking at the magazine story.

15   All I knew was the capital of California, because Sacramento was the name of the street we lived on in Chinatown. "Nairobi!" I guessed, saying the most foreign word I could think of. She checked to see if that was possibly one way to pronounce "Helsinki" before showing me the answer.

The tests got harder—multiplying numbers in my head, finding the queen of hearts in a deck of cards, trying to stand on my head without using my hands, predicting the daily temperatures in Los Angeles, New York, and London.

One night I had to look at a page from the Bible for three minutes and then report everything I could remember. "Now Jehoshaphat had riches and honor in abundance and . . . that's all I remember, Ma," I said.

And after seeing my mother's disappointed face once again, something inside of me began to die. I hated the tests, the raised hopes and failed expectations. Before going to bed that night, I looked in the mirror above the bathroom sink and when I saw only my face staring back—and that it would always be this ordinary face—I began to cry. Such a sad, ugly girl! I made high-pitched noises like a crazed animal, trying to scratch out the face in the mirror.

And then I saw what seemed to be the prodigy side of me—because I had never seen that face before. I looked at my reflection, blinking so I could see more clearly. The girl staring back at me was angry, powerful. This girl and I were the same. I had new thoughts, willful thoughts, or rather thoughts filled with lots of won'ts. I won't let her change me, I promised myself. I won't be what I'm not.

20   So now on nights when my mother presented her tests, I performed listlessly, my head propped on one arm. I pretended to be bored. And I was. I got so bored I started counting the bellows of the foghorns out on the bay while my mother drilled me in other areas. The sound was comforting and reminded me of the cow jumping over the moon. And the next day, I played a game with myself, seeing if my mother would give up on me before eight bellows. After a while I usually counted only one, maybe two bellows at most. At last she was beginning to give up hope.

Two or three months had gone by without any mention of my being a prodigy again. And then one day my mother was watching *The Ed Sullivan Show* on TV. The TV was old and the sound kept shorting out. Every time my mother got halfway up from the sofa to adjust the set, the sound would go back on and Ed would be talking. As soon as she sat down, Ed would go silent again. She got up, the TV broke into loud piano music. She sat down. Silence. Up and down, back and forth, quiet and loud. It was like a stiff embraceless dance between her and the TV set. Finally she stood by the set with her hand on the sound dial.

She seemed entranced by the music, a little frenzied piano piece with this mesmerizing quality, sort of quick passages and then teasing lilting ones before it returned to the quick playful parts.

"*Ni kan,*" my mother said, calling me over with hurried hand gestures, "look here."

I could see why my mother was fascinated by the music. It was being pounded out by a little Chinese girl, about nine years old, with a Peter Pan haircut. The girl had the sauciness of a Shirley Temple. She was proudly modest like a proper Chinese child. And she also did this fancy sweep of a curtsy, so that the fluffy skirt of her white dress cascaded slowly to the floor like the petals of a large carnation.

25   In spite of these warning signs, I wasn't worried. Our family had no piano and we couldn't afford to buy one, let alone reams of sheet music and piano lessons. So I could be generous in my comments when my mother bad-mouthed the little girl on TV.

"Play note right, but doesn't sound good! No singing sound," my mother complained.

"What are you picking on her for?" I said carelessly. "She's pretty good. Maybe she's not the best, but she's trying hard." I knew almost immediately I would be sorry I said that.

"Just like you," she said. "Not the best. Because you not trying." She gave a little huff as she let go of the sound dial and sat down on the sofa.

The little Chinese girl sat down also to play an encore of "Anitra's Dance," by Grieg. I remember the song, because later on I had to learn how to play it.

30   Three days after watching *The Ed Sullivan Show,* my mother told me what my schedule would be for piano lessons and piano practice. She had talked to Mr. Chong, who lived on the first floor of our apartment building. Mr. Chong was a retired piano teacher and my mother had traded housecleaning services for weekly lessons and a piano for me to practice on every day, two hours a day, from four until six.

When my mother told me this, I felt as though I had been sent to hell. I whined and then kicked my foot a little when I couldn't stand it anymore.

"Why don't you like me the way I am? I'm *not* a genius! I can't play the piano. And even if I could, I wouldn't go on TV if you paid me a million dollars!" I cried.

My mother slapped me. "Who ask you be genius?" she shouted. "Only ask you be your best. For you sake. You think I want you be genius? Hnnh! What for! Who ask you!"

"So ungrateful," I heard her mutter in Chinese. "If she had as much talent as she has temper, she would be famous now."

35   Mr. Chong, whom I secretly nicknamed Old Chong, was very strange, always tapping his fingers to the silent music of an invisible orchestra. He looked ancient in my eyes. He had lost most of the hair on top of his head and he wore thick glasses and had eyes that always looked tired and sleepy. But he must have been younger than I thought, since he lived with his mother and was not yet married.

I met Old Lady Chong once and that was enough. She had this peculiar smell like a baby that had done something in its pants. And her fingers felt like a dead person's, like an old peach I once found in the back of the refrigerator; the skin just slid off the meat when I picked it up.

I soon found out why Old Chong had retired from teaching piano. He was deaf. "Like Beethoven!" he shouted to me. "We're both listening only in our head!" And he would start to conduct his frantic silent sonatas.

Our lessons went like this. He would open the book and point to different things, explaining their purpose: "Key! Treble! Bass! No sharps or flats! So this is C major! Listen now and play after me!"

And then he would play the C scale a few times, a simple chord, and then, as if inspired by an old, unreachable itch, he gradually added more notes and running trills and a pounding bass until the music was really something quite grand.

40   I would play after him, the simple scale, the simple chord, and then I just played some nonsense that sounded like a cat running up and down on top of garbage cans. Old Chong smiled and applauded and then said, "Very good! But now you must learn to keep time!"

So that's how I discovered that Old Chong's eyes were too slow to keep up with the wrong notes I was playing. He went through the motions in half-time. To help me keep rhythm, he stood behind me, pushing down on my right shoulder for every beat. He balanced pennies on top of my wrists so I would keep them still as I slowly played scales and arpeggios. He had me curve my hand around an apple and keep that shape when playing chords. He marched stiffly to show me how to make each finger dance up and down, staccato like an obedient little soldier.

He taught me all these things, and that was how I also learned I could be lazy and get away with mistakes, lots of mistakes. If I hit the wrong notes because I hadn't practiced enough, I never corrected myself. I just kept playing in rhythm. And Old Chong kept conducting his own private reverie.

So maybe I never really gave myself a fair chance. I did pick up the basics pretty quickly, and I might have become a good pianist at that young age. But I was so determined not to try, not to be anybody different that I learned to play only the most ear-splitting preludes, the most discordant hymns.

Over the next year I practiced like this, dutifully in my own way. And then one day I heard my mother and her friend Lindo Jong both talking in a loud bragging tone of voice so others could hear. It was after church, and I was leaning against the brick wall wearing a dress with stiff white petticoats. Auntie Lindo's daughter, Waverly, who was about my age, was standing farther down the wall about five feet away. We had grown up together and shared all the closeness of two sisters squabbling over crayons and dolls. In other words, for the most part, we hated each other. I thought she was snotty. Waverly Jong had gained a certain amount of fame as "Chinatown's Littlest Chinese Chess Champion."

45   "She bring home too many trophy," lamented Auntie Lindo that Sunday. "All day she play chess. All day I have no time do nothing but dust off her winnings." She threw a scolding look at Waverly, who pretended not to see her.

"You lucky you don't have this problem," said Auntie Lindo with a sigh to my mother.

And my mother squared her shoulders and bragged: "Our problem worser than yours. If we ask Jing-mei wash dish, she hear nothing but music. It's like you can't stop this natural talent."

And right then, I was determined to put a stop to her foolish pride.

A few weeks later, Old Chong and my mother conspired to have me play in a talent show which would be held in the church hall. By then, my parents had saved up enough to buy me a secondhand piano, a black Wurlitzer spinet with a scarred bench. It was the showpiece of our living room.

50   For the talent show, I was to play a piece called "Pleading Child" from Schumann's *Scenes from Childhood.* It was a simple, moody piece that sounded more difficult than it was. I was supposed to memorize the whole thing, playing the repeat parts twice to make the piece sound longer. But I dawdled over it, playing a few bars and then cheating, looking up to see what notes followed. I never really listened to what I was playing. I daydreamed about being somewhere else, about being someone else.

The part I liked to practice best was the fancy curtsy: right foot out, touch the rose on the carpet with a pointed foot, sweep to the side, left leg bends, look up and smile.

My parents invited all the couples from the Joy Luck Club to witness my debut. Auntie Lindo and Uncle Tin were there. Waverly and her two older brothers had also come. The first two rows were filled with children both younger and older than I was. The littlest ones got to go first. They recited simple nursery rhymes, squawked out tunes on miniature violins, twirled Hula Hoops, pranced in pink ballet tutus, and when they bowed or curtsied, the audience would sigh in unison, "Awww," and then clap enthusiastically.

When my turn came, I was very confident. I remember my childish excitement. It was as if I knew, without a doubt, that the prodigy side of me really did exist. I had no fear whatsoever, no nervousness. I remember thinking to myself, This is it! This is it! I looked out over the audience, at my mother's blank face, my father's yawn, Auntie Lindo's stiff-lipped smile, Waverly's sulky expression. I had on a white dress layered with sheets of lace, and a pink bow in my Peter Pan haircut. As I sat down I envisioned people jumping to their feet and Ed Sullivan rushing up to introduce me to everyone on TV.

And I started to play. It was so beautiful. I was so caught up in how lovely I looked that at first I didn't worry how I would sound. So it was a surprise to me when I hit the first wrong note and I realized something didn't sound quite right. And then I hit another and another followed that. A chill started at the top of my head and began to trickle down. Yet I couldn't stop playing, as though my hands were bewitched. I kept thinking my fingers would adjust themselves back, like a train switching to the right track. I played this strange jumble through two repeats, the sour notes staying with me all the way to the end.

55   When I stood up, I discovered my legs were shaking. Maybe I had just been nervous and the audience, like Old Chong, had seen me go through the right motions and had not heard anything wrong at all. I swept my right foot out, went down on my knee, looked up and smiled. The room was quiet, except for Old Chong, who was beaming and shouting, "Bravo! Bravo! Well done!" But then I saw my mother's face, her stricken face. The audience clapped weakly, and as I walked back to my chair, with my whole face quivering as I tried not to cry, I heard a little boy whisper loudly to his mother, "That was awful," and the mother whispered back, "Well, she certainly tried."

And now I realized how many people were in the audience, the whole world it seemed. I was aware of eyes burning into my back. I felt the shame of my mother and father as they sat stiffly throughout the rest of the show.

We could have escaped during intermission. Pride and some strange sense of honor must have anchored my parents to their chairs. And so we watched it all: the eighteen-year-old boy with a fake moustache who did a magic show and juggled flaming hoops while riding a unicycle. The breasted girl with white makeup who sang from *Madame Butterfly* and got honorable mention. And the eleven-year-old boy who won first prize playing a tricky violin song that sounded like a busy bee.

After the show, the Hsus, the Jongs, and the St. Clairs from the Joy Luck Club, came up to my mother and father.

"Lots of talented kids," Auntie Lindo said vaguely, smiling broadly.

60   "That was somethin' else," said my father, and I wondered if he was referring to me in a humorous way, or whether he even remembered what I had done.

Waverly looked at me and shrugged her shoulders. "You aren't a genius like me," she said matter-of-factly. And if I hadn't felt so bad, I would have pulled her braids and punched her stomach.

But my mother's expression was what devastated me: a quiet, blank look that said she had lost everything. I felt the same way, and it seemed as if everybody were now coming up, like gawkers at the scene of an accident, to see what parts were actually missing. When we got on the bus to go home, my father was humming the busy-bee tune and my mother was silent. I kept thinking she wanted to wait until we got home before shouting at me. But when my father unlocked the door to our apartment, my mother walked in and then went to the back, into the bedroom. No accusations. No blame. And in a way, I felt disappointed. I had been waiting for her to start shouting, so I could shout back and cry and blame her for all my misery.

I assumed my talent-show fiasco meant I never had to play the piano again. But two days later, after school, my mother came out of the kitchen and saw me watching TV.

"Four clock," she reminded me as if it were any other day. I was stunned, as though she were asking me to go through the talent-show torture again. I wedged myself more tightly in front of the TV.

65   "Turn off TV," she called from the kitchen five minutes later.

I didn't budge. And then I decided. I didn't have to do what my mother said anymore. I wasn't her slave. This wasn't China. I had listened to her before and look what happened. She was the stupid one.

She came out from the kitchen and stood in the arched entryway of the living room. "Four clock," she said once again, louder.

"I'm not going to play anymore," I said nonchalantly. "Why should I? I'm not a genius."

She walked over and stood in front of the TV. I saw her chest was heaving up and down in an angry way.

70   "No!" I said, and I now felt stronger, as if my true self had finally emerged. So this was what had been inside me all along.

"No! I won't!" I screamed.

She yanked me by the arm, pulled me off the floor, snapped off the TV. She was frighteningly strong, half pulling, half carrying me toward the piano as I kicked the throw rugs under my feet. She lifted me up and onto the hard bench. I was sobbing by now, looking at her bitterly. Her chest was heaving even more and her mouth was open, smiling crazily as if she were pleased I was crying.

"You want me to be someone that I'm not!" I sobbed. "I'll never be the kind of daughter you want me to be!"

"Only two kinds of daughters," she shouted in Chinese. "Those who are obedient and those who follow their own mind! Only one kind of daughter can live in this house. Obedient daughter!"

75   "Then I wish I wasn't your daughter. I wish you weren't my mother," I shouted. As I said these things I got scared. It felt like worms and toads and slimy things crawling out of my chest, but it also felt good, as if this awful side of me had surfaced, at last.

"Too late change this," said my mother shrilly.

And I could sense her anger rising to its breaking point. I wanted to see it spill over. And that's when I remembered the babies she had lost in China, the ones we never talked about. "Then I wish I'd never been born!" I shouted. "I wish I were dead! Like them."

It was as if I had said the magic words. Alakazam!—and her face went blank, her mouth closed, her arms went slack, and she backed out of the room, stunned, as if she were blowing away like a small brown leaf, thin, brittle, lifeless.

It was not the only disappointment my mother felt in me. In the years that followed, I failed her so many times, each time asserting my own will, my right to fall short of expectations. I didn't get straight As. I didn't become class president. I didn't get into Stanford. I dropped out of college.

80   For unlike my mother, I did not believe I could be anything I wanted to be. I could only be me.

And for all those years, we never talked about the disaster at the recital or my terrible accusations afterward at the piano bench. All of that remained unchecked, like a betrayal that was now unspeakable. So I never found a way to ask her why she had hoped for something so large that failure was inevitable.

And even worse, I never asked her what frightened me the most: Why had she given up hope?

For after our struggle at the piano, she never mentioned my playing again. The lessons stopped. The lid to the piano was closed, shutting out the dust, my misery, and her dreams.

So she surprised me. A few years ago, she offered to give me the piano, for my thirtieth birthday. I had not played in all those years. I saw the offer as a sign of forgiveness, a tremendous burden removed.

85   "Are you sure?" I asked shyly. "I mean, won't you and Dad miss it?"

"No, this your piano," she said firmly. "Always your piano. You only one can play."

"Well, I probably can't play anymore," I said. "It's been years."

"You pick up fast," said my mother, as if she knew this was certain. "You have natural talent. You could been genius if you want to."

"No I couldn't."

90   "You just not trying," said my mother. And she was neither angry nor sad. She said it as if to announce a fact that could never be disproved. "Take it," she said.

But I didn't at first. It was enough that she had offered it to me. And after that, every time I saw it in my parents' living room, standing in front of the bay windows, it made me feel proud, as if it were a shiny trophy I had won back.

Last week I sent a tuner over to my parents' apartment and had the piano reconditioned, for purely sentimental reasons. My mother had died a few months before and I had been getting things in order for my father, a little bit at a time. I put the jewelry in special silk pouches. The sweaters she had knitted in yellow, pink, bright orange—all the colors I hated—I put those in moth-proof boxes. I found some old Chinese silk dresses, the kind with little slits up the sides. I rubbed the old silk against my skin, then wrapped them in tissue and decided to take them home with me.

After I had the piano tuned, I opened the lid and touched the keys. It sounded even richer than I remembered. Really, it was a very good piano. Inside the bench were the same exercise notes with handwritten scales, the same secondhand music books with their covers held together with yellow tape.

I opened up the Schumann book to the dark little piece I had played at the recital. It was on the left-hand side of the page, "Pleading Child." It looked more difficult than I remembered. I played a few bars, surprised at how easily the notes came back to me.

95   And for the first time, or so it seemed, I noticed the piece on the right-hand side. It was called "Perfectly Contented." I tried to play this one as well. It had a lighter melody but the same flowing rhythm and turned out to be quite easy. "Pleading Child" was shorter but slower; "Perfectly Contented" was longer, but faster. And after I played them both a few times, I realized they were two halves of the same song.

 ## MAKING CONNECTIONS

1. To what extent does your own experience in a parent-child relationship affect your response to the mother-daughter relationship in this story?
2. The narrator, Jing-Mei, is the protagonist in this story. How does her point of view affect how and what we are told?
3. Describe Jing-Mei. What is the primary conflict she struggles with? Is it external? Internal? Both? Explain. Why is she so resistant to her mother's wishes?
4. Describe her mother. How would she characterize Jing-Mei? What does she want for her daughter? How does her own background influence that?
5. When Jing-Mei shouts at her mother that she wishes she was not her daughter, she recalls, "As I said [this] I got scared. It felt like worms and toads and slimy things crawling out of my chest, but it also felt good, as if this awful side of me had surfaced, at last." What do you think she means?
6. After her mother dies, Jing-Mei is reunited with her piano. What does she realize about herself, her mother, and their relationship?

MAKING AN ARGUMENT

1. To what extent do cultural differences lead to the central conflict in "Two Kinds"? To what extent are these differences generational or based on the differing circumstances of where the mother and daughter grew up? Write about the impact of cultural and generational differences on the relationship of the mother and daughter in this story. Cite the text of the story for support.

EUDORA WELTY [1909–2001]

The daughter of an insurance salesman, Eudora Welty graduated from the University of Wisconsin in 1929 and studied advertising at the Columbia University Graduate School of Business. She was born and lived most of her long life in Jackson, Mississippi. Welty wrote many novels, including The Optimist's Daughter, *which won the Pulitzer Prize in 1972, and numerous essays, but she is best known for her short stories. Internationally recognized for her writing—and photography—she was inducted into the French Legion d'Honneur. Though her stories are almost always set in a specific geographic locale—the small towns of the Mississippi delta—Welty's best stories uncover aspects of the human experience that are universal.*

A WORN PATH   [1941]

It was December—a bright frozen day in the early morning. Far out in the country there was an old Negro woman with her head tied in a red rag, coming along a path through the pinewoods. Her name was Phoenix Jackson. She was very old and small and she walked slowly in the dark pine shadows, moving a little from side to side in her steps, with the balanced heaviness and lightness of a pendulum in a grandfather clock. She carried a thin, small cane made from an umbrella, and with this she kept tapping the frozen earth in front of her. This made a grave and persistent noise in the still air, that seemed meditative like the chirping of a solitary little bird.

She wore a dark striped dress reaching down to her shoe tops, and an equally long apron of bleached sugar sacks, with a full pocket: all neat and tidy, but every time she took a step she might have fallen over her shoelaces, which dragged from her unlaced shoes. She looked straight ahead. Her eyes were blue with age. Her skin had a pattern all its own of numberless branching wrinkles and as though a whole little tree stood in the middle of her forehead, but a golden color ran underneath, and the two knobs of her cheeks were illuminated by a yellow burning under the dark. Under the red rag her hair came down on her neck in the frailest of ringlets, still black, and with an odor like copper.

Now and then there was a quivering in the thicket. Old Phoenix said, "Out of my way, all you foxes, owls, beetles, jack rabbits, coons, and wild animals! . . . Keep out from under these feet, little bob-whites. . . . Keep the big wild hogs out of my path. Don't let none of those come running my direction. I got a long way." Under her small black-freckled hand her cane, limber as a buggy whip, would switch at the brush as if to rouse up any hiding things.

On she went. The woods were deep and still. The sun made the pine needles almost too bright to look at, up where the wind rocked. The cones dropped as light as feathers. Down in the hollow was the mourning dove—it was not too late for him.

5   The path ran up a hill. "Seem like there is chains about my feet, time I get this far," she said, in the voice of argument old people keep to use with themselves. "Something always take a hold of me on this hill—pleads I should stay."

After she got to the top she turned and gave a full, severe look behind her where she had come. "Up through pines," she said at length. "Now down through oaks."

Her eyes opened their widest, and she started down gently. But before she got to the bottom of the hill a bush caught her dress.

Her fingers were busy and intent, but her skirts were full and long, so that before she could pull them free in one place they were caught in another. It was not possible to allow the dress to tear. "I in the thorny bush," she said. "Thorns, you doing your appointed work. Never want to let folks pass, no sir. Old eyes thought you was a pretty little *green* bush."

Finally, trembling all over, she stood free, and after a moment dared to stoop for her cane.

10   Sun so high!" she cried, leaning back and looking, while the thick tears went over her eyes. "The time getting all gone here."

At the foot of this hill was a place where a log was laid across the creek.

"Now comes the trial," said Phoenix.

Putting her right foot out, she mounted the log and shut her eyes. Lifting her skirt, leveling her cane fiercely before her, like a festival figure in some parade, she began to march across. Then she opened her eyes and she was safe on the other side.

"I wasn't as old as I thought," she said.

15   But she sat down to rest. She spread her skirts on the bank around her and folded her hands over her knees. Up above her was a tree in a pearly cloud of mistletoe. She did not dare to close her eyes, and when a little boy brought her a little plate with a slice of marble-cake on it she spoke to him. "That would be acceptable," she said. But when she went to take it there was just her own hand in the air.

So she left that tree, and had to go through a barbed-wire fence. There she had to creep and crawl, spreading her knees and stretching her fingers like a baby trying to climb the steps. But she talked loudly to herself: she could not let her dress be torn now, so late in the day, and she could not pay for having her arm or leg sawed off if she got caught fast where she was.

At last she was safe through the fence and risen up out in the clearing. Big dead trees, like black men with one arm, were standing in the purple stalks of the withered cotton field. There sat a buzzard.

"Who you watching?"

In the furrow she made her way along.

20   "Glad this not the season for bulls," she said, looking sideways, "and the good Lord made his snakes to curl up and sleep in the winter. A pleasure I don't see no two-headed snake coming around that tree, where it come once. It took a while to get by him, back in the summer."

She passed through the old cotton and went into a field of dead corn. It whispered and shook and was taller than her head. "Through the maze now," she said, for there was no path.

Then there was something tall, black, and skinny there, moving before her.

At first she took it for a man. It could have been a man dancing in the field. But she stood still and listened, and it did not make a sound. It was as silent as a ghost.

"Ghost," she said sharply, "who be you the ghost of? For I have heard of nary death close by."

25   But there was no answer—only the ragged dancing in the wind.

She shut her eyes, reached out her hand, and touched a sleeve. She found a coat and inside that an emptiness, cold as ice.

"You scarecrow," she said. Her face lighted. "I ought to be shut up for good," she said with laughter. "My senses is gone. I too old. I the oldest people I ever know. Dance, old scarecrow," she said, "while I dancing with you."

She kicked her foot over the furrow, and with mouth drawn down, shook her head once or twice in a little strutting way. Some husks blew down and whirled in streamers about her skirts.

Then she went on, parting her way from side to side with the cane, through the whispering field. At last she came to the end, to a wagon track where the silver grass blew between the red ruts. The quail were walking around like pullets, seeming all dainty and unseen.

30   "Walk pretty," she said. "This the easy place. This the easy going."

She followed the track, swaying through the quiet bare fields, through the little strings of trees silver in their dead leaves, past cabins silver from weather, with the doors and windows boarded shut, all like old women under a spell sitting there. "I walking in their sleep," she said, nodding her head vigorously.

In a ravine she went where a spring was silently flowing through a hollow log. Old Phoenix bent and drank. "Sweet-gum makes the water sweet," she said, and drank more. "Nobody know who made this well, for it was here when I was born."

The track crossed a swampy part where the moss hung as white as lace from every limb. "Sleep on, alligators, and blow your bubbles." Then the track went into the road.

Deep, deep the road went down between the high green-colored banks. Overhead the live-oaks met, and it was as dark as a cave.

35   A black dog with a lolling tongue came up out of the weeds by the ditch. She was meditating, and not ready, and when he came at her she only hit him a little with her cane. Over she went in the ditch, like a little puff of milk-weed.

Down there, her senses drifted away. A dream visited her, and she reached her hand up, but nothing reached down and gave her a pull. So she lay there and presently went to talking. "Old woman," she said to herself, "that black dog come up out of the weeds to stall you off, and now there he sitting on his fine tail, smiling at you."

A white man finally came along and found her—a hunter, a young man, with his dog on a chain.

"Well, Granny!" he laughed. "What are you doing there?"

"Lying on my back like a June-bug waiting to be turned over, mister," she said, reaching up her hand.

40   He lifted her up, gave her a swing in the air, and set her down. "Anything broken, Granny?"

"No sir, them old dead weeds is springy enough," said Phoenix, when she had got her breath. "I thank you for your trouble."

"Where do you live, Granny?" he asked, while the two dogs were growling at each other.

"Away back yonder, sir, behind the ridge. You can't even see it from here."

"On your way home?"

45   "No, sir, I going to town."

"Why, that's too far! That's as far as I walk when I come out myself, and I get something for my trouble." He patted the stuffed bag he carried, and there hung down a little closed claw. It was one of the bob-whites, with its beak hooked bitterly to show it was dead. "Now you go on home, Granny!"

"I bound to go to town, mister," said Phoenix. "The time come around."

He gave another laugh, filling the whole landscape. "I know you old colored people! Wouldn't miss going to town to see Santa Claus!"

But something held old Phoenix very still. The deep lines in her face went into a fierce and different radiation. Without warning, she had seen with her own eyes a flashing nickel fall out of the man's pocket onto the ground.

50   "How old are you, Granny?" he was saying.

"There is no telling, mister," she said, "no telling."

Then she gave a little cry and clapped her hands and said, "Git on away from here, dog! Look! Look at that dog!" She laughed as if in admiration. "He ain't scared of nobody. He a big black dog." She whispered, "Sic him!"

"Watch me get rid of that cur," said the man. "Sic him, Pete! Sic him!"

Phoenix heard the dogs fighting, and heard the man running and throwing sticks. She even heard a gunshot. But she was slowly bending forward by that time, further and further forward, the lids stretched down over her eyes, as if she were doing this in her sleep. Her chin was lowered almost to her knees. The yellow palm of her hand came out from the fold of her apron. Her fingers slid down and along the ground under the piece of money with the grace and care they would have in lifting an egg from under a sitting hen. Then she slowly straightened up, she stood erect, and the nickel was in her apron pocket. A bird flew by. Her lips moved. "God watching me the whole time. I come to stealing."

55   The man came back, and his own dog panted about them. "Well, I scared him off that time," he said, and then he laughed and lifted his gun and pointed it at Phoenix.

She stood straight and faced him.

"Doesn't the gun scare you?" he said, still pointing it.

"No, sir, I seen plenty go off closer by, in my day, and for less than what I done," she said, holding utterly still.

He smiled, and shouldered the gun. "Well, Granny," he said, "you must be a hundred years old, and scared of nothing. I'd give you a dime if I had any money with me. But you take my advice and stay home, and nothing will happen to you."

60   "I bound to go on my way, mister," said Phoenix. She inclined her head in the red rag. Then they went in different directions, but she could hear the gun shooting again and again over the hill.

She walked on. The shadows hung from the oak trees to the road like curtains. Then she smelled wood-smoke, and smelled the river, and she saw a steeple and the cabins on their steep steps. Dozens of little black children whirled around her. There ahead was Natchez shining. Bells were ringing. She walked on.

In the paved city it was Christmas time. There were red and green electric lights strung and crisscrossed everywhere, and all turned on in the daytime. Old Phoenix would have been lost if she had not distrusted her eyesight and depended on her feet to know where to take her.

She paused quietly on the sidewalk where people were passing by. A lady came along in the crowd, carrying an armful of red-, green-, and silver-wrapped presents; she gave off perfume like the red roses in hot summer, and Phoenix stopped her.

"Please, missy, will you lace up my shoe?" She held up her foot.

65   "What do you want, Grandma?"

"See my shoe," said Phoenix. "Do all right for out in the country, but wouldn't look right to go in a big building."

"Stand still then, Grandma," said the lady. She put her packages down on the sidewalk beside her and laced and tied both shoes tightly.

"Can't lace 'em with a cane," said Phoenix. "Thank you, missy, I doesn't mind asking a nice lady to tie up my shoe, when I gets out on the street."

Moving slowly and from side to side, she went into the big building and into a tower of steps, where she walked up and around and around until her feet knew to stop.

70   She entered a door, and there she saw nailed up on the wall the document that had been stamped with the gold seal and framed in the gold frame, which matched the dream that was hung up in her head.

"Here I be," she said. There was a fixed and ceremonial stiffness over her body.

"A charity case, I suppose," said an attendant who sat at the desk before her.

But Phoenix only looked above her head. There was sweat on her face, the wrinkles in her skin shone like a bright net.

"Speak up, Grandma," the woman said. "What's your name? We must have your history, you know. Have you been here before? What seems to be the trouble with you?"

75   Old Phoenix only gave a twitch to her face as if a fly were bothering her.

"Are you deaf?" cried the attendant.

But then the nurse came in.

"Oh, that's just old Aunt Phoenix," she said. "She doesn't come for herself—she has a little grandson. She makes these trips just as regular as clockwork. She lives away back off the old Natchez Trace." She bent down. "Well, Aunt Phoenix, why don't you just take a seat? We won't keep you standing after your long trip." She pointed.

The old woman sat down, bolt upright in the chair.

80   "Now, how is the boy?" asked the nurse.

Old Phoenix did not speak.

"I said, how is the boy?"

But Phoenix only waited and stared straight ahead, her face very solemn and withdrawn into rigidity.

"Is his throat any better?" asked the nurse. "Aunt Phoenix, don't you hear me? Is your grandson's throat any better since the last time you came for the medicine?"

85   With her hands on her knees, the old woman waited, silent, erect and motionless, just as if she were in armor.

"You mustn't take up our time this way, Aunt Phoenix," the nurse said. "Tell us quickly about your grandson, and get it over. He isn't dead, is he?"

At last there came a flicker and then a flame of comprehension across her face, and she spoke.

"My grandson. It was my memory had left me. There I sat and forgot why I made my long trip."

"Forgot?" The nurse frowned. "After you came so far?"

90   Then Phoenix was like an old woman begging a dignified forgiveness for waking up frightened in the night. "I never did go to school, I was too old at the Surrender,"

she said in a soft voice. "I'm an old woman without an education. It was my memory fail me. My little grandson, he is just the same, and I forgot it in the coming."

"Throat never heals, does it?" said the nurse, speaking in a loud, sure voice to Old Phoenix. By now she had a card with something written on it, a little list. "Yes. Swallowed lye. When was it—January—two—three years ago—"

Phoenix spoke unasked now. "No, missy, he not dead, he just the same. Every little while his throat begin to close up again, and he not able to swallow. He not get his breath. He not able to help himself. So the time come around, and I go on another trip for the soothing medicine."

"All right. The doctor said as long as you came to get it, you could have it," said the nurse. "But it's an obstinate case."

"My little grandson, he sit up there in the house all wrapped up, waiting by himself," Phoenix went on. "We is the only two left in the world. He suffer and it don't seem to put him back at all. He got a sweet look. He going to last. He wear a little patch quilt and peep out holding his mouth open like a little bird. I remembers so plain now. I not going to forget him again, no, the whole enduring time. I could tell him from all the others in creation."

95 "All right." The nurse was trying to hush her now. She brought her a bottle of medicine. "Charity," she said, making a check mark in a book.

Old Phoenix held the bottle close to her eyes and then carefully put it into her pocket.

"I thank you," she said.

"It's Christmas time, Grandma," said the attendant. "Could I give you a few pennies out of my purse?"

"Five pennies is a nickel," said Phoenix stiffly.

100 "Here's a nickel," said the attendant.

Phoenix rose carefully and held out her hand. She received the nickel and then fished the other nickel out of her pocket and laid it beside the new one. She stared at her palm closely, with her head on one side.

Then she gave a tap with her cane on the floor.

"This is what come to me to do," she said. "I going to the store and buy my child a little windmill they sells, made out of paper. He going to find it hard to believe there such a thing in the world. I'll march myself back where he waiting, holding it straight up in this hand."

She lifted her free hand, gave a little nod, turned round, and walked out of the doctor's office. Then her slow step began on the stairs, going down.

MAKING CONNECTIONS

1. The Phoenix is a bird that, according to legend, lived for hundreds of years, burned itself to ashes on a funeral pyre, and then rose from the ashes to live again. Why do you think the protagonist of "A Worn Path" is named Phoenix?
2. Based on what you learn about Phoenix in the story, what is her background?
3. What is your response to the hunter she meets on the path? What is his role in the story?

4. What is the central conflict or struggle in this story? What are the obstacles against Phoenix? How does she overcome them?
5. It has been suggested that Phoenix has a special relationship with nature. Cite specific passages in the story where natural objects or creatures appear along her journey.
6. In what way is "A Worn Path" an appropriate title for this story?

MAKING AN ARGUMENT

1. Like so many stories, "A Worn Path" is the story of a journey. In what ways is this journey a metaphor for the entire life of the protagonist? Write about the extent to which this story is about the *journey* of Phoenix rather than her destination. Reread the story carefully and cite the text for support.

◆ POETRY ◆

CONNECTING THROUGH COMPARISON: REMEMBRANCE

The two poems that follow address a subtheme of this section: remembrance of family and friends. Read and discussed together, they invite comparison and connections—not only with each other—but with similar experiences of your own.

ELIZABETH GAFFNEY [B. 1953]

Elizabeth Gaffney's poems have appeared in Wordsmith, Southern Poetry Review, College English, Descant, Wind, *and other publications. A graduate of Fordham University, she has a Ph.D. from the State University of New York at Stony Brook and teaches at SUNY Westchester Community College. She lives in Pelham, New York, with her husband and three children.*

LOSSES THAT TURN UP IN DREAMS   [1992]

The notebook I left on a windowsill
in Keating Hall two years ago
floats back to me full of poems.
The silver pin shaped like a bird's wings,
my mother's gold chain   5
stolen with the burnished purse I loved,
its leather worn to smoothness
from years of use—in dreams
appear again my homing pigeons.

Their familiar feel reassures me   10
that nothing's ever gone for good;
the sunglasses, pens, umbrellas,
the scarf of red and blue challis,
the lost socks, the trivial objects
I weep for are losses so palpable,   15

all equal in the land of dreams,
where the baby I lost one October night
comes home to nest, poor ghost,
and my mother, grandmother, uncles
crowd small rooms, and I am one   20
with the tree that bloomed on my birthday,
a daughter, filling up with milk and love.

WILLIAM SHAKESPEARE   [1564–1616]

(See biography on p. 537)

WHEN TO THE SESSIONS OF SWEET SILENT
THOUGHT (SONNET NO. 30)   [1609]

When to the sessions° of sweet silent thought
I summon° up remembrance of things past,
I sigh the lack of many a thing I sought,
And with old woes new wail my dear times waste:
Then can I drown an eye (un-used to flow)   5
For precious friends hid in death's dateless° night,
And weep afresh love's long since canceled° woe,
And moan the expense of many a vanished sight,
Then can I grieve at grievances foregone,
And heavily from woe to woe tell o'er   10
The sad account of fore-bemoaned moan,
Which I new pay, as if not paid before.
But the while I think on thee (dear friend)
All losses are restored, and sorrows end.

1 **sessions** as in court sessions
2 **summon** as in a legal summons
6 **dateless** endless
7 **canceled** as in a paid-up debt

▶ MAKING CONNECTIONS

1. In "Losses That Turn Up in Dreams," what losses is the speaker talking about?
2. In what way are the objects that she mentions "homing pigeons"? Can you think of objects in your own life that are "homing pigeons"?

3. What does she mean by "I am one / with the tree that bloomed on my birth-day"?
4. In "Sonnet No. 30," what does the speaker mean by "weep afresh love's long since canceled woe"?
5. To what extent do either or both poems remind you of your own experience? Compare the two poems. How are they alike? How different?

MAKING AN ARGUMENT

1. While both poems address a similar topic, they were written nearly four hundred years apart and their structures, rhythm and rhyme, diction, and use of poetic language are quite different. Write about the differences and similarities of these elements in these poems and their impact on content. Cite the language of both poems for support.

JULIA ALVAREZ   [B. 1950]

Though Julia Alvarez was born in New York City, she spent her childhood in the Dominican Republic. When she was ten, she returned with her parents to New York City, where she attended public schools. Confused and lonely (she spoke only Spanish), she struggled until high school, where she encountered an English teacher who encouraged her to write of her experiences as a stranger to the United States and its language. This experience was transform-ing, and she discovered her love of writing. She went on to study at Middlebury College, where she currently teaches, and later earned an M.F.A. from Syracuse University. She has published three books of poetry, Homecoming *(1984),* The Other Side/El Otro Lado *(1995), and* The Woman I Kept to Myself *(2004), and four novels,* How the Garcia Girls Lost Their Accents *(1991),* In the Time of the Butterflies *(1994),* !Yo! *(1996), and* In the Name of Salome *(2000).*

DUSTING   [1984]

Each morning I wrote my name
On the dusty cabinet, then crossed
The dining table in script, scrawled
In capitals on the backs of chairs,
Practicing signatures like scales   5
While mother followed, squirting
Linseed from a burping can
Into a crumpled-up flannel.

She erased my fingerprints
From the bookshelf and rocker,   10

Polished mirrors on the desk
Scribbled with my alphabets.
My name was swallowed in the towel
With which she jewelled the table tops.
The grain surfaced in the oak   15
And the pine grew luminous.
But I refused with every mark
To be like her, anonymous.

MAKING CONNECTIONS

1. The speaker's attitude toward her mother seems to be revealed in the
   poem's final word. What effect did the speaker's final comment have on
   you? Were you expecting the poem to end this way?
2. In what sense is the mother "anonymous"? Why do you think the speaker
   refuses to be like her?
3. Compare this poem with "The Youngest Daughter" on page 282.

MAKING AN ARGUMENT

1. Based on the description in this poem, write a different ending for this
   poem. Generate a different list of words that could have been used to
   describe the mother. Write about the ways that these words change the
   overall effect of the poem and its meaning. Carefully cite the original language of the poem for support.

ROBERT FROST [1874–1963]

*Robert Frost was born in San Francisco, California, to a
headmaster and schoolteacher who met at a tiny private
school in Pennsylvania. When his father died of tuberculosis in 1885, his mother returned the family to New
England. Frost attended a local high school where,
together with the woman he would eventually marry,
Elinor White, he served as class valedictorian. It was in
high school, where he was known as the class poet, that
Frost seriously began writing poetry. In the many years that followed, Frost continued to write while he attended college (short stints at Dartmouth and
Harvard) and held a series of odd jobs, including work as a cobbler, journalist,
teacher, and at a cotton mill. From 1900 to 1905, he lived on a farm in Derry,
New Hampshire, purchased for him by his grandfather, but financial hardships—*

he and Elinor had five children by this point—forced him to return to teaching. In 1912, frustrated by his inability to publish in the United States, Frost moved his family to England, where he published his first two books of poetry: A Boy's Will *(1913) and* North of Boston *(1914). By the time he returned to the United States in 1915, he was well on his way to becoming the most famous American poet of the century. In 1961, an infirm Frost read his poem "The Gift Outright" at the inauguration of President John F. Kennedy. His poetry, which takes much of its inspiration from the countryside of New England, is often deceptively simple, as it artfully and effortlessly weaves together traditional metrical forms with collo-quial American speech.*

MENDING WALL   [1914]

Something there is that doesn't love a wall,
That sends the frozen-ground-swell under it,
And spills the upper boulders in the sun;
And makes gaps even two can pass abreast.
The work of hunters is another thing: 5
I have come after them and made repair
Where they have left not one stone on a stone,
But they would have the rabbit out of hiding,
To please the yelping dogs. The gaps I mean,
No one has seen them made or heard them made,   10
But at spring mending-time we find them there.
I let my neighbor know beyond the hill;
And on a day we meet to walk the line
And set the wall between us once again.
We keep the wall between us as we go.   15
To each the boulders that have fallen to each.
And some are loaves and some so nearly balls
We have to use a spell to make them balance:
"Stay where you are until our backs are turned!"
We wear our fingers rough with handling them.   20
Oh, just another kind of outdoor game,
One on a side. It comes to little more:
There where it is we do not need the wall:
He is all pine and I am apple orchard.
My apple trees will never get across   25
And eat the cones under his pines, I tell him.
He only says, "Good fences make good neighbors."
Spring is the mischief in me, and I wonder
If I could put a notion in his head:
"*Why* do they make good neighbors? Isn't it   30
Where there are cows? But here there are no cows.
Before I built a wall I'd ask to know

What I was walling in or walling out,
And to whom I was like to give offense.
Something there is that doesn't love a wall,   35
That wants it down." I could say "Elves" to him,
But it's not elves exactly, and I'd rather
He said it for himself. I see him there
Bringing a stone grasped firmly by the top
In each hand, like an old-stone savage armed.   40
He moves in darkness as it seems to me,
Not of woods only and the shade of trees.
He will not go behind his father's saying,
And he likes having thought of it so well
He says again, "Good fences make good neighbors."   45

MAKING CONNECTIONS

1. Have you ever felt walled in or out? Explain.
2. To what extent is the wall in this poem symbolic?
3. What is the "Something" in "Something there is that doesn't love a wall"?
4. How would you interpret the line "He moves in darkness as it seems to me"?

MAKING AN ARGUMENT

1. Does the speaker in the poem agree that "Good fences make good neigh-bors"? He says of his neighbor: "He moves in darkness as it seems to me." But why does he remind his neighbor when it's time to mend the wall? Write an interpretation of this poem. Carefully cite the text of the poem for support.

SEAMUS HEANEY [B. 1939]

Sometimes referred to as Ireland's greatest poet since Yeats, Seamus Heaney was born on a farm in County Derry in Northern Ireland. He graduated from Queen's University in Belfast in 1961. He published his first book of poetry, Eleven Poems, in 1965. Electric Light (2001) is his most recent. He was awarded the Nobel Prize in 1995. Currently he divides his time between Dublin and the United States, where he holds a teaching position at Harvard University. The rich, and often violent, history of Ireland and its people is the concern of much of his poetry. His critically acclaimed verse translation of Beowulf *was published in 2000.* The Burial at Thebes, *a version of Sophocles's* Antigone, *was published in 2004.*

DIGGING [1965]

Between my finger and my thumb
The squat pen rests; snug as a gun.

Under my window, a clean rasping sound
When the spade sinks into gravelly ground:
My father, digging. I look down   5

Till his straining rump among the flowerbeds
Bends low, comes up twenty years away
Stooping in rhythm through potato drills
Where he was digging.

The coarse boot nestled on the lug, the shaft   10
Against the inside knee was levered firmly.
He rooted out tall tops, buried the bright edge deep
To scatter new potatoes that we picked
Loving their cool hardness in our hands.

By God, the old man could handle a spade.   15
Just like his old man.

My grandfather cut more turf in a day
Than any other man on Toner's bog.
Once I carried him milk in a bottle
Corked sloppily with paper. He straightened up   20
To drink it, then fell to right away

Nicking and slicing neatly, heaving sods
Over his shoulder, going down and down
For the good turf. Digging.

The cold smell of potato mould, the squelch and slap   25
Of soggy peat, the curt cuts of an edge
Through living roots awaken in my head.
But I've no spade to follow men like them.

Between my finger and my thumb
The squat pen rests.   30
I'll dig with it.

MAKING CONNECTIONS

1. What kind of work did the speaker's father and grandfather do? To what
   extent is your response to this poem influenced by the work of your parents or grandparents?
2. The speaker begins the poem by saying, "The squat pen rests; snug as a
   gun." But in the last stanza he says of the squat pen, "I'll dig with it." What
   kind of work does he do and what does he mean?

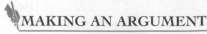

MAKING AN ARGUMENT

1. Do you think the speaker in the poem is suggesting that "we should define ourselves by the work we do?" Write about the extent to which this poem suggests that and whether or not you think it's appropriate. Cite the text of the poem for support.

PHILIP LARKIN [1922–1985]

Philip Larkin was born to a working-class family in Coventry, an industrial city in northern England. He attended Oxford University on a scholarship, and afterward served for many years as the librarian at the University of Hull. Though he wrote novels and was an astute critic of both music—jazz, in particular—and literature, Larkin is remembered today as one of England's most influential postwar poets. In his poems, which are often called anti-Romantic, Larkin takes a witty, sophisticated, and tough-minded approach to traditional poetic subjects.

THIS BE THE VERSE   [1971]

They fuck you up, your mum and dad.
    They may not mean to, but they do.
They fill you with the faults they had
    And add some extra, just for you.

But they were fucked up in their turn   5
    By fools in old-style hats and coats,
Who half the time were soppy-stern
    And half at one another's throats.

Man hands on misery to man.
    It deepens like a coastal shelf.   10
Get out as early as you can.
    And don't have any kids yourself.

MAKING CONNECTIONS

1. What is the tone of this poem? Were you surprised by it, and the message? Why?
2. Discuss the effect of the rhythm and rhyme scheme on the content of the poem. Do you think it helps to convey its meaning? How so?

MAKING AN ARGUMENT

1. Take a position in response to the conclusion of this whimsical but provocative poem. To what extent is the advice at the end of the poem realistic? Do you agree with it? If yes, why? If not, write an ending you believe is more realistic and explain why you prefer it. Cite the text of the poem for support.

MICHAEL LASSELL [B. 1947]

Michael Lassell is the author of six books of poetry, fiction, and nonfiction, including A Flame for the Touch That Matters *(1998) and* Decade Dance *(1990), which won a Lambda Literary Award. He is also the editor of five books, including (with Elena Georgiou)* The World in Us: Lesbian and Gay Poetry of the Next Wave *(2000) and* Elton John and Tim Rice's Aida: The Making of a Broadway Show *(2000). He holds degrees from Colgate University, California Institute of the Arts, and Yale, and lives in New York City, where he is the features editor of* Metropolitan Home *magazine. His most recent book,* Disney on Broadway, *was published in 2002.*

HOW TO WATCH YOUR BROTHER DIE [1990]

for Carl Morse

When the call comes, be calm.
Say to your wife, "My brother is dying. I have to fly
to California."
Try not to be shocked that he already looks like
a cadaver.   5
Say to the young man sitting by your brother's side,
"I'm his brother."
Try not to be shocked when the young man says,
"I'm his lover. Thanks for coming."

Listen to the doctor with a steel face on.   10
Sign the necessary forms.
Tell the doctor you will take care of everything.
Wonder why doctors are so remote.

Watch the lover's eyes as they stare into
your brother's eyes as they stare into   15
space.
Wonder what they see there.
Remember the time he was jealous and
opened your eyebrow with a sharp stick.

Forgive him out loud
even if he can't
understand you.
Realize the scar will be
all that's left of him.   20

Over coffee in the hospital cafeteria   25
say to the lover, "You're an extremely good-looking
young man."
Hear him say,
"I never thought I was good enough looking to
deserve your brother."   30

Watch the tears well up in his eyes. Say,
"I'm sorry, I don't know what it means to be
the lover of another man."
Hear him say,
"It's just like a wife, only the commitment is   35
deeper because the odds against you are so much
greater."
Say nothing, but
take his hand like a brother's.

Drive to Mexico for unproved drugs that might   40
help him live longer.
Explain what they are to the border guard.
Fill with rage when he informs you,
"You can't bring those across."

Begin to grow loud.   45
Feel the lover's hand on your arm
restraining you. See in the guard's eye
how much a man can hate another man.
Say to the lover, "How can you stand it?"
Hear him say, "You get used to it."   50
Think of one of your children getting used to
another man's hatred.

Call your wife on the telephone. Tell her,
"He hasn't much time.
I'll be home soon." Before you hang up, say,   55
"How could anyone's commitment be deeper than
a husband and wife?" Hear her say,
"Please. I don't want to know all the details."

When he slips into an irrevocable coma,
hold his lover in your arms while he sobs,   60
no longer strong. Wonder how much longer

you will be able to be strong.
Feel how it feels to hold a man in your arms
whose arms are used to holding men.
Offer God anything to bring your brother back.   65
Know you have nothing God could possibly want.
Curse God, but do not
abandon Him.

Stare at the face of the funeral director
when he tells you he will not   70
embalm the body for fear of
contamination. Let him see in your eyes
how much a man can hate another man.

Stand beside a casket covered in flowers,
white flowers. Say,   75
"Thank you for coming," to each of several
hundred men
who file past in tears, some of them
holding hands. Know that your brother's life
was not what you imagined. Overhear two   80
mourners say, "I wonder who'll be next?" and
"I don't care anymore,
as long as it isn't you."

Arrange to take an early flight home,
his lover will drive you to the airport.   85
When your flight is announced say,
awkwardly, "If I can do anything, please
let me know." Do not flinch when he says,
"Forgive yourself for not wanting to know him
after he told you. He did."   90
Stop and let it soak in. Say,
"He forgave me, or he knew himself?"
"Both," the lover will say, not knowing what else
to do. Hold him like a brother while he
kisses you on the cheek. Think that   95
you haven't been kissed by a man since
your father died. Think,
"This is no moment not to be strong."

Fly first class and drink Scotch. Stroke
your split eyebrow with a finger and   100
think of your brother alive. Smile
at the memory and think
how your children will feel in your arms,
warm and friendly and without challenge.

 MAKING CONNECTIONS

1. What do you think of the title of the poem? Is this how to watch your brother die? Explain.
2. Who is the "you" to whom the speaker addresses himself?
3. What does the speaker mean by "See in the guard's eye / how much a man can hate another man"? What other images of love or hate can you find in the poem?
4. The poem concludes with "think / how your children will feel in your arms, / warm and friendly and without challenge." Is this a fitting conclusion? Explain.

MAKING AN ARGUMENT

1. The author of this poem is gay, but the speaker in the poem is heterosexual and is not always comfortable with what he encounters. What kind of impact does this speaker have on the content of the poem? To what extent would this be a different poem if the speaker were gay? Write about the effectiveness of narration in this poem. Cite the text of the poem for support.

LI-YOUNG LEE [B. 1957]

Li-Young Lee was born in Jakarta, Indonesia. He came to the United States in 1964 at the age of seven, when his father, a physician and minister, was forced to flee Indonesia due to political persecution. He attended the University of Pittsburgh, the University of Arizona, and the State University of New York at Brockport. His volumes of poetry include Rose *(1986) and* The City in Which I Love You *(1990). In 1994, he published a book of his memoirs,* The Winged Seed. *His most recent book of poems,* Book of My Nights, *was published in 2001. He lives in Chicago.*

THE GIFT   [1986]

To pull the metal splinter from my palm
my father recited a story in a low voice.
I watched his lovely face and not the blade.
Before the story ended he removed
the iron sliver I thought I'd die from.   5

I can't remember the tale
but hear his voice still, a well

of dark water, a prayer.
And I recall his hands,
two measures of tenderness   10
he laid against my face,
the flames of discipline
he raised above my head.

Had you entered that afternoon
you would have thought you saw a man   15
planting something in a boy's palm,
a silver tear, a tiny flame.
Had you followed that boy
you would have arrived here,
where I bend over my wife's right hand.   20

Look how I shave her thumbnail down
so carefully she feels no pain.
Watch as I lift the splinter out.
I was seven when my father
took my hand like this,   25
and I did not hold that shard
between my fingers and think,
Metal that will bury me,
christen it Little Assassin,
Ore Going Deep for My Heart,   30
And I did not lift up my wound and cry,

Death visited here!
I did what a child does
when he's given something to keep,
I kissed my father.   35

 ## MAKING CONNECTIONS

1. What is "the gift"? Can you remember a time when someone gave you a "gift" like this? Explain.
2. How do you think the italicized phrases *"Metal that will bury me"* and *"Death visited here!"* fit in this poem? Are there any other phrases that stand out for you?

MAKING AN ARGUMENT

1. Like "Those Winter Sundays" (p. 13), "My Papa's Waltz" (p. 281), or "The Road" (p. 243), this poem is about a father-son relationship. On the surface, its tone and conclusion seem quite different, yet there is one similarity that all share. Each of these sons has been "given something to keep." Write about what each son has been given and cite the text of each work to support your view.

JANICE MIRIKITANI [B. 1938]

Like many Japanese-Americans of her generation, Janice Mirikitani was incarcerated with her family in an internment camp during World War II. She was educated at UCLA and the University of California of Berkeley, where she first developed her interests in the arts, both from creative and administrative perspectives. During her career, she has managed numerous social and arts programs, public and private, including San Francisco's famous Glide Foundation. She has published three collections of poetry: Awake in the River *(1978),* Shedding Silence *(1987), and* We, the Dangerous *(1994).*

FOR MY FATHER   [1987]

He came over the ocean
carrying Mt. Fuji on
his back/Tule Lake on his chest
hacked through the brush
of deserts   5
and made them grow
strawberries

we stole berries
from the stem
we could not afford them   10
for breakfast

his eyes held
nothing
as he whipped us
for stealing.   15

the desert had dried
his soul.

wordless
he sold
the rich,   20
full berries
to hakujin°
whose children
pointed at our eyes

hakujin white people

they ate fresh   25
strawberries
on corn flakes.
Father,
i wanted to scream
at your silence.   30
Your strength
was a stranger
i could never touch.

iron
in your eyes   35
to shield
the pain
to shield desert-like wind
from patches
of strawberries   40
grown
from
tears.

MAKING CONNECTIONS

1. The speaker says that her father "came over the ocean / carrying Mt. Fuji on
   his back." What do you think she means?
2. Later in the poem, she addresses her father directly and says, "Your strength
   / was a stranger / I could never touch." What do you think she is saying
   about their relationship? What has she been missing?
3. Have you ever had this kind of response to a parent or authority figure in
   your life? Explain.
4. Compare this poem to the parent-child relationship in "Those Winter
   Sundays" (p. 13) or the "The Road" on page 243.

MAKING AN ARGUMENT

1. The poem is written in the past tense and contains a number of strong
   images. Is the adult speaker angry or appreciative? Based on the content of
   the poem, what do you believe she feels? Is there a clear message here? Write
   about the narrative tone and imagery in this poem and its effectiveness in
   conveying the poem's meaning. Cite the text of the poem for support.

SHARON OLDS [B. 1942]

*Born in San Francisco, California, Sharon Olds graduated
from Stanford University in 1964 and earned a Ph.D. from
Columbia University in 1972. She published her first book
of poetry,* Satan Says, *in 1980, but it was not until her
second,* The Dead and the Living, *which won the National
Book Critics Circle Award in 1985, that her reputation as
an important voice was firmly established. Her poetry,
which is often intensely personal, is noted for its candor
and power. Her book of poems,* Blood, Tin, and Straw, *was published in 1999 and
her latest book of poems,* The Unswept Room, *in 2002. She teaches creative writing at New York University.*

35/10   [1984]

Brushing out my daughter's dark
silken hair before the mirror
I see the grey gleaming on my head,
the silver-haired servant behind her. Why is it
just as we begin to go   5
they begin to arrive, the fold in my neck
clarifying as the fine bones of her
hips sharpen? As my skin shows
its dry pitting, she opens like a small
pale flower on the tip of a cactus;   10
as my last chances to bear a child
are falling through my body, the duds among them,
her purse of eggs, round and
firm as hard-boiled yolks, is about
to snap its clasp. I brush her tangled   15
fragrant hair at bedtime. It's an old
story—the oldest we have on our planet—
the story of replacement.

MAKING CONNECTIONS

1. What does the title of the poem refer to? How do the numbers "35/10"
   match the specific comparisons of the poem?
2. In what way is it "an old / story—the oldest we have on our planet"? How
   does it play itself out in your own life?
3. Compare this mother-daughter relationship with that in "Dusting" on page 267.

MAKING AN ARGUMENT

1. Like the title, much of this poem is a comparison and contrast. Write about what's being compared and the effectiveness of images, metaphors, and similes that are used. Cite the text of the poem for support.

THEODORE ROETHKE [1908–1963]

Theodore Roethke was a native of Saginaw, Michigan, where his father owned a greenhouse. After graduating from the University of Michigan, he did graduate work at Harvard, taught at a number of universities, and became a poet-in-residence at the University of Washington in 1948. The poem "My Papa's Waltz" is taken from his second volume of poems, The Lost Son *(1948). During the course of a long career, he won two National Book Awards, and in 1954 received the Pulitzer Prize for his book of poems* The Waking: Poems 1933–1953.

MY PAPA'S WALTZ [1942]

The whiskey on your breath
Could make a small boy dizzy;
But I hung on like death
Such waltzing was not easy.

We romped until the pans   5
Slid from the kitchen shelf;
My mother's countenance
Could not unfrown itself.

The hand that held my wrist
Was battered on one knuckle;   10
At every step you missed
My right ear scraped a buckle.

You beat time on my head
With a palm caked hard by dirt,
Then waltzed me off to bed   15
Still clinging to your shirt.

MAKING CONNECTIONS

1. Do you think this is a good or bad memory for the speaker? Explain. To what extent is your response to this poem affected by your own experience with a parent?
2. What is the mother's response to the dancing and why does she respond this way?
3. How does this father compare with the fathers in "Those Winter Sundays" on page 13 or "For My Father" on page 278?

MAKING AN ARGUMENT

1. The speaker in this poem narrates in the past tense—not from the perspective of the small boy in the poem. If it were told from the perspective of the small boy, how would it change? Write about the effectiveness of narration and imagery in this poem. Cite the text of the poem for support.

CATHY SONG [B. 1955]

Cathy Song was born in Honolulu, Hawaii, to a Korean father and a Chinese mother. She graduated from Wellesley College in 1975, and received an M.A. from Boston College in 1981. She currently lives in Hawaii, when she is not teaching creative writing on the mainland. Her first book, The Picture Bride, *from which "The Youngest Daughter" is taken, was published in 1983.* Frameless Windows, Squares of Light, *her second, was published in 1991.* School Figures *appeared in 1994, and her latest collection of poems,* The Land of Bliss, *was published in 2001.*

THE YOUNGEST DAUGHTER   [1983]

The sky has been dark
for many years.
My skin has become as damp
and pale as rice paper
and feels the way   5
mother's used to before the drying sun
parched it out there in the fields.

Lately, when I touch my eyelids,
my hands react as if

I had just touched something   10
hot enough to burn.
My skin, aspirin colored,
tingles with migraine. Mother
has been massaging the left side of my face
especially in the evenings   15
when the pain flares up.

This morning
her breathing was graveled,
her voice gruff with affection
when I wheeled her into the bath.   20
She was in a good humor,
making jokes about her great breasts,
floating in the milky water
like two walruses,
flaccid and whiskered around the nipples.   25
I scrubbed them with a sour taste
in my mouth, thinking:
six children and an old man
have sucked from these brown nipples.

I was almost tender   30
when I came to the blue bruises
that freckle her body,
places where she has been injecting insulin
for thirty years. I soaped her slowly,
she sighed deeply, her eyes closed.   35
It seems it has always
been like this: the two of us
in this sunless room,
the splashing of the bathwater.

In the afternoons   40
when she has rested,
she prepares our ritual of tea and rice,
garnished with a shred of gingered fish,
a slice of pickled turnip,
a token for my white body.   45
We eat in the familiar silence.
She knows I am not to be trusted,
even now planning my escape.
As I toast to her health
with the tea she has poured,   50
a thousand cranes curtain the window,
fly up in a sudden breeze.

MAKING CONNECTIONS

1. What does she mean by "She knows I am not to be trusted, / even now planning my escape"? Do you think the narrator should be having these feelings? Explain.
2. Describe the speaker's reciprocal relationship with her mother. What keeps the mother and daughter bound to each other? What power do they have over each other? What lines in the poem support your view?
3. Compare this mother-daughter relationship with that in "Dusting" on page 267 and "35/10" on page 280.

MAKING AN ARGUMENT

1. One of the most striking images in this poem follows the speaker's toast to her mother's health in the last stanza, and is contained in the lines "a thousand cranes curtain the window, / fly up in a sudden breeze." How does that image compare with other images the speaker presents? Write about the effectiveness of the imagery in this poem and the impact it has on the poem's meaning. Cite the text of the poem for support.

◆ DRAMA ◆

TENNESSEE WILLIAMS [1911–1983]

Tennessee Williams was born in Columbus, Mississippi, and moved with his family to St. Louis, Missouri, when he was twelve. The troubled family of The Glass Menagerie *resembles Williams's own—his mother was a faded southern beauty, his sister suffered from intense shyness, and Williams himself, a frustrated writer, worked at a series of low-paying, unsatisfying jobs. After years of struggling,* The Glass Menagerie *opened on Broadway to tremendous acclaim in 1945, and Williams was instantly established as an important new voice in the theater. Lonely women inhabiting a world of dreams, much like Amanda in* The Glass Menagerie, *are central figures in many of his greatest plays, including* A Streetcar Named Desire, *which won the Pulitzer Prize in 1947, and* Summer and Smoke *(1948). His other major works include the Pulitzer Prize–winning* Cat on a Hot Tin Roof *(1955),* The Rose Tattoo *(1951),* Orpheus Descending *(1957),* Sweet Bird of Youth *(1959), and* The Night of the Iguana *(1961). Though he continued to write until his death, his later plays were less successful. Nevertheless, Williams remains one of the giants of twentieth-century drama.*

THE GLASS MENAGERIE   [1945]

CHARACTERS

AMANDA WINGFIELD, *the mother. A little woman of great but confused vitality cling-ing frantically to another time and place. Her characterization must be carefully created, not copied from type. She is not paranoiac, but her life is paranoia. There is much to admire in* AMANDA, *and as much to love and pity as there is to laugh at. Certainly she has endurance and a kind of heroism, and though her foolishness makes her unwittingly cruel at times, there is tenderness in her slight person.*

LAURA WINGFIELD, *her daughter.* AMANDA, *having failed to establish contact with reality, continues to live vitally in her illusions, but Laura's situation is even graver. A childhood illness has left her crippled, one leg slightly shorter than the other, and held in a brace. This defect need not be more than suggested on the stage. Stemming from this,* LAURA'S *separation increases till she is like a piece of her own glass collection, too exquisitely fragile to move from the shelf.*

TOM WINGFIELD, *her son. And the narrator of the play. A poet with a job in a ware-house. His nature is not remorseless, but to escape from a trap he has to act without pity.*

JIM O'CONNOR, *the gentleman caller. A nice, ordinary, young man.*

SCENE: *An alley in St. Louis.*
PART I: *Preparation for a Gentleman Caller.*
PART II: *The Gentleman Calls.*
TIME: *Now and the Past.*

SCENE I

The Wingfield apartment is in the rear of the building, one of those vast hive-like conglomerations of cellular living-units that flower as warty growths in over-crowded urban centers of lower middle-class population and are symptomatic of the impulse of this largest and fundamentally enslaved section of American soci-ety to avoid fluidity and differentiation and to exist and function as one inter-fused mass of automatism.

The apartment faces an alley and is entered by a fire escape, a structure whose name is a touch of accidental poetic truth, for all of these huge buildings are always burning with the slow and implacable fires of human desperation. The fire escape is included in the set—that is, the landing of it and steps descending from it.

The scene is memory and is therefore nonrealistic. Memory takes a lot of poetic license. It omits some details, others are exaggerated, according to the emo-tional value of the articles it touches, for memory is seated predominantly in the heart. The interior is therefore rather dim and poetic.

At the rise of the curtain, the audience is faced with the dark, grim rear wall of the Wingfield tenement. This building, which runs parallel to the footlights, is flanked on both sides by dark, narrow alleys which run into murky canyons of tangled clotheslines, garbage cans and the sinister latticework of neighboring fire escapes. It is up and down these side alleys that exterior entrances and exits are made, during the play. At the end of TOM'S opening commentary, the dark

*tenement wall slowly reveals (by means of a transparency) the interior of the
ground floor Wingfield apartment.*

Downstage is the living room, which also serves as a sleeping room for LAURA,
*the sofa unfolding to make her bed. Upstage, center, and divided by a wide arch
or second proscenium with transparent faded portieres (or second curtain), is the
dining room. In an old-fashioned what-not in the living room are seen scores of
transparent glass animals. A blown-up photograph of the father hangs on the wall
of the living room, facing the audience, to the left of the archway. It is the face of
a very handsome young man in a doughboy's First World War cap. He is gallantly
smiling, ineluctably smiling, as if to say, "I will be smiling forever."*

*The audience hears and sees the opening scene in the dining room through
both the transparent fourth wall of the building and the transparent gauze
portieres of the dining room arch. It is during this revealing scene that the fourth
wall slowly ascends, out of sight. This transparent exterior wall is not brought
down again until the very end of the play, during* TOM's *final speech.*

*The narrator is an undisguised convention of the play. He takes whatever
license with dramatic convention as is convenient to his purposes.*

TOM *enters dressed as a merchant sailor from alley, stage left, and strolls
across the front of the stage to the fire escape. There he stops and lights a cigarette.
He addresses the audience.*

TOM: Yes, I have tricks in my pocket, I have things up my sleeve. But I am the opposite of a stage magician. He gives you illusion that has the appearance of truth.
I give you truth in the pleasant disguise of illusion. To begin with, I turn back
time. I reverse it to that quaint period, the thirties, when the huge middle class
of America was matriculating in a school for the blind. Their eyes had failed
them, or they had failed their eyes, and so they were having their fingers
pressed forcibly down on the fiery Braille alphabet of a dissolving economy. In
Spain there was revolution. Here there was only shouting and confusion. In
Spain there was Guernica. Here there were disturbances of labor, sometimes
pretty violent, in otherwise peaceful cities such as Chicago, Cleveland, Saint
Louis. . . . This is the social background of the play.

[Music.]

The play is memory.
Being a memory play, it is dimly lighted, it is sentimental, it is not realistic. In
memory everything seems to happen to music. That explains the fiddle in the
wings. I am the narrator of the play, and also a character in it. The other characters are my mother, Amanda, my sister, Laura, and a gentleman caller who
appears in the final scenes. He is the most realistic character in the play, being
an emissary from a world of reality that we were somehow set apart from. But
since I have a poet's weakness for symbols, I am using this character also as a
symbol; he is the long delayed but always expected something that we live for.
There is a fifth character in the play who doesn't appear except in this larger-
than-life photograph over the mantel. This is our father who left us a long time
ago. He was a telephone man who fell in love with long distances; he gave up

his job with the telephone company and skipped the light fantastic out of town. . . . The last we heard of him was a picture postcard from Mazatlan, on the Pacific coast of Mexico, containing a message of two words—"Hello—Goodbye!" and no address. I think the rest of the play will explain itself. . . .

AMANDA'S *voice becomes audible through the portieres.*

[Legend on screen:"Où Sont les Neiges."]

He divides the portieres and enters the upstage area.

AMANDA *and* LAURA *are seated at a drop-leaf table. Eating is indicated by gestures without food or utensils.* AMANDA *faces the audience.* TOM *and* LAURA *are seated in profile.*

The interior has lit up softly and through the scrim we see AMANDA *and* LAURA *seated at the table in the upstage area.*

AMANDA [*calling*]:   Tom?

TOM: Yes, Mother.

AMANDA: We can't say grace until you come to the table!

TOM: Coming, Mother. [*He bows slightly and withdraws, reappearing a few moments later in his place at the table.*]

AMANDA [*to her son*]:   Honey, don't *push* with your *fingers.* If you have to push with something, the thing to push with is a crust of bread. And chew—chew! Animals have sections in their stomachs which enable them to digest food without mastication, but human beings are supposed to chew their food before they swallow it down. Eat food leisurely, son, and really enjoy it. A well-cooked meal has lots of delicate flavors that have to be held in the mouth for appreciation. So chew your food and give your salivary glands a chance to function!

TOM *deliberately lays his imaginary fork down and pushes his chair back from the table.*

TOM: I haven't enjoyed one bite of this dinner because of your constant directions on how to eat it. It's you that makes me rush through meals with your hawk-like attention to every bite I take. Sickening—spoils my appetite—all this discussion of animals' secretion—salivary glands—mastication!

AMANDA   [*lightly*] Temperament like a Metropolitan star! [*He rises and crosses downstage.*] You're not excused from the table.

TOM: I am getting a cigarette.

AMANDA: You smoke too much.

LAURA *rises.*

LAURA: I'll bring in the blanc mange.

He remains standing with his cigarette by the portieres during the following.

---

¹**Où Sont les Neiges [d'antan]** "Where are the snows of yesteryear?" A quotation from the French poet Francois Villon to be projected on a screen at the back of the stage.

AMANDA [*rising*]:   No, sister, no, sister—you be the lady this time and I'll be the darky.

LAURA: I'm already up.

AMANDA: Resume your seat, little sister—I want you to stay fresh and pretty—for gentlemen callers!

LAURA: I'm not expecting any gentlemen callers.

AMANDA [*crossing out to kitchenette. Airily*]:   Sometimes they come when they are least expected! Why, I remember one Sunday afternoon in Blue Mountain— [*enters kitchenette.*]

TOM: I know what's coming!

LAURA: Yes. But let her tell it.

TOM: Again?

LAURA: She loves to tell it.

AMANDA *returns with bowl of dessert.*

AMANDA: One Sunday afternoon in Blue Mountain—your mother received— *seventeen*—gentlemen callers! Why, sometimes there weren't chairs enough to accommodate them all. We had to send the nigger over to bring in folding chairs from the parish house.

TOM [*remaining at portieres*]:   How did you entertain those gentlemen callers?

AMANDA: I understood the art of conversation!

TOM: I bet you could talk.

AMANDA: Girls in those days *knew* how to talk, I can tell you.

TOM: Yes?

[*Image:* AMANDA *as a girl on a porch greeting callers.*]

AMANDA: They knew how to entertain their gentlemen callers. It wasn't enough for a girl to be possessed of a pretty face and a graceful figure—although I wasn't slighted in either respect. She also needed to have a nimble wit and a tongue to meet all occasions.

TOM: What did you talk about?

AMANDA: Things of importance going on in the world! Never anything coarse or common or vulgar. [*She addresses* Tom *as though he were seated in the vacant chair at the table though he remains by portieres. He plays this scene as though he held the book.*] My callers were gentlemen—all! Among my callers were some of the most prominent young planters of the Mississippi Delta—planters and sons of planters!

TOM *motions for music and a spot of light on* AMANDA. *Her eyes lift, her face glows, her voice becomes rich and elegiac.*

[*Screen legend: "Où Sont les Neiges."*]

There was young Champ Laughlin who later became vice president of the Delta Planters Bank. Hadley Stevenson who was drowned in Moon Lake and left his widow one hundred and fifty thousand in Government bonds. There were the Cutrere brothers, Wesley and Bates. Bates was one of my bright particular beaux! He got in a quarrel with that wild Wainright boy. They shot it out on the floor of Moon Lake Casino. Bates was shot through the stomach. Died in the ambulance on his way to Memphis. His widow was also well-provided for, came into eight or ten thousand acres, that's all. She married him on the rebound—never loved her—carried my picture on him the night he died! And there was that boy that every girl in Delta had set her cap for! That beautiful, brilliant young Fitzhugh boy from Green County!

TOM: What did he leave his widow?

AMANDA: He never married! Gracious, you talk as though all of my old admirers had turned up their toes to the daisies!

TOM: Isn't this the first you mentioned that still survives?

AMANDA: That Fitzhugh boy went North and made a fortune—came to be known as the Wolf of Wall Street! He had the Midas touch, whatever he touched turned to gold! And I could have been Mrs. Duncan J. Fitzhugh, mind you! But—I picked your *father!*

LAURA [*rising*]:   Mother, let me clear the table.

AMANDA: No dear, you go in front and study your typewriter chart. Or practice your shorthand a little. Stay fresh and pretty—It's almost time for our gentlemen callers to start arriving. [*She flounces girlishly toward the kitchenette.*] How many do you suppose we're going to entertain this afternoon?

TOM *throws down the paper and jumps up with a groan.*

LAURA [*alone in the dining room*]:   I don't believe we're going to receive any, Mother.

AMANDA [*reappearing, airily*]:   What? No one—not one? You must be joking! [LAURA *nervously echoes her laugh. She slips in a fugitive manner through the half-open portieres and draws them gently behind her. A shaft of very clear light is thrown on her face against the faded tapestry of the curtains.*] [*Music: "The Glass Menagerie" under faintly.*] [*lightly.*] Not one gentleman caller? It can't be true! There must be a flood, there must have been a tornado!

LAURA: It isn't a flood, it's not a tornado, Mother. I'm just not popular like you were in Blue Mountain. . . . [TOM *utters another groan.* LAURA *glances at him with a faint, apologetic smile. Her voice catching a little.*] Mother's afraid I'm going to be an old maid.

[The scene dims out with "The Glass Menagerie" music.]

SCENE 2

"LAURA, Haven't You Ever Liked Some Boy?"
On the dark stage the screen is lighted with the image of blue roses. Gradually LAURA'S *figure becomes apparent and the screen goes out. The music subsides.*

LAURA *is seated in the delicate ivory chair at the small clawfoot table.*

She wears a dress of soft violet material for a kimono—her hair tied back from her forehead with a ribbon.

She is washing and polishing her collection of glass.

AMANDA *appears on the fire-escape steps. At the sound of her ascent,* LAURA *catches her breath, thrusts the bowl of ornaments away and seats herself stiffly before the diagram of the typewriter keyboard as though it held her spellbound. Something has happened to* AMANDA. *It is written in her face as she climbs to the landing: a look that is grim and hopeless and a little absurd.*

She has on one of those cheap or imitation velvety-looking cloth coats with imitation fur collar. Her hat is five or six years old, one of those dreadful cloche hats that were worn in the late twenties, and she is clasping an enormous black patent-leather pocketbook with nickel clasp and initials. This is her full-dress outfit, the one she usually wears to the D.A.R.

Before entering she looks through the door.

She purses her lips, opens her eyes wide, rolls them upward and shakes her head.

Then she slowly lets herself in the door. Seeing her mother's expression LAURA *touches her lips with a nervous gesture.*

LAURA: Hello, Mother, I was—[*She makes a nervous gesture toward the chart on the wall.* AMANDA *leans against the shut door and stares at* LAURA *with a martyred look.*]

AMANDA: Deception? Deception? [*She slowly removes her hat and gloves, continuing the swift suffering stare. She lets the hat and gloves fall on the floor—a bit of acting.*]

LAURA [*shakily*]:   How was the D.A.R. meeting? [AMANDA *slowly opens her purse and removes a dainty white handkerchief which she shakes out delicately and delicately touches to her lips and nostrils.*] Didn't you go to the D.A.R. meeting, Mother?

AMANDA [*faintly, almost inaudibly*]:   —No.—No. [*then more forcibly.*] I did not have the strength—to go to the D.A.R. In fact, I did not have the courage! I wanted to find a hole in the ground and hide myself in it forever! [*She crosses slowly to the wall and removes the diagram of the typewriter keyboard. She holds it in front of her for a second, staring at it sweetly and sorrowfully— then bites her lips and tears it in two pieces.*]

LAURA [*faintly*]:   Why did you do that, Mother? [AMANDA *repeats the same procedure with the chart of the Gregg alphabet.*] Why are you—

AMANDA: Why? Why? How old are you, Laura?

LAURA: Mother, you know my age.

AMANDA: I thought that you were an adult; it seems that I was mistaken. [*She crosses slowly to the sofa and sinks down and stares at* LAURA.]

LAURA: Please don't stare at me, Mother.

AMANDA *closes her eyes and lowers her head. Count ten.*

AMANDA: What are we going to do, what is going to become of us, what is the future?

Count ten.

LAURA: Has something happened, Mother? [AMANDA *draws a long breath and takes out the handkerchief again. Dabbing process.*] Mother, has—something happened?

AMANDA: I'll be all right in a minute. I'm just bewildered—[*count five*]—by life. . . .

LAURA: Mother, I wish that you would tell me what's happened.

AMANDA: As you know, I was supposed to be inducted into my office at the D.A.R. this afternoon. [*Image: A swarm of typewriters.*] But I stopped off at Rubicam's Business College to speak to your teachers about your having a cold and ask them what progress they thought you were making down there.

LAURA: Oh. . . .

AMANDA: I went to the typing instructor and introduced myself as your mother. She didn't know who you were. Wingfield, she said. We don't have any such student enrolled at the school! I assured her she did, that you had been going to classes since early in January. "I wonder," she said, "if you could be talking about that terribly shy little girl who dropped out of school after only a few days' attendance?" "No," I said, "Laura, my daughter, has been going to school every day for the past six weeks!" "Excuse me," she said. She took the attendance book out and there was your name, unmistakably printed, and all the dates you were absent until they decided that you had dropped out of school. I still said, "No, there must have been some mistake! There must have been some mix-up in the records!" And she said, "No—I remember her perfectly now. Her hand shook so that she couldn't hit the right keys! The first time we gave a speed-test, she broke down completely—was sick at the stomach and almost had to be carried into the wash-room! After that morning she never showed up any more. We phoned the house but never got any answer"—while I was working at Famous and Barr, I suppose, demonstrating those—Oh! I felt so weak I could barely keep on my feet. I had to sit down while they got me a glass of water! Fifty dollars tuition, all of our plans—my hopes and ambitions for you—just gone up the spout, just gone up the spout like that. [LAURA *draws a long breath and gets awkwardly to her feet. She crosses to the victrola and winds it up.*] What are you doing?

LAURA: Oh! [*She releases the handle and returns to her seat.*]

AMANDA: Laura, where have you been going when you've gone out pretending that you were going to business college?

LAURA: I've just been going out walking.

AMANDA: That's not true.

LAURA: It is. I just went walking.

AMANDA: Walking? Walking? In winter? Deliberately courting pneumonia in that light coat? Where did you walk to, Laura?

LAURA: It was the lesser of two evils, Mother. [*Image: Winter scene in park.*] I couldn't go back up. I—threw up—on the floor!

AMANDA: From half past seven till after five every day you mean to tell me you walked around in the park, because you wanted to make me think that you were still going to Rubicam's Business College?

LAURA: It wasn't as bad as it sounds. I went inside places to get warmed up.

AMANDA: Inside where?

LAURA: I went in the art museum and the bird-houses at the zoo. I visited the penguins every day! Sometimes I did without lunch and went to the movies. Lately I've been spending most of my afternoons in the Jewel box, that big glass house where they raise the tropical flowers.

AMANDA: You did all this to deceive me, just for the deception? [LAURA *looks down.*] Why?

LAURA: Mother, when you're disappointed, you get that awful suffering look on your face, like the picture of Jesus' mother in the museum!

AMANDA: Hush!

LAURA: I couldn't face it.

Pause. A whisper of strings.

[Legend: "The Crust of Humility."]

AMANDA [*hopelessly fingering the huge pocketbook*]:   So what are we going to do the rest of our lives? Stay home and watch the parades go by? Amuse ourselves with the glass menagerie, darling? Eternally play those worn-out phonograph records your father left as a painful reminder of him? We won't have a business career— we've given that up because it gave us nervous indigestion! [*laughs wearily.*] What is there left but dependency all our lives? I know so well what becomes of unmarried women who aren't prepared to occupy a position. I've seen such pitiful cases in the South—barely tolerated spinsters living upon the grudging patronage of sister's husband or brother's wife!—stuck away in some little mousetrap of a room—encouraged by one in-law to visit another—little birdlike women without any nest—eating the crust of humility all their life! Is that the future that we've mapped out for ourselves? I swear it's the only alternative I can think of! It isn't a very pleasant alternative, is it? Of course—some girls *do marry.* [LAURA *twists her hands nervously.*] Haven't you ever liked some boy?

LAURA: Yes. I liked one once. [*rises.*] I came across his picture a while ago.

AMANDA   [*with some interest*]: He gave you his picture?

LAURA: No, it's in the year-book.

AMANDA [*disappointed*]:   Oh—a high-school boy.

[Screen Image: JIM as a high-school hero bearing a silver cup.]

LAURA: Yes. His name was Jim. [LAURA *lifts the heavy annual from the clawfoot table.*] Here he is in *The Pirates of Penzance.*

AMANDA [*absently*]:   The what?

LAURA: The operetta the senior class put on. He had a wonderful voice and we sat across the aisle from each other Mondays, Wednesdays and Fridays in the Aud. Here he is with the silver cup for debating! See his grin?

AMANDA [*absently*]:   He must have had a jolly disposition.

LAURA: He used to call me—Blue Roses.

[Image: Blue roses.]

AMANDA: Why did he call you such a name as that?

LAURA: When I had that attack of pleurosis—he asked me what was the matter when I came back. I said pleurosis—he thought that I said Blue Roses! So that's what he always called me after that. Whenever he saw me, he'd holler, "Hello, Blue Roses!" I didn't care for the girl that he went out with. Emily Meisenbach. Emily was the best-dressed girl at Soldan. She never struck me, though, as being sincere.... It says in the Personal Section—they're engaged. That's—six years ago! They must be married by now.

AMANDA: Girls that aren't cut out for business careers usually wind up married to some nice man. [*gets up with a spark of revival.*] Sister, that's what you'll do!

LAURA *utters a startled, doubtful laugh. She reaches quickly for a piece of glass.*

LAURA: But, Mother—

AMANDA: Yes? [*crossing to photograph.*]

LAURA [*in a tone of frightened apology*]:   I'm—crippled!

[Image: Screen.]

AMANDA: Nonsense! Laura, I've told you never, never to use that word. Why, you're not crippled, you just have a little defect—hardly noticeable, even! When people have some slight disadvantage like that, they cultivate other things to make up for it—develop charm—and vivacity—and—*charm!* That's all you have to do! [*She turns again to the photograph.*] One thing your father had plenty of—was charm!

TOM *motions to the fiddle in the wings.*

[The scene fades out with music.]

SCENE 3

[Legend on screen:"After the Fiasco—"]
TOM *speaks from the fire escape landing.*

TOM: After the fiasco at Rubicam's Business College, the idea of getting a gentleman caller for Laura began to play a more important part in Mother's calculations. It became an obsession. Like some archetype of the universal unconscious, the image of the gentleman caller haunted our small apartment.... [*Image:Young man at door with flowers.*] An evening at home rarely passed without some allusion to this image, this specter, this hope.... Even when he wasn't mentioned, his presence hung in Mother's preoccupied look and in my sister's frightened, apologetic manner—hung like a sentence passed upon the Wingfields! Mother was a woman of action as well as words. She began to take logical steps in the planned direction. Late that winter and in the early spring—realizing that extra money would be needed to properly feather the nest and plume the bird—she conducted a vigorous campaign on the telephone, roping in subscribers to one of those magazines for matrons called *The Homemaker's Companion*, the type of journal that features the serialized sublimations of ladies of letters who think in terms of delicate cuplike breasts, slim, tapering waists, rich, creamy thighs, eyes like wood smoke in autumn, fingers that soothe and caress like strains of music, bodies as powerful as Etruscan sculpture.

[Screen image: Glamor magazine cover.]

AMANDA *enters with phone on long extension cord. She is spotted in the dim stage.*

AMANDA: Ida Scott? This is Amanda Wingfield! We *missed* you at the D.A.R. last Monday! I said to myself: She's probably suffering with that sinus condition! How is that sinus condition? Horrors! Heaven have mercy!—You're a Christian martyr, yes, that's what you are, a Christian martyr! Well, I just now happened to notice that your subscription to the *Companion*'s about to expire! Yes, it expires with the next issue, honey!—just when that wonderful new serial by Bessie Mae Hopper is getting off to such an exciting start. Oh, honey, it's something that you can't miss! You remember how *Gone with the Wind* took everybody by storm? You simply couldn't go out if you hadn't read it. All everybody *talked* was Scarlett O'Hara. Well, this is a book that critics already compare to *Gone with the Wind*. It's the *Gone with the Wind* of the post–World War generation!—What?—Burning?—Oh, honey, don't let them burn, go take a look in the oven and I'll hold the wire! Heavens—I think she's hung up!

[Dim out.]

[Legend on screen: "You Think I'm in Love with Continental Shoemakers?"]

Before the stage is lighted, the violent voices of TOM *and* AMANDA *are heard. They are quarreling behind the portieres. In front of them stands* LAURA *with clenched hands and panicky expression.*

A clear pool of light on her figure throughout this scene.

TOM: What in Christ's name am I—

AMANDA [*shrilly*]:   Don't you use that—

TOM: Supposed to do!

AMANDA: Expression! Not in my—

TOM: Ohhh!

AMANDA: Presence! Have you gone out of your senses?

TOM: I have, that's true, *driven* out!

AMANDA: What is the matter with you, you—big—big—IDIOT!

TOM: Look—I've got *no thing,* no single thing—

AMANDA: Lower your voice!

TOM: In my life here that I can call my OWN! Everything is—

AMANDA: Stop that shouting!

TOM: Yesterday you confiscated my books! You had the nerve to—

AMANDA: I took that horrible novel back to the library—yes! That hideous book by that insane Mr. Lawrence. [TOM *laughs wildly.*] I cannot control the output of diseased minds or people who cater to them—[Tom laughs still more wildly.] BUT I WON'T ALLOW SUCH FILTH BROUGHT INTO MY HOUSE! No, no, no, no, no!

TOM: House, house! Who pays rent on it, who makes a slave of himself to—

AMANDA [*fairly screeching*]:   Don't you DARE to—

TOM: No, no, *I* mustn't say things! *I've* got to just—

AMANDA: Let me tell you—

TOM: I don't want to hear any more! [*He tears the portieres open. The upstage area is lit with a turgid smoky red glow.*]

AMANDA'S *hair is in metal curlers and she wears a very old bathrobe, much too large for her slight figure, a relic of the faithless Mr. Wingfield.*

An upright typewriter and a wild disarray of manuscripts are on the dropleaf table. The quarrel was probably precipitated by AMANDA'S *interruption of his creative labor. A chair lying overthrown on the floor.*

Their gesticulating shadows are cast on the ceiling by the fiery glow.

AMANDA: You *will* hear more, you—

TOM: No, I won't hear more, I'm going out!

AMANDA: You come right back in—

TOM: Out, out, out! Because I'm—

AMANDA: Come back here, Tom Wingfield! I'm not through talking to you!

TOM: Oh, go—

LAURA [*desperately*]:   Tom!

AMANDA: You're going to listen, and no more insolence from you! I'm at the end of my patience! [*He comes back toward her.*]

TOM: What do you think I'm at? Aren't I supposed to have any patience to reach the end of, Mother? I know, I know. It seems unimportant to you, what I'm *doing*—what I *want* to do—having a little *difference* between them! You don't think that—

AMANDA: I think you've been doing things that you're ashamed of. That's why you act like this. I don't believe that you go every night to the movies. Nobody goes to the movies night after night. Nobody in their right minds goes to the movies as often as you pretend to. People don't go to the movies at nearly midnight, and movies don't let out at two A.M. Come in stumbling. Muttering to yourself like a maniac! You get three hours' sleep and then go to work. Oh, I can picture the way you're doing down there. Moping, doping, because you're in no condition.

TOM [*wildly*]:   No, I'm in no condition!

AMANDA: What right have you got to jeopardize your job? Jeopardize the security of us all? How do you think we'd manage if you were—

TOM: Listen! You think I'm crazy *about* the *warehouse?* [*He bends fiercely toward her slight figure.*] You think I'm in love with the Continental Shoemakers? You think I want to spend fifty-five *years* down there in that—*celotex interior!* with—

fluorescent—tubes! Look! I'd rather somebody picked up a crowbar and battered out my brains—than go back mornings! I *go!* Every time you come in yelling that God damn "*Rise and Shine!*" "*Rise and Shine!*" I say to myself "How *lucky dead* people are!" But I get up. I *go!* For sixty-five dollars a month I give up all that I dream of doing and being *ever!* And you say self—*self's* all I ever think of. Why, listen, if self is what I thought of, Mother, I'd be where he is—GONE! [*pointing to father's picture.*] As far as the system of transportation reaches! [*He starts past her. She grabs his arm.*] Don't grab at me, Mother!

AMANDA: Where are you going?

TOM: I'm going to the *movies!*

AMANDA: I don't believe that lie!

TOM [*Crouching toward her, overtowering her tiny figure. She backs away, gasping*]:   I'm going to opium dens! Yes, opium dens, dens of vice and criminals' hangouts, Mother. I've joined the Hogan gang, I'm a hired assassin, I carry a tommy-gun in a violin case! I run a string of cathouses in the valley! They call me Killer, Killer Wingfield, I'm leading a doublelife, a simple, honest warehouse worker by day, by night a dynamic *czar* of the *underworld, Mother.* I go to gambling casinos, I spin away fortunes on the roulette table! I wear a patch over one eye and a false mustache, sometimes I put on green whiskers. On those occasions they call me—*El Diablo!* Oh, I could tell you things to make you sleepless! My enemies plan to dynamite this place. They're going to blow us all sky high some night! I'll be glad, very happy, and so will you! You'll go up, up on a broomstick, over Blue Mountain with seventeen gentlemen callers! You ugly—babbling old—*witch....*

[*He goes through a series of violent, clumsy movements, seizing his overcoat, lunging to the door, pulling it fiercely open. The women watch him, aghast. His arm catches in the sleeve of the coat as he struggles to pull it on. For a moment he is pinioned by the bulky garment. With an outraged groan he tears the coat off again, splitting the shoulders of it and hurls it across the room. It strikes against the shelf of* LAURA's *glass collection, there is a tinkle of shattering glass.* LAURA *cries out as if wounded.*]

[*Music legend: "The Glass Menagerie."*]

LAURA [*shrilly*]:   My glass!—menagerie. . . . [*She covers her face and turns away.*]

But AMANDA *is still stunned and stupefied by the "ugly witch" so that she barely notices this occurrence. Now she recovers her speech.*

AMANDA [*in an awful voice*]:   I won't speak to you—until you apologize!

[*She crosses through portieres and draws them together behind her.* TOM *is left with* LAURA. LAURA *clings weakly to the mantel with her face averted.* TOM *stares at her stupidly for a moment. Then he crosses to shelf. Drops, awkwardly to his knees to collect the fallen glass, glancing at* LAURA *as if he would speak but couldn't.*]

"The Glass Menagerie" steals in as

[*The scene dims out.*]

SCENE 4

The interior is dark. Faint light in the alley.

A deep-voiced bell in a church is tolling the hour of five as the scene commences.

TOM *appears at the top of the alley. After each solemn boom of the bell in the tower, he shakes a little noise-maker or rattle as if to express the tiny spasm of man in contrast to the sustained power and dignity of the Almighty. This and the unsteadiness of his advance make it evident that he has been drinking.*

As he climbs the few steps to the fire-escape landing light steals up inside. LAURA *appears in nightdress, observing* TOM's *empty bed in the front room.*

TOM *fishes in his pockets for the door key, removing a motley assortment of articles in the search, including a perfect shower of movie ticket stubs and an empty bottle. At last he finds the key, but just as he is about to insert it, it slips from his fingers. He strikes a match and crouches below the door.*

TOM [*bitterly*]:   One crack—and it falls through!

LAURA *opens the door.*

LAURA: Tom! Tom, what are you doing?

TOM: Looking for a door key.

LAURA: Where have you been all this time?

TOM: I have been to the movies.

LAURA: All this time at the movies?

TOM: There was a very long program. There was a Garbo picture and a Mickey Mouse and a travelogue and a newsreel and a preview of coming attractions. And there was an organ solo and a collection for the milk fund—simultaneously—which ended up in a terrible fight between a fat lady and an usher!

LAURA [*innocently*]:   Did you have to stay through everything?

TOM: Of course! And, oh, I forgot! There was a big stage show! The headliner on this stage show was Malvolio the Magician. He performed wonderful tricks, many of them, such as pouring water back and forth between pitchers. First it turned to wine and then it turned to beer and then it turned to whiskey. I know it was whiskey it finally turned into because he needed somebody to come up out of the audience to help him, and I came up—both shows! It was Kentucky Straight Bourbon. A very generous fellow, he gave souvenirs. [*He pulls from his back pocket a shimmering rainbow-colored scarf.*] He gave me this. This is his magic scarf. You can have it, Laura. You wave it over a canary cage and you get a bowl of goldfish. You wave it over the goldfish bowl and they fly away canaries. . . . But the wonderfullest trick of all was the coffin trick. We nailed him into a coffin and he got out of the coffin without removing one nail. [*He has come inside.*] There is a trick that would come in handy for me—get me out of this two-by-four situation! [*flops onto bed and starts removing shoes.*]

LAURA: Tom—Shhh!

TOM: What you shushing me for?

LAURA: You'll wake up Mother.

TOM: Goody, goody! Pay 'er back for all those "Rise an' shines." [*lies down, groaning.*] You know it don't take much intelligence to get yourself into a nailed-up coffin, Laura. But who in hell ever got himself out of one without removing one nail?

As if in answer, the father's grinning photograph lights up.

[Scene dims out.]

Immediately following: The church bell is heard striking six. At the sixth stroke the alarm clock goes off in AMANDA'S *room, and after a few moments we hear her calling: "Rise and shine! Rise and shine! Laura, go tell your brother to rise and shine!"*

TOM [*sitting up slowly*]:   I'll rise—but I won't shine.

The light increases.

AMANDA: Laura, tell your brother his coffee is ready.

LAURA *slips into front room.*

LAURA: Tom! it's nearly seven. Don't make Mother nervous. [*He stares at her stupidly. Beseechingly.*] Tom, speak to Mother this morning. Make up with her, apologize, speak to her!

TOM: She won't to me. It's her that started not speaking.

LAURA: If you just say you're sorry she'll start speaking.

TOM: Her not speaking—is that such a tragedy?

LAURA: Please—please!

AMANDA [*calling from kitchenette*]:   Laura, are you going to do what I asked you to do, or do I have to get dressed and go out myself?

LAURA: Going, going—soon as I get on my coat! [*She pulls on a shapeless felt hat with nervous, jerky movement, pleadingly glancing at* TOM. *Rushes awkwardly for coat. The coat is one of* AMANDA'S, *inaccurately made-over, the sleeves too short for* LAURA.] Butter and what else?

AMANDA [*entering upstage*]:   Just butter. Tell them to charge it.

LAURA: Mother, they make such faces when I do that.

AMANDA: Sticks and stones may break my bones, but the expression on Mr. Garfinkel's face won't harm us! Tell your brother his coffee is getting cold.

LAURA [*at door*]:   Do what I asked you, will you, will you, Tom?

He looks sullenly away.

AMANDA: Laura, go now or just don't go at all!

LAURA   [*rushing out*]: Going—going! [*A second later she cries out.* TOM *springs up and crosses to the door.* AMANDA *rushes anxiously in.* TOM *opens the door.*]

TOM: Laura?

LAURA: I'm all right. I slipped, but I'm all right.

AMANDA [*peering anxiously after her*]:   If anyone breaks a leg on those fire escape steps, the landlord ought to be sued for every cent he possesses!

[She shuts door. Remembers she isn't speaking and returns to other room.]

As TOM *enters listlessly for his coffee, she turns her back to him and stands rigidly facing the window on the gloomy gray vault of the areaway. Its light on her face with its aged but childish features is cruelly sharp, satirical as a Daumier[2] print.*

[Music Under:"Ave Maria."]

TOM *glances sheepishly but sullenly at her averted figure and slumps at the table. The coffee is scalding hot; he sips it and gasps and spits it back in the cup. At his gasp,* AMANDA *catches her breath and half turns. Then catches herself and turns back to window.*

TOM *blows on his coffee, glancing sidewise at his mother. She clears her throat.* TOM *clears his. He starts to rise. Sinks back down again, scratches his head, clears his throat again.* AMANDA *coughs.* TOM *raises his cup in both hands to blow on it, his eyes staring over the rim of it at his mother for several moments. Then he slowly sets the cup down and awkwardly and hesitantly rises from the chair.*

TOM [*hoarsely*]:   Mother. I—I apologize. Mother. [AMANDA *draws a quick, shuddering breath. Her face works grotesquely. She breaks into childlike tears.*] I'm sorry for what I said, for everything that I said, I didn't mean it.

AMANDA [*sobbingly*]:   My devotion has made me a witch and so I make myself hateful to my children!

TOM: No you *don't.*

AMANDA: I worry so much, don't sleep, it makes me nervous!

TOM [*gently*]:   I understand that.

AMANDA: I've had to put up a solitary battle all these years. But you're my right-hand bower! Don't fall down, don't fail!

TOM [*gently*]:   I try, Mother.

AMANDA [*with great enthusiasm*]:   Try and you will SUCCEED! [*The notion makes her breathless.*] Why, you—you're just *full* of natural endowments! Both of my children—they're *unusual* children! Don't you think I know it? I'm so— *proud!* Happy and—feel I've—so much to be thankful for but—promise me one thing, son!

TOM: What, Mother?

AMANDA: Promise, son, you'll—never be a drunkard!

TOM [*turns to her grinning*]:   I will never be a drunkard, Mother.

AMANDA: That's what frightened me so, that you'd be drinking! Eat a bowl of Purina!

TOM: Just coffee, Mother.

AMANDA: Shredded wheat biscuit?

TOM: No. No, Mother, just coffee.

AMANDA: You can't put in a day's work on an empty stomach. You've got ten

---

[2]**Honoré Daumier** (1808–1879) French caricaturist, painter, and sculptor who was known for the lithographs he created to mock middle-class society.

minutes—don't gulp! Drinking too-hot liquids makes cancer of the stomach. . . . Put cream in.

TOM: No, thank you.

AMANDA: To cool it.

TOM: No! No, thank you, I want it black.

AMANDA: I know, but it's not good for you. We have to do all that we can to build ourselves up. In these trying times we live in, all that we have to cling to is— each other. . . . That's why it's so important to—Tom, I—I sent out your sister so I could discuss something with you. If you hadn't spoken I would have spoken to you. [*sits down.*]

TOM [*gently*]: What is it, Mother, that you want to discuss?

AMANDA: Laura!

TOM *puts his cup down slowly.*

[*Legend on screen:"Laura."*]

[*Music:"The Glass Menagerie."*]

TOM: —Oh.—Laura . . .

AMANDA [*touching his sleeve*]: You know how Laura is. So quiet but—still water runs deep! She notices things and I think she—broods about them. [TOM *looks up.*] A few days ago I came in and she was crying.

TOM: What about?

AMANDA: You.

TOM: Me?

AMANDA: She has an idea that you're not happy here.

TOM: What gave her that idea?

AMANDA: What gives her any idea? However, you do act strangely. I—I'm not criticizing, understand *that!* I know your ambitions do not lie in the warehouse, that like everybody in the whole wide world—you've had to—make sacrifices, but—Tom—Tom—life's not easy, it calls for—Spartan endurance! There's so many things in my heart that I cannot describe to you! I've never told you but I—*loved* your father. . . .

TOM [*gently*]: I know that, Mother.

AMANDA: And you—when I see you taking after his ways! Staying out late—and— well, you *had* been drinking the night you were in that—terrifying condition! Laura says that you hate the apartment and that you go out nights to get away from it! Is that true, Tom?

TOM: No. You say there's so much in your heart that you can't describe to me. That's true of me, too. There's so much in my heart that I can't describe to *you!* So let's respect each other's—

AMANDA: But, why—*why,* Tom—are you always so *restless?* Where do you go to, nights?

TOM: I—go to the movies.

AMANDA: Why do you go to the movies so much, Tom?

Tom: I go to the movies because—I like adventure. Adventure is something I don't
have much of at work, so I go to the movies.

Amanda: But, Tom, you go to the movies *entirely* too *much!*

Tom: I like a lot of adventure.

Amanda *looks baffled, then hurt. As the familiar inquisition resumes he becomes
hard and impatient again.* Amanda *slips back into her querulous attitude toward
him.*

[Image on screen: Sailing vessel with Jolly Roger.]

Amanda: Most young men find adventure in their careers.

Tom: Then most young men are not employed in a warehouse.

Amanda: The world is full of young men employed in warehouses and offices and
factories.

Tom: Do all of them find adventure in their careers?

Amanda: They do or they do without it! Not everybody has a craze for adventure.

Tom: Man is by instinct a lover, a hunter, a fighter, and none of those instincts are
given much play at the warehouse!

Amanda: Man is by instinct! Don't quote instinct to me! Instinct is something that
people have got away from! It belongs to animals! Christian adults don't
want it!

Tom: What do Christian adults want, then, Mother?

Amanda: Superior things! Things of the mind and the spirit! Only animals have to
satisfy instincts! Surely your aims are somewhat higher than theirs! Than monkeys—pigs—

Tom: I reckon they're not.

Amanda: You're joking. However, that isn't what I wanted to discuss.

Tom [*rising*]:   I haven't much time.

Amanda   [*pushing his shoulders*]:Sit down.

Tom: You want me to punch in red at the warehouse, Mother?

Amanda: You have five minutes. I want to talk about Laura.

[Legend:"Plans and Provisions."]

Tom: All right! What about Laura?

Amanda: We have to be making plans and provisions for her. She's older than you,
two years, and nothing has happened. She just drifts along doing nothing. It
frightens me terribly how she just drifts along.

Tom: I guess she's the type that people call home girls.

Amanda: There's no such type, and if there is, it's a pity! That is unless the home is
hers, with a husband!

Tom: What?

Amanda: Oh, I can see the handwriting on the wall as plain as I see the nose in the
front of my face! It's terrifying! More and more you remind me of your father!
He was out all hours without explanation—Then *left! Goodbye!* And me with
the bag to hold. I saw that letter you got from the merchant marine. I know

what you're dreaming of. I'm not standing here blindfolded. Very well, then. Then *do* it! But not till there's somebody to take your place.

TOM: What do you mean?

AMANDA: I mean that as soon as Laura has got somebody to take care of her, married, a home of her own, independent—why, then you'll be free to go wherever you please, on land, on sea, whichever way the wind blows! But until that time you've got to look out for your sister. I don't say me because I'm old and don't matter! I say for your sister because she's young and dependent. I put her in business college—a dismal failure! Frightened her so it made her sick to her stomach. I took her over to the Young People's League at the church. Another fiasco. She spoke to nobody, nobody spoke to her. Now all she does is fool with those pieces of glass and play those worn-out records. What kind of a life is that for a girl to lead!

TOM: What can I do about it?

AMANDA: Overcome selfishness! Self, self, self is all that you ever think of! [TOM *springs up and crosses to get his coat. It is ugly and bulky. He pulls on a cap with earmuffs.*] Where is your muffler? Put your wool muffler on! [*He snatches it angrily from the closet and tosses it around his neck and pulls both ends tight.*] Tom! I haven't said what I had in mind to ask you.

TOM: I'm too late to—

AMANDA [*catching his arms—very importunately. Then shyly*]:   Down at the warehouse, aren't there some—nice young men?

TOM: No!

AMANDA: There must be—*some.*

TOM: Mother—

Gesture.

AMANDA: Find out one that's clean-living—doesn't drink and—ask him out for sister!

TOM: What?

AMANDA: For *sister!* To *meet!* Get *acquainted!*

TOM [*stamping to door*]:   Oh, my *go-osh!*

AMANDA: Will you? [*He opens door. Imploringly.*] Will you? [*He starts down*] Will you? Will you, dear?

TOM [*calling back*]:   Yes!

AMANDA *closes the door hesitantly and with a troubled but faintly hopeful expression.*

[*Screen image: Glamor magazine cover.*]

Spot AMANDA *at phone.*

AMANDA: Ella Cartwright? This is Amanda Wingfield! How are you, honey? How is that kidney condition? [*count five.*] *Horrors!* [*count five.*] You're a Christian martyr, yes, honey, that's what you are, a Christian martyr! Well, I just happened to notice in my little red book that your subscription to the *Companion* has just run out! I knew that you wouldn't want to miss out on the wonderful serial starting in this new issue. It's by Bessie Mae Hopper, the first thing she's written since *Honeymoon for Three*. Wasn't that a strange and interesting story? Well, this one is even lovelier, I believe. It has a sophisticated society background. It's all about the horsey set on Long Island!

[Fade out.]

SCENE 5

[Legend on screen:"Annunciation."] Fade with music.

It is early dusk of a spring evening. Supper has just been finished at the Wingfield apartment. AMANDA *and* LAURA *in light colored dresses are removing dishes from the table, in the upstage area, which is shadowy, their movements formalized almost as a dance or ritual, their moving forms as pale and silent as moths.*

TOM, *in white shirt and trousers, rises from the table and crosses toward the fire escape.*

AMANDA [*as he passes her*]:   Son, will you do me a favor?

TOM: What?

AMANDA: Comb your hair! You look so pretty when your hair is combed! [TOM *slouches on sofa with evening paper. Enormous caption:"Franco Triumphs."*] There is only one respect in which I would like you to emulate your father.

TOM: What respect is that?

AMANDA: The care he always took of his appearance. He never allowed himself to look untidy. [*He throws down the paper and crosses to fire escape.*] Where are you going?

TOM: I'm going out to smoke.

AMANDA: You smoke too much. A pack a day at fifteen cents a pack. How much would that amount to in a month? Thirty times fifteen is how much, Tom? Figure it out and you will be astounded at what you could save. Enough to give you a night-school course in accounting at Washington U! Just think what a wonderful thing that would be for you, son!

TOM *is unmoved by the thought.*

TOM: I'd rather smoke. [*He steps out on landing, letting the screen door slam.*]

AMANDA [*sharply*]:   I know! That's the tragedy of it. . . . [*Alone, she turns to look at her husband's picture.*]

[Dance music;"All the World Is Waiting for the Sunrise!"]

TOM [*to the audience*]:   Across the alley from us was the Paradise Dance Hall. On evenings in spring the windows and doors were open and the music came outdoors. Sometimes the lights were turned out except for a large glass sphere that hung from the ceiling. It would turn slowly about and filter the dusk with delicate rainbow colors. Then the orchestra played a waltz or a tango,

something that had a slow and sensuous rhythm. Couples would come outside, to the relative privacy of the alley. You could see them kissing behind ash
pits and telephone poles. This was the compensation for lives that passed like
mine, without any change or adventure. Adventure and change were imminent
in this year. They were waiting around the corner for all these kids. Suspended
in the mist over Berchtesgaden,[3] caught in the folds of Chamberlain's[4]
umbrella—In Spain there was Guernica! But here there was only hot swing
music and liquor, dance halls, bars, and movies, and sex that hung in the gloom
like a chandelier and flooded the world with brief, deceptive rainbows. . . . All
the world was waiting for bombardments!

AMANDA *turns from the picture and comes outside.*

AMANDA [*sighing*]:   A fire escape landing's a poor excuse for a porch. [*She spreads a
    newspaper on a step and sits down, gracefully and demurely as if she were
    settling into a swing on a Mississippi veranda.*] What are you looking at?

TOM: The moon.

AMANDA: Is there a moon this evening?

TOM: It's rising over Garfinkel's Delicatessen.

AMANDA: So it is! A little silver slipper of a moon. Have you made a wish on it yet?

TOM: Um-hum.

AMANDA: What did you wish for?

TOM: That's a secret.

AMANDA: A secret, huh? Well, I won't tell mine either. I will be just as mysterious as
    you.

TOM: I bet I can guess what yours is.

AMANDA: Is my head so transparent?

TOM: You're not a sphinx.

AMANDA: No, I don't have secrets. I'll tell you what I wished for on the moon.
    Success and happiness for my precious children! I wish for that whenever
    there's a moon, and when there isn't a moon, I wish for it, too.

TOM: I thought perhaps you wished for a gentleman caller.

AMANDA: Why do you say that?

TOM: Don't you remember asking me to fetch one?

AMANDA: I remember suggesting that it would be nice for your sister if you brought
    some nice young man from the warehouse. I think I've made that suggestion
    more than once.

TOM: Yes, you have made it repeatedly.

---

[3]**Berchtesgaden** A resort town in Bavaria, Germany, where Hitler met with the leaders of the
Third Reich to plan strategy.   [4]**Neville Chamberlain** (1869–1940) British prime minister
who believed that Hitler could be appeased, a policy that many thought led to World War II.

AMANDA: Well?

TOM: We are going to have one.

AMANDA: What?

TOM: A gentleman caller!

[The Annunciation Is Celebrated with Music.]

AMANDA *rises.*

[Image on screen: Caller with bouquet.]

AMANDA: You mean you have asked some nice young man to come over?

TOM: Yep. I've asked him to dinner.

AMANDA: You really did?

TOM: I did!

AMANDA: You did, and did he—*accept?*

TOM: He did!

AMANDA: Well, well—well, well! That's—lovely!

TOM: I thought that you would be pleased.

AMANDA: It's definite, then?

TOM: Very definite.

AMANDA: Soon?

TOM: Very soon.

AMANDA: For heaven's sake, stop putting on and tell me some things, will you?

TOM: What things do you want me to tell you?

AMANDA: Naturally I would like to know when he's *coming!*

TOM: He's coming tomorrow.

AMANDA: *Tomorrow?*

TOM: Yep. Tomorrow.

AMANDA: But, Tom!

TOM: Yes, Mother?

AMANDA: Tomorrow gives me no time!

TOM: Time for what?

AMANDA: Preparations! Why didn't you phone me at once, as soon as you asked him, the minute that he accepted? Then, don't you see, I could have been getting ready!

TOM: You don't have to make any fuss.

AMANDA: Oh, Tom, Tom, Tom, of course I have to make a fuss! I want things nice, not sloppy! Not thrown together. I'll certainly have to do some fast thinking, won't I?

TOM: I don't see why you have to think at all.

AMANDA: You just don't know. We can't have a gentleman caller in a pigsty! All my wedding silver has to be polished, the monogrammed table linen ought to be laundered! The windows have to be washed and fresh curtains put up. And how about clothes? We have to *wear* something, don't we?

TOM: Mother, this boy is no one to make a fuss over!

AMANDA: Do you realize he's the first young man we've introduced to your sister? It's terrible, dreadful, disgraceful that poor little sister has never received a single gentleman caller! Tom, come inside! [*She opens the screen door.*]

TOM: What for?

AMANDA: I want to ask you some things.

TOM: If you're going to make such a fuss, I'll call it off, I'll tell him not to come.

AMANDA: You certainly won't do anything of the kind. Nothing offends people worse than broken engagements. It simply means I'll have to work like a Turk! We won't be brilliant, but we'll pass inspection. Come on inside. [TOM *follows, groaning.*] Sit down.

TOM: Any particular place you would like me to sit?

AMANDA: Thank heavens I've got that new sofa! I'm also making payments on a floor lamp I'll have sent out! And put the chintz covers on, they'll brighten things up! Of course I'd hoped to have these walls repapered. . . . What is the young man's name?

TOM: His name is O'Connor.

AMANDA: That, of course, means fish—tomorrow is Friday! I'll have that salmon loaf—with Durkee's dressing! What does he do? He works at the warehouse?

TOM: Of course! How else would I—

AMANDA: Tom, he—doesn't drink?

TOM: Why do you ask me that?

AMANDA: Your father *did!*

TOM: Don't get started on that!

AMANDA: He *does* drink, then?

TOM: Not that I know of!

AMANDA: Make sure, be certain! The last thing I want for my daughter's a boy who drinks!

TOM: Aren't you being a little premature? Mr. O'Connor has not yet appeared on the scene!

AMANDA: But will tomorrow. To meet your sister, and what do I know about his character? Nothing! Old maids are better off than wives of drunkards!

TOM: Oh, my God!

AMANDA: Be still!

TOM [*leaning forward to whisper*]:   Lots of fellows meet girls whom they don't marry!

AMANDA: Oh, talk sensibly, Tom—and don't be sarcastic! [*She has gotten a hairbrush.*]

TOM: What are you doing?

AMANDA: I'm brushing that cowlick down! What is this young man's position at the warehouse?

TOM [*submitting grimly to the brush and the interrogation*]:   This young man's position is that of a shipping clerk, Mother.

AMANDA: Sounds to me like a fairly responsible job, the sort of a job *you* would be in if you just had more *get-up.* What is his salary? Have you got any idea?

TOM: I would judge it to be approximately eighty-five dollars a month.

AMANDA: Well—not princely, but—

TOM: Twenty more than I make.

AMANDA: Yes, how well I know! But for a family man, eighty-five dollars a month is not much more than you can just get by on. . . .

TOM: Yes, but Mr. O'Connor is not a family man.

AMANDA: He might be, mightn't he? Some time in the future?

TOM: I see. Plans and provisions.

AMANDA: You are the only young man that I know of who ignores the fact that the future becomes the present, the present the past, and the past turns into everlasting regret if you don't plan for it!

TOM: I will think that over and see what I can make of it.

AMANDA: Don't be supercilious with your mother! Tell me some more about this—what do you call him?

TOM: James D. O'Connor. The D. is for Delaney.

AMANDA: Irish on *both* sides! *Gracious!* And doesn't drink?

TOM: Shall I call him up and ask him right this minute?

AMANDA: The only way to find out about those things is to make discreet inquiries at the proper moment. When I was a girl in Blue Mountain and it was suspected that a young man drank, the girl whose attentions he had been receiving, if any girl *was,* would sometimes speak to the minister of his church, or rather her father would if her father was living, and sort of feel him out on the young man's character. That is the way such things are discreetly handled to keep a young woman from making a tragic mistake!

TOM: Then how did you happen to make a tragic mistake?

AMANDA: That innocent look of your father's had everyone fooled! He *smiled*—the world was *enchanted!* No girl can do worse than put herself at the mercy of a handsome appearance! I hope that Mr. O'Connor is not too good-looking.

TOM: No, he's not too good-looking. He's covered with freckles and hasn't too much of a nose.

AMANDA: He's not right-down homely, though?

TOM: Not right-down homely. Just medium homely, I'd say.

AMANDA: Character's what to look for in a man.

TOM: That's what I've always said, Mother.

AMANDA: You've never said anything of the kind and I suspect you would never give it a thought.

TOM: Don't be suspicious of me.

AMANDA: At least I hope he's the type that's up and coming.

TOM: I think he really goes in for self-improvement.

AMANDA: What reason have you to think so?

TOM: He goes to night school.

AMANDA [*beaming*]:   Splendid! What does he do, I mean study?

TOM: Radio engineering and public speaking!

AMANDA: Then he has visions of being advanced in the world! Any young man who studies public speaking is aiming to have an executive job some day! And radio engineering? A thing for the future! Both of these facts are very illuminating. Those are the sort of things that a mother should know concerning any young man who comes to call on her daughter. Seriously or—not.

TOM: One little warning. He doesn't know about Laura. I didn't let on that we had dark ulterior motives. I just said, why don't you come have dinner with us? He said okay and that was the whole conversation.

AMANDA: I bet it was! You're eloquent as an oyster. However, he'll know about Laura when he gets here. When he sees how lovely and sweet and pretty she is, he'll thank his lucky stars he was asked to dinner.

TOM: Mother, you mustn't expect too much of Laura.

AMANDA: What do you mean?

TOM: Laura seems all those things to you and me because she's ours and we love her. We don't even notice she's crippled any more.

AMANDA: Don't say crippled! You know that I never allow that word to be used!

TOM: But face facts, Mother. She is and—that's not all—

AMANDA: What do you mean "not all"?

TOM: Laura is very different from other girls.

AMANDA: I think the difference is all to her advantage.

TOM: Not quite all—in the eyes of others—strangers—she's terribly shy and lives in a world of her own and those things make her seem a little peculiar to people outside the house.

AMANDA: Don't say peculiar.

TOM: Face the facts. She is.

[*The dance-Hall music changes to a tango that has a minor and somewhat ominous tone.*]

AMANDA: In what way is she peculiar—may I ask?

TOM [*gently*]:   She lives in a world of her own—a world of—little glass ornaments, Mother. . . . [*Gets up.* AMANDA *remains holding brush, looking at him, troubled.*] She plays old phonograph records and—that's about all—[*He glances at himself in the mirror and crosses to door.*]

AMANDA [*sharply*]:   Where are you going?

TOM: I'm going to the movies. [*out screen door.*]

AMANDA: Not to the movies, every night to the movies! [*follows quickly to screen door.*] I don't believe you always go to the movies! [*He is gone.* AMANDA *looks worriedly after him for a moment. Then vitality and optimism return and she turns from the door. Crossing to portieres.*] Laura! Laura! [LAURA *answers from kitchenette.*]

LAURA: Yes, Mother.

AMANDA: Let those dishes go and come in front! [LAURA *appears with dish towel. Gaily.*] Laura, come here and make a wish on the moon!

LAURA   [*entering*]:Moon—moon?

AMANDA: A little silver slipper of a moon. Look over your left shoulder, Laura, and make a wish! [LAURA *looks faintly puzzled as if called out of sleep. Amanda seizes her shoulders and turns her at angle by the door.*] Now! Now, darling, *wish!*

LAURA: What shall I wish for, Mother?

AMANDA [*her voice trembling and her eyes suddenly filling with tears*]:   Happiness! Good fortune!

The violin rises and the stage dims out.

SCENE 6

[Image: High school hero.]

TOM: And so the following evening I brought Jim home to dinner. I had known Jim slightly in high school. In high school Jim was a hero. He had tremendous Irish good nature and vitality with the scrubbed and polished look of white chinaware. He seemed to move in a continual spotlight. He was a star in basketball, captain of the debating club, president of the senior class and the glee club and he sang the male lead in the annual light operas. He was always running or bounding, never just walking. He seemed always at the point of defeating the law of gravity. He was shooting with such velocity through his adolescence that you would logically expect him to arrive at nothing short of the White House by the time he was thirty. But Jim apparently ran into more interference after his graduation from Soldan. His speed had definitely slowed. Six years after he left high school he was holding a job that wasn't much better than mine.

[Image: Clerk.]

He was the only one at the warehouse with whom I was on friendly terms. I was valuable to him as someone who could remember his former glory, who had seen him win basketball games and the silver cup in debating. He knew of my secret practice of retiring to a cabinet of the washroom to work on poems when business was slack in the warehouse. He called me Shakespeare. And while the other boys in the warehouse regarded me with suspicious hostility, Jim took a humorous attitude toward me. Gradually his attitude affected the others, their hostility wore off and they also began to smile at me as people smile at an oddly fashioned dog who trots across their path at some distance.

I knew that Jim and Laura had known each other at Soldan, and I had heard Laura speak admiringly of his voice. I didn't know if Jim remembered her or not. In high school Laura had been as unobtrusive as Jim had been astonishing. If he did remember Laura, it was not as my sister, for when I asked him to dinner, he grinned and said, "You know, Shakespeare, I never thought of you as having folks!"

He was about to discover that I did. . . .

[Light upstage]

[Legend on screen:"The Accent of a Coming Foot."]

Friday evening. It is about five o'clock of a late spring evening which comes "scattering poems in the sky."

A delicate lemony light is in the Wingfield apartment.

AMANDA *has worked like a Turk in preparation for the gentleman caller. The results are astonishing. The new floor lamp with its rose-silk shade is in place, a colored paper lantern conceals the broken light fixture in the ceiling, new billowing white curtains are at the windows, chintz covers are on chairs and sofa, a pair of new sofa pillows make their initial appearance.*

Open boxes and tissue paper are scattered on the floor.

LAURA *stands in the middle with lifted arms while* AMANDA *crouches before her, adjusting the hem of the new dress, devout and ritualistic. The dress is colored and designed by memory. The arrangement of* LAURA'S *hair is changed; it is softer and more becoming. A fragile, unearthly prettiness has come out in* LAURA: *she is like a piece of translucent glass touched by light, given a momentary radiance, not actual, not lasting.*

AMANDA [*impatiently*]:   Why are you trembling?

LAURA: Mother, you've made me so nervous!

AMANDA: How have I made you nervous?

LAURA: By all this fuss! You make it seem so important!

AMANDA: I don't understand you, Laura. You couldn't be satisfied with just sitting home, and yet whenever I try to arrange something for you, you seem to resist it. [*She gets up.*] Now take a look at yourself. No, wait! Wait just a moment—I have an idea!

LAURA: What is it now?

AMANDA *produces two powder puffs which she wraps in handkerchiefs and stuffs in* LAURA'S *bosom.*

LAURA: Mother, what are you doing?

AMANDA: They call them "Gay Deceivers!"

LAURA: I won't wear them!

AMANDA: You will!

LAURA: Why should I?

AMANDA: Because, to be painfully honest, your chest is flat.

LAURA: You make it seem like we were setting a trap.

AMANDA: All pretty girls are a trap, a pretty trap, and men expect them to be. [*Legend:"A Pretty Trap."*] Now look at yourself, young lady. This is the prettiest you will ever be! I've got to fix myself now! You're going to be surprised by your mother's appearance! [*She crosses through portieres, humming gaily.*]

LAURA *moves slowly to the long mirror and stares solemnly at herself.*

A wind blows the white curtains inward in a slow, graceful motion and with a faint sorrowful sighing.

AMANDA [*off stage*]:   It isn't dark enough yet. [*She turns slowly before the mirror with a troubled look.*]

[*Legend on screen:"This Is My Sister: Celebrate Her with Strings!" Music.*]

AMANDA [*laughing, off*]:   I'm going to show you something. I'm going to make a spectacular appearance!

LAURA: What is it, Mother?

AMANDA: Possess your soul in patience—you will see! Something I've resurrected from that old trunk! Styles haven't changed so terribly much after all.... [*She parts the portieres.*] Now just look at your mother! [*She wears a girlish frock of yellowed voile with a blue silk sash. She carries a bunch of jonquils—the legend of her youth is nearly revived. Feverishly.*] This is the dress in which I led the cotillion. Won the cakewalk twice at Sunset Hill, wore one spring to the governor's ball in Jackson! See how I sashayed around the ballroom, Laura? [*She raises her skirt and does a mincing step around the room.*] I wore it on Sundays for my gentlemen callers! I had it on the day I met your father—I had malaria fever all that spring. The change of climate from East Tennessee to the Delta—weakened resistance—I had a little temperature all the time—not enough to be serious—just enough to make me restless and giddy! Invitations poured in—parties all over the Delta!—"Stay in bed," said Mother, "you have fever!"—but I just wouldn't.—I took quinine but kept on going, going!—Evenings, dances!—Afternoons, long, long rides! Picnics—lovely!—So lovely, that country in May.—All lacy with dogwood, literally flooded with jonquils!—That was the spring I had the craze for jonquils. Jonquils became an absolute obsession. Mother said, "Honey, there's no more room for jonquils." And still I kept bringing in more jonquils. Whenever, wherever I saw them, I'd say, "Stop! Stop! I see jonquils!" I made the young men help me gather the jonquils! It was a joke, Amanda and her jonquils! Finally there were no more vases to hold them, every available space was filled with jonquils. No vases to hold them? All right, I'll hold them myself! And then I—[*She stops in front of the picture. Music.*] met your father! Malaria fever and jonquils and then—this—boy.... [*She switches on the rose-colored lamp.*] I hope they get here before it starts to rain. [*She crosses upstage and places the jonquils in bowl on table.*] I gave your brother a little extra change so he and Mr. O'Connor could take the service car home.

LAURA [*with altered look*]:   What did you say his name was?

AMANDA: O'Connor.

LAURA: What is his first name?

AMANDA: I don't remember. Oh, yes, I do. It was—Jim!

LAURA *sways slightly and catches hold of a chair.*

[Legend on screen:"Not Jim!"]

LAURA [*faintly*]:   Not—Jim!

AMANDA: Yes, that was it, it was Jim! I've never known a Jim that wasn't nice!

[Music: Ominous.]

LAURA: Are you sure his name is Jim O'Connor?

AMANDA: Yes. Why?

LAURA: Is he the one that Tom used to know in high school?

AMANDA: He didn't say so. I think he just got to know him at the warehouse.

LAURA: There was a Jim O'Connor we both knew in high school—[*Then, with effort.*] If that is the one that Tom is bringing to dinner—you'll have to excuse me, I won't come to the table.

AMANDA: What sort of nonsense is this?

LAURA: You asked me once if I'd ever liked a boy. Don't you remember I showed you this boy's picture?

AMANDA: You mean the boy you showed me in the year book?

LAURA: Yes, that boy.

AMANDA: Laura, Laura, were you in love with that boy?

LAURA: I don't know, Mother. All I know is I couldn't sit at the table if it was him!

AMANDA: It won't be him! It isn't the least bit likely. But whether it is or not, you will come to the table. You will not be excused.

LAURA: I'll have to be, Mother.

AMANDA: I don't intend to humor your silliness, Laura. I've had too much from you and your brother, both! So just sit down and compose yourself till they come. Tom has forgotten his key so you'll have to let them in, when they arrive.

LAURA [*panicky*]:   Oh, Mother—*you* answer the door!

AMANDA   I[*lightly*]:'ll be in the kitchen—busy!

LAURA: Oh, Mother, please answer the door, don't make me do it!

AMANDA [*crossing into kitchenette*]:   I've got to fix the dressing for the salmon. Fuss, fuss—silliness!—over a gentleman caller!

Door swings shut. LAURA *is left alone.*

[Legend:"Terror!"]

She utters a low moan and turns off the lamp—sits stiffly on the edge of the sofa, knotting her fingers together.

[Legend on screen:"The Opening of a Door!"]

TOM *and* JIM *appear on the fire escape steps and climb to landing. Hearing their approach,* LAURA *rises with a panicky gesture. She retreats to the portieres.*

The doorbell. LAURA *catches her breath and touches her throat. Low drums.*

AMANDA [*calling*]:   Laura, sweetheart! The door!

Laura *stares at it without moving.*

JIM: I think we just beat the rain.

TOM: Uh-huh. [*He rings again, nervously.* JIM *whistles and fishes for a cigarette.*]

AMANDA [*very, very gaily*]:   Laura, that is your brother and Mr. O'Connor! Will you let them in, darling?

LAURA *crosses toward kitchenette door.*

LAURA [*breathlessly*]:   Mother—you go to the door!

AMANDA *steps out of kitchenette and stares furiously at* LAURA: *She points imperiously at the door.*

LAURA: Please, please!

AMANDA [*in a fierce whisper*]:   What is the matter with you, you silly thing?

LAURA [*desperately*]:   Please, you answer it, *please!*

AMANDA: I told you I wasn't going to humor you, Laura. Why have you chosen this moment to lose your mind?

LAURA: Please, please, please, you go!

AMANDA: You'll have to go to the door because I can't!

LAURA [*despairingly*]:   I can't either!

AMANDA: Why?

LAURA: I'm *sick!*

AMANDA: I'm sick, too—of your nonsense! Why can't you and your brother be normal people? Fantastic whims and behavior! [Tom *gives a long ring.*] Preposterous goings on! Can you give me one reason—[*calls out lyrically.*] COMING! JUST ONE SECOND!—why should you be afraid to open a door? Now you answer it, Laura!

LAURA: Oh, oh, oh . . . [*She returns through the portieres. Darts to the victrola and winds it frantically and turns it on.*]

AMANDA: Laura Wingfield, you march right to that door!

LAURA: Yes—yes, Mother!

A faraway, scratchy rendition of "Dardanella" softens the air and gives her strength to move through it. She slips to the door and draws it cautiously open. TOM *enters with caller,* JIM O'CONNOR.

TOM: Laura, this is Jim. Jim, this is my sister, Laura.

JIM [*stepping inside*]:   I didn't know that Shakespeare had a sister!

LAURA [*retreating stiff and trembling from the door*]:   How—how do you do?

JIM [*heartily extending his hand*]:   Okay!

LAURA *touches it hesitantly with hers.*

JIM: Your hand's *cold,* Laura!

LAURA: Yes, well—I've been playing the victrola. . . .

JIM: Must have been playing classical music on it! You ought to play a little hot swing music to warm you up!

LAURA: Excuse me—I haven't finished playing the victrola. . . .

She turns awkwardly and hurries into the front room. She pauses a second by the victrola. Then catches her breath and darts through the portieres like a frightened deer.

JIM [*grinning*]:   What was the matter?

TOM: Oh—with Laura? Laura is—terribly shy.

JIM: Shy, huh? It's unusual to meet a shy girl nowadays. I don't believe you ever mentioned you had a sister.

TOM: Well, now you know. I have one. Here is the *Post Dispatch*. You want a piece of it?

JIM: Uh-huh.

TOM: What piece? The comics?

JIM: Sports! [*glances at it*] Ole Dizzy Dean is on his bad behavior.

TOM [*disinterest*]:   Yeah? [*lights cigarette and crosses back to fire escape door.*]

JIM: Where are *you* going?

TOM: I'm going out on the terrace.

JIM [*goes after him*]:   You know, Shakespeare—I'm going to sell you a bill of goods!

TOM: What goods?

JIM: A course I'm taking.

TOM: Huh?

JIM: In public speaking! You and me, we're not the warehouse type.

TOM: Thanks—that's good news. But what has public speaking got to do with it?

JIM: It fits you for—executive positions!

TOM: Awww.

JIM: I tell you it's done a helluva lot for me.

[Image: Executive at desk.]

TOM: In what respect?

JIM: In every! Ask yourself what is the difference between you an' me and men in the office down front? Brains?—No!—Ability?—No! Then what? Just one little thing—

TOM: What is that one little thing?

JIM: Primarily it amounts to—social poise! Being able to square up to people and hold your own on any social level!

AMANDA [*off stage*]:   Tom?

TOM: Yes, Mother?

AMANDA: Is that you and Mr. O'Connor?

TOM: Yes, Mother.

AMANDA: Well, you just make yourselves comfortable in there.

TOM: Yes, Mother.

AMANDA: Ask Mr. O'Connor if he would like to wash his hands.

JIM: Aw—no—no—thank you—I took care of that at the warehouse. Tom—

TOM: Yes?

JIM: Mr. Mendoza was speaking to me about you.

TOM: Favorably?

JIM: What do you think?

TOM: Well—

JIM: You're going to be out of a job if you don't wake up.

TOM: I am waking up—

JIM: You show no signs.

TOM: The signs are interior.

[Image on screen: The sailing vessel with Jolly Roger again.]

TOM: I'm planning to change. [*He leans over the rail speaking with quiet exhila-
      ration. The incandescent marquees and signs of the first-run movie houses
      light his face from across the alley. He looks like a voyager.*] I'm right at the
      point of committing myself to a future that doesn't include the warehouse and
      Mr. Mendoza or even a night-school course in public speaking.

JIM: What are you gassing about?

TOM: I'm tired of the movies.

JIM: Movies!

TOM: Yes, movies! Look at them—[*a wave toward the marvels of Grand Avenue.*]
      All of those glamorous people—having adventures—hogging it all, gobbling
      the whole thing up! You know what happens? People go to the *movies* instead
      of *moving!* Hollywood characters are supposed to have all the adventures for
      everybody in America, while everybody in America sits in a dark room and
      watches them have them! Yes, until there's a war. That's when adventure
      becomes available to the masses! *Everyone's* dish, not only Gable's! Then the
      people in the dark room come out of the dark room to have some adventures
      themselves—Goody, goody—It's our turn now, to go to the South Sea Island—
      to make a safari—to be exotic, far off—But I'm not patient. I don't want to wait
      till then. I'm tired of the movies and I am *about to move!*

JIM [*incredulously*]: Move?

TOM: Yes.

JIM: When?

TOM: Soon!

JIM: Where? Where?

Theme three music Seems to Answer the Question, while TOM *thinks it over. He
searches among his pockets.*

TOM: I'm starting to boil inside. I know I seem dreamy, but inside—well, I'm boil-
      ing! Whenever I pick up a shoe, I shudder a little thinking how short life is and
      what I am doing!—Whatever that means. I know it doesn't mean shoes—
      except as something to wear on a traveler's feet [*finds paper.*] Look—

JIM: What?

TOM: I'm a member.

JIM [*reading*]: The Union of Merchant Seamen.

TOM: I paid my dues this month, instead of the light bill.

JIM: You will regret it when they turn the lights off.

TOM: I won't be here.

JIM: How about your mother?

TOM: I'm like my father. The bastard son of a bastard! See how he grins? And he's been absent going on sixteen years!

JIM: You're just talking, you drip. How does your mother feel about it?

TOM: Shhh—Here comes Mother! Mother is not acquainted with my plans!

AMANDA [*enters portieres*]:   Where are you all?

TOM: On the terrace, Mother.

They start inside. She advances to them. TOM *is distinctly shocked at her appearance. Even* JIM *blinks a little. He is making his first contact with girlish Southern vivacity and in spite of the night-school course in public speaking is somewhat thrown off the beam by the unexpected outlay of social charm.*

Certain responses are attempted by JIM *but are swept aside by* AMANDA'S *gay laughter and chatter.* TOM *is embarrassed but after the first shock* JIM *reacts very warmly. Grins and chuckles, is altogether won over.*

[*Image:* AMANDA *as a girl.*]

AMANDA [*coyly smiling, shaking her girlish ringlets*]:   Well, well, well, so this is Mr. O'Connor. Introductions entirely unnecessary. I've heard so much about you from my boy. I finally said to him, Tom—good gracious!—why don't you bring this paragon to supper? I'd like to meet this nice young man at the warehouse!—Instead of just hearing him sing your praises so much! I don't know why my son is so standoffish—that's not Southern behavior! Let's sit down and—I think we could stand a little more air in here! Tom, leave the door open. I felt a nice fresh breeze a moment ago. Where has it gone? Mmm, so warm already! And not quite summer, even. We're going to burn up when summer really gets started. However, we're having—we're having a very light supper. I think light things are better fo' this time of year. The same as light clothes are. Light clothes an' light food are what warm weather calls fo'. You know our blood gets so thick during th' winter—it takes a while fo' us to *adjust* ou'selves—when the season changes. . . . It's come so quick this year, I wasn't prepared. All of a sudden—heavens! Already summer!—I ran to the trunk an' pulled out this light dress—Terribly old! Historical almost! But feels so good—so good an' co-ol, y'know. . . .

TOM: Mother—

AMANDA: Yes, honey?

TOM: How about—supper?

AMANDA: Honey, you go ask Sister if supper is ready! You know that Sister is in full charge of supper! Tell her you hungry boys are waiting for it. [*to* Jim] Have you met Laura?

JIM: She—

AMANDA: Let you in? Oh, good, you've met already! It's rare for a girl as sweet an' pretty as Laura to be domestic! But Laura is, thank heavens, not only pretty but also very domestic. I'm not at all. I never was a bit. I never could make a thing but angel-food cake. Well, in the South we had so many servants. Gone, gone, gone. All vestiges of gracious living! Gone completely! I wasn't prepared for what the future brought me. All of my gentlemen callers were sons of planters and so of course I assumed that I would be married to one and raise my family on a large piece of land with plenty of servants. But man proposes—and woman accepts the proposal!—To vary that old, old saying a little bit—I married no planter! I married a man who worked for the telephone company!— that gallantly smiling gentleman over there! [*points to the picture.*] A telephone man who—fell in love with long distance!—Now he travels and I don't even know where!—But what am I going on for about my—tribulations! Tell me yours—I hope you don't have any! Tom?

TOM [*returning*]:   Yes, Mother?

AMANDA: Is supper nearly ready?

TOM: It looks to me like supper is on the table.

AMANDA: Let me look—[*She rises prettily and looks through portieres.*] Oh, lovely—But where is Sister?

TOM: Laura is not feeling well and she says that she thinks she'd better not come to the table.

AMANDA: What?—Nonsense!—Laura? Oh, Laura!

LAURA [*off stage, faintly*]:   Yes, Mother.

AMANDA: You really must come to the table. We won't be seated until you come to the table! Come in, Mr. O'Connor. You sit over there and I'll—Laura? Laura Wingfield! You're keeping us waiting, honey! We can't say grace until you come to the table!

The back door is pushed weakly open and LAURA *comes in. She is obviously quite faint, her lips trembling, her eyes wide and staring. She moves unsteadily toward the table.*

[Legend: "Terror!"]

Outside a summer storm is coming abruptly. The white curtains billow inward at the windows and there is a sorrowful murmur and deep blue dusk.

LAURA *suddenly stumbles—She catches a chair with a faint moan.*

TOM: Laura!

AMANDA: Laura! [*There is a clap of thunder.*] [*Legend: "Ah!"*] [*despairingly.*] Why, Laura, you are sick, darling! Tom, help your sister into the living room, dear! Sit in the living room, Laura—rest on the sofa. Well! [*to the gentleman caller.*] Standing over the hot stove made her ill!—I told her that it was just too warm this evening, but—[TOM *comes back in.* LAURA *is on the sofa.*] Is Laura all right now?

TOM: Yes.

AMANDA: What *is* that? Rain? A nice cool rain has come up! [*She gives the gentle-man caller a frightened look.*] I think we may—have grace—now . . . [Tom *looks at her stupidly.*] Tom, honey—you say grace!

TOM: Oh . . . "For these and all thy mercies—" [*They bow their heads.* AMANDA *stealing a nervous glance at* JIM. *In the living room* LAURA, *stretched on the sofa, clenches her hand to her lips, to hold back a shuddering sob.*] God's Holy Name be praised—

[*The scene dims out.*]

SCENE 7

A Souvenir

Half an hour later. Dinner is just being finished in the upstage area which is concealed by the drawn portieres.

As the curtain rises LAURA *is still huddled upon the sofa, her feet drawn under her, her head resting on a pale blue pillow, her eyes wide and mysteriously watchful. The new floor lamp with its shade of rose-colored silk gives a soft, becoming light to her face, bringing out the fragile, unearthly prettiness which usually escapes attention. There is a steady murmur of rain, but it is slackening and stops soon after the scene begins; the air outside becomes pale and luminous as the moon breaks out.*

A moment after the curtain rises, the lights in both rooms flicker and go out.

JIM: Hey, there, Mr. Light Bulb!

AMANDA *laughs nervously.*

[*Legend:"Suspension of a Public Service."*]

AMANDA: Where was Moses when the lights went out? Ha-ha. Do you know the answer to that one, Mr. O'Connor?

JIM: No, ma'am, what's the answer?

AMANDA: In the dark! [JIM *laughs appreciatively.*] Everybody sit still. I'll light the candles. Isn't it lucky we have them on the table? Where's a match? Which of you gentlemen can provide a match?

JIM: Here.

AMANDA: Thank you, sir.

JIM: Not at all, Ma'am!

AMANDA: I guess the fuse has burnt out. Mr. O'Connor, can you tell a burnt-out fuse? I know I can't and Tom is a total loss when it comes to mechanics. [*Sound: Getting up: Voices recede a little to kitchenette.*] Oh, be careful you don't bump into something. We don't want our gentleman caller to break his neck. Now wouldn't that be a fine howdy-do?

JIM: Ha-ha! Where is the fuse box?

AMANDA: Right here next to the stove. Can you see anything?

JIM: Just a minute.

AMANDA: Isn't electricity a mysterious thing? Wasn't it Benjamin Franklin who tied a key to a kite? We live in such a mysterious universe, don't we? Some people say that science clears up all the mysteries for us. In my opinion it only creates more! Have you found it yet?

JIM: No, Ma'am. All these fuses look okay to me.

AMANDA: Tom!

TOM: Yes, Mother?

AMANDA: That light bill I gave you several days ago. The one I told you we got the notices about?

TOM: Oh.—Yeah.

[Legend:"Ha!"]

AMANDA: You didn't neglect to pay it by any chance?

TOM: Why, I—

AMANDA: Didn't! I might have known it!

JIM: Shakespeare probably wrote a poem on that light bill, Mrs. Wingfield.

AMANDA: I might have known better than to trust him with it! There's such a high price for negligence in this world!

JIM: Maybe the poem will win a ten-dollar prize.

AMANDA: We'll just have to spend the remainder of the evening in the nineteenth century, before Mr. Edison made the Mazda[5] lamp!

JIM: Candlelight is my favorite kind of light.

AMANDA: That shows you're romantic! But that's no excuse for Tom. Well, we got through dinner. Very considerate of them to let us get through dinner before they plunged us into everlasting darkness, wasn't it, Mr. O'Connor?

JIM: Ha-ha!

AMANDA: Tom, as a penalty for your carelessness you can help me with the dishes.

JIM: Let me give you a hand.

AMANDA: Indeed you will not!

JIM: I ought to be good for something.

AMANDA: Good for something? [*Her tone is rhapsodic.*] *You?* Why, Mr. O'Connor, nobody, *nobody's* given me this much entertainment in years—as you have!

JIM: Aw, now, Mrs. Wingfield!

AMANDA: I'm not exaggerating, not one bit! But Sister is all by her lonesome. You go keep her company in the parlor! I'll give you this lovely old candelabrum that used to be on the altar at the church of the Heavenly Rest. It was melted a little out of shape when the church burnt down. Lightning struck it one spring. Gypsy Jones was holding a revival at the time and he intimated that the church was destroyed because the Episcopalians gave card parties.

JIM: Ha-ha.

[5]**Mazda lamp** electric lamp

AMANDA: And how about coaxing Sister to drink a little wine? I think it would be good for her! Can you carry both at once?

JIM: Sure. I'm Superman!

AMANDA: Now, Thomas, get into this apron!

The door of kitchenette swings closed on AMANDA'S *gay laughter; the flickering light approaches the portieres.*

LAURA *sits up nervously as he enters. Her speech at first is low and breathless from the almost intolerable strain of being alone with a stranger.*

[Legend: "I Don't Suppose You Remember Me at All!"]

In her first speeches in this scene, before JIM'S *warmth overcomes her paralyzing shyness,* LAURA'S *voice is thin and breathless as though she has run up a steep flight of stairs.*

JIM'S *attitude is gently humorous. In playing this scene it should be stressed that while the incident is apparently unimportant, it is to* LAURA *the climax of her secret life.*

JIM: Hello, there, Laura.

LAURA [*faintly*]:   Hello. [*She clears her throat.*]

JIM: How are you feeling now? Better?

LAURA: Yes. Yes, thank you.

JIM: This is for you. A little dandelion wine. [*He extends it toward her with extravagant gallantry.*]

LAURA: Thank you.

JIM: Drink it—but don't get drunk! [*He laughs heartily. Laura takes the glass uncertainly; laughs shyly.*] Where shall I set the candles?

LAURA: Oh—oh, anywhere . . .

JIM: How about here on the floor? Any objections?

LAURA: No.

JIM: I'll spread a newspaper under to catch the drippings. I like to sit on the floor. Mind if I do?

LAURA: Oh, no.

JIM: Give me a pillow?

LAURA: What?

JIM: A pillow!

LAURA: Oh . . . [*hands him one quickly.*]

JIM: How about you? Don't you like to sit on the floor?

LAURA: Oh—yes.

JIM: Why don't you, then?

LAURA: I—will.

JIM: Take a pillow! [LAURA *does. Sits on the other side of the candelabrum.* JIM *crosses his legs and smiles engagingly at her.*] I can't hardly see you sitting way over there.

LAURA: I can—see you.

JIM: I know, but that's not fair, I'm in the limelight. [LAURA *moves her pillow closer.*]

Good! Now I can see you! Comfortable?

LAURA: Yes.

JIM: So am I. Comfortable as a cow. Will you have some gum?

LAURA: No, thank you.

JIM: I think that I will indulge, with your permission [*musingly unwraps it and holds it up.*] Think of the fortune made by the guy that invented the first piece of chewing gum. Amazing, huh? The Wrigley Building is one of the sights of Chicago.—I saw it summer before last when I went up to the Century of Progress. Did you take in the Century of Progress?

LAURA: No, I didn't.

JIM: Well, it was quite a wonderful exposition. What impressed me most was the Hall of Science. Gives you an idea of what the future will be in America, even more wonderful than the present time is! [*Pause, Smiling at her.*] Your brother tells me you're shy. Is that right, Laura?

LAURA: I—don't know.

JIM: I judge you to be an old-fashioned type of girl. Well, I think that's a pretty good type to be. Hope you don't think I'm being too personal—do you?

LAURA [*hastily, out of embarrassment*]:   I believe I *will* take a piece of gum, if you—don't mind. [*clearing her throat.*] Mr. O'Connor, have you—kept up with your singing?

JIM: Singing? Me?

LAURA: Yes. I remember what a beautiful voice you had.

JIM: When did you hear me sing?

[Voice offstage in the pause]

VOICE [*offstage*]:   O blow, ye winds, heigh-ho.

A-roving I will go!

I'm off to my love

With a boxing glove—

Ten thousand miles away!

JIM: You say you've heard me sing?

LAURA: Oh, yes! Yes, very often . . . I—don't suppose you remember me—at all?

JIM [*smiling doubtfully*]:   You know I have an idea I've seen you before. I had that idea soon as you opened the door. It seemed almost like I was about to remember your name. But the name that I started to call you   wasn't a name! And so I stopped myself before I said it.

LAURA: Wasn't it—Blue Roses?

JIM [*springs up, grinning*]:   Blue Roses! My gosh, yes—Blue Roses! That's what I had on my tongue when you opened the door! Isn't it funny what tricks your memory plays? I didn't connect you with the high school somehow or other. But that's where it was; it was high school. I didn't even know you were Shakespeare's sister! Gosh, I'm sorry.

LAURA: I didn't expect you to. You—barely knew me!

JIM: But we did have a speaking acquaintance, huh?

LAURA: Yes, we—spoke to each other.

JIM: When did you recognize me?

LAURA: Oh, right away!

JIM: Soon as I came in the door?

LAURA: When I heard your name I thought it was probably you. I knew that Tom used to know you a little in high school. So when you came in the door—Well, then I was—sure.

JIM: Why didn't you *say* something, then?

LAURA [*breathlessly*]:   I didn't know what to say, I was—too surprised!

JIM: For goodness' sakes! You know, this sure is funny!

LAURA: Yes! Yes, isn't it, though. . . .

JIM: Didn't we have a class in something together?

LAURA: Yes, we did.

JIM: What class was that?

LAURA: It was—singing—Chorus!

JIM: Aw!

LAURA: I sat across the aisle from you in the Aud.

JIM: Aw.

LAURA: Mondays, Wednesdays, and Fridays.

JIM: Now I remember—you always came in late.

LAURA: Yes, it was so hard for me, getting upstairs. I had a brace on my leg—it clumped so loud!

JIM: I never heard any clumping.

LAURA [*wincing at the recollection*]:   To me it sounded like—thunder!

JIM: Well, well, well. I never even noticed.

LAURA: And everybody was seated before I came in. I had to walk in front of all those people. My seat was in the back row. I had to go clumping all the way up the aisle with everyone watching!

JIM: You shouldn't have been self-conscious.

LAURA: I know, but I was. It was always such a relief when the singing started.

JIM: Aw, yes, I've placed you now! I used to call you Blue Roses. How was it that I got started calling you that?

LAURA: I was out of school a little while with pleurosis. When I came back you asked me what was the matter. I said I had pleurosis—you thought I said Blue Roses. That's what you always called me after that!

JIM: I hope you didn't mind.

LAURA: Oh, no—I liked it. You see, I wasn't acquainted with many—people. . . .

JIM: As I remember you sort of stuck by yourself.

LAURA: I—I—never had much luck at—making friends.

JIM: I don't see why you wouldn't.

LAURA: Well, I—started out badly.

JIM: You mean being—

LAURA: Yes, it sort of—stood between me—

JIM: You shouldn't have let it!

LAURA: I know, but it did, and—

JIM: You were shy with people!

LAURA: I tried not to be but never could—

JIM: Overcome it?

LAURA: No, I—I never could!

JIM: I guess being shy is something you have to work out of kind of gradually.

LAURA [*sorrowfully*]:   Yes—I guess it—

JIM: Takes time!

LAURA: Yes—

JIM: People are not so dreadful when you know them. That's what you have to remember! And everybody has problems, not just you, but practically everybody has got some problems. You think of yourself as having the only problems, as being the only one who is disappointed. But just look around you and you will see lots of people as disappointed as you are. For instance, I hoped when I was going to high school that I would be further along at this time, six years later, than I am now—You remember that wonderful write-up I had in *The Torch?*

LAURA: Yes! [*She rises and crosses to table.*]

JIM: It said I was bound to succeed in anything I went into! [LAURA *returns with the annual.*] Holy Jeez! *The Torch!* [*He accepts it reverently. They smile across it with mutual wonder.* LAURA *crouches beside him and they begin to turn through it.* LAURA's *shyness is dissolving in his warmth.*]

LAURA: Here you are in Pirates of Penzance!

JIM [*wistfully*]:   I sang the baritone lead in that operetta.

LAURA [*rapidly*]:   So—*beautifully!*

JIM [*protesting*]:   Aw—

LAURA: Yes, yes—beautifully—beautifully!

JIM: You heard me?

LAURA: All three times!

JIM: No!

LAURA: Yes!

JIM: All three performances?

LAURA [*looking down*]:   Yes.

JIM: Why?

LAURA: I—wanted to ask you to—autograph my program.

JIM: Why didn't you ask me to?

LAURA: You were always surrounded by your own friends so much that I never had a chance to.

JIM: You should have just—

LAURA: Well, I—thought you might think I was—

JIM: Thought I might think you was—what?

LAURA: Oh—

JIM [*with reflective relish*]:   I was beleaguered by females in those days.

LAURA: You were terribly popular!

JIM: Yeah—

LAURA: You had such a—friendly way—

JIM: I was spoiled in high school.

LAURA: Everybody—liked you!

JIM: Including you?

LAURA: I—yes, I—I did, too—[*She gently closes the book in her lap.*]

JIM: Well, well, well!—Give me that program, Laura. [*She hands it to him. He signs it with a flourish.*] There you are—better late than never!

LAURA: Oh, I—what a—surprise!

JIM: My signature isn't worth very much right now. But some day—maybe—it will increase in value! Being disappointed is one thing and being discouraged is something else. I am disappointed but I'm not discouraged. I'm twenty-three years old. How old are you?

LAURA: I'll be twenty-four in June.

JIM: That's not old age!

LAURA: No, but—

JIM: You finished high school?

LAURA [*with difficulty*]:   I didn't go back.

JIM: You mean you dropped out?

LAURA: I made bad grades in my final examinations. [*She rises and replaces the book and the program. Her voice strained.*] How is—Emily Meisenbach getting along?

JIM: Oh, that kraut-head!

LAURA: Why do you call her that?

JIM: That's what she was.

LAURA: You're not still—going with her?

JIM: I never see her.

LAURA: It said in the Personal Section that you were—engaged!

JIM: I know, but I wasn't impressed by that—propaganda!

LAURA: It wasn't—the truth?

JIM: Only in Emily's optimistic opinion!

LAURA: Oh—

[Legend: "What Have You Done Since High School?"]

JIM *lights a cigarette and leans indolently back on his elbows smiling at* LAURA *with a warmth and charm which light her inwardly with altar candles. She remains by the table and turns in her hands a piece of glass to cover her tumult.*

JIM [*after several reflective puffs on a cigarette*]:   What have you done since high school? [*She seems not to hear him.*] Huh? [LAURA *looks up.*] I said what have you done since high school, Laura?

LAURA: Nothing much.

JIM: You must have been doing something these six long years.

LAURA: Yes.

JIM: Well, then, such as what?

LAURA: I took a business course at business college—

JIM: How did that work out?

LAURA: Well, not very—well—I had to drop out, it gave me—indigestion—

JIM *laughs gently.*

JIM: What are you doing now?

LAURA: I don't do anything—much. Oh, please don't think I sit around doing nothing! My glass collection takes up a good deal of my time. Glass is something
you have to take good care of.

JIM: What did you say—about glass?

LAURA: Collection I said—I have one—[*She clears her throat and turns away
again, acutely shy.*]

JIM [*abruptly*]:   You know what I judge to be the trouble with you? Inferiority
complex! Know what that is? That's what they call it when someone low rates
himself! I understand it because I had it, too. Although my case was not so
aggravated as yours seems to be. I had it until I took up public speaking, developed my voice, and learned that I had an aptitude for science. Before that time
I never thought of myself as being outstanding in any way whatsoever! Now
I've never made a regular study of it, but I have a friend who says I can analyze
people better than doctors that make a profession of it. I don't claim that to be
necessarily true, but I can sure guess a person's psychology, Laura! [*takes out
his gum.*] Excuse me, Laura. I always take it out when the flavor is gone. I'll use
this scrap of paper to wrap it in. I know how it is to get it stuck on a shoe.
Yep—that's what I judge to be your principal trouble. A lack of confidence in
yourself as a person. You don't have the proper amount of faith in yourself. I'm
basing that fact on a number of your remarks and also on certain observations
I've made. For instance that clumping you thought was so awful in high
school. You say that you even dreaded to walk into class. You see what you did?
You dropped out of school, you gave up an education because of a clump,
which as far as I know was practically nonexistent! A little physical defect is
what you have. Hardly noticeable even! Magnified thousands of times by imagination! You know what my strong advice to you is? Think of yourself as
superior in some way!

LAURA: In what way would I think?

JIM: Why, man alive, Laura! Just look about you a little. What do you see? A world
full of common people! All of 'em born and all of 'em going to die! Which of
them has one-tenth of your good points! Or mine! Or anyone else's, as far as
that goes—Gosh! Everybody excels in some one thing. Some in many!
[*unconsciously glances at himself in the mirror.*] All you've got to do is
discover in *what!* Take me, for instance. [*He adjusts his tie at the mirror.*] My

interest happens to lie in electro-dynamics. I'm taking a course in radio engineering at night school, Laura, on top of a fairly responsible job at the warehouse. I'm taking that course and studying public speaking.

LAURA: Ohhhh.

JIM: Because I believe in the future of television! [*turning back to her.*] I wish to
be ready to go up right along with it. Therefore I'm planning to get in on the
ground floor. In fact, I've already made the right connections and all that
remains is for the industry itself to get under way! Full steam—[*His eyes are
starry.*] *Knowledge*—Zzzzzp! *Money*—Zzzzzzp!—*Power!* That's the cycle
democracy is built on! [*His attitude is convincingly dynamic. Laura stares at
him, even her shyness eclipsed in her absolute wonder. He suddenly grins.*]
I guess you think I think a lot of myself!

LAURA: No-o-o-o, I—

JIM: Now how about you? Isn't there something you take more interest in than anything else?

LAURA: Well, I do—as I said—have my—glass collection—

A peal of girlish laughter from the kitchen.

JIM: I'm not right sure I know what you're talking about. What kind of glass is it?

LAURA: Little articles of it, they're ornaments mostly! Most of them are little animals
made out of glass, the tiniest little animals in the world. Mother calls them a
glass menagerie! Here's an example of one, if you'd like to see it! This one is
one of the oldest. It's nearly thirteen. [*He stretches out his hand.*] [*Music:"The
Glass Menagerie."*] Oh, be careful—if you breathe, it breaks!

JIM: I'd better not take it. I'm pretty clumsy with things.

LAURA: Go on, I trust you with him! [*places it in his palm.*] There now—you're
holding him gently! Hold him over the light, he loves the light! You see how
the light shines through him?

JIM: It sure does shine!

LAURA: I shouldn't be partial, but he is my favorite one.

JIM: What kind of a thing is this one supposed to be?

LAURA: Haven't you noticed the single horn on his forehead?

JIM: A unicorn, huh?

LAURA: Mmm-hmmm!

JIM: Unicorns, aren't they extinct in the modern world?

LAURA: I know!

JIM: Poor little fellow, he must feel sort of lonesome.

LAURA [*smiling*]:   Well, if he does he doesn't complain about it. He stays on a shelf
with some horses that don't have horns and all of them seem to get along
nicely together.

JIM: How do you know?

LAURA [*lightly*]:   I haven't heard any arguments among them!

JIM [*grinning*]:   No arguments, huh? Well, that's a pretty good sign! Where shall I set
him?

LAURA: Put him on the table. They all like a change of scenery once in a while!

JIM [*stretching*]:   Well, well, well, well—Look how big my shadow is when I stretch!

LAURA: Oh, oh, yes—it stretches across the ceiling!

JIM [*crossing to door*]:   I think it's stopped raining. [*opens fire escape door.*] Where does the music come from?

LAURA: From the Paradise Dance Hall across the alley.

JIM: How about cutting the rug a little, Miss Wingfield?

LAURA: Oh, I—

JIM: Or is your program filled up? Let me have a look at it. [*grasps imaginary card.*] Why, every dance is taken! I'll just have to scratch some out. [*Waltz music:"La Golondrina."*] Ahhh, a waltz! [*He executes some sweeping turns by himself then holds his arms toward* LAURA.]

LAURA [*breathlessly*]:   I—can't dance!

JIM: There you go, that inferiority stuff!

LAURA: I've never danced in my life!

JIM: Come on, try!

LAURA: Oh, but I'd step on you!

JIM: I'm not made out of glass.

LAURA: How—how—how do we start?

JIM: Just leave it to me. You hold your arms out a little.

LAURA: Like this?

JIM: A little bit higher. Right. Now don't tighten up, that's the main thing about it—relax.

LAURA [*laughing breathlessly*]:   It's hard not to.

JIM: Okay.

LAURA: I'm afraid you can't budge me.

JIM: What do you bet I can't? [*He swings her into motion.*]

LAURA: Goodness, yes, you can!

JIM: Let yourself go, now, Laura, just let yourself go.

LAURA: I'm—

JIM: Come on!

LAURA: Trying?

JIM: Not so stiff—Easy does it!

LAURA: I know but I'm—

JIM: Loosen th' backbone! There now, that's a lot better.

LAURA: Am I?

JIM: Lots, lots better! [*He moves her about the room in a clumsy waltz.*]

LAURA: Oh, my!

JIM: Ha-ha!

LAURA: Goodness, yes you can!

JIM: Ha-ha-ha! [*They suddenly bump into the table.* JIM *stops.*] What did we hit on?

LAURA: Table.

JIM: Did something fall off it? I think—

LAURA: Yes.

JIM: I hope that it wasn't the little glass horse with the horn!

LAURA: Yes.

JIM: Aw, aw, aw. Is it broken?

LAURA: Now it is just like all the other horses.

JIM: It's lost its—

LAURA: Horn! It doesn't matter. Maybe it's a blessing in disguise.

JIM: You'll never forgive me. I bet that that was your favorite piece of glass.

LAURA: I don't have favorites much. It's no tragedy, Freckles. Glass breaks so easily. No matter how careful you are. The traffic jars the shelves and things fall off them.

JIM: Still I'm awfully sorry that I was the cause.

LAURA [*smiling*]:   I'll just imagine he had an operation. The horn was removed to make him feel less—freakish! [*They both laugh.*] Now he will feel more at home with the other horses, the ones that don't have horns . . .

JIM: Ha-ha, that's very funny! [*suddenly serious.*] I'm glad to see that you have a sense of humor. You know—you're—well—very different! Surprisingly different from anyone else I know! [*His voice becomes soft and hesitant with a genuine feeling.*] Do you mind me telling you that? [LAURA *is abashed beyond speech.*] You make me feel sort of—I don't know how to put it! I'm usually pretty good at expressing things, but—This is something that I don't know how to say! LAURA *touches her throat and clears it—turns the broken unicorn in her hands.*] [*even softer*] Has anyone ever told you that you were pretty? [*Pause: Music.*] [LAURA *looks up slowly, with wonder, and shakes her head.*] Well, you are! In a very different way from anyone else. And all the nicer because of the difference, too. [*His voice becomes low and husky.* LAURA *turns away, nearly faint with the novelty of her emotions.*] I wish that you were my sister. I'd teach you to have some confidence in yourself. The different people are not like other people, but being different is nothing to be ashamed of. Because other people are not such wonderful people. They're one hundred times one thousand. You're one times one! They walk all over the earth. You just stay here. They're common as—weeds, but—you—well, you're—*Blue Roses!*

[Image on screen: Blue Roses.]

[Music changes.]

LAURA: But blue is wrong for—roses . . .

JIM: It's right for you—You're—pretty!

LAURA: In what respect am I pretty?

JIM: In all respects—believe me! Your eyes—your hair—are pretty! Your hands are pretty! [*He catches hold of her hand.*] You think I'm making this up because I'm invited to dinner and have to be nice. Oh, I could do that! I could put on an act for you, Laura, and say lots of things without being very sincere. But this time I am. I'm talking to you sincerely. I happened to notice you had this inferiority complex that keeps you from feeling comfortable with people. Somebody needs to build your confidence up and make you proud instead of shy and turning away and—blushing—Somebody ought to—ought to—kiss you. Laura! [*His hand slips slowly up her arm to her shoulder.*] [*Music Swells Tumultuously.*] [*He suddenly turns her about and kisses her on the lips. When he releases her* LAURA *sinks on the sofa with a bright, dazed look.* JIM *backs away and fishes in his pocket for a cigarette.*] [*Legend on screen: "Souvenir."*] Stumble-john! [*He lights the cigarette, avoiding her look. There is a peal of girlish laughter from* AMANDA *in the kitchen.* LAURA *slowly raises and opens her hand. It still contains the little broken glass animal. She looks at it with a tender, bewildered expression.*] Stumble-john! I shouldn't have done that—That was way off the beam. You don't smoke, do you? [*She looks up, smiling, not hearing the question. He sits beside her a little gingerly. She looks at him speechlessly—waiting. He coughs decorously and moves a little farther aside as he considers the situation and senses her feelings, dimly, with perturbation. Gently.*] Would you—care for a—mint? [*She doesn't seem to hear him but her look grows brighter even.*] Peppermint—Life Saver? My pocket's a regular drug store—wherever I go . . . [*He pops a mint in his mouth. Then gulps and decides to make a clean breast of it. He speaks slowly and gingerly.*] Laura, you know, if I had a sister like you, I'd do the same thing as Tom. I'd bring out fellows—introduce her to them. The right type of boys of a type to—appreciate her. Only—well—he made a mistake about me. Maybe I've got no call to be saying this. That may not have been the idea in having me over. But what if it was? There's nothing wrong about that. The only trouble is that in my case—I'm not in a situation to—do the right thing. I can't take down your number and say I'll phone. I can't call up next week and—ask for a date. I thought I had better explain the situation in case you misunderstood it and—hurt your feelings. . . . [*Pause. Slowly, very slowly,* Laura's *look changes, her eyes returning slowly from his to the ornament in her palm.*]

AMANDA *utters another gay laugh in the kitchen.*

LAURA [*faintly*]:   You—won't—call again?

JIM: No, Laura, I can't. [*He rises from the sofa.*] As I was just explaining, I've—got strings on me, Laura, I've—been going steady! I go out all the time with a girl named Betty. She's a home-girl like you, and Catholic, and Irish, and in a great many ways we—get along fine. I met her last summer on a moonlight boat trip up the river to Alton, on the Majestic. Well—right away from the start it was—love! [*Legend: Love!*] [LAURA *sways slightly forward and grips the arm of the sofa. He fails to notice, now enrapt in his own comfortable being.*] Being in love has made a new man of me! [*Leaning stiffly forward, clutching the arm of the sofa,* LAURA *struggles visibly with her storm. But* Jim *is oblivious, she is a long way off.*] The power of love is really pretty tremendous! Love is something that—changes the whole world, Laura! [*The storm abates a little and Laura leans back. He notices her again.*] It happened that Betty's aunt took sick, she got a wire and had to go to Centralia. So Tom—when he asked me to dinner—I naturally just accepted the invitation, not knowing that you—that he—that I—[*He stops awkwardly.*] Huh—I'm a stumble-john! [*He flops back on the sofa. The holy candles in the altar of* LAURA'S *face have been snuffed out! There is a look of almost infinite desolation.* JIM *glances at her uneasily.*] I wish that you would—say something. [*She bites her lip which was trembling and then bravely smiles. She opens her hand again on the broken glass ornament. Then she gently takes his hand and raises it level with her own. She carefully places the unicorn in the palm of his hand, then pushes his fingers closed upon it.*] What are you—doing that for? You want me to have him?—Laura? [*She nods.*] What for?

LAURA: A—souvenir . . .

She rises unsteadily and crouches beside the victrola to wind it up.

[*Legend on screen:"Things Have a Way of Turning Out So Badly."*]

[*Or image:"Gentleman Caller Waving Goodbye!—Gaily."*]

At this moment AMANDA *rushes brightly back in the front room. She bears a pitcher of fruit punch in an old-fashioned cut-glass pitcher and a plate of macaroons. The plate has a gold border and poppies painted on it.*

AMANDA: Well, well, well! Isn't the air delightful after the shower? I've made you children a little liquid refreshment. [*turns gaily to the gentleman caller.*] Jim, do you know that song about lemonade?

"Lemonade, lemonade
Made in the shade and stirred with a spade—
Good enough for any old maid!"

JIM [*uneasily*]:   Ha-ha! No—I never heard it.

AMANDA: Why, Laura! You look so serious!

JIM: We were having a serious conversation.

AMANDA: Good! Now you're better acquainted!

JIM [*uncertainly*]:   Ha-ha! Yes.

AMANDA: You modern young people are much more serious-minded than my generation. I was so gay as a girl!

JIM: You haven't changed, Mrs. Wingfield.

AMANDA: Tonight I'm rejuvenated! The gaiety of the occasion, Mr. O'Connor! [*She tosses her head with a peal of laughter. Spills lemonade.*] Oooo! I'm baptizing myself!

JIM: Here—let me—

AMANDA [*setting the pitcher down*]:   There now. I discovered we had some maraschino cherries. I dumped them in, juice and all!

JIM: You shouldn't have gone to that trouble, Mrs. Wingfield.

AMANDA: Trouble, trouble? Why it was loads of fun! Didn't you hear me cutting up in the kitchen? I bet your ears were burning! I told Tom how outdone with him I was for keeping you to himself so long a time! He should have brought you over much, much sooner! Well, now that you've found your way, I want you to be a very frequent caller! Not just occasional but all the time. Oh, we're going to have a lot of gay times together! I see them coming! Mmm, just breathe that air! So fresh, and the moon's so pretty! I'll skip back out—I know where my place is when young folks are having a—serious conversation!

JIM: Oh, don't go out, Mrs. Wingfield. The fact of the matter is I've got to be going.

AMANDA: Going, now? You're joking! Why, it's only the shank of the evening, Mr. O'Connor!

JIM: Well, you know how it is.

AMANDA: You mean you're a young workingman and have to keep workingmen's hours. We'll let you off early tonight. But only on the condition that next time you stay later. What's the best night for you? Isn't Saturday night the best night for you workingmen?

JIM: I have a couple of time clocks to punch, Mrs. Wingfield. One at morning, another one at night!

AMANDA: My, but you *are* ambitious! You work at night, too?

JIM: No, Ma'am, not work but—Betty! [*He crosses deliberately to pick up his hat. The band at the Paradise Dance Hall goes into a tender waltz.*]

AMANDA: Betty? Betty? Who's—Betty! [*There is an ominous cracking sound in the sky.*]

JIM: Oh, just a girl. The girl I go steady with! [*He smiles charmingly. The sky falls.*]

[*Legend: "The Sky Falls."*]

AMANDA [*a long-drawn exhalation*]:   Ohhh . . . Is it a serious romance, Mr. O'Connor?

JIM: We're going to be married the second Sunday in June.

AMANDA: Ohhhh—how nice! Tom didn't mention that you were engaged to be married.

JIM: The cat's not out of the bag at the warehouse yet. You know how they are. They call you Romeo and stuff like that. [*He stops at the oval mirror to put on his hat. He carefully shapes the brim and the crown to give a discreetly dashing effect.*] It's been a wonderful evening, Mrs. Wingfield. I guess this is what they mean by Southern hospitality.

AMANDA: It really wasn't anything at all.

JIM: I hope it don't seem like I'm rushing off. But I promised Betty I'd pick her up at the Wabash depot, an' by the time I get my jalopy down there her train'll be in. Some women are pretty upset if you keep 'em waiting.

AMANDA: Yes, I know—The tyranny of women! [*extends her hand.*] Goodbye, Mr. O'Connor. I wish you luck—and happiness—and success! All three of them, and so does Laura!—Don't you, Laura?

LAURA: Yes!

JIM [*taking her hand*]:   Goodbye, Laura. I'm certainly going to treasure that souvenir. And don't you forget the good advice I gave you. [*raises his voice to a cheery shout.*] So long, Shakespeare! Thanks again, ladies—good night!

He grins and ducks jauntily out.

Still bravely grimacing, AMANDA *closes the door on the gentleman caller. Then she turns back to the room with a puzzled expression. She and* LAURA *don't dare to face each other.* LAURA *crouches beside the victrola to wind it.*

AMANDA [*faintly*]:   Things have a way of turning out so badly. I don't believe that I would play the victrola. Well, well—well—Our gentleman caller was engaged to be married! Tom!

TOM [*from back*]:   Yes, Mother?

AMANDA: Come in here a minute. I want to tell you something awfully funny.

TOM [*enters with macaroon and a glass of lemonade*]:   Has the gentleman caller gotten away already?

AMANDA: The gentleman caller has made an early departure. What a wonderful joke you played on us!

TOM: How do you mean?

AMANDA: You didn't mention that he was engaged to be married.

TOM: Jim? Engaged?

AMANDA: That's what he just informed us.

TOM: I'll be jiggered! I didn't know about that.

AMANDA: That seems very peculiar.

TOM: What's peculiar about it?

AMANDA: Didn't you call him your best friend down at the warehouse?

TOM: He is, but how did I know?

AMANDA: It seems extremely peculiar that you wouldn't know your best friend was going to be married!

TOM: The warehouse is where I work, not where I know things about people!

AMANDA: You don't know things anywhere! You live in a dream; you manufacture illusions! [*He crosses to door.*] Where are you going?

TOM: I'm going to the movies.

AMANDA: That's right, now that you've had us make such fools of ourselves. The effort, the preparations, all the expense! The new floor lamp, the rug, the clothes for Laura! All for what? To entertain some other girl's fiancé! Go to the movies, go! Don't think about us, a mother deserted, an unmarried sister who's crippled and has no job! Don't let anything interfere with your selfish pleasure! Just go, go, go—to the movies!

TOM: All right, I will! The more you shout about my selfishness to me the quicker I'll go, and I won't go to the movies!

AMANDA: Go, then! Then go to the moon—you selfish dreamer!

TOM *smashes his glass on the floor. He plunges out on the fire escape, slamming the door.* LAURA *screams—cut by door.*

Dance-hall music up. TOM *goes to the rail and grips it desperately, lifting his face in the chill white moonlight penetrating the narrow abyss of the alley.*

[Legend on screen:"And So Good-bye . . . "]

TOM'S *closing speech is timed with the interior pantomime. The interior scene is played as though viewed through sound-proof glass.* AMANDA *appears to be making a comforting speech to* LAURA *who is huddled upon the sofa. Now that we cannot hear the mother's speech, her silliness is gone and she has dignity and tragic beauty.* LAURA'S *dark hair hides her face until at the end of the speech she lifts it to smile at her mother.* AMANDA'S *gestures are slow and graceful, almost dancelike, as she comforts the daughter. At the end of her speech she glances a moment at the father's picture—then withdraws through the portieres. At close of* TOM'S *speech,* LAURA *blows out the candles, ending the play.*

TOM: I didn't go to the moon, I went much further—for time is the longest distance between two places—Not long after that I was fired for writing a poem on the lid of a shoe box. I left Saint Louis. I descended the steps of this fire-escape for a last time and followed, from then on, in my father's footsteps, attempting to find in motion what was lost in space—I traveled around a great deal. The cities swept about me like dead leaves, leaves that were brightly colored but torn away from the branches. I would have stopped, but I was pursued by something. It always came upon me unawares, taking me altogether by surprise. Perhaps it was a familiar bit of music. Perhaps it was only a piece of transparent glass. Perhaps I am walking along a street at night, in some strange city, before I have found companions. I pass the lighted window of a shop where perfume is sold. The window is filled with pieces of colored glass, tiny transparent bottles in delicate colors, like bits of a shattered rainbow. Then all at once my sister touches my shoulder. I turn around and look into her eyes . . . Oh, Laura, Laura, I tried to leave you behind me, but I am more faithful than I intended to be! I reach for a cigarette, I cross the street, I run into the movies or a bar, I buy a drink, I speak to the nearest stranger—anything that can blow your candles out! [LAURA *bends over the candles.*]—for nowadays the world is lit by lightning! Blow out your candles, Laura—and so goodbye . . .

She blows the candles out.

[The scene dissolves.]

MAKING CONNECTIONS

1. Who is the central character in this play? What criteria do you use to make your determination?
2. A central issue in the play is whether Tom will obey his mother's wishes and stay in St. Louis with her and his sister. Yet, when Tom addresses us at the start of the play, he wears a merchant marine uniform, signaling that he will not choose to remain at home. Does this visual clue influence your understanding of Tom as the play develops? Instead of suspense as to whether Tom will obey his mother's wishes, what effect does this create?
3. It is presented as a fact that Laura is the recluse of the family. Yet, does it seem to you that either Amanda or Tom has many friends and acquaintances? How has Laura garnered this reputation? Is it fair or unfair?
4. Which Wingfield changes the most over the course of the play? Which one changes the least?
5. Over and over, Jim tells Laura what he would do if she were his sister. Is this an indictment of Tom as a brother? Do you think Tom does his duty by his family?
6. As Laura reveals herself to Jim, does he react in the way you expect him to? Do his reactions to Laura change what you think of Amanda and Tom?
7. In what ways is Jim different from the Wingfields? Why is Laura able to give Jim the broken horse? Do you see this as an unselfish act or as an exchange for something she has received from him?
8. Why does Tom leave home? Is either Amanda or Laura responsible? Could they have done anything to make him stay?
9. Do you think *The Glass Menagerie* is an appropriate title for this play? Explain.
10. Compare the sibling relationship in this play with that in the stories "Sonny's Blues" (p. 211) or "The Red Convertible" (p. 236).

MAKING AN ARGUMENT

1. Plays are meant to be seen more than read. Nevertheless, Williams provides detailed and vivid descriptions of the setting, characters, and stage action. Carefully reread his descriptions of the three Wingfields at the start of the play and write an essay about characterization in the play. Could you learn this much about each character solely by reading the scenes that follow? Does the play deliver the characters that Williams promises? Cite the text of the play to support your view.

◆ ESSAYS ◆

BELL HOOKS [B. 1952]

A prolific prose writer and poet who was born as Gloria Jean Watkins, bell hooks took the name of her progressive, outspoken great-grandmother. An outspoken commentator herself on issues of race, class, and gender, her books include Ain't I a Woman *(1981),* Talking Back: Thinking Feminist, Thinking Black *(1989),* Yearning: Race, Gender and Cultural Studies *(1990),* Outlaw Culture: Resisting Representation *(1994),* Bone Black: Memories of Girlhood *(1996), and* Remembered Rapture: The Writer at Work *(1999). She has taught at Yale University, Oberlin College, and CCNY.*

INSPIRED ECCENTRICITY   [1996]

There are family members you try to forget and ones that you always remember, that you can't stop talking about. They may be dead—long gone—but their presence lingers and you have to share who they were and who they still are with the world. You want everyone to know them as you did, to love them as you did.

All my life I have remained enchanted by the presence of my mother's parents, Sarah and Gus Oldham. When I was a child they were already old. I did not see that then, though. They were Baba and Daddy Gus, together for more than seventy years at the time of his death. Their marriage fascinated me. They were strangers and lovers—two eccentrics who created their own world.

More than any other family members, together they gave me a worldview that sustained me during a difficult and painful childhood. Reflecting on the eclectic writer I have become, I see in myself a mixture of these two very different but equally powerful figures from my childhood. Baba was tall, her skin so white and her hair so jet black and straight that she could have easily "passed," denying all traces of blackness. Yet the man she married was short and dark, and sometimes his skin looked like the color of soot from burning coal. In our childhood the fireplaces burned coal. It was bright heat, luminous and fierce. If you got too close it could burn you.

Together Baba and Daddy Gus generated a hot heat. He was a man of few words, deeply committed to silence—so much so that it was like a religion to him. When he spoke you could hardly hear what he said. Baba was just the opposite. Smoking an abundance of cigarettes a day, she talked endlessly. She preached. She yelled. She fussed. Often her vitriolic rage would heap itself on Daddy Gus, who would sit calmly in his chair by the stove, as calm and still as the Buddha sits. And when he had enough of her words, he would reach for his hat and walk.

5   Neither Baba nor Daddy Gus drove cars. Rarely did they ride in them. They preferred walking. And even then their styles were different. He moved slow, as though carrying a great weight; she with her tall, lean, boyish frame moved swiftly, as though there was never time to waste. Their one agreed-upon passion was fishing. Though they did not do even that together. They lived close but they created separate worlds.

In a big two-story wood frame house with lots of rooms they constructed a world that could contain their separate and distinct personalities. As children one of the first things we noticed about our grandparents was that they did not sleep in the same room. This arrangement was contrary to everything we understood about marriage. While Mama never wanted to talk about their separate worlds, Baba would tell you in a minute that Daddy Gus was nasty, that he smelled like tobacco juice, that he did not wash enough, that there was no way she would want him in her bed. And while he would say nothing nasty about her, he would merely say why would he want to share somebody else's bed when he could have his own bed to himself, with no one to complain about anything.

I loved my granddaddy's smells. Always, they filled my nostrils with the scent of happiness. It was sheer ecstasy for me to be allowed into his inner sanctum. His room was a small Van Gogh–like space off from the living room. There was no door. Old-fashioned curtains were the only attempt at privacy. Usually the curtains were closed. His room reeked of tobacco. There were treasures everywhere in that small room. As a younger man Daddy Gus did odd jobs, and sometimes even in his old age he would do a chore for some needy lady. As he went about his work, he would pick up found objects, scraps. All these objects would lie about his room, on the dresser, on the table near his bed. Unlike all other grown-ups he never cared about children looking through his things. Anything we wanted he gave to us.

Daddy Gus collected beautiful wooden cigar boxes. They held lots of the important stuff—the treasures. He had tons of little diaries that he made notes in. He gave me my first wallet, my first teeny little book to write in, my first beautiful pen, which did not write for long, but it was still a found and shared treasure. When I would lie on his bed or sit close to him, sometimes just standing near, I would feel all the pain and anxiety of my troubled childhood leave me. His spirit was calm. He gave me the unconditional love I longed for.

"Too calm," his grown-up children thought. That's why he had let this old woman rule him, my cousin BoBo would say. Even as children we knew that grown-ups felt sorry for Daddy Gus. At times his sons seemed to look upon him as not a "real man." His refusal to fight in wars was another sign to them of weakness. It was my grandfather who taught me to oppose war. They saw him as a man controlled by the whims of others, by this tall, strident, demanding woman he had married. I saw him as a man of profound beliefs, a man of integrity. When he heard their putdowns—for they talked on and on about his laziness—he merely muttered that he had no use for them. He was not gonna let anybody tell him what to do with his life.

10   Daddy Gus was a devout believer, a deacon at his church; he was one of the right-hand men of God. At church, everyone admired his calmness. Baba had no use for church. She liked nothing better than to tell us all the ways it was one big hypo-

critical place: "Why, I can find God anywhere I want to—I do not need a church." Indeed, when my grandmother died, her funeral could not take place in a church, for she had never belonged. Her refusal to attend church bothered some of her daughters, for they thought she was sinning against God, setting a bad example for the children. We were not supposed to listen when she began to damn the church and everybody in it.

Baba loved to "cuss." There was no bad word she was not willing to say. The improvisational manner in which she would string those words together was awesome. It was the goddamn sons of bitches who thought that they could fuck with her when they could just kiss her black ass. A woman of strong words and powerful metaphors, she could not read or write. She lived in the power of language. Her favorite sayings were a prelude for storytelling. It was she who told me, "Play with a puppy, he'll lick you in the mouth." When I heard this saying, I knew what was coming—a long polemic about not letting folks get too close, 'cause they will mess with you.

Baba loved to tell her stories. And I loved to hear them. She called me Glory. And in the midst of her storytelling she would pause to say, "Glory, are ya listenin'. Do you understand what I'm telling ya." Sometimes I would have to repeat the lessons I had learned. Sometimes I was not able to get it right and she would start again. When Mama felt I was learning too much craziness "over home" (that is what we called Baba's house), my visits were curtailed. As I moved into my teens I learned to keep to myself all the wisdom of the old ways I picked up over home.

Baba was an incredible quilt maker, but by the time I was old enough to really understand her work, to see its beauty; she was already having difficulty with her eyesight. She could not sew as much as in the old days, when her work was on everybody's bed. Unwilling to throw anything away, she loved to make crazy quilts, 'cause they allowed every scrap to be used. Although she would one day order patterns and make perfect quilts with colors that went together, she always collected scraps.

Long before I read Virginia Woolf's *A Room of One's Own* I learned from Baba that a woman needed her own space to work. She had a huge room for her quilting. Like every other space in the private world she created upstairs, it had her treasures, an endless array of hatboxes, feathers, and trunks filled with old clothes she had held on to. In room after room there were feather tick mattresses; when they were pulled back, the wooden slats of the bed were revealed, lined with exquisite hand-sewn quilts.

15   In all these trunks, in crevices and drawers were braided tobacco leaves to keep away moths and other insects. A really hot summer could make cloth sweat, and stains from tobacco juice would end up on quilts no one had ever used. When I was a young child, a quilt my grandmother had made kept me warm, was my solace and comfort. Even though Mama protested when I dragged that old raggedy quilt from Kentucky to Stanford, I knew I needed that bit of the South, of Baba's world, to sustain me.

Like Daddy Gus, she was a woman of her word. She liked to declare with pride, "I mean what I say and I say what I mean." "Glory," she would tell me, "nobody is better than their word—if you can't keep ya word you ain't worth nothin' in this world." She would stop speaking to folk over the breaking of their word, over lies. Our mama was not given to loud speech or confrontation. I learned all those things from Baba—"to stand up and speak up" and not to "give a good goddamn" what folk who "ain't got a pot to pee in" think. My parents were concerned with their image in the world. It was pure blasphemy for Baba to teach that it did not matter what other folks thought—"Ya have to be right with yaself in ya own heart—that's all that matters." Baba taught me to listen to my heart—to follow it. From her we learned as small children to remember our dreams in the night and to share them when we awakened. They would be interpreted by her. She taught us to listen to the knowledge in dreams. Mama would say this was all nonsense, but she too was known to ask the meaning of a dream.

In their own way my grandparents were rebels, deeply committed to radical individualism. I learned how to be myself from them. Mama hated this. She thought it was important to be liked, to conform. She had hated growing up in such an eccentric, otherworldly household. This world where folks made their own wine, their own butter, their own soap; where chickens were raised, and huge gardens were grown for canning everything. This was the world Mama wanted to leave behind. She wanted store-bought things.

Baba lived in another time, a time when all things were produced in the individual household. Everything the family needed was made at home. She loved to tell me stories about learning to trap animals, to skin, to soak possum and coon in brine, to fry up a fresh rabbit. Though a total woman of the outdoors who could shoot and trap as good as any man, she still believed every woman should sew—she made her first quilt as a girl. In her world, women were as strong as men because they had to be. She had grown up in the country and knew that country ways were the best ways to live. Boasting about being able to do anything that a man could do and better, this woman who could not read or write was confident about her place in the universe.

My sense of aesthetics came from her. She taught me to really look at things, to see underneath the surface, to see the different shades of red in the peppers she had dried and hung in the kitchen sunlight. The beauty of the ordinary, the everyday, was her feast of light. While she had no use for the treasures in my granddaddy's world, he too taught me to look for the living spirit in things—the things that are cast away but still need to be touched and cared for. Picking up a found object he would tell me its story or tell me how he was planning to give it life again.

20   Connected in spirit but so far apart in the life of everydayness, Baba and Daddy Gus were rarely civil to each other. Every shared talk begun with goodwill ended in disagreement and contestation. Everyone knew Baba just loved to fuss. She liked a good war of words. And she was comfortable using words to sting and hurt, to punish. When words would not do the job, she could reach for the strap, a long piece of black leather that would leave tiny imprints on the flesh.

There was no violence in Daddy Gus. Mama shared that he had always been that way, a calm and gentle man, full of tenderness. I remember clinging to his tenderness when nothing I did was right in my mother's eyes, when I was constantly punished. Baba was not an ally. She advocated harsh punishment. She had no use for children who would not obey. She was never ever affectionate. When we entered her house, we gave her a kiss in greeting and that was it. With Daddy Gus we could cuddle, linger in his arms, give as many kisses as desired. His arms and heart were always open.

In the back of their house were fruit trees, chicken coops, and gardens, and in the front were flowers. Baba could make anything grow. And she knew all about herbs and roots. Her home remedies healed our childhood sicknesses. Of course she thought it crazy for anyone to go to a doctor when she could tell them just what they needed. All these things she had learned from her mother, Bell Blair Hooks, whose name I would choose as my pen name. Everyone agreed that I had the temperament of this great-grandmother I would not remember. She was a sharp-tongued woman. Or so they said. And it was believed I had inherited my way with words from her.

Families do that. They chart psychic genealogies that often overlook what is right before our eyes. I may have inherited my great-grandmother Bell Hook's way with words, but I learned to use those words listening to my grandmother. I learned to be courageous by seeing her act without fear. I learned to risk because she was daring. Home and family were her world. While my grandfather journeyed down-town, visited at other folks' houses, went to church, and conducted affairs in the world, Baba rarely left home. There was nothing in the world she needed. Things out there violated her spirit.

As a child I had no sense of what it would mean to live a life, spanning so many gen-erations, unable to read or write. To me Baba was a woman of power. That she would have been extraordinarily powerless in a world beyond 1200 Broad Street was a thought that never entered my mind. I believed that she stayed home because it was the place she liked best. Just as Daddy Gus seemed to need to walk—to roam.

25   After his death it was easier to see the ways that they complemented and com-pleted each other. For suddenly, without him as a silent backdrop, Baba's spirit was diminished. Something in her was forever lonely and could not find solace. When she died, tulips, her favorite flower, surrounded her. The preacher told us that her death was not an occasion for grief, for "it is hard to live in a world where your choicest friends are gone." Daddy Gus was the companion she missed most. His pres-ence had always been the mirror of memory. Without it there was so much that could not be shared. There was no witness.

Seeing their life together, I learned that it was possible for women and men to fashion households arranged around their own needs. Power was shared. When there was an imbalance, Baba ruled the day. It seemed utterly alien to me to learn about black women and men not making families and homes together. I had not been raised in a world of absent men. One day I knew I would fashion a life using the patterns I inherited from Baba and Daddy Gus. I keep treasures in my cigar box, which still smells after all these years. The quilt that covered me as a child remains, full of ink stains and faded colors. In my trunks are braided tobacco leaves, taken from over home. They keep evil away—keep bad spirits from crossing the threshold, like the ancestors they guard and protect.

MAKING CONNECTIONS

1. Can you think of family members from whom you've learned lessons that will last a lifetime? Explain.
2. To what extent does the author "show," not just tell you about, her grand-parents and the influence they have had on her? Pick out specific details that support her description of them and the role they played in her life— and discuss their effectiveness.

3. Compare this essay to Philip Larkin's poem "This Be the Verse" on page 272 and Li-Young Lee's poem "The Gift" on page 276.

MAKING AN ARGUMENT

1. In the opening section of this theme, Carl Jung is quoted as saying that "The little world of childhood with its familiar surroundings is a model of the greater world." In "Inspired Eccentricity," bell hooks seems to agree when she says, "One day I knew I would fashion a life using the patterns I inherited from Baba and Daddy Gus." Using this essay and other works from Family and Friends, build an argument in support of or against the view that the family provides us a model of the greater world—and that we "fashion" our lives "using the patterns" we've learned at home.

MARK TWAIN [1835–1910]

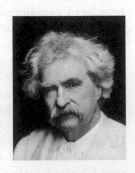

Born Samuel Longhorne Clemens in Florida, Missouri, Mark Twain was raised along the Mississippi River, in the town of Hannibal. He left school at the age of twelve, worked first in the printing trade, where he wrote occasional news stories and sketches, and then, in 1859, fulfilled his childhood dream of becoming a riverboat pilot. The Civil War put an end to commercial traffic on the river, and after a short and uncomfortable time in the Confederate army, Twain headed West to Colorado, Nevada, and finally California to seek his fortune. It was there, while working as a reporter, that he decided on his vocation as a writer and began publishing a series of popular humorous writings, including "The Celebrated Jumping Frog of Calaveras County" (1865). The publication of The Innocents Abroad *in 1869, a humorous account of his travels in Europe, established his reputation as an important literary figure, and he spent the rest of his life as one of America's most recognizable personalities. His novels include* The Adventures of Tom Sawyer *(1876),* The Prince and the Pauper *(1882),* A Connecticut Yankee in King Arthur's Court *(1889), and his masterpiece,* The Adventures of Huckleberry Finn *(1884), which Ernest Hemingway called "the best book we've had."*

ADVICE TO YOUTH   [1882]

Being told I would be expected to talk here, I inquired what sort of a talk I ought to make. They said it should be something suitable to youth—something didactic, instructive, or something in the nature of good advice. Very well. I have a few things in my mind which I have often longed to say for the instruction of the young; for it is in one's tender early years that such things will best take root and be most enduring and most valuable. First, then, I will say to you, my young friends—and I say it beseechingly, urgingly—

Always obey your parents, when they are present. This is the best policy in the long run, because if you don't they will make you. Most parents think they know better than you do, and you can generally make more by humoring that superstition than you can by acting on your own better judgment.

Be respectful to your superiors, if you have any, also to strangers, and sometimes to others. If a person offend you, and you are in doubt as to whether it was intentional or not, do not resort to extreme measures; simply watch your chance and hit him with a brick. That will be sufficient. If you shall find that he had not intended any offense, come out frankly and confess yourself in the wrong when you struck him; acknowledge it like a man and say you didn't mean to. Yes, always avoid violence; in this age of charity and kindliness, the time has gone by for such things. Leave dynamite to the low and unrefined.

Go to bed early, get up early—this is wise. Some authorities say get up with the sun; some others say get up with one thing, some with another. But a lark is really the best thing to get up with. It gives you a splendid reputation with everybody to know that you get up with the lark; and if you get the right kind of a lark, and work at him right, you can easily train him to get up at half past nine, every time—it is no trick at all.

5   Now as to the matter of lying. You want to be very careful about lying; otherwise you are nearly sure to get caught. Once caught, you can never again be, in the eyes of the good and the pure, what you were before. Many a young person has injured himself permanently through a single clumsy and illfinished lie, the result of carelessness born of incomplete training. Some authorities hold that the young ought not to lie at all. That, of course, is putting it rather stronger than necessary; still, while I cannot go quite so far as that, I do maintain, and I believe I am right, that the young ought to be temperate in the use of this great art until practice and experience shall give them that confidence, elegance, and precision which alone can make the accomplishment graceful and profitable. Patience, diligence, painstaking attention to detail—these are the requirements; these, in time, will make the student perfect; upon these, and upon these only, may he rely as the sure foundation for future eminence. Think what tedious years of study, thought, practice, experience, went to the equipment of that peerless old master who was able to impose upon the whole world the lofty and sounding maxim that "truth is mighty and will prevail"—the most majestic compound fracture of fact which any of woman born has yet achieved. For the history of our race, and each individual's experience, are sown thick with evidence that a truth is not hard to kill and that a lie told well is immortal. There is in Boston a monument of the man who discovered anaesthesia; many people are aware, in these latter days, that that man didn't discover it at all, but stole the discovery from another man. Is this truth mighty, and will it prevail? Ah no, my hearers, the monument is made of hardy material, but the lie it tells will outlast it a million years. An awkward, feeble, leaky lie is a thing which you ought to make it your unceasing study to avoid; such a lie as that has no more real permanence than an average truth. Why, you might as well tell the truth at once and be done with it. A feeble, stupid, preposterous lie will not live two years—except it be a slander upon somebody. It is indestructible, then, of course, but that is no merit of yours. A final word: begin your practice of this gracious and beautiful art early—begin now. If I had begun earlier, I could have learned how.

Never handle firearms carelessly. The sorrow and suffering that have been caused through the innocent out heedless handling of firearms by the young! Only four days ago, right in the next farmhouse to the one where I am spending the summer, a grandmother, old and gray and sweet, one of the loveliest spirits in the land, was sitting at her work, when her young grandson crept in and got down an old, battered, rusty gun which had not been touched for many years and was supposed not to be loaded, and pointed it at her, laughing and threatening to shoot. In her fright she ran screaming and pleading toward the door on the other side of the room; but as she passed him he placed the gun almost against her very breast and pulled the trigger! He had supposed it was not loaded. And he was right—it wasn't. So there wasn't any harm done. It is the only case of that kind I ever heard of. Therefore, just the same, don't you meddle with old unloaded firearms; they are the most deadly and unerring things that have ever been created by man. You don't have to take any pains at all with them; you don't have to have a rest, you don't have to have any sights on the gun, you don't have to take aim, even. No, you just pick out a relative and bang away, and you are sure to get him. A youth who can't hit a cathedral at thirty yards with a Gatling gun in three-quarters of an hour, can take up an old empty musket and bag his grandmother every time, at a hundred. Think what Waterloo would have been if one of the armies had been boys armed with old muskets supposed not to be loaded, and the other army had been composed of their female relations. The very thought of it makes one shudder.

There are many sorts of books; but good ones are the sort for the young to read. Remember that. They are a great, an inestimable, an unspeakable means of improvement. Therefore be careful in your selection, my young friends; be very careful; confine yourselves exclusively to Robertson's Sermons, Baxter's *Saint's Rest, The Innocents Abroad,* and works of that kind.

But I have said enough. I hope you will treasure up the instructions which I have given you, and make them a guide to your feet and a light to your understanding. Build your character thoughtfully and painstakingly upon these precepts, and by and by, when you have got it built, you will be surprised and gratified to see how nicely and sharply it resembles everybody else's.

 MAKING CONNECTIONS

1. Mark Twain is a great satirist. What is the tone of this essay? To what extent does Twain mean what he says? Is he serious? Explain.
2. Have you ever received advice like this? If so, have you always taken it seriously? Why or why not?
3. Do you think there is wisdom in this essay? Explain.

MAKING AN ARGUMENT

1. Twain's essay was written over a hundred years ago. If you were writing a tongue-in-cheek "Advice to Youth" today, what issues would you address? Write an essay (or write your own advice to youth) that accounts for these current issues and shows why they deserve to be satirized.

CASE STUDY IN BIOGRAPHICAL CONTEXT

Lorraine Hansberry and *A Raisin in the Sun*

The purpose of this Case Study is to provide you with biographical, historical, and cultural material for a self-contained research unit. As mentioned in Chapter 5, one popular area of literary research is inquiry into an author's life or the relationship between the author's life and work. The materials that follow contain a primary source—the play *A Raisin in the Sun*—and a number of secondary sources—a brief biography, the author's words, interviews, and articles about her and the play. By themselves or in combination with other sources, they provide a good resource for a research essay.

Knowing about the author's life or intentions is not a prerequisite for understanding and appreciating a work of literature. Good literature stands on its own and appeals to us through its own merit. Of greatest importance, for our purposes, is reading and interpreting these texts. But discovering and exploring connections between an author's background and the literature may enrich and expand your response.

Our focus in this Case Study is on playwright Lorraine Hansberry. Her story is both inspiring and tragically sad. By the time she was twenty-nine years old, *A Raisin in the Sun* was an award-winning play on Broadway, and this brilliant young playwright seemed to have a remarkable future in front of her. Before she was thirty-five years old, however, she had died of cancer.

The passages that follow her brief biography and the play contain the comments of both Lorraine Hansberry and others about her life and work. Many of her own comments, taken largely from interviews and public presentations, were organized and reprinted by her husband in a production and publication called *To Be Young, Gifted, and Black (YGB)*. The rest of her comments are taken from speeches and television interviews with Mike Wallace and Studs Terkel shortly after the Broadway debut of *A Raisin in the Sun*. The commentary of others includes a biographical tribute by friend and fellow writer James Baldwin and critical and biographical commentary about the play by Julius Lester, Anne Cheney, Steven R. Carter, and Margaret B. Wilkerson. This casebook concludes with a 1999 article by Michael Anderson that celebrates the fortieth anniversary of the play's opening.

How has Lorraine Hansberry's background, her artistic philosophy, and the influence of other writers affected her writing of *A Raisin in the Sun?* Does the play seem to fulfill her own artistic requirements? Do the characters have within them the "elements of profundity, of profound anguish"? Does the play seem to "tell the truth about people"? How do her own comments about herself compare with what others say? Is there anything in her background, for example, that may account for what Steven R. Carter in his comments calls her "artistic misstep"?

LORRAINE HANSBERRY [1930–1965]

Lorraine Hansberry was born in Chicago, Illinois, to middle-class black parents who lived on the city's South Side. When she was still a child, her father was barred from purchasing a house in a white neighborhood. He sued and pursued the case all the way to the Supreme Court, which ruled in his favor. Hansberry attended the University of Wisconsin as an undergraduate. Following college, she pursued a career as a painter, studying at the Art Institute of Chicago and in Mexico before she decided to move to New York to pursue her interest in writing. There she wrote for Freedom, *a magazine founded by the great singer-actor-turned-political-activist Paul Robeson. When her first play,* A Raisin in the Sun, *premiered at the Ethel Barrymore Theater in 1959, it was the first play written by an African-American woman to be performed on Broadway. She wrote only one other play,* The Sign in Sidney Brustien's Window *(1965), before she died of cancer at the age of thirty-four. The title of* A Raisin in the Sun *is taken from the poem "A Dream Deferred" by Langston Hughes (p. 76).*

A RAISIN IN THE SUN   [1958]

CHARACTERS IN ORDER OF APPEARANCE
RUTH YOUNGER *Walter's wife, about thirty*
TRAVIS YOUNGER *her son and Walter's*
WALTER LEE YOUNGER *(brother) Ruth's husband, mid-thirties*
BENEATHA YOUNGER *Walter's sister, about twenty*
LENA YOUNGER *(Mama) mother of Walter and Beneatha*
JOSEPH ASAGAI *Nigerian, Beneatha's suitor*
GEORGE MURCHISON *Beneatha's date, wealthy*
KARL LINDNER *white, chairman of the Clybourne Park New Neighbors Orientation Committee*
BOBO *one of Walter's business partners*
MOVING MEN
The action of the play is set in Chicago's South Side, sometime between World War II and the present.

ACT I
Scene 1. Friday morning
Scene 2. The following morning

ACT II
Scene 1. Later, the same day
Scene 2. Friday night, a few weeks later
Scene 3. Moving day, one week later

ACT III
An hour later

ACT I

SCENE 1

The Younger living room would be a comfortable and well-ordered room if it were not for a number of indestructible contradictions to this state of being. Its furnishings are typical and undistinguished and their primary feature now is that they have clearly had to accommodate the living of too many people for too many years—and they are tired. Still, we can see that at some time, a time probably no longer remembered by the family (except perhaps for Mama*) the furnishings of this room were actually selected with care and love and even hope—and brought to this apartment and arranged with taste and pride.*

That was a long time ago. Now the once loved pattern of the couch upholstery has to fight to show itself from under acres of crocheted doilies and couch covers which have themselves finally come to be more important than the upholstery. And here a table or a chair has been moved to disguise the worn places in the carpet; but the carpet has fought back by showing its weariness, with depressing uniformity, elsewhere on its surface.

Weariness has, in fact, won in this room. Everything has been polished, washed, sat on, used, scrubbed too often. All pretenses but living itself have long since vanished from the very atmosphere of this room.

Moreover, a section of this room, for it is not really a room unto itself, though the landlord's lease would make it seem so, slopes backward to provide a small kitchen area, where the family prepares the meals that are eaten in the living room proper, which must also serve as dining room. The single window that has been provided for these "two" rooms is located in this kitchen area. The sole natural light the family may enjoy in the course of a day is only that which fights its way through this little window.

At left, a door leads to a bedroom which is shared by Mama *and her daughter,* Beneatha. *At right, opposite, is a second room (which in the beginning of the life of this apartment was probably a breakfast room) which serves as a bedroom for* Walter *and his wife,* Ruth.

Time: *Sometime between World War II and the present.*

Place: *Chicago's South Side.*

At rise: *It is morning dark in the living room.* Travis *is asleep on the make-down bed at center. An alarm clock sounds from within the bedroom at right, and presently* Ruth *enters from that room and closes the door behind her. She crosses sleepily toward the window. As she passes her sleeping son she reaches down and shakes him a little. At the window she raises the shade and a dusky South Side morning light comes in feebly. She fills a pot with water and puts it on to boil. She calls to the boy, between yawns, in a slightly muffled voice.*

Ruth *is about thirty. We can see that she was a pretty girl, even exceptionally so, but now it is apparent that life has been little that she expected, and disappointment has already begun to hang in her face. In a few years, before thirty-five even, she will be known among her people as a "settled woman."*

She crosses to her son and gives him a good, final, rousing shake.

Ruth: Come on now, boy, it's seven thirty! [*Her son sits up at last, in a stupor of sleepiness.*] I say hurry up, Travis! You ain't the only person in the world got to use a bathroom! [*The child, a sturdy, handsome little boy of ten or eleven, drags himself out of the bed and almost blindly takes his towels and "today's clothes" from drawers and a closet and goes out to the bathroom, which is in an outside hall and which is shared by another family or families on the same floor.* Ruth *crosses to the bedroom door at right and opens it and calls in to her husband.*] Walter Lee! . . . It's after seven thirty! Lemme see you do some waking up in there now! [*She waits.*] You better get up from there, man! It's after seven thirty I tell you. [*She waits again.*] All right, you just go ahead and lay there and next thing you know Travis be finished and Mr. Johnson'll be in there and you'll be fussing and cussing round here like a mad man! And be late too! [*She waits, at the end of patience.*] Walter Lee—it's time for you to get up! [*She waits another second and then starts to go into the bedroom, but is apparently satisfied that her husband has begun to get up. She stops, pulls the door to, and returns to the kitchen area. She wipes her face with a moist cloth and runs her fingers through her sleep-disheveled hair in a vain effort and ties an apron around her housecoat. The bedroom door at right opens and her husband stands in the doorway in his pajamas, which are rumpled and mismated. He is a lean, intense young man in his middle thirties, inclined to quick nervous movements and erratic speech habits—and always in his voice there is a quality of indictment.*]

Walter: Is he out yet?

Ruth: What you mean *out?* He ain't hardly got in there good yet.

Walter [*wandering in, still more oriented to sleep than to a new day*]:   Well, what was you doing all that yelling for if I can't even get in there yet? [*stopping and thinking*] Check coming today?

RUTH: They *said* Saturday and this is just Friday and I hopes to God you ain't going to get up here first thing this morning and start talking to me 'bout no money—'cause I 'bout don't want to hear it.

WALTER: Something the matter with you this morning?

RUTH: No—I'm just sleepy as the devil. What kind of eggs you want?

WALTER: Not scrambled. [RUTH *starts to scramble eggs.*] Paper come? [RUTH *points impatiently to the rolled up* TRIBUNE *on the table, and he gets it and spreads it out and vaguely reads the front page.*] Set off another bomb yesterday.

RUTH [*maximum indifference*]:   Did they?

WALTER [*looking up*]:   What's the matter with you?

RUTH: Ain't nothing the matter with me. And don't keep asking me that this morning.

WALTER: Ain't nobody bothering you. [*reading the news of the day absently again*] Say Colonel McCormick is sick.

RUTH [*affecting tea-party interest*]:   Is he now? Poor thing.

WALTER [*Sighing and looking at his watch*]:   Oh, me. [*He waits.*] Now what is that boy doing in that bathroom all this time? He just going to have to start getting up earlier. I can't be being late to work on account of him fooling around in there.

RUTH [*turning on him*]:   Oh, no he ain't going to be getting up earlier no such thing! It ain't his fault that he can't get to bed no earlier nights 'cause he got a bunch of crazy good-for-nothing clowns sitting up running their mouths in what is supposed to be his bedroom after ten o'clock at night . . .

WALTER: That's what you mad about, ain't it? The things I want to talk about with my friends just couldn't be important in your mind, could they? [*He rises and finds a cigarette in her handbag on the table and crosses to the little window and looks out, smoking and deeply enjoying this first one.*]

RUTH [*almost matter of factly, a complaint too automatic to deserve emphasis*]:   Why you always got to smoke before you eat in the morning?

WALTER [*at the window*]:   Just look at 'em down there. . . . Running and racing to work . . . [*He turns and faces his wife and watches her a moment at the stove, and then, suddenly.*] You look young this morning, baby.

RUTH [*indifferently*]:   Yeah?

WALTER: Just for a second—stirring them eggs. It's gone now—just for a second it was—you looked real young again. [*then, drily*] It's gone now—you look like yourself again.

RUTH: Man, if you don't shut up and leave me alone.

WALTER [*looking out to the street again*]:   First thing a man ought to learn in life is not to make love to no colored woman first thing in the morning. You all some evil people at eight o'clock in the morning. [TRAVIS *appears in the hall doorway, almost fully dressed and quite wide awake now, his towels and pajamas across his shoulders. He opens the door and signals for his father to make the bathroom in a hurry.*]

TRAVIS [*watching the bathroom*]:   Daddy, come on! [WALTER *gets his bathroom utensils and flies out to the bathroom.*]

RUTH: Sit down and have your breakfast, Travis.

TRAVIS: Mama, this is Friday. [*gleefully*] Check coming tomorrow, huh?

RUTH: You get your mind off money and eat your breakfast.

TRAVIS [*eating*]:   This is the morning we supposed to bring the fifty cents to school.

RUTH: Well, I ain't got no fifty cents this morning.

TRAVIS: Teacher say we have to.

RUTH: I don't care what teacher say. I ain't got it. Eat your breakfast, Travis.

TRAVIS: I *am* eating.

RUTH: Hush up now and just eat! [*The boy gives her an exasperated look for her lack of understanding, and eats grudgingly.*]

TRAVIS: You think Grandmama would have it?

RUTH: No! And I want you to stop asking your grandmother for money, you hear me?

TRAVIS [*outraged*]:   Gaaaleee! I don't ask her, she just gimme it sometimes!

RUTH: Travis Willard Younger—I got too much on me this morning to be—

TRAVIS: Maybe Daddy—

RUTH: *Travis!* [*The boy hushes abruptly. They are both quiet and tense for several seconds.*]

TRAVIS [*presently*]:   Could I maybe go carry some groceries in front of the super-market for a little while after school then?

RUTH: Just hush, I said. [Travis *jabs his spoon into his cereal bowl viciously, and rests his head in anger upon his fists.*] If you through eating, you can get over there and make up your bed. [*The boy obeys stiffly and crosses the room, almost mechanically, to the bed and more or less carefully folds the covering. He carries the bedding into his mother's room and returns with his books and cap.*]

TRAVIS [*sulking and standing apart from her unnaturally*]:   I'm gone.

RUTH [*looking up from the stove to inspect him automatically*]:   Come here. [*He crosses to her and she studies his head.*] If you don't take this comb and fix this here head, you better! [TRAVIS *puts down his books with a great sigh of oppression, and crosses to the mirror. His mother mutters under her breath about his "stubbornness."*] 'Bout to march out of here with that head looking just like chickens slept in it! I just don't know where you get your stubborn ways . . . And get your jacket, too. Looks chilly out this morning.

TRAVIS [*with conspicuously brushed hair and jacket*]:   I'm gone.

RUTH: Get carfare and milk money—[*waving one finger*]—and not a single penny for no caps, you hear me?

TRAVIS [*with sullen politeness*]:   Yes'm. [*He turns in outrage to leave. His mother watches after him as in his frustration he approaches the door almost comically. When she speaks to him, her voice has become a very gentle tease.*]

RUTH [*mocking, as she thinks he would say it*]:   Oh, Mama makes me so mad some-times, I don't know what to do! [*She waits and continues to his back as he stands stock-still in front of the door.*] I wouldn't kiss that woman good-bye for nothing in this world this morning! [*The boy finally turns around and rolls his eyes at her, knowing the mood has changed and he is vindicated; he does not, however, move toward her yet.*] Not for nothing in this world! [*She finally laughs aloud at him and holds out her arms to him and we see that it is a way between them, very old and practiced. He crosses to her and allows her to embrace him warmly but keeps his face fixed with masculine rigidity. She holds him back from her presently and looks at him and runs her fingers over the features of his face. With utter gentleness—*] Now— whose little old angry man are you?

TRAVIS [*The masculinity and gruffness start to fade at last.*]:   Aw gaalee—Mama . . .

RUTH [*mimicking*]:   Aw—gaaaaalleeeee, Mama! [*She pushes him, with rough playfulness and finality, toward the door.*] Get on out of here or you going to be late.

TRAVIS [*in the face of love, new aggressiveness*]:   Mama, could I *please* go carry groceries?

RUTH: Honey, it's starting to get so cold evenings.

WALTER [*coming in from the bedroom and drawing a make-believe gun from a make-believe holster and shooting at his son*]:   What is it he wants to do?

RUTH: Go carry groceries after school at the supermarket.

WALTER: Well, let him go . . .

TRAVIS [*quickly, to the ally*]:   I *have* to—she won't gimme the fifty cents . . .

WALTER [*to his wife only*]:   Why not?

RUTH [*simply, and with flavor*]:   'Cause we don't have it.

WALTER [*to RUTH only*]:   What you tell the boy things like that for? [*reaching down into his pants with a rather important gesture*] Here, son—[*He hands the boy the coin, but his eyes are directed to his wife's.* TRAVIS *takes the money happily.*]

TRAVIS: Thanks, Daddy. [*He starts out.* RUTH *watches both of them with murder in her eyes.* WALTER *stands and stares back at her with defiance, and suddenly reaches into his pocket again on an afterthought.*]

WALTER [*without even looking at his son, still staring hard at his wife*]:   In fact, here's another fifty cents . . . Buy yourself some fruit today—or take a taxicab to school or something!

TRAVIS: Whoopee—[*He leaps up and clasps his father around the middle with his legs, and they face each other in mutual appreciation; slowly* WALTER LEE *peeks around the boy to catch the violent rays from his wife's eyes and draws his head back as if shot.*]

WALTER: You better get down now—and get to school, man.

TRAVIS [*at the door*]:   O.K. Good-bye. [*He exits.*]

WALTER [*after him, pointing with pride*]:   That's *my* boy. [*She looks at him in disgust and turns back to her work.*] You know what I was thinking 'bout in the bathroom this morning?

RUTH: No.

WALTER: How come you always try to be so pleasant!

RUTH: What is there to be pleasant 'bout!

WALTER: You want to know what I was thinking 'bout in the bathroom or not!

RUTH: I know what you thinking 'bout.

WALTER [*ignoring her*]:   'Bout what me and Willy Harris was talking about last night.

RUTH [*immediately—a refrain*]:   Willy Harris is a good-for-nothing loudmouth.

WALTER: Anybody who talks to me has got to be a good-for-nothing loudmouth, ain't he? And what you know about who is just a good-for-nothing loudmouth? Charlie Atkins was just a "good-for-nothing loudmouth" too, wasn't he! When he wanted me to go in the dry-cleaning business with him. And now—he's grossing a hundred thousand a year. A hundred thousand dollars a year! You still call *him* a loudmouth!

RUTH [*bitterly*]:   Oh, Walter Lee . . . [*She folds her head on her arms over the table.*]

WALTER [*rising and coming to her and standing over her*]:   You tired, ain't you? Tired of everything. Me, the boy, the way we live—this beat-up hole—everything. Ain't you? [*She doesn't look up, doesn't answer.*] So tired—moaning and groaning all the time, but you wouldn't do nothing to help, would you? You couldn't be on my side that long for nothing, could you?

RUTH: Walter, please leave me alone.

WALTER: A man needs for a woman to back him up . . .

RUTH: Walter—

WALTER: Mama would listen to you. You know she listen to you more than she do me and Bennie. She think more of you. All you have to do is just sit down with her when you drinking your coffee one morning and talking 'bout things like you do and—[*He sits down beside her and demonstrates graphically what he thinks her methods and tone should be.*]—you just sip your coffee, see, and say easy like that you been thinking 'bout that deal Walter Lee is so interested in, 'bout the store and all, and sip some more coffee, like what you saying ain't really that important to you—And the next thing you know, she be listening good and asking you questions and when I come home—I can tell her the details. This ain't no fly-by-night proposition, baby. I mean we figured it out, me and Willy and Bobo.

RUTH [*with a frown*]:   Bobo?

WALTER: Yeah. You see, this little liquor store we got in mind cost seventy-five thousand and we figured the initial investment on the place be 'bout thirty thousand, see. That be ten thousand each. Course, there's a couple of hundred you got to pay so's you don't spend your life just waiting for them clowns to let your license get approved—

RUTH: You mean graft?

WALTER [*frowning impatiently*]:   Don't call it that. See there, that just goes to show you what women understand about the world. Baby, don't *nothing* happen for you in this world 'less you pay *somebody* off!

RUTH: Walter, leave me alone! [*She raises her head and stares at him vigorously—then says, more quietly.*] Eat your eggs, they gonna be cold.

WALTER [*straightening up from her and looking off*]:   That's it. There you are. Man say to his woman: I got me a dream. His woman say: Eat your eggs. [*sadly, but gaining in power*] Man say: I got to take hold of this here world, baby! And a woman will say: Eat your eggs and go to work. [*passionately now*] Man say: I got to change my life, I'm choking to death, baby! And his woman say—[*in utter anguish as he brings his fists down on his thighs*]—Your eggs is getting cold!

RUTH [*softly*]:   Walter, that ain't none of our money.

WALTER [*not listening at all or even looking at her*]:   This morning, I was lookin' in the mirror and thinking about it . . . I'm thirty-five years old; I been married eleven years and I got a boy who sleeps in the living room—[*very, very quietly*]—and all I got to give him is stories about how rich white people live . . .

RUTH: Eat your eggs, Walter.

WALTER: *Damn my eggs . . . damn all the eggs that ever was!*

RUTH: Then go to work.

WALTER [*looking up at her*]:   See—I'm trying to talk to you 'bout myself—[*shaking his head with the repetition*]—and all you can say is eat them eggs and go to work.

RUTH [*wearily*]:   Honey, you never say nothing new. I listen to you every day, every night and every morning, and you never say nothing new. [*shrugging*] So you would rather *be* Mr. Arnold than be his chauffeur. So—I would *rather* be living in Buckingham Palace.

WALTER: That is just what is wrong with the colored woman in this world . . . Don't understand about building their men up and making 'em feel like they somebody. Like they can do something.

RUTH [*drily, but to hurt*]:   There *are* colored men who do things.

WALTER: No thanks to the colored woman.

RUTH: Well, being a colored woman, I guess I can't help myself none. [*She rises and gets the ironing board and sets it up and attacks a huge pile of rough-dried clothes, sprinkling them in preparation for the ironing and then rolling them into tight fat balls.*]

WALTER [*mumbling*]:   We one group of men tied to a race of women with small minds. [*his sister* BENEATHA *enters. She is about twenty, as slim and intense as her brother. She is not as pretty as her sister-in-law, but her lean, almost intellectual face has a handsomeness of its own. She wears a bright-red flannel nightie, and her thick hair stands wildly about her head. Her speech is a mixture of many things; it is different from the rest of the family's insofar as education has permeated her sense of English—and perhaps the Midwest rather than the South has finally—at last—won out in her inflection; but not altogether, because over all of it is a soft slurring and transformed use of vowels which is the decided influence of the South Side. She passes*] *through the room without looking at either* RUTH *or* WALTER *and goes to the outside door and looks, a little blindly, out to the bathroom. She sees that it has been lost to the Johnsons. She closes the door with a sleepy vengeance and crosses to the table and sits down a little defeated.*]

BENEATHA: I am going to start timing those people.

WALTER: You should get up earlier.

BENEATHA [*Her face in her hands. She is still fighting the urge to go back to bed*]:   Really—would you suggest dawn? Where's the paper?

WALTER [*pushing the paper across the table to her as he studies her almost clinically, as though he has never seen her before*]:   You a horrible-looking chick at this hour.

BENEATHA [*drily*]:   Good morning, everybody.

WALTER [*senselessly*]:   How is school coming?

BENEATHA [*in the same spirit*]:   Lovely, Lovely. And you know, biology is the greatest. [*looking up at him*] I dissected something that looked just like you yesterday.

WALTER: I just wondered if you've made up your mind and everything.

BENEATHA [*gaining in sharpness and impatience*]:   And what did I answer yesterday morning—and the day before that?

RUTH [*from the ironing board, like someone disinterested and old*]:   Don't be so nasty, Bennie.

BENEATHA [*still to her brother*]:   And the day before that and the day before that!

WALTER [*defensively*]:   I'm interested in you. Something wrong with that? Ain't many girls who decide—

WALTER AND BENEATHA [*in unison*]:   —"to be a doctor." [*silence*]

WALTER: Have we figured out yet just exactly how much medical school is going to cost?

RUTH: Walter Lee, why don't you leave that girl alone and get out of here to work?

BENEATHA [*exits to the bathroom and bangs on the door*]:   Come on out of there, please! [*She comes back into the room.*]

WALTER [*looking at his sister intently*]:   You know the check is coming tomorrow.

BENEATHA [*turning on him with a sharpness all her own*]:   That money belongs to Mama, Walter, and it's for her to decide how she wants to use it. I don't care if she wants to buy a house or a rocket ship or just nail it up somewhere and look at it. It's hers. Not ours—hers.

WALTER [*bitterly*]:   Now ain't that fine! You just got your mother's interest at heart, ain't you, girl? You such a nice girl—but if Mama got that money she can always take a few thousand and help you through school too—can't she?

BENEATHA: I have never asked anyone around here to do anything for me!

WALTER: No! And the line between asking and just accepting when the time comes is big and wide—ain't it!

BENEATHA [*with fury*]:   What do you want from me, Brother—that I quit school or just drop dead, which!

WALTER: I don't want nothing but for you to stop acting holy 'round here. Me and Ruth done made some sacrifices for you—why can't you do something for the family?

RUTH: Walter, don't be dragging me in it.

WALTER: You are in it—Don't you get up and go work in somebody's kitchen for the last three years to help put clothes on her back?

RUTH: Oh, Walter—that's not fair . . .

WALTER: It ain't that nobody expects you to get on your knees and say thank you, Brother; thank you, Ruth; thank you, Mama—and thank you, Travis, for wearing the same pair of shoes for two semesters—

BENEATHA [*dropping to her knees*]:   Well—I do—all right?—thank everybody . . . and forgive me for ever wanting to be anything at all . . . forgive me, forgive me!

RUTH: Please stop it! Your mama'll hear you.

WALTER: Who the hell told you you had to be a doctor? If you so crazy 'bout messing 'round with sick people—then go be a nurse like other women—or just get married and be quiet . . .

BENEATHA: Well—you finally got it said . . . It took you three years but you finally got it said. Walter, give up; leave me alone—it's Mama's money.

WALTER: *He was my father, too!*

BENEATHA: So what? He was mine, too—and Travis' grandfather—but the insurance money belongs to Mama. Picking on me is not going to make her give it to you to invest in any liquor stores—[*under breath, dropping into a chair*]—and I for one say, God bless Mama for that!

WALTER [*To* RUTH]:   See—did you hear? Did you hear!

RUTH: Honey, please go to work.

WALTER: Nobody in this house is ever going to understand me.

BENEATHA: Because you're a nut.

WALTER: Who's a nut?

BENEATHA: You—you are a nut. Thee is mad, boy.

WALTER [*looking at his wife and his sister from the door, very sadly*]:   The world's most backward race of people, and that's a fact.

BENEATHA [*turning slowly in her chair*]:   And then there are all those prophets who would lead us out of the wilderness—[WALTER *slams out of the house.*]—into the swamps!

RUTH: Bennie, why you always gotta be pickin' on your brother? Can't you be a little sweeter sometimes? [*Door opens.* WALTER *walks in.*]

WALTER [*to* RUTH]:   I need some money for carfare.

RUTH [*looks at him, then warms; teasing, but tenderly*]:   Fifty cents? [*She goes to her bag and gets money.*] Here, take a taxi. [Walter *exits.* MAMA *enters. She is a woman in her early sixties, full-bodied and strong. She is one of those women of a certain grace and beauty who wear it so unobtrusively that it takes a while to notice. Her dark-brown face is surrounded by the total whiteness of her hair, and, being a woman who has adjusted to many things in life and overcome many more, her face is full of strength. She has, we can see, wit and faith of a kind that keep her eyes lit and full of interest and expectancy. She is, in a word, a beautiful woman. Her bearing is perhaps most like the noble bearing of the women of the Hereros of Southwest Africa—rather as if she imagines that as she walks she still bears a basket or a vessel upon her head. Her speech, on the other hand, is as careless as her carriage is precise—she is inclined to slur everything—but her voice is perhaps not so much quiet as simply soft.*]

MAMA: Who that 'round here slamming doors at this hour? [*She crosses through the room, goes to the window, opens it, and brings in a feeble little plant growing doggedly in a small pot on the window sill. She feels the dirt and puts it back out.*]

RUTH: That was Walter Lee. He and Bennie was at it again.

MAMA: My children and they tempers. Lord, if this little old plant don't get more sun that it's been getting it ain't never going to see spring again. [*She turns from the window.*] What's the matter with you this morning, Ruth? You looks right peaked. You aiming to iron all them things? Leave some for me. I'll get to 'em this afternoon. Bennie honey, it's too drafty for you to be sitting 'round half dressed. Where's your robe?

BENEATHA: In the cleaners.

MAMA: Well, go get mine and put it on.

BENEATHA: I'm not cold, Mama, honest.

MAMA: I know—but you so thin . . .

BENEATHA [*irritably*]:   Mama, I'm not cold.

MAMA [*seeing the make-down bed as* TRAVIS *has left it*]:   Lord have mercy, look at that poor bed. Bless his heart—he tries, don't he? [*She moves to the bed* Travis *has sloppily made up.*]

RUTH: No—he don't half try at all 'cause he knows you going to come along behind him and fix everything. That's just how come he don't know how to do nothing right now—you done spoiled that boy so.

MAMA: Well—he's a little boy. Ain't supposed to know 'bout housekeeping. My baby, that's what he is. What you fix for his breakfast this morning?

RUTH [*angrily*]:   I feed my son, Lena!

MAMA: I ain't meddling—[*under breath, busy-bodyish*]: I just noticed all last week he had cold cereal, and when it starts getting this chilly in the fall a child ought to have some hot grits or something when he goes out in the cold—

RUTH [*furious*]:   I gave him hot oats—is that all right!

MAMA: I ain't meddling. [*pause*] Put a lot of nice butter on it? [RUTH *shoots her an angry look and does not reply.*] He likes lots of butter.

RUTH [*exasperated*]:   Lena—

MAMA [*To* BENEATHA: Mama *is inclined to wander conversationally sometimes*]:   What was you and your brother fussing 'bout this morning?

BENEATHA: It's not important, Mama. [*She gets up and goes to look out at the bathroom, which is apparently free, and she picks up her towels and rushes out.*]

MAMA: What was they fighting about?

RUTH: Now you know as well as I do.

MAMA   [*shaking her head*]:Brother still worrying hisself sick about that money?

RUTH: You know he is.

MAMA: You had breakfast?

RUTH: Some coffee.

MAMA: Girl, you better start eating and looking after yourself better.You almost thin as Travis.

RUTH: Lena—

MAMA: Uh-hunh?

RUTH: What are you going to do with it?

MAMA: Now don't you start, child. It's too early in the morning to be talking about money. It ain't Christian.

RUTH: It's just that he got his heart set on that store—

MAMA: You mean that liquor store that Willy Harris want him to invest in?

RUTH: Yes—

MAMA: We ain't no business people, Ruth. We just plain working folks.

RUTH: Ain't nobody business people till they go into business. Walter Lee say colored people ain't never going to start getting ahead till they start gambling on some different kinds of things in the world—investments and things.

MAMA: What done got into you, girl? Walter Lee done finally sold you on investing.

RUTH: No. Mama, something is happening between Walter and me. I don't know what it is—but he needs something—something I can't give him any more. He needs this chance, Lena.

MAMA [*frowning deeply*]:   But liquor, honey—

RUTH: Well—like Walter say—I spec people going to always be drinking themselves some liquor.

MAMA: Well—whether they drinks it or not ain't none of my business. But whether I go into business selling it to 'em is, and I don't want that on my ledger this late in life. [*stopping suddenly and studying her daughter-in-law*] Ruth Younger, what's the matter with you today? You look like you could fall over right there.

RUTH: I'm tired.

MAMA: Then you better stay home from work today.

RUTH: I can't stay home. She'd be calling up the agency and screaming at them, "My girl didn't come in today—send me somebody! My girl didn't come in!" Oh, she just have a fit . . .

MAMA: Well, let her have it. I'll just call her up and say you got the flu—

RUTH [*laughing*]:   Why the flu?

MAMA: 'Cause it sounds respectable to 'em. Something white people get, too. They know 'bout the flu. Otherwise they think you been cut up or something when you tell 'em you sick.

RUTH: I got to go in. We need the money.

MAMA: Somebody would of thought my children done all but starved to death the way they talk about money here late. Child, we got a great big old check coming tomorrow.

RUTH [*sincerely, but also self-righteously*]:   Now that's your money. It ain't got nothing to do with me. We all feel like that—Walter and Bennie and me—even Travis.

MAMA [*thoughtfully, and suddenly very far away*]:   Ten thousand dollars—

RUTH: Sure is wonderful.

MAMA: Ten thousand dollars.

RUTH: You know what you should do, Miss Lena? You should take yourself a trip somewhere. To Europe or South America or someplace—

MAMA [*throwing up her hands at the thought*]:   Oh, child!

RUTH: I'm serious. Just pack up and leave! Go on away and enjoy yourself some. Forget about the family and have yourself a ball for once in your life—

MAMA [*drily*]:   You sound like I'm just about ready to die. Who'd go with me? What I look like wandering 'round Europe by myself?

RUTH: Shoot—these here rich white women do it all the time. They don't think nothing of packing up they suitcases and piling on one of them big steamships and—swoosh!—they gone, child.

MAMA: Something always told me I wasn't no rich white woman.

RUTH: Well—what are you going to do with it then?

MAMA: I ain't rightly decided. [*Thinking. She speaks now with emphasis.*] Some of it got to be put away for Beneatha and her schoolin'—and ain't nothing going to touch that part of it. Nothing. [*She waits several seconds, trying to make up her mind about something, and looks at* RUTH *a little tentatively before going on.*] Been thinking that we maybe could meet the notes on a little old two-story somewhere, with a yard where Travis could play in the summertime, if we use part of the insurance for a down payment and everybody kind of pitch in. I could maybe take on a little day work again, few days a week—

RUTH [*studying her mother-in-law furtively and concentrating on her ironing, anxious to encourage without seeming to*]:   Well, Lord knows, we've put enough rent into this here rat trap to pay for four houses by now . . .

MAMA [*looking up at the words "rat trap" and then looking around and leaning back and sighing—in a suddenly reflective mood—*]:   "Rat trap"—yes, that's all it is. [*smiling*] I remember just as well the day me and Big Walter moved in here. Hadn't been married but two weeks and wasn't planning on living here no more than a year. [*She shakes her head at the dissolved dream.*] We was going to set away, little by little, don't you know, and buy a little place out in Morgan Park. We had even picked out the house. [*chuckling a little*] Looks right dumpy today. But Lord, child, you should know all the dreams I had 'bout buying that house and fixing it up and making me a little garden in the back—[*She waits and stops smiling.*] And didn't none of it happen. [*dropping her hands in a futile gesture*]

RUTH [*keeps her head down, ironing*]:   Yes, life can be a barrel of disappointments, sometimes.

MAMA: Honey, Big Walter would come in here some nights back then and slump down on that couch there and just look at the rug, and look at me and look at the rug and then back at me—and I'd know he was down then . . . really down. [*After a second very long and thoughtful pause; she is seeing back to times that only she can see.*]   And then, Lord, when I lost that baby—little Claude—I almost thought I was going to lose Big Walter too. Oh, that man grieved hisself! He was one man to love his children.

RUTH: Ain't nothin' can tear at you like losin' your baby.

MAMA: I guess that's how come that man finally worked hisself to death like he done. Likely he was fighting his own war with this here world that took his baby from him.

RUTH: He sure was a fine man, all right. I always liked Mr. Younger.

MAMA: Crazy 'bout his children! God knows there was plenty wrong with Walter Younger—hard-headed, mean, kind of wild with women—plenty wrong with him. But he sure loved his children. Always wanted them to have something—be something. That's where Brother gets all these notions, I reckon. Big Walter used to say, he'd get right wet in the eyes sometimes, lean his head back with the water standing in his eyes and say, "Seem like God didn't see fit to give the black man nothing but dreams—but He did give us children to make them dreams seem worth while." [*She smiles.*] He could talk like that, don't you know.

RUTH: Yes, he sure could. He was a good man, Mr. Younger.

MAMA: Yes, a fine man—just couldn't never catch up with his dreams, that's all. [Beneatha *comes in, brushing her hair and looking up to the ceiling, where the sound of a vacuum cleaner has started up.*]

BENEATHA: What could be so dirty on that woman's rugs that she has to vacuum them every single day?

RUTH: I wish certain young women 'round here who I could name would take inspiration about certain rugs in a certain apartment I could also mention.

BENEATHA [*shrugging*]:   How much cleaning can a house need, for Christ's sakes?

MAMA [*not liking the Lord's name used thus*]:   Bennie!

RUTH: Just listen to her—just listen!

BENEATHA: Oh, God!

MAMA: If you use the Lord's name just one more time—

BENEATHA [*a bit of a whine*]:   Oh, Mama—

RUTH: Fresh—just fresh as salt, this girl!

BENEATHA [*drily*]:   Well—if the salt loses its savor—

MAMA: Now that will do. I just ain't going to have you 'round here reciting the scriptures in vain—you hear me?

BENEATHA: How did I manage to get on everybody's wrong side by just walking into a room?

RUTH: If you weren't so fresh—

BENEATHA: Ruth, I'm twenty years old.

MAMA: What time you be home from school today?

BENEATHA: Kind of late. [*with enthusiasm*] Madeline is going to start my guitar lessons today. [MAMA *and* RUTH *look up with the same expression.*]

MAMA: Your *what* kind of lessons?

BENEATHA: Guitar.

RUTH: Oh, Father!

MAMA: How come you done taken it in your mind to learn to play the guitar?

BENEATHA: I just want to, that's all.

MAMA [*smiling*]:   Lord, child, don't you know what to do with yourself? How long it going to be before you get tired of this now—like you got tired of that little play-acting group you joined last year? [*looking at* RUTH] And what was it the year before that?

RUTH: The horseback-riding club for which she bought that fifty-five-dollar riding habit that's been hanging in the closet ever since!

MAMA [*to* BENEATHA]:   Why you got to flit so from one thing to another, baby?

BENEATHA [*sharply*]:   I just want to learn to play the guitar. Is there anything wrong with that?

MAMA: Ain't nobody trying to stop you. I just wonders sometimes why you has to flit so from one thing to another all the time. You ain't never done nothing with all that camera equipment you brought home—

BENEATHA: I don't flit! I—I experiment with different forms of expression—

RUTH: Like riding a horse?

BENEATHA: —People have to express themselves one way or another.

MAMA: What is it you want to express?

BENEATHA [*angrily*]:   Me! [MAMA *and* RUTH *look at each other and burst into raucous laughter*] Don't worry—I don't expect you to understand.

MAMA [*to change the subject*]:   Who you going out with tomorrow night?

BENEATHA [*with displeasure*]:   George Murchison again.

MAMA [*pleased*]:   Oh—you getting a little sweet on him?

RUTH: You ask me, this child ain't sweet on nobody but herself—[*under breath*] Express herself! [*They laugh.*]

BENEATHA: Oh—I like George all right, Mama. I mean I like him enough to go out with him and stuff, but—

RUTH [*for devilment*]:   What does and stuff mean?

BENEATHA: Mind your own business.

MAMA: Stop picking at her now, Ruth. [*a thoughtful pause, and then a suspicious sudden look at her daughter as she turns in her chair for emphasis*] What does it mean?

BENEATHA [*wearily*]:   Oh, I just mean I couldn't ever really be serious about George. He's—he's so shallow.

RUTH: Shallow—what do you mean he's shallow? He's *Rich!*

MAMA: Hush, Ruth.

BENEATHA: I know he's rich. He knows he's rich, too.

RUTH: Well—what other qualities a man got to have to satisfy you, little girl?

BENEATHA: You wouldn't even begin to understand. Anybody who married Walter could not possibly understand.

MAMA [*outraged*]:   What kind of way is that to talk about your brother?

BENEATHA: Brother is a flip—let's face it.

MAMA [*to Ruth, helplessly*]:   What's a flip?

RUTH [*glad to add kindling*]:   She's saying he's crazy.

BENEATHA: Not crazy. Brother isn't really crazy yet—he—he's an elaborate neurotic.

MAMA: Hush your mouth!

BENEATHA: As for George. Well. George looks good—he's got a beautiful car and he takes me to nice places and, as my sister-in-law says, he is probably the richest boy I will ever get to know and I even like him sometimes—but if the Youngers are sitting around waiting to see if their little Bennie is going to tie up the family with the Murchisons, they are wasting their time.

RUTH: You mean you wouldn't marry George Murchison if he asked you someday? That pretty, rich thing? Honey, I knew you was odd—

BENEATHA: No I would not marry him if all I felt for him was what I feel now. Besides, George's family wouldn't really like it.

MAMA: Why not?

BENEATHA: Oh, Mama—The Murchisons are honest-to-God-real-*live*-rich colored people, and the only people in the world who are more snobbish than rich white people are rich colored people. I thought everybody knew that. I've met Mrs. Murchison. She's a scene!

MAMA: You must not dislike people 'cause they well off, honey.

BENEATHA: Why not? It makes just as much sense as disliking people 'cause they are poor, and lots of people do that.

RUTH [*a wisdom-of-the-ages manner. To* MAMA]:   Well, she'll get over some of this—

BENEATHA: Get over it? What are you talking about, Ruth? Listen, I'm going to be a doctor. I'm not worried about who I'm going to marry yet—if I ever get married.

MAMA AND RUTH: *If!*

MAMA: Now, Bennie—

BENEATHA: Oh, I probably will . . . but first I'm going to be a doctor, and George, for one, still thinks that's pretty funny. I couldn't be bothered with that. I am going to be a doctor and everybody around here better understand that!

MAMA [*kindly*]:   'Course you going to be a doctor, honey, God willing.

BENEATHA [*drily*]:   God hasn't got a thing to do with it.

MAMA: Beneatha—that just wasn't necessary.

BENEATHA: Well—neither is God. I get sick of hearing about God.

MAMA: Beneatha!

BENEATHA: I mean it! I'm just tired of hearing about God all the time. What has He got to do with anything? Does he pay tuition?

MAMA: You 'bout to get your fresh little jaw slapped!

RUTH: That's just what she needs, all right!

BENEATHA: Why? Why can't I say what I want to around here, like everybody else?

MAMA: It don't sound nice for a young girl to say things like that—you wasn't brought up that way. Me and your father went to trouble to get you and Brother to church every Sunday.

BENEATHA: Mama, you don't understand. It's all a matter of ideas, and God is just one idea I don't accept. It's not important. I am not going out and be immoral or commit crimes because I don't believe in God. I don't even think about it. It's just that I get tired of Him getting credit for all the things the human race achieves through its own stubborn effort. There simply is no blasted God— there is only man and it is he who makes miracles! [MAMA *absorbs this speech, studies her daughter and rises slowly and crosses to* BENEATHA *and slaps her powerfully across the face. After, there is only silence and the daughter drops her eyes from her mother's face, and* MAMA *is very tall before her.*]

MAMA: Now—you say after me, in my mother's house there is still God. [*There is a long pause and* BENEATHA *stares at the floor wordlessly.* MAMA *repeats the phrase with precision and cool emotion.*] In my mother's house there is still God.

BENEATHA: In my mother's house there is still God. [*a long pause*]

MAMA [*Walking away from* BENEATHA, *too disturbed for triumphant posture. Stopping and turning back to her daughter.*]: There are some ideas we ain't going to have in this house. Not long as I am at the head of this family.

BENEATHA: Yes, ma'am. [MAMA *walks out of the room.*]

RUTH [*almost gently, with profound understanding*]: You think you a woman, Bennie—but you still a little girl. What you did was childish—so you got treated like a child.

BENEATHA: I see. [*quietly*] I also see that everybody thinks it's all right for Mama to be a tyrant. But all the tyranny in the world will never put a God in the heavens! [*She picks up her books and goes out.*]

RUTH [*goes to* MAMA'S *door*]: She said she was sorry.

MAMA [*coming out, going to her plant*]: They frightens me, Ruth. My children.

RUTH: You got good children, Lena. They just a little off sometimes—but they're good.

MAMA: No—There's something come down between me and them that don't let us understand each other and I don't know what it is. One done almost lost his mind thinking 'bout money all the time and the other done commence to talk about things I can't seem to understand in no form or fashion. What is it that's changing, Ruth?

RUTH [*soothingly, older than her years*]: Now . . . you taking it all too seriously. You just got strong-willed children and it takes a strong woman like you to keep 'em in hand.

MAMA [*looking at her plant and sprinkling a little water on it*]: They spirited all right, my children. Got to admit they got spirit—Bennie and Walter. Like this little old plant that ain't never had enough sunshine or nothing—and look at it . . . [*She has her back to* RUTH, *who has had to stop ironing and lean against something and put the back of her hand to her forehead.*]

RUTH [*trying to keep* MAMA *from noticing*]:   You . . . sure . . . loves that little old thing, don't you? . . .

MAMA: Well, I always wanted me a garden like I used to see sometimes at the back of the houses down home. This plant is close as I ever got to having one. [*She looks out of the window as she replaces the plant.*] Lord, ain't nothing as dreary as the view from this window on a dreary day, is there? Why ain't you singing this morning, Ruth? Sing that "No Ways Tired." That song always lifts me up so—[*She turns at last to see that* RUTH *has slipped quietly into a chair, in a state of semiconsciousness.*] Ruth! Ruth honey—what's the matter with you . . . Ruth!

Curtain

SCENE 2

It is the following morning; a Saturday morning, and house cleaning is in progress at the Youngers. Furniture has been shoved hither and yon and MAMA *is giving the kitchen-area walls a washing down.* BENEATHA, *in dungarees, with a handkerchief tied around her face, is spraying insecticide into the cracks in the walls. As they work, the radio is on and a South Side disk jockey program is inappropriately filling the house with a rather exotic saxophone blues.* TRAVIS, *the sole idle one, is leaning on his arms, looking out of the window.*

TRAVIS: Grandmama, that stuff Bennie is using smells awful. Can I go downstairs, please?

MAMA: Did you get all them chores done already? I ain't seen you doing much.

TRAVIS: Yes'm—finished early. Where did Mama go this morning?

MAMA [*looking at* BENEATHA]:   She had to go on a little errand.

TRAVIS: Where?

MAMA: To tend to her business.

TRAVIS: Can I go outside then?

MAMA: Oh, I guess so. You better stay right in front of the house, though . . . and keep a good lookout for the postman.

TRAVIS: Yes'm. [*He starts out and decides to give his* AUNT BENEATHA *a good swat on the legs as he passes her.*] Leave them poor little old cockroaches alone, they ain't bothering you none. [*He runs as she swings the spray gun at him both viciously and playfully.* WALTER *enters from the bedroom and goes to the phone.*]

MAMA: Look out there, girl, before you be spilling some of that stuff on that child!

TRAVIS [*teasing*]:   That's right—look out now! [*He exits.*]

BENEATHA [*drily*]:   I can't imagine that it would hurt him—it has never hurt the roaches.

MAMA: Well, little boys' hides ain't as tough as South Side roaches.

WALTER [*into phone*]:   Hello—Let me talk to Willy Harris.

MAMA: You better get over there behind the bureau. I seen one marching out of there like Napoleon yesterday.

WALTER: Hello, Willy? It ain't come yet. It'll be here in a few minutes. Did the lawyer give you the papers?

BENEATHA: There's really only one way to get rid of them, Mama—

MAMA: How?

BENEATHA: Set fire to this building.

WALTER: Good. Good. I'll be right over.

BENEATHA: Where did Ruth go, Walter?

WALTER: I don't know. [*He exits abruptly.*]

BENEATHA: Mama, where did Ruth go?

MAMA [*looking at her with meaning*]:   To the doctor, I think.

BENEATHA: The doctor? What's the matter? [*They exchange glances.*] You don't think—

MAMA [*with her sense of drama*]:   Now I ain't saying what I think. But I ain't never been wrong 'bout a woman neither. [*The phone rings.*]

BENEATHA [*at the phone*]:   Hay-lo . . . [*pause, and a moment of recognition*] Well—when did you get back! . . . And how was it? . . . Of course I've missed you—in my way . . . This morning? No . . . house cleaning and all that and Mama hates it if I let people come over when the house is like this . . . You *have?* Well, that's different . . . What is it—Oh, what the hell, come on over . . . Right, see you then.

[She hangs up.]

MAMA [*who has listened vigorously, as is her habit*]:   Who is that you inviting over here with this house looking like this? You ain't got the pride you was born with!

BENEATHA: Asagai doesn't care how houses look, Mama—he's an intellectual.

MAMA: *Who?*

BENEATHA: Asagai—Joseph Asagai. He's an African boy I met on campus. He's been studying in Canada all summer.

MAMA: What's his name?

BENEATHA: Asagai, Joseph. Ah-sah-guy . . . He's from Nigeria.

MAMA: Oh, that's the little country that was founded by slaves way back . . .

BENEATHA: No, Mama—that's Liberia.

MAMA: I don't think I never met no African before.

BENEATHA: Well, do me a favor and don't ask him a whole lot of ignorant questions about Africans. I mean, do they wear clothes and all that—

MAMA: Well, now, I guess if you think we so ignorant 'round here maybe you shouldn't bring your friends here—

BENEATHA: It's just that people ask such crazy things. All anyone seems to know about when it comes to Africa is Tarzan—

MAMA [*indignantly*]:   Why should I know anything about Africa?

BENEATHA: Why do you give money at church for the missionary work?

MAMA: Well, that's to help save people.

BENEATHA: You mean save them from *heathenism*—

MAMA [*innocently*]:   Yes.

BENEATHA: I'm afraid they need more salvation from the British and the French.

[RUTH *comes in forlornly and pulls off her coat with dejection. They both turn to look at her.*]

RUTH [*Dispiritedly*]:   Well, I guess from all the happy faces—everybody knows.

BENEATHA: You pregnant?

MAMA: Lord have mercy, I sure hope it's a little old girl. Travis ought to have a sister.

[BENEATHA *and* RUTH *give her a hopeless look for this grandmotherly enthusiasm*]

BENEATHA: How far along are you?

RUTH: Two months.

BENEATHA: Did you mean to? I mean did you plan it or was it an accident?

MAMA: What do you know about planning or not planning?

BENEATHA: Oh, Mama.

RUTH [*wearily*]:   She's twenty years old, Lena.

BENEATHA: Did you plan it, Ruth?

RUTH: Mind your own business.

BENEATHA: It is my business—where is he going to live, on the roof? [*There is silence following the remark as the three women react to the sense of it.*] Gee—I didn't mean that, Ruth, honest. Gee, I don't feel like that at all. I—I think it is wonderful.

RUTH [*dully*]:   Wonderful.

BENEATHA: Yes—really.

MAMA [*looking at* RUTH, *worried*]:   Doctor say everything going to be all right?

RUTH [*far away*]:   Yes—she says everything is going to be fine . . .

MAMA [*Immediately suspicious*]:   "She"—What doctor you went to? [Ruth *folds over, near hysteria*]

MAMA [*worriedly hovering over* RUTH]:   Ruth, honey—what's the matter with you—you sick? [RUTH *has her fists clenched on her thighs and is fighting hard to suppress a scream that seems to be rising in her.*]

BENEATHA: What's the matter with her, Mama?

MAMA [*working her fingers in* RUTH'S *shoulder to relax her*]:   She be all right. Women gets right depressed sometimes when they get her way. [*speaking softly, expertly, rapidly*] Now you just relax. That's right . . . just lean back, don't think 'bout nothing at all . . . nothing at all—

RUTH: I'm all right . . . [*The glassy-eyed look melts and then she collapses into a fit of heavy sobbing. The bell rings.*]

BENEATHA: Oh, my God—that must be Asagai.

MAMA [*to* RUTH]:   Come on now, honey. You need to lie down and rest awhile . . . then have some nice hot food. [*They exit,* RUTH'S *weight on her mother-in-law.*

BENEATHA, *herself profoundly disturbed, opens the door to admit a rather dramatic-looking young man with a large package.*]

ASAGAI: Hello, Alaiyo—

BENEATHA [*holding the door open and regarding him with pleasure*]:   Hello . . . [*long pause*] Well—come in. And please excuse everything. My mother was very upset about my letting anyone come here with the place like this.

ASAGAI [*coming into the room*]:   You look disturbed too . . . Is something wrong?

BENEATHA [*still at the door, absently*]:   Yes . . . we've all got acute ghetto-itus. [*She smiles and comes toward him, finding a cigarette and sitting.*] So—sit down! How was Canada?

ASAGAI [*a sophisticate*]:   Canadian.

BENEATHA [*looking at him*]:   I'm very glad you are back.

ASAGAI [*looking back at her in turn*]:   Are you really?

BENEATHA: Yes—very.

ASAGAI: Why—you were quite glad when I went away. What happened?

BENEATHA: You went away.

ASAGAI: Ahhhhhhhh.

BENEATHA: Before—you wanted to be so serious before there was time.

ASAGAI: How much time must there be before one knows what one feels?

BENEATHA [*Stalling this particular conversation. Her hands pressed together, in a deliberately childish gesture*]:   What did you bring me?

ASAGAI [*handing her the package*]:   Open it and see.

BENEATHA [*eagerly opening the package and drawing out some records and the colorful robes of a Nigerian woman*]:   Oh, Asagai! . . .You got them for me! . . . How beautiful . . . and the records too! [*She lifts out the robes and runs to the mirror with them and holds the drapery up in front of herself.*]

ASAGAI   [*coming to her at the mirror*]:   I shall have to teach you how to drape it properly. [*He flings the material about her for the moment and stands back to look at her.*] Ah—Oh-pay-gay-day, oh-gbah-mu-shay. [*a Yoruba exclamation for admiration*] You wear it well . . . very well . . . mutilated hair and all.

BENEATHA [*turning suddenly*]:   My hair—what's wrong with my hair?

ASAGAI [*shrugging*]:   Were you born with it like that?

BENEATHA [*reaching up to touch it*]:   No . . . of course not. [*She looks back to the mirror, disturbed.*]

ASAGAI [*smiling*]:   How then?

BENEATHA: You know perfectly well how . . . as crinkly as yours . . . that's how.

ASAGAI: And it is ugly to you that way?

BENEATHA [*quickly*]:   Oh, no—not ugly . . . [*more slowly, apologetically*] But it's so hard to manage when it's, well—raw.

ASAGAI: And so to accommodate that—you mutilate it every week?

BENEATHA: It's not mutilation!

ASAGAI [*laughing aloud at her seriousness*]:   Oh . . . please! I am only teasing you because you are so very serious about these things. [*He stands back from her and folds his arms across his chest as he watches her pulling at her hair and frowning in the mirror.*] Do you remember the first time you met me at school? . . . [*He laughs.*] You came up to me and said—and I thought you were the most serious little thing I had ever seen—you said: [*He imitates her.*] "Mr. Asagai—I want very much to talk with you. About Africa. You see, Mr. Asagai, I am looking for my *identity!*" [*He laughs.*]

BENEATHA [*turning to him, not laughing*]:   Yes—[*Her face is quizzical, profoundly disturbed.*]

ASAGAI [*still teasing and reaching out and taking her face in his hands and turning her profile to him*]:   Well . . . it is true that this is not so much a profile of a Hollywood queen as perhaps a queen of the Nile—[*a mock dismissal of the importance of the question*] But what does it matter? Assimilationism is so popular in your country.

BENEATHA [*wheeling, passionately, sharply*]:   I am not an assimilationist!

ASAGAI [*The protest hangs in the room for a moment and* ASAGAI *studies her, his laughter fading.*]:   Such a serious one. [*There is a pause.*] So—you like the robes? You must take excellent care of them—they are from my sister's personal wardrobe.

BENEATHA [*with incredulity*]:   You—you sent all the way home—for me?

ASAGAI [*with charm*]:   For you—I would do much more . . . Well, that is what I came for. I must go.

BENEATHA: Will you call me Monday?

ASAGAI: Yes . . . We have a great deal to talk about. I mean about identity and time and all that.

BENEATHA: Time?

ASAGAI: Yes. About how much time one needs to know what one feels.

BENEATHA: You never understood that there is more than one kind of feeling which can exist between a man and a woman—or, at least, there should be.

ASAGAI [*shaking his head negatively but gently*]:   No. Between a man and a woman there need be only one kind of feeling. I have that for you . . . Now even . . . right this moment . . . .

BENEATHA: I know—and by itself—it won't do. I can find that anywhere.

ASAGAI: For a woman it should be enough.

BENEATHA: I know—because that's what it says in all the novels that men write. But it isn't. Go ahead and laugh—but I'm not interested in being someone's little episode in America or—[*with feminine vengeance*]—one of them! [ASAGAI *has burst into laughter again.*] That's funny as hell, huh!

ASAGAI: It's just that every American girl I have known has said that to me. White—black—in this you are all the same. And the same speech, too!

BENEATHA [*angrily*]:   Yuk, yuk, yuk!

ASAGAI: It's how you can be sure that the world's most liberated women are not liberated at all. You all talk about it too much! [MAMA *enters and is immediately all social charm because of the presence of a guest.*]

BENEATHA: Oh—Mama—this is Mr. Asagai.

MAMA: How do you do?

ASAGAI [*total politeness to an elder*]:   How do you do, Mrs. Younger. Please forgive me for coming at such an outrageous hour on a Saturday.

MAMA: Well, you are quite welcome. I just hope you understand that our house don't always look like this. [*chatterish*] You must come again. I would love to hear all about—[*not sure of the name*]—your country. I think it's so sad the way our American Negroes don't know nothing about Africa 'cept Tarzan and all that. And all that money they pour into these churches when they ought to be helping you people over there drive out them French and Englishmen done taken away your land. [*The mother flashes a slightly superior look at her daughter upon completion of the recitation.*]

ASAGAI [*taken aback by this sudden and acutely unrelated expression of sympathy*]:   Yes . . . yes . . .

MAMA [*smiling at him suddenly and relaxing and looking him over*]:   How many miles is it from here to where you come from?

ASAGAI: Many thousands.

MAMA [*looking at him as she would* WALTER]:   I bet you don't half look after yourself, being away from your mama either. I spec you better come 'round here from time to time and get yourself some decent home-cooked meals . . .

ASAGAI [*moved*]:   Thank you. Thank you very much. [*They are all quiet, then—*] Well . . . I must go. I will call you Monday, Alaiyo.

MAMA: What's that he call you?

ASAGAI: Oh—"Alaiyo." I hope you don't mind. It is what you would call a nickname, I think. It is a Yoruba word. I am a Yoruba.

MAMA [*looking at* BENEATHA]:   I—I thought he was from—

ASAGAI [*understanding*]:   Nigeria is my country. Yoruba is my tribal origin—

BENEATHA: You didn't tell us what Alaiyo means . . . for all I know, you might be calling me Little Idiot or something . . .

ASAGAI: Well . . . let me see . . . I do not know how just to explain it . . . The sense of a thing can be so different when it changes languages.

BENEATHA: You're evading.

ASAGAI: No—really it is difficult . . . [*thinking*] It means . . . it means One for Whom Bread—Food—Is Not Enough. [*He looks at her.*] Is that all right?

BENEATHA [*understanding, softly*]:   Thank you.

MAMA [*looking from one to the other and not understanding any of it*]:   Well . . . that's nice. . . . You must come see us again—Mr.—

ASAGAI: Ah-sah-guy. . . .

MAMA: Yes . . . Do come again.

ASAGAI: Good-bye. [*He exits.*]

MAMA [*after him*]:   Lord, that's a pretty thing just went out here! [*insinuatingly, to her daughter*] Yes, I guess I see why we done commence to get so interested in Africa 'round here. Missionaries my aunt Jenny! [*She exits.*]

BENEATHA: Oh, Mama! . . . [*She picks up the Nigerian dress and holds it up to her in front of the mirror again. She sets the headdress on haphazardly and then notices her hair again and clutches at it and then replaces the headdress and frowns at herself. Then she starts to wriggle in front of the mirror as she thinks a Nigerian woman might.* TRAVIS *enters and regards her.*]

TRAVIS: You cracking up?

BENEATHA: Shut up. [*She pulls the headdress off and looks at herself in the mirror and clutches at her hair again and squinches her eyes as if trying to imagine something. Then, suddenly, she gets her raincoat and kerchief and hurriedly prepares for going out.*]

MAMA [*coming back into the room*]:   She's resting now. Travis, baby, run next door and ask Miss Johnson to please let me have a little kitchen cleanser. This here can is empty as Jacob's kettle.

TRAVIS: I just came in.

MAMA: Do as you told. [*He exits and she looks at her daughter.*] Where you going?

BENEATHA [*halting at the door*]:   To become a queen of the Nile! [*She exits in a breathless blaze of glory.* Ruth *appears in the bedroom doorway.*]

MAMA: Who told you to get up?

RUTH: Ain't nothing wrong with me to be lying in no bed for. Where did Bennie go?

MAMA [*drumming her fingers*]:   Far as I could make out—to Egypt. [RUTH *just looks at her.*] What time is it getting to?

RUTH: Ten twenty. And the mailman going to ring that bell this morning just like he done every morning for the last umpteen years. [Travis *comes in with the cleanser can.*]

TRAVIS: She say to tell you that she don't have much.

MAMA [*angrily*]:   Lord, some people I could name sure is tight-fisted! [*directing her grandson*] Mark two cans of cleanser down on the list there. If she that hard up for kitchen cleanser, I sure don't want to forget to get her none!

RUTH: Lena—maybe the woman is just short on cleanser—

MAMA [*not listening*]:   —Much baking powder as she done borrowed from me all these years, she could of done gone into the baking business! [*The bell sounds suddenly and sharply and all three are stunned—serious and silent—mid-speech. In spite of all the other conversation and distractions of the morning, this is what they have been waiting for, even* TRAVIS, *who looks helplessly from his mother to his grandmother.* RUTH *is the first to come to life again.*]

RUTH [*to* TRAVIS]:   Get down them steps, boy! [TRAVIS *snaps to life and flies out to get the mail.*]

MAMA [*her eyes wide, her hand to her breast*]:   You mean it done really come?

RUTH [*excited*]:   Oh, Miss Lena!

MAMA [*collecting herself*]:   Well . . . I don't know what we all so excited about 'round here for. We known it was coming for months.

RUTH: That's a whole lot different from having it come and being able to hold it in your hands . . . a piece of paper worth ten thousand dollars . . . [TRAVIS *bursts back into the room. He holds the envelope high above his head, like a little dancer, his face is radiant and he is breathless. He moves to his grandmother with sudden slow ceremony and puts the envelope into her hands. She accepts it, and then merely holds it and looks at it.*] Come on! Open it . . . Lord have mercy, I wish Walter Lee was here!

TRAVIS: Open it, Grandmama!

MAMA [*staring at it*]:   Now you all be quiet. It's just a check.

RUTH: Open it . . .

MAMA [*still staring at it*]:   Now don't act silly . . . We ain't never been no people to act silly 'bout no money—

RUTH [*swiftly*]:   We ain't never had none before—*open it!* [MAMA *finally makes a good strong tear and pulls out the thin blue slice of paper and inspects it closely. The boy and his mother study it raptly over* MAMA's *shoulders.*]

MAMA: Travis! [*She is counting off with doubt.*] Is that the right number of zeros?

TRAVIS: Yes'm . . . ten thousand dollars. Gaalee, Grandmama, you rich.

MAMA [*She holds the check away from her, still looking at it. Slowly her face sobers into a mask of unhappiness.*]:   Ten thousand dollars. [*She hands it to* RUTH.] Put it away somewhere, Ruth. [*She does not look at* RUTH; *her eyes seem to be seeing something somewhere very far off.*] Ten thousand dollars they give you. Ten thousand dollars.

TRAVIS [*to his mother, sincerely*]:   What's the matter with Grandmama—don't she want to be rich?

RUTH [*distractedly*]:   You go on out and play now, baby. [TRAVIS *exits.* MAMA *starts wiping dishes absently, humming intently to herself.* RUTH *turns to her, with kind exasperation.*] You've gone and got yourself upset.

MAMA [*not looking at her*]:   I spec if it wasn't for you all . . . I would just put that money away or give it to the church or something.

RUTH: Now what kind of talk is that. Mr. Younger would just be plain mad if he could hear you talking foolish like that.

MAMA [*stopping and staring off*]:   Yes . . . he sure would. [*sighing*] We got enough to do with that money, all right. [*She halts then, and turns and looks at her daughter-in-law hard;* RUTH *avoids her eyes and* MAMA *wipes her hands with finality and starts to speak firmly to* RUTH.] Where did you go today, girl?

RUTH: To the doctor.

MAMA [*impatiently*]:   Now, Ruth . . . you know better than that. Old Doctor Jones is strange enough in his way but there ain't nothing 'bout him make somebody slip and call him "she"—like you done this morning.

RUTH: Well, that's what happened—my tongue slipped.

MAMA: You went to see that woman, didn't you?

RUTH [*defensively, giving herself away*]:   What woman you talking about?

MAMA [*angrily*]:   That woman who—[Walter *enters in great excitement.*]

WALTER: Did it come?

MAMA [*quietly*]:   Can't you give people a Christian greeting before you start asking about money?

WALTER [*to Ruth*]:   Did it come? [RUTH *unfolds the check and lays it quietly before him, watching him intently with thoughts of her own.* WALTER *sits down and grasps it close and counts off the zeros.*] Ten thousand dollars—[*He turns suddenly, frantically to his mother and draws some papers out of his breast pocket.*] Mama—look. Old Willy Harris put everything on paper—

MAMA: Son—I think you ought to talk to your wife . . . I'll go on out and leave you alone if you want—

WALTER: I can talk to her later—Mama, look—

MAMA: Son—

WALTER: WILL SOMEBODY PLEASE LISTEN TO ME TODAY!

MAMA [*quietly*]:   I don't 'low no yellin' in this house, Walter Lee, and you know it— [WALTER *stares at them in frustration and starts to speak several times.*] And there ain't going to be no investing in no liquor stores. I don't aim to have to speak on that again. [*a long pause*]

WALTER: Oh—so you don't aim to have to speak on that again? So you have decided . . . [*crumpling his papers*] Well, *you* tell that to my boy tonight when you put him to sleep on the living-room couch . . . [*turning to* MAMA *and speaking directly to her*]: Yeah—and tell it to my wife, Mama, tomorrow when she has to go out of here to look after somebody else's kids. And tell it to *me*, MAMA, every time we need a new pair of curtains and I have to watch *you* go out and work in somebody's kitchen. Yeah, you tell me then! [*Walter starts out*]

RUTH: Where you going?

WALTER: I'm going out!

RUTH: Where?

WALTER: Just out of this house somewhere—

RUTH [*getting her coat*]:   I'll come too.

WALTER: I don't want you to come!

RUTH: I got something to talk to you about, Walter.

WALTER: That's too bad.

MAMA [*still quietly*]:   Walter Lee—[*She waits and he finally turns and looks at her.*] Sit down.

WALTER: I'm a grown man, Mama.

MAMA: Ain't nobody said you wasn't grown. But you still in my house and my presence. And as long as you are—you'll talk to your wife civil. Now sit down.

RUTH [*suddenly*]:   Oh, let him go on out and drink himself to death! He makes me sick to my stomach! [*She flings her coat against him.*]

WALTER [*violently*]:   And you turn mine, too, baby! [RUTH *goes into their bedroom and slams the door behind her.*] That was my greatest mistake—

MAMA [*still quietly*]:   Walter, what is the matter with you?

WALTER: Matter with me? Ain't nothing the matter with *me!*

MAMA: Yes there is. Something eating you up like a crazy man. Something more than me not giving you this money. The past few years I been watching it happen to you. You get all nervous acting and kind of wild in the eyes— [WALTER *jumps up impatiently at her words.*] I said sit there now, I'm talking to you!

WALTER: Mama—I don't need no nagging at me today.

MAMA: Seem like you getting to a place where you always tied up in some kind of knot about something. But if anybody ask you 'bout it you just yell at 'em and bust out the house and go out and drink somewheres. Walter Lee, people can't live with that. Ruth's a good, patient girl in her way—but you getting to be too much. Boy, don't make the mistake of driving that girl away from you.

WALTER: Why—what she do for me?

MAMA: She loves you.

WALTER: Mama—I'm going out. I want to go off somewhere and be by myself for a while.

MAMA: I'm sorry 'bout your liquor store, son. It just wasn't the thing for us to do. That's what I want to tell you about—

WALTER: I got to go out, Mama—[*He rises.*]

MAMA: It's dangerous, son.

WALTER: What's dangerous?

MAMA: When a man goes outside his home to look for peace.

WALTER [*beseechingly*]:   Then why can't there never be no peace in this house then?

MAMA: You done found it in some other house?

WALTER: No—there ain't no woman! Why do women always think there's a woman somewhere when a man gets restless. [*coming to her*] Mama—Mama—I want so many things. . .

MAMA: Yes, son—

WALTER: I want so many things that they are driving me kind of crazy . . . Mama— look at me.

MAMA: I'm looking at you. You a good-looking boy. You got a job, a nice wife, a fine boy and—

WALTER: A job. [*looks at her*] Mama, a job? I open and close car doors all day long. I drive a man around in his limousine and I say, "Yes, sir; no, sir; very good, sir; shall I take the Drive, sir?" Mama, that ain't no kind of job . . . that ain't nothing at all. [*very quietly*] Mama, I don't know if I can make you understand.

MAMA: Understand what, baby?

WALTER [*quietly*]:   Sometimes it's like I can see the future stretched out in front of me—just plain as day. The future, Mama. Hanging over there at the edge of my days. Just waiting for me—a big, looming blank space—full of *nothing*. Just waiting for *me*. [*pause*] Mama—sometimes when I'm downtown and I pass them cool, quiet-looking restaurants where them white boys are sitting back and talking 'bout things . . . sitting there turning deals worth millions of dollars . . . sometimes I see guys don't look much older than me—

MAMA: Son—how come you talk so much 'bout money?

WALTER [*with immense passion*]:   Because it is life, Mama!

MAMA [*quietly*]:   Oh—[*very quietly*] So now it's life. Money is life. Once upon a time freedom used to be life—now it's money. I guess the world really do change. . .

WALTER: No—it was always money, Mama. We just didn't know about it.

MAMA: No . . . something has changed. [*She looks at him.*] You something new, boy. In my time we was worried about not being lynched and getting to the North if we could and how to stay alive and still have a pinch of dignity too . . . Now here come you and Beneatha—talking 'bout things we ain't never even thought about hardly, me and your daddy. You ain't satisfied or proud of nothing we done. I mean that you had a home; that we kept you out of trouble till you was grown; that you don't have to ride to work on the back of nobody's streetcar—You my children—but how different we done become.

WALTER: You just don't understand, Mama, you just don't understand.

MAMA: Son—do you know your wife is expecting another baby? [WALTER *stands, stunned, and absorbs what his mother has said.*] That's what she wanted to talk to you about. [WALTER *sinks down into a chair.*] This ain't for me to be telling—but you ought to know. [*She waits*] I think Ruth is thinking 'bout getting rid of that child.

WALTER [*slowly understanding*]:   No—no—Ruth wouldn't do that.

MAMA: When the world gets ugly enough—a woman will do anything for her family. *The part that's already living.*

WALTER: You don't know Ruth, Mama, if you think she would do that. [Ruth *opens the bedroom door and stands there a little limp.*]

RUTH [*beaten*]:   Yes I would too, Walter, [*pause*] I gave her a five-dollar down payment. [*There is total silence as the man stares at his wife and the mother stares at her son.*]

MAMA [*presently*]:   Well—[*tightly*] Well—son, I'm waiting to hear you say something . . . I'm waiting to hear how you be your father's son. Be the man he was . . . [*pause*] Your wife say she going to destroy your child. And I'm waiting to hear you talk like him and say we a people who give children life, not who destroys them—[*She rises.*] I'm waiting to see you stand up and look like your daddy and say we done give up one baby to poverty and that we ain't going to give up nary another one . . . I'm waiting.

WALTER: Ruth—

MAMA: If you a son of mine, tell her! [WALTER *turns, looks at her and can say nothing. She continues, bitterly.*] You . . . you are a disgrace to your father's memory. Somebody get me my hat.

Curtain

ACT II
SCENE 1

TIME: *Later the same day.*

AT RISE: RUTH *is ironing again. She has the radio going. Presently* BENEATHA'S *bedroom door opens and* RUTH'S *mouth falls and she puts down the iron in fascination.*

RUTH: What have we got on tonight!

BENEATHA [*emerging grandly from the doorway so that we can see her thoroughly robed in the costume* ASAGAI *brought.*]:   You are looking at what a well-dressed Nigerian woman wears—[*She parades for* RUTH, *her hair completely hidden by the headdress; she is coquettishly fanning herself with an ornate oriental fan, mistakenly more like Butterfly than any Nigerian that ever was.*] Isn't it beautiful? [*She promenades to the radio and, with an arrogant flourish, turns off the good loud blues that is playing.*] Enough of this assimilationist junk! [RUTH *follows her with her eyes as she goes to the phonograph and puts on a record and turns and waits ceremoniously for the music to come up. Then with a shout—*] OCOMOGOSIAY! [RUTH *jumps. The music comes up, a lovely Nigerian melody.* BENEATHA *listens, enraptured, her eyes far away—"back to the past." She begins to dance.* RUTH *is dumbfounded.*]

RUTH: What kind of dance is that?

BENEATHA: A folk dance.

RUTH [*Pearl Bailey*]:   What kind of folks do that, honey?

BENEATHA: It's from Nigeria. It's a dance of welcome.

RUTH: Who you welcoming?

BENEATHA: The men back to the village.

RUTH: Where they been?

BENEATHA: How should I know—out hunting or something. Anyway, they are coming back now. . .

RUTH: Well, that's good.

BENEATHA   [*with the record*]:   *Alundi, alundi*
Alundi alunya
Jop pu a jeepua
Ang gu sooooooooooo
Ai yai yae . . .

Ayehaye—alundi . . . [WALTER *comes in during this performance; he has obviously been drinking. He leans against the door heavily and watches his sister, at first with distaste. Then his eyes look off—"back to the past"—as he lifts both his fists to the roof, screaming.*]

WALTER: YEAH . . . AND ETHIOPIA STRETCH FORTH HER HANDS AGAIN! . . .

RUTH [*drily, looking at him*]:   Yes—and Africa sure is claiming her own tonight. [*She gives them both up and starts ironing again.*]

WALTER [*all in a drunken, dramatic shout*]:   Shut up! . . . I'm digging them drums . . . them drums move me! . . . [*He makes his weaving way to his wife's face and leans in close to her.*] In my heart of hearts—[*He thumps his chest.*]—I am much warrior!

RUTH [*without even looking up*]:   In your heart of hearts you are much drunkard.

WALTER [*coming away from her and starting to wander around the room, shouting*]:   Me and Jomo . . . [*Intently, in his sister's face. She has stopped dancing to watch him in this unknown mood.*] That's my man, Kenyatta. [*Shouting and thumping his chest.*] FLAMING SPEAR! HOT DAMN! [*He is suddenly in possession of an imaginary spear and actively spearing enemies all over the room.*] OCOMOGOSIAY . . . THE LION IS WAKING . . . OWIMOWEH! [*He pulls his shirt open and leaps up on a table and gestures with his spear. The bell rings.* RUTH *goes to answer.*]

BENEATHA [*to encourage* WALTER, *thoroughly caught up with this side of him*]:   OCOMOGOSIAY, FLAMING SPEAR!

WALTER [*On the table, very far gone, his eyes pure glass sheets. He sees what we cannot, that he is a leader of his people, a great chief, a descendant of Chaka, and that the hour to march has come.*]:   Listen, my black brothers—

BENEATHA: OCOMOGOSIAY!

WALTER: —Do you hear the waters rushing against the shores of the coastlands—

BENEATHA: OCOMOGOSIAY!

WALTER: —Do you hear the screeching of the cocks in yonder hills beyond where the chiefs meet in council for the coming of the mighty war—

BENEATHA: OCOMOGOSIAY!

WALTER: —Do you hear the beating of the wings of the birds flying low over the mountains and the low places of our land—[RUTH *opens the door,* GEORGE MURCHISON *enters.*]

BENEATHA: OCOMOGOSIAY!

WALTER: —Do you hear the singing of the women, singing the war songs of our fathers to the babies in the great houses . . . singing the sweet war songs? OH, DO YOU HEAR, MY BLACK BROTHERS?

BENEATHA [*completely gone*]:   We hear you, Flaming Spear—

WALTER: Telling us to prepare for the greatness of the time—[*to* GEORGE] Black Brother! [*He extends his hand for the fraternal clasp.*]

GEORGE: Black Brother, hell!

RUTH [*having had enough, and embarrassed for the family*]:   Beneatha, you got company—what's the matter with you? Walter Lee Younger, get down off that table and stop acting like a fool . . . [WALTER *comes down off the table suddenly and makes a quick exit to the bathroom.*]

RUTH: He's had a little to drink . . . I don't know what her excuse is.

GEORGE   [*to* BENEATHA]:Look honey, we're going *to* the theatre—we're not going to be *in* it . . . so go change, huh?

RUTH: You expect this boy to go out with you looking like that?

BENEATHA [*looking at* GEORGE]:   That's up to George. If he's ashamed of his heritage—

GEORGE: Oh, don't be so proud of yourself, Bennie—just because you look eccentric.

BENEATHA: How can something that's natural be eccentric?

GEORGE: That's what being eccentric means—being natural. Get dressed.

BENEATHA: I don't like that, George.

RUTH: Why must you and your brother make an argument out of everything people
say?

BENEATHA: Because I hate assimilationist Negroes!

RUTH: Will somebody please tell me what assimila-who-ever means!

GEORGE: Oh, it's just a college girl's way of calling people Uncle Toms—but that
isn't what it means at all.

RUTH: Well, what does it mean?

BENEATHA [*cutting* GEORGE *off and staring at him as she replies to* RUTH]:   It means
someone who is willing to give up his own culture and submerge himself completely in the dominant, and in this case, *oppressive* culture!

GEORGE: Oh, dear, dear, dear! Here we go! A lecture on the African past! On our
Great West African Heritage! In one second we will hear all about the great
Ashanti empires; the great Songhay civilizations; and the great sculpture of
Benin—and then some poetry in the Bantu—and the whole monologue will
end with the word *heritage!* [*nastily*] Let's face it, baby, your heritage is noth-
ing but a bunch of raggedy-assed spirituals and some grass huts!

BENEATHA: *Grass huts!* [RUTH *crosses to her and forcibly pushes her toward the
bedroom.*] See there . . . you are standing there in your splendid ignorance talking about people who were the first to smelt iron on the face of the earth!
[RUTH *is pushing her through the door.*] The Ashanti were performing surgical operations when the English—[RUTH *pulls the door to, with* BENEATHA *on
the other side, and smiles graciously at* GEORGE. BENEATHA *opens the door and
shouts the end of the sentence defiantly at* GEORGE.]—were still tattooing
themselves with blue dragons . . . [*She goes back inside.*]

RUTH: Have a seat, George. [*They both sit.* RUTH *folds her hands rather primly on
her lap, determined to demonstrate the civilization of the family.*] Warm,
ain't it? I mean for September. [*pause*] Just like they always say about Chicago
weather: If it's too hot or cold for you, just wait a minute and it'll change. [*She
smiles happily at this cliché, of clichés.*] Everybody say it's got to do with
them bombs and things they keep setting off. [*pause*] Would you like a nice
cold beer?

GEORGE: No, thank you. I don't care for beer. [*He looks at his watch.*] I hope she
hurries up.

RUTH: What time is the show?

GEORGE: It's an eight-thirty curtain. That's just Chicago, though. In New York standard curtain time is eight forty. [*He is rather proud of this knowledge.*]

RUTH [*properly appreciating it*]:   You get to New York a lot?

GEORGE [*offhand*]:   Few times a year.

RUTH: Oh—that's nice. I've never been to New York. [WALTER *enters. We feel he has relieved himself, but the edge of unreality is still with him.*]

WALTER: New York ain't got nothing Chicago ain't. Just a bunch of hustling people all squeezed up together—being "Eastern." [*He turns his face into a screw of displeasure.*]

GEORGE: Oh—you've been?

WALTER: Plenty of times.

RUTH [*shocked at the lie*]:   Walter Lee Younger!

WALTER [*staring her down*]:   Plenty! [*pause*] What we got to drink in this house? Why don't you offer this man some refreshment. [*to* GEORGE] They don't know how to entertain people in this house, man.

GEORGE: Thank you—I don't really care for anything.

WALTER [*feeling his head; sobriety coming*]:   Where's Mama?

RUTH: She ain't come back yet.

WALTER [*looking* MURCHISON *over from head to toe, scrutinizing his carefully casual tweed sports jacket over cashmere V-neck sweater over soft eyelet shirt and tie, and soft slacks, finished off with white buckskin shoes*]:   Why all you college boys wear them fairyish-looking white shoes?

RUTH: Walter Lee! [GEORGE MURCHISON *ignores the remark.*]

WALTER [*to* RUTH]:   Well, they look crazy as hell—white shoes, cold as it is.

RUTH [*crushed*]:   You have to excuse him—

WALTER: No he don't! Excuse me for what? What you always excusing me for! I'll excuse myself when I needs to be excused! [*a pause*] They look as funny as them black knee socks Beneatha wears out of here all the time.

RUTH: It's the college *style,* Walter.

WALTER: Style, hell. She looks like she got burnt legs or something!

RUTH: Oh, Walter—

WALTER [*an irritable mimic*]:   Oh, Walter! Oh, Walter! [*to* MURCHISON] How's your old man making out? I understand you all going to buy that big hotel on the Drive?[1] [*He finds a beer in the refrigerator, wanders over to* MURCHISON, *sipping and wiping his lips with the back of his hand, and straddling a chair backwards to talk to the other man.*] Shrewd move. Your old man is all right, man. [*tapping his head and half winking for emphasis*] I mean he knows how to operate. I mean he thinks big, you know what I mean, I mean for a home,[2] you know? But I think he's kind of running out of ideas now. I'd like to talk to him. Listen, man, I got some plans that could turn this city upside down. I mean I think like he does. *Big.* Invest big, gamble big, hell, lose

---

[1]**Drive** Chicago's Outer Drive running along Lake Michigan
[2]**home** home-boy; one of us

big if you have to, you know what I mean. It's hard to find a man on this whole Southside who understands my kind of thinking—you dig? [*He scrutinizes* MURCHISON *again, drinks his beer, squints his eyes and leans in close, confidential, man to man.*] Me and you ought to sit down and talk sometimes, man. Man, I got me some ideas . . .

GEORGE [*with boredom*]:   Yeah—sometimes we'll have to do that, Walter.

WALTER [*understanding the indifference, and offended*]:   Yeah—well, when you get the time, man. I know you a busy little boy.

RUTH: Walter, please—

WALTER [*bitterly, hurt*]:   I know ain't nothing in this world as busy as you colored college boys with your fraternity pins and white shoes . . .

RUTH [*covering her face with humiliation*]:   Oh, Walter Lee—

WALTER: I see you all all the time—with the books tucked under your arms—going to your [*British* A—*a mimic*] "clahsses." And for what! What the hell you learning over there? Filling up your heads—[*counting off on his fingers*]— with the sociology and the psychology—but they teaching you how to be a man? How to take over and run the world? They teaching you how to run a rubber plantation or a steel mill? Naw—just to talk proper and read books and wear white shoes . . .

GEORGE [*looking at him with distaste, a little above it all*]:   You're all wacked up with bitterness, man.

WALTER [*intently, almost quietly, between the teeth, glaring at the boy*]:   And you—ain't you bitter, man? Ain't you just about had it yet? Don't you see no stars gleaming that you can't reach out and grab? You happy?—You contented son-of-a-bitch—you happy? You got it made? Bitter? Man, I'm a volcano. Bitter? Here I am a giant—surrounded by ants! Ants who can't even understand what it is the giant is talking about.

RUTH   [*passionately and suddenly*]:Oh, Walter—ain't you with nobody!

WALTER [*violently*]:   No! 'Cause ain't nobody with me! Not even my own mother!

RUTH: Walter, that's a terrible thing to say! [BENEATHA *enters, dressed for the evening in a cocktail dress and earrings.*]

GEORGE: Well—hey, you look great.

BENEATHA: Let's go, George. See you all later.

RUTH: Have a nice time.

GEORGE: Thanks. Good night. [*to* WALTER, *sarcastically*] Good night, *Prometheus.*

[BENEATHA *and* GEORGE *exit.*]

WALTER [*to* RUTH]:   Who is Prometheus?

RUTH: I don't know. Don't worry about it.

WALTER [*in fury, pointing after* George]:   See there—they get to a point where they can't insult you man to man—they got to go talk about something ain't nobody never heard of!

RUTH: How do you know it was an insult? [*to humor him*] Maybe Prometheus is a nice fellow.

WALTER: Prometheus! I bet there ain't even no such thing! I bet that simpleminded clown—

RUTH: Walter—[*She stops what she is doing and looks at him.*]

WALTER   [*yelling*]:   Don't start!

RUTH: Start what?

WALTER: Your nagging! Where was I? Who was I with? How much money did I spend?

RUTH [*plaintively*]:   Walter Lee—why don't we just try to talk about it . . .

WALTER [*not listening*]:   I been out talking with people who understand me. People who care about the things I got on my mind.

RUTH [*wearily*]:   I guess that means people like Willy Harris.

WALTER: Yes, people like Willy Harris.

RUTH [*with a sudden flash of impatience*]:   Why don't you all just hurry up and go into the banking business and stop talking about it!

WALTER: Why? You want to know why? 'Cause we all tied up in a race of people that don't know how to do nothing but moan, pray and have babies! [*The line is too bitter even for him and he looks at her and sits down.*]

RUTH: Oh, Walter . . . [*softy*] Honey, why can't you stop fighting me?

WALTER [*without thinking*]:   Who's fighting you? Who even cares about you? [*This line begins the retardation of his mood.*]

RUTH: Well—[*She waits a long time, and then with resignation starts to put away her things.*] I guess I might as well go on to bed . . . [*more or less to herself*] I don't know where we lost it . . . but we have . . . [*Then, to him.*] I— I'm sorry about this new baby, Walter. I guess maybe I better go on and do what I started . . . I guess I just didn't realize how bad things was with us . . . I guess I just didn't really realize—[*She starts out to the bedroom and stops.*] You want some hot milk?

WALTER: Hot milk?

RUTH: Yes—hot milk.

WALTER: Why hot milk?

RUTH: 'Cause after all that liquor you come home with you ought to have something hot in your stomach.

WALTER: I don't want no milk.

RUTH: You want some coffee then?

WALTER: No, I don't want no coffee. I don't want nothing hot to drink. [*almost plaintively*] Why you always trying to give me something to eat?

RUTH [*standing and looking at him helplessly*]:   What else can I give you, Walter Lee Younger? [*She stands and looks at him and presently turns to go out again. He lifts his head and watches her going away from him in a new mood which began to emerge when he asked her, "Who cares about you?"*]

WALTER: It's been rough, ain't it, baby? [*She hears and stops but does not turn around and he continues to her back.*] I guess between two people there ain't never as much understood as folks generally thinks there is. I mean like between me and you—[*She turns to face him.*] How we gets to the place where we scared to talk softness to each other. [*He waits, thinking hard himself.*] Why you think it got to be like that? [*He is thoughtful, almost as a child would be.*] Ruth, what is it gets into people ought to be close?

RUTH: I don't know, honey. I think about it a lot.

WALTER: On account of you and me, you mean? The way things are with us. The way something done come down between us.

RUTH: There ain't so much between us, Walter . . . Not when you come to me and try to talk to me. Try to be with me . . . a little even.

WALTER   [*total honesty*]:   Sometimes . . . sometimes . . . I don't even know how to try.

RUTH: Walter—

WALTER: Yes?

RUTH [*coming to him, gently and with misgiving, but coming to him*]:   Honey . . . life don't have to be like this. I mean sometimes people can do things so that things are better . . . You remember how we used to talk when Travis was born . . . about the way we were going to live . . . the kind of house . . . [*She is stroking his head.*] Well, it's all starting to slip away from us . . . [MAMA *enters, and* WALTER *jumps up and shouts at her.*]

WALTER: Mama, where have you been?

MAMA: My—them steps is longer than they used to be. Whew! [*She sits down and ignores him.*] How you feeling this evening, Ruth! [RUTH *shrugs, disturbed some at having been prematurely interrupted and watching her husband knowingly.*]

WALTER: Mama, where have you been all day?

MAMA [*still ignoring him and leaning on the table and changing to more comfortable shoes*]:   Where's Travis?

RUTH: I let him go out earlier and he ain't come back yet. Boy, is he going to get it!

WALTER: Mama!

MAMA [*as if she has heard him for the first time*]:   Yes, son?

WALTER: Where did you go this afternoon?

MAMA: I went downtown to tend to some business that I had to tend to.

WALTER: What kind of business?

MAMA: You know better than to question me like a child, Brother.

WALTER [*rising and bending over the table*]:   Where were you, Mama? [*bringing his fists down and shouting*] Mama, you didn't go do something with that insurance money, something crazy? [*The front door opens slowly, interrupting him, and* TRAVIS *peeks his head in, less than hopefully.*]

TRAVIS [*to his mother*]:   Mama, I—

RUTH: "Mama I" nothing! You're going to get it, boy! Get on in that bedroom and get yourself ready!

TRAVIS: But I—

MAMA: Why don't you all never let the child explain hisself.

RUTH: Keep out of it now, Lena. [MAMA *clamps her lips together, and* RUTH *advances toward her son menacingly.*]

RUTH: A thousand times I have told you not to go off like that—

MAMA [*holding out her arms to her grandson*]:   Well—at least let me tell him something. I want him to be the first one to hear . . . Come here, Travis. [*the boy obeys, gladly*] Travis—[*She takes him by the shoulder and looks into his face.*]—you know that money we got in the mail this morning?

TRAVIS: Yes'm—

MAMA: Well—what you think your grandmama gone and done with that money?

TRAVIS: I don't know, Grandmama.

MAMA [*putting her finger on his nose for emphasis*]:   She went out and she bought you a house! [*The explosion comes from* WALTER *at the end of the revelation and he jumps up and turns away from all of them in a fury.* MAMA *continues, to* TRAVIS.] You glad about the house? It's going to be yours when you get to be a man.

TRAVIS: Yeah—I always wanted to live in a house.

MAMA: All right, gimme some sugar then—[TRAVIS *puts his arms around her neck as she watches her son over the boy's shoulder. Then, to* TRAVIS, *after the embrace.*] Now when you say your prayers tonight, you thank God and your grandfather—'cause it was him who give you the house—in his way.

RUTH [*taking the boy from* MAMA *and pushing him toward the bedroom*]:   Now you get out of here and get ready for your beating.

TRAVIS: Aw, Mama—

RUTH: Get on in there—[*closing the door behind him and turning radiantly to her mother-in-law*] So you went and did it!

MAMA [*quietly, looking at her son with pain*]:   Yes, I did.

RUTH [*raising both arms classically*]:   Praise God! [*Looks at* WALTER *a moment, who says nothing. She crosses rapidly to her husband.*] Please, honey—let me be glad . . . you be glad too. [*She has laid her hands on his shoulders, but he shakes himself free of her roughly, without turning to face her.*] Oh, Walter . . . a home . . . a home. [*She comes back to* MAMA.] Well—where is it? How big is it? How much it going to cost?

MAMA: Well—

RUTH: When we moving?

MAMA [*smiling at her*]:   First of the month.

RUTH [*throwing back her head with jubilance*]:   Praise God!

MAMA [*tentatively, still looking at her son's back turned against her and* RUTH]:   It's—it's a nice house too . . . [*She cannot help speaking directly to him. An imploring quality in her voice, her manner, makes her almost like a girl now.*] Three bedrooms—nice big one for you and Ruth . . . Me and Beneatha still have to share our room, but Travis have one of his own—and [*with*

difficulty] I figure if the—new baby—is a boy, we could get one of them
double-decker outfits . . . And there's a yard with a little patch of dirt where I
could maybe get to grow me a few flowers . . . And a nice big basement. . . .

RUTH: Walter honey, be glad—

MAMA [*still to his back, fingering things on the table*]:   'Course I don't want to
make it sound fancier than it is . . . . It's just a plain little old house—but it's
made good and solid—and it will be *ours*. Walter Lee—it makes a difference
in a man when he can walk on floors that belong to *him*. . . .

RUTH: Where is it?

MAMA [*frightened at this telling*]:   Well—well—it's out there in Clybourne Park—
[RUTH'S *radiance fades abruptly, and* WALTER *finally turns slowly to face his
mother with incredulity and hostility.*]

RUTH: Where?

MAMA [*matter-of-factly*]:   Four o six Clybourne Street, Clybourne Park.

RUTH: Clybourne Park? Mama, there ain't no colored people living in Clybourne
Park.

MAMA [*almost idiotically*]:   Well, I guess there's going to be some now.

WALTER [*bitterly*]:   So that's the peace and comfort you went out and bought for us
today!

MAMA [*raising her eyes to meet his finally*]:   Son—I just tried to find the nicest
place for the least amount of money for my family.

RUTH [*trying to recover from the shock*]:   Well—well—'course I ain't one never
been 'fraid of no crackers, mind you—but—well, wasn't there no other houses
nowhere?

MAMA: Them houses they put up for colored in them areas way out all seem to cost
twice as much as other houses. I did the best I could.

RUTH [*Struck senseless with the news, in its various degrees of goodness and trouble, she sits a moment, her fists propping her chin in thought, and then she
starts to rise, bringing her fists down with vigor, the radiance spreading
from cheek to cheek again.*]:   Well—well!—All I can say is—if this is my time
in life—my time—to say good-bye—[*And she builds with momentum as she
starts to circle the room with an exuberant, almost tearfully happy
release.*]—to these Goddamned cracking walls!—[*She pounds the walls*]—
and these marching roaches!—[*She wipes at an imaginary army of marching roaches.*]—and this cramped little closet which ain't now or never was no
kitchen! . . . then I say it loud and good, Hallelujah! and good-bye misery . . .
I don't never want to see your ugly face again! [*She laughs joyously, having
practically destroyed the apartment, and flings her arms up and lets them
come down happily, slowly, reflectively, over her abdomen, aware for the
first time perhaps that the life therein pulses with happiness and not
despair.*] Lena?

MAMA [*moved, watching her happiness*]:   Yes, honey?

RUTH [*looking off*]:   Is there—is there a whole lot of sunlight?

MAMA [*understanding*]:   Yes, child, there's a whole lot of sunlight. [*long pause*]

RUTH [*collecting herself and going to the door of the room* TRAVIS *is in*]:   Well—I guess I better see 'bout Travis. [*to* MAMA] Lord, I sure don't feel like whipping nobody today! [*she exits*]

MAMA [*The mother and son are left alone now and the mother waits a long time, considering deeply, before she speaks.*]:   Son—you—you understand what I done, don't you? [WALTER *is silent and sullen.*] I—I just seen my family falling apart today . . . just falling to pieces in front of my eyes . . . We couldn't of gone on like we was today. We was going backwards 'stead of forwards—talking 'bout killing babies and wishing each other was dead . . . When it gets like that in life—you just got to do something different, push on out and do something bigger . . . [*She waits.*] I wish you say something, son . . . I wish you'd say how deep inside you you think I done the right thing—

WALTER [*crossing slowly to his bedroom door and finally turning there and speaking measuredly*]:   What you need me to say you done right for? You the head of this family. You run our lives like you want to. It was your money and you did what you wanted with it. So what you need for me to say it was all right for? [*bitterly, to hurt her as deeply as he knows is possible*] So you butchered up a dream of mine—you—who always talking 'bout your children's dreams . . .

MAMA: Walter Lee—[*He just closes the door behind him.* MAMA *sits alone, thinking heavily.*]

Curtain

SCENE 2

TIME: *Friday night. A few weeks later.*

AT RISE: *Packing crates mark the intention of the family to move.* BENEATHA *and* GEORGE *come in, presumably from an evening out again.*

GEORGE: O.K. . . . O.K., whatever you say . . . [*They both sit on the couch. He tries to kiss her. She moves away.*] Look, we've had a nice evening; let's not spoil it, huh? . . . [*He again turns her head and tries to nuzzle in and she turns away from him, not with distaste but with momentary lack of interest; in a mood to pursue what they were talking about.*]

BENEATHA: I'm trying to talk to you.

GEORGE: We always talk.

BENEATHA: Yes—and I love to talk.

GEORGE [*exasperated; rising*]:   I know it and I don't mind it sometimes . . . I want you to cut it out, see—The moody stuff, I mean. I don't like it. You're a nice-looking girl . . . all over. That's all you need, honey, forget the atmosphere. Guys aren't going to go for the atmosphere—they're going to go for what they see. Be glad for that. Drop the Garbo routine. It doesn't go with you. As for myself, I want a nice—[*groping*]—simple [*thoughtfully*]—sophisticated girl . . . not a poet—O.K.? [*She rebuffs him again and he starts to leave.*]

BENEATHA: Why are you angry?

GEORGE: Because this is stupid! I don't go out with you to discuss the nature of "quiet desperation" or to hear all about your thoughts—because the world will go on thinking what it thinks regardless—

BENEATHA: Then why read books? Why go to school?

GEORGE [*with artificial patience, counting on his fingers*]:   It's simple. You read books—to learn facts—to get grades—to pass the course—to get a degree. That's all—it has nothing to do with thoughts. [*a long pause*]

BENEATHA: I see. [*a longer pause as she looks at him*] Good night, George. [GEORGE *looks at her a little oddly, and starts to exit. He meets* MAMA *coming in.*]

GEORGE: Oh—hello, Mrs. Younger.

MAMA: Hello, George, how you feeling?

GEORGE: Fine—fine, how are you?

MAMA: Oh, a little tired. You know them steps can get you after a day's work. You all have a nice time tonight?

GEORGE: Yes—a fine time. Well, good night.

MAMA: Good night. [*He exits.* MAMA *closes the door behind her.*] Hello, honey. What you sitting like that for?

BENEATHA: I'm just sitting.

MAMA: Didn't you have a nice time?

BENEATHA: No.

MAMA: No? What's the matter?

BENEATHA: Mama, George is a fool—honest. [*She rises.*]

MAMA [*Hustling around unloading the packages she has entered with. She stops.*]:   Is he, baby?

BENEATHA: Yes. [BENEATHA *makes up* TRAVIS' *bed as she talks.*]

MAMA: You sure?

BENEATHA: Yes.

MAMA: Well—I guess you better not waste your time with no fools. [BENEATHA *looks up at her mother, watching her put groceries in the refrigerator. Finally she gathers up her things and starts into the bedroom. At the door she stops and looks back at her mother.*]

BENEATHA: Mama—

MAMA: Yes, baby—

BENEATHA: Thank you.

MAMA: For what?

BENEATHA: For understanding me this time. [*She exits quickly and the mother stands, smiling a little, looking at the place where* BENEATHA *had stood.* RUTH *enters.*]

RUTH: Now don't you fool with any of this stuff, Lena—

MAMA: Oh, I just thought I'd sort a few things out. [*The phone rings.* RUTH *answers.*]

RUTH [*at the phone*]:   Hello—Just a minute. [*goes to door*] Walter, it's Mrs. Arnold. [*Waits. Goes back to the phone. Tense.*] Hello. Yes, this is his wife speaking . . . He's lying down now. Yes . . . well, he'll be in tomorrow. He's been very sick. Yes—I know we should have called, but we were so sure he'd be able to come in today. Yes—yes, I'm very sorry. Yes . . . Thank you very much. [*She hangs up.* Walter *is standing in the doorway of the bedroom behind her.*] That was Mrs. Arnold.

WALTER [*indifferently*]:   Was it?

RUTH: She said if you don't come in tomorrow that they are getting a new man . . .

WALTER: Ain't that sad—ain't that crying sad.

RUTH: She said Mr. Arnold has had to take a cab for three days . . . Walter, you ain't been to work for three days! [*This is a revelation to her.*] Where you been, Walter Lee Younger? [WALTER *looks at her and starts to laugh.*] You're going to lose your job.

WALTER: That's right . . .

RUTH: Oh, Walter, and with your mother working like a dog every day—

WALTER: That's sad too—Everything is sad.

MAMA: What you been doing for these three days, son?

WALTER: Mama—you don't know all the things a man what got leisure can find to do in this city . . . What's this—Friday night? Well—Wednesday I borrowed Willy Harris' car and I went for a drive . . . just me and myself and I drove and drove . . . Way out . . . way past South Chicago, and I parked the car and I sat and looked at the steel mills all day long. I just sat in the car and looked at them big black chimneys for hours. Then I drove back and I went to the Green Hat. [*pause*] And Thursday—Thursday I borrowed the car again and I got in it and I pointed it the other way and I drove the other way—for hours—way, way up to Wisconsin, and I looked at the farms. I just drove and looked at the farms. Then I drove back and I went to the Green Hat. [*pause*] And today—today I didn't get the car. Today I just walked. All over the Southside. And I looked at the Negroes and they looked at me and finally I just sat down on the curb at Thirty-ninth and South Parkway and I just sat there and watched the Negroes go by. And then I went to the Green Hat. You all sad? You all depressed? And you know where I am going right now—[Ruth *goes out quietly.*].

MAMA: Oh, Big Walter, is this the harvest of our days?

WALTER: You know what I like about the Green Hat? [*He turns the radio on and a steamy, deep blues pours into the room.*] I like this little cat they got there who blows a sax . . . He blows. He talks to me. He ain't but 'bout five feet tall and he's got a conked head and his eyes is always closed and he's all music—

MAMA [*rising and getting some papers out of her handbag*]:   Walter—

WALTER: And there's this other guy who plays the piano . . . and they got a sound. I mean they can work on some music . . . They got the best little combo in the world in the Green Hat . . . You can just sit there and drink and listen to them three men play and you realize that don't nothing matter worth a damn, but just being there—

MAMA: I've helped do it to you, haven't I, son? Walter, I been wrong.

WALTER: Naw—you ain't never been wrong about nothing, Mama.

MAMA: Listen to me, now. I say I been wrong, son. That I been doing to you what the rest of the world been doing to you. [*She stops and he looks up slowly at her and she meets his eyes pleadingly.*] Walter—what you ain't understood is that I ain't got nothing, don't own nothing, ain't never really wanted nothing that wasn't for you. There ain't nothing as precious to me . . . There ain't nothing worth holding on to, money, dreams, nothing else—if it means—if it means it's going to destroy my boy. [*She puts her papers in front of him and he watches her without speaking or moving.*] I paid the man thirty-five hundred dollars down on the house. That leaves sixty-five hundred dollars. Monday morning I want you to take this money and take three thousand dollars and put it in a savings account for Beneatha's medical schooling. The rest you put in a checking account—with your name on it. And from now on any penny that come out of it or that go in it is for you to look after. For you to decide. [*She drops her hands a little helplessly.*] It ain't much, but it's all I got in the world and I'm putting it in your hands. I'm telling you to be the head of this family from now on like you supposed to be.

WALTER [*stares at the money*]:   You trust me like that, Mama?

MAMA: I ain't never stop trusting you. Like I ain't never stop loving you. [*She goes out, and* WALTER *sits looking at the money on the table as the music continues in its idiom, pulsing in the room. Finally, in a decisive gesture, he gets up, and, in mingled joy and desperation, picks up the money. At the same moment,* TRAVIS *enters for bed.*]

TRAVIS: What's the matter, Daddy? You drunk?

WALTER [*sweetly, more sweetly than we have ever known him*]:   No, Daddy ain't drunk. Daddy ain't going to never be drunk again. . . .

TRAVIS: Well, good night, Daddy. [*The father has come from behind the couch and leans over, embracing his son.*]

WALTER: Son, I feel like talking to you tonight.

TRAVIS: About what?

WALTER: Oh, about a lot of things. About you and what kind of man you going to be when you grow up. . . . Son—son, what do you want to be when you grow up?

TRAVIS: A bus driver.

WALTER [*laughing a little*]:   A what? Man, that ain't nothing to want to be!

TRAVIS: Why not?

WALTER: 'Cause, man—it ain't big enough—you know what I mean.

TRAVIS: I don't know then. I can't make up my mind. Sometimes Mama asks me that too. And sometimes when I tell her I just want to be like you—she says she don't want me to be like that and sometimes she says she does . . .

WALTER [*gathering him up in his arms*]:   You know what, Travis? In seven years you going to be seventeen years old. And things is going to be very different with us in seven years, Travis. . . . One day when you are seventeen I'll come home—home from my office downtown somewhere—

TRAVIS: You don't work in no office, Daddy.

WALTER: No—but after tonight. After what your daddy gonna do tonight, there's going to be offices—a whole lot of offices. . . .

TRAVIS: What you gonna do tonight, Daddy?

WALTER: You wouldn't understand yet, son, but your daddy's gonna make a transaction . . . a business transaction that's going to change our lives . . . That's how come one day when you 'bout seventeen years old I'll come home and I'll be pretty tired, you know what I mean, after a day of conferences and secretaries getting things wrong the way they do . . . 'cause an executive's life is hell, man—[*The more he talks the farther away he gets.*] And I'll pull the car up on the driveway . . . just a plain black Chrysler, I think, with white walls—no— black tires. More elegant. Rich people don't have to be flashy . . . though I'll have to get something a little sportier for Ruth—maybe a Cadillac convertible to do her shopping in. . . . And I'll come up the steps to the house and the gardener will be clipping away at the hedges and he'll say, "Good evening, Mr. Younger." And I'll say, "Hello, Jefferson, how are you this evening?" And I'll go inside and Ruth will come downstairs and meet me at the door and we'll kiss each other and she'll take my arm and we'll go up to your room to see you sitting on the floor with the catalogues of all the great schools in America around you. . . . All the great schools in the world! And—and I'll say, all right son—it's your seventeenth birthday, what is it you've decided? . . . Just tell me where you want to go to school and you'll *go*. Just tell me, what it is you want to be—and you'll be it. . . . Whatever you want to be—Yessir! [*He holds his arms open for* TRAVIS.] You just name it, son . . . [TRAVIS *leaps into them*] and I hand you the world! [WALTER'S *voice has risen in pitch and hysterical promise and on the last line he lifts* TRAVIS *high.*]

Blackout

SCENE 3

TIME: *Saturday, moving day, one week later.*

Before the curtain rises, RUTH'S *voice, a strident, dramatic church alto, cuts through the silence.*

It is, in the darkness, a triumphant surge, a penetrating statement of expectation; "Oh, Lord, I don't feel no ways tired! Children, oh, glory hallelujah!"

As the curtain rises we see that RUTH *is alone in the living room, finishing up the family's packing. It is moving day. She is nailing crates and tying cartons.* BENEATHA *enters, carrying a guitar case, and watches her exuberant sister-in-law.*

RUTH: Hey!

BENEATHA [*putting away the case*]:   Hi.

RUTH [*pointing at a package*]:   Honey—look in that package there and see what I found on sale this morning at the South Center. [RUTH *gets up and moves to the package and draws out some curtains.*] Lookahere—hand-turned hems!

BENEATHA: How do you know the window size out there?

RUTH [*who hadn't thought of that*]:   Oh—Well, they bound to fit something in the whole house. Anyhow, they was too good a bargain to pass up. [RUTH *slaps her head, suddenly remembering something.*] Oh, Bennie—I meant to put a special note on that carton over there. That's your mama's good china and she wants 'em to be very careful with it.

BENEATHA: I'll do it. [Beneatha *finds a piece of paper and starts to draw large letters on it.*]

RUTH: You know what I'm going to do soon as I get in that new house?

BENEATHA: What?

RUTH: Honey—I'm going to run me a tub of water up to here . . . [*with her fingers practically up to her nostrils*] And I'm going to get in it—and I am going to sit . . . and sit . . . and sit in that hot water and the first person who knocks to tell *me* to hurry up and come out—

BENEATHA: Gets shot at sunrise.

RUTH [*laughing happily*]:   You said it, sister! [*noticing how large* BENEATHA *is absentmindedly making the note*] Honey, they ain't going to read that from no airplane.

BENEATHA [*laughing herself*]:   I guess I always think things have more emphasis if they are big, somehow.

RUTH [*looking up at her and smiling*]:   You and your brother seem to have that as a philosophy of life. Lord, that man—done changed so 'round here. You know—you know what we did last night? Me and Walter Lee?

BENEATHA: What?

RUTH [*smiling to herself*]:   We went to the movies. [*looking at* BENEATHA *to see if she understands*] We went to the movies. You know the last time me and Walter went to the movies together?

BENEATHA: No.

RUTH: Me neither. That's how long it been. [*smiling again*] But we went last night. The picture wasn't much good, but that didn't seem to matter. We went—and we held hands.

BENEATHA: Oh, Lord!

RUTH: We held hands—and you know what?

BENEATHA: What?

RUTH: When we come out of the show it was late and dark and all the stores and things was closed up . . . and it was kind of chilly and there wasn't many people on the streets . . . and we was still holding hands, me and Walter.

BENEATHA: You're killing me. [WALTER *enters with a large package. His happiness is deep in him; he cannot keep still with his new-found exuberance. He is singing and wiggling and snapping his fingers. He puts his package in a corner and puts a phonograph record, which he has brought in with him, on the record player. As the music comes up he dances over to* RUTH *and tries to get her to dance with him. She gives in at last to his raunchiness and in a fit of giggling allows herself to be drawn into his mood and together they deliberately burlesque an old social dance of their youth.*]

BENEATHA [*Regarding them a long time as they dance, then drawing in her breath for a deeply exaggerated comment which she does not particularly mean.*]: Talk about—olddddddddddd—fashionedddddddd—Negroes!

WALTER [*stopping momentarily*]:   What kind of Negroes? [*He says this in fun. He is not angry with her today, nor with anyone. He starts to dance with his wife again.*]

BENEATHA: Old-fashioned.

WALTER [*as he dances with* Ruth]:   You know, when these *New Negroes* have their convention—[*pointing at his sister*]—that is going to be the chairman of the Committee on Unending Agitation. [*He goes on dancing, then stops.*] Race, race, race! . . . Girl, I do believe you are the first person in the history of the entire human race to successfully brainwash yourself. [BENEATHA *breaks up and he goes on dancing. He stops again, enjoying his tease.*] Damn, even the N double A C P takes a holiday sometimes! [BENEATHA *and* RUTH *laugh. He dances with* Ruth *some more and starts to laugh and stops and pantomimes someone over an operating table.*] I can just see that chick someday looking down at some poor cat on an operating table before she starts to slice him, saying . . . [*pulling his sleeves back maliciously*] "By the way, what are your views on civil rights down there? . . . " [*He laughs at her again and starts to dance happily. The bell sounds.*]

BENEATHA: Sticks and stones may break my bones but . . . words will never hurt me! [Beneatha *goes to the door and opens it as* WALTER *and* RUTH *go on with the clowning.* BENEATHA *is somewhat surprised to see a quiet-looking middle-aged white man in a business suit holding his hat and a briefcase in his hand and consulting a small piece of paper.*]

MAN: Uh—how do you do, miss. I am looking for a Mrs.—[*He looks at the slip of paper.*] Mrs. Lena Younger?

BENEATHA [*smoothing her hair with slight embarrassment*]:   Oh—yes, that's my mother. Excuse me. [*She closes the door and turns to quiet the other two.*] Ruth! Brother! Somebody's here. [*Then she opens the door. The man casts a curious quick glance at all of them.*] Uh—come in please.

MAN [*coming in*]:   Thank you.

BENEATHA: My mother isn't here just now. Is it business?

MAN: Yes . . . well, of a sort.

WALTER [*freely, the Man of the House*]:   Have a seat. I'm Mrs. Younger's son. I look after most of her business matters. [RUTH *and* BENEATHA *exchange amused glances.*]

MAN [*regarding* Walter, *and sitting*]:   Well—My name is Karl Lindner . . .

WALTER [*stretching out his hand*]:   Walter Younger. This is my wife—[RUTH *nods politely.*]—and my sister.

LINDNER: How do you do.

WALTER [*amiably, as he sits himself easily on a chair, leaning with interest forward on his knees and looking expectantly into the newcomer's face*]:   What can we do for you, Mr. Lindner!

LINDNER [*some minor shuffling of the hat and briefcase on his knees*]:   Well—I am a representative of the Clybourne Park Improvement Association—

WALTER [*pointing*]:   Why don't you sit your things on the floor?

LINDNER:Oh—yes. Thank you. [*He slides the briefcase and hat under the chair.*] And as I was saying—I am from the Clybourne Park Improvement Association and we have had it brought to our attention at the last meeting that you people— or at least your mother—has bought a piece of residential property at—[*He digs for the slip of paper again.*]—four o six at Clybourne Street . . .

WALTER: That's right. Care for something to drink? Ruth, get Mr. Lindner a beer.

LINDNER [*upset for some reason*]:   Oh—no, really, I mean thank you very much, but no thank you.

RUTH [*innocently*]:   Some coffee?

LINDNER: Thank you, nothing at all. [BENEATHA *is watching the man carefully.*]

LINDNER: Well, I don't know how much you folks know about our organization. [*He is a gentle man; thoughtful and somewhat labored in his manner.*] It is one of these community organizations set up to look after—oh, you know, things like block upkeep and special projects and we also have what we call our New Neighbors Orientation Committee . . .

BENEATHA [*drily*]:   Yes—and what do they do?

LINDNER [*turning a little to her and then returning the main force to* WALTER]: Well—it's what you might call a sort of welcoming committee, I guess. I mean they, we, I'm the chairman of the committee—go around and see the new people who move into the neighborhood and sort of give them the lowdown on the way we do things out in Clybourne Park.

BENEATHA [*with appreciation of the two meanings, which escape* RUTH *and* WALTER]: Uh-huh.

LINDNER: And we also have the category of what the association calls—[*He looks elsewhere.*]—uh—special community problems . . .

BENEATHA: Yes—and what are some of those?

WALTER: Girl, let the man talk.

LINDNER [*with understated relief*]:   Thank you. I would sort of like to explain this thing in my own way. I mean I want to explain to you in a certain way.

WALTER: Go ahead.

LINDNER: Yes. Well. I'm going to try to get right to the point. I'm sure we'll all appreciate that in the long run.

BENEATHA: Yes.

WALTER: Be still now!

LINDNER: Well—

RUTH [*still innocently*]:   Would you like another chair—you don't look comfortable.

LINDNER [*more frustrated than annoyed*]:   No, thank you very much. Please. Well—
to get right to the point I—[*a great breath, and he is off at last*] I am sure you
people must be aware of some of the incidents which have happened in various parts of the city when colored people have moved into certain areas—
[BENEATHA: *exhales heavily and starts tossing a piece of fruit up and down
in the air.*] Well—because we have what I think is going to be a unique type
of organization in American community life—not only do we deplore that
kind of thing—but we are trying to do something about it. [BENEATHA *stops
tossing and turns with a new and quizzical interest to the man.*] We feel—
[*gaining confidence in his mission because of the interest in the faces of the
people he is talking to*]—we feel that most of the trouble in this world, when
you come right down to it—[*He hits his knee for emphasis.*]—most of the
trouble exists because people just don't sit down and talk to each other.

RUTH [*nodding as she might in church, pleased with the remark*]:   You can say
that again, mister.

LINDNER [*more encouraged by such affirmation*]:   That we don't try hard enough
in this world to understand the other fellow's problem. The other guy's point
of view.

RUTH: Now that's right. [BENEATHA *and* WALTER *merely watch and listen with genuine interest.*]

LINDNER: Yes—that's the way we feel out in Clybourne Park. And that's why I was
elected to come here this afternoon and talk to you people. Friendly like, you
know, the way people should talk to each other and see if we couldn't find
some way to work this thing out. As I say, the whole business is a matter of
caring about the other fellow. Anybody can see that you are a nice family of
folks, hard working and honest I'm sure. [BENEATHA *frowns slightly, quizzically,
her head tilted regarding him.*] Today everybody knows what it means to be
on the outside of *something.* And of course, there is always somebody who is
out to take the advantage of people who don't always understand.

WALTER: What do you mean?

LINDNER: Well—you see our community is made of people who've worked hard as
the dickens for years to build up that little community. They're not rich and
fancy people; just hardworking, honest people who don't really have much but
those little homes and a dream of the kind of community they want to raise
their children in. Now, I don't say we are perfect and there is a lot wrong in
some of the things they want. But you've got to admit that a man, right or
wrong, has the right to want to have the neighborhood he lives in a certain
kind of way. And at the moment the overwhelming majority of our people out
there feel that people get along better, take more of a common interest in the
life of the community, when they share a common background. I want you to

believe me when I tell you that race prejudice simply doesn't enter into it. It is a matter of the people of Clybourne Park believing, rightly or wrongly, as I say, that for the happiness of all concerned that our Negro families are happier when they live in their *own* communities.

BENEATHA [*with a grand and bitter gesture*]:   This, friends, is the Welcoming Committee!

WALTER [*dumbfounded, looking at* LINDNER]:   Is this what you came marching all the way over here to tell us?

LINDNER: Well, now we've been having a fine conversation. I hope you'll hear me all the way through.

WALTER [*tightly*]:   Go ahead, man.

LINDNER: You see—in the face of all the things I have said, we are prepared to make your family a very generous offer . . .

BENEATHA: Thirty pieces and not a coin less!

WALTER: Yeah?

LINDNER [*putting on his glasses and drawing a form out of the briefcase*]:   Our association is prepared, through the collective effort of our people, to buy the house from you at a financial gain to your family.

RUTH: Lord have mercy, ain't this the living gall!

WALTER: All right, you through?

LINDNER: Well, I want to give you the exact terms of the financial arrangement—

WALTER: We don't want to hear no exact terms of no arrangements. I want to know if you got any more to tell us 'bout getting together?

LINDNER [*taking off his glasses*]:   Well—I don't suppose that you feel . . .

WALTER: Never mind how I feel—you got any more to say 'bout how people ought to sit down and talk to each other? . . . Get out of my house, man. [*He turns his back and walks to the door.*]

LINDNER [*looking around at the hostile faces and reaching and assembling his hat and briefcase*]:   Well—I don't understand why you people are reacting this way. What do you think you are going to gain by moving into a neighborhood where you just aren't wanted and where some elements—well—people can get awful worked up when they feel that their whole way of life and everything they've ever worked for is threatened.

WALTER: Get out.

LINDNER [*at the door, holding a small card*]:   Well—I'm sorry it went like this.

WALTER: Get out.

LINDNER [*almost sadly regarding* WALTER]:   You just can't force people to change their hearts, son. [*He turns and puts his card on a table and exits.* WALTER *pushes the door to with stinging hatred, and stands looking at it.* RUTH *just sits and* BENEATHA *just stands. They say nothing.* MAMA *and* TRAVIS *enter.*]

MAMA: Well—this all the packing got done since I left out of here this morning. I testify before God that my children got all the energy of the dead. What time the moving men due?

BENEATHA: Four o'clock. You had a caller, Mama. [*She is smiling, teasingly.*]

MAMA: Sure enough—who?

BENEATHA [*her arms folded saucily*]:   The Welcoming Committee. [WALTER *and* RUTH *giggle.*]

MAMA [*innocently*]:   Who?

BENEATHA: The Welcoming Committee. They said they're sure going to be glad to see you when you get there.

WALTER [*devilishly*]:   Yeah, they said they can't hardly wait to see your face. [*laughter*]

MAMA [*sensing their facetiousness*]:   What's the matter with you all?

WALTER: Ain't nothing the matter with us. We just telling you 'bout the gentleman who came to see you this afternoon. From the Clybourne Park Improvement Association.

MAMA: What he want?

RUTH [*in the same mood as* BENEATHA *and* WALTER]:   To welcome you, honey.

WALTER: He said they can't hardly wait. He said the one thing they don't have, that they just dying to have out there is a fine family of colored people! [*to* Ruth *and* Beneatha] Ain't that right!

RUTH AND BENEATHA [*mockingly*]:   Yeah! He left his card in case—[*They indicate the card, and* MAMA *picks it up and throws it on the floor—understanding and looking off as she draws her chair up to the table on which she has put her plant and some sticks and some cord.*]

MAMA: Father, give us strength. [*knowingly—and without fun*] Did he threaten us?

BENEATHA: Oh—Mama—they don't do it like that any more. He talked Brotherhood. He said everybody ought to learn how to sit down and hate each other with good Christian fellowship. [*She and* WALTER *shake hands to ridicule the remark.*]

MAMA [*sadly*]:   Lord, protect us . . .

RUTH: You should hear the money those folks raised to buy the house from us. All we paid and then some.

BENEATHA: What they think we going to do—eat 'em?

RUTH: No, honey, marry 'em.

MAMA [*shaking her head*]:   Lord, Lord, Lord . . .

RUTH: Well that's the way the crackers crumble. Joke.

BENEATHA [*laughingly noticing what her mother is doing*]:   Mama, what are you doing?

MAMA: Fixing my plant so it won't get hurt none on the way . . .

BENEATHA: Mama, you going to take that to the new house?

MAMA: Un-huh—

BENEATHA: That raggedy-looking old thing?

MAMA [*stopping and looking at her*]:   It expresses *me.*

RUTH [*with delight, to* BENEATHA]:   So there, Miss Thing! [WALTER *comes to* MAMA *suddenly and bends down behind her and squeezes her in his arms with all his strength. She is overwhelmed by the suddenness of it and, though delighted, her manner is like that of* RUTH *with* TRAVIS.]

MAMA: Look out now, boy! You make me mess up my thing here!

WALTER [*His face lit, he slips down on his knees beside her, his arms still about her.*]:   Mama . . . you know what it means to climb up in the chariot?

MAMA [*gruffly, very happy*]:   Get on away from me now . . .

RUTH [*near the gift-wrapped package, trying to catch* WALTER'S *eye*]:   Psst—

WALTER: What the old song say, Mama . . .

RUTH: Walter—Now? [*She is pointing at the package.*]

WALTER [*speaking the lines, sweetly, playfully, in his mother's face*]:
    I got wings . . . you got wings . . .
    All God's children got wings . . .

MAMA: Boy—get out of my face and do some work . . .

WALTER: *When I get to heaven gonna put on my wings, Gonna fly all over God's heaven . . .*

BENEATHA [*teasingly, from across the room*]:   Everybody talking 'bout heaven ain't going there!

WALTER [*to* RUTH, *who is carrying the box across to them*]:   I don't know, you think we ought to give her that . . . Seems to me she ain't been very appreciative around here.

MAMA [*eying the box, which is obviously a gift*]:   What is that?

WALTER [*taking it from* RUTH *and putting it on the table in front of* MAMA]:   Well— what you all think? Should we give it to her?

RUTH: Oh—she was pretty good today.

MAMA: I'll good you—[*She turns her eyes to the box again.*]

BENEATHA: Open it, Mama. [*She stands up, looks at it, turns and looks at all of them, and then presses her hands together and does not open the package.*]

WALTER [*sweetly*]:   Open it, Mama. It's for you. [MAMA *looks in his eyes. It is the first present in her life without its being Christmas. Slowly she opens her package and lifts out, one by one, a brand-new sparkling set of gardening tools.* WALTER *continues, prodding.*] Ruth made up the note—read it . . .

MAMA [*picking up the card and adjusting her glasses*]:   "To our own Mrs. Miniver—Love from Brother, Ruth and Beneatha." Ain't that lovely . . .

TRAVIS [*tugging at his father's sleeve*]:   Daddy, can I give her mine now?

WALTER: All right, son. [TRAVIS *flies to get his gift.*] Travis didn't want to go in with the rest of us, Mama. He got his own. [*somewhat amused*] We don't know what it is . . .

TRAVIS [*racing back in the room with a large hatbox and putting it in front of his grandmother*]:   Here!

MAMA: Lord have mercy, baby. You done gone and bought your grandmother a hat?

TRAVIS [*very proud*]:   Open it! [*She does and lifts out an elaborate, but very elaborate, wide gardening hat, and all the adults break up at the sight of it.*]

RUTH: Travis, honey, what is that?

TRAVIS [*who thinks it is beautiful and appropriate*]: It's a gardening hat! Like the ladies always have on in the magazines when they work in their gardens.

BENEATHA [*giggling fiercely*]: Travis—we were trying to make Mama Mrs. Miniver— not Scarlett O'Hara!

MAMA [*indignantly*]: What's the matter with you all! This here is a beautiful hat! [*absurdly*] I always wanted me one just like it! [*She pops it on her head to prove it to her grandson, and the hat is ludicrous and considerably oversized.*]

RUTH: Hot dog! Go, Mama!

WALTER [*doubled over with laughter*]: I'm sorry, Mama—but you look like you ready to go out and chop you some cotton sure enough! [*They all laugh except* MAMA, *out of deference to* TRAVIS's *feelings.*]

MAMA [*gathering the boy up to her*]: Bless your heart—this is the prettiest hat I ever owned—[WALTER, RUTH *and* BENEATHA *chime in—noisily, festively and insincerely congratulating* TRAVIS *on his gift.*] What are we all standing around here for? We ain't finished packin' yet. Bennie, you ain't packed one book. [*The bell rings.*]

BENEATHA: That couldn't be the movers . . . it's not hardly two o'clock yet— [BENEATHA *goes into her room.* MAMA *starts for door.*]

WALTER [*turning, stiffening*]: Wait—wait—I'll get it. [*He stands and looks at the door.*]

MAMA: You expecting company, son?

WALTER [*just looking at the door*]: Yeah—yeah . . . [MAMA *looks at* RUTH, *and they exchange innocent and unfrightened glances.*]

MAMA [*not understanding*]: Well, let them in, son.

BENEATHA [*from her room*]: We need some more string.

MAMA: Travis—you run to the hardware and get me some string cord. [MAMA *goes out and* WALTER *turns and looks at* RUTH. *Travis goes to a dish for money.*]

RUTH: Why don't you answer the door, man?

WALTER [*suddenly bounding across the floor to her*]: 'Cause sometimes it hard to let the future begin! [*stooping down in her face*]

> *I got wings! You got wings!*
> *All God's children got wings!*

[*He crosses to the door and throws it open. Standing there is a very slight little man in a not too prosperous business suit and with haunted frightened eyes and a hat pulled down tightly, brim up, around his forehead.* TRAVIS *passes between the men and exits.* WALTER *leans deep in the man's face, still in his jubilance.*]

> *When I get to heaven gonna put on my wings,*
> *Gonna fly all over God's heaven . . .*
> [*The little man just stares at him*]
> *Heaven—*
> [*Suddenly he stops and looks past the little man into the empty hallway.*] Where's Willy, man?

BOBO: He ain't with me.

WALTER [*not disturbed*]:   Oh—come on in. You know my wife.

BOBO [*dumbly, taking off his hat*]:   Yes—h'you, Miss Ruth.

RUTH [*quietly, a mood apart from her husband already, seeing* BOBO]:   Hello,
    Bobo.

WALTER: You right on time today . . . . Right on time. That's the way! [*He slaps* BOBO
    on his back.] Sit down . . . lemme hear. [RUTH *stands stiffly and quietly in
    back of them, as though somehow she senses death, her eyes fixed on her
    husband.*]

BOBO [*his frightened eyes on the floor, his hat in his hands*]:   Could I please get a
    drink of water, before I tell you about it, Walter Lee? [WALTER *does not take his
    eyes off the man.* RUTH *goes blindly to the tap and gets a glass of water and
    brings it to* BOBO.]

WALTER: There ain't nothing wrong, is there?

BOBO: Lemme tell you—

WALTER: Man—didn't nothing go wrong?

BOBO: Lemme tell you—Walter Lee. [*Looking at* RUTH *and talking to her more
    than to* Walter.] You know how it was. I got to tell you how it was. I mean first
    I got to tell you how it was all the way . . . I mean about the money I put in,
    Walter Lee . . .

WALTER [*with taut agitation now*]:   What about the money you put in?

BOBO: Well—it wasn't much as we told you—me and Willy—[*He stops.*] I'm sorry,
    Walter. I got a bad feeling about it. I got a real bad feeling about it . . .

WALTER: Man, what you telling me about all this for? . . . Tell me what happened in
    Springfield . . .

BOBO: Springfield.

RUTH [*like a dead woman*]:   What was supposed to happen in Springfield?

BOBO [*to her*]:   This deal that me and Walter went into with Willy—Me and Willy
    was going to go down to Springfield and spread some money 'round so's we
    wouldn't have to wait so long for the liquor license . . . That's what we were
    going to do. Everybody said that was the way you had to do, you understand,
    Miss Ruth?

WALTER: Man—what happened down there?

BOBO [*a pitiful man, near tears*]:   I'm trying to tell you, Walter.

WALTER [*screaming at him suddenly*]:   THEN TELL ME, GODDAMMIT . . . WHAT'S
    THE MATTER WITH YOU?

BOBO: Man . . . I didn't go to no Springfield, yesterday.

WALTER [*halted, life hanging in the moment*]:   Why not?

BOBO [*the long way, the hard way to tell*]:   'Cause I didn't have no reasons to . . .

WALTER: Man, what are you talking about!

BOBO: I'm talking about the fact that when I got to the train station yesterday morn-
    ing—eight o'clock like we planned . . . Man—*Willy didn't never show up.*

WALTER: Why . . . where was he . . . where is he?

BOBO: That's what I'm trying to tell you . . . I don't know . . . I waited six hours . . . I called his house . . . and I waited . . . six hours . . . I waited in that train station six hours . . . [*breaking into tears*] That was all the extra money I had in the world . . . [*looking up at* WALTER *with the tears running down his face*] Man, *Willy is gone.*

WALTER: Gone, what you mean Willy is gone? Gone where? You mean he went by himself. You mean he went off to Springfield by himself—to take care of getting the license—[*turns and looks anxiously at* RUTH] You mean maybe he didn't want too many people in on the business down there? [*looks to* RUTH *again, as before*] You know Willy got his own ways. [*looks back to* BOBO] Maybe you was late yesterday and he just went on down there without you. Maybe—maybe—he's been callin' you at home tryin' to tell you what happened or something. Maybe—maybe—he just got sick. He's somewhere—he's got to be somewhere. We just got to find him—me and you got to find him. [*grabs* BOBO *senselessly by the collar and starts to shake him*] We got to!

BOBO [*in sudden angry, frightened agony*]:   What's the matter with you, Walter! *When a cat take off with your money he don't leave you no maps!*

WALTER [*turning madly, as though he is looking for* WILLY *in the very room*]: Willy! . . . Willy . . . don't do it . . . Please don't do it . . . Man, not with that money . . . Man, please, not with that money . . . Oh, God . . . Don't let it be true . . . [*He is wandering around, crying out for* WILLY *and looking for him or perhaps for help from God.*] Man . . . I trusted you . . . Man, I put my life in your hands . . . [*He starts to crumple down on the floor as* RUTH *just covers her face in horror,* MAMA *opens the door and comes into the room, with* BENEATHA *behind her.*] Man . . . [*He starts to pound the floor with his fists, sobbing wildly.*] *That money is made out of my father's flesh* . . .

BOBO [*standing over him helplessly*]:   I'm sorry, Walter . . . [*Only* WALTER'S *sobs reply.* BOBO *puts on his hat.*] I had my life staked on this deal, too . . . [*He exits.*]

MAMA [*to* WALTER]:   Son—[*She goes to him, bends down to him, talks to his bent head.*] Son . . . Is it gone? Son, I gave you sixty-five hundred dollars. Is it gone? All of it? Beneatha's money too?

WALTER [*lifting his head slowly*]:   Mama . . . I never . . . went to the bank at all.

MAMA [*not wanting to believe him*]:   You mean . . . your sister's school money . . . you used that too . . . Walter? . . .

WALTER: Yessss! . . . All of it . . . It's all gone . . .

[*There is total silence.* RUTH *stands with her face covered with her hands;* BENEATHA *leans forlornly against a wall, fingering a piece of red ribbon from the mother's gift.* MAMA *stops and looks at her son without recognition and then, quite without thinking about it, starts to beat him senselessly in the face.* BENEATHA *goes to them and stops it.*]

BENEATHA: Mama! [MAMA *stops and looks at both of her children and rises slowly and wanders vaguely, aimlessly away from them.*]

MAMA: I seen ... him ... night after night ... come in ... and look at that rug ... and then look at me ... the red showing in his eyes ... the veins moving in his head ... I seen him grow thin and old before he was forty ... working and working and working like somebody's old horse ... killing himself ... and you—you give it all away in a day ...

BENEATHA: Mama—

MAMA: Oh, God ... [*She looks up to Him.*] Look down here—and show me the strength.

BENEATHA: Mama—

MAMA [*folding over*]:   Strength ...

BENEATHA [*plaintively*]:   MAMA ...

MAMA: Strength!

Curtain

ACT III

An hour later.

At curtain, there is a sullen light of gloom in the living room, gray light not unlike that which began the first scene of Act I.At left we can see WALTER within his room, alone with himself. He is stretched out on the bed, his shirt out and open, his arms under his head. He does not smoke, he does not cry out, he merely lies there, looking up at the ceiling, much as if he were alone in the world.

In the living room BENEATHA sits at the table, still surrounded by the now almost ominous packing crates. She sits looking off. We feel that this is a mood struck perhaps an hour before, and it lingers now, full of the empty sound of profound disappointment.We see on a line from her brother's bedroom the sameness of their attitudes. Presently the bell rings and BENEATHA rises without ambition or interest in answering. It is ASAGAI, smiling broadly, striding into the room with energy and happy expectation and conversation.

ASAGAI: I came over ... I had some free time. I thought I might help with the packing. Ah, I like the look of packing crates! A household in preparation for a journey! It depresses some people ... but for me ... it is another feeling. Something full of the flow of life, do you understand? Movement, progress ... It makes me think of Africa.

BENEATHA: Africa!

ASAGAI: What kind of a mood is this? Have I told you how deeply you move me?

BENEATHA: He gave away the money, Asagai ...

ASAGAI: Who gave away what money?

BENEATHA: The insurance money. My brother gave it away.

ASAGAI: Gave it away?

BENEATHA: He made an investment! With a man even Travis wouldn't have trusted.

ASAGAI: And it's gone?

BENEATHA: Gone!

ASAGAI: I'm very sorry ... And you, now?

BENEATHA: Me? . . . Me? . . . Me, I'm nothing . . . Me. When I was very small . . . we used to take our sleds out in the wintertime and the only hills we had were the ice-covered stone steps of some houses down the street. And we used to fill them in with snow and make them smooth and slide down them all day . . . and it was very dangerous you know . . . far too steep . . . and sure enough one day a kid named Rufus came down too fast and hit the sidewalk . . . and we saw his face just split open right there in front of us . . . And I remember standing there looking at his bloody open face thinking that was the end of Rufus. But the ambulance came and they took him to the hospital and they fixed the broken bones and they sewed it all up . . . and the next time I saw Rufus he just had a little line down the middle of his face . . . I never got over that . . . [WALTER *sits up, listening on the bed. Throughout this scene it is important that we feel his reaction at all times, that he visibly respond to the words of his sister and* ASAGAI.]

ASAGAI: What?

BENEATHA: That that was what one person could do for another, fix him up—sew up the problem, make him all right again. That was the most marvelous thing in the world . . . I wanted to do that. I always thought it was the one concrete thing in the world that a human being could do. Fix up the sick, you know— and make them whole again. This was truly being God . . .

ASAGAI: You wanted to be God?

BENEATHA: No—I wanted to cure. It used to be so important to me. I wanted to cure. It used to matter. I used to care. I mean about people and how their bodies hurt . . .

ASAGAI: And you've stopped caring?

BENEATHA: Yes—I think so.

ASAGAI: Why? [WALTER *rises, goes to the door of his room and is about to open it, then stops and stands listening, leaning on the door jamb.*]

BENEATHA: Because it doesn't seem deep enough, close enough to what ails mankind—I mean this thing of sewing up bodies or administering drugs. Don't you understand? It was a child's reaction to the world. I thought that doctors had the secret to all the hurts . . . That's the way a child sees things— or an idealist.

ASAGAI: Children see things very well sometimes—and idealists even better.

BENEATHA: I know that's what you think. Because you are still where I left off—you still care. This is what you see for the world, for Africa. You with the dreams of the future will patch up all Africa—you are going to cure the Great Sore of colonialism with Independence—

ASAGAI: Yes!

BENEATHA: Yes—and you think that one word is the penicillin of the human spirit: "Independence!" But then what?

ASAGAI: That will be the problem for another time. First we must get there.

BENEATHA: And where does it end?

ASAGAI: End? Who even spoke of an end? To life? To living?

BENEATHA: An end to misery!

ASAGAI [*smiling*]:   You sound like a French intellectual.

BENEATHA: No! I sound like a human being who just had her future taken right out of her hands! While I was sleeping in my bed in there, things were happening in this world that directly concerned me—and nobody asked me, consulted me—they just went out and did things—and changed my life. Don't you see there isn't any real progress, Asagai, there is only one large circle that we march in, around and around, each of us with our own little picture—in front of us—our own little mirage that we think is the future.

ASAGAI: That is the mistake.

BENEATHA: What?

ASAGAI: What you just said—about the circle. It isn't a circle—it is simply a long line—as in geometry, you know, one that reaches into infinity. And because we cannot see the end—we also cannot see how it changes. And it is very odd but those who see the changes are called "idealists"—and those who cannot, or refuse to think, they are the "realists." It is very strange, and amusing too, I think.

BENEATHA: You—you are almost religious.

ASAGAI: Yes . . . I think I have the religion of doing what is necessary in the world—and of worshipping man—because he is so marvelous, you see.

BENEATHA: Man is foul! And the human race deserves its misery!

ASAGAI: You see: *you* have become the religious one in the old sense. Already, and after such a small defeat, you are worshipping despair.

BENEATHA: From now on, I worship the truth—and the truth is that people are puny, small and selfish . . .

ASAGAI: Truth? Why is it that you despairing ones always think that only you have the truth? I never thought to see *you* like that. You! Your brother made a stupid, childish mistake—and you are grateful to him. So that now you can give up the ailing human race on account of it. You talk about what good is struggle; what good is anything? Where are we all going? And why are we bothering?

BENEATHA: *And you cannot answer it!* All your talk and dreams about Africa and Independence. Independence and then what? What about all the crooks and petty thieves and just plain idiots who will come into power to steal and plunder the same as before—only now they will be black and do it in the name of the new Independence—You cannot answer that.

ASAGAI [*shouting over her*]:   *I live the answer!* [*pause*] In my village at home it is the exceptional man who can even read a newspaper . . . or who ever *sees* a book at all. I will go home and much of what I will have to say will seem strange to the people of my village. . . . But I will teach and work and things will happen, slowly and swiftly. At times it will seem that nothing changes at all . . . and then again . . . the sudden dramatic events which make history leap into the future. And then quiet again. Retrogression even. Guns, murder, revolution. And I even will have moments when I wonder if the quiet was not better than all that death and hatred. But I will look about my village at the illiteracy and disease and ignorance and I will not wonder long. And perhaps . . . perhaps I will be a great man . . . I mean perhaps I will hold on to the substance of truth and find my way always with the right course . . . and perhaps for it I will be butchered in my bed some night by the servants of empire . . .

BENEATHA: *The martyr!*

ASAGAI: . . . or perhaps I shall live to be a very old man, respected and esteemed in my new nation . . . And perhaps I shall hold office and this is what I'm trying to tell you, Alaiyo; perhaps the things I believe now for my country will be wrong and outmoded, and I will not understand and do terrible things to have things my way or merely to keep my power. Don't you see that there will be young men and women, not British soldiers then, but my own black countrymen . . . to step out of the shadows some evening and slit my then useless throat? Don't you see they have always been there . . . that they always will be. And that such a thing as my own death will be an advance? They who might kill me even . . . actually replenish me!

BENEATHA: Oh, Asagai, I know all that.

ASAGAI: Good! Then stop moaning and groaning and tell me what you plan to do.

BENEATHA: Do?

ASAGAI: I have a bit of a suggestion.

BENEATHA: What?

ASAGAI [*rather quietly for him*]:   That when it is all over—that you come home with me—

BENEATHA [*slapping herself on the forehead with exasperation born of misunderstanding*]:   Oh—Asagai—at this moment you decide to be romantic!

ASAGAI   [*quickly understanding the misunderstanding*]:   My dear, young creature of the New World—I do not mean across the city—I mean across the ocean; home—to Africa.

BENEATHA [*slowly understanding and turning to him with murmured amazement*]:   To—to Nigeria?

ASAGAI: Yes! . . . [*smiling and lifting his arms playfully*]. Three hundred years later the African Prince rose up out of the seas and swept the maiden back across the middle passage over which her ancestors had come—

BENEATHA [*unable to play*]:   Nigeria?

ASAGAI: Nigeria. Home. [*coming to her with genuine romantic flippancy*] I will show you our mountains and our stars; and give you cool drinks from gourds and teach you the old songs and the ways of our people—and, in time, we will pretend that—[*very softly*]—you have only been away for a day—[*She turns her back to him, thinking. He swings her around and takes her full in his arms in a long embrace which proceeds to passion.*]

BENEATHA [*pulling away*]:   You're getting me all mixed up—

ASAGAI: Why?

BENEATHA: Too many things—too many things have happened today. I must sit down and think. I don't know what I feel about anything right this minute. [*She promptly sits down and props her chin on her fist.*]

ASAGAI [*charmed*]:   All right, I shall leave you. No—don't get up. [*touching her, gently, sweetly*] Just sit awhile and think . . . Never be afraid to sit awhile and think. [*He goes to door and looks at her.*] How often I have looked at you and said, "Ah—so this is what the New World hath finally wrought . . . " [*He exits. BENEATHA sits on alone. Presently WALTER enters from his room and starts to rummage through things, feverishly looking for something. She looks up and turns in her seat.*]

BENEATHA [*hissingly*]:   Yes—just look at what the New World hath wrought! . . .Just look! [*She gestures with bitter disgust.*] There he is! *Monsieur le petit bougeois noir*—himself! There he is—Symbol of a Rising Class! Entrepreneur! Titan of the system! [*WALTER ignores her completely and continues frantically and destructively looking for something and hurling things to the floor and tearing things out of their place in his search. BENEATHA ignores the eccentricity of his actions and goes on with the monologue of insult.*] Did you dream of yachts on Lake Michigan, Brother? Did you see yourself on that Great Day sitting down at the Conference Table, surrounded by all the mighty bald-headed men in America? All halted, waiting, breathless, waiting for your pronouncements on industry? Waiting for you—Chairman of the Board? [*WALTER finds what he is looking for—a small piece of white paper—and pushes it in his pocket and puts on his coat and rushes out without ever having looked at her. She shouts after him.*] I look at you and I see the final triumph of stupidity in the world! [*The door slams and she returns to just sitting again. RUTH comes quickly out of MAMA's room.*]

RUTH: Who was that?

BENEATHA: Your husband.

RUTH: Where did he go?

BENEATHA: Who knows—maybe he has an appointment at U.S. Steel.

RUTH [*anxiously, with frightened eyes*]:   You didn't say nothing bad to him, did you?

BENEATHA: Bad? Say anything bad to him? No—I told him he was a sweet boy and full of dreams and everything is strictly peachy keen, as the ofay[3] kids say!

[*MAMA enters from her bedroom. She is lost, vague, trying to catch hold, to make some sense of her former command of the world, but it still eludes her. A sense of waste overwhelms her gait; a measure of apology rides on her shoulders. She goes to her plant, which has remained on the table, looks at it, picks it up and takes it to the window sill and sets it outside, and she stands and looks at it a long moment. Then she closes the window, straightens her body with effort and turns around to her children.*]

[3]**ofay** white (pig Latin meaning "foe")

MAMA: Well—ain't it a mess in here, though? [*a false cheerfulness, a beginning of something*] I guess we all better stop moping around and get some work done. All this unpacking and everything we got to do. [RUTH *raises her head slowly in response to the sense of the line; and* BENEATHA *in similar manner turns very slowly to look at her mother.*] One of you all better call the moving people and tell 'em not to come.

RUTH: Tell 'em not to come?

MAMA: Of course, baby. Ain't no need in 'em coming all the way here and having to go back. They charges for that too. [*She sits down, fingers to her brow, thinking.*] Lord, ever since I was a little girl, I always remembers people saying, "Lena—Lena Eggleston, you aims too high all the time. You needs to slow down and see life a little more like it is. Just slow down some." That's what they always used to say down home—"Lord, that Lena Eggleston is a high-minded thing. She'll get her due one day!"

RUTH: No, Lena . . .

MAMA: Me and Big Walter just didn't never learn right.

RUTH: Lena, no! We gotta go. Bennie—tell her . . . [*She rises and crosses to* BENEATHA *with her arms outstretched.* BENEATHA *doesn't respond.*] Tell her we can still move . . . the notes ain't but a hundred and twenty-five a month. We got four grown people in this house—we can work . . .

MAMA [*to herself*]:   Just aimed too high all the time—

RUTH [*turning and going to* MAMA *fast—the words pouring out with urgency and desperation*]:   Lena—I'll work . . . I'll work twenty hours a day in all the kitchens in Chicago . . . I'll strap my baby on my back if I have to and scrub all the floors in America and wash all the sheets in America if I have to—but we got to move . . . We got to get out of here . . . [MAMA *reaches out absently and pats* Ruth's *hand.*]

MAMA: No—I sees things differently now. Been thinking 'bout some of the things we could do to fix this place up some. I seen a second-hand bureau over on Maxwell Street just the other day that could fit right there. [*She points to where the new furniture might go.* RUTH *wanders away from her.*] Would need some new handles on it and then a little varnish and then it look like something brand-new. And—we can put up them new curtains in the kitchen . . . Why this place be looking fine. Cheer us all up so that we forget trouble ever came . . . [*to* RUTH] And you could get some nice screens to put up in your room round the baby's bassinet . . . [*She looks at both of them, pleadingly.*] Sometimes you just got to know when to give up some things . . . and hold on to what you got. [WALTER *enters from the outside, looking spent and leaning against the door, his coat hanging from him.*]

MAMA: Where you been, son?

WALTER [*breathing hard*]:   Made a call.

MAMA: To who, son?

WALTER: To the Man.

MAMA: What man, baby?

WALTER: The Man, Mama. Don't you know who The Man is?

RUTH: Walter Lee?

WALTER: *The Man.* Like the guys in the street say—*the Man.* Captain Boss—Mistuh Charley . . . Old Captain Please Mr. Bossman . . .

BENEATHA [*suddenly*]:   Lindner!

WALTER: That's right! That's good. I told him to come right over.

BENEATHA [*fiercely, understanding*]:   For what? What do you want to see him for?

WALTER [*looking at his sister*]:   We are going to do business with him.

MAMA: What you talking 'bout, son?

WALTER: Talking 'bout life, Mama. You all always telling me to see life like it is. Well— I laid in there on my back today . . . and I figured it out. Life just like it is. Who gets and who don't get. [*He sits down with his coat on and laughs.*] Mama, you know it's all divided up. Life is. Sure enough. Between the takers and the "tooken." [*He laughs.*] I've figured it out finally. [*He looks around at them.*] Yeah. Some of us always getting "tooken." [*He laughs.*] People like Willy Harris, they don't never get "tooken." And you know why the rest of us do? 'Cause we all mixed up. Mixed up bad. We get to looking 'round for the right and the wrong; and we worry about it and cry about it and stay up nights trying to figure out 'bout the wrong and the right of things all the time . . . And all the time, man, them takers is out there operating, just taking and taking. Willy Harris? Shoot— Willy Harris don't even count. He don't even count in the big scheme of things. But I'll say one thing for old Willy Harris . . . he's taught me something. He's taught me to keep my eye on what counts in this world. Yeah—[*shouting out a little*] Thanks, Willy!

RUTH: What did you call that man for, Walter Lee!

WALTER: Called him to tell him to come on over to the show. Gonna put on a show for the man. Just what he wants to see. You see, Mama, the man came here today and he told us that them people out there where you want us to move— well they so upset they willing to pay us not to move out there. [*He laughs again.*] And—and oh, Mama—you would of been proud of the way me and Ruth and Bennie acted. We told him to get out . . . Lord have mercy! We told the man to get out. Oh, we was some proud folks this afternoon, yeah. [*He lights a cigarette.*] We were still full of that old-time stuff . . .

RUTH [*coming toward him slowly*]:   You talking 'bout taking them people's money to keep us from moving in that house?

WALTER: I ain't just talking 'bout it, baby—I'm telling you that's what's going to happen.

BENEATHA: Oh, God! Where is the bottom! Where is the real honest-to-God bottom so he can't go any farther!

WALTER: See—that's the old stuff. You and that boy that was here today. You all want everybody to carry a flag and a spear and sing some marching songs, huh? You wanna spend your life looking into things and trying to find the right and the

wrong part, huh? Yeah. You know what's going to happen to that boy someday—he'll find himself sitting in a dungeon, locked in forever—and the takers
will have the key! Forget it, baby! There ain't no causes—there ain't nothing
but taking in this world, and he who takes most is smartest—and it don't
make a damn bit of difference *how.*

MAMA: You making something inside me cry, son. Some awful pain inside me.

WALTER: Don't cry, Mama. Understand. That white man is going to walk in that door
able to write checks for more money than we ever had. It's important to him
and I'm going to help him . . . I'm going to put on the show, Mama.

MAMA: Son—I come from five generations of people who was slaves and share-
croppers—but ain't nobody in my family never let nobody pay 'em no money
that was a way of telling us we wasn't fit to walk the earth. We ain't never been
that poor. [*raising her eyes and looking at him*] We ain't never been that
dead inside.

BENEATHA: Well—we are dead now. All the talk about dreams and sunlight that goes
on in this house. All dead.

WALTER: What's the matter with you all! I didn't make this world! It was give to me
this way! Hell, yes, I want me some yachts someday! Yes, I want to hang some
real pearls 'round my wife's neck. Ain't she supposed to wear no pearls?
Somebody tell me—tell me, who decides which women is suppose to wear
pearls in this world. I tell you I am a *man*—and I think my wife should wear
some pearls in this world! [*This last line hangs a good while and* WALTER
*begins to move about the room. The word "Man" has penetrated his con-
sciousness; he mumbles it to himself repeatedly between strange agitated
pauses as he moves about.*]

MAMA: Baby, how you going to feel on the inside?

WALTER: Fine! . . . Going to feel fine . . . a man. . . .

MAMA: You won't have nothing left then, Walter Lee.

WALTER [*coming to her*]:   I'm going to feel fine, Mama. I'm going to look that son-of-
a-bitch in the eyes and say—[*He falters.*]—and say, "All right, Mr. Lindner—[*He
falters even more.*]—that's your neighborhood out there. You got the right to
keep it like you want. You got the right to have it like you want. Just write the
check and—the house is yours." And, and I am going to say—[*His voice
almost breaks.*] And you—you people just put the money in my hand and you
won't have to live next to this bunch of stinking niggers! . . . [*He straightens
up and moves away from his mother, walking around the room.*] Maybe—
maybe I'll just get down on my black knees . . . [*He does so;* RUTH *and* BENNIE
and MAMA *watch him in frozen horror.*] Captain, Mistuh, Bossman. [*He starts
crying.*] A-hee-hee-hee! [*wringing his hands in profoundly anguished imitation*] Yasssssuh! Great White Father, just gi' ussen de money, fo' God's sake,
and we's ain't gwine come out deh and dirty up yo' white folks' neighborhood
. . . [*He breaks down completely, then gets up and goes into the bedroom.*]

BENEATHA: That is not a man. That is nothing but a toothless rat.

MAMA: Yes—death done come in this here house. [*She is nodding, slowly, reflectively.*] Done come walking in my house. On the lips of my children. You what supposed to be my beginning again. You—what supposed to be my harvest. [*to* BENEATHA] You—you mourning your brother?

BENEATHA: He's no brother of mine.

MAMA: What you say?

BENEATHA: I said that that individual in that room is no brother of mine.

MAMA: That's what I thought you said. You feeling like you better than he is today? [BENEATHA *does not answer.*] Yes? What you tell him a minute ago? That he wasn't a man? Yes? You give him up for me? You done wrote his epitaph too—like the rest of the world? Well, who give you the privilege?

BENEATHA: Be on my side for once! You saw what he just did, Mama! You saw him—down on his knees. Wasn't it you who taught me—to despise any man who would do that? Do what he's going to do.

MAMA: Yes—I taught you that. Me and your daddy. But I thought I taught you something else too . . . I thought I taught you to love him.

BENEATHA: Love him? There is nothing left to love.

MAMA: There is always something left to love. And if you ain't learned that, you ain't learned nothing. [*looking at her*] Have you cried for that boy today? I don't mean for yourself and for the family 'cause we lost the money. I mean for him; what he been through and what it done to him. Child, when do you think is the time to love somebody the most; when they done good and made things easy for everybody? Well then, you ain't through learning—because that ain't the time at all. It's when he's at his lowest and can't believe in hisself 'cause the world done whipped him so. When you starts measuring somebody, measure him right, child, measure him right. Make sure you done taken into account what hills and valleys he come through before he got to wherever he is. [*Travis bursts into the room at the end of the speech, leaving the door open.*]

TRAVIS: Grandmama—the moving men are downstairs! The truck just pulled up.

MAMA [*turning and looking at him*]:   Are they, baby? They downstairs? [*She sighs and sits.* LINDNER *appears in the doorway. He peers in and knocks lightly, to gain attention, and comes in. All turn to look at him.*]

LINDNER [*hat and briefcase in hand*]:   Uh—hello . . . [RUTH *crosses mechanically to the bedroom door and opens it and lets it swing open freely and slowly as the lights come up on* WALTER *within, still in his coat, sitting at the far corner of the room. He looks up and out through the room to* LINDNER.]

RUTH: He's here. [*A long minute passes and* WALTER *slowly gets up.*]

LINDNER [*coming to the table with efficiency, putting his briefcase on the table and starting to unfold papers and unscrew fountain pens*]:   Well, I certainly was glad to hear from you people. [WALTER *has begun the trek out of the room, slowly and awkwardly, rather like a small boy, passing the back of his sleeve across his mouth from time to time.*] Life can really be so much simpler than people let it be most of the time. Well—with whom do I negotiate?

You, Mrs. Younger, or your son here? [MAMA *sits with her hands folded on her lap and her eyes closed as* WALTER *advances.* TRAVIS *goes close to* LINDNER *and looks at the papers curiously.*] Just some official papers, sonny.

RUTH: Travis, you go downstairs.

MAMA [*opening her eyes and looking into* WALTER'S]:   No. Travis, you stay right here. And you make him understand what you doing. Walter Lee. You teach him good. Like Willy Harris taught you. You show where our five generations done come to. Go ahead, son—

WALTER [*Looks down into his boy's eyes.* TRAVIS *grins at him merrily and* WALTER *draws him beside him with his arm lightly around his shoulders.*]:   Well, Mr. Lindner. [BENEATHA *turns away.*] We called you—[*There is a profound, simple groping quality in his speech.*]—because, well, me and my family [*He looks around and shifts from one foot to the other.*] Well—we are very plain people. . . .

LINDNER: Yes—

WALTER: I mean—I have worked as a chauffeur most of my life—and my wife here, she does domestic work in people's kitchens. So does my mother. I mean—we are plain people. . . .

LINDNER: Yes, Mr. Younger—

WALTER [*really like a small boy, looking down at his shoes and then up at the man*]:   And—uh—well, my father, well, he was a laborer most of his life.

LINDNER [*absolutely confused*]:   Uh, yes—

WALTER [*looking down at his toes once again*]:   My father almost beat a man to death once because this man called him a bad name or something, you know what I mean?

LINDNER: No, I'm afraid I don't.

WALTER [*finally straightening up*]:   Well, what I mean is that we come from people who had a lot of pride. I mean—we are very proud people. And that's my sister over there and she's going to be a doctor—and we are very proud—

LINDNER: Well—I am sure that is very nice, but—

WALTER [*Starting to cry and facing the man eye to eye*]:   What I am telling you is that we called you over here to tell you that we are very proud and that this is—this is my son, who makes the sixth generation of our family in this country, and that we have all thought about your offer and we have decided to move into our house because my father—my father—he earned it. [MAMA *has her eyes closed and is rocking back and forth as though she were in church, with her head nodding the amen yes.*] We don't want to make no trouble for nobody or fight no causes—but we will try to be good neighbors. That's all we got to say. [*He looks the man absolutely in the eyes.*] We don't want your money. [*He turns and walks away from the man.*]

LINDNER [*looking around at all of them*]:   I take it then that you have decided to occupy.

BENEATHA: That's what the man said.

LINDNER [*to* MAMA *in her reverie*]:   Then I would like to appeal to you, Mrs. Younger. You are older and wiser and understand things better I am sure . . .

MAMA [*rising*]:   I am afraid you don't understand. My son said we was going to move and there ain't nothing left for me to say. [*Shaking her head with double meaning.*] You know how these young folks is nowadays, mister. Can't do a thing with 'em. Good-bye.

LINDNER [*folding up his materials*]:   Well—if you are that final about it . . . There is nothing left for me to say. [*He finishes. He is almost ignored by the family, who are concentrating on* WALTER LEE. *At the door* Lindner *halts and looks around.*] I sure hope you people know what you're doing. [*He shakes his head and exits.*]

RUTH [*looking around and coming to life*]:   Well, for God's sake—if the moving men are here—LET'S GET THE HELL OUT OF HERE!

MAMA [*into action*]:   Ain't it the truth! Look at all this here mess. Ruth, put Travis' good jacket on him . . . Walter Lee, fix your tie and tuck your shirt in, you look just like somebody's hoodlum. Lord have mercy, where is my plant? [*She flies to get it amid the general bustling of the family, who are deliberately trying to ignore the nobility of the past moment.*] You all start on down . . . Travis child, don't go empty-handed . . . Ruth, where did I put that box with my skillets in it? I want to be in charge of it myself . . . I'm going to make us the biggest dinner we ever ate tonight . . . Beneatha, what's the matter with them stockings? Pull them things up, girl . . . [*The family starts to file out as two moving men appear and begin to carry out the heavier pieces of furniture, bumping into the family as they move about.*]

BENEATHA: Mama, Asagai—asked me to marry him today and go to Africa—

MAMA [*in the middle of her getting-ready activity*]:   He did? You ain't old enough to marry nobody—[*Seeing the moving men lifting one of her chairs precariously.*] Darling, that ain't no bale of cotton, please handle it so we can sit in it again. I had that chair twenty-five years . . . [*The movers sigh with exasperation and go on with their work.*]

BENEATHA [*girlishly and unreasonably trying to pursue the conversation*]:   To go to Africa, Mama—be a doctor in Africa . . .

MAMA [*distracted*]:   Yes, baby—

WALTER: Africa! What he want to go to Africa for?

BENEATHA: To practice there . . .

WALTER: Girl, if you don't get all them silly ideas out your head! You better marry yourself a man with some loot . . .

BENEATHA [*angrily, precisely as in the first scene of the play*]:   What have you got to do with who I marry!

WALTER: Plenty. Now I think George Murchison—[*He and* BENEATHA *go out yelling at each other vigorously;* BENEATHA *is heard saying that she would not marry* GEORGE MURCHISON *if he were Adam and she were Eve, etc. The anger is loud and real till their voices diminish.* RUTH *stands at the door and turns to* MAMA *and smiles knowingly.*]

MAMA [*fixing her hat at last*]:   Yeah—they something all right, my children . . .

RUTH: Yeah—they're something. Let's go, Lena.

MAMA [*stalling, starting to look around at the house*]:   Yes—I'm coming. Ruth—

RUTH: Yes?

MAMA [*quietly, woman to woman*]:   He finally come into his manhood today, didn't he? Kind of like a rainbow after the rain . . .

RUTH [*biting her lip lest her own pride explode in front of* MAMA]:   Yes, Lena. [WALTER'S *voice calls for them raucously.*]

MAMA [*waving* RUTH *out vaguely*]:   All right, honey—go on down. I be down directly.

[RUTH *hesitates, then exits.* MAMA *stands, at last alone in the living room, her plant on the table before her as the lights start to come down. She looks around at all the walls and ceilings and suddenly, despite herself, while the children call below, a great heaving thing rises in her and she puts her fist to her mouth, takes a final desperate look, pulls her coat about her, pats her hat and goes out. The lights dim down. The door opens and she comes back in, grabs her plant, and goes out for the last time.]*

Curtain

✎MAKING CONNECTIONS

1. The title of the play is taken from a line in Langston Hughes's poem "A Dream Deferred" (p. 76). Do you think *A Raisin in the Sun* is an appropriate title? Explain.

2. How are sunlight and Mama's plant used as symbols in this play? How do these objects also serve to set the mood?

3. The main characters all have different plans for the insurance money. What do you think of the process the Youngers follow in making the decision? Do you think the decision might have been made differently?

4. Does the Younger family share a common heritage with Asagai? Explain your answer with examples from the play.

5. What purpose do the scenes between George and Beneatha serve? Compare their different ideas about education, race, heritage, and the future.

6. Do you think it is necessary for Mama to entrust Walter with all the money? Why doesn't she split the money, giving Beneatha her share?

7. Do you agree with Walter's decision at the end of the play? What does he gain? What would be gained or lost by selling to Lindner? What kind of life do you expect the Youngers to find in Clybourne Park?

8. Ruth is very eager for the family to move into a house. Have you ever lived somewhere that you didn't consider a home? How does that affect a person—or a family—psychologically?

9. To what extent are the family's problems a question of bad luck, bad timing, or forces beyond their control? Provide examples.

10. Compare the relationships within the Younger family with those in other works you've read.

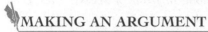

MAKING AN ARGUMENT

1. Characterization is one of the play's great strengths. Consider the dreams of Mama, Walter, Ruth and Beneatha. Beyond specific goals—like owning a liquor store—what do their dreams represent for them? What would achieving these dreams give them that seems to be missing from their lives? How does the insurance payment increase or ease the frustration they feel? To what extent are the characters themselves—in addition to the setting and their economic circumstances—responsible for the central conflict?

   Write a critical essay about the relationship between characterization and conflict in this play. Cite the text of the play to support your views.

LORRAINE HANSBERRY

IN HER OWN WORDS

On Growing Up "I was born May 19, 1930, the last of four children. Of love and my parents there is little to be written: their relationship to their children was utilitarian. We were fed and housed and dressed and outfitted with more cash than our associates and that was all. We were also vaguely taught certain vague absolutes: that we were better than no one but infinitely superior to everyone; that we were products of the proudest and most mistreated of the races of man; that there was nothing enormously difficult about life; that one succeeded as a matter of course."

"Life was not a struggle—it was something that one *did*. One won an argument because, if facts gave out, one invented them—with color! The only sinful people in the world were dull people. And above all, there were two things which were never to be betrayed: the family and the race. But of love, there was nothing ever said." (*YGB*, pp. 17–18)

"Seven years separated the nearest of my brothers and sisters and myself; I wear, I am sure, the earmarks of that familial station to this day. Little has been written or thought to my knowledge about children who occupy that place: the last born separated by an uncommon length of time from the next youngest. I suspect we are probably a race apart." (*YGB*, p. 18)

"I was given, during my grade school years, one-half the amount of education prescribed by the Board of Education of my city. This was so because the children of the Chicago ghetto were jammed into a segregated school system. I am a product of that system and one result is that—to this day—I cannot count properly. I do not add, subtract, or multiply with ease. Our teachers, devoted and indifferent alike, had to sacrifice something to make the system work at all—and in my case it was arithmetic that got put aside most often. Thus, the mind which was able to grasp university-level reading materials in the sixth and seventh grades had not been sufficiently exposed to elementary arithmetic to make even simple change in a grocery store."

"This is what is meant when we speak of the scars, the marks that the ghettoized child carries through life. To be imprisoned in the ghetto is to be forgotten—or deliberately cheated of one's birthright—at best." (*YGB,* p. 36)

"But we are all shaped, are we not, by that particular rim of the soup bowl where we swim, and I have remained throughout the balance of my life a creature formed in a community atmosphere where I was known as a 'rich' girl."

"In any case, my mother sent me to kindergarten in white fur in the middle of the depression; the kids beat me up; and I think it was from that moment I became—a rebel . . . " (*YGB,* p. 36)

"Above all, there had been an aspect of the society of the kids from the ghetto which demanded utmost respect: they fought. The girls as well as the boys. THEY FOUGHT. If you were not right with them, or sometimes even if you were, there they were of an afternoon after school, standing waiting for you in the sunshine; a little gang of them in their gym shoes, milling close together, blocking off the sidewalk, daring you to break for it and try to run to the other side of the street where, if luck prevailed, one might gain the protection of some chance passing adult. That, ultimately, was the worst thing of all to do because they always got you after that. *Always.* It was better to continue on right in their midst, feigning the courage or at least nonchalance." (*YGB,* p. 38)

"[My father] was the sort of a man who put a great deal of his money, a great deal of his extraordinary talents, and a great deal of passion into everything that we say is the American way of going after gold. He moved his family into a restricted area where no Negroes were supposed to live and proceeded to fight the case in the courts, all the way to the Supreme Court of the United States. This cost a great deal of money and involved the assistance of the NAACP attorneys and so on. It is the way of struggling that everyone says is the proper way. And it individually resulted in a decision against restrictive covenance, which is a famous case known as Hansberry vs. Lee." (From a speech at Town Hall, New York City, 1964)

On Her Motivation to Become a Playwright "My high school yearbook bears the dedication: "Englewood High trains for citizenship in a world of many different peoples. Who could better appreciate this wonderful country than our forefathers who traveled hundreds of miles from every known nation, seeking a land of freedom from discrimination of race, color, or creed." And in illustration, there is this:

The Great Branches of Man at Englewood High: in front, Mangolia Ali of East Indian Mohammedan descent; second couple, Nancy Diagre and Harold Bradley, Negroid; middle couple, Rosalind Sherr and William Krugman, Jewish religion, not a racial stock; next, Eleanor Trester and Theodore Flood, Caucasoid; extreme right, Lois Lee and Barbara Nomura, Mongoloid; rear, left, Mr. Thompson, principal.

I was reminded of Englewood by a questionnaire which came from *Show* magazine the other day . . .

THE SHAKESPEAREAN EXPERIENCE

SHOW POLL #5, February 1964

Some Questions Answered by: Robert Bolt, Jean Cocteau, T. S. Eliot, Tyrone Guthrie, Lorraine Hansberry, Joan Littlewood, Harold Pinter, Alain Robbe-Grillet, Igor Stravinsky, Harry S. Truman

QUESTION: *What was your first contact with Shakespeare?*

High school English literature classwork. We had to read and memorize speeches from *Macbeth* and *Julius Caesar* all under the auspices of a strange and bewigged teacher who we, after this induction, naturally and cruelly christened "Pale Hecate"—God rest her gentle, enraptured and igniting soul!

PALE HECATE *enters, ruler in hand, and takes her place in the classroom. She surveys the class. They come to attention as her eye falls on each in turn.*

PALE HECATE: Y'do not read, nor speak, nor write the English language! I suspect that y'do not even *think* in it! God only knows in what language y'do think, or if you think at all. 'Tis true that the *English* have done little enough with the tongue, but being the English I expect it was the best they could do. [*They giggle.*] In any case, I'll have it learned properly before a living one of y'll pass out of this class. That I will! (*Waving a composition book and indicating the grade marked in red at the top*) As for you, Miss—as for you, indeed, surely you will recognize the third letter of the alphabet, when y'have seen it?

STUDENT: *C.*

PALE HECATE: Aye, a *C* it 'tis! You're a bright and clever one now after all, aren't y'lass? [*The class snickers.*] And now, my brilliance, would you also be informing us as to what a grade signifies when it is thus put upon the page?

STUDENT: Average.

PALE HECATE: "Average." Yes, yes—and what else in your case, my iridescence? Well then, I'll be tellin' you in fine order. It stands for "cheat," my luminous one! [*The class sobers.*] For them that will do *half* when *all* is called for; for them that will slip and slide through life at the edge of their minds, never once pushing into the interior to see what wonders are hiding there—content to drift along on whatever gets them by, *cheating* themselves, *cheating* the world, *cheating* Nature! That is what the *C* means, my dear child—[*She smiles.*]—my pet [*they giggle; in rapid order she raps each on the head with her ruler.*]—my laziest *Queen of the Ethiopes!*

She exits or dims out.

QUESTION: *Which is your favorite Shakespeare play and why?*

"Favorite? It is like choosing the 'superiority' of autumn days; mingling titles permits a reply: *Othello* and *Hamlet.* Why? There is a sweetness in the former that lingers long after the tragedy is done. A kind of possibility that we suspect in man wherein even its flaw is a tribute. The latter because there remains a depth in the prince that, as we all know, constantly reengages as we mature. And it does seem that the wit remains the brightest and most instructive in all dramatic literature."

QUESTION: *What is the most important result of your familiarity with Shakespeare? What has he given you?*

"Comfort and agitation so bound together that they are inseparable. Man, as set down in the plays, is large. Enormous. Capable of anything at all. And yet fragile, too, this view of the human spirit; one feels it ought be respected and protected and loved rather fiercely.

Rollicking times, Shakespeare has given me. I love to laugh and his humor is that of everyday; of every man's foible at no man's expense. Language. At thirteen a difficult and alien tedium, those Elizabethan cadences; but soon a balm, a thrilling source of contact with life." (*YGB,* pp. 43–44)

On the Influence of Sean O'Casey (At seventeen years old, sitting in on a rehearsal of Sean O'Casey's *Juno and the Paycock*) "I remember rather clearly that my coming had been an accident. Also that I sat in the orchestra close to the stage: the orchestra of the great modern building which is the main theater plant of the University of Wisconsin. The woman's voice, the howl, the shriek of misery fitted to a wail of poetry that consumed all my senses and all my awareness of human pain, endurance and the futility of it—'Now Mrs. Madigan reappeared with her compassionate shawl and the wail rose and hummed through the tenement, through Dublin, through Ireland itself and then mingled with seas and became something born of the Irish wail that was all of us.' I remember sitting there stunned with a melody that I thought might have been sung in a different meter. The play was *Juno,* the writer Sean O'Casey—but the melody was one that I had known for a very long while."

"I was seventeen and I did not think then of *writing* the melody as *I* knew it—in a different key; but I believe it entered my consciousness and stayed there . . . ." (*YGB,* p. 65)

"I love Sean O'Casey. This, to me, is the playwright of the twentieth century accepting and using the most obvious instruments of Shakespeare, which is the human personality in its totality. O'Casey never fools you about the Irish, you see . . . the Irish drunkard, the Irish braggart, the Irish liar . . . and the genuine heroism which must naturally emerge when you tell the truth about people. This, to me, is the height of artistic perception and is the most rewarding kind of thing that can happen in drama, because when you believe people so completely—because *everybody* has their drunkards and their braggarts and their cowards, you know—then you also believe them in their moments of heroic assertion; you don't doubt them." (*YGB,* p. 69)

On Drama as a Medium "I happen to believe that the most ordinary human being . . . has within him elements of profundity, of profound anguish. You don't have to go to the kings and queens of the earth—I think the Greeks and the Elizabethans did this because it was a logical concept—but every human being is in enormous conflict about something, even if it's how to get to work in the morning and all that . . . " (Studs Terkel interview, 1959)

"I'm particularly attracted to a medium where not only do you get to do what we do in life every day—you know, talk to people—but to be very selective about the nature of the conversation. It's an opportunity to treat character in the most absolute relief, one against the other, so that everything, sympathy and conflict, is played so sharply, you know—even a little more than a novel. And I suppose it's my own private sense of drama that makes *that* appeal to me." (Studs Terkel interview, 1959)

"There's no contradiction between protest art and good art. That's an artificial argument. You either write a good play or bad play. It doesn't have too much to do with what it is about. People say that this or that minority group is so preoccupied with their problem that it diminishes their art. I've always been very pleased, and my husband also, to note that for the last two hundred years the only writers in the English language we've had to boast about are the Irish writers—who reflect an oppressed culture." (Mike Wallace interview, 1959)

On A Raisin in the Sun "Months before I had turned the last page out of the typewriter and pressed all the sheets neatly together in a pile, and gone and stretched out face down on the living room floor. I had finished a play; a play I had no reason to think or not think would ever be done; a play that I was sure no one would quite understand. . . . "

"I cannot any longer remember if I liked it or not. I have said to some that it was not my 'kind' of play; and yet it moved me to read it sometimes—and once I wept at a performance."

"I have been tongue-tied and glib and fatuous trying to answer questions which must always seem strange to a writer: 'Why did you write it?' and 'How did it come to be?'"

"The truly relevant and revealing answers are always too diffuse, too vague in time and place and specific meaning to quite try and share with people. I know— but how can I tell it." (*YGB,* p. 104)

> Hotel Taft
> New Haven, Conn.
> January 19, 1959

Dear Mother:

Well—here we are. I am sitting alone in a nice hotel room in New Haven, Conn. Downstairs, next door in the Shubert Theatre, technicians are putting the finishing touches on a living room that is supposed to be a Chicago living room. Wednesday the curtain goes up at 8 P.M. The next day the New Haven papers will say what they think of our efforts. A great deal of money has been spent and a lot of people have done some hard, hard work, and it may be the beginning of many different careers.

The actors are very good and the director is a very talented man—so if it is a poor show I won't be able to blame a soul but your youngest daughter.

Mama, it is a play that tells the truth about people, Negroes and life and I think it will help a lot of people to understand how we are just as complicated as they are—and just as mixed up—but above all, that we have among our miserable and downtrodden ranks—people who are the very essence of human dignity. That is what, after all the laughter and tears, the play is supposed to say. I hope it will make you very proud. See you soon. Love to all. (*YGB*, p. 91)

> QUESTION: *Is there a character in the play who represents Lorraine Hansberry?*

"The college student—Beneatha. I had a great deal of fun with this character. First of all I knew if the play ever got to Broadway, she would be the kind of character that people had never seen before—a Negro girl with actual pretensions of any sort—it's just unknown to theater and I also had a great deal of fun making fun of her a little bit because it's a pleasure to sit back eight years later and see yourself as you think you were. What she reflects symbolically is a very legitimate and active sentiment among American Negro intellectuals and among much larger sections of Negro life, that repudiates much of what has come to us through cultural experience and historical experience that we think is not necessarily as valid as we have been told that it is. And since the 1930s there has been quite a movement that feels that what we want now is a recognition of the beauty of things African and the beauty of things black, and this girl represents part of this development—as I do, I think." (Mike Wallace interview, 1959)

On Walter Lee's Comment:"We're all tied up in a race of people who don't know how to do nothing but moan, pray and have babies."

"He's an individual. He's one character in a play—representative of a good many people. This is inner group bitterness. When one can't speak against anyone else, one indicts one's own. It's very common. People have done this always. And he means this to hurt. It's a line that's directed toward his wife in the play. It's a way of turning the attack within for his own personal reasons. I think if you had a conversation with Walter Lee Younger, he'd have other things to tell you. But in that moment, he is trying to hurt her." (Mike Wallace interview, 1959)

On What People of Any Race Can Learn from This Play

"I have a suspicion of the universal humanity of all people. I think it is possible to reach it. And I think in the moment when they are sitting in the theater and they murmur in favor of the family and they applaud a particular action, I believe that almost every human being there genuinely wishes it to happen. To what extent that any member of the audience comes out of the theater at any time and retains the emotion of a moment within the theater I certainly couldn't begin to guess. In a much larger way, it may have affirmative effects." (Mike Wallace interview, 1959)

On the Affirmative Ending of the Play

"For me this is one of the most affirmative periods in history. I'm very pleased that those peoples in the world that I feel closest to, the colonial peoples, the African peoples, the Asian peoples, are in an insurgent mood. They are in the process of transforming the world, and I think for the better. I can't quite understand pessimism at this moment. Unless, of course, one is wedded to things that are dying out like colonialism, like racism. Walter Lee Younger and his family are necessarily tied to this international movement, whether they have consciousness of it or not, they belong to an affirmative movement in history. Anything that he does that is the least positive has implications that embrace all of us. I feel that his moving into the new house, his decision, is in a way a reply to those who say all guilt is equal, all questions lack clarity that it's hard to know what you should fight for or against, that there are things to do—that the new house has many shapes, and we must make some decisions in this country as this man does." (Mike Wallace interview, 1959)

On Mama

"This is a very strong woman. This is a woman who keeps her authority in any way that she has to, emotionally, physically, however. I think she's a great woman. But she can be wrong—terribly wrong." (Mike Wallace interview, 1959)

On What Joseph Asagai Represents in This Play

"He represents two things: he represents, first of all, the true intellectual. This is a young man who is so absolutely confident in his understanding and his perception about the world that he has no need of any of the façade of pseudo intellectuality— for any of the pretenses and the nonsense. He can already kid about all the features of intense nationalism because he's been there and he understands beyond that point. He's already concerned about the human race on a new level. He's a true, genuine intellectual. So that he doesn't have time or interest except for amusement in useless passion, in useless promenading of ideas. That's partially what he represents. The other thing that he represents is much more overt. I was aware that on a Broadway stage they have never seen an African who didn't have his shoes hanging around his neck and a bone through his nose or his ears or something. And I thought that even just theatrically speaking this would most certainly be refreshing, and what this fellow represents in the play is the emergence of an articulate and deeply conscious colonial intelligentsia in the world. " (Studs Terkel interview, 1959)

IN OTHERS' WORDS

JAMES BALDWIN

SWEET LORRAINE   [1969]

That's the way I always felt about her, and so I won't apologize for calling her that now. *She* understood it: in that far too brief a time when we walked and talked and laughed and drank together, sometimes in the streets and bars and restaurants of the Village, sometimes at her house, sometimes at my house, sometimes gracelessly fleeing the houses of others; and sometimes seeming, for anyone who didn't know us, to be having a knockdown, drag-out battle. We spent a lot of time arguing about history and tremendously related subjects in her Bleecker Street and, later Waverly Place flat. And often, just when I was certain that she was about to throw me out, as being altogether too rowdy a type, she would stand up, her hands on her hips (for these down-home sessions she always wore slacks) and pick up my empty glass as though she intended to throw it at me. Then she would walk into the kitchen, saying, with a haughty toss of her head, "Really, Jimmy. You ain't *right,* child!" With which stern put down, she would hand me another drink and launch into a brilliant analysis of just why I wasn't "right." I would often stagger down her stairs as the sun came up, usually in the middle of a paragraph and always in the middle of a laugh. That marvelous laugh. That marvelous face. I loved her, she was my sister and my comrade. Her going did not so much make me lonely as make me realize how lonely we were. We had that respect for each other which perhaps is only felt by people on the same side of the barricades, listening to the accumulating thunder of the hooves of horses and the threads of tanks.

The first time I ever saw Lorraine was at the Actors' Studio, in the winter of '57–58. She was there as an observer of the Workshop Production of *Giovanni's Room.*[1] She was way up in the bleachers, taking on some of the biggest names in the American theater because she had liked the play and they, in the main, hadn't. I was enormously grateful to her, she seemed to speak for me; and afterwards she talked to me with a gentleness and generosity never to be forgotten. A small, shy, determined person, with that strength dictated by absolutely impersonal ambition: she was not trying to "make it"—she was trying to keep the faith.

We really met, however, in Philadelphia, in 1959, when *A Raisin in the Sun* was at the beginning of its amazing career. Much has been written about this play; I personally feel that it will demand a far less guilty and constricted people than the present-day Americans to be able to assess it at all; as an historical achievement, anyway, no one can gainsay its importance. What is relevant here is that I had never in my life seen so many black people in the theater. And the reason was that never before, in the entire history of the American theater, had so much of the truth of black people's lives been seen on the stage. Black people ignored the theater because the theater had always ignored them.

But, in *Raisin,* black people recognized that house and all the people in it—the mother, the son, the daughter, and the daughter-in-law, and supplied the play with an interpretative element which could not be present in the minds of white people: a kind of claustrophobic terror, created not only by their knowledge of the house but by their knowledge of the streets. And when the curtain came down, Lorraine and I found ourselves in the backstage alley, where she was immediately mobbed. I produced a pen and Lorraine handed me her handbag and began signing autographs. "It only happens once," she said. I stood there and watched. I watched the people, who loved Lorraine for what she had brought to them; and watched Lorraine, who loved the people for what they brought to *her.* It was not, for her, a matter of being admired. She was being corroborated and confirmed. She was wise enough and honest enough to recognize that black American artists are a very special case. One is not merely an artist and one is not judged merely as an artist: the black people crowding around Lorraine, whether or not they considered her an artist, assuredly considered her a

[1]**Giovanni's Room** a novel by James Baldwin published in 1956

witness. This country's concept of art and artists has the effect, scarcely worth mentioning by now, of isolating the artist from the people. One can see the effect of this in the irrelevance of so much of the work produced by celebrated white artists; but the effect of this isolation on a black artist is absolutely fatal. He *is,* already, as a black American citizen, isolated from most of his white countrymen. At the crucial hour, he can hardly look to his artistic peers for help, for they do not know enough about him to be able to correct him. To continue to grow, to remain in touch with himself, he needs the support of that community from which, however, all of the pressures of American life incessantly conspire to remove him. And when he is effectively removed, he falls silent—and the people have lost another hope.

5   Much of the strain under which Lorraine worked was produced by her knowledge of this reality, and her determined refusal to be destroyed by it. She was a very young woman, with an overpowering vision, and fame had come to her early—she must certainly have wished, often enough, that fame had seen fit to drag its feet a little. For fame and recognition are not synonymous, especially not here, and her fame was to cause her to be criticized very harshly, very loudly, and very often by both black and white people who were unable to believe, apparently, that a really serious intention could be contained in so glamorous a frame. She took it all with a kind of astringent good humor, refusing, for example, even to consider defending herself when she was being accused of being a "slum-lord" because of her family's real-estate holdings in Chicago. I called her during that time, and all she said—with a wry laugh—was, "My God, Jimmy, do you realize you're only the second person who's called me today? And you know how my phone kept ringing *before!*" She was not surprised. She was devoted to the human race, but she was not romantic about it.

JULIUS LESTER

THE HEROIC DIMENSION IN A RAISIN IN THE SUN   [1972]

A Raisin in the Sun is no intellectual abstraction about upward mobility and conspicuous consumption. It goes right to the core of practically every black family in the ghettos of Chicago, New York, Los Angeles, and elsewhere. Whether they have a picture of Jesus, Martin Luther King, or Malcolm X on the lead-painted walls of their rat-infested tenement, all of them want to get the hell out of there as quickly as they can. Maybe black militants don't know it, or don't want to admit it, but Malcolm X made a down payment on a house in a suburban community a few weeks before he was murdered. And one surely can't accuse Malcolm of bourgeois aspirations. He merely wanted what every black wants—a home of his own adequate to his needs, at a minimum, and the fulfillment of his desires, at the most. . . . *A Raisin in the Sun* is most definitely about "human dignity" because Lorraine Hansberry is concerned with the attitude we must have toward material things if we are to be their master and not their slave. Is that attitude to be Mama's? Or is it to be Walter's? And, for blacks, locked out from these things for so long, the question is a crucial one. As blacks acquire more and more of America's material offerings, are they, too, going to be transformed by their acquisitions into mindless consumers like the majority of whites? Or are they going to continue to walk in the path of righteousness like their forebears? Lorraine Hansberry summarized it well when, in a letter, she wrote of the play:

. . . we cannot . . . very well succumb to monetary values and know the survival of certain interior aspects of man which . . . must remain if we are to loom larger than other creatures on this planet. . . . Our people fight daily and magnificently for a more comfortable material base for their lives; they desperately need and hourly sacrifice for clean homes, decent food, personal and group dignity and the abolition of terroristic violence as their children's heritage. So, in that sense, I am certainly a materialist in the first order.

However, the distortion of this aspiration surrounds us in the form of an almost maniacal lusting for "acquisitions." It seems to have absorbed the national mentality and Negroes, to be sure, have certainly been affected by it. The young man in the play, Walter Lee, is meant to symbolize their number. Consequently, in the beginning, he dreams not so much of being comfortable and imparting the most meaningful gifts to his son (education in depth, humanist values, a worship of dignity) but merely of being what it seems to him the "success" portion of humankind is— "rich." Toward this end he is willing to make an old trade; urgently willing. On the fact that some aspect of his society has brought him to this point, the core of the drama hangs.

Walter blames himself, his wife, and his mother for what he sees as his personal failure. And only at the end of the play does it become possible for him to realize that there is a puppeteer manipulating him, a puppeteer who brought him dangerously close to destroying his family and himself.

5   The climax of the play comes after Walter's deal to get a liquor license falls through. Mama Younger has made a $3,500 down payment on a house and gives the remaining money to Walter to do with as he wishes after he deposits $2,500 in a savings account for Beneatha's education. Walter, however, takes the entire $6,500 and gives it to one of his two future "partners." One of the "partners" absconds with the money. A Mr. Lindner, a white man from the neighborhood into which they are to move, comes and offers to buy the house from them for more than they would eventually pay. The whites in the neighborhood do not want a black family moving in. Previously, Walter had scornfully turned the man down. However, when he learns that his money has been stolen, he calls Mr. Lindner on the phone and tells him that they will sell the house. Mr. Lindner comes over and Walter finds that he is unable to go through with it. There is something in him—a little bit of self-respect is still left; he tells Mr. Lindner that they are going to move in. And with Walter making his first step toward being a man, a *black* man, the play ends.

Few see the heroism in Walter's simple act of assertion. Indeed, how many who have seen the play or the movie have not thought that Walter was a fool for *not* accepting the money? How one views Walter's act is a direct reflection of how much one accepts the American dream. And there is the significance of the fact that the play ends with the Youngers moving into a "white" neighborhood. To see this as a confirmation of the American dream is to accept the myth that blacks have wanted nothing more than to be integrated with whites. In actuality, the fact that the neighborhood is white is the least important thing about it. It merely happened to be the neighborhood in which Mama Younger could find a nice house she could afford. And it is this simple, practical element which has always been mistaken by whites as a desire on the part of blacks to be "integrated." But why, the question could be raised, would the Youngers persist in moving into a neighborhood where they are not wanted, where they may be subjected to harassment or even physical violence? They persist, as all blacks persist, not because it is any great honor to live among whites, but because one cannot consider himself a human being as long as he acquiesces to restrictions placed upon him by others, particularly if those restrictions are based solely on race or religion. If Walter had accepted the money, he would have been saying, in graphic language, You are right, we are niggers and don't have the right to live where we can afford to. But, with that earthy eloquence of a black still close to his roots, Walter says, "We have decided to move into our house because my father—my father—he earned it." And, in that realization, Walter learns also that it was not a black woman who castrated him. It was America and his own acceptance of America's values. No woman can make him a man. He has to do it himself.

He is a hero, a twentieth-century hero. We still long, of course, for the heroes who seemed to ride history as if it were a bronco and they were champion rodeo riders. But those heroes—if they were ever real—come from a time when life, perhaps, was somewhat less complex. But the problems that face man in the latter twentieth century are large, larger than any one of us, and the sword of a knight in armor is laughable to the dragons roaming our countryside. Our heroes are more difficult to recognize only because they appear so small beside the overwhelming enemies they must slay. But because they appear small does not mean that they are, and it does not make their acts less heroic. Walter Lee Younger has his contemporary historic counterpart in the person of a small, quiet black woman named Rosa Parks who refused to get out of a seat on a bus in Montgomery, Alabama. It would have been so easy for her to have relinquished her seat to a white person that day—as it would have been easy for Walter to have taken the money. But something in her, as in him, said No. And in that quiet dissent, both of them said Yes to human dignity. They said No to those who would define them and thereby deny their existence, and by saying No, they began to define themselves. There have been many Rosa Parks, but few of them have mysteriously set in motion a whole movement for social change. Walter Lee Younger is one of those whose act probably set nothing in motion. And that only increases its heroic dimension. In an article in *The Village Voice,* which compared Walter to Willy Loman, Lorraine Hansberry described the hero she saw in Walter Younger.

For if there are no waving flags and marching songs at the barricades as Walter marches out with his little battalion, it is not because the battle lacks nobility. On the contrary, he has picked up in his way, still imperfect and wobbly in his small view of human destiny, what I believe Arthur Miller once called "the golden thread of history." He becomes, in spite of those who are too intrigued with despair and hatred of man to see it, King Oedipus refusing to tear out his eyes, but attacking the Oracle instead. He is that last Jewish patriot manning his rifle in the burning ghetto at Warsaw; he is that young girl who swam into sharks to save a friend a few weeks ago; he is Anne Frank, still believing in people; he is the nine small heroes of Little Rock; he is Michelangelo creating David, and Beethoven bursting forth with the Ninth Symphony. He is all those things because he has finally reached out in his tiny moment and caught that sweet essence which is human dignity, and it shines like the old star-touched dream that is in his eyes.

ANNE CHENEY

THE AFRICAN HERITAGE IN A RAISIN IN THE SUN   [1984]

A moving testament to the strength and endurance of the human spirit, *A Raisin in the Sun* is a quiet celebration of the black family, the importance of African roots, the equality of women, the vulnerability of marriage, the true value of money, the survival of the individual, and the nature of man's dreams. A well-made play, *Raisin* at first seems a plea for racial tolerance or a fable of man's overcoming an insensitive society, but the simple eloquence of the characters elevates the play into a universal representation of all people's hopes, fears, and dreams.

On January 19, 1959, a timid Lorraine Hansberry wrote her mother about *Raisin:* "Mama, it is a play that tells the truth about people, Negroes and life and I think it will help a lot of people to understand how we are just as complicated as they are . . . people who are the very essence of human dignity. . . . I hope it will make you very proud." Indeed, *A Raisin in the Sun* made not only Nannie Perry Hansberry proud but also artists—both black and white. *Raisin* was the first play by a black writer ever to win the prestigious New York Drama Critics' Circle Award. The play would become "an American classic, published and produced in some thirty languages abroad and in thousands of productions across the country. . . . James Baldwin [said]: "Never before in the entire history of the American theatre had so much of the truth of Black people's lives been seen on the stage." Despite the earlier contributions of Langston Hughes, David Littlejohn wrote, "It would not be unfair in dating the emergence of a serious and mature Negro theatre in America from 1959, the date of Lorraine Hansberry's *A Raisin in the Sun*. . . . "

Today some black critics feel that *A Raisin in the Sun* is a play whose time has passed—a simplistic, halting treatment of race relations. Some are confused by Hansberry's professed nationalism, when she seems to favor integration. Harold Cruse even calls *Raisin* a "cleverly written piece of glorified soap opera." Hansberry used the traditional form of the well-made play in *Raisin,* especially observing the unities of action, place, and time. The action of the play is carefully delineated: act 1 serves as the beginning, act 2 as the middle, and act 3 as the tightly knit end. Furthermore, all action is carefully and causally related. Hansberry strictly abides by the unity of place: all action transpires in one room of the Youngers' South Side Chicago apartment. Stretching the unity of time from one day to one month (not unusual for a modern dramatist), Hansberry still maintains unity of impression with the central emotional concerns of the Younger family: Walter's search for a dream, Lena's faith in God and the family, Beneatha's hope for a new world.

Hansberry needed this rather traditional form to control the innovative ideas and themes of *Raisin.* Far from being a stereotyped or romanticized treatment of black life, the play embodies ideas that have been uncommon on the Broadway stage in any period. Resurrecting the ideas of the Harlem renaissance and anticipating the new thinking of the 1960s, Hansberry examines the importance of African roots, traditional versus innovative women, the nature of marriage, the real meaning of money, the search for human dignity. Most significantly, she addresses the sensitive question of to what extent people, in liberating themselves from the burdens of discrimination, should aspire to a white middle-class way of life.

5   During her *Freedom* years, Lorraine Hansberry continued to study African history with encouragement from Paul Robeson, W.E.B. Du Bois, and Louis Burnham. "She had spent hours of her younger years poring over maps of the African continent. . . . She was at one, texture, blood . . . with the sound of a mighty Congo drum." She imaginatively knew the lions, drumbeats, quiet sandy nights, respected the antiquity of Ethiopia founded in 1000 B.C. Stirred by Kenya and Ghana wresting control from Europe and England, Hansberry inevitably incorporated her knowledge of Africa in her first play. More than earlier playwrights, Hansberry made Africa a serious, yet natural, issue on Broadway.

In *Raisin* even George Murchison, Beneatha's beau, has an awareness of his African past. In the fever of Walter Lee's and Beneatha's mock African dance in act 2, George remarks sarcastically: "In one second we will hear all about the great Ashanti empires; the great Songhay civilizations; and the great sculpture of Benin—and then some poetry in the Bantu." George had probably learned in a college atmosphere that the Songhai empire was a powerful western African kingdom, which garnered wealth from its export of ivory and gold between 850 and 1500 A.D. (Mali and Ghana—not to be confused with the modern state of Ghana—were equally old and powerful empires.) Along the coast of Nigeria, Benin was another expansive empire, noted for its bronze and gold art objects, that came to power around 1500. Coming to power about 1700, Ashanti was still another western kingdom famous for its heroic warriors.

In the stage direction, Hansberry writes that Lena has "the noble bearing of the women of the Hereros of Southwest Africa," who were essentially a pastoral people. Thus Hansberry identifies Lena as an "earth mother," one who nurtures both her family and her plant as well as she can. But Lena reveals her total ignorance of African history by a parroting of Beneatha's earlier remarks in her politely naïve, unwittingly humorous speech to Joseph Asagai, the young Nigerian visitor: "I think it's so sad the way our American Negroes don't know nothing about Africa 'cept Tarzan and all that. And all that money they pour into these churches when they ought to be helping you people over there drive out them French and Englishmen done taken away your Land."

Most of the African material in *A Raisin in the Sun,* however, surfaces in conversations between Beneatha and Joseph Asagai. Touched by Beneatha's beauty and idealism, Asagai lovingly nicknames her Alaiyo—a Yoruban word for "One for Whom Bread—Food—Is Not Enough." In act 3, after Walter Lee has been duped out of his $6,500, Asagai visits an embittered, distraught Beneatha. Speaking of his beloved Nigeria, Asagai reveals his basic philosophy of life, of Africa: "A household in preparation of a journey . . . it is another feeling. Something full of the flow of life. . . . Movement, progress. . . . It makes me think of Africa." Perhaps he sees in Beneatha a microcosmic America—one struggling to overthrow the limitations imposed on her by an alien culture.

Asagai's village in Nigeria is one where most people cannot read, where many have not even seen a book. In the village, there are mountains and stars, cool drinks from gourds at the well, old songs, people who move slowly, anciently. But Nigeria also has guns, murder, revolution, illiteracy, disease, ignorance. Asagai understands the inevitability of change and progress in Africa; he imagines for a moment the consequences should he betray the movement. "Don't you see that . . . young men and women . . . my own black countrymen . . . [may] . . . step out of the shadows some evening and slit my then useless throat?" Rebuking Beneatha for becoming discouraged over one small frustration (Walter's losing the money), Asagai views his possible death as an advance toward freedom for himself and his people. "They who might kill me even . . . actually replenish me." Asagai's beliefs certainly contribute to Beneatha's transition from brittle idealist to a more tolerant human being.

10   In an interview with Studs Terkel (Chicago, May 2, 1959), Lorraine Hansberry referred to Joseph Asagai as her "favorite character" in *Raisin*. He represents the "true intellectual" with no pretense, no illusions. A revolutionary and nationalist, he realizes that initially black African leaders may be as corrupt as their white predecessors (Idi Amin of Uganda bore out this theory in the 1970s). Nevertheless, he shares Hansberry's conviction that "before you can start talking about what's wrong with independence, get it." More the idealist than the practical, effective leader—compared to Kenyatta and Nkrumah—Asagai is willing to die at the hands of his countrymen for the general good and freedom. (Harold Issacs suggests that his name derives from the Zulu word *asegai*, "sawed-off spear.") On a more obvious level, Asagai certainly refutes the stage stereotype of the African with "a bone through his nose, or his ears."

In *A Raisin in the Sun,* then, Africa becomes a symbol of a proud heritage and a troublesome but hopeful future. To Hansberry's great credit, Africa is a natural, at times humorous, element in the Younger family—as Walter Lee shouts "HOT DAMN! FLAMING SPEAR," as Beneatha dresses in Nigerian robes, as Mama speaks of Tarzan, churches, and Englishmen.

STEVEN R. CARTER

HANSBERRY'S ARTISTIC MISSTEP   [1994]

Unfortunately, Hansberry's vigorous, sharp, and usually intriguing characterization of Beneatha is slightly marred by her one serious artistic misstep in *A Raisin in the Sun.* This occurs when Beneatha tells Lena and Ruth about the guitar lessons she has just started and they remind her about "the horseback-riding club for which she bought that fifty-five dollar riding habit that's been hanging in the closet ever since!" On the whole, this scene portrays Beneatha's striving for self-expression with warm humor and a touch of self-mockery that almost always pleases the audiences. The problem is that only a short time earlier Walter had angrily demanded that Beneatha show more gratitude for the financial sacrifices he and Ruth have made for her, and Ruth had denied her son the fifty cents he requested for school. It is inconceivable that a woman who could refuse such a small sum to a dearly beloved son would so casually accept the squandering of a much larger contribution to a mere sister-in-law, and even if, by some miracle, she were able to accept it out of an all-embracing feminist sisterhood (which doesn't fit Ruth's overall character), she could not do so with such ease. Worse still, lightly tossing away all this money in the face of the family's dire need makes Beneatha seem monstrously selfish rather than mildly selfish as Hansberry had intended. Granted, Hansberry's main concern in the scene was the general relationship between the two older women and Beneatha, particularly their fond amusement at the younger woman's forms of self-expression, which are so different from anything they have ever done, and their vicarious delight at her ability to break free from restrictions, including that of having to weigh the cost of everything. However, on this rare occasion, by concentrating exclusively on the moment and neglecting to see its relation to previous parts of the play, Hansberry, to a small but disconcerting extent, damages the whole.

MARGARET B. WILKERSON

HANSBERRY'S AWARENESS OF CULTURE AND GENDER   [1994]

As a black writer, Hansberry was caught in a paradox of expectations. She was expected to write about that which she "knew best," the black experience, and yet that expression was doomed to be called parochial and narrow. Hansberry, however, challenged these facile categories and forced a redefinition of the term "universality," one which would include the dissonant voice of an oppressed American minority. As a young college student, she had wandered into a rehearsal of Sean O'Casey's *Juno and the Paycock*. Hearing in the wails and moans of the Irish characters a universal cry of human misery, she determined to capture that sound in the idiom of her own people—so that it could be heard by all. "One of the most sound ideas in dramatic writing," she would later conclude, "is that in order to create the universal, you must pay very great attention to the specific. Universality, I think, emerges from truthful identity of what is. . . . In other words, I think people, to the extent we accept them and believe them as who they're supposed to be, to that extent they can become everybody." Such a choice by a black writer posed an unusual challenge to the literary establishment and a divided society ill-prepared to comprehend its meaning.

"All art is ultimately social: that which agitates and that which prepares the mind for slumber," Hansberry argued, attacking another basic tenet held by traditional critics. One of the most fundamental illusions of her time and culture, she believed, is the idea that art is not and should not make a social statement. The belief in "l'art pour l'art" permeates literary and theatrical criticism, denying the integral relationship between society and art. "The writer is deceived who thinks he has some other choice. The question is not whether one will make a social statement in one's work—but only *what* the statement will say, for if it says anything at all, it will be social."

It would have been impossible for a person of her background and sensitivity to divorce herself from the momentous social and political events of the 1950s and 1960s. This period witnessed the beginning of a Cold War between the U.S. and Soviet superpowers, a rising demand by blacks for civil rights at home, and a growing intransigence by colonized peoples throughout the world. Isolation is the enemy of black writers, Hansberry believed; they are obligated to participate in the intellectual and social affairs of humankind everywhere.

This abhorrence for narrowness and parochialism led her to examine the hidden alliance between racism and sexism long before it was popular to do so, and to shape a vision cognizant of the many dimensions of colonialism and oppression.

Anticipating the women's movement of the 1970s, Hansberry was already aware of the peculiar oppression under which women lived and the particular devastation visited upon women of color.

5   With the statement "I was born black and a female," Hansberry immediately established the basis for a tension that informed her world view. Her consciousness, of both ethnicity and gender from the very beginning, brought awareness of two key forces of conflict and oppression in the contemporary world. Because she embraced these dual truths despite their implicit competition for her attention (a competition exacerbated by external pressures), her vision was expansive enough to contain and even synthesize what to others would be contradictions. Thus, she was amused in 1955 at progressive friends who protested whenever she posed "so much as an itsy-bitsy analogy between the situation, say, of the Negro people in the U.S.—and women." She was astonished to be accused by a woman of being bitter and of thinking that men are beasts simply because she expressed the view that women are oppressed. "Must I hate 'men' any more than I hate 'white people'—because some of them are savage and others commit savage acts," she asked herself. "Of course not!" she answered vehemently.

This recognition of the tension implicit in her blackness and femaleness was the starting point for her philosophical journey from the South Side of Chicago to the world community. The following quote charts the journey and the expansion of Hansberry's consciousness, which is unconstrained by culture and gender, but which at the same time refuses to diminish the importance of either.

I was born on the South Side of Chicago. I was born black and a female. I was born in a depression after one world war, and came into my adolescence during another. While I was still in my teens the first atom bombs were dropped on human beings at Nagasaki and Hiroshima. And by the time I was twenty-three years old, my government and that of the Soviet Union had entered actively into the worst conflict of nerves in human history—the Cold War.

I have lost friends and relatives through cancer, lynching, and war. I have been personally the victim of physical attack which was the offspring of racial and political hysteria. I have worked with the handicapped and seen the ravages of congenital diseases that we have not yet conquered, because we spend our time and ingenuity in far less purposeful wars; I have known persons afflicted with drug addiction and alcoholism and mental illness. I see daily on the streets of New York, street gangs and prostitutes and beggars. I have, like all of you, on a thousand occasions seen indescribable displays of man's very real inhumanity to man, and I have come to maturity, as we all must, knowing that greed and malice and indifference to human misery and bigotry and corruption, brutality, and perhaps above all else, ignorance—the prime ancient and persistent enemy of man—abound in this world.

I say all of this to say that one cannot live with sighted eyes and feeling heart and not know and react to the miseries which afflict this world.

10   Her "sighted eyes and feeling heart" were what enabled her to hear the wail of her own people in O'Casey's *Juno and the Paycock,* a play steeped in Irish history and tradition. And those eloquent moans sent her forth to capture that collective cry in a black idiom.

Hansberry's cognizance of being black and female formed the basis for her comprehensive world view. Just as she could accept fully the implications and responsibility of both blackness and femaleness, so was she also aware of the many other competing and equally legitimate causes which grow out of humankind's misery. The one issue that deeply concerned her but that she did not address publicly was homosexuality. The repressive atmosphere of the 1950s, coupled with the homophobia of the general society, including politically left organizations, caused her to suppress her writings that explored issues of sexuality and gender relations. Nevertheless, she pushed and teased boundaries by probing the nature of the individual within the specifics of culture, ethnicity, and gender. In the midst of her expansiveness, she refused to diminish the pain, suffering, or truths of any one group in order to benefit another, a factor which made her plays particularly rich and her characters thoroughly complex. Hence, she could write authentically about a black family in *A Raisin in the Sun* and yet produce, in the same instance, a play which appealed to both blacks and whites, bridging for a moment the historical and cultural gaps between them.

Her universalism, which redefines that much abused term, grew out of a deep, complex encounter with the specific terms of human experience as it occurs for blacks, women, whites, and many other groups of people. Her universalism was not facile, nor did it gloss over the things that divide people. She engaged those issues, worked through them to find whatever may be, *a priori,* the human commonality that lies beneath. It was as if she believed that one can understand and embrace the human family (with all its familial warfare) only to the extent that one can engage the truths (however partisan they may seem) of a social, cultural individual. "We must turn our eyes outward," she wrote, "but to do so we must also turn them inward toward our people and their complex and still transitory culture." When she turned inward, she saw not only color but gender as well—a prism of humanity.

MICHAEL ANDERSON

A RAISIN IN THE SUN: *A LANDMARK LESSON IN BEING BLACK*   [1999]

They had never seen anything like it. The theater critics, hurrying down the aisles under the pressure of deadline, paused at the rear of the Ethel Barrymore Theater. The date was March 11, 1959. For a few moments they stopped considering the words with which they would salute this poetically named play, *A Raisin in the Sun.* Instead, they watched the first-night audience deliver its own verdict: on its feet and willing to applaud, it seemed, for eternity.

The cast took its curtain calls—Sidney Poitier, Claudia McNeil, Ruby Dee, Diana Sands, Lonne Elder 3d, Lou Gossett Jr., Ivan Dixon, Glynn Turman, John Fiedler, Ed Hall, Douglas Turner—as the applause engulfed the theater. The stage manager opened and closed the curtain. The director, Lloyd Richards, joined his players, but the ovations swelled ever louder and more insistent: "Author! Author! Author!"

Finally, Mr. Poitier descended to a fourth-row aisle seat, where the twenty-eight-year-old playwright sat, thrilled rigid at the reception of her first produced play. On the arm of her leading man, Lorraine Hansberry took the stage.

"It was as if the audience that night uniquely understood that they had not just seen a play but had attended a historical event," the play's coproducer, Philip Rose, said recently, reminiscing about the opening on the eve of its fortieth anniversary this Thursday.

5   In that remarkable theatrical season of 1958–59, Broadway had seen Paul Newman and Geraldine Page open (the previous night) in Tennessee Williams's *Sweet Bird of Youth*, directed by Elia Kazan; Helen Hayes and Kim Stanley in *A Touch of the Poet* by Eugene O'Neill, directed by Harold Clurman; and Christopher Plummer and Raymond Massey in Archibald MacLeish's *J.B.*, also directed by Mr. Kazan.

But until that evening, Broadway had never seen a play written by a black woman, nor a play with a black director, nor a commercially produced drama about black life, rather than musicals or comedy. The Broadway premiere of *A Raisin in the Sun* was as much a milestone in the nation's social history as it was in American theater. "Never before," commented James Baldwin, "had so much of the truth of black people's lives been seen onstage."

Hansberry's story—about the black Younger family's decision to risk moving from their "rat-trap" on the South Side of Chicago to a three-bedroom house in an all-white neighborhood—interwove prescient observations about identity, feminism, and personal ethics. Unlike the wooden "problem plays" about blacks that preceded it, *A Raisin in the Sun* seemed steeped in human drama. The cruelties of racism— "What happens to a dream deferred/ Does it dry up/ Like a raisin in the sun?" in the words of the Langston Hughes poem that gave the play its title—are illuminated through the dynamics of conflict and love between mother and son, husband and wife, brother and sister.

Kenneth Tynan remarked in his review of *A Raisin in the Sun* in *The New Yorker* that "a play is not an entity in itself, it is a part of history." In that sense, the presence of the play on Broadway appeared to be a triumph of determined idealism for those involved. The 1960s would see productions of *The Blacks*, the drama by Jean Genet about racism, as well as works by the black playwrights LeRoi Jones (later Amiri Baraka) and Ed Bullins. Lonne Elder 3rd would go on to write the acclaimed 1969 play *Ceremonies in Dark Old Men*.

But in the 1950s, before the acclaim that greeted *A Raisin in the Sun*, "Broadway was not ready for a play about a black family," Mr. Richards, the director, said.

10   What Broadway knew about black people, Hansberry once told a reporter, involved "cardboard characters, cute dialect bits, or hip-swinging musicals from exotic scores." (And few enough of those: in the seventy-seven productions of the 1958–59 season, Actors Equity reported that the number of Broadway parts for black actors totaled twenty-four.)

The inspiration for *A Raisin in the Sun*, its author said, came after she had seen a play in 1956 that left her "disgusted with a whole body of material about Negroes." That night, she told her husband, Robert Nemiroff, "I'm going to write a social drama about Negroes that will be good art." But since devoting herself full-time to playwriting in 1955, she had accomplished little—drafts of three plays had gone nowhere beyond sympathetic readings by her husband and friends.

She expected much the same in the late summer of 1957, when she and Nemiroff invited company for a dinner of spaghetti and banana cream pie to their fourth-floor walk-up on Bleecker Street in Greenwich Village.

Then Nemiroff began to read from the work that had possessed his wife for nearly a year. This time it was different. "The feeling was one of excitement," Mr. Rose said, during an interview in his office on the Upper West Side of Manhattan. After an animated discussion that went on into the night, Mr. Rose called Hansberry early the next morning. "I told her," he said, " 'this play has to get done, and it has to get done on Broadway.' "

Mr. Rose would end up as a producer of nearly two dozen plays, including *Purlie Victorious* (1961), *The Owl and the Pussycat* (1964), and the musical *Shenandoah* (1975). But at the time, he was thirty-six years old and in the music business, producing and publishing. He said he had assumed that there would be difficulties in getting a work by a first-time playwright on the boards, but not that raising the money would take nearly fifteen agonizing months.

15   Networking among his friends brought a response "somewhere between admiration and pity," he said, along with donations of $50 toward what they regarded as a lost cause. Established theatrical backers were equally skeptical. "Much as some expressed admiration," Nemiroff wrote in his introduction to the Modern Library edition of *A Raisin in the Sun*, the play "was turned down by virtually every established name in the business."

The conventional wisdom was that "nobody was going to pay those prices to see "a bunch of Negroes emoting," Hansberry later said in a letter included in *To Be Young, Gifted and Black*, a collection of her writings. (Nemiroff assembled the book after Hansberry's death from cancer at thirty-four in 1965, during the run of her second Broadway play, *The Sign in Sidney Brustein's Window;* Nemiroff died in 1991.)

"Very often, the professionals were respectful, even admiring that I would think of trying to get the play on," said Mr. Rose, who is writing a book about the production. "However, they could not see where it would make any money."

He did have one ace: his friend Sidney Poitier. Already a movie star, the actor had agreed to join the cast after being "overwhelmed by the power of the material," as he wrote in his own memoir, *This Life*. "Without Sidney Poitier," Mr. Rose said, "the play would never have seen the light of day."

Mr. Poitier was also responsible for the director. "I had a pact with Sidney Poitier," Mr. Richards said in an interview at his home on the Upper West Side. It dated to their time as students of the director and drama teacher Paul Mann. "One day, after class, Sidney said, 'If I ever do anything on Broadway, I want you to direct it.' "

20   In December 1957, Mr. Poitier introduced Mr. Richards, already known as an actor, teacher, and director, to Mr. Rose and Hansberry. They clicked.

"There was no question that I wanted to do the play," Mr. Richards said, remembering that when he and his wife first read it, "We laughed and cried; it was a wonderful evening reading." Still, it was the work of a neophyte, and he and Hansberry struggled until opening night to develop her script. Although not autobiographical, the story originated from an incident in Hansberry's childhood.

Her parents, politically and socially prominent in Chicago's black upper-middle class, agreed in 1938 to take the lead in the fight against housing segregation by buying a home in an all-white neighborhood near the University of Chicago. Hansberry would always remember being an eight-year-old who was "spat at, cursed and pummeled in the daily trek to and from school." She also remembered the nights her mother patrolled their house with a loaded pistol against the "literally howling mobs" that surrounded their home and once threw bricks through their windows.

But the real story of the play, Mr. Rose said, was not the family's move to the unreceptive white neighborhood but Walter Lee Younger, the character portrayed by Mr. Poitier, "and his development, his being able to accept certain responsibilities." With this as the goal, playwright and director began their work.

Meanwhile, the tasks of production went on, including casting.

25   "*Raisin* was a big breakthrough," said Ruby Dee. "The mainstream was not welcoming for African-American actors." She signed on even though she would not have the ingenue role of Walter Lee's sister that she desired; Diana Sands got the part, while Claudia McNeil portrayed his mother. Instead, Ms. Dee would play his wife, Ruth. "Another one of those put-upon wives. And they always seemed to be named Ruth!" But, she added: "I dusted off my disappointment. This was very important. It was going to be a Broadway show."

It would be, that is, if the money could be raised. Throughout 1958, Mr. Rose sought big-money angels. "The smart money on Broadway was not involved and would not be involved," Mr. Richards said. The $75,000 budget (equivalent to more than $420,000 today) would eventually come from a group of 147 investors—"more than any play on Broadway had had up to that time," Mr. Richards said. Mr. Poitier's wife, Juanita, invested $4,000 and "about two or three people, including Harry Belafonte, put in $2,000 each," Mr. Rose said. But the most significant investor was the playwright William Gibson, whose *Two for the Seesaw* had opened a successful run with Anne Bancroft and Henry Fonda in January 1958.

"I sent him the play," Mr. Rose recalled. "He called me and said: 'This play must get on Broadway.'" With that endorsement (and Mr. Gibson's own stake of $750), his tax consultant, David J. Cogan, a previous Broadway investor who initially had rejected *A Raisin in the Sun,* signed on as coproducer, and the financing was complete. Rehearsals began on December 27, 1958.

There was only one problem: no theater on Broadway would agree to rent to *A Raisin in the Sun.* The same arguments were repeated: a white audience would not pay to see a nonmusical about blacks. The possibility of black theatergoers was dismissed out of hand. And if they did come, would white patrons stay away—perhaps even boycott other shows? In 1958, the Supreme Court's landmark school desegregation decision was four years old; not until February 1960 would the student sit-ins put the racial equality movement permanently before the nation's conscience. Even in the relatively urbane climate of the Village, an interracial couple like Hansberry and Nemiroff could expect stares and denial of service in some restaurants.

Mr. Rose said he was advised to terminate the production until he could obtain a theater. Instead, he took a gamble: he booked the traditional tryout theaters in New Haven and Philadelphia. "And I prayed a lot," he said. "But I knew if we didn't do it, nothing was going to get done. The hope was that we had something so spectacular, Broadway couldn't ignore us." His daring paid off. The rave reviews for the four-night engagement in New Haven were matched during the two-week run in Philadelphia.

30   *A Raisin in the Sun* ended up playing for nineteen months at the Ethel Barrymore on Broadway. Hansberry won the New York Drama Critics Circle Award for best play, and most of the original cast starred in the 1961 film version, directed by Daniel Petrie. The 1973 musical *Raisin* was adapted from the play and produced by Nemiroff. The play has been translated into thirty languages.

In retrospect, Mr. Rose can joke that during the prolonged incubation of *A Raisin in the Sun* he was discouraged "only about half the time." But his explanation for his stubborn determination is simple: "I believed in it. I loved the play."

A Student Essay

Sara Roell

Dr. Madden

English 102

December 12, 200X

Lorraine Hansberry and the Realism of <u>A Raisin in the Sun</u>

The issue of racism and the emergence of civil rights among black men and women is evident in Lorraine Hansberry's <u>A Raisin in the Sun</u>. The play, written in 1957, is an interesting and at times wrenching depiction of a black family's struggle to achieve the American dream and escape the constraints of poverty. When the play first opened, in the early years of the civil rights movement, there was a great deal of controversy surrounding it because it was written realistically. Situations such as a black family moving into an all-white neighborhood were not common before this time period; they were just beginning to emerge. But disagreement exists about the motivation and the goals Lorraine Hansberry had in mind when she wrote the play. Hansberry has been praised by many critics, but also widely criticized.

Harold Cruse questions Hansberry's intentions for writing the play. "She intended to write a Negro play because she could not make her stage debut with anything else" (270). During that time the theater was primarily white, forcing authors to direct their writing to reflect white ideas or beliefs. He calls Hansberry evasive about her intentions and thinks she visualizes the Negro world through a "quasi-white orientation." Essentially, Cruse believes that the author is not a force for the black community, but rather supports the drive for racial integration in which the Negro working class must give up its ethnicity. Racism is portrayed in this play, but whether or not it is displayed realistically is also questioned.

The fact that Hansberry grew up as a middle-class African American rather than a "Harlem Negro" (Cruse 270), led many people to criticize her writing as unrealistic not only with reference to racism, but to the experiences of the working-class black American as well.

Walter is a middle-aged, black man who works as a chauffeur and becomes obsessed with his dreams of a business venture to give him financial independence. Living in overcrowded conditions and unable to provide adequately for his family, he feels that as an independent business owner he will attain economic gains as well as heightened value as a human being. "It can be asked, if <u>A Raisin in the Sun</u> is oriented to reality, why does Walter willingly give up those things, i.e., independence and economic success" (Adams 109). Adams believes that this is not a black play, that the conditions of the Younger family are universal and represent many ethnic groups.

Hansberry depicted the Youngers very realistically. In the late 1950s, it would have been very unusual for a black male to escape the poverty of an urban ghetto and its resulting oppression. Uneducated and with few available resources, Walter's dream is understandable, and although it turns out to be an unwise venture, it is just this obsession that helps him to escape his oppression even before it is realized. In fact, Walter is so taken with his idealized self that he is unable to alter his plan even when faced with his mother's moral reservations. While Walter seems superficial on one level, it is understandable how this new found money could contribute to his dreams of providing for himself and his family. An example of this is his statement that he wants to provide pearls for his wife, Ruth, as other men do for their wives: ". . . who decides which women is supposed to wear pearls in this world. I tell you I am a <u>man</u> . . . "(Hansberry 403).

Racism in this play is overtly expressed through the white character, Lindner, who represents the white majority of the time and in all likelihood a white minority even now. A less obvious representation of the impact of racism is portrayed in the internal, racial conflicts of the black characters themselves, especially Walter Lee Younger and his untrustworthy friend Willy.

Walter's growth is evident as his focus changes from materialism to his conviction that his family should move into an all-white neighborhood where blacks aren't wanted. At this juncture, Walter realizes that what really gives his life worth is standing up for the principle that should be basic to all people, that every individual has a basic right to choose where and how they live. Walter's decision to go forward with the move to the all-white neighborhood represents a victory for himself as a person and a black male.

Walter finally tells Lindner that his family will move despite protests and monetary incentives. "Few see the heroism in Walter's simple act of assertion" (Lester 417) in rejecting the white neighborhood association's offer to buy them out. Lindner is representative of the white majority of this time period. However, in his initial meeting with the Younger family his discomfort is evident when he realizes that the family members are open and likable. An example of this is when Ruth says, "Would you like another chair--you don't took comfortable" (Hansberry 389). Lindner was stumbling on his words and could not get directly to the point. It is interesting that Hansberry portrayed this character as polite and unthreatening, although his message was racially motivated. Given the climate of the times and the subsequent racial strife that occurred in the United States during the 1960s, creating a character in this way took what could have been an even more politically charged issue and softened it so that a white majority could be more reflective about their own prejudices.

Although we never see or meet him, we know that Willy has a background similar to Walter's. He is a black man living in a racially oppressed ghetto. Despite the fact that he has a similar background and has the same wants and needs as his friends, he steals the money. Racism and poverty provoke thinking like this by clouding a person's vision and making him feel entitled to have something he has never had an opportunity to acquire. Willy has no illusions about getting rich through Walter's liquor store. "You know Willy got his own ways" (Hansberry 395). He is street smart and is not bound by traditional moral codes or religious ideals that probably never worked in the past for him anyway. He lives in a neighborhood where if you need something, for the most part, you either do without it or get it any way you can.

These three characters, Walter Younger, Lindner, and Willy, are all dealing with racial issues that impact on them both globally and individually. In some ways Willy and Lindner are more similar to each other than to Walter. They have learned to negotiate the racism in their environments differently, but both with narrow focus. Walter Younger, while initially focused on escaping his situation and the effect that racism had on it, ultimately rises to hurdle his internal conflicts and stand up for beliefs that give him his individual worth.

"A Raisin in the Sun is most definitely about 'human dignity,' " writes Julius Lester. "Lorraine Hansberry is concerned with the attitude we must have toward material things if we are to be their master and not their slave" (416). The play was introduced into a society just beginning to become aware of many flaws, and people were forced to change their actions and feelings about the controversial issues of that time period. The debatable issues surrounding this play are not important when considering the issues within the play. They are universal.

The struggle of Walter Lee and his family can be understood by everyone. The public reaction to the play when it was first produced is evidence of the ignorance that people had toward its issues. The embarrassing issue of racism was something America didn't want to face, but civil rights leaders, dramatists like Hansberry, or the people themselves who were suffering from it forced us to see what we didn't want to or know how to deal with. Anne Cheney suggests how Americans should view A Raisin in the Sun: "Raisin at first seems a plea for racial tolerance or a fable of man's overcoming an insensitive society, but the simple eloquence of the characters elevates the play into a universal representation of all people's hopes, fears, and dreams" (419).

[New Page]

Works Cited

Adams, George R. "Black Literature: Black Militant Drama." American Imago. Vol. 28, No. 2. New York: Association for Applied Psychoanalysis, Inc., 1971. 107-28.

Cheney, Anne. "The African Heritage in A Raisin in the Sun." Exploring Literature. Ed. Frank Madden. 3rd ed. New York: Longman, 2007. 419-421.

Cruse, Harold. Lorraine Hansberry, The Crisis of the Negro Intellectual. New York: William Morrow & Company, Inc., 1967. 267-84.

Hansberry, Lorraine. A Raisin in the Sun. Exploring Literature. Ed. Frank Madden. 3rd ed. New York: Longman, 2007. 344-407.

Lester, Julius. "The Heroic Dimension in A Raisin in the Sun." Exploring Literature. Ed. Frank Madden. 3rd ed. New York: Longman, 2007. 416-418.

EXPLORING THE LITERATURE OF FAMILY AND FRIENDS: OPTIONS FOR MAKING CONNECTIONS AND ARGUMENTS

Making Connections

1. Consider the ways in which your family or friends have affected your life. Do any of the stories, poems, plays, or essays in this section remind you of your relationships with family or friends?

   Choose one or more of these works and write a response essay that compares your experience or circumstances with those in the literature.

2. Our families and friends can influence and shape our values, our behavior, our aspirations. These values can also strongly influence our response to literature. We may agree or disagree with what an author says or what characters say or do. So, too, literature may influence us and the formation of our values about family and friends.

   Choose one or more works in this section and write an essay about the ways in which this literature either provoked your moral judgment or enabled you to learn something that influenced your values.

Making an Argument

1. In his *Theory of Psychoanalysis,* Carl Jung, a pioneer and influential theorist in the field of psychology, wrote: "The little world of childhood with its familiar surroundings is a model of the greater world. The more intensely the family has stamped its character upon the child, the more it will tend to feel and see its earlier miniature world again in the bigger world of adult life."

   Consider this quote and write a critical essay about the way in which one or more works in this section exemplify the way that early family experiences influence how we see and experience the world.

2. Over two thousand years ago, Plato wrote in *Dialogues:* "Friends have all things in common." What do you think he meant?

   Are any of the selections in this section good examples of this adage about friendship? Write a critical essay about this quote and its application to one or more works in this section.

3. Choose a quote (or quotes) in the introduction to this section, Family and Friends (pp. 203–204) and pair it (or them) with one of the longer pieces in this section that either supports it or argues against it. For example, Benjamin Spock's statement about the instincts of parents to do what is best for their children might be paired with Tennessee Williams's *The Glass Menagerie,* which might be seen as an argument against it. If we chose Jean de la Fontaine's comment about the impossibility of pleasing all the world and one's father, we might choose Janice Mirikitani's poem "For My Father" to qualify and to support la Fontaine's statement.

   Write an essay that compares or contrasts a quote (or quotes) from the introduction with a story, poem, play, or essay that supports or argues against it.

A Research Option

Janice Mirikitani's poem "For My Father," Tennessee Williams's play *The Glass Menagerie,* and bell hooks's "Inspired Eccentricity" all have something important to say about family and friends. However, each of these works springs from a very different historical, social, or political context.

Expanding our exploration of literature to include the context in which these works were produced can be an enriching and enlightening experience. Choose one or more of these or other works in this section and write a research essay that includes secondary source material about the historical, social, or political background that influenced the creation of this literature.

Writing About Connections Across Themes

Most of the literature in the text has been organized into theme sections, but good literature is much too complex to be reduced to a single broad theme. Many of the works included under Family and Friends could just as easily fit under other themes—and in many cases works arranged in other themes could fit here as well.

Choose one or more of the following works from earlier chapters or other themes and consider how they can be linked to Family and Friends—and how this combination of the work with more than one theme provides additional insight into the literature and fresh topics for writing.

"Brave We Are"—p. 977
"Everyday Use"—p. 982
"In the Waiting Room"—p. 1000
From Faith and Doubt
"Young Goodman Brown"—p. 1167
"War"—p. 1205
"The Chrysanthemums"—p. 1208
"Do Not Go Gentle into That Good Night"—p. 1238

Collaboration: Writing and Revising with Your Peers

In addition to applying your own values and standards to writing about the literature in this section, you may find it beneficial to share and discuss your work with classmates. Getting feedback from others can help you generate and clarify your ideas and revise and edit your writing more effectively.

Choose a work, a topic, or one of the options for writing about family and friends above, and work with a partner or in a small group. Exchange journal entries or response sheets, generate questions together, do a group semantic map (see pp. 41–42), or simply share and respond to each other's ideas.

After you have written a rough draft of your essay, share it with a partner or your group. Respondents should function primarily as sensitive readers and give honest, constructive responses. They should try to be aware of each writer's purpose, discuss concerns particular to each writer, and comment on the effectiveness of the essay's organization, support, clarity, and voice (for a checklist for revision, see p. 46).

In the final stage of your writing, editing and proofreading might be done in a similar fashion. A partner or group of readers might help you check for correct grammar, spelling, punctuation, and typos (a checklist for editing is on p. 49).

A Writing/Research Portfolio Option

A portfolio is a collection of your work, related materials, and commentary about your work collected over time. Gathering materials in a portfolio will provide you with resources for research and development. You can use your portfolio to collect your writing about the literature in this section, find a topic to write about, revise or add to your work, or keep multiple drafts and monitor the changes you make as you revise. Among the resources you might include:

- Your responses to the quotes and prompts about family and friends at the beginning of this section, the questions you had right after you finished reading each piece of literature, or your journal entries.

- What your classmates, instructor, or published critics had to say about the literature and how their comments may have influenced your interpretation.

- Information you have gathered from the library and the Internet about the historical, social, and political context of the work or its author.

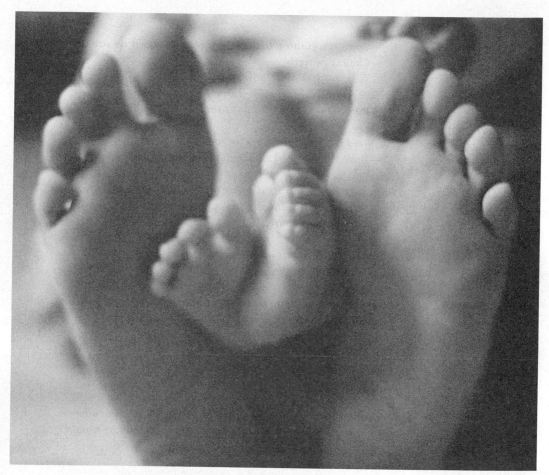

Innocence & Experience
A DIALOGUE ACROSS HISTORY

Experience is a comb which nature gives us when we are bald.
   —Chinese proverb

The life which is unexamined is not worth living.
   —Plato, 428-348 B.C., *Symposium*

The mind is always the dupe of the heart.
   —Duke Francois de La Rochefoucauld, *Maxims,* 1665

Crime like virtue has its degrees; and timid innocence was never known to blossom suddenly into extreme license.
   —Jean Racine, *Phedre,* 1677

We live and learn, but not the wiser grow.
   —John Pomfret, *Reason,* 1702

I have but one lamp by which my feet are guided, and that is the lamp of experience, [judging] the future by the past.
   —Patrick Henry, speech, 1775

Ignorance is not innocence but sin.
   —Robert Browning, *The Inn Album,* 1875

Education is an admirable thing, but it is well to remember from time to time that nothing worth knowing can be taught.
   —Oscar Wilde, "The Critic as Artist," 1890

You cannot create experience, you undergo it.
   —Albert Camus, *Notebooks,* 1935-42

The turning point in the process of growing up is when you discover the core of strength within you that survives all hurt.
   —Max Lerner, *The Unfinished Country,* 1950

Experience is not what happens to you; it is what you do with what happens to you.
   —Aldous Huxley, *Reader's Digest,* 1956

Experience is a hard teacher because [it] gives the test first, the lesson after.
   —Vernon Law, *This Week,* 1960

Tis e'er the lot of the innocent in the world to fly to the wolf for succor from the lion.
   —John Barth, *The Sot-Weed Factor,* 1960

How many roads must a man walk down / Before you call him a man?
   —Bob Dylan, "Blowin' in the Wind," 1962

All I Really Need To Know I Learned in Kindergarten
   —Robert Fulghum, book title, 1993

Our genetic heritage endows each of us with a series of emotional setpoints that determines our temperament. But the brain circuitry involved is extraordinarily malleable. . . . This means that childhood and adolescence are critical windows of opportunity for setting down the essential emotional habits that will govern our lives.
   —Daniel Goleman, *Emotional Intelligence,* 1995

INNOCENCE AND EXPERIENCE: EXPLORING YOUR OWN VALUES AND BELIEFS

What comes to mind when you hear the word *innocence*? Do you think of innocence as being "good"? Or do you think of innocence as being naïve, uninformed, or inexperienced? Is the "loss" of innocence really a loss—or is it a gain of knowledge? Does experience bring wisdom? Or is it what we do with our experiences—in ourselves and in the world—that brings wisdom? Must we learn from all experiences? Or should we try to forget some experiences and move on as best we can?

Innocence is most often associated with childhood and growing up. The world is relatively new to us as children, and our understanding of the world is relatively simple. We are very impressionable, and our hopes and expectations are often measured against the ideals that we have learned from the well-intentioned adults around us. As we make the passage from child to adult, however, we realize through experience—often abruptly and painfully—that the world is a much more complex, uncertain, and hostile place than we had imagined as children.

Our experiences remain with us for the duration of our lives. The nature of those experiences—especially our experiences growing up—can have a powerful impact on us. For better or worse, they will influence our values and our behavior. We may feel crushed and defeated by them or enlightened and strengthened by them. And as we encounter issues of innocence and experience in the literature we read, we will naturally compare them to similar circumstances in our own lives. As a preparation for reading the literature in this section, you may want to think about the way that important personal experiences have shaped your own values and beliefs.

READING AND WRITING ABOUT INNOCENCE AND EXPERIENCE

Exploring your beliefs and values and connecting your experiences with what you read is an important first step toward our ultimate goal—an appreciation of literature and the ability to think and write critically about it. Critical analysis will require rereading and reflection, writing and revising, gathering evidence, and constructing a solid argument to support your responses.

At least one aspect of the many stories, poems, plays, and essays in this section is about the impact that an experience or the loss of innocence has on characters: a young boy's overwhelming crush on his friend's older sister—and subsequent disappointment—in James Joyce's short story "Araby," a young girl's disillusionment as she realizes her "place" at a birthday party in Liliana Heker's short story "The Stolen Party," a young man's experience of the death of a sibling in Seamus Heaney's poem "Mid-Term Break," and the gruesome discoveries of police officer Edward Conlon on "The Midnight Tour." The brief quotes that open this section also give you some idea of the number of compelling emotions that are connected to innocence and experience. Issues of unrequited love, disillusionment, loneliness, loyalty, comfort, and self-realization head a long list of concerns. Any of these or other related issues might provide a fine topic for an essay.

◆ FICTION ◆

Julia Alvarez (B. 1954)

(See biography on p. 267.)

SNOW   [1991]

Our first year in New York we rented a small apartment with a Catholic school nearby, taught by the Sisters of Charity, hefty women in long black gowns and bonnets that made them look peculiar, like dolls in mourning. I liked them a lot, especially my grand-motherly fourth grade teacher, Sister Zoe. I had a lovely name, she said, and she had me teach the whole class how to pronounce it. *Yo-lan-da*. As the only immigrant in my class, I was put in a special seat in the first row by the window, apart from the other children so that Sister Zoe could tutor me without disturbing them. Slowly, she enunciated the new words I was to repeat: *laundromat, cornflakes, subway, snow*.

Soon I picked up enough English to understand holocaust was in the air. Sister Zoe explained to a wide-eyed classroom what was happening in Cuba. Russian missiles were being assembled, trained supposedly on New York City. President Kennedy, looking worried too, was on the television at home, explaining we might have to go to war against the Communists. At school, we had air-raid drills: an ominous bell would go off and we'd file into the hall, fall to the floor, cover our heads with our coats, and imagine our hair falling out, the bones in our arms going soft. At home, Mami and my sisters and I said a rosary for world peace. I heard new vocabulary: *nuclear bomb, radioactive fallout, bomb shelter*. Sister Zoe explained how it would happen. She drew a picture of a mushroom on the blackboard and dotted a flurry of chalkmarks for the dusty fallout that would kill us all.

The months grew cold, November, December. It was dark when I got up in the morning, frosty when I followed my breath to school. One morning as I sat at my desk daydreaming out the window, I saw dots in the air like the ones Sister Zoe had drawn—random at first, then lots and lots. I shrieked, "Bomb! Bomb!" Sister Zoe jerked around, her full black skirt ballooning as she hurried to my side. A few girls began to cry.

But then Sister Zoe's shocked look faded. "Why, Yolanda dear, that's snow!" She laughed. "Snow."

5   "Snow," I repeated. I looked out the window warily. All my life I had heard about the white crystals that fell out of American skies in the winter. From my desk I watched the fine powder dust the sidewalk and parked cars below. Each flake was different, Sister Zoe said, like a person, irreplaceable and beautiful.

MAKING CONNECTIONS

1. Why is the snowfall such a shocking experience for the narrator? What does she think is falling from the sky?
2. This story is told from the first-person point of view. How would it change if told in the third person?
3. At the end of this brief story, Sister Zoe tries to calm Yolanda by telling her each snowflake "was different . . . like a person, irreplaceable and beautiful." Do you think her explanation of snow is comforting? Why?

MAKING AN ARGUMENT

1. Both "Snow" and Sandra Cisneros's "Eleven" on page 26 are stories of classroom experiences told in the first person, but one narrator is an adult looking back and the other is a child "in the moment." Compare their narrative voices and write about the effectiveness of narration in each story. Cite the language of both stories for support.

TONI CADE BAMBARA [1939–1995]

Toni Cade Bambara was born in New York City and raised in the impoverished neighborhoods of Harlem and Bedford-Stuyvesant, New York, and Jersey City, New Jersey. Born Toni Cade, she added the name Bambara after discovering it as part of a signature in her great-grandmother's sketchbook. She attended Queen's College, where she majored in Theater Arts and English, graduating in 1959. Before turning to writing, she worked for the New York Department of Welfare, served as a director of recreation in a psychiatric ward, studied theater at the famous Commedia dell'Arte in Italy, ran a local community center, and earned an M.A. from the City University of New York. She began her writing career editing anthologies of black women writers and African-American stories, but first attracted attention with her collections of short stories Gorilla, My Love *(1972) and* The Sea Birds Are Still Alive *(1977). She died of cancer in 1995. Her most recent publication,* Deep Sightings and Rescue Missions: Fiction, Essays, and Conversations *(1996), was published posthumously. In an interview in* Black Women Writers at Work, *she said: "It's a tremendous responsibility—responsibility and honor—to be a writer, an artist, a cultural worker . . . One's got to see what the factory worker sees, what the prisoner sees, what the welfare children see, what the scholar sees, got to see what the ruling-class mythmakers see as well, in order to tell the truth and not get trapped."*

THE LESSON

[1972]

Back in the days when everyone was old and stupid or young and foolish and me and Sugar were the only ones just right, this lady moved on our block with nappy hair and proper speech and no makeup. And quite naturally we laughed at her, laughed the way we did at the junk man who went about his business like he was some big-time president and his sorryass horse his secretary. And we kinda hated her too, hated the way we did the winos who cluttered up our parks and pissed on our handball walls and stank up our hallways and stairs so you couldn't-halfway play hide-and-seek without a goddamn gas mask. Miss Moore was her name. The only woman on the block with no first name. And she was black as hell, cept for her feet, which were fish-white and spooky. And she was always planning these boring-ass things for us to do, us being my cousin, mostly, who lived on the block cause we all moved North the same time and to the same apartment then spread out gradual to breathe. And our parents would yank our heads into some kinda shape and crisp up our clothes so we'd be presentable for travel with Miss Moore, who always looked like she was going to church, though she never did. Which is just one of the things the grownups talked about when they talked behind her back like a dog. But when she came calling, with some sachet she'd sewed up or some gingerbread she'd made or some book, why then they'd still be too embarrassed to turn her down and we'd get handed over all spruced up. She'd been to college and said it was only right that she should take responsibility for the young ones' education, and she not even related by marriage or blood. So they'd go for it. Specially Aunt Gretchen. She was the main gofer in the family. You got some ole dumb shit foolishness you want somebody to go for, you send for Aunt Gretchen. She been screwed into the go-along for so long, it's a blood-deep natural thing with her. Which is how she got saddled with me and Sugar and junior in the first place while our mothers were in a la-de-da apartment up the block having a good ole time.

So this one day Miss Moore rounds us all up at the mailbox and it's puredee hot and she's knockin herself out about arithmetic. And school suppose to let up in summer I heard, but she don't never let up. And the starch in my pinafore scratching the shit outta me and I'm really hating this nappy-head bitch and her goddamn college degree. I'd much rather go to the pool or to the show where it's cool. So me and Sugar leaning on the mailbox being surly, which is a Miss Moore word. And Flyboy checking out what everybody brought for lunch. And Fat Butt already wasting his peanut butter-and-jelly sandwich like the pig he is. And Junebug punchin on Q.T.'s arm for potato chips. And Rosie Giraffe shifting from one hip to the other waiting for somebody to step on her foot or ask her if she from Georgia so she can kick ass, preferably Mercedes'. And Miss Moore asking us do we know what money is, like we a bunch of retards. I mean real money, she say, like it's only poker chips or monopoly papers we lay on the grocer. So right away I'm tired of this and say so. And would much rather snatch Sugar and go to the Sunset and terrorize the West Indian kids and take their hair ribbons and their money too. And Miss Moore files that remark away for next week's lesson on brotherhood, I can tell. And finally I say we oughta get to the subway cause it's cooler and besides we might meet some cute boys. Sugar done swiped her mama's lipstick, so we ready.

So we heading down the street and she's boring us silly about what things cost and what our parents make and how much goes for rent and how money ain't divided up right in this country. And then she gets to the part about we all poor and live in the slums, which I don't feature. And I'm ready to speak on that, but she steps out in the street and hails two cabs just like that. Then she hustles half the crew in with her and hands me a five-dollar bill and tells me to calculate 10 percent tip for the driver. And we're off. Me and Sugar and Junebug and Flyboy hangin out the window and hollering to everybody, putting lipstick on each other cause Flyboy a faggot anyway, and making farts with our sweaty armpits. But I'm mostly trying to figure how to spend this money. But they all fascinated with the meter ticking and Junebug starts laying bets as to how much it'll read when Flyboy can't hold his breath no more. Then Sugar lays bets as to how much it'll be when we get there. So I'm stuck. Don't nobody want to go for my plan, which is to jump out at the next light and run off to the first bar-b-que we can find. Then the driver tells us to get the hell out cause we there already. And the meter reads eighty-five cents. And I'm stalling to figure out the tip and Sugar say give him a dime. And I decide he don't need it bad as I do, so later for him. But then he tries to take off with Junebug foot still in the door so we talk about his mama something ferocious. Then we check out that we on Fifth Avenue and everybody dressed up in stockings. One lady in a fur coat, hot as it is. White folks crazy.

"This is the place," Miss Moore say, presenting it to us in the voice she uses at the museum. "Let's look in the windows before we go in."

5   "Can we steal?" Sugar asks very serious like she's getting the ground rules squared away before she plays. "I beg your pardon," say Miss Moore, and we fall out. So she leads us around the windows of the toy store and me and Sugar screamin, "This is mine, that's mine, I gotta have that, that was made for me, I was born for that," till Big Butt drowns us out.

"Hey, I'm going to buy that there."

"That there? You don't even know what it is, stupid."

"I do so," he say punchin on Rosie Giraffe. "It's a microscope."

"Whatcha gonna do with a microscope, fool?"

10   "Look at things."

"Like what, Ronald?" ask Miss Moore. And Big Butt ain't got the first notion. So here go Miss Moore gabbing about the thousands of bacteria in a drop of water and the somethin or other in a speck of blood and the million and one living things in the air around us is invisible to the naked eye. And what she say that for? Junebug go to town on that "naked" and we rolling. Then Miss Moore ask what it cost. So we all jam into the window smudgin it up and the price tag say $300. So then she ask how long'd take for Big Butt and Junebug to save up their allowances. "Too long," I say. "Yeh," adds Sugar, "outgrown it by that time." And, Miss Moore say no, you never outgrow learning instruments. "Why, even medical students and interns and," blah, blah, blah. And we ready to choke Big Butt for bringing it up in the first damn place.

"This here costs four hundred eighty dollars," say Rosie Giraffe. So we pile up all over her to see what she pointin out. My eyes tells me it's a chunk of glass cracked with something heavy, and different-color inks dripped into the splits, then the whole thing put into a oven or something. But for $480 it don't make sense.

"That's a paperweight made of semi-precious stones fused together under tremendous pressure," she explains slowly, with her hands doing the mining and all the factory work.

"So what's a paperweight?" asks Rosie Giraffe.

15   "To weigh paper with, dumbbell," say Flyboy, the wise man from the East.

"Not exactly," say Miss Moore, which is what she say when you warm or way off too. "It's to weigh paper down so it won't scatter and make your desk untidy." So right away me and Sugar curtsy to each other and then to Mercedes who is more the tidy type.

"We don't keep paper on top of the desk in my class," say Junebug, figuring Miss Moore crazy or lyin one.

"At home, then," she say. "Don't you have a calendar and a pencil case and a blotter and a letter-opener on your desk at home where you do your homework?" And she know damn well what our homes look like cause she nosys around in them every chance she gets.

"I don't even have a desk," say Junebug. "Do we?"

20   "No. And I don't get no homework neither," says Big Butt.

"And I don't even have a home," say Flyboy like he do at school to keep the white folks off his back and sorry for him. Send this poor kid to camp posters, is his specialty.

"I do," says Mercedes. "I have a box of stationery on my desk and a picture of my cat. My godmother bought the stationery and the desk. There's a big rose on each sheet and the envelopes smell like roses."

"Who wants to know about your smelly-ass stationery," say Rosie Giraffe fore I can get my two cents in.

"It's important to have a work area all your own so that...."

25   "Will you look at this sailboat, please," say Flyboy, cuttin her off and pointin to the thing like it was his.

So once again we tumble all over each other to gaze at this magnificent thing in the toy store which is just big enough to maybe sail two kittens across the pond if you strap them to the posts tight. We all start reciting the price tag like we in assembly. "Hand-crafted sailboat of fiberglass at one thousand one hundred ninety-five dollars."

"Unbelievable," I hear myself say and am really stunned. I read it again for myself just in case the group recitation put me in a trance. Same thing. For some reason this pisses me off. We look at Miss Moore and she lookin at us, waiting for I dunno what.

"Who'd pay all that when you can buy a sailboat set for a quarter at Pop's, a tube of glue for a dime, and a ball of string for eight cents? It must have a motor and a whole lot else besides," I say. "My sailboat cost me about fifty cents."

"But will it take water?" say Mercedes with her smart ass.

30   "Took mine to Alley Pond Park once," say Flyboy. "String broke. Lost it. Pity."

"Sailed mine in Central Park and it keeled over and sank. Had to ask my father for another dollar."

"And you got the strap," laugh Big Butt. "The jerk didn't even have a string on it. My old man wailed on his behind."

Little Q.T. was staring hard at the sailboat and you could see he wanted it bad.

But he too little and somebody'd just take it from him. So what the hell. "This boat for kids, Miss Moore?"

"Parents silly to buy something like that just to get all broke up," say Rosie Giraffe.

35   "That much money it should last forever," I figure.

"My father'd buy it for me if I wanted it."

"Your father, my ass," say Rosie Giraffe getting a chance to finally push Mercedes.

"Must be rich people shop here," say Q.T.

"You are a very bright boy," say Flyboy. "What was your first clue?" And he rap him on the head with the back of his knuckles, since Q.T. the only one he could get away with. Though Q.T. liable to come up behind you years later and get his licks in when you half expect it.

40   "What I want to know is," I says to Miss Moore though I never talk to her, I wouldn't give the bitch that satisfaction, "is how much a real boat costs? I figure a thousand'd get you a yacht any day."

"Why don't you check that out," she says, "and report back to the group?" Which really pains my ass. If you gonna mess up a perfectly good swim day least you could do is have some answers. "Let's go in," she say like she got something up her sleeve. Only she don't lead the way. So me and Sugar turn the corner to where the entrance is, but when we get there I kinda hang back. Not that I'm scared, what's there to be afraid of, just a toy store. But I feel funny, shame. But what I got to be shamed about? Got as much right to go in as anybody. But somehow I can't seem to get hold of the door, so I step away for Sugar to lead. But she hangs back too. And I look at her and she looks at me and this is ridiculous. I mean, damn, I have never ever been shy about doing nothing or going nowhere. But then Mercedes steps up and then Rosie Giraffe and Big Butt crowd in behind and shove, and next thing we all stuffed into the doorway with only Mercedes squeezing past us, smoothing out her jumper and walking right down the aisle. Then the rest of us tumble in like a glued-together jigsaw done all wrong. And people lookin at us. And it's like the time me and Sugar crashed into the Catholic church on a dare. But once we got in there and everything so hushed and holy and the candles and the bowin and the handker-chiefs on all the drooping heads, I just couldn't go through with the plan. Which was for me to run up to the altar and do a tap dance while Sugar played the nose flute and messed around in the holy water. And Sugar kept given me the elbow. Then later teased me so bad I tied her up in the shower and turned it on and locked her in. And she'd be there till this day if Aunt Gretchen hadn't finally figured I was lyin about the boarder takin a shower.

Same thing in the store. We all walkin on tiptoe and hardly touchin the games and puzzles and things. And I watched Miss Moore who is steady watchin us like she waitin for a sign. Like Mama Drewery watches the sky and sniffs the air and takes note of just how much slant is in the bird formation. Then me and Sugar bump smack into each other, so busy gazing at the toys, 'specially the sailboat. But we don't laugh and go into our fat-lady bump-stomach routine. We just stare at that price tag. Then Sugar run a finger over the whole boat. And I'm jealous and want to hit her. Maybe not her, but I sure want to punch somebody in the mouth.

"Watcha bring us here for, Miss Moore?"

"You sound angry, Sylvia. Are you mad about something?" Given me one of them grins like she tellin a grown-up joke that never turns out to be funny. And she's lookin very closely at me like maybe she plannin to do my portrait from memory. I'm mad, but I won't give her that satisfaction. So I slouch around the store bein very bored and say, "Let's go."

45 Me and Sugar at the back of the train watchin the tracks whizzin by large then small then gettin gobbled up in the dark. I'm thinkin about this tricky toy I saw in the store. A clown that somersaults on a bar then does chin-ups just cause you yank lightly at his leg. Cost $35. I could see me askin my mother for a $35 birthday clown. "You wanna who that costs what?" she'd say, cocking her head to the side to get a better view of the hole in my head. Thirty-five dollars could buy new bunk beds for junior and Gretchen's boy. Thirty-five dollars and the whole household could go visit Granddaddy Nelson in the country. Thirty-five dollars would pay for the rent and the piano bill too. Who are these people that spend that much for performing clowns and $1000 for toy sailboats? What kinda work they do and how they live and how come we ain't in on it? Where we are is who we are, Miss Moore always pointin out. But it don't necessarily have to be that way, she always adds then waits for somebody to say that poor people have to wake up and demand their share of the pie and don't none of us know what kind of pie she talking about in the first damn place. But she ain't so smart cause I still got her four dollars from the taxi and she sure ain't gettin it. Messin up my day with this shit. Sugar nudges me in my pocket and winks.

Miss Moore lines us up in front of the mailbox where we started from, seem like years ago, and I got a headache for thinkin so hard. And we lean all over each other so we can hold up under the draggy-ass lecture she always finishes us off with at the end before we thank her for borin us to tears. But she just looks at us like she readin tea leaves. Finally she say, "Well, what did you think of F.A.O. Schwartz?"

Rosie Giraffe mumbles, "White folks crazy."

"I'd like to go there again when I get my birthday money," says Mercedes, and we shove her out the pack so she has to lean on the mailbox by herself.

"I'd like a shower. Tiring day," say Flyboy.

50 Then Sugar surprises me by sayin, "You know, Miss Moore, I don't think all of us here put together eat in a year what that sailboat costs." And Miss Moore lights up like somebody goosed her. "And?" she say, urging Sugar on. Only I'm standin on her foot so she don't continue.

"Imagine for a minute what kind of society it is in which some people can spend on a toy what it would cost to feed a family of six or seven. What do you think?"

"I think," say Sugar pushing me off her feet like she never done before, cause I whip her ass in a minute, "that this is not much of a democracy if you ask me. Equal chance to pursue happiness means an equal crack at the dough, don't it?" Miss Moore is beside herself and I am disgusted with Sugar's treachery. So I stand on her foot one more time to see if she'll shove me. She shuts up, and Miss Moore looks at me, sorrowfully I'm thinkin. And somethin weird is goin on, I can feel it in my chest.

"Anybody else learn anything today?" lookin dead at me. I walk away and Sugar has to run to catch up and don't even seem to notice when I shrug her arm off my shoulder.

"Well, we got four dollars anyway," she says.

55   "Uh hunh."

"We could go to Hascombs and get half a chocolate layer and then go to the Sunset and still have plenty money for potato chips and ice cream sodas."

"Uh hunh."

"Race you to Hascombs," she say.

We start down the block and she gets ahead which is O.K. by me cause I'm going to the West End and then over to the Drive to think this day through. She can run if she want to and even run faster. But ain't nobody gonna beat me at nuthin.

MAKING CONNECTIONS

1. You might say that this story is told from the point of view of a "hostile witness." How did you respond to the speaker? To the events she describes? How would the story change if told from Miss Moore's point of view?
2. Describe the narrator's relationship to Sugar. In what ways is this relationship important to the narrator? How is the relationship developed throughout the story?
3. Think about the final paragraph of the story. Has the narrator changed? If so, why? What does she tell us about herself and her future?
4. What is it that Miss Moore wants these children to experience? Why does she bring poor inner-city adolescents to a store where they can't afford anything? Do you think this is an effective lesson? Explain.

MAKING AN ARGUMENT

1. In the quotations that open this theme, Aldous Huxley is quoted as saying: "Experience is not what happens to you; it is what you do with what happens to you." Do you agree? What difference would that distinction make for the children in the story? What could they "do" with this experience? Write about this quote as it applies to this story. Cite the text of the story for support.

THOMAS BULFINCH [1796-1867]

Thomas Bulfinch was born in Newton, Massachusetts, the son of one of the most prominent architects of the time. During most of his life he worked as a clerk at the Merchant's Bank of Boston, a post that allowed him the leisure to pursue his many other interests, which included writing. His most enduring works are his three collections of myths and fables, The Age of Fables *(1855),* The Age of Chivalry *(1858), and* Legends of Charlemagne *(1863),*

which are now reprinted under the title Bulfinch's Mythology. *Bulfinch's approach to the ancient myths may seem dated by twenty-first-century standards, but his learned and vigorous retellings of these tales remain timeless.*

THE MYTH OF DAEDALUS AND ICARUS   [1855]

The labyrinth from which Theseus escaped, by means of the clew of Ariadne was built by Daedalus, a most skilful artificer. It was an edifice with numberless winding passages and turnings opening into one another, and seeming to have neither beginning nor end, like the river Maeander, which returns on itself, and flows now onward, now backward, in its course to the sea. Daedalus built the labyrinth for King Minos, but afterwards lost the favor of the king, and was shut up in a tower. He contrived to make his escape from his prison, but could not leave the island by sea, as the king kept strict watch on all the vessels, and permitted none to sail without being carefully searched. "Minos may control the land and sea," said Daedalus, "but not the regions of the air. I will try that way." So he set to work to fabricate wings for himself and his young son Icarus. He wrought feathers together, beginning with the smallest and adding larger, so as to form an increasing surface. The larger ones he secured with thread and the smaller with wax, and gave the whole a gentle curvature like the wings of a bird. Icarus, the boy, stood and looked on, sometimes running to gather up the feathers which the wind had blown away, and then handling the wax and working it over with his fingers, by his play impeding his father in his labors. When at last the work was done, the artist, waving his wings, found himself buoyed upward, and hung suspended, poising himself on the beaten air. He next equipped his son in the same manner, and taught him how to fly, as a bird tempts her young ones from the lofty nest into the air. When all was prepared for flight he said, "Icarus, my son, I charge you to keep at a moderate height, for if you fly too low the damp will clog your wings, and if too high the heat will melt them. Keep near me and you will be safe." While he gave him these instructions and fitted the wings to his shoulders, the face of the father was wet with tears, and his hands trembled. He kissed the boy, not knowing that it was for the last time. Then rising on his wings, he flew off, encouraging him to follow, and looked back from his own flight to see how his son managed his wings. As they flew the ploughman stopped his work to gaze, and the shepherd leaned on his staff and watched them, astonished at the sight, and thinking they were gods who could thus cleave the air.

They passed Samos and Delos on the left and Lebynthos on the right, when the boy, exulting in his career, began to leave the guidance of his companion and soar upward as if to reach heaven. The nearness of the blazing sun softened the wax which held the feathers together, and they came off. He fluttered with his arms, but no feathers remained to hold the air. While his mouth uttered cries to his father it was submerged in the blue waters of the sea, which thenceforth was called by his name. His father cried, "Icarus, Icarus, where are you?" At last he saw the feathers floating on the water, and bitterly lamenting his own arts, he buried the body and called the land Icaria in memory of his child. Daedalus arrived safe in Sicily where he built a Temple to Apollo, and hung up his wings, an offering to the gods.

MAKING CONNECTIONS

1. Is there a lesson to be learned in this myth? Explain.
2. Daedalus warned Icarus about flying too high. Why does he bitterly lament his own arts?

MAKING AN ARGUMENT

1. Look at Brueghel's painting of this myth, *Landscape with the Fall of Icarus*, on page 686 and the two poems written in response to the painting. Does the painting capture what you felt after reading "The Myth of Daedalus and Icarus"? Do the poems? Identify the theme of the myth and write an essay comparing the effectiveness of each medium in conveying that theme. Cite the texts of the myth and the poems for support.

RALPH ELLISON [1914–1994]

Ralph Waldo Ellison was born in Oklahoma and was named after the famous nineteenth-century writer Ralph Waldo Emerson. He was educated at the Tuskegee Institute where he majored in Music. The short story below, "Battle Royal," is an excerpt from his novel Invisible Man, *which won the National Book Award in 1953 and was widely praised for its depiction of the plight of African-Americans. In addition to his fiction writing, Ellison frequently wrote essays (many of them about music) and gave interviews about race relations, and was Albert Schweitzer Professor of the Humanities at New York University. The* Collected Essays of Ralph Ellison *was published in 1995, and an unfinished novel,* Juneteenth *(completed by John Callahan), was published in 1999.*

BATTLE ROYAL   [1953]

It goes a long way back, some twenty years. All my life I had been looking for something, and everywhere I turned someone tried to tell me what it was. I accepted their answers too, though they were often in contradiction and even self-contradictory. I was naïve. I was looking for myself and asking everyone except myself questions which I, and only I, could answer. It took me a long time and much painful boomeranging of my expectations to achieve a realization everyone else appears to have been born with: That I am nobody but myself. But first I had to discover that I am an invisible man!

And yet I am no freak of nature, nor of history. I was in the cards, other things having been equal (or unequal) eighty-five years ago. I am not ashamed of my grandparents for having been slaves. I am only ashamed of myself for having at one time been ashamed. About eighty-five years ago they were told that they were free, united with others of our country in everything pertaining to the common good, and, in everything social, separate like the fingers of the hand. And they believed it. They exulted in it. They stayed in their place, worked hard, and brought up my father to do the same. But my grandfather is the one. He was an odd old guy, my grandfather, and I am told I take after him. It was he who caused the trouble. On his deathbed he called my father to him and said, "Son, after I'm gone I want you to keep up the good fight. I never told you, but our life is a war and I have been a traitor all my born days, a spy in the enemy's country ever since I give up my gun back in the Reconstruction. Live with your head in the lion's mouth. I want you to overcome 'em with yeses, undermine 'em with grins, agree 'em to death and destruction, let 'em swoller you till they vomit or bust wide open." They thought the old man had gone out of his mind. He had been the meekest of men. The younger children were rushed from the room, the shades drawn and the flame of the lamp turned so low that it sputtered on the wick like the old man's breathing. "Learn it to the younguns," he whispered fiercely; then he died.

But my folks were more alarmed over his last words than over his dying. It was as though he had not died at all, his words caused so much anxiety. I was warned emphatically to forget what he had said and, indeed, this is the first time it has been mentioned outside the family circle. It had a tremendous effect upon me, however. I could never be sure of what he meant. Grandfather had been a quiet old man who never made any trouble, yet on his deathbed he had called himself a traitor and a spy, and he had spoken of his meekness as a dangerous activity. It became a constant puzzle which lay unanswered in the back of my mind. And whenever things went well for me I remembered my grandfather and felt guilty and uncomfortable. It was as though I was carrying out his advice in spite of myself. And to make it worse, everyone loved me for it. I was praised by the most lily-white men of the town. I was considered an example of desirable conduct—just as my grandfather had been. And what puzzled me was that the old man had defined it as *treachery*. When I was praised for my conduct I felt a guilt that in some way I was doing something that was really against the wishes of the white folks, that if they had understood they would have desired me to act just the opposite, that I should have been sulky and mean, and that that really would have been what they wanted, even though they were fooled and thought they wanted me to act as I did. It made me afraid that some day they would look upon me as a traitor and I would be lost. Still I was more afraid to act any other way because they didn't like that at all. The old man's words were like a curse. On my graduation day I delivered an oration in which I showed that humility was the secret, indeed, the very essence of progress. (Not that I believed this—how could I, remembering my grandfather?—I only believed that it worked.) It was a great success. Everyone praised me and I was invited to give the speech at a gathering of the town's leading white citizens. It was a triumph for our whole community.

It was in the main ballroom of the leading hotel. When I got there I discovered that it was on the occasion of a smoker, and I was told that since I was to be there anyway I might as well take part in the battle royal to be fought by some of my schoolmates as part of the entertainment. The battle royal came first.

5   All of the town's big shots were there in their tuxedoes, wolfing down the buffet foods, drinking beer and whiskey and smoking black cigars. It was a large room with a high ceiling. Chairs were arranged in neat rows around three sides of a portable boxing ring. The fourth side was clear, revealing a gleaming space of polished floor. I had some misgivings over the battle royal, by the way. Not from a distaste for fighting, but because I didn't care too much for the other fellows who were to take part. They were tough guys who seemed to have no grandfather's curse worrying their minds. No one could mistake their toughness. And besides, I suspected that fighting a battle royal might detract from the dignity of my speech. In those pre-invisible days I visualized myself as a potential Booker T. Washington. But the other fellows didn't care too much for me either, and there were nine of them. I felt superior to them in my way, and I didn't like the manner in which we were all crowded together into the servants' elevator. Nor did they like my being there. In fact, as the warmly lighted floors flashed past the elevator we had words over the fact that I, by taking part in the fight, had knocked one of their friends out of a night's work.

We were led out of the elevator through a rococo hall into an anteroom and told to get into our fighting togs. Each of us was issued a pair of boxing gloves and ushered out into the big mirrored hall, which we entered looking cautiously about us and whispering, lest we might accidentally be heard above the noise of the room. It was foggy with cigar smoke. And already the whiskey was taking effect. I was shocked to see some of the most important men of the town quite tipsy. They were all there—bankers, lawyers, judges, doctors, fire chiefs, teachers, merchants. Even one of the more fashionable pastors. Something we could not see was going on up front. A clarinet was vibrating sensuously and the men were standing up and moving eagerly forward. We were a small tight group, clustered together, our bare upper bodies touching and shining with anticipatory sweat; while up front the big shots were becoming increasingly excited over something we still could not see. Suddenly I heard the school superintendent, who had told me to come, yell. "Bring up the shines, gentlemen! Bring up the little shines!"

We were rushed up to the front of the ballroom, where it smelled even more strongly of tobacco and whiskey. Then we were pushed into place. I almost wet my pants. A sea of faces, some hostile, some amused, ringed around us, and in the center, facing us, stood a magnificent blonde—stark naked. There was dead silence. I felt a blast of cold air chill me. I tried to back away, but they were behind me and around me. Some of the boys stood with lowered heads, trembling. I felt a wave of irrational guilt and fear. My teeth chattered, my skin turned to goose flesh, my knees knocked. Yet I was strongly attracted and looked in spite of myself. Had the price of looking been blindness, I would have looked. The hair was yellow like that of a circus kewpie doll, the face heavily powdered and rouged, as though to form an abstract mask, the eyes hollow and smeared a cool blue, the color of a baboon's butt. I felt a desire to spit upon her as my eyes brushed slowly over her body. Her breasts were firm and round as the domes of East Indian temples, and I stood so close as to see the fine skin texture and beads of pearly perspiration glistening like dew around the pink and erected buds of her nipples. I wanted at one and the same time to run from the room, to sink through the floor, or go to her and cover her from my eyes and the eyes of the others with my body; to feel the soft thighs, to caress her and destroy her, to love her and murder her, to hide from her, and yet to stroke where below the small American flag tattooed upon her belly her thighs formed a capital V. I had a notion that of all in the room she saw only me with her impersonal eyes.

And then she began to dance, a slow sensuous movement; the smoke of a hundred cigars clinging to her like the thinnest of veils. She seemed like a fair bird-girl girdled in veils calling to me from the angry surface of some gray and threatening sea. I was transported. Then I became aware of the clarinet playing and the big shots yelling at us. Some threatened us if we looked and others if we did not. On my right I saw one boy faint. And now a man grabbed a silver pitcher from a table and stepped close as he dashed ice water upon him and stood him up and forced two of us to support him as his head hung and moans issued from his thick bluish lips. Another boy began to plead to go home. He was the largest of the group, wearing dark red fighting trunks much too small to conceal the erection which projected from him as though in answer to the insinuating low-registered moans of the clarinet. He tried to hide himself with his boxing gloves.

And all the while the blonde continued dancing, smiling faintly at the big shots who watched her with fascination, and faintly smiling at our fear. I noticed a certain merchant who followed her hungrily, his lips loose and drooling. He was a large man who wore diamond studs in a shirtfront which swelled with the ample paunch underneath, and each time the blonde swayed her undulating hips he ran his hand through the thin hair of his bald head and, with his arms upheld, his posture clumsy like that of an intoxicated panda, wound his belly in a slow and obscene grind. This creature was completely hypnotized. The music had quickened. As the dancer flung herself about with a detached expression on her face, the men began reaching out to touch her. I could see their beefy fingers sink into her soft flesh. Some of the others tried to stop them and she began to move around the floor in graceful circles, as they gave chase, slipping and sliding over the polished floor. It was mad. Chairs went crashing, drinks were spilt, as they ran laughing and howling after her. They caught her just as she reached a door, raised her from the floor, and tossed her as college boys are tossed at a hazing, and above her red, fixed-smiling lips I saw the terror and disgust in her eyes, almost like my own terror and that which I saw in some of the other boys. As I watched, they tossed her twice and her soft breasts seemed to flatten against the air and her legs flung wildly as she spun. Some of the more sober ones helped her to escape. And I started off the floor, heading for the anteroom with the rest of the boys.

10   Some were still crying and in hysteria. But as we tried to leave we were stopped and ordered to get into the ring. There was nothing to do but what we were told. All ten of us climbed under the ropes and allowed ourselves to be blindfolded with broad bands of white cloth. One of the men seemed to feel a bit sympathetic and tried to cheer us up as we stood with our backs against the ropes. Some of us tried to grin. "See that boy over there?" one of the men said. "I want you to run across at the bell and give it to him right in the belly. If you don't get him, I'm going to get you. I don't like his looks." Each of us was told the same. The blindfolds were put on. Yet even then I had been going over my speech. In my mind each word was as bright as flame. I felt the cloth pressed into place, and frowned so that it would be loosened when I relaxed.

But now I felt a sudden fit of blind terror. I was unused to darkness. It was as though I had suddenly found myself in a dark room filled with poisonous cottonmouths. I could hear the bleary voices yelling insistently for the battle royal to begin.

"Get going in there!"

"Let me at that big nigger!"

I strained to pick up the school superintendent's voice, as though to squeeze some security out of that slightly more familiar sound.

15   "Let me at those black sonsabitches!" someone yelled.

"No, Jackson, no!" another voice yelled. "Here, somebody, help me hold Jack."

"I want to get at that ginger-colored nigger. Tear him limb from limb," the first voice yelled.

I stood against the ropes trembling. For in those days I was what they called ginger-colored, and he sounded as though he might crunch me between his teeth like a crisp ginger cookie.

Quite a struggle was going on. Chairs were being kicked about and I could hear voices grunting as with a terrific effort. I wanted to see, to see more desperately than ever before. But the blindfold was as tight as a thick skin-puckering scab and when I raised my gloved hands to push the layers of white aside a voice yelled, "Oh, no you don't, black bastard! Leave that alone!"

20   "Ring the bell before Jackson kills him a coon!" someone boomed in the sudden silence. And I heard the bell clang and the sound of the feet scuffling forward.

A glove smacked against my head. I pivoted, striking out stiffly as someone went past, and felt the jar ripple along the length of my arm to my shoulder. Then it seemed as though all nine of the boys had turned upon me at once. Blows pounded me from all sides while I struck out as best I could. So many blows landed upon me that I wondered if I were not the only blindfolded fighter in the ring, or if the man called Jackson hadn't succeeded in getting me after all.

Blindfolded, I could no longer control my motions. I had no dignity. I stumbled about like a baby or a drunken man. The smoke had become thicker and with each new blow it seemed to sear and further restrict my lungs. My saliva became like hot bitter glue. A glove connected with my head, filling my mouth with warm blood. It was everywhere. I could not tell if the moisture I felt upon my body was sweat or blood. A blow landed hard against the nape of my neck. I felt myself going over, my head hitting the floor. Streaks of blue light filled the black world behind the blindfold. I lay prone, pretending that I was knocked out, but felt myself seized by hands and yanked to my feet. "Get going, black boy! Mix it up!" My arms were like lead, my head smarting from blows. I managed to feel my way to the ropes and held on, trying to catch my breath. A glove landed in my midsection and I went over again, feeling as though the smoke had become a knife jabbed into my guts. Pushed this way and that by the legs milling around me, I finally pulled erect and discovered that I could see the black, sweat-washed forms weaving in the smoky-blue atmosphere like drunken dancers weaving to the rapid drum-like thuds of blows.

Everyone fought hysterically. It was complete anarchy. Everybody fought everybody else. No group fought together for long. Two, three, four, fought one, then turned to fight each other, were themselves attacked. Blows landed below the belt and in the kidney, with the gloves open as well as closed, and with my eye partly opened now there was not so much terror. I moved carefully, avoiding blows, although not too many to attract attention, fighting from group to group. The boys groped about like blind, cautious crabs crouching to protect their mid-sections, their heads pulled in short against their shoulders, their arms stretched nervously before them, with their fists testing the smoke-filled air like the knobbed feelers of hypersensitive snails. In one corner I glimpsed a boy violently punching the air and heard him scream in pain as he smashed his hand against a ring post. For a second I saw him bent over holding his hand, then going down as a blow caught his unprotected head. I played one group against the other, slipping and throwing a punch then stepping out of range while pushing the others into the melee to take the blows blindly aimed at me. The smoke was agonizing and there were no rounds, no bells at three minute intervals to relieve our exhaustion. The room spun round me, a swirl of lights, smoke, sweating bodies surrounded by tense white faces. I bled from both nose and mouth, the blood spattering upon my chest.

The men kept yelling, "Slug him, black boy! Knock his guts out!"

25   "Uppercut him! Kill him! Kill that big boy!"

Taking a fake fall, I saw a boy going down heavily beside me as though we were felled by a single blow, saw a sneaker-clad foot shoot into his groin as the two who had knocked him down stumbled upon him. I rolled out of range, feeling a twinge of nausea.

The harder we fought the more threatening the men became. And yet, I had begun to worry about my speech again. How would it go? Would they recognize my ability? What would they give me?

I was fighting automatically and suddenly I noticed that one after another of the boys was leaving the ring. I was surprised, filled with panic, as though I had been left alone with an unknown danger. Then I understood. The boys had arranged it among themselves. It was the custom for the two men left in the ring to slug it out for the winner's prize. I discovered this too late. When the bell sounded two men in tuxedoes leaped into the ring and removed the blindfold. I found myself facing Tatlock, the biggest of the gang. I felt sick at my stomach. Hardly had the bell stopped ringing in my ears than it clanged again and I saw him moving swiftly toward me. Thinking of nothing else to do I hit him smash on the nose. He kept coming, bringing the rank sharp violence of stale sweat. His face was a black bank of a face, only his eyes alive—with hate of me and aglow with a feverish terror from what had happened to us all. I became anxious. I wanted to deliver my speech and he came at me as though he meant to beat it out of me. I smashed him again and again, taking his blows as they came. Then on a sudden impulse I struck him lightly as we clinched, I whispered, "Fake like I knocked you out, you can have the prize."

"I'll break your behind," he whispered hoarsely.

30   "For *them?*"

"For *me*, sonofabitch!"

They were yelling for us to break it up and Tatlock spun me half around with a blow, and as a joggled camera sweeps in a reeling scene, I saw the howling red faces crouching tense beneath the cloud of blue-gray smoke. For a moment the world wavered, unraveled, flowed, then my head cleared and Tatlock bounced before me.

That fluttering shadow before my eyes was his jabbing left hand. Then falling forward, my head against his damp shoulder, I whispered,

"I'll make it five dollars more."

"Go to hell!"

35   But his muscles relaxed a trifle beneath my pressure and I breathed, "Seven!"

"Give it to your ma," he said, ripping me beneath the heart.

And while I still held him I butted him and moved away. I felt myself bombarded with punches. I fought back with hopeless desperation. I wanted to deliver my speech more than anything else in the world, because I felt that only these men could judge truly my ability, and now this stupid clown was ruining my chances. I began fighting carefully now, moving in to punch him and out again with my greater speed. A lucky blow to his chin and I had him going too—until I heard a loud voice yell, "I got my money on the big boy."

Hearing this, I almost dropped my guard. I was confused: Should I try to win against the voice out there? Would not this go against my speech, and was not this a moment for humility, for nonresistance? A blow to my head as I danced about sent my right eye popping like a jack-in-the-box and settled my dilemma. The room went red as I fell. It was a dream fall, my body languid and fastidious as to where to land, until the floor became impatient and smashed up to meet me. A moment later I came to. An hypnotic voice said FIVE emphatically. And I lay there, hazily watching a dark red spot of my own blood shaping itself into a butterfly, glistening and soaking into the soiled gray world of the canvas.

When the voice drawled TEN I was lifted up and dragged to a chair. I sat dazed. My eye pained and swelled with each throb of my pounding heart and I wondered if now I would be allowed to speak. I was wringing wet, my mouth still bleeding. We were grouped along the wall now. The other boys ignored me as they congratulated Tatlock and speculated as to how much they would be paid. One boy whimpered over his smashed hand. Looking up front, I saw attendants in white jackets rolling the portable ring away and placing a small square rug in the vacant space surrounded by chairs. Perhaps, I thought, I will stand on the rug to deliver my speech.

40   Then the M.C. called to us, "Come on up here boys and get your money." We ran forward to where the men laughed and talked in their chairs, waiting. Everyone seemed friendly now.

"There it is on the rug," the man said. I saw the rug covered with coins of all dimensions and a few crumpled bills. But what excited me, scattered here and there, were the gold pieces.

"Boys, it's all yours," the man said. "You get all you grab."

"That's right, Sambo," a blond man said, winking at me confidentially.

I trembled with excitement, forgetting my pain. I would get the gold and the bills, I thought. I would use both hands. I would throw my body against the boys nearest me to block them from the gold.

45   "Get down around the rug now," the man commanded, "and don't anyone touch it until I give the signal."

"This ought to be good," I heard.

As told, we got around the square rug on our knees. Slowly the man raised his freckled hand as we followed it upward with our eyes.

I heard, "These niggers look like they're about to pray!"

Then, "Ready," the man said. "Go!"

50   I lunged for a yellow coin lying on the blue design of the carpet, touching it and sending a surprised shriek to join those rising around me. I tried frantically to remove my hand but could not let go. A hot, violent force tore through my body, shaking me like a wet rat. The rug was electrified. The hair bristled up on my head as I shook myself free. My muscles jumped, my nerves jangled, writhed. But I saw that this was not stopping the other boys. Laughing in fear and embarrassment, some were holding back and scooping up the coins knocked off by the painful contortions of the others. The men roared above us as we struggled.

"Pick it up, goddamnit, pick it up!" someone called like a bass-voiced parrot. "Go on, get it!"

I crawled rapidly around the floor, picking up the coins, trying to avoid the coppers and to get greenbacks and the gold. Ignoring the shock by laughing, as I brushed the coins off quickly, I discovered that I could contain the electricity—a contradiction, but it works. Then the men began to push us onto the rug. Laughing embarrassedly, we struggled out of their hands and kept after the coins. We were all wet and slippery and hard to hold. Suddenly I saw a boy lifted into the air, glistening with sweat like a circus seal, and dropped, his wet back landing flush upon the charged rug, heard him yell and saw him literally dance upon his back, his elbows beating a frenzied tattoo upon the floor, his muscles twitching like the flesh of a horse stung by many flies. When he finally rolled off, his face was gray and no one stopped him when he ran from the floor amid booming laughter.

"Get the money," the M.C. called. "That's good hard American cash!"

And we snatched and grabbed, snatched and grabbed. I was careful not to come too close to the rug now, and when I felt the hot whiskey breath descend upon me like a cloud of foul air I reached out and grabbed the leg of a chair. It was occupied and I held on desperately.

55   "Leggo, nigger! Leggo!"

The huge face wavered down to mine as he tried to push me free. But my body was slippery and he was too drunk. It was Mr. Colcord, who owned a chain of movie houses and "entertainment palaces." Each time he grabbed me I slipped out of his hands. It became a real struggle. I feared the rug more than I did the drunk, so I held on, surprising myself for a moment by trying to topple *him* upon the rug. It was such an enormous idea that I found myself actually carrying it out. I tried not to be obvious, yet when I grabbed his leg, trying to tumble him out of the chair, he raised up roaring with laughter, and, looking at me with soberness dead in the eye, kicked me viciously in the chest. The chair leg flew out of my hand. I felt myself going and rolled. It was as though I had rolled through a bed of hot coals. It seemed a whole century would pass before I would roll free, a century in which I was seared through the deepest levels of my body to the fearful breath within me and the breath seared and heated to the point of explosion. It'll all be over in a flash, I thought as I rolled clear. It'll all be over in a flash.

But not yet, the men on the other side were waiting, red faces swollen as though from apoplexy as they bent forward in their chairs. Seeing their fingers coming toward me I rolled away as a fumbled football rolls off the receiver's fingertips, back into the coals. That time I luckily sent the rug sliding out of place and heard the coins ringing against the floor and the boys scuffling to pick them up and the M.C. calling, "All right, boys, that's all. Go get dressed and get your money."

I was limp as a dish rag. My back felt as though it had been beaten with wires.

When we had dressed the M.C. came in and gave us each five dollars, except Tatlock, who got ten for being the last in the ring. Then he told us to leave. I was not to get a chance to deliver my speech, I thought. I was going out into the dim alley in despair when I was stopped and told to go back. I returned to the ballroom, where the men were pushing back their chairs and gathering in groups to talk.

60   The M.C. knocked on a table for quiet. "Gentlemen," he said, "we almost forgot an important part of the program. A most serious part, gentlemen. This boy was brought here to deliver a speech which he made at his graduation yesterday. . . . "

"Bravo!"

"I'm told that he is the smartest boy we've got out there in Greenwood. I'm told that he knows more big words than a pocket-sized dictionary."

Much applause and laughter.

"So now, gentlemen, I want you to give him your attention."

65   There was still laughter as I faced them, my mouth dry, my eye throbbing. I began slowly, but evidently my throat was tense, because they began shouting, "Louder! Louder!"

"We of the younger generation extol the wisdom of that great leader and educator," I shouted, "who first spoke these flaming words of wisdom: 'A ship lost at sea for many days suddenly sighted a friendly vessel. From the mast of the unfortunate vessel was seen a signal: "Water, water; we die of thirst!" The answer from the friendly vessel came back: "Cast down your bucket where you are." The captain of the distressed vessel, at last heeding the injunction, cast down his bucket, and it came up full of fresh sparkling water from the mouth of the Amazon River.' And like him I say, and in his words. 'To those of my race who depend upon bettering their condition in a foreign land, or who underestimate the importance of cultivating friendly relations with the Southern white man, who is his next-door neighbor, I would say: "Cast down your bucket where you are"—cast it down in making friends in every manly way of the people of all races by whom we are surrounded. . . . '"

I spoke automatically and with such fervor that I did not realize that the men were still talking and laughing until my dry mouth, filling up with blood from the cut, almost strangled me. I coughed, wanting to stop and go to one of the tall brass, sand-filled spittoons to relieve myself, but a few of the men, especially the superintendent, were listening and I was afraid. So I gulped it down, blood, saliva and all, and continued. (What powers of endurance I had during those days! What enthusiasm! What a belief in the rightness of things!) I spoke even louder in spite of the pain. But still they talked and still they laughed, as though deaf with cotton in dirty ears. So I spoke with greater emotional emphasis. I closed my ears and swallowed blood until I was nauseated. The speech seemed a hundred times as long as before, but I could not leave out a single word. All had to be said, each memorized nuance considered, rendered. Nor was that all. Whenever I uttered a word of three or more syllables a group of voices would yell for me to repeat it. I used the phrase "social responsibility" and they yelled:

"What's the word you say, boy?"

"Social responsibility," I said.

70   "What?"

"Social . . ."

"Louder."

". . . responsibility."

"More!"

75   "Respon—"

"Repeat!"

"—sibility."

The room filled with the uproar of laughter until, no doubt, distracted by having to gulp down my blood, I made a mistake and yelled a phrase I had often seen denounced in newspaper editorials, heard debated in private.

"Social . . ."

80   "What?" they yelled.

". . . equality—"

The laughter hung smokelike in the sudden stillness. I opened my eyes, puzzled. Sounds of displeasure filled the room. The M.C. rushed forward. They shouted hostile phrases at me. But I did not understand.

A small dry mustached man in the front row blared out, "Say that slowly, son!"

"What sir?"

85   "What you just said!"

"Social responsibility, sir," I said.

"You weren't being smart, were you, boy?" he said, not unkindly.

"No, sir!"

"You sure that about 'equality' was a mistake?"

90   "Oh, yes, sir," I said. "I was swallowing blood."

"Well, you had better speak more slowly so we can understand. We mean to do right by you, but you've got to know your place at all times. All right, now, go on with your speech."

I was afraid. I wanted to leave but I wanted also to speak and I was afraid they'd snatch me down.

"Thank you, sir," I said, beginning where I had left off, and having them ignore me as before.

Yet when I finished there was a thunderous applause. I was surprised to see the superintendent come forth with a package wrapped in white tissue paper, and gesturing for quiet, address the men.

95   "Gentlemen, you see that I did not overpraise this boy. He makes a good speech and some day he'll lead his people in the proper paths. And I don't have to tell you that that is important in these days and times. This is a good, smart boy, and so to encourage him in the right direction, in the name of the Board of Education I wish to present him a prize in the form of this . . . "

He paused, removing the tissue paper and revealing a gleaming calfskin brief case.

". . . in the form of this first-class article from Shad Whitmore's shop."

"Boy," he said, addressing me, "take this prize and keep it well. Consider it a badge of office. Prize it. Keep developing as you are and some day it will be filled with important papers that will help shape the destiny of your people."

I was so moved that I could hardly express my thanks. A rope of bloody saliva forming a shape like an undiscovered continent drooled upon the leather and I wiped it quickly away. I felt an importance that I had never dreamed.

100   "Open it and see what's inside," I was told.

My fingers a-tremble, I complied, smelling the fresh leather and finding an official-looking document inside. It was a scholarship to the state college for Negroes. My eyes filled with tears and I ran awkwardly off the floor.

I was overjoyed; I did not even mind when I discovered that the gold pieces I had scrambled for were brass pocket tokens advertising a certain make of automobile.

When I reached home everyone was excited. Next day the neighbors came to congratulate me. I even felt safe from grandfather, whose deathbed curse usually spoiled my triumphs. I stood beneath his photograph with my brief case in hand and smiled triumphantly into his stolid black peasant's face. It was a face that fascinated me. The eyes seemed to follow everywhere I went.

That night I dreamed I was at a circus with him and that he refused to laugh at the clowns no matter what they did. Then later he told me to open my brief case and read what was inside and I did, finding an official envelope stamped with the state seal; and inside the envelope I found another and another, endlessly, and I thought I would fall of weariness. "Them's years," he said. "Now open that one." And I did and in it I found an engraved document containing a short message in letters of gold. "Read it," my grandfather said. "Out loud."

105   "To Whom It May Concern," I intoned. "Keep This Nigger-Boy Running."

I awoke with the old man's laughter ringing in my ears.

(It was a dream I was to remember and dream again for many years after. But at the time I had no insight into its meaning. First I had to attend college.)

MAKING CONNECTIONS

1. Have you ever found yourself in a humiliating circumstance but didn't want to protest—and wanted the approval of those who were humiliating you? If so, how did that experience affect your response to this story?
2. The narrator is the protagonist. In what way does this point of view influence how you experience the story?
3. What is the role of the naked dancer in the story?
4. To what extent is the narrator's act of delivering the speech more important to him than its message or the citizens to whom it is delivered? Why do you think he feels this way?
5. Describe the setting of the story. What aspects of the description were most effective in conveying the atmosphere?
6. Why does the audience react so strongly to the narrator's use of the terms "social responsibility" and "social equality"?
7. What is the primary conflict in the story? Is it external, internal, both? Explain.

MAKING AN ARGUMENT

1. Interpret the narrator's dream in terms of the "battle" he has just fought. What do you think the declaration in the dream "Keep This Nigger-Boy Running" means? Write an essay about the relationship between the "battle royal" the narrator has just experienced and his dream at the end. Cite the text of the story for support.

LILIANA HEKER [B. 1943]

Liliana Heker is a native of Argentina. She was editor in chief of two literary magazines, the Escarahajo de Oro, *and the* Ornitorrinco *("The Platypus"), for over twenty-five years—an era that coincided with Argentina's descent into chaos under military dictatorships. Her works include* Those That Saw the Bramble *(1966),* Zona de Clivage *(1988),* The Edges of the Real Thing *(1991), and* The Aim of History *(1996). "The Stolen Party" was published in Spanish in 1982 and translated into English by Alberto Manguel. It was also published in 1985 in a collection of short stories,* Other Fires: Short Fiction by Latin American Women. *Her latest book,* La Crueldad de La Vida, *was published in 2001.*

THE STOLEN PARTY   [1982]

As soon as she arrived she went straight to the kitchen to see if the monkey was there. It was: what a relief! She wouldn't have liked to admit that her mother had been right. *Monkeys at a birthday?* her mother had sneered. *Get away with you, believing any nonsense you're told!* She was cross, but not because of the monkey, the girl thought; it's just because of the party.

"I don't like you going," she told her. "It's a rich people's party."

"Rich people go to Heaven too," said the girl, who studied religion at school.

"Get away with Heaven," said the mother. "The problem with you, young lady, is that you like to fart higher than your ass."

5   The girl didn't approve of the way her mother spoke. She was barely nine, and one of the best in her class.

"I'm going because I've been invited," she said. "And I've been invited because Luciana is my friend. So there."

"Ah yes, your friend," her mother grumbled. She paused. "Listen, Rosaura," she said at last. "That one's not your friend. You know what you are to them? The maid's daughter, that's what."

Rosaura blinked hard: she wasn't going to cry. Then she yelled: "Shut up! You know nothing about being friends!"

Every afternoon she used to go to Luciana's house and they would both finish their homework while Rosaura's mother did the cleaning. They had their tea in the kitchen and they told each other secrets. Rosaura loved everything in the big house, and she also loved the people who lived there.

10   "I'm going because it will be the most lovely party in the whole world, Luciana told me it would. There will be a magician, and he will bring a monkey and everything."

The mother swung around to take a good look at her child, and pompously put her hands on her hips.

"Monkeys at a birthday?" she said. "Get away with you, believing any nonsense you're told!"

Rosaura was deeply offended. She thought it unfair of her mother to accuse other people of being liars simply because they were rich. Rosaura too wanted to be rich, of course. If one day she managed to live in a beautiful palace, would her mother stop loving her? She felt very sad. She wanted to go to that party more than anything else in the world.

"I'll die if I don't go," she whispered, almost without moving her lips.

15   And she wasn't sure whether she had been heard, but on the morning of the party she discovered that her mother had starched her Christmas dress. And in the afternoon, after washing her hair, her mother rinsed it in apple vinegar so that it would be all nice and shiny. Before going out, Rosaura admired herself in the mirror, with her white dress and glossy hair, and thought she looked terribly pretty.

Señora Ines also seemed to notice. As soon as she saw her, she said:

"How lovely you look today, Rosaura."

Rosaura gave her starched skirt a slight toss with her hands and walked into the party with a firm step. She said hello to Luciana and asked about the monkey. Luciana put on a secretive look and whispered into Rosaura's ear: "He's in the kitchen. But don't tell anyone, because it's a surprise."

Rosaura wanted to make sure. Carefully she entered the kitchen and there she saw it: deep in thought, inside its cage. It looked so funny that the girl stood there for a while, watching it, and later, every so often, she would slip out of the party unseen and go and admire it. Rosaura was the only one allowed into the kitchen. Señora Ines had said: "You yes, but not the others, they're much too boisterous, they might break something." Rosaura had never broken anything. She even managed the jug of orange juice, carrying it from the kitchen into the dining room. She held it carefully and didn't spill a single drop. And Señora Ines had said: "Are you sure you can manage a jug as big as that?" Of course she could manage. She wasn't a butterfingers, like the others. Like that blonde girl with the bow in her hair. As soon as she saw Rosaura, the girl with the bow had said:

20   "And you? Who are you?"

"I'm a friend of Luciana," said Rosaura.

"No," said the girl with the bow, "you are not a friend of Luciana because I'm her cousin and I know all her friends. And I don't know you."

"So what," said Rosaura. "I come here every afternoon with my mother and we do our homework together."

"You and your mother do your homework together?" asked the girl, laughing.

25   "I and Luciana do our homework together," said Rosaura, very seriously.

The girl with the bow shrugged her shoulders.

"That's not being friends," she said. "Do you go to school together?"

"No."

"So where do you know her from?" said the girl, getting impatient.

30   Rosaura remembered her mother's words perfectly. She took a deep breath.

"I'm the daughter of the employee," she said.

Her mother had said very clearly: "If someone asks, you say you're the daughter of the employee; that's all." She also told her to add: "And proud of it." But Rosaura thought that never in her life would she dare say something of the sort.

"What employee?" said the girl with the bow. "Employee in a shop?"

"No," said Rosaura angrily. "My mother doesn't sell anything in any shop, so there."

35   "So how come she's an employee?" said the girl with the bow.

Just then Señora Ines arrived saying *shh shh,* and asked Rosaura if she wouldn't mind helping serve out the hotdogs, as she knew the house so much better than the others.

"See?" said Rosaura to the girl with the bow, and when no one was looking she kicked her in the shin.

Apart from the girl with the bow, all the others were delightful. The one she liked best was Luciana, with her golden birthday crown; and then the boys. Rosaura won the sack race, and nobody managed to catch her when they played tag. When they split into two teams to play charades, all the boys wanted her for their side. Rosaura felt she had never been so happy in all her life.

But the best was still to come. The best came after Luciana blew out the candles. First the cake. Señora Ines had asked her to help pass the cake around, and Rosaura had enjoyed the task immensely, because everyone called out to her, shouting "Me, me!" Rosaura remembered a story in which there was a queen who had the power of life or death over her subjects. She had always loved that, having the power of life or death. To Luciana and the boys she gave the largest pieces, and to the girl with the bow she gave a slice so thin one could see through it.

40   After the cake came the magician, tall and bony, with a fine red cape. A true magician: he could untie handkerchiefs by blowing on them and make a chain with links that had no openings. He could guess what cards were pulled out from a pack, and the monkey was his assistant. He called the monkey "partner." "Let's see here, partner," he would say, "turn over a card." And, "Don't run away, partner: time to work now."

The final trick was wonderful. One of the children had to hold the monkey in his arms and the magician said he would make him disappear.

"What, the boy?" they all shouted.

"No, the monkey!" shouted back the magician.

Rosaura thought that this was truly the most amusing party in the whole world.

45   The magician asked a small fat boy to come and help, but the small fat boy got frightened almost at once and dropped the monkey on the floor. The magician picked him up carefully, whispered something in his ear, and the monkey nodded almost as if he understood.

"You mustn't be so unmanly, my friend," the magician said to the fat boy.

"What's unmanly?" said the fat boy.

The magician turned around as if to look for spies.

"A sissy," said the magician. "Go sit down."

50   Then he stared at all the faces, one by one. Rosaura felt her heart tremble.

"You, with the Spanish eyes," said the magician. And everyone saw that he was pointing at her.

She wasn't afraid. Neither holding the monkey, nor when the magician made him vanish; not even when, at the end, the magician flung his red cape over Rosaura's head and uttered a few magic words . . . and the monkey reappeared, chattering happily, in her arms. The children clapped furiously. And before Rosaura returned to her seat, the magician said:

"Thank you very much, my little countess."

She was so pleased with the compliment that a while later, when her mother came to fetch her, that was the first thing she told her.

55   "I helped the magician and he said to me, 'Thank you very much, my little countess.'"

It was strange because up to then Rosaura had thought that she was angry with her mother. All along Rosaura had imagined that she would say to her: "See that the monkey wasn't a lie?" But instead she was so thrilled that she told her mother all about the wonderful magician.

Her mother tapped her on the head and said: "So now we're a countess!"

But one could see that she was beaming.

And now they both stood in the entrance, because a moment ago Señora Ines, smiling, had said: "Please wait here a second."

60   Her mother suddenly seemed worried.

"What is it?" she asked Rosaura.

"What is what?" said Rosaura. "It's nothing; she just wants to get the presents for those who are leaving, see?"

She pointed at the fat boy and at a girl with pigtails who were also waiting there, next to their mothers. And she explained about the presents. She knew, because she had been watching those who left before her. When one of the girls was about to leave, Señora Ines would give her a bracelet. When a boy left, Señora Ines gave him a yo-yo. Rosaura preferred the yo-yo because it sparkled, but she didn't mention that to her mother. Her mother might have said: "So why don't you ask for one, you blockhead?" That's what her mother was like. Rosaura didn't feel like explaining that she'd be horribly ashamed to be the odd one out. Instead she said:

"I was the best-behaved at the party."

65   And she said no more because Señora Ines came out into the hall with two bags, one pink and one blue.

First she went up to the fat boy, gave him a yo-yo out of the blue bag, and the fat boy left with his mother. Then she went up to the girl and gave her a bracelet out of the pink bag, and the girl with the pigtails left as well.

Finally she came up to Rosaura and her mother. She had a big smile on her face and Rosaura liked that. Señora Ines looked down at her, then looked up at her mother, and then said something that made Rosaura proud:

"What a marvelous daughter you have, Herminia."

For an instant, Rosaura thought that she'd give her two presents: the bracelet and the yo-yo. Señora Ines bent down as if about to look for something. Rosaura also leaned forward, stretching out her arm. But she never completed the movement.

70 Señora Ines didn't look in the pink bag. Nor did she look in the blue bag. Instead she rummaged in her purse. In her hand appeared two bills.

"You really and truly earned this," she said handing them over. "Thank you for all your help, my pet."

Rosaura felt her arms stiffen, stick close to her body, and then she noticed her mother's hand on her shoulder. Instinctively she pressed herself against her mother's body. That was all. Except her eyes. Rosaura's eyes had a cold, clear look that fixed itself on Señora Ines's face.

Señora Ines, motionless, stood there with her hand outstretched. As if she didn't dare draw it back. As if the slightest change might shatter an infinitely delicate balance.

MAKING CONNECTIONS

1. Discuss the relationship between Rosaura and her mother. Do you think it's a good one? Do they learn anything from each other? Pick out passages in the story that illustrate their relationship.

2. Why do you think the story is called "The Stolen Party"? What has been "stolen"? Explain.

3. What is the point of view of this story? What impact does this narrative perspective have on the story? If the story were told by Señora Ines, how would it be different?

MAKING AN ARGUMENT

1. Is Señora Ines a rich snob? Or is she just trying to be nice to Rosaura? Or something else? Take a position and write an essay that interprets the characters, the conflict, and the theme of this story. Cite the text of the story for support.

JAMES JOYCE [1882–1941]

(See biography on p. 190.)

ARABY   [1914]

North Richmond Street, being blind, was a quiet street except at the hour when the Christian Brothers' School set the boys free. An uninhabited house of two stories stood at the blind end, detached from its neighbors in a square ground. The other houses of the street, conscious of decent lives within them, gazed at one another with brown imperturbable faces.

The former tenant of our house, a priest, had died in the back drawing-room. Air, musty from having been long enclosed, hung in all the rooms, and the waste room behind the kitchen was littered with old useless papers. Among these I found a few paper-covered books, the pages of which were curled and damp: *The Abbot,*[1] by Walter Scott, *The Devout Communicant*[2] and *The Memoirs of Vidocq*.[3] I liked the last best because its leaves were yellow. The wild garden behind the house contained a central apple-tree and a few straggling bushes under one of which I found the late tenant's rusty bicycle-pump. He had been a very charitable priest; in his will he had left all his money to institutions and the furniture of his house to his sister.

When the short days of winter came dusk fell before we had well eaten our dinners. When we met in the street the houses had grown sombre. The space of sky above us was the colour of ever-changing violet and towards it the lamps of the street lifted their feeble lanterns. The cold air stung us and we played till our bodies glowed. Our shouts echoed in the silent street. The career of our play brought us through the dark muddy lanes behind the houses where we ran the gauntlet of the rough tribes from the cottages, to the back doors of the dark dripping gardens where odours arose from the ashpits, to the dark odorous stables where a coachman smoothed and combed the horse or shook music from the buckled harness. When we returned to the street light from the kitchen windows had filled the areas. If my uncle was seen turning the corner we hid in the shadow until we had seen him safely housed. Or if Mangan's sister came out on the doorstep to call her brother in to his tea we watched her from our shadow peer up and down the street. We waited to see whether she would remain or go in and, if she remained, we left our shadow and walked up to Mangan's steps resignedly. She was waiting for us, her figure defined by the light from the half-opened door. Her brother always teased her before he obeyed and I stood by the railings looking at her. Her dress swung as she moved her body and the soft rope of her hair tossed from side to side.

Every morning I lay on the floor in the front parlour watching her door. The blind was pulled down to within an inch of the sash so that I could not be seen. When she came out on the doorstep my heart leaped. I ran to the hall, seized my books and followed her. I kept her brown figure always in my eye and, when we came near the point at which our ways diverged, I quickened my pace and passed her. This happened morning after morning. I had never spoken to her, except for a few casual words, and yet her name was like a summons to all my foolish blood.

5   Her image accompanied me even in places the most hostile to romance. On Saturday evenings when my aunt went marketing I had to go to carry some of the parcels. We walked through the flaring streets, jostled by drunken men and bargaining women, amid the curses of labourers, the shrill litanies of shop-boys who stood on guard by the barrels of pigs' cheeks, the nasal chanting of street-singers, who sang a *come-all-you* about O'Donovan Rossa, or a ballad about the troubles in our native land. These noises converged in a single sensation of life for me: I imagined that I bore my chalice safely through a throng of foes. Her name sprang to my

[1]**The Abbot** an early-nineteenth-century romantic novel   [2]**The Devout Communicant** a religious text   [3]**The Memoirs of Vidocq** the memoirs of a French secret service agent

lips at moments in strange prayers and praises which I myself did not understand. My eyes were often full of tears (I could not tell why) and at times a flood from my heart seemed to pour itself out into my bosom. I thought little of the future. I did not know whether I would ever speak to her or not or, if I spoke to her, how I could tell her of my confused adoration. But my body was like a harp and her words and gestures were like fingers running upon the wires.

One evening I went into the back drawing-room in which the priest had died. It was a dark rainy evening and there was no sound in the house. Through one of the broken panes I heard the rain impinge upon the earth, the fine incessant needles of water playing in the sodden beds. Some distant lamp or lighted window gleamed below me. I was thankful that I could see so little. All my senses seemed to desire to veil themselves and, feeling that I was about to slip from them, I pressed the palms of my hands together until they trembled, murmuring: "*O love! O love!*" many times.

At last she spoke to me. When she addressed the first words to me I was so confused that I did not know what to answer. She asked me was I going to Araby. I forget whether I answered yes or no. It would be a splendid bazaar, she said; she would love to go.

"And why can't you?" I asked.

While she spoke she turned a silver bracelet round and round her wrist. She could not go, she said, because there would be a retreat that week in her convent.[4] Her brother and two other boys were fighting for their caps and I was alone at the railings. She held one of the spikes, bowing her head towards me. The light from the lamp opposite our door caught the white curve of her neck, lit up her hair that rested there and, falling, lit up the hand upon the railing. It fell over one side of her dress and caught the white border of a petticoat, just visible as she stood at ease.

10   "It's well for you," she said.

"If I go," I said, "I will bring you something."

What innumerable follies laid waste my waking and sleeping thoughts after that evening! I wished to annihilate the tedious intervening days. I chafed against the work of school. At night in my bedroom and by day in the classroom her image came between me and the page I strove to read. The syllables of the word *Araby* were called to me through the silence in which my soul luxuriated and cast an Eastern enchantment over me. I asked for leave to go to the bazaar on Saturday night. My aunt was surprised and hoped it was not some Freemason affair. I answered few questions in class. I watched my master's face pass from amiability to sternness; he hoped I was not beginning to idle. I could not call my wandering thoughts together. I had hardly any patience with the serious work of life which, now that it stood between me and my desire, seemed to me child's play, ugly monotonous child's play.

On Saturday morning I reminded my uncle that I wished to go to the bazaar in the evening. He was fussing at the hall-stand, looking for the hat-brush, and answered me curtly:

"Yes, boy, I know."

[4]**convent** in this case a parochial school for girls

15   As he was in the hall I could not go into the front parlour and lie at the window. I left the house in bad humour and walked slowly towards the school. The air was pitilessly raw and already my heart misgave me.

When I came home to dinner my uncle had not yet been home. Still it was early. I sat staring at the clock for some time and, when its ticking began to irritate me, I left the room. I mounted the staircase and gained the upper part of the house. The high cold empty gloomy rooms liberated me and I went from room to room singing. From the front window I saw my companions playing below in the street. Their cries reached me weakened and indistinct and, leaning my forehead against the cool glass, I looked over at the dark house where she lived. I may have stood there for an hour, seeing nothing but the brown-clad figure cast by my imagination, touched discreetly by the lamplight at the curved neck, at the hand upon the railings and at the border below the dress.

When I came downstairs again I found Mrs. Mercer sitting at the fire. She was an old garrulous woman, a pawnbroker's widow, who collected used stamps for some pious purpose. I had to endure the gossip of the tea-table. The meal was prolonged beyond an hour and still my uncle did not come. Mrs. Mercer stood up to go: she was sorry she couldn't wait any longer, but it was after eight o'clock and she did not like to be out late, as the night air was bad for her. When she had gone I began to walk up and down the room, clenching my fists. My aunt said:

"I'm afraid you may put off your bazaar for this night of Our Lord."

At nine o'clock I heard my uncle's latchkey in the halldoor. I heard him talking to himself and heard the hallstand rocking when it had received the weight of his overcoat. I could interpret these signs. When he was midway through his dinner I asked him to give me the money to go to the bazaar. He had forgotten.

20   "The people are in bed and after their first sleep now," he said.

I did not smile. My aunt said to him energetically:

"Can't you give him the money and let him go? You've kept him late enough as it is."

My uncle said he was very sorry he had forgotten. He said he believed in the old saying: "All work and no play makes Jack a dull boy." He asked me where I was going and, when I had told him a second time he asked me did I know *The Arab's Farewell to His Steed*. When I left the kitchen he was about to recite the opening lines of the piece to my aunt.

I held a florin tightly in my hand as I strode down Buckingham Street towards the station. The sight of the streets thronged with buyers and glaring with gas recalled to me the purpose of my journey. I took my seat in a third-class carriage of a deserted train. After an intolerable delay the train moved out of the station slowly. It crept onward among ruinous houses and over the twinkling river. At Westland Row Station a crowd of people pressed to the carriage doors; but the porters moved them back, saying that it was a special train for the bazaar. I remained alone in the bare carriage. In a few minutes the train drew up beside an improvised wooden platform. I passed out on to the road and saw by the lighted dial of a clock that it was ten minutes to ten. In front of me was a large building which displayed the magical name.

25   I could not find any sixpenny entrance and, fearing that the bazaar would be closed, I passed in quickly through a turnstile, handing a shilling to a weary-looking

man. I found myself in a big hall girdled at half its height by a gallery. Nearly all the stalls were closed and the greater part of the hall was in darkness. I recognized a silence like that which pervades a church after a service. I walked into the center of the bazaar timidly. A few people were gathered about the stalls which were still open. Before a curtain, over which the words *Café Chantant* were written in coloured lamps, two men were counting money on a salver. I listened to the fall of the coins.

Remembering with difficulty why I had come I went over to one of the stalls and examined porcelain vases and flowered tea-sets. At the door of the stall a young lady was talking and laughing with two young gentlemen. I remarked their English accents and listened vaguely to their conversation.

"O, I never said such a thing!"

"O, but you did!"

"O, but I didn't!"

30   "Didn't she say that?"

"Yes. I heard her."

"O, there's a . . . fib!"

Observing me the young lady came over and asked me did I wish to buy anything. The tone of her voice was not encouraging; she seemed to have spoken to me out of a sense of duty. I looked humbly at the great jars that stood like eastern guards at either side of the dark entrance to the stall and murmured:

"No, thank you."

35   The young lady changed the position of one of the vases and went back to the two young men. They began to talk of the same subject. Once or twice the young lady glanced at me over her shoulder.

I lingered before her stall, though I knew my stay was useless, to make my interest in her wares seem the more real. Then I turned away slowly and walked down the middle of the bazaar. I allowed the two pennies to fall against the sixpence in my pocket. I heard a voice call from one end of the gallery that the light was out. The upper part of the hall was now completely dark.

Gazing up into the darkness I saw myself as a creature driven and derided by vanity; and my eyes burned with anguish and anger.

MAKING CONNECTIONS

1. To what extent does your own experience with a crush influence your response to this story?

2. Describe the setting of the story. How are you affected by the personification in the first paragraph? Is North Richmond street "blind" only because it's a dead-end street? Do you think the setting is an appropriate background for the boy's feelings? To what extent are the changes in setting related to his emotions?

3. Who is the narrator? How old is he at the time of the story? Is the story told in the "voice" of a child or an adult? What difference does that make in the telling and in your response?

4. What aspects of the boy's reactions illustrate his feelings for Mangan's sister? Do you think the boy's crush is believable? Do people behave like this when they are "smitten"? Explain.
5. To what extent is the Araby bazaar symbolic of the boy's crush on Mangan's sister? What other symbols can you find?

MAKING AN ARGUMENT

1. At the end of the story, the boy sees himself "as a creature driven and derided by vanity." Why? Is this a loss of innocence? Was he really in love? Is his disappointment only about love? Write an essay that interprets this story in light of Joyce's characterization of the boy, the conflict, and the outcome. Cite the text of the story for support.

JOYCE CAROL OATES [B. 1938]

Joyce Carol Oates was born into a blue-collar family in Lockport, New York, and even as a child, she was a prolific writer. Her best-known works include A Garden of Earthly Delights *(1967), the National Book Award–winning* Them *(1969), and* On Boxing *(1987). Oates currently lives in suburban New Jersey and is the Berlind Distinguished Professor of Humanities at Princeton University. Many critics have complained about the graphic violence that is often present in her work. Oates has responded:"The more violent the murders in* Macbeth, *the more relief one can feel at not having to perform them. Great art is cathartic; it is always moral." "Where Are You Going, Where Have You Been?",* *which first appeared in* The Wheel and Love and Other Stories *(1970), was the basis for the 1985 film* Smooth Talk. *She is the author of more than thirty books, and her most recent novel is* Broke Heart Blues, *published in 2005.*

WHERE ARE YOU GOING, WHERE HAVE YOU BEEN?   [1970]

For Bob Dylan

Her name was Connie. She was fifteen and she had a quick nervous giggling habit of craning her neck to glance into mirrors, or checking other people's faces to make sure her own was all right. Her mother, who noticed everything and knew everything and who hadn't much reason any longer to look at her own face, always scolded Connie about it. "Stop gawking at yourself, who are you? You think you're so pretty?" she would say. Connie would raise her eyebrows at these familiar complaints and look right through her mother, into a shadowy vision of herself as she was right at that moment: she knew she was pretty and that was everything. Her mother had been pretty once too, if you could believe those old snapshots in the album, but now her looks were gone and that was why she was always after Connie.

"Why don't you keep your room clean like your sister? How've you got your hair fixed—what the hell stinks? Hair spray? You don't see your sister using that junk."

Her sister June was twenty-four and still lived at home. She was a secretary in the high school Connie attended, and if that wasn't bad enough—with her in the same building—she was so plain and chunky and steady that Connie had to hear her praised all the time by her mother and her mother's sisters. June did this, June did that, she saved money and helped clean the house and cooked and Connie couldn't do a thing, her mind was all filled with trashy daydreams. Their father was away at work most of the time and when he came home he wanted supper and he read the newspaper at supper and after supper he went to bed. He didn't bother talking much to them, but around his bent head Connie's mother kept picking at her until Connie wished her mother was dead and she herself was dead and it was all over. "She makes me want to throw up sometimes," she complained to her friends. She had a high, breathless, amused voice which made everything she said sound a little forced, whether it was sincere or not.

There was one good thing: June went places with girl friends of hers, girls who were just as plain and steady as she, and so when Connie wanted to do that her mother had no objections. The father of Connie's best girl friend drove the girls the three miles to town and left them off at a shopping plaza, so that they could walk through the stores or go to a movie, and when he came to pick them up again at eleven he never bothered to ask what they had done.

5   They must have been familiar sights, walking around that shopping plaza in their shorts and flat ballerina slippers that always scuffed the sidewalk, with charm bracelets jingling on their thin wrists; they would lean together to whisper and laugh secretly if someone passed by who amused or interested them. Connie had long dark blond hair that drew anyone's eye to it, and she wore part of it pulled up on her head and puffed out and the rest of it she let fall down her back. She wore a pull-over jersey blouse that looked one way when she was at home and another way when she was away from home. Everything about her had two sides to it, one for home and one for anywhere that was not home: her walk that could be childlike and bobbing, or languid enough to make anyone think she was hearing music in her head, her mouth which was pale and smirking most of the time, but bright and pink on these evenings out, her laugh which was cynical and drawling at home—"Ha, ha, very funny"—but high-pitched and nervous anywhere else, like the jingling of the charms on her bracelet.

Sometimes they did go shopping or to a movie, but sometimes they went across the highway, ducking fast across the busy road, to a drive-in restaurant where older kids hung out. The restaurant was shaped like a big bottle, though squatter than a real bottle, and on its cap was a revolving figure of a grinning boy who held a hamburger aloft. One night in mid-summer they ran across, breathless with daring, and right away someone leaned out a car window and invited them over, but it was just a boy from high school they didn't like. It made them feel good to be able to ignore him. They went up through the maze of parked and cruising cars to the bright-lit, fly-infested restaurant, their faces pleased and expectant as if they were entering a sacred building that loomed out of the night to give them what haven and what blessing they yearned for. They sat at the counter and crossed their legs at the ankles, their thin shoulders rigid with excitement, and listened to the music that made everything so good: the music was always in the background like music at a church service, it was something to depend upon.

A boy named Eddie came in to talk with them. He sat backwards on his stool, turning himself jerkily around in semi-circles and then stopping and turning again, and after a while he asked Connie if she would like something to eat. She said she did and so she tapped her friend's arm on her way out—her friend pulled her face up into a brave droll look—and Connie said she would meet her at eleven, across the way. "I just hate to leave her like that," Connie said earnestly, but the boy said that she wouldn't be alone for long. So they went out to his car and on the way Connie couldn't help but let her eyes wander over the windshields and faces all around her, her face gleaming with a joy that had nothing to do with Eddie or even this place; it might have been the music. She drew her shoulders up and sucked in her breath with the pure pleasure of being alive, and just at that moment she happened to glance at a face just a few feet from hers. It was a boy with shaggy black hair, in a convertible jalopy painted gold. He stared at her and then his lips widened into a grin. Connie slit her eyes at him and turned away, but she couldn't help glancing back and there he was still watching her. He wagged a finger and laughed and said, "Gonna get you, baby," and Connie turned away again without Eddie noticing anything.

She spent three hours with him, at the restaurant where they ate hamburgers and drank Cokes in wax cups that were always sweating, and then down an alley a mile or so away, and when he left her off at five to eleven only the movie house was still open at the plaza. Her girl friend was there, talking with a boy. When Connie came up the two girls smiled at each other and Connie said, "How was the movie?" and the girl said, "*You* should know." They rode off with the girl's father, sleepy and pleased, and Connie couldn't help but look at the darkened shopping plaza with its big empty parking lot and its signs that were faded and ghostly now, and over at the drive-in restaurant where cars were still circling tirelessly. She couldn't hear the music at this distance.

Next morning June asked her how the movie was and Connie said, "So-so."

10   She and that girl and occasionally another girl went out several times a week that way, and the rest of the time Connie spent around the house—it was summer vacation—getting in her mother's way and thinking, dreaming, about the boys she met. But all the boys fell back and dissolved into a single face that was not even a face, but an idea, a feeling, mixed up with the urgent insistent pounding of the music and the humid night air of July. Connie's mother kept dragging her back to the daylight by finding things for her to do or saying, suddenly, "What's this about the Pettinger girl?"

And Connie would say nervously, "Oh, her. That dope." She always drew thick clear lines between herself and such girls, and her mother was simple and kindly enough to believe her. Her mother was so simple, Connie thought, that it was maybe cruel to fool her so much. Her mother went scuffling around the house in old bed-room slippers and complained over the telephone to one sister about the other, then the other called up and the two of them complained about the third one. If June's name was mentioned her mother's tone was approving, and if Connie's name was mentioned it was disapproving. This did not really mean she disliked Connie and actually Connie thought that her mother preferred her to June because she was prettier, but the two of them kept up a pretense of exasperation, a sense that they were tugging and struggling over something of little value to either of them. Sometimes, over coffee, they were almost friends, but something would come up—some vexation that was like a fly buzzing suddenly around their heads—and their faces went hard with contempt.

One Sunday Connie got up at eleven—none of them bothered with church— and washed her hair so that it could dry all day long, in the sun. Her parents and sister were going to a barbecue at an aunt's house and Connie said no, she wasn't interested, rolling her eyes to let her mother know just what she thought of it. "Stay home alone then," her mother said sharply. Connie sat out back in a lawn chair and watched them drive away, her father quiet and bald, hunched around so that he could back the car out, her mother with a look that was still angry and not at all softened through the windshield, and in the back seat poor old June all dressed up as if she didn't know what a barbecue was, with all the running yelling kids and the flies. Connie sat with her eyes closed in the sun, dreaming and dazed with the warmth about her as if this were a kind of love, the caresses of love, and her mind slipped over onto thoughts of the boy she had been with the night before and how nice he had been, how sweet it always was, not the way someone like June would suppose but sweet, gentle, the way it was in movies and promised in songs; and when she opened her eyes she hardly knew where she was, the back yard ran off into weeds and a fence-line of trees and behind it the sky was perfectly blue and still. The asbestos "ranch house" that was now three years old startled her—it looked small. She shook her head as if to get awake.

It was too hot. She went inside the house and turned on the radio to drown out the quiet. She sat on the edge of her bed, barefoot, and listened for an hour and a half to a program called XYZ Sunday Jamboree, record after record of hard, fast, shrieking songs she sang along with, interspersed by exclamations from "Bobby King": "An' look here you girls at Napoleon's—Son and Charley want you to pay real close attention to this song coming up!"

And Connie paid close attention herself, bathed in a glow of slow-pulsed joy that seemed to rise mysteriously out of the music itself and lay languidly about the airless little room, breathed in and breathed out with each gentle rise and fall of her chest.

15   After a while she heard a car coming up the drive. She sat up at once, startled, because it couldn't be her father so soon. The gravel kept crunching all the way in from the road—the driveway was long—and Connie ran to the window. It was a car she didn't know. It was an open jalopy, painted a bright gold that caught the sunlight opaquely. Her heart began to pound and her fingers snatched at her hair, checking it, and she whispered "Christ. Christ," wondering how bad she looked. The car came to a stop at the side door and the horn sounded four short taps as if this were a signal Connie knew.

She went into the kitchen and approached the door slowly, then hung out the screen door, her bare toes curling down off the step. There were two boys in the car and now she recognized the driver: he had shaggy, shabby black hair that looked crazy as a wig and he was grinning at her.

"I ain't late, am I?" he said.

"Who the hell do you think you are?" Connie said.

"Toldja I'd be out, didn't I?"

20   "I don't even know who you are."

She spoke sullenly, careful to show no interest or pleasure, and he spoke in a fast bright monotone. Connie looked past him to the other boy, taking her time. He had fair brown hair, with a lock that fell onto his forehead. His sideburns gave him a fierce, embarrassed look, but so far he hadn't even bothered to glance at her. Both boys wore sunglasses. The driver's glasses were metallic and mirrored everything in miniature.

"You wanta come for a ride?" he said.

Connie smirked and let her hair fall loose over one shoulder.

"Don'tcha like my car? New paint job," he said. "Hey."

25   "What?"

"You're cute."

She pretended to fidget, chasing flies away from the door.

"Don'tcha believe me, or what?" he said.

"Look, I don't even know who you are," Connie said in disgust.

30   "Hey, Ellie's got a radio, see. Mine's broke down." He lifted his friend's arm and showed her the little transistor the boy was holding, and now Connie began to hear the music. It was the same program that was playing inside the house.

"Bobby King?" she said.

"I listen to him all the time. I think he's great."

"He's kind of great," Connie said reluctantly.

"Listen, that guy's *great*. He knows where the action is."

35   Connie blushed a little, because the glasses made it impossible for her to see just what this boy was looking at. She couldn't decide if she liked him or if he was just a jerk, and so she dawdled in the doorway and wouldn't come down or go back inside. She said, "What's all that stuff painted on your car?"

"Can'tcha read it?" He opened the door very carefully, as if he was afraid it might fall off. He slid out just as carefully, planting his feet firmly on the ground, the tiny metallic world in his glasses slowing down like gelatin hardening and in the midst of it Connie's bright green blouse. "This here is my name, to begin with," he said. ARNOLD FRIEND was written in tarlike black letters on the side, with a drawing of a round grinning face that reminded Connie of a pumpkin, except it wore sunglasses. "I wanta introduce myself, I'm Arnold Friend and that's my real name and I'm gonna be your friend, honey, and inside the car's Ellie Oscar, he's kinda shy." Ellie brought his transistor radio up to his shoulder and balanced it there. "Now these numbers are a secret code, honey," Arnold Friend explained. He read off the numbers 33, 19, 17 and raised his eyebrows at her to see what she thought of that, but she didn't think much of it. The left rear fender had been smashed and around it was written, on the gleaming gold background: DONE BY CRAZY WOMAN DRIVER. Connie had to laugh at that. Arnold Friend was pleased at her laughter and looked up at her. "Around the other side's a lot more—you wanta come and see them?"

"No."

"Why not?"

"Why should I?"

40   "Don'tcha wanta see what's on the car? Don'tcha wanta go for a ride?"

"I don't know."

"Why not?"

"I got things to do."

"Like what?"

45   "Things."

He laughed as if she had said something funny. He slapped his thighs. He was standing in a strange way, leaning back against the car as if he were balancing himself. He wasn't tall, only an inch or so taller than she would be if she came down to him. Connie liked the way he was dressed, which was the way all of them dressed: tight faded jeans stuffed into black, scuffed boots, a belt that pulled his waist in and showed how lean he was, and a white pull-over shirt that was a little soiled and showed the hard small muscles of his arms and shoulders. He looked as if he probably did hard work, lifting and carrying things. Even his neck looked muscular. And his face was a familiar face, somehow: the jaw and chin and cheeks slightly darkened, because he hadn't shaved for a day or two, and the nose long and hawk-like, sniffing as if she were a treat he was going to gobble up and it was all a joke.

"Connie, you ain't telling the truth. This is your day set aside for a ride with me and you know it," he said, still laughing. The way he straightened and recovered from his fit of laughing showed that it had been all fake.

"How do you know what my name is?" she said suspiciously.

"It's Connie."

50   "Maybe and maybe not."

"I know my Connie," he said, wagging his finger. Now she remembered him even better, back at the restaurant, and her cheeks warmed at the thought of how she sucked in her breath just at the moment she passed him—how she must have looked to him. And he had remembered her. "Ellie and I come out here especially for you," he said. "Ellie can sit in back. How about it?"

"Where?"

"Where what?"

"Where're we going?"

55   He looked at her. He took off the sunglasses and she saw how pale the skin around his eyes was, like holes that were not in shadow but instead in light. His eyes were chips of broken glass that catch the light in an amiable way. He smiled. It was as if the idea of going for a ride somewhere, to some place, was a new idea to him.

"Just for a ride, Connie sweetheart."

"I never said my name was Connie," she said.

"But I know what it is. I know your name and all about you, lots of things," Arnold Friend said. He had not moved yet but stood still leaning back against the side of his jalopy. "I took a special interest in you, such a pretty girl, and found out all about you like I know your parents and sister are gone somewheres and I know where and how long they're going to be gone, and I know who you were with last night, and your best girl friend's name is Betty. Right?"

He spoke in a simple lilting voice, exactly as if he were reciting the words to a song. His smile assured her that everything was fine. In the car Ellie turned up the volume on his radio and did not bother to look around at them.

60   "Ellie can sit in the back seat," Arnold Friend said. He indicated his friend with a casual jerk of his chin, as if Ellie did not count and she should not bother with him.

"How'd you find out all that stuff?" Connie said.

"Listen: Betty Schultz and Tony Fitch and Jimmy Pettinger and Nancy Pettinger," he said, in a chant. "Raymond Stanley and Bob Hutter—"

"Do you know all those kids?"

"I know everybody."

65 "Look, you're kidding. You're not from around here."

"Sure."

"But—how come we never saw you before?"

"Sure you saw me before," he said. He looked down at his boots, as if he were a little offended. "You just don't remember."

"I guess I'd remember you," Connie said.

70 "Yeah?" He looked up at this, beaming. He was pleased. He began to mark time with the music from Ellie's radio, tapping his fists lightly together. Connie looked away from his smile to the car, which was painted so bright it almost hurt her eyes to look at it. She looked at that name, ARNOLD FRIEND. And up at the front fender was an expression that was familiar—MAN THE FLYING SAUCERS. It was an expression kids had used the year before, but didn't use this year. She looked at it for a while as if the words meant something to her that she did not yet know.

"What're you thinking about? Huh?" Arnold Friend demanded. "Not worried about your hair blowing around in the car, are you?"

"No."

"Think I maybe can't drive good?"

"How do I know?"

75 "You're a hard girl to handle. How come?" he said. "Don't you know I'm your friend? Didn't you see me put my sign in the air when you walked by?"

"What sign?"

"My sign." And he drew an X in the air, leaning out toward her. They were maybe ten feet apart. After his hand fell back to his side the X was still in the air, almost visible. Connie let the screen door close and stood perfectly still inside it, listening to the music from her radio and the boy's blend together. She stared at Arnold Friend. He stood there so stiffly relaxed, pretending to be relaxed, with one hand idly on the door handle as if he were keeping himself up that way and had no intention of ever moving again. She recognized most things about him, the tight jeans that showed his thighs and buttocks and the greasy leather boots and the tight shirt, and even that slippery friendly smile of his, that sleepy dreamy smile that all the boys used to get across ideas they didn't want to put into words. She recognized all this and also the singsong way he talked, slightly mocking, kidding, but serious and a little melancholy, and she recognized the way he tapped one fist against the other in homage to the perpetual music behind him. But all these things did not come together.

She said suddenly, "Hey, how old are you?"

His smile faded. She could see then that he wasn't a kid, he was much older—thirty, maybe more. At this knowledge her heart began to pound faster.

80 "That's a crazy thing to ask. Can'tcha see I'm your own age?"

"Like hell you are."

"Or maybe a coupla years older, I'm eighteen."

"Eighteen?" she said doubtfully.

He grinned to reassure her and lines appeared at the corners of his mouth. His teeth were big and white. He grinned so broadly his eyes became slits and she saw how thick the lashes were, thick and black as if painted with a black tarlike material. Then he seemed to become embarrassed, abruptly, and looked over his shoulder at Ellie. "*Him,* he's crazy," he said. "Ain't he a riot, he's a nut, a real character." Ellie was still listening to the music. His sunglasses told nothing about what he was thinking. He wore a bright orange shirt unbuttoned halfway to show his chest, which was a pale, bluish chest and not muscular like Arnold Friend's. His shirt collar was turned up all around and the very tips of the collar pointed out past his chin as if they were protecting him. He was pressing the transistor radio up against his ear and sat there in a kind of daze, right in the sun.

85   "He's kinda strange," Connie said.

"Hey, she says you're kinda strange! Kinda strange!" Arnold Friend cried. He pounded on the car to get Ellie's attention. Ellie turned for the first time and Connie saw with shock that he wasn't a kid either—he had a fair, hairless face, cheeks reddened slightly as if the veins grew too close to the surface of his skin, the face of a forty-year-old baby. Connie felt a wave of dizziness rise in her at this sight and she stared at him as if waiting for something to change the shock of the moment, make it all right again. Ellie's lips kept shaping words, mumbling along, with the words blasting in his ear.

"Maybe you two better go away," Connie said faintly.

"What? How come?" Arnold Friend cried. "We come out here to take you for a ride. It's Sunday." He had the voice of the man on the radio now. It was the same voice, Connie thought. "Don'tcha know it's Sunday all day and honey, no matter who you were with last night today you're with Arnold Friend and don't you forget it!— Maybe you better step out here," he said, and this last was in a different voice. It was a little flatter, as if the heat was finally getting to him.

"No. I got things to do."

90   "Hey."

"You two better leave."

"We ain't leaving until you come with us."

"Like hell I am—"

"Connie, don't fool around with me. I mean, I mean, don't fool *around,*" he said, shaking his head. He laughed incredulously. He placed his sunglasses on top of his head, carefully, as if he were indeed wearing a wig, and brought the stems down behind his ears. Connie stared at him, another wave of dizziness and fear rising in her so that for a moment he wasn't even in focus but was just a blur, standing there against his gold car, and she had the idea that he had driven up the driveway all right but had come from nowhere before that and belonged nowhere and that everything about him and even about the music that was so familiar to her was only half real.

95   "If my father comes and sees you—"

"He ain't coming. He's at the barbecue."

"How do you know that?"

"Aunt Tillie's. Right now they're—uh—they're drinking. Sitting around," he said vaguely, squinting as if he were staring all the way to town and over to Aunt Tillie's backyard. Then the vision seemed to get clear and he nodded energetically. "Yeah. Sitting around. There's your sister in a blue dress, huh? And high heels, the poor sad bitch—nothing like you, sweetheart! And your mother's helping some fat woman with the corn, they're cleaning the corn—husking the corn—"

"What fat woman?" Connie cried.

100   "How do I know what fat woman. I don't know every goddam fat woman in the world!" Arnold Friend laughed.

"Oh, that's Mrs. Hornby. . . . Who invited her?" Connie said. She felt a little light-headed. Her breath was coming quickly.

"She's too fat. I don't like them fat. I like them the way you are, honey," he said, smiling sleepily at her. They stared at each other for a while, through the screen door. He said softly, "Now what you're going to do is this: you're going to come out that door. You're going to sit up front with me and Ellie's going to sit in the back, the hell with Ellie, right? This isn't Ellie's date. You're my date. I'm your lover, honey."

"What? You're crazy—"

"Yes, I'm your lover. You don't know what that is but you will," he said. "I know that too. I know all about you. But look: it's real nice and you couldn't ask for nobody better than me, or more polite. I always keep my word. I'll tell you how it is, I'm always nice at first, the first time. I'll hold you so tight you won't think you have to try to get away or pretend anything because you'll know you can't. And I'll come inside you where it's all secret and you'll give in to me and you'll love me—"

105   "Shut up! You're crazy!" Connie said. She backed away from the door. She put her hands against her ears as if she'd heard something terrible, something not meant for her. "People don't talk like that, you're crazy," she muttered. Her heart was almost too big now for her chest and its pumping made sweat break out all over her. She looked out to see Arnold Friend pause and then take a step toward the porch lurch-ing. He almost fell. But, like a clever drunken man, he managed to catch his balance. He wobbled in his high boots and grabbed hold of one of the porch posts.

"Honey?" he said. "You still listening?"

"Get the hell out of here!"

"Be nice, honey. Listen."

"I'm going to call the police—"

110   He wobbled again and out of the side of his mouth came a fast spat curse, an aside not meant for her to hear. But even this "Christ!" sounded forced. Then he began to smile again. She watched this smile come, awkward as if he were smiling from inside a mask. His whole face was a mask, she thought wildly, tanned down onto his throat but then running out as if he had plastered make-up on his face but had forgotten about his throat.

"Honey—? Listen, here's how it is. I always tell the truth and I promise you this: I ain't coming in that house after you."

"You better not! I'm going to call the police if you—if you don't—"

"Honey," he said, talking right through her voice, "honey, I'm not coming in there but you are coming out here. You know why?"

She was panting. The kitchen looked like a place she had never seen before, some room she had run inside but which wasn't good enough, wasn't going to help her. The kitchen window had never had a curtain, after three years, and there were dishes in the sink for her to do—probably—and if you ran your hand across the table you'd probably feel something sticky there.

115   "You listening, honey? Hey?"

"—going to call the police—"

"Soon as you touch the phone I don't need to keep my promise and can come inside. You won't want that."

She rushed forward and tried to lock the door. Her fingers were shaking. "But why lock it," Arnold Friend said gently, talking right into her face. "It's just a screen door. It's just nothing." One of his boots was at a strange angle, as if his foot wasn't in it. It pointed out to the left, bent at the ankle. "I mean, anybody can break through a screen door and glass and wood and iron or anything else if he needs to, anybody at all and specially Arnold Friend. If the place got lit up with a fire honey you'd come running out into my arms, right into my arms and safe at home—like you knew I was your lover and'd stopped fooling around. I don't mind a nice shy girl but I don't like no fooling around." Part of those words were spoken with a slight rhythmic lilt, and Connie somehow recognized them—the echo of a song from last year, about a girl rushing into her boy friend's arms and coming home again—

Connie stood barefoot on the linoleum floor, staring at him. "What do you want?" she whispered.

120   "I want you," he said.

"What?"

"Seen you that night and thought, that's the one, yes sir. I never needed to look any more."

"But my father's coming back. He's coming to get me. I had to wash my hair first—" She spoke in a dry, rapid voice, hardly raising it for him to hear.

"No, your daddy is not coming and yes, you had to wash your hair and you washed it for me. It's nice and shining and all for me, I thank you, sweetheart," he said, with a mock bow, but again he almost lost his balance. He had to bend and adjust his boots. Evidently his feet did not go all the way down; the boots must have been stuffed with something so that he would seem taller. Connie stared out at him and behind him Ellie in the car, who seemed to be looking off toward Connie's right, into nothing. This Ellie said, pulling the words out of the air one after another as if he were just discovering them, "You want me to pull out the phone?"

125   "Shut your mouth and keep it shut," Arnold Friend said, his face red from bending over or maybe from embarrassment because Connie had seen his boots. "This ain't none of your business."

"What—what are you doing? What do you want?" Connie said. "If I call the police they'll get you, they'll arrest you—"

"Promise was not to come in unless you touch that phone, and I'll keep that promise," he said. He resumed his erect position and tried to force his shoulders back. He sounded like a hero in a movie, declaring something important. He spoke too loudly and it was as if he were speaking to someone behind Connie. "I ain't made plans for coming in that house where I don't belong but just for you to come out to me, the way you should. Don't you know who I am?"

"You're crazy," she whispered. She backed away from the door but did not want to go into another part of the house, as if this would give him permission to come through the door. "What do you . . . .You're crazy, you . . . ."

"Huh? What're you saying, honey?"

130   Her eyes darted everywhere in the kitchen. She could not remember what it was, this room.

"This is how it is, honey: you come out and we'll drive away, have a nice ride. But if you don't come out we're gonna wait till your people come home and then they're all going to get it."

"You want that telephone pulled out?" Ellie said. He held the radio away from his ear and grimaced, as if without the radio the air was too much for him.

"I toldja shut up, Ellie," Arnold Friend said, "you're deaf, get a hearing aid, right? Fix yourself up. This little girl's no trouble and's gonna be nice to me, so Ellie keep to yourself, this ain't your date—right? Don't hem in on me. Don't hog. Don't crush. Don't bird dog. Don't trail me," he said in a rapid meaningless voice, as if he were running through all the expressions he'd learned but was no longer sure which one of them was in style, then rushing on to new ones, making them up with his eyes closed, "Don't crawl under my fence, don't squeeze in my chipmunk hole, don't sniff my glue, suck my popsicle, keep your own greasy fingers on yourself!" He shaded his eyes and peered in at Connie, who was backed against the kitchen table. "Don't mind him honey he's just a creep. He's a dope. Right? I'm the boy for you and like I said you come out here nice like a lady and give me your hand, and nobody else gets hurt, I mean, your nice old bald-headed daddy and your mummy and your sister in her high heels. Because listen: why bring them in this?"

"Leave me alone," Connie whispered.

135   "Hey, you know that old woman down the road, the one with the chickens and stuff—you know her?"

"She's dead!"

"Dead? What? You know her?" Arnold Friend said.

"She's dead—"

"Don't you like her?"

140   "She's dead—she's—she isn't here any more—"

"But don't you like her, I mean, you got something against her? Some grudge or something?" Then his voice dipped as if he were conscious of a rudeness. He touched the sunglasses perched on top of his head as if to make sure they were still there. "Now you be a good girl."

"What are you going to do?"

"Just two things, or maybe three," Arnold Friend said. "But I promise it won't last long and you'll like me that way you get to like people you're close to. You will. It's all over for you here, so come on out. You don't want your people in any trouble, do you?"

She turned and bumped against a chair or something, hurting her leg, but she ran into the back room and picked up the telephone. Something roared in her ear, a tiny roaring, and she was so sick with fear that she could do nothing but listen to it—the telephone was clammy and very heavy and her fingers groped down to the dial but were too weak to touch it. She began to scream into the phone, into the roaring. She cried out, she cried for her mother, she felt her breath start jerking back and forth in her lungs as if it were something Arnold Friend were stabbing her with again and again with no tenderness. A noisy sorrowful wailing rose all about her and she was locked inside it the way she was locked inside the house.

145   After a while she could hear again. She was sitting on the floor with her wet back against the wall.

Arnold Friend was saying from the door, "That's a good girl. Put the phone back."

She kicked the phone away from her.

"No, honey. Pick it up. Put it back right."

She picked it up and put it back. The dial tone stopped.

150   "That's a good girl. Now come outside."

She was hollow with what had been fear, but what was now just an emptiness. All that screaming had blasted it out of her. She sat, one leg cramped under her, and deep inside her brain was something like a pinpoint of light that kept going and would not let her relax. She thought, I'm not going to see my mother again. She thought, I'm not going to sleep in my bed again. Her bright green blouse was all wet.

Arnold Friend said, in a gentle-loud voice that was like a stage voice, "The place where you came from ain't there any more, and where you had in mind to go is cancelled out. This place you are now—inside your daddy's house—is nothing but a cardboard box I can knock down any time. You know that and always did know it. You hear me?"

She thought, I have got to think. I have to know what to do.

"We'll go out to a nice field, out in the country here where it smells so nice and it's sunny," Arnold Friend said. "I'll have my arms around you so you won't need to try to get away and I'll show you what love is like, what it does. The hell with this house! It looks solid all right," he said. He ran a fingernail down the screen and the noise did not make Connie shiver, as it would have the day before. "Now put your hand on your heart, honey. Feel that? That feels solid too but we know better, be nice to me, be sweet like you can because what else is there for a girl like you but to be sweet and pretty and give in?—and get away before her people come back?"

155   She felt her pounding heart. Her hand seemed to enclose it. She thought for the first time in her life that it was nothing that was hers, that belonged to her, but just a pounding, living thing inside this body that wasn't really hers either.

"You don't want them to get hurt," Arnold Friend went on. "Now get up, honey. Get up all by yourself."

She stood up.

"Now turn this way. That's right. Come over here to me—Ellie, put that away, didn't I tell you? You dope. You miserable creepy dope," Arnold Friend said. His words were not angry but only part of an incantation. The incantation was kindly. "Now come out through the kitchen to me honey and let's see a smile, try it, you're a brave sweet little girl and now they're eating corn and hot-dogs cooked to bursting over an outdoor fire, and they don't know one thing about you and never did and honey you're better than them because not a one of them would have done this for you."

Connie felt the linoleum under her feet; it was cool. She brushed her hair back out of her eyes. Arnold Friend let go of the post tentatively and opened his arms for her, his elbows pointing in toward each other and his wrists limp, to show that this was an embarrassed embrace and a little mocking, he didn't want to make her self-conscious.

160   She put out her hand against the screen. She watched herself push the door slowly open as if she were safe back somewhere in the other doorway, watching this body and this head of long hair moving out into the sunlight where Arnold Friend waited.

"My sweet little blue-eyed girl," he said, in a half-sung sigh that had nothing to do with her brown eyes but was taken up just the same by the vast sunlit reaches of the land behind him and on all sides of him, so much land that Connie had never seen before and did not recognize except to know that she was going to it.

MAKING CONNECTIONS

1. Describe Connie. Why is she so irked by her mother's criticism and comparisons to her older sister? What is her social life like?
2. Music is a recurrent image in this story. To what kinds of music does the narrator refer and in what settings? The narrator says that for the girls "music was something to depend on." Do you think it is? Explain.
3. Describe Arnold Friend. What is your reaction to him? If he called on you, would you go with him? Explain.
4. Why does Connie eventually go with him? To what extent does she go voluntarily and to what extent is she coerced by his threat to kill her family? Does Connie have any idea what will happen to her if she goes with Friend? Explain.

MAKING AN ARGUMENT

1. Arnold Friend says to Connie, "What else is there for a girl like you but to be sweet and pretty and give in?" Do you think he's right? Interpret the characterization of Connie and make a case for why she gives in and goes with Arnold Friend. Cite the text of the story for support.

FRANK O'CONNOR (1903–1966)

Frank O'Connor was the adopted pen name of Michael Donovan, who was born in Cork, Ireland. When he was only in the fourth grade, his impoverished parents were forced to take him out of school so he could go to work. Nevertheless, while toiling at numerous odd jobs, he developed a lifelong love of reading and writing. During the "troubles" of 1918–1921, which led to an independent Ireland, O'Connor was a soldier of the Irish Republican Army. He later wrote about his experiences in his 1931 collection of short stories, Guest of the Nation. *Following the war, O'Connor worked first as a librarian and later as a director of the famous Abbey Theatre in Dublin. He then moved to the United States, where he held teaching positions at Harvard University and Northwestern University, and achieved some celebrity appearing on Sunday-*

morning television telling stories. His work—which includes stories, novels, plays,
poetry, and criticism—is noted for its humor, poetic sensibility, and superb
craftsmanship.

GUESTS OF THE NATION   [1931]

I

At dusk the big Englishman, Belcher, would shift his long legs out of the ashes and
say "Well, chums, what about it?" and Noble or me would say "All right, chum" (for
we had picked up some of their curious expressions), and the little Englishman,
Hawkins, would light the lamp and bring out the cards. Sometimes Jeremiah
Donovan would come up and supervise the game and get excited over Hawkins's
cards, which he always played badly, and shout at him as if he was one of our own,
"Ah, you divil, you, why didn't you play the tray?"

But ordinarily Jeremiah was a sober and contented poor devil like the big
Englishman, Belcher, and was looked up to only because he was a fair hand at documents, though he was slow enough even with them. He wore a small cloth hat and
big gaiters over his long pants, and you seldom saw him with his hands out of his
pockets. He reddened when you talked to him, tilting from toe to heel and back, and
looking down all the time at his big farmer's feet. Noble and me used to make fun of
his broad accent, because we were from the town.

I couldn't at the time see the point of me and Noble guarding Belcher and
Hawkins at all, for it was my belief that you could have planted that pair down any-
where from this to Claregalway and they'd have taken root there like a native weed.
I never in my short experience seen two men to take to the country as they did.

They were handed on to us by the Second Battalion when the search for them
became too hot, and Noble and myself, being young, took over with a natural feeling
of responsibility, but Hawkins made us look like fools when he showed that he
knew the country better than we did.

5   "You're the bloke they calls Bonaparte," he says to me. "Mary Brigid O'Connell
told me to ask you what you done with the pair of her brother's socks you borrowed."

For it seemed, as they explained it, that the Second used to have little evenings,
and some of the girls of the neighborhood turned in, and, seeing they were such
decent chaps, our fellows couldn't leave the two Englishmen out of them. Hawkins
learned to dance "The Walls of Limerick," "The Siege of Ennis," and "The Waves of
Tory" as well as any of them, though, naturally, we couldn't return the compliment,
because our lads at that time did not dance foreign dances on principle.

So whatever privileges Belcher and Hawkins had with the Second they just naturally took with us, and after the first day or two we gave up all pretense of keeping
a close eye on them. Not that they could have got far, for they had accents you could
cut with a knife and wore khaki tunics and overcoats with civilian pants and boots.
But it's my belief that they never had any idea of escaping and were quite content
to be where they were.

It was a treat to see how Belcher got off with the old woman of the house
where we were staying. She was a great warrant to scold, and cranky even with us,
but before ever she had a chance of giving our guests, as I may call them, a lick of her

tongue, Belcher had made her his friend for life. She was breaking sticks, and Belcher, who hadn't been more than ten minutes in the house, jumped up from his seat and went over to her.

"Allow me, madam," he says, smiling his queer little smile, "please allow me"; and he takes the bloody hatchet. She was struck too paralytic to speak, and after that, Belcher would be at her heels, carrying a bucket, a basket, or a load of turf, as the case might be. As Noble said, he got into looking before she leapt, and hot water, or any little thing she wanted, Belcher would have it ready for her. For such a huge man (and though I am five foot ten myself I had to look up at him) he had an uncommon shortness—or should I say lack?—of speech. It took us some time to get used to him, walking in and out, like a ghost, without a word. Especially because Hawkins talked enough for a platoon, it was strange to hear big Belcher with his toes in the ashes come out with a solitary "Excuse me, chum," or "That's right, chum." His one and only passion was cards, and I will say for him that he was a good cardplayer. He could have fleeced myself and Noble, but whatever we lost to him Hawkins lost to us, and Hawkins played with the money Belcher gave him.

10   Hawkins lost to us because he had too much old gab, and we probably lost to Belcher for the same reason. Hawkins and Noble would spit at one another about religion into the early hours of the morning, and Hawkins worried the soul out of Noble, whose brother was a priest, with a string of questions that would puzzle a cardinal. To make it worse, even in the treating of holy subjects, Hawkins had a deplorable tongue. I never in all my career met a man who could mix such a variety of cursing and bad language into an argument. He was a terrible man, and a fright to argue. He never did a stroke of work, and when he had no one else to talk to, he got stuck in the old woman.

He met his match in her, for one day when he tried to get her to complain profanely of the drought, she gave him a great come-down by blaming it entirely on Jupiter Pluvius (a deity neither Hawkins nor I had ever heard of, though Noble said that among the pagans it was believed that he had something to do with the rain). Another day he was swearing at the capitalists for starting the German war when the old lady laid down her iron, puckered up her little crab's mouth, and said: "Mr. Hawkins, you can say what you like about the war, and think you'll deceive me because I'm only a simple poor countrywoman, but I know what started the war. It was the Italian Count that stole the heathen divinity out of the temple in Japan. Believe me, Mr. Hawkins, nothing but sorrow and want can follow the people that disturb the hidden powers."

A queer old girl, all right.

2

We had our tea one evening, and Hawkins lit the lamp and we all sat into cards. Jeremiah Donovan came in too, and sat down and watched us for a while, and it suddenly struck me that he had no great love for the two Englishmen. It came as a great surprise to me, because I hadn't noticed anything about him before.

Late in the evening a really terrible argument blew up between Hawkins and Noble, about capitalists and priests and love of your country.

15   "The capitalists," says Hawkins with an angry gulp, "pays the priests to tell you about the next world so as you won't notice what the bastards are up to in this."

"Nonsense, man!" says Noble, losing his temper. "Before ever a capitalist was thought of, people believed in the next world."

Hawkins stood up as though he was preaching a sermon.

"Oh, they did, did they?" he says with a sneer. "They believed all the things you believe, isn't that what you mean? And you believe that God created Adam, and Adam created Shem, and Shem created Jehoshaphat. You believe all that silly old fairytale about Eve and Eden and the apple. Well, listen to me, chum. If you're entitled to hold a silly belief like that, I'm entitled to hold my silly belief—which is that the first thing your God created was a bleeding capitalist, with morality and Rolls-Royce complete. Am I right, chum?" he says to Belcher.

"You're right, chum," says Belcher with his amused smile, and got up from the table to stretch his long legs into the fire and stroke his moustache. So, seeing that Jeremiah Donovan was going, and that there was no knowing when the argument about religion would be over, I went out with him. We strolled down to the village together, and then he stopped and started blushing and mumbling and saying I ought to be behind, keeping guard on the prisoners. I didn't like the tone he took with me, and anyway I was bored with life in the cottage, so I replied by asking him what the hell we wanted guarding them at all for. I told him I'd talked it over with Noble, and that we'd both rather be out with a fighting column.

20   "What use are those fellows to us?" says I.

He looked at me in surprise and said: "I thought you knew we were keeping them as hostages."

"Hostages?" I said.

"The enemy have prisoners belonging to us," he says, "and now they're talking of shooting them. If they shoot our prisoners, we'll shoot theirs."

"Shoot them?" I said.

25   "What else did you think we were keeping them for?" he says.

"Wasn't it very unforeseen of you not to warn Noble and myself of that in the beginning?" I said.

"How was it?" says he. "You might have known it."

"We couldn't know it, Jeremiah Donovan," says I. "How could we when they were on our hands so long?"

"The enemy have our prisoners as long and longer," says he.

30   "That's not the same thing at all," says I.

"What difference is there?" says he.

I couldn't tell him, because I knew he wouldn't understand. If it was only an old dog that was going to the vet's, you'd try and not get too fond of him, but Jeremiah Donovan wasn't a man that would ever be in danger of that.

"And when is this thing going to be decided?" says I.

"We might hear tonight," he says. "Or tomorrow or the next day at latest. So if it's only hanging round here that's a trouble to you, you'll be free soon enough."

35   It wasn't the hanging round that was a trouble to me at all by this time. I had worse things to worry about. When I got back to the cottage the argument was still

on. Hawkins was holding forth in his best style, maintaining that there was no next world, and Noble was maintaining that there was; but I could see that Hawkins had had the best of it.

"Do you know what, chum?" he was saying with a saucy smile. "I think you're just as big a bleeding unbeliever as I am. You say you believe in the next world, and you know just as much about the next world as I do, which is sweet damn-all. What's heaven? You don't know. Where's heaven? You don't know. You know sweet damn-all! I ask you again, do they wear wings?"

"Very well, then," says Noble, "they do. Is that enough for you? They do wear wings."

"Where do they get them, then? Who makes them? Have they a factory for wings? Have they a sort of store where you hands in your chit and takes your bleeding wings?"

"You're an impossible man to argue with," says Noble. "Now, listen to me—" And they were off again.

40   It was long after midnight when we locked up and went to bed. As I blew out the candle I told Noble what Jeremiah Donovan was after telling me. Noble took it very quietly. When we'd been in bed about an hour he asked me did I think we ought to tell the Englishmen. I didn't think we should, because it was more than likely that the English wouldn't shoot our men, and even if they did, the brigade officers, who were always up and down with the Second Battalion and knew the Englishmen well, wouldn't be likely to want them plugged. "I think so too," says Noble. "It would be great cruelty to put the wind up them now."

"It was very unforeseen of Jeremiah Donovan anyhow," says I.

It was next morning that we found it so hard to face Belcher and Hawkins. We went about the house all day scarcely saying a word. Belcher didn't seem to notice; he was stretched into the ashes as usual, with his usual look of waiting in quietness for something unforeseen to happen, but Hawkins noticed and put it down to Noble's being beaten in the argument of the night before.

"Why can't you take a discussion in the proper spirit?" he says severely. "You and your Adam and Eve! I'm a Communist, that's what I am. Communist or anarchist, it all comes to much the same thing." And for hours he went round the house, muttering when the fit took him. "Adam and Eve! Adam and Eve! Nothing better to do with their time than picking bleeding apples!"

3

I don't know how we got through that day, but I was very glad when it was over, the tea things were cleared away, and Belcher said in his peaceable way: "Well, chums, what about it?" We sat round the table and Hawkins took out the cards, and just then I heard Jeremiah Donovan's footstep on the path and a dark presentiment crossed my mind. I rose from the table and caught him before he reached the door.

45   "What do you want?" I asked.

"I want those two soldier friends of yours," he says, getting red.

"Is that the way, Jeremiah Donovan?" I asked.

"That's the way. There were four of our lads shot this morning, one of them a boy of sixteen."

"That's bad," I said.

50   At that moment Noble followed me out, and the three of us walked down the path together, talking in whispers. Feeney, the local intelligence officer, was standing by the gate.

"What are you going to do about it?" I asked Jeremiah Donovan.

"I want you and Noble to get them out; tell them they're being shifted again; that'll be the quietest way."

"Leave me out of that," says Noble under his breath.

Jeremiah Donovan looks at him hard.

55   "All right," he says. "You and Feeney get a few tools from the shed and dig a hole by the far end of the bog. Bonaparte and myself will be after you. Don't let anyone see you with the tools. I wouldn't like it to go beyond ourselves."

We saw Feeney and Noble go round to the shed and went in ourselves. I left Jeremiah Donovan to do the explanations. He told them that he had orders to send them back to the Second Battalion. Hawkins let out a mouthful of curses, and you could see that though Belcher didn't say anything, he was a bit upset too. The old woman was for having them stay in spite of us, and she didn't stop advising them until Jeremiah Donovan lost his temper and turned on her. He had a nasty temper, I noticed. It was pitch-dark in the cottage by this time, but no one thought of lighting the lamp, and in the darkness the two Englishmen fetched their topcoats and said good-bye to the old woman.

"Just as a man makes a home of a bleeding place, some bastard at headquarters thinks you're too cushy and shunts you off," says Hawkins, shaking her hand.

"A thousand thanks, madam," says Belcher. "A thousand thanks for everything"— as though he'd made it up.

We went round to the back of the house and down towards the bog. It was only then that Jeremiah Donovan told them. He was shaking with excitement.

60   "There were four of our fellows shot in Cork this morning and now you're to be shot as a reprisal."

"What are you talking about?" snaps Hawkins. "It's bad enough being mucked about as we are without having to put up with your funny jokes."

"It isn't a joke," says Donovan. "I'm sorry, Hawkins, but it's true," and begins on the usual rigmarole about duty and how unpleasant it is.

I never noticed that people who talk a lot about duty find it much of a trouble to them.

"Oh, cut it out!" says Hawkins.

65   "Ask Bonaparte," says Donovan, seeing that Hawkins isn't taking him seriously. "Isn't it true, Bonaparte?"

"It is," I say, and Hawkins stops.

"Ah, for Christ's sake, chum."

"I mean it, chum," I say.

"You don't sound as if you meant it."

70   "If he doesn't mean it, I do," says Donovan, working himself up.

"What have you against me, Jeremiah Donovan?"

"I never said I had anything against you. But why did your people take out four of our prisoners and shoot them in cold blood?"

He took Hawkins by the arm and dragged him on, but it was impossible to make him understand that we were in earnest. I had the Smith and Wesson[1] in my pocket and I kept fingering it and wondering what I'd do if they put up a fight for it or ran, and wishing to God they'd do one or the other. I knew if they did run for it, that I'd never fire on them. Hawkins wanted to know was Noble in it, and when we said yes, he asked us why Noble wanted to plug him. Why did any of us want to plug him? What had he done to us? Weren't we all chums? Didn't we understand him and didn't he understand us? Did we imagine for an instant that he'd shoot us for all the so-and-so officers in the so-and-so British Army?

By this time we'd reached the bog, and I was so sick I couldn't even answer him. We walked along the edge of it in the darkness, and every now and then Hawkins would call a halt and begin all over again, as if he was wound up, about our being chums, and I knew that nothing but the sight of the grave would convince him that we had to do it. And all the time I was hoping that something would happen; that they'd run for it or that Noble would take over the responsibility from me. I had the feeling that it was worse on Noble than on me.

4

75   At last we saw the lantern in the distance and made towards it. Noble was carrying it, and Feeney was standing somewhere in the darkness behind him, and the picture of them so still and silent in the bogland brought it home to me that we were in earnest, and banished the last bit of hope I had.

Belcher, on recognizing Noble, said: "Hallo, chum," in his quiet way, but Hawkins flew at him at once, and the argument began all over again, only this time Noble had nothing to say for himself and stood with his head down, holding the lantern between his legs.

It was Jeremiah Donovan who did the answering. For the twentieth time, as though it was haunting his mind, Hawkins asked if anybody thought he'd shoot Noble.

"Yes, you would," says Jeremiah Donovan.

"No, I wouldn't, damn you!"

80   "You would, because you'd know you'd be shot for not doing it."

"I wouldn't, not if I was to be shot twenty times over. I wouldn't shoot a pal. And Belcher wouldn't—isn't that right, Belcher?"

"That's right, chum," Belcher said, but more by way of answering the question than of joining in the argument. Belcher sounded as though whatever unforeseen thing he'd always been waiting for had come at last.

"Anyway, who says Noble would be shot if I wasn't? What do you think I'd do if I was in his place, out in the middle of a blasted bog?"

"What would you do?" asks Donovan.

85   "I'd go with him wherever he was going, of course. Share my last bob with him and stick by him through thick and thin. No one can ever say of me that I let down a pal."

[1]**Smith and Wesson** pistol, like the Webley later

"We had enough of this," says Jeremiah Donovan, cocking his revolver. "Is there any message you want to send?"

"No, there isn't."

"Do you want to say your prayers?"

Hawkins came out with a cold-blooded remark that even shocked me and turned on Noble again.

90   "Listen to me, Noble," he says. "You and me are chums. You can't come over to my side, so I'll come over to your side. That show you I mean what I say? Give me a rifle and I'll go along with you and the other lads."

Nobody answered him. We knew that was no way out.

"Hear what I'm saying?" he says. "I'm through with it. I'm a deserter or anything else you like. I don't believe in your stuff, but it's no worse than mine. That satisfy you?"

Noble raised his head, but Donovan began to speak and he lowered it again without replying.

"For the last time, have you any messages to send?" says Donovan in a cold, excited sort of voice.

95   "Shut up, Donovan! You don't understand me, but these lads do. They're not the sort to make a pal and kill a pal. They're not the tools of any capitalist."

I alone of the crowd saw Donovan raise his Webley to the back of Hawkins's neck, and as he did so I shut my eyes and tried to pray. Hawkins had begun to say something else when Donovan fired, and as I opened my eyes at the bang, I saw Hawkins stagger at the knees and lie out flat at Noble's feet, slowly and as quiet as a kid falling asleep, with the lantern-light on his lean legs and bright farmer's boots. We all stood very still, watching him settle out in the last agony.

Then Belcher took out a handkerchief and began to tie it about his own eyes (in our excitement we'd forgotten to do the same for Hawkins), and, seeing it wasn't big enough, turned and asked for the loan of mine. I gave it to him and he knotted the two together and pointed with his foot at Hawkins.

"He's not quite dead," he says. "Better give him another."

Sure enough, Hawkins's left knee is beginning to rise. I bend down and put my gun to his head; then, recollecting myself, I get up again. Belcher understands what's in my mind.

100   "Give him his first," he says. "I don't mind. Poor bastard, we don't know what's happening to him now."

I knelt and fired. By this time I didn't seem to know what I was doing. Belcher, who was fumbling a bit awkwardly with the handkerchiefs, came out with a laugh as he heard the shot. It was the first time I heard him laugh and it sent a shudder down my back; it sounded so unnatural.

"Poor bugger!" he said quietly. "And last night he was so curious about it all. It's very queer, chums, I always think. Now he knows as much about it as they'll ever let him know, and last night he was all in the dark."

Donovan helped him to tie the handkerchiefs about his eyes. "Thanks, chum," he said. Donovan asked if there were any messages he wanted sent.

"No, chum," he says. "Not for me. If any of you would like to write to Hawkins's mother, you'll find a letter from her in his pocket. He and his mother were great chums. But my missus left me eight years ago. Went away with another fellow and took the kid with her. I like the feeling of a home, as you may have noticed, but I couldn't start again after that."

105   It was an extraordinary thing, but in those few minutes Belcher said more than in all the weeks before. It was just as if the sound of the shot had started a flood of talk in him and he could go on the whole night like that, quite happily, talking about himself. We stood round like fools now that he couldn't see us any longer. Donovan looked at Noble, and Noble shook his head. Then Donovan raised his Webley, and at that moment Belcher gives his queer laugh again. He may have thought we were talking about him, or perhaps he noticed the same thing I'd noticed and couldn't understand it.

"Excuse me, chums," he says. "I feel I'm talking the hell of a lot, and so silly, about my being so handy about a house and things like that. But this thing came on me suddenly. You'll forgive me, I'm sure."

"You don't want to say a prayer?" asked Donovan.

"No, chum," he says. "I don't think it would help. I'm ready, and you boys want to get it over."

"You understand that we're only doing our duty?" says Donovan.

110   Belcher's head was raised like a blind man's, so that you could only see his chin and the tip of his nose in the lantern-light.

"I never could make out what duty was myself," he said. "I think you're all good lads, if that's what you mean. I'm not complaining."

Noble, just as if he couldn't bear any more of it, raised his fist at Donovan, and in a flash Donovan raised his gun and fired. The big man went over like a sack of meal, and this time there was no need of a second shot.

I don't remember much about the burying, but that it was worse than all the rest because we had to carry them to the grave. It was all mad lonely with nothing but a patch of lantern-light between ourselves and the dark, and birds hooting and screeching all round, disturbed by the guns. Noble went through Hawkins's belongings to find the letter from his mother, and then joined his hands together. He did the same with Belcher. Then, when we'd filled in the grave, we separated from Jeremiah Donovan and Feeney and took our tools back to the shed. All the way we didn't speak a word. The kitchen was dark and cold as we'd left it, and the old woman was sitting over the hearth, saying her beads. We walked past her into the room, and Noble struck a match to light the lamp. She rose quietly and came to the doorway with all her cantankerousness gone.

"What did ye do with them?" she asked in a whisper, and Noble started so that the match went out in his hand.

115   "What's that?" he asked without turning round.

"I heard ye," she said.

"What did you hear?" asked Noble.

"I heard ye. Do ye think I didn't hear ye, putting the spade back in the houseen?" Noble struck another match and this time the lamp lit for him.

120   "Was that what ye did to them?" she asked.

Then, by God, in the very doorway, she fell on her knees and began praying, and after looking at her for a minute or two Noble did the same by the fireplace. I pushed my way out past her and left them at it. I stood at the door, watching the stars and listening to the shrieking of the birds dying out over the bogs. It is so strange what you feel at times like that you can't describe it. Noble says he saw everything ten times the size, as though there were nothing in the whole world but that little patch of bog with the two Englishmen stiffening into it, but with me it was as if the patch of bog where the Englishmen were was a million miles away, and even Noble and the old woman, mumbling behind me, and the birds and the bloody stars were all far away, and I was somehow very small and very lost and lonely like a child astray in the snow. And anything that happened to me afterwards, I never felt the same about again.

MAKING CONNECTIONS

1. Describe your reaction as you finished the story. Do you think they made the right choice when they shot the prisoners? Explain.
2. The prisoners become friends with their guards. To what extent is the horror of the story increased by this relationship?
3. The narrator says of his experience: ". . . anything that happened to me afterwards, I never felt the same about." Could you understand the narrator's reaction? Explain.

MAKING AN ARGUMENT

1. This is a harrowing story, but its plot is carefully crafted for maximum effectiveness. Analyze the plot of the story. To what extent does it follow a classic plot line of exposition, rising action, crisis, falling action, and resolution? Identify each element of plot in the story and write about its effectiveness in moving the story to its poignant conclusion. Cite the text of the story for support.

TWO READERS ⌣ TWO DIFFERENT VIEWS

Exploring "A&P" and Making Connections

There is nothing extraordinary about the setting, the characters, or the conflict of John Updike's short story "A&P." The setting, an A&P supermarket in suburban Massachusetts in the 1960s, is as commonplace as it gets. And we experience this setting and the story's conflict through the eyes and mind of the protagonist, Sammy, an ordinary young man enduring the monotony of working a checkout slot. But Sammy checks out more than groceries. Through his narration we view the customers and employees of the supermarket, and witness his conflict, an ordinary conflict, but one that leaves him feeling "how hard the world was going to be to me hereafter."

What is extraordinary about this story is the quality of John Updike's description and his characterization of Sammy and his dilemma. Sammy, the supermarket, the customers, his boss, and his parents come to life for us. Whether we agree or disagree with Sammy's decision, we are reminded of our own choices and their consequences. In the tradition of some of the best fiction, Updike finds the "extraordinary in the ordinary" and reveals a great deal about the hard choices of growing up.

Your Experiences and Beliefs   Before you read "A&P," it may be helpful to think about your own experiences and beliefs in relation to issues that emerge from this story: pleasing or disappointing parents, teachers, employers, or other people you respect; or staying in a job, in school, or in a relationship to avoid disappointing others; or taking responsibility for your actions. If you have ever worked in a supermarket, department store, fast-food restaurant, or similar business, try to remember what that experience was like for you. If you have ever been in charge of other employees, try to recall how that responsibility made you feel.

JOHN UPDIKE [B. 1932]

John Updike was born in Shillington, Pennsylvania. His father was a teacher, and his mother a writer. After graduating from Harvard University in 1954, Updike spent two years in England, where he studied at the Ruskin School of Drawing and Fine Art. After returning to the United States in 1955, he worked as a reporter for the New Yorker, *leaving the magazine two years later to become a full-time writer. Though he is an accomplished critic, essayist, and poet, Updike is best known for his novels, which include* The Centaur *(1963),* Couples *(1968),* S. *(1988), and* Rabbit Is Rich, *which was awarded the Pulitzer Prize in 1982. His novel* The Witches of Eastwick *(1984) was turned into a film starring Susan Sarandon and Jack Nicholson in 1987. His novel* Gertrude and Cladius *was published in 2000, and his latest novel,* Terrorist, *in 2006. Michiko Kakutani, a longtime critic for the* New York Times, *has said of Updike's fiction: "His heroes over the years, have all suffered from 'the tension and guilt of being human.' Torn between vestigial spiritual yearnings and the new imperatives of self-fulfillment, they hunger for salvation even as they submit to importunate demands of the flesh."*

A&P   [1962]

In walks these three girls in nothing but bathing suits. I'm in the third check-out slot, with my back to the door, so I don't see them until they're over by the bread. The one that caught my eye first was the one in the plaid green two-piece. She was a chunky kid, with a good tan and a sweet broad soft-looking can with those two crescents of white just under it, where the sun never seems to hit, at the top of the backs of her legs. I stood there with my hand on a box of HiHo crackers trying to remember if I rang it up or not. I ring it up again and the customer starts giving me hell. She's one of these cash-register-watchers, a witch about fifty with rouge on her cheekbones and no eyebrows, and I know it made her day to trip me up. She'd been watching cash registers for fifty years and probably never seen a mistake before.

By the time I got her feathers smoothed and her goodies into a bag—she gives me a little snort in passing, if she'd been born at the right time they would have burned her over in Salem—by the time I get her on her way the girls had circled around the bread and were coming back, without a pushcart, back my way along the counters, in the aisle between the check-outs and the Special bins. They didn't even have shoes on. There was this chunky one, with the two-piece—it was bright green and the seams on the bra were still sharp and her belly was still pretty pale so I guessed she just got it (the suit)—there was this one, with one of those chubby berry-faces, the lips all bunched together under her nose, this one, and a tall one, with black hair that hadn't quite frizzed right, and one of these sunburns right across under the eyes, and a chin that was too long—you know, the kind of girl other girls think is very "striking" and "attractive" but never quite makes it, as they very well know, which is why they like her so much—and then the third one, that wasn't quite so tall. She was the queen. She kind of led them, the other two peeking around and making their shoulders round. She didn't look around, not this queen, she just walked straight on slowly, on these long white prima donna legs. She came down a little hard on her heels, as if she didn't walk in her bare feet that much, putting down her heels and then letting the weight move along to her toes as if she was testing the floor with every step, putting a little deliberate, extra action into it. You never know for sure how girls' minds work (do you really think it's a mind in there or just a little buzz like a bee in a glass jar?), but you got the idea she had talked the other two into coming in here with her, and now she was showing them how to do it, walk slow and hold yourself straight.

She had on a kind of dirty-pink—beige maybe, I don't know—bathing suit with a little nubble all over it and, what got me, the straps were down. They were off her shoulders looped loose around the cool tops of her arms, and I guess as a result the suit had slipped a little on her, so all around the top of the cloth there was this shining rim. If it hadn't been there you wouldn't have known there could have been anything whiter than those shoulders. With the straps pushed off, there was nothing between the top of the suit and the top of her head except just *her*, this clean bare plane of the top of her chest down from the shoulder bones like a dented sheet of metal tilted in the light. I mean, it was more than pretty.

She had sort of oaky hair that the sun and salt had bleached, done up in a bun that was unraveling, and a kind of prim face. Walking into the A&P with your straps down, I suppose it's the only kind of face you *can* have. She held her head so high her neck, coming up out of those white shoulders, looked kind of stretched, but I didn't mind. The longer her neck was, the more of her there was.

5   She must have felt in the corner of her eye me and over my shoulder Stokesie in the second slot watching, but she didn't tip. Not this queen. She kept her eyes moving across the racks, and stopped, and turned so slow it made my stomach rub the inside of my apron, and buzzed to the other two, who kind of huddled against her for relief, and they all three of them went up the cat-and-dog-food-breakfast-

cereal-macaroni-rice-raisins-seasonings-spreads-spaghetti-soft-drinks-crackers-and-cookies aisle. From the third slot I look straight up this aisle to the meat counter, and I watched them all the way. The fat one with the tan sort of fumbled with the cookies, but on second thought she put the packages back. The sheep pushing their carts down the aisle—the girls were walking against the usual traffic (not that we have one-way signs or anything)—were pretty hilarious. You could see them, when Queenie's white shoulders dawned on them, kind of jerk, or hop, or hiccup, but their eyes snapped back to their own baskets and on they pushed. I bet you could set off dynamite in an A&P and the people would by and large keep reaching and checking oatmeal off their lists and muttering "Let me see, there was a third thing, began with A, asparagus, no, ah yes, applesauce!" or whatever it is they do mutter. But there was no doubt, this jiggled them. A few houseslaves in pin curlers even looked around after pushing their carts past to make sure what they had seen was correct.

You know, it's one thing to have a girl in a bathing suit down on the beach, where what with the glare nobody can look at each other much anyway, and another thing in the cool of the A&P, under the fluorescent lights, against all those stacked packages, with her feet paddling along naked over our checkerboard green-and-cream rubber-tile floor.

"Oh Daddy," Stokesie said beside me. "I feel so faint."

"Darling," I said. "Hold me tight." Stokesie's married, with two babies chalked up on his fuselage already, but as far as I can tell that's the only difference. He's twenty-two, and I was nineteen this April.

"Is it done?" he asks, the responsible married man finding his voice. I forgot to say he thinks he's going to be manager some sunny day, maybe in 1990 when it's called the Great Alexandrov and Petrooshki Tea Company or something.

10   What he meant was, our town is five miles from a beach, with a big summer colony out on the Point, but we're right in the middle of town, and the women generally put on a shirt or shorts or something before they get out of the car into the street. And anyway these are usually women with six children and varicose veins mapping their legs and nobody, including them, could care less. As I say, we're right in the middle of town, and if you stand at our front doors you can see two banks and the Congregational church and the newspaper store and three real-estate offices and about twenty-seven old freeloaders tearing up Central Street because the sewer broke again. It's not as if we're on the Cape; we're north of Boston and there's people in this town haven't seen the ocean for twenty years.

The girls had reached the meat counter and were asking McMahon something. He pointed, they pointed, and they shuffled out of sight behind a pyramid of Diet Delight peaches. All that was left for us to see was old McMahon patting his mouth and looking after them sizing up their joints. Poor kids, I began to feel sorry for them, they couldn't help it.

Now here comes the sad part of the story, at least my family says it's sad but I don't think it's sad myself. The store's pretty empty, it being Thursday afternoon, so there was nothing much to do except lean on the register and wait for the girls to show up again. The whole store was like a pinball machine and I didn't know which tunnel they'd come out of. After a while they come around out of the far aisle, around the light bulbs, records at discount of the Caribbean Six or Tony Martin Sings or some such gunk you wonder they waste the wax on, sixpacks of candy bars, and plastic toys done up in cellophane that fall apart when a kid looks at them anyway. Around they come, Queenie still leading the way, and holding a little gray jar in her hand. Slots Three through Seven are unmanned, and I could see her wondering between Stokes and me, but Stokesie with his usual luck, draws an old party in baggy gray pants who stumbles up with four giant cans of pineapple juice (what do these bums *do* with all that pineapple juice? I've often asked myself) so the girls come to me. Queenie puts down the jar and I take it into my fingers icy cold. Kingfish Fancy Herring Snacks in Pure Sour Cream: 49¢. Now her hands are empty, not a ring or a bracelet, bare as God made them, and I wonder where the money's coming from. Still with that prim look she lifts a folded dollar bill out of the hollow at the center of her nubbled pink top. The jar went heavy in my hand. Really, I thought that was so cute.

Then everybody's luck begins to run out. Lengel comes in from haggling with a truck full of cabbages on the lot and is about to scuttle into that door marked MAN-AGER behind which he hides all day when the girls touch his eye. Lengel's pretty dreary, teaches Sunday school and the rest, but he doesn't miss that much. He comes over and says, "Girls, this isn't the beach."

Queenie blushes, though maybe it's just a brush of sunburn I was noticing for the first time, now that she was so close. "My mother asked me to pick up a jar of herring snacks." Her voice kind of startled me, the way voices do when you see the people first, coming out so flat and dumb yet kind of tony, too, the way it ticked over "pick up" and "snacks." All of a sudden I slid right down her voice into her living room. Her father and the other men were standing around in ice-cream coats and bow ties and the women were in sandals picking up herring snacks on toothpicks off a big plate and they were all holding drinks the color of water with olives and sprigs of mint in them. When my parents have somebody over they get lemonade and if it's a real racy affair Schlitz in tall glasses with "They'll Do It Every Time" cartoons stenciled on.

15   "That's all right," Lengel said. "But this isn't the beach." His repeating this struck me as funny, as if it had just occurred to him, and he had been thinking all these years the A&P was a great big dune and he was the head lifeguard. He didn't like my smiling—as I say he doesn't miss much—but he concentrates on giving the girls that sad Sunday-school-superintendent stare.

Queenie's blush is no sunburn now, and the plump one in plaid, that I liked better from the back—a really sweet can—pipes up, "We weren't doing any shopping. We just came in for the one thing."

"That makes no difference," Lengel tells her, and I could see from the way his eyes went that he hadn't noticed she was wearing a two-piece before. "We want you decently dressed when you come in here."

"We *are* decent," Queenie says suddenly, her lower lip pushing, getting sore now that she remembers her place, a place from which the crowd that runs the A&P must look pretty crummy. Fancy Herring Snacks flashed in her very blue eyes.

"Girls, I don't want to argue with you. After this come in here with your shoulders covered. It's our policy." He turns his back. That's policy for you. Policy is what the kingpins want. What the others want is juvenile delinquency.

20   All this while, the customers had been showing up with their carts but, you know, sheep, seeing a scene, they had all bunched up on Stokesie, who shook open a paper bag as gently as peeling a peach, not wanting to miss a word. I could feel in the silence everybody getting nervous, most of all Lengel, who asks me, "Sammy, have you rung up this purchase?"

I thought and said, "No" but it wasn't about that I was thinking. I go through the punches, 4, 9, GROC, TOT—it's more complicated than you think, and after you do it often enough, it begins to make a little song, that you hear words to, in my case "Hello (*bing*) there, you (*gung*) hap-py pee-pul (*splat*)!"—the splat being the drawer flying out. I uncrease the bill, tenderly as you may imagine, it just having come from between the two smoothest scoops of vanilla I had ever known were there, and pass a half and a penny into her narrow pink palm, and nestle the herrings in a bag and twist its neck and hand it over, all the time thinking.

The girls, and who'd blame them, are in a hurry to get out, so I say "I quit" to Lengel quick enough for them to hear, hoping they'll stop and watch me, their unsuspected hero. They keep right on going, into the electric eye; the door flies open and they flicker across the lot to their car, Queenie and Plaid and Big Tall Goony-Goony (not that as raw material she was so bad), leaving me with Lengel and a kink in his eyebrow.

"Did you say something, Sammy?"

"I said I quit."

25   "I thought you did."

"You didn't have to embarrass them."

"It was they who were embarrassing us."

I started to say something that came out "Fiddle-de-doo." It's a saying of my grandmother's, and I know she would have been pleased.

"I don't think you know what you're saying," Lengel said.

30   "I know you don't," I said. "But I do." I pull the bow at the back of my apron and start shrugging it off my shoulders. A couple customers that had been heading for my slot begin to knock against each other, like scared pigs in a chute.

Lengel sighs and begins to look very patient and old and gray. He's been a friend of my parents for years. "Sammy, you don't want to do this to your Mom and Dad," he tells me. It's true, I don't. But it seems to me that once you begin a gesture it's fatal not to go through with it. I fold the apron, "Sammy" stitched in red on the pocket, and put it on the counter, and drop the bow tie on top of it. The bow tie is theirs, if you've ever wondered. "You'll feel this for the rest of your life," Lengel says, and I know that's true, too, but remembering how he made that pretty girl blush makes me so scrunchy inside I punch the No Sale tab and the machine whirs "pee-pul" and the drawer splats out. One advantage to this scene taking place in summer, I can follow this up with a clean exit, there's no fumbling around getting your coat and galoshes, I just saunter into the electric eye in my white shirt that my mother ironed the night before, and the door heaves itself open, and outside the sunshine is skating around on the asphalt.

I look around for my girls, but they're gone, of course. There wasn't anybody but some young married screaming with her children about some candy they didn't get by the door of a powder-blue Falcon station wagon. Looking back in the big windows, over the bags of peat moss and aluminum lawn furniture stacked on the pavement, I could see Lengel in my place in the slot, checking the sheep through. His face was dark gray and his back stiff, as if he'd just had an injection of iron, and my stomach kind of fell as I felt how hard the world was going to be to me hereafter.

MAKING CONNECTIONS

1. To what extent can you connect "A&P" with your own background and experience? How did this influence your response? If you were in Sammy's position, would you have made the same decision? Explain.
2. How would you describe Sammy? What is your reaction to his description of the girls and what he says about the customers?
3. How are you affected by the concrete description of the setting? What is the relationship between the setting and the conflict in the story or between the time period in which this is set and the conflict?
4. What do you think Sammy means when he says, "Now here comes the sad part of the story, at least my family says it's sad but I don't think it's sad myself"?

MAKING AN ARGUMENT

1. At the end of the story Sammy says, " . . . my stomach kind of fell as I felt how hard the world was going to be to me hereafter." What does he mean? What do you think he has learned from this experience? Do you think he's a hero or has simply behaved immaturely? Write an essay that makes a case for what Sammy has or has not learned from this experience—and what he does with it. Cite the text of the story for support.

TWO STUDENT ESSAYS ～ TWO DIFFERENT VIEWS

Depending on your experience of it, "A&P" is a story about many different things. You may experience it as a story about family pressure, rebellion, loss of innocence, immaturity, or any number of other issues.

In the student essays that follow, Michelle and Julie both emphasize the importance of Sammy's decision to quit, but come to different conclusions about what it means. Michelle sees it as a loss of innocence—and a realization by Sammy that his actions will have negative consequences for him and his family. Julie also sees Sammy's action as significant, but as a defining moment for the rest of his life, a clear statement that Sammy will refuse to live his life like Lengel.

Michelle McAuliffe

Dr. Madden

English 102

April 10, 200X

Ironed Shirts and Bathing Suits

We all have moments in our lives when we find ourselves alone and forced to see the world and ourselves in a new and painful light. In the short story "A&P," John Updike illustrates how a seemingly unimportant experience becomes this kind of moment in the life of his main character, Sammy.

Sammy is a lively, cynical, young guy who seems more than familiar with the grocery sciences, anatomy of the store, and psychology of the customer mind: "The girls had circled around the bread and were coming back, without a pushcart, back my way along the counters, in the aisle between the check-outs and the Special bins" (491). Sammy spends a lot of time analyzing the store and the people in it: "I bet you could set off dynamite in an A&P and the people would by and large keep reaching and checking oatmeal off their lists and muttering 'Let me see, there was a third thing, began with A, asparagus, no, ah yes, applesauce!' or whatever it is they do mutter" (492). He doesn't hesitate to pass judgment on them either: "What do these bums <u>do</u> with all that pineapple juice?" (493). This seems to be the primary mental activity of his day.

On this particular day, Sammy's focus is on three young girls who enter the store wearing bathing suits. Besides ogling their every move, he gets a kick out of how they are dressed and people's reactions to it: "You could see them, when Queenie's white shoulders dawned on them, kind of jerk, or hop, or hiccup, but their eyes snapped back to their own baskets and on they pushed" (492). But Lengel, the store manager, is not so amused. He exclaims, "Girls, this isn't the beach" (493). And the fun begins.

When the confrontation with the girls and the manager occurs, Sammy sees it as time to act instead of watching passively. We can't really say what motivates his action. It may be something noble, or simply an excuse to be rid of a stifling job. Even Sammy might not be able to tell us. He has the initial urge to quit in the presence of the girls, but when they're gone, he still feels strongly about something. Once he says he quits, it's too late to turn back. Even though Lengel, the store manager, is giving him the chance to stay, "You don't want to do this to your Mom and Dad" (494), his decision is final. Sammy admits to us that he doesn't want to do this to his parents, but adds, "It seems to me that once you begin a gesture it's fatal not to go through with it" (494). He has his personal dignity to consider. Lengel speaks prophetically when he says, "'You'll feel this for the rest of your life'" (494). Sammy knows this too, but feels his decision is one of liberation. He even likes the idea of this taking place in the summertime, so he can make a quick exit.

Sammy, however, is also aware of Lengel's reaction. He notices that "Lengel sighs and begins to look very patient and old and gray" (494). His need for a quick exit is a result of feeling some shame and guilt in the face of a family friend and an understanding man. When Sammy gets outside, the desolation of the parking lot takes away the glory of his act in the war between youth and responsibility. His righteous decision is not so simple anymore. Without something to rebel against he feels alone. Sammy may be expressing his sympathy for Lengel when he says, "I could see Lengel in my place in the slot, checking the sheep through. His face was dark gray and his back stiff, as if he'd just had an injection of iron, and my stomach kind of fell as I felt how hard the world was going to be to me hereafter" (495). He feels that Lengel and his parents, and perhaps the entire adult world, must be disappointed in him. He has let them down.

Although we can't say what immediate consequence Sammy will face, we know that he recognizes the effects of his action beyond himself. This realization of how we affect others through our actions is not a lesson to be learned in books; we must experience it. We are often surprised when we see how what we do, say, or think affects others. At moments like this we know we have learned something valuable. Although we don't always understand it, we know that it's something that will influence our outlook on life. At the end of this story, Sammy is all alone to contemplate a decision and thoughts that only a half hour before were very far from his mind. Such is the introduction of insight and wisdom into our lives--when we least expect it, and in the most unlikely situations.

[New Page]

Work Cited

Updike, John. "A&P." Exploring Literature. Ed. Frank Madden. 3rd ed. New
York: Longman, 2007. 490-495.

Julie Fitzmaurice

Dr. Madden

English 102

April 6, 200X

What Makes Sammy Quit?

In John Updike's short story "A&P," we see the world through the eyes of a nineteen-year-old. Sammy, the main character, is also the narrator, and his narration creates the tone and atmosphere of the story. When Sammy quits his job for no obvious reason we are left with a question: Why? Was it his impatience with older people, rebellion against authority, or just boredom? It was not one of these alone that made him quit, but the synergy of them all which, once in motion, could not be stopped.

First, let us consider Sammy and what we learn about his character in the story. Updike doesn't actually give us many details about him. From the text we learn that Sammy is nineteen years old and lives in a small town north of Boston, five miles from the beach. The most important key to Sammy's character, however, is how he sees everyone else.

Virtually everything we learn in this story, we learn through Sammy's thoughts. Sammy comes from a working-class background: "When my parents have somebody over they get lemonade and if it's a real racy affair Schlitz in tall glasses with 'They'll Do It Every Time' cartoons stenciled on" (493). Another indication of a working-class background is in his comment, "Now here comes the sad part of the story, at least my family says it's sad, but I don't think it's sad myself" (492). This statement tells us that Sammy's parents placed importance on his job at the A&P.

His comments about Lengel tell us more about Sammy than they do about his boss at the A&P. Lengel is older and the manager of the A&P. He teaches Sunday school and has been a friend of Sammy's parents for years. Sammy thinks Lengel is "pretty dreary," and "doesn't miss that much" (493), and describes him as giving the girls that "sad Sunday-school-superintendent stare" (493). His descriptions of the customers also tell us a lot about him: "one of these cash-register-watchers, a witch about fifty" (491), "The sheep pushing their carts down the aisle" (492), and "A few houseslaves in pin curlers" (492). These comments reveal Sammy's impatience with adults and his rebellious streak.

Sammy's description of the A&P itself turns the store into a quasi character. The A&P has its own pulse and comes alive for us. He tells us what the store looks and sounds like. The cash register even sings a song as Sammy tediously pushes its keys: "Hello (bing) there, you (gung) hap-py pee-pul (splat)!" (494). Almost everyone has experienced the setting of a food store. There is a certain universality about them. But Sammy's description of the "cat-and-dog-food-breakfast-cereal-macaroni-rice-raisins-seasonings-spreads-spaghetti-soft-drinks-crackers-and-cookies aisle" (491-492) brings this familiar place to dull but fresh life.

Sammy goes into great detail about the girls, too. Had he been busy he would not have noticed so much about them. The store was slow, and Sammy leans on the register looking at the girls. He is so bored that he sees the store as a pinball machine. The girls are the balls, and the aisles are the chutes that the balls travel through.

His detailed description has a strong impact on our reading of the story. It makes it easy for us to imagine being nineteen and working in a store on a hot summer day. Sammy describes what the atmosphere is like: "The store's pretty empty, it being Thursday afternoon, so there was nothing much to do except lean on the register and wait for the girls to show up again" (492).

At the climax of the story, when Lengel confronts the girls about their bathing suits, Sammy is already bored and frustrated to exhaustion. He thinks that Lengel is a pompous bag of wind, so he says, "'I quit'" (494). He says this to Lengel to save himself, not the girls. The girls are simply the final impetus for Sammy's quitting, he needs them as his excuse. He would like to have the girls think that he is quitting his job in indignation over the way Lengel treated them.

At this moment, Lengel is everything that Sammy detests. He represents all the things that Sammy wants to rebel against: age, authority, his working-class background, Sunday school teachers, and the voice of righteousness. He realizes that if he stays at the A&P he will become a Lengel. In one brief moment all his emotions synergize. The two words "I quit" leave his lips, and Sammy changes the course of his life forever.

[New Page]

Work Cited

Updike, John. "A&P." Exploring Literature. Ed. Frank Madden. 3rd ed. New York: Longman, 2007. 490-495.

◆ POETRY ◆

CONNECTING THROUGH COMPARISON: THE CITY

Throughout history, cities have often been identified as a prime site and source of sophistication, experience, loss of innocence—and evil activities. The two poems that follow address a subtheme of this section: the city. Read and discussed together, they invite comparisons and connections—not only with each other—but with your own experience of the evils—or positive forces—of city life.

WILLIAM BLAKE [1757-1827]

The son of a London haberdasher, William Blake received very little formal education. When he was ten he entered a drawing school, and later studied for a few months at the Royal Academy of Art. At the age of fourteen he was apprenticed to an engraver, and, after seven years, he was able to earn his living illustrating books. From his early twenties to his sixties, when he chose to devote himself exclusively to pictorial art, Blake produced books of his own poetry, which were painstakingly illustrated and hand colored, often with the help of his wife. His early books of poetry, Songs of Innocence *(1789) and* Songs of Experience *(1794), from which "London" and both versions of "The Chimney Sweeper" are taken, express Blake's rage at the social injustices of England. His later work, the so-called* Prophetic Works, *are much more difficult. In these highly symbolic and often cryptic poems, Blake created his own complicated mythological system based on his deeply held religious and spiritual beliefs. (His wife said of him: "I have very little of Mr. Blake's company; he is always in Paradise.") His now-famous verses were not very well known during his lifetime, and it is only in the past century that he has earned a wider readership.*

LONDON   [1794]

I wander through each chartered street,
Near where the chartered Thames does flow,
And mark in every face I meet
Marks of weakness, marks of woe.

In every cry of every man,   5
In every infant's cry of fear,
In every voice, in every ban,
The mind-forged manacles I hear.

How the chimney-sweeper's cry
Every black'ning church appalls   10

And the hapless soldier's sigh
Runs in blood down palace walls.

But most through midnight streets I hear
How the youthful harlot's curse
Blasts the new born infant's tear   15
And blights with plagues the marriage hearse.

WILLIAM WORDSWORTH [1770–1850]

*William Wordsworth was born in Cockermouth on the
northern tip of England's Lake District and spent much of
his childhood exploring the natural sights of this region,
which later served as the setting for many of his greatest
poems. In 1791, after attending Cambridge University he
traveled to France, where he became a supporter of the
French Revolution and met and fell in love with a French
woman, Annette Vallon, with whom he had a daughter.
Due to the political situation, Wordsworth was forced to flee France and the
couple never married. Together with his sister Dorothy, an accomplished writer
herself and later his editor, Wordsworth settled first in a rent-free cottage in
Dorsetshire, and then moved to Somersetshire to be near his friend, the poet
Samuel Taylor Coleridge. In 1798, the two men collaborated to produce* Lyrical
Ballads *(which Wordsworth revised in 1800), a collection of poetry credited with
bringing the Romantic movement to England. The enormously influential volume
was a commercial success, and Wordsworth and his sister were able to live comfortably for the rest of their lives. In 1843, he was appointed poet laureate. Today,
Wordsworth is best remembered for his deeply felt depiction of the English countryside and of the customs and common speech of its people.*

COMPOSED UPON WESTMINSTER BRIDGE, SEPTEMBER 3, 1802   [1807]

Earth has not anything to show more fair:
Dull would he be of soul who could pass by
A sight so touching in its majesty;
This City now doth, like a garment, wear
The beauty of the morning; silent, bare,   5
Ships, towers, domes, theaters, and temples lie
Open unto the fields, and to the sky;
All bright and glittering in the smokeless air.
Never did sun more beautifully steep
In his first splendor, valley, rock, or hill;   10
Ne'er saw I, never felt, a calm so deep!
The river glideth at his own sweet will:
Dear God! the very houses seem asleep;
And all that mighty heart is lying still!

MAKING CONNECTIONS

1. In "London," what are "mind-forged manacles"? Can you think of any "mind-forged manacles" that exist today?
2. What is the "youthful harlot's curse" and what does it have to do with blasting "the new born infant's tear" or plaguing "the marriage hearse"?
3. Much of Wordsworth's verse depicts the countryside, but this is a city scene in early morning. To what extent is the beauty depicted here just as majestic as—but different from—nature?
4. Have you ever been so "taken" by a "human-made" sight? Explain.

MAKING AN ARGUMENT

1. Most cities have changed to some degree for the better since the days of Blake and Wordsworth, but many of the positive and negative elements described in these poems still remain. Compare and contrast Wordsworth's vision of the city with that of Blake as expressed in "London." Bring that vision forward two hundred years and write about their views as they might apply to a modern city. Cite the text of the poems for support.

CONNECTING THROUGH COMPARISON: THE CHIMNEY SWEEPERS

The two poems that follow were both written by William Blake and address the same subject—the chimney sweeper mentioned in Blake's poem "London" above. Read and discussed together, they invite comparisons and connections with that poem and each other.

WILLIAM BLAKE [1757-1827]

(See biography on p. 500.)
"Chimney-sweeps" were usually small children (small enough to slide down chimneys) who had been either sold by their poverty-stricken parents or were orphans or illegitimate children. They were overworked, inadequately clothed—and often suffered from burns, a permanent coating of soot, deformed limbs, black lung disease, or cancer.

THE CHIMNEY SWEEPER (FROM SONGS OF INNOCENCE)   [1789]

When my mother died I was very young,
And my father sold me while yet my tongue
Could scarcely cry weep weep weep weep
So your chimneys I sweep & in soot I sleep.

There's little Tom Dacre, who cried when his head   5
That curl'd like a lambs back, was shav'd, so I said:
Hush Tom never mind it, for when your head's bare
You know that the soot cannot spoil your white hair.

And so he was quiet, & that very night,
As Tom was sleeping he had such a sight,   10
That thousands of sweepers Dick, Joe, Ned & Jack
Were all of them lock'd up in coffins of black,

And by came an Angel who had a bright key,
And he open'd the coffins & set them all free.
Then down a green plain leaping laughing they run   15
And wash in a river and shine in the Sun.

Then naked & white, all their bags left behind
They rise upon clouds, and sport in the wind
And the Angel told Tom if he'd be a good boy,
He'd have God for his father & never want joy.   20

And so Tom awoke and we rose in the dark
And got with our bags & our brushes to work
Tho' the morning was cold, Tom was happy & warm
So if all do their duty they need not fear harm.

THE CHIMNEY SWEEPER (FROM SONGS OF EXPERIENCE)   [1794]

A little black thing among the snow:
Crying weep, weep, in notes of woe!
Where are thy father & mother? say?
They are both gone up to the church to pray.

Because I was happy upon the heath   5
And smil'd among the winters snow:
They clothed me in the clothes of death,
And taught me to sing the notes of woe.

And because I am happy & dance & sing,
They think they have done me no injury: 10
And are gone to praise God & his Priest & King
Who make up a heaven of our misery.

MAKING CONNECTIONS

1. How do the structures and rhymes of each poem influence your response?
2. Identify the images in both poems and write about their effectiveness in establishing the speaker's tone. Is there a difference in tone between the two? Explain.

MAKING AN ARGUMENT

1. Write a comparison of "London" and the two versions of "The Chimney Sweeper." Is there a difference in tone among the poems? Why is the first version of "The Chimney Sweeper" a "song of innocence," and the second one a "song of experience"? Cite the text of all three poems for support.

MARGARET ATWOOD [B. 1939]

Margaret Atwood was born in Ottawa, Canada, and took extensive trips during her childhood through the wilds of Canada with her father, an entomologist. In 1962, the same year she graduated from the University of Toronto, she published her first book of poetry, Double Persephone. *She has since published numerous works of fiction, poetry, and criticism, including the novels* Surfacing *(1972),* Cat's Eye *(1988), and the futuristic* The Handmaid's Tale *(1985), which was made into a film. Her most recent novel is* The Penelopiad *(2005), a feminist account of Homer's* The Odyssey. *A fierce proponent of Canadian literature as well as an ardent feminist, Atwood has been instrumental in forging a Canadian cultural identity separate from that of England and the United States. She told an interviewer in* Ms. *magazine, "I began as a profoundly apolitical writer, but then I began to do what all novelists and some poets do: I began to describe the world around me."*

SIREN SONG   [1974]

This is the one song everyone
would like to learn: the song
that is irresistible:

the song that forces men
to leap overboard in squadrons   5
even though they see in the beached skulls

the song nobody knows
because anyone who has heard it
is dead, and others can't remember.

Shall I tell you the secret   10
and if I do, will you get me
out of this bird suit?

I don't enjoy it here
squatting on this island
looking picturesque and mythical   15

with these two feathery maniacs.
I don't enjoy singing
this trio, fatal and valuable.

I will tell the secret to you,
to you, only to you.   20
Come closer. This song

is a cry for help: Help me!
Only you, only you can,
you are unique

at last. Alas   25
it is a boring song
but it works every time.

MAKING CONNECTIONS

1. "Siren Song" alludes to Greek mythology. Who were the Sirens?
2. Who is the speaker in this version? What is her "siren song"?
3. Do you agree that the song she describes is "irresistible"? Explain.

MAKING AN ARGUMENT

1. Identify the theme of this poem and write an essay comparing it to "The
   Horse Dealer's Daughter" on page 750. Cite the text of both the poem and
   the story for support.

ROBERT FROST (1874–1963)

(See biography on p. 78.)

"OUT, OUT . . . "   [1916]

The buzz saw snarled and rattled in the yard
And made dust and dropped stove-length sticks of wood,
Sweet-scented stuff when the breeze drew across it.
And from there those that lifted eyes could count
Five mountain ranges one behind the other   5
Under the sunset far into Vermont.
And the saw snarled and rattled, snarled and rattled,
As it ran light, or had to bear a load.
And nothing happened: day was all but done.
Call it a day, I wish they might have said   10
To please the boy by giving him the half hour
That a boy counts so much when saved from work.
His sister stood beside them in her apron
To tell them "Supper." At the word, the saw,

As if to prove saws knew what supper meant,   15
Leaped out at the boy's hand, or seemed to leap—
He must have given the hand. However it was,
Neither refused the meeting. But the hand!
The boy's first outcry was a rueful laugh,
As he swung toward them holding up the hand,   20
Half in appeal, but half as if to keep
The life from spilling. Then the boy saw all—
Since he was old enough to know, big boy
Doing a man's work, though a child at heart—
He saw all spoiled. "Don't let him cut my hand off—   25
The doctor, when he comes. Don't let him, sister!"
So. But the hand was gone already.
The doctor put him in the dark of ether.
He lay and puffed his lips out with his breath.
And then—the watcher at his pulse took fright.   30
No one believed. They listened at his heart.
Little—less—nothing!—and that ended it.
No more to build on there. And they, since they
Were not the one dead, turned to their affairs.

MAKING CONNECTIONS

1. To what extent does your own experience with the death of someone young affect your response to this poem?

2. In what way does the setting of the sawmill in the poem emphasize what happens to the boy?

3. At the end of the poem, the speaker says, "And they, since they / Were not the one dead, turned to their affairs." Do you think "they" are being heartless? Why or why not?

MAKING AN ARGUMENT

1. The title of this poem is taken from Shakespeare's play *Macbeth.* When he receives the news that his young wife is dead, Macbeth begins a soliloquy that includes the line "Out, out, brief candle!" Get a copy of the play, read the entire soliloquy (*Macbeth,* Act V, scene 5), and write about the appropriateness of Frost's title and its allusion to the soliloquy by comparing and contrasting the poem with the soliloquy. Cite the text of both the poem and the soliloquy for support.

SEAMUS HEANEY

(See biography on p. 270.)

MID-TERM BREAK   [1965]

I sat all morning in the college sick bay
Counting bells knelling classes to a close.
At two o'clock our neighbors drove me home.

In the porch I met my father crying—
He had always taken funerals in his stride—   5
And Big Jim Evans saying it was a hard blow.

The baby cooed and laughed and rocked the pram
When I came in, and I was embarrassed
By old men standing up to shake my hand

And tell me they were "sorry for my trouble."   10
Whispers informed strangers I was the eldest,
Away at school, as my mother held my hand

In hers and coughed out angry tearless sighs.
At ten o'clock the ambulance arrived
With the corpse, stanched and bandaged by the nurses.   15

Next morning I went up into the room. Snowdrops
And candles soothed the bedside; I saw him
For the first time in six weeks. Paler now,

Wearing a poppy bruise on his left temple.
He lay in the four foot box as in his cot.   20
No gaudy scars, the bumper knocked him clear

A four foot box, a foot for every year.

MAKING CONNECTIONS

1. The boy is told by the old men that they are "'sorry for my trouble.'" What
   trouble is that? What's happened here?
2. To what extent is your response to this poem affected by your own experience with the death of someone very young?
3. The last line of the poem, "A four foot box, a foot for every year," stands by
   itself. What is your reaction to it? In what ways is it appropriate to wrap up
   the poem?

MAKING AN ARGUMENT

1. Both Heaney's poem and Frost's "Out, Out . . . " address the death of a boy. How they address this premature death, however, seems quite different. Analyze and interpret each poem and write a comparison of their treatment of young death. Cite the text of both poems for support.

A. E. HOUSMAN [1859–1936]

An important scholar of Latin as well as a celebrated poet, A[lfred] E[dward] Housman was born in the village of Fockbury in Worcestershire, England. A brilliant student at Oxford University, Housman inexplicably failed his final exams. Determined to redeem himself after his poor showing, he wrote scholarly articles while working at night as a civil servant in the patent office. His brilliant scholarship eventually won him positions at the University of London and Cambridge University. *During his life he published only two slim volumes of poetry,* A Shropshire Lad *(1898) and* Last Poems *(1922). His poems are tinged with melancholy, often dealing with themes of lost love and youth. His* Complete Poems, *which includes verses that were published posthumously, was published in 1956.*

WHEN I WAS ONE-AND-TWENTY   [1898]

When I was one-and-twenty
    I heard a wise man say,
'Give crowns and pounds and guineas
    But not your heart away;
Give pearls away and rubies   5
    But keep your fancy free.'
But I was one-and-twenty,
    No use to talk to me.

When I was one-and-twenty
    I heard him say again,   10
'The heart out of the bosom
    Was never given in vain;
'Tis paid with sighs a plenty
    And sold for endless rue.'
And I am two-and-twenty,   15
    And oh, 'tis true, 'tis true.

MAKING CONNECTIONS

1. What do you think of the wise man's advice in the first stanza?
2. Would you have taken his advice? Explain.
3. What's happened to the speaker? Does he regret his decision? Would you?

MAKING AN ARGUMENT

1. This poem and Edna St. Vincent Millay's "What Lips My Lips Have Kissed, and Where, and Why" on page 790 and "Love Is Not All" on page 791 are love poems. Do you think the speakers in Millay's poems would agree with the view of the speaker in this poem? Write an essay in response to that question and cite the texts of all three poems for support.

EDGAR LEE MASTERS (1869-1950)

Though he is known almost exclusively for one work, Spoon River Anthology (1915), Edgar Lee Masters was a prolific writer, and he continued publishing poetry, novels, essays, and biographies for more than thirty years after his master work was published. Consensus has been, however, that the amount of his work exceeded its quality, and his role as an influential figure in American literature is still debated. Spoon River Anthology (from which "Ernest Hyde" is taken) is a series of poignant and often ironic monologues—told from the grave—that capture the pain and confusion of life in small-town America. Members of the community—librarians, preachers, poets, atheists, society women, and others—"tell it like it is" or "was" and in the process often reveal the dirty laundry of small-town life.

SPOON RIVER ANTHOLOGY #111: ERNEST HYDE

My mind was a mirror:
It saw what it saw, it knew what it knew.
In youth my mind was just a mirror
In a rapidly flying car,
Which catches and loses bits of the landscape.
Then in time
Great scratches were made on the mirror,
Letting the outside world come in,

5

And letting my inner self look out.
For this is the birth of the soul in sorrow,   10
A birth with gains and losses.
The mind sees the world as a thing apart,
And the soul makes the world at one with itself.
A mirror scratched reflects no image—
And this is the silence of wisdom.   15

MAKING CONNECTIONS

1. Why do you think the speaker describes his mind as a "mirror"? What does
   he mean?
2. In what way do you think the "scratches" on the mirror let "the outside
   world come in" and his "inner self look out"?
3. To what extent is a mirror that reflects no image "the silence of wisdom"?

MAKING AN ARGUMENT

1. Is there no gain of wisdom without pain? The speaker seems to describe
   "experience" with the caustic image of "great scratches." Do you agree that
   worthwhile experience only comes with pain? Is it possible to learn about
   the nature of the world without pain? Write an essay in response to this
   question using the poem as a point of reference. Cite the poem for support.

EDWIN ARLINGTON ROBINSON   [1869–1935]

*Born into a wealthy New England family, Edwin Arlington
Robinson was raised in Gardiner, Maine, a small town
that later served as the model for "Tilbury Town," the setting
for many of his most famous poems. Encouraged by a
neighbor, he developed an interest in poetry and wrote
numerous original poems, as well as diligently translated
the great Greek and Roman poets. He spent two years at
Harvard University, and after failing to get his poems pub-
lished he decided to print copies of his first collection,* The Torrent and The Night
Before *(1896), himself. He mailed copies to publishers and received some favorable responses, though some found his subject matter bleak. Encouraged, he published* The Children of the Night *(1896), which contained many of what were to
become his best-known Tilbury poems (including "Richard Cory"). The collection
was considered a failure, and Robinson descended into poverty and alcoholism.
In 1902, in a stroke of luck, President Theodore Roosevelt stumbled onto a copy
of* The Children of the Night *and was taken with it, saying, "I am not sure I*

understand . . . . but I'm entirely sure that I like it." Roosevelt found Robinson a post with very few duties in the customs office in New York City, and Robinson was free to devote himself to his poetry. He stepped down from the post following the success of his 1910 collection, The Town Down the River. *In 1921, Robinson was awarded the first Pulitzer Prize for poetry for his* Collected Poems, *and was awarded two more for* The Man Who Died Twice *(1924) and* Tristam *(1927). After Robinson's death in 1935, Robert Frost, who listed Robinson as one his greatest influences, wrote of him and his often unhappy life: "His theme was unhappiness itself, but his skill was as happy as it was playful. There is that comforting thought for those who suffered to see him suffer."*

RICHARD CORY   [1896]

Whenever Richard Cory went downtown,
We people on the pavement looked at him;
He was a gentleman from sole to crown,
Clean favored, and imperially slim,

And he was always quietly arrayed,   5
And he was always human when he talked;
But still he fluttered pulses when he said,
"Good-morning," and he glittered when he walked.

And he was rich—yes, richer than a king—
And admirably schooled in every grace: 10
In fine, we thought that he was everything
To make us wish that we were in his place.

So on we worked, and waited for the light,
And went without the meat, and cursed the bread;
And Richard Cory, one calm summer night,   15
Went home and put a bullet through his head.

MAKING CONNECTIONS

1. Who is the speaker in this poem?
2. Who are "we"? Who is Richard Cory to us? What lines in the poem indicate these things?
3. What effect does the last line have on you? Were you surprised? Was it effective to wait until the last line to tell you that he killed himself? Why?

MAKING AN ARGUMENT

1. We know very little about Richard Cory from the description in this poem. Based on the little you have from the poem, tap your imagination and write a history of Richard Cory up to the last line of the poem. Who was he? How did he feel about himself and why? What motivated him to kill himself? Cite the text of the poem for support.

ANNE SEXTON (1928–1974)

Born and raised in New England, Anne Sexton attended Garland Junior College and was married at the age of twenty. She suffered the first of many mental breakdowns following the birth of her first child in 1954. After a breakdown following the birth of her second child, she began writing poetry at the suggestion of a therapist. To Bedlam and Part Way Back, *her first book of poems, was published in 1960. Her 1967 volume,* Live or Die, *was awarded the Pulitzer Prize. Though she became extraordinarily successful, Sexton continually struggled with depression. Following her divorce, she committed suicide in 1974. Like her contemporary Sylvia Plath, Sexton's powerful and often startling work has been characterized as confessional poetry, in which deeply personal topics once considered taboo in modern poetry—mental illness, religious guilt, therapy—are openly discussed.*

PAIN FOR A DAUGHTER   (1966)

Blind with love, my daughter
has cried nightly for horses,
those long-necked marchers and churners
that she has mastered, any and all,
reigning them in like a circus hand—   5
the excitable muscles and the ripe neck;
tending this summer, a pony and a foal.
She who is too squeamish to pull
a thorn from the dog's paw,
watched her pony blossom with distemper,   10
the underside of the jaw swelling
like an enormous grape.
Gritting her teeth with love,
she drained the boil and scoured it
with hydrogen peroxide until pus   15
ran like milk on the barn floor.

Blind with loss all winter,
in dungarees, a ski jacket and a hard hat,
she visits the neighbor's stable,
our acreage not zoned for barns;   20
they who own the flaming horses
and the swan-whipped thoroughbred
that she tugs at and cajoles,
thinking it will burn like a furnace
under her small-hipped English seat.   25

Blind with pain she limps home.
The thoroughbred has stood on her foot.

He rested there like a building.
He grew into her foot until they were one.
The marks of the horseshoe printed   30
into her flesh, the tips of her toes
ripped off like pieces of leather,
three toenails swirled like shells
and left to float in blood in her riding boot.

Blind with fear, she sits on the toilet,   35
her foot balanced over the washbasin,
her father, hydrogen peroxide in hand,
performing the rites of the cleansing.
She bites on a towel, sucked in breath,
sucked in and arched against the pain,   40
her eyes glancing off me where
I stand at the door, eyes locked
on the ceiling, eyes of a stranger,
and then she cries . . .
Oh my God, help me!   45
Where a child would have cried *Mama!*
Where a child would have believed *Mama!*
she bit the towel and called on God
and I saw her life stretch out . . .
I saw her torn in childbirth,   50
and I saw her, at that moment,
in her own death and I knew that she
knew.

MAKING CONNECTIONS

1. Do you think the title of the poem refers to the daughter's or the mother's pain—or both? Explain.
2. The poem seems to be divided into four sections: love, loss, pain, and fear. How are each of these emotions described in the poem?
3. At the end of the poem, the speaker says, "I knew that she / knew." What do you think the daughter knows that she did not before?

MAKING AN ARGUMENT

1. The speaker in the poem is the mother. Do you think a daughter would have the same understanding of this event? Imagine you are the daughter in this poem. Using the information and images in the poem, write about this experience from your perspective. What have you learned from this experience and why? Cite the text of the poem to support your views.

WALT WHITMAN [1819-1892]

Walt Whitman was born on an impoverished farm near the town of Huntington on Long Island, New York, and moved with his family to the then-independent city of Brooklyn. For many years, he worked in the printing trade, taking occasional writing jobs, until he landed a position as an editor of a Brooklyn newspaper. Dismissed from his editorial position because of his politics, Whitman sup-ported himself working as a carpenter and contractor, while he wrote in his spare time. In 1855, he published his own book of poetry, Leaves of Grass, *a collection of twelve poems (including* Song of Myself*), which Whitman continually expanded and revised throughout his life, publishing a final "death bed" edition in 1892. His work as a volunteer nurse during the Civil War inspired his next collection of verse,* Drum Taps *(1865), as well as his famous elegy for Abraham Lincoln, "When Lilacs Last in the Dooryard Bloom'd." Whitman spent his later years as a revered figure in Camden, New Jersey, where he was the center of a devoted band of disciples and visited by many writers from around the world. His strikingly original poetry, with its boldness of form, scope, and sub-ject matter, has influenced generations of poets. The selection below is taken from* Song of Myself *(1855), Whitman's longest—it runs over two thousand lines—and perhaps greatest poem.*

THERE WAS A CHILD WENT FORTH   [1855]

There was a child went forth every day,
And the first object he looked upon, that object he
    became,
And that object became part of him for the day or a
    certain part of the day,
Or for many years or stretching cycles of years.

The early lilacs became part of this child,   5
And grass and white and red morning-glories, and
    white and red clover, and the song of the
    phoebe-bird,
And the Third-month° lambs and the sow's pink-
    faint litter, and the mare's foal and the cow's
    calf,
And the noisy brood of the barnyard or by the mire
    of the pond-side,
And the fish suspending themselves so curiously below there,
    and the beautiful curious liquid,
And the water-plants with their graceful flat heads,   10
    all became part of him.

---

7 Third-month March

The field-sprouts of Fourth-month and Fifth-month
    became part of him,
Winter-grain sprouts and those of the light-yellow
    corn, and the esculent° roots of the garden,
And the apple-trees covered with blossoms and the
    fruit afterward, and wood-berries, and the commonest
    weeds by the road,
And the old drunkard staggering home from the outhouse
    of the tavern whence he had lately risen,
And the schoolmistress that passed on her way to   15
    the school,
And the friendly boys that passed, and the quarrel-
    some boys,
And the tidy and fresh-cheeked girls, and the bare-
    foot negro boy and girl,
And all the changes of city and country wherever he
    went.

His own parents, he that had fathered him and she
    that had conceived him in her womb and
    birthed him,
They gave this child more of themselves than that,   20
They gave him afterward every day, they became
    part of him.

The mother at home quietly placing the dishes on
    the supper-table,
The mother with mild words, clean her cap and
    gown, a wholesome odor falling off her person
    and clothes as she walks by,
The father, strong, self-sufficient, manly, mean, angered,
    unjust,
The blow, the quick loud word, the tight bargain, the crafty lure,   25
The family usages, the language, the company, the
    furniture, the yearning and swelling heart,
Affection that will not be gainsayed,° the sense of
    what is real, the thought if after all it should
    prove unreal,
The doubts of day-time and the doubts of night-
    time, the curious whether and how,
Whether that which appears so is so, or is it all
    flashes and specks?
Men and women crowding fast in the streets, if they   30
    are not flashes and specks what are they?

12 esculent edible   **27 gainsayed** denied

The streets themselves and the façades of houses,
    and goods in the windows,
Vehicles, teams, the heavy-planked wharves,
    the huge crossing at the ferries,
The village on the highland seen from afar at sunset,
    the river between,
Shadows, aureola° and mist, the light falling
    on roofs and gables of white or brown two miles off,
The schooner near by sleepily dropping down the   35
    tide, the little boat slack-towed astern,
The hurrying tumbling waves, quick-broken crests,
    slapping,
The strata of colored clouds, the long bar of maroon-
    tint away solitary by itself, the spread of
    purity it lies motionless in,
The horizon's edge, the flying sea-crow, the fragrance
    of salt marsh and shore mud,
These became part of that child who went forth
    every day, and who now goes, and will always
    go forth every day.

MAKING CONNECTIONS

1. The first six lines of the poem serve as an introduction. What do they say this poem is about? Do you agree that we become objects that we look upon—and that those objects become part of us? Explain.
2. What follows in the poem is a long list of objects, people, and events the child encounters. To what extent do each of the encounters represent something different? If you recall your own childhood, can you come up with a similar list?

MAKING AN ARGUMENT

1. Compare the style and the content of this poem with Whitman's *Song of Myself 6* on page 1239 and "When I Heard the Learn'd Astronomer" on page 83. Make believe that you have not seen Whitman's name on the poems. Analyze the three poems carefully and write an argument that makes the case that all three poems were written by the same author. Cite the text of all three for support.

31 aureola bands of light

◆ ESSAYS ◆

JUDITH ORTIZ COFER [B.1952]

The daughter of a Puerto Rican mother and a U.S. main-land father, Judith Ortiz Cofer was born in Puerto Rico but immigrated to the mainland in 1956. Educated at Augusta College and Florida Atlantic University, Cofer worked as an English teacher and bilingual instructor in Florida. Because of her bilingual upbringing, much of Cofer's work is concerned with the power of language and its uses. She has published a number of volumes of poetry and a novel, The Line of the Sun *(1989). The essay below is taken from her memoir,* Silent Dancing.

I FELL IN LOVE, OR MY HORMONES AWAKENED   [1990]

I fell in love, or my hormones awakened from their long slumber in my body, and suddenly the goal of my days was focused on one thing: to catch a glimpse of my secret love. And it had to remain secret, because I had, of course, in the great tradition of tragic romance, chosen to love a boy who was totally out of my reach. He was not Puerto Rican; he was Italian and rich. He was also an older man. He was a senior at the high school when I came in as a freshman. I first saw him in the hall, leaning casually on a wall that was the border line between girlside and boyside for under-classmen. He looked extraordinarily like a young Marlon Brando—down to the ironic little smile. The total of what I knew about the boy who starred in every one of my awkward fantasies was this: that he was the nephew of the man who owned the supermarket on my block; that he often had parties at his parents' beautiful home in the suburbs which I would hear about; that his family had money (which came to our school in many ways)—and this fact made my knees weak: and that he worked at the store near my apartment building on weekends and in the summer.

My mother could not understand why I became so eager to be the one sent out on her endless errands. I pounced on every opportunity from Friday to late Saturday afternoon to go after eggs, cigarettes, milk (I tried to drink as much of it as possible, although I hated the stuff)—the staple items that she would order from the "American" store.

Week after week I wandered up and down the aisles, taking furtive glances at the stock room in the back, breathlessly hoping to see my prince. Not that I had a plan. I felt like a pilgrim waiting for a glimpse of Mecca. I did not expect him to notice me. It was sweet agony.

One day I did see him. Dressed in a white outfit like a surgeon: white pants and shirt, white cap, and (gross sight, but not to my love-glazed eyes) blood-smeared butcher's apron. He was helping to drag a side of beef into the freezer storage area of the store. I must have stood there like an idiot, because I remember that he did see me, he even spoke to me! I could have died. I think he said, "Excuse me," and smiled vaguely in my direction.

5   After that, I *willed* occasions to go to the supermarket. I watched my mother's pack of cigarettes empty ever so slowly. I wanted her to smoke them fast. I drank milk and forced it on my brother (although a second glass for him had to be bought with my share of Fig Newton cookies which we both liked, but we were restricted to one row each). I gave my cookies up for love, and watched my mother smoke her L&M's with so little enthusiasm that I thought (God, no!) that she might be cutting down on her smoking or maybe even giving up the habit. At this crucial time!

I thought I had kept my lonely romance a secret. Often I cried hot tears on my pillow for the things that kept us apart. In my mind there was no doubt that he would never notice me (and that is why I felt free to stare at him—I was invisible). He could not see me because I was a skinny Puerto Rican girl, a freshman who did not belong to any group he associated with.

At the end of the year I found out that I had not been invisible. I learned one little lesson about human nature—adulation leaves a scent, one that we are all equipped to recognize, and no matter how insignificant the source, we seek it.

In June the nuns at our school would always arrange for some cultural extravaganza. In my freshman year it was a Roman banquet. We had been studying Greek drama (as a prelude to church history—it was at a fast clip that we galloped through Sophocles and Euripides toward the early Christian martyrs), and our young, energetic Sister Agnes was in the mood for spectacle. She ordered the entire student body (it was a small group of under 300 students) to have our mothers make us togas out of sheets. She handed out a pattern on mimeo pages fresh out of the machine. I remember the intense smell of the alcohol on the sheets of paper, and how almost everyone in the auditorium brought theirs to their noses and inhaled deeply—mimeographed handouts were the school-day buzz that the new Xerox generation of kids is missing out on. Then, as the last couple of weeks of school dragged on, the city of Paterson becoming a concrete oven, and us wilting in our uncomfortable uniforms, we labored like frantic Roman slaves to build a splendid banquet hall in our small auditorium. Sister Agnes wanted a raised dais where the host and hostess would be regally enthroned.

She had already chosen our Senator and Lady from among our ranks. The Lady was to be a beautiful new student named Sophia, a recent Polish immigrant, whose English was still practically unintelligible, but whose features, classically perfect without a trace of makeup, enthralled us. Everyone talked about her gold hair cascading past her waist, and her voice which could carry a note right up to heaven in choir. The nuns wanted her for God. They kept saying that she had vocation. We just looked at her in awe, and the boys seemed afraid of her. She just smiled and did as she was told. I don't know what she thought of it all. The main privilege of beauty is that others will do almost everything for you, including thinking.

10   Her partner was to be our best basketball player, a tall, red-haired senior whose family sent its many offspring to our school. Together, Sophia and her senator looked like the best combination of immigrant genes our community could produce. It did not occur to me to ask then whether anything but their physical beauty qualified them for the starring roles in our production. I had the highest average in the church history class, but I was given the part of one of many "Roman Citizens." I was to sit in front of the plastic fruit and recite a greeting in Latin along with the rest of the school when our hosts came into the hall and took their places on their throne.

On the night of our banquet, my father escorted me in my toga to the door of our school. I felt foolish in my awkwardly draped sheet (blouse and skirt required underneath). My mother had no great skill as a seamstress. The best she could do was hem a skirt or a pair of pants. That night I would have traded her for a peasant woman with a golden needle. I saw other Roman ladies emerging from their parents' cars looking authentic in sheets of material that folded over their bodies like the garments on a statue by Michelangelo. How did they do it? How was it that I always got it just slightly wrong, and worse, I believed that other people were just too polite to mention it. "The poor little Puerto Rican girl," I could hear them thinking. But in reality, I must have been my worst critic, self-conscious as I was.

Soon, we were all sitting at our circle of tables joined together around the dais. Sophia glittered like a golden statue. Her smile was beatific: a perfect, silent Roman lady. Her "senator" looked uncomfortable, glancing around at his buddies, perhaps waiting for the ridicule that he would surely get in the locker room later. The nuns in their black habits stood in the background watching us. What were they supposed to be, the Fates? Nubian slaves? The dancing girls did their modest little dance to tinny music from their finger cymbals, then the speeches were made. Then the grape juice "wine" was raised in a toast to the Roman Empire we all knew would fall within the week—before finals anyway.

All during the program I had been in a state of controlled hysteria. My secret love sat across the room from me looking supremely bored. I watched his every move, taking him in gluttonously. I relished the shadow of his eyelashes on his ruddy cheeks, his pouty lips smirking sarcastically at the ridiculous sight of our little play. Once he slumped down on his chair, and our sergeant-at-arms nun came over and tapped him sharply on his shoulder. He drew himself up slowly, with disdain. I loved his rebellious spirit. I believed myself still invisible to him in my "nothing" status as I looked upon my beloved. But toward the end of the evening, as we stood chanting our farewells in Latin, he looked straight across the room and into my eyes! How did I survive the killing power of those dark pupils? I trembled in a new way. I was not cold—I was burning! Yet I shook from the inside out, feeling light-headed, dizzy.

The room began to empty and I headed for the girls' lavatory. I wanted to relish the miracle in silence. I did not think for a minute that anything more would follow. I was satisfied with the enormous favor of a look from my beloved. I took my time, knowing that my father would be waiting outside for me, impatient, perhaps glowing in the dark in his phosphorescent white Navy uniform. The others would ride home. I would walk home with my father, both of us in costume. I wanted as few witnesses as possible. When I could no longer hear the crowds in the hallway, I emerged from the bathroom, still under the spell of those mesmerizing eyes.

15   The lights had been turned off in the hallway and all I could see was the lighted stairwell, at the bottom of which a nun would be stationed. My father would be waiting just outside. I nearly screamed when I felt someone grab me by the waist. But my mouth was quickly covered by someone else's mouth. I was being kissed. My first kiss and I could not even tell who it was. I pulled away to see that face not two inches away from mine. It was he. He smiled down at me. Did I have a silly expression on my face? My glasses felt crooked on my nose. I was unable to move or to speak. More gently, he lifted my chin and touched his lips to mine. This time I did not

forget to enjoy it. Then, like the phantom lover that he was, he walked away into the darkened corridor and disappeared.

I don't know how long I stood there. My body was changing right there in the hallway of a Catholic school. My cells were tuning up like musicians in an orchestra, and my heart was a chorus. It was an opera I was composing, and I wanted to stand very still and just listen. But, of course, I heard my father's voice talking to the nun. I was in trouble if he had had to ask about me. I hurried down the stairs making up a story on the way about feeling sick. That would explain my flushed face and it would buy me a little privacy when I got home.

The next day Father announced at the breakfast table that he was leaving on a six month tour of Europe with the Navy in a few weeks and that at the end of the school year my mother, my brother, and I would be sent to Puerto Rico to stay for half a year at Mamá's (my mother's mother) house. I was devastated. This was the usual routine for us. We had always gone to Mamá's to stay when Father was away for long periods. But this year it was different for me. I was in love, and . . . my heart knocked against my bony chest at this thought . . . he loved me too? I broke into sobs and left the table.

In the next week I discovered the inexorable truth about parents. They can actually carry on with their plans right through tears, threats, and the awful spectacle of a teenager's broken heart. My father left me to my mother who impassively packed while I explained over and over that I was at a crucial time in my studies and that if I left my entire life would be ruined. All she would say was, "You are an intelligent girl, you'll catch up." Her head was filled with visions of *casa*[1] and family reunions, long gossip sessions with her mamá and sisters. What did she care that I was losing my one chance at true love?

In the meantime I tried desperately to see him. I thought he would look for me too. But the few times I saw him in the hallway, he was always rushing away. It would be long weeks of confusion and pain before I realized that the kiss was nothing but a little trophy for his ego. He had no interest in me other than as his adorer. He was flattered by my silent worship of him, and he had *bestowed* a kiss on me to please himself, and to fan the flames. I learned a lesson about the battle of the sexes then that I have never forgotten: the object is not always to win, but most times simply to keep your opponent (synonymous at times with "the loved one") guessing.

20   But this is too cynical a view to sustain in the face of that overwhelming rush of emotion that is first love. And in thinking back about my own experience with it, I can be objective only to the point where I recall how sweet the anguish was, how caught up in the moment I felt, and how every nerve in my body was involved in this salute to life. Later, much later, after what seemed like an eternity of dragging the weight of unrequited love around with me, I learned to make myself visible and to relish the little battles required to win the greatest prize of all. And much later, I read and understood Camus'[2] statement about the subject that concerns both adolescent and philosopher alike: if love were easy, life would be too simple.

---

[1]*casa* home   [2]**Albert Camus** (1913–1960), French novelist and philosopher

MAKING CONNECTIONS

1. Can you recall a similar experience? If so, what did you learn from it?
2. Toward the end of the essay, the author writes: "I learned to make myself visible and to relish the little battles required to win the greatest prize of all." What do you think she means?

MAKING AN ARGUMENT

1. Both this essay and James Joyce's short story "Araby" on page 463 describe the painful experience and realization of unrequited love. Write a comparison of the two with special attention to narration, characterization, and the development of the conflict to its resolution.

EDWARD CONLON [B.1965]

Edward Conlon is a detective with the New York City Police Department. A graduate of Harvard University, he is the author of Blue Blood *(2004), which was a* New York Times *Notable Book and a nominee for the National Book Critics Circle Award. Conlon originally published "The Midnight Tour" (a chapter from* Blue Blood*) under the pseudonym* Marcus Laffey *as part of a series called "Cop Diaries" in the* New Yorker. *It was selected for publication in* The Best American Essays *of 2001.*

THE MIDNIGHT TOUR   2001

When I went to work midnights a few months ago, it was discovered that I didn't have a nickname. You need one, to talk casually over the radio: "Stix, you getting coffee?" "Chicky, did you check the roof?" "O.V., T., G.Q., can you swing by?" Nicknames never stuck to me, for some reason, and I always thought that nicknaming yourself was like talking to yourself, something that made you look foolish if you were overheard. So Hawkeye, the Hat, Hollywood, Gee Whiz, Big E., the Count, Roller Coaster, and Fierce pitched a few:

"'Hemingway'—nah, they'd know it was you."

"'Ernest' is better."

"Or 'Clancy'—he'd be a good one to have."

5   "What about 'Edgar'?"

"What from?"

"Edgar Allan Poe."

"What about 'Poe'?"

As I thought about it, the fit was neat: Poe, too, in his most famous poem, had worked, weak and weary, upon a midnight dreary. He moved to New York City in 1844, the same year that legislation created the New York City Police Department. And he wrote the first detective story ever, "The Murders in the Rue Morgue," in which the killer turns out to be a demented orangutan with a straight razor. There is also a brilliant detective, an earnest sidekick, and a mood of languor and gloom— all now hallmarks of a genre that has endured for a century and a half. Poe spent his last years in the Bronx, living and working in a cottage that is midway between where I live and where I work. I am a police officer in the Bronx, where kids sometimes call the cops "po-po." And so "Poe" it was.

10   Midnights for Edgar Allan Poe seemed less a time than a territory, a place of woefully distant vistas, as if he were stargazing from the bottom of a well. A lot of that has to do with needing sleep, I think. Everyone on the late tour lacks sleep, and this state of worn-out wakefulness while the rest of the world is dreaming tends to stimulate thoughts that meander. Each precinct has a list of "cooping-prone locations," which are out-of-the-way places, under bridges and by rail yards and the like, where bosses are supposed to check to make sure patrol cars haven't stopped in for a nap. The list is posted in the station house, and when you're tired it reads like a recommendation, a Zagat guide for secret sleep, as if it might be saying, "St. Mary's Park, with its rolling hills and abundant trees, offers superb concealment in a pastoral setting—we give it four pillows!" On midnights, we talk about sleep the way frat boys talk about sex. Did you get any last night? How was it? Nah, nah, but this weekend, believe me, I'm gonna go all night long! Although I've asked practically everyone on the tour how long it takes for your body to adjust to an upside-down life, only three people have given precise answers, which were "Two months," "Four years," and "Never." Nevermore.

I went to midnights after my old narcotics team split up. It seemed like a good interim assignment, a way station until something better came along, and I thought I could use the free time during the day. Mostly, you drive around and check things out until a job comes over the radio. There are fewer jobs than during the other tours of duty—although the jobs tend to be more substantial—and even on weekend nights they tend to taper off after two or three in the morning. You usually have to check a few buildings, and you'd probably get into trouble if you never wrote a ticket, but you have more time to yourself than on any other tour. My uncle finished his thirty-three years as a cop working midnights in the Bronx; he would have said that he liked it because the bosses leave you alone. Still, to be back on patrol feels odd sometimes, and when I think about my past and the past of this place I wonder where I'm going. It can bring on a terminal feeling.

One night, I drove with my partner to the corner of 132nd Street and Lincoln Avenue—a cooping-prone location, though that wasn't the reason for the visit— which is a dead end at the very bottom of the Bronx, with a warehouse on one side and a parking lot on the other: Across the black shimmer of the river you can see Harlem and the salt piles along the FDR. The Bronx begins here physically, and it began here historically as well; this was the site of Jonas Bronck's farmhouse. Not much is known about him: he was a Swedish sea captain who was induced to settle the area by the Dutch West India Company. A peace treaty signed at Bronck's house ended years of sporadic but bloody skirmishes between the Dutch and the Weckquasgeeks. Bronck didn't have much to do with it, but his house was the only one around. "When did he move?" my partner asked. It was a funny question, because it made me think of the Bronx as a place where people come from but not where they stay, if luck is on their side.

The Bronx was a place of slow beginnings: Bronck came here in 1639 to homestead, and at the beginning of the twentieth century there was still farmland in the South Bronx; it became citified only as the subway was built. A person alive today could have witnessed the borough's entire metropolitan career: two generations as a vibrant, blue-collar boomtown, and one as a ravaged and riotous slum. When Jimmy Carter visited Charlotte Street in September 1977, he saw vacant and collapsing buildings inhabited by junkies and packs of wild dogs. A week later, during a broadcast of the World Series at Yankee Stadium, there was a fire at a school a few blocks from the game. Millions watched it as Howard Cosell intoned, "The Bronx is burning." One of my uncles was a fireman here at the time, and he told me that they were busier than the London fire department during the Blitz.

My partner and I cruised up to 142nd Street between Willis and Brook Avenues, a block with a row of little houses on one side and a school on the other. I used to chase a lot of junkies down that street when they were buying heroin with the brand name President from the projects on the corner. A hundred years ago, the Piccirilli brothers, sculptors from Pisa, had a studio here, where they carved the statue for the Lincoln Memorial, but I don't suppose the dope was named in any commemorative spirit. Four blocks up and two over, Mother Teresa's order runs a soup kitchen and a shelter next to the Church of St. Rita, a boxy old building painted robin's-egg blue. The work the order does is holy and noble, but for us there is something embarrassing about it: nuns reassigned from leper duty in Calcutta to lend us a hand. There was a picture in the *News* a few years back of Mother Teresa and Princess Diana visiting the mission together, and one of my old partners was there, standing guard, just out of the frame. A little farther out of the frame is the building where Rayvon Evans died: a little boy whose parents kept his corpse in a closet until the fluids seeped through to the floor below and the neighbors complained. No one was ever charged with the murder, because there wasn't enough left of him to determine how he died. There is a garden dedicated to Rayvon, but no sign of the Princess or the sculptors. Memory is short here, but the past is visible all around you—at least, until the present calls you back. It can take time for your eyes to adjust.

15   Midnights tend to magnify things, to set them in sharp relief against the empty night, like gems on a black velvet cloth. You meet lonely people who seem more solitary and sorrowful at night, such as the chubby little woman who reclined in her armchair like a pasha after attempting suicide by taking three Tylenol PMs. Or the woman with dye-drowned blond hair going green, who denied trying to hurt herself, though her boyfriend confided that she had: "She slapped herself, hard." Domestic disputes are all the more squalid and small-hearted when they take place at five in the morning—like the one between two middle-aged brothers who were at each other's throats hours before their mother's funeral. The place stank and the walls

seethed with roaches. One brother had a weary and beaten dignity; he was sitting on the couch with his overcoat and an attaché case when we arrived, like a salesman who'd just lost a commission. The other brother shouted drunkenly, jerking and flailing like a dervish afflicted with some unknown neurological misfiring. They had argued because he had started drinking again.

I took the jerky one aside, to let him vent a little. His room was littered with cans of Night Train; military papers and alcohol-rehab certificates were taped to the wall. As he punched the honorable discharge to emphasize that his had been a life of accomplishment, a burst of roaches shot out from underneath. I wanted to punch his rehab diploma, to show that he still had some work to do, but I thought better of it.

My partner and I knew that we would be back if both brothers remained there, and we dreaded the idea of having to lock one of them up before the funeral, so we asked the sane brother if he wouldn't mind leaving for a while. He agreed that it was the best thing to do; we agreed that it was deeply unfair. He used to work as a security guard, and he offered us his business card. "If there's anything I can do for you gentlemen," he said, and he went out to walk until daybreak.

If some people call because they need someone—anyone—to talk to, there are others for whom we're the last people they want to see. For them, we arrive the way the Bible says Judgment will: like a thief in the night. It felt like that when we showed up to take a woman's children away. We were escorting two caseworkers from the Administration of Children's Services who had a court order to remove the one-, two-, and three-year-old kids of a crackhead I'll call Pamela. The midnight visit was a sneak attack, as she had dodged the caseworkers the day before. We were there—not to put too fine a point on it—as hired muscle.

When we knocked, a woman answered ("Who?") and then delayed ten minutes, muttering excuses ("Hold on," and "Let me get something on," and "Who is it, again?"), before surrendering to threats to kick the door down. She was just a friend, she said, helping to clean up—probably in anticipation of such a visit. Pamela was out. Yes, there were kids in the back, but they were Pamela's sister's kids, and the sister was out, too. As we looked in on the sleeping children, another woman emerged from a back bedroom, and she was equally adamant: "But those are my kids, and I'm not Pamela, I'm her sister, Lorraine! I can show you you're making a mistake!"

20   We grilled both women, but they never deviated from their story, and we could find no baby pictures or prescription bottles or anything else that would tie these children to the case. So when "Lorraine" said she could prove that they were hers if we'd let her call her mother to get her ID we agreed, as it would clearly demonstrate whether we were professional public servants doing a difficult job or dimwitted repo men hauling off the wrong crack babies.

But she didn't call for her ID, she called for reinforcements, and the apartment was soon flooded with angry women. We held the baby boy while Pamela managed to grab the two girls; then a neighbor took one of the girls as Pamela tried to get out with the other, making it all the way into the hall. More cops came, and one started after her, telling her to stop, but a neighbor blocked his way, howling, "Call the cops! Call the cops and have him arrested! He ain't leaving till the cops come and arrest him!"

The sergeant called for backup, and even more cops arrived, two of them running up twelve flights of stairs—but then one had to lie down in the stairwell, and the other was rushed to the hospital with chest pains. The press of angry bodies made the apartment hot, and some women yelled for everyone to calm down, and some women yelled the opposite, and as we tried to dress the crying kids some women tried to help in earnest, finding their jackets and socks, while others were still plainly angling to spirit them away.

When Pamela's last child had been taken, she swung at a cop, but then another cop grabbed her wrists, and her friends took her aside, and after a few more eruptions of screaming we got the kids out. One woman yelled, "This is why people hate the cops!" Although I thought very little of her and the rest of them—Mothers United for Narcotics and Neglect—she had a point: no one likes people who steal babies in the middle of the night. And we had just started our tour.

The midnight tour is also called the first platoon, the second being the day tour and the third being the four-to-twelve. You begin at 2315 hours and end at 0750. If you have Tuesday and Wednesday off one week, say, you have Tuesday, Wednesday, and Thursday off the next, and then Wednesday and Thursday the week after that. It takes some getting used to, because if you're working a Friday you don't come in Friday— you come in Thursday night. Another depressing thing about midnights is that when you finish work in the morning, at ten minutes to eight, you don't say, "See you tomorrow," which would seem soon enough; you say, "See you tonight." Tonight began yesterday, and tomorrow begins tonight, and the days become one rolling night.

25   When I first went on the job, I started out on steady four-to-twelves, Sunday to Thursday, working in a project called Morris Houses, which, with Morrisania, Butler, and Webster Houses, make up a huge complex of thirty apartment buildings called Claremont Village, in the heart of the South Bronx. On that beat, I was generally busier than I am now, when I might cover an entire precinct. I knew less local lore then, and the landmarks I navigated by were of recent relevance: the pawnshop to check after a chain snatch; the crack house where a baby overdosed; the rooftop where they fought pit bulls, sometimes throwing the loser to the street below. I still occasionally drive through this area with my partner, but even with my grasp of the neighborhood's history I'm not sure why things turned out as they did, and still less what led me here.

Morris Houses was named after Gouverneur Morris, a Revolutionary War hero, who was with Washington at Valley Forge and later established the decimal system of United States currency, proposing the words "dollar" and "cent." His half-brother Lewis was a signer of the Declaration of Independence, and tried to get the Founding Fathers to establish the nation's capital on the family estate, but the idea was more or less a nonstarter. The Morrises owned most of the South Bronx for nearly two centuries, and their name is everywhere: Morrisania, the neighborhood in the Forty-second Precinct, where my beat was; Morris Heights; Port Morris; Morris High School, which the industrialist Armand Hammer and General Colin Powell graduated from. Yet I couldn't say it means much to anyone here. The kids that Bernhard Goetz shot in 1984—four thugs who failed to recognize a subway-riding vigilante—came from Morrisania. One of them remains confined to a wheelchair, and I'd sometimes see him around; I locked up another one's sister for robbery, after a nasty girl-gang fight. I can't imagine that her mother said, upon her return from jail, "Gouverneur Morris and his half-brother Lewis must be rolling in their graves!" The Morrises made this place and helped make this nation, but they might as well have knocked up some local girls and split after the shotgun wedding, leaving nothing behind but their name.

On midnights, there is a risk of drifting within yourself, trailing off on your own weird train of thought, so that when the even weirder world intrudes it is hard not to laugh. One night not long ago, it was so slow that three patrol cars showed up for a dispute between two crackheads over a lost shopping cart. To pass the time, we conducted an investigation, asking pointed questions: What color was the cart? Do you have a receipt? It was cold, and after a while one of the cops said we should leave. But I was bored enough to want to talk to the crackheads, who relished the attention. I said to the cop, "They have issues, we can help them work through them, the relationship can come out even stronger than it was before." He looked at me and said, "Hey, I'm no Dr. Zhivago—let's get out of here."

On another job, we received a call for help from an old man and his sick wife. They seemed like good people: he had an upright, military bearing, and she was a stick figure, with plum-colored bruises all over, gasping through a nebulizer, "*Ayúdame, ayúdame, ayúdame.*" We made small talk, in broken English and Spanish, while waiting for EMS. On a shelf, there was a photograph of a young man in a police uniform, who the old man said was his son, a cop in San Juan who died at the age of thirty-four from cancer. The entire apartment was a Santería shrine: cigars laid across the tops of glasses of colorless liquid; open scissors on dishes of blue liquid; dried black bananas hanging over the threshold; Tarot cards, coins, and dice before a dozen statues of saints, including a huge Virgin Mary with a triple-headed angel at her feet. Suddenly, I thought, They keep the place up, but it's more *House Voodooful* than *House Beautiful.* The line wouldn't leave my head, so I had to pretend to cough, and walk outside.

You get in the habit of reading these scenes for signs, whether forensic or sacramental, of sin and struggle in the fallen world. Santería shrines and offerings are often placed in the corner of a room near the entrance, and in just that corner of one apartment we found a black-handled butcher knife next to blood that had not just pooled but piled, it lay so thick on the floor: dark, sedimentary layers with a clear overlay, like varnish, which I was told came from the lungs. The woman responsible for this handiwork explained why she had tried to sacrifice her brother at the household altar: "Two years ago, he broke my leg in five places. I came in tonight, he sold my couch. He killed my mother. Well, she died from him and all his nonsense." She stopped talking for a moment and tried to shift her hands in her cuffs as EMS took her brother out in a wheelchair, pale and still. "I didn't stab him," she went on. "He stabbed himself by accident, in the back, during the tussle."

30   Some objects tell simple stories of fierce violence, like the two-by-four, so bloody it looked as if it had been dipped in the stuff, that a woman had used to collect a fifty-dollar debt, or the rape victim's panties in the stairwell, covered with flies. Others are

more subtle and tentative, like the open Bible in the apartment of a woman whose brother, just home from prison, had suffered some sort of psychotic break. "He sat there reading the Bible for a while, and then he just looked up and said he was going to kill me," she said. The Bible was open to Proverbs 1:18, which states, "These men lie in wait for their own blood, they set a trap for their own lives." Maybe he'd read only the first part of the sentence. The woman's husband had just died, and next to the Bible there was a sympathy card from someone named Vendetta.

As a cop, you look for patterns—for context and connections that tell a fuller truth than a complainant may be willing to tell. Sometimes, though, the parts belong to no whole. So it was with a pair of attempted robberies, only twenty minutes and four blocks apart. Each perp was a male Hispanic, tall, slim, and young, in dark clothes, with a razor blade, though in the second robbery the perp wore a mask and a wig. And so when we came upon a tall, slim, young male Hispanic in dark clothes with a wig, mask, and razor in his pocket, in a desolate park between the two crime scenes, I reasonably expected to have solved at least one crime. Both complainants were sure, however, that he wasn't the man responsible, and we let him go.

In such cases, the solution seems out of sight but within reach, like the winning card in three-card monte. But there are other, older mysteries, and if there is a hint of a game in what unfolds you feel more like a piece than like a player. One night, we went to a routine "aided case," an old woman with a history of heart trouble, whose breath was rapid and shallow. She moaned, "Mami!" as she sat on a red velvet couch, flanked by two teenage girls. As the old lady left with EMS, my partner told me that she was raising her two granddaughters. An hour or so later, we had another aided case, a "heavy bleeder." When we went inside, a woman said, "She's in bed," and then, "It's in the tub." We checked on a teenage girl in the bedroom, who said she was fine, and then looked in the bathtub; there, nestled in the drain, was a fetus the size and color of a sprained thumb. The head was turned upward and the eyes were open and dark.

When the EMTs came—the same guys we'd met on the previous job—they asked for some plastic wrap or tinfoil, and were provided with a sandwich bag to pick it up. As we helped them put the teenage girl in the ambulance, they told us that the old lady had gone into cardiac arrest and wouldn't make it. Nothing else happened that night, and as we drove around I kept thinking that for everyone who dies another isn't necessarily born. It was late but also too early, not yet time to go home.

From the sixties through the eighties, the landscape of the Bronx was a record of public failure, high and low—from Robert Moses, who moved through the Bronx like Sherman through Georgia, evicting thousands in order to build highways, to the scavengers and predators who made ordinary life impossible for ordinary people. I've often wondered what Poe would have thought of the South Bronx at its worst— what his ghost would make of our ghost town. He wrote about loves lost to death at an early age, and set his tales in ancestral houses gone to ruin, but he might have taken to the abandoned factories and the tenements whose graffiti-covered walls had collapsed, leaving them open like doll houses. He might have said, "Don't change a thing!" Then again, such a landscape might have left little room for the imagination, or offered too much.

35   Since then, the landscape has changed for the better, and the record has been rewritten, often quickly and well. Of course, when something returned from the dead in Poe's world no good came of it, like the hideous beating of that telltale heart. On the other hand, the phrase "with a vengeance" does come to mind when I look at Suburban Place, one block from Charlotte Street, which is now the center of several blocks of well-tended ranch houses. There is something surreal about this development, with its fences and lawns, given both the area's past and its surroundings, which are still rough. You could look at it as a plot twist as unexpected as anything in Poe. You have to wait for it, and be accepting of surprise.

One night, we raced to the scene of "shots fired" from an elevated subway platform—a call that EMS workers had put over as they were driving past. A number of passersby confirmed it, but the shooter was long gone. Four hours later, with little to do in the interim except drive around in the dark, we received another job of shots fired, from an apartment right next to the El. Inside, a lovely old couple pointed out a hole in the window, and the neat chute that the bullet had cut through a hanging basket of African violets, littering stems and leaves on the floor. "I love my plants, they're my babies," the woman said, more concerned about what had happened than about what might have happened. The woman was a kind of grandmother to the neighborhood, and had been for more than a generation. There was a picture on the wall of her with Mayor Lindsay, who she said had let her have a house for a dollar a year to take care of local children. "Give your plants a big drink of water," I said. "And I'll play them some nice soothing music, too," she added. We saw where the bullet had hit the back wall— not far from Mayor Lindsay—but then had to dig around in the kitchen for a while before we found it, under the refrigerator. The heat and speed and impact had transformed the sleek missile into an odd-shaped glob, like a scoop of mashed potato, harmless and pointless. It was a big slug, probably from a .45, and had she been watering her plants it would have taken her head off. It frightened her, to be sure, but she had slept through its arrival and she would sleep again now that it was gone.

The bullet had taken less than a second to travel from the barrel into the couple's home, but in my mind the journey had taken four hours—from when the bullet was heard to when it was found—and I could picture it in slow motion, floating like a soap bubble on a windless night. Both perspectives seemed equally real, the explosive instant and the glacial glide, and I was glad to be able to see each of them, in the luxury of time. The old couple, I'm sure, were glad of it as well. My partner and I took the bullet with us, and morning arrived as we left.

MAKING CONNECTIONS

1. To what extent is this an essay about helping and supporting rather than apprehending and punishing?
2. The author is a New York City police officer. To what extent does his voice seem authentic? What does he say and what details does he include in the essay to support that authenticity?

3. A number of the events in this piece are very disturbing—and yet the writer describes them with an ironic sense of humor. Do you think humor in situations like these is appropriate? Explain.

 MAKING AN ARGUMENT

1. This essay is not only about law enforcement, it's about life in the city. Is there something about a large city like New York that makes it especially mysterious and threatening? To what extent might the kind of assertions made in Blake's poem "London" be applied to a large modern city? Is the narrative perspective in each piece different? How so? Write an essay comparing Blake's poem—and its tone—to this essay. Cite the poem and the essay for support.

DAVID SEDARIS [B. 1956]

David Sedaris is a humorist, playwright, former elf, apartment cleaner, and regular contributor to National Public Radio. His books include Barrel Fever *(1994),* Naked *(1997),* Holidays on Ice *(1998), and* Me Talk Pretty One Day *(2000), from which the essay below is taken. In 2001, he received the title "Humorist of the Year" from* Time *magazine and the Thurber Prize for American Humor. His latest book,* Dress Your Family in Corduroy and Denim *(2004), was number one on the* New York Times *Bestseller List for Nonfiction.*

THE LEARNING CURVE
[2000]

A year after my graduation from the School of the Art Institute of Chicago, a terrible mistake was made and I was offered a position teaching a writing workshop. I had never gone to graduate school, and although several of my stories had been Xeroxed and stapled, none of them had ever been published in the traditional sense of the word.

Like branding steers or embalming the dead, teaching was a profession I had never seriously considered. I was clearly unqualified, yet I accepted the job without hesitation, as it would allow me to wear a tie and go by the name of Mr. Sedaris. My father went by the same name, and though he lived a thousand miles away, I liked to imagine someone getting the two of us confused. "Wait a minute," this someone might say, "are you talking about Mr. Sedaris the retired man living in North Carolina, or Mr. Sedaris the distinguished academic?"

The position was offered at the last minute, when the scheduled professor found a better-paying job delivering pizza. I was given two weeks to prepare, a period I spent searching for a briefcase and standing before my full-length mirror, repeating the words "Hello, class, my name is Mr. Sedaris." Sometimes I'd give myself an aggressive voice and firm, athletic timbre. This was the masculine Mr. Sedaris, who wrote knowingly of flesh wounds and tractor pulls. Then there was the ragged bark of the newspaper editor, a tone that coupled wisdom with an unlimited capacity for cruelty. I tried sounding businesslike and world-weary, but when the day eventually came, my nerves kicked in and the true Mr. Sedaris revealed himself. In a voice reflecting doubt, fear, and an unmistakable desire to be loved, I sounded not like a thoughtful college professor but, rather, like a high-strung twelve-year-old girl; someone named Brittany.

My first semester I had only nine students. Hoping they might view me as professional and well prepared, I arrived bearing name tags fashioned in the shape of maple leaves. I'd cut them myself out of orange construction paper and handed them out along with a box of straight pins. My fourth-grade teacher had done the same thing, explaining that we were to take only one pin per person. This being college rather than elementary school, I encouraged my students to take as many pins as they liked. They wrote their names upon their leaves, fastened them to their breast pockets, and bellied up to the long oak table that served as our communal desk.

5   "All right then," I said. "Okay, here we go." I opened my briefcase and realized that I'd never thought beyond this moment. The orange leaves were the extent of my lesson plan, but still I searched the empty briefcase, mindful that I had stupidly armed my audience with straight pins. I guess I'd been thinking that, without provocation, my students would talk, offering their thoughts and opinions on the issues of the day. I'd imagined myself sitting on the edge of the desk, overlooking a forest of raised hands. The students would simultaneously shout to be heard, and I'd pound on something in order to silence them. "Whoa people," I'd yell. "Calm down, you'll all get your turn. One at a time, one at a time."

The error of my thinking yawned before me. A terrible silence overtook the room, and seeing no other option, I instructed my students to pull out their notebooks and write a brief essay related to the theme of profound disappointment.

I'd always hated it when a teacher forced us to invent something on the spot. Aside from the obvious pressure, it seemed that everyone had his or her own little way of doing things, especially when it came to writing. Maybe someone needed a particular kind of lamp or pen or typewriter. In my experience, it was hard to write without your preferred tools, but impossible to write without a cigarette.

I made a note to bring in some ashtrays and then I rooted through the wastepaper basket for a few empty cans. Standing beneath the prominently displayed NO SMOKING sign, I distributed the cans and cast my cigarettes upon the table, encouraging my students to go at it. This, to me, was the very essence of teaching, and I thought I'd made a real breakthrough until the class asthmatic raised his hand, saying that, to the best of his knowledge, Aristophanes had never smoked a cigarette in his life. "Neither did Jane Austen," he said. "Or the Brontës."

I jotted these names into my notebook alongside the word *Troublemaker,* and said I'd look into it. Because I was the writing teacher, it was automatically assumed that I had read every leather-bound volume in the Library of Classics. The truth was that I had read none of those books, nor did I intend to. I bluffed my way through most challenges with dim memories of the movie or miniseries based upon the book in question, but it was an exhausting exercise and eventually I learned it was easier to simply reply with a question, saying, "I know what Flaubert means to *me,* but what do *you* think of her?"

10   As Mr. Sedaris I lived in constant fear. There was the perfectly understandable fear of being exposed as a fraud, and then there was the deeper fear that my students might hate me. I imagined them calling their friends on the phone. "Guess who *I* got stuck with," they'd say. Most dull teachers at least had a few credentials to back them up. They had a philosophy and a lesson plan and didn't need to hide behind a clip-on tie and an empty briefcase.

Whenever I felt in danger of losing my authority, I would cross the room and either open or close the door. A student needed to ask permission before regulating the temperature or noise level, but I could do so whenever I liked. It was the only activity sure to remind me that I was in charge, and I took full advantage of it.

"There he goes again," my students would whisper. "What's up with him and that door?"

The asthmatic transferred to another class, leaving me with only eight students. Of these, four were seasoned smokers who took long, contemplative drags and occasionally demonstrated their proficiency by blowing ghostly concentric rings that hovered like halos above their bowed heads. The others tried as best they could, but it wasn't pretty. By the end of the second session, my students had produced nothing but ashes. Their hacking coughs and complete lack of output suggested that, for certain writers, smoking was obviously not enough.

Thinking that a clever assignment might help loosen them up, I instructed my students to write a letter to their mothers in prison. They were free to determine both the crime and the sentence, and references to cellmates were strongly encouraged.

15   The group set to work with genuine purpose and enthusiasm, and I felt proud of myself, until the quietest member of the class handed in her paper, whispering that both her father and her uncle were currently serving time on federal racketeering charges.

"I just never thought of my mom going off as well," she said. "This was just a really . . . depressing assignment."

I'd never known what an actual child-to-parent prison letter might be like, but now I had a pretty clear idea. I envisioned two convicts sharing a cell. One man stood at the sink while the other lay on a bunk, reading his mail.

"Anything interesting?" the standing man asked.

"Oh, it's from my daughter," the other man said. "She's just started college, and apparently her writing teacher is a real asshole."

20   That was the last time I asked my students to write in class. From that point on all their stories were to be written at home on the subject of their choice. If I'd had my way, we would have all stayed home and conducted the class through smoke signals. As it was, I had to find some way to pass the time and trick my students into believing that they were getting an education. The class met twice a week for two hours a day. Filling an entire session with one activity was out of the question, so I began breaking each session into a series of brief, regularly scheduled discussion periods. We began each day with Celebrity Corner. This was an opportunity for the

students to share interesting bits of information provided by friends in New York or Los Angeles who were forever claiming firsthand knowledge of a rock band's impending breakup or movie star's dark sexual secret. Luckily everyone seemed to have such a friend, and we were never short of material.

Celebrity Corner was followed by the Feedbag Forum, my shameless call for easy, one-pot dinner recipes, the type favored by elderly aunts and grandmothers whose dental status demanded that all meat fall from the bone without provocation. When asked what Boiled Beef Arkansas had to do with the craft of writing, I did not mention my recent purchase of a Crock-Pot; rather, I lied through my rotten teeth, explaining that it wasn't the recipe itself but the pacing that was of interest to the writer.

After the Feedbag Forum it was time for Pillow Talk, which was defined as "an opportunity for you to discuss your private sex lives in a safe, intellectual environment." The majority of my students were reluctant to share their experiences, so arrangements were made with the audiovisual department. I then took to wheeling in a big color television so that we might spend an hour watching *One Life to Live*. This was back when Victoria Buchanan passed out at her twentieth high-school reunion and came to remembering that rather than graduating with the rest of her class, she had instead hitchhiked to New York City, where she'd coupled with a hippie and given birth to a long lost daughter. It sounds far fetched, but like a roast forsaken in the oven or a rescheduled dental appointment, childbirth is one of those minor details that tends to slip the minds of most soap opera characters. It's a personality trait you've just got to accept.

On *General Hospital* or *Guiding Light* a similar story might come off as trite or even laughable. This, though, was *One Life to Live,* and no one could suddenly recall the birth of a child quite like Erika Slezak, who played both Victoria Buchanan and her alternate personality, Nicole Smith. I'd been in the habit of taping the show and watching it every night while eating dinner. Now that I was an academic, I could watch it in class and use the dinner hour to catch up on *All My Children.* A few students grumbled, but again I assured them that this was all part of my master plan.

Word came from the front office that there had been some complaints regarding my use of class time. This meant I'd have to justify my daily screenings with a homework assignment. Now the students were to watch an episode and write what I referred to as a "guessay," a brief prediction of what might take place the following day.

25   "Remember that this is not Port Charles or Pine Valley," I said. "This is Llanview, Pennsylvania, and we're talking about the Buchanan family."

It actually wasn't a bad little assignment. While the dialogue occasionally falters, you have to admire daytime dramas for their remarkable attention to plot. Yes, there were always the predictable kidnappings and summer love triangles, but a good show could always surprise you with something as simple as the discovery of an underground city. I'd coached my students through half a dozen episodes, giving them background information and explaining that missing children do not just march through the door ten minutes after the critical delivery flashback. The inevitable reunion must unfold delicately and involve at least two-thirds of the cast.

I thought I'd effectively conveyed the seriousness of the assignment. I thought that in my own way I had actually taught them something, so I was angry when their papers included such predictions as "the long-lost daughter turns out to be a vampire" and "the next day Vicki chokes to death while eating a submarine sandwich." The vampire business smacked of *Dark Shadows* reruns, and I refused to take it seriously. But choking to death on a sandwich, that was an insult. Victoria was a Buchanan and would never duck into a sub shop, much less choke to death in a single episode. Especially on a Wednesday. Nobody dies on a Wednesday—hadn't these people learned anything?

In the past I had tried my hardest to be understanding, going so far as to allow the conjugation of nouns and the use of such questionable words as *whateverishly*. This though, was going too far. I'd taught the Buchanans' Llanview just as my colleagues had taught Joyce's Dublin or Faulkner's Mississippi, but that was over now. Obviously certain people didn't deserve to watch TV in the middle of the afternoon. If my students wanted to stare at the walls for two hours a day, then fine, from here on out we'd just stick to the basics.

I don't know who invented the template for the standard writing workshop, but whoever it was seems to have struck the perfect balance between sadism and masochism. Here is a system designed to eliminate pleasure for everyone involved. The idea is that a student turns in a story, which is then read and thoughtfully critiqued by everyone in the class. In my experience the process worked, in that the stories were occasionally submitted, Xeroxed, and distributed hand to hand. They were folded into purses and knapsacks, but here the system tended to break down. Come critique time, most students behaved as if the assignment had been to confine the stories in a dark, enclosed area and test their reaction to sensory deprivation. Even if the papers were read out loud in class, the discussions were usually brief, as the combination of good manners and complete lack of interest kept most workshop participants from expressing their honest opinions.

30   With a few notable exceptions, most of the stories were thinly veiled accounts of the author's life as he or she attempted to complete the assignment. Roommates were forever stepping out of showers, and waitresses appeared out of nowhere to deliver the onion rings and breakfast burritos that stained the pages of the manuscripts. The sloppiness occasionally bothered me, but I had no room to complain. This was an art school, and the writing workshop was commonly known as the easiest way to fulfill one's mandatory English credits. My students had been admitted because they could admirably paint or sculpt or videotape their bodies in exhausting detail, and wasn't that enough? They told funny, compelling stories about their lives, but committing the details to paper was, for them, a chore rather than an aspiration. The way I saw it, if my students were willing to pretend I was a teacher, the least I could do was return the favor and pretend that they were writers. Even if someone had used his real name and recounted, say, a recent appointment with an oral surgeon, I would accept the story as pure fiction, saying, "So tell us, Dean, how did you come up with this person?"

The student might mumble, pointing to the bloodied cotton wad packed against his swollen gum, and I'd ask, "When did you decide that your character should seek treatment for his impacted molar?" This line of questioning allowed the authors to feel creative and protected anyone who held an unpopular political opinion.

"Let me get this straight," one student said. "You're telling me that if I say something out loud, it's me saying it, but if I write the exact same thing on paper, it's somebody else, right?"

"Yes," I said. "And we're calling that fiction."

The student pulled out his notebook, wrote something down, and handed me a
sheet of paper that read, "That's the stupidest fucking thing I ever heard in my life."
35   They were a smart group.

As Mr. Sedaris I made it a point to type up a poorly spelled evaluation of each
submitted story. I'd usually begin with the high points and end, a page or two later,
by dispensing such sage professional advice as "Punctuation never hurt anyone" or
"Think verbs!" I tended to lose patience with some of the longer dream sequences,
but for the most part we all got along, and the students either accepted or politely
ignored my advice.

Trouble arose only when authors used their stories to vindicate themselves
against a great hurt or perceived injustice. This was the case with a woman whom
the admissions office would have labeled a "returning student," meaning that her
social life did not revolve around the cafeteria. The woman was a good fifteen years
older than me and clearly disapproved of my teaching methods. She never contributed to Pillow Talk or the Feedbag Forum, and I had good reason to suspect it
was she who had complained about the *One Life to Live* episodes. With the teenage
freshmen, I stood a chance, but there was nothing I could do to please someone who
regularly complained that she'd wasted enough time already. The class was divided
into two distinct groups, with her on one side and everyone else on the other. I'd
tried everything except leg irons, but nothing could bring the two sides together. It
was a real problem.

The returning student had recently come through a difficult divorce, and
because her pain was significant, she wrongly insisted that her writing was significant as well. Titled something along the lines of "I Deserve Another Chance," her
story was not well received by the class. Following the brief group discussion, I
handed her my written evaluation, which she quietly skimmed over before raising
her hand.

"Yes," she said. "If you don't mind, I have a little question." She lit a cigarette and
spent a moment identifying with the smoldering match. "Who are *you*," she asked.
"I mean, just who in the hell are you to tell *me* that *my* story has no ending?"

40   It was a worthwhile question that was bound to be raised sooner or later. I'd
noticed that her story had ended in midsentence, but that aside, who was I to offer
criticism to anyone, especially in regard to writing? I'd meant to give the issue some
serious thought, but there had been shirts to iron and name tags to make and,
between one thing and another, I managed to put it out of my mind.

The woman repeated the question, her voice breaking. "Just who . . . in the stinking hell do you think . . . you are?"

"Can I give you an answer tomorrow?" I asked.

"No," she barked. "I want to know now. Who do you think you are?"

Judging from their expressions, I could see that the other side of the class was
entertaining the same question. Doubt was spreading through the room like the cold

germs seen in one of those slow-motion close-ups of a sneeze. I envisioned myself
burning on a pyre of dream sequences, and then the answer came to me.

45   "Who am I?" I asked. "I am the only one who is paid to be in this room." This
was nothing I'd necessarily want to embroider on a pillow, but still, once the answer
left my mouth, I embraced it as a perfectly acceptable teaching philosophy. My previous doubts and fears evaporated, as now I knew that I could excuse anything. The
new Mr. Sedaris would never again back down or apologize. From here on out, I'd
order my *students* to open and close the door and let *that* remind me that I was in
charge. We could do whatever I wanted because I was a certified professional—it
practically said so right there on my paycheck. My voice deepened as I stood to
straighten my tie. "All right then," I said. "Does anyone else have a stupid question for
Mr. Sedaris?"

The returning student once again raised her hand. "It's a personal question, I
know, but exactly how much is the school paying you to be in this room?"

I answered honestly, and then, for the first time since the beginning of the
school year, my students came together as one. I can't recall which side started it, I
remember only that the laughter was so loud, so violent and prolonged that Mr.
Sedaris had to run and close the door so that the real teachers could conduct their
business in peace.

 ## MAKING CONNECTIONS

1. The title of this humorous essay is "The Learning Curve." What is a "learning
   curve"? How does it fit this piece?
2. It is not as easy to pick up humor in print as it is when you actually see or
   hear the person telling the story. When did you first realize the author was
   not "serious"? What cues in the text indicate that? Is there a consistent style
   to this humor that helps you anticipate or appreciate the humor? Explain.
3. To what extent does your own experience as a writing student help you
   appreciate the plight of the teacher and students? Pick out the events that
   you thought were especially funny and explain what made them humorous
   to you.
4. Compare this essay to Mark Twain's "Advice to Youth" on page 340.

MAKING AN ARGUMENT

1. To what extent is it possible to make serious points in a humorous essay?
   Most authors treat the passage from innocence to experience seriously. This
   essay treats it humorously. Which do you prefer? Write about your preference as it applies to this work and other works in this section. Cite the texts
   of the work(s) for support.

CASE STUDY IN THEATRICAL CONTEXT

Hamlet and Performance

INTERPRETATION AND PERFORMANCE

The purpose of this Case Study is to demonstrate the possibility of multiple interpretations and to present Hamlet *in the context of an influential critic's view and commentary on productions of the play.* It has been an emphasis throughout this book that literature prompts multiple interpretations. Nowhere is this more apparent than in great works of drama and the process actors go through as they prepare to "interpret" the characters they play.

As readers of literature, we may interpret characters by asking who they are and what they say and do. We can distance ourselves from the work, examine the facts, judge the characters and their actions, and see them as part of a coherent whole. Actors, too, may begin with an objective analysis of characters they play, but rather than distancing themselves from the action and observing characters from outside, they must move inside the play and the characters and immerse themselves in the action.

For an actor, reading a play requires a much closer look—so close that it means looking from the inside out. Questions about characterization shift from "Who is he or she?" to "Who am I?" "When is this occurring in my life?" "How do I feel about being here?" "What do I want?" Answering questions like this requires a great deal of work, but it results in a comprehensive analysis and thorough interpretation of character—an interpretation that links actor and playwright in the creative process.

Multiple Interpretations of *Hamlet*

It is hard to imagine any character in dramatic literature who is discussed, interpreted or performed more often than Hamlet. And yet no two Hamlets are identical. From the time of Shakespeare and the first actor who played the role, Richard Burbage, to the present, we are just as likely to identify the character Hamlet with the actor playing the role as with the playwright. Hamlet's words may belong to Shakespeare, but the interpretation of the character belongs to Laurence Olivier, Derek Jacobi, Mel Gibson, Kenneth Branagh, and many other actors who have played the role. While we are likely to say that we prefer one or some of these interpretations more than others, we are not likely to say that one interpretation is right and the others wrong. In this respect, examining different but supportable interpretations can give us an insight into the many views possible when reading other forms of literature as well.

WILLIAM SHAKESPEARE [1564–1616]

Though William Shakespeare is the most famous writer ever to have written in English, details of his life are surprisingly sketchy. It is known that he was born in the town of Stratford-on-Avon, where he probably attended the local grammar school, and that he married Anne Hathaway in 1582. By 1592, he was an actor and playwright in London, associated with the Lord Chamberlain's Men, the most successful acting troupe of the time. In 1593 and 1594, he published two long mythological poems, Venus and Adonis *and* The Rape of Lucrece. *His astonishing sequence of sonnets, some of the most beautiful poetry ever created, were published in 1609, though they were probably written from 1592–1594, when the theaters were shut because of the plague. By 1597, he was able to buy a large house in Stratford and apparently retired there in 1610. His works for the theater, which were not published until after his death, number thirteen comedies (including* A Midsummer's Night Dream, Twelfth Night, *and* The Merchant of Venice), *ten tragedies (including* Romeo and Juliet, Macbeth, Julius Caesar, Othello, *and* Hamlet), *ten history plays, and four romances (including* The Tempest). *Ben Jonson, a playwright who was Shakespeare's contemporary and rival, wrote of him: "He was not of an age, but for all time!"*

HAMLET, PRINCE OF DENMARK

DRAMATIS PERSONAE

GHOST of Hamlet, the former King of Denmark

CLAUDIUS, King of Denmark, the former King's brother

GERTRUDE, Queen of Denmark, widow of the former King and now wife of
      Claudius

HAMLET, Prince of Denmark, son of the late King and of Gertrude

POLONIUS, *councillor to the King*

LAERTES, *his son*

OPHELIA, *his daughter*

REYNALDO, *his servant*

HORATIO, *Hamlet's friend and fellow student*

VOLTIMAND,
CORNELIUS,
ROSENCRANTZ,
GUILDENSTERN,   } *members of the Danish court*
OSRIC,
A GENTLEMAN,
A LORD,

BERNARDO,
FRANCISCO,   } *officers and soldiers on watch*
MARCELLUS,

FORTINBRAS, *Prince of Norway*
CAPTAIN IN HIS ARMY
THREE OR FOUR PLAYERS, *taking the roles of* PROLOGUE, PLAYER KING, PLAYER
        QUEEN, AND LUCIANUS
TWO MESSENGERS
FIRST SAILOR
TWO CLOWNS, *a gravedigger and his companion*
PRIEST
FIRST AMBASSADOR *from England*
Lords, Soldiers, Attendants, Guards, other Players, Followers of Laertes, other Sailors,
        another Ambassador or Ambassadors from England

SCENE: *Denmark*

[**Act 1.1** *Enter* BERNARDO *and* FRANCISCO, *two sentinels (meeting)*].°

BERNARDO: Who's there?

FRANCISCO: Nay, answer me.° Stand and unfold yourself.°

BERNARDO: Long live the King!

FRANCISCO: Bernardo?

BERNARDO: He.   5

FRANCISCO: You come most carefully upon your hour.

BERNARDO: 'Tis now struck twelve. Get thee to bed, Francisco.

FRANCISCO: For this relief much thanks. 'Tis bitter cold,
        And I am sick at heart.

BERNARDO: Have you had quiet guard?   10

FRANCISCO: Not a mouse stirring.

BERNARDO: Well, good night.
        If you do meet Horatio and Marcellus,
        The rivals° of my watch, bid them make haste.

1.1s.d. Location: Elsinore castle. A guard platform.   2 me (Francisco emphasizes that he
is the sentry currently on watch.)   **unfold yourself** reveal your identity   **14 rivals** partners

[Enter HORATIO *and* MARCELLUS.*]*

FRANCISCO: I think I hear them.—Stand, ho! Who is there?   15

HORATIO: Friends to this ground.°

MARCELLUS: And liegemen to the Dane.°

FRANCISCO: Give° you good night.

MARCELLUS: O, farewell, honest soldier. Who hath relieved you?

FRANCISCO: Bernardo hath my place. Give you good night.   20

[Exit FRANCISCO. *]*

MARCELLUS: Holla! Bernardo!

BERNARDO: Say, what, is Horatio there?

HORATIO: A piece of him.

BERNARDO: Welcome, Horatio. Welcome, good Marcellus.

HORATIO: What, has this thing appeared again tonight?   25

BERNARDO: I have seen nothing.

MARCELLUS: Horatio says 'tis but our fantasy,°

And will not let belief take hold of him

Touching this dreaded sight twice seen of us.

Therefore I have entreated him along°   30

With us to watch° the minutes of this night,

That if again this apparition come

He may approve° our eyes and speak to it.

HORATIO: Tush, tush, 'twill not appear.

BERNARDO: Sit down awhile,

And let us once again assail your ears,   35

That are so fortified against our story,

What° we have two nights seen.

HORATIO: Well, sit we down,

And let us hear Bernardo speak of this.

BERNARDO: Last night of all,°

When yond same star that's westward from the pole°   40

Had made his° course t' illume° that part of heaven

Where now it burns, Marcellus and myself,

The bell then beating one—

[Enter GHOST.*]*

MARCELLUS: Peace, break thee off! Look where it comes again!

BERNARDO: In the same figure like the King that's dead.   45

---

16 ground country, land   **17 liegemen to the Dane** men sworn to serve the Danish king
18 Give i.e., may God give   **27 fantasy** imagination   **30 along** to come along   **31 watch** keep
watch during   **33 approve** corroborate   **37 What** with what   **39 Last . . . all** i.e., this very last
night (Emphatic.)   **40 pole** polestar, north star   **41 his** its   **illume** illuminate

MARCELLUS: Thou art a scholar.° Speak to it, Horatio.

BERNARDO: Looks 'a° not like the King? Mark it, Horatio.

HORATIO: Most like. It harrows me with fear and wonder.

BERNARDO: It would be spoke to.°

MARCELLUS: Speak to it, Horatio.

HORATIO: What art thou that usurp'st° this time of night,   50

    Together with that fair and warlike form

    In which the majesty of buried Denmark°

    Did sometime° march? By heaven, I charge thee, speak!

MARCELLUS: It is offended.

BERNARDO: See, it stalks away.

HORATIO: Stay! Speak, speak! I charge thee, speak!   55

[Exit GHOST.*]*

MARCELLUS: 'Tis gone and will not answer.

BERNARDO: How now, Horatio? You tremble and look pale.

    Is not this something more than fantasy?

    What think you on 't?°

HORATIO: Before my God, I might not this believe   60

    Without the sensible° and true avouch°

    Of mine own eyes.

MARCELLUS: Is it not like the King?

HORATIO: As thou art to thyself.

    Such was the very armor he had on

    When he the ambitious Norway° combated.   65

    So frowned he once when, in an angry parle,°

    He smote the sledded° Polacks° on the ice.

    'Tis strange.

MARCELLUS: Thus twice before, and jump° at this dead hour,

    With martial stalk° hath he gone by our watch.   70

HORATIO: In what particular thought to work° I know not,

    But in the gross and scope° of mine opinion

    This bodes some strange eruption to our state.

MARCELLUS: Good now,° sit down, and tell me, he that knows,

    Why this same strict and most observant watch   75

    So nightly toils° the subject° of the land,

---

46 scholar one learned enough to know how to question a ghost properly   **47 'a** he
49 It . . . to (It was commonly believed that a ghost could not speak until spoken to.)
50 usurp'st wrongfully takes over   **52 buried Denmark** the buried King of Denmark
53 sometime formerly   **59 on 't** of it   **61 sensible** confirmed by the senses   **avouch** warrant, evidence   **65 Norway** King of Norway   **66 parle** parley   **67 sledded** traveling on sleds
Polacks Poles   **69 jump** exactly   **70 stalk** stride   **71 to work** i.e., to collect my thoughts and
try to understand this   **72 gross and scope** general drift   **74 Good now** (An expression
denoting entreaty or expostulation.)   **76 toils** causes to toil   **subject** subjects

And why such daily cast° of brazen cannon
And foreign mart° for implements of war,
Why such impress° of shipwrights, whose sore task
Does not divide the Sunday from the week.   80
What might be toward,° that this sweaty haste
Doth make the night joint-laborer with the day?
Who is 't that can inform me?

HORATIO: That can I;
  At least, the whisper goes so. Our last king,
Whose image even but now appeared to us,   85
Was, as you know, by Fortinbras of Norway,
Thereto pricked on° by a most emulate° pride,°
Dared to the combat; in which our valiant Hamlet—
For so this side of our known world° esteemed him—
Did slay this Fortinbras; who by a sealed° compact   90
Well ratified by law and heraldry
Did forfeit, with his life, all those his lands
Which he stood seized° of, to the conqueror;
Against the° which a moiety competent°
Was gagèd° by our king, which had returned°   95
To the inheritance° of Fortinbras
Had he been vanquisher, as, by the same cov'nant°
And carriage of the article designed,°
His fell to Hamlet. Now, sir, young Fortinbras,
Of unimprovèd mettle° hot and full,   100
Hath in the skirts° of Norway here and there
Sharked up° a list° of lawless resolutes°
For food and diet° to some enterprise°
That hath a stomach° in 't, which is no other—
As it doth well appear unto our state—   105
But to recover of us, by strong hand
And terms compulsatory, those foresaid lands

---

77 cast casting   **78 mart** buying and selling   **79 impress** impressment, conscription
81 toward in preparation   **87 pricked on** incited   **emulate** emulous, ambitious   **Thereto . . .
pride** (Refers to old Fortinbras, not the Danish King.)   **89 this . . . world** i.e., all Europe, the
Western world   **90 sealed** certified, confirmed   **93 seized** possessed   **94 Against the** in return
for   **moiety competent** corresponding portion   **95 gagèd** engaged, pledged
had returned would have passed   **96 inheritance** possession   **97 cov'nant** i.e., the sealed compact of line 90   **98 carriage . . . designed** carrying out of the article or clause drawn up to cover
the point   **100 unimprovèd mettle** untried, undisciplined spirits   **101 skirts** outlying regions,
outskirts   **102 Sharked up** gathered up, as a shark takes fish   **list** i.e., troop   **resolutes** des-
peradoes   **103 For food and diet** i.e., they are to serve as *food,* or "*means,*" *to* some
enterprise also they serve in return for the rations they get   **104 stomach** (1) a spirit of daring
(2) an appetite that is fed by the *lawless resolutes*

So by his father lost. And this, I take it,
Is the main motive of our preparations,
The source of this our watch, and the chief head°   110
Of this posthaste and rummage° in the land.

BERNARDO: I think it be no other but e'en so.
Well may it sort° that this portentous figure
Comes arméd through our watch so like the King
That was and is the question° of these wars.   115

HORATIO: A mote° it is to trouble the mind's eye.
In the most high and palmy° state of Rome,
A little ere the mightiest Julius fell,
The graves stood tenantless, and the sheeted° dead
Did squeak and gibber in the Roman streets;   120
As° stars with trains° of fire and dews of blood,
Disasters° in the sun; and the moist star°
Upon whose influence Neptune's° empire stands°
Was sick almost to doomsday° with eclipse.
And even the like precurse° of feared events,   125
As harbingers° preceding still° the fates
And prologue to the omen° coming on,
Have heaven and earth together demonstrated
Unto our climatures° and countrymen.

[Enter GHOST.*]*

But soft,° behold! Lo, where it comes again!   130
I'll cross° it, though it blast° me. *[It spreads his° arms.]*
        Stay, *illusion!*
If thou hast any sound or use of voice,
Speak to me!
If there be any good thing to be done
That may to thee do ease and grace to me,   135
Speak to me!
If thou art privy to° thy country's fate,
Which, happily,° foreknowing may avoid,

---

110 head source   **111 rummage** bustle, commotion   **113 sort** suit   **115 question** focus of contention   **116 mote** speck of dust   **117 palmy** flourishing   **119 sheeted** shrouded **121 As** (This abrupt transition suggests that matter is possibly omitted between lines 120 and 121.)   **trains** trails   **122 Disasters** unfavorable signs or aspects   **moist star** i.e., moon, governing tides   **123 Neptune** god of the sea   **stands** depends   **124 sick . . . doomsday** (See Matthew 24:29 and Revelation 6:12.)   **125 precurse** heralding, foreshadowing   **126 harbingers** forerunners   **still** continually   **127 omen** calamitous event   **129 climatures** regions   **130 soft** i.e., enough, break off   **131 cross** stand in its path, confront   **blast** wither, strike with a curse **s.d. his** its   **137 privy to** in on the secret of   **138 happily** haply, perchance

O, speak!
Or if thou hast uphoarded in thy life   140
Extorted treasure in the womb of earth,
For which, they say, you spirits oft walk in death,
Speak of it! [*The cock crows.*] Stay and speak!—Stop it, Marcellus.

MARCELLUS: Shall I strike at it with my partisan?°
HORATIO: Do, if it will not stand. [*They strike at it.*]   145
BERNARDO: 'Tis here!
HORATIO: 'Tis here!

[Exit GHOST.*]*

MARCELLUS: 'Tis gone.
We do it wrong, being so majestical,
To offer it the show of violence,   150
For it is as the air invulnerable,
And our vain blows malicious mockery.

BERNARDO: It was about to speak when the cock crew.
HORATIO: And then it started like a guilty thing
Upon a fearful summons. I have heard   155
The cock, that is the trumpet° to the morn,
Doth with his lofty and shrill-sounding throat
Awake the god of day, and at his warning,
Whether in sea or fire, in earth or air,
Th' extravagant and erring° spirit hies°   160
To his confine; and of the truth herein
This present object made probation.°

MARCELLUS: It faded on the crowing of the cock.
Some say that ever 'gainst° that season comes
Wherein our Savior's birth is celebrated,   165
This bird of dawning singeth all night long,
And then, they say, no spirit dare stir abroad;
The nights are wholesome, then no planets strike,°
No fairy takes,° nor witch hath power to charm,
So hallowed and so gracious° is that time.   170

HORATIO: So have I heared and do in part believe it.
But, look, the morn in russet mantle clad
Walks o'er the dew of yon high eastward hill.
Break we our watch up, and by my advice

---

144 partisan long-handled spear   **156 trumpet** trumpeter   **160 extravagant and erring** wandering beyond bounds (The words have similar meaning.)   **hies** hastens
162 probation proof   **164 'gainst** just before   **168 strike** destroy by evil influence
169 takes bewitches   **170 gracious** full of grace

Let us impart what we have seen tonight   175
Unto young Hamlet; for upon my life,
This spirit, dumb to us, will speak to him.
Do you consent we shall acquaint him with it,
As needful in our loves, fitting our duty?

MARCELLUS: Let's do 't, I pray, and I this morning know   180
        Where we shall find him most conveniently.

[Exeunt.]

*[Act **1.2** Flourish. Enter* CLAUDIUS, *King of Denmark,* GERTRUDE *the Queen, (the)
Council, as*° POLONIUS *and his son* LAERTES, HAMLET, *cum aliis*° *(including* VOLTIMAND
and CORNELIUS*).]*

KING: Though yet of Hamlet our° dear brother's death
        The memory be green, and that it us befitted
        To bear our hearts in grief and our whole kingdom
        To be contracted in one brow of woe,
        Yet so far hath discretion fought with nature   5
        That we with wisest sorrow think on him
        Together with remembrance of ourselves.
        Therefore our sometime° sister, now our queen,
        Th' imperial jointress° to this warlike state,
        Have we, as 'twere with a defeated joy—   10
        With an auspicious and a dropping eye,°
        With mirth in funeral and with dirge in marriage,
        In equal scale weighing delight and dole°—
        Taken to wife: Nor have we herein barred
        Your better wisdoms, which have freely gone   15
        With this affair along. For all, our thanks.
        Now follows that you know° young Fortinbras,
        Holding a weak supposal° of our worth,
        Or thinking by our late dear brother's death
        Our state to be disjoint and out of frame,   20
        Co-leaguèd with° this dream of his advantage,°
        He hath not failed to pester us with message
        Importing° the surrender of those lands
        Lost by his father, with all bonds° of law,

1.2 s.d. Location: The castle. as i.e., such as, including   **cum aliis** with others   **1 our** my
(The royal "we"; also in the following lines.)   **8 sometime** former   **9 jointress** woman possessing property with her husband   **11 With . . . eye** with one eye smiling and the other weeping   **13 dole** grief   **17 that you know** what you know already, that; or, that you be informed
as follows   **18 weak supposal** low estimate   **21 Co-leaguèd with** joined to, allied with
dream . . . advantage illusory hope of having the advantage (His only ally is this hope.)
23 Importing pertaining to   **24 bonds** contracts

To our most valiant brother. So much for him.   25
Now for ourself and for this time of meeting.
Thus much the business is: we have here writ
To Norway, uncle of young Fortinbras—
Who, impotent° and bed-rid, scarcely hears
Of this his nephew's purpose—to suppress   30
His° further gait° herein, in that the levies,
The lists, and full proportions are all made
Out of his subject;° and we here dispatch
You, good Cornelius, and you, Voltimand,
For bearers of this greeting to old Norway,   35
Giving to you no further personal power
To business with the King more than the scope
Of these dilated° articles allow. [*He gives a paper.*]
Farewell, and let your haste commend your duty.°
CORNELIUS, VOLTIMAND: In that, and all things, will we show our duty.   40
KING: We doubt it nothing.° Heartily farewell.

[*Exeunt* VOLTIMAND *and* CORNELIUS.]

And now, Laertes, what's the news with you?
You told us of some suit; what is 't, Laertes?
You cannot speak of reason to the Dane°
And lose your voice.° What wouldst thou beg, Laertes,   45
That shall not be my offer, not thy asking?
The head is not more native° to the heart,
The hand more instrumental° to the mouth,
Than is the throne of Denmark to thy father.
What wouldst thou have, Laertes?
LAERTES: My dread lord,   50
Your leave and favor° to return to France,
From whence though willingly I came to Denmark
To show my duty in your coronation,
Yet now I must confess, that duty done,
My thoughts and wishes bend again toward France   55
And bow them to your gracious leave and pardon.°

---

29 impotent helpless   **31 His** i.e., Fortinbras'   **gait** proceeding   **33 31–33 in that . . . sub-ject** since the levying of troops and supplies is drawn entirely from the King of Norway's own subjects   **38 dilated** set out at length   **39 let . . . duty** let your swift obeying of orders, rather than mere words, express your dutifulness   **41 nothing** not at all   **44 the Dane** the Danish king   **45 lose your voice** waste your speech   **47 native** closely connected, related   **48 instrumental** serviceable   **51 leave and favor** kind permission   **56 bow . . . pardon** entreatingly make a deep bow, asking your permission to depart

KING: Have you your father's leave? What says Polonius?

POLONIUS: H'ath,° my lord, wrung from me my slow leave

    By laborsome petition, and at last

    Upon his will I sealed° my hard° consent.   60

    I do beseech you, give him leave to go.

KING: Take thy fair hour,° Laertes. Time be thine,

    And thy best graces spend it at thy will!°

    But now, my cousin° Hamlet, and my son—

HAMLET: A little more than kin, and less than kind.°   65

KING: How is it that the clouds still hang on you?

HAMLET: Not so, my lord. I am too much in the sun.°

QUEEN: Good Hamlet, cast thy nighted color° off,

    And let thine eye look like a friend on Denmark.°

    Do not forever with thy vailèd lids°   70

    Seek for thy noble father in the dust.

    Thou know'st 'tis common,° all that lives must die,

    Passing through nature to eternity.

HAMLET: Ay, madam, it is common.

QUEEN: If it be,

    Why seems it so particular° with thee?   75

HAMLET: Seems, madam? Nay, it is. I know not "seems."

    'Tis not alone my inky cloak, good Mother,

    Nor customary° suits of solemn black,

    Nor windy suspiration° of forced breath,

    No, nor the fruitful° river in the eye,   80

    Nor the dejected havior° of the visage,

    Together with all forms, moods,° shapes of grief,

    That can denote me truly. These indeed seem,

    For they are actions that a man might play.

    But I have that within which passes show;   85

    These but the trappings and the suits of woe.

---

58 H'ath he has   **60 sealed** (as if sealing a legal document)   **hard** reluctant   **62 Take thy fair hour** enjoy your time of youth   **63 And . . . will** and may your finest qualities guide the way you choose to spend your time   **64 cousin** any kin not of the immediate family   **65 A little . . . kind** i.e., closer than an ordinary nephew (since I am stepson), and yet more separated in natural feeling (with pun on *kind* meaning "affectionate" and "natural," "lawful." This line is often read as an aside, but it need not be. The King chooses perhaps not to respond to Hamlet's cryptic and bitter remark.)   **67 the sun** i.e., the sunshine of the King's royal favor (with pun on *son*)   **68 nighted color** (1) mourning garments of black (2) dark melancholy   **69 Denmark** the King of Denmark   **70 vailèd lids** lowered eyes   **72 common** of universal occurrence (But Hamlet plays on the sense of "vulgar" in line 74.)   **75 particular** personal   **78 customary** (1) socially conventional (2) habitual with me   **79 suspiration** sighing   **80 fruitful** abundant   **81 havior** expression   **82 moods** outward expression of feeling

KING: 'Tis sweet and commendable in your nature, Hamlet,
    To give these mourning duties to your father.
    But you must know your father lost a father,
    That father lost, lost his, and the survivor bound   90
    In filial obligation for some term
    To do obsequious° sorrow. But to persever°
    In obstinate condolement° is a course
    Of impious stubbornness. 'Tis unmanly grief.
    It shows a will most incorrect to heaven,   95
    A heart unfortified,° a mind impatient,
    An understanding simple° and unschooled.
    For what we know must be and is as common
    As any the most vulgar thing to sense,°
    Why should we in our peevish opposition   100
    Take it to heart? Fie, 'tis a fault to heaven,
    A fault against the dead, a fault to nature,
    To reason most absurd, whose common theme
    Is death of fathers, and who still° hath cried,
    From the first corpse° till he that died today,   105
    "This must be so." We pray you, throw to earth
    This unprevailing° woe and think of us
    As of a father; for let the world take note,
    You are the most immediate° to our throne,
    And with no less nobility of love   110
    Than that which dearest father bears his son
    Do I impart toward° you. For° your intent
    In going back to school° in Wittenberg,°
    It is most retrograde° to our desire,
    And we beseech you bend you° to remain   115
    Here in the cheer and comfort of our eye,
    Our chiefest courtier, cousin, and our son.
QUEEN: Let not thy mother lose her prayers, Hamlet.
    I pray thee, stay with us, go not to Wittenberg.
HAMLET: I shall in all my best° obey you, madam.   120

---

92 obsequious suited to obsequies or funerals   **persever** persevere   **93 condolement** sorrowing   **96 unfortified** i.e., against adversity   **97 simple** ignorant   **99 As . . . sense** as the most ordinary experience   **104 still** always   **105 the first corpse** (Abel's)   **107 unprevailing** unavailing, useless   **109 most immediate** next in succession   **112 impart toward** i.e., bestow my affection on   **For** as for   **113 to school** i.e., to your studies   **Wittenberg** famous German university founded in 1502   **114 retrograde** contrary   **115 bend you** incline yourself   **120 in all my best** to the best of my ability

KING: Why, 'tis a loving and a fair reply.
　　　　Be as ourself in Denmark. Madam, come.
　　　　This gentle and unforced accord of Hamlet
　　　　Sits smiling to° my heart, in grace° whereof
　　　　No jocund° health that Denmark drinks today　　　　　　125
　　　　But the great cannon to the clouds shall tell,
　　　　And the King's rouse° the heaven shall bruit again,°
　　　　Respeaking earthly thunder.° Come away.

[Flourish. Exeunt all but HAMLET.*]*

HAMLET: O, that this too too sullied° flesh would melt,
　　　　Thaw, and resolve itself into a dew!　　　　　　　　　130
　　　　Or that the Everlasting had not fixed
　　　　His canon° 'gainst self-slaughter! O God, God,
　　　　How weary, stale, flat, and unprofitable
　　　　Seem to me all the uses° of this world!
　　　　Fie on 't, ah fie! 'Tis an unweeded garden　　　　　　135
　　　　That grows to seed. Things rank and gross in nature
　　　　Possess it merely.° That it should come to this!
　　　　But two months dead—nay, not so much, not two.
　　　　So excellent a king, that was to° this
　　　　Hyperion° to a satyr,° so loving to my mother　　　　　140
　　　　That he might not beteem° the winds of heaven
　　　　Visit her face too roughly. Heaven and earth,
　　　　Must I remember? Why, she would hang on him
　　　　As if increase of appetite had grown
　　　　By what it fed on, and yet within a month—　　　　　　145
　　　　Let me not think on 't; frailty, thy name is woman!—
　　　　A little month, or ere° those shoes were old
　　　　With which she followed my poor father's body,
　　　　Like Niobe;° all tears, why she, even she—
　　　　O God, a beast, that wants discourse of reason,°　　　　150
　　　　Would have mourned longer—married with my uncle,
　　　　My father's brother, but no more like my father

---

124 to i.e., at　**grace** thanksgiving　**125 jocund** merry　**127 rouse** drinking of a draft of liquor　**bruit again** loudly echo　**128 thunder** i.e., of trumpet and kettledrum, sounded when the King drinks; see 1.4.8-12　**129 sullied** defiled (The early quartos read *sallied;* the Folio, *solid.*)　**132 canon** law　**134 all the uses** the whole routine　**137 merely** completely　**139 to** in comparison to　**140 Hyperion** Titan sun-god, father of Helios　**satyr** a lecherous creature of classical mythology, half-human but with a goat's legs, tail, ears, and horns　**141 beteem** allow　**147 or ere** even before　**149 Niobe** Tantalus' daughter, Queen of Thebes, who boasted that she had more sons and daughters than Leto; for this, Apollo and Artemis, children of Leto, slew her fourteen children. She was turned by Zeus into a stone that continually dropped tears.　**150 wants . . . reason** lacks the faculty of reason

Than I to Hercules. Within a month,
Ere yet the salt of most unrighteous tears
Had left the flushing in her gallèd° eyes,   155
She married. O, most wicked speed, to post°
With such dexterity to incestuous° sheets!
It is not, nor it cannot come to good.
But break, my heart, for I must hold my tongue.

[Enter HORATIO, MARCELLUS *and* BERNARDO.*]*

HORATIO: Hail to your lordship!
HAMLET: I am glad to see you well.   160
    Horatio!—or I do forget myself.
HORATIO: The same, my lord, and your poor servant ever.
HAMLET: Sir, my good friend; I'll change that name° with you.
    And what make you from° Wittenberg, Horatio?
    Marcellus.   165
MARCELLUS: My good lord.
HAMLET: I am very glad to see you. [*To* Bernardo.] Good even, sir.—
    But what in faith make you from Wittenberg?
HORATIO: A truant disposition, good my lord.
HAMLET: I would not hear your enemy say so,   170
    Nor shall you do my ear that violence
    To make it truster of your own report
    Against yourself. I know you are no truant.
    But what is your affair in Elsinore?
    We'll teach you to drink deep ere you depart.   175
HORATIO: My lord, I came to see your father's funeral.
HAMLET: I prithee, do not mock me, fellow student;
    I think it was to see my mother's wedding.
HORATIO: Indeed, my lord, it followed hard° upon.
HAMLET: Thrift, thrift, Horatio! The funeral baked meats°   180
    Did coldly° furnish forth the marriage tables.
    Would I had met my dearest° foe in heaven
    Or ever° I had seen that day, Horatio!
    My father!—Methinks I see my father.
HORATIO: Where, my lord?
HAMLET: In my mind's eye, Horatio.   185
HORATIO: I saw him once. 'A° was a goodly king.

---

155 gallèd irritated, inflamed   **156 post** hasten   **157 incestuous** (In Shakespeare's day, the
marriage of a man like Claudius to his deceased brother's wife was considered incestuous.)
163 change that name i.e., give and receive reciprocally the name of "friend" (rather than talk
of "servant")   **164 make you from** are you doing away from   **179 hard** close   **180 baked
meats** meat pies   **181 coldly** i.e., as cold leftovers   **182 dearest** closest (and therefore deadliest)   **183 Or ever** before   **186 'A** he

HAMLET: 'A was a man. Take him for all in all,
    I shall not look upon his like again.

HORATIO: My lord, I think I saw him yesternight.

HAMLET: Saw? Who?   190

HORATIO: My lord, the King your father.

HAMLET: The King my father?

HORATIO: Season your admiration° for a while
    With an attent° ear till I may deliver,
    Upon the witness of these gentlemen,   195
    This marvel to you.

HAMLET: For God's love, let me hear!

HORATIO: Two nights together had these gentlemen,
    Marcellus and Bernardo, on their watch,
    In the dead waste° and middle of the night,
    Been thus encountered. A figure like your father,   200
    Armèd at point° exactly, cap-á-pie,°
    Appears before them, and with solemn march
    Goes slow and stately by them. Thrice he walked
    By their oppressed and fear-surprisèd eyes
    Within his truncheon's° length, whilst they, distilled°   205
    Almost to jelly with the act° of fear,
    Stand dumb and speak not to him. This to me
    In dreadful° secrecy impart they did,
    And I with them the third night kept the watch,
    Where, as they had delivered, both in time,   210
    Form of the thing, each word made true and good,
    The apparition comes. I knew your father;
    These hands are not more like.

HAMLET: But where was this?

MARCELLUS: My lord, upon the platform where we watch.

HAMLET: Did you not speak to it?

HORATIO: My lord, I did,   215
    But answer made it none. Yet once methought
    It lifted up its head and did address
    Itself to motion, like as it would speak;°
    But even then° the morning cock crew loud,

---

193 Season your admiration restrain your astonishment   **194 attent** attentive   **199 dead waste** desolate stillness   **201 at point** correctly in every detail   **cap-á-pie** from head to foot   **205 truncheon** officer's staff   **distilled** dissolved   **206 act** action, operation   **208 dreadful** full of dread   **217–218 did . . . speak** began to move as though it were about to speak   **219 even then** at that very instant

And at the sound it shrunk in haste away   220
And vanished from our sight.

HAMLET: 'Tis very strange.

HORATIO: As I do live, my honored lord, 'tis true,
And we did think it writ down in our duty
To let you know of it.

HAMLET: Indeed, indeed, sirs. But this troubles me.   225
Hold you the watch tonight?

ALL: We do, my lord.

HAMLET: Armed, say you?

ALL: Armed, my lord.

HAMLET: From top to toe?

ALL: My lord, from head to foot.   230

HAMLET: Then saw you not his face?

HORATIO: O, yes, my lord, he wore his beaver° up.

HAMLET: What° looked he, frowningly?

HORATIO: A countenance more in sorrow than in anger.

HAMLET: Pale or red?   235

HORATIO: Nay, very pale.

HAMLET: And fixed his eyes upon you?

HORATIO: Most constantly.

HAMLET: I would I had been there.

HORATIO: It would have much amazed you.   240

HAMLET: Very like, very like. Stayed it long?

HORATIO: While one with moderate haste might tell° a hundred.

MARCELLUS, BERNARDO: Longer, longer.

HORATIO: Not when I saw 't.

HAMLET: His beard was grizzled°—no?   245

HORATIO: It was, as I have seen it in his life,
A sable silvered.°

HAMLET: I will watch tonight.
Perchance 'twill walk again.

HORATIO: I warrant° it will.

HAMLET: If it assume my noble father's person,
I'll speak to it though hell itself should gape   250
And bid me hold my peace. I pray you all,
If you have hitherto concealed this sight,
Let it be tenable° in your silence still,
And whatsoever else shall hap tonight,

---

232 beaver visor on the helmet   **233 What** how   **242 tell** count   **245 grizzled** gray
247 sable silvered black mixed with white   **248 warrant** assure you   **253 tenable** held

Give it an understanding but no tongue.   255
I will requite your loves. So, fare you well.
Upon the platform twixt eleven and twelve
I'll visit you.

ALL: Our duty to your honor.
HAMLET: Your loves, as mine to you. Farewell.

[Exeunt (all but HAMLET*).]*

My father's spirit in arms! All is not well.   260
I doubt° some foul play. Would the night were come!
Till then sit still, my soul. Foul deeds will rise,
Though all the earth o'erwhelm them, to men's eyes.

[Exit.]

[Act 1.3 Enter LAERTES *and* OPHELIA, *his sister.]°*

LAERTES: My necessaries are embarked. Farewell.
And, sister, as the winds give benefit
And convoy is assistant,° do not sleep
But let me hear from you.

OPHELIA: Do you doubt that?

LAERTES: For Hamlet, and the trifling of his favor,   5
Hold it a fashion and a toy in blood,°
A violet in the youth of primy° nature,
Forward,° not permanent, sweet, not lasting,
The perfume and suppliance° of a minute—
No more.

OPHELIA: No more but so?

LAERTES: Think it no more.   10
For nature crescent° does not grow alone
In thews° and bulk, but as this temple° waxes
The inward service of the mind and soul
Grows wide withal.° Perhaps he loves you now,
And now no soil° nor cautel° doth besmirch   15
The virtue of his will,° but you must fear,
His greatness weighed,° his will is not his own.
For he himself is subject to his birth.
He may not, as unvalued persons do,

---

261 doubt suspect   **1.3 s.d. Location: Polonius' chambers   3 convoy is assistant** means
of conveyance are available   **6 toy in blood** passing amorous fancy   **7 primy** in its prime,
springtime   **8 Forward** precocious   **9 suppliance** supply, filler   **11 crescent** growing,
waxing   **12 thews** bodily strength   **temple** i.e., body   **14 Grows wide withal** grows along
with it   **15 soil** blemish   **cautel** deceit   **16 will** desire   **17 His greatness weighed** if you
take into account his high position

Carve° for himself, for on his choice depends   20
The safety and health of this whole state,
And therefore must his choice be circumscribed
Unto the voice and yielding° of that body
Whereof he is the head. Then if he says he loves you,
It fits your wisdom so far to believe it   25
As he in his particular act and place°
May give his saying deed, which is no further
Than the main voice° of Denmark goes withal.°
Then weigh what loss your honor may sustain
If with too credent° ear you list° his songs,   30
Or lose your heart, or your chaste treasure open
To his unmastered importunity.
Fear it, Ophelia, fear it, my dear sister,
And keep you in the rear of your affection,°
Out of the shot and danger of desire.   35
The chariest° maid is prodigal enough
If she unmask° her beauty to the moon.°
Virtue itself scapes not calumnious strokes.
The canker galls° the infants of the spring
Too oft before their buttons° be disclosed,°   40
And in the morn and liquid dew° of youth
Contagious blastments° are most imminent.
Be wary then; best safety lies in fear.
Youth to itself rebels,° though none else near.
OPHELIA: I shall the effect of this good lesson keep   45
As watchman to my heart. But, good my brother,
Do not, as some ungracious° pastors do,
Show me the steep and thorny way to heaven,
Whiles like a puffed° and reckless libertine
Himself the primrose path of dalliance treads,   50
And recks° not his own rede.°

[Enter POLONIUS.]

---

20 Carve i.e., choose   **23 voice and yielding** assent, approval   **26 in . . . place** in his particular restricted circumstances   **28 main voice** general assent   **withal** along with   **30**
credent credulous   **list** listen to   **34 keep . . . affection** don't advance as far as your affection
might lead you (A military metaphor.)   **36 chariest** most scrupulously modest   **37 If she**
unmask if she does no more than show her beauty   **moon** (Symbol of chastity.)   **39 canker**
galls canker-worm destroys   **40 buttons** buds   **disclosed** opened   **41 liquid dew** i.e., time
when dew is fresh and bright   **42 blastments** blights   **44 Youth . . . rebels** youth is inherently
rebellious   **47 ungracious** ungodly   **49 puffed** bloated, or swollen with pride   **51 recks**
heeds   **rede** counsel

LAERTES: O, fear me not.°
            I stay too long. But here my father comes.
            A double° blessing is a double grace;
            Occasion smiles upon a second leave.°
POLONIUS: Yet here, Laertes? Aboard, aboard, for shame!   55
            The wind sits in the shoulder of your sail,
            And you are stayed for. There—my blessing with thee!
            And these few precepts in thy memory
            Look° thou character.° Give thy thoughts no tongue,
            Nor any unproportioned° thought his° act.   60
            Be thou familiar,° but by no means vulgar.°
            Those friends thou hast, and their adoption tried,°
            Grapple them unto thy soul with hoops of steel,
            But do not dull thy palm° with entertainment
            Of each new-hatched, unfledged courage.° Beware   65
            Of entrance to a quarrel, but being in,
            Bear 't that° th' opposèd may beware of thee.
            Give every man thy ear, but few thy voice;
            Take each man's censure,° but reserve thy judgment.
            Costly thy habit° as thy purse can buy,   70
            But not expressed in fancy;° rich, not gaudy,
            For the apparel oft proclaims the man,
            And they in France of the best rank and station
            Are of a most select and generous chief in that.°
            Neither a borrower nor a lender be,   75
            For loan oft loses both itself and friend,
            And borrowing dulleth edge of husbandry.°
            This above all: to thine own self be true,
            And it must follow, as the night the day,
            Thou canst not then be false to any man.   80
            Farewell. My blessing season° this in thee!

---

fear me not don't worry on my account   **53 double** (Laertes has already bid his father good-bye.)   **54 Occasion . . . leave** happy is the circumstance that provides a second leave-taking (The goddess Occasion, or Opportunity, smiles.)   **59 Look** be sure that   **character** inscribe   **60 unproportioned** badly calculated, intemperate   **his** its   **61 familiar** sociable   **vulgar** common   **62 and their adoption tried** and also their suitability for adoption as friends having been tested   **64 dull thy palm** i.e., shake hands so often as to make the gesture meaningless   **65 courage** young man of spirit   **67 Bear 't that** manage it so that   **69 censure** opinion, judgment   **70 habit** clothing   **71 fancy** excessive ornament, decadent fashion   **74 Are . . . that** are of a most refined and well-bred preeminence in choosing what to wear   **77 husbandry** thrift   **81 season** mature

LAERTES: Most humbly do I take my leave, my lord.

POLONIUS: The time invests° you. Go, your servants tend.°

LAERTES: Farewell, Ophelia, and remember well

What I have said to you.   85

OPHELIA: 'Tis in my memory locked,

And you yourself shall keep the key of it.

LAERTES: Farewell.

[Exit LAERTES.*]*

POLONIUS: What is 't, Ophelia, he hath said to you?

OPHELIA: So please you, something touching the Lord Hamlet.   90

POLONIUS: Marry,° well bethought.

'Tis told me he hath very oft of late

Given private time to you, and you yourself

Have of your audience been most free and bounteous.

If it be so—as so 'tis put on° me,   95

And that in way of caution—I must tell you

You do not understand yourself so clearly

As it behooves° my daughter and your honor.

What is between you? Give me up the truth.

OPHELIA: He hath, my lord, of late made many tenders°   100

Of his affection to me.

POLONIUS: Affection? Pooh! You speak like a green girl,

Unsifted° in such perilous circumstance.

Do you believe his tenders, as you call them?

OPHELIA: I do not know, my lord, what I should think.   105

POLONIUS: Marry, I will teach you. Think yourself a baby

That you have ta'en these tenders for true pay

Which are not sterling.° Tender° yourself more dearly,

Or—not to crack the wind° of the poor phrase,

Running it thus—you'll tender me a fool.°   110

OPHELIA: My lord, he hath importuned me with love

In honorable fashion.

POLONIUS: Ay, fashion° you may call it. Go to,° go to.

---

83 invests besieges, presses upon   **tend** attend, wait   **91 Marry** i.e., by the Virgin Mary (A mild oath.)   **95 put on** impressed on, told to   **98 behooves** befits   **100 tenders** offers **103 Unsifted** i.e., untried   **108 sterling** legal currency   **Tender** hold, look after, offer   **109 crack the wind** i.e., run it until it is broken-winded   **110 tender me a fool** (1) show yourself to me as a fool (2) show me up as a fool (3) present me with a grandchild (*Fool* was a term of endearment for a child.)   **113 fashion** mere form, pretense   **Go to** (An expression of impatience.)

OPHELIA: And hath given countenance° to his speech, my lord,
    With almost all the holy vows of heaven.   115
POLONIUS: Ay, springes° to catch woodcocks.° I do know,
    When the blood burns, how prodigal° the soul
    Lends the tongue vows. These blazes, daughter,
    Giving more light than heat, extinct in both
    Even in their promise as it° is a-making,   120
    You must not take for fire. From this time
    Be something° scanter of your maiden presence.
    Set your entreatments° at a higher rate
    Than a command to parle.° For Lord Hamlet,
    Believe so much in him° that he is young,   125
    And with a larger tether may he walk
    Than may be given you. In few,° Ophelia,
    Do not believe his vows, for they are brokers,°
    Not of that dye° which their investments° show,
    But mere implorators° of unholy suits,   130
    Breathing° like sanctified and pious bawds,
    The better to beguile. This is for all:°
    I would not, in plain terms, from this time forth
    Have you so slander° any moment° leisure
    As to give words or talk with the Lord Hamlet.   135
    Look to 't, I charge you. Come your ways.°
OPHELIA: I shall obey, my lord.

[Exeunt.]

[Act 1.4 Enter HAMLET, HORATIO, *and* MARCELLUS.*]°*

HAMLET: The air bites shrewdly,° it is very cold.
HORATIO: It is a nipping and an eager° air.
HAMLET: What hour now?
HORATIO: I think it lacks of° twelve.
MARCELLUS: No, it is struck.

---

114 **countenance** credit, confirmation   116 **springes** snares   **woodcocks** birds easily
caught; here used to connote gullibility   117 **prodigal** prodigally   120 **it** i.e., the promise
122 **something** somewhat   123 **entreatments** negotiations for surrender (A military term.)
124 **parle** discuss terms with the enemy (Polonius urges his daughter, in the metaphor of military language, not to meet with Hamlet and consider giving in to him merely because he requests
an interview.)   125 **so . . . him** this much concerning him   127 **In few** briefly
128 **brokers** go-betweens, procurers   129 **dye** color or sort   **investments** clothes (The vows
are not what they seem.)   130 **mere implorators** out and out solicitors   131 **Breathing**
speaking   132 **for all** once for all, in sum   134 **slander** abuse, misuse   **moment** moment's
136 **Come your ways** come along   1.4 s.d. Location: The guard platform   1 **shrewdly**
keenly, sharply   2 **eager** biting   3 **lacks of** is just short of

HORATIO: Indeed? I heard it not.
      It then draws near the season°   5
      Wherein the spirit held his wont° to walk.

[A flourish of trumpets, and two pieces° go off (within).]

      What does this mean, my lord?
HAMLET: The King doth wake° tonight and takes his rouse,°
      Keeps wassail,° and the swaggering upspring° reels,°
      And as he drains his drafts of Rhenish° down,   10
      The kettledrum and trumpet thus bray out
      The triumph of his pledge.°
HORATIO: It is a custom?
HAMLET: Ay, marry, is 't,
      But to my mind, though I am native here
      And to the manner° born, it is a custom   15
      More honored in the breach than the observance.°
      This heavy-headed revel east and west°
      Makes us traduced and taxed of° other nations.
      They clepe° us drunkards, and with swinish phrase°
      Soil our addition;° and indeed it takes   20
      From our achievements, though performed at height,°
      The pith and marrow of our attribute.°
      So, oft it chances in particular men,
      That for° some vicious mole of nature° in them,
      As in their birth—wherein they are not guilty,   25
      Since nature cannot choose his° origin—
      By their o'ergrowth of some complexion,°
      Oft breaking down the pales° and forts of reason,
      Or by some habit that too much o'erleavens°
      The form of plausive° manners, that these men,   30
      Carrying, I say, the stamp of one defect,
      Being nature's livery° or fortune's star,°

---

5 season time   **6 held his wont** was accustomed   **s.d. pieces** i.e., of ordnance, cannon
8 wake stay awake and hold revel   **takes his rouse** carouses   **9 wassail** carousal   **upspring**
wild German dance   **reels** dances   **10 Rhenish** Rhine wine   **12 The triumph . . . pledge**
i.e., his feat in draining the wine in a single draft   **15 manner** custom (of drinking)   **16 More
. . . observance** better neglected than followed   **17 east and west** i.e., everywhere   **18 taxed
of** censured by   **19 clepe** call   **with swinish phrase** i.e., by calling us swine   **20 addition**
reputation   **21 at height** outstandingly   **22 The pith . . . attribute** the essence of the reputation that others attribute to us   **24 for** on account of   **mole of nature** natural blemish in
one's constitution   **26 his** its   **27 their o'ergrowth . . . complexion** the excessive growth
in individuals of some natural trait   **28 pales** palings, fences (as of a fortification)
29 o'erleavens induces a change throughout (as yeast works in dough)   **30 plausive** pleasing
32 nature's livery sign of one's servitude to nature   **fortune's star** the destiny that chance
brings

His virtues else,° be they as pure as grace,
As infinite as man may undergo,°
Shall in the general censure° take corruption   35
From that particular fault. The dram of evil
Doth all the noble substance often dout
To his own scandal.°

[Enter GHOST.*]*

HORATIO: Look, my lord, it comes!
HAMLET: Angels and ministers° of grace defend us!
Be thou° a spirit of health° or goblin damned,   40
Bring° with thee airs from heaven or blasts from hell,
Be thy intents° wicked or charitable,
Thou com'st in such a questionable° shape
That I will speak to thee. I'll call thee Hamlet,
King, father, royal Dane. O, answer me!   45
Let me not burst in ignorance, but tell
Why thy canonized° bones, hearsèd° in death,
Have burst their cerements;° why the sepulcher
Wherein we saw thee quietly inurned°
Hath oped his ponderous and marble jaws   50
To cast thee up again. What may this mean,
That thou, dead corpse, again in complete steel,°
Revisits thus the glimpses of the moon,°
Making night hideous, and we fools of nature°
So horridly to shake our disposition°   55
With thoughts beyond the reaches of our souls?
Say, why is this? Wherefore? What should we do?

[The GHOST *beckons* HAMLET.*]*

HORATIO: It beckons you to go away with it,
As if it some impartment° did desire
To you alone.

---

33 His virtues else i.e., the other qualities of *these men* (line 30)   **34 may undergo** can sustain   **35 general censure** general opinion that people have of him   **36–38 The dram . . . scandal** i.e., the small drop of evil blots out or works against the noble substance of the whole and brings it into disrepute. To *dout* is to blot out. (A famous crux.)   **39 ministers of grace** messengers of God   **40 Be thou** whether you are   **spirit of health** good angel   **41 Bring** whether you bring   **42 Be thy intents** whether your intentions are   **43 questionable** inviting question   **47 canonized** buried according to the canons of the church   **hearsèd** coffined   **48 cerements** grave clothes   **49 inurned** entombed   **52 complete steel** full armor   **53 glimpses of the moon** pale and uncertain moonlight   **54 fools of nature** mere men, limited to natural knowledge and subject to nature   **55 So . . . disposition** to distress our mental composure so violently   **59 impartment** communication

MARCELLUS: Look with what courteous action   60
It wafts you to a more removèd ground.
But do not go with it.
HORATIO: No, by no means.
HAMLET: It will not speak. Then I will follow it.
HORATIO: Do not, my lord!
HAMLET: Why, what should be the fear?
I do not set my life at a pin's fee,°   65
And for my soul, what can it do to that,
Being a thing immortal as itself?
It waves me forth again. I'll follow it.
HORATIO: What if it tempt you toward the flood,° my lord,
Or to the dreadful summit of the cliff   70
That beetles o'er° his° base into the sea,
And there assume some other horrible form
Which might deprive your sovereignty of reason°
And draw you into madness? Think of it.
The very place puts toys of desperation,°   75
Without more motive, into every brain
That looks so many fathoms to the sea
And hears it roar beneath.
HAMLET: It wafts me still.—Go on, I'll follow thee.
MARCELLUS: You shall not go, my lord.   *[They try to stop him.]*
HAMLET: Hold off your hands!   80
HORATIO: Be ruled. You shall not go.
HAMLET: My fate cries out,°
And makes each petty° artery° in this body
As hardy as the Nemean lion's° nerve.°
Still am I called. Unhand me, gentlemen.
By heaven, I'll make a ghost of him that lets° me!   85
I say, away!—Go on, I'll follow thee.
[Exeunt GHOST *and* HAMLET.*]*

HORATIO: He waxes desperate with imagination.
MARCELLUS: Let's follow. 'Tis not fit thus to obey him.

---

65 fee value   **69 flood** sea   **71 beetles o'er** overhangs threateningly (like bushy eyebrows)
his its   **73 deprive . . . reason** take away the rule of reason over your mind   **75 toys of desperation** fancies of desperate acts, i.e., suicide   **81 My fate cries out** my destiny summons me
82 petty weak   **artery** (through which the vital spirits were thought to have been conveyed)
83 Nemean lion one of the monsters slain by Hercules in his twelve labors   **nerve** sinew
85 lets hinders

HORATIO: Have after.° To what issue° will this come?

MARCELLUS: Something is rotten in the state of Denmark.   90

HORATIO: Heaven will direct it.°

MARCELLUS: Nay, let's follow him.

[Exeunt.]

[Act 1.5 Enter GHOST *and* HAMLET.*]*°

HAMLET: Whither wilt thou lead me? Speak. I'll go no further.

GHOST: Mark me.

HAMLET: I will.

GHOST: My hour is almost come,
     When I to sulfurous and tormenting flames
     Must render up myself.

HAMLET: Alas, poor ghost!

GHOST: Pity me not, but lend thy serious hearing   5
     To what I shall unfold.

HAMLET: Speak. I am bound° to hear.

GHOST: So art thou to revenge, when thou shalt hear.

HAMLET: What?

GHOST: I am thy father's spirit,   10
     Doomed for a certain term to walk the night,
     And for the day confined to fast° in fires,
     Till the foul crimes° done in my days of nature°
     Are burnt and purged away. But that° I am forbid
     To tell the secrets of my prison house,   15
     I could a tale unfold whose lightest word
     Would harrow up° thy soul, freeze thy young blood,
     Make thy two eyes like stars start from their spheres,°
     Thy knotted and combinèd locks° to part,
     And each particular hair to stand on end   20
     Like quills upon the fretful porcupine.
     But this eternal blazon° must not be
     To ears of flesh and blood. List, list, O, list!
     If thou didst ever thy dear father love—

---

89 Have after let's go after him   **issue** outcome   **91 it** i.e., the outcome   **1.5 s.d. Location: The battlements of the castle   7 bound** (1) ready (2) obligated by duty and fate (The Ghost, in line 8, answers in the second sense.)   **12 fast** do penance by fasting   **13 crimes** sins   **of nature** as a mortal   **14 But that** were it not that   **17 harrow up** lacerate, tear   **18 spheres** i.e., eye-sockets, here compared to the orbits or transparent revolving spheres in which, according to Ptolemaic astronomy, the heavenly bodies were fixed   **19 knotted . . . locks** hair neatly arranged and confined   **22 eternal blazon** revelation of the secrets of eternity

HAMLET: O God!   25

GHOST: Revenge his foul and most unnatural murder.

HAMLET: Murder?

GHOST: Murder most foul, as in the best° it is,

But this most foul, strange, and unnatural.

HAMLET: Haste me to know't, that I, with wings as swift   30

As meditation or the thoughts of love,

May sweep to my revenge.

GHOST: I find thee apt;

And duller shouldst thou be° than the fat° weed

That roots itself in ease on Lethe° wharf,

Wouldst thou not stir in this. Now, Hamlet, hear.   35

'Tis given out that, sleeping in my orchard,°

A serpent stung me. So the whole ear of Denmark

Is by a forgèd process° of my death

Rankly abused.° But know, thou noble youth,

The serpent that did sting thy father's life   40

Now wears his crown.

HAMLET: O, my prophetic soul! My uncle!

GHOST: Ay, that incestuous, that adulterate° beast,

With witchcraft of his wit, with traitorous gifts°—

O wicked wit and gifts, that have the power   45

So to seduce!—won to his shameful lust

The will of my most seeming-virtuous queen.

O Hamlet, what a falling off was there!

From me, whose love was of that dignity

That it went hand in hand even with the vow°   50

I made to her in marriage, and to decline

Upon a wretch whose natural gifts were poor

To° those of mine!

But virtue, as it° never will be moved,

Though lewdness court it in a shape of heaven,°   55

So lust, though to a radiant angel linked,

Will sate itself in a celestial bed°

And prey on garbage.

But soft, methinks I scent the morning air.

28 in the best even at best   **33 shouldst thou be** you would have to be   **fat** torpid, lethargic   **34 Lethe** the river of forgetfulness in Hades   **36 orchard** garden   **38 forgèd process** falsified account   **39 abused** deceived   **43 adulterate** adulterous   **44 gifts** (1) talents (2) presents   **50 even with the vow** with the very vow   **53 To** compared to   **54 virtue, as it** as virtue   **55 shape of heaven** heavenly form   **57 sate . . . bed** cease to find sexual pleasure in a virtuously lawful marriage

Brief let me be. Sleeping within my orchard,   60
My custom always of the afternoon,
Upon my secure° hour thy uncle stole,
With juice of cursèd hebona° in a vial,
And in the porches of my ears° did pour
The leprous distillment,° whose effect   65
Holds such an enmity with blood of man
That swift as quicksilver it courses through
The natural gates and alleys of the body,
And with a sudden vigor it doth posset°
And curd, like eager° droppings into milk,   70
The thin and wholesome blood. So did it mine,
And a most instant tetter° barked° about,
Most lazar-like,° with vile and loathsome crust,
All my smooth body.
Thus was I, sleeping, by a brother's hand   75
Of life, of crown, of queen at once dispatched,°
Cut off even in the blossoms of my sin,
Unhouseled,° disappointed,° unaneled,°
No reckoning° made, but sent to my account
With all my imperfections on my head.   80
O, horrible! O, horrible, most horrible!
If thou hast nature° in thee, bear it not.
Let not the royal bed of Denmark be
A couch for luxury° and damnèd incest.
But, howsoever thou pursues this act,   85
Taint not thy mind nor let thy soul contrive
Against thy mother aught. Leave her to heaven
And to those thorns that in her bosom lodge,
To prick and sting her. Fare thee well at once.
The glowworm shows the matin° to be near,   90
And 'gins to pale his° uneffectual fire.
Adieu, adieu, adieu! Remember me.

---

62 secure confident, unsuspicious   **63 hebona** a poison (The word seems to be a form of
ebony, though it is thought perhaps to be related to *benbane,* a poison, or to *ebenus,* "yew.")
64 porches of my ears ears as a porch or entrance of the body   **65 leprous distillment** dis-
tillation causing leprosylike disfigurement   **69 posset** coagulate, curdle   **70 eager** sour, acid
72 tetter eruption of scabs   **barked** recovered with a rough covering, like bark on a tree
73 lazar-like leperlike   **76 dispatched** suddenly deprived   **78 Unhouseled** without having
received the Sacrament   **disappointed** unready (spiritually) for the last journey   **unaneled**
without having received extreme unction   **79 reckoning** settling of accounts   **82 nature** i.e.,
the promptings of a son   **84 luxury** lechery   **90 matin** morning   **91 his** its

[Exit.]

HAMLET: O all you host of heaven! O earth! What else?
            And shall I couple° hell? O, fie! Hold,° hold, my heart,
            And you, my sinews, grow not instant° old,   95
            But bear me stiffly up. Remember thee?
            Ay, thou poor ghost, whiles memory holds a seat
            In this distracted globe.° Remember thee?
            Yea, from the table° of my memory
            I'll wipe away all trivial fond° records,   100
            All saws° of books, all forms,° all pressures° past
            That youth and observation copied there,
            And thy commandment all alone shall live
            Within the book and volume of my brain,
            Unmixed with baser matter. Yes, by heaven!   105
            O most pernicious woman!
            O villain, villain, smiling, damnèd villain!
            My tables°—meet it is° I set it down
            That one may smile, and smile, and be a villain.
            At least I am sure it may be so in Denmark.   110

[Writing.]

            So uncle, there you are.° Now to my word:
            It is "Adieu, adieu! Remember me."
            I have sworn't.

[Enter HORATIO *and* MARCELLUS.*]*

HORATIO: My lord, my lord!
MARCELLUS: Lord Hamlet!   115
HORATIO: Heavens secure him!°
HAMLET: So be it.
MARCELLUS: Hilo, ho, ho, my lord!
HAMLET: Hilo, ho, ho, boy! Come, bird, come.°
MARCELLUS: How is 't, my noble lord?   120
HORATIO: What news, my lord?
HAMLET: O, wonderful!
HORATIO: Good my lord, tell it
HAMLET: No, you will reveal it.

94 couple add   **Hold** hold together   **95 instant** instantly   **98 globe** (1) head (2) world
99 table tablet, slate   **100 fond** foolish   **101 saws** wise sayings   **forms** shapes or images
copied onto the slate; general ideas   **pressures** impressions stamped   **108 tables** writing
tablets   **meet it is** it is fitting   **111 there you are** i.e., there, I've written that down against you
116 secure him keep him safe   **119 Hilo . . . come** (A falconer's call to a hawk in air. Hamlet
mocks the hallooing as though it were a part of hawking.)

HORATIO: Not I, my lord, by heaven.   125

MARCELLUS: Nor I, my lord.

HAMLET: How say you, then, would heart of man once° think it?

    But you'll be secret?

HORATIO, MARCELLUS: Ay, by heaven, my lord.

HAMLET: There's never a villain dwelling in all Denmark

    But he's an arrant° knave.   130

HORATIO: There needs no ghost, my lord, come from the grave

    To tell us this.

HAMLET: Why, right, you are in the right.

    And so, without more circumstance° at all,

    I hold it fit that we shake hands and part,

    You as your business and desire shall point you—   135

    For every man hath business and desire,

    Such as it is—and for my own poor part,

    Look you, I'll go pray,

HORATIO: These are but wild and whirling words, my lord.

HAMLET: I am sorry they offend you, heartily;   140

    Yes, faith, heartily.

HORATIO: There's no offense, my lord.

HAMLET: Yes, but Saint Patrick,° but there is, Horatio,

    And much offense° too. Touching this vision here,

    It is an honest ghost,° that let me tell you.

    For your desire to know what is between us,   145

    O'ermaster 't as you may. And now, good friends,

    As you are friends, scholars, and soldiers,

    Give me one poor request.

HORATIO: What is 't, my lord? We will.

HAMLET: Never make known what you have seen tonight.   150

HORATIO, MARCELLUS: My lord, we will not.

HAMLET: Nay, but swear 't.

HORATIO: In faith, my lord, not I.°

MARCELLUS: Nor I, my lord, in faith.

HAMLET: Upon my sword.°   [*He holds out his sword.*]   155

---

127 once ever   **130 arrant** thoroughgoing   **133 circumstance** ceremony, elaboration
142 Saint Patrick The keeper of Purgatory and patron saint of all blunders and confusion.
143 offense (Hamlet deliberately changes Horatio's "no offense taken" to "an offense against all decency.")   **144 an honest ghost** i.e., a real ghost and not an evil spirit   **153 In faith . . . I** i.e.,
I swear not to tell what I have seen (Horatio is not refusing to swear.)   **155 sword** i.e., the hilt in the form of a cross

MARCELLUS: We have sworn, my lord, already.°

HAMLET: Indeed, upon my sword, indeed.

GHOST [*cries under the stage*]:   Swear.

HAMLET: Ha, ha, boy, sayst thou so? Art thou there, truepenny?°

    Come on, you hear this fellow in the cellarage.   160

    Consent to swear.

HORATIO: Propose the oath, my lord.

HAMLET: Never to speak of this that you have seen,

    Swear by my sword.

GHOST [*beneath*]:   Swear.   [*They swear.*°]

HAMLET: *Hic et ubique?*° Then we'll shift our ground.   165

[He moves to another spot.]

    Come hither, gentlemen,

    And lay your hands again upon my sword.

    Swear by my sword

    Never to speak of this that you have heard.

GHOST [*beneath*]:   Swear by his sword.   [*They swear.*]   170

HAMLET: Well said, old mole. Canst work i' th' earth so fast?

    A worthy pioneer!°—Once more removed, good friends.

[He moves again.]

HORATIO: O day and night, but this is wondrous strange!

HAMLET: And therefore as a stranger° give it welcome.

    There are more things in heaven and earth, Horatio,   175

    Than are dreamt of in your philosophy.°

    But come;

    Here, as before, never, so help you mercy,°

    How strange or odd soe'er I bear myself—

    As I perchance hereafter shall think meet   180

    To put an antic° disposition on—

    That you, at such times seeing me, never shall,

---

156 We . . . already i.e., we swore in *faith*   **159 truepenny** honest old fellow   **164 s.d. They swear** (Seemingly they swear here, and at lines 170 and 190, as they lay their hands on Hamlet's sword. Triple oaths would have particular force; these three oaths deal with what they have seen, what they have heard, and what they promise about Hamlet's *antic disposition.*   **165 *Hic et ubique*** here and everywhere (Latin.)   **172 pioneer** foot soldier assigned to dig tunnels and excavations   **174 as a stranger** i.e., needing your hospitality   **176 your philosophy** this subject called "natural philosophy" or "science" that people talk about   **178 so help you mercy** as you hope for God's mercy when you are judged   **181 antic** fantastic

With arms encumbered° thus, or this headshake,
Or by pronouncing of some doubtful phrase
As "Well, we know," or "We could, an if° we would,"   185
Or "If we list° to speak," or "There be, an if they might,"
Or such ambiguous giving out,° to note°
That you know aught° of me—this do swear,
So grace and mercy at your most need help you.
GHOST [*beneath*]:   Swear.   [*They swear.*]   190
HAMLET: Rest, rest, perturbèd spirit! So, gentlemen,
With all my love I do commend me to you;°
And what so poor a man as Hamlet is
May do t' express his love and friending° to you,
God willing, shall not lack.° Let us go in together,   195
And still° your fingers on your lips, I pray.
The time° is out of joint. O cursèd spite°
That ever I was born to set it right!

[They wait for him to leave first.]

Nay, come, let's go together.°

[Exeunt.]

*[*Act 2.1 *Enter old* POLONIUS *with his man* (REYNALDO).*]°*

POLONIUS: Give him this money and these notes, Reynaldo.

[He gives money and papers.]

REYNALDO: I will, my lord.
POLONIUS: You shall do marvelous° wisely, good Reynaldo,
Before you visit him, to make inquire°
Of his behavior.
REYNALDO: My lord, I did intend it.   5
POLONIUS: Marry, well said, very well said. Look you, sir,
Inquire me first what Danskers° are in Paris,
And how, and who, what means,° and where they keep,°

---

183 encumbered folded   **185 an if** if   **186 list** wished **There . . . might** i.e., there are people
here (we, in fact) who could tell news if we were at liberty to do so   **187 giving out** intimation
note draw attention to the fact   **188 aught** i.e., something secret   **192 do . . . you** entrust
myself to you   **194 friending** friendliness   **195 lack** be lacking   **196 still** always   **197 The
time** the state of affairs   **spite** i.e., the spite of Fortune   **199 let's go together** (Probably they
wait for him to leave first, but he refuses this ceremoniousness.)   **2.1 s.d. Location: Polonius'
chambers   3 marvelous** marvelously   **4 inquire** inquiry   **7 Danskers** Danes   **8 what
means** what wealth (they have)   **keep** dwell

What company, at what expense; and finding
By this encompassment° and drift° of question   10
That they do know my son, come you more nearer
Than your particular demands will touch it.°
Take you,° as 'twere, some distant knowledge of him,
As thus, "I know his father and his friends,
And in part him." Do you mark this, Reynaldo?   15

REYNALDO: Ay, very well, my lord.

POLONIUS: "And in part him, but," you may say, "not well.
But if 't be he I mean, he's very wild,
Addictcd so and so," and there put on° him
What forgeries° you please—marry, none so rank°   20
As may dishonor him, take heed of that,
But, sir, such wanton,° wild, and usual slips
As are companions noted and most known
To youth and liberty.

REYNALDO: As gaming, my lord.   25

POLONIUS: Ay, or drinking, fencing, swearing,
Quarreling, drabbing°—you may go so far.

REYNALDO: My lord, that would dishonor him.

POLONIUS: Faith, no, as you may season° it in the charge.
You must not put another scandal on him   30
That he is open to incontinency;°
That's not my meaning. But breathe his faults so quaintly°
That they may seem the taints of liberty,°
The flash and outbreak of a fiery mind,
A savageness in unreclaimèd blood,   35
Of general assault.°

REYNALDO: But, my good lord—

POLONIUS: Wherefore should you do this?

REYNALDO: Ay, my lord, I would know that.

POLONIUS: Marry, sir, here's my drift,
And I believe it is a fetch of warrant.°   40
You laying these slight sullies on my son,

---

10 encompassment roundabout talking   **drift** gradual approach or course   **11–12 come . . .
it** you will find out more this way than by asking pointed questions (*particular demands*)
13 Take you assume, pretend   **19 put on** impute to   **20 forgeries** invented tales   **rank** gross
22 wanton sportive, unrestrained   **27 drabbing** whoring   **29 season** temper, soften
31 incontinency habitual sexual excess   **32 quaintly** artfully, subtly   **33 taints of liberty**
faults resulting from free living   **35–36 A savageness . . . assault** a wildness in untamed youth
that assails all indiscriminately   **41 fetch of warrant** legitimate trick

As 'twere a thing a little soiled wi' the working,°
Mark you,
Your party in converse,° him you would sound,°   45
Having ever° seen in the prenominate crimes°
The youth you breathe° of guilty, be assured
He closes with you in this consequence:°
"Good sir," or so, or "friend," or "gentleman,"
According to the phrase or the addition°   50
Of man and country.

REYNALDO: Very good, my lord.

POLONIUS: And then, sir, does 'a this—'a does—what was I about to say? By the
Mass, I was about to say something. Where did I leave?

REYNALDO: At "closes in the consequence."   55

POLONIUS: At "closes in the consequence," ay, marry.
He closes thus: "I know the gentleman,
I saw him yesterday," or "th' other day,"
Or then, or then, with such or such, "and as you say,
There was 'a gaming," "there o'ertook in 's rouse,"°   60
"There falling out° at tennis," or perchance
"I saw him enter such a house of sale,"
Videlicet° a brothel, or so forth. See you now,
Your bait of falsehood takes this carp° of truth;
And thus do we of wisdom and of reach,°   65
With windlasses° and with assays of bias,°
By indirections find directions° out.
So by my former lecture and advice
Shall you my son. You have° me, have you not?

REYNALDO: My lord, I have.

POLONIUS: God b' wi'° ye; fare ye well.   70

REYNALDO: Good my lord.

POLONIUS: Observe his inclination in yourself.°

REYNALDO: I shall, my lord.

---

43 soiled wi' the working soiled by handling while it is being made, i.e., by involvement in the
ways of the world   **45 converse** conversation   **sound** i.e., sound out   **46 Having ever** if he has
ever   **prenominate crimes** before-mentioned offenses   **47 breathe** speak   **48 closes . . .
consequence** takes you into his confidence in some fashion, as follows   **50 addition** title
60 o'er-took in 's rouse overcome by drink   **61 falling out** quarreling   **63 Videlicet** namely
64 carp a fish   **65 reach** capacity, ability   **66 windlasses** i.e., circuitous paths. (Literally, circuits
made to head off the game in hunting.)   **assays of bias** attempts through indirection (like the
curving path of the bowling ball, which is biased or weighted to one side)   **67 directions** i.e., the
way things really are   **69 have** understand   **70 b' wi'** be with   **72 in yourself** in your own
person (as well as by asking questions)

POLONIUS: And let him ply his music.
REYNALDO: Well, my lord.   75
POLONIUS: Farewell.

[Exit REYNALDO.*]*

[Enter OPHELIA.*]*

                              How now, Ophelia, what's the matter?
OPHELIA: O my lord, my lord, I have been so affrighted!
POLONIUS: With what, i' the name of God?
OPHELIA: My lord, as I was sewing in my closet,°
            Lord Hamlet, with his doublet° all unbraced,°   80
            No hat upon his head, his stockings fouled,
            Ungartered, and down-gyvèd° to his ankle,
            Pale as his shirt, his knees knocking each other,
            And with a look so piteous in purport°
            As if he had been loosèd out of hell   85
            To speak of horrors—he comes before me.
POLONIUS: Mad for thy love?
OPHELIA: My lord, I do not know,
            But truly I do fear it.
POLONIUS: What said he?
OPHELIA: He took me by the wrist and held me hard.
            Then goes he to the length of all his arm,   90
            And, with his other hand thus o'er his brow
            He falls to such perusal of my face
            As° 'a would draw it. Long stayed he so.
            At last, a little shaking of mine arm
            And thrice his head thus waving up and down,   95
            He raised a sigh so piteous and profound
            As it did seem to shatter all his bulk°
            And end his being. That done, he lets me go,
            And with his head over his shoulder turned
            He seemed to find his way without his eyes,   100
            For out o' doors he went without their helps,
            And to the last bended their light on me.
POLONIUS: Come, go with me. I will go seek the King.
            This is the very ecstasy° of love,

---

79 **closet** private chamber   80 **doublet** close-fitting jacket   **unbraced** unfastened   82 **down-gyvèd** fallen to the ankles (like gyves or fetters)   84 **in purport** in what it expressed   93 **As** as if (also in line 97)   97 **bulk** body   104 **ecstasy** madness

Whose violent property° fordoes° itself   105
And leads the will to desperate undertakings
As oft as any passion under heaven
That does afflict our natures. I am sorry.
What, have you given him any hard words of late?

OPHELIA: No, my good lord, but as you did command   110
     I did repel his letters and denied
     His access to me.

POLONIUS: That hath made him mad.
     I am sorry that with better heed and judgment
     I had not quoted° him. I feared he did but trifle
     And meant to wrack° thee. But beshrew my jealousy!°   115
     By heaven, it is as proper to our age°
     To cast beyond° ourselves in our opinions
     As it is common for the younger sort
     To lack discretion. Come, go we to the King.
     This must be known,° which, being kept close,° might move   120
     More grief to hide than hate to utter love.°
     Come.

[Exeunt.]

*[Act **2.2** Flourish. Enter* KING *and* QUEEN, ROSENCRANTZ, *and* GUILDENSTERN *(with others).]°*

KING: Welcome, dear Rosencrantz and Guildenstern.
     Moreover that° we much did long to see you,
     The need we have to use you did provoke
     Our hasty sending. Something have you heard
     Of Hamlet's transformation—so call it,   5
     Sith nor° th' exterior nor the inward man
     Resembles that° it was. What it should be,
     More than his father's death, that thus hath put him
     So much from th' understanding of himself,
     I cannot dream of. I entreat you both   10
     That, being of so young days° brought up with him,
     And sith so neighbored to° his youth and havior,°

---

105 property nature   **fordoes** destroys   **114 quoted** observed   **115 wrack** ruin, seduce **beshrew my jealousy** a plague upon my suspicious nature   **116 proper . . . age** characteristic of us (old) men   **117 cast beyond** overshoot, miscalculate (A metaphor from hunting.) **120 known** made known (to the King)   **close** secret   **120–121 might . . . love** i.e., might cause more grief (because of what Hamlet might do) by hiding the knowledge of Hamlet's strange behavior to Ophelia than unpleasantness by telling it   **2.2 s.d. Location: The castle 2 Moreover that** besides the fact that   **6 Sith nor** since neither   **7 that** what   **11 of . . . days** from such early youth   **12 And sith so neighbored to** and since you are (or, and since that time you are) intimately acquainted with   **havior** demeanor

That you vouchsafe your rest° here in our court
Some little time, so by your companies
To draw him on to pleasures, and to gather   15
So much as from occasion° you may glean,
Whether aught to us unknown afflicts him thus
That, opened,° lies within our remedy.

QUEEN: Good gentlemen, he hath much talked of you,
And sure I am two men there is not living   20
To whom he more adheres. If it will please you
To show us so much gentry° and good will
As to expend your time with us awhile
For the supply and profit of our hope,°
Your visitation shall receive such thanks   25
As fits a king's remembrance.°

ROSENCRANTZ: Both Your Majesties
Might, by the sovereign power you have of° us,
Put your dread° pleasures more into command
Than to entreaty.

GUILDENSTERN: But we both obey,
And here give up ourselves in the full bent°   30
To lay our service freely at your feet,
To be commanded.

KING: Thanks, Rosencrantz and gentle Guildenstern.

QUEEN: Thanks, Guildenstern and gentle Rosencrantz.
And I beseech you instantly to visit
My too much changèd son. Go, some of you,   35
And bring these gentlemen where Hamlet is.

GUILDENSTERN: Heavens make our presence and our practices°
Pleasant and helpful to him!

QUEEN: Ay, amen!

[Exeunt ROSENCRANTZ *and* GUILDENSTERN *(with some attendants).]*

[Enter POLONIUS.*]*

POLONIUS: Th' ambassadors from Norway, my good lord,   40
Are joyfully returned.

KING: Thou still° hast been the father of good news.

---

13 vouchsafe your rest please to stay   **16 occasion** opportunity   **18 opened** being revealed
22 gentry courtesy   **24 supply . . . hope** aid and furtherance of what we hope for   **26 As fits
. . . remembrance** as would be a fitting gift of a king who rewards true service   **27 of** over
28 dread inspiring awe   **30 in . . . bent** to the utmost degree of our capacity (An archery
metaphor.)   **38 practices** doings   **42 still** always

POLONIUS: Have I, my lord? I assure my good liege
 I hold° my duty, as° I hold my soul,
 Both to my God and to my gracious king;   45
 And I do think, or else this brain of mine
 Hunts not the trail of policy° so sure
 As it hath used to do, that I have found
 The very cause of Hamlet's lunacy.

KING: O, speak of that! That do I long to hear.   50

POLONIUS: Give first admittance to th' ambassadors.
 My news shall be the fruit° to that great feast.

KING: Thyself do grace° to them and bring them in.

[Exit POLONIUS.*]*

 He tells me, my dear Gertrude, he hath found
 The head and source of all your son's distemper. 55

QUEEN: I doubt° it is no other but the main,°
 His father's death and our o'erhasty marriage.

[Enter Ambassadors VOLTIMAND *and* CORNELIUS, *with* POLONIUS.*]*

KING: Well, we shall sift him.°—Welcome, my good friends!
 Say, Voltimand, what from our brother° Norway?

VOLTIMAND: Most fair return of greetings and desires.° 60
 Upon our first,° he sent out to suppress
 His nephew's levies, which to him appeared
 To be a preparation 'gainst the Polack,
 But, better looked into, he truly found
 It was against Your Highness. Whereat grieved 65
 That so his sickness, age, and impotence°
 Was falsely borne in hand,° sends out arrests°
 On Fortinbras, which he, in brief, obeys,
 Receives rebuke from Norway, and in fine°
 Makes vow before his uncle never more 70
 To give th' assay° of arms against Your Majesty.
 Whereon old Norway, overcome with joy,
 Gives him three thousand crowns in annual fee
 And his commission to employ those soldiers,

---

44 hold maintain **as** firmly as **47 policy** sagacity **52 fruit** dessert **53 grace** honor (punning on *grace* said before a *feast*, line 52) **56 doubt** fear, suspect **main** chief point, principal concern **58 sift him** question Polonius closely **59 brother** fellow king **60 desires** good wishes **61 Upon our first** at our first words on the business **66 impotence** helplessness **67 borne in hand** deluded, taken advantage of **arrests** orders to desist **69 in fine** in conclusion **71 give th' assay** make trial of strength, challenge

So levied as before, against the Polack,   75
With an entreaty, herein further shown, [*giving a paper*]
That it might please you to give quiet pass
Through your dominions for this enterprise
On such regards of safety and allowance°
As therein are set down.

KING: It likes° us well,   80
And at our more considered° time we'll read,
Answer, and think upon this business.
Meantime we thank you for your well-took labor.
Go to your rest; at night we'll feast together.
Most welcome home!

                                        [*Exeunt* AMBASSADORS.]

POLONIUS: This business is well ended.   85
My liege, and madam, to expostulate°
What majesty should be, what duty is,
Why day is day, night night, and time is time,
Were nothing but to waste night, day, and time.
Therefore, since brevity is the soul of wit,°   90
And tediousness the limbs and outward flourishes,
I will be brief. Your noble son is mad.
Mad call I it, for, to define true madness.
What is 't but to be nothing else but mad?
But let that go.
QUEEN: More matter, with less art.   95
POLONIUS: Madam. I swear I use no art at all.
That he's mad, 'tis true; 'tis true 'tis pity.
And pity 'tis 'tis true—a foolish figure,°
But farewell it, for I will use no art.
Mad let us grant him, then, and now remains   100
That we find out the cause of this effect,
Or rather say, the cause of this defect,
For this effect defective comes by cause.°
Thus it remains, and the remainder thus.
Perpend.°   105
I have a daughter—have while she is mine—
Who, in her duty and obedience, mark,

---

78 On . . . allowance i.e., with such considerations for the safety of Denmark and permission
for Fortinbras   **80 likes** pleases   **81 considered** suitable for deliberation   **86 expostulate**
expound, inquire into   **90 wit** sense or judgment   **98 figure** figure of speech   **103 For . . .
cause** i.e., for this defective behavior, this madness, has a cause   **105 Perpend** consider

Hath given me this. Now gather and surmise.°
[*He reads the letter.*] "To the celestial and my soul's idol, the most
beautified Ophelia"—   110
That's an ill phrase, a vile phrase; "beautified" is a vile phrase. But
you shall hear. Thus: [*He reads.*]
"In her excellent white bosom,° these,° etc."

QUEEN: Came this from Hamlet to her?

POLONIUS: Good madam, stay° awhile, I will be faithful.°   [*He reads.*]   115

"Doubt thou the stars are fire,
    Doubt that the sun doth move,
Doubt° truth to be a liar,
    But never doubt I love.

O dear Ophelia, I am ill at these numbers.° I have not art to   120
reckon° my groans. But that I love thee best, O most best, believe it.
Adieu.
Thine evermore, most dear lady, whilst this machine° is to him,
                                                                Hamlet."

This in obedience hath my daughter shown me,   125
And, more above,° hath his solicitings,
As they fell out° by° time, by means, and place,
All given to mine ear.°

KING: But how hath she
Received his love?

POLONIUS: What do you think of me?

KING: As of a man faithful and honorable.   130

POLONIUS: I would fain° prove so. But what might you think,
When I had seen this hot love on the wing—
As I perceived it, I must tell you that,
Before my daughter told me—what might you,
Or my dear Majesty your queen here, think,   135
If I had played the desk or table book,°
Or given my heart a winking,° mute and dumb,
Or looked upon this love with idle sight?°
What might you think? No, I went round° to work,

---

108 gather and surmise draw your own conclusions   **113 In . . . bosom** (The letter is poetically addressed to her heart.)   **these** i.e., the letter   **115 stay** wait   **faithful** i.e., in reading
the letter accurately   **118 Doubt** suspect   **120 ill . . . numbers** unskilled at writing verses
121 reckon (1) count (2) number metrically, scan   **123 machine** i.e., body   **126 more above**
moreover   **127 fell out** occurred   **by** according to   **128 given . . . ear** i.e., told me about
131 fain gladly   **136 played . . . table book** i.e., remained shut up, concealing the information
137 given . . . winking closed the eyes of my heart to this   **138 with idle sight** complacently
or incomprehendingly   **139 round** roundly, plainly

And my young mistress thus I did bespeak:°   140
"Lord Hamlet is a prince out of thy star;°
This must not be." And then I prescripts° gave her,
That she should lock herself from his resort,°
Admit no messengers, receive no tokens.
Which done, she took the fruits of my advice;   145
And he, repellèd—a short tale to make—
Fell into a sadness, then into a fast,
Thence to a watch,° thence into a weakness,
Thence to a lightness,° and by this declension°
Into the madness wherein now he raves,   150
And all we° mourn for.

KING [*to the* QUEEN]:   Do you think 'tis this?

QUEEN: It may be, very like.

POLONIUS: Hath there been such a time—I would fain know that—
That I have positively said "'Tis so,"
When it proved otherwise?

KING: Not that I know.   155

POLONIUS: Take this from this,° if this be otherwise.
If circumstances lead me, I will find
Where truth is hid, though it were hid indeed
Within the center.°

KING: How may we try° it further?

POLONIUS: You know sometimes he walks four hours together   160
Here in the lobby.

QUEEN: So he does indeed.

POLONIUS: At such a time I'll loose° my daughter to him.
Be you and I behind an arras° then.
Mark the encounter. If he love her not
And be not from his reason fall'n thereon,°   165
Let me be no assistant for a state,
But keep a farm and carters.°

KING: We will try it.

[Enter HAMLET *(reading on a book).]*

---

140 bespeak address   **141 out of thy star** above your sphere, position   **142 prescripts**
orders   **143 his resort** his visits   **148 watch** state of sleeplessness   **149 lightness** light-
headedness   **declension** decline, deterioration (with a pun on the grammatical sense)   **151**
all we all of us, or, into everything that we   **156 Take this from this** (The actor probably gestures, indicating that he means his head from his shoulders, or his staff of office or chain from his
hands or neck, or something similar.)   **159 center** middle point of the earth (which is also the
center of the Ptolemaic universe)   **try** test, judge   **162 loose** (as one might release an animal
that is being mated)   **163 arras** hanging, tapestry   **165 thereon** on that account   **167 carters**
wagon drivers

QUEEN: But look where sadly° the poor wretch comes reading.

POLONIUS: Away, I do beseech you both, away.

I'll board° him presently.° O, give me leave.°   170

[Exeunt KING *and* QUEEN *(with attendants).]*

How does my good Lord Hamlet?

HAMLET: Well, God-a-mercy.°

POLONIUS: Do you know me, my lord?

HAMLET: Excellent well. You are a fishmonger.°

POLONIUS: Not I, my lord.   175

HAMLET: Then I would you were so honest a man.

POLONIUS: Honest, my lord?

HAMLET: Ay, sir. To be honest, as this world goes, is to be one man picked out
of ten thousand.

POLONIUS: That's very true, my lord.   180

HAMLET: For if the sun breed maggots in a dead dog, being a good kissing
carrion°—Have you a daughter?

POLONIUS: I have, my lord.

HAMLET: Let her not walk i' the sun.° Conception° is a blessing, but as your
daughter may conceive, friend, look to 't.   185

POLONIUS [*aside*]:   How say you by that? Still harping on my daughter. Yet he
knew me not at first; 'a° said I was a fishmonger. 'A is far gone. And truly
in my youth I suffered much extremity for love, very near this. I'll speak to
him again.—What do you read, my lord?

HAMLET: Words, words, words.   190

POLONIUS: What is the matter,° my lord?

HAMLET: Between who?

POLONIUS: I mean, the matter that you read, my lord.

HAMLET: Slanders, sir; for the satirical rogue says here that old men have gray
beards, that their faces are wrinkled, their eyes purging° thick amber° and   195
plum-tree gum, and that they have a plentiful lack of wit,° together with
most weak hams. All which, sir, though I most powerfully and potently
believe, yet I hold it not honesty° to have it thus set down, for yourself, sir,
shall grow old° as I am, if like a crab you could go backward.

---

168 sadly seriously   **170 board** accost   **presently** at once   **give me leave** i.e., excuse me,
leave me alone (Said to those he hurries offstage, including the King and Queen.)   **172 God-a-
mercy** God have mercy, i.e., thank you   **174 fishmonger** fish merchant   **181–182 a good
kissing carrion** i.e., a good piece of flesh for kissing, or for the sun to kiss   **184 i' the sun** in
public (with additional implication of the sunshine of princely favors)   **Conception** (1) understanding (2) pregnancy   **187 'a** he   **191 matter** substance (But Hamlet plays on the sense of
"basis for a dispute.")   **195 purging** discharging   **amber** i.e., resin, like the resinous   **196 wit**
understanding   **198 honesty** decency, decorum   **199 old** as old

POLONIUS [*aside*]:   Though this be madness, yet there is method in 't.—Will   200
you walk out of the air,° my lord?

HAMLET: Into my grave.

POLONIUS: Indeed, that's out of the air. [*Aside.*] How pregnant° sometimes his
replies are! A happiness° that often madness hits on, which reason and
sanity could not so prosperously° be delivered of. I will leave him and   205
suddenly° contrive the means of meeting between him and my daughter.—
My honorable lord, I will most humbly take my leave of you.

HAMLET: You cannot, sir, take from me anything that I will more willingly
part withal°—except my life, except my life, except my life.

[*Enter* GUILDENSTERN *and* ROSENCRANTZ.]

POLONIUS: Fare you well, my lord.   210

HAMLET: These tedious old fools!°

POLONIUS: You go to seek the Lord Hamlet. There he is.

ROSENCRANTZ [*to* POLONIUS]:   God save you, sir!

[*Exit* POLONIUS.]

GUILDENSTERN: My honored lord!

ROSENCRANTZ: My most dear lord!   215

HAMLET: My excellent good friends! How dost thou, Guildenstern? Ah,
Rosencrantz! Good lads, how do you both?

ROSENCRANTZ: As the indifferent° children of the earth.

GUILDENSTERN: Happy in that we are not overhappy.
On Fortune's cap we are not the very button.   220

HAMLET: Nor the soles of her shoe?

ROSENCRANTZ: Neither, my lord.

HAMLET: Then you live about her waist, or in the middle of her favors?°

GUILDENSTERN: Faith, her privates we.°

HAMLET: In the secret parts of Fortune? O, most true, she is a strumpet.°   225
What news?

ROSENCRANTZ: None, my lord, but the world's grown honest.

HAMLET: Then is doomsday near. But your news is not true. Let me question more
in particular. What have you, my good friends, deserved at the hands of
Fortune that she sends you to prison hither?   230

---

201 out of the air (The open air was considered dangerous for sick people.)   **203 pregnant**
quick-witted, full of meaning   **204 happiness** felicity of expression   **205 prosperously** successfully   **206 suddenly** immediately   **209 withal** with   **211 old fools** i.e., old men like
Polonius   **218 indifferent** ordinary, at neither extreme of fortune or misfortune   **223 favors**
i.e., sexual favors   **224 her privates we** i.e., (1) we are sexually intimate with Fortune, the fickle
goddess who bestows her favors indiscriminately (2) we are her private citizens   **225 strumpet**
prostitute (A common epithet for indiscriminate Fortune; see line 439.)

GUILDENSTERN: Prison, my lord?

HAMLET: Denmark's a prison.

ROSENCRANTZ: Then is the world one.

HAMLET: A goodly one, in which there are many confines,° wards,° and dun-
geons, Denmark being one o' the worst.   235

ROSENCRANTZ: We think not so, my lord.

HAMLET: Why then 'tis none to you, for there is nothing either good or bad but
thinking makes it so. To me it is a prison.

ROSENCRANTZ: Why then, your ambition makes it one. 'Tis too narrow for your
mind.   240

HAMLET: O God, I could be bounded in a nutshell and count myself a king of
infinite space, were it not that I have bad dreams.

GUILDENSTERN: Which dreams indeed are ambition, for the very substance of
the ambitious° is merely the shadow of a dream.

HAMLET: A dream itself is but a shadow.   245

ROSENCRANTZ: Truly, and I hold ambition of so airy and light a quality that it is
but a shadow's shadow.

HAMLET: Then are our beggars bodies,° and our monarchs and outstretched°
heroes the beggars' shadows. Shall we to the court? For, by my fay,° I
cannot reason.   250

ROSENCRANTZ, GUILDENSTERN: We'll wait upon° you.

HAMLET: No such matter. I will not sort° you with the rest of my servants, for,
to speak to you like an honest man, I am most dreadfully attended.° But,
in the beaten way° of friendship, what make° you at Elsinore?

ROSENCRANTZ: To visit you, my lord, no other occasion.   255

HAMLET: Beggar that I am, I am even poor in thanks; but I thank you, and sure,
dear friends, my thanks are too dear a halfpenny.° Were you not sent for?
Is it your own inclining? Is it a free° visitation? Come, come, deal justly
with me. Come, come. Nay, speak.

GUILDENSTERN: What should we say, my lord?   260

---

234 **confines** places of confinement   **wards** cells   243–244 **the very . . . ambitious** that
seemingly very substantial thing that the ambitious pursue   248 **bodies** i.e., solid substances
rather than shadows (since beggars are not ambitious)   **outstretched** (1) far-reaching in their
ambition (2) elongated as shadows   249 **fay** faith   251 **wait upon** accompany, attend (But
Hamlet uses the phrase in the sense of providing menial service.)   252 **sort** class, categorize
253 **dreadfully attended** waited upon in slovenly fashion   254 **beaten way** familiar path,
tried-and-true course   **make** do   257 **too dear a halfpenny** (1) too expensive at even a halfpenny, i.e., of little worth (2) too expensive *by* a halfpenny in return for worthless kindness
258 **free** voluntary

HAMLET: Anything but to the purpose.° You were sent for, and there is a kind of
confession in your looks which your modesties° have not craft enough to
color.° I know the good King and Queen have sent for you.

ROSENCRANTZ: To what end, my lord?

HAMLET: That you must teach me. But let me conjure° you, by the rights of our   265
fellowship, by the consonancy of our youth,° by the obligation of our
ever-preserved love, and by what more dear a better° proposer could
charge° you withal, be even° and direct with me whether you were sent
for or no.

ROSENCRANTZ [*aside to* GUILDENSTERN]:   What say you?   270

HAMLET [*aside*]:   Nay, then, I have an eye of° you.—If you love me, hold not off.°

GUILDENSTERN: My lord, we were sent for.

HAMLET: I will tell you why; so shall my anticipation prevent your discovery,°
and your secrecy to the King and Queen molt no feather,° I have of late—
but wherefore I know not—lost all my mirth, forgone all custom of exer-   275
cises; and indeed it goes so heavily with my disposition that this goodly
frame, the earth, seems to me a sterile promontory; this most excellent
canopy, the air, look you, this brave° o'erhanging firmament, this majestical roof fretted° with golden fire, why, it appeareth nothing to me but a
foul and pestilent congregation° of vapors. What a piece of work° is a   280
man! How noble in reason, how infinite in faculties, in form and moving
how express° and admirable, in action how like an angel, in apprehen-
sion° how like a god! The beauty of the world, the paragon of animals!
And yet, to me, what is this quintessence° of dust? Man delights not me—
no, nor woman neither, though by your smiling you seem to say so.   285

ROSENCRANTZ: My lord, there was no such stuff in my thoughts.

HAMLET: Why did you laugh, then, when I said man delights not me?

ROSENCRANTZ: To think, my lord, if you delight not in man, what Lenten
entertainment° the players shall receive from you. We coted° them on
the way, and hither are they coming to offer you service.   290

261 Anything but to the purpose anything except a straightforward answer (Said ironically.)
262 modesties sense of shame   **263 color** disguise   **265 conjure** adjure, entreat   **266 the
consonancy of our youth** our closeness in our younger days   **267 better** more skillful
268 charge urge   **even** straight, honest   **271 of** on   **hold not off** don't hold back   **273 so
. . . discovery** in that way my saying it first will spare you from revealing the truth   **274 molt
no feather** i.e., not diminish in the least   **278 brave** splendid   **279 fretted** adorned (with fret-
work, as in a vaulted ceiling)   **280 congregation** mass   **piece of work** masterpiece
282 express well-framed, exact, expressive   **282–283 apprehension** power of comprehend-
ing   **284 quintessence** the fifth essence of ancient philosophy, beyond earth, water, air, and fire,
supposed to be the substance of the heavenly bodies and to be latent in all things   **288–289
Lenten entertainment** meager reception (appropriate to Lent)   **289 coted** overtook and
passed by

HAMLET: He that plays the king shall be welcome; His Majesty shall have trib-
ute° of° me. The adventurous knight shall use his foil and target,° the lover
shall not sigh gratis,° the humorous man° shall end his part in peace,° the
clown shall make those laugh whose lungs are tickle o' the sear,° and the
lady shall say her mind freely, or the blank verse shall halt° for 't. What   295
players are they?

ROSENCRANTZ: Even those you were wont to take such delight in, the
tragedians° of the city.

HAMLET: How chances it they travel? Their residence,° both in reputation
and profit, was better both ways.   300

ROSENCRANTZ: I think their inhibition° comes by the means of the late°
innovation.°

HAMLET: Do they hold the same estimation they did when I was in the city?
Are they so followed?

ROSENCRANTZ: No, indeed are they not.   305

HAMLET: How comes it? Do they grow rusty?

ROSENCRANTZ: Nay, their endeavor keeps° in the wonted° pace. But there is, sir,
an aerie° of children, little eyases,° that cry out on the top of question°
and are most tyrannically° clapped for 't. These are now the fashion, and
so berattle° the common stages°—so they call them—that many wearing   310
rapiers° are afraid of goose quills° and dare scarce come thither.

HAMLET: What, are they children? Who maintains 'em? How are they escoted?°
Will they pursue the quality° no longer than they can sing?° Will they not
say afterwards, if they should grow themselves to common° players—as it
is most like,° if their means are no better°—their writers do them wrong   315
to make them exclaim against their own succession?°

---

292 tribute (1) applause (2) homage paid in money   **of** from   **foil and target** sword and shield
293 gratis for nothing   **humorous man** eccentric character, dominated by one trait or "humor"
293–294 in peace i.e., with full license   **294–295 tickle o' the sear** easy on the trigger, ready
to laugh easily (A sear is part of a gunlock.)   **295 halt** limp   **298 tragedians** actors
299 residence remaining in their usual place, i.e., in the city   **301 inhibition** formal prohibition
(from acting plays in the city)   **301 late** recent   **302 innovation** i.e., the new fashion in satirical plays performed by boy actors in the "private" theaters; or possibly a political uprising; or the
strict limitations set on the theaters in London in 1600   **307 keeps** continues   **wonted** usual
308 aerie nest   **eyases** young hawks   **cry . . . question** speak shrilly, dominating the controversy (in decrying the public theaters)   **309 tyrannically** outrageously   **310 berattle** berate,
clamor against   **common stages** public theaters   **310–311 many wearing rapiers** i.e., many
men of fashion, afraid to patronize the common players for fear of being satirized by the poets
writing for the boy actors   **311 goose quills** i.e., pens of satirists   **312 escoted** maintained
313 quality (acting) profession   **no longer . . . sing** i.e., only until their voices change
314 common regular, adult   **315 like** likely   **if . . . better** if they find no better way to support
themselves   **316 succession** i.e., future careers

ROSENCRANTZ: Faith, there has been much to-do° on both sides, and the nation
holds it no sin to tar° them to controversy. There was for a while no
money bid for argument unless the poet and the player went to cuffs in
the question.°   320

HAMLET: Is 't possible?

GUILDENSTERN: O, there has been much throwing about of brains.

HAMLET: Do the boys carry it away?°

ROSENCRANTZ: Ay, that they do, my lord—Hercules and his load too.°

HAMLET: It is not very strange; for my uncle is King of Denmark, and those that   325
would make mouths° at him while my father lived give twenty, forty, fifty,
a hundred ducats° apiece for his picture in little.° 'Sblood,° there is
something in this more than natural, if philosophy° could find it out.

[A flourish (of trumpets within).]

GUILDENSTERN: There are the players.

HAMLET: Gentlemen, you are welcome to Elsinore. Your hands, come then. Th'   330
appurtenance° of welcome is fashion and ceremony. Let me comply° with
you in this garb,° lest my extent° to the players, which, I tell you, must
show fairly outwards,° should more appear like entertainment° than yours.
You are welcome. But my uncle-father and aunt-mother are deceived.   335

GUILDENSTERN: In what, my dear lord?

HAMLET: I am but mad north-north-west.° When the wind is southerly I
know a hawk from a handsaw.°

[Enter POLONIUS.*]*

POLONIUS: Well be with you, gentlemen!

HAMLET: Hark you, Guildenstern, and you too; at each ear a hearer. That great
baby you see there is not yet out of his swaddling clouts.°   340

---

317 to-do ado   **318 tar** set on (as dogs)   **318–320 There . . . question** i.e., for a while, no
money was offered by the acting companies to playwrights for the plot to a play unless the satirical poets who wrote for the boys and the adult actors came to blows in the play itself
323 carry it away i.e., win the day   **324 Hercules . . . load** (Thought to be an allusion to the
sign of the Globe Theatre, which was Hercules bearing the world on his shoulders.)
312–324 How . . . load too (The passage, omitted from the early quartos, alludes to the so-
called War of the Theaters, 1599–1602, the rivalry between the children's companies and the
adult actors.)   **326 mouths** faces   **327 ducats** gold coins   **in little** in miniature   **'Sblood**
by God's (Christ's) blood   **328 philosophy** i.e., scientific inquiry   **331 appurtenance** proper
accompaniment   **comply** observe the formalities of courtesy   **332 garb** i.e., manner   **my
extent** that which I extend, i.e., my polite behavior   **333 show fairly outwards** show every
evidence of cordiality   **entertainment** a (warm) reception   **337 north-north-west** just off
true north, only partly   **338 hawk . . . handsaw** i.e., two very different things, though also perhaps meaning a mattock (or *hack*) and a carpenter's cutting tool, respectively; also birds, with a
play on *hernshaw*, or heron   **340 swaddling clouts** cloths in which to wrap a newborn baby

ROSENCRANTZ: Haply° he is the second time come to them, for they say an old
    man is twice a child.

HAMLET: I will prophesy he comes to tell me of the players. Mark it.—You say
    right, sir, o' Monday morning, 'twas then indeed.   345

POLONIUS: My lord, I have news to tell you.

HAMLET: My lord, I have news to tell you. When Roscius° was an actor in
    Rome—

POLONIUS: The actors are come hither, my lord.

HAMLET: Buzz,° buzz!   350

POLONIUS: Upon my honor—

HAMLET: Then came each actor on his ass.

POLONIUS: The best actors in the world, either for tragedy, comedy, history,
    pastoral, pastoral-comical, historical-pastoral, tragical-historical, tragical-
    comical-historical-pastoral, scene individable,° or poem unlimited.°   355
    Seneca° cannot be too heavy, nor Plautus° too light. For the law of writ
    and the liberty,° these° are the only men.

HAMLET: O Jephthah, judge of Israel,° what a treasure hadst thou!

POLONIUS: What a treasure had he, my lord?

HAMLET: Why,   360

    "One fair daughter, and no more,
    The which he lovèd passing° well."

POLONIUS [ASIDE]:   Still on my daughter.

HAMLET: Am I not i' the right, old Jephthah?

POLONIUS: If you call me Jephthah, my lord, I have a daughter that I love   365
    passing well.

HAMLET: Nay, that follows not.

POLONIUS: What follows then, my lord?

HAMLET: Why,

    "As by lot,° God wot,"°   370

and then, you know,

    "It came to pass, as most like° it was"—
the first row° of the pious chanson° will show you more, for look
where my abridgement° comes.

---

342 Haply perhaps   **347 Roscius** a famous Roman actor who died in 62 B.C.   **350 Buzz** (An
interjection used to denote stale news.)   **355 scene individable** a play observing the unity of
place; or perhaps one that is unclassifiable, or performed without intermission   **poem unlimited** a play disregarding the unities of time and place; one that is all-inclusive   **356 Seneca** writer
of Latin tragedies   **Plautus** writer of Latin comedy   **356–357 law . . . liberty** dramatic composition both according to the rules and disregarding the rules   **these** i.e., the actors
358 Jephthah . . . Israel (Jephthah had to sacrifice his daughter; see Judges 11. Hamlet goes on
to quote from a ballad on the theme.)   **362 passing** surpassingly   **370 lot** chance   **wot** knows
372 like likely, probable   **373 row** stanza   **chanson** ballad, song   **374 my abridgment** something that cuts short my conversation; also, a diversion

[Enter the PLAYERS.*]*

You are welcome, masters; welcome, all. I am glad to see thee well. 375
Welcome, good friends. O, old friend! Why, thy face is valanced° since I
saw thee last. Com'st thou to beard° me in Denmark? What, my young
lady° and mistress! By 'r Lady,° your ladyship is nearer to heaven than
when I saw you last, by the altitude of a chopine.° Pray God your voice,
like a piece of uncurrent° gold, be not cracked within the ring.° Masters, 380
you are all welcome. We'll e'en to 't° like French falconers, fly at anything
we see. We'll have a speech straight.° Come, give us a taste of your quality.° Come, a passionate speech.

FIRST PLAYER: What speech, my good lord?

HAMLET: I heard thee speak me a speech once, but it was never acted, or if it 385
was, not above once, for the play, I remember, pleased not the million; 'twas
caviar to the general.° But it was—as I received it, and others, whose
judgments in such matters cried in the top of° mine—an excellent play,
well digested° in the scenes, set down with as much modesty° as cunning.°
I remember one said there were no sallets° in the lines to make the matter 390
savory, nor no matter in the phrase that might indict° the author of affectation, but called it an honest method, as wholesome as sweet, and by very
much more handsome° than fine.° One speech in 't I chiefly loved: 'twas
Aeneas' tale to Dido, and thereabout of it especially when he speaks of
Priam's slaughter.° If it live in your memory, begin at this line: let me see, let 395
me see—
    "The rugged Pyrrhus,° like th' Hyrcanian beast"°—
'Tis not so. It begins with Pyrrhus:
    "The rugged° Pyrrhus, he whose sable° arms,

376 valanced fringed (with a beard)   **377 beard** confront, challenge (with obvious pun)
377–378 young lady i.e., boy playing women's parts   **378 By 'r Lady** by Our Lady
379 chopine thick-soled shoe of Italian fashion   **380 uncurrent** not passable as lawful coinage
cracked . . . ring i.e., changed from adolescent to male voice, no longer suitable for women's
roles (Coins featured rings enclosing the sovereign's head; if the coin was cracked within this
ring, it was unfit for currency.)   **381 e'en to 't** go at it   **382 straight** at once   **383 quality** professional skill   **387 caviar to the general** caviar to the multitude, i.e., a choice dish too elegant
for coarse tastes   **388 cried in the top of** i.e., spoke with greater authority than
389 digested arranged, ordered   **modesty** moderation, restraint   **cunning** skill   **390 sallets**
i.e., something savory, spicy improprieties   **391 indict** convict   **393 handsome** well-propor-
tioned   **fine** elaborately ornamented, showy   **395 Priam's slaughter** the slaying of the ruler
of Troy, when the Greeks finally took the city   **397 Pyrrhus** a Greek hero in the Trojan War, also
known as Neoptolemus, son of Achilles—another avenging son   **Hyrcanian beast** i.e., tiger
(On the death of Priam, see Virgil, *Aeneid*, 2.506 ff.; compare the whole speech with Marlowe's
Dido Queen of Carthage, 2.1.214. ff. On the Hyrcanian tiger, see *Aeneid*, 4.366-367. Hyrcania is
on the Caspian Sea.)   **399 rugged** shaggy, savage   **sable** black (for reasons of camouflage
during the episode of the Trojan horse)

Black as his purpose, did the night resemble   400
When he lay couchèd° in the ominous horse,°
Hath now this dread and black complexion smeared
With heraldry more dismal.° Head to foot
Now is he total gules,° horridly tricked°
With blood of fathers, mothers, daughters, sons,   405
Baked and impasted° with the parching streets,°
That lend a tyrannous° and a damnèd light
To their lord's° murder. Roasted in wrath and fire,
And thus o'ersizèd° with coagulate gore,
With eyes like carbuncles,° the hellish Pyrrhus   410
Old grandsire Priam seeks."
So proceed you.
POLONIUS: 'Fore God, my lord, well spoken, with good accent and good
discretion.
FIRST PLAYER: "Anon he finds him
Striking too short at Greeks. His antique° sword,   415
Rebellious to his arm, lies where it falls,
Repugnant° to command. Unequal matched,
Pyrrhus at Priam drives, in rage strikes wide,
But with the whiff and wind of his fell° sword
Th' unnervèd° father falls. Then senseless Ilium,°   420
Seeming to feel this blow, with flaming top
Stoops to his° base, and with a hideous crash
Takes prisoner Pyrrhus' ear. For, lo! His sword,
Which was declining° on the milky° head
Of reverend Priam, seemed i' th' air to stick.   425
So as a painted° tyrant Pyrrhus stood,
And, like a neutral to his will and matter,°
Did nothing.
But as we often see against° some storm
A silence in the heavens, the rack° stand still,   430

401 **couchèd** concealed   **ominous horse** fateful Trojan horse, by which the Greeks gained
access to Troy   403 **dismal** ill-omened   404 **total gules** entirely red (A heraldic term.)
tricked spotted and smeared (Heraldic.)   406 **impasted** crusted, like a thick paste   **with . . .
streets** by the parching heat of the streets (because of the fires everywhere)   407 **tyrannous**
cruel   408 **their lord's** i.e., Priam's   409 **o'ersizèd** covered as with size or glue
410 **carbuncles** large fiery-red precious stones thought to emit their own light   415 **antique**
ancient, long-used   417 **Repugnant** disobedient, resistant   419 **fell** cruel   420 **unnervèd**
strengthless   **senseless Ilium** inanimate citadel of Troy   422 **his** its   424 **declining**
descending   **milky** white-haired   426 **painted** i.e., painted in a picture   427 **like . . . matter**
i.e., as though suspended between his intention and its fulfillment   429 **against** just before
430 **rack** mass of clouds

The bold winds speechless, and the orb° below
As hush as death, anon the dreadful thunder
Doth rend the region,° so, after Pyrrhus' pause,
A rousèd vengeance sets him new a-work
And never did the Cyclops'° hammers fall   435
On Mars's armor forged for proof eterne°
With less remorse° than Pyrrhus' bleeding sword
Now falls on Priam.
Out, out, thou strumpet Fortune! All you gods
In general synod° take away her power!   440
Break all the spokes and fellies° from her wheel,
And bowl the round nave° down the hill of heaven°
As low as to the fiends!"

POLONIUS: This is too long.

HAMLET: It shall to the barber's with your beard.—Prithee, say on. He's   445
for a jig° or a tale of bawdry, or he sleeps. Say on; come to
Hecuba.°

FIRST PLAYER: "But who, ah woe! had° seen the moblèd° queen"—

HAMLET: "The moblèd queen"?

POLONIUS: That's good. "Moblèd queen" is good.   450

FIRST PLAYER: "Run barefoot up and down, threat'ning the flames°
With bisson rheum,° a clout° upon that head
Where late° the diadem stood, and, for a robe,
About her lank and all o'erteemèd° loins
A blanket, in the alarm of fear caught up—   455
Who this had seen, with tongue in venom steeped,
'Gainst Fortune's state° would treason have pronounced.°
But if the gods themselves did see her then
When she saw Pyrrhus make malicious sport
In mincing with his sword her husband's limbs,   460
The instant burst of clamor that she made,
Unless things mortal move them not at all,
Would have made milch° the burning eyes of heaven,°
And passion° in the gods."

---

431 orb globe, earth   **433 region** sky   **435 Cyclops** giant armor makers in the smithy of
Vulcan   **436 proof eterne** eternal resistance to assault   **437 remorse** pity   **440 synod**
assembly   **441 fellies** pieces of wood forming the rim of a wheel   **442 nave** hub   **hill of
heaven** Mount Olympus   **446 jig** comic song and dance often given at the end of a play
447 Hecuba wife of Priam   **448 who . . . had** anyone who had (also in line 456)   **moblèd**
muffled   **451 threat'ning the flames** i.e., weeping hard enough to dampen the flames
452 bisson rheum blinding tears   **clout** cloth   **453 late** lately   **454 all o'erteemèd** utterly
worn out with bearing children   **457 state** rule, managing   **pronounced** proclaimed
463 milch milky, moist with tears   **burning eyes of heaven** i.e., heavenly bodies   **464
passion** overpowering emotion

POLONIUS: Look whe'er° he has not turned his color and has tears in 's eyes.   465
Prithee, no more.

HAMLET: 'Tis well; I'll have thee speak out the rest of this soon.—Good my lord,
will you see the players well bestowed?° Do you hear, let them be well
used, for they are the abstract° and brief chronicles of the time. After your
death you were better have a bad epitaph than their ill report while you   470
live.

POLONIUS: My lord, I will use them according to their desert.

HAMLET: God's bodikin,° man, much better. Use every man after his desert, and
who shall scape whipping? Use them after° your own honor and dignity.
The less they deserve, the more merit is in your bounty. Take them in.   475

POLONIUS: Come, sirs.

[Exit.]

HAMLET: Follow him, friends. We'll hear a play tomorrow. [*As they start to
leave,* HAMLET *detains the* FIRST PLAYER.] Dost thou hear me, old friend? Can
you play *The Murder of Gonzago?*

FIRST PLAYER: Ay, my lord.   480

HAMLET: We'll ha 't° tomorrow night. You could, for a need, study° a speech of
some dozen or sixteen lines which I would set down and insert in 't,
could you not?

FIRST PLAYER: Ay, my lord.

HAMLET: Very well. Follow that lord, and look you mock him not.   485

[Exeunt PLAYERS.*]* My good friends, I'll leave you till night. You are welcome to
Elsinore.

ROSENCRANTZ: Good my lord!

*[Exeunt (*ROSENCRANTZ *and* GUILDENSTERN*).]*

HAMLET: Ay, so, goodbye to you.—Now I am alone.
O, what a rogue and peasant slave am I!   490
Is it not monstrous that this player here,
But° in a fiction, in a dream of passion,
Could force his soul so to his own conceit°
That from her working° all his visage wanned,°
Tears in his eyes, distraction in his aspect,°   495
A broken voice, and his whole function suiting

465 whe'er whether   **468 bestowed** lodged   **469 abstract** summary account   **473 God's
bodikin** by God's (Christ's) little body, *bodykin* (Not to be confused with *bodkin,* "dagger.")
474 after according to   **481 ha 't** have it   **study** memorize   **492 But** merely   **493 force . . .
conceit** bring his innermost being so entirely into accord with his conception (of the role)
494 from her working as a result of, or in response to, his soul's activity   **wanned** grew pale
495 aspect look, glance

With forms to his conceit?° And all for nothing!
For Hecuba!
What's Hecuba to him, or he to Hecuba,
That he should weep for her? What would he do   500
Had he the motive and the cue for passion
That I have? He would drown the stage with tears
And cleave the general ear° with horrid° speech,
Make mad the guilty and appall° the free,°
Confound the ignorant,° and amaze° indeed   505
The very faculties of eyes and ears. Yet I,
A dull and muddy-mettled° rascal, peak°
Like John-a-dreams,° unpregnant of° my cause,
And can say nothing—no, not for a king
Upon whose property° and most dear life   510
A damned defeat° was made. Am I a coward?
Who calls me villain? Breaks my pate° across?
Plucks off my beard and blows it in my face?
Tweaks me by the nose? Gives me the lie i' the throat°
As deep as to the lungs? Who does me this?   515
Ha, 'swounds,° I should take it; for it cannot be
But I am pigeon-livered° and lack gall
To make oppression bitter,° or ere this
I should ha' fatted all the region kites°
With this slave's offal.° Bloody, bawdy villain!   520
Remorseless,° treacherous, lecherous, kindless° villain!
O, vengeance!
Why, what an ass am I! This is most brave,°
That I, the son of a dear father murdered,
Prompted to my revenge by heaven and hell,   525
Must like a whore unpack my heart with words
And fall a-cursing, like a very drab,°

496–497 his whole ... conceit all his bodily powers responding with actions to suit his
thought   **503 the general ear** everyone's ear   **horrid** horrible   **504 appall** (literally, make
pale.)   **free** innocent   **505 Confound the ignorant** i.e., dumbfound those who know nothing of the crime that has been committed   **amaze** stun   **507 muddy-mettled** dull-spirited
peak mope, pine   **508 John-a-dreams** a sleepy, dreaming idler   **unpregnant of** not quickened by   **510 property** i.e., the crown; also character, quality   **511 damned defeat** damnable
act of destruction   **512 pate** head   **514 Gives ... throat** calls me an out-and-out liar
516 'swounds by his (Christ's) wounds   **517 pigeon-livered** (The pigeon or dove was popularly supposed to be mild because it secreted no gall.)   **518 bitter** i.e., bitter to me
519 region kites kites (birds of prey) of the air   **520 offal** entrails   **521 Remorseless** pitiless   **kindless** unnatural   **523 brave** fine, admirable (Said ironically.)   **527 drab** whore

A scullion!° Fie upon 't, foh! About,° my brains!
Hum, I have heard
That guilty creatures sitting at a play   530
Have by the very cunning° of the scene°
They have proclaimed their malefactions;
For murder, though it have no tongue, will speak
With most miraculous organ. I'll have these players   535
Play something like the murder of my father
Before mine uncle. I'll observe his looks;
I'll tent° him to the quick.° If 'a do blench,°
I know my course. The spirit that I have seen
May be the devil, and the devil hath power   540
T' assume a pleasing shape; yea, and perhaps,
Out of my weakness and my melancholy,
As he is very potent with such spirits,°
Abuses° me to damn me. I'll have grounds
More relative° than this. The play's the thing   545
Wherein I'll catch the conscience of the King.

[Exit.]

[Act 3.1 Enter KING, QUEEN, POLONIUS, OPHELIA, ROSENCRANTZ, GUILDERNSTERN, lords.]°

KING: And can you by no drift of conference°
        Get from him why he puts on this confusion,
        Grating so harshly all his days of quiet
        With turbulent and dangerous lunacy?

ROSENCRANTZ: He does confess he feels himself distracted,   5
        But from what cause 'a will by no means speak.

GUILDENSTERN: Nor do we find him forward° to be sounded,°
        But with a crafty madness keeps aloof
        When we would bring him on to some confession
        Of his true state.

QUEEN: Did he receive you well?   10

ROSENCRANTZ: Most like a gentleman.

GUILDENSTERN: But with much forcing of his disposition.°

528 scullion menial kitchen servant (apt to be foul-mouthed)   **About** about it, to work   **531 cunning** art, skill   **scene** dramatic presentation   **532 presently** at once   **538 tent** probe **the quick** the tender part of a wound, the core   **blench** quail, flinch   **543 spirits** humors (of melancholy)   **544 Abuses** deludes   **545 relative** cogent, pertinent   **3.1 s.d. Location: The castle   1 drift of conference** directing of conversation   **7 forward** willing   **sounded** questioned   **12 disposition** inclination

ROSENCRANTZ: Niggard° of question,° but of our demands
     Most free in his reply.

QUEEN: Did you assay° him
     To any pastime?   15

ROSENCRANTZ: Madam, it so fell out that certain players
     We o'erraught° on the way. Of these we told him,
     And there did seem in him a kind of joy
     To hear of it. They are here about the court,
     And, as I think, they have already order   20
     This night to play before him.

POLONIUS: 'Tis most true,
     And he beseeched me to entreat Your Majesties
     To hear and see the matter.

KING: With all my heart, and it doth much content me
     To hear him so inclined.   25
     Good gentlemen, give him a further edge°
     And drive his purpose into these delights.

ROSENCRANTZ: We shall, my lord.

[Exeunt ROSENCRANTZ *and* GUILDENSTERN.*]*

KING: Sweet Gertrude, leave us too,
     For we have closely° sent for Hamlet hither,
     That he, as 'twere by accident, may here   30
     Affront° Ophelia.
     Her father and myself, lawful espials,°
     Will so bestow ourselves that seeing, unseen,
     We may of their encounter frankly judge,
     And gather by him, as he is behaved,   35
     If 't be th' affliction of his love or no
     That thus he suffers for.

QUEEN: I shall obey you.
     And for your part, Ophelia, I do wish
     That your good beauties be the happy cause
     Of Hamlet's wildness. So shall I hope your virtues   40
     Will bring him to his wonted° way again,
     To both your honors.

OPHELIA: Madam, I wish it may.

[Exit QUEEN.*]*

13 Niggard stingy   **question** conversation   **14 assay** try to win   **17 o'erraught** overtook
26 edge incitement   **29 closely** privately   **31 Affront** confront, meet   **32 espials** spies
41 wonted accustomed

POLONIUS: Ophelia, walk you here.—Gracious,° so please you,
　　　We will bestow° ourselves. [*To* OPHELIA.] Read on this book,

　　　　　　　　　　　　　　　　　　[giving her a book]

　　　That show of such an exercise° may color°　　　　　　　45
　　　Your loneliness.° We are oft to blame in this—
　　　'Tis too much proved°—that with devotion's visage
　　　And pious action we do sugar o'er
　　　The devil himself.
KING [*aside*]:   O 'tis too true!　　　　　　　　　　　　50
　　　How smart a lash that speech doth give my conscience!
　　　The harlot's cheek, beautied with plastering art,
　　　Is not more ugly to° the thing° that helps it
　　　Than is my deed to my most painted word.
　　　O heavy burden!　　　　　　　　　　　　　　　55
POLONIUS: I hear him coming. Let's withdraw, my lord.

[The KING *and* POLONIUS *withdraw.°]*

[Enter HAMLET. *(*OPHELIA *pretends to read a book.)]*

HAMLET: To be, or not to be, that is the question:
　　　Whether 'tis nobler in the mind to suffer
　　　The slings° and arrows of outrageous fortune,
　　　Or to take arms against a sea of troubles　　　　　　　60
　　　And by opposing end them. To die, to sleep—
　　　No more—and by a sleep to say we end
　　　The heartache and the thousand natural shocks
　　　That flesh is heir to. 'Tis a consummation
　　　Devoutly to be wished. To die, to sleep;　　　　　　　65
　　　To sleep, perchance to dream. Ay, there's the rub,°
　　　For in that sleep of death what dreams may come,
　　　When we have shuffled° off this mortal coil,°
　　　Must give us pause. There's the respect°
　　　That makes calamity of so long life.°　　　　　　　　70

---

43 Gracious Your Grace (i.e., the King)　**44 bestow** conceal　**45 exercise** religious exercise (The book she reads is one of devotion.)　**color** give a plausible appearance to　**46 loneliness** being alone　**47 too much proved** too often shown to be true, too often practiced　**53 to** compared to　**the thing** i.e., the cosmetic　**s.d. withdraw** (The King and Polonius may retire behind an arras. The stage directions specify that they "enter" again near the end of the scene.)　**59 slings** missiles　**66 rub** (Literally, an obstacle in the game of bowls.)　**68 shuffled** sloughed, cast　**coil** turmoil　**69 respect** consideration　**70 of . . . life** so long-lived, something we willingly endure for so long (also suggesting that long life is itself a calamity)

For who would bear the whips and scorns of time,
Th' oppressor's wrong, the proud man's contumely,°
The pangs of disprized° love, the law's delay,
The insolence of office,° and the spurns°
That patient merit of th' unworthy takes,° 75
When he himself might his quietus° make
With a bare bodkin?° Who would fardels° bear,
To grunt and sweat under a weary life,
But that the dread of something after death,
The undiscovered country from whose bourn° 80
No traveler returns, puzzles the will,
And makes us rather bear those ills we have
Than fly to others that we know not of?
Thus conscience does make cowards of us all;
And thus the native hue° of resolution 85
Is sicklied o'er with the pale cast° of thought,
And enterprises of great pitch° and moment°
With this regard° their currents° turn awry
And lose the name of action.—Soft you° now,
The fair Ophelia. Nymph, in thy orisons° 90
Be all my sins remembered.

OPHELIA: Good my lord,
How does your honor for this many a day?

HAMLET: I humbly thank you; well, well, well.

OPHELIA: My lord, I have remembrances of yours,
That I have longèd long to redeliver. 95
I pray you, now receive them.   [*She offers tokens.*]

HAMLET: No, not I, I never gave you aught.

OPHELIA: My honored lord, you know right well you did,
And with them words of so sweet breath composed
As made the things more rich. Their perfume lost, 100
Take these again, for to the noble mind
Rich gifts wax poor when givers prove unkind.
There, my lord.   [*She gives tokens.*]

HAMLET: Ha, ha! Are you honest?°

---

72 contumely insolent abuse   **73 disprized** unvalued   **74 office** officialdom   **spurns** insults
75 of . . . takes receives from unworthy persons   **76 quietus** acquittance; here, death   **77 a
bare bodkin** a mere dagger, unsheathed   **fardels** burdens   **80 bourn** frontier, boundary   **85
native hue** natural color, complexion   **86 cast** tinge, shade of color   **87 pitch** height (as of a
falcon's flight)   **moment** importance   **88 regard** respect, consideration   **currents** courses
89 Soft you i.e., wait a minute, gently   **90 orisons** prayers   **104 honest** (1) truthful (2) chaste

OPHELIA: My lord?   105

HAMLET: Are you fair?°

OPHELIA: What means your lordship?

HAMLET: That if you be honest and fair, your honesty° should admit no discourse° to your beauty.

OPHELIA: Could beauty, my lord, have better commerce° than with honesty?   110

HAMLET: Ay, truly, for the power of beauty will sooner transform honesty from what it is to a bawd than the force of honesty can translate beauty into his° likeness. This was sometime° a paradox,° but now the time° gives it proof. I did love you once.

OPHELIA: Indeed, my lord, you made me believe so.   115

HAMLET: You should not have believed me, for virtue cannot so inoculate° our old stock but we shall relish of it.° I loved you not.

OPHELIA: I was the more deceived.

HAMLET: Get thee to a nunnery.° Why wouldst thou be a breeder of sinners? I am myself indifferent honest,° but yet I could accuse me of such things   120 that it were better my mother had not borne me: I am very proud, revengeful, ambitious, with more offenses at my beck° than I have thoughts to put them in, imagination to give them shape, or time to act them in. What should such fellows as I do crawling between earth and heaven? We are arrant knaves all; believe none of us. Go thy ways to a   125 nunnery. Where's your father?

OPHELIA: At home, my lord.

HAMLET: Let the doors be shut upon him, that he may play the fool nowhere but in 's own house. Farewell.

OPHELIA: O, help him, you sweet heavens!   130

HAMLET: If thou dost marry, I'll give thee this plague for thy dowry: be thou as chaste as ice, as pure as snow, thou shalt not escape calumny. Get thee to a nunnery, farewell. Or, if thou wilt needs marry, marry a fool, for wise men know well enough what monsters° you° make of them. To a nunnery, go, and quickly too. Farewell.

OPHELIA: Heavenly powers, restore him!   135

---

106 fair (1) beautiful (2) just, honorable   **108 your honesty** your chastity   **109 discourse** to familiar dealings with   **110 commerce** dealings, intercourse   **113 his** its   **sometime** formerly **a paradox** a view opposite to commonly held opinion   **the time** the present age   **116 inoculate** graft, be engrafted to   **117 but . . . it** that we do not still have about us a taste of the old stock (i.e., retain our sinfulness)   **119 nunnery** convent (with possibly an awareness that the word was also used derisively to denote a brothel)   **120 indifferent honest** reasonably virtuous   **122 beck** command   **134 monsters** (An allusion to the horns of a cuckold.)   **you** i.e., you women

HAMLET: I have heard of your paintings too, well enough. God hath given you
one face, and you make yourselves another. You jig,° you amble,° and you
lisp, you nickname God's creatures,° and make your wantonness your
ignorance.° Go to, I'll no more on 't;° it hath made me mad. I say we will   140
have no more marriage. Those that are married already—all but one—shall
live. The rest shall keep as they are. To a nunnery, go.

[Exit.]

OPHELIA: O, what a noble mind is here o'erthrown!
 The courtier's, soldier's, scholar's, eye, tongue, sword,
 Th' expectancy° and rose° of the fair state,   145
 The glass of fashion and the mold of form,°
 Th' observed of all observers,° quite, quite down!
 And I, of ladies most deject and wretched,
 That sucked the honey of his music° vows,
 Now see that noble and most sovereign reason   150
 Like sweet bells jangled out of tune and harsh,
 That unmatched form and feature of blown° youth
 Blasted° with ecstasy.° O, woe is me,
 T' have seen what I have seen, see what I see!

[Enter KING *and* POLONIUS.*]*

KING: Love? His affections° do not that way tend;   155
 Nor what he spake, though it lacked form a little,
 Was not like madness. There's something in his soul
 O'er which his melancholy sits on brood,°
 And I do doubt° the hatch and the disclose°
 Will be some danger; which for to prevent,   160
 I have in quick determination
 Thus set it down:° he shall with speed to England
 For the demand of° our neglected tribute.
 Haply the seas and countries different
 With variable objects° shall expel   165
 This something-settled matter in his heart,°

---

138 jig dance   **amble** move coyly   **139 you nickname . . . creatures** i.e., you give trendy
names to things in place of their God-given names   **139–140 make . . . ignorance** i.e., excuse
your affectation on the grounds of pretended ignorance   **140 on 't** of it   **145 expectancy**
hope   **145 rose** ornament   **146 The glass . . . form** the mirror of true fashioning and the pattern of courtly behavior   **147 Th' observed . . . observers** i.e., the center of attention and
honor in the court   **149 music** musical, sweetly uttered   **152 blown** blooming   **153 Blasted**
withered   **ecstasy** madness   **155 affections** emotions, feelings   **158 sits on brood** sits like
a bird on a nest, about to *hatch* mischief (line 159)   **159 doubt** fear   **disclose** disclosure, hatch-
ing   **162 set it down** resolved   **163 For . . . of** to demand   **165 variable objects** various
sights and surroundings to divert him   **166 This something . . . heart** the strange matter
settled in his heart

Whereon his brains still° beating puts him thus
From fashion of himself.° What think you on 't
POLONIUS: It shall do well. But yet do I believe
 The origin and commencement of his grief   170
 Sprung from neglected love.—How now, Ophelia?
 You need not tell us what Lord Hamlet said;
 We heard it all.—My lord, do as you please,
 But, if you hold it fit, after the play
 Let his queen-mother° all alone entreat him   175
 To show his grief. Let her be round° with him;
 And I'll be placed, so please you, in the ear
 Of all their conference. If she find him not,°
 To England send him, or confine him where
 Your wisdom best shall think.
KING: It shall be so.   180
 Madness in great ones must not unwatched go.

[Exeunt.]

*[Act **3.2** Enter* HAMLET *and three of the* PLAYERS.*]*°

HAMLET: Speak the speech, I pray you, as I pronounced it to you, trippingly on
 the tongue. But if you mouth it, as many of our players° do, I had as lief°
 the town crier spoke my lines. Nor do not saw the air too much with
 your hand, thus, but use all gently; for in the very torrent, tempest, and, as
 I may say, whirlwind of your passion, you must acquire and beget a 5
 temperance that may give it smoothness. O, it offends me to the soul to
 hear a robustious° periwig-pated° fellow tear a passion to tatters, to very
 rags, to split the ears of the groundlings,° who for the most part are capable of° nothing but inexplicable dumb shows° and noise. I would have
 such a fellow whipped for o'erdoing Termagant.° It out-Herods Herod.° 10
 Pray you, avoid it.
FIRST PLAYER: I warrant your honor.

---

167 still continually   **168 From . . . himself** out of his natural manner   **175 queen-mother**
queen and mother   **176 round** blunt   **178 find him not** fails to discover what is troubling
him   **3.2 s.d. Location: The castle   2 our players** players nowadays   **I had as lief** I would
just as soon   **7 robustious** violent, boisterous   **periwig-pated** wearing a wig   **8 groundlings**
spectators who paid least and stood in the yard of the theater   **8–9 capable of** able to understand   **9 dumb shows** mimed performances, often used before Shakespeare's time to precede
a play or each act   **10 Termagant** a supposed deity of the Mohammedans, not found in any
English medieval play but elsewhere portrayed as violent and blustering   **Herod** Herod of Jewry
(A character in *The Slaughter of the Innocents* and other cycle plays. The part was played with
great noise and fury.)

HAMLET: Be not too tame neither, but let your own discretion be your tutor. Suit the action to the word, the word to the action, with this special observance, that you o'erstep not the modesty° of nature. For anything so   15
o'erdone is from° the purpose of playing, whose end, both at the first and now, was and is to hold as 't were the mirror up to nature, to show virtue her feature, scorn° her own image, and the very age and body of the time° his° form and pressure.° Now this overdone or come tardy off,° though it makes the unskillful° laugh, cannot but make the judicious grieve, the   20
censure of the which one° must in your allowance° o'erweigh a whole theater of others. O, there be players that I have seen play, and heard others praise, and that highly, not to speak it profanely,° that, neither having th' accent of Christians° nor the gait of Christian, pagan, nor man,° have so strutted and bellowed that I have thought some of nature's journeymen°   25
had made men and not made them well, they imitated humanity so abominably.°

FIRST PLAYER: I hope we have reformed that indifferently° with us, sir.

HAMLET: O, reform it altogether. And let those that play your clowns speak no more than is set down for them; for there be of them° that will themselves   30
laugh, to set on some quantity of barren° spectators to laugh too, though in the meantime some necessary question of the play be then to be considered. That's villainous, and shows a most pitiful ambition in the fool that uses it. Go make you ready.

[Exeunt PLAYERS.*]*

[Enter POLONIUS, GUILDENSTERN *and* ROSENCRANTZ.*]*

How now, my lord, will the King hear this piece of work?   35

POLONIUS: And the Queen too, and that presently.°

HAMLET: Bid the players make haste.

[Exit POLONIUS.*]*

Will you two help to hasten them?

ROSENCRANTZ: Ay, my lord.

[Exeunt they two.]

---

15 modesty restraint, moderation   **16 from** contrary to   **18 scorn** i.e., something foolish and deserving of scorn   **the very . . . time** i.e., the present state of affairs   **19 his** its   **pressure** stamp, impressed character   **come tardy off** inadequately done   **20 the unskillful** those lacking in judgment   **20–21 the censure . . . one** the judgment of even one of whom   **21 your allowance** your scale of values   **23 not . . . profanely** (Hamlet anticipates his idea in lines 25–27 that some men were not made by God at all.)   **24 Christians** i.e., ordinary decent folk   **nor man** i.e., nor any human being at all   **25 journeymen** laborers who are not yet masters in their trade   **27 abominably** (Shakespeare's usual spelling, *abhominably*, suggests a literal though etymologically incorrect meaning, "removed from human nature.")   **28 indifferently** tolerably   **30 of them** some among them   **31 barren** i.e., of wit   **36 presently** at once

HAMLET: What ho, Horatio!

[Enter HORATIO.*]*

HORATIO: Here, sweet lord, at your service.   40

HAMLET: Horatio, thou art e'en as just a man

As e'er my conversation coped withal.°

HORATIO: O, my dear lord—

HAMLET: Nay, do not think I flatter,

For what advancement may I hope from thee

That no revenue hast but thy good spirits   45

To feed and clothe thee? Why should the poor be flattered?

No, let the candied° tongue lick absurd pomp,

And crook the pregnant° hinges of the knee

Where thrift° may follow fawning. Dost thou hear?

Since my dear soul was mistress of her choice   50

And could of men distinguish her election,°

Sh' hath sealed thee° for herself, for thou hast been

As one, in suffering all, that suffers nothing,

A man that Fortune's buffets and rewards

Hast ta'en with equal thanks; and blest are those   55

Whose blood° and judgment are so well commeddled°

That they are not a pipe for Fortune's finger

To sound what stop° she please. Give me that man

That is not passion's slave, and I will wear him

In my heart's core, ay, in my heart of heart,   60

As I do thee.—Something too much of this.—

There is a play tonight before the King.

One scene of it comes near the circumstance

Which I have told thee of my father's death.

I prithee, when thou seest that act afoot,   65

Even with the very comment of thy soul°

Observe my uncle. If his occulted° guilt

Do not itself unkennel° in one speech,

It is a damnèd° ghost that we have seen,

And my imaginations are as foul   70

As Vulcan's stithy.° Give him heedful note,

---

42 my . . . withal my dealings encountered   **47 candied** sugared, flattering   **48 pregnant** compliant   **49 thrift** profit   **51 could . . . election** could make distinguishing choices among persons   **52 sealed thee** (Literally, as one would seal a legal document to mark possession.)   **56 blood** passion   **commeddled** commingled   **58 stop** hole in a wind instrument for controlling the sound   **66 very . . . soul** your most penetrating observation and consideration   **67 occulted** hidden   **68 unkennel** (As one would say of a fox driven from its lair.)   **69 damnèd** in league with Satan   **71 stithy** smithy, place of stiths (anvils)

For I mine eyes will rivet to his face,
And after we will both our judgments join
In censure of his seeming.°

HORATIO: Well, my lord.
If 'a steal aught° the whilst this play is playing   75
And scape detecting, I will pay the theft.

[(Flourish.) Enter trumpets and kettledrums, KING, QUEEN, POLONIUS OPHELIA, (ROSENCRANTZ, GUILDENSTERN, and other lords, with guards carrying torches).]

HAMLET: They are coming to the play. I must be idle.°
Get you a place. [*The* KING, QUEEN, *and courtiers sit.*]

KING: How fares our cousin° Hamlet?

HAMLET: Excellent, i' faith, of the chameleon's dish:° I eat the air, promise-   80
crammed. You cannot feed capons° so.

KING: I have nothing with° this answer, Hamlet. These words are not mine.°

HAMLET: No, nor mine now.° [*To* POLONIUS.] My lord, you played once i' th' university, you say?

POLONIUS: That did I, my lord, and was accounted a good actor.   85

HAMLET: What did you enact?

POLONIUS: I did enact Julius Caesar. I was killed i' the Capitol; Brutus killed me.

HAMLET: It was a brute° part° of him to kill so capital a calf° there.—Be the
players ready?

ROSENCRANTZ: Ay, my lord. They stay upon° your patience.   90

QUEEN: Come hither, my dear Hamlet, sit by me.

HAMLET: No, good Mother, here's metal° more attractive.

POLONIUS [*to the* KING]:   O, ho, do you mark that?

HAMLET: Lady, shall I lie in your lap?

[Lying down at OPHELIA's *feet.]*

OPHELIA: No, my lord.   95

HAMLET: I mean, my head upon your lap?

OPHELIA: Ay, my lord.

---

74 censure of his seeming judgment of his appearance or behavior   **75 If 'a steal aught** if he gets away with anything   **77 idle** (1) unoccupied (2) mad   **79 cousin** i.e., close relative   **80 chameleon's dish** (Chameleons were supposed to feed on air. Hamlet deliberately misinterprets the King's *fares* as "feeds." By his phrase *eat the air* he also plays on the idea of feeding himself with the promise of succession, of being the *heir*.)   **81 capons** roosters castrated and *crammed* with feed to make them succulent   **82 have . . . with** make nothing of, or gain nothing from   **are not mine** do not respond to what I asked   **83 nor mine now** (Once spoken, words are proverbially no longer the speaker's own—and hence should be uttered warily.)   **88 brute** (The Latin meaning of *brutus,* "stupid," was often used punningly with the name Brutus.)   **part** (1) deed (2) role   **calf** fool   **90 stay upon** await   **92 metal** substance that is attractive, i.e., magnetic, but with suggestion also of *mettle,* "disposition"

HAMLET: Do you think I meant country matters?°

OPHELIA: I think nothing, my lord.

HAMLET: That's a fair thought to lie between maids' legs. 100

OPHELIA: What is, my lord?

HAMLET: Nothing.°

OPHELIA: You are merry, my lord.

HAMLET: Who, I?

OPHELIA: Ay, my lord. 105

HAMLET: O God, your only jig maker.° What should a man do but be merry? For look you how cheerfully my mother looks, and my father died within 's° two hours.

OPHELIA: Nay, 'tis twice two months, my lord.

HAMLET: So long? Nay then, let the devil wear black, for I'll have a suit of sables.° O heavens! Die two months ago, and not forgotten yet? Then 110 there's hope a great man's memory may outlive his life half a year. But, by 'r Lady, 'a must build churches, then, or else shall 'a suffer not thinking on,° with the hobbyhorse, whose epitaph is "For O, for O, the hobbyhorse is forgot."°

[The trumpets sound. Dumb show follows.]

[Enter a King and a Queen [very lovingly]; the Queen embracing him, and he her. (She kneels, and makes show of protestation unto him.) He takes her up, and declines his head upon her neck. He lies him down upon a bank of flowers. She, seeing him asleep, leaves him. Anon comes in another man, takes off his crown, kisses it, pours poison in the sleeper's ears, and leaves him. The Queen returns, finds the King dead, makes passionate action. The Poisoner with some three or four come in again, seem to condole with her. The dead body is carried away. The Poisoner woos the Queen with gifts; she seems harsh awhile, but in the end accepts love.]

[Exeunt PLAYERS.*]*

98 country matters sexual intercourse (making a bawdy pun on the first syllable of *country*) **102 Nothing** the figure zero or naught, suggesting the female sexual anatomy. (*Thing* not infrequently has a bawdy connotation of male or female anatomy, and the reference here could be male.) **106 only jig maker** very best composer of jigs, i.e., pointless merriment (Hamlet replies sardonically to Ophelia's observation that he is merry by saying, "If you're looking for someone who is really merry, you've come to the right person.") **107 within 's** within this (i.e., these) **109–110 suit of sables** garments trimmed with the fur of the sable and hence suited for a wealthy person, not a mourner (but with a pun on *sable,* "black," ironically suggesting mourning once again) **112–113 suffer ... on** undergo oblivion **113–114 For ... forgot** (verse of a song occurring also in *Love's Labor's Lost,* 3.1.27–28. The hobbyhorse was a character made up to resemble a horse and rider, appearing in the morris dance and such May-game sports. This song laments the disappearance of such customs under pressure from the Puritans.)

OPHELIA: What means this, my lord?   115

HAMLET: Marry, this' miching mallico;° it means mischief.

OPHELIA: Belike° this show imports the argument° of the play.

[Enter PROLOGUE.]

HAMLET: We shall know by this fellow. The players cannot keep counsel;° they'll

    tell all.

OPHELIA: Will 'a tell us what this show meant?   120

HAMLET: Ay, or any show that you will show him. Be not you° ashamed to show,

    he'll not shame to tell you what it means.

OPHELIA: You are naught,° you are naught. I'll mark the play.

PROLOGUE: For us, and for our tragedy,

    Here stooping° to your clemency,   125

    We beg your hearing patiently.

[Exit.]

HAMLET: Is this a prologue, or the posy of a ring?°

OPHELIA: 'Tis brief, my lord.

HAMLET: As woman's love.

[Enter (two PLAYERS as) King and Queen.]

PLAYER KING: Full thirty times hath Phoebus' cart° gone round   130

    Neptune's salt wash° and Tellus'° orbèd ground,

    And thirty dozen moons with borrowed° sheen

    About the world have times twelve thirties been,

    Since love our hearts and Hymen° did our hands

    Unite commutual° in most sacred bands.°   135

PLAYER QUEEN: So many journeys may the sun and moon

    Make us again count o'er ere love be done!

    But, woe is me, you are so sick of late,

    So far from cheer and from your former state,

    That I distrust° you. Yet, though I distrust,   140

    Discomfort° you, my lord, it nothing° must.

    For women's fear and love hold quantity;°

---

116 this' miching mallico this is sneaking mischief   **117 Belike** probably   **argument** plot   **118 counsel** secret   **121 Be not you** provided you are not   **123 naught** indecent (Ophelia is reacting to Hamlet's pointed remarks about not being ashamed to show all.)   **125 stooping** bowing   **127 posy . . . ring** brief motto in verse inscribed in a ring   **130 Phoebus' cart** the sun-god's chariot, making its yearly cycle   **131 salt wash** the sea   **131 Tellus** goddess of the earth, of the *orbèd ground*   **132 borrowed** i.e., reflected   **134 Hymen** god of matrimony   **135 commutual** mutually   **135 bands** bonds   **140 distrust** am anxious about   **141 Discomfort** distress   **nothing** not at all   **142 hold quantity** keep proportion with one another

In neither aught, or in extremity.°
Now, what my love is, proof° hath made you know,
And as my love is sized,° my fear is so.   145
Where love is great, the littlest doubts are fear;
Where little fears grow great, great love grows there.

PLAYER KING: Faith, I must leave thee, love, and shortly too;
My operant powers° their functions leave to do.°
And thou shalt live in this fair world behind,°   150
Honored, beloved; and haply one as kind
For husband shalt thou—

PLAYER QUEEN: O, confound the rest!
Such love must needs be treason in my breast.
In second husband let me be accurst!
None° wed the second but who° killed the first.   155

HAMLET: Wormwood,° wormwood.

PLAYER QUEEN: The instances° that second marriage move°
Are base respects of thrift,° but none of love.
A second time I kill my husband dead
When second husband kisses me in bed.   160

PLAYER KING: I do believe you think what now you speak,
But what we do determine oft we break.
Purpose is but the slave to memory,°
Of violent birth, but poor validity,°
Which° now, like fruit unripe, sticks on the tree,   165
But fall unshaken when they mellow be.
Most necessary 'tis that we forget
To pay ourselves what to ourselves is debt.°
What to ourselves in passion we propose,
The passion ending, doth the purpose lose.   170
The violence of either grief or joy
Their own enactures° with themselves destroy.
Where joy most revels, grief doth most lament;

---

143 In . . . extremity i.e., women fear and love either too little or too much, but the two, fear and love, are equal in either case   144 proof experience   145 sized in size   149 operant powers vital functions   leave to do cease to perform   150 behind after I have gone   155 None i.e., let no woman   but who except the one who   156 Wormwood i.e., how bitter. (Literally, a bitter-tasting plant.)   157 instances motives   move motivate   158 base . . . thrift ignoble considerations of material prosperity   163 Purpose . . . memory our good intentions are subject to forgetfulness   164 validity strength, durability   165 Which i.e., purpose   167–168 Most . . . debt it's inevitable that in time we forget the obligations we have imposed on ourselves   172 enactures fulfillments

Grief joys, joy grieves, on slender accident.°
This world is not for aye,° nor 'tis not strange   175
That even our loves should with our fortunes change;
For 'tis a question left us yet to prove,
Whether love lead fortune, or else fortune love.
The great man down,° you mark his favorite flies;
The poor advanced makes friends of enemies.°   180
And hitherto° doth love on fortune tend;°
For who not needs° shall never lack a friend,
And who in want° a hollow friend doth try°
Directly seasons him° his enemy.
But, orderly to end where I begun,   185
Our wills and fates do so contrary run°
That our devices still° are overthrown;
Our thoughts are ours, their ends° none of our own.
So think thou wilt no second husband wed,
But die thy thoughts when thy first lord is dead.   190

PLAYER QUEEN: Nor° earth to me give food, nor heaven light,
Sport and repose lock from me day and night,°
To desperation turn my trust and hope,
An anchor's cheer° in prison be my scope!°
Each opposite that blanks° the face of joy   195
Meet what I would have well and it destroy!°
Both here and hence° pursue me lasting strife
If, once a widow, ever I be wife!

HAMLET: If she should break it now!

173–174 Where . . . accident the capacity for extreme joy and grief go together, and often one extreme is instantly changed into its opposite on the slightest provocation   **175 aye** ever   **179 down** fallen in fortune   **180 The poor . . . enemies** when one of humble station is promoted, you see his enemies suddenly becoming his friends   **181 hitherto** up to this point in the argument, or, to this extent   **tend** attend   **182 who not needs** he who is not in need (of wealth)   **183 who in want** he who, being in need   **try** test (his generosity)   **184 seasons him** ripens him into   **186 Our . . . run** what we want and what we get go so contrarily   **187 devices still** intentions continually   **188 ends** results   **191 Nor** let neither   **192 Sport . . . night** may day deny me its pastimes and night its repose   **194 anchor's cheer** anchorite's or hermit's fare   **my scope** the extent of my happiness   **195 blanks** causes to blanch or grow pale   **195–196 Each . . . destroy** may every adverse thing that causes the face of joy to turn pale meet and destroy everything that I desire to see prosper   **197 hence** in the life hereafter

PLAYER KING: 'Tis deeply sworn. Sweet, leave me here awhile;   200
    My spirits° grow dull, and fain I would beguile
    The tedious day with sleep.
PLAYER QUEEN: Sleep rock thy brain,
    And never come mischance between us twain!

[(He sleeps.) Exit (PLAYER QUEEN).]

HAMLET: Madam, how like you this play?
QUEEN: The lady doth protest too much,° methinks.   205
HAMLET: O, but she'll keep her word.
KING: Have you heard the argument?° Is there no offense in 't?
HAMLET: No, no, they do but jest,° poison in jest. No offense° i' the world.
KING: What do you call the play?
HAMLET: *The Mousetrap.* Marry, how? Tropically.° This play is the image of a   210
    murder done in Vienna. Gonzago is the Duke's° name, his wife, Baptista.
    You shall see anon. 'Tis a knavish piece of work, but what of that? Your
    Majesty, and we that have free° souls, it touches us not. Let the galled
    jade° wince, our withers° are unwrung.°

[Enter LUCIANUS.]

    This is one Lucianus, nephew to the King.   215
OPHELIA: You are as good as a chorus,° my lord.
HAMLET: I could interpret° between you and your love, if I could see the pup-
    pets dallying.°
OPHELIA: You are keen,° my lord, you are keen.
HAMLET: It would cost you a groaning to take off mine edge.   220
OPHELIA: Still better, and worse.°
HAMLET: So° you mis-take° your husbands. Begin, murder; leave thy damnable
    faces and begin. Come, the croaking raven doth bellow for revenge.

201 spirits vital spirits   **205 doth . . . much** makes too many promises and protestations
207 argument plot   **208 jest** make believe   **207–208 offense . . . offense** cause for objection . . . actual injury, crime   **210 Tropically** figuratively (The First Quarto reading, *trapically,*
suggests a pun on *trap* in *Mousetrap.*)   **211 Duke's** i.e., King's (A slip that may be due to
Shakespeare's possible source, the alleged murder of the Duke of Urbino by Luigi Gonzaga in
1538.)   **213 free** guiltless   **213–214 galled jade** horse whose hide is rubbed by saddle or harness   **214 withers** the part between the horse's shoulder blades   **unwrung** not rubbed sore
216 chorus (In many Elizabethan plays, the forthcoming action was explained by an actor
known as the "chorus"; at a puppet show, the actor who spoke the dialogue was known as an
"interpreter," as indicated by the lines following.)   **217 interpret** (1) ventriloquize the dialogue,
as in puppet show (2) act as pander   **218 puppets dallying** (With suggestion of sexual play,
continued in *keen,* "sexually aroused," *groaning,* "moaning in pregnancy," and *edge,* "sexual
desire" or "impetuosity.")   **219 keen** sharp, bitter   **221 Still . . . worse** more keen, always
bettering what other people say with witty wordplay, but at the same time more offensive   **222
So** even thus (in marriage)   **mis-take** take falseheartedly and cheat on (The marriage vows say
"for better, for worse.")

LUCIANUS: Thoughts black, hands apt, drugs fit, and time agreeing,
    Confederate season,° else° no creature seeing,°   225
    Thou mixture rank, of midnight weeds collected,
    With Hecate's ban° thrice blasted, thrice infected,
    Thy natural magic and dire property°
    On wholesome life usurp immediately.

[He pours the poison into the sleeper's ear.]

HAMLET: 'A poisons him i' the garden for his estate.° His° name's Gonzago. The   230
    story is extant, and written in very choice Italian. You shall see anon how
    the murderer gets the love of Gonzago's wife.

*[*CLAUDIUS *rises.]*

OPHELIA: The King rises.
HAMLET: What, frighted with false fire?°
QUEEN: How fares my lord?   235
POLONIUS: Give o'er the play.
KING: Give me some light. Away!
POLONIUS: Lights, lights, lights!

[Exeunt all but HAMLET *and* HORATIO.*]*

HAMLET: "Why, let the strucken deer go weep,
        The hart ungallèd° play.   240
    For some must watch,° while some must sleep;
        Thus runs the world away."°
    Would not this,° sir, and a forest of feathers°—if the rest of my fortunes
    turn Turk with° me—with two Provincial roses° on my razed° shoes, get
    me a fellowship in a cry° of players?°   245
HORATIO: Half a share.
HAMLET: A whole one, I.
    "For thou dost know, O Damon° dear,

---

225 Confederate season the time and occasion conspiring (to assist the murderer)   **else** otherwise   **seeing** seeing me   **227 Hecate's ban** the curse of Hecate, the goddess of witchcraft   **228 dire property** baleful quality   **230 estate** i.e., the kingship   **His** i.e., the King's   **234 false fire** the blank discharge of a gun loaded with powder but no shot   **240 ungallèd** unafflicted   **241 watch** remain awake   **242 Thus . . . away** thus the world goes   **239–242 Why . . . away** (Probably from an old ballad, with allusion to the popular belief that a wounded deer retires to weep and die; compare with *As You Like It,* 2.1.33–66.)   **243 this** i.e., the play   **feathers** (Allusion to the plumes that Elizabethan actors were fond of wearing.)   **244 turn Turk with** turn renegade against, go back on   **Provincial roses** rosettes of ribbon, named for roses grown in a part of France   **razed** with ornamental slashing   **245 cry** pack (of hounds)   **fellowship . . . players** partnership in a theatrical company   **248 Damon** the friend of Pythias, as Horatio is friend of Hamlet; or, a traditional pastoral name

        This realm dismantled° was
        Of Jove himself, and now reigns here   250
        A very, very—pajock."°

HORATIO: You might have rhymed.

HAMLET: O good Horatio, I'll take the ghost's word for a thousand pound. Didst perceive?

HORATIO: Very well, my lord.   255

HAMLET: Upon the talk of the poisoning?

HORATIO: I did very well note him.

[Enter ROSENCRANTZ *and* GUILDENSTERN.*]*

HAMLET: Aha! Come, some music! Come, the recorders.°
        "For if the King like not the comedy,
        Why then, belike, he likes it not, perdy."°   260
    Come, some music.

GUILDENSTERN: Good my lord, vouchsafe me a word with you.

HAMLET: Sir, a whole history.

GUILDENSTERN: The King, sir—

HAMLET: Ay, sir, what of him?   265

GUILDENSTERN: Is in his retirement° marvelous distempered.°

HAMLET: With drink, sir?

GUILDENSTERN: No, my lord, with choler.°

HAMLET: Your wisdom should show itself more richer to signify this to the doctor, for me to put him to his purgation° would perhaps plunge him   270 into more choler.

GUILDENSTERN: Good my lord, put your discourse into some frame° and start° not so wildly from my affair.

HAMLET: I am tame, sir. Pronounce.

GUILDENSTERN: The Queen, your mother, in most great affliction of spirit, hath   275 sent me to you.

HAMLET: You are welcome.

---

249 dismantled stripped, divested   **249–251 This realm . . . pajock** i.e., Jove, representing divine authority and justice, has abandoned this realm to its own devices, leaving in his stead only a peacock or vain pretender to virtue (though the rhyme-word expected in place of *pajock* or "peacock" suggests that the realm is now ruled over by an "ass")   **258 recorders** wind instruments of the flute kind   **260 perdy** (A corruption of the French *par dieu,* "by God")   **266 retirement** withdrawal to his chambers   **distempered** out of humor (But Hamlet deliberately plays on the wider application to any illness of mind or body, as in line 296, especially to drunkenness.)   **268 choler** anger (But Hamlet takes the word in its more basic humoral sense of "bilious disorder.")   **270 purgation** (Hamlet hints at something going beyond medical treatment to bloodletting and the extraction of confession.)   **272 frame** order   **273 start** shy or jump away (like a horse; the opposite of *tame* in line 274)

GUILDENSTERN: Nay, good my lord, this courtesy is not of the right breed.° If it
  shall please you to make me a wholesome answer, I will do your mother's
  commandment; if not, your pardon° and my return shall be the end of my   280
  business.

HAMLET: Sir, I cannot.

ROSENCRANTZ: What, my lord?

HAMLET: Make you a wholesome answer; my wit's diseased. But, sir, such
  answer as I can make, you shall command, or rather, as you say, my mother.   285
  Therefore no more, but to the matter. My mother, you say—

ROSENCRANTZ: Then thus she says: your behavior hath struck her into amazement and admiration.°

HAMLET: O wonderful son, that can so stonish a mother! But is there no sequel
  at the heels of this mother's admiration? Impart.   290

ROSENCRANTZ: She desires to speak with you in her closet° ere you go to bed.

HAMLET: We shall obey, were she ten times our mother. Have you any further
  trade with us?

ROSENCRANTZ: My lord, you once did love me.

HAMLET: And do still, by these pickers and stealers.°   295

ROSENCRANTZ: Good my lord, what is your cause of distemper? You do surely
  bar the door upon your own liberty° if you deny° your griefs to your
  friend.

HAMLET: Sir, I lack advancement.

ROSENCRANTZ: How can that be, when you have the voice of the King himself   300
  for your succession in Denmark?

HAMLET: Ay, sir, but "While the grass grows"°—the proverb is something°
  musty.

[Enter the PLAYERS° *with recorders.]*

  O, the recorders. Let me see one. [*He takes a recorder.*]
  To withdraw° with you: why do you go about to recover the wind° of me,   305
  as if you would drive me into a toil?°

GUILDENSTERN: O, my lord, if my duty be too bold, my love is too
  unmannerly.°

HAMLET: I do not well understand that.° Will you play upon this pipe?

---

278 breed (1) kind (2) breeding, manners   **280 pardon** permission to depart   **288
admiration** bewilderment   **291 closet** private chamber   **295 pickers and stealers** i.e., hands
(So called from the catechism, "to keep my hands from picking and stealing.")   **297 liberty** i.e.,
being freed from *distemper,* line 296; but perhaps with a veiled threat as well   **deny** refuse to
share   **302 While . . . grows** (The rest of the proverb is "the silly horse starves"; Hamlet may
not live long enough to succeed to the kingdom.)   **something** somewhat   **s.d. Players** actors
305 withdraw speak privately   **recover the wind** get to the windward side (thus driving the
game into the *toil,* or "net")   **306 toil** snare   **307–308 If . . . unmannerly** if I am using an
unmannerly boldness, it is my love that occasion it   **309 I . . . that** i.e., I don't understand how
genuine love can be unmannerly

GUILDENSTERN: My lord, I cannot.   310

HAMLET: I pray you.

GUILDENSTERN: Believe me, I cannot.

HAMLET: I do beseech you.

GUILDENSTERN: I know no touch of it, my lord.

HAMLET: It is as easy as lying. Govern these ventages° with your fingers and   315
thumb, give it breath with your mouth, and it will discourse most eloquent
music. Look you, these are the stops.

GUILDENSTERN: But these cannot I command to any utterance of harmony. I have
not the skill.

HAMLET: Why, look you now, how unworthy a thing you make of me! You   320
would play upon me, you would seem to know my stops, you would
pluck out the heart of my mystery, you would sound° me from my lowest
note to the top of my compass,° and there is much music, excellent voice,
in this little organ,° yet cannot you make it speak. 'Sblood, do you think I
am easier to be played on than a pipe? Call me what instrument you will,   325
though you can fret° me, you cannot play upon me.

[Enter POLONIUS.*]*

God bless you, sir!

POLONIUS: My lord, the Queen would speak with you, and presently.°

HAMLET: Do you see yonder cloud that's almost in shape of a camel?

POLONIUS: By the Mass and 'tis, like a camel indeed.   330

HAMLET: Methinks it is like a weasel.

POLONIUS: It is backed like a weasel.

HAMLET: Or like a whale.

POLONIUS: Very like a whale.

HAMLET: Then I will come to my mother by and by.° *[Aside.]* They fool me° to   335
the top of my bent.°—I will come by and by.

POLONIUS: I will say so.

[Exit.]

HAMLET: "By and by" is easily said. Leave me, friends.

[Exeunt all but HAMLET.*]*

'Tis now the very witching time° of night,
When churchyards yawn and hell itself breathes out   340

---

315 **ventages** finger-holes or *stops* (line 317) of the recorder   322 **sound** (1) fathom (2) produce sound in   323 **compass** range (of voice)   324 **organ** musical instrument   326 **fret** irritate (with a quibble on *fret,* meaning the piece of wood, gut, or metal that regulates the fingering
on an instrument)   328 **presently** at once   335 **by and by** quite soon   **fool me** trifle with
me, humor my fooling   336 **top of my bent** limit of my ability or endurance (Literally, the
extent to which a bow may be bent.)   339 **witching time** time when spells are cast and evil
is abroad

Contagion to this world. Now could I drink hot blood
And do such bitter business as the day
Would quake to look on. Soft, now to my mother.
O heart, lose not thy nature!° Let not ever
The soul of Nero° enter this firm bosom.   345
Let me be cruel, not unnatural;
I will speak daggers to her, but use none.
My tongue and soul in this be hypocrites:
How in my words soever° she be shent,°
To give them seals° never my soul consent!   350

[Exit.]

*[Act **3.3** Enter* KING, ROSENCRANTZ, *and* GUILDENSTERN.*]°*

KING: I like him° not, nor stands it safe with us
To let his madness range. Therefore prepare you.
I your commission will forthwith dispatch,°
And he to England shall along with you.
The terms of our estate° may not endure   5
Hazard so near 's as doth hourly grow
Out of his brows.°
GUILDENSTERN: We will ourselves provide.
Most holy and religious fear° it is
To keep those many many bodies safe
That live and feed upon Your Majesty.   10
ROSENCRANTZ: The single and peculiar° life is bound
With all the strength and armor of the mind
To keep itself from noyance,° but much more
That spirit upon whose weal depends and rests
The lives of many. The cess° of majesty   15
Dies not alone, but like a gulf° doth draw
What's near it with it; or it is a massy° wheel
Fixed on the summit of the highest mount,
To whose huge spokes ten thousand lesser things
Are mortised° and adjoined, which, when it falls,°   20

---

344 **nature** natural feeling   345 **Nero** murderer of his mother, Agrippina   349 **How . . .
soever** however much by my words   **shent** rebuked   350 **give them seals** i.e., confirm them
with deeds   **3.3 s.d. Location: The castle   1 him** i.e., his behavior   **3 dispatch** prepare,
cause to be drawn up   **5 terms of our estate** circumstances of my royal position   **7 Out of his
brows** i.e., from his brain, in the form of plots and threats   **8 religious fear** sacred concern
11 single and peculiar individual and private   **13 noyance** harm   **15 cess** decease, cessation
16 gulf whirlpool   **17 massy** massive   **20 mortised** fastened (as with a fitted joint)   **when
it falls** i.e., when it descends, like the wheel of Fortune, bringing a king down with it

Each small annexment, petty consequence,°
Attends° the boisterous ruin. Never alone
Did the King sigh, but with a general groan.

KING: Arm° you, I pray you, to this speedy voyage,
For we will fetters put about this fear,   25
Which now goes too free-footed.

ROSENCRANTZ: We will haste us.

[Exeunt gentlemen (ROSENCRANTZ and GUILDENSTERN).]

[Enter POLONIUS.]

POLONIUS: My lord, he's going to his mother's closet.
Behind the arras° I'll convey myself
To hear the process.° I'll warrant she'll tax him home,°
And, as you said—and wisely was it said—   30
'Tis meet° that some more audience than a mother,
Since nature makes them partial, should o'erhear
The speech, of vantage.° Fare you well, my liege.
I'll call upon you ere you go to bed
And tell you what I know.

KING: Thanks, dear my lord.   35

[Exit (POLONIUS).]

O, my offense is rank! It smells to heaven.
It hath the primal eldest curse° upon 't,
A brother's murder. Pray can I not,
Though inclination be as sharp as will;°
My stronger guilt defeats my strong intent,   40
And like a man to double business bound°
I stand in pause where I shall first begin,
And both neglect. What if this cursèd hand
Were thicker than itself with brother's blood,
Is there not rain enough in the sweet heavens   45
To wash it white as snow? Whereto serves mercy

---

21 Each . . . consequence i.e., every hanger-on and unimportant person or thing connected with the King   **22 Attends** participates in   **24 Arm** prepare   **28 arras** screen of tapestry placed around the walls of household apartments (On the Elizabethan stage, the arras was presumably over a door or discovery space in the tiring-house facade.)   **29 process** proceedings **tax him home** reprove him severely   **31 meet** fitting   **33 of vantage** from an advantageous place, or, in addition   **37 the primal eldest curse** the curse of Cain, the first murderer; he killed his brother Abel   **39 Though . . . will** though my desire is as strong as my determination **41 bound** (1) destined (2) obliged (The King wants to repent and still enjoy what he has gained.)

But to confront the visage of offense?°
And what's in prayer but this twofold force,
To be forestallèd° ere we come to fall,
Or pardoned being down? Then I'll look up.   50
My fault is past. But O, what form of prayer
Can serve my turn? "Forgive me my foul murder"?
That cannot be, since I am still possessed
Of those effects for which I did the murder:
My crown, mine own ambition, and my Queen.   55
May one be pardoned and retain th' offense?°
In the corrupted currents° of this world
Offense's gilded hand° may shove by° justice,
And oft 'tis seen the wicked prize° itself
Buys out the law. But 'tis not so above.   60
There° is no shuffling,° there the action lies°
In his° true nature, and we ourselves compelled,
Even to the teeth and forehead° of our faults,
To give in° evidence. What then? What rests?°
Try what repentance can. What can it not?   65
Yet what can it, when one cannot repent?
O wretched state, O bosom black as death,
O limèd° soul that, struggling to be free,
Art more engaged!° Help, angels! Make assay.°
Bow, stubborn knees, and heart with strings of steel,   70
Be soft as sinews of the newborn babe!
All may be well.

[He kneels.]

[Enter HAMLET.*]*

HAMLET: Now might I do it pat,° now 'a is a-praying;
And now I'll do 't. [*He draws his sword.*] And so 'a goes to heaven,
And so am I revenged. That would be scanned:°   75
A villain kills my father, and for that,

46–47 Whereto ... offense what function does mercy serve other than to meet sin face to face?   **49 forestallèd** prevented (from sinning)   **56 th' offense** the thing for which one offended   **57 currents** courses   **58 gilded hand** hand offering gold as a bribe   **shove by** thrust aside   **59 wicked prize** prize won by wickedness   **61 There** i.e., in heaven   **shuffling** escape by trickery   **the action lies** the accusation is made manifest (A legal metaphor.)   **62 his** its   **63 to the teeth and forehead** face to face, concealing nothing   **64 give in** provide   **rests** remains   **68 limèd** caught as with birdlime, a sticky substance used to ensnare birds   **69 engaged** entangled   **assay** trial (Said to himself.)   **73 pat** opportunely   **75 would be scanned** needs to be looked into, or, would be interpreted as follows

I, his sole son, do this same villain send
To heaven.
Why, this is hire and salary, not revenge.
'A took my father grossly, full of bread,°   80
With all his crimes broad blown,° as flush° as May;
And how his audit° stands who knows save° heaven?
But in our circumstance and course of thought°
'Tis heavy with him. And am I then revenged,
To take him in the purging of his soul,   85
When he is fit and seasoned° for his passage?
No!
Up, sword, and know thou a more horrid hent.°

                                        [He puts up his sword.]

When he is drunk asleep, or in his rage,°
Or in th' incestuous pleasure of his bed,   90
At game,° a-swearing, or about some act
That has no relish° of salvation in 't—
Then trip him, that his heels may kick at heaven,
And that his soul may be as damned and black
As hell, whereto it goes. My mother stays.°   95
This physic° but prolongs thy sickly days.

[Exit.]

KING: My words fly up, my thoughts remain below.
         Words without thoughts never to heaven go.

[Exit.]

[Act 3.4 *Enter* (QUEEN) GERTRUDE *and* POLONIUS.*]*°

POLONIUS: 'A will come straight. Look you lay home° to him.
             Tell him his pranks have been too broad° to bear with,

---

80 grossly, full of bread i.e., enjoying his worldly pleasures rather than fasting (See Ezekiel 16:49.)   **81 crimes broad blown** sins in full bloom   **flush** vigorous   **82 audit** account   **save** except for   **83 in . . . thought** as we see it from our mortal perspective   **86 seasoned** matured, readied   **88 know . . . hent** await to be grasped by me on a more horrid occasion   **hent** act of seizing   **89 drunk . . . rage** dead drunk, or in a fit of sexual passion   **91 game** gambling   **92 relish** trace, savor   **95 stays** awaits (me)   **96 physic** purging (by prayer), or, Hamlet's postponement of the killing   **3.4 s.d. Location:** The Queen's private chamber   **1 lay home** thrust to the heart, reprove him soundly   **2 broad** unrestrained

And that Your Grace hath screened and stood between
Much heat° and him. I'll shroud° me even here.
Pray you, be round° with him.   5

HAMLET [*within*]:   Mother, Mother, Mother!

QUEEN: I'll warrant you, fear me not.
Withdraw, I hear him coming.

                                          [POLONIUS *hides behind the arras.*]

[*Enter* HAMLET.]

HAMLET: Now, Mother, what's the matter?

QUEEN: Hamlet, thou hast thy father° much offended.   10

HAMLET: Mother, you have my father much offended.

QUEEN: Come, come, you answer with an idle° tongue.

HAMLET: Go, go, you question with a wicked tongue.

QUEEN: Why, how now, Hamlet?

HAMLET: What's the matter now?

QUEEN: Have you forgot me?°

HAMLET: No, by the rood,° not so: 15
You are the Queen, your husband's brother's wife,
And—would it were not so!—you are my mother.

QUEEN: Nay, then, I'll set those to you that can speak.°

HAMLET: Come, come, and sit you down; you shall not budge.
You go not till I set you up a glass   20
Where you may see the inmost part of you.

QUEEN: What wilt thou do? Thou wilt not murder me?
Help, ho!

POLONIUS [*behind the arras*]:   What ho! Help!

HAMLET: [*drawing*]:   How now? A rat? Dead for a ducat,° dead!   25

                                          [*He thrusts his rapier through the arras.*]

POLONIUS [*behind the arras*]:   O, I am slain!   [*He falls and dies.*]

QUEEN: O me, what hast thou done?

HAMLET: Nay, I know not. Is it the King?

QUEEN: O, what a rash and bloody deed is this!

HAMLET: A bloody deed—almost as bad, good Mother,
As kill a King, and marry with his brother.   30

QUEEN: As kill a King!

---

4 Much heat i.e., the King's anger   **shroud** conceal (with ironic fitness to Polonius' imminent
death. The word is only in the First Quarto: the Second Quarto and the Folio read "silence.")   **5
round** blunt   **10 thy father** i.e., your stepfather, Claudius   **12 idle** foolish   **14 forgot me** i.e.,
forgotten that I am your mother   **15 rood** cross of Christ   **18 speak** i.e., to someone so rude
25 Dead for a ducat i.e., I bet a ducat he's dead; or, a ducat is his life's fee

HAMLET: Ay, lady, it was my word.

[He parts the arras and discovers POLONIUS.*]*

Thou wretched, rash, intruding fool, farewell!
I took thee for thy better. Take thy fortune.
Thou find'st to be too busy° is some danger.—
Leave wringing of your hands. Peace, sit you down,   35
And let me wring your heart, for so I shall,
If it be made of penetrable stuff,
If damnèd custom° have not brazed° it so
That it be proof° and bulwark against sense.°

QUEEN: What have I done, that thou dar'st wag thy tongue   40
In noise so rude against me?

HAMLET: Such an act
That blurs the grace and blush of modesty,
Calls virtue hypocrite, takes off the rose
From the fair forehead of an innocent love
And sets a blister° there, makes marriage vows   45
As false as dicers' oaths. O, such a deed
As from the body of contraction° plucks
The very soul, and sweet religion makes°
A rhapsody° of words. Heaven's face does glow
O'er this solidity and compound mass   50
With tristful visage, as against the doom,
Is thought-sick at the act.°

QUEEN: Ay me, what act,
That roars so loud and thunders in the index?°

HAMLET [*showing her two likenesses*]:   Look here upon this picture, and on this,
The counterfeit presentment° of two brothers.   55
See what a grace was seated on this brow:
Hyperion's° curls, the front° of Jove himself,
An eye like Mars° to threaten and command,
A station° like the herald Mercury°
New-lighted° on a heaven-kissing hill—   60

---

34 busy nosey   **38 damnèd custom** habitual wickedness   **brazed** brazened, hardened   **39
proof** armor   **sense** feeling   **45 sets a blister** i.e., brands as a harlot   **47 contraction** the
marriage contract   **48 sweet religion makes** i.e., makes marriage vows   **49 rhapsody** senseless string   **49–52 Heaven's . . . act** heaven's face blushes at this solid world compounded of
the various elements, with sorrowful face as though the day of doom were near, and is sick with
horror at the deed (i.e., Gertrude's marriage)   **53 index** table of contents, prelude or preface
55 counterfeit presentment portrayed representation   **57 Hyperion's** the sungod's   **front**
brow   **58 Mars** god of war   **59 station** manner of standing   **Mercury** winged messenger of
the gods   **60 New-lighted** newly alighted

A combination and a form indeed
Where every god did seem to set his seal°
To give the world assurance of a man.
This was your husband. Look you now what follows:
Here is your husband, like a mildewed ear,°   65
Blasting° his wholesome brother. Have you eyes?
Could you on this fair mountain leave° to feed
And batten° on this moor?° Ha, have you eyes?
You cannot call it love, for at your age
The heyday° in the blood° is tame, it's humble,   70
And waits upon the judgment, and what judgment
Would step from this to this? Sense,° sure, you have,
Else could you not have motion, but sure that sense
Is apoplexed,° for madness would not err,°
Nor sense to ecstasy was ne'er so thralled,   75
But° it reserved some quantity of choice
To serve in such a difference.° What devil was 't
That thus hath cozened° you at hoodman-blind?°
Eyes without feeling, feeling without sight,
Ears without hands or eyes, smelling sans° all,   80
Or but a sickly part of one true sense
Could not so mope.° O shame, where is thy blush?
Rebellious hell,
If thou canst mutine° in a matron's bones,
To flaming youth let virtue be as wax   85
And melt in her own fire.° Proclaim no shame
When the compulsive ardor gives the charge,
Since frost itself as actively doth burn,
And reason panders will.°

---

62 set his seal i.e., affix his approval   **65 ear** i.e., of grain   **66 Blasting** blighting   **67 leave**
cease   **68 batten** gorge   **moor** barren or marshy ground (suggesting also "dark-skinned")
70 heyday state of excitement   **blood** passion   **72 Sense** perception through the five senses
(the functions of the middle or sensible soul)   **74 apoplexed** paralyzed (Hamlet goes on to
explain that, without such a paralysis of will, mere madness would not so err, nor would the five
senses so enthrall themselves to ecstasy or lunacy; even such deranged states of mind would be
able to make the obvious choice between Hamlet Senior and Claudius.)   **err** so err   **76 But** but
that   **77 To ... difference** to help in making a choice between two such men   **78 cozened**
cheated   **hoodman-blind** blindman's buff (In this game, says Hamlet, the devil must have
pushed Claudius toward Gertrude while she was blindfolded.)   **80 sans** without   **82 mope**
be dazed, act aimlessly   **84 mutine** incite mutiny   **85–86 be as wax ... fire** melt like a candle
or stick of sealing wax held over the candle flame   **86–89 Proclaim ... will** call it no shameful business when the compelling ardor of youth delivers the attack, i.e., commits lechery, since
the *frost* of advanced age burns with as active a fire of lust and reason perverts itself by foment-
ing lust rather than restraining it

QUEEN: O Hamlet, speak no more!   90
    Thou turn'st mine eyes into my very soul,
    And there I see such black and grainèd° spots
    As will not leave their tinct.°

HAMLET: Nay, but to live
    In the rank sweat of an enseamèd° bed,
    Stewed° in corruption, honeying and making love   95
    Over the nasty sty!

QUEEN: O, speak to me no more!
    These words like daggers enter in my ears.
    No more, sweet Hamlet!

HAMLET: A murderer and a villain,
    A slave that is not twentieth part the tithe°   100
    Of your precedent lord,° a vice° of kings,
    A cutpurse of the empire and the rule,
    That from a shelf the precious diadem stole
    And put it in his pocket!

QUEEN: No more!   105

[Enter GHOST *(in his nightgown).]*

HAMLET: A king of shreds and patches°—
    Save me, and hover o'er me with your wings,
    You heavenly guards! What would your gracious figure?

QUEEN: Alas, he's mad!

HAMLET: Do you not come your tardy son to chide,   110
    That, lapsed° in time and passion, lets go by
    Th' important° acting of your dread command?
    O, say!

GHOST: Do not forget. This visitation
    Is but to whet thy almost blunted purpose.   115
    But look, amazement° on thy mother sits.
    O, step between her and her fighting soul!
    Conceit° in weakest bodies strongest works.
    Speak to her, Hamlet.

HAMLET: How is it with you, lady?

---

92 grainèd dyed in grain, indelible   **93 leave their tinct** surrender their color
94 enseamèd saturated in the grease and filth of passionate lovemaking   **95 Stewed** soaked,
bathed (with a suggestion of "stew," brothel)   **100 tithe** tenth part   **101 precedent lord**
former husband   **vice** buffoon (A reference to the Vice of the morality plays.)   **106 shreds and
patches** i.e., motley, the traditional costume of the clown or fool   **111 lapsed** delaying
112 important importunate, urgent   **116 amazement** distraction   **118 Conceit** imagination

QUEEN: Alas, how is 't with you,   120
    That you do bend your eye on vacancy,
    And with th' incorporal° air do hold discourse?
    Forth at your eyes your spirits wildly peep,
    And, as the sleeping soldiers in th' alarm,°
    Your bedded° hair, like life in excrements,°   125
    Start up and stand on end. O gentle son,
    Upon the heat and flame of thy distemper°
    Sprinkle cool patience. Whereon do you look?
HAMLET: On him, on him! Look you how pale he glares!
    His form and cause conjoined,° preaching to stones,   130
    Would make them capable.°—Do not look upon me,
    Lest with this piteous action you convert
    My stern effects.° Then what I have to do
    Will want true color—tears perchance for blood.°
QUEEN: To whom do you speak this?   135
HAMLET: Do you see nothing there?
QUEEN: Nothing at all, yet all that is I see.
HAMLET: Nor did you nothing hear?
QUEEN: No, nothing but ourselves.
HAMLET: Why, look you there, look how it steals away!   140
    My father, in his habit° as° he lived!
    Look where he goes even now out at the portal!

[Exit GHOST.*]*

QUEEN: This is the very° coinage of your brain.
    This bodiless creation ecstasy
    Is very cunning in.°   145
HAMLET: Ecstasy?
    My pulse as yours doth temperately keep time,
    And makes as healthful music. It is not madness
    That I have uttered. Bring me to the test,
    And I the matter will reword,° which madness   150

---

122 incorporal immaterial   **124 as ... alarm** like soldiers called out of sleep by an alarm
125 bedded laid flat   **like life in excrements** i.e., as though hair, an outgrowth of the body,
had a life of its own (Hair was thought to be lifeless because it lacks sensation, and so its standing on end would be unnatural and ominous.)   **127 distemper** disorder   **130 His ...
conjoined** his appearance joined to his cause for speaking   **131 capable** receptive
132–133 convert ... effects divert me from my stern duty   **134 want ... blood** lack plau-
sibility so that (with a play on the normal sense of *color*) I shall shed colorless tears instead of
blood   **141 habit** clothes   **as** as when   **143 very** mere   **144–145 This ... in** madness is
skillful in creating this kind of hallucination   **150 reword** repeat word for word

Would gambol° from. Mother, for love of grace,
Lay not that flattering unction° to your soul
That not your trespass but my madness speaks.
It will but skin° and film the ulcerous place,
Whiles rank corruption, mining° all within,   155
Infects unseen. Confess yourself to heaven,
Repent what's past, avoid what is to come,
And do not spread the compost° on the weeds
To make them ranker. Forgive me this my virtue;°
For in the fatness° of these pursy° times   160
Virtue itself of vice must pardon beg,
Yea, curb° and woo for leave° to do him good.

QUEEN: O Hamlet, thou hast cleft my heart in twain.

HAMLET: O, throw away the worser part of it,
And live the purer with the other half.   165
Good night. But go not to my uncle's bed;
Assume a virtue, if you have it not.
That monster, custom, who all sense doth eat,°
Of habits devil,° is angel yet in this,
That to the use of actions fair and good   170
He likewise gives a frock or livery°
That aptly° is put on. Refrain tonight,
And that shall lend a kind of easiness
To the next abstinence; the next more easy;
For use° almost can change the stamp of nature,°   175
And either° . . . the devil, or throw him out
With wondrous potency. Once more, good night;
And when you are desirous to be blest,
I'll blessing beg of you.° For this same lord,

[pointing to POLONIUS.*]*

I do repent; but heaven hath pleased it so   180
To punish me with this, and this with me,

---

151 gambol skip away   **152 unction** ointment   **154 skin** grow a skin for   **155 mining** working under the surface   **158 compost** manure   **159 this my virtue** my virtuous talk in reproving you   **160 fatness** grossness   **pursy** flabby, out of shape   **162 curb** bow, bend the knee   **leave** permission   **168 who . . . eat** which consumes all proper or natural feeling, all sensibility   **169 Of habits devil** devil-like in prompting evil habits   **171 livery** an outer appearance, a customary garb (and hence a predisposition easily assumed in time of stress)   **172 aptly** readily   **175 use** habit   **the stamp of nature** our inborn traits   **176 And either** (A defective line, usually emended by inserting the word *master* after *either,* following the Fourth Quarto and early editors.)   **178–179 when . . . you** i.e., when you are ready to be penitent and seek God's blessing, I will ask your blessing as a dutiful son should

That I must be their scourge and minister.°
I will bestow° him, and will answer° well
The death I gave him. So, again, good night.
I must be cruel only to be kind.   185
This° bad begins, and worse remains behind.°
One word more, good lady.

QUEEN: What shall I do?

HAMLET: Not this by no means that I bid you do:
Let the bloat° King tempt you again to bed,
Pinch wanton° on your cheek, call you his mouse,   190
And let him, for a pair of reechy° kisses,
Or paddling° in your neck with his damned fingers,
Make you to ravel all this matter out°
That I essentially am not in madness,
But mad in craft.° 'Twere good° you let him know,   195
For who that's but a Queen, fair, sober, wise,
Would from a paddock,° from a bat, a gib,°
Such dear concernings° hide? Who would do so?
No, in despite of sense and secrecy,°
Unpeg the basket° on the house's top,   200
Let the birds fly, and like the famous ape,°
To try conclusions,° in the basket creep
And break your own neck down.°

QUEEN: Be thou assured, if words be made of breath,
And breath of life, I have no life to breathe   205
What thou hast said to me.

HAMLET: I must to England. You know that?

QUEEN: Alack,
I had forgot. 'Tis so concluded on.

HAMLET: There's letters sealed, and my two schoolfellows,
Whom I will trust as I will adders fanged,   210

182 their scourge and minister i.e., agent of heavenly retribution (By *scourge,* Hamlet also suggests that he himself will eventually suffer punishment in the process of fulfilling heaven's will.) **183 bestow** stow, dispose of **answer** account or pay for **186 This** i.e., the killing of Polonius **behind** to come **189 bloat** bloated **190 Pinch wanton** i.e., leave his love pinches on your cheeks, branding you as wanton **191 reechy** dirty, filthy **192 paddling** fingering amorously **193 ravel . . . out** unravel, disclose **195 in craft** by cunning **good** (Said sarcastically; also the following eight lines.) **197 paddock** toad **gib** tomcat **198 dear concernings** important affairs **199 sense and secrecy** secrecy that common sense requires **200 Unpeg the basket** open the cage, i.e., let out the secret **201 famous ape** (In a story now lost.) **202 try conclusions** test the outcome (in which the ape apparently enters a cage from which birds have been released and then tries to fly out of the cage as they have done, falling to its death) **203 down** in the fall; utterly

They bear the mandate; they must sweep my way
And marshal me to knavery.° Let it work.°
For 'tis the sport to have the enginer°
Hoist with° his own petard,° and 't shall go hard
But I will° delve one yard below their mines°   215
And blow them at the moon. O, 'tis most sweet
When in one line° two crafts° directly meet.
This man shall set me packing.°
I'll lug the guts into the neighbor room.
Mother, good night indeed. This counselor   220
Is now most still, most secret, and most grave,
Who was in life a foolish prating knave.—
Come, sir, to draw toward an end° with you.—
Good night, Mother.

[Exeunt (separately, HAMLET *dragging in* POLONIUS*).]*

*[***Act 4.1** *Enter* KING *and* QUEEN,° *with* ROSENCRANTZ *and* GUILDENSTERN*.]*°

KING: There's matter° in these sighs, these profound heaves.°
     You must translate; 'tis fit we understand them.
     Where is your son?
QUEEN: Bestow this place on us a little while.

[Exeunt ROSENCRANTZ *and* GUILDENSTERN*.]*

     Ah, mine own lord, what have I seen tonight!   5
KING: What, Gertrude? How does Hamlet?
QUEEN: Mad as the sea and wind when both contend
     Which is the mightier. In his lawless fit,
     Behind the arras hearing something stir,
     Whips out his rapier, cries, "A rat, a rat!"   10

211–212 sweep . . . knavery sweep a path before me and conduct me to some *knavery* or treachery prepared for me   **212 work** proceed   **213 enginer** maker of military contrivances **214 Hoist with** blown up by   **petard** an explosive used to blow in a door or make a breach **214–215 't shall . . . will** unless luck is against me, I will   **215 mines** tunnels used in warfare to undermine the enemy's emplacements; Hamlet will countermine by going under their mines **217 in one line** i.e., mines and countermines on a collision course, or the countermines directly below the mines   **crafts** acts of guile, plots   **218 set me packing** set me to making schemes, and set me to lugging (him), and, also, send me off in a hurry   **223 draw . . . end** finish up (with a pun on *draw,* "pull")   **4.1 s.d Location: The castle**   **s.d. Enter . . . Queen** (Some editors argue that Gertrude never exits in 3.4 and that the scene is continuous here, as suggested in the Folio, but the Second Quarto marks an entrance for her and at line 35 Claudius speaks of Gertrude's *closet* as though it were elsewhere. A short time has elapsed, during which the King has become aware of her highly wrought emotional state.)   **1 matter** significance   **heaves** heavy sighs

And in this brainish apprehension° kills
The unseen good old man.

KING: O heavy° deed!
It had been so with us,° had we been there.
His liberty is full of threats to all—
To you yourself, to us, to everyone.   15
Alas, how shall this bloody deed be answered?°
It will be laid to us, whose providence°
Should have kept short,° restrained, and out of haunt°
This mad young man. But so much was our love,
We would not understand what was most fit,   20
But, like the owner of a foul disease,
To keep it from divulging,° let it feed
Even on the pith of life. Where is he gone?

QUEEN: To draw apart the body he hath killed,
O'er whom his very madness, like some ore°   25
Among a mineral° of metals base,
Shows itself pure: 'a weeps for what is done.

KING: O Gertrude, come away!
The sun no sooner shall the mountains touch
But we will ship him hence, and this vile deed   30
We must with all our majesty and skill
Both countenance° and excuse.—Ho, Guildenstern!

[Enter ROSENCRANTZ *and* GUILDENSTERN.*]*

Friends both, go join you with some further aid.
Hamlet in madness hath Polonius slain,
And from his mother's closet hath he dragged him.   35
Go seek him out, speak fair, and bring the body
Into the chapel. I pray you, haste in this.

[Exeunt ROSENCRANTZ *and* GUILDENSTERN.*]*

Come, Gertrude, we'll call up our wisest friends
And let them know both what we mean to do
And what's untimely done°   40
Whose whisper o'er the world's diameter,°
As level° as the cannon to his blank,°

11 brainish apprehension headstrong conception   **12 heavy** grievous   **13 us** i.e., me (The royal "we"; also in line 15.)   **16 answered** explained   **17 providence** foresight   **18 short** i.e., on a short tether   **out of haunt** secluded   **22 divulging** becoming evident   **25 ore** vein of gold   **26 mineral** mine   **32 countenance** put the best face on   **40 And . . . done** (A defective line; conjectures as to the missing words include *So, haply, slander* [Capell and others]; *For, haply, slander* [Theobald and others]; and *So envious slander* [Jenkins].)   **41 diameter** extent from side to side   **42 As level** with as direct aim   **his blank** its target at point-blank range

Transports his poisoned shot, may miss our name
And hit the woundless° air. O, come away!
My soul is full of discord and dismay.   45

[Exeunt.]

[Act 4.2 Enter HAMLET.*]*°

HAMLET: Safely stowed.

ROSENCRANTZ, GUILDENSTERN [*within*]:   Hamlet! Lord Hamlet!

HAMLET: But soft, what noise? Who calls on Hamlet? O, here they come.

[Enter ROSENCRANTZ *and* GUILDENSTERN.*]*

ROSENCRANTZ: What have you done, my lord, with the dead body?

HAMLET: Compounded it with dust, whereto 'tis kin.   5

ROSENCRANTZ: Tell us where 'tis, that we may take it thence
And bear it to the chapel.

HAMLET: Do not believe it.

ROSENCRANTZ: Believe what?

HAMLET: That I can keep your counsel and not mine own.° Besides, to be   10
demanded of° a sponge, what replication° should be made by the son of
a king?

ROSENCRANTZ: Take you me for a sponge, my lord?

HAMLET: Ay, sir, that soaks up the King's countenance,° his rewards, his
authorities.° But such officers do the King best service in the end. He   15
keeps them, like an ape, an apple, in the corner of his jaw, first mouthed
to be last swallowed. When he needs what you have gleaned, it is but
squeezing you, and, sponge, you shall be dry again.

ROSENCRANTZ: I understand you not, my lord.

HAMLET: I am glad of it. A knavish speech sleeps in° a foolish ear.   20

ROSENCRANTZ: My lord, you must tell us where the body is and go with us to the
King.

HAMLET: The body is with the King, but the King is not with the body.°
The King is a thing—

---

44 woundless invulnerable   **4.2 s.d. Location: The castle**   **10 That . . . own** i.e., that I can
follow your advice (by telling where the body is) and still keep my own secret   **11 demanded
of** questioned by   **replication** reply   **14 countenance** favor   **15 authorities** delegated
power, influence   **20 sleeps in** has no meaning to   **23 The . . . body** (Perhaps alludes to the
legal commonplace of "the king's two bodies," which drew a distinction between the sacred
office of kingship and the particular mortal who possessed it at any given time. Hence, although
Claudius' body is necessarily a part of him, true kingship is not contained in it. Similarly, Claudius
will have Polonius' body when it is found, but there is no kingship in this business either.)

GUILDENSTERN: A thing, my lord?   25

HAMLET: Of nothing.° Bring me to him. Hide fox, and all after!°

[Exeunt (running).]

*[***Act 4.3*** Enter* KING, *and two or three.]*°

KING: I have sent to seek him, and to find the body.

How dangerous is it that this man goes loose!

Yet must not we put the strong law on him.

He's loved of° the distracted° multitude,

Who like not in their judgment, but their eyes,°   5

And where 'tis so, th' offender's scourge° is weighed,°

But never the offense. To bear all smooth and even,°

This sudden sending him away must seem

Deliberate pause.° Diseases desperate grown

By desperate appliance° are relieved,   10

Or not at all.

[Enter ROSENCRANTZ, GUILDENSTERN, *and all the rest.]*

How now, what hath befall'n?

ROSENCRANTZ: Where the dead body is bestowed, my lord,

We cannot get from him.

KING: But where is he?

ROSENCRANTZ: Without, my lord; guarded, to know your pleasure.

KING: Bring him before us.   15

ROSENCRANTZ: Ho! Bring in the lord.

[They enter (with HAMLET).]*

KING: Now, Hamlet, where's Polonius?

HAMLET: At supper.

KING: At supper? Where?

HAMLET: Not where he eats, but where 'a is eaten. A certain convocation of   20
politic worms° are e'en° at him. Your worm° is your only emperor for
diet.° We fat all creatures else to fat us, and we fat ourselves for maggots.
Your fat king and your lean beggar is but variable service°—two dishes,
but to one table. That's the end.

---

26 Of nothing (1) of no account (2) lacking the essence of kingship, as in lines 23–24 and note
Hide . . . after (An old signal cry in the game of hide-and-seek, suggesting that Hamlet now runs
away from them.)   **4.3 s.d. Location: The castle**   **4 of** by   **distracted** fickle, unstable   **5
Who . . . eyes** who choose not by judgment but by appearance   **6 scourge** punishment
(Literally, blow with a whip.)   **weighed** sympathetically considered   **7 To . . . even** to
manage the business in an unprovocative way   **9 Deliberate pause** carefully considered
action   **10 appliance** remedies   **21 politic worms** crafty worms (suited to a master spy like
Polonius)   **e'en** even now   **Your worm** your average worm (Compare *your fat king and your
lean beggar* in line 23.)   **22 diet** food, eating (with a punning reference to the Diet of Worms,
a famous *convocation* held in 1521)   **23 variable service** different courses of a single meal

KING: Alas, alas!   25

HAMLET: A man may fish with the worm that hath eat° of a king, and eat of the
    fish that hath fed of that worm.

KING: What dost thou mean by this?

HAMLET: Nothing but to show you how a king may go a progress° through the
    guts of a beggar.   30

KING: Where is Polonius?

HAMLET: In heaven. Send thither to see. If your messenger find him not there,
    seek him i' th' other place yourself. But if indeed you find him not within
    this month, you shall nose him as you go up the stairs into the lobby.

KING: [to some attendants] Go seek him there.   35

HAMLET: 'A will stay till you come.

[Exeunt attendants.]

KING: Hamlet, this deed, for thine especial safety—
    Which we do tender,° as we dearly° grieve
    For that which thou hast done—must send thee hence
    With fiery quickness. Therefore prepare thyself.   40
    The bark° is ready, and the wind at help,
    Th' associates tend,° and everything is bent°
    For England.

HAMLET: For England!

KING: Ay, Hamlet.   45

HAMLET: Good.

KING: So is it, if thou knew'st our purposes.

HAMLET: I see a cherub° that sees them. But come, for England!
    Farewell, dear mother.

KING: Thy loving father, Hamlet.   50

HAMLET: My mother. Father and mother is man and wife, man and wife is one
    flesh, and so, my mother. Come, for England!

[Exit.]

KING: Follow him at foot;° tempt him with speed aboard.
    Delay it not. I'll have him hence tonight.
    Away! For everything is sealed and done   55
    That else leans on° th' affair. Pray you, make haste.

[Exeunt all but the KING.*]*

26 **eat** eaten (Pronounced et.)   29 **progress** royal journey of state   38 **tender** regard, hold
dear   **dearly** intensely   41 **bark** sailing vessel   42 **tend** wait   **bent** in readiness   48 **cherub**
(Cherubim are angels of knowledge. Hamlet hints that both he and heaven are onto Claudius'
tricks.)   53 **at foot** close behind, at heel   56 **leans on** bears upon, is related to

And, England,° if my love thou hold'st at aught°—
As my great power thereof may give thee sense,°
Since yet thy cicatrice° looks raw and red
After the Danish sword, and thy free awe°   60
Pays homage to us—thou mayst not coldly set°
Our sovereign process,° which imports at full,°
By letters congruing° to that effect,
The present° death of Hamlet. Do it, England,
For like the hectic° in my blood he rages,   65
And thou must cure me. Till I know 'tis done,
Howe'er my haps,° my joys were ne'er begun.

[Exit.]

*[**Act 4.4** Enter* FORTINBRAS *with his army over the stage.]*°

FORTINBRAS: Go, Captain, from me greet the Danish king.
Tell him that by his license° Fortinbras
Craves the conveyance of° a promised march
Over his kingdom. You know the rendezvous.
If that His Majesty would aught with us,   5
We shall express our duty° in his eye;°
And let him know so.
CAPTAIN: I will do 't, my lord.
FORTINBRAS: Go softly° on.

[Exeunt all but the CAPTAIN.*]*

[Enter HAMLET, ROSENCRANTZ, *(*GUILDENSTERN,*) etc.]*

HAMLET: Good sir, whose powers° are these?   10
CAPTAIN: They are of Norway, sir.
HAMLET: How purposed, sir, I pray you?
CAPTAIN: Against some part of Poland.
HAMLET: Who commands them, sir?
CAPTAIN: The nephew to old Norway, Fortinbras.   15
HAMLET: Goes it against the main° of Poland, sir,
Or for some frontier?

57 England i.e., King of England   **at aught** at any value   **58 As . . . sense** for so my great power may give you a just appreciation of the importance of valuing my love   **59 cicatrice** scar **60 free awe** voluntary show of respect   **61 coldly set** regard with indifference **62 process** command   **imports at full** conveys specific directions for   **63 congruing** agreeing   **64 present** immediate   **65 hectic** persistent fever   **67 haps** fortunes   **4.4 s.d. Location: The coast of Denmark   2 license** permission   **3 the conveyance of** escort during   **6 duty** respect   **eye** presence   **9 softly** slowly, circumspectly   **10 powers** forces **16 main** main part

CAPTAIN: Truly to speak, and with no addition,°
    We go to gain a little patch of ground
    That hath in it no profit but the name.   20
    To pay° five ducats, five, I would not farm it;°
    Nor will it yield to Norway or the Pole
    A ranker° rate, should it be sold in fee.°
HAMLET: Why, then the Polack never will defend it.
CAPTAIN: Yes, it is already garrisoned.   25
HAMLET: Two thousand souls and twenty thousand ducats
    Will not debate° the question of this straw.°
    This is th' impostume° of much wealth and peace,
    That inward breaks, and shows no cause without
    Why the man dies. I humbly thank you, sir.   30
CAPTAIN: God b' wi' you, sir.

[Exit.]

ROSENCRANTZ: Will 't please you go, my lord?
HAMLET: I'll be with you straight. Go a little before.

                                  [Exeunt all except HAMLET.*]*

    How all occasions do inform against° me
    And spur my dull revenge! What is a man,
    If his chief good and market of° his time   35
    Be but to sleep and feed? A beast, no more.
    Sure he that made us with such large discourse,°
    Looking before and after,° gave us not
    That capability and godlike reason
    To fust° in us unused. Now, whether it be   40
    Bestial oblivion,° or some craven° scruple
    Of thinking too precisely° on th' event°—
    A thought which, quartered, hath but one part wisdom
    And ever three parts coward—I do not know
    Why yet I live to say "This thing's to do,"   45
    Sith° I have cause, and will, and strength, and means
    To do 't. Examples gross° as earth exhort me:
    Witness this army of such mass and charge,°
    Led by a delicate and tender° prince,

---

18 addition exaggeration   **21 To pay** i.e., for a yearly rental of   **farm it** take a lease of it   **23 ranker** higher   **in fee** fee simple, outright   **27 debate . . . straw** settle this trifling matter   **28 impostume** abscess   **33 inform against** denounce, betray; take shape against   **35 market of** profit of, compensation for   **37 discourse** power of reasoning   **38 Looking before and after** able to review past events and anticipate the future   **40 fust** grow moldy   **41 oblivion** forgetfulness   **craven** cowardly   **42 precisely** scrupulously   **event** outcome   **46 Sith** since   **47 gross** obvious   **48 charge** expense   **49 delicate and tender** of fine and youthful qualities

Whose spirit with divine ambition puffed   50
Makes mouths° at the invisible event,°
Exposing what is mortal and unsure
To all that fortune, death, and danger dare,°
Even for an eggshell. Rightly to be great
Is not to stir without great argument,   55
But greatly to find quarrel in a straw
When honor's at the stake.° How stand I, then,
That have a father killed, a mother stained,
Excitements of° my reason and my blood,
And let all sleep, while to my shame I see   60
The imminent death of twenty thousand men
That for a fantasy° and trick° of fame
Go to their graves like beds, fight for a plot°
Whereon the numbers cannot try the cause,°
Which is not tomb enough and continent°   65
To hide the slain? O, from this time forth
My thoughts be bloody or be nothing worth!

[Exit.]

*[*Act 4.5 *Enter* HORATIO, *(*QUEEN*)* GERTRUDE, *and a* GENTLEMAN.*]°*

QUEEN: I will not speak with her.
GENTLEMAN: She is importunate,
     Indeed distract.° Her mood will needs be pitied.
QUEEN: What would she have?
GENTLEMAN: She speaks much of her father, says she hears
     There's tricks° i' the world, and hems,° and beats her heart,°   5
     Spurns enviously at straws,° speaks things in doubt°
     That carry but half sense. Her speech is nothing,
     Yet the unshapèd use° of it doth move
     The hearers to collection;° they yawn° at it,
     And botch° the words up fit to their own thoughts,   10

---

51 Makes mouths makes scornful faces   **invisible event** unforeseeable outcome   **53 dare**
could do (to him)   **54–57 Rightly . . . stake** true greatness does not normally consist of rushing into action over some trivial provocation; however, when one's honor is involved, even a trifling insult requires that one respond greatly   **57 at the stake** (A metaphor from gambling or
bear-baiting.)   **59 Excitements of** promptings by   **62 fantasy** fanciful caprice, illusion
trick trifle, deceit   **63 plot** plot of ground   **64 Whereon . . . cause** on which there is insufficient room for the soldiers needed to engage in a military contest   **65 continent** receptacle;
container   **4.5 s.d. Location: The castle**   **2 distract** distracted   **5 tricks** deceptions
hems makes "hmm" sounds   **heart** i.e., breast   **6 Spurns . . . straws** kicks spitefully, takes
offense at trifles   **in doubt** obscurely   **8 unshapèd use** incoherent manner   **9 collection**
inference, a guess at some sort of meaning   **yawn** gape, wonder; grasp (The Folio reading, *aim*,
is possible.)   **10 botch** patch

Which,° as her winks and nods and gestures yield° them,
Indeed would make one think there might be thought,°
Though nothing sure, yet much unhappily.°

HORATIO: 'Twere good she were spoken with, for she may strew
    Dangerous conjectures in ill-breeding° minds.   15

QUEEN: Let her come in.   *[Exit* Gentleman.*]*
    [Aside.] To my sick soul, as sin's true nature is,
    Each toy° seems prologue to some great amiss.°
    So full of artless jealousy is guilt,
    It spills itself in fearing to be spilt.°   20

[Enter OPHELIA° *(distracted).]*

OPHELIA: Where is the beauteous majesty of Denmark?

QUEEN: How now, Ophelia?

OPHELIA *[she sings]:*
    "How should I your true love know
        From another one?
    By his cockle hat° and staff,   25
        And his sandal shoon."°

QUEEN: Alas, sweet lady, what imports this song?

OPHELIA: Say you? Nay, pray you, mark.
    "He is dead and gone, lady,   *[Song.]*
        He is dead and gone;   30
    At his head a grass-green turf,
        At his heels a stone."
    O, ho!

QUEEN: Nay, but Ophelia—

OPHELIA: Pray you, mark.   *[Sings.]*   35
    "White his shroud as the mountain snow"—

[Enter KING.*]*

QUEEN: Alas, look here, my lord.

OPHELIA: "Larded° with sweet flowers;   *[Song.]*
    Which bewept to the ground did not go
        With true-love showers."°   40

KING: How do you, pretty lady?

11 Which which words   **yield** deliver, represent   **12 thought** intended   **13 unhappily**
unpleasantly near the truth, shrewdly   **15 ill-breeding** prone to suspect the worst and to make
mischief   **18 toy** trifle   **amiss** calamity   **19–20 So . . . split** guilt is so full of suspicion that
it unskillfully betrays itself in fearing betrayal   **s.d. Enter Ophelia** (In the First Quarto, Ophelia
enters, "playing on a lute, and her hair down, singing.")   **25 cockle hat** hat with cockle-shell
stuck in it as a sign that the wearer had been a pilgrim to the shrine of Saint James of Compostela
in Spain   **26 shoon** shoes   **38 Larded** decorated   **40 showers** i.e., tears

OPHELIA: Well, God 'ild° you! They say the owl° was a baker's daughter. Lord, we know what we are, but know not what we may be. God be at your table!

KING: Conceit° upon her father.   45

OPHELIA: Pray let's have no words of this; but when they ask you what it means, say you this:

    "Tomorrow is Saint Valentine's day,   [*Song.*]
       All in the morning betime,°
    And I a maid at your window,   50
       To be your Valentine.
    Then up he rose, and donned his clothes,
       And dupped° the chamber door,
    Let in the maid, that out a maid
       Never departed more."   55

KING: Pretty Ophelia—

OPHELIA: Indeed, la, without an oath, I'll make an end on 't: [*Sings.*]
    "By Gis° and by Saint Charity,
       Alack, and fie for shame!
    Young men will do 't, if they come to 't;   60
       By Cock,° they are to blame.
    Quoth she, 'Before you tumbled me,
       You promised me to wed.' "
  He answers:
    " 'So would I ha' done, by yonder sun,   65
       An° thou hadst not come to my bed.' "

KING: How long hath she been thus?

OPHELIA: I hope all will be well. We must be patient, but I cannot choose but weep to think they would lay him i' the cold ground. My brother shall know of it. And so I thank you for your good counsel. Come, my coach!   70
Good night, ladies, good night, sweet ladies, good night, good night.

[Exit.]

KING [*to* HORATIO]:   Follow her close. Give her good watch, I pray you.
                                      [Exit HORATIO.*]*

  O, this is the poison of deep grief; it springs
  All from her father's death—and now behold!
  O Gertrude, Gertrude,   75
  When sorrows come, they come not single spies,°

---

42 God 'ild God yield or reward   **owl** (Refers to a legend about a baker's daughter who was turned into an owl for being ungenerous when Jesus begged a loaf of bread.)   **45 Conceit** brooding   **49 betime** early   **53 dupped** did up, opened   **58 Gis** Jesus   **61 Cock** (A perversion of "God" in oaths; here also with a quibble on the slang word for penis.)   **66 An** if **76 spies** scouts sent in advance of the main force

But in battalions. First, her father slain;
Next, your son gone, and he most violent author
Of his own just remove;° the people muddied,°
Thick and unwholesome in their thoughts and whispers   80
For good Polonius' death—and we have done but greenly,°
In hugger-mugger° to inter him; poor Ophelia
Divided from herself and her fair judgment,
Without the which we are pictures or mere beasts;
Last, and as much containing° as all these,   85
Her brother is in secret come from France,
Feeds on this wonder, keeps himself in clouds,°
And wants° not buzzers° to infect his ear
With pestilent speeches of his father's death,
Wherein necessity,° of matter beggared,°   90
Will nothing stick our person to arraign
In ear and ear.° O my dear Gertrude, this,
Like to a murdering piece,° in many places
Gives me superfluous death.°   *[A noise within.]*

QUEEN: Alack, what noise is this?   95

KING: Attend!°

Where is my Switzers?° Let them guard the door.

[Enter MESSENGER.*]*

What is the matter?

MESSENGER: Save yourself, my lord!
The ocean, overpeering of his list,°
Eats not the flats° with more impetuous° haste   100
Than young Laertes, in a riotous head,°
O'erbears your officers. The rabble call him lord,
And, as° the world were now but to begin,
Antiquity forgot, custom not known,
The ratifiers and props of every word,°   105

---

79 remove removal   **muddied** stirred up, confused   **81 greenly** in an inexperienced way,
foolishly   **82 hugger-mugger** secret haste   **85 as much containing** as full of serious matter
87 Feeds . . . clouds feeds his resentment or shocked grievance, holds himself inscrutable and
aloof amid all this rumor   **88 wants** lacks   **buzzers** gossipers, informers   **90 necessity** i.e.,
the need to invent some plausible explanation   **of matter beggared** unprovided with facts
91–92 Will . . . ear will not hesitate to accuse my (royal) person in everybody's ears   **93
murdering piece** cannon loaded so as to scatter its shot   **94 Gives . . . death** kills me over and
over   **96 Attend** i.e., guard me   **97 Switzers** Swiss guards, mercenaries   **99 overpeering of
his list** overflowing its shore, boundary   **100 flats** i.e., flatlands near shore   **impetuous** violent (perhaps also with the meaning of *impiteous* [*impitious,* Q2], "pitiless.")   **101 head** insur-
rection   **103 as** as if   **105 The ratifiers . . . word** i.e., *antiquity* (or tradition) and *custom*
ought to confirm (*ratify*) and underprop our every word or promise

They cry, "Choose we! Laertes shall be king!"
Caps,° hands, and tongues applaud it to the clouds,
"Laertes shall be king, Laertes king!"

QUEEN: How cheerfully on the false trail they cry!   *[A noise within.]*
O, this is counter,° you false Danish dogs!   110

[Enter LAERTES *with others.]*

KING: The doors are broke.

LAERTES: Where is this King?—Sirs, stand you all without.

ALL: No, let's come in.

LAERTES: I pray you, give me leave.

ALL: We will, we will.   115

LAERTES: I thank you. Keep the door. [*Exeunt followers.*] O thou vile king,
Give me my father!

QUEEN [*restraining him*]:   Calmly, good Laertes.

LAERTES: That drop of blood that's calm proclaims me bastard,
Cries cuckold to my father, brands the harlot   120
Even here, between° the chaste unsmirchèd brow
Of my true mother.

KING: What is the cause, Laertes,
That thy rebellion looks so giantlike?
Let him go, Gertrude. Do not fear our° person.
There's such divinity doth hedge° a king   125
That treason can but peep to what it would,°
Acts little of his will.° Tell me, Laertes,
Why thou art thus incensed. Let him go, Gertrude.
Speak, man.

LAERTES: Where is my father?

KING: Dead.

QUEEN: But not by him.

KING: Let him demand his fill.   130

LAERTES: How came he dead? I'll not be juggled with.°
To hell, allegiance! Vows, to the blackest devil!
Conscience and grace, to the profoundest pit!
I dare damnation. To this point I stand,°
That both the worlds I give to negligence,°   135

---

107 Caps (The caps are thrown in the air.)   **110 counter** (A hunting term, meaning to follow the
trail in a direction opposite to that which the game has taken.)   **121 between** in the middle of
124 fear our fear for my   **125 hedge** protect, as with a surrounding barrier   **126 can . . . would**
can only peep furtively, as through a barrier, at what it would intend   **127 Acts . . . will** (but)
performs little of what it intends   **131 juggled with** cheated, deceived   **134 To . . . stand** I am
resolved in this   **135 both . . . negligence** i.e., both this world and the next are of no consequence to me

Let come what comes, only I'll be revenged
Most throughly° for my father.

KING: Who shall stay you?

LAERTES: My will, not all the world's.°

And for° my means, I'll husband them so well   140
They shall go far with little.

KING: Good Laertes,
If you desire to know the certainty
Of your dear father, is 't writ in your revenge
That, swoopstake,° you will draw both friend and foe,
Winner and loser?   145

LAERTES: None but his enemies.

KING: Will you know them, then?

LAERTES: To his good friends thus wide I'll ope my arms,
And like the kind life-rendering pelican°
Repast° them with my blood.

KING: Why, now you speak   150
Like a good child and a true gentleman.
That I am guiltless of your father's death,
And am most sensibly° in grief for it,
It shall as level° to your judgment 'pear
As day does to your eye.   [A noise within.]   155

LAERTES: How now, what noise is that?

[Enter OPHELIA.]

KING: Let her come in.

LAERTES: O heat, dry up my brains! Tears seven times salt
Burn out the sense and virtue° of mine eye!
By heaven, thy madness shall be paid with weight°
Till our scale turn the beam.° O rose of May!   160
Dear maid, kind sister, sweet Ophelia!
O heavens, is 't possible a young maid's wits
Should be as mortal as an old man's life?
Nature is fine in° love, and where 'tis fine
It sends some precious instance° of itself   165
After the thing it loves.°

---

137 **throughly** thoroughly   139 **My will . . . world's** I'll stop (stay) when my will is accomplished, not for anyone else's   140 **for** as for   144 **swoopstake** i.e., indiscriminately (Literally, taking all stakes on the gambling table at once. *Draw* is also a gambling term, meaning "take from.")   149 **pelican** (Refers to the belief that the female pelican fed its young with its own blood.)   150 **Repast** feed   153 **sensibly** feelingly   154 **level** plain   158 **virtue** faculty, power   159 **paid with weight** repaid, avenged equally or more   160 **beam** crossbar of a balance   164 **fine in** refined by   165 **instance** token   166 **After . . . loves** i.e., into the grave, along with Polonius

OPHELIA: *[Song.]*

     "They bore him barefaced on the bier,

        Hey non nonny, nonny, hey nonny,

           And in his grave rained many a tear—"

    Fare you well, my dove!   170

LAERTES: Hadst thou thy wits and didst persuade° revenge,

    It could not move thus.

OPHELIA: You must sing "A-down a-down," and you "call him a-down-a."° O, how

    the wheel° becomes it! It is the false steward° that stole his master's

    daughter.   175

LAERTES: This nothing's more than matter.°

OPHELIA: There's rosemary,° that's for remembrance; pray you, love, remember.

    And there is pansies;° that's for thoughts.

LAERTES: A document° in madness, thoughts and remembrance fitted.

OPHELIA: There's fennel° for you, and columbines.° There's rue° for you,   180

    and here's some for me; we may call it herb of grace o' Sundays. You

    must wear your rue with a difference.° There's a daisy.°

    I would give you some violets,° but they withered all when my father

    died. They say 'a made a good end—

    [Sings.] "For bonny sweet Robin is all my joy."   185

LAERTES: Thought° and affliction, passion,° hell itself,

    She turns to favor° and to prettiness.

OPHELIA: *[Song.]*

    "And will 'a not come again?

    And will 'a not come again?

       No, no, he is dead.   190

       Go to thy deathbed,

    He never will come again.

    "His beard was as white as snow,

    All flaxen was his poll.°

171 persuade argue cogently for   **173 You . . . a-down-a** (Ophelia assigns the singing of refrains, like her own "Hey non nonny," to others present.)   **174 wheel** spinning wheel as accompaniment to the song, or refrain   **false steward** (The story is unknown.)   **176 This , , , matter** this seeming nonsense is more eloquent than sane utterance   **177 rosemary** (Used as a symbol of remembrance both at weddings and at funerals.)   **178 pansies** (Emblems of love and courtship; perhaps from French *pensées*, "thoughts.")   **179 document** instruction, lesson   **180 fennel** (Emblem of flattery.)   **columbines** (Emblems of unchastity or ingratitude.)   **rue** (Emblem of repentance—a signification that is evident in its popular name, *herb of grace.*)   **182 with a difference** (A device used in heraldry to distinguish one family from another on the coat of arms, here suggesting that Ophelia and the others have different causes of sorrow and repentance; perhaps with a play on rue in the sense of "ruth," "pity.")   **daisy** (Emblem of dissembling, faithlessness.)   **183 violets** (Emblems of faithfulness.)   **186 Thought** melancholy **passion** suffering   **187 favor** grace, beauty   **194 poll** head

He is gone, he is gone,   195
  And we cast away moan.
God ha' mercy on his soul!"
And of all Christian souls, I pray God. God b' wi' you.

[Exit, followed by GERTRUDE.]

LAERTES: Do you see this, O God?

KING: Laertes, I must commune with your grief,   200
Or you deny me right. Go but apart,
Make choice of whom° your wisest friends you will,
And they shall hear and judge twixt you and me.
If by direct or by collateral hand°
They find us touched,° we will our kingdom give,   205
Our crown, our life, and all that we call ours
To you in satisfaction; but if not,
Be you content to lend your patience to us,
And we shall jointly labor with your soul
To give it due content.

LAERTES: Let this be so.   210
His means of death, his obscure funeral—
No trophy,° sword, nor hatchment° o'er his bones,
No noble rite, nor formal ostentation°—
Cry to be heard, as 'twere from heaven to earth,
That° I must call 't in question.°

KING: So you shall,   215
And where th' offense is, let the great ax fall.
I pray you, go with me.

[Exeunt.]

*[**Act 4.6** Enter* HORATIO *and others.]*°

HORATIO: What are they that would speak with me?

GENTLEMAN: Seafaring men, sir. They say they have letters for you.

HORATIO: Let them come in.

            [Exit Gentleman.]

I do not know from what part of the world
I should be greeted, if not from Lord Hamlet.   5

[Enter SAILORS.]

---

202 whom whichever of **204 collateral hand** indirect agency **205 us touched** me implicated **212 trophy** memorial **hatchment** tablet displaying the armorial bearings of a
deceased person **213 ostentation** ceremony **215 That** so that **call 't in question** demand
an explanation **4.6 s.d. Location: The castle**

FIRST SAILOR: God bless you, sir.

HORATIO: Let him bless thee too.

FIRST SAILOR: 'A shall, sir, an 't° please him. There's a letter for you, sir—it came
from th' ambassador° that was bound for England—if your name be
Horatio, as I am let to know it is.   [*He gives a letter.*]   10

HORATIO [*reads*]:   "Horatio, when thou shalt have overlooked° this, give these
fellows some means° to the King; they have letters for him. Ere we were
two days old at sea, a pirate of very warlike appointment° gave us chase.
Finding ourselves too slow of sail, we put on a compelled valor, and in the
grapple I boarded them. On the instant they got clear of our ship, so I   15
alone became their prisoner. They have dealt with me like thieves of
mercy,° but they knew what they did: I am to do a good turn for them. Let
the King have the letters I have sent, and repair° thou to me with as
much speed as thou wouldest fly death. I have words to speak in thine ear
will make thee dumb, yet are they much too light for the bore° of the   20
matter. These good fellows will bring thee where I am. Rosencrantz and
Guildenstern hold their course for England. Of them I have much to tell
thee. Farewell.

He that thou knowest thine, Hamlet."

Come, I will give you way° for these your letters,
And do 't the speedier that you may direct me   25
To him from whom you brought them.

[*Exeunt.*]

[**Act 4.7** *Enter* KING *and* LAERTES.]°

KING: Now must your conscience my acquittance seal,°
And you must put me in your heart for friend,
Sith° you have heard, and with a knowing ear,
That he which hath your noble father slain
Pursued my life.

LAERTES: It well appears. But tell me   5
Why you proceeded not against these feats°
So crimeful and so capital° in nature,
As by your safety, greatness, wisdom, all things else,
You mainly° were stirred up.

---

8 an 't if it   **9 th' ambassador** (Evidently Hamlet. The sailor is being circumspect.)   **11
overlooked** looked over   **12 means** means of access   **13 appointment** equipage   **15–17
thieves of mercy** merciful thieves   **18 repair** come   **20 bore** caliber, i.e., importance   **24 way**
means of access   **4.7** s.d. **Location: The castle   1 my acquittance seal** confirm or acknowledge
my innocence   **3 Sith** since   **6 feats** acts   **7 capital** punishable by death   **9 mainly** greatly

KING: O, for two special reasons,
      Which may to you perhaps seem much unsinewed,°
      But yet to me they're strong. The Queen his mother
      Lives almost by his looks, and for myself—
      My virtue or my plague, be it either which—
      She is so conjunctive° to my life and soul   15
      That, as the star moves not but in his° sphere,°
      I could not but by her. The other motive
      Why to a public count° I might not go
      Is the great love the general gender° bear him,
      Who, dipping all his faults in their affection,   20
      Work° like the spring° that turneth wood to stone,
      Convert his gyves° to graces, so that my arrows,
      Too slightly timbered° for so loud° a wind,
      Would have reverted° to my bow again
      But not where I had aimed them.   25
LAERTES: And so have I a noble father lost,
      A sister driven into desperate terms,°
      Whose worth, if praises may go back° again,
      Stood challenger on mount° of all the age
      For her perfections. But my revenge will come.   30
KING: Break not your sleeps for that. You must not think
      That we are made of stuff so flat and dull
      That we can let our beard be shook with danger
      And think it pastime. You shortly shall hear more.
      I loved your father, and we love ourself;   35
      And that, I hope, will teach you to imagine—

[Enter MESSENGER *with letters.]*

      How now? What news?
MESSENGER: Letters, my lord, from Hamlet:
      This to Your Majesty, this to the Queen.

[He gives letters.]

---

11 unsinewed weak   **15 conjunctive** closely united (An astronomical metaphor.)   **16 his**
its   **sphere** one of the hollow spheres in which, according to Ptolemaic astronomy, the planets were supposed to move   **18 count** account, reckoning, indictment   **19 general gender**
common people   **21 Work** operate, act   **spring** i.e., a spring with such a concentration of lime
that it coats a piece of wood with limestone, in effect gilding and petrifying it   **22 gyves** fetters
(which, gilded by the people's praise, would look like badges of honor)   **23 slightly timbered**
light   **loud** (suggesting public outcry on Hamlet's behalf)   **24 reverted** returned   **27 terms**
state, condition   **28 go back** i.e., recall what she was   **29 on mount** set up on high

KING: From Hamlet? Who brought them?   40

MESSENGER: Sailors, my lord, they say. I saw them not.

They were given me by Claudio. He received them

Of him that brought them.

KING: Laertes, you shall hear them.—

Leave us.

[Exit MESSENGER.*]*

[*He reads.*] "High and mighty, you shall know I am set naked° on your   45

kingdom. Tomorrow shall I beg leave to see your kingly eyes, when I

shall, first asking your pardon,° thereunto recount the occasion of my

sudden and more strange return.   Hamlet."

What should this mean? Are all the rest come back?

Or is it some abuse,° and no such thing?°   50

LAERTES: Know you the hand?

KING: 'Tis Hamlet's character.° "Naked!"

And in a postscript here he says "alone."

Can you devise° me?

LAERTES: I am lost in it, my lord. But let him come.

It warms the very sickness in my heart   55

That I shall live and tell him to his teeth,

"Thus didst thou."°

KING: If it be so, Laertes—

As how should it be so? How otherwise?°—

Will you be ruled by me?

LAERTES: Ay, my lord,

So° you will not o'errule me to a peace.   60

KING: To thine own peace. If he be now returned,

As checking at° his voyage, and that° he means

No more to undertake it, I will work him

To an exploit, now ripe in my device,°

Under the which he shall not choose but fall;   65

And for his death no wind of blame shall breathe,

But even his mother shall uncharge the practice°

And call it accident.

LAERTES: My lord, I will be ruled,

---

45 naked destitute, unarmed, without following   **47 pardon** permission   **50 abuse** deceit   **no such thing** not what it appears   **51 character** handwriting   **53 devise** explain to   **57 Thus didst thou** i.e., here's for what you did to my father   **58 As . . . otherwise** how can this (Hamlet's return) be true? Yet how otherwise than true (since we have the evidence of his letter)?   **60 So** provided that   **62 checking at** i.e., turning aside from (like a falcon leaving the quarry to fly at a chance bird)   **that** if   **64 device** devising, invention   **67 uncharge the practice** acquit the stratagem of being a plot

The rather if you could devise it so
That I might be the organ.°

KING: It falls right.   70
You have been talked of since your travel much,
And that in Hamlet's hearing, for a quality
Wherein they say you shine. Your sum of parts°
Did not together pluck such envy from him
As did that one, and that, in my regard,   75
Of the unworthiest siege.°

LAERTES: What part is that, my lord?

KING: A very ribbon in the cap of youth,
Yet needful too, for youth no less becomes°
The light and careless livery that it wears   80
Than settled age his sables° and his weeds°
Importing health and graveness.° Two months since
Here was a gentleman of Normandy.
I have seen myself, and served against, the French,
And they can well° on horseback, but this gallant   85
Had witchcraft in 't; he grew unto his seat,
And to such wondrous doing brought his horse
As had he been incorpsed and demi-natured°
With the brave beast. So far he topped° my thought
That I in forgery° of shapes and tricks   90
Come short of what he did.

LAERTES: A Norman was 't?

KING: A Norman.

LAERTES: Upon my life, Lamord.

KING: The very same.

LAERTES: I know him well. He is the brooch° indeed
And gem of all the nation.   95

KING: He made confession° of you,
And gave you such a masterly report
For art and exercise in your defense,°
And for your rapier most especial,

---

70 **organ** agent, instrument   73 **Your . . . parts** i.e., all your other virtues   76 **unworthiest siege** least important rank   79 **no less becomes** is no less suited by   81 **his sables** its rich robes furred with sable   **weeds** garments   82 **Importing . . . graveness** signifying a concern for health and dignified prosperity; also, giving an impression of comfortable prosperity   85 **can well** are skilled   88 **As . . . demi-natured** as if he had been of one body and nearly of one nature (like the centaur)   89 **topped** surpassed   90 **forgery** imagining   94 **brooch** ornament   96 **confession** testimonial, admission of superiority   98 **For . . . defense** with respect to your skill and practice with your weapon

That he cried out 'twould be a sight indeed   100
If one could match you. Th' escrimers° of their nation,
He swore, had neither motion, guard, nor eye
If you opposed them. Sir, this report of his
Did Hamlet so envenom with his envy
That he could nothing do but wish and beg   105
Your sudden° coming o'er, to play° with you.
Now, out of this—

LAERTES: What out of this, my lord?

KING: Laertes, was your father dear to you?
Or are you like the painting of a sorrow,
A face without a heart?

LAERTES: Why ask you this?   110

KING: Not that I think you did not love your father,
But that I know love is begun by time,°
And that I see, in passages of proof,°
Time qualifies° the spark and fire of it.
There lives within the very flame of love   115
A kind of wick or snuff° that will abate it,
And nothing is at a like goodness still,°
For goodness, growing to a pleurisy,°
Dies in his own too much.° That° we would do,
We should do when we would; for this "would" changes   120
And hath abatements° and delays as many
As there are tongues, are hands, are accidents,°
And then this "should" is like a spendthrift sigh,°
That hurts by easing.° But, to the quick o' th' ulcer:°
Hamlet comes back. What would you undertake   125
To show yourself in deed your father's son
More than in words?

LAERTES: To cut his throat i' the church.

---

101 escrimers fencers   **106 sudden** immediate   **play** fence   **112 begun by time** i.e., created by the right circumstance and hence subject to change   **113 passages of proof** actual instances that prove it   **114 qualifies** weakens, moderates   **116 snuff** the charred part of a candlewick   **117 nothing . . . still** nothing remains at a constant level of perfection   **118 pleurisy** excess, plethora (Literally, a chest inflammation.)   **119 in . . . much** of its own excess   **That** that which   **121 abatements** diminutions   **122 As . . . accidents** as there are tongues to dissuade, hands to prevent, and chance events to intervene   **123 spendthrift sigh** (An allusion to the belief that sighs draw blood from the heart.)   **124 hurts by easing** i.e., costs the heart blood and wastes precious opportunity even while it affords emotional relief   **quick o' th' ulcer** i.e., heart of the matter

KING: No place, indeed, should murder sanctuarize;°
    Revenge should have no bounds. But good Laertes,
    Will you do this,° keep close within your chamber.   130
    Hamlet returned shall know you are come home.
    We'll put on those shall° praise your excellence
    And set a double varnish on the fame
    The Frenchman gave you, bring you in fine° together,
    And wager on your heads. He, being remiss,°   135
    Most generous,° and free from all contriving,
    Will not peruse the foils, so that with ease,
    Or with a little shuffling, you may choose
    A sword unbated,° and in a pass of practice°
    Requite him for your father.

LAERTES: I will do 't,   140
    And for that purpose I'll anoint my sword.
    I bought an unction° of a mountebank°
    So mortal that, but dip a knife in it,
    Where it draws blood no cataplasm° so rare,
    Collected from all simples° that have virtue°   145
    Under the moon,° can save the thing from death
    That is but scratched withal. I'll touch my point
    With this contagion, that if I gall° him slightly,
    It may be death.

KING: Let's further think of this,
    Weigh what convenience both of time and means   150
    May fit us to our shape.° If this should fail,
    And that our drift look through our bad performance,°
    'Twere better not assayed. Therefore this project
    Should have a back or second, that might hold
    If this did blast in proof.° Soft, let me see.   155
    We'll make a solemn wager on your cunnings°—
    I ha 't!

---

128 sanctuarize protect from punishment (Alludes to the right of sanctuary with which certain religious places were invested.)   **130 Will you do this** if you wish to do this   **132 put on those shall** arrange for some to   **134 in fine** finally   **135 remiss** negligently unsuspicious **136 generous** noble-minded   **139 unbated** not blunted having no button   **pass of practice** treacherous thrust   **142 unction** ointment   **mountebank** quack doctor   **144 cataplasm** plaster or poultice   **145 simples** herbs   **virtue** potency   **146 Under the moon** i.e., anywhere (with reference perhaps to the belief that herbs gathered at night had a special power)   **148 gall** graze, wound   **151 shape** part we propose to act   **152 drift . . . performance** intention should be made visible by our bungling   **155 blast in proof** burst in the test (like a cannon) **156 cunnings** respective skills

When in your motion you are hot and dry—
As° make your bouts more violent to that end—
And that he calls for drink, I'll have prepared him   160
A chalice for the nonce,° whereon but sipping,
If he by chance escape your venomed stuck,°
Our purpose may hold there. [*A cry within.*] But stay, what noise?

[*Enter* QUEEN.]

QUEEN: One woe doth tread upon another's heel,
So fast they follow. Your sister's drowned, Laertes.   165

LAERTES: Drowned! O, where?

QUEEN: There is a willow grows askant° the brook,
That shows his hoar leaves° in the glassy stream;
Therewith fantastic garlands did she make
Of crowflowers, nettles, daisies, and long purples,°   170
That liberal° shepherds give a grosser name,°
But our cold° maids do dead men's fingers call them.
There on the pendent° boughs her crownet° weeds
Clamb'ring to hang, an envious sliver° broke,
When down her weedy° trophies and herself   175
Fell in the weeping brook. Her clothes spread wide,
And mermaidlike awhile they bore her up,
Which time she chanted snatches of old lauds,°
As one incapable of° her own distress,
Or like a creature native and endued°   180
Unto that element. But long it could not be
Till that her garments, heavy with their drink,
Pulled the poor wretch from her melodious lay
To muddy death.

LAERTES: Alas, then she is drowned?

QUEEN: Drowned, drowned.   185

LAERTES: Too much of water hast thou, poor Ophelia,
And therefore I forbid my tears. But yet
It is our trick;° nature her custom holds,
Let shame say what it will. [*He weeps.*] When these are gone,

---

159 As i.e., and you should   **161 nonce** occasion   **162 stuck** thrust (From *stoccado*, a fencing term.)   **167 askant** aslant   **168 hoar leaves** white or gray undersides of the leaves   **170 long purples** early purple orchids   **171 liberal** free-spoken   **a grosser name** (The testicleresembling tubers of the orchid, which also in some cases resemble *dead men's fingers,* have earned various slang names like "dogstones" and "cullions.")   **172 cold** chaste   **173 pendent** over-hanging   **crownet** made into a chaplet or coronet   **174 envious sliver** malicious branch   **175 weedy** i.e., of plants   **178 lauds** hymns   **179 incapable of** lacking capacity to apprehend   **180 endued** adapted by nature   **188 It is our trick** i.e., weeping is our natural way (when sad)

The woman will be out.° Adieu, my lord.   190
I have a speech of fire that fain would blaze,
But that this folly douts° it.   [*Exit.*]
KING: Let's follow, Gertrude.
How much I had to do to calm his rage!
Now fear I this will give it start again;
Therefore let's follow.   195

[Exeunt.]

[Act 5.1 *Enter two* CLOWNS° *(with spades and mattocks).]°*

FIRST CLOWN: Is she to be buried in Christian burial, when she willfully seeks
her own salvation?°
SECOND CLOWN: I tell thee she is; therefore make her grave straight.° The
crowner° hath sat on her,° and finds it° Christian burial.
FIRST CLOWN: How can that be, unless she drowned herself in her own defense?   5
SECOND CLOWN: Why, 'tis found so.°
FIRST CLOWN: It must be *se offendendo,*° it cannot be else. For here lies the
point: if I drown myself wittingly, it argues an act, and an act hath three
branches—it is to act, to do, and to perform. Argal,° she drowned herself
wittingly.   10
SECOND CLOWN: Nay, but hear you, goodman° delver—
FIRST CLOWN: Give me leave. Here lies the water; good. Here stands the man;
good. If the man go to this water and drown himself, it is, will he, nill he,°
he goes, mark you that. But if the water come to him and drown him, he
drowns not himself. Argal, he that is not guilty of his own death shortens   15
not his own life.
SECOND CLOWN: But is this law?
FIRST CLOWN: Ay, marry, is 't—crowner's quest° law.
SECOND CLOWN: Will you ha' the truth on 't? If this had not been a gentle-
woman, she should have been buried out o' Christian burial.   20

189–190 When . . . out when my tears are all shed, the woman in me will be expended, satisfied   **192 douts** extinguishes (The Second Quarto reads "drowns.")   **5.1 s.d. Location: A
churchyard   Clowns** rustics   **2 salvation** (A blunder for "damnation," or perhaps a suggestion that Ophelia was taking her own shortcut to heaven.)   **3 straight** straightway, immediately
(But with a pun on *strait*, "narrow.")   **4 crowner** coroner   **sat on her** conducted an inquest
on her case   **finds it** gives his official verdict that her means of death was consistent with   **6
found so** determined so in the coroner's verdict   **7 *se offendendo*** (A comic mistake for *se
defendendo,* a term used in verdicts of justifiable homicide.)   **9 Argal** (Corruption of *ergo,*
"therefore.")   **11 goodman** (An honorific title often used with the name of a profession or craft.)
13–14 will he, nill he whether he will or no, willy-nilly   **18 quest** inquest

FIRST CLOWN: Why, there thou sayst.° And the more pity that great folk should have countenance° in this world to drown or hang themselves, more than their even-Christian.° Come, my spade. There is no ancient° gentlemen but gardeners, ditchers, and grave makers. They hold up° Adam's profession.   25

SECOND CLOWN: Was he a gentleman?

FIRST CLOWN: 'A was the first that ever bore arms.°

SECOND CLOWN: Why, he had none.

FIRST CLOWN: What, art a heathen? How dost thou understand the Scripture? The Scripture says Adam digged. Could he dig without arms?° I'll put   30 another question to thee. If thou answerest me not to the purpose, confess thyself°—

SECOND CLOWN: Go to.

FIRST CLOWN: What is he that builds stronger than either the mason, the ship-wright, or the carpenter?   35

SECOND CLOWN: The gallows maker, for that frame° outlives a thousand tenants.

FIRST CLOWN: I like thy wit well, in good faith. The gallows does well.° But how does it well? It does well to those that do ill. Now thou dost ill to say the gallows is built stronger than the church. Argal, the gallows may do well to thee. To 't again, come.   40

SECOND CLOWN: "Who builds stronger than a mason, a shipwright, or a carpenter?"

FIRST CLOWN: Ay, tell me that, and unyoke.°

SECOND CLOWN: Marry, now I can tell.

FIRST CLOWN: To 't.   45

SECOND CLOWN: Mass,° I cannot tell.

[Enter HAMLET *and* HORATIO *(at a distance).]*

FIRST CLOWN: Cudgel thy brains no more about it, for your dull ass will not mend his pace with beating; and when you are asked this question next, say "a grave maker." The houses he makes lasts till doomsday. Go get thee in and fetch me a stoup° of liquor.   50

[Exit SECOND CLOWN. FIRST CLOWN *digs.]*

[Song.]

---

21 there thou sayst i.e., that's right   **22 countenance** privilege   **23 even-Christian** fellow Christians   **ancient** going back to ancient times   **24 hold up** maintain   **27 bore arms** (To be entitled to bear a coat of arms would make Adam a gentleman, but as one who bore a spade, our common ancestor was an ordinary delver in the earth.)   **30 arms** i.e., the arms of the body **32 confess thyself** (The saying continues, "and be hanged.")   **36 frame** (1) gallows (2) structure   **37 does well** (1) is an apt answer (2) does a good turn   **43 unyoke** i.e., after this great effort, you may unharness the team of your wits   **46 Mass** by the Mass   **50 stoup** two-quart measure

"In youth, when I did love, did love,°
　　　Methought it was very sweet,
　　　To contract—O—the time for—a—my behove,°
　　O, methought there—a—was nothing—a—meet."°

HAMLET:　Has this fellow no feeling of his business, 'a° sings in gravemaking?　　55

HORATIO:　Custom hath made it in him a property of easiness.°

HAMLET:　'Tis e'en so. The hand of little employment hath the daintier sense.°

FIRST CLOWN:　　　　　　　　　　　　　　　　　　　　*[Song.]*
　　　　　　　"But age with his stealing steps
　　　　　　　　Hath clawed me in his clutch,
　　　　　　　　And hath shipped me into the land,°　　　　　60
　　　　　　　　As if I had never been such."

[He throws up a skull.]

HAMLET:　That skull had a tongue in it and could sing once. How the knave
jowls° it to the ground, as if 'twere Cain's jawbone, that did the first
murder! This might be the pate of a politician,° which this ass now o'erreaches,° one that would circumvent God, might it not?　　　　65

HORATIO:　It might, my lord.

HAMLET:　Or of a courtier, which could say, "Good morrow, sweet lord! How
dost thou, sweet lord?" This might be my Lord Such-a-one, that praised my
Lord Such-a-one's horse when 'a meant to beg it, might it not?

HORATIO:　Ay, my lord.　　　　70

HAMLET:　Why, e'en so, and now my Lady Worm's, chapless,° and knocked about
the mazard° with a sexton's spade. Here's fine revolution,° an° we had the
trick to see° 't. Did these bones cost no more the breeding but° to play at
loggets° with them? Mine ache to think on 't.

FIRST CLOWN:　　　　　　　　　　　　　　　　　　　*[Song.]*
　　　　　"A pickax and a spade, a spade,　　　　75
　　　　　　For and° a shrouding sheet;
　　　　　　O, a pit of clay for to be made
　　　　　　For such a guest is meet."

---

51 In . . . love (This and the two following stanzas, with nonsensical variations, are from a
poem attributed to Lord Vaux and printed in *Tottel's Miscellany,* 1557. The *O* and *a* [for "ah"]
seemingly are the grunts of the digger.)　　**53 To contract . . . behove** i.e., to shorten the time
for my own advantage (Perhaps he means to *prolong* it.)　　**54 meet** suitable, i.e., more suitable
55 'a that he　　**56 property of easiness** something he can do easily and indifferently
57 daintier sense more delicate sense of feeling　　**60 into the land** i.e., toward my grave (But
note the lack of rhyme in *steps, land.*)　　**63 jowls** dashes (with a pun on *jowl*, "jawbone")
64 politician schemer, plotter　　**64–65 o'erreaches** circumvents, gets the better of (with a quibble on the literal sense)　　**71 chapless** having no lower jaw　　**72 mazard** i.e., head (Literally, a
drinking vessel.)　　**revolution** turn of Fortune's wheel, change　　**an** if　　**73 trick to see** knack
of seeing　　**cost . . . but** involve so little expense and care in upbringing that we may
74 loggets a game in which pieces of hard wood shaped like Indian clubs or bowling pins are
thrown to lie as near as possible to a stake　　**76 For and** and moreover

[He throws up another skull.]

HAMLET: There's another. Why may not that be the skull of a lawyer? Where be
his quiddities° now, his quillities,° his cases, his tenures,° and his tricks?   80
Why does he suffer this mad knave now to knock him about the sconce°
with a dirty shovel, and will not tell him of his action of battery?° Hum, this
fellow might be in 's time a great buyer of land, with his statutes, his
recognizances,° his fines, his double° vouchers,° his recoveries.° Is this the
fine of his fines and the recovery of his recoveries, to have his fine pate full   85
of fine dirt?° Will his vouchers vouch him no more of his purchases, and
double ones too, than the length and breadth of a pair of indentures?° The
very conveyances° of his lands will scarcely lie in this box,° and must th'
inheritor° himself have no more, ha?

HORATIO: Not a jot more, my lord.   90

HAMLET: Is not parchment made of sheepskins?

HORATIO: Ay, my lord, and of calves' skins too.

HAMLET: They are sheep and calves which seek out assurance in that.° I will
speak to this fellow.—Whose grave's this, sirrah?°

FIRST CLOWN: Mine, sir.   *[Sings.]*   95

"O, pit of clay for to be made
For such a guest is meet."

HAMLET: I think it be thine, indeed, for thou liest in 't.

FIRST CLOWN: You lie out on 't, sir, and therefore 'tis not yours. For my part,
I do not lie in 't, yet it is mine.   100

HAMLET: Thou dost lie in 't, to be in 't and say it is thine. 'Tis for the dead, not
for the quick;° therefore thou liest.

FIRST CLOWN: 'Tis a quick lie, sir; 'twill away again from me to you.

HAMLET: What man dost thou dig it for?

FIRST CLOWN: For no man, sir.   105

HAMLET: What woman, then?

FIRST CLOWN: For none, neither.

80 quiddities subtleties, quibbles (From Latin *quid,* "a thing.")   **quillities** verbal niceties, subtle
distinctions (Variation of *quiddities.*)   **tenures** the holding of a piece of property or office, or
the conditions or period of such holding   **81 sconce** head   **82 action of battery** lawsuit about
physical assault   **83–84 statutes . . . recognizances** legal documents guaranteeing a debt by
attaching land and property   **84 double** signed by two signatories   **vouchers** guarantees of
the legality of a title to real estate   **fines . . . recoveries** ways of converting entailed estates into
"fee simple" or freehold   **85–86 fine of his fines . . . fine pate . . . fine dirt** end of his legal
maneuvers . . . elegant head . . . minutely sifted dirt   **87 pair of indentures** legal document
drawn up in duplicate on a single sheet and then cut apart on a zigzag line so that each pair was
uniquely matched (Hamlet may refer to two rows of teeth or dentures.)   **88 conveyances**
deeds   **box** (1) deed box (2) coffin ("Skull" has been suggested.)   **89 inheritor** possessor,
owner   **93 assurance in that** safety in legal parchments   **94 sirrah** (A term of address to infe-
riors.)   **102 quick** living

HAMLET: Who is to be buried in 't?

FIRST CLOWN: One that was a woman, sir, but, rest her soul, she's dead.

HAMLET: How absolute° the knave is! We must speak by the card,° or   110
equivocation° will undo us. By the Lord, Horatio, this three years I have
took° note of it: the age is grown so picked° that the toe of the peasant
comes so near the heel of the courtier, he galls his kibe.°—How long
hast thou been grave maker?

FIRST CLOWN: Of all the days i' the year, I came to 't that day that our last king   115
Hamlet overcame Fortinbras.

HAMLET: How long is that since?

FIRST CLOWN: Cannot you tell that? Every fool can tell that. It was that very day
that young Hamlet was born—he that is mad and sent into England.

HAMLET: Ay, marry, why was he sent into England?   120

FIRST CLOWN: Why, because 'a was mad. 'A shall recover his wits there, or if 'a
do not, 'tis no great matter there.

HAMLET: Why?

FIRST CLOWN: 'Twill not be seen in him there. There the men are as mad as he.

HAMLET: How came he mad?   125

FIRST CLOWN: Very strangely, they say.

HAMLET: How strangely?

FIRST CLOWN: Faith, e'en with losing his wits.

HAMLET: Upon what ground?°

FIRST CLOWN: Why, here in Denmark. I have been sexton here, man and boy, thirty   130
years.

HAMLET: How long will a man lie i' th' earth ere he rot?

FIRST CLOWN: Faith, if 'a be not rotten before 'a die—as we have many pocky°
corpses nowadays, that will scarce hold the laying in°—'a will last you°
some eight year or nine year. A tanner will last you nine year.   135

HAMLET: Why he more than another?

---

110 absolute strict, precise   **by the card** i.e., with precision (Literally, by the mariner's com-
pass-card, on which the points of the compass were marked.)   **111 equivocation** ambiguity in
the use of terms   **112 took** taken   **picked** refined, fastidious   **113 galls his kibe** chafes the
courtier's chilblain   **129 ground** cause (But, in the next line, the gravedigger takes the word in
the sense of "land," "country.")   **134 pocky** rotten, diseased (Literally, with the pox, or syphilis.)
hold the laying in hold together long enough to be interred   **134–135 last you** last (*You* is
used colloquially here and in the following lines.)

FIRST CLOWN: Why, sir, his hide is so tanned with his trade that 'a will keep out water a great while, and your water is a sore° decayer of your whoreson° dead body. [*He picks up a skull.*] Here's a skull now hath lien you° i'th' earth three-and-twenty years.   140

HAMLET: Whose was it?

FIRST CLOWN: A whoreson mad fellow's it was. Whose do you think it was?

HAMLET: Nay, I know not.

FIRST CLOWN: A pestilence on him for a mad rogue! 'A poured a flagon of Rhenish° on my head once. This same skull, sir, was, sir, Yorick's skull, the 145 King's jester.

HAMLET: This?

FIRST CLOWN: E'en that.

HAMLET: Let me see. [*He takes the skull.*] Alas, poor Yorick! I knew him, Horatio, a fellow of infinite jest, of most excellent fancy. He hath bore° me 150 on his back a thousand times, and now how abhorred in my imagination it is! My gorge rises° at it. Here hung those lips that I have kissed I know not how oft. Where be your gibes now? Your gambols, your songs, your flashes of merriment that were wont° to set the table on a roar? Not one now, to mock your own grinning?° Quite chopfallen?° Now get you to my 155 lady's chamber and tell her, let her paint an inch thick, to this favor° she must come. Make her laugh at that. Prithee, Horatio, tell me one thing.

HORATIO: What's that, my lord?

HAMLET: Dost thou think Alexander looked o' this fashion i' th' earth?

HORATIO: E'en so. 160

HAMLET: And smelt so? Pah! [*He throws down the skull.*]

HORATIO: E'en so, my lord.

HAMLET: To what base uses we may return, Horatio! Why may not imagination trace the noble dust of Alexander till 'a find it stopping a bunghole?°

HORATIO: 'Twere to consider too curiously° to consider so. 165

HAMLET: No, faith, not a jot, but to follow him thither with modesty° enough, and likelihood to lead it. As thus: Alexander died, Alexander was buried, Alexander returneth to dust, the dust is earth, of earth we make loam,° and why of that loam whereto he was converted might they not stop a beer barrel? 170

Imperious° Caesar, dead and turned to clay,

138 **sore** i.e., terrible, great   138–139 **whoreson** i.e., vile, scurvy   139 **lien you** lain (See the note at line 134.)   145 **Rhenish** Rhine wine   150 **bore** borne   152 **My gorge rises** i.e., I feel nauseated   154 **were wont** used   155 **mock your own grinning** mock at the way your skull seems to be grinning (just as you used to mock at yourself and those who grinned at you) **chopfallen** (1) lacking the lower jaw (2) dejected   156 **favor** aspect, appearance   164 **bunghole** hole for filling or emptying a cask   165 **curiously** minutely   166 **modesty** plausible moderation   169 **loam** mortar consisting chiefly of moistened clay and straw   171 **Imperious** imperial

Might stop a hole to keep the wind away.
O, that that earth which kept the world in awe
Should patch a wall t' expel the winter's flaw!°

[Enter KING, QUEEN, LAERTES, *and the corpse (of* OPHELIA, *in procession, with* PRIEST, *lords, etc.).]*

But soft,° but soft awhile! Here comes the King,   175
The Queen, the courtiers. Who is this they follow?
And with such maimèd° rites? This doth betoken
The corpse they follow did with desperate hand
Fordo° its own life. 'Twas of some estate.°
Couch we° awhile and mark.   180

[He and HORATIO *conceal themselves.* OPHELIA'S *body is taken to the grave.]*

LAERTES: What ceremony else?
HAMLET [*to* HORATIO]:   That is Laertes, a very noble youth. Mark.
LAERTES: What ceremony else?
PRIEST: Her obsequies have been as far enlarged
As we have warranty.° Her death was doubtful,   185
And but that great command o'ersways the order°
She should in ground unsanctified been lodged°
Till the last trumpet. For° charitable prayers,
Shards,° flints, and pebbles should be thrown on her.
Yet here she is allowed her virgin crants,°   190
Her maiden strewments,° and the bringing home
Of bell and burial.°
LAERTES: Must there no more be done?
PRIEST: No more be done.
We should profane the service of the dead
To sing a requiem and such rest° to her   195
As to peace-parted souls.°
LAERTES: Lay her i' th' earth,
And from her fair and unpolluted flesh
May violets° spring! I tell thee, churlish priest,

---

174 **flaw** gust of wind   175 **soft** i.e., wait, be careful   177 **maimèd** mutilated, incomplete
179 **Fordo** destroy   **estate** rank   180 **Couch we** let's hide, lie low   185 **warranty** i.e., ecclesiastical authority   186 **great . . . order** orders from on high overrule the prescribed procedures   187 **She should . . . lodged** she should have been buried in unsanctified ground   188 **For** in place of   189 **Shards** broken bits of pottery   190 **crants** garlands betokening maidenhood   191 **strewments** flowers strewn on a coffin   191–192 **bringing . . . burial** laying the body to rest, to the sound of the bell   195 **such rest** i.e., to pray for such rest   196 **peace-parted souls** those who have died at peace with God   198 **violets** (See 4.5.183 and note.)

A ministering angel shall my sister be
When thou liest howling.°
HAMLET [*to* HORATIO]:   What, the fair Ophelia!   200
QUEEN [*scattering flowers*]:   Sweets to the sweet! Farewell.
I hoped thou shouldst have been my Hamlet's wife.
I thought thy bride-bed to have decked, sweet maid,
And not t' have strewed thy grave.
LAERTES: O, treble woe
Fall ten times treble on that cursèd head   205
Whose wicked deed thy most ingenious sense°
Deprived thee of! Hold off the earth awhile,
Till I have caught her once more in mine arms.

[He leaps into the grave and embraces OPHELIA.*]*

Now pile your dust upon the quick and dead,
Till of this flat a mountain you have made   210
T' o'ertop old Pelion or the skyish head
Of blue Olympus.°
HAMLET [*coming forward*]:   What is he whose grief
Bears such an emphasis,° whose phrase of sorrow
Conjures the wandering stars° and makes them stand   215
Like wonder-wounded° hearers? This is I,
Hamlet the Dane.°
LAERTES [*grappling with him*°]:   The devil take thy soul!
HAMLET: Thou pray'st not well.
I prithee, take thy fingers from my throat,   220
For though I am not splenitive° and rash,
Yet have I in me something dangerous,
Which let thy wisdom fear. Hold off thy hand.
KING: Pluck them asunder.
QUEEN: Hamlet, Hamlet!
ALL: Gentlemen!   225

---

200 howling i.e., in hell   **206 ingenious sense** a mind that is quick, alert, of fine qualities
211–212 Pelion . . . Olympus sacred mountains in the north of Thessaly; see also *Ossa,* below,
at line 245   **214 emphasis** i.e., rhetorical and florid emphasis (*Phrase* has a similar rhetorical
connotation.)   **215 wandering stars** planets   **216 wonder-wounded** struck with amazement
217 the Dane (This title normally signifies the King; see 1.1.17 and note.)   **s.d. grappling
with him** The testimony of the First Quarto that *"Hamlet leaps in after Laertes"* and the "Elegy
on Burbage" ("Oft have I seen him leap into the grave") seem to indicate one way in which this
fight was staged; however, the difficulty of fitting two contenders and Ophelia's body into a confined space (probably the trapdoor) suggests to many editors the alternative, that Laertes jumps
out of the grave to attack Hamlet.)   **221 splenitive** quick-tempered

HORATIO: Good my lord, be quiet.

[HAMLET and LAERTES are parted.]

HAMLET: Why, I will fight with him upon this theme
    Until my eyelids will no longer wag.°

QUEEN: O my son, what theme?   230

HAMLET: I loved Ophelia. Forty thousand brothers
    Could not with all their quantity of love
    Make up my sum. What wilt thou do for her?

KING: O, he is mad, Laertes.

QUEEN: For love of God, forbear him.°   235

HAMLET: 'Swounds,° show me what thou'lt do.
    Woo 't° weep? Woo 't fight? Woo 't fast? Woo 't tear thyself?
    Woo 't drink up° eisel?° Eat a crocodile?°
    I'll do 't. Dost come here to whine?
    To outface me with leaping in her grave?   240
    Be buried quick° with her, and so will I.
    And if thou prate of mountains, let them throw
    Millions of acres on us, till our ground,
    Singeing his pate° against the burning zone,°
    Make Ossa° like a wart! Nay, an° thou'lt mouth,°   245
    I'll rant as well as thou.

QUEEN: This is mere° madness,
    And thus awhile the fit will work on him;
    Anon, as patient as the female dove
    When that her golden couplets° are disclosed,°
    His silence will sit drooping.

HAMLET: Hear you, sir,   250
    What is the reason that you use me thus?
    I loved you ever. But it is no matter.
    Let Hercules himself do what he may,
    The cat will mew, and dog will have his day.°

[Exit HAMLET.]

---

229 wag move (A fluttering eyelid is a conventional sign that life has not yet gone.)   **235
forbear him** leave him alone   **236 'Swounds** by His (Christ's) wounds   **237 Woo 't** wilt thou
238 drink up drink deeply   **eisel** vinegar   **crocodile** (Crocodiles were tough and dangerous,
and were supposed to shed hypocritical tears.)   **241 quick** alive   **244 his pate** its head, i.e.,
top   **burning zone** zone in the celestial sphere containing the sun's orbit, between the trop-
ics of Cancer and Capricorn   **245 Ossa** another mountain in Thessaly (In their war against the
Olympian gods, the giants attempted to heap Ossa on Pelion to scale Olympus.)   **an** if   **mouth**
i.e., rant   **246 mere** utter   **249 golden couplets** two baby pigeons, covered with yellow down
disclosed hatched   **253–254 Let . . . day** i.e., (1) even Hercules couldn't stop Laertes' theatrical rant (2) I, too, will have my turn; i.e., despite any blustering attempts at interference, every
person will sooner or later do what he or she must do

KING: I pray thee, good Horatio, wait upon him.   255

[(Exit) HORATIO.*]*

[*To* LAERTES.] Strengthen your patience in° our last night's speech;
We'll put the matter to the present push.°—
Good Gertrude, set some watch over your son.—
This grave shall have a living° monument.
An hour of quiet° shortly shall we see;   260
Till then, in patience our proceeding be.

[Exeunt.]

*[Act **5.2** Enter* HAMLET *and* HORATIO.*]*°

HAMLET: So much for this, sir; now shall you see the other.°
You do remember all the circumstance?

HORATIO: Remember it, my lord!

HAMLET: Sir, in my heart there was a kind of fighting
That would not let me sleep. Methought I lay   5
Worse than the mutines° in the bilboes.° Rashly,°
And praised be rashness for it—let us know°
Our indiscretion° sometimes serves us well
When our deep plots do pall,° and that should learn° us
There's a divinity that shapes our ends,   10
Rough-hew° them how we will—

HORATIO: That is most certain.

HAMLET: Up from my cabin,
My sea-gown° scarfed° about me, in the dark
Groped I to find out them,° had my desire,
Fingered° their packet, and in fine° withdrew   15
To mine own room again, making so bold,
My fears forgetting manners, to unseal
Their grand commission; where I found, Horatio—
Ah, royal knavery!—an exact command,
Larded° with many several° sorts of reasons   20

256 in i.e., by recalling **257 present push** immediate test **259 living** lasting (For Laertes' private understanding, Claudius also hints that Hamlet's death will serve as such a monument.) **260 hour of quiet** time free of conflict **5.2 s.d. Location: The castle** **1 see the other** hear the other news **6 mutines** mutineers **bilboes** shackles **rashly** on impulse (This adverb goes with lines 12 ff.) **7 know** acknowledge **8 indiscretion** lack of foresight and judgment (not an indiscreet act) **9 pall** fail, falter, go stale **learn** teach **11 Rough-hew** shape roughly **13 sea-gown** seaman's coat **scarfed** loosely wrapped **14 them** i.e., Rosencrantz and Guildenstern **15 Fingered** pilfered, pinched **in fine** finally, in conclusion **20 Larded** garnished **several** different

Importing° Denmark's health and England's too,
With, ho! such bugs° and goblins in my life,°
That on the supervise,° no leisure bated,°
No, not to stay° the grinding of the ax,
My head should be struck off.

HORATIO: Is 't possible?   25

HAMLET [*giving a document*]:   Here's the commission. Read it at more leisure.
But wilt thou hear now how I did proceed?

HORATIO: I beseech you.

HAMLET: Being thus benetted round with villainies—
Ere I could make a prologue to my brains,   30
They had begun the play°—I sat me down,
Devised a new commission, wrote it fair.°
I once did hold it, as our statists° do,
A baseness° to write fair, and labored much
How to forget that learning; but, sir, now   35
It did me yeoman's° service. Wilt thou know
Th' effect° of what I wrote?

HORATIO: Ay, good my lord.

HAMLET: An earnest conjuration° from the King,
As England was his faithful tributary,
As love between them like the palm° might flourish,   40
As peace should still° her wheaten garland° wear
And stand a comma° 'tween their amities,
And many suchlike "as"es° of great charge,°
That on the view and knowing of these contents,
Without debatement further more or less,   45
He should those bearers put to sudden death,
Not shriving time° allowed.

HORATIO: How was this sealed?

HAMLET: Why, even in that was heaven ordinant.°
I had my father's signet° in my purse,
Which was the model° of that Danish seal;   50

---

21 Importing relating to   **22 bugs** bugbears, hobgoblins   **in my life** i.e., to be feared if I were allowed to live   **23 supervise** reading   **leisure bated** delay allowed   **24 stay** await   **30–31 Ere . . . play** before I could consciously turn my brain to the matter, it had started working on a plan   **32 fair** in a clear hand   **33 statists** statesmen   **34 baseness** i.e., lower-class trait   **36 yeoman's** i.e., substantial, faithful, loyal   **37 effect** purport   **38 conjuration** entreaty   **40 palm** (An image of health; see Psalm 92:12.)   **41 still** always   **wheaten garland** (Symbolic of fruitful agriculture, of peace and plenty.)   **42 comma** (Indicating continuity, link.)   **43 "as"es** (1) the "whereases" of a formal document (2) asses   **charge** (1) import (2) burden (appropriate to asses)   **47 shriving time** time for confession and absolution   **48 ordinant** directing   **49 signet** small seal   **50 model** replica

Folded the writ° up in the form of th' other,
Subscribed° it, gave 't th' impression,° placed it safely,
The changeling° never known. Now, the next day
Was our sea fight, and what to this was sequent°
Thou knowest already.   55

HORATIO: So Guildenstern and Rosencrantz go to 't.

HAMLET: Why, man, they did make love to this employment.
They are not near my conscience. Their defeat°
Does by their own insinuation° grow.
'Tis dangerous when the baser° nature comes   60
Between the pass° and fell° incensèd points
Of mighty opposites.°

HORATIO: Why, what a king is this!

HAMLET: Does it not, think thee, stand me now upon°—
He that hath killed my king and whored my mother,
Popped in between th' election° and my hopes,   65
Thrown out his angle° for my proper° life,
And with such cozenage°—is 't not perfect conscience
To quit° him with this arm? And is 't not to be damned
To let this canker° of our nature come
In° further evil?   70

HORATIO: It must be shortly known to him from England
What is the issue of the business there.

HAMLET: It will be short. The interim is mine,
And a man's life's no more than to say "one."°
But I am very sorry, good Horatio,   75
That to Laertes I forgot myself,
For by the image of my cause I see
The portraiture of his. I'll court his favors.
But, sure, the bravery° of his grief did put me
Into a tow'ring passion.

HORATIO: Peace, who comes here?   80

[Enter a Courtier (OSRIC).]

OSRIC: Your lordship is right welcome back to Denmark.

---

51 writ writing   **52 Subscribed** signed (with forged signature)   **impression** i.e., with a wax seal
53 changeling i.e., substituted letter (Literally, a fairy child substituted for a human one.)   **54 was
sequent** followed   **58 defeat** destruction   **59 insinuation** intrusive intervention, sticking their
noses in my business   **60 baser** of lower social station   **61 pass** thrust   **fell** fierce   **62
opposites** antagonists   **63 stand me now upon** become incumbent on me now   **65 election**
(The Danish monarch was "elected" by a small number of high-ranking electors.)   **66 angle** fish-
hook   **proper** very   **67 cozenage** trickery   **68 quit** requite, pay back
69 canker ulcer   **69–70 come In** grow into   **74 a man's . . . "one"** one's whole life occupies
such a short time, only as long as it takes to count to 1   **79 bravery** bravado

HAMLET: I humbly thank you, sir. [*To* HORATIO.] Dost know this water fly?

HORATIO: No, my good lord.

HAMLET: Thy state is the more gracious, for 'tis a vice to know him. He hath
much land, and fertile. Let a beast be lord of beasts, and his crib° shall   85
stand at the King's mess.° 'Tis a chuff,° but, as I say, spacious in the
possession of dirt.

OSRIC: Sweet lord, if your lordship were at leisure, I should impart a thing to
you from His Majesty.

HAMLET: I will receive it, sir, with all diligence of spirit.   90
Put your bonnet° to his° right use; 'tis for the head.

OSRIC: I thank your lordship, it is very hot.

HAMLET: No, believe me, 'tis very cold. The wind is northerly.

OSRIC: It is indifferent° cold, my lord, indeed.

HAMLET: But yet methinks it is very sultry and hot for my complexion.°   95

OSRIC: Exceedingly, my lord. It is very sultry, as 'twere—I cannot tell how. My
lord, His Majesty bade me signify to you that 'a has laid a great wager on
your head. Sir, this is the matter—

HAMLET: I beseech you, remember.

[Hamlet moves him to put on his hat.]

OSRIC: Nay, good my lord; for my ease,° in good faith. Sir, here is newly come to   100
court Laertes—believe me, an absolute° gentleman, full of most excellent
differences,° of very soft society° and great showing.° Indeed, to speak
feelingly° of him, he is the card° or calendar° of gentry,° for you shall find
in him the continent of what part a gentleman would see.°

HAMLET: Sir, his definement° suffers no perdition° in you,° though I know to   105
divide him inventorially° would dozy° th' arithmetic of memory, and yet but
yaw° neither° in respect of° his quick sail. But, in the verity of extolment,° I
take him to be a soul of great article,° and his infusion° of such dearth and

---

85 crib manger   **85–86 Let . . . mess** i.e., if a man, no matter how beastlike, is as rich in live-
stock and possessions as Osric, he may eat at the King's table   **86 chuff** boor, churl (The Second
Quarto spelling, *chough,* is a variant spelling that also suggests the meaning here of "chattering
jackdaw.")   **91 bonnet** any kind of cap or hat   **his** its   **94 indifferent** somewhat   **95
complexion** temperament   **100 for my ease** (A conventional reply declining the invitation to
put his hat back on.)   **101 absolute** perfect   **102 differences** special qualities   **soft society**
agreeable manners   **great showing** distinguished appearance   **103 feelingly** with just perception   **card** chart, map   **calendar** guide   **gentry** good breeding   **104 the continent . . .
see** one who contains in him all the qualities a gentleman would like to see (A *continent* is that
which contains.)   **105 definement** definition (Hamlet proceeds to mock Osric by throwing his
lofty diction back at him.)   **perdition** loss, diminution   **you** your description   **106 divide him
inventorially** enumerate his graces   **dozy** dizzy   **107 yaw** swing unsteadily off course (Said
of a ship.)   **neither** for all that   **in respect of** in comparison with   **107–108 in . . .
extolment** in true praise (of him)   **108 of great article** one with many articles in his inventory
infusion essence, character infused into him by nature

rareness° as, to make true diction° of him, his semblable° is his mirror and
who else would trace° him his umbrage,° nothing more.   110

OSRIC: Your lordship speaks most infallibly of him.

HAMLET: The concernancy,° sir? Why do we wrap the gentleman in our more
rawer breath?°

OSRIC: Sir?

HORATIO: Is 't not possible to understand in another tongue?° You will do 't,°   115
sir, really.

HAMLET: What imports the nomination° of this gentleman?

OSRIC: Of Laertes?

HORATIO [TO HAMLET]:   His purse is empty already; all 's golden words are spent.

HAMLET: Of him, sir.   120

OSRIC: I know you are not ignorant—

HAMLET: I would you did, sir. Yet in faith if you did, it would not much approve°
me. Well, sir?

OSRIC: You are not ignorant of what excellence Laertes is—

HAMLET: I dare not confess that, lest I should compare with him in excellence.   125
But to know a man well were to know himself.°

OSRIC: I mean, sir, for° his weapon; but in the imputation laid on him by them,°
in his meed° he's unfellowed.°

HAMLET: What's his weapon?

OSRIC: Rapier and dagger.   130

HAMLET: That's two of his weapons—but well.°

OSRIC: The King, sir, hath wagered with him six Barbary horses, against the
which he° has impawned,° as I take it, six French rapiers and poniards,°
with their assigns,° as girdle, hangers,° and so.° Three of the carriages,° in
faith, are very dear to fancy,° very responsive° to the hilts, most delicate°   135
carriages, and of very liberal conceit.°

---

109 dearth and rareness rarity   **make true diction** speak truly   **semblable** only true likeness
110 who ... trace any other person who would wish to follow   **umbrage** shadow   **112
concernancy** import, relevance   **113 rawer breath** unrefined speech that can only come short in
praising him   **115 to understand ... tongue** i.e., for you, Osric, to understand when someone else
speaks your language. (Horatio twits Osric for not being able to understand the kind of flowery
speech he himself uses, when Hamlet speaks in such a vein. Alternatively, all this could be said to
Hamlet.)   **You will do 't** i.e., you can if you try, or, you may well have to try (to speak plainly)   **117
nomination** naming   **123 approve** commend   **125–126 I dare ... himself** I dare not boast of
knowing Laertes' excellence lest I seem to imply a comparable excellence in myself. Certainly, to
know another person well, one must know oneself.   **127 for** i.e., with   **127–128 imputation ...
them** reputation given him by others   **128 meed** merit   **unfellowed** unmatched   **131 but well**
but never mind   **133 he** i.e., Laertes   **impawned** staked, wagered   **poniards** daggers   **134
assigns** appurtenances   **hangers** straps on the sword belt (*girdle*), from which the sword hung
and so and so on   **carriages** (An affected way of saying *hangers;* literally, gun carriages.)   **135 dear
to fancy** delightful to the fancy   **responsive** corresponding closely, matching or well adjusted
delicate (i.e., in workmanship.)   **136 liberal conceit** elaborate design

HAMLET: What call you the carriages?

HORATIO [*to* HAMLET]:   I knew you must be edified by the margent° ere you had done.

OSRIC: The carriages, sir, are the hangers.   140

HAMLET: The phrase would be more germane to the matter if we could carry a cannon by our sides; I would it might be hangers till then. But, on: six Barbary horses against six French swords, their assigns, and three liberal-conceited carriages; that's the French bet against the Danish. Why is this impawned, as you call it?   145

OSRIC: The King, sir, hath laid,° sir, that in a dozen passes° between yourself and him, he shall not exceed you three hits. He hath laid on twelve for nine, and it would come to immediate trial, if your lordship would vouchsafe the answer.°

HAMLET: How if I answer no?   150

OSRIC: I mean, my lord, the opposition of your person in trial.

HAMLET: Sir, I will walk here in the hall. If it please His Majesty, it is the breathing time° of day with me. Let° the foils be brought, the gentleman willing, and the King hold his purpose. I will win for him an I can; if not, I will gain nothing but my shame and the odd hits.   155

OSRIC: Shall I deliver you° so?

HAMLET: To this effect, sir—after what flourish your nature will.

OSRIC: I commend° my duty to your lordship.

HAMLET: Yours, yours. [*Exit* OSRIC.] 'A does well to commend it himself; there are no tongues else for 's turn.°   160

HORATIO: This lapwing° runs away with the shell on his head.

HAMLET: 'A did comply with his dug° before 'a sucked it. Thus has he—and many more of the same breed that I know the drossy° age dotes on— only got the tune° of the time and, out of an habit of encounter,° a kind of

---

138 margent margin of a book, place for explanatory notes   **146 laid** wagered   **passes** bouts (The odds of the betting are hard to explain. Possibly the King bets that Hamlet will win at least five out of twelve, at which point Laertes raises the odds against himself by betting he will win nine.) **149 vouchsafe the answer** be so good as to accept the challenge (Hamlet deliberately takes the phrase in its literal sense of replying.)   **153 breathing time** exercise period   Let i.e., if   **156 deliver you** report what you say   **158 commend** commit to your favor (A conventional salutation, but Hamlet wryly uses a more literal meaning, "recommend," "praise," in line 159.)   **160 for 's turn** for his purposes, i.e., to do it for him   **161 lapwing** (A proverbial type of youthful forwardness. Also, a bird that draws intruders away from its nest and was thought to run about with its head in the shell when newly hatched; a seeming reference to Osric's hat.)   **162 comply . . . dug** observe ceremonious formality toward his nurse's or mother's teat   **163 drossy** laden with scum and impurities, frivolous   **164 tune** temper, mood, manner of speech   **an habit of encounter** a demeanor in conversing (with courtiers of his own kind)

yeasty° collection,° which carries them through and through the most   165
fanned and winnowed opinions;° and do° but blow them to their trial, the
bubbles are out.°   *[Enter a* LORD.]

LORD: My lord, His Majesty commended him to you by young Osric, who
brings back to him that you attend him in the hall. He sends to know if
your pleasure hold to play with Laertes, or that° you will take longer   170
time.

HAMLET: I am constant to my purposes; they follow the King's pleasure. If his
fitness speaks, mine is ready;° now or whensoever, provided I be so able
as now.

LORD: The King and Queen and all are coming down.   175

HAMLET: In happy time.°

LORD: The Queen desires you to use some gentle entertainment° to Laertes
before you fall to play.

HAMLET: She well instructs me.

                                                                        [Exit Lord.]

HORATIO: You will lose, my lord.   180

HAMLET: I do not think so. Since he went into France, I have been in continual
practice; I shall win at the odds. But thou wouldst not think how ill all's
here about my heart; but it is no matter.

HORATIO: Nay, good my lord—

HAMLET: It is but foolery, but it is such a kind of gaingiving° as would perhaps   185
trouble a woman.

HORATIO: If your mind dislike anything, obey it. I will forestall their repair°
hither and say you are not fit.

HAMLET: Not a whit, we defy augury. There is special providence in the fall of
a sparrow. If it be now, 'tis not to come; if it be not to come, it will be now;   190
if it be not now, yet it will come. The readiness is all. Since no man of aught
he leaves knows, what is 't to leave betimes? Let be.°

[A table prepared. (Enter) trumpets, drums, and officers with cushions; KING, QUEEN,
*(*OSRIC,*) and all the state; foils, daggers, (and wine borne in;) and* LAERTES.]

KING: Come, Hamlet, come and take this hand from me.

[The KING *puts* LAERTES' *hand into* HAMLET'S.]

---

165 yeasty frothy   **collection** i.e., of current phrases   **165–166 carries ... opinions** sustains
them right through the scrutiny of persons whose opinions are select and refined (Literally, like
grain separated from its chaff. Osric is both the chaff and the bubbly froth on the surface of the
liquor that is soon blown away.)   **166 and do** yet do   **166–167 blow ... out** test them by
merely blowing on them, and their bubbles burst   **170 that** if   **172–173 If ... ready** if he
declares his readiness, my convenience waits on his   **176 In happy time** (A phrase of courtesy
indicating that the time is convenient.)   **177 entertainment** greeting   **185 gaingiving** misgiving   **187 repair** coming   **191–192 Since ... Let be** since no one has knowledge of what
he is leaving behind, what does an early death matter after all? Enough; don't struggle against it.

HAMLET [*to* LAERTES]:   Give me your pardon, sir. I have done you wrong,
    But pardon 't as you are a gentleman.   195
    This presence° knows,
    And you must needs have heard, how I am punished°
    With a sore distraction. What I have done
    That might your nature, honor, and exception°
    Roughly awake, I here proclaim was madness.   200
    Was 't Hamlet wronged Laertes? Never Hamlet.
    If Hamlet from himself be ta'en away,
    And when he's not himself does wrong Laertes,
    Then Hamlet does it not, Hamlet denies it.
    Who does it, then? His madness. If 't be so,   205
    Hamlet is of the faction° that is wronged;
    His madness is poor Hamlet's enemy.
    Sir, in this audience
    Let my disclaiming from a purposed evil
    Free me so far in your most generous thoughts   210
    That I have° shot my arrow o'er the house
    And hurt my brother.
LAERTES: I am satisfied in nature,°
    Whose motive° in this case should stir me most
    To my revenge. But in my terms of honor
    I stand aloof, and will no reconcilement   215
    Till by some elder masters of known honor
    I have a voice° and precedent of peace°
    To keep my name ungored.° But till that time
    I do receive your offered love like love,
    And will not wrong it.
HAMLET: I embrace it freely,   220
    And will this brothers' wager frankly° play. —
    Give us the foils. Come on.
LAERTES: Come, one for me.
HAMLET: I'll be your foil,° Laertes. In mine ignorance
    Your skill shall, like a star i' the darkest night,
    Stick fiery off° indeed.
LAERTES: You mock me, sir.   225
HAMLET: No, by this hand.

---

196 presence royal assembly   **197 punished** afflicted   **199 exception** disapproval   **206**
faction party   **211 That I have** as if I had   **212 in nature** i.e., as to my personal feelings   **213**
motive prompting   **217 voice** authoritative pronouncement   **of peace** for reconciliation
218 name ungored reputation unwounded   **221 frankly** without ill feeling or the burden of
rancor   **223 foil** thin metal background which sets a jewel off (with pun on the blunted rapier
for fencing)   **225 Stick fiery off** stand out brilliantly

KING: Give them the foils, young Osric. Cousin Hamlet,
     You know the wager?

HAMLET: Very well, my lord.
     Your Grace has laid the odds o'° the weaker side.

KING: I do not fear it; I have seen you both.   230
     But since he is bettered,° we have therefore odds.

LAERTES: This is too heavy. Let me see another.

[He exchanges his foil for another.]

HAMLET: This likes me° well. These foils have all a length?

[They prepare to play.]

OSRIC: Ay, my good lord.

KING: Set me the stoups of wine upon that table.   235
     If Hamlet give the first or second hit,
     Or quit in answer of the third exchange,°
     Let all the battlements their ordnance fire.
     The King shall drink to Hamlet's better breath,°
     And in the cup an union° shall he throw   240
     Richer than that which four successive kings
     In Denmark's crown have worn. Give me the cups,
     And let the kettle° to the trumpet speak,
     The trumpet to the cannoneer without,
     The cannons to the heavens, the heaven to earth,   245
     "Now the King drinks to Hamlet." Come, begin.

                                              [Trumpets the while.]
     And you, the judges, bear a wary eye.

HAMLET: Come on, sir.

LAERTES: Come, my lord.   *[They play.* HAMLET *scores a hit.]*

HAMLET: One.   250

LAERTES: No.

HAMLET: Judgment.

OSRIC: A hit, a very palpable hit.

[Drum, trumpets, and shot. Flourish. A piece goes off.]

LAERTES: Well, again.

KING: Stay, give me drink. Hamlet, this pearl is thine.

                          [He drinks, and throws a pearl in HAMLET'S *cup.]*

     Here's to thy health. Give him the cup.   255

---

229 laid the odds o' bet on, backed   **231 is bettered** has improved; is the odds-on favorite
(Laertes' handicap is the "three hits" specified in line 147.)   **233 likes me** pleases me   **237 Or
. . . exchange** i.e., or requites Laertes in the third bout for having won the first two   **239 better
breath** improved vigor   **240 union** pearl (So called, according to Pliny's *Natural History,* 9,
because pearls are *unique,* never identical.)   **243 kettle** kettledrum

HAMLET: I'll play this bout first. Set it by awhile.

    Come. [*They play.*] Another hit; what say you?

LAERTES: A touch, a touch, I do confess 't.

KING: Our son shall win.

QUEEN: He's fat° and scant of breath.

    Here, Hamlet, take my napkin,° rub thy brows.   260

    The Queen carouses° to thy fortune, Hamlet.

HAMLET: Good, madam!

KING: Gertrude, do not drink.

QUEEN: I will, my lord, I pray you pardon me.   *[She drinks.]*

KING: [*aside*] It is the poisoned cup. It is too late.   265

HAMLET: I dare not drink yet, madam; by and by.

QUEEN: Come, let me wipe thy face.

LAERTES: [*to* KING] My lord, I'll hit him now.

KING: I do not think 't.

LAERTES: [*aside*] And yet it is almost against my conscience.

HAMLET: Come, for the third, Laertes. You do but dally.   270

    I pray you, pass° with your best violence;

    I am afeard you make a wanton of me.°

LAERTES: Say you so? Come on.   *[They play.]*

OSRIC: Nothing neither way.

LAERTES: Have at you now!

*[*LAERTES *wounds* HAMLET; *then, in scuffling, they change rapiers,° and* HAMLET *wounds* LAERTES.]*

KING: Part them! They are incensed.   275

HAMLET: Nay, come, again.   *[The* QUEEN *falls.]*

OSRIC: Look to the Queen there, ho!

HORATIO: They bleed on both sides. How is it, my lord?

OSRIC: How is 't, Laertes?

LAERTES: Why, as a woodcock° to mine own springe,° Osric;

    I am justly killed with mine own treachery.   280

HAMLET: How does the Queen?

KING: She swoons to see them bleed.

QUEEN: No, no, the drink, the drink—O my dear Hamlet—

    The drink, the drink! I am poisoned.   *[She dies.]*

HAMLET: O villainy! Ho, let the door be locked!

    Treachery! Seek it out.   285

---

259 fat not physically fit, out of training   **260 napkin** handkerchief   **261 carouses** drinks a toast   **271 pass** thrust   **272 make . . . me** i.e., treat me like a spoiled child, trifle with me   **s.d. in scuffling, they change rapiers** (This stage direction occurs in the Folio. According to a widespread stage tradition, Hamlet receives a scratch, realizes that Laertes' sword is unbated, and accordingly forces an exchange.)   **279 woodcock** a bird, a type of stupidity or as a decoy   **springe** trap, snare

[Laertes falls. Exit OSRIC.*]*

LAERTES: It is here, Hamlet. Hamlet, thou art slain.
No med'cine in the world can do thee good;
In thee there is not half an hour's life.
The treacherous instrument is in thy hand,
Unbated° and envenomed. The foul practice°   290
Hath turned itself on me. Lo, here I lie,
Never to rise again. Thy mother's poisoned.
I can no more. The King, the King's to blame.

HAMLET: The point envenomed too? Then, venom, to thy work.

[He stabs the KING.*]*

ALL: Treason! Treason!   295

KING: O, yet defend me, friends! I am but hurt.

HAMLET: *[forcing the* KING *to drink.]*
Here, thou incestuous, murderous, damnèd Dane,
Drink off this potion. Is thy union° here?
Follow my mother.   *[The* KING *dies.]*

LAERTES: He is justly served.
It is a poison tempered° by himself.   300
Exchange forgiveness with me, noble Hamlet.
Mine and my father's death come not upon thee,
Nor thine on me!   *[He dies.]*

HAMLET: Heaven make thee free of it! I follow thee.
I am dead, Horatio. Wretched Queen, adieu!   305
You that look pale and tremble at this chance,°
That are but mutes° or audience to this act,
Had I but time—as this fell° sergeant,° Death,
Is strict° in his arrest°—O, I could tell you—
But let it be. Horatio, I am dead;   310
Thou livest. Report me and my cause aright
To the unsatisfied.

HORATIO: Never believe it.
I am more an antique Roman° than a Dane.
Here's yet some liquor left.

[He attempts to drink from the poisoned cup. HAMLET *prevents him.]*

---

290 Unbated not blunted with a button   **practice** plot   **298 union** pearl (See line 240; with grim puns on the word's other meanings: marriage, shared death.)**300 tempered** mixed   **306 chance** mischance   **307 mutes** silent observers (Literally, actors with nonspeaking parts.)   **308 fell** cruel   **sergeant** sheriffs officer   **309 strict** (1) severely just (2) unavoidable   **arrest** (1) taking into custody (2) stopping my speech   **313 Roman** (Suicide was an honorable choice for many Romans as an alternative to a dishonorable life.)

HAMLET: As thou'rt a man,
        Give me the cup! Let go! By heaven, I'll ha 't.   315
        O God, Horatio, what a wounded name,
        Things standing thus unknown, shall I leave behind me!
        If thou didst ever hold me in thy heart,
        Absent thee from felicity awhile,
        And in this harsh world draw thy breath in pain   320
        To tell my story.   *[A march afar off (and a volley within).]*
        What warlike noise is this?

[Enter OSRIC.]

OSRIC: Young Fortinbras, with conquest come from Poland,
        To th' ambassadors of England gives
        This warlike volley.
HAMLET: O, I die, Horatio!   325
        The potent poison quite o'ercrows° my spirit.
        I cannot live to hear the news from England,
        But I do prophesy th' election lights
        On Fortinbras. He has my dying voice.°
        So tell him, with th' occurrents° more and less   330
        Which have solicited°—the rest is silence.   *[He dies.]*
HORATIO: Now cracks a noble heart. Good night, sweet prince,
        And flights of angels sing thee to thy rest!
                                [March within.]
        Why does the drum come hither?

*[Enter FORTINBRAS, with the (English) AMBASSADORS (with drum, colors, and atten-
dants).]*

FORTINBRAS: Where is this sight?
HORATIO: What is it you would see?   335
        If aught of woe or wonder, cease your search.
FORTINBRAS: This quarry° cries on havoc.° O proud Death,
        What feast° is toward° in thine eternal cell,
        That thou so many princes at a shot
        So bloodily hast struck?
FIRST AMBASSADOR: The sight is dismal,   340
        And our affairs from England come too late.
        The ears are senseless that should give us hearing,
        To tell him his commandment is fulfilled,

---

326 o'ercrows triumphs over (like the winner in a cockfight) **329 voice** vote **330 occurrents**
events, incidents **331 solicited** moved, urged (Hamlet doesn't finish saying what the events have
prompted—presumably, his acts of vengeance, or his reporting of those events to Fortinbras.) **337
quarry** heap of dead **cries on havoc** proclaims a general slaughter **338 feast** i.e., Death feast-
ing on those who have fallen **toward** in preparation

That Rosencrantz and Guildenstern are dead.
Where should we have our thanks?

HORATIO: Not from his° mouth,   345
Had it th' ability of life to thank you.
He never gave commandment for their death.
But since, so jump° upon this bloody question,°
You from the Polack wars, and you from England,
And here arrived, give order that these bodies   350
High on a stage° be placèd to the view,
And let me speak to th' yet unknowing world
How these things came about. So shall you hear
Of carnal, bloody, and unnatural acts,
Of accidental judgments,° casual° slaughters,   355
Of deaths put on° by cunning and forced cause,°
And, in this upshot, purposes mistook
Fall'n on th' inventors' heads. All this can I
Truly deliver.

FORTINBRAS: Let us haste to hear it,
And call the noblest to the audience.   360
For me, with sorrow I embrace my fortune.
I have some rights of memory° in this kingdom,
Which now to claim my vantage° doth invite me.

HORATIO: Of that I shall have also cause to speak,
And from his mouth whose voice will draw on more.°   365
But let this same be presently° performed,
Even while men's minds are wild, lest more mischance
On° plots and errors happen.

FORTINBRAS: Let four captains
Bear Hamlet, like a soldier, to the stage,
For he was likely, had he been put on,°   370
To have proved most royal; and for his passage,°
The soldiers' music and the rite of war
Speak° loudly for him.
Take up the bodies. Such a sight as this
Becomes the field,° but here shows much amiss.   375
Go bid the soldiers shoot.

[Exeunt (marching, bearing off the dead bodies; a peal of ordnance is shot off).]

345 his i.e., Claudius'   **348 jump** precisely, immediately   **question** dispute, affair
351 stage platform   **355 judgments** retributions   **casual** occurring by chance   **356 put on**
instigated   **forced cause** contrivance   **362 of memory** traditional, remembered, unforgotten
363 vantage favorable opportunity   **365 voice ... more** vote will influence still others
366 presently immediately   **368 On** on the basis of; on top of   **370 put on** i.e., invested in
royal office and so put to the test   **371 passage** i.e., from life to death   **373 Speak** (let them)
speak   **375 Becomes the field** suits the field of battle

MAKING CONNECTIONS

1. What is your reaction to Hamlet at the beginning of the play? Do you think his response to his father's death and mother's marriage is excessive? Explain.
2. If you were in his situation, do you think you would have responded in the same way? Why or why not?
3. What is your response to Claudius at the beginning of the play? Does he seem to be an effective leader, loving stepfather to Hamlet, loving husband to Gertrude? Explain.
4. What is your response to Hamlet's mother, Gertrude? Does she seem to be a loving mother to Hamlet? Do you think she understands why he is so angry? Explain.
5. Describe Polonius, Laertes, and Ophelia. To what extent is this a loving family? A dysfunctional family?
6. Pick out Hamlet's soliloquies throughout the play. Is there a pattern in what Hamlet says about himself and his dilemma?
7. Do you think Hamlet procrastinates too much? Is the play he arranges necessary? Should he have killed Claudius at his first opportunity? Explain.
8. Is Hamlet all good? Do you think that his treatment of Ophelia was fair? Are any of his other actions questionable? Explain.
9. At the beginning of the play we are told, "Something is rotten in the state of Denmark." Is all well at the end of the play? Explain.
10. Choose a scene from the play and discuss why it is important in light of the whole play.

MAKING AN ARGUMENT

1. Read the Ernest Jones essay "Hamlet's and the Oedipus Complex" on page 669 and and write an argument in support of it or against it. Carefully cite both the article and the text of the play in support of your view.
2. Like Shakespeare's other plays, most of this play is dramatic poetry. Choose examples of poetic language from *Hamlet* that are particularly effective in prompting strong emotion, developing character, building conflict, or advancing the plot. Write an essay that describes why the language is so effective. Cite the text of the play for support.

Desperately Seeking *Hamlet:* Four Interpretations

Over the past sixty years, some of the best performances of *Hamlet* have been recorded on film and video. Perhaps the four most popular of these productions are Laurence Olivier's 1948 film, which won the Academy Award for best picture; Derek Jacobi's 1979 *Hamlet,* produced as part of the monumental BBC Shakespeare series; Mel Gibson's portrayal in a popular 1990 Franco Zeffirelli production; and Kenneth Branagh's 1996 star-studded extravaganza. Their performances—their different, but justifiable interpretations—illustrate the complexities of the character and demonstrate the validity of multiple perspectives.

Let's look briefly at these four versions and examine each actor's interpretation of the famous "To be, or not to be" soliloquy. Because this soliloquy is so familiar to the general public, even to those who have never seen the play, it is a major challenge for an actor. Like the role of Hamlet itself, this soliloquy demands a unique interpretation. Both actors and audience often recognize in its rendering a microcosm of the character himself.

Olivier's **Hamlet**   The oldest, but not the most traditional, of these versions is Laurence Olivier's 1948 film. Revered by many purists as the definitive version, it is in many ways the least pure. The film opens with a reductive voice-over that claims, "This is the story of a man who could not make up his mind." While it is not unusual for directors to cut lines in this four-hour-long play, Olivier has, in addition, cut two important characters, Rosencrantz and Guildenstern. The fog-shrouded setting and powerful orchestral music seem omnipresent. And instead of preceding Hamlet's encounter with Ophelia with  his "To be, or not to be" soliloquy, Olivier has switched the order of Shakespeare's text. In this version, Hamlet's speech follows and seems influenced by their painful meeting.

We move into his soliloquy as we move away from a sobbing, disconsolate Ophelia, who has thrown herself at the foot of the castle steps where Hamlet has just exited. The camera follows the path of her extended arm up the winding, cold stone stairs—higher and higher—as the music rises and we are hurled into the swirling dark clouds above the castle, then down to the crashing sea and jagged rocks below. The camera shifts slowly to the back of Hamlet's head and seems to bore deeper and deeper into his skull as we hear powerful string music and see an impression of the pulsing, swirling chaos of the sea embedded on the lobes of his brain. And he has not even begun to speak.

When he does speak, he is accompanied by the sounds of the chaotic sea below and powerful orchestral music in the background. He delivers the first part of the speech looking out over the castle wall to the sea below and seems mesmerized by what he sees and says. He produces a dagger and closes his eyes while we hear the "To die, to sleep . . . " section as a voice-over. He snaps out of his reverie when he cries out, "perchance to dream." The music stops and he delivers the rest of the soliloquy to the crashing of the waves beneath him. While he speaks he peruses the sea and points the dagger at himself. As he concludes the soliloquy, he drops the dagger and it falls ominously to the rocks far below. He rises from his precarious perch on the castle wall, finishes the speech, and walks off into the fog.

Jacobi's **Hamlet**   The BBC video production of 1979 is a very complete version of the play and follows the original order of Shakespeare's text. For Derek Jacobi this means starting the "To be, or not to be" soliloquy from scratch without the momentum of the previous scene to build on. As he begins his soliloquy, therefore, Hamlet remains unaware of the interloping Polonius and Claudius and the "by chance" encounter with Ophelia they have planned for him.

Jacobi enters a quiet, empty room, notices us (the audience), and approaches to speak with us. There is no music in the background—just Jacobi and Shakespeare's words. He looks at us, confides in us. He is earnest and philosophical. He seems to ask questions with his statements, and to seek answers while feeling our concern. His is a youthful sadness and confusion—not a deep obsessive depression like Olivier's. Halfway through the soliloquy, we catch a glimpse of Ophelia approaching in the background. But Jacobi's eyes remain on us throughout. Like Olivier, he shows us his dagger as he contemplates death but looks, too, at the picture of his dead father.

On "lose the name of action," he returns the dagger to its case and greets the "fair Ophelia"—first with enthusiasm and affection, then with disappointment and suspicion as he notices the book she is reading is upside down.

Gibson's Hamlet

Like Olivier's *Hamlet*, Franco Zeffirelli's 1989 film of the play with Mel Gibson as Hamlet takes a few liberties with Shakespeare's text. Here too, the Ophelia encounter and the "To be, or not to be" soliloquy are reversed from their original order. Hamlet's painful scene with Ophelia precedes his speech, and his realization that "it hath made me mad" seems to say more about his anger than his sanity.

Mel Gibson takes his soliloquy "on the run"—busying himself with other tasks while he speaks to us—not entirely surprising for an actor who is not used to doing Shakespeare. Perhaps the most difficult task in performing Shakespeare's work is delivering a soliloquy head-on with the audience—with nothing between the actor and the audience but the words. Having Gibson keep physically busy while he relates his thoughts fits the energy of this Hamlet. His is a visceral, physical Hamlet who doesn't sit still for much. As he enters a large family crypt below the castle, his perusal of the tombs seems "to give him pause" even before he speaks. Rather than confiding in us as Jacobi does, he seems to be thinking out loud to himself. While he speaks and moves, he pauses to view and touch the reclining statues on top of the tombs. He leans against them, kneels at them, sits on the floor by them as he ponders the big questions of life and death. He seems energized by his musings and almost bounds up the stairs toward the light as he finishes his soliloquy and leaves the crypt.

Branagh's Hamlet

Kenneth Branagh's 1996 four-hour-long production of *Hamlet* is lavish. The play is set in the nineteenth century at a magnificent palace (actually, England's Blenheim Palace). The indoor scenes include a throne room surrounded by mirrored walls, overlooked by a gallery, and divided by an elevated walkway. There are two-way mirrors and concealed chambers and corridors. There are movie stars galore. And this production definitively answers the question "Was Ophelia sleeping with Hamlet?" by showing Ophelia sleeping with Hamlet.

Like the production itself, the setting for Branagh's "To be, or not to be" soliloquy is opulent—a glorious mirrored-in throne room. Like Shakespeare's text and the

BBC production, and unlike the Olivier and Zeffirelli versions, this scene precedes the Ophelia encounter. Branagh enters the huge, empty room and walks slowly across it, footsteps echoing loudly. He turns, looks directly at a mirror—behind which Claudius and Polonius are hiding to listen in on the subsequent Ophelia encounter. He speaks quickly but clearly, his voice almost a whisper. He moves closer and closer to the mirror as he speaks—thus moving closer and closer to the hiding interlopers, who see him clearly through the two-way mirror. Is he speaking to himself or to them? He unsheaths a dagger on "bare bodkin" and points it at his reflection in the mirror and Claudius on the other side of the mirror—now only a hand's length away. Claudius shudders.

As the soliloquy ends, Ophelia crosses the long hall. Hamlet approaches her with affection and a gentle hug and kiss, which gradually turns to anger as she tries to return his gifts and he suspects her duplicity.

From Part to Whole, from Whole to Part

Thinking about and analyzing the interpretations of these actors and directors can tell us much about interpreting literature. Many legitimate interpretations are possible. We would not say that one was correct and the others wrong. We might say that we preferred one to the others—or preferred a different one to any presented here.

But we might also conclude that no one scene could show us all of a character. Olivier's interpretation of this soliloquy seems to show us an obsessed, deeply depressed Hamlet close to suicide. Though we can say that this speech tells us a lot about Hamlet, we cannot say that that is all there is to this Hamlet unless we place the speech in the context of all his other speeches and actions. And so it is with Jacobi's earnest and likable Hamlet, Gibson's energetic and sad Hamlet, or Branagh's quick and angry Hamlet. If we characterize any of these Hamlets solely on his behavior as he delivers this one soliloquy, we may be ignoring evidence in other parts of the play that tells us about aspects of the character not revealed in this scene.

So, too, our interpretation of this soliloquy, like an actor's preparation and interpretation of this speech, should be informed by our whole vision of Hamlet—the whole character as we have seen him throughout the play.

A Student Essay—Explication and Analysis of the "To be, or not to be" Soliloquy

Charles Chiang

Dr. Madden

English 102

November 16, 200X

Hamlet: Connecting with the Audience

In this play, the emotional impact of Hamlet's death results less from his nobility than from his fragility and humanity. It is the human side of

Hamlet that touches us and thereby makes his death seem more tragic. Shakespeare creates empathy between Hamlet and the audience in a number of ways but accomplishes the task best with the "To be, or not to be" soliloquy. In this speech, which best demonstrates Hamlet's humanity, Shakespeare connects Hamlet to his audience with thoughts that cross the mind of every person at one time or another.

Even without the obvious closeness between the character of Hamlet and the audience that comes from the very nature of the soliloquy, the "To be, or not to be" soliloquy is so ingeniously crafted to appeal to the audience that we ignore the minor discrepancies that might come from careful analysis.

> For who would bear the whips and scorns of time,
> Th' oppressor's wrong, the proud man's contumely,
> The pangs of disprized love, the law's delay,
> The insolence of office, and the spurns
> That patient merit of th' unworthy takes. (3.1.71–75)

In this passage, Shakespeare (through Hamlet) is able to connect with us by using the tactic of a common denominator. Unreturned love ("disprized love"), injustice ("law's delay"), and bureaucracy ("insolence of office") are all experiences that are familiar even to us today. However, are these really experiences that Hamlet has suffered himself? The answer is no.

Hamlet was the prince of Denmark and lived a life of privilege. His only known romantic interest was Ophelia, who obviously returned his affections. Throughout the play almost every request he makes is granted. People are constantly doting on him and waiting on him hand and foot. While this may seem to be a burden to him, it is one the average person is unfamiliar with and one that would naturally distance Hamlet from us. Yet we ignore this reality because the soliloquy is so superbly written.

Shakespeare first manages to manipulate us with the brilliant introduction of the soliloquy:

> To be, or not to be, that is the question:
> Whether 'tis nobler in the mind to suffer
> The slings and arrows of outrageous fortune,
> Or to take arms against a sea of troubles
> And by opposing, end them. (3.1.57–61)

When first contemplating the subject, Hamlet weighs what choices are involved in suicide. On one side, there are "the slings and arrows of outrageous fortune," which we probably interpret as the death of Hamlet's father, the subsequent marriage of his uncle and mother, the appearance of the ghost, and the revelation that his uncle killed his father.

This series of events, added to the betrayal of Hamlet's childhood friends Rosencrantz and Guildenstern, would qualify as both "outrageous fortune" and "a sea of troubles" to most people because they are not everyday occurrences to anyone. However, there is no resemblance between these events and the common experiences described in the passage above, yet Shakespeare is somehow able to join these two different sets of experiences together and create a bond between Hamlet and the audience.

Shakespeare does this by using logic and a subtle shift in language in the intervening passage between the two sections:

> To die, to sleep--
> No more--and by a sleep to say we end
> The heartache and the thousand natural shocks
> That flesh is heir to. 'Tis a consummation
> Devoutly to be wished. To die, to sleep;
> To sleep, perchance to dream. Ay, there's the rub,
> For in that sleep of death what dreams may come,
> When we have shuffled off this mortal coil,
> Must give us pause. There's the respect
> That makes calamity of so long life. (3.1.61-70)

First, Shakespeare has Hamlet take a commonsense and almost childlike approach to suicide by comparing it to sleep, an everyday experience. We buy into this argument because death is like a "no more" sleep, a sleep without any waking. Hamlet continues with his logic by asking: If death is like sleep, are there dreams in death? Moreover, he implies there might be nightmares in death, thereby making suicide not an escape from unpleasant experiences.

However, in this progression of logic, Hamlet takes a more familiar tone with the audience. It is not "I" but "we," and Hamlet is no longer ending "the slings and arrows of outrageous fortune" or "a sea of troubles," but now refers to the end of "the heartache and the thousand natural shocks that flesh is heir to." Thus Shakespeare has shifted our thoughts from Hamlet's situation and mortality to our own.

As if he is still trying to distract us from the true topic, himself, Hamlet continues with the logic and reasoning of suicide:

> But that the dread of something after death,
>
> The undiscovered country from whose bourn
>
> No traveler returns, puzzles the will,
>
> And makes us rather bear those ills we have
>
> Than fly to others that we know not of?
>
> Thus conscience does make cowards of us all;
>
> And thus the native hue of resolution
>
> Is sicklied o'er with the pale cast of thought,
>
> And enterprises of great pitch and moment
>
> With this regard their currents turn awry
>
> And lose the name of action. (3.1.79-89)

Hamlet, like the audience, is afraid of the great unknown of death and that is why he will not commit suicide. However, Hamlet does suspect what death is like because of his experience with his father's ghost. If Hamlet does kill himself without first avenging his father's death, a terrible fate may await him in the afterlife. Though not addressed in this speech, there is also the Christian taboo against suicide and the punishment of going to hell for committing the sin.

It can be suggested that Hamlet knows that death is a fate worse than living, and that his true dilemma lies with deciding to act or go against his uncle. Instead, Hamlet is trying in a roundabout way to tell us that he is a coward for not acting. Like a real person trying to reveal a personal secret and shame, Hamlet hems and haws around the topic, hints at, and then hopes we can guess what he is really talking about. With either explanation, Hamlet still connects and bonds with us.

What the "To be, or not to be" soliloquy accomplishes is to bring Hamlet to the level of the audience by allowing both audience and prince to connect with a common interest--suicide. When subtext and nuances are combined, the audience (and reader) is able to sympathize with the character, thereby making his death seem more tragic.

Hamlet's death, unlike the deaths of most fictional characters, and even some real people, evokes an authentic response from us because of the emotional and personal connection. This was best demonstrated in our class, where our initial response to the ending was more numbness than sadness. This reaction was like the initial reaction to a real death--numbness, disbelief, and denial.

Despite the fact that the play is a tragedy, there is a sense of disbelief and denial when Hamlet dies, and not because he dies so senselessly. Shakespeare defies the conventions of the time and his own standards because Hamlet lacked the tragic flaw that doomed other tragic heroes. Hamlet's only flaw was to be human. So if Hamlet can die just because he is all too human, isn't Shakespeare forcing us to confront our own mortality? In "denying" Hamlet's death, the audience is denying its own mortality as if a real person has died.

[New Page]

Work Cited

Shakespeare, William. Hamlet. Exploring Literature. Ed. Frank Madden. 3rd
    ed. New York: Longman, 2007. 537-661.

A Critic's Influential Interpretation

ERNEST JONES

HAMLET'S OEDIPUS COMPLEX

In short, the whole picture presented by Hamlet, his deep depression, the hopeless note in his attitude towards the world and towards the value of life, his dread of death, his repeated reference to bad dreams, his self-accusations, his desperate efforts to get away from the thoughts of his duty, and his vain attempts to find an excuse for his procrastination: all this unequivocally points to a *tortured conscience,* to some hidden ground for shirking his task, a ground which he dare not or cannot avow to himself.

Extensive studies of the past half century, inspired by Freud, have taught us that a psychoneurosis means a state of mind where the person is unduly, and often painfully, driven or thwarted by the "unconscious" part of his mind, that buried part that was once the infant's mind and still lives on side by side with the adult mentality that has developed out of it and should have taken its place. It signifies *internal* mental conflict. We have here the reason why it is impossible to discuss intelligently the state of mind of anyone suffering from a psychoneurosis, whether the description is of a living person or an imagined one, without correlating the manifestations with what must have operated in his infancy and is *still operating*. That is what I propose to attempt here.

For some deep-seated reason, which is to him unacceptable, Hamlet is plunged into anguish at the thought of his father being replaced in his mother's affections by someone else. It is as if his devotion to his mother had made him so jealous for her affection that he had found it hard enough to share this even with his father and could not endure to share it with still another man. Against this thought, however, suggestive as it is, may be urged three objections. First, if it were in itself a full state-ment of the matter, Hamlet would have been aware of the jealousy, whereas we have concluded that the mental process we are seeking is hidden from him. Secondly, we see in it no evidence of the arousing of an old and forgotten memory. And, thirdly, Hamlet is being deprived by Claudius of no greater share in the Queen's affection than he had been by his own father, for the two brothers made exactly similar claims in this respect—namely, those of a loved husband. The last-named objection, however, leads us to the heart of the situation. How if, in fact, Hamlet had in years gone by, as a child, bitterly resented having had to share his mother's affection even with his own father, had regarded him as a rival, and had secretly wished him out of the way so that he might enjoy undisputed and undisturbed the monopoly of that affection? If such thoughts had been present in his mind in childhood days they evidently would have been "repressed," and all traces of them obliterated, by filial piety and other educative influences. The actual realization of his early wish in the death of his father at the hands of a jealous rival would then have stimulated into activity these "repressed" memories, which would have produced, in the form of depression and other suffer-ing, an obscure aftermath of his childhood's conflict. This is at all events the mecha-nism that is actually found in the real Hamlets who are investigated psychologically.

The explanation, therefore, of the delay and self-frustration exhibited in the endeavour to fulfil his father's demand for vengeance is that to Hamlet the thought of incest and parricide combined is too intolerable to be borne. One part of him tries to carry out the task, the other flinches inexorably from the thought of it. How fain would he blot it out in that "bestial oblivion" which unfortunately for him his con-science contemns. He is torn and tortured in an insoluble inner conflict.

5   Now comes the father's death and the mother's second marriage. The associa-tion of the idea of sexuality with his mother, buried since infancy, can no longer be concealed from his consciousness. As Bradley well says: "Her son was forced to see in her action not only an astounding shallowness of feeling, but an eruption of coarse sensuality, 'rank and gross,' speeding post-haste to its horrible delight." Feelings which once, in the infancy of long ago, were pleasurable desires can now, because of his repressions, only fill him with repulsion. The long "repressed" desire to take his father's place in his mother's affection is stimulated to unconscious activ-ity by the sight of someone usurping this place exactly as he himself had once longed to do. More, this someone was a member of the same family, so that the actual usurpation further resembled the imaginary one in being incestuous. Without his being in the least aware of it these ancient desires are ringing in his mind, are once more struggling to find conscious expression, and need such an expenditure of

energy again to "repress" them that he is reduced to the deplorable mental state he himself so vividly depicts.

There follows the Ghost's announcement that the father's death was a willed one, was due to murder. Hamlet, having at the moment his mind filled with natural indignation at the news, answers normally enough with the cry (Act I, Sc. 5):

> Haste me to know't, that I with wings as swift
> As meditation or the thoughts of love,
> May sweep to my revenge.

The momentous words follow revealing who was the guilty person, namely a relative who had committed the deed at the bidding of lust. Hamlet's second guilty wish had thus also been realized by his uncle, namely to procure the fulfilment of the first—the possession of the mother—by a personal deed, in fact by murder of the father. The two recent events, the father's death and the mother's second marriage, seemed to the world to have no inner causal relation to each other, but they represented ideas which in Hamlet's unconscious phantasy had always been closely associated. These ideas now in a moment forced their way to conscious recognition in spite of all "repressing forces," and found immediate expression in his almost reflex cry: "O my prophetic soul! My uncle?" The frightful truth his unconscious had already intuitively divined, his consciousness had now to assimiliate as best it could. For the rest of the interview Hamlet is stunned by the effect of the internal conflict thus re-awakened, which from now on never ceases, and into the essential nature of which he never penetrates.

HAMLET ON SCREEN

BERNICE W. KLIMAN

THE BBC HAMLET

With *Hamlet,* the producers of the BBC Shakespeare Plays have finally met the demands of Shakespeare-on-television by choosing a relatively bare set, conceding only a few richly detailed movable panels and props to shape key locales. By avoiding both location and realistic settings, they point up the natural affinity between Shakespeare's stage and the undisguised sound set. This starkness of setting admits poetry, heightened intensity—and "what not that's sweet and happy."

The producers have thus made a valid choice from among television's three faces: one, broadcast films whether made for television or not, which exploit location settings, long shots, and all the clichés we associate with movies, including sudden shifts of space and time and full use of distance, from the most extreme long shots to "eyes only" closeups; two, studio-shot television drama with naturalistic settings, such as the hospital corridors and middle-class living rooms of sitcoms and soap operas, mostly in mid- to close-shots, often interspersed, to be sure, with a bit of stock footage of highways and skylines to establish a realistic environment. This second style varies from a close representation of real action to frankly staged action, where canned laughter or even shadowy glimpses of the studio audience can heighten the staged effect. Three, there is bare space with little or no effort made to disguise that this is a televised activity with a television crew out of sight but nearby. News broadcasts, talk shows and some television drama fit into this third category. Because of its patently unrepresentational quality, this last type offers the most freedom in shooting style. To all three kinds of settings we bring particular expectations in response to their conventions.

Shakespeare's plays work best in the last kind of television space, I believe, because it avoids the clash between realism and poetry, between the unity often expected in realistic media and the disunity and ambiguity of many of the plays, especially *Hamlet*. Yet, while closest to the kind of stage Shakespeare wrote for, the bare television set can be stretched through creative camera work. For example, when Hamlet follows the ghost in the BBC play, the two repeatedly walk across the frame and out of it, first from one direction, then from another; framing fosters the illusion of extended space. Freeing this *Hamlet* from location (as in the BBC *As You Like It*) and from realistic sets (as in the BBC *Measure for Measure*—however well those sets worked for that play) allows the play to be as inconsistent as it is, with, as Bernard Beckerman has so brilliantly explained in *Shakespeare at the Globe, 1599–1609,* a rising and falling action in each individual scene rather than through the course of the drama as a whole. It also allows for acting, the bravura kind that Derek Jacobi is so capable of.

Although gradually coalescing like the pointillism of impressionistic paintings into a subtly textured portrait, at first his mannerisms suggesting madness seem excessive. It is to be expected, perhaps, that Hamlet is a bit unhinged after the ghost scene, but Jacobi's rapid, hard blows to his forehead with the flat of his hand as he says "My tables" recall the desperation of Lear's cry: "O, let me not be mad, not mad, sweet heaven." And soon after, following the last couplet of the scene, Hamlet, maniacally playful, widens his eyes and points, pretending to see the ghost again, then guffaws at Marcellus's fears. Even more unsettling is his laughter when he is alone, as while he is saying "The play's the thing / Wherein I'll catch the conscience of the King." More significantly, he breaks up his own "Mousetrap" by getting right into the play, destroying the distance between audience and stage (a very real raked proscenium-arch stage), spoiling it as a test, because Claudius has a right to be incensed at Hamlet's behavior. Of course, Hamlet does so because Claudius never gives himself away, an unusual and provocative but not impossible interpretation. Thus, Claudius can only have the court's sympathy as he calmly calls for light and uses it to examine Hamlet closely. Hamlet, in response, covers his face, then laughs.

5   Hamlet himself thinks he is mad. To Ophelia he says, as if the realization had suddenly struck him, "It *bath* made me mad [emphasis his]" (III.i.147). To his mother he stresses the word "essentially" in "I *essentially* am not in madness" (III.iv.187). That is, in all essential matters he can be considered sane, though mad around the edges. This indeed turns out to be the explanation.

However doubtful about Hamlet's sanity Jacobi's acting leaves us, in this production this question does not seem to make a difference because it does not have a bearing on the tragedy, and this is true at least partly because in each scene on this nonrealistic set we seem to start anew, ready to let Hamlet's behavior tell us if he is mad or not. Moreover, if Hamlet is mad, it is not so totally as to obscure reason or sensibility. Far from it. It is more as if exacerbated reason and sensibility sometimes tip him into madness. This madness is no excuse for action or delay; it is simply part of the suffering that Hamlet is heir to.

Hamlet, then, is left to struggle against himself—surely where Shakespeare intended the struggle to abide. One of the conflicts in this Hamlet results from his affinity, perhaps, more to the bureaucratic Claudius who handles war-scares with diplomacy and who sits at a desk while brooding over his sins than to the warlike King Hamlet who comes in full armor. Hamlet may admire Fortinbras but is himself more like the bookish Horatio. Through nuance of gesture, through body movement, through a face that is indeed a map of all emotions, Jacobi shapes a Hamlet who loves his father too much to disregard his command, yet who cannot hate his stepfather enough to attend to it. Because Jacobi conveys so fully Hamlet's aloneness and vulnerability, one could be struck, for the first time, by the ghost's silence about his son. There is no declaration of love, no concern about Hamlet's ascension to the throne. Hamlet is doomed, it seems, to care about those who consistently care more for others than for him.

All of this production's richness and suggestiveness was realized not only because Jacobi is a marvelous actor—as indeed he is—but also because within the set's spareness that acting could unfold, an acting style that subsumes and transcends the "real." This production's space tells us what is possible for television presentations of Shakespeare. The more bare the set, it seems, the more glowing the words, the more immediate our apprehension of the enacted emotion.

CLAIRE BLOOM

PLAYING GERTRUDE ON TELEVISION

It's very hard to play because strangely enough Gertrude has very few lines; I've always known it was a wonderful part and it *is*, but when you come to play it you realise you have to find many ways around the fact that she in actual fact says little!

You come to rehearse a part like this with certain preconceived notions, which you usually leave! I can only describe them as a battering ram—you knock down the first wall then what is inside is something quite different from what you'd imagined. I was convinced that she was guilty, not of the murder, but certainly that she had found out from Claudius that he had killed her husband. But there's nothing in the text that bears that out and many things that contradict it. I had thought it would make her less of a victim, more of a performer in the world, but [she laughs at herself] it isn't so. Like anyone if you live with a man, she must know there was something more, but I now believe that when Hamlet confronts her with "as kill a king . . . ay, madam, it was my word," it's the first time she's realised. I think from then on she knows and she must accept the fact that Claudius did it, and there is a change in their relationship. But there isn't a break—you don't break with someone suddenly like that. It changes; perhaps if they'd lived another twenty years they would have drifted apart. But there isn't a complete withdrawal. The hold they have on each other is too strong for that to happen. That caused me great difficulty; the scene after the closet scene is with Claudius, when he repeats twice "Gertrude, come away," and she does-n't reply. It's very mysterious. It's a kind of underwritten scene until you realise, or I realised, that there is no real choice for her. For the moment she doesn't go with him, but the next day she does. Hamlet knows it when he says, "Go not to my uncle's bed." She never replies and says "I won't"; she just says, "Thou hast cleft my heart in twain." She's a woman who goes with whatever is happening at the time. She's a weak-willed woman, but most of us are weak-willed if we're in the power of some-body who is very strong—and Claudius and Hamlet are both pretty strong fellows.

The "mysterious" scene with Claudius was one of the hardest to deal with in rehearsal. . . . We tried backwards, forwards, upside down and inside out and didn't really find it until a couple of days before we shot it. The minute we found it we knew it was the right one, but at other times we'd go away saying, "We've got it," then both Patrick and I would come in the next day depressed and say to Rodney, "Could we please do that scene again because it doesn't make sense when you think about it." There are questions that I'm sure have been asked by every cast of every *Hamlet* since Burbage[1] and for Gertrude they are: Was there a decision to go with Claudius or not to go with Claudius? How far was she lying about Hamlet's madness? I do think part of her believes he's mad, but when she says to the king "He's mad," I think that's protection, or overstating a fact she believes is possibly true. And of course she withholds information from Claudius; she says, "Behind the arras hearing something stir . . . [he] kills the unseen good old man," but she *doesn't* say he said "Is it the king?" That is a very important bit of information which she certainly does-n't pass on!

STANLEY KAUFFMANN

BRANAGH'S HAMLET

Kenneth Branagh wins two victories in *Hamlet* (Castle Rock [1996]). He has made a vital, exciting film; and he has triumphed over the obstacles he put in his own way.

Let's first rejoice in the virtues. Branagh confirms what was known from the opening shot of *Henry V:* he has fine cinematic skills. His directing keeps *Hamlet* flowing, endows scenes that might become static with germane movement. Many of his touches illuminate. One of them: Hamlet comes into a huge mirrored room in the palace, sees himself full-length and, after a moment, begins "To be or not to be." Two selves speak that speech and give it an added edge.

Then there's the text itself. Branagh has used the complete First Folio text, has included a scene from the Second Quarto that is not in the Folio, to make a film that runs four hours plus intermission. I could find only a few alterations, trifles com-pared with the chopped, twisted, insulting text that Olivier used in his 155-minute

---

[1]**Burbage** Richard Burbage (c. 1567–1619), the first actor to play Shakespeare's Hamlet.

version. Branagh's film looks splendid. He sets it in the mid-nineteenth century—with Blenheim Palace serving as the exterior of Elsinore—and Alex Byrne's costumes fully exploit the period. The cinematographer, Alex Thomson, using 70-mm wide-screen format, has nonetheless created lighting that seems naturally evolved from the hundreds of candles. And as for the music, Patrick Doyle again does wonders. He wrote the scores for Branagh's two previous Shakespeare films, and here again he provides music that rises unobtrusively to benefit scene after scene.

Every supporting role of significance has been superbly cast and is superbly played. I can't imagine a better Claudius than Derek Jacobi, who brings to it force and cunning and manipulative charm. The sequences in which he converts the furious Laertes from enemy to accomplice are masterpieces of guile manifested as honesty. (Jacobi, by the way, was the first Hamlet that Branagh ever saw; and years later Jacobi directed Branagh in a theater production.)

5   Jacobi is no surprise: Julie Christie is. This Golden Girl of the 1960s virtually disappeared for a while, then reappeared in a London production of Pinter's *Old Times.* She was so dull that I thought she was being used just for her name. But here, as Gertrude, she is emotionally rich. She brings to the role the apt quality of overblown sex object, and, presumably with Branagh's help, she completely fulfills the woman. In Gertrude's key moment, the closet scene, Christie bursts with the frightened despair of a guilty woman who thinks that her behavior may have driven her son mad.

Kate Winslet, dear to us already through *Sense and Sensibility* and *Jude,* gives Ophelia the kind of vulnerability that almost invites the man she loves to wound her. Polonius gets the obtuse officiousness that he needs from Richard Briers. It's immediately clear why Horatio, done by Nicholas Farrell, is Hamlet's dearest friend; anybody would want him for a friend. Laertes, a role always in danger of being as much of a blowhard as his father, Polonius, is realized in his confusions by Michael Maloney. Branagh, as he did in *Much Ado About Nothing,* has sprinkled some American actors through his cast. The best of these is Charlton Heston as the Player King, sounding and (even) looking plummy, home at last.

Hamlet is unique in Shakespeare. I can think of no other role in the plays in which an actor is so compelled, commanded, to present *himself.* Macbeth, Othello, Iago, the Richards and the Henrys—run through the roster, and always the actor selects and nurtures what there is in his imagination and experience and technique that will make the man come alive. No such selections for Hamlet. The whole actor is the whole character. So, when we see a Hamlet, we are looking at an actor in a unique way.

Branagh's Hamlet—or, one might say, Hamlet's Branagh—is attractive, keen, nobly intended, tender with regret for Ophelia, torn with disgust for the chicaneries of the world, fiery, quite susceptible to cracking into frenzy. (In appearance, he is fair—not Olivier's platinum blond—with a somewhat darker moustache and goatee.)

This is a man we could meet and understand. What this Hamlet lacks is what possibly we could not understand: his sense of falling upward into the metaphysical. This is what is sometimes called the "poetic" nature of Hamlet, this linkage with a spirit walking the earth in quest of purgation; and this linkage, in mystery and awe and uncertainty, leads to what Granville Barker called "a tragedy of inaction." Branagh's Hamlet doesn't attain this quality; it doesn't quite seem to be in him. Not long ago Ralph Fiennes, burdened with an unworthy director and cast, nevertheless did a Hamlet on Broadway that took us out into the spheres. Not Branagh. Every word he speaks is true. But in Hamlet that is not quite enough.

10   Now the lesser aspects of the film. First, the obverse side of Branagh's directing skill. He is too eager for spectacle, even if it's pointless or harmful. When Gertrude and Claudius exit at the end of the first court scene, confetti rains down on them. For the moment, it's startling, pretty. Then we wonder who planned it and who threw it. Answer: the director. When the Ghost speaks to Hamlet, the earth splits and flames leap. Is this God overseeing unpurged souls? Or the special effects department? Rosencrantz and Guildenstern arrive on a toy locomotive. Who put that model train and tracks on the palace grounds? Old King Hamlet? Claudius? Or the director? When Hamlet and Laertes duel, the civilized sport explodes into Errol Flynn antics, with ropes and chandeliers—another directorial intrusion. Branagh sets the whole film in winter, which allows for some breathtaking vistas but makes us wonder why the old king was sleeping outdoors in his snow-covered orchard on the afternoon of his murder and how the brookside flowers could be present when Ophelia drowns.

Another obverse side, one that may sound odd: the use of the complete text. Admirable though it is in Branagh to aim at "classic" status, not every word is helpful today, especially in a film. To hear Marcellus discourse on "the bird of dawning" at Christmastime, just after the Ghost's second appearance, is a soft indulgence in Elizabethan folklore. To hear Gertrude include a small dirty joke, about "long purples," when she tells Laertes of his sister's death is to coddle the lad from Stratford who couldn't always keep rustic humor out of his plays. And the sad fact is that, when Shakespeare takes time out from drama for moral commentary, the result is sometimes mere homiletics. Hamlet's speech about "the dram of evil" is not only a brusque lapse in the action, it captures perfectly the quality in Shakespeare that Bernard Shaw called "the atmosphere of the rented pew."

Sex. Branagh has searched for chances to get it into the film. While Polonius is warning Ophelia to be careful in her behavior with Hamlet, to avoid the prince completely, Branagh includes flashback shots of her and Hamlet naked in bed together. Presumably Branagh takes his license from the bawdy song that Ophelia later sings when she is mad—"Young men will do't if they come to't," etc.—a song that is usually viewed as the raving of a sexually repressed virgin. Whether or not Hamlet and Ophelia actually had an affair is possibly arguable, but what seems clear is that, if they have made love, it detracts considerably from the fierce, Savonarola-like outburst of the "get thee to a nunnery" passages.

Then, too, Polonius is given a visiting whore in the scene with Reynaldo, who is apparently her pimp. (Ophelia bursts in without knocking—fortuitously, just after Reynaldo and the whore leave.) Branagh's purpose is to lend irony to the old man's instructions to Reynaldo, about checking on Laertes's behavior in Paris, but the episode smacks of opportunism.

Politics. Of course Hamlet is, among other elements, a political play. One cause for Hamlet's hatred of Claudius is that his uncle has "popp'd in between th'election and my hopes." Branagh's use of the mid-century period affords the ambiance of the "Age of Metternich," but it misplaces in time the Denmark-England-Norway-Poland relationships of the original. Further, Branagh distorts the political action of the closing scenes. Early in the play we learn that the young Fortinbras of Norway wants to reconquer some lands that his country lost to Denmark, but the Norwegian king dissuades him. Fortinbras swears never to attack Denmark, but he will ask for the right of passage through Denmark to attack Poland. Toward the end of the play Fortinbras leads an army into Denmark and sends a messenger to Claudius to ask for that right of passage.

15   Incomprehensibly, in Branagh's film, Fortinbras then attacks Elsinore. (Real reason: Branagh wants to heat up the film's closing moments.) Shots of this violence are intercut with the Hamlet-Laertes duel. Just as Hamlet dies, the Norwegian soldiers burst into the court, destroying as they come. Fortinbras ought to feel a bit foolish, not only having broken his word but to find out that, just before Hamlet expired, the prince named him as his successor. ("He has my dying voice.") Instead, Fortinbras is shown as a glowering conqueror moderately disturbed by the prince's death. The very last shot is of old King Hamlet's statue being toppled and smashed. Why did Branagh choose that shot as the moment toward which the entire film moved?

Some other points might be called matters of interpretation—Claudius's slapping of Hamlet in anger at the chaffing about Polonius's corpse, the straitjacketing of Ophelia in a padded cell—but one Branagh touch seems just plain misreading. Claudius (in Act III, Scene 1) says he has "closely sent for Hamlet" so that the prince can meet Ophelia while Claudius and Polonius are hidden and watching. They do hide, Hamlet enters, finds the chamber empty though he has been sent for, muses aloud while waiting ("To be or not to be"). Then Ophelia enters—the girl who, for days, has been forbidden to see him. And it was the king who summoned him here. Surely, in simple reason, Hamlet must be suspicious that this is a set-up from the moment she appears. Instead, Branagh plays it merely petulantly until, after the nunnery speech, he hears a noise behind the door and the deception dawns on him. Branagh's treatment not only makes Hamlet less acute than we are, it takes the bite out of "Are you honest?"

Interpretations and innovations have different weights in a Shakespeare film from such matters in a theater production. When I saw Ingmar Bergman's production of *Hamlet,* with his sluttish Ophelia wandering through scenes in which Shakespeare forgot to include her, I was relieved that Bergman had not filmed it. Branagh's film, warts and all, will be with us for some time to come.

On the whole, this is good news. Though his *Henry V* and *Much Ado About Nothing* were closer to perfection, *Hamlet* is more difficult in every way. Flaws, problems, bumps, yes; but the film surpasses them finally through Branagh's talent and the talents of his colleagues. And, not to be slighted, there is Branagh's infectious joy—the right word even for *Hamlet*—in doing Shakespeare.

RUSSELL JACKSON (B. 1949)

A FILM DIARY OF THE SHOOTING
OF KENNETH BRANAGH'S HAMLET   1996

WEDNESDAY 3 JANUARY REHEARSALS BEGIN

First morning in Shepperton. This may be one of the major British studios but it's not, on first sight, impressive. Located in a semi-suburban hinterland southwest of London, it seems at first like an industrial estate, a jumble of sheds, hangars, workshops, and what look like builders' yards, with a mansion trapped in the middle of it all like a genteel hostage from Edwardian England. . . .

We're in the elegant boardroom of the old house, round a long green-baize covered table. First session is with Derek Jacobi (Claudius) and Julie Christie (Gertrude), plus Ken, Orlando Seale (his "acting double"), Annie Wotton (Script Supervisor), Simon Mosley (First A.D.), and Hugh Cruttwell.

Ken distributes phials [vials] of a herbal "Rescue Remedy" (only half a joke, admitting nervous apprehension). Everyone has read the screenplay, and the actors have already had some discussion of their roles with Ken, but these days of rehearsal before we begin shooting will give everyone time for reappraisal, adjustments, and (most important) finding out how the story will be told by *this* company of actors, in *these* circumstances. We won't start with a read-through; better to edge toward the play. We discuss royal families (including the current one), privacy, politics, and draw toward a reading of the scenes when Claudius and Gertrude are together. There's talk about the issue of complicity between them (not at all, so far as murder is concerned) and the "essential" Claudius, which she took (and part of him still takes) as loving, kind, a "good" man. Derek goes along with this, though he and Hugh Cruttwell remind us of Hamlet's very different point of view. Gertrude and Claudius feel responsible for Hamlet but Claudius has another agenda she knows nothing about—concerning the potential threat posed by her son.

After lunch the Polonius family join us, with Horatio. By now we feel able to discuss frankly and simply (and off the record) our own experiences of family, bereavement, grief. (This is not just to canvass ideas about the emotions of the play to draw on them in performance: it also establishes common ground among us.) Then we try to imagine an "ideal" family, successful and well-balanced according to current middle-class notions, professional but not competitive, materially well-off but not showy—which (we agree) turns out quite repulsive. Then on to the Polonius family.

5   Polonius (Richard Briers) was promoted by new king. Laertes (Michael Maloney) is in Paris getting the gentlemanly accomplishments (N.B. not at Wittenberg). Ophelia (Kate Winslett) and Hamlet have been having an affair (yes, they have been to bed together, because we want this relationship to be as serious as possible) since the death of Hamlet senior. (Effect of a surge of feeling in time of bereavement and crisis?)

THURSDAY 4–MONDAY 8 JANUARY

We work through scenes, trying various approaches, finding snags, problems, opportunities. Ophelia's motivations in returning Hamlet's love tokens are considered: she is going further than Polonius suggested in any instructions we have heard, and whatever her father and the king expect from this confrontation, she has her own agenda (perhaps to find out why Hamlet is behaving this way to her, to put him on the spot?). The kinder and more circumspect Polonius seems, the harder it will be for her to betray him—hence her lying to Hamlet ("Where's your father?—At home, my lord"). In "To be or not to be" Ken wants to show Hamlet alone with his mirror image(s) in the vast space of the mirrored hall. He has to be careful not to give the soliloquy an energy or momentum that it does not need—those qualities are coming soon enough in what follows when he encounters Ophelia. Ken steers Derek toward seeming even more vulnerable as Claudius, "quietly anxious" about Hamlet after "nunnery" scene, rarely openly angry, even when Rosencrantz and Guildenstern have screwed up. So, when he does flare up, becomes desperate, it will be more shocking.

On 8 January we go over each actor's list of their character's priorities. Claudius has specific aims: inspiring confidence and trust in himself; loving Gertrude; making Hamlet look indulgent and neurotic (and thus defusing him); creating a new, strong, triumphalist Denmark (a military regime). Gertrude's aims are more general: decorum, sense of behaving properly in public; *noblesse oblige,* etiquette; sense of culture, confidence; loving Hamlet. Old Hamlet (Brian Blessed) points out that when he was alive he never let Claudius see how little he mattered—there has to be an underlying bitterness in what Claudius has done to get the crown as well as intense love for Gertrude. We consider different ways of showing these relationships in a short flashback—perhaps Old Hamlet and his son playing chess while Gertrude and Claudius watch, or some other activity (perhaps outdoors) that will focus their various feelings for each other.

From *Hamlet.* Screenplay and Introduction by
Kenneth Branagh. Film diary by Russell Jackson.

EXPLORING THE LITERATURE OF INNOCENCE AND EXPERIENCE: MAKING CONNECTIONS AND ARGUMENTS

❦MAKING CONNECTIONS

1. Consider the ways in which personal experiences have influenced your life. Do any of the stories, poems, plays, or essays in this section remind you of your own experiences or the circumstances of your life? Choose one or more of these works and write a response essay that compares your experience or circumstances with those in the literature.
2. Our personal experiences can affect how we see the world and the formation of our values. These values can strongly influence our response to literature. We may agree or disagree with what an author says or what characters say or do. So, too, this literature may influence us and help to form our ideas about innocence and experience. Write an essay about the ways in which one or more works in this section helped you learn something about innocence and experience.

❦MAKING AN ARGUMENT

1. Over two thousand years ago, Plato wrote in the *Symposium,* "The life which is unexamined is not worth living." Do you agree? Consider this quote, and write an essay about the value of examining or reflecting on a personal experience in one or more works in this section.
2. Oscar Wilde has written that ". . . it is well to remember from time to time that nothing worth knowing can be taught." Do you agree?

Write about this quote as it applies to the experience of a character in one or more works in this section.

3. Choose a quote (or quotes) in the introduction to this section, "Innocence and Experience," and pair it (or them) with one of the longer pieces in this section that either supports or argues against it. For example, La Rochefoucauld's maxim "The mind is always the dupe of the heart" might be compared to James Joyce's "Araby." Or Huxley's comment that "Experience is not what happens to you; it is what you do with what happens to you" might be compared with Liliana Heker's "The Stolen Party."

A Research Option

Toni Cade Bambara's "The Lesson," Seamus Heaney's, "Mid-Term Break," Shakespeare's *Hamlet,* and David Sedaris's "The Learning Curve" all have something to say about innocence and experience. Each of these works, however, springs from a very different historical, social, or political context.

Expanding our exploration of literature to include the context in which these works were produced can be an enriching and enlightening experience. Choose one or more of these or other works in this section and write a research essay that includes secondary source material about the historical, social, or political background of the literature.

Writing About Connections Across Themes

Most of the literature in the text has been organized into theme sections, but good literature is much too complex to be reduced to a single broad theme. Many of the works included under Innocence and Experience could just as easily fit under other themes—and in many cases works arranged in other themes or chapters could fit here as well.

Choose one or more of the following works from earlier chapters or other themes and consider how they can be linked to Innocence and Experience—and how this combination of the work with more than one theme provides additional insight into the literature and fresh topics for writing.

From Chapter 1
  "Advice to My Son"—p. 9
  "Zimmer in Grade School"—p. 11
  "Not Waving but Drowning"—p. 12
  "Those Winter Sundays"—p. 13
  "Barbie Doll"—p. 14
  "Ballad of Birmingham"—p. 17
From Chapter 2
  "Incident"—p. 24
  "Eleven"—p. 26

Collaboration: Writing and Revising with Your Peers

In addition to applying your own values and standards to writing about the literature in this section, you may find it beneficial to share and discuss your work with classmates. Getting feedback from others can help you generate and clarify your ideas and revise and edit your writing more effectively.

Choose a work, a topic, or one of the above options for writing about innocence and experience, and work with a partner or in a small group. Exchange journal entries or response sheets, generate questions together, do a group semantic map (see p. 41), or simply share and respond to each other's ideas.

After you have written a rough draft of your essay, share it with a partner or your group. Respondents should function primarily as sensitive readers and give honest, constructive responses. They should try to be aware of each writer's purpose, discuss concerns particular to each writer, and comment on the effectiveness of the essay's organization, support, clarity, and voice. (For a comprehensive checklist for revision, see p. 46).

In the final stage of your writing, editing and proofreading might be done in a similar fashion. A partner or group readers might help you check for correct grammar, spelling, punctuation, and typos. (A comprehensive checklist for editing is on p. 49).

A Writing/Research Portfolio Option

A portfolio is a collection of your work, related materials, and commentary about your work collected over time. Gathering materials in a portfolio will provide you with resources for research and development. You can use your portfolio to collect your writing about the literature in this section, find a topic to write about, revise or add to your work, or keep multiple drafts and monitor the changes you make as you revise.

Among the resources you might include:

- Your responses to the quotes and prompts about innocence and experience at the beginning of this section, the questions you had right after you finished reading each piece of literature, and your journal entries.

- What your classmates, instructor, or published critics had to say about the literature and how their comments may have influenced your interpretation.

- Information you have gathered from the library and the Internet about the historical, social, and political context of the work or its author.

CASE STUDY IN AESTHETIC CONTEXT

Poetry and Painting

The purpose of this Case Study is to provide you with an opportunity to compare two forms of art, painting and poetry. Long before the advent of writing, people recorded their innermost feelings and impulses in images painted on cave walls. In fact, a number of cave paintings found in South Africa are nearly thirty thousand years old. Throughout history, artists have celebrated great writing by sculpting, painting, and drawing their responses to literature. The work of Homer, Shakespeare, Dickens, Joyce, and many other writers has inspired sculpture, painting, and illustration. Art inspires art. Conversely then, it's not surprising that poems are inspired by great paintings. Viewed and read together, the eight paintings that follow and the poems written in response to them invite comparisons and connections—not only with each other—but with your own experience of the subject they address.

In one way or another, these paintings and poems have something to say about many different themes and are not limited to time and place. Like the brief quotations that open the thematic units, these paintings and poems are a dialogue across history. W. H. Auden's modern poem "Musée des Beaux Arts" responds to Brueghel's sixteenth-century *Landscape with the Fall of Icarus,* itself a response to ancient Greek mythology. And Alan Devenish's "Icarus Again" is a 1999 poem written in response to the ancient myth, the paintings and poems it has inspired over the ages, and the tragedies of modern life. Native American N. Scott Momaday's modern poem "Before an Old Painting of the Crucifixion" is inspired by *Crucifixion,* a work by sixteenth-century Italian painter Tintoretto; Edward Hopper's painting *Nighthawks* and the poem it prompts, Samuel Yellen's "Nighthawks," are both modern pieces; van Gogh's nineteenth-century *Starry Night* evokes Anne Sexton's twentieth-century "The Starry Night"; Jan Vermeer's *The Loveletter* speaks across three hundred years to Sandra Nelson, who answers with her poem "When a Woman Holds a Letter." The painter of *Dance,* Henri Matisse, produced his painting more than eighty years before the poet Natalie Safir, interprets it in "Matisse's Dance." Mary Ellen LeClair's "The Clark Institute: Labor Day, 1999" is inspired by *The Gleaners,* an 1857 painting by Jean-Francois Millet. Adrienne Rich had not been born when Edwin Romanzo Elmer painted his *Mourning Picture* in memory of his young daughter Effie. Yet Rich's response to the painting, "Mourning Picture," brings Effie back to life as the mournful speaker of the poem.

Whatever they hold in common, each painting and poem is an individual work. So before you read the poems, look at each of the paintings separately and write your own response. On the next page are prompts and questions that may help you organize your responses.

FIRST RESPONSES: PAINTING AND POETRY

1. Before you read its accompanying poem, write your own response to each of the paintings.

   - As you look at the painting, write down what strikes you first. How does it make you feel? What do you like most about it? Do you find anything disturbing?
   - Do you sense a prevailing mood or tone? How do the colors affect you?

2. When you finish recording your responses to the painting, read the companion poem.

   - Compare your response to the painting with the poet's response. How are they similar? How are they different?
   - Has the poet mentioned anything that is not included in your response? Have you raised issues that the poet has not?

3. Compare and contrast the poem with the painting.

   - Are the details of each the same? What details are contained in the poem that are not in the painting? What details are in the painting but not in the poem?
   - Do the painting and the poem seem to be saying the same thing? If not, how do they differ? Which do you prefer?
   - Has reading the poem revised your response to the painting? If so, how?

Following the paintings and poems in the glossy insert, is the process (page 701) and product (page 704) of a Student's Comparison and Contrast Essay—and questions for Making Connections and Making an Argument on page 708 that build on the prompts above. You may find the student model and the questions useful for writing essays about the poems and paintings in this section.

Making
Connections
with Painting
and Poetry

Pieter Brueghel the Elder (Dutch, 1520–1569). *Landscape with the Fall of Icarus.* Musée
Royaux des Beaux-Arts, Brussels, Belgium. Photo: Scala/Art Resource, NY.

W. H. AUDEN   [1907–1973]

MUSÉE DES BEAUX ARTS   [1940]

About suffering they were never wrong,
The Old Masters: how well they understood
Its human position; how it takes place
While someone else is eating or opening a window or just walking dully along;
How, when the aged are reverently, passionately waiting   5
For the miraculous birth, there always must be
Children who did not specially want it to happen, skating
On a pond at the edge of the wood:
They never forgot
That even the dreadful martyrdom must run its course   10
Anyhow in a corner, some untidy spot
Where the dogs go on with their doggy life and the torturer's horse
Scratches its innocent behind on a tree.

In Brueghel's *Icarus,* for instance: how everything turns away
Quite leisurely from the disaster; the ploughman may   15
Have heard the splash, the forsaken cry,
But for him it was not an important failure; the sun shone
As it had to on the white legs disappearing into the green
Water; and the expensive delicate ship that must have seen
Something amazing, a boy falling out of the sky,   20
Had somewhere to get to and sailed calmly on.

ALAN DEVENISH [B. 1947]

ICARUS AGAIN   [1999]

You'd think we'd have enough of falling
since that sunny day high off the coast of Crete. Air disasters
appalling and impersonal. The bomber's hate
made potent with a bit of plastic and some altitude. Spacecrafts
with schoolteachers aboard—exploding over and over   5
again. The parents aghast at the pure Icarian sky of Florida
suddenly emptied of their child.

What is myth if not an early version of what's been happening
all along? (The arrogance of flight brought down
by faulty gaskets.)   10

As Auden would have it: the way we plow through life
head bent to the furrow while tragedy falls from the sky.

Bruegel shows only the legs—flailing and white—scissoring
into a pitiless green sea.

Williams treats a distant casualty in his clinical   15
little sketch. (Did the astronauts feel their fall
or breathe instantly the killing fumes?)

Matisse plays it another way. It's color—Icarus' love
for color and who can blame him? His poor heart
waxing red as he falls through blue and what might be   20
a scatter of sunbursts or a vision of war—the enemy
aces sighting Icarus in their crosshairs over France.

In Ovid the line that never fails to move me is
And he saw the wings on the waves . . .

The way it comes to the father. His lofty design reduced to this   25
little detritus as he hovers in the left-hand corner of the myth
grieving wingbeats wrinkling the surface of the sea.

Even in bad prints of the Bruegel I can't help feeling sorry
for this kid. And dismay at our constant clumsiness. Our light
heart pulling us down. Love itself believing against all gravity   30
that what we say is what is bound to happen. How foolish to trust
our waxen wings and how foolish not to.

Jacopo Tintoretto (Italian, 1518–1549). *Crucifixion*, Scuola Grande di San Rocco, Venice, Italy/Erich Lessing/Art Resource, NY.

N. Scott Momaday [B. 1934]

BEFORE AN OLD PAINTING OF THE CRUCIFIXION

The Mission Carmel,
June, 1960

I ponder how He died, despairing once.
I've heard the cry subside in vacant skies,
In clearings where no other was. Despair,
Which, in the vibrant wake of utterance,
Resides in desolate calm, preoccupies,   5
Though it is still. There is no solace there.

That calm inhabits wilderness, the sea,
And where no peace inheres but solitude;
Near death it most impends. It was for Him,
Absurd and public in His agony,   10
Inscrutably itself, nor misconstrued,
Nor metaphrased in art or pseudonym:

A vague contagion. Old, the mural fades . . .
Reminded of the fainter sea I scanned,
I recollect: How mute in constancy!   15
I could not leave the wall of palisades
Till cormorants returned my eyes on land.
The mural but implies eternity:

Not death, but silence after death is change.
Judean hills, the endless afternoon,   20
The farther groves and arbors seasonless
But fix the mind within the moment's range.
Where evening would obscure our sorrow soon,
There shines too much a sterile loveliness.

No imprecision of commingled shade,   25
No shimmering deceptions of the sun,
Herein no semblances remark the cold
Unhindered swell of time, for time is stayed.
The Passion wanes into oblivion,
And time and timelessness confuse, I'm told.   30

These centuries removed from either fact
Have lain upon the critical expanse
And been of little consequence. The void
Is calendared in stone; the human act,
Outrageous, is in vain. The hours advance   35
Like flecks of foam borne landward and destroyed.

Edward Hopper (American, 1882–1967). *Nighthawks*. 1942. Oil on canvas, 84.1 x 152.4 cm. Friends of American Art Collection, 1942.51. © 2000 The Art Institute of Chicago. All rights reserved.

SAMUEL YELLEN [B. 1906]

NIGHTHAWKS [1951]

The place is the corner of Empty and Bleak,
The time is night's most desolate hour,
The scene is Al's Coffee Cup or the Hamburger Tower,
The persons in this drama do not speak.

We who peer through that curve of plate glass 5
Count three nighthawks seated there—patrons of life:
The counterman will be with you in a jiff,
The thick white mugs were never meant for demitasse.

The single man whose hunched back we see
Once put a gun to his head in Russian roulette, 10
Whirled the chamber, pulled the trigger, won the bet,
And now lives out his *x* years' guarantee.

And facing us, the two central characters
Have finished their coffee, and have lit
A contemplative cigarette; 15
His hand lies close, but not touching hers.

Not long ago together in a darkened room,
Mouth burned mouth, flesh beat and ground
On ravaged flesh, and yet they found
No local habitation and no name. 20

Oh, are we not lucky to be none of these!
We can look on with complacent eye:
Our satisfactions satisfy,
Our pleasures, our pleasures please.

Vincent van Gogh (Dutch, 1853–1890.) *Starry Night.* 1889. Oil on canvas. 29 x 36 ¼" (73.7 x 92.1 cm). The Museum of Modern Art, New York. Acquired through the Lillie P. Bliss Bequest (472.1941). Photo: The Museum of Modern Art/Licensed by SCALA/Art Resource, NY.

ANNE SEXTON [1928-1975]

THE STARRY NIGHT   [1961]

That does not keep me from having a terrible need of—shall I say the word—
religion. Then I go out at night to paint the stars.
    —Vincent van Gogh in a letter to his brother

The town does not exist
except where one black-haired tree slips
up like a drowned woman into the hot sky.
The town is silent. The night boils with eleven stars
Oh starry starry night! This is how   5
I want to die.

It moves. They are all alive.
Even the moon bulges in its orange irons
to push children, like a god, from its eye.
The old unseen serpent swallows up the stars.   10
Oh starry starry night! This is how
I want to die:

into that rushing beast of the night,
sucked up by that great dragon, to split
from my life with no flag,   15
no belly,
no cry.

Henri Matisse (French, 1869–1954). *Dance* (first version). Paris (March 1909). Oil on canvas, 8' 6 ½"
x 12' 9 ½" (259.7 390.1 cm). Gift of Nelson A. Rockefeller in honor of Alfred H. Barr. Jr. Photograph
© The Museum of Modern Art/Licensed by Scala/Art Resource, New York. © 2002 Succession H.
Matisse, Paris/Artists Rights Society (ARS), New York.

NATALIE SAFIR (1935–)

MATISSE'S DANCE   [1990]

A break in the circle dance of naked women,
dropped stitch between the hands
of the slender figure stretching too hard
to reach her joyful sisters.

Spirals of glee sail from the arms   5
of the tallest woman. She pulls
the circle around with her fire.
What has she found that she doesn't
keep losing, her torso
a green-burning torch?   10

Grass mounds curve ripely beneath
two others who dance beyond the blue.
Breasts swell and multiply and
rhythms rise to a gallop.

Hurry, frightened one and grab on—before   15
the stitch is forever lost, before the dance
unravels and a black sun swirls from that space.

Jean-Francois Millet (French, 1814–1875). *The Gleaners,* 1857. Oil on canvas, 83.6 x 111 cm. Musée d'Orsay, Paris, France. Inv.: RF 592. Photo: Jean Schormans/Réunion des Musées Nationaux/Art Resource, NY.

Mary Ellen LeClair

The Clark Institute: Labor Day, 1999

We bend with the outcast women
Over stubble, searching for leftovers after the August harvest
In the backlight affluent villagers mound
Their hay into sun-streaked stacks.

We watch French peasant women,   5
Hands swollen from labor,
Searching for last yellow filaments.

They work in half light,
Faces browned, heads scarved in red, delft blue,
Sabots planted firmly on the umber land.   10

Millet's autumnal laborers give
Luminous windows into time.
Then toward the end of his life, a shift—

Nature without workers,
Only yellow haystacks, moon-filled fields.   15
He lifts up the earth, its people.

He plucks the quiet of country days,
The old callings, cowherd, shepherd, cooper,
The old stories of the land, how

Boaz loved Ruth, the gleaner, in   20
That still time of humans toiling out hard lives
With dignity. We almost touch them.

I remember my own grandfather,
I remember his hands, browned and cracked,
From a lifetime of work on the farm   25
His father homesteaded.
When I was little,
He played the violin for me with those hands.

The last time I saw him
I was a junior at boarding school,   30
He gave me a silver dollar
As if I were ten.

Now as we leave the twentieth century,
We are all gleaners
In the autumn fields,   35
Looking for chaffs of hay, of wheat, of light.

Edwin Romanzo Elmer (1850–1923). *Mourning Picture,* 1890. Oil on canvas, 27 ¹⁵/₁₆ x 36 in. (70.9 x 91.4 cm). Smith College Museum of Art, Northampton, Massachusetts. Purchased 1953.

ADRIENNE RICH [B. 1929]

MOURNING PICTURE   [1965]

The picture was painted by Edwin Romanzo Elmer (1850–1923) as a memorial to his daughter Effie. In the poem it is the dead girl who speaks.

They have carried the mahogany chair and the cane rocker
out under the lilac bush,
and my father and mother darkly sit there, in black clothes.
Our clapboard house stands fast on its hill,
my doll lies in her wicker pram   5
gazing at western Massachusetts.
This was our world,
I could remake each shaft of grass
feeling its rasp on my fingers,
draw out the map of every lilac leaf   10
or the net of vines on my father's
grief tranced hand.
Out of my head, half-bursting,
still filling, the dream condenses—
shadows, crystals, ceilings, meadows, globes of dew.   15
Under the dull green of the lilacs, out in the light
carving each spoke of the pram, the turned porch-pillars,
under high early-summer clouds,
I am Effie, visible and invisible,
remembering and remembered.   20

They will move from the house,
give the toys and pets away.
Mute and rigid with loss my mother
will ride the train to Baptist Corner,
the silk-spool will run bare.   25
I tell you, the thread that bound us lies
faint as a web in the dew.
Should I make you, world, again,
could I give back the leaf its skeleton, the air
its early-summer cloud, the house   30
its noonday presence, shadowless,
and leave *this* out? I am Effie, you were my dream.

Jan Vermeer (Dutch, 1632–1675). *The Loveletter.* c. 1670. Oil on canvas 44 x
38.5 cm. © Rijksmuseum Amsterdam.

SANDRA NELSON [B. 1951]

WHEN A WOMAN HOLDS A LETTER   [1993]

It is always from a man. Jan Vermeer
knows this as he paints the dark
note in Clarissa's right hand;
her left strangling the fretted neck coming
from the pear-shaped body of his   5
mandolin. Her upturned eyes may be tied
to a ferris wheel of sparrows' biting love.
Or she may feel the heavy curve of his instrument
against her stomach and her eyes
instinctively flip up to heaven to see   10
if anyone is watching. I am
probably wrong. There *is* another woman
behind her (a washer-woman whose head
is wrapped in a wimple to keep out the dirt).
Perhaps it is to her that Clarissa's eyes roll.   15

A STUDENT'S COMPARISON AND CONTRAST ESSAY: PROCESS AND PRODUCT

On the following pages we follow Barbara Pfister's process as she generates ideas for her comparison and contrast essay about Vincent van Gogh's *Starry Night* and Anne Sexton's poem. At the core of this process are journal responses and semantic maps. By completing her written response and semantic map after viewing the painting—before she reads Sexton's poem—she comes up with her own interpretation of the painting. When she finally reads Sexton's poem, she has two sources to compare it with, the painting and her own interpretation—giving her a base from which to respond to the poem—and enriching the content of her subsequent essay.

Barbara Pfister's Semantic Map in Response to van Gogh's painting Starry Night

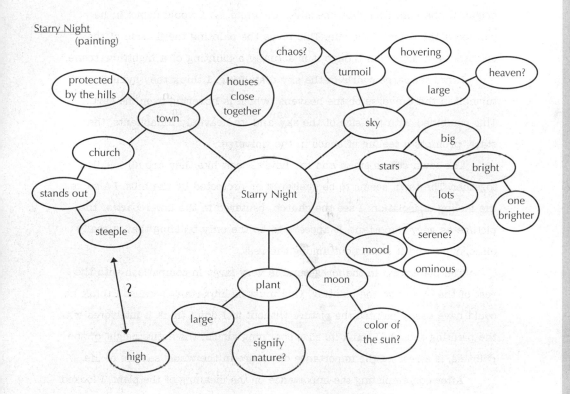

Barbara's Journal Response to van Gogh's Painting Starry Night

When I first looked at this painting, the overall impression I got was ominous and quiet, but not gloomy. The feeling was of both foreboding and powerful beauty at the same time.

I liked the short brushstrokes he used to paint this scene. They give the feeling of separate and distinct pieces that together make up the whole. The colors in the picture depict a night sky, but at the same time appear as vivid as day.

The sky takes up a major portion of the painting and it stands out quite vividly. I love the way van Gogh painted the stars. They appear to be very large and bright, not little pinpoints in the sky as we usually see them. Their size and brightness stress their importance in the picture. I think he is symbolizing the greatness of heaven or the universe. There is one star that is especially bright in the lower part of the sky and I feel this must mean something but I'm not sure exactly what.

The crescent shaped moon is painted as if it were as large and as bright as the sun. He didn't use silver or white, as I would depict it; he painted it the color of the sun. This gives the painting the illusion of the brightness of day, even though it is actually a painting of a nighttime scene.

I find the large swirls in the sky disturbing. I think they symbolize turmoil in the universe or the heavens, which is hovering over the earth. This combined with the size of the sky and its heavenly inhabitants, the stars, prompts a feeling of chaos in the universe.

The town seems small and the houses look like they are all huddled together. The town seems to be sheltered or protected by the hills. I also get the feeling of isolation. I see the church, centered in the lower part of the picture as very important. It appears to be the only building that is really discernible, and it stands out among the rest.

The plant seen in the foreground is very large in comparison with the rest of the objects in the painting. This must be important, because I think he could have easily painted the picture without it. I don't think it interferes with the painting though. I think its size, spanning almost the entire height of the painting, is stressing the importance of nature in the whole scheme of life.

After contemplating the importance or the meaning of the plant, I looked at the town and the church again. Maybe it is symbolic that the plant reaches all the way to the sky, signifying the relationship between nature and the heavens. The plant also seems to spear right through the swirling turmoil in the night. The steeple of the church, in comparison, barely reaches the horizon. I wonder if this is intentional and therefore, symbolic, or merely a coincidence.

I can summarize my feelings in a few different ways. The colors he used seem to imply that the heavens at night are as bright and clear as day, and perhaps that is how our understanding of the universe should be. With reference to the plant and the church, another idea is that people can only make a small attempt to understand the heavens or the universe, while nature is at one with the universe.

Barbara's Semantic Map in Response to Anne Sexton's poem "The Starry Night"

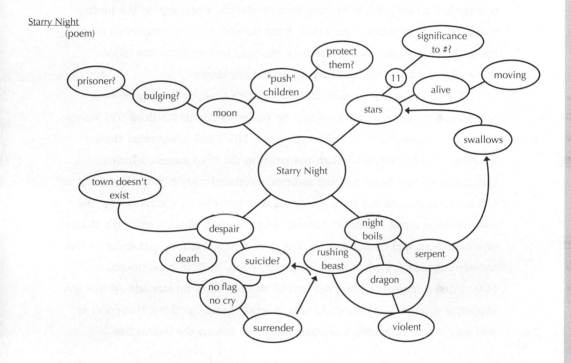

Starry Night
(poem)

Barbara's Journal Response to Anne Sexton's poem "The Starry Night"

My initial reaction after reading this poem was one of despair and gloom. It projects an overall feeling of death or possibly suicide. The wording used throughout the poem is very vivid and somewhat violent in nature.

When the poet starts off the poem with the line "The town does not exist" (1), I got the impression of a dream, which led me to an initially pleasant feeling which would not last long as I read further. In examining the first three lines together, I feel the speaker is saying the town only exists in the eyes of death--the drowned woman. Is the poet questioning our view of reality? Maybe we can only see the truth of the universe in death.

I liked the description of the stars "boiling" in the sky. It created a very vivid picture in my mind. The way the poet gives the stars and the moon life is wonderful, saying the stars are alive and moving. Personalizing the moon was a bit confusing at first. I can remember as a child hearing the usual fairy tales of "the man in the moon." The image of the moon given in the poem was initially very different from my childhood memory. The description in the poem is at first kind of violent, when saying the moon wants "to push children, like a god, from its eye" (9). On examining these lines further though, I think the poet is trying to symbolize the moon protecting children from the turmoil and chaos above.

The theme of death, most probably suicide I feel, is steadily present throughout the poem. I was intrigued by the repetition of the lines "Oh starry night! This is how / I want to die" (5, 6; 11, 12). I feel this carried the common thread of death through the poem to the third stanza, which elaborated on that death and the feelings associated with it. From beginning to end in the poem, the sky or the heavens are described in a violent way. The poet uses the words "serpent," "beast," and "dragon," which creates the illusion of a dangerous and deadly animal. The poet depicts death as surrender to that threatening creature when she writes "sucked up by that great dragon . . . " (14). I find it interesting that the last three lines show no struggle against the menacing creature she described. This is what makes me think this poem is probably a view of suicide, describing someone lacking the will to live.

A Student Essay—Comparison and Contrast

Barbara Pfister

Dr. Madden

English 102

February 9, 200X

Quiet Contemplation or Silent Desperation?

Examining art in the written word or in a painting can be a very personal experience. We bring our own, sometimes very different, responses and interpretations to each work that we study or explore. As there seems to be no one correct interpretation, I find that keeping an open mind and looking at others' views may open up new avenues of thought.

I examined my responses to both Vincent van Gogh's <u>Starry Night</u> and the poem "The Starry Night" written by Anne Sexton. I found a few similar ideas, and some very interesting differences. It is apparent that the poet had a very different response to the painting than I did.

When I first looked at the painting, the overall impression I got was ominous and quiet, but not gloomy. There was a feeling of both foreboding and powerful beauty at the same time. The short brushstrokes he used to paint the scene gave the feeling of separate and distinct pieces that together make up the whole. My initial reaction after reading the poem was one of despair and gloom. It projected an overall feeling of death or possibly suicide. The wording used throughout the poem is very vivid and seemed somewhat violent in nature.

The colors I see in the picture depict a night sky, but at the same time appear as vivid as day. The sky, taking up a major portion of the painting, stands out quite vividly. I love the way van Gogh painted the stars. They appear to be very large and bright, not little pinpoints in the sky as we usually see them. In the poem, however, I found the description of the stars "boiling" in the sky captivating, but different from my reaction. It created a very vivid picture in my mind, and I liked the way the poet gave the stars life, saying they are alive and moving. Similar to the poet's description of the stars, I found the large swirls in the sky of the painting somewhat disturbing. I think they symbolize turmoil in the universe or the heavens, and that discord is hovering over the earth. This combined with the size of the sky and its heavenly dwellers, the stars, prompts a feeling of chaos in the universe.

The crescent shaped moon in the painting is as large and as bright as the sun. Van Gogh didn't use silver or white, as I would portray it; he painted it the color of the sun. Anne Sexton's personalization of the moon was a bit confusing for me at first. I can remember as a child hearing the usual fairy tales of "the man in the moon." The image of the moon given in the poem was initially very different from my amiable childhood memory. The description in the poem is at first rather violent, when declaring that the moon wants "to push children, like a god, from its eye" (9). On examining these lines further though, I think the poet is trying to symbolize the moon protecting children from the turmoil and chaos above.

The town, as it is portrayed in the painting, seems small and the houses look like they are all huddled together. The town seems to be sheltered or protected by the hills, but this also hints at an uneasy feeling of isolation. The church was not mentioned at all in the poem. I see the church, centered in the lower part of the picture, as being very symbolic. It appears to be the only building that is really discernible; it stands out among the rest.

When the poet started the poem with the line "The town does not exist" (1), I got the initially pleasant impression of a dream, which would not last long as I read further. The poet describes the plant shown in the painting as a "drowned woman." In examining the first three lines of the poem together, I feel the speaker is saying the town only exists in the eyes of death, the drowned woman. Is the poet questioning our view of reality? Perhaps we can only see the reality of the universe in the act of death.

I had a very different impression when contemplating the plant in the painting. It is very large in comparison with the rest of the objects pictured. This must be significant, because I think he could have easily painted the picture without it, if he felt it was in the way. I don't think it interferes with the painting though. I think its size, spanning almost the entire height of the painting, is stressing the importance of nature in the whole scheme of life. This is very different from the poet's interpretation of the meaning of the plant.

After contemplating the significance of the plant, I looked at the town and the church again. Maybe it is symbolic that the plant reaches all the way to the sky, signifying the relationship between nature and the heavens. The plant also seems to spear right through the swirling turmoil in the night. The steeple of the church, in comparison, barely reaches the horizon. I wonder if this is intentional and therefore, very symbolic, or merely a coincidence.

The theme of death, most probably suicide I feel, is steadily present throughout the poem. I was intrigued by the repetition of the lines "Oh starry night! This is how / I want to die" (5, 6; 11,12). I feel this carried the common thread of death through the poem to the third stanza, which elaborated on that death and the feelings associated with it. From beginning to end in the poem, the sky or the heavens are described in a violent way, much different than the contemplative way I interpreted them. The poet uses the words "serpent," "beast," and "dragon," which creates the illusion of a dangerous and deadly animal. The poet depicts death as surrender to that threatening creature, when she writes, "sucked up by that great dragon . . . " (14). I found it interesting that the last three lines show no struggle against the menacing creature that she described. This apathy is what makes me think this poem is probably a view of suicide, describing someone lacking the will to live. There is a silent desperation in the poem. This is strikingly different when compared to the impression the painting left in my mind.

My overall feeling of the painting is more of a quiet contemplation about the relationship between mankind and the universe. The colors van Gogh used seem to imply that the heavens at night are as bright and clear as day, and perhaps that is how our understanding of the universe should be. When looking at the symbolism of the plant and the church, another notion is that people can only make a small attempt to understand the heavens or the universe, as symbolized by the church barely reaching the horizon. The plant, representing nature, is at one with the universe as it breaks through and spans the turmoil seen in the heavens.

If our understanding of the universe is as shallow as van Gogh has pictured it, perhaps that is the same desperation that Anne Sexton sees in the painting. This may explain the futility of life she described in her poem. From a broader perspective, these two different interpretations may actually be more similar than they seem.

[New Page]

Works Cited

Sexton, Anne. "The Starry Night." Exploring Literature. Ed. Frank Madden.
    3rd ed. New York: Longman, 2007. 693.

van Gogh, Vincent. Starry Night. Exploring Literature. Ed. Frank Madden.
    3rd ed. New York: Longman, 2007. 692.

EXPLORING POETRY AND PAINTING: OPTIONS FOR MAKING CONNECTIONS AND ARGUMENTS

MAKING CONNECTIONS

1. Choose a painting and write a response to your viewing. Go back and re-view the painting again. Write another response. Compare your first response with your second response. Did your re-viewing change your response? If so, how?

2. Do any of the poems or paintings in this section remind you of your own experiences or circumstances in your life? If so, choose one or more of these works and write a response essay that compares your experiences or circumstances with those in the poem and/or painting.

3. Many factors, including personal experiences, influence our perspective and can strongly influence our response to poems and paintings. Conversely, the way we are affected by a poem or painting may change our perspective. Write an essay about the way in which one or more poems and/or paintings in this section gave you a new insight and influenced your thinking.

MAKING AN ARGUMENT

1. Interpreting a painting, like interpreting a poem, requires attention to details. Choose one of the paintings in this section and write an interpretive essay. Analyze the "text" of the painting the way you would a literary text. Identify what visual elements of the painting support your interpretation.

2. Choose a painting and a poem and write an essay that compares the poet's response to the painting with your own. Cite the text of the poem and the details of the painting for support.

3. Pick a poem that agrees with your view of a painting in this section and write an argument that supports the poet's interpretation. Cite the text of the poem as well as details in the painting to support your argument.

4. Choose a painting, a poem, and another work of literature in the text that seem to treat the same theme, and write a thematic critical essay. In addition to writing about the three works, explore the theme and state why—and in what ways—the painting and literature exemplify the theme so well.

Research Option

Expanding our exploration of poems and paintings to include the context in which these works were produced can be an enriching and enlightening experience. Choose a painting and one or more poems in this section, and write a research essay that includes secondary source material about the historical, social, or political background of the works.

Women & Men

Women & Men
A DIALOGUE ACROSS HISTORY

The gate of the subtle and profound female / Is the root of Heaven and Earth. / It is continuous, and seems to be always existing. / Use it and you will never wear out.
  —Lao-tzu, *Tao te Ching,* c. 550 B.C.

A woman is always a fickle, unstable thing.
  —Vergil, *Eclogues,* 37 B.C.

The education of women should always be relative to that of men. To please, to be useful to us, to make us love and esteem them, to educate us when young, to take care of us when grown up; to advise, to console us, to render our lives easy and agreeable. These are the duties of women at all times, and what they should be taught in their infancy.
  —Jean Jacques Rousseau, *Emile,* 1762

It would be an endless task to trace the variety of meannesses, cares, and sorrows into which women are plunged by the prevailing opinion that they were created rather to feel than reason, and that all power they obtain must be obtained by their charms and weakness.
  —Mary Wollstonecraft, *A Vindication of the Rights of Women,* 1792

We hold these truths to be self-evident, that all men and women *are created equal.*
  —Elizabeth Cady Stanton, *Declaration of Sentiments,* 1848

With women the heart argues, not the mind.
  —Matthew Arnold, *Merope,* 1858

The great question . . . which I have not been able to answer, despite my thirty years of research into the feminine soul, is "What does a woman want?"
  —Sigmund Freud, 1930

The usual masculine disillusionment is discovering that a woman has a brain.
—Margaret Mitchell, *Gone with the Wind*, 1936

We know of no culture that has said articulately, that there is no difference between men and women except in the way they contribute to the creation of the next generation.
—Margaret Mead, *Male and Female*, 1948

This has always been a man's world, and none of the reasons hitherto brought forward in explanation of this fact has seemed adequate.
—Simone de Beauvoir, *The Second Sex*, 1949

A girl should not expect special privileges because of her sex, but neither should she "adjust" to prejudice and discrimination. She must learn to compete . . . not as a woman, but as a human being.
—Betty Friedan, *The Feminine Mystique*, 1963

If women had wives to keep house for them, to stay home with vomiting children, to get the car fixed, fight with the painters, run to the supermarket, reconcile the bank statements, listen to everyone's problems, cater the dinner parties, and nourish the spirit each night, just imagine the possibilities for expansion—the number of books that would be written, companies started, professorships filled, political offices that would be held, by women.
—Gail Sheehy, *Passages*, 1976

Depriving millions of gay American adults the marriages of their choice, and the rights that flow from marriage, denies equal protection of the law. They, their families and friends, together with fair-minded people everywhere, should demand an end to this monstrous injustice.
—Thomas Stoddard, *Gay Marriages: Make Them Legal*, 1988

We have defective mythologies that ignore masculine depth of feeling, assign men a place in the sky instead of earth, and teach obedience to the wrong powers. . . .
—Robert Bly, *Iron John*, 1990

We all want, above all, to be heard—but not merely to be heard. We want to be understood—heard for what we think we are saying, for what we know we meant. With increased understanding of the ways women and men use language should come a decrease in the frequency of the complaint, You just don't understand.
—Deborah Tannen, *You Just Don't Understand*, 1990

WOMEN AND MEN: EXPLORING YOUR OWN VALUES AND BELIEFS

"Can't live with them, can't live without them." We've heard this statement directed at both men and women. What is more compelling, more passionate, or more divisive than a debate about women and men? It's a debate that has been going on since humans have existed. Beyond our reproductive functions, are there significant differences between men and women? Are we intellectually and emotionally different? Should there be a different role for each gender?

Throughout most of history, women have been treated as inferior to men. It is only within the past two hundred years or so that women have had a voice loud enough to be acknowledged. While Elizabeth Cady Stanton's statement of 150 years ago "We hold these truths to be self-evident, that all *men and women* are created equal" may seem "self-evident" to us today, it has been less than one hundred years since women have even had the right to vote in this country. Although it is still not clear that women have been given equal opportunity in all areas, it is obvious how far women have come. Many men, however, now find themselves confused, frustrated, and even "bashed" by the emergence of women and the blurring of gender roles. If women's roles have been redefined, what about the roles of men?

Your gender may influence your aspirations or the expectations others have for you, the encouragement you receive for education and career goals, marriage and family, even your involvement in sports. It probably influences the formation of your values. And it certainly influences your view of the opposite sex. As a preparation for reading the literature in this section, you may find it helpful to think about your own values and beliefs about gender.

READING AND WRITING ABOUT WOMEN AND MEN

Exploring your beliefs and values and connecting your experience with what you read is an important first step toward our ultimate goal—an appreciation of literature and the ability to think and write critically about it. Critical analysis will require rereading and reflection, writing and revising, gathering evidence, and constructing a solid argument to support your responses.

At least one aspect of the many stories, poems, plays, and essays that follow is the way that gender determines how men and women define themselves and each other—and the impact that has on their relationships: a demented lover in Robert Browning's poem "Porphyria's Lover," a woman's discovery that her marriage has kept her a child in Henrik Ibsen's drama *A Doll's House,* and Bruno Bettelheim's essay on the psychological meaning of the Cinderella fairy tale. The brief quotes that open this section also give you some idea of the number of compelling ethical, political, and social arguments connected to gender. Equal rights and opportunity, intellectual equality, stereotyping, bigotry, arrogance, and styles of communication head a long list of concerns. Any of these or other related issues might provide a fine topic for building an argument and writing an essay.

◆ FICTION ◆

ANTON CHEKHOV [1860–1904]

*One of the first practitioners of the modern short story
and the modern play, Anton Pavlovich Chekhov was born
in the town of Taganrog, near the Black Sea, in Russia. His
grandfather was a serf who bought his family's freedom.
Chekhov attended the University of Moscow on a scholarship, eventually earning a degree in medicine. In an effort
to support himself and his impoverished family during
this period, Chekhov began writing short pieces, first
sketches and jokes, and later short stories for newspapers and journals. By 1886,
Chekhov had gained enough recognition to make writing his chief interest and
occupation. His long association with the famed Moscow Arts Theater began with
its acclaimed production of* The Seagull *in 1898 (which had had a disastrous premiere two years earlier in St. Petersburg), and continued with productions of his
greatest plays,* The Three Sisters, Uncle Vanya, *and* The Cherry Orchard. *In his
later years, which were plagued by ill health, Chekhov married Olga Knipper, a
star of the theater company. He died in 1904 of tuberculosis. His short stories,
which he continued to write even after he became a successful playwright, are
characterized not only by their economical prose style, but by a love of humanity that is often set against a pervading mood of sadness.*

THE LADY WITH THE PET DOG   [1899]

Translated by Avrahm Yarmolinsky

I

A new person, it was said, had appeared on the esplanade: a lady with a pet dog.
Dmitry Dmitrich Gurov, who had spent a fortnight at Yalta and had got used to the
place, had also begun to take an interest in new arrivals. As he sat in Vernet's con-
fectionery shop, he saw, walking on the esplanade, a fair-haired young woman of
medium height, wearing a beret; a white Pomeranian was trotting behind her.

And afterwards he met her in the public garden and in the square several times
a day. She walked alone, always wearing the same beret and always with the white
dog; no one knew who she was and everyone called her simply "the lady with the
pet dog."

"If she is here alone without husband or friends," Gurov reflected, "it wouldn't
be a bad thing to make her acquaintance."

He was under forty, but he already had a daughter twelve years old, and two sons
at school. They had found a wife for him when he was very young, a student in his
second year, and by now she seemed half as old again as he. She was a tall, erect
woman with dark eyebrows, stately and dignified and, as she said of herself,

intellectual. She read a great deal, used simplified spelling in her letters, called her husband, not Dmitry, but Dimitry, while he privately considered her of limited intelligence, narrow-minded, dowdy, was afraid of her, and did not like to be at home. He had begun being unfaithful to her long ago—had been unfaithful to her often and, probably for that reason, almost always spoke ill of women, and when they were talked of in his presence used to call them "the inferior race."

5   It seemed to him that he had been sufficiently tutored by bitter experience to call them what he pleased, and yet he could not have lived without "the inferior race" for two days together. In the company of men he was bored and ill at ease, he was chilly and uncommunicative with them; but when he was among women he felt free, and knew what to speak to them about and how to comport himself; and even to be silent with them was no strain on him. In his appearance, in his character, in his whole make-up there was something attractive and elusive that disposed women in his favor and allured them. He knew that, and some force seemed to draw him to them, too.

Oft-repeated and really bitter experience had taught him long ago that with decent people—particularly Moscow people—who are irresolute and slow to move, every affair which at first seems a light and charming adventure inevitably grows into a whole problem of extreme complexity, and in the end a painful situation is created. But at every new meeting with an interesting woman this lesson of experience seemed to slip from his memory, and he was eager for life, and everything seemed so simple and diverting.

One evening while he was dining in the public garden the lady in the beret walked up without haste to take the next table. Her expression, her gait, her dress, and the way she did her hair told him that she belonged to the upper class, that she was married, that she was in Yalta for the first time and alone, and that she was bored there. The stories told of the immorality in Yalta are to a great extent untrue; he despised them, and knew that such stories were made up for the most part by persons who would have been glad to sin themselves if they had had the chance; but when the lady sat down at the next table three paces from him, he recalled these stories of easy conquests, of trips to the mountains, and the tempting thought of a swift, fleeting liaison, a romance with an unknown woman of whose very name he was ignorant suddenly took hold of him.

He beckoned invitingly to the Pomeranian, and when the dog approached him, shook his finger at it. The Pomeranian growled; Gurov threatened it again.

The lady glanced at him and at once dropped her eyes.

10   "He doesn't bite," she said and blushed.

"May I give him a bone?" he asked; and when she nodded he inquired affably, "Have you been in Yalta long?"

"About five days."

"And I am dragging out the second week here."

There was a short silence.

15   "Time passes quickly, and yet it is so dull here!" she said, not looking at him.

"It's only the fashion to say it's dull here. A provincial will live in Belyov or Zhizdra and not be bored, but when he comes here it's 'Oh, the dullness! Oh, the dust!' One would think he came from Granada."

She laughed. Then both continued eating in silence, like strangers, but after dinner they walked together and there sprang up between them the light banter of people who are free and contented, to whom it does not matter where they go or what they talk about. They walked and talked of the strange light on the sea: the water was a soft, warm, lilac color, and there was a golden band of moonlight upon it. They talked of how sultry it was after a hot day. Gurov told her that he was a native of Moscow, that he had studied languages and literature at the university, but had a post in a bank; that at one time he had trained to become an opera singer but had given it up, that he owned two houses in Moscow. And he learned from her that she had grown up in Petersburg, but had lived in S＿＿＿＿ since her marriage two years previously, that she was going to stay in Yalta for about another month, and that her husband, who needed a rest, too, might perhaps come to fetch her. She was not certain whether her husband was a member of a Government Board or served on a Zemstvo Council, and this amused her. And Gurov learned that her name was Anna Sergeyevna.

Afterwards in his room at the hotel he thought about her—and was certain that he would meet her the next day. It was bound to happen. Getting into bed he recalled that she had been a schoolgirl only recently, doing lessons like his own daughter; he thought how much timidity and angularity there was still in her laugh and her manner of talking with a stranger. It must have been the first time in her life that she was alone in a setting in which she was followed, looked at, and spoken to for one secret purpose alone, which she could hardly fail to guess. He thought of her slim, delicate throat, her lovely gray eyes.

"There's something pathetic about her, though," he thought, and dropped off.

II

20   A week had passed since they had struck up an acquaintance. It was a holiday. It was close indoors, while in the street the wind whirled the dust about and blew people's hats off. One was thirsty all day, and Gurov often went into the restaurant and offered Anna Sergeyevna a soft drink or ice cream. One did not know what to do with oneself.

In the evening when the wind had abated they went out on the pier to watch the steamer come in. There were a great many people walking about the dock; they had come to welcome someone and they were carrying bunches of flowers. And two peculiarities of a festive Yalta crowd stood out: the elderly ladies were dressed like young ones and there were many generals.

Owing to the choppy sea, the steamer arrived late, after sunset, and it was a long time tacking about before it put in at the pier. Anna Sergeyevna peered at the steamer and the passengers through her lorgnette as though looking for acquaintances, and whenever she turned to Gurov her eyes were shining. She talked a great deal and asked questions jerkily, forgetting the next moment what she had asked; then she lost her lorgnette in the crush.

The festive crowd began to disperse; it was now too dark to see people's faces; there was no wind any more, but Gurov and Anna Sergeyevna still stood as though waiting to see someone else come off the steamer. Anna Sergeyevna was silent now, and sniffed her flowers without looking at Gurov.

"The weather has improved this evening," he said. "Where shall we go now? Shall we drive somewhere?"

25   She did not reply.

Then he looked at her intently, and suddenly embraced her and kissed her on the lips, and the moist fragrance of her flowers enveloped him; and at once he looked round him anxiously, wondering if anyone had seen them.

"Let us go to your place," he said softly. And they walked off together rapidly.

The air in her room was close and there was the smell of the perfume she had bought at the Japanese shop. Looking at her, Gurov thought: "What encounters life offers!" From the past he preserved the memory of carefree, good-natured women whom love made gay and who were grateful to him for the happiness he gave them, however brief it might be; and of women like his wife who loved without sincerity, with too many words, affectedly, hysterically, with an expression that it was not love or passion that engaged them but something more significant; and of two or three others, very beautiful, frigid women, across whose faces would suddenly flit a rapacious expression—an obstinate desire to take from life more than it could give, and these were women no longer young, capricious, unreflecting, domineering, unintelligent, and when Gurov grew cold to them their beauty aroused his hatred, and the lace on their lingerie seemed to him to resemble scales.

But here there was the timidity, the angularity of inexperienced youth, a feeling of awkwardness; and there was a sense of embarrassment, as though someone had suddenly knocked at the door. Anna Sergeyevna, "the lady with the pet dog," treated what had happened in a peculiar way, very seriously, as though it were her fall—so it seemed, and this was odd and inappropriate. Her features drooped and faded, and her long hair hung down sadly on either side of her face; she grew pensive and her dejected pose was that of a Magdalene in a picture by an old master.

30   "It's not right," she said. "You don't respect me now, you first of all."

There was a watermelon on the table. Gurov cut himself a slice and began eating it without haste. They were silent for at least half an hour.

There was something touching about Anna Sergeyevna; she had the purity of a well-bred, naive woman who has seen little of life. The single candle burning on the table barely illuminated her face, yet it was clear that she was unhappy.

"Why should I stop respecting you, darling?" asked Gurov. "You don't know what you're saying."

"God forgive me," she said, and her eyes filled with tears. "It's terrible."

35   "It's as though you were trying to exonerate yourself."

"How can I exonerate myself? No. I am a bad, low woman; I despise myself and I have no thought of exonerating myself. It's not my husband but myself I have deceived. And not only just now; I have been deceiving myself for a long time. My husband may be a good, honest man, but he is a flunkey! I don't know what he does, what his work is, but I know he is a flunkey! I was twenty when I married him. I was tormented by curiosity; I wanted something better. 'There must be a different sort of life,' I said to myself. I wanted to live! To live, to live! Curiosity kept eating at me— you don't understand, but I swear to God I could no longer control myself; something was going on in me; I could not be held back. I told my husband I was ill, and came here. And here I have been walking about as though in a daze, as though I were mad; and now I have become a vulgar, vile woman whom anyone may despise."

Gurov was already bored with her; he was irritated by her naive tone, by her repentance, so unexpected and so out of place, but for the tears in her eyes he might have thought she was joking or play-acting.

"I don't understand, my dear," he said softly. "What do you want?"

She hid her face on his breast and pressed close to him.

40   "Believe me, believe me, I beg you," she said, "I love honesty and purity, and sin is loathsome to me; I don't know what I'm doing. Simple people say, 'The Evil One has led me astray.' And I may say of myself now that the Evil One has led me astray."

"Quiet, quiet," he murmured.

He looked into her fixed, frightened eyes, kissed her, spoke to her softly and affectionately, and by degrees she calmed down, and her gaiety returned; both began laughing.

Afterwards when they went out there was not a soul on the esplanade. The town with its cypresses looked quite dead, but the sea was still sounding as it broke upon the beach; a single launch was rocking on the waves and on it a lantern was blinking sleepily.

They found a cab and drove to Oreanda.

45   "I found out your surname in the hall just now; it was written on the board— von Dideritz," said Gurov. "Is your husband German?"

"No; I believe his grandfather was German, but he is Greek Orthodox himself."

At Oreanda they sat on a bench not far from the church, looked down at the sea, and were silent. Yalta was barely visible through the morning mist; white clouds rested motionlessly on the mountaintops. The leaves did not stir on the trees, cicadas twanged, and the monotonous muffled sound of the sea that rose from below spoke of the peace, the eternal sleep awaiting us. So it rumbled below when there was no Yalta, no Oreanda here; so it rumbles now, and it will rumble as indifferently and as hollowly when we are no more. And in this constancy, in this complete indifference to the life and death of each of us, there lies, perhaps, a pledge of our eternal salvation, of the unceasing advance of life upon earth, of unceasing movement towards perfection. Sitting beside a young woman who in the dawn seemed so lovely, Gurov, soothed and spellbound by these magical surroundings—the sea, the mountains, the clouds, the wide sky—thought how everything is really beautiful in this world when one reflects: everything except what we think or do ourselves when we forget the higher aims of life and our own human dignity.

A man strolled up to them—probably a guard—looked at them and walked away. And this detail, too, seemed so mysterious and beautiful. They saw a steamer arrive from Feodosia, its lights extinguished in the glow of dawn.

"There is dew on the grass," said Anna Sergeyevna, after a silence.

50   "Yes, it's time to go home."

They returned to the city.

Then they met every day at twelve o'clock on the esplanade, lunched and dined together, took walks, admired the sea. She complained that she slept badly, that she had palpitations, asked the same questions, troubled now by jealousy and now by the fear that he did not respect her sufficiently. And often in the square or the public garden, when there was no one near them, he suddenly drew her to him and kissed her passionately. Complete idleness, these kisses in broad daylight exchanged furtively in dread of someone's seeing them, the heat, the smell of the sea, and the continual flitting before his eyes of idle, well-dressed, well-fed people, worked a complete change in him; he kept telling Anna Sergeyevna how beautiful she was, how seductive, was urgently passionate; he would not move a step away from her, while she was often pensive and continually pressed him to confess that he did not respect her, did not love her in the least, and saw in her nothing but a common woman. Almost every evening rather late they drove somewhere out of town, to Oreanda or to the waterfall; and the excursion was always a success, the scenery invariably impressed them as beautiful and magnificent.

They were expecting her husband, but a letter came from him saying that he had eye-trouble, and begging his wife to return home as soon as possible. Anna Sergeyevna made haste to go.

"It's a good thing I am leaving," she said to Gurov. "It's the hand of Fate!"

55   She took a carriage to the railway station, and he went with her. They were driving the whole day. When she had taken her place in the express, and when the second bell had rung, she said, "Let me look at you once more—let me look at you again. Like this."

She was not crying but was so sad that she seemed ill and her face was quivering.

"I shall be thinking of you—remembering you," she said. "God bless you; be happy. Don't remember evil against me. We are parting forever—it has to be, for we ought never to have met. Well, God bless you."

The train moved off rapidly, its lights soon vanished, and a minute later there was no sound of it, as though everything had conspired to end as quickly as possible that sweet trance, that madness. Left alone on the platform, and gazing into the dark distance, Gurov listened to the twang of the grasshoppers and the hum of the telegraph wires, feeling as though he had just waked up. And he reflected, musing, that there had now been another episode or adventure in his life, and it, too, was at an end, and nothing was left of it but a memory. He was moved, sad, and slightly remorseful: this young woman whom he would never meet again had not been happy with him; he had been warm and affectionate with her, but yet in his manner, his tone, and his caresses there had been a shade of light irony, the slightly coarse arrogance of a happy male who was, besides, almost twice her age. She had constantly called him kind, exceptional, high-minded; obviously he had seemed to her different from what he really was, so he had involuntarily deceived her.

Here at the station there was already a scent of autumn in the air; it was a chilly evening.

60   "It is time for me to go north, too," thought Gurov as he left the platform. "High time!"

III

At home in Moscow the winter routine was already established; the stoves were heated, and in the morning it was still dark when the children were having breakfast and getting ready for school, and the nurse would light the lamp for a short time.

There were frosts already. When the first snow falls, on the first day the sleighs are out, it is pleasant to see the white earth, the white roofs; one draws easy, delicious breaths, and the season brings back the days of one's youth. The old limes and birches, white with hoar-frost, have a good-natured look; they are closer to one's heart than cypresses and palms, and near them one no longer wants to think of mountains and the sea.

Gurov, a native of Moscow, arrived there on a fine frosty day, and when he put on his fur coat and warm gloves and took a walk along Petrovka, and when on Saturday night he heard the bells ringing, his recent trip and the places he had visited lost all charm for him. Little by little he became immersed in Moscow life, greedily read three newspapers a day, and declared that he did not read the Moscow papers on principle. He already felt a longing for restaurants, clubs, formal dinners, anniversary celebrations, and it flattered him to entertain distinguished lawyers and actors, and to play cards with a professor at the physicians' club. He could eat a whole portion of meat stewed with pickled cabbage and served in a pan, Moscow style.

A month or so would pass and the image of Anna Sergeyevna, it seemed to him, would become misty in his memory, and only from time to time he would dream of her with her touching smile as he dreamed of others. But more than a month went by, winter came into its own, and everything was still clear in his memory as though he had parted from Anna Sergeyevna only yesterday. And his memories glowed more and more vividly. When in the evening stillness the voices of his children preparing their lessons reached his study, or when he listened to a song or to an organ playing in a restaurant, or when the storm howled in the chimney, suddenly everything would rise up in his memory; what had happened on the pier and the early morning with the mist on the mountains, and the steamer coming from Feodosia, and the kisses. He would pace about his room a long time, remembering and smiling; then his memories passed into reveries, and in his imagination the past would mingle with what was to come. He did not dream of Anna Sergeyevna, but she followed him about everywhere and watched him. When he shut his eyes he saw her before him as though she were there in the flesh, and she seemed to him lovelier, younger, tenderer than she had been, and he imagined himself a finer man than he had been in Yalta. Of evenings she peered out at him from the bookcase, from the fireplace, from the corner—he heard her breathing, the caressing rustle of her clothes. In the street he followed the women with his eyes, looking for someone who resembled her.

Already he was tormented by a strong desire to share his memories with someone. But in his home it was impossible to talk of his love, and he had no one to talk to outside; certainly he could not confide in his tenants or in anyone at the bank. And what was there to talk about? He hadn't loved her then, had he? Had there been anything beautiful, poetical, edifying, or simply interesting in his relations with Anna Sergeyevna? And he was forced to talk vaguely of love, of women, and no one guessed what he meant; only his wife would twitch her black eyebrows and say, "The part of a philanderer does not suit you at all, Dimitry."

65   One evening, coming out of the physicians' club with an official with whom he had been playing cards, he could not resist saying:

"If you only knew what a fascinating woman I became acquainted with at Yalta!"

The official got into his sledge and was driving away, but turned suddenly and shouted:

"Dmitry Dmitrich!"

"What is it?"

70   "You were right this evening: the sturgeon was a bit high."

These words, so commonplace, for some reason moved Gurov to indignation, and struck him as degrading and unclean. What savage manners, what mugs! What stupid nights, what dull, humdrum days! Frenzied gambling, gluttony, drunkenness, continual talk always about the same thing! Futile pursuits and conversations always about the same topics take up the better part of one's time, the better part of one's strength, and in the end there is left a life clipped and wingless, an absurd mess, and there is no escaping or getting away from it—just as though one were in a madhouse or a prison.

Gurov, boiling with indignation, did not sleep all night. And he had a headache all the next day. And the following nights too he slept badly; he sat up in bed, thinking, or paced up and down his room. He was fed up with his children, fed up with the bank; he had no desire to go anywhere or to talk of anything.

In December during the holidays he prepared to take a trip and told his wife he was going to Petersburg to do what he could for a young friend—and he set off for S____. What for? He did not know, himself. He wanted to see Anna Sergeyevna and talk with her, to arrange a rendezvous if possible.

He arrived at S____ in the morning, and at the hotel took the best room, in which the floor was covered with gray army cloth, and on the table there was an inkstand, gray with dust and topped by a figure on horseback, its hat in its raised hand and its head broken off. The porter gave him the necessary information: von Dideritz lived in a house of his own on Staro-Goncharnaya Street, not far from the hotel: he was rich and lived well and kept his own horses; everyone in the town knew him. The porter pronounced the name: "Dridiritz."

75   Without haste Gurov made his way to Staro-Goncharnaya Street and found the house. Directly opposite the house stretched a long gray fence studded with nails.

"A fence like that would make one run away," thought Gurov, looking now at the fence, now at the windows of the house.

He reflected: this was a holiday, and the husband was apt to be at home. And in any case, it would be tactless to go into the house and disturb her. If he were to send her a note, it might fall into her husband's hands, and that might spoil everything. The best thing was to rely on chance. And he kept walking up and down the street and along the fence, waiting for the chance. He saw a beggar go in at the gate and heard the dogs attack him; then an hour later he heard a piano, and the sound came to him faintly and indistinctly. Probably it was Anna Sergeyevna playing. The front door opened suddenly, and an old woman came out, followed by the familiar white Pomeranian. Gurov was on the point of calling to the dog, but his heart began beating violently, and in his excitement he could not remember the Pomeranian's name.

He kept walking up and down, and hated the gray fence more and more, and by now he thought irritably that Anna Sergeyevna had forgotten him, and was perhaps already diverting herself with another man, and that that was very natural in a young woman who from morning till night had to look at that damn fence. He went back to his hotel room and sat on the couch for a long while, not knowing what to do, then he had dinner and a long nap.

"How stupid and annoying all this is!" he thought when he woke and looked at the dark windows: it was already evening. "Here I've had a good sleep for some reason. What am I going to do at night?"

80   He sat on the bed, which was covered with a cheap gray blanket of the kind seen in hospitals, and he twitted himself in his vexation:

"So there's your lady with the pet dog. There's your adventure. A nice place to cool your heels in."

That morning at the station a playbill in large letters had caught his eye. *The Geisha* was to be given for the first time. He thought of this and drove to the theater.

"It's quite possible that she goes to first nights," he thought.

The theater was full. As in all provincial theaters, there was a haze above the chandelier, the gallery was noisy and restless; in the front row, before the beginning of the performance the local dandies were standing with their hands clasped behind their backs; in the Governor's box the Governor's daughter, wearing a boa, occupied the front seat, while the Governor himself hid modestly behind the portiere and only his hands were visible; the curtain swayed; the orchestra was a long time tuning up. While the audience was coming in and taking their seats, Gurov scanned the faces eagerly.

85   Anna Sergeyevna, too, came in. She sat down in the third row, and when Gurov looked at her his heart contracted, and he understood clearly that in the whole world there was no human being so near, so precious, and so important to him; she, this little, undistinguished woman, lost in a provincial crowd, with a vulgar lorgnette in her hand, filled his whole life now, was his sorrow and his joy, the only happiness that he now desired for himself, and to the sounds of the bad orchestra, of the miserable local violins, he thought how lovely she was. He thought and dreamed.

A young man with small side-whiskers, very tall and stooped, came in with Anna Sergeyevna and sat down beside her; he nodded his head at every step and seemed to be bowing continually. Probably this was the husband whom at Yalta, in an access of bitter feeling, she had called a flunkey. And there really was in his lanky figure, his side-whiskers, his small bald patch, something of a flunkey's retiring manner; his smile was mawkish, and in his buttonhole there was an academic badge like a waiter's number.

During the first intermission the husband went out to have a smoke; she remained in her seat. Gurov, who was also sitting in the orchestra, went up to her and said in a shaky voice, with a forced smile:

"Good evening!"

She glanced at him and turned pale, then looked at him again in horror, unable to believe her eyes, and gripped the fan and the lorgnette tightly together in her hands, evidently trying to keep herself from fainting. Both were silent. She was sitting, he was standing, frightened by her distress and not daring to take a seat beside her. The violins and the flute that were being tuned up sang out. He suddenly felt frightened: it seemed as if all the people in the boxes were looking at them. She got up and went hurriedly to the exit; he followed her, and both of them walked blindly along the corridors and up and down stairs, and figures in the uniforms prescribed for magistrates, teachers, and officials of the Department of Crown Lands, all wearing badges, flitted before their eyes, as did also ladies, and fur coats on hangers; they were conscious of drafts and the smell of stale tobacco. And Gurov, whose heart was beating violently, thought:

90   "Oh, Lord! Why are these people here and this orchestra!"

And at that instant he suddenly recalled how when he had seen Anna Sergeyevna off at the station he had said to himself that all was over between them and that they would never meet again. But how distant the end still was!

On the narrow, gloomy staircase over which it said "To the Amphitheatre," she stopped.

"How you frightened me!" she said, breathing hard, still pale and stunned. "Oh, how you frightened me! I am barely alive. Why did you come? Why?"

"But do understand, Anna, do understand—" he said hurriedly, under his breath. "I implore you, do understand—"

95   She looked at him with fear, with entreaty, with love; she looked at him intently, to keep his features more distinctly in her memory.

"I suffer so," she went on, not listening to him. "All this time I have been thinking of nothing but you; I live only by the thought of you. And I wanted to forget, to forget; but why, oh, why have you come?"

On the landing above them two high school boys were looking down and smoking, but it was all the same to Gurov; he drew Anna Sergeyevna to him and began kissing her face and hands.

"What are you doing, what are you doing!" she was saying in horror, pushing him away. "We have lost our senses. Go away today; go away at once—I conjure you by all that is sacred, I implore you—People are coming this way!"

Someone was walking up the stairs.

100   "You must leave," Anna Sergeyevna went on in a whisper. "Do you hear, Dmitry Dmitrich? I will come and see you in Moscow. I have never been happy; I am unhappy now, and I never, never shall be happy, never! So don't make me suffer still more! I swear I'll come to Moscow. But now let us part. My dear, good, precious one, let us part!"

She pressed his hand and walked rapidly downstairs, turning to look round at him, and from her eyes he could see that she really was unhappy. Gurov stood for a while, listening, then when all grew quiet, he found his coat and left the theater.

IV

And Anna Sergeyevna began coming to see him in Moscow. Once every two or three months she left S_____ telling her husband that she was going to consult a doctor about a woman's ailment from which she was suffering—and her husband did and did not believe her. When she arrived in Moscow she would stop at the Slavyansky Bazar Hotel, and at once send a man in a red cap to Gurov. Gurov came to see her, and no one in Moscow knew of it.

Once he was going to see her in this way on a winter morning (the messenger had come the evening before and not found him in). With him walked his daughter, whom he wanted to take to school; it was on the way. Snow was coming down in big wet flakes.

"It's three degrees above zero,[1] and yet it's snowing," Gurov was saying to his daughter. "But this temperature prevails only on the surface of the earth; in the upper layers of the atmosphere there is quite a different temperature."

105   "And why doesn't it thunder in winter, papa?"

He explained that, too. He talked, thinking all the while that he was on his way to a rendezvous, and no living soul knew of it, and probably no one would ever know. He had two lives, an open one, seen and known by all who needed to know it, full of conventional truth and conventional falsehood, exactly like the lives of his friends and acquaintances; and another life that went on in secret. And through some strange, perhaps accidental, combination of circumstances, everything that was of interest and importance to him, everything that was essential to him, everything about which he felt sincerely and did not deceive himself, everything that consti-tuted the core of his life, was going on concealed from others; while all that was false, the shell in which he hid to cover the truth—his work at the bank, for instance, his discussions at the club, his references to the "inferior race," his appearances at anniversary celebrations with his wife—all that went on in the open. Judging others by himself, he did not believe what he saw, and always fancied that every man led his real, most interesting life under cover of secrecy as under cover of night. The per-sonal life of every individual is based on secrecy, and perhaps it is partly for that reason that civilized man is so nervously anxious that personal privacy should be respected.

Having taken his daughter to school, Gurov went on to the Slavyansky Bazar Hotel. He took off his fur coat in the lobby, went upstairs, and knocked gently at the door. Anna Sergeyevna, wearing his favorite gray dress, exhausted by the journey and by waiting, had been expecting him since the previous evening. She was pale, and looked at him without a smile, and had hardly entered when she flung herself on his breast. That kiss was a long, lingering one, as though they had not seen one another for two years.

"Well, darling, how are you getting on there?" he asked. "What news?"

"Wait; I'll tell you in a moment—I can't speak."

110   She could not speak; she was crying. She turned away from him, and pressed her handkerchief to her eyes.

"Let her have her cry; meanwhile I'll sit down," he thought, and he seated him-self in an armchair.

Then he rang and ordered tea, and while he was having his tea she remained standing at the window with her back to him. She was crying out of sheer agitation, in the sorrowful consciousness that their life was so sad; that they could only see each other in secret and had to hide from people like thieves! Was it not a broken life?

"Come, stop now, dear!" he said.

It was plain to him that this love of theirs would not be over soon, that the end of it was not in sight. Anna Sergeyevna was growing more and more attached to

---

[1]**three degrees above zero** about thirty-seven degrees Fahrenheit

him. She adored him, and it was unthinkable to tell her that their love was bound to come to an end some day; besides, she would not have believed it!

115   He went up to her and took her by the shoulders, to fondle her and say something diverting, and at that moment he caught sight of himself in the mirror.

His hair was already beginning to turn gray. And it seemed odd to him that he had grown so much older in the last few years, and lost his looks. The shoulders on which his hands rested were warm and heaving. He felt compassion for this life, still so warm and lovely, but probably already about to begin to fade and wither like his own. Why did she love him so much? He always seemed to women different from what he was, and they loved in him not himself, but the man whom their imagination created and whom they had been eagerly seeking all their lives; and afterwards, when they saw their mistake, they loved him nevertheless. And not one of them had been happy with him. In the past he had met women, come together with them, parted from them, but he had never once loved; it was anything you please, but not love. And only now when his head was gray he had fallen in love, really, truly—for the first time in his life.

Anna Sergeyevna and he loved each other as people do who are very close and intimate, like man and wife, like tender friends; it seemed to them that Fate itself had meant them for one another, and they could not understand why he had a wife and she a husband; and it was as though they were a pair of migratory birds, male and female, caught and forced to live in different cages. They forgave each other what they were ashamed of in their past, they forgave everything in the present, and felt that this love of theirs had altered them both.

Formerly in moments of sadness he had soothed himself with whatever logical arguments came into his head, but now he no longer cared for logic; he felt profound compassion, he wanted to be sincere and tender.

"Give it up now, my darling," he said. "You've had your cry; that's enough. Let us have a talk now, we'll think up something."

120   Then they spent a long time taking counsel together, they talked of how to avoid the necessity for secrecy, for deception, for living in different cities, and not seeing one another for long stretches of time. How could they free themselves from these intolerable fetters?

"How? How?" he asked, clutching his head. "How?"

And it seemed as though in a little while the solution would be found, and then a new and glorious life would begin; and it was clear to both of them that the end was still far off, and that what was to be most complicated and difficult for them was only just beginning.

▼MAKING CONNECTIONS

1. Why do you think that most of the action takes place away from Moscow?
2. What attracts Gurov to Anna Sergeyevna in the first place? During their time in Yalta, she is concerned with whether or not he respects her. Does he?
3. There are no scenes between Gurov and his wife. Why? Would it change how you feel about Gurov and Anna Sergeyevna if you knew more about his wife? Explain.

4. What does the last paragraph mean? What has happened to make the time ahead "to be most complicated and difficult"? To what extent does the story end on a positive note? In what way has this relationship changed since the story began? Do you think it has a future? Explain and cite the text for support.

MAKING AN ARGUMENT

1. Do you think that infidelity is ever justified? Do you think it's justified in this case? To what extent do Gurov and Anna behave nobly? Write an argument for or against the behavior of Gurov and Anna in this story. In addition to your own beliefs, cite the text of the story for support.

CHARLOTTE PERKINS GILMAN [1860-1935]

Charlotte Perkins Gilman was born in Hartford, Connecticut. Because her father, the writer Frederick Beecher Perkins, abandoned the family when she was only an infant, she was often left in the company of relatives, who included Harriet Beecher Stowe, the author of Uncle Tom's Cabin, *and the feminist activists Isabella Beecher Hooker and Catherine Beecher. These women instilled in Gilman the ideas of equality and independence, which formed the basis for the political activism that made her famous later in life. Though she wrote numerous works about the conditions of women, her reputation as a writer of literature rests almost solely on her short story "The Yellow Wallpaper," which adds a feminist twist to the psychological horror story pioneered by Edgar Allan Poe. The story, written in 1892, was based on her own experiences. During her unhappy first marriage, Gilman suffered a severe depression following the birth of her daughter. A noted doctor of the time prescribed a regimen of bed rest and minimal intellectual stimulation. Her condition only worsened. Eventually she rebelled, and taking responsibility for her own cure, separated from her husband and moved to California. In 1900, she married again, this time happily to her cousin George Houghton Gilman. She remained active politically until she took her own life in 1935, after fighting a losing battle with breast cancer.*

THE YELLOW WALLPAPER
[1892]

It is very seldom that mere ordinary people like John and myself secure ancestral halls for the summer.

A colonial mansion, a hereditary estate, I would say a haunted house and reach the height of romantic felicity—but that would be asking too much of fate!

Still I will proudly declare that there is something queer about it.

Else, why should it be let so cheaply? And why have stood so long untenanted?

5   John laughs at me, of course, but one expects that.

John is practical in the extreme. He has no patience with faith, an intense horror of superstition, and he scoffs openly at any talk of things not to be felt and seen and put down in figures.

John is a physician, and *perhaps*—(I would not say it to a living soul, of course, but this is dead paper and a great relief to my mind)—*perhaps* that is one reason I do not get well faster.

You see, he does not believe I am sick! And what can one do?

If a physician of high standing, and one's own husband, assures friends and relatives that there is really nothing the matter with one but temporary nervous depression—a slight hysterical tendency—what is one to do?

10   My brother is also a physician, and also of high standing, and he says the same thing.

So I take phosphates or phosphites—whichever it is—and tonics, and air and exercise, and journeys, and am absolutely forbidden to "work" until I am well again.

Personally, I disagree with their ideas.

Personally, I believe that congenial work, with excitement and change, would do me good.

But what is one to do?

15   I did write for a while in spite of them: but it *does* exhaust me a good deal—having to be so sly about it, or else meet with heavy opposition.

I sometimes fancy that in my condition, if I had less opposition and more society and stimulus—but John says the very worst thing I can do is to think about my condition, and I confess it always makes me feel bad.

So I will let it alone and talk about the house.

The most beautiful place! It is quite alone, standing well back from the road, quite three miles from the village. It makes me think of English places that you read about, for there are hedges and walls and gates that lock, and lots of separate little houses for the gardeners and people.

There is a *delicious* garden! I never saw such a garden—large and shady, full of box-bordered paths, and lined with long grape-covered arbors with seats under them.

20   There were greenhouses, but they are all broken now.

There was some legal trouble, I believe, something about the heirs and co-heirs; anyhow, the place has been empty for years.

That spoils my ghostliness, I am afraid, but I don't care—there is something strange about the house—I can feel it.

I even said so to John one moonlight evening, but he said what I felt was a draught, and shut the window.

I get unreasonably angry with John sometimes. I'm sure I never used to be so sensitive. I think it is due to this nervous condition.

25   But John says if I feel so I shall neglect proper self-control; so I take pains to control myself—before him, at least, and that makes me very tired.

I don't like our room a bit. I wanted one downstairs that opened onto the piazza and had roses all over the window, and such pretty old-fashioned chintz hangings! But John would not hear of it.

He said there was only one window and not room for two beds, and no near room for him if he took another.

He is very careful and loving, and hardly lets me stir without special direction.

I have a schedule prescription for each hour in the day; he takes all care from me, and so I feel basely ungrateful not to value it more.

30   He said he came here solely on my account, that I was to have perfect rest and all the air I could get. "Your exercise depends on your strength, my dear," said he, "and your food somewhat on your appetite; but air you can absorb all the time." So we took the nursery at the top of the house.

It is a big, airy room, the whole floor nearly, with windows that look all ways, and air and sunshine galore. It was nursery first, and then playroom and gymnasium, I should judge, for the windows are barred for little children, and there are rings and things in the walls.

The paint and paper look as if a boys' school had used it. It is stripped off—the paper—in great patches all around the head of my bed, about as far as I can reach, and in a great place on the other side of the room low down. I never saw a worse paper in my life. One of those sprawling, flamboyant patterns committing every artistic sin.

It is dull enough to confuse the eye in following, pronounced enough to constantly irritate and provoke study, and when you follow the lame uncertain curves for a little distance they suddenly commit suicide—plunge off at outrageous angles, destroy themselves in unheard-of contradictions.

The color is repellent, almost revolting: a smouldering unclean yellow, strangely faded by the slow-turning sunlight. It is a dull yet lurid orange in some places, a sickly sulphur tint in others.

35   No wonder the children hated it! I should hate it myself if I had to live in this room long.

There comes John, and I must put this away—he hates to have me write a word.

We have been here two weeks, and I haven't felt like writing before, since that first day.

I am sitting by the window now, up in this atrocious nursery, and there is nothing to hinder my writing as much as I please, save lack of strength.

John is away all day, and even some nights when his cases are serious.

40   I am glad my case is not serious!

But these nervous troubles are dreadfully depressing.

John does not know how much I really suffer. He knows there is no reason to suffer, and that satisfies him.

Of course it is only nervousness. It does weigh on me so not to do my duty in any way!

I meant to be such a help to John, such a real rest and comfort, and here I am a comparative burden already!

45   Nobody would believe what an effort it is to do what little I am able—to dress and entertain, and order things.

It is fortunate Mary is so good with the baby. Such a dear baby!

And yet I *cannot* be with him, it makes me so nervous.

I suppose John never was nervous in his life. He laughs at me so about this wallpaper!

At first he meant to repaper the room, but afterward he said that I was letting it get the better of me, and that nothing was worse for a nervous patient than to give way to such fancies.

50   He said that after the wallpaper was changed it would be the heavy bedstead, and then the barred windows, and then that gate at the head of the stairs, and so on.

"You know the place is doing you good," he said, "and really, dear, I don't care to renovate the house just for a three months' rental."

"Then do let us go downstairs," I said, "there are such pretty rooms there."

Then he took me in his arms and called me a blessed little goose, and said he would go down to the cellar, if I wished, and have it whitewashed into the bargain.

But he is right enough about the beds and windows and things.

55   It is as airy and comfortable a room as anyone need wish, and, of course, I would not be so silly as to make him uncomfortable just for a whim.

I'm really getting quite fond of the big room, all but that horrid paper.

Out of one window I can see the garden—those mysterious deep-shaded arbors, the riotous old-fashioned flowers, and bushes and gnarly trees.

Out of another I get a lovely view of the bay and a little private wharf belonging to the estate. There is a beautiful shaded lane that runs down there from the house. I always fancy I see people walking in these numerous paths and arbors, but John has cautioned me not to give way to fancy in the least. He says that with my imaginative power and habit of story-making, a nervous weakness like mine is sure to lead to all manner of excited fancies, and that I ought to use my will and good sense to check the tendency. So I try.

I think sometimes that if I were only well enough to write a little it would relieve the press of ideas and rest me.

60   But I find I get pretty tired when I try.

It is so discouraging not to have any advice and companionship about my work. When I get really well, John says we will ask Cousin Henry and Julia down for a long visit; but he says he would as soon put fireworks in my pillowcase as to let me have those stimulating people about now.

I wish I could get well faster.

But I must not think about that. This paper looks to me as if it *knew* what a vicious influence it had!

There is a recurrent spot where the pattern lolls like a broken neck and two bulbous eyes stare at you upside down.

65   I get positively angry with the impertinence of it and the everlastingness. Up and down and sideways they crawl, and those absurd, unblinking eyes are everywhere. There is one place where two breadths didn't match, and the eyes go all up and down the line, one a little higher than the other.

I never saw so much expression in an inanimate thing before, and we all know how much expression they have! I used to lie awake as a child and get more entertainment and terror out of blank walls and plain furniture than most children could find in a toystore.

I remember what a kindly wink the knobs of our big, old bureau used to have, and there was one chair that always seemed like a strong friend.

I used to feel that if any of the other things looked too fierce I could always hop into that chair and be safe.

The furniture in this room is no worse than inharmonious, however, for we had to bring it all from downstairs. I suppose when this was used as a playroom they had to take the nursery things out, and no wonder! I never saw such ravages as the children have made here.

70 The wallpaper, as I said before, is torn off in spots, and it sticketh closer than a brother—they must have had perseverance as well as hatred.

Then the floor is scratched and gouged and splintered, the plaster itself is dug out here and there, and this great heavy bed which is all we found in the room, looks as if it had been through the wars.

But I don't mind it a bit—only the paper.

There comes John's sister. Such a dear girl as she is, and so careful of me! I must not let her find me writing.

She is a perfect and enthusiastic housekeeper, and hopes for no better profession. I verily believe she thinks it is the writing which made me sick!

75 But I can write when she is out, and see her a long way off from these windows.

There is one that commands the road, a lovely shaded winding road, and one that just looks off over the country. A lovely country, too, full of great elms and velvet meadows.

This wallpaper has a kind of sub-pattern in a different shade, a particularly irritating one, for you can only see it in certain lights, and not clearly then.

But in the places where it isn't faded and where the sun is just so—I can see a strange, provoking, formless sort of figure that seems to skulk about behind that silly and conspicuous front design.

There's sister on the stairs!

80 Well, the Fourth of July is over! The people are all gone and I am tired out. John thought it might do me good to see a little company, so we just had Mother and Nellie and the children down for a week.

Of course I didn't do a thing. Jennie sees to everything now.

But it tired me all the same.

John says if I don't pick up faster he shall send me to Weir Mitchell[1] in the fall.

But I don't want to go there at all. I had a friend who was in his hands once, and she says he is just like John and my brother, only more so!

85 Besides, it is such an undertaking to go so far.

I don't feel as if it was worth while to turn my hand over for anything, and I'm getting dreadfully fretful and querulous.

I cry at nothing, and cry most of the time.

Of course I don't when John is here, or anybody else, but when I am alone.

And I am alone a good deal just now. John is kept in town very often by serious cases, and Jennie is good and lets me alone when I want her to.

90 So I walk a little in the garden or down that lovely lane, sit on the porch under the roses, and lie down up here a good deal.

[1]**Weir Mitchell** a physician known for his "rest cure" for psychoneurosies

I'm getting really fond of the room in spite of the wallpaper. Perhaps *because* of the wallpaper.

It dwells in my mind so!

I lie here on this great immovable bed—it is nailed down, I believe—and follow that pattern about by the hour. It is as good as gymnastics, I assure you. I start, we'll say, at the bottom, down in the corner over there where it has not been touched, and I determine for the thousandth time that I *will* follow that pointless pattern to some sort of a conclusion.

I know a little of the principle of design, and I know this thing was not arranged on any laws of radiation, or alternation, or repetition, or symmetry, or anything else that I ever heard of.

95 It is repeated, of course, by the breadths, but not otherwise.

Looked at in one way each breadth stands alone; the bloated curves and flourishes—a kind of "debased Romanesque" with delirium tremens go waddling up and down in isolated columns of fatuity.

But, on the other hand, they connect diagonally, and the sprawling outlines run off in great slanting waves of optic horror, like a lot of wallowing sea-weeds in full chase.

The whole thing goes horizontally, too, at least it seems so, and I exhaust myself in trying to distinguish the order of its going in that direction.

They have used a horizontal breadth for a frieze, and that adds wonderfully to the confusion.

100 There is one end of the room where it is almost intact, and there, when the crosslights fade and the low sun shines directly upon it, I can almost fancy radiation after all—the interminable grotesque seems to form around a common center and rush off in headlong plunges of equal distraction.

It makes me tired to follow it. I will take a nap, I guess.

I don't know why I should write this.

I don't want to.

I don't feel able.

105 And I know John would think it absurd. But I *must* say what I feel and think in some way—it is such a relief.

But the effort is getting to be greater than the relief!

Half the time now I am awfully lazy, and lie down ever so much. John says I mustn't lose my strength, and has me take cod liver oil and lots of tonics and things, to say nothing of ale and wine and rare meat.

Dear John! He loves me very dearly, and hates to have me sick. I tried to have a real earnest reasonable talk with him the other day, and tell him how I wish he would let me go and make a visit to Cousin Henry and Julia.

But he said I wasn't able to go, nor able to stand it after I got there: and I did not make out a very good case for myself, for I was crying before I had finished.

110 It is getting to be a great effort for me to think straight. Just this nervous weakness, I suppose.

And dear John gathered me up in his arms, and just carried me upstairs and laid me on the bed, and sat by me and read to me till it tired my head.

He said I was his darling and his comfort and all he had, and that I must take care of myself for his sake, and keep well.

He says no one but myself can help me out of it, that I must use my will and self-control and not let any silly fancies run away with me.

There's one comfort—the baby is well and happy, and does not have to occupy this nursery with the horrid wallpaper.

115   If we had not used it, that blessed child would have! What a fortunate escape! Why, I wouldn't have a child of mine, an impressionable little thing, live in such a room for worlds.

I never thought of it before, but it is lucky that John kept me here after all. I can stand it so much easier than a baby, you see.

Of course I never mention it to them any more—I am too wise—but I keep watch for it all the same.

There are things in that paper that nobody knows but me, or ever will.

Behind that outside pattern the dim shapes get clearer every day.

120   It is always the same shape, only very numerous.

And it is like a woman stooping down and creeping about behind that pattern. I don't like it a bit. I wonder—I begin to think—I wish John would take me away from here!

It is so hard to talk with John about my case, because he is so wise, and because he loves me so.

But I tried last night.

It was moonlight. The moon shines in all around just as the sun does.

125   I hate to see it sometimes, it creeps so slowly, and always comes in by one window or another.

John was asleep and I hated to waken him, so I kept still and watched the moonlight on that undulating wallpaper till I felt creepy.

The faint figure behind seemed to shake the pattern, just as if she wanted to get out.

I got up softly and went to feel and see if the paper *did* move, and when I came back John was awake.

"What is it, little girl?" he said. "Don't go walking about like that—you'll get cold."

130   I thought it was a good time to talk, so I told him that I really was not gaining here, and that I wished he would take me away.

"Why darling!" said he, "our lease will be up in three weeks, and I can't see how to leave before."

"The repairs are not done at home, and I cannot possibly leave town just now. Of course if you were in any danger, I could and would, but you really are better, dear, whether you can see it or not. I am a doctor, dear, and I know. You are gaining flesh and color, your appetite is better, I feel really much easier about you."

"I don't weigh a bit more," said I, "nor as much; and my appetite may be better in the evening when you are here but it is worse in the morning when you are away!"

"Bless her little heart!" said he with a big hug. "She shall be as sick as she pleases! But now let's improve the shining hours by going to sleep, and talk about it in the morning!"

135 "And you won't go away?" I asked gloomily.

"Why, how can I, dear? It is only three weeks more and then we will take a nice little trip of a few days while Jennie is getting the house ready. Really, dear, you are better!"

"Better in body perhaps—" I began, and stopped short, for he sat up straight and looked at me with such a stern, reproachful look that I could not say another word.

"My darling," said he, "I beg of you, for my sake and for our child's sake, as well as for your own, that you will never for one instant let that idea enter your mind! There is nothing so dangerous, so fascinating, to a temperament like yours. It is a false and foolish fancy. Can you not trust me as a physician when I tell you so?"

So of course I said no more on that score, and we went to sleep before long. He thought I was asleep first, but I wasn't and lay there for hours trying to decide whether that front pattern and the back pattern really did move together or separately.

140 On a pattern like this, by daylight, there is a lack of sequence, a defiance of law, that is a constant irritant to a normal mind.

The color is hideous enough, and unreliable enough, and infuriating enough, but the pattern is torturing.

You think you have mastered it, but just as you get well under way in following, it turns a back-somersault and there you are. It slaps you in the face, knocks you down, and tramples upon you. It is like a bad dream.

The outside pattern is a florid arabesque, reminding one of a fungus. If you can imagine a toadstool in joints, an interminable string of toadstools, budding and sprouting in endless convolutions—why, that is something like it.

That is, sometimes!

145 There is one marked peculiarity about this paper, a thing nobody seems to notice but myself, and that is that it changes as the light changes.

When the sun shoots in through the east window—I always watch for that first long, straight ray—it changes so quickly that I never can quite believe it.

That is why I watch it always.

By moonlight—the moon shines in all night when there is a moon—I wouldn't know it was the same paper.

At night in any kind of light, in twilight, candlelight, lamplight, and worst of all by moonlight, it becomes bars! The outside pattern, I mean, and the woman behind it is as plain as can be.

150 I didn't realize for a long time what the thing was that showed behind, that dim sub-pattern, but now I am quite sure it is a woman.

By daylight she is subdued, quiet. I fancy it is the pattern that keeps her so still. It is so puzzling. It keeps me quiet by the hour.

I lie down ever so much now. John says it is good for me, and to sleep all I can.

Indeed he started the habit by making me lie down for an hour after each meal.

It is a very bad habit, I am convinced, for you see, I don't sleep.

155 And that cultivates deceit, for I don't tell them I'm awake—oh, no!

The fact is I am getting a little afraid of John.

He seems very queer sometimes, and even Jennie has an inexplicable look.

It strikes me occasionally, just as a scientific hypothesis, that perhaps it is the paper!

I have watched John when he did not know I was looking, and come into the room suddenly on the most innocent excuses, and I've caught him several times *looking at the paper!* And Jennie too. I caught Jennie with her hand on it once.

160   She didn't know I was in the room, and when I asked her in a quiet, a very quiet voice, with the most restrained manner possible, what she was doing with the paper, she turned around as if she had been caught stealing, and looked quite angry—asked me why I should frighten her so!

Then she said that the paper stained everything it touched, that she had found yellow smooches on all my clothes and John's, and she wished we would be more careful!

Did not that sound innocent? But I know she was studying that pattern, and I am determined that nobody shall find it out but myself!

Life is very much more exciting now than it used to be. You see I have something more to expect, to look forward to, to watch. I really do eat better, and am more quiet than I was.

John is so pleased to see me improve! He laughed a little the other day, and said I seemed to be flourishing in spite of my wallpaper.

165   I turned it off with a laugh. I had no intention of telling him it was *because* of the wallpaper—he would make fun of me. He might even want to take me away.

I don't want to leave now until I have found it out. There is a week more, and I think that will be enough.

I'm feeling so much better!

I don't sleep much at night, for it is so interesting to watch developments, but I sleep a good deal during the daytime.

In the daytime it is tiresome and perplexing.

170   There are always new shoots on the fungus, and new shades of yellow all over it. I cannot keep count of them, though I have tried conscientiously.

It is the strangest yellow, that wallpaper! It makes me think of all the yellow things I ever saw—not beautiful ones like buttercups, but old foul, bad yellow things.

But there is something else about that paper—the smell! I noticed it the moment we came into the room, but with so much air and sun it was not bad. Now we have had a week of fog and rain, and whether the windows are open or not, the smell is here.

It creeps all over the house.

I find it hovering in the dining-room, skulking in the parlor, hiding in the hall, lying in wait for me on the stairs.

175   It gets into my hair.

Even when I go to ride, if I turn my head suddenly and surprise it—there is that smell!

Such a peculiar odor, too! I have spent hours in trying to analyze it, to find what it smelled like.

It is not bad—at first—and very gentle, but quite the subtlest, most enduring odor I ever met.

In this damp weather it is awful, I wake up in the night and find it hanging over me.

180   It used to disturb me at first. I thought seriously of burning the house—to reach the smell.

But now I am used to it. The only thing I can think of that it is like is the *color* of the paper! A yellow smell.

There is a very funny mark on this wall, low down, near the mopboard. A streak that runs round the room. It goes behind every piece of furniture, except the bed, a long, straight, even *smooch,* as if it had been rubbed over and over.

I wonder how it was done and who did it, and what they did it for. Round and round and round—round and round and round—it makes me dizzy!

I really have discovered something at last.

185   Through watching so much at night, when it changes so, I have finally found out.

The front pattern *does* move—and no wonder! The woman behind shakes it!

Sometimes I think there are a great many women behind, and sometimes only one, and she crawls around fast, and her crawling shakes it all over.

Then in the very bright spots she keeps still, and in the very shady spots she just takes hold of the bars and shakes them hard.

And she is all the time trying to climb through. But nobody could climb through that pattern—it strangles so: I think that is why it has so many heads.

190   They get through, and then the pattern strangles them off and turns them upside down, and makes their eyes white!

If those heads were covered or taken off it would not be half so bad.

I think that woman gets out in the daytime!

And I'll tell you why—privately—I've seen her!

I can see her out of every one of my windows!

195   It is the same woman, I know, for she is always creeping, and most women do not creep by daylight.

I see her in that long shaded lane, creeping up and down. I see her in those dark grape arbors, creeping all around the garden.

I see her on that long road under the trees, creeping along, and when a carriage comes she hides under the blackberry vines.

I don't blame her a bit. It must be very humiliating to be caught creeping by daylight!

I always lock the door when I creep by daylight. I can't do it at night, for I know John would suspect something at once.

200   And John is so queer now, that I don't want to irritate him. I wish he would take another room! Besides, I don't want anybody to get that woman out at night but myself.

I often wonder if I could see her out of all the windows at once.

But, turn as fast as I can, I can only see out of one at one time.

And though I always see her, she *may* be able to creep faster than I can turn! I have watched her sometimes away off in the open country, creeping as fast as a cloud shadow in a wind.

If only that top pattern could be gotten off from the under one! I mean to try it, little by little.

205   I have found out another funny thing, but I shan't tell it this time! It does not do to trust people too much.

There are only two more days to get this paper off, and I believe John is beginning to notice. I don't like the look in his eyes.

And I heard him ask Jennie a lot of professional questions about me. She had a very good report to give.

She said I slept a good deal in the daytime.

John knows I don't sleep very well at night, for all I'm so quiet!

210   He asked me all sorts of questions, too, and pretended to be very loving and kind.

As if I couldn't see through him!

Still, I don't wonder he acts so, sleeping under this paper for three months.

It only interests me, but I feel sure John and Jennie are affected by it.

Hurrah! This is the last day, but it is enough. John is to stay in town over night, and won't be out until this evening.

215   Jennie wanted to sleep with me—the sly thing; but I told her I should undoubtedly rest better for a night all alone.

That was clever, for really I wasn't alone a bit! As soon as it was moonlight and that poor thing began to crawl and shake the pattern, I got up and ran to help her.

I pulled and she shook. I shook and she pulled, and before morning we had peeled off yards of that paper.

A strip about as high as my head and half around the room.

And then when the sun came and that awful pattern began to laugh at me, I declared I would finish it today!

220   We go away tomorrow, and they are moving all my furniture down again to leave things as they were before.

Jennie looked at the wall in amazement, but I told her merrily that I did it out of pure spite at the vicious thing.

She laughed and said she wouldn't mind doing it herself, but I must not get tired.

How she betrayed herself that time!

But I am here, and no person touches this paper but Me—not *alive!*

225   She tried to get me out of the room—it was too patent! But I said it was so quiet and empty and clean now that I believed I would lie down again and sleep all I could, and not to wake me even for dinner—I would call when I woke.

So now she is gone, and the servants are gone, and the things are gone, and there is nothing left but that great bedstead nailed down, with the canvas mattress we found on it.

We shall sleep downstairs tonight, and take the boat home tomorrow.

I quite enjoy the room, now it is bare again.

How those children did tear about here!

230   This bedstead is fairly gnawed!

But I must get to work.

I have locked the door and thrown the key down into the front path.

I don't want to go out, and I don't want to have anybody come in, till John comes. I want to astonish him.

235   I've got a rope up here that even Jennie did not find. If that woman does get out, and tries to get away, I can tie her!

But I forgot I could not reach far without anything to stand on!

This bed will *not* move!

I tried to lift and push it until I was lame, and then I got so angry I bit off a little piece at one corner—but it hurt my teeth.

Then I peeled off all the paper I could reach standing on the floor. It sticks horribly and the pattern just enjoys it! All those strangled heads and bulbous eyes and waddling fungus growths just shriek with derision!

240   I am getting angry enough to do something desperate. To jump out of the window would be admirable exercise, but the bars are too strong even to try.

Besides I wouldn't do it. Of course not. I know well enough that a step like that is improper and might be misconstrued.

I don't like to *look* out of the windows even—there are so many of those creeping women, and they creep so fast.

I wonder if they all come out of that wallpaper as I did?

But I am securely fastened now by my well-hidden rope—you don't get *me* out in the road there!

245   I suppose I shall have to get back behind the pattern when it comes night, and that is hard!

It is so pleasant to be out in this great room and creep around as I please!

I don't want to go outside. I won't, even if Jennie asks me to.

For outside you have to creep on the ground, and everything is green instead of yellow.

But here I can creep smoothly on the floor, and my shoulder just fits in that long smooch around the wall, so I cannot lose my way.

250   Why, there's John at the door!

It is no use, young man, you can't open it!

How he does call and pound!

Now he's crying to Jennie for an axe.

It would be a shame to break down that beautiful door!

255   "John, dear!" said I in the gentlest voice, "The key is down by the front steps, under a plantain leaf!"

That silenced him for a few moments.

Then he said, very quietly indeed, "Open the door, my darling!"

"I can't," said I. "The key is down by the front door under a plantain leaf!" And then I said it again, several times, very gently and slowly, and said it so often that he had to go and see, and he got it of course, and came in. He stopped short by the door.

"What is the matter?" he cried. "For God's sake, what are you doing!"

260   I kept on creeping just the same, but I looked at him over my shoulder.

"I've got out at last," said I, "in spite of you and Jane. And I've pulled off most of the paper, so you can't put me back!"

Now why should that man have fainted? But he did, and right across my path by the wall, so that I had to creep over him every time!

MAKING CONNECTIONS

1. The narrator is the main character in the story. To what extent does this influence what you are told in this story? Can you describe the narrator? Do you think she is reliable? Explain.

2. Describe her relationship with her husband, John. What is he like? How does he treat her?

3. What kind of illness does the narrator say she has? What does her physician-husband prescribe as a cure? Do you think it's an appropriate cure? Why or why not?

4. In what way is the yellow wallpaper symbolic in this story? To what extent does the narrator's description of it change as the story progresses? Do you see any other symbols in the story?

5. Who is the woman in the wallpaper? What connection does she have to the narrator? To what extent is the yellow wallpaper an appropriate metaphor in this story? Would another color make a difference?

6. To what extent does the narrator change as the story progresses? What are the indications of that in the story? Near the end of the story, the narrator says, "I've got out at last." Has she? Explain.

MAKING AN ARGUMENT

1. Gilman indicated that this story was written in response to a "rest cure" she was given for her own severe, multiyear bout of depression—a rest cure that prohibited her from writing and limited her to "two hours intellectual life a day." She said that this advice nearly drove her insane, and it was only by returning to her writing that she was able to recover. In the light of this information—and what you know of attitudes toward women when the story was published in 1892—write an interpretation of the story. Cite the text of the story and its historical context for support.

BESSIE HEAD (1937–1986)

*One of Africa's most prominent writers, Bessie Head was born in South Africa in 1937 but spent most of her adult life in Botswana. Her major novels—*When Rain Clouds Gather, Maru, *and* A Question of Power—*and* Collector of Treasures, *a collection of thirteen short stories from which the story "Life" is taken, were written in Botswana during this period. The child of an "illicit" union between a Scottish woman and a black man, Head was taken from her mother at birth and raised in a foster home until the age of thirteen. For the most part, her works deal with race and sex discrimination, refugees, African history, poverty, and interpersonal relationships in postcolonial Africa.*

LIFE   [1977]

In 1963, when the borders were first set up between Botswana and South Africa, pending Botswana's independence in 1966, all Botswana-born citizens had to return home. Everything had been mingled up in the old colonial days, and the traffic of people to and fro between the two countries had been a steady flow for years and years. More often, especially if they were migrant labourers working in the mines, their period of settlement was brief, but many people had settled there in permanent employment. It was these settlers who were disrupted and sent back to village life in a mainly rural country. On their return they brought with them bits and bits of a foreign culture and city habits which they had absorbed. Village people reacted in their own way; what they liked, and was beneficial to them—they absorbed, for instance, the faith-healing cult churches which instantly took hold like wildfire— what was harmful to them, they rejected. The murder of Life had this complicated undertone of rejection.

Life had left the village as a little girl of ten years old with her parents for Johannesburg. They had died in the meanwhile, and on Life's return, seventeen years later, she found, as was village custom, that she still had a home in the village. On mentioning that her name was Life Morapedi, the villagers immediately and obligingly took her to the Morapedi yard in the central part of the village. The family yard had remained intact, just as they had left it, except that it looked pathetic in its desolation. The thatch of the mud huts had patches of soil over them where the ants had made their nests; the wooden poles that supported the rafters of the huts had tilted to an angle as their base had been eaten through by the ants. The rubber hedge had grown to a disproportionate size and enclosed the yard in a gloom of shadows that kept out the sunlight. Weeds and grass of many seasonal rains entangled them-selves in the yard.

Life's future neighbours, a group of women, continued to stand near her.

'We can help you to put your yard in order,' they said kindly. 'We are very happy that a child of ours has returned home.'

5   They were impressed with the smartness of this city girl. They generally wore old clothes and kept their very best things for special occasions like weddings, and even then those best things might just be ordinary cotton prints. The girl wore an expensive cream costume of linen material, tailored to fit her tall, full figure. She had a bright, vivacious friendly manner and laughed freely and loudly. Her speech was rapid and a little hysterical but that was in keeping with her whole personality.

'She is going to bring us a little light,' the women said among themselves, as they went off to fetch their work tools. They were always looking 'for the light' and by that they meant that they were ever alert to receive new ideas that would freshen up the ordinariness and everydayness of village life.

A woman who lived near the Morapedi yard had offered Life hospitality until her own yard was set in order. She picked up the shining new suitcases and preceded Life to her own home, where Life was immediately surrounded with all kinds of endearing attentions—a low stool was placed in a shady place for her to sit on; a little girl came shyly forward with a bowl of water for her to wash her hands; and fol-lowing on this, a tray with a bowl of meat and porridge was set before her so that she could revive herself after her long journey home. The other women briskly entered her yard with hoes to scratch out the weeds and grass, baskets of earth and buckets of water to re-smear the mud walls, and they had found two idle men to rectify the precarious tilt of the wooden poles of the mud hut. These were the sort of gestures people always offered, but they were pleased to note that the newcomer seemed to have an endless stream of money which she flung around generously. The work party in her yard would suggest that the meat of a goat, slowly simmering in a great iron pot, would help the work to move with a swing, and Life would immediately produce the money to purchase the goat and also tea, milk, sugar, pots of porridge or anything the workers expressed a preference for, so that those two weeks of making Life's yard beautiful for her seemed like one long wedding-feast; people usually only ate that much at weddings.

'How is it you have so much money, our child?' one of the women at last asked, curiously.

'Money flows like water in Johannesburg,' Life replied, with her gay and hysterical laugh. 'You just have to know how to get it.'

10   The women received this with caution. They said among themselves that their child could not have lived a very good life in Johannesburg. Thrift and honesty were the dominant themes of village life and everyone knew that one could not be honest and rich at the same time; they counted every penny and knew how they had acquired it—with hard work. They never imagined money as a bottomless pit without end; it always had an end and was hard to come by in this dry, semi-desert land. They predicted that she would soon settle down—intelligent girls got jobs in the post office sooner or later.

Life had had the sort of varied career that a city like Johannesburg offered a lot of black women. She had been a singer, beauty queen, advertising model, and prostitute. None of these careers were available in the village—for the illiterate women there was farming and housework; for the literate, teaching, nursing, and clerical work. The first wave of women Life attracted to herself were the farmers and housewives. They were the intensely conservative hard-core centre of village life. It did not take them long to shun her completely because men started turning up in an unending stream. What caused a stir of amazement was that Life was the first and the only woman in the village to make a business out of selling herself. The men were paying her for her services. People's attitude to sex was broad and generous—it was recognised as a necessary part of human life, that it ought to be available whenever possible like food and water, or else one's life would be extinguished or one would get dreadfully ill. To prevent these catastrophes from happening, men and women generally had quite a lot of sex but on a respectable and human level, with financial considerations coming in as an afterthought. When the news spread around that this had now become a business in Life's yard, she attracted to herself a second wave of women—the beer-brewers of the village.

The beer-brewing women were a gay and lovable crowd who had emancipated themselves some time ago. They were drunk every day and could be seen staggering around the village, usually with a wide-eyed, illegitimate baby hitched on to their hips. They also talked and laughed loudly and slapped each other on the back and had developed a language all their own:

'Boyfriends, yes. Husbands, uh, uh, no. Do this! Do that! We want to rule ourselves.'

But they too were subject to the respectable order of village life. Many men passed through their lives but they were all for a time steady boyfriends. The usual arrangement was:

15   'Mother, you help me and I'll help you.'

This was just so much eye-wash. The men hung around, lived on the resources of the women, and during all this time they would part with about R2.00[1] of their own money. After about three months a tally-up would be made:

'Boyfriend,' the woman would say. 'Love is love and money is money. You owe me money.' And he'd never be seen again, but another scoundrel would take his place. And so the story went on and on. They found their queen in Life and like all queens, they set her activities apart from themselves; they never attempted to extract money from the constant stream of men because they did not know how, but they liked her yard. Very soon the din and riot of a Johannesburg township was duplicated, on a minor scale, in the central part of the village. A transistor radio blared the day long. Men and women reeled around drunk and laughing and food and drink flowed like milk and honey. The people of the surrounding village watched this phenomenon with pursed lips and commented darkly:

'They'll all be destroyed one day like Sodom and Gomorrah.'

Life, like the beer-brewing women, had a language of her own too. When her friends expressed surprise at the huge quantities of steak, eggs, liver, kidneys, and rice they ate in her yard—the sort of food they too could now and then afford but would not dream of purchasing—she replied in a carefree, off-hand way: 'I'm used to handling big money.' They did not believe it; they were too solid to trust to this kind of luck which had such shaky foundations, and as though to offset some doom that might be just around the corner they often brought along their own scraggy, village chickens reared in their yards, as offerings for the day's round of meals. And one of Life's philosophies on life, which they were to recall with trembling a few months later, was: 'My motto is: live fast, die young, and have a good-looking corpse.' All this was said with the bold, free joy of a woman who had broken all the social taboos. They never followed her to those dizzy heights.

20   A few months after Life's arrival in the village, the first hotel with its pub opened. It was initially shunned by all the women and even the beer-brewers considered they hadn't fallen *that* low yet—the pub was also associated with the idea of selling oneself. It became Life's favourite business venue. It simplified the business of making appointments for the following day. None of the men questioned their behaviour, nor how such an unnatural situation had been allowed to develop—they could get all the sex they needed for free in the village, but it seemed to fascinate them that they should pay for it for the first time. They had quickly got to the stage where they communicated with Life in short-hand language:

'When?' And she would reply: 'Ten o'clock.' 'When?' 'Two o'clock.' 'When?' 'Four o'clock,' and so on.

And there would be the roar of cheap small talk and much buttock slapping. It was her element and her feverish, glittering, brilliant black eyes swept around the bar, looking for everything and nothing at the same time.

[1]**R2.00** two rand. Rand is the monetary unit of South Africa.

Then one evening death walked quietly into the bar. It was Lesego, the cattle-man, just come in from his cattle-post, where he had been occupied for a period of three months. Men built up their own, individual reputations in the village and Lesego's was one of the most respected and honoured. People said of him: 'When Lesego has got money and you need it, he will give you what he has got and he won't trouble you about the date of payment. . . ' He was honoured for another reason also—for the clarity and quiet indifference of his thinking. People often found difficulty in sorting out issues or the truth in any debatable matter. He had a way of keeping his head above water, listening to an argument and always pro-nouncing the final judgement: 'Well, the truth about this matter is . . .' He was also one of the most successful cattle-men with a balance of R7.000 in the bank, and whenever he came into the village he lounged around and gossiped or attended vil-lage kgotla meetings, so that people had a saying: 'Well, I must be getting about my business. I'm not like Lesego with money in the bank.'

As usual, the brilliant radar eyes swept feverishly around the bar. They did the rounds twice that evening in the same manner, each time coming to a dead stop for a full second on the thin, dark concentrated expression of Lesego's face. There wasn't any other man in the bar with that expression; they all had sheepish, inane-looking faces. He was the nearest thing she had seen for a long time to the Johannesburg gangsters she had associated with—the same small, economical ges-tures, the same power and control. All the men near him quietened down and began to consult with him in low earnest voices; they were talking about the news of the day which never reached the remote cattle-posts. Whereas all the other men had to approach her, the third time her radar eyes swept round he stood his ground, turned his head slowly, and then jerked it back slightly in a silent command:

25   'Come here.'

She moved immediately to his end of the bar.

'Hullo,' he said, in an astonishingly tender voice and a smile flickered across his dark, reserved face. That was the sum total of Lesego, that basically he was a kind and tender man, that he liked women and had been so successful in that sphere that he took his dominance and success for granted. But they looked at each other from their own worlds and came to fatal conclusions—she saw in him the power and maleness of the gangsters; he saw the freshness and surprise of an entirely new kind of woman. He had left all his women after a time because they bored him, and like all people who live an ordinary humdrum life, he was attracted to that undertone of hysteria in her.

Very soon they stood up and walked out together. A shocked silence fell upon the bar. The men exchanged looks with each other and the way these things com-municate themselves, they knew that all the other appointments had been can-celled while Lesego was there. And as though speaking their thoughts aloud, Sianana, one of Lesego's friends, commented: 'Lesego just wants to try it out like we all did because it is something new. He won't stay there when he finds out that it is rotten to the core.'

But Sianana was to find out that he did not fully understand his friend. Lesego was not seen at his usual lounging-places for a week and when he emerged again it was to announce that he was to marry. The news was received with cold hostility. Everyone talked of nothing else; it was as impossible as if a crime was being

committed before their very eyes. Sianana once more made himself the spokesman.
He waylaid Lesego on his way to the village kgotla:

30   'I am much surprised by the rumours about you, Lesego,' he said bluntly. 'You
can't marry that woman. She's a terrible fuck-about!'

Lesego stared back at him steadily, then he said in his quiet, indifferent way:
'Who isn't here?'

Sianana shrugged his shoulders. The subtleties were beyond him; but whatever
else was going on it wasn't commercial, it was human, but did that make it any
better? Lesego liked to bugger up an argument like that with a straightforward
point. As they walked along together Sianana shook his head several times to indicate that something important was eluding him, until at last with a smile, Lesego
said: 'She has told me all about her bad ways. They are over.'

Sianana merely compressed his lips and remained silent.

Life made the announcement too, after she was married, to all her beer-brewing
friends: 'All my old ways are over,' she said. 'I have now become a woman.'

35   She still looked happy and hysterical. Everything came to her too easily, men,
money, and now marriage. The beer-brewers were not slow to point out to her
with the same amazement with which they had exclaimed over the steak and eggs,
that there were many women in the village who had cried their eyes out over
Lesego. She was very flattered.

Their lives, at least Lesego's, did not change much with marriage. He still liked
lounging around the village; the rainy season had come and life was easy for the
cattle-men at this time because there was enough water and grazing for the animals.
He wasn't the kind of man to fuss about the house and during this time he only
made three pronouncements about the house-hold. He took control of all the
money. She had to ask him for it and state what it was to be used for. Then he didn't
like the transistor radio blaring the whole day long.

'Women who keep that thing going the whole day have nothing in their heads,'
he said.

Then he looked down at her from a great height and commented finally and quietly: 'If you go with those men again, I'll kill you.'

This was said so indifferently and quietly, as though he never really expected his
authority and dominance to encounter any challenge.

40   She hadn't the mental equipment to analyse what had hit her, but something
seemed to strike her a terrible blow behind the head. She instantly succumbed to the
blow and rapidly began to fall apart. On the surface, the everyday round of village life
was deadly dull in its even, unbroken monotony; one day slipped easily into another,
drawing water, stamping corn, cooking food. But within this there were enormous
tugs and pulls between people. Custom demanded that people care about each other,
and all day long there was this constant traffic of people in and out of each other's lives.
Someone had to be buried; sympathy and help were demanded for this event—there
were money loans, new-born babies, sorrow, trouble, gifts. Lesego had long been the
king of this world; there was, every day, a long string of people, wanting something or
wanting to give him something in gratitude for a past favour. It was the basic strength
of village life. It created people whose sympathetic and emotional responses were

always fully awakened, and it rewarded them by richly filling in a void that was one big, gaping yawn. When the hysteria and cheap rowdiness were taken away, Life fell into the yawn; she had nothing inside herself to cope with this way of life that had finally caught up with her. The beer-brewing women were still there; they still liked her yard because Lesego was casual and easy-going and all that went on in it now—like the old men squatting in corners with gifts: 'Lesego, I had good luck with my hunting today. I caught two rabbits and I want to share one with you. . . '—was simply the Tswana way of life they too lived. In keeping with their queen's new status, they said:

'We are women and must do something.'

They collected earth and dung and smeared and decorated Life's courtyard. They drew water for her, stamped her corn, and things looked quite ordinary on the surface because Lesego also liked a pot of beer. No one noticed the expression of anguish that had crept into Life's face. The boredom of the daily round was almost throttling her to death and no matter which way she looked, from the beer-brewers to her husband to all the people who called, she found no one with whom she could communicate what had become an actual physical pain. After a month of it, she was near collapse. One morning she mentioned her agony to the beer-brewers: 'I think I have made a mistake. Married life doesn't suit me.'

And they replied sympathetically: 'You are just getting used to it. After all it's a different life in Johannesburg.'

The neighbours went further. They were impressed by a marriage they thought could never succeed. They started saying that one never ought to judge a human being who was both good and bad, and Lesego had turned a bad woman into a good woman which was something they had never seen before. Just as they were saying this and nodding their approval, Sodom and Gomorrah started up all over again. Lesego had received word late in the evening that the new born calves at his cattle-post were dying, and early the next morning he was off again in his truck.

45   The old, reckless wild woman awakened from a state near death with a huge sigh of relief. The transistor blared, the food flowed again, the men and women reeled around dead drunk. Simply by their din they beat off all the unwanted guests who nodded their heads grimly. When Lesego came back they were going to tell him this was no wife for him.

Three days later Lesego unexpectedly was back in the village. The calves were all anaemic and they had to be brought in to the vet for an injection. He drove his truck straight through the village to the vet's camp. One of the beer-brewers saw him and hurried in alarm to her friend.

'The husband is back,' she whispered fearfully, pulling Life to one side.

'Agh,' she replied irritably.

She did dispel the noise, the men, and the drink, but a wild anger was driving her to break out of a way of life that was like death to her. She told one of the men she'd see him at six o'clock. At about five o'clock Lesego drove into the yard with the calves. There was no one immediately around to greet him. He jumped out of the truck and walked to one of the huts, pushing open the door. Life was sitting on the bed. She looked up silently and sullenly. He was a little surprised but his mind was still distracted by the calves. He had to settle them in the yard for the night.

50   'Will you make some tea,' he said. 'I'm very thirsty.'

'There's no sugar in the house,' she said. 'I'll have to get some.'

Something irritated him but he hurried back to the calves and his wife walked out of the yard. Lesego had just settled the calves when a neighbour walked in, he was very angry.

'Lesego,' he said bluntly. 'We told you not to marry that woman. If you go to the yard of Radithobolo now you'll find her in bed with him. Go and see for yourself that you may leave that bad woman!'

Lesego stared quietly at him for a moment, then at his own pace as though there were no haste or chaos in his life, he went to the hut they used as a kitchen. A tin full of sugar stood there. He turned and found a knife in the corner, one of the large ones he used for slaughtering cattle, and slipped it into his shirt. Then at his own pace he walked to the yard of Radithobolo. It looked deserted, except that the door of one of the huts was partially open and one closed. He kicked open the door of the closed hut and the man within shouted out in alarm. On seeing Lesego he sprang cowering into a corner. Lesego jerked his head back indicating that the man should leave the room. But Radithobolo did not run far. He wanted to enjoy himself so he pressed himself into the shadows of the rubber hedge. He expected the usual husband-and-wife scene—the irate husband cursing at the top of his voice; the wife, hysterical in her lies and self-defence. Only Lesego walked out of the yard and he held in his hand a huge, blood-stained knife. On seeing the knife Radithobolo immediately fell to the ground in a dead faint. There were a few people on the footpath and they shrank into the rubber hedge at the sight of that knife.

55   Very soon a wail arose. People clutched at their heads and began running in all directions crying yo! yo! in their shock. It was some time before anyone thought of calling the police. They were so disordered because murder, outright and violent, was a most uncommon and rare occurrence in village life. It seemed that only Lesego kept cool that evening. He was sitting quietly in his yard when the whole police force came tearing in. They looked at him in horror and began to thoroughly upbraid him for looking so unperturbed.

'You have taken a human life and you are cool like that!' they said angrily. 'You are going to hang by the neck for this. It's a serious crime to take a human life.'

He did not hang by the neck. He kept that cool, head-above-water indifferent look, right up to the day of his trial. Then he looked up at the judge and said calmly: 'Well, the truth about this matter is, I had just returned from the cattle-post. I had had trouble with my calves that day. I came home late and being thirsty, asked my wife to make me tea. She said there was no sugar in the house and left to buy some. My neighbour, Mathata, came in after this and said that my wife was not at the shops but in the yard of Radithobolo. He said I ought to go and see what she was doing in the yard of Radithobolo. I thought I would check up about the sugar first and in the kitchen I found a tin full of it. I was sorry and surprised to see this. Then a fire seemed to fill my heart. I thought that if she was doing a bad thing with Radithobolo as Mathata said, I'd better kill her because I cannot understand a wife who could be so corrupt . . . .'

Lesego had been doing this for years, passing judgement on all aspects of life in his straightforward, uncomplicated way. The judge, who was a white man, and therefore not involved in Tswana custom and its debates, was as much impressed by

Lesego's manner as all the village men had been.

'This is a crime of passion,' he said sympathetically. 'So there are extenuating circumstances. But it is still a serious crime to take a human life so I sentence you to five years imprisonment . . . '

60   Lesego's friend, Sianana, who was to take care of his business affairs while he was in jail, came to visit Lesego still shaking his head. Something was eluding him about the whole business, as though it had been planned from the very beginning.

'Lesego,' he said, with deep sorrow. 'Why did you kill that fuck-about? You had legs to walk away. You could have walked away. Are you trying to show us that rivers never cross here? There are good women and good men but they seldom join their lives together. It's always this mess and foolishness . . . '

A song by Jim Reeves was very popular at that time: *That's What Happens When Two Worlds Collide.* When they were drunk, the beer-brewing women used to sing it and start weeping. Maybe they had the last word on the whole affair.

MAKING CONNECTIONS

1. Describe Life. What do you think motivates her? What does she want? What details in the story support your views?
2. What is the attitude of the women in the village toward Life? What is the attitude of the men? Do they trust her? Why or why not? Would you trust her? Explain.
3. Describe Lesego. Why is Life attracted to him? Why is Lesego attracted to her? Do you think this is a good match? Are you surprised that Life eventually decides, "Married life doesn't suit me"? Explain.
4. Were you surprised at Lesego's response to Life's infidelity? Why? Do you agree with the song that the beer-brewing women sing, "That's What Happens When Two Worlds Collide"? Why or why not?

MAKING AN ARGUMENT

1. Lesego receives a prison sentence of five years for the murder of Life. Do you think that was just? Write an argument for or against the judge's decision. Cite the text of the story for support.

ERNEST HEMINGWAY [1899–1961]

Ernest Hemingway was born in Oak Park, Illinois, and began his writing career as a newspaper reporter, where he claimed to have learned the fundamentals of writing: short sentences, short first paragraphs, vigorous English, and smoothness. He was an active participant in World War I, the Spanish Civil War, and World War II, and often used his personal experiences as the source of his work. His writing includes A Farewell to Arms *(1929),* For Whom the

Bell Tolls (1940), and The Old Man and the Sea *(1952). He was a Pulitzer Prize winner and received the Nobel Prize for literature in 1954. His direct, spare writing style, exemplified in the short story below, was a major influence on many writers in the twentieth century.*

HILLS LIKE WHITE ELEPHANTS [1927]

The hills across the valley of the Ebro were long and white. On this side there was no shade and no trees and the station was between two lines of rails in the sun. Close against the side of the station there was the warm shadow of the building and a curtain, made of strings of bamboo beads, hung across the open door into the bar, to keep out flies. The American and the girl with him sat at a table in the shade, outside the building. It was very hot and the express from Barcelona would come in forty minutes. It stopped at this junction for two minutes and went on to Madrid.

"What should we drink?" the girl asked. She had taken off her hat and put it on the table.

"It's pretty hot," the man said.

"Let's drink beer."

5   "Dos cervezas," the man said into the curtain.

"Big ones?" a woman asked from the doorway.

"Yes. Two big ones."

The woman brought two glasses of beer and two felt pads. She put the felt pads and the beer glasses on the table and looked at the man and the girl. The girl was looking off at the line of hills. They were white in the sun and the country was brown and dry.

"They look like white elephants," she said.

10   "I've never seen one," the man drank his beer.

"No, you wouldn't have."

"I might have," the man said. "Just because you say I wouldn't have doesn't prove anything."

The girl looked at the bead curtain. "They've painted something on it," she said. "What does it say?"

"Anis del Toro. It's a drink."

15   "Could we try it?"

The man called "Listen" through the curtain. The woman came out from the bar.

"Four reales."

"We want two Anis del Toro."

"With water?"

20   "Do you want it with water?"

"I don't know," the girl said. "Is it good with water?"

"It's all right."

"You want them with water?" asked the woman.

"Yes, with water."

25   "It tastes like licorice," the girl said and put the glass down.

"That's the way with everything."

"Yes," said the girl. "Everything tastes of licorice. Especially all the things you've waited so long for, like absinthe."

"Oh, cut it out."

"You started it," the girl said. "I was being amused. I was having a fine time."

30   "Well, let's try and have a fine time."

"All right. I was trying. I said the mountains looked like white elephants. Wasn't that bright?"

"That was bright."

"I wanted to try this new drink. That's all we do, isn't it—look at things and try new drinks?"

"I guess so."

35   The girl looked across at the hills.

"They're lovely hills," she said. "They don't really look like white elephants. I just meant the coloring of their skin through the trees."

"Should we have another drink?"

"All right."

The warm wind blew the bead curtain against the table.

40   "The beer's nice and cool," the man said.

"It's lovely," the girl said.

"It's really an awfully simple operation, Jig," the man said. "It's not really an operation at all."

The girl looked at the ground the table legs rested on.

"I know you wouldn't mind it, Jig. It's really not anything. It's just to let the air in."

45   The girl did not say anything.

"I'll go with you and I'll stay with you all the time. They just let the air in and then it's all perfectly natural."

"Then what will we do afterward?"

"We'll be fine afterward. Just like we were before."

"What makes you think so?"

50   "That's the only thing that bothers us. It's the only thing that's made us unhappy."

The girl looked at the bead curtain, put her hand out and took hold of two of the strings of beads.

"And you think then we'll be all right and be happy."

"I know we will. You don't have to be afraid. I've known lots of people that have done it."

"So have I," said the girl. "And afterward they were all so happy."

55   "Well," the man said, "if you don't want to you don't have to. I wouldn't have you do it if you didn't want to. But I know it's perfectly simple."

"And you really want to?"

"I think it's the best thing to do. But I don't want you to do it if you don't really want to."

"And if I do it you'll be happy and things will be like they were and you'll love me?"

"I love you now. You know I love you."

60   "I know. But if I do it, then it will be nice again if I say things are like white elephants, and you'll like it?"

"I'll love it. I love it now but I just can't think about it. You know how I get when I worry."

"If I do it you won't ever worry?"

"I won't worry about that because it's perfectly simple."

"Then I'll do it. Because I don't care about me."

65 "What do you mean?"

"I don't care about me."

"Well, I care about you."

"Oh, yes. But I don't care about me. And I'll do it and then everything will be fine."

"I don't want you to do it if you feel that way."

70 The girl stood up and walked to the end of the station. Across, on the other side, were fields of grain and trees along the banks of the Ebro. Far away, beyond the river, were mountains. The shadow of a cloud moved across the field of grain and she saw the river through the trees.

"And we could have all this," she said. "And we could have everything and every day we make it more impossible."

"What did you say?"

"I said we could have everything."

"We can have everything."

75 "No, we can't."

"We can have the whole world."

"No, we can't."

"We can go everywhere."

"No, we can't. It isn't ours any more."

80 "It's ours."

"No, it isn't. And once they take it away, you never get it back."

"But they haven't taken it away."

"We'll wait and see."

"Come on back in the shade," he said. "You mustn't feel that way."

85 "I don't feel any way," the girl said. "I just know things."

"I don't want you to do anything that you don't want to do—"

"Nor that isn't good for me," she said. "I know. Could we have another beer?"

"All right. But you've got to realize—"

"I realize," the girl said. "Can't we maybe stop talking?"

90 They sat down at the table and the girl looked across at the hills on the dry side of the valley and the man looked at her and at the table.

"You've got to realize," he said, "that I don't want you to do it if you don't want to. I'm perfectly willing to go through with it if it means anything to you."

"Doesn't it mean anything to you? We could get along."

"Of course it does. But I don't want anybody but you. I don't want any one else. And I know it's perfectly simple."

"Yes, you know it's perfectly simple."

95 "It's all right for you to say that, but I do know it."

"Would you do something for me now?"

"I'd do anything for you."

"Would you please please please please please please please stop talking?"

He did not say anything but looked at the bags against the wall of the station. There were labels on them from all the hotels where they had spent nights.

100 "But I don't want you to," he said, "I don't care anything about it."

"I'll scream," the girl said.

The woman came out through the curtains with two glasses of beer and put them down on the damp felt pads. "The train comes in five minutes," she said.

"What did she say?" asked the girl.

"That the train is coming in five minutes."

105 The girl smiled brightly at the woman, to thank her.

"I'd better take the bags over to the other side of the station," the man said. She smiled at him.

"All right. Then come back and we'll finish the beer."

He picked up the two heavy bags and carried them around the station to the other tracks. He looked up the tracks but could not see the train. Coming back, he walked through the barroom, where people waiting for the train were drinking. He drank an Anis at the bar and looked at the people. They were all waiting reasonably for the train. He went out through the bead curtain. She was sitting at the table and smiled at him.

"Do you feel better?" he asked.

110 "I feel fine," she said. "There's nothing wrong with me. I feel fine."

MAKING CONNECTIONS

1. What are the man and woman discussing? Do you have strong feelings about this topic? If so, how does that influence your response? If you were placed in this situation, what would you say or do?
2. From what narrative perspective or point of view is the story told? What difference does it make to the story and how does it affect your response?
3. How old are the man and the woman? Have they known each other long? Are there differences in their levels of life experience? How did they meet? What kind of past relationship has led up to their present situation? What details in the story support your description of the couple?
4. What is a "white elephant"? What is significant in the woman's initial comparison of the hills to white elephants? To what extent are her later thoughts revealed through her comment that they "don't really look like white elephants. I just meant the coloring of their skin through the trees"?
5. Some researchers have suggested that men and women talk to each other with different intentions. Do you see any indication of this in the story? How are you affected by the language of the conversation?

MAKING AN ARGUMENT

1. What does the conversation between the man and the woman tell you about these characters and their relationship? Do they both want the same thing? Why do they place so much emphasis on having "a fine time"? How do you think they would define "a fine time"? Do you think "fine times" are enough to keep them together? Write an essay that analyzes these characters and this relationship—and its future. Cite the text of the story for support.

D. H. LAWRENCE [1885–1930]

D[avid] H[erbert] Lawrence was born in Nottinghamshire, England. In the largely autobiographical novel Sons and Lovers *(1913), Lawrence wrote about his difficult childhood as the son of a coarse (and often drunken) coal miner and an overprotective and demanding mother. After earning a teaching degree while on a scholarship at Nottingham University College in 1908, Lawrence taught school while he worked on his first novel,* The White Peacock *(1911), and published his first poems and short stories in the* English Review. *In 1912, he quit teaching after meeting and falling in love with Frieda von Richthofen, the sister of the German flying ace, the Red Baron. They were married in 1914, following her divorce. In 1915, Lawrence published his novel* The Rainbow, *a story of three generations of a family in Nottinghamshire. Like much of his following work, the novel was extremely controversial for its frank depiction of sexual relationships and was banned by the English courts. Lawrence spent the rest of his life in self-imposed exile with his wife, traveling around the world. Though he wrote numerous novels, poems, and essays, many critics consider Lawrence's best work to be his short stories.*

THE HORSE DEALER'S DAUGHTER   [1922]

"Well, Mabel, and what are you going to do with yourself?" asked Joe, with foolish flippancy. He felt quite safe himself. Without listening for an answer, he turned aside, worked a grain of tobacco to the tip of his tongue and spat it out. He did not care about anything, since he felt safe himself.

The three brothers and the sister sat round the desolate breakfast table, attempting some sort of desultory consultation. The morning's post had given the final tap to the family fortune, and all was over. The dreary dining room itself, with its heavy mahogany furniture, looked as if it were waiting to be done away with.

But the consultation amounted to nothing. There was a strange air of ineffectuality about the three men, as they sprawled at table, smoking and reflecting vaguely on their own condition. The girl was alone, a rather short, sullen-looking young woman of twenty-seven. She did not share the same life as her brothers. She would have been good-looking, save for the impassive fixity of her face, "bull-dog," as her brothers called it.

There was a confused tramping of horses' feet outside. The three men all sprawled round in their chairs to watch. Beyond the dark hollybushes that separated the strip of lawn from the highroad, they could see a cavalcade of shire horses swinging out of their own yard, being taken for exercise. This was the last time. These were the last horses that would go through their hands. The young men watched with critical, callous looks. They were all frightened at the collapse of their lives, and the sense of disaster in which they were involved left them no inner freedom.

5   Yet they were three fine, well-set fellows enough. Joe, the eldest, was a man of thirty-three, broad and handsome in a hot, flushed way. His face was red, he twisted his black moustache over a thick finger, his eyes were shallow and restless. He had

a sensual way of uncovering his teeth when he laughed, and his bearing was stupid. Now he watched the horses with a glazed look of helplessness in his eyes, a certain stupor of downfall.

The great draught-horses swung past. They were tied head to tail, four of them, and they heaved along to where a lane branched off from the highroad, planting their great hoofs floutingly in the fine black mud, swinging their great rounded haunches sumptuously, and trotting a few sudden steps as they were led into the lane, round the corner. Every movement showed a massive, slumbrous strength, and a stupidity which held them in subjection. The groom at the head looked back, jerking the leading rope. And the cavalcade moved out of sight up the lane, the tail of the last horse, bobbed up tight and stiff, held out taut from the swinging great haunches as they rocked behind the hedges in a motion like sleep.

Joe watched with glazed hopeless eyes. The horses were almost like his own body to him. He felt he was done for now. Luckily he was engaged to a woman as old as himself, and therefore her father, who was steward of a neighboring estate, would provide him with a job. He would marry and go into harness. His life was over, he would be a subject animal now.

He turned uneasily aside, the retreating steps of the horses echoing in his ears. Then, with foolish restlessness, he reached for the scraps of bacon-rind from the plates, and making a faint whistling sound, flung them to the terrier that lay against the fender. He watched the dog swallow them, and waited till the creature looked into his eyes. Then a faint grin came on his face, and in a high, foolish voice he said:

"You won't get much more bacon, shall you, you little bitch?"

10   The dog faintly and dismally wagged its tail, then lowered its haunches, circled round, and lay down again.

There was another helpless silence at the table. Joe sprawled uneasily in his seat, not willing to go till the family conclave was dissolved. Fred Henry, the second brother, was erect, clean-limbed, alert. He had watched the passing of the horses with more sangfroid. If he was an animal, like Joe, he was an animal which controls, not one which is controlled. He was master of any horse, and he carried himself with a well-tempered air of mastery. But he was not master of the situations of life. He pushed his coarse brown moustache upwards, off his lip, and glanced irritably at his sister, who sat impassive and inscrutable.

"You'll go and stop with Lucy for a bit, shan't you?" he asked. The girl did not answer.

"I don't see what else you can do," persisted Fred Henry.

"Go as a skivvy," Joe interpolated laconically.

15   The girl did not move a muscle.

"If I was her, I should go in for training for a nurse," said Malcolm, the youngest of them all. He was the baby of the family, a young man of twenty-two, with a fresh, jaunty *museau*.[1]

But Mabel did not take any notice of him. They had talked at her and round her for so many years, that she hardly heard them at all.

---

[1]**museau** muzzle or snout; slang for "face"

The marble clock on the mantelpiece softly chimed the half-hour, the dog rose uneasily from the hearthrug and looked at the party at the breakfast table. But still they sat on in ineffectual conclave.

"Oh, all right," said Joe suddenly, apropos of nothing. "I'll get a move on."

20   He pushed back his chair, straddled his knees with a downward jerk, to get them free, in horsey fashion, and went to the fire. Still he did not go out of the room; he was curious to know what the others would do or say. He began to charge his pipe, looking down at the dog and saying, in a high, affected voice:

"Going wi' me? Going wi' me are ter? Tha'rt goin' further than tha counts on just now, dost hear?"

The dog faintly wagged its tail, the man stuck out his jaw and covered his pipe with his hands, and puffed intently, losing himself in the tobacco, looking down all the while at the dog with an absent brown eye. The dog looked at him in mournful distrust. Joe stood with his knees stuck out, in real horsey fashion.

"Have you had a letter from Lucy?" Fred Henry asked of his sister.

"Last week," came the neutral reply.

25   "And what does she say?"

There was no answer.

"Does she *ask* you to go and stop there?" persisted Fred Henry.

"She says I can if I like."

"Well, then, you'd better. Tell her you'll come on Monday."

30   This was received in silence.

"That's what you'll do then, is it?" said Fred Henry, in some exasperation.

But she made no answer. There was a silence of futility and irritation in the room. Malcolm grinned fatuously.

"You'll have to make up your mind between now and next Wednesday," said Joe loudly, "or else find yourself lodgings on the kurbstone."

The face of the young woman darkened, but she sat on immutable.

35   "Here's Jack Fergusson!" exclaimed Malcolm, who was looking aimlessly out of the window.

"Where?" exclaimed Joe, loudly.

"Just gone past."

"Coming in?"

Malcolm craned his neck to see the gate.

40   "Yes," he said.

There was a silence. Mabel sat on like one condemned, at the head of the table. Then a whistle was heard from the kitchen. The dog got up and barked sharply. Joe opened the door and shouted:

"Come on."

After a moment a young man entered. He was muffled up in overcoat and a purple woolen scarf, and his tweed cap, which he did not remove, was pulled down on his head. He was of medium height, his face was rather long and pale, his eyes looked tired.

"Hello, Jack! Well, Jack!" exclaimed Malcolm and Joe. Fred Henry merely said, "Jack."

45   "What's doing?" asked the newcomer, evidently addressing Fred Henry.

"Same. We've got to be out by Wednesday. Got a cold?"

"I have—got it bad, too."

"Why don't you stop in?"

"*Me* stop in? When I can't stand on my legs, perhaps I shall have a chance." The young man spoke huskily. He had a slight Scotch accent.

50   "It's a knock-out, isn't it," said Joe, boisterously, "if a doctor goes round croaking with a cold. Looks bad for the patients, doesn't it?"

The young doctor looked at him slowly.

"Anything the matter with *you*, then?" he asked sarcastically.

"Not as I know of. Damn your eyes. I hope not. Why?"

"I thought you were very concerned about the patients, wondered if you might be one yourself."

55   "Damn it, no, I've never been patient to no flaming doctor, and hope I never shall be," returned Joe.

At this point Mabel rose from the table, and they all seemed to become aware of her existence. She began putting the dishes together. The young doctor looked at her, but did not address her. He had not greeted her. She went out of the room with the tray, her face impassive and unchanged.

"When are you off then, all of you?" asked the doctor.

"I'm catching the eleven-forty," replied Malcolm. "Are you goin down wi' th' trap, Joe?"

"Yes, I've told you I am going down wi' th' trap, haven't I?"

60   "We'd better be getting her in then. So long, Jack, if I don't see you before I go," said Malcolm, shaking hands.

He went out, followed by Joe, who seemed to have his tail between his legs.

"Well, this is the devil's own," exclaimed the doctor, when he was left alone with Fred Henry. "Going before Wednesday, are you?"

"That's the orders," replied the other.

"Where, to Northampton?"

65   "That's it."

"The devil!" exclaimed Fergusson, with quiet chagrin.

And there was silence between the two.

"All settled up, are you?" asked Fergusson.

"About."

70   There was another pause.

"Well, I shall miss yer, Freddy, boy," said the young doctor.

"And I shall miss thee, Jack," returned the other.

"Miss you like hell," mused the doctor.

Fred Henry turned aside. There was nothing to say. Mabel came in again, to finish clearing the table.

75   "What are *you* going to do, then, Miss Pervin?" asked Fergusson. "Going to your sister's, are you?"

Mabel looked at him with her steady, dangerous eyes, that always made him uncomfortable, unsettling his superficial ease.

"No," she said.

"Well, what in the name of fortune are *you* going to do? Say what you mean to do," cried Fred Henry, with futile intensity.

But she only averted her head, and continued her work. She folded the white table-cloth, and put on the chenile cloth.

80   "The sulkiest bitch that ever trod!" muttered her brother.

But she finished her task with perfectly impassive face, the young doctor watching her interestedly all the while. Then she went out.

Fred Henry stared after her, clenching his lips, his blue eyes fixing in sharp antagonism, as he made a grimace of sour exasperation.

"You could bray her into bits, and that's all you'd get out of her," he said in a small, narrowed tone.

The doctor smiled faintly.

85   "What's she *going* to do, then?" he asked.

"Strike me if I know!" returned the other.

There was a pause. Then the doctor stirred.

"I'll be seeing you to-night, shall I?" he said to his friend.

"Ay—where's it to be? Are we going over to Jessdale?"

90   "I don't know. I've got such a cold on me. I'll come round to the Moon and Stars, anyway."

"Let Lizzie and May miss their night for once, eh?"

"That's it—if I feel as I do now."

"All's one—"

The two young men went through the passage and down to the back door together. The house was large, but it was servantless now, and desolate. At the back was a small bricked house-yard, and beyond that a big square, graveled fine and red, and having stables on two sides. Sloping, dank, winter-dark fields stretched away on the open sides.

95   But the stables were empty. Joseph Pervin, the father of the family, had been a man of no education, who had become a fairly large horse dealer. The stables had been full of horses, there was a great turmoil and come-and-go of horses and of dealers and grooms. Then the kitchen was full of servants. But of late things had declined. The old man had married a second time, to retrieve his fortunes. Now he was dead and everything was gone to the dogs, there was nothing but debt and threatening.

For months, Mabel had been servantless in the big house, keeping the home together in penury for her ineffectual brothers. She had kept house for ten years. But previously it was with unstinted means. Then, however brutal and coarse everything was, the sense of money had kept her proud, confident. The men might be foul-mouthed, the women in the kitchen might have bad reputations, her brothers might have illegitimate children. But so long as there was money, the girl felt herself established, and brutally proud, reserved.

No company came to the house, save dealers and coarse men. Mabel had no associates of her own sex, after her sister went away. But she did not mind. She went regularly to church, she attended to her father. And she lived in the memory of her mother, who had died when she was fourteen, and whom she had loved. She had loved her father, too, in a different way, depending upon him, and feeling secure in him, until at the age of fifty-four he married again. And then she had set hard against him. Now he had died and left them all hopelessly in debt.

She had suffered badly during the period of poverty. Nothing, however, could shake the curious sullen, animal pride that dominated each member of the family. Now, for Mabel, the end had come. Still she would not cast about her. She would follow her own way just the same. She would always hold the keys of her own situation. Mindless and persistent, she endured from day to day. Why should she think? Why should she answer anybody? It was enough that this was the end, and there was no way out. She need not pass any more darkly along the main street of the small town, avoiding every eye. She need not demean herself any more, going into the shops and buying the cheapest food. This was at an end. She thought of nobody, not even of herself. Mindless and persistent, she seemed in a sort of ecstasy to be coming nearer to her fulfillment, her own glorification, approaching her dead mother, who was glorified.

In the afternoon she took a little bag, with shears and sponge and a small scrubbing brush, and went out. It was a gray, wintry day, with saddened, dark green fields and an atmosphere blackened by the smoke of foundries not far off. She went quickly, darkly along the causeway, heeding nobody, through the town to the churchyard.

100   There she always felt secure, as if no one could see her, although as a matter of fact she was exposed to the stare of every one who passed along under the churchyard wall. Nevertheless, once under the shadow of the great looming church, among the graves, she felt immune from the world, reserved within the thick churchyard wall as in another country.

Carefully she clipped the grass from the grave, and arranged the pinky white, small chrysanthemums in the tin cross. When this was done, she took an empty jar from a neighboring grave, brought water, and carefully, most scrupulously sponged the marble head-stone and the coping-stone.

It gave her sincere satisfaction to do this. She felt in immediate contact with the world of her mother. She took minute pains, went through the park in a state bordering on pure happiness, as if in performing this task she came into a subtle, intimate connection with her mother. For the life she followed here in the world was far less real than the world of death she inherited from her mother.

The doctor's house was just by the church. Fergusson, being a mere hired assistant, was slave to the country-side. As he hurried now to attend to the out-patients in the surgery, glancing across the graveyard with his quick eyes, he saw the girl at her task at the grave. She seemed so intent and remote, it was like looking into another world. Some mystical element was touched in him. He slowed down as he walked, watching her as if spellbound.

She lifted her eyes, feeling him looking. Their eyes met. And each looked away again at once, each feeling, in some way, found out by the other. He lifted his cap and passed on down the road. There remained distinct in his consciousness, like a vision, the memory of her face, lifted from the tombstone in the churchyard, and looking at him with slow, large, portentous eyes. It *was* portentous, her face. It seemed to mesmerize him. There was a heavy power in her eyes which laid hold of his whole being, as if he had drunk some powerful drug. He had been feeling weak and done before. Now the life came back into him, he felt delivered from his own fretted, daily self.

105   He finished his duties at the surgery as quickly as might be, hastily filling up the bottles of the waiting people with cheap drugs. Then, in perpetual haste, he set off again to visit several cases in another part of his round, before tea-time. At all times he preferred to walk if he could, but particularly when he was not well. He fancied the motion restored him.

The afternoon was falling. It was gray, deadened, and wintry, with a slow, moist, heavy coldness sinking in and deadening all the faculties. But why should he think or notice? He hastily climbed the hill and turned across the dark green fields, following the black cindertrack. In the distance, across a shallow dip in the country, the small town was clustered like smouldering ash, a tower, a spire, a heap of low, raw, extinct houses. And on the nearest fringe of the town, sloping into the dip, was Oldmeadow, the Pervins's house. He could see the stables and the outbuildings distinctly, as they lay towards him on the slope. Well, he would not go there many more times! Another resource would be lost to him, another place gone: the only company he cared for in the alien, ugly little town he was losing. Nothing but work, drudgery, constant hastening from dwelling to dwelling among the colliers and the ironworkers. It wore him out, but at the same time he had a craving for it. It was a stimulant to him to be in the homes of the working people, moving as it were through the innermost body of their life. His nerves were excited and gratified. He could come so near, into the very lives of the rough, inarticulate, powerfully emotional men and women. He grumbled, he said he hated the hellish hole. But as a matter of fact it excited him, the contact with the rough, strongly-feeling people was a stimulant applied direct to his nerves.

Below Oldmeadow, in the green, shallow, soddened hollow of fields, lay a square, deep pond. Roving across the landscape, the doctor's quick eye detected a figure in black passing through the gate of the field, down towards the pond. He looked again. It would be Mabel Pervin. His mind suddenly became alive and attentive.

Why was she going down there? He pulled up on the path on the slope above, and stood staring. He could just make sure of the small black figure moving in the hollow of the failing day. He seemed to see her in the midst of such obscurity, that he was like a clairvoyant, seeing rather with the mind's eye than with ordinary sight. Yet he could see her positively enough, while he kept his eye attentive. He felt, if he looked away from her, in the thick, ugly falling dusk, he would lose her altogether.

He followed her minutely as she moved, direct and intent, like something transmitted rather than stirring in voluntary activity, straight down the field towards the pond. There she stood on the bank for a moment. She never raised her head. Then she waded slowly into the water.

110   He stood motionless as the small black figure walked slowly and deliberately towards the center of the pond, very slowly, gradually moving deeper into the motionless water, and still moving forward as the water got up to her breast. Then he could see her no more in the dusk of the dead afternoon.

"There!" he exclaimed. "Would you believe it?"

And he hastened straight down, running over the wet soddened fields, pushing through the hedges, down into the depression of callous wintry obscurity. It took him several minutes to come to the pond. He stood on the bank, breathing heavily. He could see nothing. His eyes seemed to penetrate the dead water. Yes, perhaps that was the dark shadow of her black clothing beneath the surface of the water.

He slowly ventured into the pond. The bottom was deep, soft clay, he sank in, and the water clasped dead cold round his legs. As he stirred he could smell the cold, rotten clay that fouled up into the water. It was objectionable in his lungs. Still, repelled and yet not heeding, he moved deeper into the pond. The cold water rose over his thighs, over his loins, upon his abdomen. The lower part of his body was all sunk in the hideous cold element. And the bottom was so deeply soft and uncertain he was afraid of pitching with his mouth underneath. He could not swim, and was afraid.

He crouched a little, spreading his hands under the water and moving them round, trying to feel for her. The dead cold pond swayed upon his chest. He moved again, a little deeper, and again, with his hands underneath, he felt all around under the water. And he touched her clothing. But it evaded his fingers. He made a desperate effort to grasp it.

115 And so doing he lost his balance and went under, horribly, suffocating in the foul earthy water, struggling madly for a few moments. At last, after what seemed an eternity, he got his footing, rose again into the air and looked around. He gasped, and knew he was in the world. Then he looked at the water. She had risen near him. He grasped her clothing, and drawing her nearer, turned to take his way to land again.

He went very slowly, carefully, absorbed in the slow progress. He rose higher, climbing out of the pond. The water was now only about his legs: he was thankful, full of relief to be out of the clutches of the pond. He lifted her and staggered on to the bank, out of the horror of wet, gray clay.

He laid her down on the bank. She was quite unconscious and running with water. He made the water come from her mouth, he worked to restore her. He did not have to work very long before he could feel the breathing begin again in her: she was breathing naturally. He worked a little longer. He could feel her live beneath his hands: she was coming back. He wiped her face, wrapped her in his overcoat, looked round into the dim, dark gray world, then lifted her and staggered down the bank and across the fields.

It seemed an unthinkably long way, and his burden so heavy he felt he would never get to the house. But at last he was in the stable-yard, and then in the house-yard. He opened the door and went into the house. In the kitchen he laid her down on the hearthrug, and called. The house was empty. But the fire was burning in the grate.

Then again he kneeled to attend to her. She was breathing regularly, her eyes were wide open and as if conscious, but there seemed something missing in her look. She was conscious in herself, but unconscious of her surroundings.

120 He ran upstairs, took blankets from a bed, and put them before the fire to warm. Then he removed her saturated, earthy-smelling clothing, rubbed her dry with a towel, and wrapped her naked in the blankets. Then he went into the dining-room, to look for spirits. There was a little whisky. He drank a gulp himself, and put some into her mouth.

The effect was instantaneous. She looked full into his face, as if she had been seeing him for some time, and yet had only just become conscious of him.

"Dr. Fergusson?" she said.

"What?" he answered.

He was divesting himself of his coat, intending to find some dry clothing upstairs. He could not bear the smell of the dead, clayey water, and he was mortally afraid of his own health.

125   "What did I do?" she asked.

"Walked into the pond," he replied. He had begun to shudder like one sick, and could hardly attend to her. Her eyes remained full on him, he seemed to be going dark in his mind, looking back at her helplessly. The shuddering became quieter in him, his life came back in him, dark and unknowing, but strong again.

"Was I out of my mind?" she asked, while her eyes were fixed on him all the time.

"Maybe, for the moment," he replied. He felt quiet, because his strength came back. The strange fretful strain had left him.

"Am I out of my mind now?" she asked.

130   "Are you?" he reflected a moment. "No," he answered truthfully. "I don't see that you are." He turned his face aside. He was afraid now, because he felt dazed, and felt dimly that her power was stronger than his, in this issue. And she continued to look at him fixedly all the time. "Can you tell me where I shall find some dry things to put on?" he asked.

"Did you dive into the pond for me?" she asked.

"No," he answered. "I walked in. But I went in overhead as well."

There was silence for a moment. He hesitated. He very much wanted to go upstairs to get into dry clothing. But there was another desire in him. And she seemed to hold him. His will seemed to have gone to sleep, and left him, standing there slack before her. But he felt warm inside himself. He did not shudder at all, though his clothes were sodden on him.

"Why did you?" she asked.

135   "Because I didn't want you to do such a foolish thing," he said.

"It wasn't foolish," she said, still gazing at him as she lay on the floor, with a sofa cushion under her head. "It was the right thing to do. *I* knew best, then."

"I'll go and shift these wet things," he said. But still he had not the power to move out of her presence, until she sent him. It was as if she had the life of his body in her hands, and he could not extricate himself. Or perhaps he did not want to.

Suddenly she sat up. Then she became aware of her own immediate condition. She felt the blankets about her, she knew her own limbs.

For a moment it seemed as if her reason were going. She looked round, with wild eye, as if seeking something. He stood still with fear. She saw her clothing lying scattered.

140   "Who undressed me?" she asked, her eyes resting full and inevitable on his face.

"I did," he replied, "to bring you round."

For some moments she sat and gazed at him awfully, her lips parted.

"Do you love me, then?" she asked.

He only stood and stared at her, fascinated. His soul seemed to melt.

145   She shuffled forward on her knees, and put her arms round him, round his legs, as he stood there, pressing her breasts against his knees and thighs, clutching him with strange, convulsive certainty, pressing his thighs against her, drawing him to her

face, her throat, as she looked up at him with flaring, humble eyes of transfiguration, triumphant in first possession.

"You love me," she murmured, in strange transport, yearning and triumphant and confident. "You love me. I know you love me, I know."

And she was passionately kissing his knees, through the wet clothing, passionately and indiscriminately kissing his knees, his legs, as if unaware of everything.

He looked down at the tangled wet hair, the wild, bare, animal shoulders. He was amazed, bewildered, and afraid. He had never thought of loving her. He had never wanted to love her. When he rescued her and restored her, he was a doctor, and she was a patient. He had had no single personal thought of her. Nay, this introduction of the personal element was very distasteful to him, a violation of his professional honor. It was horrible to have her there embracing his knees. It was horrible. He revolted from it, violently. And yet—and yet—he had not the power to break away.

She looked at him again, with the same supplication of powerful love, and that same transcendent, frightening light of triumph. In view of the delicate flame which seemed to come from her face like a light, he was powerless. And yet he had never intended to love her. He had never intended. And something stubborn in him could not give way.

150   "You love me," she repeated, in a murmur of deep, rhapsodic assurance. "You love me."

Her hands were drawing him, drawing him down to her. He was afraid, even a little horrified. For he had, really, no intention of loving her. Yet her hands were drawing him towards her. He put out his hand quickly to steady himself, and grasped her bare shoulder. A flame seemed to burn the hand that grasped her soft shoulder. He had no intention of loving her: his whole will was against his yielding. It was horrible. And yet wonderful was the touch of her shoulders, beautiful the shining of her face. Was she perhaps mad? He had a horror of yielding to her. Yet something in him ached also.

He had been staring away at the door, away from her. But his hand remained on her shoulder. She had gone suddenly very still. He looked down at her. Her eyes were now wide with fear, with doubt, the light was dying from her face, a shadow of terrible grayness was returning. He could not bear the touch of her eyes' question upon him, and the look of death behind the question.

With an inward groan he gave way, and let his heart yield towards her. A sudden gentle smile came on his face. And her eyes, which never left his face, slowly, slowly filled with tears. He watched the strange water rise in her eyes, like some slow fountain coming up. And his heart seemed to burn and melt away in his breast.

He could not bear to look at her any more. He dropped on his knees and caught her head with his arms and pressed her face against his throat. She was very still. His heart, which seemed to have broken, was burning with a kind of agony in his breast. And he felt her slow, hot tears wetting his throat. But he could not move.

155   He felt the hot tears wet his neck and the hollows of his neck, and he remained motionless, suspended through one of man's eternities. Only now it had become indispensable to him to have her face pressed close to him; he could never let her go again. He could never let her head go away from the close clutch of his arm. He wanted to remain like that for ever, with his heart hurting him in a pain that was also

life to him. Without knowing, he was looking down on her damp, soft brown hair.

Then, as it were suddenly, he smelt the horrid stagnant smell of that water. And at the same moment she drew away from him and looked at him. Her eyes were wistful and unfathomable. He was afraid of them, and he fell to kissing her, not knowing what he was doing. He wanted her eyes not to have that terrible, wistful, unfathomable look.

When she turned her face to him again, a faint delicate flush was glowing, and there was again dawning that terrible shining of joy in her eyes, which really terrified him, and yet which he now wanted to see, because he feared the look of doubt still more.

"You love me?" she said, rather faltering.

"Yes." The word cost him a painful effort. Not because it wasn't true. But because it was too newly true, the *saying* seemed to tear open again his newly torn heart. And he hardly wanted it to be true, even now.

160 She lifted her face to him, and he bent forward and kissed her on the mouth, gently, with the one kiss that is an eternal pledge. And as he kissed her his heart strained again in his breast. He never intended to love her. But now it was over. He had crossed over the gulf to her, and all that he had left behind had shriveled and become void.

After the kiss, her eyes again slowly filled with tears. She sat still, away from him, with her face drooped aside, and her hands folded in her lap. The tears fell very slowly. There was complete silence. He too sat there motionless and silent on the hearthrug. The strange pain of his heart that was broken seemed to consume him. That he should love her? That this was love! That he should be ripped open in this way! Him, a doctor! How they would all jeer if they knew! It was agony to him to think they might know.

In the curious naked pain of the thought he looked again to her. She was sitting there drooped into a muse. He saw a tear fall, and his heart flared hot. He saw for the first time that one of her shoulders was quite uncovered, one arm bare, he could see one of her small breasts; dimly, because it had become almost dark in the room.

"Why are you crying?" he asked, in an altered voice.

She looked up at him, and behind her tears the consciousness of her situation for the first time brought a dark look of shame to her eyes.

165 "I'm not crying, really," she said, watching him half frightened.

He reached his hand, and softly closed it on her bare arm.

"I love you! I love you!" he said in a soft, low vibrating voice, unlike himself.

She shrank, and dropped her head. The soft, penetrating grip of his hand on her arm distressed her. She looked up at him.

"I want to go," she said. "I want to go and get you some dry things."

170 "Why?" he said. "I'm all right."

"But I want to go," she said. "And I want you to change your things."

He released her arm, and she wrapped herself in the blanket, looking at him rather frightened. And still she did not rise.

"Kiss me," she said wistfully.

He kissed her, but briefly, half in anger.

175   Then, after a second, she rose nervously, all mixed up in the blanket. He watched her in her confusion, as she tried to extricate herself and wrap herself up so that she could walk. He watched her relentlessly, as she knew. And as she went, the blanket trailing, and as he saw a glimpse of her feet and her white leg, he tried to remember her as she was when he had wrapped her in the blanket. But then he didn't want to remember, because she had been nothing to him then, and his nature revolted from remembering her as she was when she was nothing to him.

A tumbling, muffled noise from within the dark house startled him. Then he heard her voice:—"There are clothes." He rose and went to the foot of the stairs, and gathered up the garments she had thrown down. Then he came back to the fire, to rub himself down and dress. He grinned at his own appearance when he had finished.

The fire was sinking, so he put on coal. The house was now quite dark, save for the light of a street-lamp that shone in faintly from beyond the holly trees. He lit the gas with matches he found on the mantelpiece. Then he emptied the pockets of his own clothes, and threw all his wet things in a heap into the scullery. After which he gathered up her sodden clothes, gently, and put them in a separate heap on the copper-top in the scullery.

It was six o'clock on the clock. His own watch had stopped. He ought to go back to the surgery. He waited, and still she did not come down. So he went to the foot of the stairs and called:

"I shall have to go."

180   Almost immediately he heard her coming down. She had on her best dress of black voile, and her hair was tidy, but still damp. She looked at him—and in spite of herself, smiled.

"I don't like you in those clothes," she said.

"Do I look a sight?" he answered.

They were shy of one another.

"I'll make you some tea," she said.

185   "No, I must go."

"Must you?" And she looked at him again with the wide, strained, doubtful eyes. And again, from the pain of his breast, he knew how he loved her. He went and bent to kiss her, gently, passionately, with his heart's painful kiss.

"And my hair smells so horrible," she murmured in distraction. "And I'm so awful, I'm so awful! Oh, no, I'm too awful." And she broke into bitter, heart-broken sobbing. "You can't want to love me, I'm horrible."

"Don't be silly, don't be silly," he said, trying to comfort her, kissing her, holding her in his arms. "I want you, I want to marry you, we're going to be married, quickly, quickly—tomorrow if I can."

But she only sobbed terribly, and cried:

190   "I feel awful. I feel awful. I feel I'm horrible to you."

"No, I want you, I want you," was all he answered, blindly, with that terrible intonation which frightened her almost more than her horror lest he should *not* want her.

MAKING CONNECTIONS

1. In what way is the setting of the story a factor? How would you describe the surroundings and their effect on Mabel and Fergusson?
2. Describe Mabel. What is her everyday existence like? How is she treated by her father and brothers? In what ways does she differ from them?
3. Describe Fergusson. What is his everyday existence like?
4. Pick out the images, emotions, and language that are used to describe love in this story.
5. At the end of the story Fergusson cries out, "I want you, I want you." Why does he seem to want Mabel so much? Do you think they are really in love? Explain.

MAKING AN ARGUMENT

1. To what extent are the "earthy" setting and the hard life of the characters important factors in this story? Write about the internal and external conflict in this story and its relationship to setting and characterization. Cite the text of the story for support.

BOBBIE ANN MASON [B. 1940]

Bobbie Ann Mason grew up in rural Kentucky on a dairy farm. An excellent student, Mason was encouraged in her studies by her parents, who never finished high school. She attended college at the University of Kentucky, where she majored in journalism, and later earned an M.A. from the State University of Kentucky, where she majored in journalism, an M.A. from the State University of New York at Binghamton, and a Ph.D. from the University of Connecticut. Her first collection of short stories, Shiloh and Other Stories *(1982), was enormously well received, winning the Ernest Hemingway Foundation Award in 1982 for the year's most distinguished work of fiction. Her 1985 novel,* In Country, *was made into a film. A collection of stories,* Zigzagging Down a Wild Trail, *appeared in 2001, and her latest novel,* An Atomic Romance, *was published in 2005. Mason has described her work, which is usually set in the South and filled with popular culture references, as "southern Gothic going to the supermarket."*

SHILOH   [1982]

Leroy Moffitt's wife, Norma Jean, is working on her pectorals. She lifts three-pound dumbbells to warm up, then progresses to a twenty-pound barbell. Standing with her legs apart, she reminds Leroy of Wonder Woman.

"I'd give anything if I could just get these muscles to where they're real hard," says Norma Jean. "Feel this arm. It's not as hard as the other one."

"That's 'cause you're right-handed," says Leroy, dodging as she swings the barbell in an arc.

"Do you think so?"

5   "Sure."

Leroy is a truckdriver. He injured his leg in a highway accident four months ago, and his physical therapy, which involves weights and a pulley, prompted Norma Jean to try building herself up. Now she is attending a body-building class. Leroy has been collecting temporary disability since his tractor-trailer jackknifed in Missouri, badly twisting his left leg in its socket. He has a steel pin in his hip. He will probably not be able to drive his rig again. It sits in the backyard, like a gigantic bird that has flown home to roost. Leroy has been home in Kentucky for three months, and his leg is almost healed, but the accident frightened him and he does not want to drive any more long hauls. He is not sure what to do next. In the meantime, he makes things from craft kits. He started by building a miniature log cabin from notched Popsicle sticks. He varnished it and placed it on the TV set, where it remains. It reminds him of a rustic Nativity scene. Then he tried string art (sailing ships on black velvet), a macramé owl kit, a snap-together B-17 Flying Fortress, and a lamp made out of a model truck, with a light fixture screwed in the top of the cab. At first the kits were diversions, something to kill time, but now he is thinking about building a full-scale log house from a kit. It would be considerably cheaper than building a regular house, and besides, Leroy has grown to appreciate how things are put together. He has begun to realize that in all the years he was on the road he never took time to examine anything. He was always flying past scenery.

"They won't let you build a log cabin in any of the new subdivisions," Norma Jean tells him.

"They will if I tell them it's for you," he says, teasing her. Ever since they were married, he has promised Norma Jean he would build her a new home one day. They have always rented, and the house they live in is small and nondescript. It does not even feel like a home, Leroy realizes now.

Norma Jean works at the Rexall drugstore, and she has acquired an amazing amount of information about cosmetics. When she explains to Leroy the three stages of complexion care, involving creams, toners, and moisturizers, he thinks happily of other petroleum products—axle grease, diesel fuel. This is a connection between him and Norma Jean. Since he has been home, he has felt unusually tender about his wife and guilty over his long absences. But he can't tell what she feels about him. Norma Jean has never complained about his traveling; she has never made hurt remarks, like calling his truck a "widow-maker." He is reasonably certain she has been faithful to him, but he wishes she would celebrate his permanent homecoming more happily. Norma Jean is often startled to find Leroy at home, and he thinks she seems a little disappointed about it. Perhaps he reminds her too much of the early days of their marriage, before he went on the road. They had a child who died as an infant, years ago. They never speak about their memories of Randy, which have almost faded, but now that Leroy is home all the time, they sometimes feel awkward around each other, and Leroy wonders if one of them should mention the child. He has the feeling that they are waking up out of a dream together—that they must create a new marriage, start afresh. They are lucky they are still married. Leroy has read that for most people losing a child destroys the marriage—or else he heard this on *Donahue*. He can't always remember where he learns things anymore.

10   At Christmas, Leroy bought an electric organ for Norma Jean. She used to play the piano when she was in high school. "It don't leave you," she told him once. "It's like riding a bicycle."

The new instrument had so many keys and buttons that she was bewildered by it at first. She touched the keys tentatively, pushed some buttons, then pecked out "Chopsticks." It came out in an amplified fox-trot rhythm, with marimba sounds.

"It's an orchestra!" she cried.

The organ had a pecan-look finish and eighteen preset chords, with optional flute, violin, trumpet, clarinet, and banjo accompaniments. Norma Jean mastered the organ almost immediately. At first she played Christmas songs. Then she bought *The Sixties Songbook* and learned every tune in it, adding variations to each with the rows of brightly colored buttons.

"I didn't like these old songs back then," she said. "But I have this crazy feeling I missed something."

15   "You didn't miss a thing," said Leroy.

Leroy likes to lie on the couch and smoke a joint and listen to Norma Jean play "Can't Take My Eyes Off You" and "I'll Be Back." He is back again. After fifteen years on the road, he is finally settling down with the woman he loves. She is still pretty. Her skin is flawless. Her frosted curls resemble pencil trimmings.

Now that Leroy has come home to stay, he notices how much the town has changed. Subdivisions are spreading across western Kentucky like an oil slick. The sign at the edge of town says "Pop: 11,500"—only seven hundred more than it said twenty years before. Leroy can't figure out who is living in all the new houses. The farmers who used to gather around the courthouse square on Saturday afternoons to play checkers and spit tobacco juice have gone. It has been years since Leroy has thought about the farmers, and they have disappeared without his noticing.

Leroy meets a kid named Stevie Hamilton in the parking lot at the new shopping center. While they pretend to be strangers meeting over a stalled car, Stevie tosses an ounce of marijuana under the front seat of Leroy's car. Stevie is wearing orange jogging shoes and a T-shirt that says CHATTAHOOCHEE SUPER-RAT. His father is a prominent doctor who lives in one of the expensive subdivisions in a new white-columned brick house that looks like a funeral parlor. In the phone book under his name there is a separate number, with the listing "Teenagers."

"Where do you get this stuff?" asks Leroy. "From your pappy?"

20   "That's for me to know and you to find out," Stevie says. He is slit-eyed and skinny.

"What else you got?"

"What you interested in?"

"Nothing special. Just wondered."

Leroy used to take speed on the road. Now he has to go slowly. He needs to be mellow. He leans back against the car and says, "I'm aiming to build me a log house, soon as I get time. My wife, though, I don't think she likes the idea."

25   "Well, let me know when you want me again," Stevie says. He has a cigarette in his cupped palm, as though sheltering it from the wind. He takes a long drag, then stomps it on the asphalt and slouches away.

Stevie's father was two years ahead of Leroy in high school. Leroy is thirty-four. He married Norma Jean when they were both eighteen, and their child Randy was born a few months later, but he died at the age of four months and three days. He would be about Stevie's age now. Norma Jean and Leroy were at the drive-in, watching a double feature (*Dr. Strangelove* and *Lover Come Back*), and the baby was sleeping in the back seat. When the first movie ended, the baby was dead. It was the sudden infant death syndrome. Leroy remembers handing Randy to a nurse at the emergency room, as though he were offering her a large doll as a present. A dead baby feels like a sack of flour. "It just happens sometimes," said the doctor, in what Leroy always recalls as a nonchalant tone. Leroy can hardly remember the child anymore, but he still sees vividly a scene from *Dr. Strangelove* in which the President of the United States was talking in a folksy voice on the hot line to the Soviet premier about the bomber accidentally headed toward Russia. He was in the War Room, and the world map was lit up. Leroy remembers Norma Jean standing catatonically beside him in the hospital and himself thinking: Who is this strange girl? He had forgotten who she was. Now scientists are saying that crib death is caused by a virus. Nobody knows anything, Leroy thinks. The answers are always changing.

When Leroy gets home from the shopping center, Norma Jean's mother, Mabel Beasley, is there. Until this year, Leroy has not realized how much time she spends with Norma Jean. When she visits, she inspects the closets and then the plants, informing Norma Jean when a plant is droopy or yellow. Mabel calls the plants "flowers," although there are never any blooms. She also notices if Norma Jean's laundry is piling up. Mabel is a short, overweight woman whose tight, brown-dyed curls look more like a wig than the actual wig she sometimes wears. Today she has brought Norma Jean an off-white dust ruffle she made for the bed; Mabel works in a custom-upholstery shop.

"This is the tenth one I made this year," Mabel says. "I got started and couldn't stop."

"It's real pretty," says Norma Jean.

30   "Now we can hide things under the bed," says Leroy, who gets along with his mother-in-law primarily by joking with her. Mabel has never really forgiven him for disgracing her by getting Norma Jean pregnant. When the baby died, she said that fate was mocking her.

"What's that thing?" Mabel says to Leroy in a loud voice, pointing to a tangle of yarn on a piece of canvas.

Leroy holds it up for Mabel to see. "It's my needlepoint," he explains. "This is a *Star Trek* pillow cover."

"That's what a woman would do," says Mabel. "Great day in the morning!"

"All the big football players on TV do it," he says.

35   "Why, Leroy, you're always trying to fool me. I don't believe you for one minute. You don't know what to do with yourself—that's the whole trouble. Sewing!"

"I'm aiming to build us a log house," says Leroy. "Soon as my plans come."

"Like *heck* you are," says Norma Jean. She takes Leroy's needlepoint and shoves it into a drawer. "You have to find a job first. Nobody can afford to build now anyway."

Mabel straightens her girdle and says, "I still think before you get tied down y'all ought to take a little run to Shiloh."

"One of these days, Mama," Norma Jean says impatiently.

40 Mabel is talking about Shiloh, Tennessee. For the past few years, she has been urging Leroy and Norma Jean to visit the Civil War battleground there. Mabel went there on her honeymoon—the only real trip she ever took. Her husband died of a perforated ulcer when Norma Jean was ten, but Mabel, who was accepted into the United Daughters of the Confederacy in 1975, is still preoccupied with going back to Shiloh.

"I've been to kingdom come and back in that truck out yonder," Leroy says to Mabel, "but we never yet set foot in that battleground. Ain't that something? How did I miss it?"

"It's not even that far," Mabel says.

After Mabel leaves, Norma Jean reads to Leroy from a list she has made. "Things you could do," she announces. "You could get a job as a guard at Union Carbide, where they'd let you set on a stool. You could get on at the lumberyard. You could do a little carpenter work, if you want to build so bad. You could—"

"I can't do something where I'd have to stand up all day."

45 "You ought to try standing up all day behind a cosmetics counter. It's amazing that I have strong feet, coming from two parents that never had strong feet at all." At the moment Norma Jean is holding on to the kitchen counter, raising her knees one at a time as she talks. She is wearing two-pound ankle weights.

"Don't worry," says Leroy. "I'll do something."

"You could truck calves to slaughter for somebody. You wouldn't have to drive any big old truck for that."

"I'm going to build you this house," says Leroy. "I want to make you a real home."

"I don't want to live in any log cabin."

50 "It's not a cabin. It's a house."

"I don't care. It looks like a cabin."

"You and me together could lift those logs. It's just like lifting weights."

Norma Jean doesn't answer. Under her breath, she is counting. Now she is marching through the kitchen. She is doing goose steps.

Before his accident, when Leroy came home he used to stay in the house with Norma Jean, watching TV in bed and playing cards. She would cook fried chicken, picnic ham, chocolate pie—all his favorites. Now he is home alone much of the time. In the mornings, Norma Jean disappears, leaving a cooling place in the bed. She eats a cereal called Body Buddies, and she leaves the bowl on the table, with the soggy tan balls floating in a milk puddle. He sees things about Norma Jean that he never realized before. When she chops onions, she stares off into a corner, as if she can't bear to look. She puts on her house slippers almost precisely at nine o'clock every evening and nudges her jogging shoes under the couch. She saves bread heels for the birds. Leroy watches the birds at the feeder. He notices the peculiar way goldfinches fly past the window. They close their wings, then fall, then spread their wings to catch and lift themselves. He wonders if they close their eyes when they fall. Norma Jean closes her eyes when they are in bed. She wants the lights turned out. Even then, he is sure she closes her eyes.

55   He goes for long drives around town. He tends to drive a car rather carelessly. Power steering and an automatic shift make a car feel so small and inconsequential that his body is hardly involved in the driving process. His injured leg stretches out comfortably. Once or twice he has almost hit something, but even the prospect of an accident seems minor in a car. He cruises the new subdivisions, feeling like a criminal rehearsing for a robbery. Norma Jean is probably right about a log house being inappropriate here in the new subdivision. All the houses look grand and complicated. They depress him.

One day when Leroy comes home from a drive he finds Norma Jean in tears. She is in the kitchen making a potato and mushroom-soup casserole, with grated cheese topping. She is crying because her mother caught her smoking.

"I didn't hear her coming. I was standing here puffing away pretty as you please," Norma Jean says, wiping her eyes.

"I knew it would happen sooner or later," says Leroy, putting his arm around her.

"She don't know the meaning of the word 'knock,'" says Norma Jean. "It's a wonder she hadn't caught me years ago."

60   "Think of it this way," Leroy says. "What if she caught me with a joint?"

"You better not let her!" Norma Jean shrieks. "I'm warning you, Leroy Moffitt!"

"I'm just kidding. Here, play me a tune. That'll help you relax."

Norma Jean puts the casserole in the oven and sets the timer. Then she plays a ragtime tune, with horns and banjo, as Leroy lights up a joint and lies on the couch, laughing to himself about Mabel's catching him at it. He thinks of Stevie Hamilton— a doctor's son pushing grass. Everything is funny. The whole town seems crazy and small. He is reminded of Virgil Mathis, a boastful policeman Leroy used to shoot pool with. Virgil recently led a drug bust in a back room at a bowling alley, where he seized ten thousand dollars worth of marijuana. The newspaper had a picture of him holding up the bags of grass and grinning widely. Right now, Leroy can imagine Virgil breaking down the door and arresting him with a lungful of smoke. Virgil would probably have been alerted to the scene because of all the racket Norma Jean is making. Now she sounds like a hard-rock band. Norma Jean is terrific. When she switches to a Latin-rhythm version of "Sunshine Superman," Leroy hums along. Norma Jean's foot goes up and down, up and down.

"Well, what do you think?" Leroy says, when Norma Jean pauses to search through her music.

65   "What do I think about what?"

His mind has gone blank. Then he says, "I'll sell my rig and build us a house." That wasn't what he wanted to say. He wanted to know what she thought—what she *really* thought—about them.

"Don't start in on that again," says Norma Jean. She begins playing "Who'll Be the Next in Line?"

Leroy used to tell hitchhikers his whole life story—about his travels, his hometown, the baby. He would end with a question: "Well, what do you think?" It was just a rhetorical question. In time, he had the feeling that he'd been telling the same story over and over to the same hitchhikers. He quit talking to hitchhikers when he realized how his voice sounded—whining and self-pitying, like some teenage-tragedy song. Now Leroy has the sudden impulse to tell Norma Jean about himself, as if he had just met her. They have known each other so long they have forgotten a lot about each other. They could become reacquainted. But when the oven timer goes off and she runs to the kitchen, he forgets why he wants to do this.

The next day, Mabel drops by. It is Saturday and Norma Jean is cleaning. Leroy is studying the plans of his log house, which have finally come in the mail. He has them spread out on the table—big sheets of stiff blue paper, with diagrams and numbers printed in white. While Norma Jean runs the vacuum, Mabel drinks coffee. She sets her coffee cup on a blueprint.

70   "I'm just waiting for time to pass," she says to Leroy, drumming her fingers on the table.

As soon as Norma Jean switches off the vacuum, Mabel says in a loud voice. "Did you hear about the datsun dog that killed the baby?"

Norma Jean says, "The word is 'dachshund.'"

"They put the dog on trial. It chewed the baby's legs off. The mother was in the next room all the time." She raises her voice. "They thought it was neglect."

Norma Jean is holding her ears. Leroy manages to open the refrigerator and get some Diet Pepsi to offer Mabel. Mabel still has some coffee and she waves away the Pepsi.

75   "Datsuns are like that," Mabel says. "They're jealous dogs. They'll tear a place to pieces if you don't keep an eye on them."

"You better watch out what you're saying, Mabel," says Leroy.

"Well, facts is facts."

Leroy looks out the window at his rig. It is like a huge piece of furniture gathering dust in the backyard. Pretty soon it will be an antique. He hears the vacuum cleaner. Norma Jean seems to be cleaning the living room rug again.

Later, she says to Leroy. "She just said that about the baby because she caught me smoking. She's trying to pay me back."

80   "What are you talking about?" Leroy says, nervously shuffling blueprints.

"You know good and well," Norma Jean says. She is sitting in a kitchen chair with her feet up and her arms wrapped around her knees. She looks small and helpless. She says, "The very idea, her bringing up a subject like that! Saying it was neglect."

"She didn't mean that," Leroy says.

"She might not have *thought* she meant it. She always says things like that. You don't know how she goes on."

"But she didn't really mean it. She was just talking."

85   Leroy opens a king-sized bottle of beer and pours it into two glasses, dividing it carefully. He hands a glass to Norma Jean and she takes it from him mechanically. For a long time, they sit by the kitchen window watching the birds at the feeder.

Something is happening. Norma Jean is going to night school. She has graduated from her six-week body-building course, and now she is taking an adult-education course in composition at Paducah Community College. She spends her evenings out-lining paragraphs.

"First, you have a topic sentence," she explains to Leroy. "Then you divide it up. Your secondary topic has to be connected to your primary topic."

To Leroy, this sounds intimidating. "I never was any good in English," he says.

"It makes a lot of sense."

90   "What are you doing this for, anyhow?"

She shrugs. "It's something to do." She stands up and lifts her dumbbells a few times.

"Driving a rig, nobody cared about my English."   .

"I'm not criticizing your English."

Norma Jean used to say, "If I lose ten minutes' sleep, I just drag all day." Now she stays up late, writing compositions. She got a B on her first paper—a how-to theme on soup-based casseroles. Recently Norma Jean has been cooking unusual foods—tacos, lasagna, Bombay chicken. She doesn't play the organ anymore, though her second paper was called "Why Music Is Important to Me." She sits at the kitchen table, concentrating on her outlines, while Leroy plays with his log house plans, practicing with a set of Lincoln Logs. The thought of getting a truck-load of notched, numbered logs scares him, and he wants to be prepared. As he and Norma Jean work together at the kitchen table, Leroy has the hopeful thought that they are sharing something, but he knows he is a fool to think this. Norma Jean is miles away. He knows he is going to lose her. Like Mabel, he is just waiting for time to pass.

95   One day, Mabel is there before Norma Jean gets home from work, and Leroy finds himself confiding in her. Mabel, he realizes, must know Norma Jean better than he does.

"I don't know what's got into that girl," Mabel says. "She used to go to bed with the chickens. Now you say she's up all hours. Plus her a-smoking. I like to died."

"I want to make her this beautiful home," Leroy says, indicating the Lincoln Logs. "I don't think she even wants it. Maybe she was happier with me gone."

"She don't know what to make of you, coming home like this."

"Is that it?"

100   Mabel takes the roof off his Lincoln Log cabin. "You couldn't get *me* in a log cabin," she says. "I was raised in one. It's no picnic, let me tell you."

"They're different now," says Leroy.

"I tell you what," Mabel says, smiling oddly at Leroy.

"What?"

"Take her on down to Shiloh. Y'all need to get out together, stir a little. Her brain's all balled up over them books."

105   Leroy can see traces of Norma Jean's features in her mother's face. Mabel's worn face has the texture of crinkled cotton, but suddenly she looks pretty. It occurs to Leroy that Mabel has been hinting all along that she wants them to take her with them to Shiloh.

"Let's all go to Shiloh," he says. "You and me and her. Come Sunday."

Mabel throws up her hand in protest. "Oh, no, not me. Young folks want to be by theirselves."

When Norma Jean comes in with groceries, Leroy says excitedly, "Your mama here's been dying to go to Shiloh for thirty-five years. It's about time we went, don't you think?"

"I'm not going to butt in on anybody's second honeymoon," Mabel says.

110   "Who's going on a honeymoon, for Christ's sake?" Norma Jean says loudly.

"I never raised no daughter of mine to talk that-a-way," Mabel says.

"You ain't seen nothing yet," says Norma Jean. She starts putting away boxes and cans, slamming cabinet doors.

"There's a log cabin at Shiloh," Mabel says. "It was there during the battle. There's bullet holes in it."

"When are you going to *shut up* about Shiloh, Mama?" asks Norma Jean.

115   "I always thought Shiloh was the prettiest place, so full of history," Mabel goes on. "I just hoped y'all could see it once before I die, so you could tell me about it." Later, she whispers to Leroy, "You do what I said. A little change is what she needs."

"Your name means 'the king,'" Norma Jean says to Leroy that evening. He is trying to get her to go to Shiloh, and she is reading a book about another century.

"Well, I reckon I ought to be right proud."

"I guess so."

"Am I still king around here?"

120   Norma Jean flexes her biceps and feels them for hardness. "I'm not fooling around with anybody, if that's what you mean," she says.

"Would you tell me if you were?"

"I don't know."

"What does your name mean?"

"It was Marilyn Monroe's real name."

125   "No kidding!"

"Norma comes from the Normans. They were invaders," she says. She closes her book and looks hard at Leroy. "I'll go to Shiloh with you if you'll stop staring at me."

On Sunday, Norma Jean packs a picnic and they go to Shiloh. To Leroy's relief Mabel says she does not want to come with them. Norma Jean drives, and Leroy, sitting beside her, feels like some boring hitchhiker she has picked up. He tries some conversation, but she answers him in monosyllables. At Shiloh, she drives aimlessly through the park, past bluffs and trails and steep ravines. Shiloh is an immense place, and Leroy cannot see it as a battleground. It is not what he expected. He thought it would look like a golf course. Monuments are everywhere, showing through the thick clusters of trees. Norma Jean passes the log cabin Mabel mentioned. It is surrounded by tourists looking for bullet holes.

"That's not the kind of log house I've got in mind," says Leroy apologetically.

"I know *that*."

130   "This is a pretty place. Your mama was right."

"It's O.K.," says Norma Jean. "Well, we've seen it. I hope she's satisfied." They burst out laughing together.

At the park museum, a movie on Shiloh is shown every half hour, but they decide that they don't want to see it. They buy a souvenir Confederate flag for Mabel, and then they find a picnic spot near the cemetery. Norma Jean has brought a picnic cooler, with pimento sandwiches, soft drinks, and Yodels. Leroy eats a sandwich and then smokes a joint, hiding it behind the picnic cooler. Norma Jean has quit smoking altogether. She is picking cake crumbs from the cellophane wrapper, like a fussy bird.

Leroy says, "So the boys in gray ended up in Corinth. The Union soldiers zapped 'em finally. April 7, 1862."

135   They both know that he doesn't know any history. He is just talking about some of the historical plaques they have read. He feels awkward, like a boy on a date with an older girl. They are still just making conversation.

"Corinth is where Mama eloped to," says Norma Jean.

They sit in silence and stare at the cemetery for the Union dead and, beyond, at a tall cluster of trees. Campers are parked nearby, bumper to bumper, and small children in bright clothing are cavorting and squealing. Norma Jean wads up the cake wrapper and squeezes it tightly in her hand. Without looking at Leroy, she says, "I want to leave you."

Leroy takes a bottle of Coke out of the cooler and flips off the cap. He holds the bottle poised near his mouth but cannot remember to take a drink. Finally he says, "No, you don't."

"Yes, I do."

140   "I won't let you."

"You can't stop me."

"Don't do me that way."

Leroy knows Norma Jean will have her own way. "Didn't I promise to be home from now on?" he says.

"In some ways, a woman prefers a man who wanders," says Norma Jean. "That sounds crazy, I know."

145   "You're not crazy."

Leroy remembers to drink from his Coke. Then he says, "Yes, you *are* crazy. You and me could start all over again. Right back at the beginning."

"We *have* started all over again," says Norma Jean. "And this is how it turned out."

"What did I do wrong?"

"Nothing."

150   "Is this one of those women's lib things?" Leroy asks.

"Don't be funny."

The cemetery, a green slope dotted with white markers, looks like a subdivision site. Leroy is trying to comprehend that his marriage is breaking up, but for some reason he is wondering about white slabs in a graveyard.

"Everything was fine till Mama caught me smoking," says Norma Jean, standing up. "That set something off."

"What are you talking about?"

155   "She won't leave me alone—*you* won't leave me alone." Norma Jean seems to be crying, but she is looking away from him. "I feel eighteen again. I can't face that all over again." She starts walking away. "No, it *wasn't* fine. I don't know what I'm saying. Forget it."

Leroy takes a lungful of smoke and closes his eyes as Norma Jean's words sink in. He tries to focus on the fact that thirty-five hundred soldiers died on the grounds around him. He can only think of that war as a board game with plastic soldiers. Leroy almost smiles, as he compares the Confederates' daring attack on the Union camps and Virgil Mathis's raid on the bowling alley. General Grant, drunk and furious, shoved the Southerners back to Corinth, where Mabel and Jet Beasley were married years later, when Mabel was still thin and good-looking. The next day, Mabel and Jet visited the battleground, and then Norma Jean was born, and then she married Leroy and they had a baby, which they lost, and now Leroy and Norma Jean are here at the same battleground. Leroy knows he is leaving out a lot. He is leaving out the insides of history. History was always just names and dates to him. It occurs to him that building a house of logs is similarly empty—too simple. And the real inner workings of a marriage, like most of history, have escaped him. Now he sees that building a log house is the dumbest idea he could have had. It was clumsy of him to think Norma Jean would want a log house. It was a crazy idea. He'll have to think of something else, quickly. He will wad the blueprints into tight balls and fling them into the lake. Then he'll get moving again. He opens his eyes. Norma Jean has moved away and is walking through the cemetery, following a serpentine brick path.

Leroy gets up to follow his wife, but his good leg is asleep and his bad leg still hurts him. Norma Jean is far away, walking rapidly toward the bluff by the river, and he tries to hobble toward her. Some children run past him, screaming noisily. Norma Jean has reached the bluff, and she is looking out over the Tennessee River. Now she turns toward Leroy and waves her arms. Is she beckoning to him? She seems to be doing an exercise for her chest muscles. The sky is unusually pale—the color of the dust ruffle Mabel made for their bed.

MAKING CONNECTIONS

1. To what extent does your own background or experience influence your response to this story? Have you ever had the experience of "growing away" from someone? Explain.

2. The two main characters, Leroy and Norma Jean, seem to change as the story progresses. What do you think is happening to each of them? To their relationship?

3. Norma Jean and Leroy don't seem to have much to say to each other. Why? Are there times when you expect them to say more? What do you think remains unsaid?

4. Shiloh was the site of a major Civil War battle won by Union forces. Do you think this is an appropriate setting for this story? Explain.

MAKING AN ARGUMENT

1. It's clear that Norma Jean has changed in ways that make it very difficult for her to stay with Leroy. If you were a marriage counselor, and Norma Jean and Leroy came to you for help, what would you suggest to them? Would you suggest they stay together? Do you think this relationship should be saved? Write an argument for or against the continuance of this marriage. Cite the text of the story for evidence to support your view.

ROSARIO MORALES [B. 1930]

With her daughter Aurora Levins Morales, Rosario Morales coauthored Getting Home Alive, *a collection of poetry and prose published in 1986 and described by one critic as the most important book to come out of the Puerto Rican diaspora in a generation. It is considered a landmark in U.S.-Puerto Rican literature.* "The Day It Happened" *was published in* Callaloo.

THE DAY IT HAPPENED

[1992]

The day it happened I was washing my hair. I had long hair then that went halfway down my back and I washed it once a week and rinsed it with lemon juice "to bring out the blond highlights" Mami said. Then I'd set it into pincurls that took an age to do because there was so much to wind around and around my finger. But if Mami was in a good mood, and she looked like she might be that day, she curled the back for me. I usually did all this on Saturday so I would look great for church on Sunday, and for a date Saturday night if I ever had one. ¡ojala!

Naturally the moment when it all began I was rinsing the big soapy mess. Nosy Maria was leaning out the window drying her dark red fingernails in the breeze when Josie stepped out of our apartment house doorway with a suitcase in her hand. Maria sucked in her breath so hard the sound brought my mother who took one look, crossed herself, or so Maria says, and started praying. Someone needed to pray for Josie. It was five o'clock and Ramón was due home any minute.

I wouldn't have known anything about any of this if Olga next door hadn't rung our doorbell and banged on the door just when Mami was too deep in prayer to hear and Maria was leaning out over the sill with her eyes bugging out. I cursed, very quietly of course, because if Mami or Papi heard me curse I'd get a slap across my face. I wrapped my sopping head in a towel and opened the door to Olga's "Oh my goodness, oh my dear. Oh honey, did you see? Look out the window this minute. I wouldn't have believed it if I hadn't seen it with my own two eyes. That poor little kid. I hate to think . . . " and on and on as we crossed the apartment to look out on the street.

Little Mikey from across the way was telling the rest of the kids how he'd found a taxi for Josie the minute he'd hit Southern Boulevard and how he'd hailed it and how the driver had let him ride back to Brook Street in the front seat—even though all of them had seen him arrive and step out with his back stiff with pride. Meantime Josie was back down in the street with Doña Toña from across the hall and Betty Murphy upstairs right behind her, all of them loaded down with two lamps, a typewriter and a big box of books. Doña Toña was muttering something we couldn't hear up here on the second story but it was probably either the prayer I was hearing on my right or the ". . . hurry oh hurry oh God he'll be here any minute are you mad girl, are you mad" that came at me from the left.

5   It was hard not to be scared as well as glad that Josie was packing up and leaving Ramón. They'd been married only six months but already they were in a pattern,

like the Garcias down the block who did everything the same way on the same day, all year. Ramón worked late till seven every week day and five on Saturday. When he arrived he expected a good dinner to be on the table at the right temperature exactly five minutes after he walked in the door. He yelled if she didn't get it right and sometimes even if she did.

Saturday evening they went out to a party or the bar down the avenue, both of them dressed up and Ramón looking proud and cheerful for a change. Josie always looked great. She's so cute. Small and plump with long lashes on her dark eyes and, get this, naturally curly hair. She smiled a lot when she was happy but she hadn't been happy lately and not at all since she got pregnant. I wasn't supposed to know this. God, I was almost thirteen! But Maria, who was fourteen and a half and thought she was twenty, listened in on conversations in the living room by opening the door a sliver and she told me all about it.

Saturday nights there was sure to be a fight. Either it was that Josie was "no fun, a man can't be a man with such a wet rag around." Or it was that Josie was "a tramp. Why else was that guy staring at you, eating you up with his eyes?" The first time it happened, soon after they moved in, it woke me up from a deep sleep and I was so scared I crept into Maria's bed. I'd never heard such yelling in my life. When my parents fight it's during the day and in angry whispers. It sounds like a snake convention in my parents' bedroom. That's bad enough. Maria and I get real nervous and nothing's right until they make up and talk in normal voices again. But Ramón could be heard right through the floor at two in the morning. And then he took to throwing things and then he started hitting her. The first time that happened Josie didn't go to morning mass at St. Francis and Mami went down to her apartment to see if she was sick or something. Josie came to the door with a big bruise on her face. After that Mami went to fetch her every Sunday and stayed with her if she was too ashamed to go to church.

After she found out she was pregnant Josie had talked it over with Doña Toña and Doña Toña had talked it over with Mami and by and by we all knew she was scared he would hurt the little baby growing inside of her and worried about the child growing up with Ramón for a father. He expected too much of everyone and little kids hurt so when a parent thinks whatever they do is all wrong. Ha! Tell that to Mami and Papi, will you.

I don't think there was anyone in the neighborhood on Ramón's side not even Joe who liked to bully his wife and daughters but didn't realize he did or Tito who talked all the time about "wearing the pants in this family." Ramón was too much, even for them. Josie was so clearly a fine person, a quiet homebody, a sweetypie. Ramón was out of his mind, that's what most of us thought. I mean you had to be to be so regularly mean to a person who adored you. And she did, at least at first. You could see it in the way she looked at him, boasted about his strength, his good job, his brains. The way she excused his temper. "He can't help himself. He doesn't mean it."

10   And now she was packed up and sitting in the taxi. Waiting for him to come home, I guess. That was too much for Mami and she scooted out the door with Olga, Maria, Papi, no less, and me right behind her with that soaked blue towel

wrapped sloppily around my head. "Ai Mamita! Jesus, Maria y José. Jesus Maria y José," came faintly up the stairs in the front of the hurrying line. I knew Mami and I knew she meant to stand in front of Josie to protect her from that bully and, sure as shooting, Papi was going to protect Mami who was going so fast in her house slippers she almost fell down except that Olga gripped her hard and kept her upright.

When we streamed out the door into the small crowd that had gathered by now it was to see Ramón coming down the street with a sour look on his face. He looked up once or twice but mostly just stared at his feet as he strode up the block. He swept past us and almost into the house the way he did when he came home weary from the shipyard and the long ride home. He would have missed seeing Josie for sure, as I was praying he would, except that she called to him.

"Ramón," she said in her soft voice, stepping out of the taxi. "Ramón." He looked up and around then, took in the crowd, the taxi with a tall lamp lying on the back seat and Josie in her good suit. He stood looking at all this and especially at Josie for a long time. When he spoke it was only to Josie, as if we weren't there at all. He had to clear his throat to say "Josie?"

I was totally surprised and confused. He sounded so small, you know. So uncertain. It was Josie looked tall now and hard. If I hadn't known what I knew I would've said Josie was the bully in the family. She looked him straight in the eye and said stiffly, as if they were lines someone had given her to memorize, "I warned you. I said I would leave if you ever hit me again. I am not safe with you. Our child is not safe with you. I'm going now. I left arroz con pollo on the stove and the electric bill on the table." He didn't answer so she turned to hug Doña Toña and Mami before sitting herself back down. It was then that Ramón acted. Before I could blink he'd hurled himself at her, thrown himself on his knees and gripped her around her stockinged legs. "No! No te vayas. Tu no comprendes. Eres muy joven para comprender. Tu no puedes dejarme asi. Estamos casados para la vida. Te amo para siempre, para siempre. Josita, mi amor, no te vayas. Si te vas me mato. Te lo juro. No te puedes ir. No te puedes ir. . . " and on and on in a hoarse voice while Josie stood there frozen, fear on her face. There was no sound but Maria whispering occasional translations into Olga's impatient ear "Don't go." "You're too young to understand." "We're married for life." "I'll love you always." "I'll kill myself, I swear it."

It went on forever, Josie standing there, Ramón kneeling, all of us listening, tears running down my face, Josie's face, Mami's face. It was Olga who ended it, who walked up to Ramón, knelt down beside him, put an arm around him, and started talking, telling him Josie was a mother now and had to think about what was best for her baby, that it was his baby too, that he had to let her go now so she could bear a baby healthy in body and soul, that she knew he loved Josie, that his love would let him do what was best for them all. He was crying now, arguing with her while he slowly let go while he said he never could let her go that she was his whole life, that he would die without her, while Josie kissed Toña quickly on the cheek and climbed in next to the taxi driver who sat there looking the way I probably looked, dazed, like he'd stumbled into a movie screen and couldn't get out. She had to tell him to drive off.

MAKING CONNECTIONS

1. Who is the narrator? How does her point of view influence your response to the story?
2. Describe Ramón. Why is Josie leaving him? Why is Josie upset that she is pregnant?
3. Why does Ramón sound so small when he realizes Josie is leaving? Do you believe what he says in response? Explain.
4. Do you think Josie will eventually take Ramón back? Do you think she should? Why or why not?
5. Compare Josie with Nora Helmer in *A Doll's House* (p. 856). Do you think she is more or less justified in leaving her husband than Nora? Explain.

MAKING AN ARGUMENT

1. Research the subject of spousal abuse. Based on what you learn, write an argument for or against Josie giving Ramón another chance. Cite what you've learned through your research as well as the story to support your position.

◆ POETRY ◆

CONNECTING THROUGH COMPARISON: BE MY LOVE

The three poems that follow address a subtheme of this section: proposals of love. Read and discussed together, they invite comparison and connections—not only with each other—but with similar experiences of your own.

CHRISTOPHER MARLOWE [1564-1593]

Christopher Marlowe was a contemporary of Shakespeare and one of the most successful playwrights and poets of the Elizabethan era, but his career was cut short when he was murdered in a tavern brawl. His major plays include Tamburlaine the Great *(1587),* Dr. Faustus *(1588), and* Edward II *(1592).*

THE PASSIONATE SHEPHERD TO HIS LOVE   [1599]

Come live with me and be my love
And we will all the pleasures prove

That valleys, groves, hills, and fields
Woods, or steepy mountain yields.

And we will sit upon the rocks,   5
Seeing the shepherds feed their flocks,
By shallow rivers to whose falls
Melodious birds sing madrigals.

And I will make thee beds of roses
And a thousand fragrant posies,   10
A cap of flowers, and a kirtle°
Embroidered with leaves of myrtle;

A gown made of the finest wool
Which from our pretty lambs we pull;
Fair lined slippers for the cold,   15
With buckles of the purest gold;

A belt of straw and ivy buds,
With coral clasps and amber studs:
And if these pleasures may thee move
Come live with me and be my love.   20

The shepherds' swains° shall dance and sing
For thy delight each May morning:
If these delights thy mind may move
Then live with me and be my love.

11 kirtle a long gown   **21 swains** boy servants

WALTER RALEIGH [1552–1618]

*Walter Raleigh is best known as an adventurer, explorer,
and adviser to Queen Elizabeth I. He organized expedi-
tions to North America, founded a settlement in Virginia,
and introduced tobacco to Europe. Involved in political
intrigue for much of his career, he was imprisoned for
thirteen years in the Tower of London and was eventually
executed by James I. "The Nymph's Reply to the Shepherd"
was written in response to Christopher Marlowe's "The
Passionate Shepherd to His Love," on the previous page.*

THE NYMPH'S REPLY TO THE SHEPHERD   [1600]

If all the world were young,
And truth in every shepherd's tongue,

These pretty pleasures might me move
To live with thee and be thy love.

Time drives the flocks from field to fold   5
When rivers rage and rocks grow cold,
And Philomel° becometh dumb;
The rest complains of cares to come.

The flowers do fade, and wanton fields
To wayward winter reckoning yields;   10
A honey tongue, a heart of gall,
Is fancy's spring, but sorrow's fall.

Thy gowns, thy shoes, thy bed of roses,
Thy cap, thy kirtle,° and thy posies
Soon break, soon winter, soon forgotten—   15
In folly ripe, in season rotten.

Thy belt of straw and ivy buds,
Thy coral clasps and amber studs,
All these in me no means can move
To come to thee and be thy love.   20

But could youth last and love still breed,
Had joys no date nor age no need,
Then these delights my mind might move
To come with thee and be thy love.

7 Philomel nightingale bird   **14 kirtle** a long gown

ANDREW MARVELL   [1621–1678]

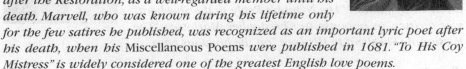

Andrew Marvell was born in the town of Hull and attended Cambridge University, graduating in 1638. During the English civil war, he held posts as a tutor in the family of an important general on the Parliamentary side, and as a secretary to the poet Milton. During the war, in 1659, Marvell was elected to Parliament and served, even after the Restoration, as a well-regarded member until his death. Marvell, who was known during his lifetime only for the few satires he published, was recognized as an important lyric poet after his death, when his Miscellaneous Poems *were published in 1681. "To His Coy Mistress" is widely considered one of the greatest English love poems.*

TO HIS COY MISTRESS   [1641]

Had we but world enough, and time,
This coyness, lady, were no crime.
We would sit down, and think which way

To walk, and pass our long love's day.
Thou by the Indian Ganges' side   5
Shoudst rubies find: I by the tide
Of Humber° would complain. I would
Love you ten years before the flood,
And you should, if you please, refuse
Till the conversion of the Jews.°   10
My vegetable love° should grow
Vaster than empires and more slow;
An hundred years should go to praise
Thine eyes, and on thy forehead gaze;
Two hundred to adore each breast,   15
But thirty thousand to the rest;
An age at least to every part,
And the last age should show your heart.
For, lady, you deserve this state,
Nor would I love at lower rate.   20
    But at my back I always hear
Time's winged chariot hurrying near;
And yonder all before us lie
Deserts of vast eternity.
Thy beauty shall no more be found;   25
Nor, in thy marble vault, shall sound
My echoing song, then worms shall try
That long-preserved virginity,
And your quaint honor turn to dust,
And into ashes all my lust: 30
The grave's a fine and private place,
But none, I think, do there embrace.
    Now therefore, while the youthful hue
Sits on thy skin like morning dew
And while thy willing soul transpires°   35
At every pore with instant fires,
Now let us sport us while we may,
And now, like amorous birds of prey,
Rather at once our time devour
Than languish in his slow-chapped° power.   40
Let us roll all our strength and all
Our sweetness up into one ball,
And tear our pleasures with rough strife
Through the iron gates of life:
Thus, though we cannot make our sun   45
Stand still, yet we will make him run.

---

7 **Humber** the river that runs through Marvell's native town, Hull   **10 the conversion of the Jews** supposedly to occur at the end of time   **11 vegetable love** growing slowly   **35 transpires** breathes **40 slow-chapped** devouring slowly

MAKING CONNECTIONS

1. In "The Passionate Shepherd to His Love," what does the shepherd want? What does he offer?
2. Do you think he is being realistic? Explain.
3. Do you agree with "The Nymph's Reply to the Shepherd"? Explain.
4. Why doesn't the speaker give the shepherd what he wants? How does her vision of reality differ from his? What reality does she recognize that he does not?
5. What does the speaker in "To His Coy Mistress" want? Why does he think he should have it?
6. "To His Coy Mistress" is divided into three parts. Discuss the content of each section and describe how the speaker builds his argument.
7. What images does the speaker use to dramatize his points?

MAKING AN ARGUMENT

1. Do you find Marvell's argument in "To His Coy Mistress" sincere and convincing? How do you imagine the speaker in "The Nymph's Reply to the Shepherd" might respond to the speaker in "To His Coy Mistress"? Take a position for or against Marvell's poem and write an essay that supports your view. Cite the text of the poems for support.

MAYA ANGELOU   [B. 1928]

Maya Angelou was born Marguerite Johnson in St. Louis, Missouri, and lived with her grandmother in Stamps, Arkansas. She studied music, dance, and drama, and also became a writer. She became very involved in the black civil rights movement, and from 1963 to 1966 she lived in Ghana. Angelou is known for her many volumes of autobiographical novels, the first of which is I Know Why the Caged Bird Sings *(1969). Her six works of poetry are* Just Give Me a Cool Drink of Water 'Fore I Die *(1971),* Oh Pray My Wings Are Gonna Fit Me Well *(1975),* And Still I Rise *(1978),* Shaker, Why Don't You Sing? *(1983),* Now Sheba Sings the Song *(1987), and* I Shall Not Be Moved *(1990). She read her poem "On the Pulse of Morning" at the inauguration ceremony for President Bill Clinton in 1990. In the same year, a collection of Angelou's essays,* Wouldn't Take Nothing for My Journey, *was published. She teaches at Wake Forest University, and in 2002 she published her autobiography,* A Song Flung Up to Heaven.

PHENOMENAL WOMAN   [1978]

Pretty women wonder where my secret lies.
I'm not cute or built to suit a fashion model's size
But when I start to tell them,

They think I'm telling lies.
I say,
It's in the reach of my arms,
The span of my hips,
The stride of my step,
The curl of my lips.
I'm a woman
Phenomenally.
Phenomenal woman,
That's me.

I walk into a room
Just as cool as you please,
And to a man,
The fellows stand or
Fall down on their knees.
Then they swarm around me,
A hive of honey bees.
I say,
It's the fire in my eyes,
And the flash of my teeth,
The swing in my waist,
And the joy in my feet.
I'm a woman
Phenomenally.
Phenomenal woman,
That's me.

Men themselves have wondered
What they see in me.
They try so much
But they can't touch
My inner mystery.
When I try to show them
They say they still can't see.
I say,
It's in the arch of my back,
The sun of my smile,
The ride of my breasts,
The grace of my style.
I'm a woman
Phenomenally.
Phenomenal woman,
That's me.

Now you understand
Just why my head's not bowed.
I don't shout or jump about

Or have to talk real loud.
When you see me passing   50
It ought to make you proud.
I say,
It's in the click of my heels,
The bend of my hair,
The palm of my hand,   55
The need for my care.
'Cause I'm a woman
Phenomenally.
Phenomenal woman,
That's me.   60

MAKING CONNECTIONS

1. What is so "phenomenal" about the speaker? What lines in the poem indicate that?
2. Do you think the speaker in this poem thinks "too much" of herself? Explain.

MAKING AN ARGUMENT

1. Write a comparison of this poem with "Barbie Doll" on page 14. To what extent do you think the "girlchild" of that poem might have become a phenomenal woman? Cite the text of both poems for support.

MARGARET ATWOOD [B. 1939]

(See biography on p. 504.)

YOU FIT INTO ME   [1971]

you fit into me
like a hook into an eye

a fish hook
an open eye

MAKING CONNECTIONS

1. The "hook" and the "eye" combo is the simile here. Is there more than one definition of a hook and an eye? Explain. Given the type of hook and type of eye in the second stanza, how would you describe the attitude of the speaker toward this relationship?
2. The first stanza introduces the second. The second is an abrupt shift. Is this combination effective? Explain.

MAKING AN ARGUMENT

1. Interpret the "hook" and "eye" combo in the poem and write about how the simile applies to relationships in other works of literature in this section ("The Day It Happened" on p. 773, "Shiloh" on p. 762, "The Proposal" on p. 813, or others). Cite the text of the literature for support.

ELIZABETH BARRETT BROWNING [1806-1861]

Elizabeth Barrett Browning was born in Durham, England, the oldest of eleven children, and at fifteen suffered a spinal injury that left her partially paralyzed. In 1845 she met Robert Browning and the two fell in love. They were forced to elope, however, because of her extremely possessive father. A very popular poet during her lifetime, she published many volumes of poetry, including her most famous collection, Sonnets from the Portuguese, *love poems written to her husband. "How Do I Love Thee?" is one of the sonnets in this collection.*

HOW DO I LOVE THEE?

[1850]

How do I love thee? Let me count the ways.
I love thee to the depth and breadth and height
My soul can reach, when feeling out of sight
For the ends of being and ideal grace.
I love thee to the level of every day's   5
Most quiet need, by sun and candle-light.
I love thee freely, as men strive for right.
I love thee purely, as they turn from praise.
I love thee with the passion put to use
In my old griefs, and with my childhood's faith.   10
I love thee with a love I seemed to lose
With my lost saints. I love thee with the breath,
Smiles, tears, of all my life; and, if God choose,
I shall but love thee better after death.

MAKING CONNECTIONS

1. The sentiments expressed in this poem are very idealistic. Do you think the depth of love described in this poem is possible? Is the poem too sentimental? Explain.

2. This poem is written in answer to the question it poses: "How Do I Love Thee?" With specific reference to the text of the poem, pick out passages and discuss the effectiveness of the speaker's language as she answers that question.

✎ MAKING AN ARGUMENT

1. Both this poem and Edna St. Vincent Millay's "Love Is Not All" (p. 791) are
   love sonnets. But what they say about love—and how they say it—differ in
   many ways. Which do you prefer and why? Write an essay that compares
   and contrasts the two poems. Consider both content and form, and cite the
   text of both poems for support.

ROBERT BROWNING [1812–1889]

*The son of a banker, Robert Browning was born in a
suburb of London, and first learned the joy of reading in
his father's vast library. He published his first collection of
poems,* Pauline, *in 1833, and over the next thirty years followed it with numerous other volumes, which, though
they contained some of his greatest works, were financially unsuccessful. In 1846, in one of the most famous
matches in literary history, he married the celebrated
poet Elizabeth Barrett, page 783, who wrote the sonnet that begins "How do I
love thee?" to him. Because of her ill health and to escape her overbearing
father, the couple moved to Italy. After her death in 1861, he returned to
England and wrote* The Ring and the Book *(1868–1869), a long narrative poem
about a famous seventeenth-century murder case. The poem was Browning's
first major success and brought him the wide recognition and respect that had
thus far eluded him. Many of his best regarded poems, including "Porphyria's
Lover," take the form of dramatic monologues, in which the poet creates a character who reveals himself or herself while delivering an extended speech, often
to a silent listener.*

PORPHYRIA'S LOVER   [1834]

The rain set early in tonight,
   The sullen wind was soon awake,
It tore the elm-tops down for spite,
   And did its worst to vex the lake:
I listened with heart fit to break.   5
   When glided in Porphyria; straight
She shut the cold out and the storm,
   And kneeled and made the cheerless grate
Blaze up, and all the cottage warm;
   Which done, she rose, and from her form   10
Withdrew the dripping cloak and shawl,
   And laid her soiled gloves by, untied
Her hat and let the damp hair fall,
   And, last, she sat down by my side

And called me. When no voice replied,   15
    She put my arm about her waist,
And made her smooth white shoulder bare,
    And all her yellow hair displaced,
And, stooping, made my cheek lie there,
    And spread, o'er all, her yellow hair,   20
Murmuring how she loved me—she
    Too weak, for all her heart's endeavor,
To set its struggling passion free
    From pride, and vainer ties dissever,
And give herself to me forever.   25
    But passion sometimes would prevail,
Nor could tonight's gay feast restrain
    A sudden thought of one so pale
For love of her, and all in vain:
    So, she was come through wind and rain.   30
Be sure I looked up at her eyes
    Happy and proud; at last I knew
Porphyria worshiped me: surprise
    Made my heart swell, and still it grew
While I debated what to do.   35
    That moment she was mine, mine, fair,
Perfectly pure and good: I found
    A thing to do, and all her hair
In one long yellow string I wound
    Three times her little throat around,   40
And strangled her. No pain felt she;
    I am quite sure she felt no pain.
As a shut bud that holds a bee,
    I warily opened her lids: again
Laughed the blue eyes without a stain.   45
    And I untightened next the tress
About her neck; her cheek once more
    Blushed bright beneath my burning kiss:
I propped her head up as before,
    Only, this time my shoulder bore   50
Her head, which droops upon it still:
    The smiling rosy little head,
So glad it has its utmost will,
    That all it scorned at once is fled,
And I, its love, am gained instead!   55
    Porphyria's love: she guessed not how
Her darling one wish would be heard.
    And thus we sit together now,
And all night long we have not stirred,
    And yet God has not said a word!   60

MAKING CONNECTIONS

1. What details set the mood early in the poem?
2. Paraphrase the speaker's argument. According to him, why is it appropriate to strangle Porphyria? Interpret the last line of the poem. Is the speaker showing consciousness of guilt?
3. Compare the love described in this poem with that described in Elizabeth Barrett Browning's "How Do I Love Thee?" (p. 783).
4. Compare the speaker in this poem with Emily in Faulkner's "A Rose for Emily" (p. 956).

MAKING AN ARGUMENT

1. This poem is a dramatic monologue told from the speaker's point of view. What difference does that make? Imagine that you are a newspaper reporter or a police officer investigating the case. How would you describe this scene? Based on your interpretation of the poem, write a history of the speaker and his relationship with Porphyria. Cite the text of the poem for support.

NIKKI GIOVANNI [B. 1943]

One of the most prominent poets to emerge from the black literary movement of the 1960s, Nikki Giovanni was born in Knoxville, Tennessee. Her father was a probation officer, and her mother a social worker. Growing up, she was particularly close to her maternal grandmother and spent summers with her in Knoxville even after her family moved to Cincinnati, Ohio. It was while she was at Fisk University in Nashville that she grew politically aware, serving in Fisk's chapter of the SNCC (Student Non-Violent Coordinating Committee), which promoted the concept of "black power" in confronting the social and economic problems of the time. Her first books of poetry, Black Feeling and Black Talk *(1968),* Black Judgment *(1968), and* Re: Creation *(1970) were enormously successful and brought her much acclaim. A vibrant personality, she has toured the United States giving lectures and reading her poetry, and has recorded numerous albums of her poetry, including* Truth Is on Its Way, *which was the best-selling spoken-word album of 1971. Though her more recent work is more introspective and less political, she remains deeply committed to the transforming power of poetry. She has said: "If everybody became a poet, the world would be so much better." Her latest book of poetry,* Quilting the Black-Eyed Pea: Poems and Not Quite Poems, *was published in 2002. She is a University Distinguished Professor at Virginia Tech.*

WOMAN   [1978]

she wanted to be a blade
of grass amid the fields
but he wouldn't agree
to be the dandelion

she wanted to be a robin singing   5
through the leaves
but he refused to be
her tree

she spun herself into a web
and looking for a place to rest   10
turned to him
but he stood straight
declining to be her corner

she tried to be a book
but he wouldn't read   15

she turned herself into a bulb
but he wouldn't let her grow

she decided to become
a woman
and though he still refused   20
to be a man
she decided it was all
right.

✎ MAKING CONNECTIONS

1. When we "personify" objects or animals, we give them human characteristics. Where does this reversal of personification occur in the poem and how
   does it affect you?
2. Compare this poem to "Barbie Doll" (p. 14), "Phenomenal Woman" (p. 780),
   or "Ella, in a Square Apron, Along Highway 80" (p. 788).

✎ MAKING AN ARGUMENT

1. Identify each of the metaphors for the woman and the man and write about
   the kind of relationship they create. Would it have been better if he was the
   things she wanted him to be—or not? Take a position and cite the text of
   the poem to support your view.

JUDY GRAHN [B. 1940]

Judy Grahn was born in Chicago, Illinois. Her father worked as a cook, and her mother was a photographer's assistant. In her twenties, Grahn worked in a series of odd jobs, including short-order cook, artist's model, and nurse's aide before starting the Women's Press Collective with artist Wendy Cadden in Oakland, California, in 1969. In the 1980s, although she was already a well-established poet, she returned to school at San Francisco State University and earned a B.A. degree. She currently teaches in the New College of California in San Francisco, where she helped create the Gay and Lesbian Studies department. Her publications include The Work of a Common Woman: The Collected Poetry of Judy Grahn, 1964-1977 *(1978),* The Queen of Wands *(1982), and a collection of nonfiction,* Blood and Bread and Roses *(1986).*

ELLA, IN A SQUARE APRON, ALONG HIGHWAY 80   [1971]

She's a copperheaded waitress,
tired and sharp-worded, she hides
her bad brown tooth behind a wicked
smile, and flicks her ass
out of habit, to fend off the pass   5
that passes for affection.
She keeps her mind the way men
keep a knife—keen to strip the game
down to her size. She has a thin spine,
swallows her eggs cold, and tells lies.   10
She slaps a wet rag at the truck drivers
if they should complain. She understands
the necessity for pain, turns away
the smaller tips, out of pride, and
keeps a flask under the counter. Once,   15
she shot a lover who misused her child.
Before she got out of jail, the courts had pounced
and given the child away. Like some isolated lake,
her flat blue eyes take care of their own stark
bottoms. Her hands are nervous, curled, ready   20
to scrape.
The common woman is as common
as a rattlesnake.

⚜ MAKING CONNECTIONS

1. Who is Ella? What words or phrases in the poem help you to see her?
2. What does the speaker mean by "The common woman is as common / as a rattlesnake"? How has the speaker in the poem defined "common"? Can

you think of people in your own experience that this definition of "common" might be applied to? Explain.

MAKING AN ARGUMENT

1. Write a comparison of the character description in this poem with "Barbie Doll" (p. 14), "Phenomenal Woman" (p. 780), and "Woman" (p. 787). Analyze the language used to create the images in the texts of each poem to support your view.

ESSEX HEMPHILL (1957–1995)

The primary focus of Essex Hemphill's writing is the difficult plight of black gay men, and his books include a collection of writings by black gay men, Brother to Brother *(1991). The poem below is taken from his book* Ceremonies: Prose and Poetry *(1992). Hemphill died of AIDS-related illness at the age of thirty-eight.*

COMMITMENTS

(1992)

I will always be there
When the silence is exhumed.
When the photographs are examined
I will be pictured smiling
among siblings, parents,   5
nieces and nephews.

In the background of the photographs
the hazy smoke of barbecue,
a checkered red-and-white tablecloth
laden with blackened chicken,   10
glistening ribs, paper plates,
bottles of beer, and pop.

In the photos
the smallest children
are held by their parents.   15
My arms are empty, or around
the shoulders of unsuspecting aunts
expecting to throw rice at me someday.

Or picture tinsel, candles,
ornamented, imitation trees,   20
or another table, this one

set for Thanksgiving,
a turkey steaming the lens.

My arms are empty
in those photos, too,   25
so empty they would break around a lover.

I am always there
for critical emergencies,
graduations,
the middle of the night.   30

I am the invisible son.
In the family photos
nothing appears out of character.
I smile as I serve my duty.

MAKING CONNECTIONS

1. What does the speaker mean by "I will always be there"? In what way will
   he always be there?
2. The speaker says that his arms are around "the shoulders of unsuspecting
   aunts." What are they unsuspecting of?
3. To what extent is the speaker the "invisible son"? How can he be invisible if
   he's in the photographs?

MAKING AN ARGUMENT

1. How does the narrative perspective in this poem compare with that in
   "How to Watch Your Brother Die" on page 273? Who are the speakers in
   each poem—and what difference does it make? Write a comparative essay
   about the two poems that includes the relationship between narrative perspective and theme. Cite the text of each poem for support.

EDNA ST. VINCENT MILLAY [1892–1950]

*Edna St. Vincent Millay was born in Rockland, Maine, and
began writing poetry as a child. After graduating from
Vassar College in 1917, she moved to New York City, where
she quickly became a noted figure in the bustling arts
scene of Greenwich Village. She published her first book of
poetry, the acclaimed* Renascence and Other Poems, *that
same year. In 1923, she won the Pulitzer Prize for* The
Harp Weaver and Other Poems. *Her later poetry, which
became increasingly political, never received the same acclaim as her early work,*

and, after 1940, when she suffered a nervous breakdown, she wrote very little. She died in 1950, feeling that she had been largely forgotten. After her death, the publication of her collected poems in 1956 restored her position as one of the most accomplished poets of the century.

WHAT LIPS MY LIPS HAVE KISSED, AND WHERE, AND WHY   [1923]

What lips my lips have kissed, and where, and why,
I have forgotten, and what arms have lain
Under my head till morning; but the rain
Is full of ghosts tonight, that tap and sigh
Upon the glass and listen for reply,   5
And in my heart there stirs a quiet pain
For unremembered lads that not again
Will turn to me at midnight with a cry.
Thus in the winter stands the lonely tree,
Nor knows what birds have vanished one by one,   10
Yet knows its boughs more silent than before:
I cannot say what loves have come and gone,
I only know that summer sang in me
A little while, that in me sings no more.

LOVE IS NOT ALL   [1931]

Love is not all; it is not meat nor drink
Nor slumber nor a roof against the rain;
Nor yet a floating spar to men that sink
And rise and sink and rise and sink again;
Love cannot fill the thickened lung with breath,   5
Nor clean the blood, nor set the fractured bone;
Yet many a man is making friends with death
Even as I speak, for lack of love alone.
It well may be that in a difficult hour,
Pinned down by pain and moaning for release   10
Or nagged by want past resolution's power,
I might be driven to sell your love for peace,
Or trade the memory of this night for food.
It well may be. I do not think I would.

MAKING CONNECTIONS

1. How would you respond to the title "What Lips My Lips Have Kissed, and Where, and Why"?
2. What do you think the speaker means when she says, "I only know that summer sang in me / A little while, that in me sings no more"?
3. What role does irony play in "Love Is Not All"?

MAKING AN ARGUMENT

1. Write a comparison of Millay's sonnet "Love Is Not All" with Shakespeare's "Sonnet No. 29" (p. 82). Include an analysis of structure, rhyme, rhythm, and imagery—and their effectiveness in conveying the content of each poem.

PABLO NERUDA (1904–1973)

A revered and influential poet, Pablo Neruda was born in Chile, where he remained politically active until his death. His poetry often mixes his views on political oppression with passionate lyrics about romantic love. His many works include Twenty Love Poems and a Song of Despair *(1924),* Spain in the Heart *(1937),* The Captain's Verses *(1952), and* Memorial of Isla Negra *(1964). He was awarded the Nobel Prize for literature in 1971.*

THE FICKLE ONE   (1972)

Translated by Donald D. Walsh

My eyes went away from me
following a dark girl
who went by.

She was made of black mother-of-pearl,
made of dark-purple grapes,   5
and she lashed my blood
with her tail of fire.

After them all
I go.

A pale blond went by   10
like a golden plant
swaying her gifts.
And my mouth went
like a wave
discharging on her breast   15
lightning bolts of blood.

After them all
I go.

But to you, without my moving,
without seeing you, distant you,   20
go my blood and my kisses,
my dark one and my fair one,
my tall one and my little one,

my broad one and my slender one,
my ugly one, my beauty,   25
made of all the gold
and of all the silver,
made of all the wheat
and of all the earth,
made of all the water   30
of the sea waves.
Made for my arms,
made for my kisses,
made for my soul.

MAKING CONNECTIONS

1. What does the speaker mean by "After them all / I go"? To what extent do you think he actually goes?
2. Do you approve of his wandering attentions? Explain.
3. Compare this poem to "Sex Without Love" below.

MAKING AN ARGUMENT

1. The speaker's tone and the nature of his language differ in the section that begins "But to you, . . . " To whom does he seem to be addressing this section—and this poem? Are you convinced by his explanation? Write an argument of your own that agrees or disagrees with his position. Cite your own reasons and the text of the poem (and/or other poems) for support.

SHARON OLDS [B. 1942]

(See biography on p. 280.)

SEX WITHOUT LOVE

[1984]

How do they do it, the ones who make love
without love? Beautiful as dancers,
gliding over each other like ice-skaters
over the ice, fingers hooked
inside each other's bodies, faces   5
red as steak, wine, wet as the
children at birth whose mothers are going to
give them away. How do they come to the
come to the come to the God come to the
still waters, and not love   10
the one who came there with them, light
rising slowly as steam off their joined

skin? These are the true religious,
the purists, the pros, the ones who will not
accept a false Messiah, love the   15
priest instead of the God. They do not
mistake the lover for their own pleasure,
they are like great runners, they know they are alone
with the road surface, the cold, the wind,
the fit of their shoes, their over-all cardio-   20
vascular health—just factors; like the partner
in the bed, and not the truth, which is the
single body alone in the universe
against its own best time.

MAKING CONNECTIONS

1. What is the tone of this poem? How would you characterize the speaker's attitude?
2. In what way do the lovers glide "over each other like ice-skaters / over the ice"?
3. What is the purpose of the stammered "come to the" in lines 8 and 9?
4. We are regularly bombarded by popular media, especially through advertising, with "sex without love." Do you see this as a problem? Does it matter? Explain.

MAKING AN ARGUMENT

1. What is the "truth" referred to at the end of the poem? How would you describe it in your own words? Identify and write about the images in this poem, what you think they mean, and the way that these images "add up" to the "truth" of this poem. Cite the text of the poem for support.

SYLVIA PLATH [1932-1963]

Encouraged by her mother, Sylvia Plath began writing poetry as a precocious child in Boston, publishing her first poem in the Boston Traveller *when she was only eight years old. That same year her father died, an event that haunted her for the rest of her life. Like the protagonist in her autobiographical novel* The Bell Jar *(1963), she was a star student at Smith College, became a guest editor of a fashion magazine, and moved for a short time to New York City. When she returned home, she suffered the first of her serious mental breakdowns and attempted suicide. She was institutionalized for over a year and received electric shock treatments. When she returned to Smith she again excelled, winning a Fulbright scholarship to England after her final year. While studying at Cambridge she met and fell in love with the English poet Ted Hughes.*

*Married in 1956, the couple eventually settled in the English countryside and pro-
duced two children. The marriage was a difficult one, and the couple separated in
1962. Once again Plath entered a severe depression, committing suicide in 1963.
Her greatest work dates to the tortured final years of her life, when she was able
to channel her energies into highly personal, ironic, and often terrifying poems.
Her* Collected Poems, *edited by Ted Hughes, appeared in 1981 and was awarded
the Pulitzer Prize.*

MIRROR

[1963]

I am silver and exact. I have no preconceptions.
Whatever I see I swallow immediately
Just as it is, unmisted by love or dislike.
I am not cruel, only truthful—
The eye of a little god, four-cornered.   5
Most of the time I meditate on the opposite wall.
It is pink, with speckles. I have looked at it so long
I think it is a part of my heart. But it flickers.
Faces and darkness separate us over and over.

Now I am a lake. A woman bends over me.   10
Searching my reaches for what she really is.
Then she turns to those liars, the candles or the moon.
I see her back, and reflect it faithfully.
She rewards me with tears and an agitation of hands.
I am important to her. She comes and goes.   15
Each morning it is her face that replaces the darkness.
In me she has drowned a young girl, and in me an old woman
Rises toward her day after day, like a terrible fish.

MAKING CONNECTIONS

1. Discuss the personification of the mirror in the poem. The mirror has a
   voice. How does the mirror describe itself? Cite lines from the text of the
   poem to support your response.
2. To what extent is the mirror honest? In what way are "the candles or the
   moon" liars? What rises toward her "like a terrible fish"?

MAKING AN ARGUMENT

1. To what extent do the mirror and the lake help the woman discover who
   she is? In what way do they interfere with her self-discovery? Are the
   mirror and the lake responsible for what she sees? Write about the woman
   in this poem. What do you think her problem is? Compare her to characters
   in other poems in this section. Cite the text of this poem and/or other
   poems for support.

ALBERTO RIOS [B. 1952]

A bilingual native of Nogales, Arizona (where he could stand with one foot in the United States and the other in Mexico at the same time), Alberto Rios's father came from Mexico and his mother from England. He has received Guggenheim and National Endowment for the Arts Fellowships, and his books of poetry include Whispering to Fool the Wind *(1981), for which he won the Walt Whitman Award,* The Live Orchard Woman *(1990),* Pig Cookies and Other Stories *(1995), and* The Smallest Muscle in the Human Body *(2002). He is the Regents Professor of English at Arizona State University, where he teaches Creative Writing.*

THE PURPOSE OF ALTAR BOYS   [1982]

Tonio told me at catechism
the big part of the eye
admits good, and the little
black part is for seeing
evil—his mother told him   5
who was a widow and so
an authority on such things.
That's why at night
the black part gets bigger.
That's why kids can't go out   10
at night, and at night
girls take off their clothes
and walk around their
bedrooms or jump on their
beds or wear only sandals   15
and stand in their windows.
I was the altar boy
who knew about these things,
whose mission on some Sundays
was to remind people of   20
the night before as they
knelt for Holy Communion.
To keep Christ from falling
I held the metal plate
under chins,   25
while on the thick
red carpet of the altar
I dragged my feet
and waited for the precise
moment: plate to chin   30
I delivered without expression

the Holy Electric Shock,
the kind that produces
a really large swallowing
and makes people think.   35
I thought of it as justice.
But on other Sundays the fire
in my eyes was different,
my mission somehow changed.
I would hold the metal plate   40
a little too hard
against those certain same
nervous chins, and I
I would look
with authority down   45
the tops of white dresses.

MAKING CONNECTIONS

1. Who is the speaker? What is the tone of the poem?
2. What does he mean in lines 19-21 that his "mission on some Sundays / was to remind people of / the night before"?
3. He says that on other Sundays his mission changed. How so?

MAKING AN ARGUMENT

1. Identify and write about the images in this poem. To what extent does being an altar boy serve a larger purpose than what is indicated in the poem? What is that purpose? Cite the text of the poem to support your view.

CONNECTING THROUGH COMPARISON: SHALL I COMPARE THEE?

The three poems that follow address a subtheme of this section: the adequacy—or inadequacy—of language to describe a lover. Read and discussed together, they invite comparisons and connections—not only with each other—but with similar experiences of your own.

WILLIAM SHAKESPEARE [1564-1616]

(See biography on p. 537.)

SHALL I COMPARE THEE TO A SUMMER'S DAY? (SONNET NO. 18)   [1609]

Shall I compare thee to a summer's day?
Thou art more lovely and more temperate:
Rough winds do shake the darling buds of May,

And summer's lease hath all too short a date;
Sometime too hot the eye of heaven shines,
And often is his gold complexion dimm'd;
And every fair from fair sometime declines,
By chance or nature's changing course untrimm'd;
But thy eternal summer shall not fade
Nor lose possession of that fair thou ow'st;
Nor shall Death brag thou wand'rest in his shade,
When in eternal lines to time thou grow'st;
So long as men can breathe or eyes can see,
So long lives this, and this gives life to thee.

MY MISTRESS' EYES ARE NOTHING LIKE THE SUN (SONNET NO. 130)   [1609]

My mistress' eyes are nothing like the sun;
Coral is far more red than her lips' red;
If snow be white, why then her breasts are dun;
If hairs be wires, black wires grow on her head.
I have seen roses damasked,° red and white,   5
But no such roses see I in her cheeks;
And in some perfumes is there more delight
Than in the breath that from my mistress reeks.°
I love to hear her speak, yet well I know
That music hath a far more pleasing sound;   10
I grant I never saw a goddess go;°
My mistress, when she walks, treads on the ground.
And yet, by heaven, I think my love as rare
As any she belied with false compare.

5 damasked of mingled red and white   **8 reeks** (in Shakespeare's time) to emit vapour   **11**
go walk

HOWARD MOSS [1922–1987]

Howard Moss was a poet, critic, and dramatist, and in 1971 he received the National Book Award for poetry for his Selected Poems. *He was the poetry editor for the* New Yorker *magazine for more than thirty years.*

SHALL I COMPARE THEE TO A SUMMER'S DAY?   [1976]

Who says you're like one of the dog days?
You're nicer. And better.
Even in May, the weather can be gray,
And a summer sub-let doesn't last forever.
Sometimes the sun's too hot;   5
Sometimes it is not.
Who can stay young forever?
People break their necks or just drop dead!
But you? Never!
If there's just one condensed reader left   10
Who can figure out the abridged alphabet,
After you're dead and gone,
In this poem you'll live on!

MAKING CONNECTIONS

1. In Sonnet No. 18, do you think the speaker should compare his beloved to a summer's day? Why or why not?
2. In many of Shakespeare's sonnets, a dilemma is presented in the first eight lines—a turning point and solution in the next six. To what extent is that the case here?
3. What is the tone of the Howard Moss poem? Compare and contrast it with Shakespeare's.
4. Compare and contrast both of these poems with "My Mistress' Eyes Are Nothing Like the Sun."
5. According to the speaker in Sonnet No. 130, his mistress's eyes, lips, breasts, hair, cheeks, breath, voice, and walk don't stand up to nature very well. Do you think he is insulting her? Explain.
6. In what way do the last two lines reverse the first ten?

MAKING AN ARGUMENT

1. To what extent are these sonnets not about love but about the limitations of language? Write a comparison of the three poems that focuses on the use of language and its inability to capture and convey the qualities of the beloved. Cite all three poems to support your view.

CONNECTING AND COMPARING ACROSS GENRES: CINDERELLA

The fairy tale, the poem, and the essay that follow address a subtheme of this section: the Cinderella fairy tale and what it means. Read and discussed together, they invite comparisons and connections—not only with each other—but with your own experience of this classic tale.

JACOB LUDWIG KARL GRIMM [1785-1863]
AND WILHELM KARL GRIMM [1786-1859]

The Brothers Grimm are best known today for their collection of children's tales known popularly as Grimm's fairy tales, though during their lifetimes they were both renowned as scholars of the German language. They derived most of the fairy tales in their volume not from written sources, but by interviewing German peasants.

CINDERELLA   [1812]

Translated by Margaret Hunt and James Stern

The wife of a rich man fell sick, and as she felt that her end was drawing near, she called her only daughter to her bedside and said: "Dear child, be good and pious, and then the good God will always protect you, and I will look down on you from heaven and be near you." Thereupon she closed her eyes and departed. Every day the maiden went out to her mother's grave and wept, and she remained pious and good. When winter came the snow spread a white sheet over the grave, and by the time the spring sun had drawn it off again, the man had taken another wife.

The woman had brought with her into the house two daughters, who were beautiful and fair of face, but vile and black of heart. Now began a bad time for the poor step-child. "Is the stupid goose to sit in the parlor with us?" they said. "He who wants to eat bread must earn it; out with the kitchen-wench." They took her pretty clothes away from her, put an old grey bedgown on her, and gave her wooden shoes. "Just look at the proud princess, how decked out she is!" they cried, and laughed, and led her into the kitchen. There she had to do hard work from morning till night, get up before daybreak, carry water, light fires, cook and wash. Besides this, the sisters did her every imaginable injury—they mocked her and emptied her peas and lentils into the ashes, so that she was forced to sit and pick them out again. In the evening when she had worked till she was weary she had no bed to go to, but had to sleep by the hearth in the cinders. And as on that account she always looked dusty and dirty, they called her Cinderella.

It happened that the father was once going to the fair, and he asked his two step-daughters what he should bring back for them. "Beautiful dresses," said one, "pearls and jewels," said the second. "And you, Cinderella," said he, "what will you have?" "Father, break off for me the first branch which knocks against your hat on your way home." So he bought beautiful dresses, pearls and jewels for his two step-daughters, and on his way home, as he was riding through a green thicket, a hazel twig brushed against him and knocked off his hat. Then he broke off the branch and took it with him. When he reached home he gave his step-daughters the things which they had wished for, and to Cinderella he gave the branch from the hazel bush. Cinderella thanked him, went to her mother's grave and planted the branch on it, and wept so much that the tears fell down on it and watered it. And it grew and became a handsome tree. Thrice a day Cinderella went and sat beneath it, and wept and prayed, and a little white bird always came on the tree, and if Cinderella expressed a wish, the bird threw down to her what she had wished for.

It happened, however, that the King gave orders for a festival which was to last three days, and to which all the beautiful young girls in the county were invited, in order that his son might choose himself a bride. When the two step-sisters heard that they too were to appear among the number, they were delighted, called Cinderella and said: "Comb our hair for us, brush our shoes and fasten our buckles, for we are going to the wedding at the King's palace." Cinderella obeyed, but wept, because she too would have liked to go with them to the dance, and begged her step-mother to allow her to do so. "You go, Cinderella!" said she; "covered in dust and dirt as you are, and would go to the festival? You have no clothes and shoes, and yet would dance!" As, however, Cinderella went on asking, the step-mother said at last: "I have emptied a dish of lentils into the ashes for you, if you have picked them out again in two hours, you shall go with us." The maiden went through the backdoor into the garden, and called: "You tame pigeons, you turtle-doves, and all you birds beneath the sky, come and help me to pick

> The good into the pot,
> The bad into the crop."

5   Then two white pigeons came in by the kitchen-window, and afterwards the turtle-doves, and at last all the birds beneath the sky, came whirring and crowding in, and alighted amongst the ashes. And the pigeons nodded with their heads and began pick, pick, pick, pick, and the rest began also pick, pick, pick, pick, and gathered all the good grains into the dish. Hardly had one hour passed before they had finished, and all flew out again. Then the girl took the dish to her step-mother, and was glad, and believed that now she would be allowed to go with them to the festival. But the step-mother said: "No, Cinderella, you have no clothes and you cannot dance; you would only be laughed at." And as Cinderella wept at this, the step-mother said: "If you can pick two dishes of lentils out of the ashes for me in one hour, you shall go with us." And she thought to herself: "That she most certainly cannot do again." When the step-mother had emptied the two dishes of lentils amongst the ashes, the maiden went through the back-door into the garden and cried: "You tame pigeons, you turtle-doves, and all you birds beneath the sky, come and help me to pick

> The good into the pot,
> The bad into the crop."

Then two white pigeons came in by the kitchen-window, and afterwards the turtle-doves, and at length all the birds beneath the sky, came whirring and crowding in, and alighted amongst the ashes. And the doves nodded with their heads and began pick, pick, pick, pick, and the others began also pick, pick, pick, pick, and gathered all the good seeds into the dishes, and before half an hour was over they had already finished, and all flew out again. Then the maiden carried the dishes to the step-mother and was delighted, and believed that she might now go with them to the festival. But the step-mother said: "All this will not help; you cannot go with us, for you have no clothes and cannot dance; we should be ashamed of you!" On this she turned her back on Cinderella, and hurried away with her two proud daughters.

As no one was now at home, Cinderella went to her mother's grave beneath the hazel tree, and cried:

> "Shiver and quiver, little tree,
> Silver and gold throw down over me."

Then the bird threw a gold and silver dress down to her, and slippers embroidered with silk and silver. She put on the dress with all speed, and went to the festival. Her step-sisters and the step-mother however did not know her, and thought she must be a foreign princess, for she looked so beautiful in the golden dress. They never once thought of Cinderella, and believed that she was sitting at home in the dirt, picking lentils out of the ashes. The prince approached her, took her by the hand and danced with her. He would dance with no other maiden, and never let loose of her hand, and if any one else came to invite her, he said: "This is my partner."

She danced till it was evening, and then she wanted to go home. But the King's son said: "I will go with you and bear you company," for he wished to see to whom the beautiful maiden belonged. She escaped from him, however, and sprang into the pigeon-house. The King's son waited until her father came, and then he told him that the unknown maiden had leapt into the pigeon-house. The old man thought: "Can it be Cinderella?" and they had to bring him an axe and a pickaxe that he might hew the pigeon-house to pieces, but no one was inside it. And when they got home Cinderella lay in her dirty clothes among the ashes, and a dim little oil-lamp was burning on the mantle-piece, for Cinderella had jumped quickly down from the back of the pigeon-house and had run to the little hazel-tree, and there she had taken off her beautiful clothes and laid them on the grave, and the bird had taken them away again, and then she had seated herself in the kitchen amongst the ashes in her grey gown.

10   Next day when the festival began afresh, and her parents and the step-sisters had gone once more, Cinderella went to the hazel-tree and said:

> "Shiver and quiver, little tree,
> Silver and gold throw down over me."

Then the bird threw down a much more beautiful dress than on the preceding day. And when Cinderella appeared at the festival in this dress, every one was astonished at her beauty. The King's son had waited until she came, and instantly took her by the hand and danced with no one but her. When others came and invited her he said: "This is my partner." When evening came she wished to leave, and the King's son followed her and wanted to see into which house she went. But she sprang away from him, and into the garden behind the house. Therein stood a beautiful tall tree on which hung the most magnificent pears. She clambered so nimbly between the branches like a squirrel that the King's son did not know where she was gone. He waited until her father came, and said to him: "The unknown maiden has escaped from me, and I believe she has climbed up the pear-tree." The father thought: "Can it be Cinderella?" and had an axe brought and cut the tree down, but no one was on it. And when they got into the kitchen, Cinderella lay there among the ashes, as usual, for she had jumped down on the other side of the tree, had taken the beautiful dress to the bird on the little hazel-tree, and put on her grey gown.

On the third day, when the parents and sisters had gone away, Cinderella went once more to her mother's grave and said to the little tree:

> "Shiver and quiver, little tree,
> Silver and gold throw down over me."

And now the bird threw down to her a dress which was more splendid and magnificent than any she had yet had, and the slippers were golden. And when she went to the festival in the dress, no one knew how to speak for astonishment. The King's son danced with her only, and if any one invited her to dance, he said: "This is my partner."

When evening came, Cinderella wished to leave, and the King's son was anxious to go with her, but she escaped from him so quickly that he could not follow her. The King's son, however, had employed a ruse, and had caused the whole staircase to be smeared with pitch, and there, when she ran down, had the maiden's left slipper remained stuck. The King's son picked it up, and it was small and dainty, and all golden. Next morning, he went with it to the father, and said to him: "No one shall be my wife but she whose foot this golden slipper fits." Then were the two sisters glad, for they had pretty feet. The eldest went with the shoe into her room and wanted to try it on, and her mother stood by. But she could not get her big toe into it, and the shoe was too small for her. Then her mother gave her a knife and said: "Cut the toe off; when you are Queen you will no more need to go on foot." The maiden cut the toe off, forced the foot into the shoe, swallowed the pain, and went out to the King's son. Then he took her on his horse as his bride and rode away with her. They were obliged, however, to pass the grave, and there, on the hazel-tree, the two little pigeons sat on it and cried:

> "Turn and peep, turn and peep,
> There's blood within the shoe,
> The shoe it is too small for her,
> The true bride waits for you."

Then he looked at her foot and saw how the blood was trickling from it. He turned his horse round and took the false bride home again, and said she was not the true one, and that the other sister was to put the shoe on. Then this one went into her chamber and got her toes safely into the shoe, but her heel was too large. So her mother gave her a knife and said: "Cut a bit off your heel; when you are Queen you will have no more need to go on foot." The maiden cut a bit off her heel, forced her foot into the shoe, swallowed the pain, and went out to the King's son. He took her on his horse as his bride, and rode away with her, but when they passed by the hazel-tree, the two little pigeons sat on it and cried:

> "Turn and peep, turn and peep,
> There's blood within the shoe,
> The shoe it is too small for her,
> The true bride waits for you."

He looked down at her foot and saw how the blood was running out of her shoe, and how it had stained her white stocking quite red. Then he turned his horse and took the false bride home again. "This also is not the right one," said he, "have you no other daughter?" "No," said the man, "there is still a little stunted kitchen-wench which my late wife left behind her, but she cannot possibly be the bride." The King's son said he was to send her up to him; but the mother answered: "Oh no, she is much too dirty, she cannot show herself!" But he absolutely insisted on it, and Cinderella had to be called. She first washed her hands and face clean, and then went and bowed down before the King's son, who gave her the golden shoe. Then she seated herself on a stool, drew her foot out of the heavy wooden shoe, and put it into the slipper, which fitted like a glove. And when she rose up and the King's son looked at her face he recognized the beautiful maiden who had danced with him and cried: "That is the true bride!" The step-mother and the two sisters were horrified and became pale with rage; he, however, took Cinderella on his horse and rode away with her. As they passed by the hazel tree, the two white doves cried:

> "Turn and peep, turn and peep,
> No blood is in the shoe,
> The shoe is not too small for her,
> The true bride rides with you,"

and when they had cried that, the two came flying down and placed themselves on Cinderella's shoulders, one on the right, the other on the left, and remained sitting there.

15   When the wedding with the King's son was to be celebrated, the two false sisters came and wanted to get into favor with Cinderella and share her good fortune. When the betrothed couple went to church, the elder was at the right side and the younger at the left, and the pigeons pecked out one eye from each of them. Afterwards as they came back, the elder was at the left, and the younger at the right, and then the pigeons pecked out the other eye from each. And thus, for their wickedness and falsehood, they were punished with blindness all their days.

ANNE SEXTON [1928–1974]

(See biography on p. 512.)

CINDERELLA   [1970]

You always read about it:
the plumber with twelve children
who wins the Irish Sweepstakes.
From toilets to riches.
That story.   5

Or the nursemaid,
some luscious sweet from Denmark
who captures the oldest son's heart.
From diapers to Dior.
That story.   10

Or a milkman who serves the wealthy,
eggs, cream, butter, yogurt, milk,
the white truck like an ambulance
who goes into real estate
and makes a pile.   15
From homogenized to martinis at lunch.

Or the charwoman
who is on the bus when it cracks up
and collects enough from the insurance.
From mops to Bonwit Teller.   20
That story.

Once
the wife of a rich man was on her deathbed
and she said to her daughter Cinderella:
Be devout. Be good. Then I will smile   25
down from heaven in the seam of a cloud.
The man took another wife who had
two daughters, pretty enough
but with hearts like blackjacks.
Cinderella was their maid.   30
She slept on the sooty hearth each night
and walked around looking like Al Jolson.
Her father brought presents home from town,
jewels and gowns for the other women
but the twig of a tree for Cinderella.   35
She planted that twig on her mother's grave
and it grew to a tree where a white dove sat.
Whenever she wished for anything the dove
would drop it like an egg upon the ground.
The bird is important, my dears, so heed him.   40

Next came the ball, as you all know.
It was a marriage market.
The prince was looking for a wife.
All but Cinderella were preparing
and gussying up for the big event.   45
Cinderella begged to go too.
Her stepmother threw a dish of lentils
into the cinders and said: Pick them
up in an hour and you shall go.
The white dove brought all his friends;   50
all the warm wings of the fatherland came,
and picked up the lentils in a jiffy.
No, Cinderella, said the stepmother,
you have no clothes and cannot dance.
That's the way with stepmothers.   55

Cinderella went to the tree at the grave
and cried forth like a gospel singer:
Mama! Mama! My turtledove,
send me to the prince's ball!
The bird dropped down a golden dress   60
and delicate little gold slippers.
Rather a large package for a simple bird.
So she went. Which is no surprise.
Her stepmother and sisters didn't
recognize her without her cinder face   65
and the prince took her hand on the spot
and danced with no other the whole day.

As nightfall came she thought she'd better
get home. The prince walked her home
and she disappeared into the pigeon house 70
and although the prince took an axe and broke
it open she was gone. Back to her cinders.
These events repeated themselves for three days.
However on the third day the prince
covered the palace steps with cobbler's wax 75
and Cinderella's gold shoe stuck upon it.
Now he would find whom the shoe fit
and find his strange dancing girl for keeps.
He went to their house and the two sisters
were delighted because they had lovely feet. 80
The eldest went into a room to try the slipper on
but her big toe got in the way so she simply
sliced it off and put on the slipper;
The prince rode away with her until the white dove
told him to look at the blood pouring forth. 85
That is the way with amputations.
They don't just heal up like a wish.
The other sister cut off her heel
but the blood told as blood will.
The prince was getting tired.   90

He began to feel like a shoe salesman.
But he gave it one last try.
This time Cinderella fit into the shoe
like a love letter into its envelope.

At the wedding ceremony   95
he two sisters came to curry favor
and the white dove pecked their eyes out.
Two hollow spots were left
like soup spoons.

Cinderella and the prince   100
lived, they say, happily ever after,
like two dolls in a museum case
never bothered by diapers or dust,
never arguing over the timing of an egg,
never telling the same story twice,   105
never getting a middle-aged spread,
their darling smiles pasted on for eternity
Regular Bobbsey Twins.
That story.

BRUNO BETTELHEIM [1903–1996]

Austrian-born psychologist, educator, and author Bruno Bettelheim came to the United States in 1939, after surviving a series of German concentration camps. He wrote about his experience in the widely read and enormously influential Individual and Mass Behavior in Extreme Situations *(1943). Once in America, Bettelheim established himself as an expert on the psychology of children, publishing works such as* Love Is Not Enough *(1950),* The Children of the Dream *(1969),* A Home for the Heart *(1974), and* Surviving and Other Essays *(1979). "Cinderella" is taken from* The Uses of Enchantment *(1976), in which Bettelheim discusses the psychosocial importance of fairy tales.*

CINDERELLA   [1976]

By all accounts, "Cinderella" is the best-known fairy tale, and probably also the best-liked. It is quite an old story; when first written down in China during the ninth century A.D., it already had a history. The unrivaled tiny foot size as a mark of extraordinary virtue, distinction, and beauty, and the slipper made of precious material are facets which point to an Eastern, if not necessarily Chinese, origin. The modern hearer does not connect sexual attractiveness and beauty in general with extreme smallness of the foot, as the ancient Chinese did, in accordance with their practice of binding women's feet.

"Cinderella," as we know it, is experienced as a story about the agonies and hopes which form the essential content of sibling rivalry; and about the degraded heroine winning out over her siblings who abused her. Long before Perrault gave "Cinderella" the form in which it is now widely known, "having to live among the ashes" was a symbol of being debased in comparison to one's siblings, irrespective of sex. In Germany, for example, there were stories in which such an ash-boy later becomes king, which parallels Cinderella's fate. "Aschenputtel" is the title of the Brothers Grimm's version of the tale. The term originally designated a lowly, dirty kitchenmaid who must tend to the fireplace ashes.

There are many examples in the German language of how being forced to dwell among the ashes was a symbol not just of degradation, but also of sibling rivalry, and of the sibling who finally surpasses the brother or brothers who have debased him. Martin Luther[1] in his *Table Talks* speaks about Cain as the God-forsaken evildoer who is powerful, while pious Abel is forced to be his ash-brother (*Aschebrüdel*), a mere nothing, subject to Cain; in one of Luther's sermons he says that Esau was forced into the role of Jacob's ash-brother. Cain and Abel, Jacob and Esau are Biblical examples of one brother being suppressed or destroyed by the other.

The fairy tale replaces sibling relations with relations between step-siblings—perhaps a device to explain and make acceptable an animosity which one wishes would not exist among true siblings. Although sibling rivalry is universal and "natural" in the sense that it is the negative consequence of being a sibling, this same relation also generates equally as much positive feeling between siblings, highlighted in fairy tales such as "Brother and Sister."

5   No other fairy tale renders so well as the "Cinderella" stories the inner experiences of the young child in the throes of sibling rivalry, when he feels hopelessly outclassed by his brothers and sisters. Cinderella is pushed down and degraded by her stepsisters; her interests are sacrificed to theirs by her (step)mother; she is expected to do the dirtiest work and although she performs it well, she receives no credit for it; only more is demanded of her. This is how the child feels when devastated by the miseries of sibling rivalry. Exaggerated though Cinderella's tribulations and degradations may seem to the adult, the child carried away by sibling rivalry feels, "That's me; that's how they mistreat me, or would want to; that's how little they think of me." And there are moments—often long time periods—when for inner reasons a child feels this way even when his position among his siblings may seem to give him no cause for it.

When a story corresponds to how the child feels deep down—as no realistic narrative is likely to do—it attains an emotional quality of "truth" for the child. The events of "Cinderella" offer him vivid images that give body to his overwhelming but nevertheless often vague and nondescript emotions; so these episodes seem more convincing to him than his life experiences.

The term "sibling rivalry" refers to a most complex constellation of feelings and their causes. With extremely rare exceptions, the emotions aroused in the person subject to sibling rivalry are far out of proportion to what his real situation with his sisters and brothers would justify, seen objectively. While all children at times suffer greatly from sibling rivalry, parents seldom sacrifice one of the children to the others, nor do they condone the other children's persecuting one of them. Difficult as objective judgments are for the young child—nearly impossible when his emotions are aroused—even he in his more rational moments "knows" that he is not treated as badly as Cinderella. But the child often feels mistreated, despite all his "knowledge" to the contrary. That is why he believes in the inherent truth of "Cinderella," and then he also comes to believe in her eventual deliverance and vic-

---

[1]**Martin Luther** (1483-1546) German leader of the Protestant Reformation and Lutheranism

tory. From her triumph he gains the exaggerated hopes for his future which he needs to counteract the extreme misery he experiences when ravaged by sibling rivalry.

Despite the name "sibling rivalry," this miserable passion has only incidentally to do with a child's actual brothers and sisters. The real source of it is the child's feelings about his parents. When a child's older brother or sister is more competent than he, this arouses only temporary feelings of jealousy. Another child being given special attention becomes an insult only if the child fears that, in contrast, he is thought little of by his parents, or feels rejected by them. It is because of such an anxiety that one or all of a child's sisters or brothers may become a thorn in his flesh. Fearing that in comparison to them he cannot win his parents' love and esteem is what inflames sibling rivalry. This is indicated in stories by the fact that it matters little whether the siblings actually possess greater competence. The Biblical story of Joseph tells that it is jealousy of parental affection lavished on him which accounts for the destructive behavior of his brothers. Unlike Cinderella's, Joseph's parent does not participate in degrading him, and, on the contrary, prefers him to his other children. But Joseph, like Cinderella, is turned into a slave, and, like her, he miraculously escapes and ends by surpassing his siblings.

Telling a child who is devastated by sibling rivalry that he will grow up to do as well as his brothers and sisters offers little relief from his present feelings of dejection. Much as he would like to trust our assurances, most of the time he cannot. A child can see things only with subjective eyes, and comparing himself on this basis to his siblings, he has no confidence that he, on his own, will someday be able to fare as well as they. If he could believe more in himself, he would not feel destroyed by his siblings no matter what they might do to him, since then he could trust that time would bring about a desired reversal of fortune. But since the child cannot, on his own, look forward with confidence to some future day when things will turn out all right for him, he can gain relief only through fantasies of glory—a domination over his siblings—which he hopes will become reality through some fortunate event.

10   Whatever our position within the family, at certain times in our lives we are beset by sibling rivalry in some form or other. Even an only child feels that other children have some great advantages over him, and this makes him intensely jealous. Further, he may suffer from the anxious thought that if he did have a sibling, his parents would prefer this other child to him. "Cinderella" is a fairy tale which makes nearly as strong an appeal to boys as to girls, since children of both sexes suffer equally from sibling rivalry, and have the same desire to be rescued from their lowly position and surpass those who seem superior to them.

On the surface, "Cinderella" is as deceptively simple as the story of Little Red Riding Hood, with which it shares greatest popularity. "Cinderella" tells about the agonies of sibling rivalry, of wishes coming true, of the humble being elevated, of true merit being recognized even when hidden under rags, of virtue rewarded and evil punished—a straightforward story. But under this overt content is concealed a welter of complex and largely unconscious material, which details of the story allude to just enough to set our unconscious associations going. This makes a contrast between surface simplicity and underlying complexity which arouses deep interest in the story and explains its appeal to the millions over centuries. To begin gaining an understanding of these hidden meanings, we have to penetrate behind the obvious sources of sibling rivalry discussed so far.

As mentioned before, if the child could only believe that it is the infirmities of his age which account for his lowly position, he would not have to suffer so wretchedly from sibling rivalry, because he could trust the future to right matters. When he thinks that his degradation is deserved, he feels his plight is utterly hopeless. Djuna Barnes's perceptive statement about fairy tales—that the child knows something about them which he cannot tell (such as that he likes the idea of Little Red Riding Hood and the wolf being in bed together)—could be extended by dividing fairy tales into two groups: one group where the child responds only unconsciously to the inherent truth of the story and thus cannot tell about it; and another large number of tales where the child preconsciously or even consciously knows what the "truth" of the story consists of and thus could tell about it, but does not want to let on that he knows. Some aspects of "Cinderella" fall into the latter category. Many children believe that Cinderella probably deserves her fate at the beginning of the story, as they feel they would, too; but they don't want anyone to know it. Despite this, she is worthy at the end to be exalted, as the child hopes he will be too, irrespective of his earlier shortcomings.

Every child believes at some period of his life—and this is not only at rare moments—that because of his secret wishes, if not also his clandestine actions, he deserves to be degraded, banned from the presence of others, relegated to a netherworld of smut. He fears this may be so, irrespective of how fortunate his situation may be in reality. He hates and fears those others—such as his siblings—whom he believes to be entirely free of similar evilness, and he fears that they or his parents will discover what he is really like, and then demean him as Cinderella was by her family. Because he wants others—most of all, his parents—to believe in his innocence, he is delighted that "everybody" believes in Cinderella's. This is one of the great attractions of this fairy tale. Since people give credence to Cinderella's goodness, they will also believe in his, so the child hopes. And "Cinderella" nourishes this hope, which is one reason it is such a delightful story.

Another aspect which holds large appeal for the child is the vileness of the stepmother and stepsisters. Whatever the shortcomings of a child may be in his own eyes, these pale into insignificance when compared to the stepsisters' and stepmother's falsehood and nastiness. Further, what these stepsisters do to Cinderella justifies whatever nasty thoughts one may have about one's siblings: they are so vile that anything one may wish would happen to them is more than justified. Compared to their behavior, Cinderella is indeed innocent. So the child, on hearing her story, feels he need not feel guilty about his angry thoughts.

15   On a very different level—and reality considerations coexist easily with fantastic exaggerations in the child's mind—as badly as one's parents or siblings seem to treat one, and much as one thinks one suffers because of it, all this is nothing compared to Cinderella's fate. Her story reminds the child at the same time how lucky he is, and how much worse things could be. (Any anxiety about the latter possibility is relieved, as always in fairy tales, by the happy ending.)

The behavior of a five-and-a-half-year-old girl, as reported by her father, may illustrate how easily a child may feel that she is a "Cinderella." This little girl had a younger sister of whom she was very jealous. The girl was very fond of "Cinderella," since the story offered her material with which to act out her feelings, and because without the story's imagery she would have been hard pressed to comprehend and express them. This little girl had used to dress very neatly and liked pretty clothes, but she became unkempt and dirty. One day when she was asked to fetch some salt, she said as she was doing so, "Why do you treat me like Cinderella?"

Almost speechless, her mother asked her, "Why do you think I treat you like Cinderella?"

"Because you make me do all the hardest work in the house!" was the little girl's answer. Having thus drawn her parents into her fantasies, she acted them out more openly, pretending to sweep up all the dirt, etc. She went even further, playing that she prepared her little sister for the ball. But she went the "Cinderella" story one better, based on her unconscious understanding of the contradictory emotions fused into the "Cinderella" role, because at another moment she told her mother and sister, "You shouldn't be jealous of me just because I am the most beautiful in the family."

This shows that behind the surface humility of Cinderella lies the conviction of her superiority to mother and sisters, as if she would think: "You can make me do all the dirty work, and I pretend that I am dirty, but within me I know that you treat me this way because you are jealous of me because I am so much better than you." This conviction is supported by the story's ending, which assures every "Cinderella" that eventually she will be discovered by her prince.

20   Why does the child believe deep within himself that Cinderella deserves her dejected state? This question takes us back to the child's state of mind at the end of the oedipal period. Before he is caught in oedipal entanglements, the child is convinced that he is lovable, and loved, if all is well within his family relationships. Psychoanalysis describes this stage of complete satisfaction with oneself as "primary narcissism." During this period the child feels certain that he is the center of the universe, so there is no reason to be jealous of anybody.

The oedipal disappointments which come at the end of this developmental stage cast deep shadows of doubt on the child's sense of his worthiness. He feels that if he were really as deserving of love as he had thought, then his parents would never be critical of him or disappoint him. The only explanation for parental criticism the child can think of is that there must be some serious flaw in him which accounts for what he experiences as rejection. If his desires remain unsatisfied and his parents disappoint him, there must be something wrong with him or his desires, or both. He cannot yet accept that reasons other than those residing within him could have an impact on his fate. In his oedipal jealousy, wanting to get rid of the parent of the same sex had seemed the most natural thing in the world, but now the child realizes that he cannot have his own way, and that maybe this is so because the desire was wrong. He is no longer so sure that he is preferred to his siblings, and he begins to suspect that this may be due to the fact that *they* are free of any bad thoughts or wrongdoing such as his.

All this happens as the child is gradually subjected to ever more critical attitudes as he is being socialized. He is asked to behave in ways which run counter to his natural desires, and he resents this. Still he must obey, which makes him very angry. This anger is directed against those who make demands, most likely his parents; and this is another reason to wish to get rid of them, and still another reason to feel guilty about such wishes. This is why the child also feels that he deserves to be chastised for his feelings, a punishment he believes he can escape only if nobody learns what he is thinking when he is angry. The feeling of being unworthy to be loved by his parents at a time when his desire for their love is very strong leads to the fear of rejection, even when in reality there is none. This rejection fear compounds the anxiety that others are preferred and also may be preferable—the root of sibling rivalry.

MAKING CONNECTIONS

1. Did you find anything different about the Grimm brothers' fairy tale of Cinderella than the one you are used to reading or viewing?
2. How are you affected by the harsh punishment that Cinderella's stepsisters receive? Do you think they deserve it?
3. Do these gruesome details change the impact of the story? Why do you think they have been removed in the modern version of this fairy tale?
4. Compare Anne Sexton's poem of "Cinderella" with the Grimm brothers' version.
5. Who is the speaker in this version? How does the speaker's "voice" differ from that of the narrator in the Grimm version? What words or phrases exemplify that difference? How are you affected by the repetition of the phrase "That story"?
6. The last stanza of Sexton's poem is a variation on the usual ending of a fairy tale. What is its tone? To what extent does it emphasize the tone of the entire poem?
7. Bettelheim argues that children without siblings—as well as older siblings—respond to the Cinderella story in the same way that younger siblings do. Explain his argument. Do you find it convincing? Or do you think that if "Cinderella" is about sibling rivalry, then younger siblings, older siblings, and "only" children would respond to the story in different ways?
8. Do you think that boys respond to Cinderella's plight in the same way that girls do? Why or why not?
9. Do you think Bettelheim's interpretation of the Cinderella tale pertains to the Sexton poem as well? Why or why not? Does Sexton seem to think that the tale is about sibling rivalry?

MAKING AN ARGUMENT

1. Write an argument that agrees or disagrees with Bettelheim's essay that "Cinderella" is a tale "about the agonies and hopes which form the essential content of sibling rivalry." If you disagree, then what do you think the tale is about and why? Cite the text of both "Cinderella" and Bettelheim's essay for support.

◆ DRAMA ◆

ANTON CHEKHOV [1860–1904]

(See biography on p. 713.)

THE PROPOSAL   [1889]

Translated by Paul Schmidt

CHARACTERS
STEPÁN STEPÁNICH CHUBUKÓV, *a landowner*
NATÁLIA STEPÁNOVNA [NATÁSHA], *his daughter*
IVÁN VASSÍLIEVICH LÓMOV, *their neighbor*

The action takes place in CHUBUKÓV's *farmhouse.*
A room in CHUBUKÓV's *farmhouse. Enter* LÓMOV, *wearing a tailcoat and white gloves.* CHUBUKÓV *goes to meet him.*

CHUBUKÓV: By God, if it isn't my old friend Iván Vassílievich! Glad to see you, boy, glad to see you. [*Shakes his hand*] This is certainly a surprise, and that's a fact. How are you doing?

LÓMOV: Oh, thanks a lot. And how are you? Doing, I mean?

CHUBUKÓV: We get by, my boy, we get by. Glad to know you think of us occasionally and all the rest of it. Have a seat, boy, be my guest, glad you're here, and that's a fact. Don't want to forget your old friends and neighbors, you know. But why so formal, boy? What's the occasion? You're all dressed up and everything— you on your way to a party, or what?

LÓMOV: No, I only came to see you, Stepán Stepánich.

CHUBUKÓV: But why the fancy clothes, boy? You look like you're still celebrating New Year's Eve!

LÓMOV: Well, I'll tell you. [*Takes his arm*] You see, Stepán Stepánich, I hope I'm not disturbing you, but I came to ask you a little favor. This isn't the first time I've, uh, had occasion, as they say, to ask you for help, and I want you to know that I really admire you when I do it. . . . Er, what I mean is . . . Look, you have to excuse me, Stepán Stepánich, this is making me very nervous. I'll just take a little drink of water, if it's all right with you. [*Takes a drink of water*]

CHUBUKÓV [*Aside*]:   He wants me to lend him some money. I won't. [*To him*] So! What exactly are you here for, hm? A big strong boy like you.

LÓMOV: You see, I really have the greatest respect for you, Stepán Respéctovich— excuse me, I mean Stepán Excúsemevich. What I mean is—I'm really nervous, as you can plainly see. . . . Well, what it all comes down to is this: you're the only person who can give me what I want and I know I don't deserve it of course that goes without saying and I haven't any real right to it either—

CHUBUKÓV: Now, my boy, you don't have to beat about the bush with me. Speak right up. What do you want?

LÓMOV: All right, I will. I will. Well, what I came for is, I came to ask for the hand of your daughter Natásha.

CHUBUKÓV [*Overjoyed*]:   Oh, mama! Iván Vassílievich, say it again! I don't think I caught that last part!

LÓMOV: I came to ask—

CHUBUKÓV: Lover boy! Buddy boy! I can't tell you how happy I am and everything. And that's a fact. And all the rest of it. [*Gives him a bear hug*] I've always hoped this would happen. It's a longtime dream come true. [*Sheds a tear*] I have always loved you, boy, just like you were my own son, and you know it. God bless you both and all the rest of it. This is a dream come true. But why am I standing here like a big dummy? Happiness has got my tongue, that's what's happened, happiness has got my tongue. Oh, from the bottom of my heart. . . You wait right here, I'll go get Natásha and whatever.

LÓMOV [*Intense concern*]:   What do you think, Stepán Stepánich? Do you think she'll say yes?

CHUBUKÓV: Big, good-looking fellow like you—how could she help herself? Of course she'll say yes, and that's a fact. She's like a cat in heat. And all the rest of it. Don't go away, I'll be right back. [*Exit*]

LÓMOV: It must be cold in here. I'm starting to shiver, just like I was going to take an exam. The main thing is, you have to make up your mind. You just keep thinking about it, you argue back and forth and talk a lot and wait for the ideal woman or for true love, you'll never get married. Brr . . . it's cold in here. Natásha is a very good housekeeper, she's kind of good-looking, she's been to school . . . What more do I need? I'm starting to get that hum in my ears again; it must be my nerves. [*Drinks some water*] And I can't just *not* get married. First of all, I'm already thirty-five, and that's about what they call the turning point. Second of all, I have to start leading a regular, normal life. There's something wrong with my heart—I've got a *murmur;* I'm always nervous as a tick, and the least little thing can drive me crazy. Like right now, for instance. My lips are starting to shudder, and this little whatsit keeps twitching in my right eyelid. But the worst thing about me is sleep. I mean, I don't. I go to bed, and as soon as I start falling asleep, all of a sudden something in my left side goes *drrrk!* and it pounds right up into my shoulder and my head. . . . I jump out of bed like crazy and walk around for a while and then I lie down again and as soon as I start falling asleep all of a sudden something in my left side goes *drrrk!* And that happens twenty times a night—

[Enter Natásha]

NATÁSHA: Oh, it's you. It's just you, and Papa said go take a look in the other room, somebody wants to sell you something. Oh, well. How are you anyway?

LÓMOV: How do you do, Natásha?

NATÁSHA: You'll have to excuse me, I'm still in my apron. We were shelling peas. How come you haven't been by to see us for so long? Sit down. . . .

[They both sit.]

You feel like something to eat?

LÓMOV: No, thanks. I ate already.

NATÁSHA: You smoke? Go ahead if you want to; here's some matches. Beautiful day today, isn't it? And yesterday it was raining so hard the men in the hay-fields couldn't do a thing. How many stacks you people got cut so far? You know what happened to me? I got so carried away I had them cut the whole meadow, and now I'm sorry I did—the hay's going to rot. Oh, my! Look at you! What've you got on those fancy clothes for? Well, if you aren't something! You going to a party, or what? You know, you're looking kind of cute these days. . . . Anyway, what are you all dressed up for?

LÓMOV [*A bit nervous*]:   Well, you see, Natásha . . . well, the fact is I decided to come ask you to . . . to listen to what I have to say. Of course, you'll probably be sort of surprised and maybe get mad, but I . . . [*Aside*] It's awful cold in here.

NATÁSHA: So . . . so what did you come for, huh? [*Pause*] Huh?

LÓMOV: I'll try to make this brief. Now, Natásha, you know, we've known each other for a long time, ever since we were children, and I've had the pleasure of knowing your entire family. My poor dead aunt and her husband—as you know, I inherited my land from them—they always had the greatest respect for your father and your poor dead mother. The Lómovs and the Chubukóvs have always been on very friendly terms, almost like we were related. And besides—well, you already know this—and besides, your land and mine are right next door to each other. Take my Meadowland, for instance. It lies right alongside of your birch grove.

NATÁSHA: Excuse me. I don't mean to interrupt you, but I think you said "my Meadowland." Are you saying that Meadowland belongs to you?

LÓMOV: Well, yes; as a matter of fact, I am.

NATÁSHA: Well, I never! Meadowland belongs to us, not you!

LÓMOV: No, Natásha. Meadowland is mine.

NATÁSHA: Well, that's news to me. Since when is it yours?

LÓMOV: What do you mean, since when? I'm talking about the little pasture they call Meadowland, the one that makes a wedge between your birch grove and Burnt Swamp.

NATÁSHA: Yes, I know the one you mean. But it's ours.

LÓMOV: Natásha, I think you're making a mistake. That field belongs to me.

NATÁSHA: Iván Vassílich, do you realize what you're saying? And just how long has it belonged to you?

LÓMOV: What do you mean, how long? As far as I know, it's always been mine.

NATÁSHA: Now wait just a minute. Excuse me, but—

LÓMOV: It's all very clearly marked on the deeds, Natásha. Now, it's true there was some argument about it back a ways, but nowadays everybody knows it belongs to me. So there's no use arguing about it. You see, what happened was, my aunt's grandmother let your grandfather's tenants have that field free of charge for an indefinite time in exchange for their making bricks for her. So your grandfather's people used that land for free for about forty years and they started to think it was theirs, but then, when it turned out what the real situation was—

NATÁSHA: My grandfather and my great-grandfather both always said that the land went as far as Burnt Swamp, which means Meadowland belongs to us. So what's the point of arguing about it? I think you're just being rude.

LÓMOV: I can show you the papers, Natálya Stepánovna!

NATÁSHA: Oh, you're just teasing! You're trying to pull my leg! This is all a big joke, isn't it? We've owned that land for going on three hundred years, and all of a sudden you say it doesn't belong to us. Excuse me, Iván Vassílich, excuse me, but I can't believe you said that. And believe me, I don't care one bit about that old meadow: it's only twenty acres, it's not worth three hundred rubles, even, but that's not the point. It's the injustice of it that hurts. And I don't care what anybody says—injustice is something I just can't put up with.

LÓMOV: But you didn't listen to what I was saying! Please! Your grandfather's tenants, as I was trying very politely to point out to you, made bricks for my aunt's grandmother. Now, my aunt's grandmother just wanted to make things easier and—

NATÁSHA: Grandmother, grandfather, father—what difference does it all make? The field belongs to us, and that's that.

LÓMOV: That field belongs to me!

NATÁSHA: That field belongs to us! You can go on about your grandmother until you're blue in the face, you can wear fifteen fancy coats—it still belongs to us! It's ours, ours, ours! I don't want anything that belongs to you, but I do want to keep what's my own, thank you very much!

LÓMOV: Natálya Stepánovna, I don't care about that field either; I don't need that field; I'm talking about the principle of the thing. If you want the field, you can have it. I'll give it to you.

NATÁSHA: If there's any giving to be done, I'll do it! That field belongs to me! Iván Vassílich, I have never gone through anything this crazy in all my life! Up till now I've always thought of you as a good neighbor, a real friend—last year we even lent you our threshing machine, which meant that we were threshing *our* wheat in November—and now all of a sudden you start treating us like Gypsies. *You'll* give *me* my own field? Excuse me, but that is a pretty unneighborly thing to do. In fact, in my opinion, it's downright insulting!

LÓMOV: So in your opinion I'm some kind of claim jumper, you mean? Look, lady, I have never tried to take anybody else's land, and I'm not going to let anybody try to tell me I did, not even you. [*Runs to the table and takes a drink of water*] Meadowland is mine!

NATÁSHA: You lie! It's ours!

LÓMOV: It's mine!

NATÁSHA: You lie! I'll show you! I'll send my mowers out there today!

LÓMOV: You'll what!

NATÁSHA: I said I'll have my mowers out there today, and they'll hay that field flat!

LÓMOV: You do, and I'll break their necks!

NATÁSHA: You wouldn't dare!

LÓMOV [*Clutches his chest*]:   Meadowland is mine! You understand? Mine!

NATÁSHA: Please don't shout. You can scream and carry on all you want in your own house, but as long as you're in mine, try to behave like a gentleman.

LÓMOV: I tell you, if I didn't have these murmurs, these awful pains, these veins throbbing in my temples, I wouldn't be talking like this. [*Shouts*] Meadowland is mine!

NATÁSHA: Ours!

LÓMOV: Mine!

NATÁSHA: Ours!

LÓMOV: Mine!

[Enter CHUBUKÓV.*]*

CHUBUKÓV: What's going on? What are you both yelling for?

NATÁSHA: Papa, will you please explain to this gentleman just who owns Meadowland, him or us?

CHUBUKÓV: Lover boy, Meadowland belongs to us.

LÓMOV: I beg your pardon, Stepán Stepánich, how can it belong to you? Think what you're saying! My aunt's grandmother let your grandfather's people have that land to use free of charge, temporarily, and they used that land for forty years and started thinking it was theirs, but it turned out what the problem was—

CHUBUKÓV: Allow me, sweetheart. You're forgetting that the reason those people didn't pay your granny and all the rest of it was because there was *already* a real problem about just who *did* own the meadow. And everything. But nowadays every dog in the village knows it belongs to us, and that's a fact. I don't think you've ever seen the survey map—

LÓMOV: Look, I can prove to you that Meadowland belongs to me!

CHUBUKÓV: No you can't, lover boy.

LÓMOV: I can too!

CHUBUKÓV: Oh, for crying out loud! What are you shouting for? You can't prove anything by shouting, and that's a fact. Look, I am not interested in taking any of your land, and neither am I interested in giving away any of my own. Why should I?

And if it comes down to it, lover boy, if you want to make a case out of this, or anything like that, I'd just as soon give it to the peasants as give it to you. So there!

LÓMOV: You're not making any sense. What gives you the right to give away someone else's land?

CHUBUKÓV: I'll be the judge of whether I have the right or not! The fact is, boy, I am not used to being talked to in that tone of voice and all the rest of it. I am twice your age, boy, and I'll ask you to talk to me without getting so excited and whatever.

LÓMOV: No! You think I'm just stupid, and you're making fun of me! You stand there and tell me my own land belongs to you, and then you expect me to be calm about it and talk as if nothing had happened! That's not the way good neighbors behave, Stepán Stepánich! You are not a neighbor, you are a *usurper!*

CHUBUKÓV: I'm a *what?* What did you call me?

NATÁSHA: Papa, you send our mowers out to Meadowland right this very minute!

CHUBUKÓV: You, boy! What did you just call me?

NATÁSHA: Meadowland belongs to us, and I'll never give it up—never, never, never!

LÓMOV: We'll see about that! I'll take you to court, and then we'll see who it belongs to!

CHUBUKÓV: To court! Well, you just go right ahead, boy, you take us to court! I dare you! Oh, now I get it, you were just waiting for a chance to take us to court and all the rest of it! And whatever! It's inbred, isn't it? Your whole family was like that—they couldn't wait to start suing. They were always in court! And that's a fact!

LÓMOV: You leave my family out of this! The Lómovs were all decent, law-abiding citizens, every one of them, not like some people I could name, who were arrested for embezzlement—your uncle, for instance!

CHUBUKÓV: Every single one of the Lómovs was crazy! All of them!

NATÁSHA: All of them! Every single one!

CHUBUKÓV: Your uncle was a falling-down drunk, and that's a fact! And your aunt, the youngest one, she used to run around with an architect! An architect! And that's a fact!

LÓMOV: And your mother was a hunchback! [*Clutches his chest*] Oh, my God, I've got a pain in my side . . . my head's beginning to pound! Oh, my God, give me some water!

CHUBUKÓV: And your father was a gambler and a glutton!

NATÁSHA: And your aunt was a tattletale; she was the worst gossip in town!

LÓMOV: My left leg is paralyzed. . . . And you're a sneak! Oh, my heart! And everybody knows that during the elections, you people . . . I've got spots in front of my eyes. . . . Where's my hat?

NATÁSHA: You're low! And lousy! And cheap!

CHUBUKÓV: You are a lowdown two-faced snake in the grass, and that's a fact! An absolute fact!

LÓMOV: Here's my hat! My heart! How do I get out of here . . . where's the door? I think I'm dying . . . I can't move my leg. [*Heads for the door*]

CHUBUKÓV [*Following him*]:   And don't you ever set foot in this house again!

NATÁSHA: And you just take us to court! Go ahead, see what happens!

[Exit Lómov, staggering.]

CHUBUKÓV [*Walks up and down in agitation*]:   He can go to hell!

NATÁSHA: What a creep! See if I ever trust a neighbor again after this!

CHUBUKÓV: Crook!

NATÁSHA: Creep! He takes over somebody else's land and then has the nerve to threaten them!

CHUBUKÓV: And would you believe that wig-worm, that chicken-brain, had the nerve to come here and propose? Hah? He proposed!

NATÁSHA: He proposed what?

CHUBUKÓV: What? He came here to propose to you!

NATÁSHA: To propose? To me? Why didn't you tell me that before!

CHUBUKÓV: That's why he was all dressed up in that stupid coat! What a silly sausage!

NATÁSHA: Me? He came to propose to me? Oh, my God, my God! [*Collapses into a chair and wails*] Oh, make him come back! Make him come back! Oh, please, make him come back! [*She has hysterics*]

CHUBUKÓV: What's the matter? What's the matter with you? [*Smacks his head*] Oh, my God, what have I done! I ought to shoot myself! I ought to be hanged! I ought to be tortured to death!

NATÁSHA: I think I'm going to die! Make him come back!

CHUBUKÓV: All right! Just stop screaming! Please! [*Runs out*]

NATÁSHA [*Alone, wailing*]:   What have we done? Oh, make him come back! Make him come back!

CHUBUKÓV [*Reenters*]:   He's coming, he's coming back and everything, goddamn it! You talk to him yourself this time; I can't. . . . And that's a fact!

NATÁSHA [*Wailing*]:   Make him come back!

CHUBUKÓV: I just told you, he *is* coming back. Oh, God almighty, what an ungrateful assignment, being the father of a grown-up girl! I'll slit my throat, I swear I'll slit my throat! We yell at the man, we insult him, we chase him away . . . and it's all your fault. It's your fault!

NATÁSHA: No, it's your fault!

CHUBUKÓV: All right, I'm sorry, it's my fault. Or whatever.

[Lómov appears in the doorway.]

   This time you do the talking yourself! [*Exit*]

LÓMOV [*Entering, exhausted*]:   I'm having a heart murmur, it's awful, my leg is paralyzed . . . my left side is going *drrrk!*

NATÁSHA: You'll have to excuse us, Iván Vassílich—we got a little bit carried away. . . . Anyway, I just remembered, Meadowland belongs to you after all.

LÓMOV: There's something wrong with my heart—it's beating too loud. . . . Meadowland is mine? These little whatsits are twitching in both my eyelids. . . .

NATÁSHA: It's your—Meadowland is all yours. Here, sit down.

[They both sit.]

>   We made a mistake.

LÓMOV: It was always just the principle of the thing. I don't care about the land, but I do care about the principle of the thing.

NATÁSHA: I know, the principle of the thing. . . . Why don't we talk about something else?

LÓMOV: And besides, I really can prove it. My aunt's grandmother let your grandfather's tenants have that field—

NATÁSHA: That's enough! I think we should change the subject. *[Aside]* I don't know where to start. . . . *[To* LÓMOV*]* How's the hunting? Are you going hunting anytime soon?

LÓMOV: Oh, yes, geese and grouse hunting, Natásha, geese and grouse. I was thinking of going after the harvest is in. Oh, by the way, did I tell you? The worst thing happened to me! You know my old hound Guesser? Well, he went lame on me.

NATÁSHA: Oh, that's terrible! What happened?

LÓMOV: I don't know; he must have dislocated his hip, or maybe he got into a fight with some other dogs and got bit. *[Sighs]* And he was the best hound dog, not to mention how much he cost. I got him from Mirónov, and I paid a hundred and twenty-five for him.

NATÁSHA *[Beat]*:   Iván Vassílich, you paid too much.

LÓMOV *[Beat]*:   I thought I got him pretty cheap. He's a real good dog.

NATÁSHA: Papa paid only eighty-five for his hound dog Messer, and Messer is a lot better than your old Guesser!

LÓMOV: Messer is better than Guesser? What do you mean? *[Laughs]* Messer is better than Guesser!

NATÁSHA: Of course he's better! I mean, he's not full grown yet, he's still a pup, but when it comes to a bark and a bite, nobody has a better dog.

LÓMOV: Excuse me, Natásha, but I think you're forgetting something. He's got an underslung jaw, and a dog with an underslung jaw can never be a good retriever.

NATÁSHA: An underslung jaw? That's the first I ever heard of it!

LÓMOV: I'm telling you, his lower jaw is shorter than his upper.

NATÁSHA: What did you do, measure it?

LÓMOV: Of course I measured it! I grant you he's not so bad on point, but you tell him to go fetch, and he can barely—

NATÁSHA: In the first place, our Messer is a purebred from a very good line—he's the son of Pusher and Pisser, so that limp-foot mutt of yours couldn't touch him for breeding. Besides which, your dog is old and ratty and full of fleas—

Lómov: He may be old, but I wouldn't take five of your Messers for him. How can you even say that? Guesser is a real hound, and that Messer is a joke, he's not even worth worrying about. Every old fart in the country's got a dog just like your Messer—there's a mess of them everywhere you look! You paid twenty rubles, you paid too much!

Natásha: Iván Vassílich, for some reason you are being perverse on purpose. First you think Meadowlands belongs to you, now you think Guesser is better than Messer. I don't think much of a man who doesn't say what he knows to be a fact. You know perfectly well that Messer is a hundred times better than that . . . that dumb Guesser of yours. So why do you keep saying the opposite?

Lómov: You must think I'm either blind or stupid! Can't you understand that your Messer has an underslung jaw!

Natásha: It's not true!

Lómov: He has an underslung jaw!

Natásha [*Shouting*]:   It's not true!

Lómov: What are you shouting for?

Natásha: What are you lying for? I can't stand any more of this. You ought to be getting ready to put your old Guesser out of his misery, and here you are comparing him to our Messer!

Lómov: You'll have to excuse me, I can't go on with this conversation. I'm having a heart murmur.

Natásha: This just goes to prove what I've always known: the hunters who talk the most are the ones who know the least.

Lómov: Will you please do me a favor and just shut up. . . . My heart is starting to pound. . . . [*Shouts*] Shut up!

Natásha: I will not shut up until you admit that Messer is a hundred times better than Guesser!

Lómov: He's a hundred times worse! I hope he croaks, your Messer. . . . My head . . . my eyes . . . my shoulders . . .

Natásha: And your dumb old Guesser doesn't need to croak—he's dead already!

Lómov: Shut up! [*Starts to cry*] I'm having a heart attack!

Natásha: I will not shut up!

[*Enter* Chubukóv.]

Chubukóv: Now what's the matter?

Natásha: Papa, will you please tell us frankly, on your honor, who's a better dog: Guesser or Messer?

Lómov: Stepán Stepánich, I just want to know one thing: does your Messer have an underslung jaw or doesn't he? Yes or no?

Chubukóv: Well? So what if he does? What difference does it make? Anyway, there isn't a better dog in the whole county, and that's a fact.

LÓMOV: But you don't think my Guesser is better? On your honor!

CHUBUKÓV: Now, loverboy, don't get all upset; just wait a minute. Please. Your Guesser has his good points and whatever. He's a thoroughbred, got a good stance, nice round hindquarters, all the rest of it. But that dog, if you really want to know, boy, has got two vital defects: he's old and he's got a short bite.

LÓMOV: You'll have to excuse me, I'm having another heart murmur. Let's just look at the facts, shall we? All I'd like you to do is just think back to that time at the field trials when my Guesser kept up with the count's dog Fresser. They were going ear to ear, and your Messer was a whole half mile behind.

CHUBUKÓV: He was behind because one of the count's men whopped him with his whip!

LÓMOV: That's not the point! All the other dogs were after the fox, and your Messer was chasing a sheep!

CHUBUKÓV: That's not true! Now listen, boy, I have a very quick temper, as you very well know, and that's a fact, so I think we should keep this discussion very short. He whopped him because none of the rest of you can stand watching other people's dogs perform! You're all rotten with envy! Even you, buddy boy, even you! The fact is, all somebody has to do is point out that somebody's dog is better than your Guesser, and right away you start in with this and that and all the rest of it. I happen to remember exactly what happened!

LÓMOV: And I remember too!

CHUBUKÓV [*Mimics him*]:   "And I remember too!" What do you remember?

LÓMOV: My heart murmur . . . My leg is paralyzed . . . I can't move . . .

NATÁSHA [*Mimics him*]:   "My heart murmur!" What kind of hunter are you? You'd do better in the kitchen catching cockroaches instead of out hunting foxes! A heart murmur!

CHUBUKÓV: She's right—what kind of hunter are you? You and your heart murmur should stay home instead of galloping cross-country, and that's a fact. You say you like to hunt; all you really want to do is ride around arguing and interfering with other people's dogs and whatever. You are *not,* and that's a fact, a hunter.

LÓMOV: And what makes you think you're a hunter? The only reason you go hunting is so you can get in good with the count! My heart! You're a sneak!

CHUBUKÓV: I'm a what? A sneak! [*Shouts*] Shut up!

LÓMOV: A sneak!

CHUBUKÓV: You young whippersnapper! You puppy!

LÓMOV: You rat! You rickety old rat!

CHUBUKÓV: You shut up, or I'll give you a tailful of buckshot! You snoop!

LÓMOV: Everybody knows your poor dead wife—oh, my heart!—used to beat you. My legs . . . my head . . . I see spots . . . I'm going to faint, I'm going to faint!

CHUBUKÓV: And everyone knows your housekeeper has you tied to her apron strings!

LÓMOV: Wait wait wait . . . here it comes! A heart attack! My shoulder just came undone—where's my shoulder? I'm going to die! [*Collapses into a chair*] Get a doctor! [*Faints*]

CHUBUKÓV: Whippersnapper! Milk sucker! Snoop! You make me sick! [*Drinks some water*] Sick!

NATÁSHA: What kind of a hunter are you? You can't even ride a horse! [*To* CHUBUKÓV] Papa! What's the matter with him? Papa! Look at him, Papa! [*Screeching*] Iván Vassílich! He's dead!

CHUBUKÓV: I'm sick! I can't breathe . . . give me some air!

NATÁSHA: He's dead! [*Shakes* LÓMOV's *shoulders*] Iván Vassílich! Iván Vassílich! What have we done? He's dead! [*Collapses into the other chair*] Get a doctor! Get a doctor! [*She has hysterics*]

CHUBUKÓV: Oh, now what? What's the matter with you?

NATÁSHA [*Wailing*]:   He's dead! He's dead!

CHUBUKÓV: Who's dead? [*Looks at* LÓMOV] Oh, my God, he *is* dead! Oh, my God! Get some water! Get a doctor! [*Puts glass to* LÓMOV's *mouth*] Here, drink this. . . . He's not drinking it. . . . That means he's really dead . . . and everything! Oh, what a mess! I'll kill myself! I'll kill myself! Why did I wait so long to kill myself? What am I waiting for right now? Give me a knife! Lend me a gun! [LÓMOV *stirs*] I think he's going to live! Here, drink some water. That's the way.

LÓMOV: Spots . . . everything is all spots . . . it's all cloudy. . . . Where am I?

CHUBUKÓV: Just get married as soon as you can and then get out of here! She says yes! [*Joins* LÓMOV's *and* NATÁSHA's *hands*] She says yes and all the rest of it. I give you both my blessing and whatever. Only please just leave me in peace!

LÓMOV: Huh? Wha'? [*Starts to get up*] Who?

CHUBUKÓV: She says yes! All right? Go ahead and kiss her. . . . And then get the hell out of here!

NATÁSHA [*Moaning*]:   He's alive. . . . Yes, yes, I say yes. . . .

CHUBUKÓV: Go ahead, give him a kiss.

LÓMOV: Huh? Who?

[Natásha kisses him.]

Oh, that's very nice. . . . Excuse me, but what's happening? Oh, yes, I remember now. . . . My heart . . . those spots. . . . I'm so happy, Natásha! [*Kisses her hand*] My leg is still paralyzed. . . .

NATÁSHA: I'm . . . I'm very happy too.

CHUBUKÓV: And I'm getting a weight off my shoulders. Oof!

NATÁSHA: But all the same—you can admit it now, can't you?—Messer is better than Guesser.

LÓMOV: He's worse!

NATÁSHA: He's better!

CHUBUKÓV: And they lived happily ever after! Bring on the champagne!

LÓMOV: He's worse!

NATÁSHA: Better! Better! Better!

CHUBUKÓV [*Tries to make himself heard*]:   Champagne! Bring on the champagne!

Curtain.

MAKING CONNECTIONS

1. It doesn't take long in this comedy to identify the basic personality traits of Natásha and Lómov. To what extent does their relationship remind you of relationships you know?
2. All of the characters in this play seem to have the same objective in mind. Why is it so hard, then, for them to reach it? Given their reactions to each other, why do they want this marriage to happen?
3. This play is a comedy. What makes it funny? Does Chekhov make any serious points about human nature here? Explain.
4. Is this a good match? Can you predict what this relationship will be like in five years? Explain.

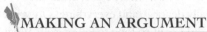

MAKING AN ARGUMENT

1. Opposites attract. Or do they? They do in this play, but do they in real life? And do opposites make a good long-term relationship? Using your own knowledge, this play, and other literature that you have read, write an argument one way or the other. Cite the text of the literature for support.

CONNECTING AND COMPARING ACROSS GENRES: FICTION AND DRAMA

The two works that follow address a subtheme of this section: comparing fiction and drama. Susan Glaspell tells the same story in two different genres, a one-act play, "Trifles," and a short story, "A Jury of Her Peers." Read and discussed together, they invite connections and comparisons.

SUSAN GLASPELL [1882–1948]

Susan Keating Glaspell was born in Davenport, Iowa, and attended Drake University. After working for a time as a reporter, she decided to devote herself to writing fiction, publishing two well-regarded novels, Glory of the Conquered *(1909) and* The Visioning *(1911). In 1913, she married George Cram Cook, a stage director. Together, they moved to Provincetown, Massachusetts, and founded the Provincetown Players, one of the first influential noncom-mercial theaters in the country. The theater provided an artistic home to many illustrious writers of the time, including Edna St. Vincent Millay and Eugene O'Neill. Glaspell wrote a number of plays for the Players, often with feminist themes. In her later years she wrote, among other works, a biography of her husband,* The Road to the Temple *(1927), and* Alison's House, *which won the Pulitzer Prize in 1930. In the original Provincetown Players production of her best-known*

play, Trifles *(1916), Susan Glaspell took the role of Mrs. Hale. The short story "A Jury of Her Peers" was published in 1917.*

TRIFLES

[1916]

Scene: The kitchen in the now abandoned farmhouse of JOHN WRIGHT, *a gloomy kitchen, and left without having been put in order—unwashed pans under the sink, a loaf of bread outside the breadbox, a dish towel on the table—other signs of incompleted work. At the rear the outer door opens, and the* SHERIFF *comes in, followed by the* COUNTY ATTORNEY *and* HALE: *The* SHERIFF *and* HALE *are men in middle life, the* COUNTY ATTORNEY *is a young man; all are much bundled up and go at once to the stove. They are followed by the two women—the* SHERIFF 's *wife,* MRS. PETERS, *first; she is a slight wiry woman, a thin nervous face.* MRS. HALE *is larger and would ordinarily be called more comfortable looking, but she is disturbed now and looks fearfully about as she enters. The women have come in slowly and stand close together near the door.*

COUNTY ATTORNEY [*at the stove rubbing his hands*]:   This feels good. Come up to the fire, ladies.

MRS. PETERS [*after taking a step forward*]:   I'm not—cold.

SHERIFF [*unbuttoning his overcoat and stepping away from the stove as if to the beginning of official business*]:   Now, Mr. Hale, before we move things about, you explain to Mr. Henderson just what you saw when you came here yesterday morning.

COUNTY ATTORNEY [*crossing down to left of the table*]:   By the way, has anything been moved? Are things just as you left them yesterday?

SHERIFF [*looking about*]:   It's just the same. When it dropped below zero last night, I thought I'd better send Frank out this morning to make a fire for us—[*sits right of center table*] no use getting pneumonia with a big case on, but I told him not to touch anything except the stove—and you know Frank.

COUNTY ATTORNEY: Somebody should have been left here yesterday.

SHERIFF: Oh—yesterday. When I had to send Frank to Morris Center for that man who went crazy—I want you to know I had my hands full yesterday. I knew you could get back from Omaha by today, and as long as I went over everything here myself—

COUNTY ATTORNEY: Well, Mr. Hale, tell just what happened when you came here yesterday morning.

HALE [*crossing down to above table*]:   Harry and I had started to town with a load of potatoes. We came along the road from my place and as I got here, I said, "I'm going to see if I can't get John Wright to go in with me on a party telephone." I spoke to Wright about it once before and he put me off, saying folks talked too much anyway, and all he asked was peace and quiet—I guess you know about how much he talked himself; but I thought maybe if I went to the house and talked about it before his wife, though I said to Harry that I didn't know as what his wife wanted made much difference to John—

COUNTY ATTORNEY: Let's talk about that later, Mr. Hale. I do want to talk about that, but tell now just what happened when you got to the house.

HALE: I didn't hear or see anything; I knocked at the door, and still it was all quiet inside. I knew they must be up, it was past eight o'clock. So I knocked again, and I thought I heard somebody say, "Come in." I wasn't sure, I'm not sure yet, but I opened the door—this door [*indicating the door by which the two women are still standing*] and there in that rocker—[*pointing to it*] sat Mrs. Wright.

[*They all look at the rocker.*]

COUNTY ATTORNEY: What—was she doing?

HALE: She was rockin' back and forth. She had her apron in her hand and was kind of—pleating it.

COUNTY ATTORNEY: And how did she—look?

HALE: Well, she looked queer.

COUNTY ATTORNEY: How do you mean—queer?

HALE: Well, as if she didn't know what she was going to do next. And kind of done up.

COUNTY ATTORNEY: How did she seem to feel about your coming?

HALE: Why, I don't think she minded—one way or other. She didn't pay much attention. I said, "How do, Mrs. Wright, it's cold, ain't it?" And she said, "Is it?"—and went on kind of pleating at her apron. Well, I was surprised; she didn't ask me to come up to the stove, or to set down, but just sat there, not even looking at me, so I said, "I want to see John." And then she—laughed. I guess you would call it a laugh. I thought of Harry and the team outside, so I said a little sharp: "Can't I see John?" "No," she says, kind o' dull like. "Ain't he home?" says I. "Yes," says she, "he's home." "Then why can't I see him?" I asked her, out of patience. "'Cause he's dead," says she. "*Dead?*" says I. She just nodded her head, not getting a bit excited, but rockin' back and forth. "Why—where is he?" says I, not knowing what to say. She just pointed upstairs—like that [*himself pointing to the room above*]. I got up, with the idea of going up there. I walked from there to here—then I says, "Why, what did he die of?" "He died of a rope around his neck," says she, and just went on pleatin' at her apron. Well, I went out and called Harry. I thought I might—need help. We went upstairs, and there he was lyin'—

COUNTY ATTORNEY: I think I'd rather have you go into that upstairs, where you can point it all out. Just go on now with the rest of the story.

HALE: Well, my first thought was to get that rope off. I looked . . . [*stops, his face twitches.*] . . . but Harry, he went up to him, and he said, "No, he's dead all right, and we'd better not touch anything." So we went back downstairs. She was still sitting that same way. "Has anybody been notified?" I asked. "No," says she, unconcerned. "Who did this, Mrs. Wright?" said Harry. He said it businesslike—and she stopped pleatin' of her apron. "I don't know," she says. "You don't *know?*" says Harry. "No," says she, "Weren't you sleepin' in the bed with him?" says Harry. "Yes," says she, "but I was on the inside." "Somebody slipped a rope round his neck and strangled him, and you didn't wake up?" says Harry. "I didn't wake up," she said after him. We must 'a looked as if we didn't see how that could be, for after a minute she said, "I sleep sound." Harry was going to ask her more questions but I said maybe we ought to let her tell her story first to the coroner, or the Sheriff, so Harry went fast as he could to Rivers' place, where there's a telephone.

COUNTY ATTORNEY: And what did Mrs. Wright do when she knew that you had gone for the coroner?

HALE: She moved from that chair to this one over here [*pointing to a small chair in the corner*] and just sat there with her hands held together and looking down. I got a feeling that I ought to make some conversation, so I said I had come in to see if John wanted to put in a telephone, and at that she started to laugh, and then she stopped and looked at me—scared. [*The* COUNTY ATTORNEY, *who has had his notebook out, makes a note.*] I dunno, maybe it wasn't scared. I wouldn't like to say it was. Soon Harry got back, and then Dr. Lloyd came, and you, Mr. Peters, and so I guess that's all I know that you don't.

COUNTY ATTORNEY [*looking around*]:   I guess we'll go upstairs first—and then out to the barn and around there. [*to the* SHERIFF] You're convinced that there was nothing important here—nothing that would point to any motive?

SHERIFF: Nothing here but kitchen things.

[*The* COUNTY ATTORNEY, *after again looking around the kitchen, opens the door of a cupboard closet. He gets up on a chair and looks on a shelf. Pulls his hand away, sticky.*]

COUNTY ATTORNEY: Here's a nice mess.

[*The women draw nearer.*]

MRS. PETERS [*to the other woman*]:   Oh, her fruit; it did freeze. [*to the* County Attorney] She worried about that when it turned so cold. She said the fire'd go out and her jars would break.

SHERIFF: Well, can you beat the women! Held for murder and worryin' about her preserves.

COUNTY ATTORNEY: I guess before we're through she may have something more serious than preserves to worry about.

HALE: Well, women are used to worrying over trifles.

[*The two women move a little closer together.*]

COUNTY ATTORNEY [*with the gallantry of a young politician*]:   And yet, for all their worries, what would we do without the ladies? [*The women do not unbend. He goes to the sink, takes a dipperful of water from the pail and pouring it into a basin, washes his hands. Starts to wipe them on the roller towel, turns it for a cleaner place.*] Dirty towels! [*kicks his foot against the pans under the sink.*] Not much of a housekeeper, would you say: ladies?

MRS. HALE [*stiffly*]:   There's a great deal of work to be done on a farm.

COUNTY ATTORNEY: To be sure. And yet [*with a little bow to her*] I know there are some Dickson county farmhouses which do not have such roller towels.

[*He gives it a pull to expose its full length again.*]

MRS. HALE: Those towels get dirty awful quick. Men's hands aren't always as clean as they might be.

COUNTY ATTORNEY: Ah, loyal to your sex, I see. But you and Mrs. Wright were neighbors. I suppose you were friends, too.

MRS. HALE [*shaking her head*]:   I've not seen much of her of late years. I've not been in this house—it's more than a year.

COUNTY ATTORNEY: And why was that? You didn't like her?

MRS. HALE: I liked her all well enough. Farmers' wives have their hands full, Mr. Henderson. And then—

COUNTY ATTORNEY: Yes—?

MRS. HALE [*looking about*]:   It never seemed a very cheerful place.

COUNTY ATTORNEY: No—it's not cheerful. I shouldn't say she had the homemaking instinct.

MRS. HALE: Well, I don't know as Wright had, either.

COUNTY ATTORNEY: You mean that they didn't get on very well?

MRS. HALE: No, I don't mean anything. But I don't think a place'd be any cheerfuler for John Wright's being in it.

COUNTY ATTORNEY: I'd like to talk more of that a little later. I want to get the lay of things upstairs now.

[*He goes to the left, where three steps lead to a stair door.*]

SHERIFF: I suppose anything Mrs. Peters does'll be all right. She was to take in some clothes for her, you know, and a few little things. We left in such a hurry yesterday.

COUNTY ATTORNEY: Yes, but I would like to see what you take, Mrs. Peters, and keep an eye out for anything that might be of use to us.

MRS. PETERS: Yes, Mr. Henderson.

[*The women listen to the men's steps on the stairs, then look about the kitchen.*]

MRS. HALE: I'd hate to have men coming into my kitchen, snooping around and criticizing.

[*She arranges the pans under sink which the* COUNTY ATTORNEY *had shoved out of place.*]

MRS. PETERS: Of course it's no more than their duty.

MRS. HALE: Duty's all right, but I guess that deputy Sheriff that came out to make the fire might have got a little of this on. [*gives the roller towel a pull*] Wish I'd thought of that sooner. Seems mean to talk about her for not having things slicked up when she had to come away in such a hurry.

MRS. PETERS [*who has gone to a small table in the left rear corner of the room, and lifted one end of a towel that covers a pan*]:   She had bread set.

[*Stands still.*]

MRS. HALE [*Eyes fixed on a loaf of bread beside the breadbox, which is on a low shelf at the other side of the room, moves slowly toward it.*]:   She was going to put this in there. [*Picks up loaf, then abruptly drops it. In a manner of returning to familiar things.*] It's a shame about her fruit. I wonder if it's all gone. [*gets up on the chair and looks.*] I think there's some here that's all right, Mrs. Peters. Yes—here; [*holding it toward the window*] this is cherries, too. [*looking again*] I declare I believe that's the only one. [*Gets down, bottle in her hand. Goes to the sink and wipes it off on the outside.*] She'll feel awful bad after all her hard work in the hot weather. I remember the afternoon I put up my cherries last summer.

[*She puts the bottle on the big kitchen table, center of the room. With a sigh, is about to sit down in the rocking-chair. Before she is seated realizes what chair it is; with a slow look at it, steps back. The chair which she has touched rocks back and forth.*]

MRS. PETERS: Well, I must get those things from the front room closet. [*She goes to the door at the right, but after looking into the other room, steps back.*] You coming with me, Mrs. Hale? You could help me carry them.

[*They go into the other room; reappear,* MRS. PETERS *carrying a dress and skirt,* MRS. HALE *following with a pair of shoes.*]

MRS. PETERS: My, it's cold in there.

[*She puts the clothes on the big table, and hurries to the stove.*]

MRS. HALE [*examining the skirt*]:   Wright was close. I think maybe that's why she kept so much to herself. She didn't even belong to the Ladies Aid. I suppose she felt she couldn't do her part, and then you don't enjoy things when you feel shabby. She used to wear pretty clothes and be lively, when she was Minnie Foster, one of the town girls singing in the choir. But that—oh, that was thirty years ago. This all you was to take in?

MRS. PETERS: She said she wanted an apron. Funny thing to want, for there isn't much to get you dirty in jail, goodness knows. But I suppose just to make her feel more natural. She said they was in the top drawer in this cupboard. Yes, here. And then her little shawl that always hung behind the door. [*opens stair door and looks*] Yes, here it is.

[*Quickly shuts door leading upstairs.*]

MRS. HALE [*abruptly moving toward her*]:   Mrs. Peters?
MRS. PETERS: Yes, Mrs. Hale?
MRS. HALE: Do you think she did it?
MRS. PETERS [*in a frightened voice*]:   Oh, I don't know.

MRS. HALE: Well, I don't think she did. Asking for an apron and her little shawl. Worrying about her fruit.

MRS. PETERS [*starts to speak, glances up, where footsteps are heard in the room above. In a low voice*]:   Mr. Peters says it looks bad for her. Mr. Henderson is awful sarcastic in speech and he'll make fun of her sayin' she didn't wake up.

MRS. HALE: Well, I guess John Wright didn't wake when they was slipping that rope under his neck.

MRS. PETERS: No, it's strange. It must have been done awful crafty and still. They say it was such a—funny way to kill a man, rigging it all up like that.

MRS. HALE: That's just what Mr. Hale said. There was a gun in the house. He says that's what he can't understand.

MRS. PETERS: Mr. Henderson said coming out that what was needed for the case was a motive; something to show anger, or—sudden feeling.

MRS. HALE [*who is standing by the table*]:   Well, I don't see any signs of anger around here. [*She puts her hand on the dish towel which lies on the table, stands looking down at the table, one half of which is clean, the other half messy.*] It's wiped to here. [*Makes a move as if to finish work, then turns and looks at loaf of bread outside the breadbox. Drops towel. In that voice of coming back to familiar things.*] Wonder how they are finding things upstairs? I hope she had it a little more red-up up there. You know, it seems kind of sneaking. Locking her up in town and then coming out here and trying to get her own house to turn against her!

MRS. PETERS: But, Mrs. Hale, the law is the law.

MRS. HALE: I s'pose 'tis. [*unbuttoning her coat*] Better loosen up your things, Mrs. Peters. You won't feel them when you go out.

[*MRS. PETERS takes off her fur tippet, goes to hang it on hook at the back of room, stands looking at the under part of the small corner table.*]

MRS. PETERS: She was piecing a quilt.

[*She brings the large sewing basket and they look at the bright pieces.*]

MRS. HALE: It's log cabin pattern. Pretty, isn't it? I wonder if she was goin' to quilt or just knot it?

[*Footsteps have been heard coming down the stairs. The SHERIFF enters, followed by HALE and the COUNTY ATTORNEY.*]

SHERIFF: They wonder if she was going to quilt it or just knot it.

[*The men laugh; the women look abashed.*]

COUNTY ATTORNEY [*rubbing his hands over the stove*]:   Frank's fire didn't do much up there, did it? Well, let's go out to the barn and get that cleared up.

[*The men go outside.*]

MRS. HALE [*resentfully*]:   I don't know as there's anything so strange, our takin' up our time with little things while we're waiting for them to get the evidence.

[*She sits down at the big table, smoothing out a block with decision.*] I don't see as it's anything to laugh about.

MRS. PETERS [*apologetically*]:   Of course they've got awful important things on their minds.

[*Pulls up a chair and joins* MRS. HALE *at the table.*]

MRS. HALE [*examining another block*]:   Mrs. Peters, look at this one. Here, this is the one she was working on, and look at the sewing! All the rest of it has been so nice and even. And look at this! It's all over the place! Why, it looks as if she didn't know what she was about!

[*After she has said this, they look at each other, then start to glance back at the door. After an instant* MRS. HALE *has pulled at a knot and ripped the sewing.*]

MRS. PETERS: Oh, what are you doing, Mrs. Hale?

MRS. HALE [*mildly*]:   Just pulling out a stitch or two that's not sewed very good. [*threading a needle*] Bad sewing always made me fidgety.

MRS. PETERS [*nervously*]:   I don't think we ought to touch things.

MRS. HALE: I'll just finish up this end. [*suddenly stopping and leaning forward*] Mrs. Peters?

MRS. PETERS: Yes, Mrs. Hale?

MRS. HALE: What do you suppose she was so nervous about?

MRS. PETERS: Oh—I don't know. I don't know as she was nervous. I sometimes sew awful queer when I'm just tired. [MRS. HALE *starts to say something, looks at* Mrs. Peters, *then goes on sewing.*] Well, I must get these things wrapped up. They may be through sooner than we think. [*putting apron and other things together*] I wonder where I can find a piece of paper, and string.

MRS. HALE: In that cupboard, maybe.

MRS. PETERS [*looking in cupboard*]:   Why, here's a birdcage. [*holds it up*] Did she have a bird, Mrs. Hale?

MRS. HALE: Why, I don't know whether she did or not—I've not been here for so long. There was a man around last year selling canaries cheap, but I don't know as she took one; maybe she did. She used to sing real pretty herself.

MRS. PETERS [*glancing around*]:   Seems funny to think of a bird here. But she must have had one, or why should she have a cage? I wonder what happened to it.

MRS. HALE: I s'pose maybe the cat got it.

MRS. PETERS.   No, she didn't have a cat. She's got that feeling some people have about cats—being afraid of them. My cat got in her room, and she was real upset and asked me to take it out.

MRS. HALE: My sister Bessie was like that. Queer, ain't it?

MRS. PETERS [*examining the cage*]:   Why, look at this door. It's broke. One hinge is pulled apart.

MRS. HALE [*looking, too*]:   Looks as if someone must have been rough with it.

MRS. PETERS: Why, yes.

[She brings the cage forward and puts it on the table.]

MRS. HALE: I wish if they're going to find any evidence they'd be about it. I don't like this place.

MRS. PETERS: But I'm awful glad you came with me, Mrs. Hale. It would be lonesome for me sitting here alone.

MRS. HALE: It would, wouldn't it? *[dropping her sewing]* But I tell you what I do wish, Mrs. Peters. I wish I had come over sometimes when *she* was here. I—*[looking around the room]*—wish I had.

MRS. PETERS: But of course you were awful busy, Mrs. Hale—your house and your children.

MRS. HALE: I could've come. I stayed away because it weren't cheerful—and that's why I ought to have come. I—I've never liked this place. Maybe because it's down in a hollow and you don't see the road. I dunno what it is, but it's a lonesome place and always was. I wish I had come over to see Minnie Foster sometimes. I can see now—

[Shakes her head.]

MRS. PETERS: Well, you mustn't reproach yourself, Mrs. Hale. Somehow we just don't see how it is with other folks until—something comes up.

MRS. HALE: Not having children makes less work—but it makes a quiet house, and Wright out to work all day, and no company when he did come in. Did you know John Wright, Mrs. Peters?

MRS. PETERS: Not to know him; I've seen him in town. They say he was a good man.

MRS. HALE: Yes—good; he didn't drink, and kept his word as well as most, I guess, and paid his debts. But he was a hard man, Mrs. Peters. Just to pass the time of day with him—*[shivers]* Like a raw wind that gets to the bone. *[pauses, her eye falling on the cage]* I should think she would 'a wanted a bird. But what do you suppose went with it?

MRS. PETERS: I don't know, unless it got sick and died.

[She reaches over and swings the broken door, swings it again; both women watch it.]

MRS. HALE: You weren't raised round here, were you? *[Mrs. Peters shakes her head.]* You didn't know—her?

MRS. PETERS: Not till they brought her yesterday.

MRS. HALE: She—come to think of it, she was kind of like a bird herself—real sweet and pretty, but kind of timid and—fluttery. How—she—did—change. *[silence; then as if struck by a happy thought and relieved to get back to everyday things.]* Tell you what, Mrs. Peters; why don't you take the quilt in with you? It might take up her mind.

MRS. PETERS: Why, I think that's a real nice idea, Mrs. Hale. There couldn't possibly be any objection to it, could there? Now, just what would I take? I wonder if her patches are in here—and her things.

[They look in the sewing basket.]

MRS. HALE: Here's some red. I expect this has got sewing things in it [*brings out a fancy box*] What a pretty box. Looks like something somebody would give you. Maybe her scissors are in here. [*Opens box. Suddenly puts her hand to her nose.*] Why—[Mrs. Peters *bends nearer, then turns her face away.*] There's something wrapped up in this piece of silk.

MRS. PETERS: Why, this isn't her scissors.

MRS. HALE [*lifting the silk*]:   Oh, Mrs. Peters—it's—

[*Mrs. Peters bends closer.*]

MRS. PETERS: It's the bird.

MRS. HALE [*jumping up*]:   But, Mrs. Peters—look at it. Its neck! Look at its neck! It's all—other side *to*.

MRS. PETERS: Somebody—wrung—its neck.

[*Their eyes meet. A look of growing comprehension, of horror. Steps are heard outside.* MRS. HALE *slips box under quilt pieces, and sinks into her chair. Enter* SHERIFF *and* COUNTY ATTORNEY. MRS. PETERS *rises.*]

COUNTY ATTORNEY [*as one turning from serious things to little pleasantries*]:   Well, ladies, have you decided whether she was going to quilt it or knot it?

MRS. PETERS: We think she was going to—knot it.

COUNTY ATTORNEY: Well, that's interesting, I'm sure. [*seeing the birdcage*] Has the bird flown?

MRS. HALE [*putting more quilt pieces over the box*]:   We think the—cat got it.

COUNTY ATTORNEY [*preoccupied*]:   Is there a cat?

[*Mrs. Hale glances in a quick covert way at* Mrs. Peters.]

MRS. PETERS: Well, not *now*. They're superstitious, you know. They leave.

COUNTY ATTORNEY [*to* SHERIFF PETERS, *continuing an interrupted conversation*]:   No sign at all of anyone having come from the outside. Their own rope. Now let's go up again and go over it piece by piece. [*They start upstairs.*] It would have to have been someone who knew just the—

[*Mrs. Peters sits down. The two women sit there not looking at one another, but as if peering into something and at the same time holding back. When they talk now it is the manner of feeling their way over strange ground, as if afraid of what they are saying, but as if they cannot help saying it.*]

MRS. HALE: She liked the bird. She was going to bury it in that pretty box.

MRS. PETERS [*in a whisper*]:   When I was a girl—my kitten—there was a boy took a hatchet, and before my eyes—and before I could get there—[*covers her face an instant*] If they hadn't held me back, I would have—[*catches herself, looks upstairs where steps are heard, falters weakly*]—hurt him.

MRS. HALE [*with a slow look around her*]:   I wonder how it would seem never to have had any children around. [*pause*] No, Wright wouldn't like the bird—a thing that sang. She used to sing. He killed that, too.

MRS. PETERS [*moving uneasily*]:   We don't know who killed the bird.

MRS. HALE: I knew John Wright.

MRS. PETERS: It was an awful thing was done in this house that night, Mrs. Hale. Killing a man while he slept, slipping a rope around his neck that choked the life out of him.

MRS. HALE: His neck. Choked the life out of him.

[Her hand goes out and rests on the birdcage.]

MRS. PETERS [*with a rising voice*]:   We don't know who killed him. We don't know.

MRS. HALE [*her own feeling not interrupted*]:   If there'd been years and years of nothing, then a bird to sing to you, it would be awful—still, after the bird was still.

MRS. PETERS [*something within her speaking*]:   I know what stillness is. When we homesteaded in Dakota, and my first baby died—after he was two years old, and me with no other then—

MRS. HALE [*moving*]:   How soon do you suppose they'll be through, looking for evidence?

MRS. PETERS: I know what stillness is. [*pulling herself back—*] The law has got to punish crime, Mrs. Hale.

MRS. HALE [*not as if answering that*]:   I wish you'd seen Minnie Foster when she wore a white dress with blue ribbons and stood up there in the choir and sang. [*a look around the room*] Oh, I *wish* I'd come over here once in a while! That was a crime! That was a crime! Who's going to punish that?

MRS. PETERS [*looking upstairs*]:   We mustn't—take on.

MRS. HALE: I might have known she needed help! I know how things can be—for women. I tell you, it's queer, Mrs. Peters. We live close together and we live far apart. We all go through the same things—it's all just a different kind of the same thing. [*brushes her eyes, noticing the bottle of fruit, reaches out for it*] If I was you, I wouldn't tell her her fruit was gone. Tell her it ain't. Tell her it's all right. Take this in to prove it to her. She—she may never know whether it was broke or not.

MRS. PETERS [*Takes the bottle, looks about for something to wrap it in; takes petticoat from the clothes brought from the other room, very nervously begins winding this around the bottle. In a false voice.*]:   My, it's a good thing the men couldn't hear us. Wouldn't they just laugh! Getting all stirred up over a little thing like a—dead canary. As if that could have anything to do with—with—wouldn't they *laugh!*

[The men are heard coming downstairs.]

MRS. HALE [*under her breath*]:   Maybe they would—maybe they wouldn't.

COUNTY ATTORNEY: No, Peters, it's all perfectly clear except a reason for doing it. But you know juries when it comes to women. If there was some definite thing. Something to show—something to make a story about—a thing that would connect up with this strange way of doing it—

[The women's eyes meet for an instant. Enter HALE *from outer door.]*

HALE: Well, I've got the team around. Pretty cold out there.

COUNTY ATTORNEY: I'm going to stay here awhile by myself. [*to the* SHERIFF] You can send Frank out for me, can't you? I want to go over everything. I'm not satisfied that we can't do better.

SHERIFF: Do you want to see what Mrs. Peters is going to take in? [*The* LAWYER *goes to the table, picks up the apron, laughs.*]

COUNTY ATTORNEY: Oh, I guess they're not very dangerous things the ladies have picked up. [*Moves a few things about, disturbing the quilt pieces which cover the box. Steps back.*] No, Mrs. Peters doesn't need supervising. For that matter, a Sheriff's wife is married to the law. Ever think of it that way, Mrs. Peters?

MRS. PETERS: Not—just that way.

SHERIFF [*chuckling*]:   Married to the law. [*moves down right door to the other room*] I just want you to come in here a minute, George. We ought to take a look at these windows.

COUNTY ATTORNEY [*scoffingly*]:   Oh windows!

SHERIFF: We'll be right out, Mr. Hale. [Hale *goes outside. The* SHERIFF *follows the* County Attorney *into the other room. Then* MRS. HALE *rises, hands tight together, looking intensely at* MRS. PETERS, *whose eyes take a slow turn, finally meeting* Mrs. Hale'*s. A moment* Mrs. Hale *holds her, then her own eyes point the way to where the box is concealed. Suddenly* Mrs. Peters *throws back quilt pieces and tries to put the box in the bag she is carrying. It is too big. She opens box, starts to take the bird out, cannot touch it, goes to pieces, stands there helpless. Sound of a knob turning in the other room.* MRS. HALE *snatches the box and puts it in the pocket of her big coat. Enter* COUNTY ATTORNEY *and* SHERIFF.]

COUNTY ATTORNEY [*crosses to up left door facetiously*]:   Well, Henry, at least we found out that she was not going to quilt it. She was going to—what is it you call it, ladies?

MRS. HALE [*standing center below table facing front, her hand against her pocket*]:   We call it—knot it, Mr. Henderson.

Curtain

A JURY OF HER PEERS   [1917]

When Martha Hale opened the storm-door and got a cut of the north wind, she ran back for her big woolen scarf. As she hurriedly wound that round her head her eye made a scandalized sweep of her kitchen. It was no ordinary thing that called her away—it was probably farther from ordinary than anything that had ever happened in Dickson County. But what her eye took in was that her kitchen was in no shape for leaving: her bread all ready for mixing, half the flour sifted and half unsifted.

She hated to see things half done; but she had been at that when the team from town stopped to get Mr. Hale, and then the sheriff came running in to say his wife wished Mrs. Hale would come too—adding, with a grin, that he guessed she was getting scarey and wanted another woman along. So she had dropped everything right where it was.

"Martha!" now came her husband's impatient voice. "Don't keep folks waiting out here in the cold."

She again opened the storm-door, and this time joined the three men and the one woman waiting for her in the big two-seated buggy.

5   After she had the robes tucked around her she took another look at the woman who sat beside her on the back seat. She had met Mrs. Peters the year before at the county fair, and the thing she remembered about her was that she didn't seem like a sheriff's wife. She was small and thin and didn't have a strong voice. Mrs. Gorman, sheriff's wife before Gorman went out and Peters came in, had a voice that somehow seemed to be backing up the law with every word. But if Mrs. Peters didn't look like a sheriff's wife, Peters made it up in looking like a sheriff. He was to a dot the kind of man who could get himself elected sheriff—a heavy man with a big voice, who was particularly genial with the law-abiding, as if to make it plain that he knew the difference between criminals and non-criminals. And right there it came into Mrs. Hale's mind, with a stab, that this man who was so pleasant and lively with all of them was going to the Wrights' now as a sheriff.

"The country's not very pleasant this time of year," Mrs. Peters at last ventured, as if she felt they ought to be talking as well as the men.

Mrs. Hale scarcely finished her reply, for they had gone up a little hill and could see the Wright place now, and seeing it did not make her feel like talking. It looked very lonesome this cold March morning. It had always been a lonesome-looking place. It was down in a hollow, and the poplar trees around it were lonesome-looking trees. The men were looking at it and talking about what had happened. The county attorney was bending to one side of the buggy, and kept looking steadily at the place as they drew up to it.

"I'm glad you came with me," Mrs. Peters said nervously, as the two women were about to follow the men in through the kitchen door.

Even after she had her foot on the door-step, her hand on the knob, Martha Hale had a moment of feeling she could not cross that threshold. And the reason it seemed she couldn't cross it now was simply because she hadn't crossed it before. Time and time again it had been in her mind, "I ought to go over and see Minnie Foster"—she still thought of her as Minnie Foster, though for twenty years she had been Mrs. Wright. And then there was always something to do and Minnie Foster would go from her mind. But *now* she could come.

10   The men went over to the stove. The women stood close together by the door. Young Henderson, the county attorney, turned around and said, "Come up to the fire, ladies."

Mrs. Peters took a step forward, then stopped. "I'm not—cold," she said.

And so the two women stood by the door, at first not even so much as looking around the kitchen.

The men talked for a minute about what a good thing it was, the sheriff had sent his deputy out that morning to make a fire for them, and then Sheriff Peters stepped back from the stove, unbuttoned his outer coat, and leaned his hands on the kitchen table in a way that seemed to mark the beginning of official business. "Now, Mr. Hale," he said in a sort of semi-official voice, "before we move things about, you tell Mr. Henderson just what it was you saw when you came here yesterday morning."

The county attorney was looking around the kitchen.

15   "By the way," he said, "has anything been moved?" He turned to the sheriff. "Are things just as you left them yesterday?"

Peters looked from cupboard to sink; from that to a small worn rocker a little to one side of the kitchen table.

"It's just the same."

"Somebody should have been left here yesterday," said the county attorney.

"Oh—yesterday," returned the sheriff, with a little gesture as of yesterday having been more than he could bear to think of. "When I had to send Frank to Morris Center for that man who went crazy—let me tell you. I had my hands full yesterday. I knew you could get back from Omaha by today, George, and as long as I went over everything here myself—"

20   "Well, Mr. Hale," said the county attorney, in a way of letting what was past and gone go, "tell just what happened when you came here yesterday morning."

Mrs. Hale, still leaning against the door, had that sinking feeling of the mother whose child is about to speak a piece. Lewis often wandered along and got things mixed up in a story. She hoped he would tell this straight and plain, and not say unnecessary things that would just make things harder for Minnie Foster. He didn't begin at once, and she noticed that he looked queer—as if standing in that kitchen and having to tell what he had seen there yesterday morning made him almost sick.

"Yes, Mr. Hale?" the county attorney reminded.

"Harry and I had started to town with a load of potatoes," Mrs. Hale's husband began.

Harry was Mrs. Hale's oldest boy. He wasn't with them now, for the very good reason that those potatoes never got to town yesterday and he was taking them this morning, so he hadn't been home when the sheriff stopped to say he wanted Mr. Hale to come over to the Wright place and tell the county attorney his story there, where he could point it all out. With all Mrs. Hale's other emotions came the fear now that maybe Harry wasn't dressed warm enough—they hadn't any of them realized how that north wind did bite.

25   "We come along this road," Hale was going on, with a motion of his hand to the road over which they had just come, "and as we got in sight of the house I says to Harry, 'I'm goin' to see if I can't get John Wright to take a telephone.' You see," he explained to Henderson, "unless I can get somebody to go in with me they won't come out this branch road except for a price I can't pay. I'd spoke to Wright about it once before; but he put me off, saying folks talked too much anyway, and all he asked was peace and quiet—guess you know about how much he talked himself. But I thought maybe if I went to the house and talked about it before his wife, and said all the women-folks liked the telephones, and that in this lonesome stretch of road it would be a good thing—well, I said to Harry that that was what I was going

to say—though I said at the same time that I didn't know as what his wife wanted made much difference to John—"

Now there he was!—saying things he didn't need to say. Mrs. Hale tried to catch her husband's eye, but fortunately the county attorney interrupted with:

"Let's talk about that a little later, Mr. Hale. I do want to talk about that, but I'm anxious now to get along to just what happened when you got here."

When he began this time, it was very deliberately and carefully:

"I didn't see or hear anything. I knocked at the door. And still it was all quiet inside. I knew they must be up—it was past eight o'clock. So I knocked again, louder, and I thought I heard somebody say, 'Come in.' I wasn't sure—I'm not sure yet. But I opened the door—this door," jerking a hand toward the door by which the two women stood, "and there, in that rocker"—pointing to it—"sat Mrs. Wright."

30   Everyone in the kitchen looked at the rocker. It came into Mrs. Hale's mind that that rocker didn't look in the least like Minnie Foster—the Minnie Foster of twenty years before. It was a dingy red, with wooden rungs up the back, and the middle rung was gone, and the chair sagged to one side.

"How did she—look?" the county attorney was inquiring.

"Well," said Hale, "she looked—queer."

"How do you mean—queer?"

As he asked it he took out a note-book and pencil. Mrs. Hale did not like the sight of that pencil. She kept her eye fixed on her husband, as if to keep him from saying unnecessary things that would go into that note-book and make trouble.

35   Hale did speak guardedly, as if the pencil had affected him too.

"Well, as if she didn't know what she was going to do next. And kind of—done up."

"How did she seem to feel about your coming?"

"Why, I don't think she minded—one way or other. She didn't pay much attention. I said, 'Ho' do, Mrs. Wright? It's cold, ain't it?' And she said, 'Is it?'—and went on pleatin' at her apron.

"Well, I was surprised. She didn't ask me to come up to the stove, or to sit down, but just set there, not even lookin' at me. And so I said: 'I want to see John.'

40   "And then she—laughed. I guess you would call it a laugh.

"I thought of Harry and the team outside, so I said, a little sharp, 'Can I see John?' 'No,' says she—kind of dull like. 'Ain't he home?' says I. Then she looked at me. 'Yes,' says she, 'he's home.' 'Then why can't I see him?' I asked her, out of patience with her now. 'Cause he's dead' says she, just as quiet and dull—and fell to pleatin' her apron. 'Dead?' says I, like you do when you can't take in what you've heard.

"She just nodded her head, not getting a bit excited, but rockin' back and forth.

"Why—where is he?' says I, not knowing *what* to say.

"She just pointed upstairs—like this"—pointing to the room above.

45   "I got up, with the idea of going up there myself. By this time I—didn't know what to do. I walked from there to here; then I says: 'Why, what did he die of?'

" 'He died of a rope around his neck,' says she; and just went on pleatin' at her apron."

Hale stopped speaking, and stood staring at the rocker, as if he were still seeing the woman who had sat there the morning before. Nobody spoke; it was as if every one were seeing the woman who had sat there the morning before.

"And what did you do then?" the county attorney at last broke the silence.

"I went out and called Harry. I thought I might—need help. I got Harry in, and we went upstairs." His voice fell almost to a whisper. "There he was—lying over the—"

50 "I think I'd rather have you go into that upstairs," the county attorney interrupted, "where you can point it all out. Just go on now with the rest of the story."

"Well, my first thought was to get that rope off. It looked—"

He stopped, his face twitching.

"But Harry, he went up to him, and he said, 'No, he's dead all right, and we'd better not touch anything.' So we went downstairs.

"She was still sitting that same way. 'Has anybody been notified?' I asked. 'No,' says she, unconcerned.

55 " 'Who did this, Mrs. Wright?' said Harry. He said it businesslike, and she stopped pleatin' at her apron. 'I don't know,' she says. 'You don't *know?*' says Harry. 'Weren't you sleepin' in the bed with him?' 'Yes,' says she, 'but I was on the inside.' 'Somebody slipped a rope round his neck and strangled him, and you didn't wake up?' says Harry. 'I didn't wake up,' she said after him.

"We may have looked as if we didn't see how that could be, for after a minute she said, 'I sleep sound.'

"Harry was going to ask her more questions, but I said maybe that weren't our business; maybe we ought to let her tell her story first to the coroner or the sheriff. So Harry went fast as he could over to High Road—the Rivers' place, where there's a telephone."

"And what did she do when she knew you had gone for the coroner?" The attorney got his pencil in his hand all ready for writing.

"She moved from that chair to this one over here"—Hale pointed to a small chair in the corner—"and just sat there with her hands held together and looking down. I got a feeling that I ought to make some conversation, so I said I had come in to see if John wanted to put in a telephone; and at that she started to laugh, and then she stopped and looked at me—scared."

60 At the sound of a moving pencil the man who was telling the story looked up.

"I dunno—maybe it wasn't scared," he hastened: "I wouldn't like to say it was. Soon Harry got back, and then Dr. Lloyd came, and you, Mr. Peters, and so I guess that's all I know that you don't."

He said that last with relief, and moved a little, as if relaxing. Everyone moved a little. The county attorney walked toward the stair door.

"I guess we'll go upstairs first—then out to the barn and around there."

He paused and looked around the kitchen.

65 "You're convinced there was nothing important here?" he asked the sheriff. "Nothing that would—point to any motive?"

The sheriff too looked all around, as if to re-convince himself.

"Nothing here but kitchen things," he said, with a little laugh for the insignificance of kitchen things.

The county attorney was looking at the cupboard—a peculiar, ungainly structure, half closet and half cupboard, the upper part of it being built in the wall, and the lower part just the old-fashioned kitchen cupboard. As if its queerness attracted him, he got a chair and opened the upper part and looked in. After a moment he drew his hand away sticky.

"Here's a nice mess," he said resentfully.

70 The two women had drawn nearer, and now the sheriff's wife spoke.

"Oh—her fruit," she said, looking to Mrs. Hale for sympathetic understanding. She turned back to the county attorney and explained: "She worried about that when it turned so cold last night. She said the fire would go out and her jars might burst."

Mrs. Peters' husband broke into a laugh.

"Well, can you beat the women! Held for murder, and worrying about her preserves!"

The young attorney set his lips.

75 "I guess before we're through with her she may have something more serious than preserves to worry about."

"Oh, well," said Mrs. Hale's husband, with good-natured superiority, "women are used to worrying over trifles."

The two women moved a little closer together. Neither of them spoke. The county attorney seemed suddenly to remember his manners—and think of his future.

"And yet," said he, with the gallantry of a young politician, "for all their worries, what would we do without the ladies?"

The women did not speak, did not unbend. He went to the sink and began washing his hands. He turned to wipe them on the roller towel—whirled it for a cleaner place.

80 "Dirty towels! Not much of a housekeeper, would you say, ladies?"

He kicked his foot against some dirty pans under the sink.

"There's a great deal of work to be done on a farm," said Mrs. Hale stiffly.

"To be sure. And yet"—with a little bow to her—"I know there are some Dickson County farm-houses that do not have such roller towels." He gave it a pull to expose its full length again.

"Those towels get dirty awful quick. Men's hands aren't always as clean as they might be."

85 "Ah, loyal to your sex, I see," he laughed. He stopped and gave her a keen look. "But you and Mrs. Wright were neighbors. I suppose you were friends, too."

Martha Hale shook her head.

"I've seen little enough of her of late years. I've not been in this house—it's more than a year."

"And why was that? You didn't like her?"

"I liked her well enough," she replied with spirit. "Farmers' wives have their hands full, Mr. Henderson. And then"—She looked around the kitchen.

90 "Yes?" he encouraged.

"It never seemed a very cheerful place," said she, more to herself than to him.

"No," he agreed; "I don't think anyone would call it cheerful. I shouldn't say she had the home-making instinct."

"Well, I don't know as Wright had, either," she muttered.

"You mean they didn't get on very well?" he was quick to ask.

95   "No; I don't mean anything," she answered, with decision. As she turned a little away from him, she added: "But I don't think a place would be any the cheerfuler for John Wright's bein' in it."

"I'd like to talk to you about that a little later, Mrs. Hale," he said. "I'm anxious to get the lay of things upstairs now."

He moved toward the stair door, followed by the two men.

"I suppose anything Mrs. Peters does'll be all right?" the sheriff inquired. "She was to take in some clothes for her, you know—and a few little things. We left in such a hurry yesterday."

The county attorney looked at the two women they were leaving alone there among the kitchen things.

100   "Yes—Mrs. Peters," he said, his glance resting on the woman who was not Mrs. Peters, the big farmer woman who stood behind the sheriff's wife. "Of course Mrs. Peters is one of us," he said, in a manner of entrusting responsibility. "And keep your eye out, Mrs. Peters, for anything that might be of use. No telling; you women might come upon a clue to the motive—and that's the thing we need."

Mr. Hale rubbed his face after the fashion of a show man getting ready for a pleasantry.

"But would the women know a clue if they did come upon it?" he said; and, having delivered himself of this, he followed the others through the stair door.

The women stood motionless and silent, listening to the footsteps, first upon the stairs, then in the room above them.

Then, as if releasing herself from something strange, Mrs. Hale began to arrange the dirty pans under the sink, which the county attorney's disdainful push of the foot had deranged.

105   "I'd hate to have men comin' into my kitchen," she said testily—"snoopin' round and criticizin'."

"Of course it's no more than their duty," said the sheriff's wife, in her manner of timid acquiescence.

"Duty's all right," replied Mrs. Hale bluffly; "but I guess that deputy sheriff that come out to make the fire might have got a little of this on." She gave the roller towel a pull. "Wish I'd thought of that sooner! Seems mean to talk about her for not having things slicked up, when she had to come away in such a hurry."

She looked around the kitchen. Certainly it was not "slicked up." Her eye was held by a bucket of sugar on a low shelf. The cover was off the wooden bucket, and beside it was a paper bag—half full.

Mrs. Hale moved toward it.

110   "She was putting this in there," she said to herself—slowly.

She thought of the flour in her kitchen at home—half sifted, half not sifted. She had been interrupted, and had left things half done. What had interrupted Minnie Foster? Why had that work been left half done? She made a move as if to finish it,—unfinished things always bothered her,—and then she glanced around and saw that Mrs. Peters was watching her—and she didn't want Mrs. Peters to get that feeling she had got of work begun and then—for some reason—not finished.

"It's a shame about her fruit," she said, and walked toward the cupboard that the county attorney had opened, and got on the chair, murmuring: "I wonder if it's all gone."

It was a sorry enough looking sight, but "Here's one that's all right," she said at last. She held it toward the light. "This is cherries, too." She looked again. "I declare I believe that's the only one."

With a sigh, she got down from the chair, went to the sink, and wiped off the bottle.

115   "She'll feel awful bad, after all her hard work in the hot weather. I remember the afternoon I put up my cherries last summer."

She set the bottle on the table, and, with another sigh, started to sit down in the rocker. But she did not sit down. Something kept her from sitting down in that chair. She straightened—stepped back, and, half turned away, stood looking at it, seeing the woman who had sat there "pleatin' at her apron."

The thin voice of the sheriff's wife broke in upon her: "I must be getting those things from the front-room closet." She opened the door into the other room, started in, stepped back. "You coming with me, Mrs. Hale?" she asked nervously. "You—you could help me get them."

They were soon back—the stark coldness of that shut-up room was not a thing to linger in.

"My!" said Mrs. Peters, dropping the things on the table and hurrying to the stove.

120   Mrs. Hale stood examining the clothes the woman who was being detained in town had said she wanted.

"Wright was close!" she exclaimed, holding up a shabby black skirt that bore the marks of much making over. "I think maybe that's why she kept so much to herself. I s'pose she felt she couldn't do her part; and then, you don't enjoy things when you feel shabby. She used to wear pretty clothes and be lively—when she was Minnie Foster, one of the town girls, singing in the choir. But that—oh, that was twenty years ago."

With a carefulness in which there was something tender, she folded the shabby clothes and piled them at one corner of the table. She looked up at Mrs. Peters, and there was something in the other woman's look that irritated her.

"She don't care," she said to herself. "Much difference it makes to her whether Minnie Foster had pretty clothes when she was a girl."

Then she looked again, and she wasn't so sure; in fact, she hadn't at any time been perfectly sure about Mrs. Peters. She had that shrinking manner, and yet her eyes looked as if they could see a long way into things.

125   "This all you was to take in?" asked Mrs. Hale.

"No," said the sheriff's wife; "she said she wanted an apron. Funny thing to want," she ventured in her nervous little way, "for there's not much to get you dirty in jail, goodness knows. But I suppose just to make her feel more natural. If you're used to wearing an apron—. She said they were in the bottom drawer of this cupboard. Yes—here they are. And then her little shawl that always hung on the stair door."

She took the small gray shawl from behind the door leading upstairs, and stood a minute looking at it.

Suddenly Mrs. Hale took a quick step toward the other woman.

"Mrs. Peters!"

130   "Yes, Mrs. Hale?"

"Do you think she—did it?"

A frightened look blurred the other things in Mrs. Peters' eyes.

"Oh, I don't know," she said, in a voice that seemed to shrink away from the subject.

"Well, I don't think she did," affirmed Mrs. Hale stoutly. "Asking for an apron, and her little shawl. Worryin' about her fruit."

135   "Mr. Peters says—" Footsteps were heard in the room above; she stopped, looked up, then went on in a lowered voice: "Mr. Peters says—it looks bad for her. Mr. Henderson is awful sarcastic in speech, and he's going to make fun of her saying she didn't—wake up."

For a moment Mrs. Hale had no answer. Then, "Well, I guess John Wright didn't wake up—when they was slippin' that rope under his neck," she muttered.

"No, it's *strange,*" breathed Mrs. Peters. "They think it was such a—funny way to kill a man."

She began to laugh; at sound of the laugh, abruptly stopped.

"That's just what Mr. Hale said," said Mrs. Hale, in a resolutely natural voice. "There was a gun in the house. He says that's what he can't understand."

140   "Mr. Henderson said, coming out, that what was needed for the case was a motive. Something to show anger—or sudden feeling."

"Well, I don't see any signs of anger around here," said Mrs. Hale, "I don't—"

She stopped. It was as if her mind tripped on something. Her eye was caught by a dish-towel in the middle of the kitchen table. Slowly she moved toward the table. One half of it was wiped clean, the other half messy. Her eyes made a slow, almost unwilling turn to the bucket of sugar and the half empty bag beside it. Things begun—and not finished.

After a moment she stepped back, and said, in that manner of releasing herself:

"Wonder how they're finding things upstairs? I hope she had it a little more red up up there. You know,"—she paused, and feeling gathered,—"it seems kind of *sneaking:* locking her up in town and coming out here to get her own house to turn against her!"

145   "But, Mrs. Hale," said the sheriff's wife, "the law is the law."

"I s'pose 'tis," answered Mrs. Hale shortly.

She turned to the stove, saying something about that fire not being much to brag of. She worked with it a minute, and when she straightened up she said aggressively:

"The law is the law—and a bad stove is a bad stove. How'd you like to cook on this?"—pointing with the poker to the broken lining. She opened the oven door and started to express her opinion of the oven; but she was swept into her own thoughts, thinking of what it would mean, year after year, to have that stove to wrestle with. The thought of Minnie Foster trying to bake in that oven—and the thought of her never going over to see Minnie Foster—.

She was startled by hearing Mrs. Peters say: "A person gets discouraged—and loses heart."

150   The sheriff's wife had looked from the stove to the sink—to the pail of water which had been carried in from outside. The two women stood there silent, above them the footsteps of the men who were looking for evidence against the woman

who had worked in that kitchen. That look of seeing into things, of seeing through a thing to something else, was in the eyes of the sheriff's wife now. When Mrs. Hale next spoke to her, it was gently:

"Better loosen up your things, Mrs. Peters. We'll not feel them when we go out."

Mrs. Peters went to the back of the room to hang up the fur tippet she was wearing. A moment later she exclaimed, "Why, she was piecing a quilt," and held up a large sewing basket piled high with quilt pieces.

Mrs. Hale spread some of the blocks on the table.

"It's log-cabin pattern," she said, putting several of them together, "Pretty, isn't it?"

155   They were so engaged with the quilt that they did not hear the footsteps on the stairs. Just as the stair door opened Mrs. Hale was saying:

"Do you suppose she was going to quilt it or just knot it?"

The sheriff threw up his hands.

"They wonder whether she was going to quilt it or just knot it!"

There was a laugh for the ways of women, a warming of hands over the stove, and then the county attorney said briskly:

160   "Well, let's go right out to the barn and get that cleared up."

"I don't see as there's anything so strange," Mrs. Hale said resentfully, after the outside door had closed on the three men—"our taking up our time with little things while we're waiting for them to get the evidence. I don't see as it's anything to laugh about."

"Of course they've got awful important things on their minds," said the sheriff's wife apologetically.

They returned to an inspection of the blocks for the quilt. Mrs. Hale was looking at the fine, even sewing, and preoccupied with thoughts of the woman who had done that sewing, when she heard the sheriff's wife say, in a queer tone:

"Why, look at this one."

165   She turned to take the block held out to her.

"The sewing," said Mrs. Peters, in a troubled way, "All the rest of them have been so nice and even—but—this one. Why, it looks as if she didn't know what she was about!"

Their eyes met—something flashed to life, passed between them; then, as if with an effort, they seemed to pull away from each other. A moment Mrs. Hale sat there, her hands folded over that sewing which was so unlike all the rest of the sewing. Then she had pulled a knot and drawn the threads.

"Oh, what are you doing, Mrs. Hale?" asked the sheriff's wife, startled.

"Just pulling out a stitch or two that's not sewed very good," said Mrs. Hale mildly.

170   "I don't think we ought to touch things," Mrs. Peters said, a little helplessly.

"I'd just finish up this end," answered Mrs. Hale, still in that mild, matter-of-fact fashion.

She threaded a needle and started to replace bad sewing with good. For a little while she sewed in silence. Then, in that thin, timid voice, she heard:

"Mrs. Hale!"

"Yes, Mrs. Peters?"

175 "What do you suppose she was so—nervous about?"

"Oh, I don't know," said Mrs. Hale, as if dismissing a thing not important enough to spend much time on. "I don't know as she was—nervous. I sew awful queer sometimes when I'm just tired."

She cut a thread, and out of the corner of her eye looked up at Mrs. Peters. The small, lean face of the sheriff's wife seemed to have tightened up. Her eyes had that look of peering into something. But next moment she moved, and said in her thin, indecisive way:

"Well, I must get those clothes wrapped. They may be through sooner than we think. I wonder where I could find a piece of paper—and string."

"In that cupboard, maybe," suggested Mrs. Hale, after a glance around.

180 One piece of the crazy sewing remained unripped. Mrs. Peters' back turned, Martha Hale now scrutinized that piece, compared it with the dainty, accurate sewing of the other blocks. The difference was startling. Holding this block made her feel queer, as if the distracted thoughts of the woman who had perhaps turned to it to try and quiet herself were communicating themselves to her.

Mrs. Peters' voice roused her.

"Here's a bird-cage," she said. "Did she have a bird, Mrs. Hale?"

"Why, I don't know whether she did or not." She turned to look at the cage Mrs. Peters was holding up. "I've not been here in so long." She sighed. "There was a man round last year selling canaries cheap—but I don't know as she took one. Maybe she did. She used to sing real pretty herself."

Mrs. Peters looked around the kitchen.

185 "Seems kind of funny to think of a bird here." She half laughed—an attempt to put up a barrier. "But she must have had one—or why would she have a cage? I wonder what happened to it."

"I suppose maybe the cat got it," suggested Mrs. Hale, resuming her sewing.

"No; she didn't have a cat. She's got that feeling some people have about cats—being afraid of them. When they brought her to our house yesterday, my cat got in the room, and she was real upset and asked me to take it out."

"My sister Bessie was like that," laughed Mrs. Hale.

The sheriff's wife did not reply. The silence made Mrs. Hale turn round. Mrs. Peters was examining the bird-cage.

190 "Look at this door," she said slowly. "It's broke. One hinge has been pulled apart."

Mrs. Hale came nearer.

"Looks as if someone must have been—rough with it."

Again their eyes met—startled, questioning, apprehensive. For a moment neither spoke nor stirred. Then Mrs. Hale, turning away, said brusquely:

"If they're going to find any evidence, I wish they'd be about it. I don't like this place."

195 "But I'm awful glad you came with me, Mrs. Hale." Mrs. Peters put the bird-cage on the table and sat down. "It would be lonesome for me—sitting here alone."

"Yes, it would, wouldn't it?" agreed Mrs. Hale, a certain determined naturalness in her voice. She had picked up the sewing, but now it dropped in her lap, and she murmured in a different voice: "But I tell you what I *do* wish, Mrs. Peters. I wish I had come over sometimes when she was here. I wish—I had."

"But of course you were awful busy, Mrs. Hale. Your house—and your children."

"I could've come," retorted Mrs. Hale shortly. "I stayed away because it weren't cheerful—and that's why I ought to have come. I"—she looked around—"I've never liked this place. Maybe because it's down in a hollow and you don't see the road. I don't know what it is, but it's a lonesome place, and always was. I wish I had come over to see Minnie Foster sometimes. I can see now—" She did not put it into words.

"Well, you mustn't reproach yourself," counseled Mrs. Peters. "Somehow, we just don't see how it is with other folks till—something comes up."

200   "Not having children makes less work," mused Mrs. Hale, after a silence, "but it makes a quiet house—and Wright out to work all day—and no company when he did come in. Did you know John Wright, Mrs. Peters?"

"Not to know him. I've seen him in town. They say he was a good man."

"Yes—good," conceded John Wright's neighbor grimly. "He didn't drink, and kept his word as well as most, I guess, and paid his debts. But he was a hard man, Mrs. Peters. Just to pass the time of day with him—." She stopped, shivered a little. "Like a raw wind that gets to the bone." Her eye fell upon the cage on the table before her, and she added, almost bitterly: "I should think she would've wanted a bird!"

Suddenly she leaned forward, looking intently at the cage. "But what do you s'pose went wrong with it?"

"I don't know," returned Mrs. Peters; "unless it got sick and died."

205   But after she said it she reached over and swung the broken door. Both women watched it as if somehow held by it.

"You didn't know—her?" Mrs. Hale asked, a gentler note in her voice.

"Not till they brought her yesterday," said the sheriff's wife.

"She—come to think of it, she was kind of like a bird herself. Real sweet and pretty, but kind of timid and—fluttery. How—she—did—change."

That held her for a long time. Finally, as if struck with a happy thought and relieved to get back to everyday things, she exclaimed:

210   "Tell you what, Mrs. Peters, why don't you take the quilt in with you? It might take up her mind."

"Why, I think that's a real nice idea, Mrs. Hale," agreed the sheriff's wife, as if she too were glad to come into the atmosphere of a simple kindness. "There couldn't possibly be any objection to that, could there? Now, just what will I take? I wonder if her patches are in here—and her things?"

They turned to the sewing basket.

"Here's some red," said Mrs. Hale, bringing out a roll of cloth. Underneath that was a box. "Here, maybe her scissors are in here—and her things." She held it up. "What a pretty box! I'll warrant that was something she had a long time ago—when she was a girl."

She held it in her hand a moment; then, with a little sigh, opened it.

215   Instantly her hand went to her nose.

"Why—!"

Mrs. Peters drew nearer—then turned away.

"There's something wrapped up in this piece of silk," faltered Mrs. Hale.

"This isn't her scissors," said Mrs. Peters, in a shrinking voice.

220   Her hand not steady, Mrs. Hale raised the piece of silk. "Oh, Mrs. Peters!" she cried. "It's—"

Mrs. Peters bent closer.

"It's the bird," she whispered.

"But, Mrs. Peters!" cried Mrs. Hale. "*Look* at it! Its *neck*—look at its neck! It's all—other side *to.*"

She held the box away from her.

225   The sheriff's wife again bent closer.

"Somebody wrung its neck," said she, in a voice that was slow and deep.

And then again the eyes of the two women met—this time clung together in a look of dawning comprehension, of growing horror. Mrs. Peters looked from the dead bird to the broken door of the cage. Again their eyes met. And just then there was a sound at the outside door.

Mrs. Hale slipped the box under the quilt pieces in the basket, and sank into the chair before it. Mrs. Peters stood holding to the table. The county attorney and the sheriff came in from outside.

"Well, ladies," said the county attorney, as one turning from serious things to little pleasantries, "have you decided whether she was going to quilt it or knot it?"

230   "We think," began the sheriff's wife in a flurried voice, "that she was going to—knot it."

He was too preoccupied to notice the change that came in her voice on that last.

"Well, that's very interesting, I'm sure," he said tolerantly. He caught sight of the bird-cage. "Has the bird flown?"

"We think the cat got it," said Mrs. Hale in a voice curiously even.

He was walking up and down, as if thinking something out.

235   "Is there a cat?" he asked absently.

Mrs. Hale shot a look up at the sheriff's wife.

"Well, not *now,*" said Mrs. Peters. "They're superstitious, you know; they leave."

She sank into her chair.

The county attorney did not heed her. "No sign at all of anyone having come in from the outside," he said to Peters, in the manner of continuing an interrupted conversation. "Their own rope. Now let's go upstairs again and go over it, piece by piece. It would have to have been someone who knew just the—"

240   The stair door closed behind them and their voices were lost.

The two women sat motionless, not looking at each other, but as if peering into something and at the same time holding back. When they spoke now it was as if they were afraid of what they were saying, but as if they could not help saying it.

"She liked the bird," said Martha Hale, low and slowly. "She was going to bury it in that pretty box."

"When I was a girl," said Mrs. Peters, under her breath, "my kitten—there was a boy took a hatchet, and before my eyes—before I could get there—" She covered her face an instant. "If they hadn't held me back I would have"—she caught herself, looked upstairs where footsteps were heard, and finished weakly—"hurt him."

Then they sat without speaking or moving.

245   "I wonder how it would seem," Mrs. Hale at last began, as if feeling her way over strange ground—"never to have had any children around?" Her eyes made a slow sweep of the kitchen, as if seeing what that kitchen had meant through all the years. "No, Wright wouldn't like the bird," she said after that—"a thing that sang. She used to sing. He killed that too." Her voice tightened.

Mrs. Peters moved uneasily.

"Of course we don't know who killed the bird."

"I knew John Wright," was Mrs. Hale's answer.

"It was an awful thing was done in this house that night, Mrs. Hale," said the sheriff's wife. "Killing a man while he slept—slipping a thing round his neck that choked the life out of him."

250   Mrs. Hale's hand went out to the bird-cage.

"His neck. Choked the life out of him."

"We don't *know* who killed him," whispered Mrs. Peters wildly. "We don't *know.*"

Mrs. Hale had not moved. "If there had been years and years of—nothing, then a bird to sing to you, it would be awful—still—after the bird was still."

It was as if something within her not herself had spoken, and it found in Mrs. Peters something she did not know as herself.

255   "I know what stillness is," she said, in a queer, monotonous voice. "When we homesteaded in Dakota, and my first baby died—after he was two years old—and me with no other then—"

Mrs. Hale stirred.

"How soon do you suppose they'll be through looking for the evidence?"

"I know what stillness is," repeated Mrs. Peters, in just that same way. Then she too pulled back. "The law has got to punish crime, Mrs. Hale," she said in her tight little way.

"I wish you'd seen Minnie Foster," was the answer, "when she wore a white dress with blue ribbons, and stood up there in the choir and sang."

260   The picture of that girl, the fact that she had lived neighbor to that girl for twenty years, and had let her die for lack of life, was suddenly more than she could bear.

"Oh, I *wish* I'd come over here once in a while!" she cried. "That was a crime! That was a crime. Who's going to punish that?"

"We mustn't take on," said Mrs. Peters, with a frightened look toward the stairs.

"I might 'a' *known* she needed help! I tell you, it's *queer,* Mrs. Peters. We live close together, and we live far apart. We all go through the same things—it's all just a different kind of the same thing! If it weren't—why do you and I *understand?* Why do we *know*—what we know this minute?"

She dashed her hand across her eyes. Then, seeing the jar of fruit on the table she reached for it and choked out:

265   "If I was you I wouldn't *tell* her her fruit was gone! Tell her it *ain't.* Tell her it's all right—all of it. Here—take this in to prove it to her! She—she may never know whether it was broke or not."

She turned away.

Mrs. Peters reached out for the bottle of fruit as if she were glad to take it—as if touching a familiar thing, having something to do, could keep her from something else. She got up, looked about for something to wrap the fruit in, took a petticoat from the pile of clothes she had brought from the front room, and nervously started winding that round the bottle.

"My!" she began, in a high, false voice, "it's a good thing the men couldn't hear us! Getting all stirred up over a little thing like a—dead canary." She hurried over that. "As if that could have anything to do with—with—My, wouldn't they *laugh?*"

Footsteps were heard on the stairs.

270   "Maybe they would," muttered Mrs. Hale—"maybe they wouldn't."

"No, Peters," said the county attorney incisively; "it's all perfectly clear, except the reason for doing it. But you know juries when it comes to women. If there was some definite thing—something to show. Something to make a story about. A thing that would connect up with this clumsy way of doing it."

In a covert way Mrs. Hale looked at Mrs. Peters. Mrs. Peters was looking at her. Quickly they looked away from each other. The outer door opened and Mr. Hale came in.

"I've got the team round now," he said. "Pretty cold out there."

"I'm going to stay here awhile by myself," the county attorney suddenly announced. "You can send Frank out for me, can't you?" he asked the sheriff. "I want to go over everything. I'm not satisfied we can't do better."

275   Again, for one brief moment, the two women's eyes found one another.

The sheriff came up to the table.

"Did you want to see what Mrs. Peters was going to take in?"

The county attorney picked up the apron. He laughed.

"Oh, I guess they're not very dangerous things the ladies have picked out."

280   Mrs. Hale's hand was on the sewing basket in which the box was concealed. She felt that she ought to take her hand off the basket. She did not seem able to. He picked up one of the quilt blocks which she had piled on to cover the box. Her eyes felt like fire. She had a feeling that if he took up the basket she would snatch it from him.

But he did not take it up. With another little laugh, he turned away, saying:

"No; Mrs. Peters doesn't need supervising. For that matter, a sheriff's wife is married to the law. Ever think of it that way, Mrs. Peters?"

Mrs. Peters was standing beside the table. Mrs. Hale shot a look up at her; but she could not see her face. Mrs. Peters had turned away. When she spoke, her voice was muffled.

"Not—just that way," she said.

285   "Married to the law!" chuckled Mrs. Peters' husband. He moved toward the door into the front room, and said to the county attorney:

"I just want you to come in here a minute, George. We ought to take a look at these windows."

"Oh—windows," said the county attorney scoffingly.

"We'll be right out, Mr. Hale," said the sheriff to the farmer, who was still waiting by the door.

Hale went to look after the horses. The sheriff followed the county attorney into the other room. Again—for one final moment—the two women were alone in that kitchen.

290   Martha Hale sprang up, her hands tight together, looking at that other woman, with whom it rested. At first she could not see her eyes, for the sheriff's wife had not turned back, since she turned away at that suggestion of being married to the law. But now Mrs. Hale made her turn back. Her eyes made her turn back. Slowly, unwillingly, Mrs. Peters turned her head until her eyes met the eyes of the other woman. There was a moment when they held each other in a steady, burning look in which there was no evasion or flinching. Then Martha Hale's eyes pointed the way to the basket in which was hidden the thing that would make certain the conviction of the other woman—that woman who was not there and yet who had been there with them all through the hour.

For a moment Mrs. Peters did not move. And then she did it. With a rush forward, she threw back the quilt pieces, got the box, tried to put it in her handbag. It was too big. Desperately she opened it, started to take the bird out. But there she broke—she could not touch the bird. She stood there helpless, foolish.

There was the sound of a knob turning in the inner door. Martha Hale snatched the box from the sheriff's wife, and got it in the pocket of her big coat just as the sheriff and the county attorney came back into the kitchen.

"Well, Henry," said the county attorney facetiously, "at least we found out that she was not going to quilt it. She was going to—what is it you call it, ladies?"

Mrs. Hale's hand was against the pocket of her coat.

295   "We call it—knot it, Mr. Henderson."

MAKING CONNECTIONS— "A JURY OF HER PEERS" AND "TRIFLES"

1. Which title do you prefer, "A Jury of Her Peers" or "Trifles"? Which one conveys more of the complexities of the conflict? The short story was published a year after the play. Does it show? Explain.

2. In many ways, the central characters of the short story and the play are John Wright and his wife, neither of whom appear in the story or onstage. What is the effect of learning about them through other characters? How would this story and play be different if they included the scenes leading up to the death of John Wright?

3. Why don't Mrs. Peters and Mrs. Hale reveal the evidence they discover? Do they think it would help or hinder Mrs. Wright's case?

4. If all the evidence were to come to light, do you think that it would matter whether or not Mrs. Wright were tried by a jury composed of all women versus a jury composed of all men? Explain.

5. Given the attitudes of the men, how would you describe the values of this culture? What are these women supposed to know? What do they really know?

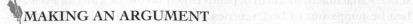

MAKING AN ARGUMENT

1. Which form, fiction or drama, do you prefer as the vehicle for this story? Why? What does one have that the other lacks? Do you think either could have been written more effectively? Analyze the effectiveness of each and write an argument in favor of one form or the other. Cite the text of both play and story to support your view.

❖ ESSAYS ❖

SEI SHŌNAGAN [c. 966–c. 1017]

Sei Shōnagan was a lady-in-waiting at the court of the Japanese empress during the end of the tenth century. Renowned for her beauty and wit, she left the court following the death of the empress and married a provincial governor. Following his death, she became a Buddhist nun. "A Lover's Departure" is taken from The Pillow Book, *her famous "notebook" filled with over three hundred entries made up of anecdotes, poems, and reflections of life in the royal court.*

A LOVER'S DEPARTURE   [c. 990]

A lover who is leaving at dawn announces that he has to find his fan and his paper. "I know I put them somewhere last night," he says. Since it is pitch dark, he gropes about the room, bumping into the furniture and muttering, "Strange! Where on earth can they be?" Finally he discovers the objects. He thrusts the paper into the breast of his robe with a great rustling sound; then he snaps open his fan and busily fans away with it. Only now is he ready to take his leave. What charmless behavior! "Hateful" is an understatement.

Equally disagreeable is the man who, when leaving in the middle of the night, takes care to fasten the cord of his headdress. This is quite unnecessary; he could perfectly well put it gently on his head without tying the cord. And why must he spend time adjusting his cloak or hunting costume? Does he really think someone may see him at this time of night and criticize him for not being impeccably dressed?

A good lover will behave as elegantly at dawn as at any other time. He drags himself out of bed with a look of dismay on his face. The lady urges him on: "Come, my friend, it's getting light. You don't want anyone to find you here." He gives a deep sigh, as if to say that the night has not been nearly long enough and that it is agony to leave. Once up, he does not instantly pull on his trousers. Instead he comes close to the lady and whispers whatever was left unsaid during the night. Even when he is dressed, he still lingers, vaguely pretending to be fastening his sash.

Presently he raises the lattice, and the two lovers stand together by the side door while he tells her how he dreads the coming day, which will keep them apart; then he slips away. The lady watches him go, and this moment of parting will remain among her most charming memories.

5   Indeed, one's attachment to a man depends largely on the elegance of his leave-taking. When he jumps out of bed, scurries about the room, tightly fastens his trouser-sash, rolls up the sleeves of his Court cloak, overrode, or hunting costume, stuffs his belongings into the breast of his robe and then briskly secures the outer sash—one really begins to hate him.

MAKING CONNECTIONS

1. This piece is more than a thousand years old. Does it seem old and out of date to you? Explain.
2. To what extent does this piece tell you as much about the narrator as about the subject she addresses? What is she like? How can you tell?

MAKING AN ARGUMENT

1. The narrator says that "one's attachment to a man depends largely on the elegance of his leave-taking." Can you think of other circumstances and behaviors that influence one's attachment to a person—man or woman? Write an essay that identifies a different circumstance and type of behavior and how it solidifies our "attachment"—or at least tells us a lot about the quality of a person.

VIRGINIA WOOLF   [1882–1941]

Virginia Woolf was born in London, England. Her father, Leslie Stephen, was a prominent scholar, and through him Woolf was introduced to many of the leading lights of the Victorian age. Unlike her brothers, who were sent to college, she was educated at home in her father's massive library. After his death, she and her sister, Vanessa Bell, moved to London, where they became the center of the so-called "Bloomsbury Group," informal gatherings of the era's most important intellectuals, including E. M. Forster and John Maynard Keynes. Throughout her life, Woolf was acutely aware of what she felt was the inferior status accorded her as a woman, and this theme runs throughout much of her work. A pioneer in the technique of "stream of consciousness," she is best known for her experimental novels, including Mrs. Dalloway *(1925),* To the Lighthouse *(1927),* Orlando *(1928), and* The Waves *(1931). After suffering a series of nervous breakdowns during which she feared she was going insane, Woolf committed suicide in 1941. "If Shakespeare Had a Sister" is taken from her 1929 classic feminist work,* A Room of One's Own.

IF SHAKESPEARE HAD A SISTER   [1929]

It would have been impossible, completely and entirely, for any woman to have written the plays of Shakespeare in the age of Shakespeare. Let me imagine, since facts are so hard to come by, what would have happened had Shakespeare had a wonderfully gifted sister, called Judith, let us say. Shakespeare himself went, very probably—his mother was an heiress—to the grammar school, where he may have learnt Latin—Ovid, Virgil and Horace—and the elements of grammar and logic. He was, it is well known, a wild boy who poached rabbits, perhaps shot a deer, and had, rather sooner than he should have done, to marry a woman in the neighborhood, who bore him a child rather quicker than was right. That escapade sent him to seek his fortune in London. He had, it seemed, a taste for the theatre; he began by holding horses at the stage door. Very soon he got work in the theatre, became a successful actor, and lived at the hub of the universe, meeting everybody, knowing everybody, practicing his art on the boards, exercising his wits in the streets, and even getting access to the palace of the queen. Meanwhile his extraordinarily gifted sister, let us suppose, remained at home. She was as adventurous, as imaginative, as agog to see the world as he was. But she was not sent to school. She had no chance of learning grammar and logic, let alone of reading Horace and Virgil. She picked up a book now and then, one of her brother's perhaps, and read a few pages. But then her parents came in and told her to mend the stockings or mind the stew and not moon about with books and papers. They would have spoken sharply but kindly, for they were substantial people who knew the conditions of life for a woman and loved their daughter—indeed, more likely than not she was the apple of her father's eye. Perhaps she scribbled some pages up in an apple loft on the sly, but was careful to hide them or set fire to them. Soon, however, before she was out of her teens, she was to be betrothed to the son of a neighboring woolstapler. She cried out that marriage was hateful to her, and for that she was severely beaten by her father. Then he ceased to scold her. He begged her instead not to hurt him, not to shame him in this matter of her marriage. He would give her a chain of beads or a fine petticoat, he said; and there were tears in his eyes. How could she disobey him? How could she break his heart? The force of her own gift alone drove her to it. She made up a small parcel of her belongings, let herself down by a rope one summer's night and took the road to London. She was not seventeen. The birds that sang in the hedge were not more musical than she was. She had the quickest fancy, a gift like her brother's, for the tune of words. Like him, she had a taste for the theatre. She stood at the stage door; she wanted to act, she said. Men laughed in her face. The manager—a fat, loose-lipped man—guffawed. He bellowed something about poodles dancing and women acting—no woman, he said, could possibly be an actress. He hinted—you can imagine what. She could get no training in her craft. Could she even seek her dinner in a tavern or roam the streets at midnight? Yet her genius was for fiction and lusted to feed abundantly upon the lives of men and women and the study of their ways. At last—for she was very young, oddly like Shakespeare the poet in her face, with the same grey eyes and rounded brows—at last Nick Greene the actor-manager took pity on her; she found herself with child by that gentleman and so—who shall measure the heat and violence of the poet's heart when caught and tangled in a woman's body?—killed herself one winter's night and lies buried at some crossroads where the omnibuses now stop outside the Elephant and Castle.

That, more or less, is how the story would run, I think, if a woman in Shakespeare's day had had Shakespeare's genius. But for my part, I agree with the deceased bishop, if such he was—it is unthinkable that any woman in Shakespeare's day should have had Shakespeare's genius. For genius like Shakespeare's is not born among labouring, uneducated, servile people. It was not born in England among the Saxons and the Britons. It is not born today among the working classes. How, then, could it have been born among women whose work began, according to Professor Trevelyan, almost before they were out of the nursery, who were forced to it by their parents and held to it by all the power of law and custom? Yet genius of a sort must have existed among women as it must have existed among the working classes. Now and again an Emily Brontë or a Robert Burns blazes out and proves its presence. But certainly it never got itself on to paper. When, however, one reads of a witch being ducked, of a woman possessed by devils, of a wise woman selling herbs, or even of a very remarkable man who had a mother, then I think we are on the track of a lost novelist, a suppressed poet, of some mute and inglorious Jane Austen, some Emily Brontë who dashed her brains out on the moor or mopped and mowed about the highways crazed with the torture that her gift had put her to. Indeed, I would venture to guess that Anon, who wrote so many poems without signing them, was often a woman.

MAKING CONNECTIONS

1. Why does Woolf create a sister for Shakespeare? What basic point is she trying to make?
2. In what ways does she indicate that Judith would have been deprived of the opportunities that William had?

MAKING AN ARGUMENT

1. If Shakespeare were alive today and had a sister, she could do whatever she wanted to. Or could she? Write an argument that agrees or disagrees with the proposition "Women today have equal opportunity to become or to do whatever their potential will allow." Cite evidence from your own knowledge and/or literature in this section or elsewhere to support your views.

CASE STUDY IN HISTORICAL CONTEXT

Women in Culture and History

The purpose of this case study is to provide you with material for a self-contained research unit. As outlined in Chapter 5, one popular area of literary research is inquiry into the social, historical, or cultural background of a work. The materials that follow contain a primary source—the play *A Doll's House*—and a number of secondary sources—a brief biography, the playwright's comments, a changed ending for one production, letters and articles that reflect the attitudes of that period, and an essay describing the plight of women over the last millennium. By themselves, or in combination with other sources, they provide a good resource for a research essay. The best literature has a universal, timeless quality. It speaks to us across time and culture and appeals to our humanity. Being aware of the historical and cultural context from which literature springs can enrich our understanding of it and lead to greater insight.

A number of the stories and plays in this section depict the lives of women in the late nineteenth and early twentieth centuries. Their actions and reactions are strongly motivated by the cultural imperatives of their time. Though we still struggle with issues of social justice at the beginning of the twenty-first century, it is impossible for us to fully appreciate the impact of these imperatives on people who lived in those times. But a look at some sample letters, notes, newspaper columns, and excerpts from speeches and essays—the historical and cultural artifacts—may give us a better feel for the assumptions about women that dominated that era.

With the exception of our final essay, "The Rest of the Story," published by Natalie Zemon Davis and Jill Ker Conway in 1999, all of the selections that follow are more than a century old. The letters of John and Abigail Adams are more than two hundred years old, and seem to draw the battle lines for the prolonged struggle for women's rights that followed. On the eve of one rebellion, Abigail Adams forecasts another if the men creating the new "code of laws" are not "more generous and favorable" to women than their ancestors have been. In its own way, each of the other selections acts for or against that rebellion. A German husband's letter to his uncooperative wife illustrates the righteousness and arrogance of the male role in marriage. Having severed one bond of slavery herself, Sojourner Truth encourages and inspires women to overcome another in her speech to a women's rights meeting in Ohio.

855

Adding to their other pieces in this section, Henrik Ibsen and Charlotte Perkins Gilman show us their views of women's rights from another angle. Ibsen's "notes" for the play *A Doll's House,* a changed ending he wrote reluctantly for a German production of the play, and his speech to the Norwegian League for Women's Rights inject some interesting complications into our understanding of his intentions. Charlotte Perkins Stetson (Gilman), writing in a very different voice than the speaker in her short story "The Yellow Wallpaper," makes her case for women's rights in an excerpt from her scholarly essay "Women and Economics."

Elizabeth Cady Stanton writes about the compelling need for women to be given their "birthright of self-sovereignty." And in the latest of the nineteenth-century pieces, two journalists, Wibur Fisk Tillet and Dorothy Dix, assess the progress made by women in the nineteenth century. Tillet believes much progress has been made—as long as women don't develop masculine qualities and wander outside the home. Dix, a pioneer advice-to-women columnist for a New Orleans newspaper, *The Daily Picayune,* is a bit more feisty and realistic with her assessment.

At the end of the nineteenth century, 134 years after Abigail Adams's letter, it's clear that her prophesied rebellion was still going strong. It's sobering to realize, however, that twenty more years would pass before women even had the right to vote.

In addition to the pieces that follow the play, you may inform your response further by reading Virginia Woolf's twentieth-century essay "If Shakespeare Had a Sister" on page 853. This essay complements and supports similar concerns expressed so long ago.

HENRIK IBSEN [1828–1906]

Henrik Ibsen was born in the seaport town of Skien, Norway. When he was still a child, his father, once a prosperous businessman, lost his fortune and the family was reduced to poverty. As a teenager, Ibsen was apprenticed to a pharmacist and briefly studied medicine, but soon found himself employed as a stage manager in a small regional theater. He turned to writing historical plays, and enjoyed some success. Moving to the capital city of Christiania (now Oslo), Ibsen managed the Norwegian Theater. When the theater failed in 1864, due in part to lack of government support, a disillusioned Ibsen left Norway and spent over twenty years living in continental Europe. His greatest plays, including A Doll's House, Ghosts, An Enemy of the People, The Wild Duck, *and* Hedda Gabler, *date to this period. These highly realistic plays revolutionized modern drama by wedding characters of psychological depth to thoughtful plots concerning the age's most pressing social problems. His later plays* John Gabriel Borkman *(1896) and* When We Dead Awaken *(1899), which he wrote after his triumphant return to Norway in 1891, were heavily symbolic and poetic. Ibsen suffered a stroke in 1900, which left him unable to write.*

A DOLL'S HOUSE   [1879]

Translated by James McFarlane

CHARACTERS

TORVALD HELMER, *A LAWYER*
NORA, *HIS WIFE*
DR. RANK
MRS. KRISTINE LINDE
NILS KROGSTAD
ANNE MARIE, *THE NURSEMAID*
HELENE, *THE MAID*
THE HELMERS' THREE CHILDREN
A PORTER

The action takes place in the Helmers' flat.

ACT I

A pleasant room, tastefully but not expensively furnished. On the back wall, one door on the right leads to the entrance hall, a second door on the left leads to HELMER'S *study. Between these two doors, a piano. In the middle of the left wall, a door; and downstage from it, a window. Near the window a round table with armchairs and a small sofa. In the right wall, upstage, a door; and on the same wall downstage, a porcelain stove with a couple of armchairs and a rocking chair. Between the stove and the door a small table. Etchings on the walls. A whatnot with china and other small objects d'art; a small bookcase with books in handsome bindings. Carpet on the floor; a fire burns in the stove. A winter's day.*

The front doorbell rings in the hall; a moment later, there is the sound of the front door being opened. NORA *comes into the room, happily humming to herself. She is dressed in her outdoor things, and is carrying lots of parcels which she then puts down on the table, right. She leaves the door into the hall standing open; a* PORTER *can be seen outside holding a Christmas tree and a basket; he hands them to the* MAID *who has opened the door for them.*

NORA: Hide the Christmas tree away carefully, Helene. The children mustn't see it
  till this evening when it's decorated. [*To the* Porter, *taking out her purse.*]
  How much?
PORTER: Fifty öre.
NORA: There's a crown. Keep the change.

"A Doll's House," © *James McFarlane 1961. Reprinted from* Henrik Ibsen: Four
Major Plays, *translated by James McFarlane and Jens Arup (Oxford World Classics,
1998.) By permission of Oxford University Press.*

[The PORTER *thanks her and goes.* NORA *shuts the door. She continues to laugh quietly and happily to herself as she takes off her things. She takes a bag of macaroons out of her pocket and eats one or two; then she walks stealthily across and listens at her husband's door.]*

NORA:　Yes, he's in.

[She begins humming again as she walks over to the table, right.]

HELMER *[in his study]*:　Is that my little skylark chirruping out there?

NORA *[busy opening some of the parcels]*:　Yes, it is.

HELMER:　Is that my little squirrel frisking about?

NORA:　Yes!

HELMER:　When did my little squirrel get home?

NORA:　Just this minute. *[She stuffs the bag of macaroons in her pocket and wipes her mouth.]* Come on out, Torvald, and see what I've bought.

HELMER:　I don't want to be disturbed! *[A moment later, he opens the door and looks out, his pen in his hand.]* "Bought," did you say? All that? Has my little spendthrift been out squandering money again?

NORA:　But, Torvald, surely this year we can spread ourselves just a little. This is the first Christmas we haven't had to go carefully.

HELMER:　Ah, but that doesn't mean we can afford to be extravagant, you know.

NORA:　Oh yes, Torvald, surely we can afford to be just a little bit extravagant now, can't we? Just a teeny-weeny bit. You are getting quite a good salary now, and you are going to earn lots and lots of money.

HELMER:　Yes, after the New Year. But it's going to be three whole months before the first pay cheque comes in.

NORA:　Pooh! We can always borrow in the meantime.

HELMER:　Nora! *[Crosses to her and takes her playfully by the ear.]* Here we go again, you and your frivolous ideas! Suppose I went and borrowed a thousand crowns today, and you went and spent it all over Christmas, then on New Year's Eve a slate fell and hit me on the head and there I was....

NORA *[putting her hand over his mouth]*:　Sh! Don't say such horrid things.

HELMER:　Yes, but supposing something like that did happen . . . what then?

NORA:　If anything as awful as that did happen, I wouldn't care if I owed anybody anything or not.

HELMER:　Yes, but what about the people I'd borrowed from?

NORA:　Them? Who cares about them! They are only strangers!

HELMER:　Nora, Nora! Just like a woman! Seriously though, Nora, you know what I think about these things. No debts! Never borrow! There's always something inhibited, something unpleasant, about a home built on credit and borrowed money. We two have managed to stick it out so far, and that's the way we'll go on for the little time that remains.

NORA *[walks over to the stove]*:　Very well, just as you say, Torvald.

HELMER [*following her*]:   There, there! My little singing bird mustn't go drooping her wings, eh? Has it got the sulks, that little squirrel of mine? [*Takes out his wallet.*] Nora, what do you think I've got here?

NORA [*quickly turning round*]:   Money!

HELMER: There! [*He hands her some notes*]. Good heavens, I know only too well how Christmas runs away with the housekeeping.

NORA [*counts*]:   Ten, twenty, thirty, forty. Oh, thank you, thank you, Torvald! This will see me quite a long way.

HELMER: Yes, it'll have to.

NORA: Yes, yes, I'll see that it does. But come over here, I want to show you all the things I've bought. And so cheap! Look, some new clothes for Ivar . . . and a little sword. There's a horse and a trumpet for Bob. And a doll and a doll's cot for Emmy. They are not very grand but she'll have them all broken before long anyway. And I've got some dress material and some handkerchiefs for the maids. Though, really, dear old Anne Marie should have had something better.

HELMER: And what's in this parcel here?

NORA [*shrieking*]:   No, Torvald! You mustn't see that till tonight!

HELMER: All right. But tell me now, what did my little spendthrift fancy for herself?

NORA: For me? Puh, I don't really want anything.

HELMER: Of course you do. Anything reasonable that you think you might like, just tell me.

NORA: Well, I don't really know. As a matter of fact, though, Torvald . . .

HELMER: Well?

NORA [*toying with his coat buttons, and without looking at him*]:   If you did want to give me something, you could . . . you could always. . .

HELMER: Well, well, out with it!

NORA [*quickly*]:   You could always give me money, Torvald. Only what you think you could spare. And then I could buy myself something with it later on.

HELMER: But Nora . . .

NORA: Oh, please, Torvald dear! Please! I beg you. Then I'd wrap the money up in some pretty gilt paper and hang it on the Christmas tree. Wouldn't that be fun?

HELMER: What do we call my pretty little pet when it runs away with all the money?

NORA: I know, I know, we call it a spendthrift. But please let's do what I said, Torvald. Then I'll have a bit of time to think about what I need most. Isn't that awfully sensible, now, eh?

HELMER [*smiling*]:   Yes, it is indeed—that is, if only you really could hold on to the money I gave you, and really did buy something for yourself with it. But it just gets mixed up with the housekeeping and frittered away on all sorts of useless things, and then I have to dig into my pocket all over again.

NORA: Oh but, Torvald. . . .

HELMER: You can't deny it, Nora dear. [*Puts his arm round her waist.*] My pretty little pet is very sweet, but it runs away with an awful lot of money. It's incredible how expensive it is for a man to keep such a pet.

NORA: For shame! How can you say such a thing? As a matter of fact I save everything I can.

HELMER [*laughs*]: Yes, you are right there. Everything you *can*. But you simply can't.

NORA [*hums and smiles quietly and happily*]: Ah, if you only knew how many expenses the likes of us skylarks and squirrels have, Torvald!

HELMER: What a funny little one you are! Just like your father. Always on the lookout for money, wherever you can lay your hands on it; but as soon as you've got it, it just seems to slip through your fingers. You never seem to know what you've done with it. Well, one must accept you as you are. It's in the blood. Oh yes, it is, Nora. That sort of thing is hereditary.

NORA: Oh, I only wish I'd inherited a few more of Daddy's qualities.

HELMER: And I wouldn't want my pretty little songbird to be the least bit different from what she is now. But come to think of it, you look rather . . . rather . . . how shall I put it? . . . rather guilty today. . . .

NORA: Do I?

HELMER: Yes, you do indeed. Look me straight in the eye.

NORA [*looks at him*]: Well?

HELMER [*wagging his finger at her*]: My little sweet-tooth surely didn't forget herself in town today?

NORA: No, whatever makes you think that?

HELMER: She didn't just pop into the confectioner's for a moment?

NORA: No, I assure you, Torvald . . . !

HELMER: Didn't try sampling the preserves?

NORA: No, really I didn't.

HELMER: Didn't go nibbling a macaroon or two?

NORA: No, Torvald, honestly, you must believe me . . . !

HELMER: All right then! It's really just my little joke. . . .

NORA [*crosses to the table*]: I would never dream of doing anything you didn't want me to.

HELMER: Of course not, I know that. And then you've given me your word. . . . [*Crosses to her.*] Well then, Nora dearest, you shall keep your little Christmas secrets. They'll all come out tonight, I dare say, when we light the tree.

NORA: Did you remember to invite Dr. Rank?

HELMER: No. But there's really no need. Of course he'll come and have dinner with us. Anyway, I can ask him when he looks in this morning. I've ordered some good wine. Nora, you can't imagine how I am looking forward to this evening.

NORA: So am I. And won't the children enjoy it, Torvald!

HELMER: Oh, what a glorious feeling it is, knowing you've got a nice, safe job, and a good fat income. Don't you agree? Isn't it wonderful, just thinking about it?

NORA: Oh, it's marvelous!

HELMER: Do you remember last Christmas? Three whole weeks beforehand you shut yourself up every evening till after midnight making flowers for the Christmas tree and all the other splendid things you wanted to surprise us with. Ugh, I never felt so bored in all my life.

NORA: I wasn't the least bit bored.

HELMER [*smiling*]:   But it turned out a bit of an anticlimax, Nora.

NORA: Oh, you are not going to tease me about that again! How was I to know the cat would get in and pull everything to bits?

HELMER: No, of course you weren't. Poor little Nora! All you wanted was for us to have a nice time—and it's the thought behind it that counts, after all. All the same, it's a good thing we've seen the back of those lean times.

NORA: Yes, really it's marvelous.

HELMER: Now there's no need for me to sit here all on my own, bored to tears. And you don't have to strain your dear little eyes, and work those dainty little fingers to the bone. . . .

NORA [*clapping her hands*]:   No, Torvald, I don't, do I? Not any more. Oh, how marvelous it is to hear that! [*Takes his arm.*] Now I want to tell you how I've been thinking we might arrange things, Torvald. As soon as Christmas is over. . . . [*The door-bell rings in the hall.*] Oh, there's the bell. [*Tidies one or two things in the room.*] It's probably a visitor. What a nuisance!

HELMER: Remember I'm not at home to callers.

MAID [*in the doorway*]:   There's a lady to see you, ma'am.

NORA: Show her in, please.

MAID [*to* HELMER]:   And the doctor's just arrived, too, sir.

HELMER: Did he go straight into my room?

MAID: Yes, he did, sir.

[HELMER *goes into his study. The* MAID *shows in* MRS. LINDE, *who is in traveling clothes, and closes the door after her.*]

MRS. LINDE [*subdued and rather hesitantly*]:   How do you do, Nora?

NORA [*uncertainly*]:   How do you do?

MRS. LINDE: I'm afraid you don't recognize me.

NORA: No, I don't think I . . . And yet I seem to . . .   [*Bursts out suddenly.*] Why! Kristine! Is it really you?

MRS. LINDE: Yes, it's me.

NORA: Kristine! Fancy not recognizing you again! But how was I to, when . . . [*Gently.*] How you've changed, Kristine!

MRS. LINDE: I dare say I have. In nine . . . ten years. . . .

NORA: Is it so long since we last saw each other? Yes, it must be. Oh, believe me these last eight years have been such a happy time. And now you've come up to town, too? All that long journey in wintertime. That took courage.

MRS. LINDE: I just arrived this morning on the steamer.

NORA: To enjoy yourself over Christmas, of course. How lovely! Oh, we'll have such fun, you'll see. Do take off your things. You are not cold, are you? [*Helps her.*] There now! Now let's sit down here in comfort beside the stove. No, here, you take the armchair, I'll sit here on the rocking chair. [*Takes her hands.*] Ah, now you look a bit more like your old self again. It was just that when I first saw you. . . . But you are a little paler, Kristine . . . and perhaps even a bit thinner!

MRS. LINDE: And much, much older, Nora.

NORA: Yes, perhaps a little older . . . very, very little, not really very much. [*Stops suddenly and looks serious.*] Oh, what a thoughtless creature I am, sitting here chattering on like this! Dear, sweet Kristine, can you forgive me?

MRS. LINDE: What do you mean, Nora?

NORA [*gently*]:   Poor Kristine, of course you're a widow now.

MRS. LINDE: Yes, my husband died three years ago.

NORA: Oh, I remember now. I read about it in the papers. Oh, Kristine, believe me I often thought at the time of writing to you. But I kept putting it off, something always seemed to crop up.

MRS. LINDE: My dear Nora, I understand so well.

NORA: No, it wasn't very nice of me, Kristine. Oh, you poor thing, what you must have gone through. And didn't he leave you anything?

MRS. LINDE: No.

NORA: And no children?

MRS. LINDE: No.

NORA: Absolutely nothing?

MRS. LINDE: Nothing at all . . . not even a broken heart to grieve over.

NORA [*looks at her incredulously*]:   But, Kristine, is that possible?

MRS. LINDE [*smiles sadly and strokes* NORA's *hair*]:   Oh, it sometimes happens, Nora.

NORA: So utterly alone. How terribly sad that must be for you. I have three lovely children. You can't see them for the moment, because they're out with their nanny. But now you must tell me all about yourself. . . .

MRS. LINDE: No, no, I want to hear about you.

NORA: No, you start. I won't be selfish today. I must think only about your affairs today. But there's just one thing I really must tell you. Have you heard about the great stroke of luck we've had in the last few days?

MRS. LINDE: No. What is it?

NORA: What do you think? My husband has just been made Bank Manager!

MRS. LINDE: Your husband? How splendid!

NORA: Isn't it tremendous! It's not a very steady way of making a living, you know, being a lawyer, especially if he refuses to take on anything that's the least bit shady—which of course is what Torvald does, and I think he's quite right. You can imagine how pleased we are! He starts at the Bank straight after New Year, and he's getting a big salary and lots of commission. From now on we'll be able to live quite differently . . . we'll do just what we want. Oh, Kristine, I'm so happy and relieved. I must say it's lovely to have plenty of money and not have to worry. Isn't it?

MRS. LINDE: Yes. It must be nice to have enough, at any rate.

NORA: No, not just enough, but pots and pots of money.

MRS. LINDE [*smiles*]:   Nora, Nora, haven't you learned any sense yet? At school you used to be an awful spendthrift.

NORA: Yes, Torvald still says I am. [*Wags her finger.*] But little Nora isn't as stupid as everybody thinks. Oh, we haven't really been in a position where I could afford to spend a lot of money. We've both had to work.

MRS. LINDE: You too?

NORA: Yes, odd jobs—sewing, crochetwork, embroidery and things like that. [*Casually.*] And one or two other things, besides. I suppose you know that Torvald left the Ministry when we got married. There weren't any prospects of promotion in his department, and of course he needed to earn more money than he had before. But the first year he wore himself out completely. He had to take on all kinds of extra jobs, you know, and he found himself working all hours of the day and night. But he couldn't go on like that; and he became seriously ill. The doctors said it was essential for him to go South.

MRS. LINDE: Yes, I believe you spent a whole year in Italy, didn't you?

NORA: That's right. It wasn't easy to get away, I can tell you. It was just after I'd had Ivar. But of course we had to go. Oh, it was an absolutely marvelous trip. And it saved Torvald's life. But it cost an awful lot of money, Kristine.

MRS. LINDE: That I can well imagine.

NORA: Twelve hundred dollars. Four thousand eight hundred crowns. That's a lot of money, Kristine.

MRS. LINDE: Yes, but in such circumstances, one is very lucky if one has it.

NORA: Well, we got it from Daddy, you see.

MRS. LINDE: Ah, that was it. It was just about then your father died, I believe, wasn't it?

NORA: Yes, Kristine, just about then. And do you know, I couldn't even go and look after him. Here was I expecting Ivar any day. And I also had poor Torvald, gravely ill, on my hands. Dear, kind Daddy! I never saw him again, Kristine. Oh, that's the saddest thing that has happened to me in all my married life.

MRS. LINDE: I know you were very fond of him. But after that you left for Italy?

NORA: Yes, we had the money then, and the doctors said it was urgent. We left a month later.

MRS. LINDE: And your husband came back completely cured?

NORA: Fit as a fiddle!

MRS. LINDE: But . . . what about the doctor?

NORA: How do you mean?

MRS. LINDE: I thought the maid said something about the gentleman who came at the same time as me being a doctor.

NORA: Yes, that was Dr. Rank. But this isn't a professional visit. He's our best friend and he always looks in at least once a day. No, Torvald has never had a day's illness since. And the children are fit and healthy, and so am I. [*Jumps up and claps her hands.*] Oh God, oh God, isn't it marvelous to be alive, and to be happy, Kristine! . . . Oh, but I ought to be ashamed of myself . . . Here I go on talking about nothing but myself. [*She sits on a low stool near* Mrs. Linde *and lays her arms on her lap.*] Oh, please, you mustn't be angry with me! Tell me, is it really true that you didn't love your husband? What made you marry him, then?

MRS. LINDE: My mother was still alive; she was bedridden and helpless. And then I had my two young brothers to look after as well. I didn't think I would be justified in refusing him.

NORA: No, I dare say you are right. I suppose he was fairly wealthy then?

MRS. LINDE: He was quite well off, I believe. But the business was shaky. When he died, it went all to pieces, and there just wasn't anything left.

NORA: What then?

MRS. LINDE: Well, I had to fend for myself, opening a little shop, running a little school, anything I could turn my hand to. These last three years have been one long relentless drudge. But now it's finished, Nora. My poor dear mother doesn't need me any more, she's passed away. Nor the boys either; they're at work now, they can look after themselves.

NORA: What a relief you must find it. . . .

MRS. LINDE: No, Nora! Just unutterably empty. Nobody to live for any more. [*Stands up restless.*] That's why I couldn't stand it any longer being cut off up there. Surely it must be a bit easier here to find something to occupy your mind. If only I could manage to find a steady job of some kind, in an office perhaps. . . .

NORA: But, Kristine, that's terribly exhausting; and you look so worn out even before you start. The best thing for you would be a little holiday at some quiet little resort.

MRS. LINDE [*crosses to the window*]:   I haven't any father I can fall back on for the money, Nora.

NORA [*rises*]:   Oh, please, you mustn't be angry with me!

MRS. LINDE [*goes to her*]:   My dear Nora, you mustn't be angry with me either. That's the worst thing about people in my position, they become so bitter. One has nobody to work for, yet one has to be on the look-out all the time. Life has to go on, and one starts thinking only of oneself. Believe it or not, when you told me the good news about your step up, I was pleased not so much for your sake as for mine.

NORA: How do you mean? Ah, I see. You think Torvald might be able to do something for you.

MRS. LINDE: Yes, that's exactly what I thought.

NORA: And so he shall, Kristine. Just leave things to me. I'll bring it up so cleverly . . . I'll think up something to put him in a good mood. Oh, I do so much want to help you.

MRS. LINDE: It is awfully kind of you, Nora, offering to do all this for me, particularly in your case, where you haven't known much trouble or hardship in your own life.

NORA: When I . . . ? I haven't known much . . . ?

MRS. LINDE [*smiling*]:   Well, good heavens, a little bit of sewing to do and a few things like that. What a child you are, Nora!

NORA [*tosses her head and walks across the room*]:   I wouldn't be too sure of that, if I were you.

MRS. LINDE: Oh?

NORA: You're just like the rest of them. You all think I'm useless when it comes to anything really serious. . . .

MRS. LINDE: Come, come. . . .

NORA: You think I've never had anything much to contend with in this hard world.

MRS. LINDE: Nora dear, you've only just been telling me all the things you've had to put up with.

NORA: Pooh! They were just trivialities! [*Softly.*] I haven't told you about the really big thing.

MRS. LINDE: What big thing? What do you mean?

NORA: I know you rather tend to look down on me, Kristine. But you shouldn't, you know. You are proud of having worked so hard and so long for your mother.

MRS. LINDE: I'm sure I don't look down on anybody. But it's true what you say: I am both proud and happy when I think of how I was able to make Mother's life a little easier towards the end.

NORA: And you are proud when you think of what you have done for your brothers, too.

MRS. LINDE: I think I have every right to be.

NORA: I think so too. But now I'm going to tell you something, Kristine. I too have something to be proud and happy about.

MRS. LINDE: I don't doubt that. But what is it you mean?

NORA: Not so loud. Imagine if Torvald were to hear! He must never on any account . . . nobody must know about it, Kristine, nobody but you.

MRS. LINDE: But what is it?

NORA: Come over here. [*She pulls her down on the sofa beside her.*] Yes, Kristine, I too have something to be proud and happy about. I was the one who saved Torvald's life.

MRS. LINDE: Saved. . . ? How. . . ?

NORA: I told you about our trip to Italy. Torvald would never have recovered but for that. . . .

MRS. LINDE: Well? Your father gave you what money was necessary. . . .

NORA [*smiles*]:   That's what Torvald thinks, and everybody else. But. . .

MRS. LINDE: But . . . ?

NORA: Daddy never gave us a penny. I was the one who raised the money.

MRS. LINDE: You? All that money?

NORA: Twelve hundred dollars. Four thousand eight hundred crowns. What do
   you say to that!

MRS. LINDE: But, Nora, how was it possible? Had you won a sweepstake or something?

NORA [*contemptuously*]: A sweepstake? Pooh! There would have been nothing to
   it then.

MRS. LINDE: Where did you get it from, then?

NORA [*hums and smiles secretively*]: H'm, tra-la-la!

MRS. LINDE: Because what you couldn't do was borrow it.

NORA: Oh? Why not?

MRS. LINDE: Well, a wife can't borrow without her husband's consent.

NORA [*tossing her head*]: Ah, but when it happens to be a wife with a bit of a sense
   for business . . . a wife who knows her way about things, then. . . .

MRS. LINDE: But, Nora, I just don't understand. . . .

NORA: You don't have to. I haven't said I did borrow the money. I might have got
   it some other way. [*Throws herself back on the sofa.*] I might even have got it
   from some admirer. Anyone as reasonably attractive as I am. . . .

MRS. LINDE: Don't be so silly!

NORA: Now you must be dying of curiosity, Kristine.

MRS. LINDE: Listen to me now, Nora dear—you haven't done anything rash, have
   you?

NORA [*sitting up again*]: Is it rash to save your husband's life?

MRS. LINDE: I think it was rash to do anything without telling him. . . .

NORA: But the whole point was that he mustn't know anything. Good heavens,
   can't you see! He wasn't even supposed to know how desperately ill he was.
   It was me the doctors came and told his life was in danger, that the only way
   to save him was to go South for a while. Do you think I didn't try talking him
   into it first? I began dropping hints about how nice it would be if I could be
   taken on a little trip abroad, like other young wives. I wept, I pleaded. I told
   him he ought to show some consideration for my condition, and let me have
   a bit of my own way. And then I suggested he might take out a loan. But at that
   he nearly lost his temper, Kristine. He said I was being frivolous, that it was his
   duty as a husband not to give in to all these whims and fancies of mine—as I
   do believe he called them. All right, I thought, somehow you've got to be
   saved. And it was then I found a way. . . .

MRS. LINDE: Did your husband never find out from your father that the money
   hadn't come from him?

NORA: No, never. It was just about the time Daddy died. I'd intended letting him into
   the secret and asking him not to give me away. But when he was so ill . . . I'm
   sorry to say it never became necessary.

MRS. LINDE: And you never confided in your husband?

NORA: Good heavens, how could you ever imagine such a thing! When he's so
   strict about such matters! Besides, Torvald is a man with a good deal of pride—

it would be terribly embarrassing and humiliating for him if he thought he owed anything to me. It would spoil everything between us; this happy home of ours would never be the same again.

MRS. LINDE: Are you never going to tell him?

NORA [*reflectively, half smiling*]:   Oh yes, some day perhaps . . . in many years time, when I'm no longer as pretty as I am now. You mustn't laugh! What I mean of course is when Torvald isn't quite so much in love with me as he is now, when he's lost interest in watching me dance, or get dressed up, or recite. Then it might be a good thing to have something in reserve. . . . [*Breaks off.*] What nonsense! That day will never come. Well, what have you got to say to my big secret, Kristine? Still think I'm not much good for anything? One thing, though, it's meant a lot of worry for me, I can tell you. It hasn't always been easy to meet my obligations when the time came. You know in business there is something called quarterly interest, and other things called installments, and these are always terribly difficult things to cope with. So what I've had to do is save a little here and there, you see, wherever I could. I couldn't really save anything out of the housekeeping, because Torvald has to live in decent style. I couldn't let the children go about badly dressed either—I felt any money I got for them had to go on them alone. Such sweet little things!

MRS. LINDE: Poor Nora! So it had to come out of your own allowance?

NORA: Of course. After all, I was the one it concerned most. Whenever Torvald gave me money for new clothes and such-like, I never spent more than half. And always I bought the simplest and cheapest things. It's a blessing most things look well on me, so Torvald never noticed anything. But sometimes I did feel it was a bit hard, Kristine, because it is nice to be well dressed, isn't it?

MRS. LINDE: Yes, I suppose it is.

NORA: I have had some other sources of income, of course. Last winter I was lucky enough to get quite a bit of copying to do. So I shut myself up every night and sat and wrote through to the small hours of the morning. Oh, sometimes I was so tired, so tired. But it was tremendous fun all the same, sitting there working and earning money like that. It was almost like being a man.

MRS. LINDE: And how much have you been able to pay off like this?

NORA: Well, I can't tell exactly. It's not easy to know where you are with transactions of this kind, you understand. All I know is I've paid off just as much as I could scrape together. Many's the time I was at my wit's end. [*Smiles.*] Then I used to sit here and pretend that some rich old gentleman had fallen in love with me. . . .

MRS. LINDE: What! What gentleman?

NORA: Oh, rubbish! . . . and that now he had died, and when they opened his will, there in big letters were the words; "My entire fortune is to be paid over, immediately and in cash, to charming Mrs. Nora Helmer."

MRS. LINDE: But my dear Nora—who is this man?

NORA: Good heavens, don't you understand? There never was any old gentleman; it was just something I used to sit here pretending, time and time again, when I didn't know where to turn next for money. But it doesn't make very much difference; as far as I'm concerned, the old boy can do what he likes, I'm tired of him; I can't be bothered any more with him or his will. Because now all my worries are over. [*Jumping up.*] Oh God, what a glorious thought, Kristine! No more worries! Just think of being without a care in the world . . . being able to romp with the children, and making the house nice and attractive, and having things just as Torvald likes to have them! And then spring will soon be here, and blue skies. And maybe we can go away somewhere. I might even see something of the sea again. Oh, yes! When you're happy, life is a wonderful thing!

[The doorbell is heard in the hall.]

MRS. LINDE [*gets up*]:   There's the bell. Perhaps I'd better go.

NORA: No, do stay, please. I don't suppose it's for me; it's probably somebody for Torvald. . .

MAID [*in the doorway*]:   Excuse me, ma'am, but there's a gentleman here wants to see Mr. Helmer, and I didn't quite know . . . because the doctor is in there. . . .

NORA: Who is the gentleman?

KROGSTAD [*in the doorway*]:   It's me, Mrs. Helmer.

[MRS. LINDE starts, then turns away to the window.]

NORA [*tense, takes a step towards him and speaks in a low voice*]:   You? What is it? What do you want to talk to my husband about?

KROGSTAD: Bank matters . . . in a manner of speaking. I work at the bank, and I hear your husband is to be the new manager. . . .

NORA: So it's. . .

KROGSTAD: Just routine business matters, Mrs. Helmer. Absolutely nothing else.

NORA: Well then, please go into his study.

[She nods impassively and shuts the hall door behind him; then she walks across and sees to the stove.]

MRS. LINDE: Nora . . . who was that man?

NORA: His name is Krogstad.

MRS. LINDE: So it really was him.

NORA: Do you know the man?

MRS. LINDE: I used to know him . . . a good many years ago. He was a solicitor's clerk in our district for a while.

NORA: Yes, so he was.

MRS. LINDE: How he's changed!

NORA: His marriage wasn't a very happy one, I believe.

MRS. LINDE: He's a widower now, isn't he?

NORA: With a lot of children. There, it'll burn better now.

[She closes the stove door and moves the rocking chair a little to one side.]

MRS. LINDE: He does a certain amount of business on the side, they say?

NORA: Oh? Yes, it's always possible. I just don't know. . . . But let's not think about business . . . it's all so dull.

*[*DR. RANK *comes in from* HELMER'S *study.]*

DR. RANK *[still in the doorway]*:   No, no, Torvald, I won't intrude. I'll just look in on your wife for a moment. *[Shuts the door and notices* MRS. LINDE.*]* Oh, I beg your pardon. I'm afraid I'm intruding here as well.

NORA: No, not at all! *[Introduces them.]* Dr. Rank . . . Mrs. Linde.

RANK: Ah! A name I've often heard mentioned in this house. I believe I came past you on the stairs as I came in.

MRS. LINDE: I have to take things slowly going upstairs. I find it rather a trial.

RANK: Ah, some little disability somewhere, eh?

MRS. LINDE: Just a bit run down, I think, actually.

RANK: Is that all? Then I suppose you've come to town for a good rest—doing the rounds of the parties?

MRS. LINDE: I have come to look for work.

RANK: Is that supposed to be some kind of sovereign remedy for being run down?

MRS. LINDE: One must live, Doctor.

RANK: Yes, it's generally thought to be necessary.

NORA: Come, come, Dr. Rank. You are quite as keen to live as anybody.

RANK: Quite keen, yes. Miserable as I am, I'm quite ready to let things drag on as long as possible. All my patients are the same. Even those with a moral affliction are no different. As a matter of fact, there's a bad case of that kind in talking with Helmer at this very moment. . .

MRS. LINDE *[softly]*:   Ah!

NORA: Whom do you mean?

RANK: A person called Krogstad—nobody you would know. He's rotten to the core. But even he began talking about having to *live,* as though it were something terribly important.

NORA: Oh? And what did he want to talk to Torvald about?

RANK: I honestly don't know. All I heard was something about the Bank.

NORA: I didn't know that Krog . . . that this Mr. Krogstad had anything to do with the Bank.

RANK: Oh yes, he's got some kind of job down there. *[To* Mrs. Linde.*]* I wonder if you've got people in your part of the country too who go rushing round sniffing out cases of moral corruption, and then installing the individuals concerned in nice, well-paid jobs where they can keep them under observation. Sound, decent people have to be content to stay out in the cold.

MRS. LINDE: Yet surely it's the sick who most need to be brought in.

RANK *[shrugs his shoulders]*:   Well, there we have it. It's that attitude that's turning society into a clinic.

[NORA, *lost in her own thoughts, breaks into smothered laughter and claps her hands.*]

RANK: Why are you laughing at that? Do you know in fact what society is?

NORA: What do I care about your silly old society? I was laughing about something quite different . . . something frightfully funny. Tell me, Dr. Rank, are all the people who work at the Bank dependent on Torvald now?

RANK: Is that what you find so frightfully funny?

NORA [*smiles and hums*]:   Never you mind! Never you mind! [*Walks about the room.*] Yes, it really is terribly amusing to think that we . . . that Torvald now has power over so many people. [*She takes the bag out of her pocket.*] Dr. Rank, what about a little macaroon?

RANK: Look at this, eh? Macaroons. I thought they were forbidden here.

NORA: Yes, but these are some Kristine gave me.

MRS. LINDE: What? I . . . ?

NORA: Now, now, you needn't be alarmed. You weren't to know that Torvald had forbidden them. He's worried in case they ruin my teeth, you know. Still . . . what's it matter once in a while! Don't you think so, Dr. Rank? Here! [*She pops a macaroon into his mouth.*] And you too, Kristine. And I shall have one as well; just a little one . . . or two at the most. [*She walks about the room again.*] Really I am so happy. There's just one little thing I'd love to do now.

RANK: What's that?

NORA: Something I'd love to say in front of Torvald.

RANK: Then why can't you?

NORA: No, I daren't. It's not very nice.

MRS. LINDE: Not very nice?

RANK: Well, in that case it might not be wise. But to us, I don't see why . . . What is this you would love to say in front of Helmer?

NORA: I would simply love to say: "Damn."

RANK: Are you mad!

MRS. LINDE: Good gracious, Nora . . . !

RANK: Say it! Here he is!

NORA [*hiding the bag of macaroons*]:   Sh! Sh!

[HELMER *comes out of his room, his overcoat over his arm and his hat in his hand.*]

NORA [*going over to him*]:   Well, Torvald dear, did you get rid of him?

HELMER: Yes, he's just gone.

NORA: Let me introduce you. This is Kristine, who has just arrived in town . . . .

HELMER: Kristine . . . ? You must forgive me, but I don't think I know . . .

NORA: Mrs. Linde, Torvald dear. Kristine Linde.

HELMER: Ah, indeed. A school friend of my wife's, presumably.

MRS. LINDE: Yes, we were girls together.

NORA: Fancy, Torvald, she's come all this long way just to have a word with you.

HELMER: How is that?

MRS. LINDE: Well, it wasn't really. . . .

NORA: The thing is, Kristine is terribly clever at office work, and she's frightfully keen on finding a job with some efficient man, so that she can learn even more . . . .

HELMER: Very sensible, Mrs. Linde.

NORA: And then when she heard you'd been made Bank Manager—there was a bit in the paper about it—she set off at once. Torvald please! You *will* try and do something for Kristine, won't you? For my sake?

HELMER: Well, that's not altogether impossible. You are a widow, I presume?

MRS. LINDE: Yes.

HELMER: And you've had some experience in business?

MRS. LINDE: A fair amount.

HELMER: Well, it's quite probable I can find you a job, I think . . . .

NORA [*clapping her hands*]:   There, you see!

HELMER: You have come at a fortunate moment, Mrs. Linde . . .

MRS. LINDE: Oh, how can I ever thank you . . . ?

HELMER: Not a bit. [*He puts on his overcoat.*] But for the present I must ask you to excuse me. . . .

RANK: Wait. I'm coming with you.

[*He fetches his fur coat from the hall and warms it at the stove.*]

NORA: Don't be long, Torvald dear.

HELMER: Not more than an hour, that's all.

NORA: Are you leaving too, Kristine?

MRS. LINDE [*putting on her things*]:   Yes, I must go and see if I can't find myself a room.

HELMER: Perhaps we can all walk down the road together.

NORA [*helping her*]:   What a nuisance we are so limited for space here. I'm afraid it just isn't possible . . . .

MRS. LINDE: Oh, you mustn't dream of it! Goodbye, Nora dear, and thanks for everything.

NORA: Goodbye for the present. But . . . you'll be coming back this evening, of course. And you too, Dr. Rank? What's that? If you are up to it? Of course you'll be up to it. Just wrap yourself up well.

[*They go out, talking, into the hall; children's voices can be heard on the stairs.*]

NORA: Here they are! Here they are! [*She runs to the front door and opens it. Anne Marie, the nursemaid, enters with* THE CHILDREN.] Come in! Come in! [*She bends down and kisses them.*] Ah! my sweet little darlings. . . . You see them, Kristine? Aren't they lovely!

RANK: Don't stand here chattering in this draught!

HELMER: Come along, Mrs. Linde. The place now becomes unbearable for anybody except mothers.

[DR. RANK, HELMER and MRS. LINDE go down the stairs: the NURSEMAID comes into the room with THE CHILDREN, then NORA, shutting the door behind her.]

NORA: How fresh and bright you look! My, what red cheeks you've got! Like apples and roses. [*During the following, the children keep chattering away to her.*] Have you had a nice time? That's splendid. And you gave Emmy and Bob a ride on your sledge? Did you now! Both together! Fancy that! There's a clever boy, Ivar. Oh, let me take her a little while, Anne Marie. There's my sweet little baby-doll! [*She takes the youngest of THE CHILDREN from the NURSEMAID and dances with her.*] All right, Mummy will dance with Bobby too. What? You've been throwing snowballs? Oh, I wish I'd been there. No, don't bother, Anne Marie, I'll help them off with their things. No, please, let me—I like doing it. You go on in, you look frozen. You'll find some hot coffee on the stove. [*The NURSEMAID goes into the room, left. NORA takes off THE CHILDREN's coats and hats and throws them down anywhere, while THE CHILDREN all talk at once.*] Really! A great big dog came running after you? But he didn't bite. No, the doggies wouldn't bite my pretty little dollies. You mustn't touch the parcels, Ivar! What are they? Wouldn't you like to know! No, no, that's nasty. Now? Shall we play something? What shall we play? Hide and seek? Yes, let's play hide and seek. Bob can hide first. Me first? All right, let me hide first.

[She and THE CHILDREN play, laughing and shrieking, in this room and in the adjacent room on the right. Finally NORA hides under the table; THE CHILDREN come rushing in to look for her but cannot find her; they hear her stifled laughter, rush to the table, lift up the tablecloth and find her. Tremendous shouts of delight. She creeps out and pretends to frighten them. More shouts. Meanwhile there has been a knock at the front door, which nobody has heard. The door half opens, and Krogstad can be seen. He waits a little; the game continues.]

KROGSTAD: I beg your pardon, Mrs. Helmer . . . .

NORA [*turns with a stifled cry and half jumps up*]:   Ah! What do you want?

KROGSTAD: Excuse me. The front door was standing open. Somebody must have forgotten to shut it . . . .

NORA [*standing up*]:   My husband isn't at home, Mr. Krogstad.

KROGSTAD: I know.

NORA: Well . . . what are you doing here?

KROGSTAD: I want a word with you.

NORA: With . . . ? [*Quietly, to THE CHILDREN.*] Go to Anne Marie. What? No, the strange man won't do anything to Mummy. When he's gone we'll have another game. [*She leads THE CHILDREN into the room, left, and shuts the door after them; tense and uneasy.*] You want to speak to me?

KROGSTAD: Yes, I do.

NORA: Today? But it isn't the first of the month yet . . . .

KROGSTAD: No, it's Christmas Eve. It depends entirely on you what sort of Christmas you have.

NORA: What do you want? Today I can't possibly. . . .

KROGSTAD: Let's not talk about that for the moment. It's something else. You've got a moment to spare?

NORA: Yes, I suppose so, though. . . .

KROGSTAD: Good. I was sitting in Olsen's café, and I saw your husband go down the road. . .

NORA: Did you?

KROGSTAD: . . . with a lady.

NORA: Well?

KROGSTAD: May I be so bold as to ask whether that lady was a Mrs. Linde?

NORA: Yes.

KROGSTAD: Just arrived in town?

NORA: Yes, today.

KROGSTAD: And she's a good friend of yours?

NORA: Yes, she is. But I can't see . . .

KROGSTAD: I also knew her once.

NORA: I know.

KROGSTAD: Oh? So you know all about it. I thought as much. Well, I want to ask you straight: is Mrs. Linde getting a job in the Bank?

NORA: How dare you cross-examine me like this, Mr. Krogstad? You, one of my husband's subordinates? But since you've asked me, I'll tell you. Yes, Mrs. Linde has got a job. And I'm the one who got it for her, Mr. Krogstad. Now you know.

KROGSTAD: So my guess was right.

NORA [*walking up and down*]:   Oh, I think I can say that some of us have a little influence now and again. Just because one happens to be a woman, that doesn't mean. . . . People in subordinate positions, ought to take care they don't offend anybody . . . who . . . him . . . .

KROGSTAD: . . . has influence?

NORA: Exactly.

KROGSTAD [*changing his tone*]:   Mrs. Helmer, will you have the goodness to use your influence on my behalf?

NORA: What? What do you mean?

KROGSTAD: Will you be so good as to see that I keep my modest little job at the Bank?

NORA: What do you mean? Who wants to take it away from you?

KROGSTAD: Oh, you needn't try and pretend to me you don't know. I can quite see that this friend of yours isn't particularly anxious to bump up against me. And I can also see now whom I can thank for being given the sack.

NORA: But I assure you. . . .

KROGSTAD: All right, all right. But to come to the point: there's still time. And I advise you to use your influence to stop it.

NORA: But, Mr. Krogstad, I *have* no influence.

KROGSTAD: Haven't you? I thought just now you said yourself . . .

NORA: I didn't mean it that way, of course. Me? What makes you think I've got any influence of that kind over my husband?

KROGSTAD: I know your husband from our student days. I don't suppose he is any more steadfast than other married men.

NORA: You speak disrespectfully of my husband like that and I'll show you the door.

KROGSTAD: So the lady's got courage.

NORA: I'm not frightened of you any more. After New Year's I'll soon be finished with the whole business.

KROGSTAD [*controlling himself*]:   Listen to me, Mrs. Helmer. If necessary I shall fight for my little job in the Bank as if I were fighting for my life.

NORA: So it seems.

KROGSTAD: It's not just for the money, that's the last thing I care about. There's something else . . . well, I might as well out with it. You see it's like this. You know as well as anybody that some years ago I got myself mixed up in a bit of trouble.

NORA: I believe I've heard something of the sort.

KROGSTAD: It never got as far as the courts; but immediately it was as if all paths were barred to me. So I started going in for the sort of business you know about. I had to do something, and I think I can say I haven't been one of the worst. But now I have to get out of it. My sons are growing up; for their sake I must try and win back what respectability I can. That job in the Bank was like the first step on the ladder for me. And now your husband wants to kick me off the ladder again, back into the mud.

NORA: But in God's name, Mr. Krogstad, it's quite beyond my power to help you.

KROGSTAD: That's because you haven't the will to help me. But I have ways of making you.

NORA: You wouldn't go and tell my husband I owe you money?

KROGSTAD: Suppose I did tell him?

NORA: It would be a rotten shame. [*Half choking with tears.*] That secret is all my pride and joy—why should he have to hear about it in this nasty, horrid way . . . hear about it from *you*. You would make things horribly unpleasant for me. . . .

KROGSTAD: Merely unpleasant?

NORA [*vehemently*]:   Go on, do it then! It'll be all the worse for you. Because then my husband will see for himself what a bad man you are, and then you certainly won't be able to keep your job.

KROGSTAD: I asked whether it was only a bit of domestic unpleasantness you were afraid of?

NORA: If my husband gets to know about it, he'll pay off what's owing at once. And then we'd have nothing more to do with you.

KROGSTAD [*taking a pace towards her*]:   Listen, Mrs. Helmer, either you haven't a very good memory, or else you don't understand much about business. I'd better make the position a little bit clearer for you.

NORA: How do you mean?

KROGSTAD: When your husband was ill, you came to me for the loan of twelve hundred dollars.

NORA: I didn't know of anybody else.

KROGSTAD: I promised to find you the money. . . .

NORA: And you did find it.

KROGSTAD: I promised to find you the money on certain conditions. At the time you were so concerned about your husband's illness, and so anxious to get the money for going away with, that I don't think you paid very much attention to all the incidentals. So there is perhaps some point in reminding you of them. Well, I promised to find you the money against an IOU which I drew up for you.

NORA: Yes, and which I signed.

KROGSTAD: Very good. But below that I added a few lines, by which your father was to stand security. This your father was to sign.

NORA: Was to . . . ? He did sign it.

KROGSTAD: I had left the date blank. The idea was that your father was to add the date himself when he signed it. Remember?

NORA: Yes, I think. . . .

KROGSTAD: I then gave you the IOU to post to your father. Wasn't that so?

NORA: Yes.

KROGSTAD: Which of course you did at once. Because only about five or six days later you brought it back to me with your father's signature. I then paid out the money.

NORA: Well? Haven't I paid the installments regularly?

KROGSTAD: Yes, fairly. But . . . coming back to what we were talking about . . . that was a pretty bad period you were going through then, Mrs. Helmer.

NORA: Yes, it was.

KROGSTAD: Your father was seriously ill, I believe.

NORA: He was very near the end.

KROGSTAD: And died shortly afterwards?

NORA: Yes.

KROGSTAD: Tell me, Mrs. Helmer, do you happen to remember which day your father died? The exact date, I mean.

NORA: Daddy died on 29 September.

KROGSTAD: Quite correct. I made some inquiries. Which brings up a rather curious point [*takes out a paper*] which I simply cannot explain.

NORA: Curious . . . ? I don't know . . .

KROGSTAD: The curious thing is, Mrs. Helmer, that your father signed this document three days after his death.

NORA: What? I don't understand. . . .

KROGSTAD: Your father died on 29 September. But look here. Your father has dated his signature 2 October. Isn't that rather curious, Mrs. Helmer? [Nora *remains silent.*] It's also remarkable that the words '2 October' and the year are not in your father's handwriting, but in a handwriting I rather think I recognize. Well, perhaps that could be explained. Your father might have forgotten to date his signature, and then somebody else might have made a guess at the date later, before the fact of your father's death was known. There is nothing wrong in that. What really matters is the signature. And *that* is of course genuine, Mrs. Helmer? It really was your father who wrote his name here?

NORA [*after a moment's silence, throws her head back and looks at him defiantly*]:   No, it wasn't. It was me who signed father's name.

KROGSTAD: Listen to me. I suppose you realize that that is a very dangerous confession?

NORA: Why? You'll soon have all your money back.

KROGSTAD: Let me ask you a question: why didn't you send that document to your father?

NORA: It was impossible. Daddy was ill. If I'd asked him for his signature, I'd have to tell him what the money was for. Don't you see, when he was as ill as that I couldn't go and tell him that my husband's life was in danger. It was simply impossible.

KROGSTAD: It would have been better for you if you had abandoned the whole trip.

NORA: No, that was impossible. This was the thing that was to save my husband's life. I couldn't give it up.

KROGSTAD: But did it never strike you that this was fraudulent . . . ?

NORA: That wouldn't have meant anything to me. Why should I worry about you? I couldn't stand you, not when you insisted on going through with all those cold-blooded formalities, knowing all the time what a critical state my husband was in.

KROGSTAD: Mrs. Helmer, it's quite clear you still haven't the faintest idea what it is you've committed. But let me tell you, my own offence was no more and no worse than that, and it ruined my entire reputation.

NORA: You? Are you trying to tell me that you once risked everything to save your wife's life?

KROGSTAD: The law takes no account of motives.

NORA: Then they must be very bad laws.

KROGSTAD: Bad or not, if I produce this document in court, you'll be condemned according to them.

NORA: I don't believe it. Isn't a daughter entitled to try and save her father from worry and anxiety on his deathbed? Isn't a wife entitled to save her husband's life? I might not know very much about the law, but I feel sure of one thing: it must say somewhere that things like this are allowed. You mean to say you don't know that—you, when it's your job? You must be a rotten lawyer, Mr. Krogstad.

KROGSTAD: That may be. But when it comes to business transactions—like the sort between us two—perhaps you'll admit I know something about them? Good.

Now you must please yourself. But I tell you this: if I'm pitched out a second time, you are going to keep me company.

[He bows and goes out through the hall.]

NORA [*stands thoughtfully for a moment, then tosses her head*]:   Rubbish! He's just trying to scare me. I'm not such a fool as all that. [*Begins gathering up* THE CHILDREN's *clothes; after a moment she stops.*] Yet . . . ? No, it's impossible! I did it for love, didn't I?

THE CHILDREN [*in the doorway, left*]:   Mummy, the gentleman's just gone out of the gate.

NORA: Yes, I know. But you mustn't say anything to anybody about that gentleman. You hear? Not even to Daddy!

THE CHILDREN: All right, Mummy. Are you going to play again?

NORA: No, not just now.

THE CHILDREN: But Mummy, you promised!

NORA: Yes, but I can't just now. Off you go now, I have a lot to do. Off you go, my darlings. [*She herds them carefully into the other room and shuts the door behind them. She sits down on the sofa, picks up her embroidery and works a few stitches, but soon stops.*] No! [*She flings her work down, stands up, goes to the hall door and calls out.*] Helene! Fetch the tree in for me, please. [*She walks across to the table, left, and opens the drawer; again pauses.*] No, really, it's quite impossible!

MAID [*with the Christmas tree*]:   Where shall I put it, ma'am?

NORA: On the floor there, in the middle.

MAID: Anything else you want me to bring?

NORA: No, thank you. I've got what I want.

[The MAID *has put the tree down and goes out.]*

NORA [*busy decorating the tree*]:   Candles here . . . and flowers here—Revolting man! It's all nonsense! There's nothing to worry about. We'll have a lovely Christmas tree. And I'll do anything you want me to, Torvald; I'll sing for you, dance for you . . . .

*[*HELMER, *with a bundle of documents under his arm, comes in by the hall door.]*

NORA: Ah, back again already?

HELMER: Yes. Anybody been?

NORA: Here? No.

HELMER: That's funny. I just saw Krogstad leave the house.

NORA: Oh? O yes, that's right. Krogstad was here a minute.

HELMER: Nora, I can tell by your face he's been asking you to put a good word in for him.

NORA: Yes.

HELMER: And you were to pretend it was your own idea? You were to keep quiet about his having been here. He asked you to do that as well, didn't he?

NORA: Yes, Torvald. But . . .

HELMER: Nora, Nora, what possessed you to do a thing like that? Talking to a person
like him, making him promises? And then on top of everything, to tell me a lie!

NORA: A lie . . . ?

HELMER: Didn't you say that nobody had been here? [*Wagging his finger at her.*]
Never again must my little song-bird do a thing like that! Little song-birds
must keep their pretty little beaks out of mischief; no chirruping out of tune!
[*Puts his arm round her waist.*] Isn't that the way we want things to be? Yes,
of course it is. [*Lets her go.*] So let's say no more about it. [*Sits down by the
stove.*] Ah, nice and cozy here!

[*He glances through his papers.*]

NORA [*busy with the Christmas tree, after a short pause*]:   Torvald!

HELMER: Yes.

NORA: I'm so looking forward to the fancy dress ball at the Stenborgs on Boxing Day.

HELMER: And I'm terribly curious to see what sort of surprise you've got for me.

NORA: Oh, it's too silly.

HELMER: Oh?

NORA: I just can't think of anything suitable. Everything seems so absurd, so pointless.

HELMER: Has my little Nora come to that conclusion?

NORA [*behind his chair, her arms on the chair-back*]:   Are you very busy, Torvald?

HELMER: Oh . . . .

NORA: What are all those papers?

HELMER: Bank matters.

NORA: Already?

HELMER: I have persuaded the retiring manager to give me authority to make any
changes in organization or personnel I think necessary. I have to work on it
over the Christmas week. I want everything straight by the New Year.

NORA: So that was why that poor Krogstad . . . .

HELMER: Hm!

NORA [*still leaning against the back of the chair, running her fingers through his
hair*]:   If you hadn't been so busy, Torvald, I'd have asked you to do me an
awfully big favor.

HELMER: Let me hear it. What's it to be?

NORA: Nobody's got such good taste as you. And the thing is I do so want to look
my best at the fancy dress ball. Torvald, couldn't you give me some advice and
tell me what you think I ought to go as, and how I should arrange my costume?

HELMER: Aha! So my impulsive little woman is asking for somebody to come to her
rescue, eh?

NORA: Please, Torvald, I never get anywhere without your help.

HELMER: Very well, I'll think about it. We'll find something.

NORA: That's sweet of you. [*She goes across to the tree again; pause.*] How pretty these red flowers look.—Tell me, was it really something terribly wrong this man Krogstad did?

HELMER: Forgery. Have you any idea what that means?

NORA: Perhaps circumstances left him no choice?

HELMER: Maybe. Or perhaps, like so many others, he just didn't think. I am not so heartless that I would necessarily want to condemn a man for a single mistake like that.

NORA: Oh no, Torvald, of course not!

HELMER: Many a man might be able to redeem himself, if he honestly confessed his guilt and took his punishment.

NORA: Punishment?

HELMER: But that wasn't the way Krogstad chose. He dodged what was due to him by a cunning trick. And that's what has been the cause of his corruption.

NORA: Do you think it would . . . ?

HELMER: Just think how a man with a thing like that on his conscience will always be having to lie and cheat and dissemble; he can never drop the mask, not even with his own wife and children. And the children—that's the most terrible part of it, Nora.

NORA: Why?

HELMER: A fog of lies like that in a household, and it spreads disease and infection to every part of it. Every breath the children take in that kind of house is reeking with evil germs.

NORA [*closer behind him*]:   Are you sure of that?

HELMER: My dear Nora, as a lawyer I know what I'm talking about. Practically all juvenile delinquents come from homes where the mother is dishonest.

NORA: Why mothers particularly?

HELMER: It's generally traceable to the mothers, but of course fathers can have the same influence. Every lawyer knows that only too well. And yet there's Krogstad been poisoning his own children for years with lies and deceit. That's the reason I call him morally depraved. [*Holds out his hands to her.*] That's why my sweet little Nora must promise me not to try putting in any more good words for him. Shake hands on it. Well? What's this? Give me your hand. There now! That's settled. I assure you I would have found it impossible to work with him. I quite literally feel physically sick in the presence of such people.

NORA [*draws her hand away and walks over to the other side of the Christmas tree*]:   How hot it is in here! And I still have such a lot to do.

HELMER [*stands up and collects his papers together*]:   Yes, I'd better think of getting some of this read before dinner. I must also think about your costume. And I might even be able to lay my hands on something to wrap in gold paper and hang on the Christmas tree. [*He lays his hand on her head.*] My precious little singing bird.

[He goes into his study and shuts the door behind him.]

NORA *[quietly, after a pause]*:   Nonsense! It can't be. It's impossible. It *must* be impossible.

MAID *[in the doorway, left]*:   The children keep asking so nicely if they can come in and see Mummy.

NORA: No, no, don't let them in! You stay with them, Anne Marie.

MAID: Very well, ma'am.

[She shuts the door.]

NORA *[PALE WITH TERROR]*:   Corrupt my children . . . ! Poison my home? *[Short pause; she throws back her head.]* It's not true! It could never, never be true!

ACT II

The same room. In the corner beside the piano stands the Christmas tree, stripped, bedraggled and with its candles burnt out. NORA'S *outdoor things lie on the sofa.* NORA, *alone there, walks about restlessly; at last she stops by the sofa and picks up her coat.*

NORA *[putting her coat down again]*:   Somebody's coming! *[Crosses to the door, listens.]* No, it's nobody. Nobody will come today, of course, Christmas Day— nor tomorrow, either. But perhaps . . . . *[She opens the door and looks out.]* No, nothing in the letter box; quite empty. *[Comes forward.]* Oh, nonsense! He didn't mean it seriously. Things like that can't happen. It's impossible. Why, I have three small children.

[The NURSEMAID *comes from the room, left, carrying a big cardboard box.]*

NURSE MAID: I finally found it, the box with the fancy dress costumes.

NORA: Thank you. Put it on the table, please.

NURSE MAID *[does this]*:   But I'm afraid they are in an awful mess.

NORA: Oh, if only I could rip them up into a thousand pieces!

NURSE MAID: Good heavens, they can be mended all right, with a bit of patience.

NORA: Yes, I'll go over and get Mrs. Linde to help me.

NURSE MAID: Out again? In this terrible weather? You'll catch your death of cold, Ma'am.

NORA: Oh, worse things might happen.—How are the children?

NURSE MAID: Playing with their Christmas presents, poor little things, but . . .

NORA: Do they keep asking for me?

NURSE MAID: They are so used to being with their Mummy.

NORA: Yes, Anne Marie, from now on I can't be with them as often as I was before.

NURSE MAID: Ah well, children get used to anything in time.

NORA: Do you think so? Do you think they would forget their Mummy if she went away for good?

NURSE MAID: Good gracious—for good?

NORA: Tell me, Anne Marie—I've often wondered—how on earth could you bear to hand your child over to strangers?

NURSE MAID: Well, there was nothing else for it when I had to come and nurse my little Nora.

NORA: Yes but . . . how could you *bring* yourself to do it?

NURSE MAID: When I had the chance of such a good place? When a poor girl's been in trouble she must make the best of things. Because *he* didn't help, the rotter.

NORA: But your daughter will have forgotten you.

NURSE MAID: Oh no, she hasn't. She wrote to me when she got confirmed, and again when she glt married.

NORA [*pulling her arms round her neck*]:   Dear old Anne Marie, you were a good mother to me when I was little.

NURSE MAID: My poor little Nora never had any other mother but me.

NORA: And if my little ones only had you, I know you would. . . . Oh, what am I talking about! [*She opens the box.*] Go in to them. I must . . . Tomorrow I'll let you see how pretty I am going to look.

NURSE MAID: Ah, there'll be nobody at the ball as pretty as my Nora.

[*She goes into the room, left.*]

NORA [*begins unpacking the box, but soon throws it down*]:   Oh, if only I dare go out. If only I could be sure nobody would come. And that nothing would happen in the meantime here at home. Rubbish—nobody's going to come. I mustn't think about it. Brush this muff. Pretty gloves, pretty gloves! I'll put it right out of my mind. One, two, three, four, five, six. . . . [*Screams.*] Ah, they are coming. . . . [*She starts towards the door, but stops irresolute. Mrs. Linde comes from the hall, where she has taken off her things.*] Oh, it's you, Kristine. There's nobody else out there, is there? I'm so glad you've come.

MRS. LINDE: I heard you'd been over looking for me.

NORA: Yes, I was just passing. There's something you must help me with. Come and sit beside me on the sofa here. You see, the Stenborgs are having a fancy dress party upstairs tomorrow evening, and now Torvald wants me to go as a Neapolitan fisher lass and dance the tarantella. I learned it in Capri, you know.

MRS. LINDE: Well, well! So you are going to do a party piece?

NORA: Torvald says I should. Look, here's the costume, Torvald had it made for me down there. But it's got all torn and I simply don't know. . . .

MRS. LINDE: We'll soon have that put right. It's only the trimming come away here and there. Got a needle and thread? Ah, here's what we are after.

NORA: It's awfully kind of you.

MRS. LINDE: So you are going to be all dressed up tomorrow, Nora? Tell you what— I'll pop over for a minute to see you in all your finery. But I'm quite forgetting to thank you for the pleasant time we had last night.

NORA [*gets up and walks across the room*]:   Somehow I didn't think yesterday was as nice as things generally are.—You should have come to town a little earlier, Kristine.—Yes, Torvald certainly knows how to make things pleasant about the place.

MRS. LINDE: You too, I should say. You are not your father's daughter for nothing. But tell me, is Dr. Rank always as depressed as he was last night?

NORA: No, last night it was rather obvious. He's got something seriously wrong with him, you know. Tuberculosis of the spine, poor fellow. His father was a horrible man, who used to have mistresses and things like that. That's why the son was always ailing, right from being a child.

MRS. LINDE [*lowering her sewing*]:   But my dear Nora, how do you come to know about things like that?

NORA [*walking about the room*]:   Huh! When you've got three children, you get these visits from . . . women who have had a certain amount of medical training. And you hear all sorts of things from them.

MRS. LINDE [*begins sewing again; short silence*]:   Does Dr. Rank call in every day?

NORA: Every single day. He was Torvald's best friend as a boy, and he's a good friend of mine, too. Dr. Rank is almost like one of the family.

MRS. LINDE: But tell me—is he really genuine? What I mean is: doesn't he sometimes rather turn on the charm?

NORA: No, on the contrary. What makes you think that?

MRS. LINDE: When you introduced me yesterday, he claimed he'd often heard my name in this house. But afterwards I noticed your husband hadn't the faintest idea who I was. Then how is it that Dr. Rank should. . . .

NORA: Oh yes, it was quite right what he said, Kristine. You see Torvald is so terribly in love with me that he says he wants me all to himself. When we were first married, it even used to make him sort of jealous if I only as much as mentioned any of my old friends from back home. So of course I stopped doing it. But I often talk to Dr. Rank about such things. He likes hearing about them.

MRS. LINDE: Listen, Nora! In lots of ways you are still a child. Now, I'm a good deal older than you, and a bit more experienced. I'll tell you something: I think you ought to give up all this business with Dr. Rank.

NORA: Give up what business?

MRS. LINDE: The whole thing, I should say. Weren't you saying yesterday something about a rich admirer who was to provide you with money. . . .

NORA: One who's never existed, I regret to say. But what of it?

MRS. LINDE: Has Dr. Rank money?

NORA: Yes, he has.

MRS. LINDE: And no dependents?

NORA: No, nobody. But . . . ?

MRS. LINDE: And he comes to the house every day?

NORA: Yes, I told you.

MRS. LINDE: But how can a man of his position want to pester you like this?

NORA: I simply don't understand.

MRS. LINDE: Don't pretend, Nora. Do you think I don't see now who you borrowed the twelve hundred from?

NORA: Are you out of your mind? Do you really think that? A friend of ours who comes here every day? The whole situation would have been absolutely intolerable.

MRS. LINDE: It *really* isn't him?

NORA: No, I give you my word. It would never have occurred to me for one moment.... Anyway, he didn't have the money to lend then. He didn't inherit it till later.

MRS. LINDE: Just as well for you, I'd say, my dear Nora.

NORA: No, it would never have occurred to me to ask Dr. Rank.... All the same I'm pretty certain if I were to ask him . . .

MRS. LINDE: But of course you won't.

NORA: No, of course not. I can't ever imagine it being necessary. But I'm quite certain if ever I were to mention it to Dr. Rank. . . .

MRS. LINDE: Behind your husband's back?

NORA: I have to get myself out of that other business. That's also behind his back. I must get myself out of that.

MRS. LINDE: Yes, that's what I said yesterday. But . . .

NORA [*walking up and down*]:   A man's better at coping with these things than a woman. . . .

MRS. LINDE: Your own husband, yes.

NORA: Nonsense! [*Stops.*] When you've paid everything you owe, you do get your IOU back again, don't you?

MRS. LINDE: Of course.

NORA: And you can tear it up into a thousand pieces and burn it—the nasty, filthy thing!

MRS. LINDE [*looking fixedly at her, puts down her sewing and slowly rises*]:   Nora, you are hiding something from me.

NORA: Is it so obvious?

MRS. LINDE: Something has happened to you since yesterday morning. Nora, what is it?

NORA [*going towards her*]:   Kristine! [*Listens.*] Hush! There's Torvald back. Look, you go and sit in there beside the children for the time being. Torvald can't stand the sight of mending lying about. Get Anne Marie to help you.

MRS. LINDE [*gathering a lot of the things together*]:   All right, but I'm not leaving until we have thrashed this thing out.

[*She goes into the room, left; at the same time Helmer comes in from the hall.*]

NORA [*goes to meet him*]:   I've been longing for you to be back, Torvald, dear.

HELMER: Was that the dressmaker . . . ?

NORA: No, it was Kristine; she's helping me with my costume. I think it's going to look very nice . . .

HELMER: Wasn't that a good idea of mine, now?

NORA: Wonderful! But wasn't it also nice of me to let you have your way?

HELMER [*taking her under the chin*]:   Nice of you—because you let your husband have his way? All right, you little rogue, I know you didn't mean it that way. But I don't want to disturb you. You'll be wanting to try the costume on, I suppose.

NORA: And I dare say you've got work to do?

HELMER: Yes. [*Shows her a bundle of papers.*] Look at this. I've been down at the Bank. . . .

[*He turns to go into his study.*]

NORA: Torvald!

HELMER [*stopping*]:   Yes.

NORA: If a little squirrel were to ask ever so nicely . . . ?

HELMER: Well?

NORA: Would you do something for it?

HELMER: Naturally I would first have to know what it is.

NORA: Please, if only you would let it have its way, and do what it wants, it'd scamper about and do all sorts of marvelous tricks.

HELMER: What is it?

NORA: And the pretty little skylark would sing all day long. . . .

HELMER: Huh! It does that anyway.

NORA: I'd pretend I was an elfin child and dance a moonlight dance for you, Torvald.

HELMER: Nora—I hope it's not that business you started on this morning?

NORA [*coming closer*]:   Yes, it is, Torvald. I implore you!

HELMER: You have the nerve to bring that up again?

NORA: Yes, yes, you *must* listen to me. You must let Krogstad keep his job at the Bank.

HELMER: My dear Nora, I'm giving his job to Mrs. Linde.

NORA: Yes, it's awfully sweet of you. But couldn't you get rid of somebody else in the office instead of Krogstad?

HELMER: This really is the most incredible obstinacy! Just because you go and make some thoughtless promise to put in a good word for him, you expect me . . .

NORA: It's not that, Torvald. It's for your own sake. That man writes in all the nastiest papers, you told me that yourself. He can do you no end of harm. He terrifies me to death. . . .

HELMER: Aha, now I see. It's your memories of what happened before that are frightening you.

NORA: What do you mean?

HELMER: It's your father you are thinking of.

NORA: Yes . . . yes, that's right. You remember all the nasty insinuations those wicked people put in the papers about Daddy? I honestly think they would have had him dismissed if the Ministry hadn't sent you down to investigate, and you hadn't been so kind and helpful.

HELMER: My dear little Nora, there is a considerable difference between your father
and me. Your father's professional conduct was not entirely above suspicion.
Mine is. And I hope it's going to stay that way as long as I hold this position.

NORA: But nobody knows what some of these evil people are capable of. Things
could be so nice and pleasant for us here, in the peace and quiet of our
home—you and me and the children, Torvald! That's why I implore you. . . .

HELMER: The more you plead for him, the more impossible you make it for me to
keep him on. It's already known down at the Bank that I am going to give
Krogstad his notice. If it ever got around that the new manager had been
talked over by his wife. . . .

NORA: What of it?

HELMER: Oh, nothing! As long as the little woman gets her own stubborn way . . . !
Do you want me to make myself a laughing stock in the office? . . . Give people
the idea that I am susceptible to any kind of outside pressure? You can imagine
how soon I'd feel the consequences of that! Anyway, there's one other consideration that makes it impossible to have Krogstad in the Bank as long as I am
manager.

NORA: What's that?

HELMER: At a pinch I might have overlooked his past lapses. . . .

NORA: Of course you could, Torvald!

HELMER: And I'm told he's not bad at his job, either. But we knew each other rather
well when we were younger. It was one of those rather rash friendships that
prove embarrassing in later life. There's no reason why you shouldn't know we
were once on terms of some familiarity. And he, in his tactless way, makes no
attempt to hide the fact, particularly when other people are present. On the
contrary, he thinks he has every right to treat me as an equal, with his "Torvald
this" and "Torvald that" every time he opens his mouth. I find it extremely irritating, I can tell you. He would make my position at the Bank absolutely intolerable.

NORA: Torvald, surely you aren't serious?

HELMER: Oh? Why not?

NORA: Well, it's all so petty.

HELMER: What's that you say? Petty? Do you think I'm petty?

NORA: No, not at all, Torvald dear! And that's why . . .

HELMER: Doesn't make any difference! . . . You call my motives petty; so I must be
petty too. Petty! Indeed! Well, we'll put a stop to that, once and for all. [*He
opens the hall door and calls.*] Helene!

NORA: What are you going to do?

HELMER [*searching among his papers*]:   Settle things. [*The* MAID *comes in.*] See this
letter? I want you to take it down at once. Get hold of a messenger and get him
to deliver it. Quickly. The address is on the outside. There's the money.

MAID: Very good, sir.

[*She goes with the letter.*]

HELMER [*putting his papers together*]:   There now, my stubborn little miss.

NORA [*breathless*]:   Torvald . . . what was that letter?

HELMER: Krogstad's notice.

NORA: Get it back, Torvald! There's still time! Oh, Torvald, get it back! Please for my sake, for your sake, for the sake of the children! Listen, Torvald, please! You don't realize what it can do to us.

HELMER: Too late.

NORA: Yes, too late.

HELMER: My dear Nora, I forgive you this anxiety of yours, although it is actually a bit of an insult. Oh, but it is, I tell you! It's hardly flattering to suppose that anything this miserable pen-pusher wrote could frighten *me!* But I forgive you all the same, because it is rather a sweet way of showing how much you love me. [*He takes her in his arms.*] This is how things must be, my own darling Nora. When it comes to the point, I've enough strength and enough courage, believe me, for whatever happens. You'll find I'm man enough to take everything on myself.

NORA [*terrified*]:   What do you mean?

HELMER: Everything, I said. . . .

NORA [*in command of herself*]:   That is something you shall never, never do.

HELMER: All right, then we'll share it, Nora—as man and wife. That's what we'll do. [*Caressing her.*] Does that make you happy now? There, there, don't look at me with those eyes, like a little frightened dove. The whole thing is sheer imagination.—Why don't you run through the tarantella and try out the tambourine? I'll go into my study and shut both the doors, then I won't hear anything. You can make all the noise you want. [*Turns in the doorway.*] And when Rank comes, tell him where he can find me.

[*He nods to her, goes with his papers into his room, and shuts the door behind him.*]

NORA [*wild-eyed with terror, stands as though transfixed*]:   He's quite capable of doing it! He would do it! No matter what, he'd do it.—No, never in this world! Anything but that! Help? Some way out . . . ? [*The doorbell rings in the hall.*] Dr. Rank . . . ! Anything but that, anything! [*She brushes her hands over her face, pulls herself together and opens the door into the hall. DR. RANK is standing outside hanging up his fur coat. During what follows it begins to grow dark.*] Hello, Dr. Rank. I recognized your ring. Do you mind not going in to Torvald just yet, I think he's busy.

RANK: And you?

[*DR. RANK comes into the room and she closes the door behind him.*]

NORA: Oh, you know very well I've always got time for you.

RANK: Thank you. A privilege I shall take advantage of as long as I am able.

NORA: What do you mean—as long as you are able?

RANK: Does that frighten you?

NORA: Well, it's just that it sounds so strange. Is anything likely to happen?

RANK: Only what I have long expected. But I didn't think it would come quite so soon.

NORA [*catching at his arm*]: What have you found out? Dr. Rank, you must tell me!

RANK: I'm slowly sinking. There's nothing to be done about it.

NORA [*with a sigh of relief*]: Oh, it's *you* you're . . . ?

RANK: Who else? No point in deceiving oneself. I am the most wretched of all my patients, Mrs. Helmer. These last few days I've made a careful analysis of my internal economy. Bankrupt! Within a month I shall probably be lying rotting up there in the churchyard.

NORA: Come now, what a ghastly thing to say!

RANK: The whole damned thing is ghastly. But the worst thing is all the ghastliness that has to be gone through first. I only have one more test to make; and when that's done I'll know pretty well when the final disintegration will start. There's something I want to ask you. Helmer is a sensitive soul; he loathes anything that's ugly. I don't want him visiting me. . . .

NORA: But Dr. Rank. . . .

RANK: On no account must he. I won't have it. I'll lock the door on him.—As soon as I'm absolutely certain of the worst, I'll send you my visiting card with a black cross on it. You'll know then the final horrible disintegration has begun.

NORA: Really, you are being quite absurd today. And here was I hoping you would be in a thoroughly good mood.

RANK: With death staring me in the face? Why should I suffer for another man's sins? What justice is there in that? Somewhere, somehow, every single family must be suffering some such cruel retribution. . . .

NORA [*stopping up her ears*]: Rubbish! Do cheer up!

RANK: Yes, really the whole thing's nothing but a huge joke. My poor innocent spine must do penance for my father's gay subaltern life.

NORA [*by the table, left*]: Wasn't he rather partial to asparagus and *pâté de foie gras?*

RANK: Yes, he was. And truffles.

NORA: Truffles, yes. And oysters, too, I believe?

RANK: Yes, oysters, oysters, of course.

NORA: And all the port and champagne that goes with them. It does seem a pity all these delicious things should attack the spine.

RANK: Especially when they attack a poor spine that never had any fun out of them.

NORA: Yes, that is an awful pity.

RANK [*looks at her sharply*]: Hm. . . .

NORA [*after a pause*]: Why did you smile?

RANK: No, it was you who laughed.

NORA: No, it was you who smiled, Dr. Rank!

RANK [*getting up*]: You are a bigger rascal than I thought you were.

NORA: I feel full of mischief today.

RANK: So it seems.

NORA [*putting her hands on his shoulders*]:   Dear, dear Dr. Rank, you mustn't go and die on Torvald and me.

RANK: You wouldn't miss me for long. When you are gone, you are soon forgotten.

NORA [*looking at him anxiously*]:   Do you think so?

RANK: People make new contacts, then . . .

NORA: Who make new contacts?

RANK: Both you and Helmer will, when I'm gone. You yourself are already well on the way, it seems to me. What was this Mrs. Linde doing here last night?

NORA: Surely you aren't jealous of poor Kristine?

RANK: Yes, I am. She'll be my successor in this house. When I'm done for, I can see this woman. . . .

NORA: Hush! Don't talk so loud, she's in there.

RANK: Today as well? There you are, you see!

NORA: Just to do some sewing on my dress. Good Lord, how absurd you are! [*She sits down on the sofa.*] Now Dr. Rank, cheer up. You'll see tomorrow how nicely I can dance. And you can pretend I'm doing it just for you—and for Torvald as well, of course. [*She takes various things out of the box.*] Come here, Dr. Rank. I want to show you something.

RANK [*sits*]:   What is it?

NORA: Look!

RANK: Silk stockings.

NORA: Flesh-coloured! Aren't they lovely! Of course, it's dark here now, but tomorrow. . . . No, no, no, you can only look at the feet. Oh well, you might as well see a bit higher up, too.

RANK: Hm. . . .

NORA: Why are you looking so critical? Don't you think they'll fit?

RANK: I couldn't possibly offer any informed opinion about that.

NORA [*looks at him for a moment*]:   Shame on you. [*Hits him lightly across the ear with the stockings.*] Take that! [*Folds them up again.*]

RANK: And what other delights am I to be allowed to see?

NORA: Not another thing. You are too naughty. [*She hums a little and searches among her things.*]

RANK [*after a short pause*]:   Sitting here so intimately like this with you, I can't imagine . . . I simply cannot conceive what would have become of me if I had never come to this house.

NORA [*smiles*]:   Yes, I rather think you do enjoy coming here.

RANK [*in a low voice, looking fixedly ahead*]:   And the thought of having to leave it all . . .

NORA: Nonsense. You aren't leaving.

RANK [*in the same tone*]:   . . . without being able to leave behind even the slightest token of gratitude, hardly a fleeting regret even . . . nothing but an empty place to be filled by the first person that comes along.

NORA: Supposing I were to ask you to . . . ? No . . .

RANK: What?

NORA: . . . to show me the extent of your friendship . . .

RANK: Yes?

NORA: I mean . . . to do me a tremendous favor. . . .

RANK: Would you really, for once, give me that pleasure?

NORA: You have no idea what it is.

RANK: All right, tell me.

NORA: No, really I can't, Dr. Rank. It's altogether too much to ask . . . because I need your advice and help as well. . . .

RANK: The more the better. I cannot imagine what you have in mind. But tell me anyway. You do trust me, don't you?

NORA: Yes, I trust you more than anybody I know. You are my best and my most faithful friend. I know that. So I will tell you. Well then, Dr. Rank, there is something you must help me to prevent. You know how deeply, how passionately Torvald is in love with me. He would never hesitate for a moment to sacrifice his life for my sake.

RANK [*bending towards her*]:   Nora. . . do you think he's the only one who. . . ?

NORA [*stiffening slightly*]:   Who. . . ?

RANK: Who wouldn't gladly give his life for your sake.

NORA [*sadly*]:   Oh!

RANK: I swore to myself you would know before I went. I'll never have a better opportunity. Well, Nora! Now you know. And now you know too that you can confide in me as in nobody else.

NORA [*rises and speaks evenly and calmly*]:   Let me past.

RANK [*makes way for her, but remains seated*]:   Nora. . . .

NORA [*in the hall doorway*]:   Helene, bring the lamp in, please. [*Walks over to the stove.*] Oh, my dear Dr. Rank, that really was rather horrid of you.

RANK [*getting up*]:   That I have loved you every bit as much as anybody? Is *that* horrid?

NORA: No, but that you had to go and tell me. When it was all so unnecessary. . . .

RANK: What do you mean? Did you know. . . ?

[*The Maid comes in with the lamp, puts it on the table, and goes out again.*]

RANK: Nora. . . Mrs. Helmer. . . I'm asking you if you knew?

NORA: How can I tell whether I did or didn't. I simply can't tell you. . . . Oh, how could you be so clumsy, Dr. Rank! When everything was so nice.

RANK: Anyway, you know now that I'm at your service, body and soul. So you can speak out.

NORA [*looking at him*]:   After this?

RANK: I beg you to tell me what it is.

NORA: I can tell you nothing now.

RANK: You must. You can't torment me like this. Give me a chance—I'll do anything that's humanly possible.

NORA: You can do nothing for me now. Actually, I don't really need any help. It's all just my imagination, really it is. Of course! [*She sits down in the rocking chair, looks at him and smiles.*] I must say, you are a nice one, Dr. Rank! Don't you feel ashamed of yourself, now the lamp's been brought in?

RANK: No, not exactly. But perhaps I ought to go—for good?

NORA: No, you mustn't do that. You must keep coming just as you've always done. You know very well Torvald would miss you terribly.

RANK: And *you?*

NORA: I always think it's tremendous fun having you.

RANK: That's exactly what gave me wrong ideas. I just can't puzzle you out. I often used to feel you'd just as soon be with me as with Helmer.

NORA: Well, you see, there are those people you love and those people you'd almost rather *be* with.

RANK: Yes, there's something in that.

NORA: When I was a girl at home, I loved Daddy best, of course. But I also thought it great fun if I could slip into the maids' room. For one thing they never preached at me. And they always talked about such exciting things.

RANK: Aha! So it's their role I've taken over!

NORA [*jumps up and crosses to him*]:   Oh, my dear, kind Dr. Rank, I didn't mean that at all. But you can see how it's a bit with Torvald as it was with Daddy. . . .

[*The* MAID *comes in from the hall.*]

MAID: Please, ma'am. . . !

[*She whispers and hands her a card.*]

NORA [*glances at the card*]:   Ah!

[*She puts it in her pocket.*]

RANK: Anything wrong?

NORA: No, no, not at all. It's just. . . it's my new costume. . . .

RANK: How is that? There's your costume in there.

NORA: That one, yes. But this is another one. I've ordered it. Torvald mustn't hear about it. . .

RANK: Ah, so that's the big secret, is it!

NORA: Yes, that's right. Just go in and see him, will you? He's in the study. Keep him occupied for the time being. . . .

RANK: Don't worry. He shan't escape me.

[*He goes into Helmer's study.*]

NORA [*to the* MAID]:   Is he waiting in the kitchen?

MAID: Yes, he came up the back stairs. . . .

NORA: But didn't you tell him somebody was here?

MAID: Yes, but it was no good.

NORA: Won't he go?

MAID: No, he won't till he's seen you.

NORA: Let him in, then. But quietly. Helene, you mustn't tell anybody about this. It's a surprise for my husband.

MAID: I understand, ma'am. . . .

[She goes out.]

NORA: Here it comes! What I've been dreading! No, no, it can't happen, it *can't* happen.

[She walks over and bolts HELMER*'s door. The* MAID *opens the hall door for* KROGSTAD *and shuts it again behind him. He is wearing a fur coat, overshoes, and a fur cap.]*

NORA *[goes towards him]*:   Keep your voice down, my husband is at home.

KROGSTAD: What if he is?

NORA: What do you want with me?

KROGSTAD: To find out something.

NORA: Hurry, then. What is it?

KROGSTAD: You know I've been given notice.

NORA: I couldn't prevent it, Mr. Krogstad, I did my utmost for you, but it was no use.

KROGSTAD: Has your husband so little affection for you? He knows what I can do to you, yet he dares. . . .

NORA: You don't imagine he knows about it!

KROGSTAD: No, I didn't imagine he did. It didn't seem a bit like my good friend Torvald Helmer to show that much courage. . . .

NORA: Mr. Krogstad, I must ask you to show some respect for my husband.

KROGSTAD: Oh, sure! All due respect! But since you are so anxious to keep this business quiet, Mrs. Helmer, I take it you now have a rather clearer idea of just what it is you've done, than you had yesterday.

NORA: Clearer than *you* could ever have given me.

KROGSTAD: Yes, being as I am such a rotten lawyer. . . .

NORA: What do *you* want with me?

KROGSTAD: I just wanted to see how things stood, Mrs. Helmer. I've been thinking about you all day. Even a mere money-lender, a hack journalist, a—well, even somebody like me has a bit of what you might call feeling.

NORA: Show it then. Think of my little children.

KROGSTAD: Did you or your husband think of mine? But what does it matter now? There was just one thing I wanted to say: you needn't take this business too seriously. I shan't start any proceedings, for the present.

NORA: Ah, I knew you wouldn't.

KROGSTAD: The whole thing can be arranged quite amicably. Nobody need know. Just the three of us.

NORA: My husband must never know.

KROGSTAD: How can you prevent it? Can you pay off the balance?

NORA: No, not immediately.

KROGSTAD: Perhaps you've some way of getting hold of the money in the next few days.

NORA: None I want to make use of.

KROGSTAD: Well, it wouldn't have been very much help to you if you had. Even if you stood there with the cash in your hand and to spare, you still wouldn't get your IOU back from me now.

NORA: What are you going to do with it?

KROGSTAD: Just keep it—have it in my possession. Nobody who isn't implicated need know about it. So if you are thinking of trying any desperate remedies. . .

NORA: Which I am. . . .

KROGSTAD: . . . if you happen to be thinking of running away. . .

NORA: Which I am!

KROGSTAD: . . . or anything worse. . .

NORA: How did you know?

KROGSTAD: . . . forget it!

NORA: How did you know I was thinking of *that?*

KROGSTAD: Most of us think of *that,* to begin with. I did, too; but I didn't have the courage. . . .

NORA [*tonelessly*]:   I haven't either.

KROGSTAD [*relieved*]:   So you haven't the courage either, eh?

NORA: No, I haven't! I haven't!

KROGSTAD: It would also be very stupid. There'd only be the first domestic storm to get over. . . . I've got a letter to your husband in my pocket here. . . .

NORA: And it's all in there?

KROGSTAD: In as tactful a way as possible.

NORA [*quickly*]:   He must never read that letter. Tear it up. I'll find the money somehow.

KROGSTAD: Excuse me, Mrs. Helmer, but I've just told you. . . .

NORA: I'm not talking about the money I owe you. I want to know how much you are demanding from my husband, and I'll get the money.

KROGSTAD: I want no money from your husband.

NORA: What do you want?

KROGSTAD: I'll tell you. I want to get on my feet again, Mrs. Helmer; I want to get to the top. And your husband is going to help me. For the last eighteen months I've gone straight; all that time it's been hard going; I was content to work my way up, step by step. Now I'm being kicked out, and I won't stand for being taken back again as an act of charity. I'm going to get to the top, I tell you. I'm going back into that Bank—with a better job. Your husband is going to create a new vacancy, just for me. . . .

NORA: He'll never do that!

KROGSTAD: He will do it. I know him. He'll do it without so much as a whimper. And once I'm in there with him, you'll see what's what. In less than a year I'll be his right-hand man. It'll be Nils Krogstad, not Torvald Helmer, who'll be running that Bank.

NORA: You'll never live to see that day!

KROGSTAD: You mean you. . . ?

NORA: Now I have the courage.

KROGSTAD: You can't frighten me! A precious pampered little thing like you. . . .

NORA: I'll show you! I'll show you!

KROGSTAD: Under the ice, maybe? Down in the cold, black water? Then being washed up in the spring, bloated, hairless, unrecognizable. . . .

NORA: You can't frighten me.

KROGSTAD: You can't frighten me, either. People don't do that sort of thing, Mrs. Helmer. There wouldn't be any point to it, anyway, I'd still have him right in my pocket.

NORA: Afterwards? When I'm no longer. . .

KROGSTAD: Aren't you forgetting that your reputation would then be entirely in my hands? [NORA *stands looking at him, speechless.*] Well, I've warned you. Don't do anything silly. When Helmer gets my letter, I expect to hear from him. And don't forget: it's him who is forcing me off the straight and narrow again, your own husband! That's something I'll never forgive him for. Goodbye, Mrs. Helmer.

[*He goes out through the hall.* NORA *crosses to the door, opens it slightly, and listens.*]

NORA: He's going. He hasn't left the letter. No, no, that would be impossible! [*Opens the door further and further.*] What's he doing? He's stopped outside. He's not going down the stairs. Has he changed his mind? Is he. . . ? [*A letter falls into the letter box. Then* KROGSTAD'*s footsteps are heard receding as he walks downstairs.* NORA *gives a stifled cry, runs across the room to the sofa table; pause.*] In the letter box! [*She creeps stealthily across to the hall door.*] There it is! Torvald, Torvald! It's hopeless now!

MRS. LINDE [*comes into the room, left, carrying the costume*]:   There, I think that's everything. Shall we try it on?

NORA [*in a low, hoarse voice*]:   Kristine, come here.

MRS. LINDE [*throws the dress down on the sofa*]:   What's wrong with you? You look upset.

NORA: Come here. Do you see that letter? There, look! Through the glass in the letter box.

MRS. LINDE: Yes, yes, I can see it.

NORA: It's a letter from Krogstad.

MRS. LINDE: Nora! It was Krogstad who lent you the money!

NORA: Yes. And now Torvald will get to know everything.

MRS. LINDE: Believe me, Nora, it's best for you both.

NORA: But there's more to it than that. I forged a signature. . . .

MRS. LINDE: Heavens above!

NORA: Listen, I want to tell you something, Kristine, so you can be my witness.

MRS. LINDE: What do you mean, "witness"? What do you want me to. . . ?

NORA: If I should go mad . . . which might easily happen. . .

MRS. LINDE: Nora!

NORA: Or if anything happened to me . . . which meant I couldn't be here. . . .

MRS. LINDE: Nora, Nora! Are you out of your mind?

NORA: And if somebody else wanted to take it all upon himself, the whole blame, you understand. . . .

MRS. LINDE: Yes, yes. But what makes you think. . . ?

NORA: Then you must testify that it isn't true, Kristine. I'm not out of my mind; I'm quite sane now. And I tell you this: nobody else knew anything, I alone was responsible for the whole thing. Remember that!

MRS. LINDE: I will. But I don't understand a word of it.

NORA: Why should you? You see, something miraculous is going to happen.

MRS. LINDE: Something miraculous?

NORA: Yes, a miracle. But something so terrible as well, Kristine—oh, it must never happen, not for anything.

MRS. LINDE: I'm going straight over to talk to Krogstad.

NORA: Don't go. He'll only do you harm.

MRS. LINDE: There was a time when he would have done anything for me.

NORA: Him!

MRS. LINDE: Where does he live?

NORA: How do I know. . . ? Wait a minute. [*She feels in her pocket.*] Here's his card. But the letter, the letter. . . !

HELMER [*from his study, knocking on the door*]:   Nora!

NORA [*cries out in terror*]:   What's that? What do you want?

HELMER: Don't be frightened. We're not coming in. You've locked the door. Are you trying on?

NORA: Yes, yes, I'm trying on. It looks so nice on me, Torvald.

MRS. LINDE [*who has read the card*]:   He lives just round the corner.

NORA: It's no use. It's hopeless. The letter is there in the box.

MRS. LINDE: Your husband keeps the key?

NORA: Always.

MRS. LINDE: Krogstad must ask for his letter back unread, he must find some sort of excuse. . . .

NORA: But this is just the time that Torvald generally. . .

MRS. LINDE: Put him off! Go in and keep him busy. I'll be back as soon as I can.

[*She goes out hastily by the hall door. NORA walks over to HELME'S door, opens it and peeps in.*]

NORA: Torvald!

HELMER [*in the study*]:   Well, can a man get into his own living room again now? Come along, Rank, now we'll see . . . [*In the doorway.*] But what's this?

NORA: What, Torvald dear?

HELMER: Rank led me to expect some kind of marvelous transformation.

RANK [*in the doorway*]:   That's what I thought too, but I must have been mistaken.

NORA: I'm not showing myself off to anybody before tomorrow.

HELMER: Nora dear, you look tired. You haven't been practicing too hard?

NORA: No, I haven't practiced at all yet.

HELMER: You'll have to, though.

NORA: Yes, I certainly must, Torvald. But I just can't get anywhere without your help: I've completely forgotten it.

HELMER: We'll soon polish it up.

NORA: Yes, do help me, Torvald. Promise? I'm so nervous. All those people. . . .You must devote yourself exclusively to me this evening. Pens away! Forget all about the office! Promise me, Torvald dear!

HELMER: I promise. This evening I am wholly and entirely at your service . . . helpless little thing that you are. Oh, but while I remember, I'll just look first. . .

[He goes towards the hall door.]

NORA: What do you want out there?

HELMER: Just want to see if there are any letters.

NORA: No, don't, Torvald!

HELMER: Why not?

NORA: Torvald, *please!* There aren't any.

HELMER: Just let me see.

[He starts to go. NORA, *at the piano, plays the opening bars of the tarantella.]*

HELMER [*at the door, stops*]:   Aha!

NORA: I shan't be able to dance tomorrow if I don't rehearse it with you.

HELMER [*walks to her*]:   Are you really so nervous, Nora dear?

NORA: Terribly nervous. Let me run through it now. There's still time before supper. Come and sit here and play for me, Torvald dear. Tell me what to do, keep me right—as you always do.

HELMER: Certainly, with pleasure, if that's what you want.

[He sits at the piano. NORA *snatches the tambourine out of the box, and also a long gaily coloured shawl which she drapes round herself, then with a bound she leaps forward.]*

NORA [*shouts*]:   Now play for me! Now I'll dance!

*[*HELMER *plays and* NORA *dances;* DR. RANK *stands at the piano behind* HELMER *and looks on.]*

HELMER [*playing*]:   Not so fast! Not so fast!

NORA: I can't help it.

HELMER: Not so wild, Nora!

NORA: This is how it has to be.

HELMER [*stops*]:   No, no, that won't do at all.

NORA [*laughs and swings the tambourine*]:   Didn't I tell you?

RANK: Let me play for her.

HELMER [*gets up*]:   Yes, do. Then I'll be better able to tell her what to do.

[RANK sits down at the piano and plays. NORA dances more and more wildly. HELMER stands by the stove giving her repeated directions as she dances; she does not seem to hear them. Her hair comes undone and falls about her shoulders; she pays no attention and goes on dancing. MRS. LINDE enters.]

MRS. LINDE [*standing as though spellbound in the doorway*]:   Ah. . .!

NORA [*dancing*]:   See what fun we are having, Kristine.

HELMER: But my dear darling Nora, you are dancing as though your life depended on it.

NORA: It does.

HELMER: Stop, Rank! This is sheer madness. Stop, I say.

[RANK stops playing and NORA comes to a sudden halt.]

HELMER [*crosses to her*]:   I would never have believed it. You have forgotten everything I ever taught you.

NORA [*throwing away the tambourine*]:   There you are, you see.

HELMER: Well, some more instruction is certainly needed there.

NORA: Yes, you see how necessary it is. You must go on coaching me right up to the last minute. Promise me, Torvald?

HELMER: You can rely on me.

NORA: You mustn't think about anything else but me until after tomorrow . . . mustn't open any letters . . . mustn't touch the letter box.

HELMER: Ah, you are still frightened of what that man might . . .

NORA: Yes, yes, I am.

HELMER: I can see from your face there's already a letter there from him.

NORA: I don't know. I think so. But you mustn't read anything like that now. We don't want anything horrid coming between us until all this is over.

RANK [*softly to HELMER*]:   I shouldn't cross her.

HELMER [*puts his arm round her*]:   The child must have her way. But tomorrow night, when your dance is done. . . .

NORA: Then you are free.

MAID [*in the doorway, right*]:   Dinner is served, madam.

NORA: We'll have champagne, Helene.

MAID: Very good, madam.

[She goes.]

HELMER: Aha! It's to be quite a banquet, eh?

NORA: With champagne flowing until dawn. [*Shouts.*] And some macaroons, Helene . . . lots of them, for once in a while.

HELMER [*seizing her hands*]:   Now, now, not so wild and excitable! Let me see you being my own little singing bird again.

NORA: Oh yes, I will. And if you'll just go in . . . you, too, Dr. Rank. Kristine, you must help me to do my hair.

RANK [*softly, as they leave*]:   There isn't anything . . . anything as it were, impending, is there?

HELMER: No, not at all, my dear fellow. It's nothing but these childish fears I was
  telling you about.

[They go out to the right.]

NORA: Well?

MRS. LINDE: He's left town.

NORA: I saw it in your face.

MRS. LINDE: He's coming back tomorrow evening. I left a note for him.

NORA: You shouldn't have done that. You must let things take their course. Because
  really it's a case for rejoicing, waiting like this for the miracle.

MRS. LINDE: What is it you are waiting for?

NORA: Oh, you wouldn't understand. Go and join the other two. I'll be there in a
  minute.

*[*MRS. LINDE *goes into the dining-room.* NORA *stands for a moment as though to collect herself, then looks at her watch.]*

NORA: Five. Seven hours to midnight. Then twenty-four hours till the next midnight.
  Then the tarantella will be over. Twenty-four and seven? Thirty-one hours to
  live.

HELMER [*in the doorway, right*]:   What's happened to our little sky-lark?

NORA [*running towards him with open arms*]:   Here she is!

ACT III

*The same room. The round table has been moved to the center of the room, and
the chairs placed round it. A lamp is burning on the table. The door to the hall
stands open. Dance music can be heard coming from the floor above.* MRS. LINDE
*is sitting by the table, idly turning over the pages of a book; she tries to read, but
does not seem able to concentrate. Once or twice she listens, tensely, for a sound
at the front door.*

MRS. LINDE [*looking at her watch*]:   Still not here. There isn't much time left. I only
  hope he hasn't . . . [*She listens again.*] Ah, there he is. [*She goes out into the
  hall, and cautiously opens the front door. Soft footsteps can be heard on the
  stairs. She whispers.*] Come in. There's nobody here.

KROGSTAD [*in the doorway*]:   I found a note from you at home. What does it all
  mean?

MRS. LINDE: I *had* to talk to you.

KROGSTAD: Oh? And did it have to be here, in this house?

MRS. LINDE: It wasn't possible over at my place, it hasn't a separate entrance. Come
  in. We are quite alone. The maid's asleep and the Helmers are at a party
  upstairs.

KROGSTAD [*comes into the room*]:   Well, well! So the Helmers are out dancing
  tonight! Really?

MRS. LINDE: Yes, why not?

KROGSTAD: Why not indeed!

MRS. LINDE: Well then, Nils. Let's talk.

KROGSTAD: Have we two anything more to talk about?

MRS. LINDE: We have a great deal to talk about.

KROGSTAD: I shouldn't have thought so.

MRS. LINDE: That's because you never really understood me.

KROGSTAD: What else was there to understand, apart from the old, old story? A heartless woman throws a man over the moment something more profitable offers itself.

MRS. LINDE: Do you really think I'm so heartless? Do you think I found it easy to break it off?

KROGSTAD: Didn't you?

MRS. LINDE: You didn't really believe that?

KROGSTAD: If that wasn't the case, why did you write to me as you did?

MRS. LINDE: There was nothing else I could do. If I had to make the break, I felt in duty bound to destroy any feeling that you had for me.

KROGSTAD [*clenching his hands*]:   So that's how it was. And all that . . . was for money!

MRS. LINDE: You mustn't forget I had a helpless mother and two young brothers. We couldn't wait for you, Nils. At that time you hadn't much immediate prospect of anything.

KROGSTAD: That may be. But you had no right to throw me over for somebody else.

MRS. LINDE: Well, I don't know. Many's the time I've asked myself whether I was justified.

KROGSTAD [*more quietly*]:   When I lost you, it was just as if the ground had slipped away from under my feet. Look at me now; a broken man clinging to the wreck of his life.

MRS. LINDE: Help might be near.

KROGSTAD: It was near. Then you came along and got in the way.

MRS. LINDE: Quite without knowing, Nils. I only heard today it's you I'm supposed to be replacing at the Bank.

KROGSTAD: If you say so, I believe you. But now you do know, aren't you going to withdraw?

MRS. LINDE: No, that wouldn't benefit you in the slightest.

KROGSTAD: Benefit, benefit. . . ! I would do it just the same.

MRS. LINDE: I have learned to go carefully. Life and hard, bitter necessity have taught me that.

KROGSTAD: And life has taught me not to believe in pretty speeches.

MRS. LINDE: Then life has taught you a very sensible thing. But deeds are something you surely must believe in?

KROGSTAD: How do you mean?

MRS. LINDE: You said you were like a broken man clinging to the wreck of his life.

KROGSTAD: And I said it with good reason.

MRS. LINDE: And I am like a broken woman clinging to the wreck of her life. Nobody to care about, and nobody to care for.

KROGSTAD: It was your own choice.

MRS. LINDE: At the time there was no other choice.

KROGSTAD: Well, what of it?

MRS. LINDE: Nils, what about us two castaways joining forces?

KROGSTAD: What's that you say?

MRS. LINDE: Two of us on one wreck surely stand a better chance than each on his own.

KROGSTAD: Kristine!

MRS. LINDE: Why do you suppose I came to town?

KROGSTAD: You mean, you thought of me?

MRS. LINDE: Without work I couldn't live. All my life I have worked, for as long as I can remember; that has always been my one great joy. But now I'm completely alone in the world, and feeling horribly empty and forlorn. There's no pleasure in working only for yourself. Nils, give me somebody and something to work for.

KROGSTAD: I don't believe all this. It's only a woman's hysteria, wanting to be all magnanimous and self-sacrificing.

MRS. LINDE: Have you ever known me hysterical before?

KROGSTAD: Would you really do this? Tell me—do you know all about my past?

MRS. LINDE: Yes.

KROGSTAD: And you know what people think about me?

MRS. LINDE: Just now you hinted you thought you might have been a different person with me.

KROGSTAD: I'm convinced I would.

MRS. LINDE: Couldn't it still happen?

KROGSTAD: Kristine! You know what you are saying, don't you? Yes, you do. I can see you do. Have you really the courage . . . ?

MRS. LINDE: I need someone to mother, and your children need a mother. We two need each other. Nils, I have faith in what, deep down, you are. With you I can face anything.

KROGSTAD [*seizing her hands*]:   Thank you, thank you, Kristine. And I'll soon have everybody looking up to me, or I'll know the reason why. Ah, but I was forgetting. . . .

MRS. LINDE: Hush! The tarantella! You must go!

KROGSTAD: Why? What is it?

MRS. LINDE: You hear that dance upstairs? When it's finished they'll be coming.

KROGSTAD: Yes, I'll go. It's too late to do anything. Of course, you know nothing about what steps I've taken against the Helmers.

MRS. LINDE: Yes, Nils, I do know.

KROGSTAD: Yet you still want to go on. . . .

MRS. LINDE: I know how far a man like you can be driven by despair.

KROGSTAD: Oh, if only I could undo what I've done!

MRS. LINDE: You still can. Your letter is still there in the box.

KROGSTAD: Are you sure?

MRS. LINDE: Quite sure. But . . .

KROGSTAD [*regards her searchingly*]:   Is that how things are? You want to save your friend at any price? Tell me straight. Is that it?

MRS. LINDE: When you've sold yourself *once* for other people's sake, you don't do it again.

KROGSTAD: I shall demand my letter back.

MRS. LINDE: No, no.

KROGSTAD: Of course I will, I'll wait here till Helmer comes. I'll tell him he has to give me my letter back . . . that it's only about my notice . . . that he mustn't read it. . . .

MRS. LINDE: No, Nils, don't ask for it back.

KROGSTAD: But wasn't that the very reason you got me here?

MRS. LINDE: Yes, that was my first terrified reaction. But that was yesterday, and it's quite incredible the things I've witnessed in this house in the last twenty-four hours. Helmer must know everything. This unhappy secret must come out. Those two must have the whole thing out between them. All this secrecy and deception, it just can't go on.

KROGSTAD: Well, if you want to risk it. . . . But one thing I can do, and I'll do it at once. . . .

MRS. LINDE [*listening*]:   Hurry! Go, go! The dance has stopped. We aren't safe a moment longer.

KROGSTAD: I'll wait for you downstairs.

MRS. LINDE: Yes, do. You must see me home.

KROGSTAD: I've never been so incredibly happy before.

[He goes out by the front door. The door out into the hall remains standing open.]

MRS. LINDE [*tidies the room a little and gets her hat and coat ready*]:   How things change! How things change! Somebody to work for . . . to live for. A home to bring happiness into. Just let me get down to it. . . . I wish they'd come. . . . [*Listens.*] Ah, there they are. . . . Get my things.

[She takes her coat and hat. The voices of HELMER *and* NORA *are heard outside. A key is turned and* HELMER *pushes* NORA *almost forcibly into the hall. She is dressed in the Italian costume, with a big black shawl over it. He is in evening dress, and over it a black cloak, open.]*

NORA [*still in the doorway, reluctantly*]:   No, no, not in here! I want to go back up again. I don't want to leave so early.

HELMER: But my dearest Nora . . .

NORA: Oh, please, Torvald, I beg you. . . . *Please,* just for another hour.

HELMER: Not another minute, Nora my sweet. You remember what we agreed. There now, come along in. You'll catch cold standing there.

[He leads her, in spite of her resistance, gently but firmly into the room.]

MRS. LINDE: Good evening.

NORA: Kristine!

HELMER: Why, Mrs. Linde. You here so late?

MRS. LINDE: Yes. You must forgive me but I did so want to see Nora all dressed up.

NORA: Have you been sitting here waiting for me?

MRS. LINDE: Yes, I'm afraid I wasn't in time to catch you before you went upstairs. And I felt I couldn't leave again without seeing you.

HELMER [*removing* NORA'S *shawl*]:   Well take a good look at her. I think I can say she's worth looking at. Isn't she lovely, Mrs. Linde?

MRS. LINDE: Yes, I must say. . . .

HELMER: Isn't she quite extraordinarily lovely? That's what everybody at the party thought, too. But she's dreadfully stubborn . . . the sweet little thing! And what shall we do about that? Would you believe it, I nearly had to use force to get her away.

NORA: Oh Torvald, you'll be sorry you didn't let me stay, even for half an hour.

HELMER: You hear that, Mrs. Linde? She dances her tarantella, there's wild applause—which was well deserved, although the performance was perhaps rather realistic . . . I mean, rather more so than was strictly necessary from the artistic point of view. But anyway! The main thing is she was a success, a tremendous success. Was I supposed to let her stay after that? Spoil the effect? No thank you! I took my lovely little Capri girl—my capricious little Capri girl, I might say—by the arm, whisked her once round the room, a curtsey all round, and then—as they say in novels—the beautiful vision vanished. An exit should always be effective, Mrs. Linde. But I just can't get Nora to see that. Phew! It's warm in here. [*He throws his cloak over a chair and opens the door to his study.*] What? It's dark. Oh yes, of course. Excuse me. . . .

[He goes in and lights a few candles.]

NORA [*quickly, in a breathless whisper*]:   Well?

MRS. LINDE [*softly*]:   I've spoken to him.

NORA: And . . . ?

MRS. LINDE: Nora . . . you must tell your husband everything.

NORA [*tonelessly*]:   I knew it.

MRS. LINDE: You've got nothing to fear from Krogstad. But you must speak.

NORA: I won't.

MRS. LINDE: Then the letter will.

NORA: Thank you, Kristine. Now I know what's to be done. Hush . . . !

HELMER [*comes in again*]:   Well, Mrs. Linde, have you finished admiring her?

MRS. LINDE: Yes. And now I must say good night.

HELMER: Oh, already? Is this yours, this knitting?

MRS. LINDE [*takes it*]:   Yes, thank you. I nearly forgot it.

HELMER: So you knit, eh?

MRS. LINDE: Yes.

HELMER: You should embroider instead, you know.

MRS. LINDE: Oh? Why?

HELMER: So much prettier. Watch! You hold the embroidery like this in the left hand, and then you take the needle in the right hand, like this, and you describe a long, graceful curve. Isn't that right?

MRS. LINDE: Yes, I suppose so. . . .

HELMER: Whereas knitting on the other hand just can't help being ugly. Look! Arms pressed into the sides, the knitting needles going up and down—there's something Chinese about it. . . . Ah, that was marvelous champagne they served tonight.

MRS. LINDE: Well, good night, Nora! And stop being so stubborn.

HELMER: Well said, Mrs. Linde!

MRS. LINDE: Good night, Mr. Helmer.

HELMER [*accompanying her to the door*]:   Good night, good night! You'll get home all right, I hope? I'd be only too pleased to. . . . But you haven't far to walk. Good night, good night! [*She goes; he shuts the door behind her and comes in again.*] There we are, got rid of her at last. She's a frightful bore, that woman.

NORA: Aren't you very tired, Torvald?

HELMER: Not in the least.

NORA: Not sleepy?

HELMER: Not at all. On the contrary, I feel extremely lively. What about you? Yes, you look quite tired and sleepy.

NORA: Yes, I'm very tired. I just want to fall straight off to sleep.

HELMER: There you are, you see! Wasn't I right in thinking we shouldn't stay any longer?

NORA: Oh, everything you do is right.

HELMER [*kissing her forehead*]:   There's my little sky-lark talking common sense. Did you notice how gay Rank was this evening?

NORA: Oh, was he? I didn't get a chance to talk to him.

HELMER: I hardly did either. But it's a long time since I saw him in such a good mood. [*Looks at* NORA *for a moment or two, then comes nearer her.*] Ah, it's wonderful to be back in our own home again, and quite alone with you. How irresistibly lovely you are, Nora!

NORA: Don't look at me like that, Torvald!

HELMER: Can't I look at my most treasured possession? At all this loveliness that's mine and mine alone, completely and utterly mine.

NORA [*walks round to the other side of the table*]:   You mustn't talk to me like that tonight.

HELMER [*following her*]:   You still have the tarantella in your blood, I see. And that makes you even more desirable. Listen! The guests are beginning to leave now. [*Softly.*] Nora . . . soon the whole house will be silent.

NORA: I should hope so.

HELMER: Of course you do, don't you, Nora my darling? You know, whenever I'm out at a party with you . . . do you know why I never talk to you very much, why I always stand away from you and only steal a quick glance at you now and then . . . do you know why I do that? It's because I'm pretending we are secretly in love, secretly engaged and nobody suspects there is anything between us.

NORA: Yes, yes. I know your thoughts are always with me, of course.

HELMER: And when it's time to go, and I lay your shawl round those shapely, young shoulders, round the exquisite curve of your neck . . . I pretend that you are my young bride, that we are just leaving our wedding, that I am taking you to our new home for the first time . . . to be alone with you for the first time . . . quite alone with your young and trembling loveliness! All evening I've been longing for you, and nothing else. And as I watched you darting and swaying in the tarantella, my blood was on fire . . . I couldn't bear it any longer . . . and that's why I brought you down here with me so early. . . .

NORA: Go away, Torvald! Please leave me alone. I won't have it.

HELMER: What's this? It's just your little game isn't it, my little Nora. Won't! Won't! Am I not your husband . . . ?

[There is a knock on the front door.]

NORA [*startled*]:   Listen . . . !

HELMER [*going towards the hall*]:   Who's there?

RANK [*outside*]:   It's me. Can I come in for a minute?

HELMER [*in a low voice, annoyed*]:   Oh, what does he want now? [*Aloud*] Wait a moment. [*He walks across and opens the door.*] How nice of you to look in on your way out.

RANK: I fancied I heard your voice and I thought I would just look in. [*He takes a quick glance round.*] Ah yes, this dear, familiar old place! How cozy and comfortable you've got things here, you two.

HELMER: You seemed to be having a pretty good time upstairs yourself.

RANK: Capital! Why shouldn't I? Why not make the most of things in this world? At least as much as one can, and for as long as one can. The wine was excellent . . .

HELMER: Especially the champagne.

RANK: You noticed that too, did you? It's incredible the amount I was able to put away.

NORA: Torvald also drank a lot of champagne this evening.

RANK: Oh?

NORA: Yes, and that always makes him quite merry.

RANK: Well, why shouldn't a man allow himself a jolly evening after a day well spent?

HELMER: Well spent? I'm afraid I can't exactly claim that.

RANK [*clapping him on the shoulder*]:   But I can, you see!

NORA: Dr. Rank, am I right in thinking you carried out a certain laboratory test today?

RANK: Exactly.

HELMER: Look at our little Nora talking about laboratory tests!

NORA: And may I congratulate you on the result?

RANK: You may indeed.

NORA: So it was good?

RANK: The best possible, for both doctor and patient—certainty!

NORA [*quickly and searchingly*]:   Certainty?

RANK: Absolute certainty. So why shouldn't I allow myself a jolly evening after that?

NORA: Quite right, Dr. Rank.

HELMER: I quite agree. As long as you don't suffer for it in the morning.

RANK: Well, you never get anything for nothing in this life.

NORA: Dr. Rank . . . you are very fond of masquerades, aren't you?

RANK: Yes, when there are plenty of amusing disguises. . . .

NORA: Tell me, what shall we two go as next time?

HELMER: There's frivolity for you . . . thinking about the next time already!

RANK: We two? I'll tell you. You must go as Lady Luck. . . .

HELMER: Yes, but how do you find a costume to suggest *that?*

RANK: Your wife could simply go in her everyday clothes. . . .

HELMER: That was nicely said. But don't you know what you would be?

RANK: Yes, my dear friend, I know exactly what I shall be.

HELMER: Well?

RANK: At the next masquerade, I shall be invisible.

HELMER: That's a funny idea!

RANK: There's a big black cloak . . . haven't you heard of the cloak of invisibility? That comes right down over you, and then nobody can see you.

HELMER [*suppressing a smile*]:   Of course, that's right.

RANK: But I'm clean forgetting what I came for. Helmer, give me a cigar, one of the dark Havanas.

HELMER: With the greatest of pleasure.

[*He offers his case.*]

RANK [*takes one and cuts the end off*]:   Thanks.

NORA [*strikes a match*]:   Let me give you a light.

RANK: Thank you. [*She holds out the match and he lights his cigar.*] And now, goodbye!

HELMER: Goodbye, goodbye, my dear fellow!

NORA: Sleep well, Dr. Rank.

RANK: Thank you for that wish.

NORA: Wish me the same.

RANK: You? All right, if you want me to. . . . Sleep well. And thanks for the light.

[He nods to them both, and goes.]

HELMER [*subdued*]:   He's had a lot to drink.

NORA [*absently*]:   Very likely.

*[*HELMER *takes a bunch of keys out of his pocket and goes out into the hall.]*

NORA: Torvald . . . what do you want there?

HELMER: I must empty the letter box, it's quite full. There'll be no room for the papers in the morning. . . .

NORA: Are you going to work tonight?

HELMER: You know very well I'm not. Hello, what's this? Somebody's been at the lock.

NORA: At the lock?

HELMER: Yes, I'm sure of it. Why should that be? I'd hardly have thought the maids . . . ? Here's a broken hairpin. Nora, it's one of yours. . . .

NORA [*quickly*]:   It must have been the children. . . .

HELMER: Then you'd better tell them not to. Ah . . . there . . . I've managed to get it open. [*He takes the things out and shouts into the kitchen.*] Helene! . . . Helene, put the light out in the hall. [*He comes into the room again with the letters in his hand and shuts the hall door.*] Look how it all mounts up. [*Runs through them.*] What's this?

NORA: The letter! Oh no, Torvald, no!

HELMER: Two visiting cards . . . from Dr. Rank.

NORA: From Dr. Rank?

HELMER [*looking at them*]:   Dr. Rank, Medical Practitioner. They were on top. He must have put them in as he left.

NORA: Is there anything on them?

HELMER: There's a black cross above his name. Look. What an uncanny idea. It's just as if he were announcing his own death.

NORA: He is.

HELMER: What? What do you know about it? Has he said anything to you?

NORA: Yes. He said when these cards came, he would have taken his last leave of us. He was going to shut himself up and die.

HELMER: Poor fellow! Of course I knew we couldn't keep him with us very long. But so soon. . . . And hiding himself away like a wounded animal.

NORA: When it has to happen, it's best that it should happen without words. Don't you think so, Torvald?

HELMER [*walking up and down*]:   He had grown so close to us. I don't think I can imagine him gone. His suffering and his loneliness seemed almost to provide a background of dark cloud to the sunshine of our lives. Well, perhaps it's all for the best. For him at any rate. [*Pauses.*] And maybe for us as well, Nora. Now there's just the two of us. [*Puts his arms round her.*] Oh, my darling wife, I can't hold you close enough. You know, Nora . . . many's the time I wish you were threatened by some terrible danger so I could risk everything, body and soul, for your sake.

NORA [*tears herself free and says firmly and decisively*]:   Now you must read your letters, Torvald.

HELMER: No, no, not tonight. I want to be with you, my darling wife.

NORA: Knowing all the time your friend is dying . . . ?

HELMER: You are right. It's been a shock to both of us. This ugly thing has come between us . . . thoughts of death and decay. We must try to free ourselves from it. Until then . . . we shall go our separate ways.

NORA [*her arms round his neck*]:   Torvald . . . good night! Good night!

HELMER [*kisses her forehead*]:   Goodnight, my little singing bird. Sleep well, Nora, I'll just read through my letters.

[He takes the letters into his room and shuts the door behind him.]

NORA [*gropes around her, wild-eyed, seizes* HELMER's *cloak, wraps it round herself, and whispers quickly, hoarsely, spasmodically*]:   Never see him again. Never, never, never. [*Throws her shawl over her head.*] And never see the children again either. Never, never. Oh, that black icy water. Oh, that bottomless . . . ! If only it were all over! He's got it now. Now he's reading it. Oh no, no! Not yet! Torvald, goodbye . . . and my children. . . .

[She rushes out in the direction of the hall; at the same moment HELMER *flings open his door and stands there with an open letter in his hand.]*

HELMER: Nora!

NORA [*shrieks*]:   Ah!

HELMER: What is this? Do you know what is in this letter?

NORA: Yes, I know. Let me go! Let me out!

HELMER [*holds her back*]:   Where are you going?

NORA [*trying to tear herself free*]:   You mustn't try to save me, Torvald!

HELMER [*reels back*]:   True! Is it true what he writes? How dreadful! No, no, it can't possibly be true.

NORA: It *is* true. I loved you more than anything else in the world.

HELMER: Don't come to me with a lot of paltry excuses!

NORA [*taking a step towards him*]:   Torvald . . . !

HELMER: Miserable woman . . . what is this you have done?

NORA: Let me go. I won't have you taking the blame for me. You mustn't take it on yourself.

HELMER: Stop play-acting! [*Locks the front door.*] You are staying here to give an account of yourself. Do you understand what you have done? Answer me! Do you understand?

NORA [*looking fixedly at him, her face hardening*]:   Yes, now I'm really beginning to understand.

HELMER [*walking up and down*]:   Oh, what a terrible awakening this is. All these
eight years . . . this woman who was my pride and joy . . . a hypocrite, a liar,
worse than that, a criminal! Oh, how utterly squalid it all is! Ugh! Ugh! [*Nora
remains silent and looks fixedly at him.*] I should have realized something like
this would happen. I should have seen it coming. All your father's irresponsible
ways. . . . Quiet! All your father's irresponsible ways are coming out in you. No
religion, no morals, no sense of duty. . . . Oh, this is my punishment for turning a
blind eye to him. It was for your sake I did it, and this is what I get for it.

NORA: Yes, this.

HELMER: Now you have ruined my entire happiness, jeopardized my whole future.
It's terrible to think of. Here I am, at the mercy of a thoroughly unscrupulous
person; he can do whatever he likes with me, demand anything he wants,
order me about just as he chooses . . . and I daren't even whimper. I'm done
for, a miserable failure, and it's all the fault of a feather-brained woman!

NORA: When I've left this world behind, you will be free.

HELMER: Oh, stop pretending! Your father was just the same, always ready with fine
phrases. What good would it do me if you left this world behind, as you put it?
Not the slightest bit of good. He can still let it all come out, if he likes; and if he
does, people might even suspect me of being an accomplice in these criminal
acts of yours. They might even think I was the one behind it all, that it was I
who pushed you into it! And it's you I have to thank for this . . . and when I've
taken such good care of you, all our married life. Now do you understand what
you have done to me?

NORA [*coldly and calmly*]:   Yes.

HELMER: I just can't understand it, it's so incredible. But we must see about putting
things right. Take that shawl off. Take it off, I tell you! I must see if I can't find
some way or other of appeasing him. The thing must be hushed up at all
costs. And as far as you and I are concerned, things must appear to go on
exactly as before. But only in the eyes of the world, of course. In other words
you'll go on living here; that's understood. But you will not be allowed to
bring up the children, I can't trust you with them. . . . Oh, that I should have to
say this to the woman I loved so dearly, the woman I still. . . . Well, that must be
all over and done with. From now on, there can be no question of happiness.
All we can do is save the bits and pieces from the wreck, preserve appearances. . . . [*The front door-bell rings.* HELMER *gives a start.*] What's that? So
late? How terrible, supposing. . . . If he should . . . ? Hide, Nora! Say you are not
well.

[*Nora stands motionless. Helmer walks across and opens the door into the hall.*]

MAID [*half dressed, in the hall*]:   It's a note for Mrs. Helmer.

HELMER: Give it to me. [*He snatches the note and shuts the door.*] Yes, it's from him.
You can't have it. I want to read it myself.

NORA: You read it then.

HELMER [*by the lamp*]:   I hardly dare. Perhaps this is the end, for both of us. Well, I must know. [*He opens the note hurriedly, reads a few lines, looks at another enclosed sheet, and gives a cry of joy.*] Nora! [NORA *looks at him inquiringly.*] Nora! I must read it again. Yes, yes, it's true! I am saved! Nora, I am saved!

NORA: And me?

HELMER: You too, of course, we are both saved, you as well as me. Look, he's sent your IOU back. He sends his regrets and apologies for what he has done. . . . His luck has changed. . . . Oh, what does it matter what he says. We are saved, Nora! Nobody can do anything to you now. Oh, Nora, Nora . . . but let's get rid of this disgusting thing first. Let me see. . . .   [*He glances at the IOU.*] No, I don't want to see it. I don't want it to be anything but a dream. [*He tears up the IOU and both letters, throws all the pieces into the stove and watches them burn.*] Well, that's the end of that. He said in his note you'd known since Christmas Eve. . . . You must have had three terrible days of it, Nora.

NORA: These three days haven't been easy.

HELMER: The agonies you must have gone through! When the only way out seemed to be. . . . No, let's forget the whole ghastly thing. We can rejoice and say: It's all over! It's all over! Listen to me, Nora! You don't seem to understand: it's all over! Why this grim look on your face? Oh, poor little Nora, of course I understand. You can't bring yourself to believe I've forgiven you. But I have, Nora, I swear it. I forgive you everything. I know you did what you did because you loved me.

NORA: That's true.

HELMER: You loved me as a wife should love her husband. It was simply that you didn't have the experience to judge what was the best way of going about things. But do you think I love you any the less for that; just because you don't know how to act on your own responsibility? No, no, you just lean on me, I shall give you all the advice and guidance you need. I wouldn't be a proper man if I didn't find a woman doubly attractive for being so obviously helpless. You mustn't dwell on the harsh things I said in that first moment of horror, when I thought everything was going to come crashing down about my ears. I have forgiven you, Nora, I swear it! I have forgiven you!

NORA: Thank you for your forgiveness.

[*She goes out through the door, right.*]

HELMER: No, don't go! [*He looks through the doorway.*] What are you doing in the spare room?

NORA: Taking off this fancy dress.

HELMER [*standing at the open door*]:   Yes, do. You try and get some rest, and set your mind at peace again, my frightened little songbird. Have a good long sleep; you know you are safe and sound under my wing. [*Walks up and down near the door.*] What a nice, cozy little home we have here, Nora! Here you can find refuge. Here I shall hold you like a hunted dove I have rescued unscathed from the cruel talons of the hawk, and calm your poor beating heart. And that will come, gradually, Nora, believe me. Tomorrow you'll see everything quite differently. Soon everything will be just as it was before. You won't need me to keep on telling you I've forgiven you; you'll feel convinced of it in your own heart. You don't really imagine me ever thinking of turning you out, or even of reproaching you? Oh, a real man isn't made that way, you know, Nora. For a man, there's something indescribably moving and very satisfying in knowing that he has forgiven his wife—forgiven her, completely and genuinely, from the depths of his heart. It's as though it made her his property in a double sense: he has, as it were, given her a new life, and she becomes in a way both his wife and at the same time his child. That is how you will seem to me after today, helpless, perplexed little thing that you are. Don't you worry your pretty little head about anything, Nora. Just you be frank with me, and I'll make all the decisions for you. . . . What's this? Not in bed? You've changed your things?

NORA [*in her everyday dress*]:   Yes, Torvald, I've changed.

HELMER: What for? It's late.

NORA: I shan't sleep tonight.

HELMER: But my dear Nora. . . .

NORA [*looks at her watch*]:   It's not so terribly late. Sit down, Torvald. We two have a lot to talk about.

[*She sits down at one side of the table.*]

HELMER: Nora, what is all this? Why so grim?

NORA: Sit down. It'll take some time. I have a lot to say to you.

HELMER [*sits down at the table opposite her*]:   You frighten me, Nora. I don't understand you.

NORA: Exactly. You don't understand me. And I have never understood you, either—until tonight. No, don't interrupt. I just want you to listen to what I have to say. We are going to have things out, Torvald.

HELMER: What do you mean?

NORA: Isn't there anything that strikes you about the way we two are sitting here?

HELMER: What's that?

NORA: We have now been married eight years. Hasn't it struck you this is the first time you and I, man and wife, have had a serious talk together?

HELMER: Depends what you mean by "serious."

NORA: Eight whole years—no, more, ever since we first knew each other—and never have we exchanged one serious word about serious things.

HELMER: What did you want me to do? Get you involved in worries that you couldn't possibly help me to bear?

NORA: I'm not talking about worries. I say we've never once sat down together and seriously tried to get to the bottom of anything.

HELMER: But, my dear Nora, would that have been a thing for you?

NORA: That's just it. You have never understood me . . . I've been greatly wronged, Torvald. First by my father, and then by you.

HELMER: What! Us two! The two people who loved you more than anybody?

NORA [*shakes her head*]:   You two never loved me. You only thought how nice it was to be in love with me.

HELMER: But, Nora, what's this you are saying?

NORA: It's right, you know, Torvald. At home, Daddy used to tell me what he thought, then I thought the same. And if I thought differently, I kept quiet about it, because he wouldn't have liked it. He used to call me his baby doll, and he played with me as I used to play with my dolls. Then I came to live in your house. . . .

HELMER: What way is that to talk about our marriage?

NORA [*imperturbably*]:   What I mean is: I passed out of Daddy's hands into yours. You arranged everything to your tastes, and I acquired the same tastes. Or I pretended to . . . I don't really know . . . I think it was a bit of both, sometimes one thing and sometimes the other. When I look back, it seems to me I have been living here like a beggar, from hand to mouth. I lived by doing tricks for you, Torvald. But that's the way you wanted it. You and Daddy did me a great wrong. It's your fault that I've never made anything of my life.

HELMER: Nora, how unreasonable . . . how ungrateful you are! Haven't you been happy here?

NORA: No, never. I thought I was, but I wasn't really.

HELMER: Not . . . not happy!

NORA: No, just gay. And you've always been so kind to me. But our house has never been anything but a playroom. I have been your doll wife, just as at home I was Daddy's doll child. And the children in turn have been my dolls. I thought it was fun when you came and played with me, just as they thought it was fun when I went and played with them. That's been our marriage, Torvald.

HELMER: There is some truth in what you say, exaggerated and hysterical though it is. But from now on it will be different. Playtime is over; now comes the time for lessons.

NORA: Whose lessons? Mine or the children's?

HELMER: Both yours and the children's, my dear Nora.

NORA: Ah, Torvald, you are not the man to teach me to be a good wife for you.

HELMER: How can you say that?

NORA: And what sort of qualifications have I to teach the children?

HELMER: Nora!

NORA: Didn't you say yourself, a minute or two ago, that you couldn't trust me with that job?

HELMER: In the heat of the moment! You shouldn't pay any attention to that.

NORA: On the contrary, you were quite right. I'm not up to it. There's another problem needs solving first. I must take steps to educate myself. You are not the man to help me there. That's something I must do on my own. That's why I'm leaving you.

HELMER [*jumps up*]:   What did you say?

NORA: If I'm ever to reach any understanding of myself and the things around me, I must learn to stand alone. That's why I can't stay here with you any longer.

HELMER: Nora! Nora!

NORA: I'm leaving here at once. I dare say Kristine will put me up for tonight. . . .

HELMER: You are out of your mind! I won't let you! I forbid you!

NORA: It's no use forbidding me anything now. I'm taking with me my own personal belongings. I don't want anything of yours, either now or later.

HELMER: This is madness!

NORA: Tomorrow I'm going home—to what used to be my home, I mean. It will be easier for me to find something to do there.

HELMER: Oh, you blind, inexperienced . . .

NORA: I must set about *getting* experience, Torvald.

HELMER: And leave your home, your husband and your children? Don't you care what people will say?

NORA: That's no concern of mine. All I know is that this is necessary for me.

HELMER: This is outrageous! You are betraying your most sacred duty.

NORA: And what do you consider to be my most sacred duty?

HELMER: Does it take me to tell you that? Isn't it your duty to your husband and your children?

NORA: I have another duty equally sacred.

HELMER: You have not. What duty might *that* be?

NORA: My duty to myself.

HELMER: First and foremost, you are a wife and mother.

NORA: That I don't believe any more. I believe that first and foremost I am an individual, just as much as you are—or at least I'm going to try to be. I know most people agree with you, Torvald, and that's also what it says in books. But I'm not content any more with what most people say, or with what it says in books. I have to think things out for myself, and get things clear.

HELMER: Surely you are clear about your position in your own home? Haven't you an infallible guide in questions like these? Haven't you your religion?

NORA: Oh, Torvald, I don't really know what religion is.

HELMER: What do you say!

NORA: All I know is what Pastor Hansen said when I was confirmed. He said religion was this, that and the other. When I'm away from all this and on my own, I'll go into that, too. I want to find out whether what Pastor Hansen told me was right—or at least whether it's right for *me.*

HELMER: This is incredible talk from a young woman! But if religion cannot keep you on the right path, let me at least stir your conscience. I suppose you do have some moral sense? Or tell me—perhaps you don't?

NORA: Well, Torvald, that's not easy to say. I simply don't know. I'm really very confused about such things. All I know is my ideas about such things are very different from yours. I've also learnt that the law is different from what I thought;

but I simply can't get it into my head that that particular law is right. Apparently a woman has no right to spare her old father on his deathbed, or to save her husband's life, even. I just don't believe it.

HELMER: You are talking like a child. You understand nothing about the society you live in.

NORA: No, I don't. But I shall go into that too. I must try to discover who is right, society or me.

HELMER: You are ill, Nora. You are delirious. I'm half inclined to think you are out of your mind.

NORA: Never have I felt so calm and collected as I do tonight.

HELMER: Calm and collected enough to leave your husband and children?

NORA: Yes.

HELMER: Then only one explanation is possible.

NORA: And that is?

HELMER: You don't love me any more.

NORA: Exactly.

HELMER: Nora! Can you say that!

NORA: I'm desperately sorry, Torvald. Because you have always been so kind to me. But I can't help it. I don't love you any more.

HELMER [*struggling to keep his composure*]:   Is that also a "calm and collected" decision you've made?

NORA: Yes, absolutely calm and collected. That's why I don't want to stay here.

HELMER: And can you also account for how I forfeited your love?

NORA: Yes, very easily. It was tonight, when the miracle didn't happen. It was then I realized you weren't the man I thought you were.

HELMER: Explain yourself more clearly. I don't understand.

NORA: For eight years I have been patiently waiting. Because, heavens, I knew miracles didn't happen every day. Then this devastating business started, and I became absolutely convinced the miracle *would* happen. All the time Krogstad's letter lay there, it never so much as crossed my mind that you would ever submit to that man's conditions. I was absolutely convinced you would say to him: Tell the whole wide world if you like. And when that was done . . .

HELMER: Yes, then what? After I had exposed my own wife to dishonor and shame . . . !

NORA: When that was done, I was absolutely convinced you would come forward and take everything on yourself, and say: I am the guilty one.

HELMER: Nora!

NORA: You mean I'd never let you make such a sacrifice for my sake? Of course not. But what would my story have counted for against yours?—That was the miracle I went in hope and dread of. It was to prevent it that I was ready to end my life.

HELMER: I would gladly toil day and night for you, Nora, enduring all manner of sorrow and distress. But nobody sacrifices his *honor* for the one he loves.

NORA: Hundreds and thousands of women have.

HELMER: Oh, you think and talk like a stupid child.

NORA: All right. But you neither think nor talk like the man I would want to share my life with. When you had got over your fright—and you weren't concerned about me but only about what might happen to you—and when all danger was past, you acted as though nothing had happened. I was your little skylark again, your little doll, exactly as before; except you would have to protect it twice as carefully as before, now that it had shown itself to be so weak and fragile. [*Rises.*] Torvald, that was the moment I realized that for eight years I'd been living with a stranger, and had borne him three children. . . . Oh, I can't bear to think about it! I could tear myself to shreds.

HELMER [*sadly*]:   I see. I see. There is a tremendous gulf dividing us. But, Nora, is there no way we might bridge it?

NORA: As I am now, I am no wife for you.

HELMER: I still have it in me to change.

NORA: Perhaps . . . if you have your doll taken away.

HELMER: And be separated from you! No, no, Nora, the very thought of it is inconceivable.

NORA [*goes into the room, right*]:   All the more reason why it must be done.

[*She comes back with her outdoor things and a small traveling bag, which she puts on the chair beside the table.*]

HELMER: Nora, Nora, not now! Wait till the morning.

NORA [*putting on her coat*]:   I can't spend the night in a strange man's room.

HELMER: Couldn't we go on living here like brother and sister . . . ?

NORA [*tying on her hat*]:   You know very well that wouldn't last. [*She draws the shawl round her.*] Goodbye, Torvald. I don't want to see the children. I know they are in better hands than mine. As I am now, I can never be anything to them.

HELMER: But some day, Nora, some day . . . ?

NORA: How should I know? I've no idea what I might turn out to be.

HELMER: But you are my wife, whatever you are.

NORA: Listen, Torvald, from what I've heard, when a wife leaves her husband's house as I am doing now, he is absolved by law of all responsibility for her. I can at any rate free you from all responsibility. You must not feel in any way bound, any more than I shall. There must be full freedom on both sides. Look, here's your ring back. Give me mine.

HELMER: That too?

NORA: That too.

HELMER: There it is.

NORA: Well, that's the end of that. I'll put the keys down here. The maids know where everything is in the house—better than I do, in fact. Kristine will come in the morning after I've left to pack up the few things I brought with me from home. I want them sent on.

HELMER: The end! Nora, will you never think of me?

NORA: I dare say I'll often think about you and the children and this house.

HELMER: May I write to you, Nora?

NORA: No, never. I won't let you.

HELMER: But surely I can send you . . .

NORA: Nothing, nothing.

HELMER: Can't I help you if ever you need it?

NORA: I said no. I don't accept things from strangers.

HELMER: Nora, can I never be anything more to you than a stranger?

NORA [*takes her bag*]:   Ah, Torvald, only by a miracle of miracles . . .

HELMER: Name it, this miracle of miracles!

NORA: Both you and I would have to change to the point where. . . . Oh, Torvald, I don't believe in miracles any more.

HELMER: But I *will* believe. Name it! Change to the point where . . . ?

NORA: Where we could make a real marriage of our lives together. Goodbye!

[*She goes out through the hall door.*]

HELMER [*sinks down on a chair near the door, and covers his face with his hands*]: Nora! Nora! [*He rises and looks round.*] Empty! She's gone! [*With sudden hope.*] The miracle of miracles . . . ?

[*The heavy sound of a door being slammed is heard from below.*]

MAKING CONNECTIONS

1. To what extent was your response to this play influenced by your own background or experience?
2. What kind of relationship do the Helmers have? In what way do their conversations early in the play tell us almost everything there is to know about their relationship?
3. To what extent is Nora a victim of society? Of Torvald? Of herself?
4. Who is Mrs. Linde and how does she differ from Nora?
5. What is your response to Krogstad? To what extent is he a victim of society?
6. Consider the kinds of statements that are made about marriage by the past experience of supporting characters (Mrs. Linde, Krogstad, Ann Marie) in this play.
7. What kind of relationship do Krogstad and Mrs. Linde have? Compare it to the Helmers' relationship.
8. What is the role of Dr. Rank in the play? To what extent does he know Nora better than Torvald? Why is Nora so upset when he confesses his love for her?
9. What is the theme of the play? What objects or actions in the play seem symbolic of the play's theme?
10. Is the play still relevant? Are there relationships like this today? Explain.
11. What conventions of society are being criticized in the play? Consider Ibsen's statements on pages 918–920. What is your response to his views in light of your response to the play?

MAKING AN ARGUMENT

1. How do you feel about Nora leaving Torvald and their children at the end of the play? Do you think she has a choice? Consider Ibsen's changed ending on page 919. Which ending do you prefer? Write an argument for or against Nora's action at the end of the play. Cite the text of the play for support.
2. Many women today still feel the frustrations of Nora Helmer. For them, the world still seems made for men. The specific conditions of Nora's problem are out of date, but *A Doll's House* remains the classic statement of the problem. With this in mind, bring Ibsen's play into the twenty first century and write about Nora's situation now. In addition to your own experience, consider examples from other literature, television, and movies.

THE ADAMS LETTERS [1776]

From Abigail to John
Braintree
March 31, 1776

——I long to hear that you have declared an independancy (sic)—and by the way in the new Code of Laws which I suppose it will be necessary for you to make I desire you would Remember the Ladies and be more generous and favorable to them than your ancestors. Do not put such unlimited powers into the hands of the Husbands. Remember all Men would be tyrants if they could. If perticular (sic) care and attention is not paid to the Laidies (sic) we are determined to foment a Rebellion, and will not hold ourselves bound by any Laws in which we have no voice, or Representation.

That your Sex are Naturally Tyrannical is a Truth so thoroughly established as to admit of no dispute, but such of you as wish to be happy willingly give up the harsh title of Master for the more tender and endearing one of Friend. Why then, not put it out of power of the vicious and the Lawless to use us with cruelty and indignity with impunity. Men of Sense in all Ages abhor those customs which treat us only as the vassals of your Sex. Regard us then as Beings placed by providence under your protection and in imitation of the Supreem (sic) Being make use of that power only for our happiness.

From John to Abigail
April 14, 1776

As to your extraordinary Code of Laws, I cannot but laugh. We have been told that our Struggle has loosened the bands of Government everywhere. The Children and Apprentices were disobedient—that schools and Colledges (sic) were grown turbulent—that Indians slighted their Guardians and Negroes grew insolent to their Masters. But your Letter was the first Intimation that another Tribe more numerous and powerfull (sic) than all the rest were grown discontented.—This is rather too coarse a Compliment but you are so saucy, I won't blot it out.

Depend upon it, We know better than to repeal our Masculine systems. Altho (sic) they are in full Force, you know they are little more than Theory. We dare not exert our Power in its full Latitude. We are obliged to go fair, and softly, and in Practice you know We are the subjects. We have only the Name of Masters, and rather than give this, which would compleatly (sic) subject us to the Despotism of the Peticoat, I hope General Washington, and all our Brave Heroes would fight.

A Husband's Letter to His Wife   [1844]

June 23, 1844

Dear Wife,

You have sinned greatly—and maybe I too; but this much is certain: Adam sinned after Eve had already sinned. So it is with us; you, alone, carry the guilt of all the misfortune which, however, I helped to enlarge later by my behavior. Listen now, since I still believe certain things to be necessary in order that we may have a peaceful life. If we want not only to be content for a day but forever, you will have to follow my wishes. So examine yourself and determine if you are strong enough to conquer your false ambitions and your stubbornness to submit to all the conditions, the fulfillment of which I cannot ignore. Every sensible person will tell you that all I ask of you is what is easily understood. If you insist on remaining stubborn, then do not return to my house, for you will never be happy with me; your husband, children, and the entire city threaten indifference or even contempt.

But if you decide to act *sensibly and correctly, that is justly and kindly,* then be certain that many in the world will envy you.

I am including here the paper which I read to you in front of the rabbi; ask anyone in your residence if the wishes expressed by me are not quite reasonable, and are of a kind to which every wife can agree for the welfare of domestic happiness. In any case, act in a way you think best.

5   When you decide to return, write to tell me on which day and hour you depart from Berlin and give me your itinerary whether by way of Kuestrin and Pinne or by way of Wollstein. I will then meet you at Wollstein or Pinne. I expect you will bring Solomon with you.

Don't travel unprepared. If you need money, ask your father.

May God enlighten your heart and mind.

I remain your so far unhappy, [Marcus]

Greetings to my parents, brothers, and sisters; also your brother. Show them what you wish, this letter, the enclosure, whatever you want. The children are fortunately healthy,

If you want to return with joy and peace, write me by return mail. In that case, I would rather send you a carriage. Maybe Madam Fraenkel will come along. . . .

(Enclosure)

10   My wife promises—for which every wife is obligated to her husband—to follow my wishes in everything and to strictly obey my orders. It is already self-evident that our marital relations have often been disturbed by the fact that my wife does not follow my

wishes but believes herself to be entitled to act on her own, even if this is totally against my orders. In order not to have to remind my wife every second what my wishes are regarding homemaking and public conduct—wishes which I have often expressed—I want to make here a few rules which shall serve as a code of conduct. A home is best run if the work for each hour is planned ahead of time, if possible.

Servants get up no later than 5:00 A.M. in summer and 6:00 A.M. in winter, the children an hour later. The cook prepares breakfast. The nursemaid puts out clothes for every child, prepares water and sponge, cleans the combs, etc. The cook should stay in the kitchen unless there is time to clean the rooms. At least once a week the rooms should be cleaned whenever possible, but not all on the same day.

Every Wednesday, the people in the house should do a laundry. Every last Wednesday in the month, there shall be a large laundry with an outside washer-woman. At least every Monday, the seamstress shall come into the house to fix what is necessary.

Every Thursday or Friday, bread is baked for the week; I think it is best to buy grain and have it ground, but to knead it at home.

Every Friday special bread (Barches) should be bought for the evening meal.

15   The kitchen list will be prepared and discussed every Thursday evening, jointly, by me and my wife; but my wish is to be decisive.

After this, provisions are to be bought every Friday at the market. For this purpose, my wife, herself, will go to the market on Fridays, accompanied by a servant; she can substitute a special woman who does errands (*Faktorfrau*) if she wishes, but not a servant.

All expenditures have to be written down daily and punctually.

The children receive a bath every Thursday evening. The children's clothes must be kept in a specially appointed chest, with a separate compartment for each child with the child's name upon it. The boys' suits and girls' dresses are to be kept separately. To keep used laundry, there must be a hamper easily accessible. Equally important is the food storage box in which provisions are kept in order, locked and safe from vermin.

The kitchen should be kept in order. Once a week all woodwork and copper must be scoured. The lights and lamps have to be cleaned daily. Toward servants, one has to be strict and just. Therefore, one should not call them names which aren't suitable for a decent wife. One should give them enough nourishing food. Disobedience and obstinacy are to be referred to me.

20   My wife will never make visits in my absence. However, she should visit the synagogue every Saturday—at least once a month; also she should go for a walk with the children at least once a week.

SOJOURNER TRUTH

AIN'T I A WOMAN   [1851]

This impromptu speech given by Sojourner Truth, a freed slave, was recorded with her own commentary by Frances Gage at a woman's rights convention in Ohio.

"WALL, CHILERN, WHAR DAR IS SO MUCH racket dar must be somethin' out o' kilter. I tink dat 'twixt de niggers of de Souf and de womin at de Norf, all talkin' 'bout rights, de white men will be in a fix pretty soon. But what's all dis here talkin' 'bout?

"Dat man ober dar say dat womin needs to be helped into carriages, and lifted ober ditches, and to hab de best place everywhar. Nobody eber helps me into carriages, or ober mud puddles, or gibs me any best place!" And raising herself to her full height, and her voice to a pitch like rolling thunder, she asked, 'And an't I a woman? Look at me! Look at my arm! (and she bared her right arm to the shoulder, showing her tremendous muscular power). I have ploughed, and planted, and gathered into barns, and no man could head me! And an't I a woman? I could work as much and eat as much as a man—when I could get it—and bear de lash as well! And an't I a woman? I have borne thirteen chilern, and seen 'em mos' all sold off to slavery, and when I cried out with my mother's grief, none but Jesus heard me! And an't I a woman?

"Den dey talks 'bout dis ting in de head; what dis dey call it?" ("Intellect," whispered someone near.) "Dat's it, honey. What's dat got to do wid womin's rights or nigger's rights? If my cup won't hold but a pint, and yourn holds a quart, wouldn't ye be mean not to let me have my little half-measure full?" And she pointed her significant finger, and sent a keen glance at the minister who had made the argument. The cheering was long and loud.

5   "Den dat little man in black dar, he say women can't have as much rights as men, 'cause Christ wan't a woman! Whar did your Christ come from?" Rolling thunder couldn't have stilled that crowd, as did those deep, wonderful tones, as she stood there with outstretched arms and eyes of fire. Raising her voice still louder, she repeated, "Whar did your Christ come from? From God and a, woman! Man had nothin' to do wid Him." Oh, what a rebuke that was to that little man.

Turning again to another objector, she took up the defense of Mother Eve. I cannot follow her through it all. It was pointed, and witty, and solemn; eliciting at almost every sentence deafening applause; and she ended by asserting: "If de fust woman God ever made was strong enough to turn de world upside down all alone, dese women togedder (and she glanced her eye over the platform) ought to be able to turn it back, and get it right side up again! And now dey is asking to do it, de men better let 'em." Long-continued cheering greeted this. "'Bleeged to ye for hearin' on me, and now ole Sojourner han't got nothin' more to say."

Amid roars of applause, she returned to her corner, leaving more than one of us with streaming eyes, and hearts beating with gratitude. She had taken us up in her strong arms and carried us safely over the slough of difficulty turning the whole tide in our favor. I have never in my life seen anything like the magical influence that subdued the mobbish spirit of the day, and turned the sneers and jeers of an excited crowd into notes of respect and admiration. Hundreds rushed up to shake hands with her, and congratulate the glorious old mother, and bid her God-speed on her mission of "testifyin' agin concerning the wickedness of this 'ere people."

HENRIK IBSEN

NOTES FOR THE MODERN TRAGEDY   [1878]

There are two kinds of spiritual law, two kinds of conscience, one in man and another, altogether different, in woman. They do not understand each other; but in practical life the woman is judged by man's law, as though she were not a woman but a man.

The wife in the play ends by having no idea of what is right or wrong; natural feeling on the one hand and belief in authority on the other have altogether bewildered her.

A woman cannot be herself in the society of the present day, which is an exclusively masculine society, with laws framed by men and with a judicial system that judges feminine conduct from a masculine point of view.

She has committed forgery, and she is proud of it; for she did it out of love for her husband, to save his life. But this husband with his commonplace principles of honor is on the side of the law and looks at the question from the masculine point of view.

5   Spiritual conflicts. Oppressed and bewildered by the belief in authority, she loses faith in her moral right and ability to bring up her children. Bitterness. A mother in modern society, like certain insects who go away and die when she has done her duty in the propagation of the race. Love of life, of home, of husband and children and family. Now and then a womanly shaking off of her thoughts. Sudden return of anxiety and terror. She must bear it all alone. The catastrophe approaches, inexorably, inevitably. Despair, conflict, and destruction.

THE CHANGED ENDING OF A DOLL'S HOUSE FOR A GERMAN PRODUCTION
[1880]

NORA: . . . . Where we could make a real marriage out of our lives together. Goodbye. [*Begins to go.*]

HELMER: Go then! [*Seizes her arm.*] But first you shall see your children for the last time!

NORA: Let me go! I will not see them! I cannot!

HELMER [*draws her over to the door, left*]:   You shall see them. [*Opens the door and says softly.*] Look, there they are asleep, peaceful and carefree. Tomorrow, when they wake up and call for their mother, they will be—motherless.

NORA [*trembling*]:   Motherless. . . !

HELMER: As you once were.

NORA: Motherless! [*Struggles with herself, lets her traveling bag fall, and says.*] Oh, this is a sin against myself, but I cannot leave them. [*Half sinks down by the door.*]

HELMER [*joyfully, but softly*]:   Nora!

[*The Curtain Falls.*]

SPEECH AT THE BANQUET OF THE NORWEGIAN LEAGUE FOR WOMEN'S RIGHTS
[1898]

Christiania, May 26, 1898

I am not a member of the Women's Rights League. Whatever I have written has been without any conscious thought of making propaganda. I have been more the poet and less the social philosopher than people generally seem inclined to believe. I thank you for the toast, but must disclaim the honor of having consciously worked for the women's rights movement. I am not even quite clear as to just what this women's rights movement really is. To me it has seemed a problem of mankind in general. And if you read my books carefully you will understand this. True enough, it is desirable to solve the woman problem, along with all the others; but that has not been the whole purpose. My task has been the *description of humanity.* To be sure, whenever such a description is felt to be reasonably true, the reader will read his own feelings and sentiments into the work of the poet. These are then attributed to the poet; but incorrectly so. Every reader remolds the work beautifully and neatly, each according to his own personality. Not only those who write but also those who read are poets. They are collaborators. They are often more poetical than the poet himself.

ELIZABETH CADY STANTON

EXCERPT FROM "THE SOLITUDE OF SELF" [1892]

The strongest reason for giving woman all the opportunities for higher education, for the full development of her faculties, her forces of mind and body; for giving her the most enlarged freedom of thought and action; a complete emancipation from all forms of bondage, of custom, dependence, superstition; from all the crippling influences of fear—is the solitude and personal responsibility of her own individual life. The strongest reason why we ask for woman a voice in the government under which she lives; in the religion she is asked to believe; equality in social life, where she is the chief factor; a place in the trades and professions, where she may earn her bread, is because of her birthright to self-sovereignty; because, as an individual, she must rely on herself. No matter how much women prefer to lean, to be protected and supported, nor how much men desire to have them do so, they must make the voyage of life alone, and for safety in an emergency, they must know something of the laws of navigation. To guide our own craft, we must be captain, pilot, engineer; with chart and compass to stand at the wheel; to watch the winds and waves, and know when to take in the sail, and to read the signs in the firmament over all. It matters not whether the solitary voyager is man or woman; nature, having endowed them equally, leaves them to their own skill and judgment in the hour of danger, and, if not equal to the occasion, alike they perish.

   To appreciate the importance of fitting every human soul for independent action, think for a moment of the immeasurable solitude of self. We come into the world alone, unlike all who have gone before us, we leave it alone, under circumstances peculiar to ourselves. No mortal ever has been, no mortal ever will be like the soul just launched on the sea of life. There can never again be just such a combination of prenatal influences; never again just such environments as make up the infancy, youth and manhood of this one. Nature never repeats herself, and the possibilities of one human soul will never be found in another. No one has ever found two blades of ribbon grass alike, and no one will ever find two human beings alike. Seeing, then, that what must be the infinite diversity in human character, we can in a measure appreciate the loss to a nation when any class of the people is uneducated and unrepresented in the government.

WILBUR FISK TILLETT

EXCERPT FROM "SOUTHERN WOMANHOOD" [1891]

The growing respectability of self-support in woman is everywhere recognized as one of the healthiest signs of the times. The number of vocations open to women is constantly on the increase. Some modes of self-support are, and always will be, socially more respectable than others. In the report for 1888 of the Commissioner of Labor concerning the number and condition of working-women in the large cities is the following concerning Charleston, South Carolina:

> In no other Southern city has the exclusion of women from business been so rigid and the tradition that respectability is forfeited by manual labor so influential and powerful. Proud and well-born women have practised great self-denial at ill-paid conventional pursuits in preference to independence in untrodden paths. The embargo against self-support, however, has to some extent been lifted, and were there a larger number of remunerative occupations open to women, the rush to avail of them would show how ineffectual the old traditions have become.

A similar report of 1890 would show rapid changes and advances in public sentiment concerning the respectability of self-support in women, and would reveal that the "embargo" had, in most parts of the South at least, been entirely removed.

If we look at the South as a whole, and not at individual portions of it, it is unquestionably true that the great changes which the past thirty years have witnessed have wrought most favorably upon the intellectual life of Southern womanhood. The conditions under which Southern women now live are far more favorable for developing literary women than those existing in the days of slavery. In 1869 a volume was published by Mr. James Wood Davidson entitled "The Living Writers of the South," in which 241 writers are noticed, of which number 75 are women and 166 are men. Of the 241 named, 40 had written only for newspapers and magazines, while 201 had published one or more volumes, aggregating 739 in all. Although this book was published only four years after the close of the war, it was even then true that from two thirds to three fourths of the volumes mentioned in it as having been published by women—not to speak of the others—had been written and published after the opening of the war. They had been called forth by the war and the trying experiences following it. Whether the changed conditions under which we live have anything to do with it, it is nevertheless certainly true that there have been more literary women developed in the South in the thirty years since the war than in all our previous history.

It is Victor Hugo who has called this "the century of woman." It is certainly an age that has witnessed great changes in the life, education, and labor of women everywhere; and these changes have all been in the direction of enlarging the sphere of woman's activities, increasing her liberties, and opening up possibilities to her life hitherto restricted to man. It is a movement limited to no land and to no race. So far as this movement may have any tendency to take woman out of her true place in the home, to give her man's work to do and to develop masculine qualities in her, it finds no sympathy in the South. The Southern woman loves the retirement of home, and shrinks from everything that would tend to bring her into the public gaze.

DOROTHY DIX

THE AMERICAN WIFE   [1898]

It always seems to the American woman that the wives of other countries, who are held up for her admiration and imitation, have rather the easiest time of it. It would be comparatively simple to make yourself a decorative object to adorn a man's house, if that were all that was expected of you. It would be simple enough to accomplish marvels of cooking and housekeeping if that were the chief end of life. It is when one attempts to combine the useful and the ornamental—to be a Dresden statuette in the parlor and a reliable range in the kitchen—that the situation becomes trying, and calls for genuine ability. Yet this is what we expect of the average American wife, merely as a matter of course. She must be a paragon of domesticity, an ornament in society, a wonder in finance and a light in the literary circle to which she belongs.

In our curious social system, many things are left to her that the men attend to in other countries. For one thing, her husband expects her to assume all authority and management of the home and family. He doesn't want to be bothered about it. When he makes the money he feels he has done his whole duty, and he leaves the rest to her. When he comes home, tired out, after a day's work, he wants to rest, to read his paper, to think out some scheme in which he is interested. If his wife has any idea of leaning on his superior judgment and asking his advice about domestic problems she is very soon undeceived. "Great Scotts, Mary," is the impatient reply, "can't you manage your own affairs? I haven't got time to see about it. Settle it yourself."

It is the same way about the children. The American father is generally a devoted parent, but he wants his wife to do the managing and disciplining. In the brief hours he is at home, the little ones are his playthings, and he spoils them, and indulges them with a happy sense that he has no responsibility about it and that their mother will have to do the subsequent disciplining. She is responsible for their mental and physical well-being. She decides on the schools, and what they shall study, what colleges they shall attend, and all the rest of it. The average American John has a well-founded belief that his Mary is the smartest woman in the world, and knows what she is about, and so, at last, when she announces that the children need to go to Europe to study this or that, he consents through mere force of habit. He is so much in the way of letting her decide things it doesn't occur to him he could raise a dissenting voice.

To her, too, he leaves the matter of society. She dominates it, and runs it, and an American married man's social position depends entirely on his wife. If she is ambitious he climbs meekly up the social ladder in her wake; if she is not ambitious, they sit comfortably and contentedly down on the lower rungs, and stay there. He feels that he would be a bungler in the game of society, and he simply backs her hand for all it is worth. He pays for the house in the fashionable neighborhood of her choice, and for her entertainments, but he leaves all the rest to "mother and the girls." They must attend to the intricate social machinery, that he admits is a necessity, and is perfectly willing to support with anything but his own presence.

WOMEN AND SUICIDE   [1899]

The claim recently put boldly forth by a distinguished lawyer that a person has a right to die, when by means of disease or misfortune life becomes a burden, has provoked renewed discussion of the suicide question, and it is interesting, in this connection, to note that by far the larger number of suicides are among men. Women seldom take their own lives, and so we have the curious and contradictory spectacle of the sex that is universally accounted the braver and stronger, flinging themselves out of the world to avoid its troubles, while the weaklings patiently bear theirs on to the bitter end.

Nothing is more common than for the man who has speculated with other people's money and lost, and so brought ruin and disgrace on his family, to commit suicide. In fact, after reading of the trusted cashier going wrong, in one column, we almost expect to read in the next that he shot himself. No thought apparently comes to him of having any duty to stay and help lift the misery he brought on innocent people. In times of great financial stress, when a rich man has everything swept away, he, too, often solves the question of the future for himself by suicide, leaving his wife and little children to face a situation for which they are wholly unprepared. You never hear of a woman committing suicide and leaving her little children to the cruel mercies of the world, because she has lost her property. Instead, she feels more than ever that they need her care, and her help, and that she would be incapable of the unmentionable baseness of deserting them in such a crisis.

Yet if suicide is ever justifiable, it is for woman far more than men. She is always handicapped in the race of life. Sometimes with bodily infirmities, sometimes with mental idiosyncrasies, always by lack of training and business experience. Hard as poverty is for a man, it is harder still for a woman. Desperate as the struggle for existence is for him, it is still more desperate for her, limited by narrower opportunities, and rewarded with lesser pay. Terrible as are the tortures suffered by many a poor wretch, they are no worse than the life-long martyrdom that many a woman endures with never a thought of doing anything but bearing them with Christian fortitude and resignation until God's own hand sets her free.

There are many reasons why this state of affairs should exist. Woman's whole life is one long lesson in patience and submission. She must always give in. Men feel that they are born to command, to force circumstances to their will, and when circumstances can no longer be forced or bent, and they must yield to untoward fate, too many yield to the desire to avoid the misery they see before them by sneaking out of life. It is always a coward's deed. The babe salutes life with a wail, and the dying man takes leave of it with a groan. Between there is no time that has not its own troubles, and cares, and sorrows, and it is our part to bear them with courage, and it should be part of our pride in our sex that so many women sustain this brave attitude towards life under circumstances that might well tempt them to play the coward's part.

CHARLOTTE PERKINS STETSON (GILMAN)

EXCERPT FROM "WOMEN AND ECONOMICS"   [1899]

Worse than the check set upon the physical activities of women has been the restriction of their power to think and judge for themselves. The extended use of the human will and its decisions is conditioned upon free, voluntary action. In her rudimentary position, woman was denied the physical freedom which underlies all knowledge, she was denied the mental freedom which is the path to further wisdom, she was denied the moral freedom of being mistress of her own action and of learning by the merciful law of consequences what was right and what was wrong; and she has remained, perforce, undeveloped in the larger judgment of ethics.

Her moral sense is large enough, morbidly large, because in this tutelage she is always being praised or blamed for her conduct. She lives in a forcing-bed of sensitiveness to moral distinctions, but the broad judgment that alone can guide and govern this sensitiveness she has not. Her contribution to moral progress has added to the anguish of the world the fierce sense of sin and shame, the desperate desire to do right, the fear of wrong; without giving it the essential help of a practical wisdom and a regulated will. Inheriting with each generation the accumulating forces of our social nature, set back in each generation by the conditions of the primitive human female, women have become vividly self-conscious centres of moral impulse, but poor guides as to the conduct which alone can make that impulse useful and build the habit of morality into the constitution of the race.

Recognizing her intense feeling on moral lines, and seeing in her the rigidly preserved virtues of faith, submission, and self-sacrifice,—qualities which in the Dark Ages were held to be the first of virtues,—we have agreed of late years to call woman the moral superior of man. But the ceaseless growth of human life, social life, has developed in him new virtues, later, higher, more needful; and the moral nature of woman, as maintained in this rudimentary stage by her economic dependence, is a continual check to the progress of the human soul. The main feature of her life—the restriction of her range of duty to the love and service of her own immediate family—acts upon us continually as a retarding influence, hindering the expansion of the spirit of social love and service on which our very lives depend. It keeps the moral standard of the patriarchal era still before us, and blinds our eyes to the full duty of man.

An intense self-consciousness, born of the ceaseless contact of close personal relation; an inordinate self-interest, bred by the constant personal attention and service of this relation; a feverish, torturing, moral sensitiveness, without the width and clarity of vision of a full-grown moral sense; a thwarted will, used to meek surrender, cunning evasion, or futile rebellion; a childish, wavering, short-range judgment, handicapped by emotion; a measureless devotion to one's own sex relatives, and a maternal passion swollen with the full strength of the great social heart, but denied social expression,—such psychic qualities as these, born in us all, are the inevitable result of the sexuo-economic relation.

5   It is not alone upon woman, and, through her, upon the race, that the ill-effects may be observed. Man, as master, has suffered from his position also. The lust for power and conquest, natural to the male of any species, has been fostered in him to an enormous degree by this cheap and easy lordship. His dominance is not that of one chosen as best fitted to rule or of one ruling by successful competition with "foemen worthy of his steel"; but it is a sovereignty based on the accident of sex, and holding over such helpless and inferior dependants as could not question or oppose. The easy superiority that needs no striving to maintain it; the temptation to cruelty always begotten by irresponsible power; the pride and self-will which surely accompany it,—these qualities have been bred into the souls of men by their side of the relation. When man's place was maintained by brute force, it made him more brutal: when his place was maintained by purchase, by the power of economic necessity, then he grew into the merciless use of such power as distinguishes him to-day.

Yet here, as in the other evil results of the sexuo-economic relation, we can see the accompanying good that made the condition necessary in its time; and we can follow the beautiful results of our present changes with comforting assurance. A healthy, normal moral sense will be ours, freed from its exaggerations and contradictions; and, with that clear perception, we shall no longer conceive of the ethical process as something outside of and against nature, but as the most natural thing in the world.

Where now we strive and agonize after impossible virtues, we shall then grow naturally and easily into those very qualities; and we shall not even think of them as especially commendable. Where our progress hitherto has been warped and hindered by the retarding influence of surviving rudimentary forces, it will flow on smoothly and rapidly when both men and women stand equal in economic relation. When the mother of the race is free, we shall have a better world, by the easy right of birth and by the calm, slow, friendly forces of social evolution.

Natalie Zemon Davis and Jill Ker Conway

The Rest of the Story   [1999]

For all their drama and insight, traditional histories of the last thousand years fall short. Written mostly by men, they introduced women into the standard parade of wars, revolutions, monarchs and parliaments only at moments like their ascension to inherited thrones or religious authority. In the nineteenth century, most male historians compounded the problem by making women's history sound as though women had only then begun making headway.

Women's history has more to it than that. Women have always questioned their subordination and often found ways around it. Further, some institutions important in the lives of women that seem timeless, like monogamous marriage, are in fact rooted in the last thousand years; some ostensibly modern movements reach far back in time. Indeed, many turning points on the thousand-year time line of women's history are little known or little understood. The following brief account of that history describes the rest of the story.

Who Says Men Are Closer to God?

Are women and men more alike than they are different? And where they are different, are women inferior or superior? Such questions have been debated since biblical times, and especially in the years after 1000. Some medieval theologians—male, that is—taught that woman was not created in God's image. But that could not be true, abbesses and nuns objected, for they had felt Christ's "imprint of resemblance" on them. Hildegard of Bingen, a nun in the Rhineland in the twelfth century, insisted that women's "weakness" did not refer to spiritual capacities. A woman could mortify the flesh and draw close to God as well as any man.

Such women accepted the general view that the universe was organized into realms of higher and lower: angels over humans, humans over animals, nobles over commoners, soul over body. But when it came to men over women, women balked. Christine de Pizan, poet and moralist at the French court, said in her "Book of the City of Ladies" of 1405 that God had created men and women with equal potential.

If men had stronger bodies, women had freer and sharper minds, if they were just educated. Against the old medical idea that women had a hungry womb—that is, a sexual appetite less controllable than men's—Christine countered that women were by nature virtuous and modest.

5   The hottest debates about male-female relations in medieval Europe turned on celibacy. In the tenth and eleventh centuries, many priests were married, and their wives had access to the sacred. In a turning point in women's history, the eleventh-century reforms of Pope Gregory VII did away with clerical marriage in the Roman Church. These reforms inaugurated ten centuries in which sexually active males—and all women—were forbidden to perform important liturgical functions. A spiritual demotion it may have been, but it also confirmed an ideal of the celibate life, leaving nuns like Hildegard of Bingen scope for high ascetic devotions.

One Man, One Wife

The church put all its force behind insisting on monogamous, permanent marriage. An important step was declaring the full doctrine of marriage as a religious sacrament in 1215. Getting the doctrine accepted by lay people was another matter. Among the landed classes, men lived with concubines instead of, or along with, wives and cast their women aside at will. Only when the great families decided that the church's rule would help keep feudal property together did they go along.

Then in the sixteenth century, the Protestant Reformation did away with marriage as a religious sacrament and allowed for divorce. Yet it legitimated marriage all the more by allowing clergymen to wed and doing away with celibate nunneries and monasteries. In Europe, prostitution was made illegal in both Catholic and Protestant cities. It was still practiced, of course, as was concubinage, especially between European settlers in America and their female slaves. But monogamous marriage remained the triumphant cultural ideal.

According to religious teaching and secular law, the wife was "subject" to her husband, and her property was under his control. He was to rule her justly and not be cruel. Moderate beating was permissible, though some Protestant pastors preached against using it at all, and Ashkenazic rabbis disagreed about whether it was grounds for divorce. Divorce was not an easy out: a single woman with children could scarcely survive. Marriage was a frame that most women accepted, hoping for affectionate unions. What we today would call lesbian couples lived as married partners in the seventeenth and eighteenth centuries, one cross-dressing as a man. Protofeminists chronicled abuses in marriage, but did not reject the notion of "subjection" outright until the eighteenth century. A seventeenth-century male feminist said that wives should defer to their husbands not because the men were truly superior, but to keep the peace.

Nine Babies, Three Adults

More worrisome to women than subjection was procreation. For most of the millennium, the pattern was many births, many deaths. Given the poor food and poor health, it was not always easy to get and stay pregnant. Many infants, even among the wealthy, died at birth. In seventeenth-century France, a long-lived peasant mother might bring nine children to term; half might survive till age five, and she could rejoice if two or three reached adulthood. Under these circumstances, the local midwife was consulted much more often for medicines to conceive than for those to abort. Only in the late seventeenth century, when a better food supply in Western Europe allowed more children to survive, did couples start to limit the number of their children.

10   The model of man over woman had some effect in every sphere, forcing women to find means to cope or resist. Female wage earners were paid less than men; the women improvised new ways to stitch, smuggle, peddle or beg. Male surgeons began to deliver babies in the wealthy families in the seventeenth century; midwives defended their female turf in the village, claiming their dexterous hands would do better than the surgeon's forceps.

Does "Man" Include Woman?

Since the days of Hildegard of Bingen, women had tried for a larger role in religion. The witchcraft prosecutions that swept Europe and then New England in the fifteenth through seventeenth centuries threatened that initiative: among the many thousands executed, women outnumbered men everywhere, at least four to one. To rulers and churchmen seeking control, the sorceress with her pact with the devil was the symbol of secret revolt. Out of jealousy, infertile village women even accused other women. Meanwhile, during the Counter Reformation, energetic women founded teaching orders that brought instruction to many girls other than nuns; contemplative orders were reformed by leaders like Teresa of Avila. Her autobiography, a profound account of a woman's interior and mystical life, was read as eagerly as Augustine's "Confessions."

Jewish women followed their own leader in the women's gallery of the synagogue; one Yiddish prayer visualized women studying Torah in Paradise. Protestant women expanded their Bible reading, but it was especially radical sects like the Quakers who challenged the limits on women. Margaret Fell wrote her 1666 tract, "Women's Speaking Justified," against Paul's admonition that women should keep silent in church. Women "led by the Spirit of God" could preach "Christ in the Male and Female is one."

For centuries, women had been queens, some of whom, like Elizabeth I of England, sustained authority by combining "masculine" and "feminine" styles of rulership. But no woman served in the law courts or chancelleries of late medieval and early modern monarchies. If a woman wanted to fight in the royal army, she had to do so disguised as a man. Joan of Arc, openly leading soldiers into battle to save France, was an exception in her day—and she ended up burned at the stake.

Most political action of women was taken informally through conversations and coquetry at court and as sponsors of the salons that arose in many cities in the seventeenth century. More open influence came about through increased literacy and printing. By the eighteenth century, women of diverse views were contributing to the abundant pamphlet literature on public affairs. The English historian Catharine Sawbridge Macaulay published tracts defending authors' copyright, frequently elected parliaments and the rights of the American colonies. As for the illiterate women of the lower classes in England, France and the Netherlands, their only lever of protest was joining in street riots.

15   All these forms of political action came together in the French Revolution, and some new ones were added as women made public political speeches and joined the army openly. The new philosophy of rational natural rights placed all men on an

equal footing in regard to citizenship and the law. But did "men" include women? The French playwright Olympe de Gouges insisted that it did in her "Declaration of the Rights of Woman," in 1791, as did Mary Wollstonecraft the following year in "A Vindication of the Rights of Woman." Others did not want women to have so much of a share in political life. Men of the revolution said that women should stay home and rear their sons to be good citizens. Even evangelical women encouraged their sisters to seek reform through religion and leave matters of state to men. It would be the new American republic where the issues of women's status would play out most vigorously over the next century.

"The Slavery of Marriage"

When enlightenment ideas came to America, the debate about women's rights found a new context, since the most powerful form of social hierarchy there was not gender but race. And the American Constitution, by dispensing with hereditary rank and monarchical institutions, immediately granted women a new role: teaching republican values to young Americans. The new republic opened many avenues to women: social, economic, political, educational and religious. Evangelical Christianity made the home, not the church, the site of religious instruction.

As women increasingly assumed this responsibility, they also began teaching outside the home and stressed the need for women's schools. In the first half of the nineteenth century, Emma Willard's Troy Female Seminary and Catharine Beecher's Hartford Female Seminary became thriving institutions, followed by Mary Lyon's Mount Holyoke Female Seminary. By midcentury, it was clear that tax revenues should be spent to educate girls as well as boys, at least in New York and New England. By the 1870s, many public universities admitted women, and elite women's colleges like Smith and Wellesley were established. In 1894, feminist donors to Johns Hopkins Medical School used their gifts to compel the admission of women.

Still, far into the first half of the twentieth century, many professional schools continued to bar women, and when they were admitted, discrimination drove them to lower-status professional fields. Female doctors were steered toward public health, lawyers to social work, language scholars to library cataloguing, scientists to high-school teaching.

Within the white middle-class family, education and religious responsibility for children improved women's status through the nineteenth century. By the 1830s, magazines analyzing life from a woman's point of view began to flourish in North America. In Europe, female writers of philosophical insight, from George Eliot to Virginia Woolf in the early twentieth century and on up to Simone de Beauvoir, steadily clarified women's issues. But mostly, wives were still considered their husbands' subordinates.

20   American feminists wishing to convey their critique of marriage often did so through the lens of slavery, the most volatile public issue of the mid- and late nineteenth century. "The investigation of the rights of the slave has led me to a better understanding of my own," wrote Angelina Grimk, a Southern abolitionist. "I have found the Anti-Slavery cause to be the high school of morals in our land. Now if rights are founded in the nature of our moral being, then the mere circumstance of sex does not give to man higher rights and responsibilities than to woman."

Though they didn't participate in elections, American women believed that they had access to the political system through the right to petition Congress. But as the conflict over abolition escalated, it became clear that women's petitions were not being heard. The right to vote was moved to the top of the list. Female reformers like Elizabeth Cady Stanton and Anna Howard Shaw combined spell-binding oratory with noisy street politics. Stanton was well known, for instance, for her lecture The Slavery of Marriage. The argument for suffrage then became more expedient: white women's votes would balance those of newly enfranchised black males and immigrants. The majority that ratified the nineteenth Amendment in 1920 was built on these racist grounds.

New Experts in Mothering: Men

Meanwhile, biological science was replacing theology as the language for discussing the differences between women and men. The popularity of Darwinian thought and the discovery of the endocrine system anchored the discussion firmly in science. Nor were such discussions purely theoretical, for by the 1920s women and men began to inhabit the same workplace. Even so, the young women taking clerical jobs in corporate offices were considered little threat, for it was thought that their hormones would drive them to maternity and service rather than wealth and power.

The new economic forces at work in America radically altered the role of women as workers, mothers and wives. Industrialization had created jobs for women in factories and textile mills in the mid-1800s. At the same time, the fruits of industrialization—mass-produced clothing and foods—gave middle-class mothers a new role: manager of household consumption. But many female responsibilities were subject to male guidance at the turn of the century. In the new field of child studies, male experts like G. Stanley Hall even tried to make mothering a science.

Isolation made mothers willing recipients of such expertise. The middle class had begun its flight from the city in the mid-nineteenth century, and by its close servants were being replaced by new labor-saving household equipment. So suburban women were alone with their children. Whereas in the eighteenth century the family was a partnership for spouses and children, the twentieth-century family became based on intimacy. Greater life expectancy meant that marriages lasted longer, well past a woman's childbearing years. As infant mortality declined, the family became more child-centered, and private insurance and pensions, as well as governmental assistance, made older parents less dependent on working children.

25   The emotional tone of marriages also changed with the rise of the corporation and the profession. Increasingly, the vocations of middle-class men excluded their families. This prompted a movement for more accessible divorce, along with longer marriages, increased mobility and the growing ideal of emotional and sexual fulfillment between spouses.

Not-So-Equal Rights

Sigmund Freud and other pioneers of psychology profoundly affected the status of women by arguing that an acceptance of gender difference was a prerequisite for mental health. From the 1920s through the 1970s, women with political, scientific or intellectual interests were stigmatized as neurotic, while men involved in the more feminine realms like the arts were considered less than fully male. The family dynamic laid out by Freud, based on latent erotic attachments, encouraged sons to overcome their mother complexes by becoming strong and independent.

Daughters, meanwhile, were encouraged to replace their love for their fathers by finding a male romantic partner rather than by developing an independent self. In time, however, feminist interpretations of difference developed. In the 1970s, Nancy Chodorow reworked Freud's Oedipal system to point out that the strongest erotic gratification a female infant receives comes from a same-sex relationship with her mother, raising questions about the inevitability of female dependence on males.

In the political sphere, meanwhile, female voting didn't change party power structures, and women began developing parallel institutions like the National Woman's Party, in 1916. Its 1923 drive for an equal rights amendment failed, just as its successor failed in the 1970s, partly because Americans, including women, remained resistant to the idea of a woman as President. Once again, feminists created parallel structures to support female candidates, like Emily's List (Early Money Is Like Yeast). Where once the rare women elected to public office were typically the widows of male officeholders, the election of women became unremarkable, though even now they comprise only a fraction of Congress and high state officials.

In the 1960s, feminists began to focus on changing the composition of high-status professions. Once access to graduate education was won, feminist scholars pushed to change patterns of research and teaching so that women were no longer regarded as a failed model of the male norm, but as a norm themselves. In so doing, they helped ignite the culture wars of the 1980s and 90s. And by the end of the 90s, women constituted 60 percent of college graduates. Even so, on leaving school they still face the continuing reality of the glass ceiling.

Inflation, rising economic expectations and women's quest for professional equality after World War II produced the reinvention of the nanny—a movement promptly challenged by the argument that only birth mothers could care effectively for their children. A successful dual-track life as mother and professional, therefore, required heroic energy or a flouting of this conventional wisdom. Two careers within one family often meant a commuter marriage, which may have seemed new but which echoed the old aristocratic pattern: spouses parted by attendance at court and by journeys to distant estates or remote colonies. But now there is a big difference: a woman's property and income do not necessarily belong to her husband.

30   While feminist interpretations of gender difference gained favor in the 1970s, and while lesbian feminists argued in the 1980s for difference with a difference, claiming the superiority of same-sex relationships, a strong backlash arose in conservative quarters. This was marked not only by a denigration of feminism but also by an elevation of macho versions of male power and fresh assertions of difference. Such arguments were once again located in theology by Christian, Jewish and Islamic fundamentalists. Meanwhile, new debates about gender difference emerged in brain research. While female and male synapses might fire the same way, doubters insisted that there must surely be a difference in the circuitry. Questions about differences in wiring are a new form of debate that goes back to the medieval question about whether women have souls.

The New Terrain
So what has happened to women over the past thousand years? Western women and their children have made astonishing gains in health and life expectancy, though most of their non-Western sisters have not yet shared those benefits. The scope of

women's work has expanded vastly, much of it paying well enough so that women with children can survive. Women in the West have secured access to education beyond the wildest dreams of their medieval counterparts. Women's athletic prowess has captured public imagination, and a female general is no longer a novelty.

But what of the mixed outcomes? Feminist spirituality today provides a powerful leaven within some Christian, Jewish and Islamic communities, but others still forbid female participation, and the loss of the institutional structure once provided by female religious orders has shrunk the territory controlled by women. The reduced number of women's colleges has had a similar effect. Women's reproductive lives, though, are now managed by technologies subject to male control. The ability to detect the sex of a fetus can result in higher abortion rates for female infants, whereas in medieval society the girl babies at least had a chance to be born. Sexual freedoms have enlarged the sphere of pleasure, but with them have come unresolved problems about sexual behavior.

What will be the new terrain for addressing the issues of likeness and difference? What new strategies will women develop to dismantle exclusively male hierarchies? The cognitive sciences will most likely inherit the role of theology in arguing about differences between male and female. Still, the global rise of religious fundamentalism will counter women's efforts to secure equal footing. And among women worldwide there will remain stark differences about how to achieve a better life.

But argument—and laughter—about the relationship between women and men will never end. Our physical bodies are cultural texts that are constantly revised, and no single formulation of the relationship between the sexes can last.

A Student Essay

Trisa Hayes

Dr. Madden

English 102

December 20, 200X

The Age of Living Dolls

When I was a little girl, I desperately wanted a doll house. After my persistent begging, whining, and promise making, my parents finally gave in and bought me one. I spent hours playing with my doll, the new house, and all its tiny furniture. I loved it simply because I had sole control over all aspects of my doll's life: when she would eat, where she would shop, what she would wear, what time she would go to bed. These were things my parents had control over in my life.

Playing with my doll was fun until the newness wore off; after that I only played with her when I was bored. The rest of the time she just sat in her house, lifeless and waiting patiently for the next string of activities I would plan for her.

Over the years my parents and others encouraged me to make my own decisions no matter how big they were, and having the freedom to do so is something I'll never take for granted again. After reading Henrik Ibsen's A Doll's House and Kate Chopin's "The Story of an Hour," I saw what life could be like through the eyes of women who are treated like dolls. These stories are an illustration of women's roles and the dilemmas they faced in society during the nineteenth century.

The protagonist in A Doll's House is Nora, a simple housewife who is treated like a five-year-old by her husband Torvald. It appears at first that the only thing Nora is capable of is mirroring what her husband wishes to see in her. Because he expects her to be like a pet, she flutters and twitters about the room like a helpless bird, or takes on the characteristics of a small woodland creature that relies entirely on a much larger beast for its safety. As I continued to read about her incomprehensible submissiveness, I found myself getting angrier and angrier. First she hides her macaroons because Torvald doesn't want her to have sweets. Then there's my favorite example; Nora tells Torvald, "Oh, everything you do is right" (902). Her spineless actions are infuriating.

Torvald's overwhelming male chauvinistic attitude only intensified my frustrations. When Nora approaches him on Krogstad's behalf, Torvald insists he will have to replace him and gives this revealing excuse: "If it ever got around that the new manager had been talked over by his wife . . . " (885). And when Nora tells him he is always right, he responds, "There's my little sky-lark talking common sense" (902).

But this is 1879, and Nora and Torvald are only filling the female/male roles that are socially acceptable at that time. It is a man's world, with only male views and male rules. What gives men the right to tell women how to behave? Nothing. They are just the physically stronger of the two sexes. As Charlotte Perkins Stetson says in "Women and Economics," published in 1899, a man's role in relation to women is "a sovereignty based on the accident of sex" (924). But Nora is growing tired of being treated like mindless property and snaps to Mrs. Linde, "You're just like the rest of them. You all think I'm useless when it comes to anything really serious . . . " (865).

When Torvald opens Krogstad's letter, she is so terrified of him, she wants to escape from the house before he has a chance to confront her. He grabs her arm and declares with great despair and rage, "I'm done for, a miserable failure, and it's all the fault of a feather-brained woman!" (907). This is hardly a way for him to show his gratitude to the woman who saved his life. As soon as Torvald receives the next letter and returned IOU from Krogstad, he cries "I am saved!" (908) and digs himself into a deeper hole in Nora's eyes when he adds, "There's something indescribably moving and very satisfying in knowing that he has forgiven his wife. . . . It's as though it made her his property in a double sense: he has, as it were, given her new life, and she becomes in a way both his wife and at the same time his child" (909). Torvald's response has provided Nora with a revelation about Torvald and about herself. She begins to discover how very little she knows about herself and the world around her. She isn't even aware of her own interests because she has always been so eager to please her husband.

His unsavory responses present her with a new dilemma. Should she abandon her family and comfortable home for a sense of self-worth? Or should she stay and sacrifice any future prospects of happiness? I can't imagine being forced to believe that it's a woman's duty to maintain a man's happiness even if it costs her own. Furthermore, Nora had to consider how others would treat her if she left, for back then women absolutely, positively did not go against the grain of society's expectations unless they were fully prepared to endure vicious slurs and be shunned by respected members of the community, lifelong friends, and in some instances even their own families.

Then, with a mature demeanor, Nora sits down with her husband to have a serious discussion for the first time. The tide of power shifts as she reveals her observations of their life together. She explains to him how both he and her father have treated her like a doll, and that now she is certain of what she needs to do. She announces to Torvald that she is leaving him. He is dumbfounded but attempts to reason with her by reminding her of her "sacred duty" to him and their children, but she unleashes her pent up feelings on him: "I'm not content any more with what most people say, or with what it says in books. I have to think things out for myself, and get things clear" (911). "I must try to discover who is right, society or me" (912). And she leaves to try to discover the choices and opportunities for those who are not confined to a child's boundaries.

Kate Chopin, who was born in 1851 and died in 1904, probably witnessed such struggles firsthand. The signs of her times were expressed through her writing, specifically through "The Story of an Hour." It's evident that throughout history many women have walked in Nora's shoes, thus the fight for the right to vote. But most women of her time didn't dare acknowledge the slightest dissatisfaction with their roles as wives and mothers, much less have the courage to leave. "The Story of an Hour" is the story of such a woman.

Her story is about a woman who has just found out that her husband has died in a railroad disaster. At first she is in shock, void of all emotion. And then without warning she begins to cry hysterically. After her sister Josephine succeeds in calming her somewhat, she retreats to the solitude of her room to collect her thoughts. Then, after a sincere struggle to maintain the specific emotions that society expects her to have over the loss of her husband, she finally succumbs to her true feelings by uttering softly to herself, "Free, free, free!" (68).

Her sister, out of concern, begs her to open the door. She "breathed a quick prayer that life might be long. It was only yesterday she had thought with a shudder that life might be long" (68). Then, almost in a tranquil state, she rises to let Josephine in and agrees to accompany her downstairs. But as they descend the front door unlocks and in walks her husband, completely unscathed and very much alive. She instantly dies of a heart attack at the sight of her husband. The doctors say she died from a "joy that kills" (69), but nothing could be further from the truth. She and Nora, though worlds apart in some ways, share a common bond. They both have a burning desire to be free, to break the mold of their doll-like lives.

It's frightening to read about all the stifling rules and regulations women had to follow back then. Just thinking about it makes me claustrophobic. The sad part is that there are still an astounding number of women in our country who are forced to obey each and every command given to them by their husbands, no matter how humiliating or dehumanizing. The ability to think as an individual is gradually stripped and they become more and more lifeless, mindless dolls every day.

  I am deeply grateful to the women who believed that they deserved more in life than that. Because of these two stories, I have a new respect and understanding of the women that lived in the nineteenth century, a time I think of as "the age of the living dolls." For without these pioneering women who struggled through and endured many hardships to obtain basic human rights, life for women now would only be something to be endured and not enjoyed.

[New Page]

Works Cited

Chopin, Kate. "The Story of an Hour." Exploring Literature. Ed. Frank
  Madden. 3rd ed. New York: Longman, 2007. 67-69.

Ibsen, Henrik. A Doll's House. Exploring Literature. Ed. Frank Madden. 3rd
  ed. New York: Longman, 2007. 857-914.

Stetson (Gilman), Charlotte Perkins. Excerpt from "Women and Economics."
  Exploring Literature. Ed. Frank Madden. 3rd ed. New York: Longman,
  2007. 923-925.

EXPLORING THE LITERATURE OF WOMEN AND MEN: OPTIONS FOR MAKING CONNECTIONS AND ARGUMENTS

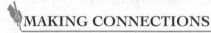

MAKING CONNECTIONS

1. Consider the ways your gender or the gender of those you know has affected your life. Do any of the stories, poems, plays, or essays in this section remind you of your own experiences or the circumstances of your life? Choose one or more of these works and write a response essay that compares your experience or circumstances with those in the literature.

2. Our own values about gender can affect how we see the world and strongly influence our response to literature. We may agree or disagree with what an author says or what characters say or do. So too, literature may influence us and the formation of our values about gender. Write an essay about the ways in which one or more works in this section either provoked a moral judgment on your part or helped you learn something.

❦MAKING AN ARGUMENT

1. Over two hundred years ago, Mary Wollstonecraft in *A Vindication of the Rights of Women* wrote: "It would be an endless task to trace the variety of meannesses, cares, and sorrows into which women are plunged by the prevailing opinion that they were created rather to feel than reason, and that all power they obtain must be obtained by their charms and weakness." Consider this quote, and write an essay about how this kind of stereotyping has influenced the way women are treated or behave in one or more works in this section.

2. In the best-selling book *Iron John,* Robert Bly wrote: "We have defective mythologies that ignore masculine depth of feeling, assign men a place in the sky instead of earth, teach obedience to the wrong powers, and entangle men and women in systems of industrial domination." Write about this quote as it applies to the roles of men in one or more works in this section.

3. Choose a quote (or quotes) in the introduction to this section, Women and Men (pp. 710–711), and pair it (or them) with one of the longer pieces in this section that either supports it or argues against it. For example, Rousseau's quote about the education (training) of women might be paired with Virginia Woolf's essay "If Shakespeare Had a Sister," which argues against it. On the other hand, if you choose Gail Sheehy's quote about the plight of the modern married woman, you might choose the Woolf essay to exemplify and support the point Sheehy is making.

    Write an essay that compares or contrasts a quote (or quotes) from the introduction with a story, poem, play, or essay that supports or argues against it.

A Research Option

Anton Chekhov's "The Lady with the Pet Dog," Andrew Marvell's poem "To His Coy Mistress," Henrik Ibsen's play *A Doll's House,* and Virginia Woolf's essay "If Shakespeare Had a Sister" all have something important to say about relationships between men and women. Each of these works, however, springs from a very different historical, social, or political context. Expanding our exploration of literature to include the context in which these works were produced can be an enriching and enlightening experience.

Choose one or more of these or other works in this section and write a research essay that includes secondary source material about the historical, social, or political background of the literature.

Writing About Connections Across Themes

Most of the literature in the text has been organized into theme sections, but good literature is much too complex to be reduced to a single broad theme. Many of the

works included under Women and Men could just as easily fit under other themes—
and in many cases works arranged in other themes could fit here as well.

Choose one or more of the following works from earlier chapters or other
themes and consider how they can be linked to Women and Men—and how this
combination of the work with more than one theme provides additional insight into
the literature and fresh topics for writing.

From Chapter 1
   "Barbie Doll"—p. 14
From Chapter 2
   "Mothers"—p. 31
From Chapter 3
   "The Story of an Hour"—p. 67
   "Meeting at Night"—p. 75
   "Parting at Morning"—p. 75
   "Simile"—p. 76
From Chapter 5
   "Eveline"—p. 190
From Family and Friends
   "Marriage Is a Private Affair"—p. 206
   "How to Watch Your Brother Die"—p. 273
   "The Youngest Daughter"—p. 282
   A Raisin in the Sun—p. 344
From Innocence and Experience
   "Araby"—p. 463
   "Where Are You Going, Where Have You Been?"—p. 468
   "Siren Song"—p. 504
   "When I Was One-and-Twenty"—p. 508
   "I Fell in Love, or My Hormones Awakened"—p. 517
From Culture and Identity
   "Désirée's Baby"—p. 951
   "A Rose for Emily"—p. 956
   "Girl"—p. 963
   "I Want to Die While You Love Me"—p. 1132
   "Sweat"—p. 1132
From Faith and Doubt
   "Young Goodman Brown"—p. 1167
   "The Chrysanthemums"—p. 1208
   "Patterns"—p. 1241
   "Wild Night, Wild Nights!"—p. 1309

Collaboration: Writing and Revising with Your Peers

In addition to applying your own values and standards to writing about the literature
in this section, you may find it beneficial to share and discuss your work with classmates. Getting feedback from others can help you generate and clarify your ideas
and revise and edit your writing more effectively

Choose a work, topic, or one of the options for writing about women and men above, and work with a partner or in a small group. Exchange journal entries or response sheets, generate questions together, do a group semantic map (see pp. 36–43), or simply share and respond to each other's ideas.

After you have written a rough draft of your essay, share it with a partner or your group. Respondents should function primarily as sensitive readers and give honest, constructive responses. They should try to be aware of each writer's purpose, discuss concerns particular to each writer, and comment on the effectiveness of the essay's organization, support, clarity, and voice (for a comprehensive checklist for revision, see p. 46).

In the final stage of your writing, editing and proofreading might be done in a similar fashion. A partner or a group of readers might help you check for correct grammar, spelling, punctuation, and typos (a comprehensive checklist for editing is on p. 49).

A Writing/Research Portfolio Option

A portfolio is a collection of your work, related materials, and commentary about your work collected over time. Gathering materials in a portfolio will provide you with resources for research and development. You can use your portfolio to collect your writing about the literature in this section, to find a topic to write about, to revise or add to your work, or to keep multiple drafts and monitor the changes you make as you revise. Among the resources you might include:

- Your responses to the quotes and prompts about women and men at the beginning of this section, the questions you had right after you finished reading each work of literature, and your journal entries.

- What your classmates, instructor, or published critics had to say about the literature and how their comments may have influenced your interpretation.

- Information you have gathered from the library and the Internet about the historical, social, and political context of the work or its author.

Culture & Identity

Culture and Identity
A DIALOGUE ACROSS HISTORY

Better one's own duty, [though] imperfect, / Than another's duty well performed.
  —from the *Bhagavad Gita*, c. 250 B.C.–250 A.D.

Man is born a barbarian, and only raises himself above the beast by culture.
  —Baltasar Gracian, *The Art of Worldly Wisdom*, 1647

The great law of culture is: Let each become all that he was created capable of being.
  —Thomas Carlyle, *Critical Essays*, 1827

Instead of boiling up individuals into the species, I would draw a chalk line round every individuality, and preach to it to keep within that, and preserve and cultivate its identity.
  —Jane Welsh Carlyle, letter, 1845

If a man does not keep pace with his companions, perhaps it is because he hears a different drummer. Let him step to the music which he hears, however measured or far away.
  —Henry David Thoreau, *Walden*, 1854

It is not the consciousness of men that determines their existence, but on the contrary it is their social existence that determines their consciousness.
  —Karl Marx, *Critique of Political Economy*, 1859

I'm Nobody! Who are you? / Are you—Nobody—too?
  —Emily Dickinson, c. 1861

When I found that I had crossed that line [during her first escape from slavery], I looked at my hands to see if I was the same person. There was such a glory over everything.
  —Harriet Tubman, her biography, 1868

Knowledge of [another] culture should sharpen our ability to scrutinize more steadily, to appreciate more lovingly, our own.

    —Margaret Mead, *Coming of Age in Somoa*, 1928

The most powerful obstacle to culture . . . is the tendency to aggression, [which is] an innate, independent, instinctual disposition in man.

    —Sigmund Freud, *Civilization and Its Discontents*, 1930

From the moment of his birth the customs into which [an individual] is born shape his experience and behavior. By the time he can talk, he is the little creature of his culture.

    —Ruth Benedict, *Patterns of Culture*, 1934

I wouldn't want to belong to any club that would accept me as a member.

    —Groucho Marx, c. 1935

Men can starve from a lack of self-realization as much as . . . from a lack of bread.

    —Richard Wright, *Native Son*, 1940

It is thus with most of us; we are what other people say we are. We know ourselves chiefly by hearsay.

    —Eric Hoffer, *The Passionate State of Mind*, 1954

We become what we are only by the radical and profound rejection of what others have said about us.

    —Jean Paul Sartre, preface to Frantz Fanon's *Wretched of the Earth*, 1961

I have a dream that one day on the red hills of Georgia the sons of former slaves and the sons of former slaveowners will be able to sit down together at the table of brotherhood.

    —Martin Luther King, Jr., speech, 1963

[Culture] is a product of man: he projects himself into it, he recognizes himself in it; that critical mirror alone offers him his image.

    —Jean Paul Sartre, *The Words*, 1964

I began to feel oddly detached. I was "there"; but I was also looking at myself being there. . . . I had learned much about the ways actors worked . . . the small signs and tags that they offered to display emotions they might not feel. [And] I began to feel that I was performing my life instead of living it.

    —Pete Hamill, *A Drinking Life*, 1994

CULTURE AND IDENTITY: EXPLORING YOUR OWN VALUES AND BELIEFS

What comes to mind when you hear the word *culture?* In everyday conversation, this word is often used to evaluate people rather than to identify their background. So it's common to hear people depicted as "cultured" as being praised for their good taste, aesthetic appreciation, behavior, or character. But our use of the term *culture* here, as reflected in the quotes on the previous pages and in the literature that follows, is based on a more formal definition. For our purposes, *culture* represents the shared attitudes, the values, or the behavioral patterns of a social or ethnic group.

Culture and identify are closely related. Cultural values and institutions play a big part in shaping who we are. Our ethnicity, families, geographic location, religious background, economic resources, education, and other factors influence how we see the world. But are we who we are exclusively because of our cultural backgrounds? Or are we who we are ultimately because of conscious choices we make as individuals? Are we responsible only to ourselves for our actions, or do we have an added responsibility to others in society?

The elusive answers to these questions are at the heart of our search for identity. Whether we seek our personal identity by marching to the beat of Thoreau's "different drummer," celebrate our common humanity at Martin Luther King, Jr.'s "table of brotherhood," or recognize in ourselves the cultural traditions and values we carry with us, we spend much of our lives finding our place in the world and our sense of who we are.

How we respond to literature, too, is often influenced by our sense of cultural and personal identity—how we see ourselves, our backgrounds, and our circumstances reflected in what we read. As a preparation for reading the literature in this section, you may find it helpful to think about your own beliefs about culture and identity.

READING AND WRITING ABOUT CULTURE AND IDENTITY

Exploring your beliefs and values and connecting your experience with what you read is an important first step toward our ultimate goal—an appreciation of literature and the ability to think and write critically about it. Critical analysis will require rereading and reflection, writing and revising, gathering evidence, and constructing a solid argument to support your responses.

At least one aspect of the many stories, poems, plays, and essays in this section is about the impact that culture and identity have on the characters: W. H. Auden's satirical tribute to an "identityless" hero in his poem "The Unknown Citizen"; the struggle of migrant farm workers in Luis Valdez's play *Los Vendidos;* and Frederick Douglass's valiant efforts to educate himself in the hostile atmosphere of slavery in the essay "Learning to Read and Write." The brief quotes that open this section also give you some idea of the number of compelling ethical, political, and social arguments that are connected to culture and identity. Civil rights, equal opportunity, stereotyping, bigotry, oppression, social pressure and individual conscience, community and anonymity, and responsibility and self-realization head a long list of concerns. Any of these or other related issues might provide a fine topic for building an argument and writing an essay.

◆ FICTION ◆

T. CORAGHESSAN BOYLE [B. 1948]

T. Coraghessan Boyle is the author of fifteen books of fiction, including the novel Drop City *(2003) and his most recent collection,* After the Plague *(2002). He received his B.A. in English and History from SUNY Potsdam in 1968, his M.F.A. from the University of Iowa Writers' Workshop in 1974, and a Ph.D. in Nineteenth-Century British Literature from the University of Iowa in 1977. He has been a member of the English Department at the University of Southern California since 1978. His stories have appeared in most of the major American magazines, including the* New Yorker, Harper's, Esquire, The Atlantic Monthly, Playboy, The Paris Review, GQ, Antaeus, *and* Granta, *and he has been the recipient of a number of literary awards. He currently lives near Santa Barbara, California, with his wife and three children.*

GREASY LAKE   [1985]

It's about a mile down on the dark side of Route 8.
                              —Bruce Springsteen

There was a time when courtesy and winning ways went out of style, when it was good to be bad, when you cultivated decadence like a taste. We were all dangerous characters then. We wore torn-up leather jackets, slouched around with toothpicks in our mouths, sniffed glue and ether and what somebody claimed was cocaine. When we wheeled our parents' whining station wagons out onto the street we left a patch of rubber half a block long. We drank gin and grape juice, Tango, Thunderbird, and Bali Hai. We were nineteen. We were bad. We read André Gide[1] and struck elaborate poses to show that we didn't give a shit about anything. At night, we went up to Greasy Lake.

Through the center of town, up the strip, past the housing developments and shopping malls, street lights giving way to the thin streaming illumination of the headlights, trees crowding the asphalt in a black unbroken wall: that was the way out to Greasy Lake. The Indians had called it Wakan, a reference to the clarity of its waters. Now it was fetid and murky, the mud banks glittering with broken glass and strewn with beer cans and the charred remains of bonfires. There was a single ravaged island a hundred yards from shore, so stripped of vegetation it looked as if the

[1]**André Gide** controversial French writer (1869-1951) whose novels, including *The Counterfeiters* and *Lafcadio's Adventurers,* often show individuals in conflict with accepted morality

air force had strafed it. We went up to the lake because everyone went there, because we wanted to snuff the rich scent of possibility on the breeze, watch a girl take off her clothes and plunge into the festering murk, drink beer, smoke pot, howl at the stars, savor the incongruous full-throated roar of rock and roll against the primeval susurrus of frogs and crickets. This was nature.

I was there one night, late, in the company of two dangerous characters. Digby wore a gold star in his right ear and allowed his father to pay his tuition at Cornell; Jeff was thinking of quitting school to become a painter/musician/head-shop proprietor. They were both expert in the social graces, quick with a sneer, able to manage a Ford with lousy shocks over a rutted and gutted blacktop road at eighty-five while rolling a joint as compact as a Tootsie Roll Pop stick. They could lounge against a bank of booming speakers and trade "man's" with the best of them or roll out across the dance floor as if their joints worked on bearing. They were slick and quick and they wore their mirror shades at breakfast and dinner, in the shower, in closets and caves. In short, they were bad.

I drove. Digby pounded the dashboard and shouted along with Toots & the Maytals while Jeff hung his head out the window and streaked the side of my mothers Bel Air with vomit. It was early June, the air soft as a hand on your cheek, the third night of summer vacation. The first two nights we'd been out till dawn, looking for something we never found. On this, the third night, we'd cruised the strip sixty-seven times, been in and out of every bar and club we could think of in a twenty-mile radius, stopped twice for bucket chicken and forty-cent hamburgers, debated going to a party at the house of a girl Jeff's sister knew, and chucked two dozen raw eggs at mailboxes and hitchhikers. It was 2:00 A.M.; the bars were closing. There was nothing to do but take a bottle of lemon-flavored gin up to Greasy Lake.

5   The taillights of a single car winked at us as we swung into the dirt lot with its tufts of weed and washboard corrugations; '57 Chevy, mint, metallic blue. On the far side of the lot, like the exoskeleton of some gaunt chrome insect, a chopper leaned against its kickstand. And that was it for excitement; some junkie halfwit biker and a car freak pumping his girlfriend. Whatever it was we were looking for, we weren't about to find it at Greasy Lake. Not that night.

But then all of a sudden Digby was fighting for the wheel. "Hey, that's Tony Lovett's car! Hey!" he shouted, while I stabbed at the brake pedal and the Bel Air nosed up to the gleaming bumper of the parked Chevy. Digby leaned on the horn, laughing, and instructed me to put my bright lights on. I flicked on the brights. This was hilarious. A joke. Tony would experience premature withdrawal and expect to be confronted by grim-looking state troopers with flashlights. We hit the horn, strobed the lights, and then jumped out of the car to press our witty faces to Tony's windows; for all we knew we might even catch a glimpse of some little fox's tit, and then we could slap backs with red-faced Tony, roughhouse a little, and go on to new heights of adventure and daring.

The first mistake, the one that opened the whole floodgate, was losing my grip on the keys. In the excitement, leaping from the car with the gin in one hand and a roach clip in the other, I spilled them in the grass—in the dark, rank, mysterious nighttime grass of Greasy Lake. This was a tactical error, as damaging and irreversible in its way as Westmoreland's decision to dig in at Khe Sanh.[2] I felt it like a jab of intuition, and I stopped there by the open door, peering vaguely into the night that puddled up round my feet.

The second mistake—and this was inextricably bound up with the first—was identifying the car as Tony Lovett's. Even before the very bad character in greasy jeans and engineer boots ripped out of the driver's door, I began to realize that this chrome blue was much lighter than the robin's-egg of Tony's car, and that Tony's car didn't have rear-mounted speakers. Judging from their expressions, Digby and Jeff were privately groping toward the same inevitable and unsettling conclusion as I was.

In any case, there was no reasoning with this bad greasy character—clearly he was a man of action. The first lusty Rockette[3] kick of his steel-toed boot caught me under the chin, chipped my favorite tooth, and left me sprawled in the dirt. Like a fool, I'd gone down on one knee to comb the stiff cracked grass for my keys, my mind making connections in the most dragged-out, testudineous way, knowing that things had gone wrong, that I was in a lot of trouble, and that the lost ignition key was my grail and my salvation. The three or four succeeding blows were mainly absorbed by my right buttock and the tough piece of bone at the base of my spine.

10   Meanwhile, Digby vaulted the kissing bumpers and delivered a savage kung-fu blow to the greasy character's collarbone. Digby had just finished a course in martial arts for phys-ed credit and had spent the better part of the past two nights telling us apocryphal tales of Bruce Lee types and of the raw power invested in lightning blows shot from coiled wrists, ankles, and elbows. The greasy character was unimpressed. He merely backed off a step, his face like a Toltec mask, and laid Digby out with a single whistling roundhouse blow . . . but by now Jeff had got into the act, and I was beginning to extricate myself from the dirt, a tinny compound of shock, rage, and impotence wadded in my throat.

Jeff was on the guy's back, biting his ear. Digby was on the ground, cursing. I went for the tire iron I kept under the driver's seat. I kept it there because bad characters always keep tire irons under the driver's seat, for just such an occasion as this. Never mind that I hadn't been involved in a fight since sixth grade, when a kid with a sleepy eye and two streams of mucus descending from his nostrils hit me in the knee with a Louisville slugger,[4] never mind that I'd touched the tire iron exactly twice before, to change tires: it was there. And I went for it.

I was terrified. Blood was beating in my ears, my hands were shaking, my heart turning over like a dirtbike in the wrong gear. My antagonist was shirtless, and a single cord of muscle flashed across his chest as he bent forward to peel Jeff from his back like a wet overcoat. "Motherfucker," he spat, over and over, and I was aware

---

[2]**Westmoreland's decision** . . . **Khe Sanh** General William C. Westmoreland commanded U.S. troops in Vietnam (1964–1968). In late 1967 the North Vietnamese and Viet Cong forces attacked Khe Sanh (or Khesanh) with a show of strength, causing Westmoreland to expend great effort to defend a plateau of relatively little tactical importance.   [3]**Rockette** member of a dancing troupe in the stage show at Radio City Music Hall, New York, famous for its ability to kick fast and high with wonderful coordination.   [4]**Louisville slugger** a brand of baseball bat

in that instant that all four of us—Digby, Jeff, and myself included—were chanting, "motherfucker, motherfucker," as if it were a battle cry. (What happened next? the detective asks the murderer from beneath the turned-down brim of his porkpie hat. I don't know, the murderer says, something came over me. Exactly.)

Digby poked the flat of his hand in the bad character's face and I came at him like a kamikaze, mindless, raging, stung with humiliation—the whole thing, from the initial boot in the chin to this murderous primal instant involving no more than sixty hyperventilating, gland-flooding seconds—I came at him and brought the tire iron down across his ear. The effect was instantaneous, astonishing. He was a stunt man and this was Hollywood, he was a big grimacing toothy balloon and I was a man with a straight pin. He collapsed. Wet his pants. Went loose in his boots.

A single second, big as a zeppelin, floated by. We were standing over him in a circle, gritting our teeth, jerking our necks, our limbs and hands and feet twitching with glandular discharges. No one said anything. We just stared down at the guy, the car freak, the lover, the bad greasy character laid low. Digby looked at me; so did Jeff. I was still holding the tire iron, a tuft of hair clinging to the crook like dandelion fluff, like down. Rattled, I dropped it in the dirt, already envisioning the headlines, the pitted faces of the police inquisitors, the gleam of handcuffs, clank of bars, the big black shadows rising from the back of the cell . . . when suddenly a raw torn shriek cut through me like all the juice in all the electric chairs in the country.

15   It was the fox. She was short, barefoot, dressed in panties and a man's shirt. "Animals!" she screamed, running at us with her fists clenched and wisps of blow-dried hair in her face. There was a silver chain round her ankle, and her toenails flashed in the glare of the headlights. I think it was the toenails that did it. Sure, the gin and the cannabis and even the Kentucky Fried may have had a hand in it, but it was the sight of those flaming toes that set us off—the toad emerging from the loaf in *Virgin Spring*,[5] lipstick smeared on a child; she was already tainted. We were on her like Bergman's deranged brothers—see no evil, hear none, speak none—panting, wheezing, tearing at her clothes, grabbing for flesh. We were bad characters, and we were scared and hot and three steps over the line—anything could have happened.

It didn't.

Before we could pin her to the hood of the car, our eyes masked with lust and greed and the purest primal badness, a pair of headlights swung into the lot. There we were, dirty, bloody, guilty, dissociated from humanity and civilization, the first of the Ur-crimes behind us, the second in progress, shreds of nylon panty and spandex brassiere dangling from our fingers, our flies open, lips licked—there we were, caught in the spotlight. Nailed.

We bolted. First for the car, and then, realizing we had no way of starting it, for the woods. I thought nothing. I thought escape. The headlights came at me like accusing fingers. I was gone.

Ram-bam-bam, across the parking lot, past the chopper and into the feculent undergrowth of the lake's edge, insects flying up in my face, weeds whipping, frogs and snakes and red-eyed turtles splashing off into the night: I was already ankle-deep in muck and tepid water and still going strong. Behind me, the girl's screams rose in

[5]*Virgin Spring* film by Swedish director Ingmar Bergman

intensity, disconsolate, incriminating, the screams of the Sabine women,[6] the Christian martyrs, Anne Frank[7] dragged from the garret. I kept going, pursued by the cries, imagining cops and bloodhounds. The water was up to my knees when I realized what I was doing: I was going to swim for it. Swim the breadth of Greasy Lake and hide myself in the thick clot of woods on the far side. They'd never find me there.

20   I was breathing in sobs, in gasps. The water lapped at my waist as I looked out over the moon-burnished ripples, the mats of algae that clung to the surface like scabs. Digby and Jeff had vanished. I paused. Listened. The girl was quieter now, screams tapering to sobs, but there were male voices, angry, excited, and the high-pitched ticking of the second car's engine. I waded deeper, stealthy, hunted, the ooze sucking at my sneakers. As I was about to take the plunge—at the very instant I dropped my shoulder for the first slashing stroke—I blundered into something. Something unspeakable, obscene, something soft, wet, moss-grown. A patch of weed? A log? When I reached out to touch it, it gave like a rubber duck, it gave like flesh.

In one of those nasty little epiphanies, for which we are prepared by films and TV and childhood visits to the funeral home to ponder the shrunken painted forms of dead grandparents, I understood what it was that bobbed there so inadmissibly in the dark. Understood, and stumbled back in horror and revulsion, my mind yanked in six different directions (I was nineteen, a mere child, an infant, and here in the space of five minutes I'd struck down one greasy character and blundered into the waterlogged carcass of a second), thinking, The keys, the keys, why did I have to go and lose the keys? I stumbled back, but the muck took hold of my feet—a sneaker snagged, balance lost—and suddenly I was pitching face forward into the buoyant black mass, throwing out my hands in desperation while simultaneously conjuring the image of reeking frogs and muskrats revolving in slicks of their own deliquescing juices. AAAAArrrgh! I shot from the water like a torpedo, the dead man rotating to expose a mossy beard and eyes as cold as the moon. I must have shouted out, thrashing around in the weeds, because the voices behind me suddenly became animated.

"What was that?"

"It's them, it's them: they tried to, tried to . . . *rape* me!" Sobs.

A man's voice, flat Midwestern accent. "You sons of bitches, we'll kill you!" Frogs, crickets.

25   Then another voice, harsh, r-less, Lower East Side: "Motherfucker!" I recognized the verbal virtuosity of the bad greasy character in the engineer boots. Tooth chipped, sneakers gone, coated in mud and slime and worse, crouching breathless in

---

[6]**Sabine women** members of an ancient tribe in Italy, according to legend, forcibly carried off by the early Romans under Romulus to be their wives. The incident is depicted in a famous painting, *The Rape of the Sabine Women,* by seventeenth-century French artist Nicolas Poussin. [7]**Anne Frank** German Jewish girl (1929–1945) whose diary written during the Nazi occupation of the Netherlands later became world famous. She hid with her family in a secret attic in Amsterdam, but was caught by storm troopers and sent to the concentration camp at Belsen, where she died.

the weeds waiting to have my ass thoroughly and definitively kicked and fresh from the hideous stinking embrace of a three-days-dead-corpse, I suddenly felt a rush of joy and vindication: the son of a bitch was alive! Just as quickly, my bowels turned to ice. "Come on out of there, you pansy mothers!" the bad greasy character was screaming. He shouted curses till he was out of breath.

The crickets started up again, then the frogs. I held my breath. All at once was a sound in the reeds, a swishing, a splash: thunk-a-thunk. They were throwing rocks. The frogs fell silent. I cradled my head. Swish, swish, thunk-a-thunk. A wedge of feldspar the size of a cue ball glanced off my knee. I bit my finger.

It was then that they turned to the car. I heard a door slam, a curse, and then the sound of the headlights shattering—almost a good-natured sound, celebratory, like corks popping from the necks of bottles. This was succeeded by the dull booming of the fenders, metal on metal, and then the icy crash of the windshield. I inched forward, elbows and knees, my belly pressed to the muck, thinking of guerrillas and commandos and *The Naked and the Dead*.[8] I parted the weeds and squinted the length of the parking lot.

The second car—it was a Trans-Am—was still running, its high beams washing the scene in a lurid stagy light. Tire iron flailing, the greasy bad character was laying into the side of my mother's Bel Air like an avenging demon, his shadow riding up the trunks of the trees. Whomp. Whomp. Whomp-whomp. The other two guys— blond types, in fraternity jackets—were helping out with tree branches and skull-sized boulders. One of them was gathering up bottles, rocks, muck, candy wrappers, used condoms, poptops, and other refuse and pitching it through the window of the driver's side. I could see the fox, a white bulb behind the windshield of the '57 Chevy. "Bobby," she whined over the thumping, "come *on.*" The greasy character paused a moment, took one good swipe at the left taillight, and then heaved the tire iron halfway across the lake. Then he fired up the '57 and was gone.

Blond head nodded at blond head. One said something to the other, too low for me to catch. They were no doubt thinking that in helping to annihilate my mother's car they'd committed a fairly rash act, and thinking too that there were three bad characters connected with that very car watching them from the woods. Perhaps other possibilities occurred to them as well—police, jail cells, justices of the peace, reparations, lawyers, irate parents, fraternal censure. Whatever they were thinking, they suddenly dropped branches, bottles, and rocks and sprang for their car in unison, as if they'd choreographed it. Five seconds. That's all it took. The engine shrieked, the tires squealed, a cloud of dust rose from the rutted lot and then settled back on darkness.

30   I don't know how long I lay there, the bad breath of decay all around me, my jacket heavy as a bear, the primordial ooze subtly reconstituting itself to accommodate my upper thighs and testicles. My jaws ached, my knee throbbed, my coccyx was on fire. I contemplated suicide, wondered if I'd need bridgework, scraped the recesses of my brain for some sort of excuse to give my parents—a tree had fallen on the car, I was blinded by a bread truck, hit and run, vandals had got to it while we

---

[8]*The Naked and the Dead* novel (1948) by Norman Mailer, of U.S. Army life in World War II

were playing chess at Digby's. Then I thought of the dead man. He was probably the only person on the planet worse off than I was. I thought about him, fog on the lake, insects chirring eerily, and felt the tug of fear, felt the darkness opening up inside me like a set of jaws. Who was he, I wondered, this victim of time and circumstance bobbing sorrowfully in the lake at my back. The owner of the chopper, no doubt, a bad older character come to this. Shot during a murky drug deal, drowned while drunkenly frolicking in the lake. Another headline. My car was wrecked; he was dead.

When the eastern half of the sky went from black to cobalt and the trees began to separate themselves from the shadows, I pushed myself up from the mud and stepped out into the open. By now the birds had begun to take over for the crickets, and dew lay slick on the leaves. There was a smell in the air, raw and sweet at the same time, the smell of the sun firing buds and opening blossoms. I contemplated the car. It lay there like a wreck along the highway, like a steel sculpture left over from a vanished civilization. Everything was still. This was nature.

I was circling the car, as dazed and bedraggled as the sole survivor of an air blitz, when Digby and Jeff emerged from the trees behind me. Digby's face was crosshatched with smears of dirt; Jeff's jacket was gone and his shirt was torn across the shoulder. They slouched across the lot, looking sheepish, and silently came up beside me to gape at the ravaged automobile. No one said a word. After a while Jeff swung open the driver's door and began to scoop the broken glass and garbage off the seat. I looked at Digby. He shrugged. "At least they didn't slash the tires," he said.

It was true: the tires were intact. There was no windshield, the headlights were staved in, and the body looked as if it had been sledge-hammered for a quarter a shot at the county fair, but the tires were inflated to regulation pressure. The car was drivable. In silence, all three of us bent to scrape the mud and shattered glass from the interior. I said nothing about the biker. When we were finished, I reached in my pocket for the keys, experienced a nasty stab of recollection, cursed myself, and turned to search the grass. I spotted them almost immediately, no more than five feet from the open door, glinting like jewels in the first tapering shaft of sunlight. There was no reason to get philosophical about it: I eased into the seat and turned the engine over.

It was at that precise moment that the silver Mustang with the flame decals rumbled into the lot. All three of us froze; then Digby and Jeff slid into the car and slammed the door. We watched as the Mustang rocked and bobbed across the ruts and finally jerked to a halt beside the forlorn chopper at the far end of the lot. "Let's go," Digby said. I hesitated, the Bel Air wheezing beneath me.

35   Two girls emerged from the Mustang. Tight jeans, stiletto heels, hair like frozen fur. They bent over the motorcycle, paced back and forth aimlessly, glanced once or twice at us, and then ambled over to where the reeds sprang up in a green fence round the perimeter of the lake. One of them cupped her hands to her mouth. "Al," she called. "Hey, Al!"

"Come on," Digby hissed. "Let's get out of here."

But it was too late. The second girl was picking her way across the lot, un-steady on her heels, looking up at us and then away. She was older—twenty-five or -six— and as she came closer we could see there was something wrong with her: she was stoned or drunk, lurching now and waving her arms for balance. I gripped the steering wheel as if it were the ejection lever of a flaming jet, and Digby spat out my name, twice, terse and impatient.

"Hi," the girl said.

We looked at her like zombies, like war veterans, like deaf-and-dumb pencil peddlers.

40   She smiled, her lips cracked and dry. "Listen," she said, bending from the waist to look in the window, "you guys seen Al?" Her pupils were pinpoints, her eyes glass. She jerked her neck. "That's his bike over there—Al's. You seen him?"

Al. I didn't know what to say. I wanted to get out of the car and retch, I wanted to go home to my parents' house and crawl into bed. Digby poked me in the ribs. "We haven't seen anybody," I said.

The girl seemed to consider this, reaching out a slim veiny arm to brace herself against the car. "No matter," she said, slurring the *t's*, "he'll turn up." And then, as if she'd just taken stock of the whole scene—the ravaged car and our battered faces, the desolation of the place—she said: "Hey, you guys look like some pretty bad characters—been fightin', huh?" We stared straight ahead, rigid as catatonics. She was fumbling in her pocket and muttering something. Finally she held out a handful of tablets in glassine wrappers: "Hey, you want to party, you want to do some of these with me and Sarah?"

I just looked at her. I thought I was going to cry. Digby broke the silence. "No, thanks," he said, leaning over me. "Some other time."

I put the car in gear and it inched forward with a groan, shaking off pellets of glass like an old dog shedding water after a bath, heaving over the ruts on its worn springs, creeping toward the highway. There was a sheen of sun on the lake. I looked back. The girl was still standing there, watching us, her shoulders slumped, hand outstretched.

MAKING CONNECTIONS

1. This story is told from the first-person point of view. How would it be different if described from a more detached perspective? Do you think it would change the way you feel about the characters and what they do? Explain.
2. How would you describe the setting and the "culture" of the story? How important is it?
3. Are Digby and Jeff dynamic characters? To what extent do you think they change as a result of this incident?

MAKING AN ARGUMENT

1. Compare the narrator at the beginning and end of the story. Has he changed? To what extent does he deal with people and events differently? Do you think he will ever be the same as he was before? Write an essay that traces the characterization of the narrator over the course of the story. Cite the text of the story for support.

KATE CHOPIN [1851–1904]

Kate Chopin was born in St. Louis, Missouri. Her father, an Irish immigrant, became a successful businessman. Her mother was a prominent member of the French-Creole community and traveled in exclusive social circles. Chopin attended Catholic school, was much admired for her beauty and wit, and at nineteen, married Creole cotton broker Oscar Chopin. The couple settled first in New Orleans and, following the collapse of Oscar's business, moved to his family's plantations in Natchitoches Parish. Following his unexpected death in 1883, at a doctor's suggestion, Chopin began writing. Her stories, which are set among the Creole people of the Louisiana bayou, were collected and published in two anthologies, Bayou Folk *(1894) and* A Night in Arcadie *(1897). Her greatest work, the novel* The Awakening *(1899), which tells the story of an extramarital affair, was denounced as obscene and was largely ignored until it was reevaluated by critics, beginning in the 1930s, who praised it for its emotional honesty and beautiful prose.*

DÉSIRÉE'S BABY   [1892]

As the day was pleasant, Madame Valmondé drove over to L'Abri to see Désirée and the baby.

It made her laugh to think of Désirée with a baby. Why, it seemed but yesterday that Désirée was little more than a baby herself; when Monsieur in riding through the gateway of Valmondé had found her lying asleep in the shadow of the big stone pillar.

The little one awoke in his arms and began to cry for "Dada." That was as much as she could do or say. Some people thought she might have strayed there of her own accord, for she was of the toddling age. The prevailing belief was that she had been purposely left by a pary of Texans, whose canvas-covered wagon, late in the day, had crossed the ferry that Coton Maïs kept, just below the plantation. In time Madame Valmondé abandoned every speculation but the one that Désirée had been sent to her by a beneficent Providence to be the child of her affection, seeing that she was without child of the flesh. For the girl grew to be beautiful and gentle, affectionate and sincere—the idol of Valmondé.

It was no wonder, when she stood one day against the stone pillar in whose shadow she had lain asleep, eighteen years before, that Armand Aubigny riding by and seeing her there, had fallen in love with her. That was the way all the Aubignys fell in love, as if struck by a pistol shot. The wonder was that he had not loved her before; for he had known her since his father brought him home from Paris, a boy of eight, after his mother died there. The passion that awoke in him that day, when he saw her at the gate, swept along like an avalanche, or like a prairie fire, or like anything that drives headlong over all obstacles.

5   Monsieur Valmondé grew practical and wanted things well considered: that is, the girl's obscure origin. Armand looked into her eyes and did not care. He was reminded that she was nameless. What did it matter about a name when he could give her one of

the oldest and proudest in Louisiana? He ordered the *corbeille* from Paris, and contained himself with what patience he could until it arrived; then they were married.

Madame Valmondé had not seen Désirée and the baby for four weeks. When she reached L'Abri she shuddered at the first sight of it, as she always did. It was a sad looking place, which for many years had not know the gentle presence of a mistress, old Monsieur Aubigny having married and buried his wife in France, and she having loved her own land too well ever to leave it. The roof came down steep and black like a cowl, reaching out beyond the wide galleries that encircled the yellow stuc-coed house. Big, solemn oaks grew close to it, and their thick-leaved, far-reaching branches shadowed it like a pall. Young Aubigny's rule was a strict one, too, and under it his Negroes had forgotten how to be gay, as they had been during the old master's easy-going and indulgent lifetime.

The young mother was recovering slowly, and lay full length, in her soft white muslins and laces, upon a couch. The baby was beside her, upon her arm, where it had fallen asleep, at her breast. The yellow nurse woman sat beside a window fan-ning herself.

Madame Valmondé bent her portly figure over Désirée and kissed her, holding her an instant tenderly in her arms. Then she turned to the child.

"This is not the baby!" she exclaimed, in startled tones. French was the language spoken at Valmondé in those days.

10 "I knew you would be astonished," laughed Désirée, "at the way he has grown. The little *cochon de lait!* Look at his legs, mamma, and his hands and fingernails,— real finger-nails. Zandrine had to cut them this morning. Isn't is true, Zandrine?"

The woman bowed her turbaned head majestically, "Maïs si, Madame."

"And the way he cries," went on Désirée, "is deafening. Armand heard him the other day as far away as La Blanche's cabin."

Madame Valmondé had never removed her eyes from the child. She lifted it and walked with it over to the window that was lightest. She scanned the baby narrowly, then looked as searchingly at Zandrine, whose face was turned to gaze across the fields.

"Yes, the child has grown, has changed," said Madame Valmondé, slowly, as she replaced it beside its mother. "What does Armand say?"

15 Désirée's face became suffused with a glow that was happiness itself.

"Oh, Armand is the proudest father in the parish, I believe, chiefly because it is a boy to bear his name; though he says not,—that he would have loved a girl as well. But I know it isn't true. I know he says that to please me. And mamma," she added, drawing Madame Valmondé's head down to her, and speaking in a whisper, "he hasn't punished one of them—not one of them—since baby is born. Even Négrillon, who pretended to have burnt his leg that he might rest from work—he only laughed and said Négrillon was a great scamp. Oh, mamma, I'm so happy; it frightens me."

What Désirée said was true. Marriage, and later the birth of his son, had softened Arman Aubigny's imperious and exacting nature greatly. This was what made the gentle Désirée so happy, for she loved him desperately. When he frowned she trem-bled, but loved him. When he smiled, she asked no greater blessing of God. But Armand's dark, handsome face had not often been disfigured by frowns since the day he fell in love with her.

When the baby was about three months old, Désirée awoke one day to the con-viction that there was something in the air menacing her peace. It was at first too subtle to grasp. It had only been a disquieting suggestion; an air of mystery among the blacks; unexpected visits from far-off neighbors who could hardly account for their coming. Then a strange, an awful change in her husband's manner, which she dared not ask him to explain. When he spoke to her, it was with averted eyes, from which the old love-light seemed to have gone out. He absented himself from home; and when there, avoided her presence and that of her child, without excuse. And the very spirit of Satan seemed suddenly to take hold of him in his dealings with the slaves. Désirée was miserable enough to die.

She sat in her room, one hot afternoon, in her *peignoir,* listlessly drawing through her fingers the strands of her long, silky brown hair that hung about her shoulders. The baby, half naked, lay asleep upon her own great mahogany bed, that was like a sumptuous throne, with its satin lined halfcanopy. One of LaBlanche's little quadroon boys—half naked too—stood fanning the child slowly with a fan of peacock feathers. Désirée's eyes had been fixed absently and sadly upon the baby, while she was striving to penetrate the threatening mist that she felt closing about her. She looked from her child to the boy who stood beside him, and back again; over and over. "Ah!" It was a cry that she could not help, which she was not conscious of having uttered. The blood turned like ice in her veins, and a clammy moisture gathered upon her face.

20   She tried to speak to the little quadroon boy; but no sound would come, at first. When he heard his name uttered, he looked up, and his mistress was pointing to the door. He laid aside the great, soft fan, and obediently stole away, over the polished floor, on his bare tiptoes.

She stayed motionless, with gaze riveted upon her child, and her face the picture of fright.

Presently her husband entered the room, and without noticing her, went to a table and began to search among some papers which covered it.

"Armand," she called to him, in a voice which must have stabbed him, if he was human. But he did not notice. "Armand," she said again. Then she rose and tottered toward him. "Armand," she panted once more, clutching his arm, "look at our child. What does it mean? Tell me."

He coldly but gently loosened her fingers from about his arm and thrust the hand away from him. "Tell me what it means!" she cried despairingly.

25   "It means," he answered lightly, "that the child is not white; it means that you are not white."

A quick conception of all that this accusation meant for her nerved her with unwonted courage to deny it. "It is a lie; it is not true, I am white! Look at my hair, it is brown; and my eyes are gray. Armand, you know they are gray. And my skin is fair," seizing his wrist. "Look at my hand; whiter than yours, Armand," she laughed hysterically.

"As white as LaBlanche's," he returned cruelly; and went away leaving her alone with their child.

When she could hold a pen in her hand, she sent a despairing letter to Madame Valmondé.

"My mother, they tell me I am not white. Armand has told me I am not white. For God's sake tell them it is not true. You must know it is not true. I shall die. I must die. I cannot be so unhappy, and live."

30   The answer that came was as brief.

"My own Désirée: Come home to Valmondé; back to your mother who loves you. Come with your child."

When the letter reached Désirée she went with it to her husband's study, and laid it open upon the desk before which he sat. She was like a stone image: silent, white, motionless after she placed it there.

In silence he ran his cold eyes over the written words. He said nothing.

"Shall I go Armand?" she asked in tones sharp with agonized suspense.

"Yes, go."

35   "Do you want me to go?"

"Yes, I want you to go."

He thought Almighty God had dealt cruelly and unjustly with him; and felt, somehow, that he was paying Him back in kind when he stabbed thus into his wife's soul. Moreover he no longer loved her, because of the unconscious injury she had brought upon his home and his name.

She turned away like one stunned by a blow, and walked slowly towards the door, hoping he would call her back.

"Good-by, Armand," she moaned.

40   He did not answer her. That was his last blow at fate.

Désirée went in search of her child. Zandrine was pacing the somber gallery with it. She took the little one from the nurse's arms with no word of explanation, and descending the steps, walked away, under the live-oak branches.

It was an October afternoon; the sun was just sinking. Out in the still fields the Negroes were picking cotton.

Désirée had not changed the thin white garment nor the slippers which she wore. Her hair was uncovered and the sun's rays brought a golden gleam from its brown meshes. She did not take the broad, beaten road which led to the far-off plantation of Valmondé. She walked across a deserted field, where the stubble bruised her tender feet, so delicately shod, and tore her thin gown to shreds.

She disappeared among the reeds and willows that grew thick along the banks of the deep, sluggish bayou; and she did not come back again.

45   Some weeks later there was a curious scene enacted at L'Abri. In the center of the smoothly swept back yard was a great bonfire. Armand Aubigny sat in the wide hallway that commanded a view of the spectacle; and it was he who dealt out to a half dozen Negroes the material which kept this fire ablaze.

A graceful cradle of willow, with all its dainty furbishings, was laid upon the pyre, which had already been fed with the richness of a priceless *layette*. Then there were silk gowns, and velvet and satin ones added to these; laces, too, and embroideries; bonnets and gloves, for the *corbeille* had been of rare quality.

The last thing to go was a tiny bundle of letters; innocent little scribblings that Désirée had sent to him during the days of their espousal. There was the remnant of one back in the drawer from which he took them. But it was not Désirée's; it was part of an old letter from his mother to his father. He read it. She was thanking God for the blessing of her husband's love:—

"But, above all," she wrote, "night and day, I thank the good God for having arranged our lives that our dear Armand will never know that his mother, who adores him, belongs to the race that is cursed with the brand of slavery."

MAKING CONNECTIONS

1. What causes Armand's change in attitude toward Désirée? To what extent does the prevailing culture influence his attitude? Why does what he think he's discovered about Désirée matter so much to him?
2. What happens to Désirée and the baby? What evidence in the text of the story indicates that?
3. What does Armand discover about himself as he destroys all traces of Désirée? Do you think he will be as tough on himself as he was on Désirée? Do you think he should be? What do you think he will do?
4. How does the author mislead us into thinking that Désirée is responsible for the mixed race of the child?

MAKING AN ARGUMENT

1. This story is a good example of situational irony. What is ironic about this story? Do you think it's credible that events would come together like this? Using this story—and at least one other story in this section, write about the impact of irony in literature. Cite the texts of the stories for support.

WILLIAM FAULKNER [1897–1962]

William Faulkner was born into a genteel Southern family and was raised in Oxford, Mississippi, where he attended the University of Mississippi. Following World War I, during which he served in the Canadian air force, he settled in Oxford, Mississippi, and worked for a time in the post office until he was forced to resign—he was lax in his duties and often became absorbed in writing or reading. By 1930 he had published a book of verse and a number of novels, including two of his greatest, The Sound and The Fury *(1929) and* As I Lay Dying *(1930), but he did not reach a wide readership until the publication of the novel* Sanctuary, *in 1931. Fifteen of his novels, as well as many of his short stories, are set in fictional Yoknapatawpha County, Mississippi, and concern themselves with the interconnected fortunes of a group of families of different social classes from the Civil War to modern times. Other major works include:* Light in August *(1932),* Absalom! Absalom! *(1936),* The Hamlet *(1940), and* Collected Stories *(1950). Faulkner was awarded the Nobel Prize in 1950. When asked about his inspiration for "A Rose for Emily," which originally appeared in* These Thirteen *(1931), a collection of short stories, Faulkner said: "That came from a picture of the strand of hair on the pillow. It was a ghost story, simply a picture of a strand of hair on the pillow in the abandoned house."*

A ROSE FOR EMILY   [1931]

I

When Miss Emily Grierson died, our whole town went to her funeral: the men through a sort of respectful affection for a fallen monument, the women mostly out of curiosity to see the inside of her house, which no one save an old manservant— a combined gardener and cook—had seen in at least ten years.

It was a big, squarish frame house that had once been white, decorated with cupolas and spires and scrolled balconies in the heavily lightsome style of the seventies, set on what had once been our most select street. But garages and cotton gins had encroached and obliterated even the august names of that neighborhood; only Miss Emily's house was left, lifting its stubborn and coquettish decay above the cotton wagons and the gasoline pumps—an eyesore among eyesores. And now Miss Emily had gone to join the representatives of those august names where they lay in the cedar-bemused cemetery among the ranked and anonymous graves of Union and Confederate soldiers who fell at the battle of Jefferson.

Alive, Miss Emily had been a tradition, a duty, and a care; a sort of hereditary obligation upon the town, dating from that day in 1894 when Colonel Sartoris, the mayor—he who fathered the edict that no Negro woman should appear on the streets without an apron—remitted her taxes, the dispensation dating from the death of her father on into perpetuity. Not that Miss Emily would have accepted charity. Colonel Sartoris invented an involved tale to the effect that Miss Emily's father had loaned money to the town, which the town, as a matter of business, preferred this way of repaying. Only a man of Colonel Sartoris' generation and thought could have invented it, and only a woman could have believed it.

When the next generation, with its more modern ideas, became mayors and aldermen, this arrangement created some little dissatisfaction. On the first of the year they mailed her a tax notice. February came, and there was no reply. They wrote her a formal letter, asking her to call at the sheriff's office at her convenience. A week later the mayor wrote her himself, offering to call or to send his car for her, and received in reply a note on paper of an archaic shape, in a thin, flowing calligraphy in faded ink, to the effect that she no longer went out at all. The tax notice was also enclosed, without comment.

5   They called a special meeting of the Board of Aldermen. A deputation waited upon her, knocked at the door through which no visitor had passed since she ceased giving china-painting lessons eight or ten years earlier. They were admitted by the old Negro into a dim hall from which a staircase mounted into still more shadow. It smelled of dust and disuse—a close, dank smell. The Negro led them into the parlor. It was furnished in heavy, leather-covered furniture. When the Negro opened the blinds of one window, they could see that the leather was cracked; and when they sat down, a faint dust rose sluggishly about their thighs, spinning with slow motes in the single sunray. On a tarnished gilt easel before the fireplace stood a crayon portrait of Miss Emily's father.

They rose when she entered—a small, fat woman in black, with a thin gold chain descending to her waist and vanishing into her belt, leaning on an ebony cane with a tarnished gold head. Her skeleton was small and spare; perhaps that was why what would have been merely plumpness in another was obesity in her. She looked bloated, like a body long submerged in motionless water, and of that pallid hue. Her eyes, lost in the fatty ridges of her face, looked like two small pieces of coal pressed into a lump of dough as they moved from one face to another while the visitors stated their errand.

She did not ask them to sit. She just stood in the door and listened quietly until the spokesman came to a stumbling halt. Then they could hear the invisible watch ticking at the end of the gold chain.

Her voice was dry and cold. "I have no taxes in Jefferson. Colonel Sartoris explained it to me. Perhaps one of you can gain access to the city records and satisfy yourselves."

"But we have. We are the city authorities, Miss Emily. Didn't you get a notice from the sheriff, signed by him?"

10   "I received a paper, yes," Miss Emily said. "Perhaps he considers himself the sheriff . . . . I have no taxes in Jefferson."

"But there is nothing on the books to show that, you see. We must go by the—"

"See Colonel Sartoris. I have no taxes in Jefferson."

"But, Miss Emily—"

"See Colonel Sartoris." (Colonel Sartoris had been dead almost ten years.) "I have no taxes in Jefferson. Tobe!" The Negro appeared. "Show these gentlemen out."

II

15 So she vanquished them, horse and foot, just as she had vanquished their fathers thirty years before about the smell. That was two years after her father's death and a short time after her sweetheart—the one we believed would marry her—had deserted her. After her father's death she went out very little; after her sweetheart went away, people hardly saw her at all. A few of the ladies had the temerity to call, but were not received, and the only sign of life about the place was the Negro man—a young man then—going in and out with a market basket.

"Just as if a man—any man—could keep a kitchen properly," the ladies said; so they were not surprised when the smell developed. It was another link between the gross, teeming world and the high and mighty Griersons.

A neighbor, a woman, complained to the mayor, Judge Stevens, eighty years old.

"But what will you have me do about it, madam?" he said.

"Why, send her word to stop it," the woman said. "Isn't there a law?"

20   "I'm sure that won't be necessary," Judge Stevens said. "It's probably just a snake or a rat that nigger of hers killed in the yard. I'll speak to him about it."

The next day he received two more complaints, one from a man who came in diffident deprecation. "We really must do something about it, Judge, I'd be the last one in the world to bother Miss Emily, but we've got to do something." That night the Board of Aldermen met—three gray-beards and one younger man, a member of the rising generation.

"It's simple enough," he said. "Send her word to have her place cleaned up. Give her a certain time to do it in, and if she don't . . . "

"Dammit, sir," Judge Stevens said, "will you accuse a lady to her face of smelling bad?"

So the next night, after midnight, four men crossed Miss Emily's lawn and slunk about the house like burglars, sniffing along the base of the brickwork and at the cellar openings while one of them performed a regular sowing motion with his hand out of a sack slung from his shoulder. They broke open the cellar door and sprinkled lime there, and in all the outbuildings. As they recrossed the lawn, a window that had been dark was lighted and Miss Emily sat in it, the light behind her, and her upright torso motionless as that of an idol. They crept quietly across the lawn and into the shadow of the locusts that lined the street. After a week or two the smell went away.

25   That was when people had begun to feel really sorry for her. People in our town remembering how old lady Wyatt, her great-aunt, had gone completely crazy at last, believed that the Griersons held themselves a little too high for what they really were. None of the young men were quite good enough for Miss Emily and such. We had long thought of them as a tableau; Miss Emily a slender figure in white in the background, her father a spraddled silhouette in the foreground, his back to her and clutching a horsewhip, the two of them framed by the backflung front door. So when she got to be thirty and was still single, we were not pleased exactly, but vindicated; even with insanity in the family she wouldn't have turned down all of her chances if they had really materialized.

When her father died, it got about that the house was all that was left to her; and in a way, people were glad. At last they could pity Miss Emily. Being left alone, and a pauper, she had become humanized. Now she too would know the old thrill and the old despair of a penny more or less.

The day after his death all the ladies prepared to call at the house and offer condolence and aid, as is our custom. Miss Emily met them at the door, dressed as usual and with no trace of grief on her face. She told them that her father was not dead. She did that for three days, with the ministers calling on her, and the doctors, trying to persuade her to let them dispose of the body. Just as they were about to resort to law and force, she broke down, and they buried her father quickly.

We did not say she was crazy then. We believed she had to do that. We remembered all the young men her father had driven away, and we knew that with nothing left, she would have to cling to that which had robbed her, as people will.

III

She was sick for a long time. When we saw her again, her hair was cut short, making her look like a girl, with a vague resemblance to those angels in colored church windows—sort of tragic and serene.

30   The town had just let the contracts for paving the sidewalks, and in the summer after her father's death they began to work. The construction company came with niggers and mules and machinery, and a foreman named Homer Barron, a Yankee—a big, dark, ready man, with a big voice and eyes lighter than his face. The little boys would follow in groups to hear him cuss the niggers, and the niggers singing in time to the rise and fall of picks. Pretty soon he knew everybody in town. Whenever you heard a lot of laughing anywhere about the square, Homer Barron would be in the

center of the group. Presently we began to see him and Miss Emily on Sunday after-noons driving in the yellow-wheeled buggy and the matched team of bays from the livery stable.

At first we were glad that Miss Emily would have an interest, because the ladies all said, "Of course a Grierson would not think seriously of a Northerner, a day laborer." But there were still others, older people, who said that even grief could not cause a real lady to forget *noblesse oblige*—without calling it *noblesse oblige*. They just said, "Poor Emily. Her kinsfolk should come to her." She had some kin in Alabama; but years ago her father had fallen out with them over the estate of old lady Wyatt, the crazy woman, and there was no communication between the two fami-lies. They had not even been represented at the funeral.

And as soon as the old people said, "Poor Emily," the whispering began. "Do you suppose it's really so?" they said to one another. "Of course it is. What else could. . . . " This behind their hands; rustling of craned silk and satin behind jalousies closed upon the sun of Sunday afternoon as the thin, swift clop-clop-clop of the matched team passed: "Poor Emily."

She carried her head high enough—even when we believed that she was fallen. It was as if she demanded more than ever the recognition of her dignity as the last Grierson; as if it had wanted that touch of earthiness to reaffirm her imperviousness. Like when she bought the rat poison, the arsenic. That was over a year after they had begun to say "Poor Emily," and while the two female cousins were visiting her.

"I want some poison," she said to the druggist. She was over thirty then, still a slight woman, though thinner than usual, with cold, haughty black eyes in a face the flesh of which was strained across the temples and about the eyesockets as you imagine a lighthouse-keeper's face ought to look. "I want some poison," she said.

35   "Yes, Miss Emily. What kind? For rats and such? I'd recom—"

"I want the best you have. I don't care what kind."

The druggist named several. "They'll kill anything up to an elephant. But what you want is—"

"Arsenic." Miss Emily said. "Is that a good one?"

"Is . . . arsenic? Yes ma'am. But what you want—"

40   "I want arsenic."

The druggist looked down at her. She looked back at him, erect, her face like a strained flag. "Why, of course," the druggist said. "If that's what you want. But the law requires you to tell what you are going to use it for."

Miss Emily just stared at him, her head tilted back in order to look him eye for eye, until he looked away and went and got the arsenic and wrapped it up. The Negro delivery boy brought her the package; the druggist didn't come back. When she opened the package at home there was written on the box, under the skull and bones: "For rats."

IV

So the next day we all said, "She will kill herself"; and we said it would be the best thing. When she had first begun to be seen with Homer Barron, we had said, "She will marry him." Then we said, "She will persuade him yet," because Homer himself had remarked—he liked men, and it was known that he drank with the younger men in the Elks' Club—that he was not a marrying man. Later we said, "Poor Emily," behind the jalousies as they passed on Sunday afternoon in the glittering buggy, Miss Emily with her head high and Homer Barron with his hat cocked and a cigar in his teeth, reins and whip in a yellow glove.

Then some of the ladies began to say that it was a disgrace to the town and a bad example to the young people. The men did not want to interfere, but at last the ladies forced the Baptist minister—Miss Emily's people were Episcopal—to call upon her. He would never divulge what happened during that interview, but he refused to go back again. The next Sunday they again drove about the streets, and the following day the minister's wife wrote to Miss Emily's relations in Alabama.

45   So she had blood-kin under her roof again and we sat back to watch developments. At first nothing happened. Then we were sure that they were to be married. We learned that Miss Emily had been to the jeweler's and ordered a man's toilet set in silver, with the letters H.B. on each piece. Two days later we learned that she had bought a complete outfit of men's clothing, including a nightshirt, and we said, "They are married." We were really glad. We were glad because the two female cousins were even more Grierson than Miss Emily had ever been.

So we were surprised when Homer Barron—the streets had been finished some time since—was gone. We were a little disappointed that there was not a public blowing-off, but we believed that he had gone on to prepare for Miss Emily's coming, or to give her a chance to get rid of the cousins. (By that time it was a cabal, and we were all Miss Emily's allies to help circumvent the cousins.) Sure enough, after another week they departed. And, as we had expected all along, within three days Homer Barron was back in town. A neighbor saw the Negro man admit him at the kitchen door at dusk one evening.

And that was the last we saw of Homer Barron. And of Miss Emily for some time. The Negro man went in and out with the market basket, but the front door remained closed. Now and then we would see her at a window for a moment, as the men did that night when they sprinkled the lime, but for almost six months she did not appear on the streets. Then we knew that this was to be expected too; as if that quality of her father which had thwarted her woman's life so many times had been too virulent and too furious to die.

When we next saw Miss Emily, she had grown fat and her hair was turning gray. During the next few years it grew grayer and grayer until it attained an even pepper-and-salt iron-gray, when it ceased turning. Up to the day of her death at seventy-four it was still that vigorous iron-gray, like the hair of an active man.

From that time on her front door remained closed, save for a period of six or seven years, when she was about forty, during which she gave lessons in china-painting. She fitted up a studio in one of the downstairs rooms, where the daughters and granddaughters of Colonel Sartoris' contemporaries were sent to her with the same regularity and in the same spirit that they were sent on Sundays with a twenty-five cent piece for the collection plate. Meanwhile her taxes had been remitted.

50   Then the newer generation became the backbone and the spirit of the town, and the painting pupils grew up and fell away and did not send their children to her with boxes of color and tedious brushes and pictures cut from the ladies' magazines. The front door closed upon the last one and remained closed for good. When the

town got free postal delivery, Miss Emily alone refused to let them fasten the metal numbers above her door and attach a mailbox to it. She would not listen to them.

Daily, monthly, yearly we watched the Negro grow grayer and more stooped, going in and out with the market basket. Each December we sent her a tax notice, which would be returned by the post office a week later, unclaimed. Now and then we could see her in one of the downstairs windows—she had evidently shut up the top floor of the house—like the carven torso of an idol in a niche, looking or not looking at us, we could never tell which. Thus she passed from generation to generation—dear, inescapable, impervious, tranquil, and perverse.

And so she died. Fell ill in the house filled with dust and shadows, with only a doddering Negro man to wait on her. We did not even know she was sick; we had long since given up trying to get any information from the Negro. He talked to no one, probably not even to her, for his voice had grown harsh and rusty, as if from disuse.

She died in one of the downstairs rooms, in a heavy walnut bed with a curtain, her gray head propped on a pillow yellow and moldy with age and lack of sunlight.

V

The Negro met the first of the ladies at the front door and let them in, with their hushed, sibilant voices and their quick, curious glances, and then he disappeared. He walked right through the house and out the back and was not seen again.

55   The two female cousins came at once. They held the funeral on the second day, with the town coming to look at Miss Emily beneath a mass of bought flowers, with the crayon face of her father musing profoundly above the bier and the ladies sibilant and macabre; and the very old men—some in their brushed Confederate uniforms—on the porch and the lawn, talking of Miss Emily as if she had been a contemporary of theirs, believing that they had danced with her and courted her perhaps, confusing time with its mathematical progression, as the old do, to whom all the past is not a diminishing road, but, instead, a huge meadow which no winter ever quite touches, divided from them now by the narrow bottleneck of the most recent decade of years.

Already we knew that there was one room in that region above stairs which no one had seen in forty years, and which would have to be forced. They waited until Miss Emily was decently in the ground before they opened it.

The violence of breaking down the door seemed to fill this room with pervading dust. A thin, acrid pall as of the tomb seemed to lie everywhere upon this room decked and furnished as for a bridal: upon the valance curtains of faded rose color, upon the rose-shaded lights, upon the dressing table, upon the delicate array of crystal and the man's toilet things backed with tarnished silver, silver so tarnished that the monogram was obscured. Among them lay a collar and tie, as if they had just been removed, which, lifted, left upon the surface a pale crescent in the dust. Upon a chair hung the suit, carefully folded; beneath it the two mute shoes and the discarded socks.

The man himself lay in the bed.

For a long while we just stood there, looking down at the profound and fleshless grin. The body had apparently once lain in the attitude of an embrace, but now the long sleep that outlasts love, that conquers even the grimace of love, had cuck-olded him. What was left of him, rotted beneath what was left of the nightshirt, had become inextricable from the bed in which he lay; and upon him and upon the pillow beside him lay that even coating of the patient and biding dust.

60   Then we noticed that in the second pillow was the indentation of a head. One of us lifted something from it, and leaning forward, that faint and invisible dust dry and acrid in the nostrils, we saw a long strand of iron-gray hair.

MAKING CONNECTIONS

1. Who is the narrator? How does the narrator's unusual point of view (third person but from the perspective of "we") influence what you know in the story? What difference does it make that the story is told in flashbacks instead of from beginning to end? What is the narrator's attitude toward Emily?
2. How do you feel about Emily Grierson? What is her conflict?
3. Who is Homer Barron? How does his characterization differ from Emily's?
4. At the end of the story, what is the significance of the iron-gray strand of hair on the second pillow? Are there indications earlier in the story that foreshadow this outcome?
5. Why is Emily such a formidable force in the town? Why does she seem to get away with so much?
6. To what extent is this a story about change—or the inability to change?

MAKING AN ARGUMENT

1. The culture of the setting (the town, the era, Mississippi) is essential to this story. Write an argument that demonstrates the strong relationship between culture/setting and the characterization and conflict in this story. Cite the text of the story (and other stories if appropriate) for support.

JAMAICA KINCAID (B. 1949)

Jamaica Kincaid, whose given name was Elaine Potter Richardson, was born in St. John's Antigua, an island in the West Indies. She left the rural island when she was sev-enteen and went to New York City to work as an au pair. She studied photography at the New School in New York and attended Franconia College in New Hampshire. Much of her work is drawn from her own experiences, both as a child in Antigua and as an immigrant in the United States. Her works include a collection of short stories, At the Bottom of the River *(1983); two novels,* Annie John *(1985) and* Lucy *(1990); and a book of essays,* A

Small Place *(1988). Her most recent work,* Autobiography of My Mother, *appeared in 1995. She currently divides her time between New York City, where she has worked for many years as a staff writer for the* New Yorker, *and Bennington College in Vermont, where she is a lecturer.*

GIRL   [1978]

Wash the white clothes on Monday and put them on the stone heap; wash the color clothes on Tuesday and put them on the clothes-line to dry; don't walk barehead in the hot sun; cook pumpkin fritters in very hot sweet oil; soak your little clothes right after you take them off; when buying cotton to make yourself a nice blouse, be sure that it doesn't have gum on it, because that way it won't hold up well after a wash; soak salt fish overnight before you cook it; is it true that you sing benna in Sunday school? always eat your food in such a way that it won't turn someone else's stomach; on Sundays try to walk like a lady and not like the slut you are so bent on becoming; don't sing benna in Sunday school; you mustn't speak to wharf-rat boys, not even to give directions; don't eat fruits on the street—flies will follow you; *but I don't sing benna on Sundays at all and never in Sunday school;* this is how to sew on a button; this is how to make a buttonhole for the button you have just sewed on; this is how to hem a dress when you see the hem coming down and so to prevent yourself from looking like the slut I know you are so bent on becoming; this is how you iron your father's khaki shirt so that it doesn't have a crease; this is how you iron your fathers' khaki pants so that they don't have a crease; this is how you grow okra—far from the house, because okra tree harbors red ants; when you are growing dasheen, make sure it gets plenty of water or else it makes your throat itch when you are eating it; this is how you sweep a corner; this is how you sweep a whole house; this is how you sweep a yard; this is how you smile to someone you don't like too much; this is how you smile at someone you don't like at all; this is how you smile to someone you like completely; this is how you set a table for tea; this is how you set a table for dinner; this is how you set a table for dinner with an important guest; this is how you set a table for lunch; this is how you set a table for breakfast; this is how to behave in the presence of men who don't know you very well, and this way they won't recognize immediately the slut I have warned you against becoming; be sure to wash every day, even if it is with your own spit; don't squat down to play marbles—you are not a boy, you know; don't pick people's flowers—you might catch something; don't throw stones at blackbirds, because it might not be a blackbird at all; this is how to make a bread pudding; this is how to make doukona; this is how to make pepper pot; this is how to make a good medicine for a cold; this is how to make a good medicine to throw away a child before it even becomes a child; this is how to catch a fish; this is how to throw back a fish you don't like, and that way something bad won't fall on you; this is how to bully a man; this is how a man bullies you; this is how to love a man, and if this doesn't work there are other ways, and if they don't work don't feel too bad about giving up; this is how to spit up in the air if you feel like it, and this is how to move quick so that it doesn't fall on you; this is how to make ends meet; always squeeze bread to make sure it's fresh; *but what if the baker won't let me feel the bread?* you mean to say that after all you are really going to be the kind of woman who the baker won't let near the bread?

MAKING CONNECTIONS

1. Describe the point of view and voice in this story. Who is the narrator? What effect does the nonstop advice—in a nonstop sentence—have on you?
2. Who is making the italicized comments? What difference do they make to you?
3. How would you describe this relationship?

MAKING AN ARGUMENT

1. Given the nature of the language, this seems to be a story from the author's native culture, but to what extent is this a cross-cultural comment on the relationship between mothers and daughters in general? Pick out the elements of this monologue that reveal the mother and daughter and write an argument that shows how it might apply to your own—or any other—culture.

THOMAS KING [B. 1943]

Thomas King was born in Sacramento, California, and moved to Canada in 1980. He is a novelist and broadcaster who often writes about Canada's First Nations and is an outspoken advocate for First Nations causes. His ancestry is Cherokee, German, and Greek. His work includes Medicine River *(1990),* A Coyote Columbus Story *(1992),* Green Grass, Running Water *(1993),* Coyotes Sing to the Moon *(1998),* Truth and Bright Water *(1999), and* Dreadful Water Shows Up *(2002). He lives in Guelph, Ontario, is an English professor at the University of Guelph, and is the creator of* Dead Dog Cafe, *a CBC Radio One series.*

BORDERS

[1993]

When I was twelve, maybe thirteen, my mother announced that we were going to go to Salt Lake City to visit my sister who had left the reserve, moved across the line, and found a job. Laetitia had not left home with my mother's blessing, but over time my mother had come to be proud of the fact that Laetitia had done all of this on her own.

"She did real good," my mother would say.

Then there were the fine points to Laetitia's going. She had not, as my mother liked to tell Mrs. Manyfingers, gone floating after some man like a balloon on a string. She hadn't snuck out of the house, either, and gone to Vancouver or Edmonton or Toronto to chase rainbows down alleys. And she hadn't been pregnant.

"She did real good."

5   I was seven or eight when Laetitia left home. She was seventeen. Our father was
from Rocky Boy on the American side.

"Dad's American," Laetitia told my mother, "so I can go and come as I please."

"Send us a postcard."

Laetitia packed her things, and we headed for the border. Just outside of Milk
River, Laetitia told us to watch for the water tower.

"Over the next rise. It's the first thing you see."

10   "We got a water tower on the reserve," my mother said.

"There's a big one in Lethbridge, too."

"You'll be able to see the tops of the flagpoles, too. That's where the border is."

When we got to Coutts, my mother stopped at the convenience store and
bought her and Laetitia a cup of coffee. I got an Orange Crush.

"This is real lousy coffee."

"You're just angry because I want to see the world."

15   "It's the water. From here on down, they got lousy water."

"I can catch the bus from Sweetgrass. You don't have to lift a finger."

"You're going to have to buy your water in bottles if you want good coffee."

There was an old wooden building about a block away, with a tall sign in the
yard that said "Museum." Most of the roof had been blown away. Mom told me to go
and see when the place was open. There were boards over the windows and doors.
You could tell that the place was closed, and I told Mom so, but she said to go and
check anyway. Mom and Laetitia stayed by the car. Neither one of them moved. I sat
down on the steps of the museum and watched them, and I don't know that they
ever said anything to each other. Finally, Laetitia got her bag out of the trunk and gave
Mom a hug.

I wandered back to the car. The wind had come up, and it blew Laetitia's hair
across her face. Mom reached out and pulled the strands out of Laetitia's eyes, and
Laetitia let her.

20   "You can still see the mountain from here," my mother told Laetitia in Blackfoot.

"Lots of mountains in Salt Lake," Laetitia told her in English.

"The place is closed," I said. "Just like I told you."

Laetitia tucked her hair into her jacket and dragged her bag down the road to
the brick building with the American flag flapping on a pole. When she got to
where the guards were waiting, she turned, put the bag down, and waved to us. We
waved back. Then my mother turned the car around, and we came home.

We got postcards from Laetitia regular, and, if she wasn't spreading jelly on the
truth, she was happy. She found a good job and rented an apartment with a pool.

25   "And she can't even swim," my mother told Mrs. Manyfingers.

Most of the postcards said we should come down and see the city, but whenever I mentioned this, my mother would stiffen up.

So I was surprised when she bought two new tires for the car and put on her
blue dress with the green and yellow flowers. I had to dress up, too, for my mother
did not want us crossing the border looking like Americans. We made sandwiches
and put them in a big box with pop and potato chips and some apples and bananas
and a big jar of water.

"But we can stop at one of those restaurants, too, right?"

"We maybe should take some blankets in case you get sleepy."

30   "But we can stop at one of those restaurants, too, right?"

The border was actually two towns, though neither one was big enough to amount to anything. Coutts was on the Canadian side and consisted of the convenience store and gas station, the museum that was closed and boarded up, and a motel. Sweetgrass was on the American side, but all you could see was an overpass that arched across the highway and disappeared into the prairies. Just hearing the names of these towns, you would expect that Sweetgrass, which is a nice name and sounds like it is related to other places such as Medicine Hat and Moose Jaw and Kicking Horse Pass, would be on the Canadian side, and that Coutts, which sounds abrupt and rude, would be on the American side. But this was not the case.

Between the two borders was a duty-free shop where you could buy cigarettes and liquor and flags. Stuff like that.

We left the reserve in the morning and drove until we got to Coutts.

"Last time we stopped here," my mother said, "you had an Orange Crush. You remember that?"

35   "Sure," I said. "That was when Laetitia took off."

"You want another Orange Crush?"

"That means we're not going to stop at a restaurant, right?"

My mother got a coffee at the convenience store, and we stood around and watched the prairies move in the sunlight. Then we climbed back in the car. My mother straightened the dress across her thighs, leaned against the wheel, and drove all the way to the border in first gear, slowly, as if she were trying to see through a bad storm or riding high on black ice.

The border guard was an old guy. As he walked to the car, he swayed from side to side, his feet set wide apart, the holster on his hip pitching up and down. He leaned into the window, looked into the back seat, and looked at my mother and me.

40   "Morning, ma'am."

"Good morning."

"Where you heading?"

"Salt Lake City."

"Purpose of your visit?"

45   "Visit my daughter."

"Citizenship?"

"Blackfoot," my mother told him.

"Ma'am?"

"Blackfoot," my mother repeated.

50   "Canadian?"

"Blackfoot."

It would have been easier if my mother had just said "Canadian" and been done with it, but I could see she wasn't going to do that. The guard wasn't angry or anything. He smiled and looked towards the building. Then he turned back and nodded.

"Morning, ma'am."

"Good morning."

55   "Any firearms or tobacco?"

"No."

"Citizenship?"

"Blackfoot."

He told us to sit in the car and wait, and we did. In about five minutes, another guard came out with the first man. They were talking as they came, both men swaying back and forth like two cowboys headed for a bar or a gunfight.

60   "Morning, ma'am."

"Good morning."

"Cecil tells me you and the boy are Blackfoot."

"That's right."

"Now, I know that we got Blackfeet on the American side and the Canadians got Blackfeet on their side. Just so we can keep our records straight, what side do you come from?"

65   I knew exactly what my mother was going to say, and I could have told them if they had asked me.

"Canadian side or American side?" asked the guard.

"Blackfoot side," she said.

It didn't take them long to lose their sense of humor, I can tell you that. The one guard stopped smiling altogether and told us to park our car at the side of the building and come in.

We sat on a wood bench for about an hour before anyone came over to talk to us. This time it was a woman. She had a gun, too.

70   "Hi," she said. "I'm Inspector Pratt. I understand there is a little misunderstanding."

"I'm going to visit my daughter in Salt Lake City," my mother told her. "We don't have any guns or beer."

"It's a legal technicality, that's all."

"My daughter's Blackfoot, too."

The woman opened a briefcase and took out a couple of forms and began to write on one of them. "Everyone who crosses our border has to declare their citizenship. Even Americans. It helps us keep track of the visitors we get from the various countries."

75   She went on like that for maybe fifteen minutes, and a lot of the stuff she told us was interesting.

"I can understand how you feel about having to tell us your citizenship, and here's what I'll do. You tell me, and I won't put it down on the form. No-one will know but you and me."

Her gun was silver. There were several chips in the wood handle and the name "Stella" was scratched into the metal butt.

We were in the border office for about four hours, and we talked to almost everyone there. One of the men bought me a Coke. My mother brought a couple of sandwiches in from the car. I offered part of mine to Stella, but she said she wasn't hungry.

I told Stella that we were Blackfoot and Canadian, but she said that that didn't count because I was a minor. In the end, she told us that if my mother didn't declare her citizenship, we would have to go back to where we came from. My mother stood up and thanked Stella for her time. Then we got back in the car and drove to the Canadian border, which was only about a hundred yards away.

80   I was disappointed. I hadn't seen Laetitia for a long time, and I had never been to Salt Lake City. When she was still at home, Laetitia would go on and on about Salt Lake City. She had never been there, but her boyfriend Lester Tallbull had spent a year in Salt Lake at a technical school.

     "It's a great place," Lester would say. "Nothing but blondes in the whole state."

     Whenever he said that, Laetitia would slug him on his shoulder hard enough to make him flinch. He had some brochures on Salt Lake and some maps, and every so often the two of them would spread them out on the table.

     "That's the temple. It's right downtown. You got to have a pass to get in."

     "Charlotte says anyone can go in and look around."

85   "When was Charlotte in Salt Lake? Just when the hell was Charlotte in Salt Lake?"

     "Last year."

     "This is Liberty Park. It's got a zoo. There's good skiing in the mountains."

     "Got all the skiing we can use," my mother would say. "People come from all over the world to ski at Banff. Cardston's got a temple, if you like those kinds of things."

     "Oh, this one is real big," Lester would say. "They got armed guards and everything."

90   "Not what Charlotte says."

     "What does she know?"

     Lester and Laetitia broke up, but I guess the idea of Salt Lake stuck in her mind.

     The Canadian border guard was a young woman, and she seemed happy to see us. "Hi," she said. "You folks sure have a great day for a trip. Where are you coming from?"

     "Standoff."

95   "Is that in Montana?"

     "No."

     "Where are you going?"

     "Standoff."

     The woman's name was Carol and I don't guess she was any older than Laetitia. "Wow, you both Canadians?"

100   "Blackfoot."

     "Really? I have a friend I went to school with who is Blackfoot. Do you know Mike Harley?"

     "No."

     "He went to school in Lethbridge, but he's really from Browning."

     It was a nice conversation and there were no cars behind us, so there was no rush.

105   "You're not bringing any liquor back, are you?"

     "No."

     "Any cigarettes or plants or stuff like that?"

     "No."

     "Citizenship?"

110   "Blackfoot."

     "I know," said the woman, "and I'd be proud of being Blackfoot if I were Blackfoot. But you have to be American or Canadian."

When Laetitia and Lester broke up, Lester took his brochures and maps with him, so Laetitia wrote to someone in Salt Lake City, and, about a month later, she got a big envelope of stuff. We sat at the table and opened up all the brochures, and Laetitia read each one out loud.

"Salt Lake City is the gateway to some of the world's most magnificent skiing.

"Salt Lake City is the home of one of the newest professional basketball franchises, the Utah Jazz.

115   "The Great Salt Lake is one of the natural wonders of the world."

It was kind of exciting seeing all those color brochures on the table and listening to Laetitia read all about how Salt Lake City was one of the best places in the entire world.

"That Salt Lake City place sounds too good to be true," my mother told her.

"It has everything."

120   "We got everything right here."

"It's boring here."

"People in Salt Lake City are probably sending away for brochures of Calgary and Lethbridge and Pincher Creek right now."

In the end, my mother would say that maybe Laetitia should go to Salt Lake City, and Laetitia would say that maybe she would.

We parked the car to the side of the building and Carol led us into a small room on the second floor. I found a comfortable spot on the couch and flipped through some back issues of *Saturday Night* and *Alberta Report*.

When I woke up, my mother was just coming out of another office. She didn't say a word to me. I followed her down the stairs and out to the car. I thought we were going home, but she turned the car around and drove back towards the American border, which made me think we were going to visit Laetitia in Salt Lake City after all. Instead she pulled into the parking lot of the duty-free store and stopped.

125   "We going to see Laetitia?"

"No."

"We going home?"

Pride is a good thing to have, you know. Laetitia had a lot of pride, and so did my mother. I figured that someday, I'd have it, too.

"So where are we going?"

130   Most of that day, we wandered around the duty-free store, which wasn't very large. The manager had a name tag with a tiny American flag on one side and a tiny Canadian flag on the other. His name was Mel. Towards evening, he began suggesting that we should be on our way. I told him we had nowhere to go, that neither the Americans nor the Canadians would let us in. He laughed at that and told us that we should buy something or leave.

The car was not very comfortable, but we did have all that food and it was April, so even if it did snow as it sometimes does on the prairies, we wouldn't freeze. The next morning my mother drove to the American border.

It was a different guard this time, but the questions were the same. We didn't spend as much time in the office as we had the day before. By noon, we were back at the Canadian border. By two we were back in the duty-free shop parking lot.

The second night in the car was not as much fun as the first, but my mother seemed in good spirits, and, all in all, it was as much an adventure as an inconvenience. There wasn't much food left and that was a problem, but we had lots of water as there was a faucet at the side of the duty-free shop.

One Sunday, Laetitia and I were watching television. Mom was over at Mrs. Manyfingers's. Right in the middle of the program, Laetitia turned off the set and said she was going to Salt Lake City, that life around here was too boring. I had wanted to see the rest of the program and really didn't care if Laetitia went to Salt Lake City or not. When Mom got home, I told her what Laetitia had said.

135   What surprised me was how angry Laetitia got when she found out that I had told Mom.

"You got a big mouth."

"That's what you said."

"What I said is none of your business."

"I didn't say anything."

140   "Well, I'm going for sure, now."

That weekend, Laetitia packed her bags, and we drove her to the border.

Mel turned out to be friendly. When he closed up for the night and found us still parked in the lot, he came over and asked us if our car was broken down or something. My mother thanked him for his concern and told him that we were fine, that things would get straightened out in the morning.

"You're kidding," said Mel. "You'd think they could handle the simple things."

"We got some apples and a banana," I said, "but we're all out of ham sandwiches."

"You know, you read about these things, but you just don't believe it. You just don't believe it."

145   "Hamburgers would be even better because they got more stuff for energy."

My mother slept in the back seat. I slept in the front because I was smaller and could lie under the steering wheel. Late that night, I heard my mother open the car door. I found her sitting on her blanket leaning against the bumper of the car.

"You see all those stars," she said. "When I was a little girl, my grandmother used to take me and my sisters out on the prairies and tell us stories about all the stars."

"Do you think Mel is going to bring us any hamburgers?"

"Every one of those stars has a story. You see that bunch of stars over there that look like a fish?"

150   "He didn't say no."

"Coyote went fishing, one day. That's how it all started." We sat out under the stars that night, and my mother told me all sorts of stories. She was serious about it, too. She'd tell them slow, repeating parts as she went, as if she expected me to remember each one.

Early the next morning, the television vans began to arrive, and guys in suits and women in dresses came trotting over to us, dragging microphones and cameras and lights behind them. One of the vans had a table set up with orange juice and sandwiches and fruit. It was for the crew, but when I told them we hadn't eaten for a while, a really skinny blonde woman told us we could eat as much as we wanted.

They mostly talked to my mother. Every so often one of the reporters would come over and ask me questions about how it felt to be an Indian without a country. I told them we had a nice house on the reserve and that my cousins had a couple of horses we rode when we went fishing. Some of the television people went over to the American border, and then they went to the Canadian border.

Around noon, a good-looking guy in a dark blue suit and an orange tie with little ducks on it drove up in a fancy car. He talked to my mother for a while, and, after they were done talking, my mother called me over, and we got into our car. Just as my mother started the engine, Mel came over and gave us a bag of peanut brittle and told us that justice was a damn hard thing to get, but that we shouldn't give up.

155   I would have preferred lemon drops, but it was nice of Mel anyway.

"Where are we going now?"

"Going to visit Laetitia."

The guard who came out to our car was all smiles. The television lights were so bright they hurt my eyes, and, if you tried to look through the windshield in certain directions, you couldn't see a thing.

"Morning, ma'am."

160   "Good morning."

"Where you heading?"

"Salt Lake City."

"Purpose of your visit?"

"Visit my daughter."

165   "Any tobacco, liquor, or firearms?"

"Don't smoke."

"Any plants or fruit?"

"Not any more."

"Citizenship?"

170   "Blackfoot."

The guard rocked back on his heels and jammed his thumbs into his gun belt. "Thank you," he said, his fingers patting the butt of the revolver. "Have a pleasant trip."

My mother rolled the car forward, and the television people had to scramble out of the way. They ran alongside the car as we pulled away from the border, and, when they couldn't run any farther, they stood in the middle of the highway and waved and waved and waved.

We got to Salt Lake City the next day. Laetitia was happy to see us, and, that first night, she took us out to a restaurant that made really good soups. The list of pies took up a whole page. I had cherry. Mom had chocolate. Laetitia said that she saw us on television the night before and, during the meal, she had us tell her the story over and over again.

Laetitia took us everywhere. We went to a fancy ski resort. We went to the temple. We got to go shopping in a couple of large malls, but they weren't as large as the one in Edmonton, and Mom said so.

175   After a week or so, I got bored and wasn't at all sad when my mother said we should be heading back home. Laetitia wanted us to stay longer, but Mom said no,

that she had things to do back home and that, next time, Laetitia should come up and visit. Laetitia said she was thinking about moving back, and Mom told her to do as she pleased, and Laetitia said that she would.

On the way home, we stopped at the duty-free shop, and my mother gave Mel a green hat that said "Salt Lake" across the front. Mel was a funny guy. He took the hat and blew his nose and told my mother that she was an inspiration to us all. He gave us some more peanut brittle and came out into the parking lot and waved at us all the way to the Canadian border.

It was almost evening when we left Coutts. I watched the border through the rear window until all you could see were the tops of the flagpoles and the blue water tower, and then they rolled over a hill and disappeared.

MAKING CONNECTIONS

1. Why do you think the story moves back and forth between the border scenes and the talk about Salt Lake City? Discuss the relationship between the structure of the story and its content.
2. What happens at the end of the story? Why are they finally allowed to cross the border? Why does Mel say the narrator's mother is "an inspiration to us all"? Is she? Explain.
3. Compare this story to Gloria Anzaldúa's "To Live in the Borderlands Means You" on page 998.

MAKING AN ARGUMENT

1. When asked about her citizenship, the narrator's mother insists on identifying the two of them as "Blackfoot." Why? Given all the trouble it seems to cause, would it have been better if she simply said, "Canadian"? Write an argument that agrees or disagrees with her refusal to declare her citizenship. Cite the text of the story for support.

GABRIEL GARCIA MARQUEZ [B. 1928]

Gabriel Garcia Marquez was born in Aracataca, Colombia. Marquez published "A Very Old Man with Enormous Wings" as part of his first book, Leaf Storm and Other Stories, *in 1955. Typical of his fiction, including "A Very Old Man with Enormous Wings," is the mingling of realistic fiction and magical or fantastic elements. The author of several novels and collections of stories, including the internationally best-selling* One Hundred Years of Solitude (1967) *and* Love in the Time of Cholera, (1986) *he was awarded the Nobel Prize for literature in 1982. His latest book,* Memories of My Melancholy Whores, *was published in 2004.*

A VERY OLD MAN WITH ENORMOUS WINGS [1955]

Translated by Gregory Rabassa

On the third day of rain they had killed so many crabs inside the house that Pelayo had to cross his drenched courtyard and throw them into the sea, because the newborn child had a temperature all night and they thought it was due to the stench. The world had been sad since Tuesday. Sea and sky were a single ash-gray thing and the sands of the beach, which on March nights glimmered like powdered light, had become a stew of mud and rotten shellfish. The light was so weak at noon that when Pelayo was coming back to the house after throwing away the crabs, it was hard for him to see what it was that was moving and groaning in the rear of the courtyard. He had to go very close to see that it was an old man, a very old man, lying face down in the mud, who, in spite of his tremendous efforts, couldn't get up, impeded by his enormous wings.

Frightened by that nightmare, Pelayo ran to get Elisenda, his wife, who was putting compresses on the sick child, and he took her to the rear of the courtyard. They both looked at the fallen body with mute stupor. He was dressed like a rag-picker. There were only a few faded hairs left on his bald skull and very few teeth in his mouth, and his pitiful condition of a drenched great-grandfather had taken away any sense of grandeur he might have had. His huge buzzard wings, dirty and half-plucked, were forever entangled in the mud. They looked at him so long and so closely that Pelayo and Elisenda very soon overcame their surprise and in the end found him familiar. Then they dared speak to him, and he answered in an incomprehensible dialect with a strong sailor's voice. That was how they skipped over the inconvenience of the wings and quite intelligently concluded that he was a lonely castaway from some foreign ship wrecked by the storm. And yet, they called in a neighbor woman who knew everything about life and death to see him, and all she needed was one look to show them their mistake.

"He's an angel," she told them. "He must have been coming for the child, but the poor fellow is so old that the rain knocked him down."

On the following day everyone knew that a flesh-and-blood angel was held captive in Pelayo's house. Against the judgment of the wise neighbor woman, for whom angels in those times were the fugitive survivors to a celestial conspiracy, they did not have the heart to club him to death. Pelayo watched over him all afternoon from the kitchen, armed with his bailiff's club, and before going to bed he dragged him out of the mud and locked him up with the hens in the wire chicken coop. In the middle of the night, when the rain stopped, Pelayo and Elisenda were still killing crabs. A short time afterward the child woke up without a fever and with a desire to eat. Then they felt magnanimous and decided to put the angel on a raft with fresh water and provisions for three days and leave him to his fate on the high seas. But when they went out into the courtyard with the first light of dawn, they found the whole neighborhood in front of the chicken coop having fun with the angel, without the slightest reverence, tossing him things to eat through the openings in the wire as if he weren't a supernatural creature but a circus animal.

5   Father Gonzaga arrived before seven o'clock, alarmed at the strange news. By that time onlookers less frivolous than those at dawn had already arrived and they were making all kinds of conjectures concerning the captive's future. The simplest

among them thought that he should be named mayor of the world. Others of sterner mind felt that he should be promoted to the rank of five-star general in order to win all wars. Some visionaries hoped that he could be put to stud in order to implant on earth a race of winged wise men who could take charge of the universe. But Father Gonzaga, before becoming a priest, had been a robust woodcutter. Standing by the wire, he reviewed his catechism in an instant and asked them to open the door so that he could take a close look at that pitiful man who looked more like a huge decrepit hen among the fascinated chickens. He was lying in a corner drying his open wings in the sunlight among the fruit peels and breakfast leftovers that the early risers have thrown him. Alien to the impertinences of the world, he only lifted his antiquarian eyes and murmured something in his dialect when Father Gonzaga went into the chicken coop and said good morning to him in Latin. The parish priest had his first suspicion of an impostor when he saw that he did not understand the language of God or know how to greet His ministers. Then he noticed that seen close up he was much too human: he had an unbearable smell of the outdoors, the back side of his wings was strewn with parasites and his main feathers had been mistreated by terrestrial winds, and nothing about him measured up to the proud dignity of angels. Then he came out of the chicken coop and in a brief sermon warned the curious against the risks of being ingenuous. He reminded them that the devil had the bad habit of making use of carnival tricks in order to confuse the unwary. He argued that if wings were not the essential element in determining the difference between a hawk and an airplane, they were even less so in the recognition of angels. Nevertheless, he promised to write a letter to his bishop so that the latter would write to his primate so that the latter would write to the Supreme Pontiff in order to get the final verdict from the highest courts.

His prudence fell on sterile hearts. The news of the captive angel spread with such rapidity that after a few hours the courtyard had the bustle of a marketplace, and they had to call in troops with fixed bayonets to disperse the mob that was about to knock the house down. Elisenda, her spine all twisted from sweeping up so much marketplace trash, then got the idea of fencing in the yard and charging five cents admission to see the angel.

The curious came from far away. A traveling carnival arrived with a flying acrobat who buzzed over the crowd several times, but no one paid any attention to him because his wings were not those of an angel, but rather, those of a sidereal[1] bat. The most unfortunate invalids on earth came in search of health: a poor woman who since childhood had been counting her heartbeats and had run out of numbers; a Portuguese man who couldn't sleep because the noise of the stars disturbed him; a sleepwalker who got up at night to undo the things he had done while awake; and many others with less serious ailments. In the midst of that shipwreck disorder that made the earth tremble, Pelayo and Elisenda were happy with fatigue, for in less than a week they had crammed their rooms with money and the line of pilgrims waiting their turn to enter still reached beyond the horizon.

[1]**sidereal** coming from the stars

The angel was the only one who took no part in his own act. He spent his time trying to get comfortable in his borrowed nest, befuddled by the hellish heat of the oil lamps and sacramental candles that had been placed along the wire. At first they tried to make him eat some mothballs, which, according to the wisdom of the wise neighbor woman, were the food prescribed for angels. But he turned them down, just as he turned down the papal lunches that the penitents brought him, and they never found out whether it was because he was an angel or because he was an old man that in the end he ate nothing but eggplant mush. His only supernatural virtue seemed to be patience. Especially during the first days, when the hens pecked at him, searching for the stellar parasites that proliferated in his wings, and the cripples pulled out feathers to touch their defective parts with, and even the merciful threw stones at him, trying to get him to rise so they could see him standing. The only time they succeeded in arousing him was when they burned his side with an iron for branding steers, for he had been motionless for so many hours that they thought he was dead. He awoke with a start, ranting in his hermetic language and with tears in his eyes, and he flapped his wings a couple of times, which brought on a whirlwind of chicken dung and lunar dust and a gale of panic that did not seem to be of this world. Although many thought that his reaction had been one not of rage but of pain, from then on they were careful not to annoy him, because the majority understood that his passivity was not that of a hero taking his ease but that of a cataclysm in repose.

Father Gonzaga held back the crowd's frivolity with formulas of maidservant inspiration while awaiting the arrival of a final judgment on the nature of the captive. But the mail from Rome showed no sense of urgency. They spent their time finding out if the prisoner had a navel, if his dialect had any connection with Aramaic, how many times he could fit on the head of a pin, or whether he wasn't just a Norwegian with wings. Those meager letters might have come and gone until the end of time if a providential event had not put an end to the priest's tribulations.

10   It so happened that during those days, among so many other carnival attractions, there arrived in town the traveling show of the woman who had been changed into a spider for having disobeyed her parents. The admission to see her was not only less than the admission to see the angel, but people were permitted to ask her all manner of questions about her absurd state and to examine her up and down so that no one would ever doubt the truth of her horror. She was a frightful tarantula the size of a ram and with the head of a sad maiden. What was most heart-rending, however, was not her outlandish shape but the sincere affliction with which she recounted the details of her misfortune. While still practically a child she had sneaked out of her parents' house to go to a dance, and while she was coming back through the woods after having danced all night without permission, a fearful thunderclap rent the sky in two and through the crack came the lightning bolt of brimstone that changed her into a spider. Her only nourishment came from the meatballs that charitable souls chose to toss into her mouth. A spectacle like that, full of so much human truth and which was such a fearful lesson, was bound to defeat without even trying that of a haughty angel who scarcely deigned to look at mortals. Besides, the few miracles attributed to the angel showed a certain mental disorder, like the blind man who didn't recover his sight but grew three new teeth, or the paralytic who didn't get to walk but almost won the lottery, and the leper whose sores sprouted sunflowers. Those consolation miracles, which were more like mocking fun, had already ruined the angel's reputation when the

woman who had been changed into a spider finally crushed him completely. That was how Father Gonzaga was cured forever of his insomnia and Pelayo's courtyard went back to being as empty as during the time it had rained for three days and crabs walked through the bedrooms.

The owners of the house had no reason to lament. With the money they saved they built a two-story mansion with balconies and gardens and high netting so that crabs wouldn't get in during the winter, and with iron bars on the windows so that angels wouldn't get in. Pelayo also set up a rabbit warren close to town and gave up his job as bailiff for good, and Elisenda bought some satin pumps with high heels and many dresses of iridescent silk, the kind worn on Sunday by the most desirable women in those times. The chicken coop was the only thing that didn't receive any attention. If they washed it down with creolin and burned tears of myrrh inside it every so often, it was not in homage to the angel but to drive away the dung heap stench that still hung everywhere like a ghost and was turning the new house into an old one. At first, when the child learned to walk, they were careful that he not get too close to the chicken coop. But then they began to lose their fears and got used to the smell, and before the child got his second teeth he'd gone inside the chicken coop to play, where the wires were falling apart. The angel was no less standoffish with him than with other mortals, but he tolerated the most ingenious infamies with the patience of a dog who had no illusions. They both came down with chicken pox at the same time. The doctor who took care of the child couldn't resist the temptation to listen to the angel's heart, and he found so much whistling in the heart and so many sounds in his kidneys that it seemed impossible for him to be alive. What surprised him most, however, was the logic of his wings. They seemed so natural on that completely human organism that he couldn't understand why other men didn't have them too.

When the child began school it had been some time since the sun and rain had caused the collapse of the chicken coop. The angel went dragging himself about here and there like a stray dying man. They would drive him out of the bedroom with a broom and a moment later find him in the kitchen. He seemed to be in so many places at the same time that they grew to think that he'd been duplicated, that he was reproducing himself all through the house, and the exasperated and unhinged Elisenda shouted that it was awful living in that hell full of angels. He could scarcely eat and his antiquarian eyes had also become so foggy that he went about bumping into posts. All he had left were the bare cannulae[2] of his last feathers. Pelayo threw a blanket over him and extended him the charity of letting him sleep in the shed, and only then did they notice that he had a temperature at night, and was delirious with the tongue twisters of an old Norwegian. That was one of the few times they became alarmed, for they thought he was going to die and not even the wise neighbor woman had been able to tell them what to do with dead angels.

And yet he not only survived his worst winter, but seemed improved with the first sunny days. He remained motionless for several days in the farthest corner of the courtyard, where no one would see him, and at the beginning of December some large, stiff feathers began to grow on his wings, the feathers of a scarecrow, which

---

[2]**cannulae** the tubular pieces by which feathers are attached to a body

looked more like another misfortune of decrepitude. But he must have known the reason for those changes, for he was quite careful that no one should notice them, that no one should hear the sea chanteys that he sometimes sang under the stars. One morning Elisenda was cutting some bunches of onions for lunch when a wind that seemed to come from the high seas blew into the kitchen. Then she went to the window and caught the angel in his first attempts at flight. They were so clumsy that his fingernails opened a furrow in the vegetable patch and he was on the point of knocking the shed down with the ungainly flapping that slipped on the light and couldn't get a grip on the air. But he did manage to gain altitude. Elisenda let out a sigh of relief, for herself and for him, when she saw him pass over the last houses, holding himself up in some way with the risky flapping of a senile vulture. She kept watching him even when she was through cutting the onions and she kept on watching until it was no longer possible for her to see him, because then he was no longer an annoyance in her life but an imaginary dot on the horizon of the sea.

MAKING CONNECTIONS

1. How were you affected by Marquez's mingling of fantastic and realistic elements?
2. Does the description of this angel bother you? Does it meet your expectations for what an angel should be? Explain.
3. There are many humorous elements to this story. Do you think the story has anything meaningful to say about reality? Explain.

MAKING AN ARGUMENT

1. This story comes from a literary tradition called "magical realism"—fiction that blends realistic or ordinary details and events with those that are magical or fantastic. Identify those elements in the story that you consider to be fantastic and/or satirical, and write about their effectiveness in conveying the theme of the story. Cite the text of the story for support.

TAHIRA NAQVI [B. 1945]

Originally from Lahore, Pakistan, Tahira Naqvi is now settled in the United States with her family. She taught English for thirteen years at Western Connecticut State University before moving to Westchester County and subsequently to a teaching position at Westchester Community College. She has taught Urdu literature at Columbia University and New York University. In addition, she is a writer of English fiction and a translator of Urdu. Her own short fiction has been widely anthologized, and a first collection of short stories, titled Attar of Roses and Other Stories of Pakistan, *appeared in*

1997. A second collection, Dying in a Strange Country, *was published in 2001. She recently completed her first novel.*

Brave We Are   [2001]

"Mom, Ammi," he asks, the little boy Kasim who is my son, who has near-black eyes and whose buck teeth give him a Bugs Bunny look when his mouth is open, as it is now, in query. "What does hybrid mean?"

"Hybrid?" I'm watching the water in the pot very closely; the tiny bubbles quivering restlessly on its surface indicate it's about to come to boil. Poised over the pot, clutching a batch of straw-colored Prince spaghetti, is my hand, suspended, warm from the steam and waiting for the moment when the bubbles will suddenly and turbulently come to life.

I'm not fussy about brands, especially where spaghetti is concerned (it's all pasta, after all), but I wish there was one which would fit snugly at the outset into my largest pot. As things stand now, the strands bend uncomfortably, contort, embroiling themselves in something of a struggle within the confines of the pot once they've been dropped into the boiling water. Some day of course, I will have a pot large enough to accommodate all possible lengths and varieties.

"Yeah, hybrid. Do you know what it means?"

5   The note of restive insistence in his voice compels me to tear my gaze away from the water. Kasim's face looks darker now than when he left for school this morning. Perhaps running up the steep driveway with the March wind lashing against his lean nine-year-old frame has forced the blood to rush to his face. Flushed, his face reminds me he's still only a child, 'only ten, just a baby,' as my mother often says when I sometimes take him to task in her presence, arguing with him as if he were a man behaving like a child.

A new spelling word? Such a difficult word for a fourth-grader. "Are you studying plants?"

"No, but can you tell me what it means?" Impatient, so impatient, so like the water that's hissing and tumbling in the pot, demanding immediate attention. He slides against the kitchen counter and hums, his fingers beating an indecipherable rhythm on the Formica, his eyes raised above mine, below mine, behind me, to the window outside which white, lavender and gray have mingled to become a muddied brown. Just as he reaches for the cookie jar I quickly throw in the spaghetti.

"Well, that's a hard word. Let me see." Helplessly I watch as he breaks off a Stella Doro biscuit in his mouth and crumbs disperse in a steady fall-out, over the counter, on the kitchen tile, some getting caught in his blue-and-green striped sweater, like flies in a spider's web. "It's a sort of mixture, a combination of different sorts of things," I say wisely, with the absolute knowledge that 'things' is susceptible to misinterpretation. I rack my brain for a good example. If I don't hurry up with one he's going to move away with the notion that his mother doesn't know what hybrid means.

"You mean if you mix orange juice with lemonade it's going to become hybrid juice?" The idea has proved ticklish, he smiles, crumbs from the Stella Doro dangling on the sides of his face; they obviously don't bother him as much as they bother me. I lean forward and rub a hand around his mouth just as he lunges toward the cookie jar again. He squirms and recoils at the touch of my ministering hand. Another biscuit is retrieved. I turn down the heat under the spaghetti to medium and start chopping onions.

10   Today I'm making spaghetti the way my mother makes it in Lahore, like pulao, the way I used to make it after I got married and was just learning to cook for a husband who had selective tastes in food. That was about the only thing I could make then so I worked hard to embellish and innovate. There, we call it noodles, although it's unmistakably spaghetti, with no tomato sauce or meatballs in or anywhere near it, no cheese either, and no one has heard of mozzarella or romano. The idea of cheese with our recipe would surprise the people in Lahore; even the ones with the most adventurous palates will cringe.

"Well, that too." And why not? My eyes smart from the sharpness of the onions, tears fill my eyes and spill over my cheeks. I turn away from the chopping board. "The word is used when you breed two different kinds of plants or animals, it's called cross-breeding." I snaffle. This gets harder. I know his knowledge of breeding is limited and 'cross isn't going to help at all.

"What's cross-whatyoumaycallit?"

An example. One that will put the seal on hybrid forever. So he can boast his mother knows everything.

I wipe my watering eyes with a paper napkin and turn to the onions again. These, chopped thinly, are for the ground beef which will be cooked with small green peas, cubed potatoes and cut-leaf spinach and will be spiced with coriander, garlic, cumin, a touch of turmeric and half-inch long bristly strands of fresh ginger root. I'll throw the beef into the spaghetti when it's done and my husband and I alone will eat what I make. My children like spaghetti the way it should be, the way it is, in America.

15   Moisture runs down my cheeks and my eyes smart. I place the knife down on the chopping board, tear out another sheet from the roll of Bounty towels on my right and rub my eyes and nose with it, my attention driven to the stark, brown limbs of trees outside as I wipe my face. The kitchen window that I now face as I do innumerable times during the day, faithfully reflects the movements of time and seasons of the small town in Connecticut where we live, compelling the spirit to buoyancy or, when the tones on its canvas are achromatous and dark, to melancholy, to sadness. Today, the sun is visible again and the white of the snow is distinguishable from the lavender of the bare, thin, stalky birches, unhealthy because we haven't tended them well. Sharply the sun cuts shadows on the clean, uncluttered snow.

Why does snow in February always remind me of February in Lahore? Incongruent, disparate, the seasons have so little in common. March is spring, grass so thick your foot settles into it, roses that bloom firm, their curves fleshy, the colors like undisturbed paint on an artist's palette, the air timberous, weaving in and out of swishing tree branches with *the sar, sar, sar* of a string instrument. Why do I turn to Eileen, my cleaning lady, and say, "Eileen do you know it's spring in Lahore?" She looks up from the pot she's scrubbing in the kitchen sink with a good-humored smile. "No kidding? Really?" she asks, as if she didn't already know, as if she hadn't already heard it from me before.

An example, yes. "Now take an apple. A farmer can cross-breed a Macintosh apple with a Golden Yellow and get something which is a little bit like both. That will be a hybrid apple." I look closely at the boy's face for some signs of comprehension.

"You mean the apple's going to have a new name, like Macintosh Yellow?" he asks, his forehead creased thoughtfully.

"Yes." Relieved, I return to the onions, making a mental note to check the spaghetti soon, which, languorously swelled now, will have to be taken off from the stove and drained.

20   "But what about animals? You said there's *crosswhatyoumaycallit* in animals too." He sprawls against the counter, up and down, right and left, like a gymnast.

"Yes there is. A cow from one family may be bred with a steer from another family and they'll end up with a calf that's a bit like the two of them." I wash my hands and he skips on the floor, dance-like steps, his arms raised.

"But man's an animal too, teacher says. Do people also cross . . . *umm* . . . breed?"

He's humming again. I know the tune now: *"Suzie Q/ Suzie Q/ I love you/ 0 Suzie Q!"* It's from a song on his older brother Haider's tape, a catchy tune, sort of stays with you and you can't stop humming it. Both Haider and my younger son, Asghar, were amused when I showed an interest in the song. What do I know about music, their kind of music? Once, nearly two years ago, I tried to bribe Haider to memorize a ghazal by the poet Ghalib. The greatest Urdu poet of the subcontinent, I said passionately, the most complex. Egged on by the fifty dollars I was offering, he mastered the first verse by listening to a tape of ghazals sung by Mehdi Hasan.

> *Yeh naa thi hamari qismet ke visal-e-yaar ho*
> *Agar aurjeete rehte yehi intizar hota*
> It was not fated that I should meet my beloved,
> Life will merely prolong the waiting

Then, unable to sustain his interest, despite the now a thirty-dollar verse rate, Haider abandoned the project.

25   "The words are too hard," he complained when I protested, somewhat angrily. "The music's easy, but I can't keep up with the lyrics."

And I would have given him the money too. Actually I had decided to give him all of it after he had moved on to the second verse.

"Does that mean Mary is also hybrid?" Kasim's voice crashes into my thoughts of Suzie Q with a loud boom.

I lower the heat under the spaghetti—so what if it's a bit overdone. The yellow-white strands jump at each other in frantic embraces, hurried, as if there's no time to be lost.

"Mary? What are you talking about?" I know exactly what he's talking about. His vagueness passes through the sieve in my head and comes out as clarity. I fill in any blanks, uncannily, never ceasing to be surprised at the way this peculiar magic works.

30   "You know, Mary Khan, Dr. Khan's daughter? She's in my class Mom, you know her."

Yes, I know Mary well. Her full name is Marium. Her father, Amjad Khan and my husband, Ali, were together in the same medical school in Lahore, they graduated the same year, they completed residencies together at the same hospital in New York, where Amjad met and married Helen, a nurse. Helen is English. She's a few years older than I, very tall, almost a half-inch taller than Amjad, and has sleek, golden hair. We're good friends, Helen and I, and at least once a week we meet for lunch at a restaurant, an activity we decided to call 'sampling restaurants for later.' Over salmon lasagna or papadi chat and dosa or tandoori chicken she'll tell me how difficult Amjad is when it comes to their children, how upset he is that their son has taken it upon himself to date without his father's consent or approval. I'll shake my head and try to explain that Amjad might have dated *her*, but like a good Muslim father, he can't accept that his son can have girlfriends. "Wait till Mary is older," I say with my hand on Helen's arm, "the Muslim father in him will drop all his masks." Together we do what most women do quite unabashedly: spend a great deal of time talking about husbands.

When Mary was born Amjad said, "We're going to call her Marium, it's a name everyone knows." Familiar and convenient is what he meant, since it's tri-religious. That doesn't sound right, but if we can say bisexual, surely we can say tri-religious-religious too. Why not? After all Islam, Christianity and Judaism all profess a claim to this name. However, before the child was quite one 'Marium' was shortened permanently to Mary.

Kasim is at the breakfast table now, some of his earlier energy dissipated. A small piece of biscuit lies forlornly before him on the table and he fusses with it slowly, obviously unwilling to pop the last bit in his mouth, content just to play with it.

"You know, her mother's English and her father's Pakistani like Dad, and she's got blue eyes and black hair."

35   "Yes, she does have lovely blue eyes and they look so pretty with her dark hair." I grapple with something to blunt the sharpness of his next question which I anticipate and I know I cannot repel.

"Well, then she's hybrid too, isn't she?" He's looking straight at me. His eyes are bright with the defiance of someone who knows he's scored a point.

Brave we are, we who answer questions that spill forth artlessly from the mouths of nine-year-old purists, questions that can neither be waved nor dismissed with flippant ambiguity. Vigilant and alert, we must be ready with our answers.

"Technically speaking she is, I mean, wait, you can say she is." I lift a hand and stop him before he says more. "But we don't use the word for people." The firmness in my voice sounds forced. "Don't say anything to her, okay?"

"Why? Is it a swear?"

40   "No!" I hasten with denial. "Of course not. It's just a word we don't use for people, that's all. Understand?"

"But what do you call them then?" He persists. "Mary's like the apple, isn't she? Isn't she? Her name's Mary Khan, isn't it?"

"Yes, Kas, it is. But there's nothing wrong with that name, a name's a name." Kasim looks contemplative. I know he's saying to himself, *Mom doesn't really know, but Mary's a hybrid, she's got blue eyes and black hair.*

"She's a person Kasim, not an apple. Anyway, you didn't tell me where you heard that word. Is it on your spelling list for this week?"

"No, Mrs. Davis was reading us something about plants in the *Weekly Reader.* It's not homework." He shrugs, abandons the Stella Doro and humming, leaves the kitchen.

45   "Get to homework now," I call after him, wondering if there's an equivalent of 'hybrid' in Urdu, a whole word, not one or two strung together in a phrase to mean the same thing. Offhand I can't think of one.

Without meaning to I throw in some oregano into the boiling spaghetti. I shouldn't have done that. How's oregano going to taste in the company of coriander and cumin? Well, no matter, it's too late anyway.

After I've drained the spaghetti I will take some out for the meat mixture, saving the rest for my children. Then I'll add to our portion, my husband's and mine, the beef and vegetable mixture and turn everything over ever so gently, making sure that the spaghetti isn't squelched. The strands must remain smooth, elusive, separate.

MAKING CONNECTIONS

1. In giving her explanation, what is the narrator's conflict? What is she concerned about? Should she be? Would you be in this circumstance? Explain.
2. Describe the "voice" of the narrator. How has she "shown" what is told? What details in the story help to give you a picture of the setting and the difficulty of the situation?

MAKING AN ARGUMENT

1. To what extent is the meal the narrator is preparing a metaphor for what she is explaining? What does she mean in the last line of the story by "The strands must remain smooth, elusive, separate"? Do you agree? Interpret the theme of the story and take a position on the closing metaphor. Cite the text of the story for support.

ALICE WALKER [B. 1944]

Alice Walker was one of eight children born in rural Georgia to sharecropper parents and was particularly close to her mother. Walker first attended Spelman College, and then transferred to Sarah Lawrence, where she earned a B.A. in 1965. In 1967, she married a white civil rights lawyer (they have since divorced), and the couple settled in Jackson, Mississippi, where they were the first legally married interracial couple in the city. The following year, while she was teaching at Jackson State University, she published the first of her seven volumes of concise and unsentimental verse, Once. *Though she first attracted national attention with her edition of* I Love Myself When I Am Laughing *(1979), an anthology of essays about Zora Neale Hurston, it was her novel* The Color Purple, *the story of a black woman's struggle in the early twentieth century, that made her the literary equivalent of a superstar. Her other novels include* The Temple of My Familiar *(1989) and* Possessing the Secret of Joy *(1992). Her most recent book is* Now Is the Time to Open Your Heart *(2005). Walker currently resides in southern California.*

EVERYDAY USE

[1973]

For Your Grandmama

I will wait for her in the yard that Maggie and I made so clean and wavy yesterday afternoon. A yard like this is more comfortable than most people know. It is not just a yard. It is like an extended living room. When the hard clay is swept clean as a floor and the fine sand around the edges lined with tiny, irregular grooves anyone can come and sit and look up into the elm tree and wait for the breezes that never come inside the house.

Maggie will be nervous until after her sister goes: she will stand hopelessly in corners homely and ashamed of the burn scars down her arms and legs, eyeing her sister with a mixture of envy and awe. She thinks her sister has held life always in the palm of one hand, that "no" is a word the world never learned to say to her.

You've no doubt seen those TV shows where the child who has "made it" is confronted, as a surprise, by her own mother and father, tottering in weakly from backstage. (A pleasant surprise, of course: What would they do if parent and child came on the show only to curse out and insult each other?) On TV mother and child embrace and smile into each other's faces. Sometimes the mother and father weep, the child wraps them in her arms and leans across the table to tell how she would not have made it without their help. I have seen these programs.

Sometimes I dream a dream in which Dee and I are suddenly brought together on a TV program of this sort. Out of a dark and soft-seated limousine I am ushered into a bright room filled with many people. There I meet a smiling, gray, sporty man like Johnny Carson who shakes my hand and tells me what a fine girl I have. Then we are on the stage and Dee is embracing me with tears in her eyes. She pins on my dress a large orchid, even though she has told me once that she thinks orchids are tacky flowers.

5   In real life I am a large, big-boned woman with rough, man-working hands. In the winter I wear flannel nightgowns to bed and overalls during the day. I can kill and clean a hog as mercilessly as a man. My fat keeps me hot in zero weather. I can work outside all day, breaking ice to get water for washing; I can eat pork liver cooked over the open fire minutes after it comes steaming from the hog. One winter I knocked a bull calf straight in the brain between the eyes with a sledge hammer and had the meat hung up to chill before nightfall. But of course all this does not show on television. I am the way my daughter would want me to be: a hundred pounds lighter, my skin like an uncooked barley pancake. My hair glistens in the hot bright lights. Johnny Carson has much to do to keep up with my quick and witty tongue.

But that is a mistake. I know even before I wake up. Who ever knew a Johnson with a quick tongue? Who can even imagine me looking a strange white man in the eye? It seems to me I have talked to them always with one foot raised in flight, with my head turned in whichever way is farthest from them. Dee, though. She would always look anyone in the eye. Hesitation was no part of her nature.

"How do I look, Mama?" Maggie says, showing just enough of her thin body enveloped in pink skirt and red blouse for me to know she's there, almost hidden by the door.

"Come out into the yard," I say.

Have you ever seen a lame animal, perhaps a dog run over by some careless person rich enough to own a car, sidle up to someone who is ignorant enough to be kind to him? That is the way my Maggie walks. She has been like this, chin on chest, eyes on ground, feet in shuffle, ever since the fire that burned the other house to the ground.

10   Dee is lighter than Maggie, with nicer hair and a fuller figure. She's a woman now, though sometimes I forget. How long ago was it that the other house burned? Ten, twelve years? Sometimes I can still hear the flames and feel Maggie's arms sticking to me, her hair smoking and her dress falling off her in little black papery flakes. Her eyes seemed stretched open, blazed open by the flames reflected in them. And Dee. I see her standing off under the sweet gum tree she used to dig gum out of, a look of concentration on her face as she watched the last dingy gray board of the house fall in toward the red-hot brick chimney. Why don't you do a dance around the ashes? I'd wanted to ask her. She had hated the house that much.

I used to think she hated Maggie, too. But that was before we raised the money, the church and me, to send her to Augusta to school. She used to read to us without pity; forcing words, lies, other folks' habits, whole lives upon us two, sitting trapped and ignorant underneath her voice. She washed us in a river of make-believe, burned us with a lot of knowledge we didn't necessarily need to know. Pressed us to her with the serious way she read, to shove us away at just the moment, like dimwits, we seemed about to understand.

Dee wanted nice things. A yellow organdy dress to wear to her graduation from high school; black pumps to match a green suit she'd made from an old suit somebody gave me. She was determined to stare down any disaster in her efforts. Her eyelids would not flicker for minutes at a time. Often I fought off the temptation to shake her. At sixteen she had a style of her own: and knew what style was.

I never had an education myself. After second grade the school was closed down. Don't ask me why: in 1927 colored asked fewer questions than they do now. Sometimes Maggie reads to me. She stumbles along good-naturedly but can't see well. She knows she is not bright. Like good looks and money, quickness passed her by. She will marry John Thomas (who has mossy teeth in an earnest face) and then I'll be free to sit here and I guess just sing church songs to myself. Although I never was a good singer. Never could carry a tune. I was always better at a man's job. I used to love to milk till I was hooked in the side in '49. Cows are soothing and slow and don't bother you, unless you try to milk them the wrong way.

I have deliberately turned my back on the house. It is three rooms, just like the one that burned, except the roof is tin; they don't make shingle roofs any more. There are no real windows, just some holes cut in the sides, like the portholes in a ship, but not round and not square, with rawhide holding the shutters up on the outside. This house is in a pasture, too, like the other one. No doubt when Dee sees it she will want to tear it down. She wrote me once that no matter where we "choose" to live, she will manage to come see us. But she will never bring her friends. Maggie and I thought about this and Maggie asked me, "Mama, when did Dee ever *have* any friends?"

15   She had a few. Furtive boys in pink shirts hanging about on washday after school. Nervous girls who never laughed. Impressed with her they worshiped the well-turned phrase, the cute shape, the scalding humor that erupted like bubbles in lye. She read to them.

When she was courting Jimmy T she didn't have much time to pay to us, but turned all her faultfinding power on him. *He flew* to marry a cheap gal from a family of ignorant flashy people. She hardly had time to recompose herself.

When she comes I will meet—but there they are!

Maggie attempts to make a dash for the house, in her shuffling way, but I stay her with my hand. "Come back here," I say. And she stops and tries to dig a well in the sand with her toe.

It is hard to see them clearly through the strong sun. But even the first glimpse of leg out of the car tells me it is Dee. Her feet were always neat-looking, as if God himself had shaped them with a certain style. From the other side of the car comes a short, stocky man. Hair is all over his head a foot long and hanging from his chin like a kinky mule tail. I hear Maggie suck in her breath. "Uhnnnh," is what it sounds like. Like when you see the wriggling end of a snake just in front of your foot on the road. "Uhnnnh."

20   Dee next. A dress down to the ground, in this hot weather. A dress so loud it hurts my eyes. There are yellows and oranges enough to throw back the light of the sun. *I* feel my whole face warming from the heat waves it throws out. Earrings, too, gold and hanging down to her shoulders. Bracelets dangling and making noises when she moves her arm up to shake the folds of the dress out of her armpits. The dress is loose and flows, and as she walks closer, I like it. I hear Maggie go "Uhnnnh" again. It is her sister's hair. It stands straight up like the wool on a sheep. It is black as night and around the edges are two long pigtails that rope about like small lizards disappearing behind her ears.

"Wa-su-zo-Tean-o!" she says, coming on in that gliding way the dress makes her move. The short stocky fellow with the hair to his navel is all grinning and he follows up with "Asalamalakim, my mother and sister!" He moves to hug Maggie but she falls back, right up against the back of my chair. I feel her trembling there and when I look up I see the perspiration falling off her chin.

"Don't get up," says Dee. Since I am stout it takes something of a push. You can see me trying to move a second or two before I make it. She turns, showing white heels through her sandals, and goes back to the car. Out she peeks next with a Polaroid. She stoops down quickly and lines up picture after picture of me sitting there in front of the house with Maggie cowering behind me. She never takes a shot without making sure the house is included. When a cow comes nibbling around the edge of the yard she snaps it and me and Maggie *and* the house. Then she puts the Polaroid in the back seat of the car, and comes up and kisses me on the forehead.

Meanwhile Asalamalakim is going through the motions with Maggie's hand. Maggie's hand is as limp as a fish, and probably as cold, despite the sweat, and she keeps trying to pull it back. It looks like Asalamalakim wants to shake hands but wants to do it fancy. Or maybe he don't know how people shake hands. Anyhow, he soon gives up on Maggie.

"Well," I say. "Dee."

25   "No, Mama," she says. "Not Dee, Wangero Leewanika Kemanjo!"

"What happened to 'Dee'?" I wanted to know.

"She's dead," Wangero said. "I couldn't bear it any longer being named after the people who oppress me."

"You know as well as me you was named after your aunt Dicie," I said. Dicie is my sister. She named Dee. We called her "Big Dee" after Dee was born.

"But who was *she* named after?" asked Wangero.

30   "I guess after Grandma Dee," I said.

"And who was she named after?" asked Wangero.

"Her mother," I said, and saw Wangero was getting tired. "That's about as far back as I can trace it," I said. Though, in fact, I probably could have carried it back beyond the Civil War through the branches.

"Well," said Asalamalakim, "there you are."

"Uhnnnh," I heard Maggie say.

35   "There I was not," I said, "before 'Dicie' cropped up in our family, so why should I try to trace it that far back?"

He just stood there grinning, looking down on me like somebody inspecting a Model A car. Every once in a while he and Wangero sent eye signals over my head.

"How do you pronounce this name?" I asked.

"You don't have to call me by it if you don't want to," said Wangero.

"Why shouldn't I?" I asked. "If that's what you want us to call you, we'll call you."

40   "I know it might sound awkward at first," said Wangero.

"I'll get used to it," I said. "Ream it out again."

Well, soon we got the name out of the way. Asalamalakim had a name twice as long and three times as hard. After I tripped over it two or three times he told me to just call him Hakim-a-barber. I wanted to ask him was he a barber, but I didn't really think he was, so I didn't ask.

"You must belong to those beef-cattle peoples down the road," I said. They said "Asalamalakim" when they met you, too, but they didn't shake hands. Always too busy: feeding the cattle, fixing the fences, putting up saltlick shelters, throwing down hay. When the white folks poisoned some of the herd the men stayed up all night with rifles in their hands. I walked a mile and a half just to see the sight.

Hakim-a-barber said, "I accept some of their doctrines, but farming and raising cattle is not my style." (They didn't tell me, and I didn't ask, whether Wangero [Dee] had really gone and married him.)

45   We sat down to eat and right away he said he didn't eat collards and pork was unclean. Wangero, though, went on through the chitlins and corn bread, the greens and everything else. She talked a blue streak over the sweet potatoes. Everything delighted her. Even the fact that we still used the benches her daddy made for the table when we couldn't afford to buy chairs.

"Oh, Mama!" she cried. Then turned to Hakim-a-barber. "I never knew how lovely these benches are. You can feel the rump prints," she said, running her hands underneath her and along the bench. Then she gave a sigh and her hand closed over Grandma Dee's butter dish. "That's it!" she said. "I knew there was something I wanted to ask you if I could have." She jumped up from the table and went over in the corner where the churn stood, the milk in it clabber by now. She looked at the churn and looked at it.

"This churn top is what I need," she said. "Didn't Uncle Buddy whittle it out of a tree you all used to have?"

"Yes," I said.

"Uh huh," she said happily. "And I want the dasher, too."

50   "Uncle Buddy whittle that, too?" asked the barber.

Dee (Wangero) looked up at me.

"Aunt Dee's first husband whittled the dash," said Maggie so low you almost couldn't hear her. "His name was Henry, but they called him Stash."

"Maggie's brain is like an elephant's," Wangero said, laughing. "I can use the churn top as a centerpiece for the alcove table," she said, sliding a plate over the churn, "and I'll think of something artistic to do with the dasher."

When she finished wrapping the dasher the handle stuck out. I took it for a moment in my hands. You didn't even have to look close to see where hands pushing the dasher up and down to make butter had left a kind of sink in the wood. In fact, there were a lot of small sinks; you could see where thumbs and fingers had sunk into the wood. It was beautiful light yellow wood, from a tree that grew in the yard where Big Dee and Stash had lived.

55   After dinner Dee (Wangero) went to the trunk at the foot of my bed and started rifling through it. Maggie hung back in the kitchen over the dishpan. Out came Wangero with two quilts. They had been pieced by Grandma Dee and then Big Dee and me had hung them on the quilt frames on the front porch and quilted them. One was in the Lone Star pattern. The other was Walk Around the Mountain. In both of them were scraps of dresses Grandma Dee had worn fifty and more years ago. Bits and pieces of Grandpa Jarrell's Paisley shirts. And one teeny faded blue piece, about the size of a penny matchbox, that was from Great Grandpa Ezra's uniform that he wore in the Civil War.

"Mama," Wangero said sweet as a bird. "Can I have these old quilts?"

I heard something fall in the kitchen, and a minute later the kitchen door slammed.

"Why don't you take one or two of the others?" I asked. "These old things was just done by me and Big Dee from some tops your grandma pieced before she died."

"No," said Wangero. "I don't want those. They are stitched around the border by machine."

60   "That'll make them last better," I said.

"That's not the point," said Wangero. "These are all pieces of dresses Grandma used to wear. She did all this stitching by hand. Imagine!" She held the quilts securely in her arms, stroking them.

"Some of the pieces, like those lavender ones, come from old clothes her mother handed down to her," I said, moving up to touch the quilts. Dee (Wangero) moved back just enough so that I couldn't reach the quilts. They already belonged to her.

"Imagine!" she breathed again, clutching them closely to her bosom.

"The truth is," I said, "I promised to give them quilts to Maggie, for when she marries John Thomas."

65   She gasped like a bee had stung her.

"Maggie can't appreciate these quilts!" she said. "She'd probably be backward enough to put them to everyday use."

"I reckon she would," I said. "God knows I been saving 'em for long enough with nobody using 'em. I hope she will!" I didn't want to bring up how I had offered Dee (Wangero) a quilt when she went away to college. Then she had told me they were old-fashioned, out of style.

"But they're *priceless!*" she was saying now, furiously; for she has a temper. "Maggie would put them on the bed and in five years they'd be in rags. Less than that!"

"She can always make some more," I said. "Maggie knows how to quilt."

70   Dee (Wangero) looked at me with hatred. "You just will not understand. The point is these quilts, *these* quilts!"

"Well," I said, stumped. "What would *you* do with them?"

"Hang them," she said. As if that was the only thing you *could* do with quilts.

Maggie by now was standing in the door. I could almost hear the sound her feet made as they scraped over each other.

"She can have them, Mama," she said, like somebody used to never winning anything, or having anything reserved for her. "I can 'member Grandma Dee without the quilts."

75   I looked at her hard. She had filled her bottom lip with checkerbeny snuff and it gave her face a kind of dopey, hangdog look. It was Grandma Dee and Big Dee who taught her how to quilt herself. She stood there with her scarred hands hidden in the folds of her skirt. She looked at her sister with something like fear but she wasn't mad at her. This was Maggie's portion. This was the way she knew God to work.

When I looked at her like that something hit me in the top of my head and ran down to the soles of my feet, just like when I'm in church and the spirit of God touches me and I get happy and shout. I did something I never had done before: hugged Maggie to me, then dragged her on into the room, snatched the quilts out of Miss Wangero's hands and dumped them into Maggie's lap. Maggie just sat there on my bed with her mouth open.

"Take one or two of the others," I said to Dee.

But she turned without a word and went out to Hakim-a-barber.

"You just don't understand," she said, as Maggie and I came out to the car.

80   "What don't I understand?" I wanted to know.

"Your heritage," she said. And then she turned to Maggie, kissed her, and said, "You ought to try to make something of yourself, too, Maggie. It's really a new day for us. But from the way you and Mama still live you'd never know it."

She put on some sunglasses that hid everything above the tip of her nose and her chin.

Maggie smiled; maybe at the sunglasses. But a real smile, not scared. After we watched the car dust settle I asked Maggie to bring me a dip of snuff. And then the two of us sat there just enjoying, until it was time to go in the house and go to bed.

MAKING CONNECTIONS

1. This story is told from Mama's point of view. In what way does that affect how and what you are told? If the story were told from Dee's point of view, how would it differ? Cite some examples from the text.

2. The setting of "Everyday Use" seems to mean something different to each of the characters. What does it mean to Mama? To Dee? To Maggie?

3. How does Maggie's character change in the course of the story? What do you think prompts this change?

4. If you were in Dee's situation, would you have acted differently? Would you see the quilt as a valuable artifact or something to be used every day? Explain.
5. Is the title of the story appropriate? How so? How would you define *everyday use?*

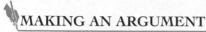

MAKING AN ARGUMENT

1. Consider the different views of cultural identity represented by Mama and Dee. Mama sees her cultural identity expressed personally and locally, whereas Dee sees it expressed more impersonally and globally. Is one more important than the other? Take a position on this issue and write an essay that argues for one position or the other (or both). Cite the text of the story for support.

◆ POETRY ◆

CONNECTING THROUGH COMPARISON: THE MASK WE WEAR

The three poems that follow address a subtheme of this section: the mask we wear. Read and discussed together, they invite comparisons and connections—not only with each other—but with your own experience.

W. H. AUDEN [1907–1973]

W[ystan] H[ugh] Auden was born in York, England, and edu-cated at Oxford University. Like many intellectuals of his generation, his left-wing politics led him to serve on the loy-alist side of the Spanish Civil War, but Auden quickly became disillusioned after witnessing the destruction and looting of Roman Catholic churches and returned to England. He immigrated to America in 1939, becoming a citizen in 1946. In 1947, he coined the term "the Age of Anxiety" in a long poem of the same name, which has since served as a shorthand term for the intel-lectual mood of the mid-twentieth century. His early work is characterized by his sharp wit and facility with elaborate verse forms. His later work, influenced by his reawakening interest in Christianity, became increasingly religious in tone.

THE UNKNOWN CITIZEN   [1940]

To
SOCIAL SECURITY ACCOUNT NUMBER 067-01-9818
THIS MARBLE MONUMENT IS ERECTED BY THE STATE

He was found by the Bureau of Statistics to be
One against whom there was no official complaint,
And all the reports on his conduct agree

That, in the modern sense of an old-fashioned word, he was a saint,
For in everything he did he served the Greater Community.   5
Except for the war, till the day he retired
He worked in one factory and never got fired,
But satisfied his employers, Fudge Motors, Inc.,
Yet was neither a scab nor odd in his views,
For his Union reports that he paid his dues   10
(Our report on his Union says it was sound),
And our Social Psychology workers found
He was popular with his mates and liked a drink.
The Press are convinced that he bought a paper every day,
And that his reactions to advertisements were normal in every way.   15
Policies taken out in his name prove that he was fully insured,
And a certificate shows that he was once in hospital but left it cured.
Both *Producer's Research* and *High Grade Living* declare
He was fully sensible to the advantages of the Installment Plan,
And had everything necessary to the Modern Man—   20
A victrola, a radio, a car, and a frigidaire.
Our investigators into Public Opinion are content
That he held the proper opinions for the time of year;
When there was peace, he was for peace; when there was war, he went.
He was married and added five children to the population,   25
Which, our eugenist says, was the right number for a parent of his generation,
And our teachers report that he never interfered with their education.
Was he free? Was he happy? The question is absurd;
Had anything been wrong, we should certainly have heard.

PAUL LAURENCE DUNBAR [1872–1906]

*Paul Laurence Dunbar was born and raised in Dayton,
Ohio. Both of his parents had been slaves. Dunbar excelled
in high school, where he was the only African-American in
his class, and served both as the class president and class
poet. While in high school, he worked as an editor at the*
Dayton Tattler, *a short-lived newspaper for blacks. His wid-
owed mother's financial situation ruled out college, and,
unable to find a position as a writer because of his race,
he was forced to find work at a number of jobs (including one as an elevator
operator) that allowed him the leisure to continue writing and publishing poems.
By 1892 he had earned enough recognition that he could pursue a literary
career. He wrote prolifically but was plagued by ill health. In 1906, at the age of
thirty-three, he died of tuberculosis. Though he is best known for his poems, which
were the first to incorporate African-American speech, Dunbar published numerous novels, short stories, and essays.*

WE WEAR THE MASK

We wear the mask that grins and lies,
It hides our cheeks and shades our eyes—
This debt we pay to human guile;
With torn and bleeding hearts we smile,
And mouth with myriad subtleties.   5

Why should the world be over-wise,
In counting all our tears and sighs?
Nay, let them only see us, while
    We wear the mask.

We smile, but, O great Christ, our cries   10
To thee from tortured souls arise.
We sing, but oh the clay is vile
Beneath our feet, and long the mile;
But let the world dream otherwise,
    We wear the mask!   15

T. S. ELIOT [1888–1965]

Born to a wealthy family in St. Louis, Missouri, T[homas]
S[tearns] Eliot attended Harvard University, where he stud-
ied Literature as an undergraduate, and, as a graduate
student, Sanskrit and Philosophy. After further studies at
the Sorbonne and Oxford University, he settled in England
in 1915, taking a job first at an insurance company and
later in publishing, becoming a British citizen in 1926.
Eliot, with his first volume of poetry, Prufrock and Other
Observations *(1917), and the 1922 publication of* The Waste Land, *transformed*
the landscape of modern poetry, shattering literary conventions in order to give
voice to what he felt was the spiritual emptiness of the modern world. An influ-
ential critic, he also wrote verse plays, including Murder in the Cathedral *(1935)*
and The Cocktail Party *(1949). He was awarded the Nobel Prize in 1948. Recent*
biographies of Eliot have not always treated him kindly, and there is much schol-
arly debate on the extent and importance of his anti-Semitism. Nevertheless, Eliot
remains perhaps the most influential poet of the twentieth century.

THE LOVE SONG OF J. ALFRED PRUFROCK

S'io credessi che mia risposta fosse
A persona che mai tornasse al mondo,
Questa fiamma staria senza più scosse.
Ma per ciò che giammai di questo fondo

Non tornò vivo alcun, s'i'odo il vero,
Senza tema d'infamia ti rispondo.°   5

Let us go then, you and I,
When the evening is spread out against the sky
Like a patient etherised upon a table;
Let us go, through certain half-deserted streets,   10
The muttering retreats
Of restless nights in one-night cheap hotels
And sawdust restaurants with oyster-shells:
Streets that follow like a tedious argument
Of insidious intent   15
To lead you to an overwhelming question . . .
Oh, do not ask, "What is it?"
Let us go and make our visit.

In the room the women come and go
Talking of Michelangelo.°   20

The yellow fog that rubs its back upon the window-panes,
The yellow smoke that rubs its muzzle on the window-panes,
Licked its tongue into the corners of the evening,
Lingered upon the pools that stand in drains,
Let fall upon its back the soot that falls from chimneys,   25
Slipped by the terrace, made a sudden leap,
And seeing that it was a soft October night,
Curled once about the house, and fell asleep.

And indeed there will be time
For the yellow smoke that slides along the street   30
Rubbing its back upon the window-panes;
There will be time, there will be time
To prepare a face to meet the faces that you meet;
There will be time to murder and create,
And time for all the works and days° of hands   35
That lift and drop a question on your plate;
Time for you and time for me,
And time yet for a hundred indecisions,

6 The statement introducing the confession of the poet Guido da Montefeltro in Dante's *Inferno* (1321), canto xxcii, 61–66. "If I thought I was speaking to someone who would go back to the world, this flame would shake no more. But since nobody has ever gone back alive from this place, if what I hear is true. I answer you without fear of infamy." **20 Michelangelo** (1474–1564) the most famous artist of the Italian Renaissance **35 works and days** possibly an allusion to *Works and Days,* a poem giving practical advice on farming by the Greek poet Hesiod (eighth century B.C.)

And for a hundred visions and revisions,
Before the taking of a toast and tea.   40

In the room the women come and go
Talking of Michelangelo.

And indeed there will be time
To wonder, "Do I dare?" and, "Do I dare?"
Time to turn back and descend the stair,   45
With a bald spot in the middle of my hair—
[They will say: "How his hair is growing thin!"]
My morning coat, my collar mounting firmly to the chin,
My necktie rich and modest, but asserted by a simple pin—
[They will say: "But how his arms and legs are thin!"]   50
Do I dare
Disturb the universe?
In a minute there is time
For decisions and revisions which a minute will reverse.

For I have known them all already, known them all—   55
Have known the evenings, mornings, afternoons,
I have measured out my life with coffee spoons;
I know the voices dying with a dying fall
Beneath the music from a farther room.
    So how should I presume?   60

And I have known the eyes already, known them all—
The eyes that fix you in a formulated phrase,
And when I am formulated, sprawling on a pin,
When I am pinned and wriggling on the wall,
Then how should I begin   65
To spit out all the butt-ends of my days and ways?
    And how should I presume?

And I have known the arms already, known them all—
Arms that are braceleted and white and bare
[But in the lamplight, downed with light brown hair!°]   70
Is it perfume from a dress
That makes me so digress?
Arms that lie along a table, or wrap about a shawl.
    And should I then presume?
    And how should I begin?   75

. . . . .

70 see Shakespeare's *Twelfth Night* (1623), Act I, scene I, 1–4

Shall I say, I have gone at dusk through narrow streets
And watched the smoke that rises from the pipes
Of lonely men in shirt-sleeves, leaning out of windows? . . .

I should have been a pair of ragged claws
Scuttling across the floors of silent seas.   80

And the afternoon, the evening, sleeps so peacefully!
Smoothed by long fingers,
Asleep . . . tired . . . or it malingers,
Stretched on the floor, here beside you and me.
Should I, after tea and cakes and ices,   85
Have the strength to force the moment to its crisis?
But though I have wept and fasted, wept and prayed,
Though I have seen my head [grown slightly bald] brought in upon a platter,°
I am no prophet—and here's no great matter;
I have seen the moment of my greatness flicker,   90
And I have seen the eternal Footman hold my coat, and snicker,
And in short, I was afraid.

And would it have been worth it, after all,
After the cups, the marmalade, the tea,
Among the porcelain, among some talk of you and me,   95
Would it have been worth while,
To have bitten off the matter with a smile,
To have squeezed the universe into a ball°
To roll it toward some overwhelming question,
To say: "I am Lazarus,° come from the dead.   100
Come back to tell you all, I shall tell you all"—
If one, settling a pillow by her head,
      Should say: "That is not what I meant at all.
      That is not it, at all."

And would it have been worth it, after all,   105
Would it have been worth while,
After the sunsets and the dooryards and the sprinkled streets,
After the novels, after the teacups, after the skirts that trail along the floor—
And this, and so much more?—
It is impossible to say just what I mean!   110
But as if a magic lantern threw the nerves in patterns on a screen:
Would it have been worth while

88 an allusion to John the Baptist, the New Testament prophet, whose head was presented to
Queen Herodias on a charger, Matthew 14:3-11   98 see Andrew Marvell's "To His Coy Mistress,"
lines 41-42, page 778.   100 Lazarus the man raised by Jesus from the dead, John 11:1-44

If one, settling a pillow or throwing off a shawl,
And turning toward the window, should say:
   "That is not it at all,   115
   That is not what I meant, at all."

. . . . .

No! I am not Prince Hamlet, nor was meant to be;
Am an attendant lord, one that will do
To swell a progress, start a scene or two,
Advise the prince; no doubt, an easy tool,   120
Deferential, glad to be of use,
Politic, cautious, and meticulous;
Full of high sentence, but a bit obtuse;
At times, indeed, almost ridiculous—
Almost, at times, the Fool.   125

I grow old . . . I grow old . . .
I shall wear the bottoms of my trousers rolled.

Shall I part my hair behind? Do I dare to eat a peach?
I shall wear white flannel trousers, and walk upon the beach.
I have heard the mermaids singing, each to each.   130

I do not think that they will sing to me.

I have seen them riding seaward on the waves
Combing the white hair of the waves blown back
When the wind blows the water white and black.

We have lingered in the chambers of the sea   135
By sea-girls wreathed with seaweed red and brown
Till human voices wake us, and we drown.

 ## MAKING CONNECTIONS

1. What is the tone of "The Unknown Citizen"? What lines in the poem indicate this?
2. This poem was written in 1940, so a few of the unknown citizen's possessions are not state-of-the-art and need to be updated to present-day equivalents. What do our possessions say about us and about our culture?
3. Based on what is said about him, who is "the Unknown Citizen"? Was he "free"? Was he "happy"? Are these questions absurd?
4. In "We Wear the Mask," who is the "we" the speaker refers to?
5. What does the "mask" look like? What are the different forms it takes?
6. To what extent does Dunbar's background and the year in which the poem was published amplify its content?

7. What is the tone of "The Love Song of J. Alfred Prufrock"? How does the language in the poem convey that tone? Is this a love song, as the title indicates?

8. Who is J. Alfred Prufrock? What is his world like? He says, "I have measured out my life with coffee spoons." What do you think he means? Find other images in the poem that convey his self-image.

9. What does he mean when he says, "Do I dare / Disturb the universe?" What is he afraid of?

10. Do you ever feel that you have "To prepare a face to meet the faces that you meet"? If so, to what extent does that help you understand J. Alfred Prufrock—and this poem?

11. Compare and contrast the three poems. Compare them also to "Zimmer in Grade School" on page 11.

MAKING AN ARGUMENT

1. To what extent do the "masks" we wear result from the cultural imperatives that surround us and form our identities? Write an essay that identifies these cultural pressures and indicates how they "form" the subjects in these three poems—and us. Cite the text of the poems for support.

SHERMAN ALEXIE [B. 1966]

Sherman Alexie achieved the goal of having ten books of poetry and fiction published before he turned thirty. His very first book, The Business of Fancydancing *(1992) was chosen as a* New York Times *Notable Book of the Year and reviewer James R. Kincaid wrote:"Mr. Alexie's is one of the major lyric voices of our time." Alexie's latest poetry collection is* One Stick Song *(2000) (Hanging Loose) and his latest fiction collection is* The Toughest Indian in the World (2000) *(Atlantic Monthly Press). The film* Smoke Signals, *for which he wrote a script adapted from one of the short stories in his book* The Lone Ranger and Tonto Fistfight in Heaven *(1993), has won rave reviews and large audiences. In 2002, he made his directorial debut with the film of* The Business of Fancydancing. *His most recent book is a collection of poetry,* Dangerous Astronomy, *published in 2005.*

Alexie's poems and stories have appeared widely, and he has read from his work in virtually every state as well as in several European countries. Among many awards, he has won a Lila Wallace-Reader's Digest Writer's Award, an American Book Award, and a Creative Writing Fellowship from the National Endowment for the Arts.

An enrolled Spokane/Coeur d'Alene Indian, Alexie was born on the Spokane reservation in Wellpinit, Washington, in 1966. He is very active in the American Indian community and frequently gives workshops. He lives in Seattle with his wife and son.

On the Amtrak from Boston to New York City   [1993]

The white woman across the aisle from me says, "Look,
look at all the history, that house
on the hill there is over two hundred years old,"
as she points out the window past me

into what she has been taught. I have learned   5
little more about American history during my few days
back East than what I expected and far less
of what we should all know of the tribal stories

whose architecture is 15,000 years older
than the corners of the house that sits   10
museumed on the hill. "Walden Pond,"°
the woman on the train asks, "Did you see Walden Pond?"

and I don't have a cruel enough heart to break
her own by telling her there are five Walden Ponds
on my little reservation out West   15
and at least a hundred more surrounding Spokane,

the city I pretend to call my home. "Listen,"
I could have told her. "I don't give a shit
about Walden. I know the Indians were living stories
around that pond before Walden's grandparents were born   20

and before his grandparents' grandparents were born.
I'm tired of hearing about Don-fucking-Henley° saving it too,
because that's redundant. If Don Henley's brothers and sisters
and mothers and fathers hadn't come here in the first place

then nothing would need to be saved."   25
But I didn't say a word to the woman about Walden
Pond because she smiled so much and seemed delighted
that I thought to bring her an orange juice

back from the food car. I respect elders
of every color. All I really did was eat   30
my tasteless sandwich, drink my Diet Pepsi
and nod my head whenever the woman pointed out

another little piece of her country's history
while I, as all Indians have done
since this war began, made plans   35
for what I would do and say the next time

somebody from the enemy thought I was one of their own.

11 Walden Pond the place where Henry David Thoreau (1817–1862) lived and about which he
wrote his most famous book, *Walden* (1854)   **22 Don Henley** a rock singer who helped protect Walden from commercial development

⚲MAKING CONNECTIONS

1. What is the significance of the title? Do you think the Amtrak between Boston and New York is an appropriate setting? Why or why not?
2. In what way is the speaker's Native American heritage a factor in this poem? The speaker refers to the passenger on the train as "the white woman." What does his word choice tell you about his tone and point of view?

⚲MAKING AN ARGUMENT

1. Given how annoyed he is by her reference to Walden Pond, why doesn't the speaker say something to the woman? Why does he refer to the white woman as "the enemy"? Write an argument that agrees or disagrees with his position. Cite the text of the poem—and your own informed knowledge—for support.

GLORIA ANZALDÚA [1942–2004]

Gloria Anzaldúa was born in southern Texas of Mexican, Native American, and Anglo ancestry. Her mixed background served as the major influence on her writing. She taught at the University of Texas at Austin, San Francisco State University, the University of California at Santa Cruz, and Vermont College. Her last book is entitled This Bridge We Call Home: Radical Visions for Transformation (2002). *"To Live in the Borderlands Means You" is taken from her critically acclaimed book* Borderlands / LaFrontera: The New Mestiza (1987).

TO LIVE IN THE BORDERLANDS MEANS YOU   [1987]

[To live in the Borderlands means you]
are neither *hispana india negra española*
ni gabacha,° *eres mestiza, mulata,* half-breed
caught in the crossfire between camps
while carrying all five races on your back   5
not knowing which side to turn to, run from;

To live in the Borderlands means knowing
    that the *india* in you,
    betrayed for 500 years,
    is no longer speaking to you,   10

---

3 gabacha a white woman

that *mexicanas* call you *rajetas,*°
that denying the Anglo inside you
is as bad as having denied
the Indian or Black;

Cuando vives en la frontera   15
people walk through you, the wind steals your voice,
you're a *burra, buey,* scapegoat,
forerunner of a new race,
half and half—both woman and man, neither—
a new gender;   20

To live in the Borderlands means to
put *chile* in the borscht,
eat whole wheat *tortillas,*
speak Tex-Mex with a Brooklyn accent;
be stopped by *la migra* at the border checkpoints;   25

Living in the Borderlands means you fight hard to
resist the gold elixir beckoning from the bottle,
the pull of the gun barrel,
the rope crushing the hollow of your throat;

In the Borderlands   30
you are the battleground
where enemies are kin to each other;
you are at home, a stranger,
the border disputes have been settled
the volley of shots have shattered the truce   35
you are wounded, lost in action
dead, fighting back;

To live in the Borderlands means
the mill with the razor white teeth wants to shred off
your olive-red skin, crush out the kernel, your heart   40
pound you pinch you roll you out
smelling like white bread but dead;

To survive the Borderlands
you must live *sin fronteras*
be a crossroads.   45

11 rajetas "split"

MAKING CONNECTIONS

1. What are the "Borderlands"? Is this solely a geographical location? To what
   extent do you, your family, or your friends live in the Borderlands?

2. How are you affected by the mixture of English and Spanish words in the text of the poem? To what extent is this mixture especially appropriate in this poem?

3. In the last stanza, what does the speaker mean by "To survive the Borderlands / you must . . . / be a crossroads"?

MAKING AN ARGUMENT

1. Both the speaker in this poem and the narrator of the short story "Borders" on page 964 see themselves culturally "on the border"—in a location and a dominant culture physically—but not ethnically or emotionally. Write a comparison of the two pieces and address the issue of cultural identification. Cite the text of both pieces for support.

ELIZABETH BISHOP [1911-1979]

Elizabeth Bishop was born in Worcester, Massachusetts. Her father died when she was still an infant, and her mother suffered a serious mental breakdown and was institutionalized. Bishop was raised first by her mother's family in Nova Scotia, and then, when she was six, by her father's parents, who lived in Worcester. Sickly and shy, she spent most of her childhood immersed in books, before attending boarding school during her teens. While at Vassar College, her poetry attracted the attention of a librarian, who introduced Bishop to the poet Marianne Moore. Moore became Bishop's mentor, and her influence can be seen in Bishop's early work. Following graduation, Bishop lived in Key West for nine years, and then moved to Brazil, where she lived for almost twenty years. Returning to the United States in 1966, she held positions at the University of Washington and the Massachusetts Institute of Technology before settling at Harvard University, where she was teaching when she died. Her collections of poetry include North and South *(1946),* A Cold Spring *(winner of the Pulitzer Prize in 1956),* Complete Poems *(winner of the National Book Award in 1970), and* Geography III *(1977). She was also a respected travel writer, publishing numerous volumes, including* Questions of Travel *(1965) and* Brazil *(1967). Considered a "poet's poet," Bishop's poems are characterized by a spare style and a distinctive, ironic voice.*

IN THE WAITING ROOM   [1976]

In Worcester, Massachusetts,
I went with Aunt Consuelo
to keep her dentist's appointment
and sat and waited for her
in the dentist's waiting room.   5

It was winter. It got dark
early. The waiting room
was full of grown-up people,
arctics and overcoats,
lamps and magazines.   10
My aunt was inside
what seemed like a long time
and while I waited I read
the *National Geographic*
(I could read) and carefully   15
studied the photographs:
the inside of a volcano,
black, and full of ashes;
then it was spilling over
in rivulets of fire.   20
Osa and Martin Johnson
dressed in riding breeches,
laced boots, and pith helmets.
A dead man slung on a pole
—"Long Pig," the caption said.   25
Babies with pointed heads
wound round and round with string;
black, naked women with necks
wound round and round with wire
like the necks of light bulbs.   30
Their breasts were horrifying.
I read it right straight through.
I was too shy to stop.
And then I looked at the cover
the yellow margins, the date.   35
Suddenly, from inside,
came an *oh!* of pain
—Aunt Consuelo's voice—
not very loud or long.

I wasn't at all surprised;   40
even then I knew she was
a foolish, timid woman.
I might have been embarrassed,
but wasn't. What took me
completely by surprise   45
was that it was *me:*
my voice, in my mouth.
Without thinking at all
I was my foolish aunt,
I—we—were falling, falling,   50

our eyes glued to the cover
of the *National Geographic,*
February, 1918.

I said to myself: three days
and you'll be seven years old
I was saying it to stop
the sensation of falling off
the round, turning world
into cold, blue-black space.
But I felt: you are an *I,*
you are an *Elizabeth,*
you are one of *them.*
Why should you be one, too?
I scarcely dared to look
to see what it was I was.
I gave a sidelong glance
—I couldn't look any higher—
at shadowy gray knees,
trousers and skirts and boots
and different pairs of hands
lying under the lamps.
I knew that nothing stranger
had ever happened, that nothing
stranger could ever happen.

Why should I be my aunt,
or me, or anyone?
What similarities—
boots, hands, the family voice
I felt in my throat, or even
the *National Geographic*
and those awful hanging breasts—
held us all together
or made us all just one?
How—I didn't know any
word for it—how "unlikely". . .
How had I come to be here,
like them, and overhear
a cry of pain that could have
got loud and worse but hadn't?
The waiting room was bright
and too hot. It was sliding
beneath a big black wave,
another, and another.

Then I was back in it.
The War was on. Outside,

in Worcester, Massachusetts,
were night and slush and cold,
and it was still the fifth
of February, 1918.

MAKING CONNECTIONS

1. Who is the speaker? How old is she? Does it matter? Explain.
2. What does the sound of Aunt Consuelo's voice reveal to her?
3. What do you think the speaker means by "But I felt: you are an *I*, / you are an *Elizabeth*, / you are one of *them*"? Have you ever had a similar experience? Explain.
4. In the last stanza, she says, "Then I was back in it." Where has she been? What is she "back in"?

MAKING AN ARGUMENT

1. Write about the way the narrator is experiencing a revelation about her identity that can't be explained in rational terms but is compelling and quite real in her mind and emotions. Cite the text for items that seem to prompt the narrator's reactions.

GWENDOLYN BROOKS [1917–2000]

Born in Topeka, Kansas, Gwendolyn Brooks was raised on the South Side of Chicago. She graduated from Wilson Junior College in 1936, and married in 1939. Though Brooks began writing poetry as a child, she did not find her vocation until she entered a poetry workshop at a local community arts center in the early 1940s. Influenced by Langston Hughes and other poets of the Harlem Renaissance, Brooks attempted to wed the familiar idiom and rhythms of the colloquial speech of Chicago's South Side to the traditional poetic forms she encountered in the workshop. Her first collection of poetry, A Street in Bronzeville, *appeared in 1945. In 1949, with the publication of* Annie Allen, *she became the first African-American woman awarded the Pulitzer Prize. After attending a conference of African-American writers at Fisk University in 1967, Brooks became convinced that "black poets should write as blacks, about blacks, and address themselves to blacks." As a result, she became a devoted teacher of writing, particularly in the African-American community, and abandoned her New York publisher in favor of small African-American presses. In addition to numerous volumes of poetry, she published children's books; a novel,* Maud Martha *(1953); and an autobiography,* Report from Part I *(1972); and received over fifty honorary degrees.*

WE REAL COOL

[1960]

The Pool Players.
Seven at the Golden Shovel.

We real cool. We
Left school. We

Lurk late. We   5
Strike straight. We

Sing sin. We
Thin gin. We

Jazz June. We
Die soon.   10

MAKING CONNECTIONS

1. Who is the speaker in this poem?
2. No sentence in the poem is more than three words long, and almost every
   line ends with the same word. What does that diction say about the speaker
   in the poem?
3. Were you surprised by the last line? Explain.

MAKING AN ARGUMENT

1. This is a very brief poem that makes a strong statement about culture/soci-
   ety and individual responsibility. What is its point? Write about the effectiveness of the "we" speaker and the relationship between rhyme and rhythm
   in conveying the poem's theme. Cite the text of the poem for support.

E. E. CUMMINGS [1894-1962]

E[dwin] E[stlin] Cummings was born in Cambridge,
Massachusetts. He began writing poetry as a child, and
claimed that he wrote at least one poem a day between the
ages of eight and twenty-two. He attended Harvard
University, earning a B.A. in 1915 and an M.A. in 1916.
During World War I, he served as an ambulance driver
and was confined for a time in a French internment camp
for what proved to be a mistaken suspicion of treason. In
1922, he wrote of these experiences in his novel The Enormous Room, *which*
proved to be a great critical success. In the 1920s, he published the collections of
poetry—including & *(1925),* XLI Poems *(1925), and* is 5 *(1926)—that would*
establish him as America's foremost avant-garde poet. His Complete Poems: 1910

to 1962 was published in 1980. Though his poems employ slang, dialect, and all kinds of typographical games, they are often much more accessible than they immediately appear.

ANYONE LIVED IN A PRETTY HOW TOWN   [1940]

anyone lived in a pretty how town
(with up so floating many bells down)
spring summer autumn winter
he sang his didn't he danced his did.

Women and men (both little and small)   5
cared for anyone not at all
they sowed their isn't they reaped their same
sun moon stars rain

children guessed (but only a few
and down they forgot as up they grew   10
autumn winter spring summer)
that noone loved him more by more

when by now and tree by leaf
she laughed his joy she cried his grief,
bird by snow and stir by still   15
anyone's any was all to her

someones married their everyones
laughed their cryings and did their dance
(sleep wake hope and then) they
said their nevers they slept their dream   20

stars rain sun moon
(and only the snow can begin to explain
how children are apt to forget to remember
with up so floating many bells down)

one day anyone died i guess   25
(and noone stooped to kiss his face)
busy folk buried them side by side
little by little and was by was

all by all and deep by deep
and more by more they dream their sleep   30
noone and anyone earth by april
wish by spirit and if by yes.

Women and men (both dong and ding)
summer autumn winter spring
reaped their sowing and went their came   35
sun moon stars rain

MAKING CONNECTIONS

1. Who is "anyone"?
2. How was your reading affected by the unusual style of the writing? Pick out some lines and describe what you think they mean.

MAKING AN ARGUMENT

1. What do you think the poem means? Why do you think Cummings wrote the poem in this unusual style? Does it help to convey its meaning? Do you think he should have written it in a more conventional form? Write an analysis of this poem and take a position in favor of or against the author's writing style. Cite the text of the poem for support.

MARTIN ESPADA [B. 1957]

Martin Espada was born in Brooklyn, New York, of Puerto Rican ancestry. He has received many awards including two National Endowment for the Arts fellowships, a PEN/Revson fellowship, and the Paterson Poetry Prize for Rebellion in the Circle of a Lover's Hands (1990). *His latest book of poems,* Amazon Astronomer in Hell's Kitchen, *was published in 2001. He worked as a tenant lawyer for six years, often defending the civil rights of immigrants. He is currently a Professor of English at the University of Massachusetts at Amherst.*

LATIN NIGHT AT THE PAWN SHOP   [1987]

Chelsea, Massachusetts
Christmas, 1987

The apparition of a salsa band
gleaming in the Liberty Loan
pawnshop window:

Golden trumpet.
silver trombone,
congas, maracas, tambourine,   5
all with price tags dangling
like the city morgue ticket
on a dead man's toe.

MAKING CONNECTIONS

1. In what way does Christmas provide an important context for this poem?
2. Make a list of important items of your own. To what extent do these items represent you?

MAKING AN ARGUMENT

1. Identify each of the items you see in the poem and its importance in the picture. In what way are their price tags "like the city morgue ticket / on a dead man's toe"? Write a comparison of this poem with "The Unknown Citizen" (p. 989) that indicates the importance of possessions in each poem—and in our culture. Cite the text of both poems for support.

PAT MORA [B. 1942]

Pat Mora was born in El Paso, Texas. Her father was an ophthalmologist and her mother, a homemaker. Mora earned her B.A. from Texas Western College in 1963, and an M.A. in 1967 from the University of Texas at El Paso. She taught for many years at both the high school and university levels, but now devotes herself completely to her poetry. Chants, *her first volume of verse, was published in 1984, and she has since published three additional collec-tions:* Borders *(1986),* Communion *(1991), and* Holy Water *(1995). Her latest publication is* House of Houses *(2002). "For a variety of complex reasons," she told* Contemporary Authors, *"anthologized American literature does not reflect the ethnic diversity of the United States. I write, in part, because Hispanic perspectives need to be part of our literary heritage; I want to be part of that validation process. I also write because I am fascinated by the pleasure and power of words."*

IMMIGRANTS   [1986]

wrap their babies in the American flag,
feed them mashed hot dogs and apple pie,
name them Bill and Daisy,
buy them blonde dolls that blink blue
eyes or a football and tiny cleats   5
before the baby can even walk,
speak to them in thick English,
    hallo, babee, hallo,
whisper in Spanish or Polish
when the babies sleep, whisper   10
in a dark parent bed, that dark
parent fear, "Will they like
our boy, our girl, our fine american
boy, our fine american girl?"

MAKING CONNECTIONS

1. Discuss the different voices represented in the poem. How many are there? What do they represent?

2. To whom is the speaker saying, "wrap their babies in the American flag"?
3. What does she mean by "that dark / parent fear"?

MAKING AN ARGUMENT

1. Do you think America is a "melting pot"? Do you think it should be? Compare this poem to the short stories "Two Kinds" on page 250 and "Brave We Are" on page 978 and write about the different issues that are raised in each selection. Cite the texts of all three for support.

EDWIN ARLINGTON ROBINSON [1869–1935]

(See biography on p. 510.)

MR. FLOOD'S PARTY [1896]

Old Eben Flood, climbing alone one night
Over the hill between the town below
And the forsaken upland hermitage
That held as much as he should ever know
On earth again of home, paused warily. 5
The road was his with not a native near;
And Eben, having leisure, said aloud,
For no man else in Tilbury Town to hear:

"Well, Mr. Flood, we have the harvest moon
Again, and we may not have many more; 10
The bird is on the wing, the poet says,
And you and I have said it here before.
Drink to the bird." He raised up to the light
The jug that he had gone so far to fill,
And answered huskily: "Well, Mr. Flood, 15
Since you propose it, I believe I will."

Alone, as if enduring to the end
A valiant armor of scarred hopes outworn,
He stood there in the middle of the road
Like Roland's ghost winding a silent horn. 20
Below him, in the town among the trees,
Where friends of other days had honored him,
A phantom salutation of the dead
Rang thinly till old Eben's eyes were dim.

Then, as a mother lays her sleeping child 25
Down tenderly, fearing it may awake,
He set the jug down slowly at his feet
With trembling care, knowing that most things break;

And only when assured that on firm earth
It stood, as the uncertain lives of men   30
Assuredly did not, he paced away,
And with his hand extended paused again:

"Well, Mr. Flood, we have not met like this
In a long time; and many a change has come
To both of us, I fear, since last it was   35
We had a drop together. Welcome home!"
Convivially returning with himself,
Again he raised the jug up to the light:
And with an acquiescent quaver said:
"Well, Mr. Flood, if you insist, I might.   40

"Only a very little, Mr. Flood—
For auld lang syne. No more, sir; that will do."
So, for the time, apparently it did,
And Eben evidently thought so too;
For soon amid the silver loneliness   45
Of night he lifted up his voice and sang,
Secure, with only two moons listening,
Until the whole harmonious landscape rang—

"For auld lang syne." The weary throat gave out,
The last word wavered; and the song being done,   50
He raised again the jug regretfully
And shook his head, and was again alone.
There was not much that was ahead of him,
And there was nothing in the town below—
Where strangers would have shut the many doors   55
That many friends had opened long ago.

 ## MAKING CONNECTIONS

1. Who is the audience for Mr. Flood's oration?
2. Why do you think "strangers would have shut the many doors / That many friends had opened long ago"?
3. Does this poem remind you of anyone you know or of people you've seen or met? Explain.

MAKING AN ARGUMENT

1. We often see the lonely plight of elderly people described in news stories. To what extent is experiencing it through a poem a different experience? If Mr. Flood is a sympathetic character in this poem, what makes him so? Write about poetry—and this poem—as a particularly effective form for conveying Mr. Flood's plight. Cite the text of the poem for support.

JOHN UPDIKE [B. 1932]

(See biography on p. 490.)

EX-BASKETBALL PLAYER   [1958]

Pearl Avenue runs past the high-school lot,
Bends with the trolley tracks, and stops, cut off
Before it has a chance to go two blocks,
At Colonel McComsky Plaza. Berth's Garage
Is on the corner facing west, and there,   5
Most days, you'll find Flick Webb, who helps Berth out.

Flick stands tall among the idiot pumps—
Five on a side, the old bubble-head style,°
Their rubber elbows hanging loose and low.
One's nostrils are two S's, and his eyes   10
An E and O.° And one is squat, without
A head at all—more of a football type.

Once Flick played for the high-school team, the Wizards.
He was good: in fact, the best. In '46
He bucketed three hundred ninety points,   15
A county record still. The ball loved Flick.
I saw him rack up thirty-eight or forty
In one home game. His hands were like wild birds.

He never learned a trade, he just sells gas,
Checks oil, and changes flats. Once in a while,   20
As a gag, he dribbles an inner tube,
But most of us remember anyway.
His hands are fine and nervous on the lug wrench.
It makes no difference to the lug wrench, though.

Off work, he hangs around Mae's luncheonette.   25
Grease-gray and kind of coiled, he plays pinball,
Smokes those thin cigars, nurses lemon phosphates.
Flick seldom says a word to Mae, just nods
Beyond her face toward bright applauding tiers
Of Necco Wafers, Nibs, and Juju Beads.   30

MAKING CONNECTIONS

1. Describe Flick Webb. To what extent do the images in the poem bring him
    to life? Give some examples.

8 bubble-head style Gasoline pumps from this era had rounded tops.   **11 ESSO** brand of gasoline (now called Exxon)

2. Who is the speaker in the poem? What point of view does he represent? If
   Flick was the speaker in the poem, how do you think it would change?
3. Discuss the structure of the poem. To what extent do each of the five stanzas represent a different aspect of Flick's life?

MAKING AN ARGUMENT

1. Write a comparison of this poem with A. E. Housman's "To an Athlete
   Dying Young" on page 1233. Cite the text of both poems for support.

WILLIAM CARLOS WILLIAMS [1883-1961]

*William Carlos Williams was born in Rutherford, New
Jersey. While attending high school in New York City,
where he focused most of his energies on math and science, he first discovered his love for writing poetry. He
skipped a traditional college education at his parents'
insistence and went directly to medical school at the
University of Pennsylvania. While completing his studies,
he came into contact with Ezra Pound, then a graduate
student, who would become his lifelong friend and critic, and Hilda Doolitle
(the poet H.D.). Pound and H.D. introduced Williams to the imagist movement,
which rejected rigid and ordered poetry in favor of simple phrases and an
embrace of the ordinary. Over the next forty years, though he practiced medicine full time, Williams wrote volumes of poetry, often finding inspiration in
the stories of his patients, jotting poems on prescription pads or between
appointments turning to a typewriter he kept in his office. His publications
include* Collected Poems *(1934);* Later Collected Poems *(1950); a five-volume
poem about a nearby city in New Jersey,* Paterson *(1946–1958); a collection of
experimental plays,* Many Loves and Other Plays *(1961); a series of novels; and
numerous short stories and essays. His final book of poems,* Pictures from
Brueghel and Other Poems, *was awarded the Pulitzer Prize in 1963. With his
innovative use of free verse, his embrace of American speech, and his insistence on the importance of the commonplace, Williams profoundly influenced
the course of American poetry.*

AT THE BALL GAME   [1923]

The crowd at the ball game
is moved uniformly

by a spirit of uselessness
which delights them—

all the exciting detail   5
of the chase

and the escape, the error
the flash of genius—

all to no end save beauty
the eternal—

So in detail they, the crowd,
are beautiful

for this
to be warned against

saluted and defied—
It is alive, venomous

it smiles grimly
its words cut—

The flashy female with her
mother, gets it—

The Jew gets it straight—it
is deadly, terrifying—

It is the Inquisition, the
Revolution

It is the beauty itself
that lives

day by day in them
idly—

This is
the power of their faces

It is summer, it is the solstice
the crowd is

cheering, the crowd is laughing
in detail

permanently, seriously
without thought

10

15

20

25

30

35

MAKING CONNECTIONS

1. The setting of this poem is a baseball game. Is this a poem about baseball? Explain.
2. What do you think the references to "the flashy female," "the Jew," "the Inquisition," and "the Revolution" mean?
3. What does the speaker mean by "the crowd is laughing / in detail / permanently, seriously / without thought"? Who is the crowd?

MAKING AN ARGUMENT

1. What is the place of crowds in our contemporary culture? Do you think they are as dangerous as Williams' poem implies? Identify the points that Williams makes in his poem and write about the impact that crowds and "crowd mentalities" have on cultural and political aspects of our society. Cite the text of the poem for support.

WILLIAM BUTLER YEATS [1865-1939]

Considered one of the greatest poets of the twentieth century, William Butler Yeats was born in Dublin, Ireland. Following in the footsteps of his father, a well-known painter, Yeats studied art for a time in Dublin and London, but gradually turned his focus to writing. While still a young man, Yeats became politically active in the movement for an independent Ireland. In 1899, he was an instrumental figure in the formation of the Irish National Theatre (now the Abbey Theatre), writing a number of verse plays for the theater and encouraging other important playwrights, including John Synge, to do likewise. He served as a senator in the newly established Irish Free State from 1922 to 1928. In 1923, he became the first Irishman awarded the Nobel Prize. Though he wrote poetry filled with the sights, sounds, and folklore of his native land throughout his life, much of his greatest work dates to his final years, when he combined his Irish perspective with a deeply felt spiritual sense and symbolic system. "The Lake Isle of Innisfree" was written in 1893 and, like much of Yeats's early poetry, is deeply Romantic in its outlook.

THE LAKE ISLE OF INNISFREE [1893]

I will arise and go now, and go to Innisfree,
And a small cabin build there, of clay and wattles° made:
Nine bean-rows will I have there, a hive for the honey-bee,
And live alone in the bee-loud glade.

And I shall have some peace there, for peace comes dropping slow,   5
Dropping from the veils of the morning to where the cricket sings;
There midnight's all a glimmer, and noon a purple glow,
And evening full of the linnet's wings.

I will arise and go now, for always night and day
I hear lake water lapping with low sounds by the shore;   10
While I stand on the roadway, or on the pavements gray,
I hear it in the deep heart's core.

2 wattles twigs woven together

MAKING CONNECTIONS

1. List the parts of Yeats's refuge at Innisfree. Identify the qualities that make each of them a contributing factor to the whole of his ideal escape there.
2. In what way does the alternating rhyme scheme of the lines in each stanza affect your response to the content?
3. What does he mean by "I hear it in the deep heart's core"?

MAKING AN ARGUMENT

1. Yeats was a student living in the city of London when he wrote this poem. To what extent do you think that might have influenced the ideal nature of his images? Write a comparison of this poem with "A Man Said to the Universe" (p. 1225). Which view of nature do you prefer? Cite the text of both poems for support.

CONNECTING THROUGH COMPARISON: WHAT IS POETRY?

The three poems that follow address a subtheme of this section: What is poetry? Read and discussed together, they invite comparisons and connections—not only with each other—but with your own experience of reading and writing about poetry.

ARCHIBALD MACLEISH [1892–1982]

Born in Glencoe, Illinois, Archibald MacLeish attended Yale University as an undergraduate, where he published poems in the Yale Review, *though he later earned a law degree from Harvard University. In 1923, he abandoned his lucrative law career and moved to Paris with his young family to pursue writing. In Paris, he came into contact with many of the greatest poets of the age including Ezra Pound and T. S. Eliot, who greatly influenced his work. In 1932, after returning to the United States, he won the first of his three Pulitzer Prizes for "Conquistador" (1932), an epic poem about Cortez's sixteenth-century expedition to Mexico. In 1939, MacLeish was appointed Librarian of Congress, and during World War II, he held a number of important political posts, including assistant secretary of state. In his later years he won two more Pulitzer Prizes, the first for his* New and Collected Poems 1917–1952 (1952), *and the second for his verse drama* J.B. (1958), *a modern retelling of the story of Job. In his later years, MacLeish taught at Harvard before retiring to Amherst, Massachusetts. "Ars Poetica" is Latin for "the art of poetry."*

ARS POETICA [1926]

A poem should be palpable and mute
As a globed fruit,

Dumb
As old medallions to the thumb,

Silent as the sleeve-worn stone   5
Of casement ledges where the moss has grown—

A poem should be wordless
As the flight of birds.

A poem should be motionless in time
As the moon climbs,   10

Leaving, as the moon releases
Twig by twig the night-entangled trees,

Leaving, as the moon behind the winter leaves,
Memory by memory the mind—

A poem should be motionless in time   15
As the moon climbs.

A poem should be equal to:
Not true.

For all the history of grief
An empty doorway and a maple leaf   20

For love
The leaning grasses and two lights above the sea—

A poem should not mean
But be.

LAWRENCE FERLINGHETTI [B. 1919]

*Lawrence Ferlinghetti was born in Yonkers, New York. His
father died before he was born, and his mother was institutionalized following a severe mental breakdown.
Shuttled between relatives, he lived in France and a public
orphanage before settling with a rich family in Bronxville,
New York, where his aunt was working as a governess.
After attending the University of North Carolina, where he
majored in Journalism, Ferlinghetti enlisted in the Navy.*

During World War II, he served as a commander in the Normandy invasion, and afterward took advantage of the G.I. Bill, earning an M.A. from Columbia University in 1948 and a Ph.D. from the Sorbonne in Paris in 1951. A prolific poet, playwright, and editor, Ferlinghetti's most famous work continues to be his collection of poems A Coney Island of the Mind *(1958), which, with its embrace of open form and colloquial speech, is considered one of the key works of the Beat movement. "Constantly Risking Absurdity" is taken from* A Coney Island of the Mind.

CONSTANTLY RISKING ABSURDITY   [1958]

<pre>
        Constantly risking absurdity
                        and death
            whenever he performs
                        above the heads
                            of his audience   5
        the poet like an acrobat
                    climbs on rime
                    to a high wire of his own making
        and balancing on eyebeams
                        above a sea of faces   10
                paces his way
                    to the other side of day
            performing entrechats
                    and sleight-of-foot tricks
        and other high theatrics   15
                    and all without mistaking
            any thing
                    for what it may not be
        For he's the super realist
                        who must perforce perceive   20
                taut truth
                    before the taking of each stance or step
        in his supposed advance
                        toward that still higher perch
        where Beauty stands and waits   25
                        with gravity
                            to start her death-defying leap
        And he
                a little charleychaplin man
                        who may or may not catch   30
                her fair eternal form
                        spreadeagled in the empty air
                of existence
</pre>

BILLY COLLINS [B. 1941]

Billy Collins is the author of six books of poetry, and his work has appeared in a variety of publications, including Poetry, American Poetry Review, American Scholar, Harper's, Paris Review, *and the* New Yorker. *He has received fellowships from the National Endowment for the Arts and the Guggenheim Foundation, and in 1992 he was chosen to serve as "Literary Lion" by the New York Public Library. He teaches at Lehman College, of the City University of New York, and lives in Somers, New York. In 2000, he was named U.S. Poet Laureate. His latest collection of poetry is* Nine Horses *(2002). His latest book is an anthology of contemporary poems for use in schools,* A Turning Back to Poetry *(2003).*

INTRODUCTION TO POETRY   [1988]

I ask them to take a poem
and hold it up to the light
like a color slide

or press an ear against its hive.

I say drop a mouse into a poem   5
and watch him probe his way out,

or walk inside the poem's room
and feel the walls for a light switch.

I want them to water-ski
across the surface of a poem   10
waving at the author's name on the shore.

But all they want to do
is tie the poem to a chair with a rope
and torture a confession out of it.

They begin beating it with a hose   15
to find out what it really means.

MAKING CONNECTIONS

1. In "Ars Poetica," summarize each of the three things that the speaker says "a poem should be."
2. Do you agree with this definition? Explain.
3. The speaker in Ferlinghetti's poem compares a poet to an acrobat. In what way is the structure of the poem like acrobatics? Does the comparison work for you?

4. To what extent is the poet a "super realist" who tries to catch "Beauty"?
5. The speaker in Billy Collins's poem is describing students who are reading a poem. Do the students do what he hopes they will? Do you when you read a poem? Explain.

MAKING AN ARGUMENT

1. MacLeish addresses what a poem is; Ferlinghetti writes about what a poet does; and Collins writes about what readers do with a poem. In what way do all three respond to the question "What is poetry?" Cite the texts of the poems for support.

✦ DRAMA ✦

SOPHOCLES [C. 496–406 B.C.]

Considered during his lifetime one of the three great Athenian tragic playwrights (the other two being Aeschylus and Euripides), Sophocles is believed to have written over 120 plays, though only seven of his tragedies have survived to modern times (Ajax, Antigonê, Oedipus the King, Electra, Philoctetes, The Trachinian Women, and Oedipus at Colonus). A popular figure throughout his long life, he served in a series of public offices, including those of general and priest, during a century that witnessed Athens's rise to power and its subsequent decline. Oedipus Rex (sometimes called Oedipus Tyrannus or Oedipus the King), Sophocles's retelling of the legend of Oedipus, was probably written in 429 B.C. The play has been held in high esteem since ancient times, when Aristotle cited the play as the perfect example of tragedy in his famous treatise on poetry, the Poetics.

OEDIPUS REX

[C. 429 B.C.]

AN ENGLISH VERSION BY DUDLEY FITTS AND ROBERT FITZGERALD

CHARACTERS
OEDIPUS
A PRIEST
CREÓN
TEIRESIAS
IOCASTÊ
MESSENGER
SHEPHERD OF LAÏOS
SECOND MESSENGER
CHORUS OF THEBAN ELDERS

Scene: Before the palace of OEDIPUS, *king of Thebes. A central door and two lateral doors open onto a platform which runs the length of the facade. On the platform, right and left, are altars; and three steps lead down into the "orchestra," or chorus ground. At the beginning of the action these steps are crowded by* SUPPLIANTS *who have brought branches and chaplets of olive leaves and who lie in various attitudes of despair.* OEDIPUS *enters.*

PROLOGUE

OEDIPUS: My children, generations of the living
    In the line of Kadmos,° nursed at his ancient hearth,
    Why have you strewn yourselves before these altars
    In supplication, with your boughs and garlands?
    The breath of incense rises from the city   5
    With a sound of prayer and lamentation.
                              Children,
    I would not have you speak through messengers,
    And therefore I have come myself to hear you—
    I, Oedipus who bear the famous name.
    [*To a* PRIEST.] You, there, since you are eldest in the company,   10
    Speak for them all, tell me what preys upon you,
    Whether you come in dread, or crave some blessing:
    Tell me, and never doubt that I will help you
    In every way I can; I should be heartless
    Were I not moved to find you suppliant here.   15

PRIEST: Great Oedipus, O powerful King of Thebes!
    You see how all the ages of our people
    Cling to your altar steps: here are boys
    Who can barely stand alone, and here are priests
    By weight of age, as I am a priest of God,   20
    And young men chosen from those yet unmarried;
    As for the others, all that multitude,
    They wait with olive chaplets in the squares,
    At the two shrines of Pallas,° and where Apollo°
    Speaks in the glowing embers.
                      Your own eyes   25
    Must tell you: Thebes is in her extremity
    And cannot lift her head from the surge of death.
    A rust consumes the buds and fruits of the earth;
    The herds are sick; children die unborn,

2 Kadmos according to legend, the founder of Thebes   **24 Pallas** Athena, Zeus's daughter and the goddess of wisdom   **Apollo** Zeus' son and the god of poetry and prophecy

And labor is vain. The god of plague and pyre   30
Raids like detestable lightning through the city,
And all the house of Kadmos is laid waste,
All emptied, and all darkened: Death alone
Battens upon the misery of Thebes.

You are not one of the immortal gods, we know;   35
Yet we have come to you to make our prayer
As to the man of all men best in adversity
And wisest in the ways of God. You saved us
From the Sphinx,° that flinty singer, and the tribute
We paid to her so long; yet you were never   40
Better informed than we, nor could we teach you:
It was some god breathed in you to set us free.

Therefore, O mighty King, we turn to you:
Find us our safety, find us a remedy,
Whether by counsel of the gods or the men.   45
A king of wisdom tested in the past
Can act in a time of troubles, and act well.
Noblest of men, restore
Life to your city! Think how all men call you
Liberator for your triumph long ago;   50
Ah, when your years of kingship are remembered,
Let them not say *We rose, but later fell*—
Keep the State from going down in the storm!
Once, years ago, with happy augury,
You brought us fortune; be the same again!   55
No man questions your power to rule the land:
But rule over men, not over a dead city!
Ships are only hulls, citadels are nothing,
When no life moves in the empty passageways.

OEDIPUS: Poor children! You may be sure I know   60
All that you longed for in your coming here.
I know that you are deathly sick; and yet,
Sick as you are, not one is as sick as I.
Each of you suffers in himself alone
His anguish, not another's; but my spirit   65
Groans for the city, for myself, for you.

I was not sleeping, you are not waking me.
No, I have been in tears for a long while
And in my restless thought walked many ways.

39 The Sphinx a monster with a lion's body, bird's wings, and woman's face

In all my search, I found one helpful course,   70
And that I have taken: I have sent Creon,
Son of Menoikeus, brother of the Queen,
To Delphi, Apollo's place of revelation,
To learn there, if he can,
What act or pledge of mine may save the city.   75
I have counted the days, and now, this very day,
I am troubled, for he has overstayed his time.
What is he doing? He has been gone too long.
Yet whenever he comes back, I should do ill
To scant whatever hint the god may give.   80

PRIEST: It is a timely promise. At this instant
They tell me Creon is here.

OEDIPUS: O Lord Apollo!
May his news be fair as his face is radiant!

PRIEST: It could not be otherwise: he is crowned with bay,
The chaplet is thick with berries.

OEDIPUS: We shall soon know;   85
He is near enough to hear us now.

[Enter CREON.]

                              O Prince:
Brother: son of Menoikeus:
What answer do you bring us from the god?

CREON: It is favorable. I can tell you, great afflictions
Will turn out well, if they are taken well.   90

OEDIPUS: What was the oracle? These vague words
Leave me still hanging between hope and fear.

CREON: Is it your pleasure to hear me with all these
Gathered around us? I am prepared to speak,
But should we not go in?

OEDIPUS: Let them all hear it.   95
It is for them I suffer, more than myself.

CREON: Then I will tell you what I heard at Delphi.

In plain words
The god commands us to expel from the land of Thebes
An old defilement that it seems we shelter.   100
It is a deathly thing, beyond expiation.
We must not let it feed upon us longer.

OEDIPUS: What defilement? How shall we rid ourselves of it?

CREON: By exile or death, blood for blood. It was
Murder that brought the plague-wind on the city.   105

OEDIPUS: Murder of whom? Surely the god has named him?

CREON: My lord: long ago Laïos was our king,
    Before you came to govern us.

OEDIPUS: I know;
    I learned of him from others; I never saw him.

CREON: He was murdered; and Apollo commands us now   110
    To take revenge upon whoever killed him.

OEDIPUS: Upon whom? Where are they? Where shall we find a clue
    To solve that crime, after so many years?

CREON: Here in this land, he said.

                    If we make enquiry,
    We may touch things that otherwise escape us.   115

OEDIPUS: Tell me: Was Laïos murdered in his house,
    Or in the fields, or in some foreign country?

CREON: He said he planned to make a pilgrimage.
    He did not come home again.

OEDIPUS: And was there no one,
    No witness, no companion, to tell what happened?   120

CREON: They were all killed but one, and he got away
    So frightened that he could remember one thing only.

OEDIPUS: What was that one thing? One may be the key
    To everything, if we resolve to use it.

CREON: He said that a band of highwaymen attacked them.   125
    Outnumbered them, and overwhelmed the King.

OEDIPUS: Strange, that a highwayman should be so daring—
    Unless some faction here bribed him to do it.

CREON: We thought of that. But after Laïos' death
    New troubles arose and we had no avenger.   130

OEDIPUS: What troubles could prevent your hunting down the killers?

CREON: The riddling Sphinx's song
    Made us deaf to all mysteries but her own.

OEDIPUS: Then once more I must bring what is dark to light.
    It is most fitting that Apollo shows,   135
    As you do, this compunction for the dead.
    You shall see how I stand by you, as I should,
    To avenge the city and the city's god,
    And not as though it were for some distant friend,
    But for my own sake, to be rid of evil.   140
    Whoever killed King Laïos might—who knows?—
    Decide at any moment to kill me as well.
    By avenging the murdered king I protect myself.
    Come, then, my children: leave the altar steps,
    Lift up your olive boughs!

                  One of you go   145

And summon the people of Kadmos to gather here.
I will do all that I can; you may tell them that.

[Exit a PAGE.*]*

So, with the help of God,
We shall be saved—or else indeed we are lost.

PRIEST: Let us rise, children. It was for this we came,   150
And now the King has promised it himself.
Phoibos° has sent us an oracle; may he descend
Himself to save us and drive out the plague.

[Exeunt OEDIPUS *and* CREON *into the palace by the central door. The* PRIEST *and the*
SUPPLIANTS *disperse right and left. After a short pause the Chorus enters the orchestra.]*

PÁRODOS°

Strophe° 1

Chorus: What is God singing in his profound
Delphi of gold and shadow?
What oracle for Thebes, the sunwhipped city?
Fear unjoints me, the roots of my heart tremble.
Now I remember, O Healer, your power, and wonder;   5
Will you send doom like a sudden cloud, or weave it
Like nightfall of the past?
Speak, speak to us, issue of holy sound:
Dearest to our expectancy: be tender!

Antistrophe° 1

Let me pray to Athenê, the immortal daughter of Zeus,   10
And to Artemis her sister
Who keeps her famous throne in the market ring,
And to Apollo, bowman at the far butts of heaven—

O gods, descend! Like three streams leap against
The fires of our grief, the fires of darkness;   15
Be swift to bring us rest!

As in the old time from the brilliant house
Of air you stepped to save us, come again!

Strophe 2

Now our afflictions have no end,
Now all our stricken host lies down   20

152 **Phoibos** Phoebus Apollo   **s.d. Párodos** the entrance song of the chorus   **s.d. Strophe**
sung as the chorus moves from stage right to stage left   **s.d. Antistrophe** sung as the chorus
moves from stage left to stage right

And no man fights off death with his mind;

The noble plowland bears no grain,

And groaning mothers cannot bear—

See, how our lives like birds take wing,

Like sparks that fly when a fire soars,   25

To the shore of the god of evening.

Antistrophe 2

The plague burns on, it is pitiless

Though pallid children laden with death

Lie unwept in the stony ways,

And old gray women by every path   30

Flock to the strand about the altars

There to strike their breasts and cry

Worship of Phoibos in wailing prayers:

Be kind, God's golden child!

Strophe 3

There are no swords in this attack by fire,   35

No shields, but we are ringed with cries.

Send the besieger plunging from our homes

Into the vast sea-room of the Atlantic

Or into the waves that foam eastward of Thrace—

For the day ravages what the night spares—   40

Destroy our enemy, lord of the thunder!

Let him be riven by lightning from heaven!

Antistrophe 3

Phoibos Apollo, stretch the sun's bowstring,

That golden cord, until it sing for us,

Flashing arrows in heaven!

                        Artemis,° Huntress,   45

Race with flaring lights upon our mountains!

O scarlet god, O golden-banded brow,

O Theban Bacchos° in a storm of Maenads,°

[Enter OEDIPUS, *center.]*

Whirl upon Death, that all the Undying hate!

Come with blinding cressets, come in joy!   50

---

45 Artemis the goddess of the hunt   **48 Bacchos . . . Maenads** the god of wine and revelry
with his female attendants

SCENE 1

OEDIPUS: Is this your prayer? It may be answered. Come,
        Listen to me, act as the crisis demands,
        And you shall have relief from all these evils.

        Until now I was a stranger to this tale,
        As I had been a stranger to the crime.   5
        Could I track down the murderer without a clue?
        But now, friends,
        As one who became a citizen after the murder,
        I make this proclamation to all Thebans:
        If any man knows by whose hand Laïos, son of Labdakos,   10
        Met his death, I direct that man to tell me everything,
        No matter what he fears for having so long withheld it.
        Let it stand as promised that no further trouble
        Will come to him, but he may leave the land in safety.

        Moreover: If anyone knows the murderer to be foreign,   15
        Let him not keep silent: he shall have his reward from me.
        However, if he does conceal it, if any man
        Fearing for his friend or for himself disobeys this edict,
        Hear what I propose to do:
        I solemnly forbid the people of this country,   20
        Where power and throne are mine, ever to receive that man
        Or speak to him, no matter who he is, or let him
        Join in sacrifice, lustration, or in prayer.
        I decree that he be driven from every house,
        Being, as he is, corruption itself to us: the Delphic   25
        Voice of Zeus has pronounced this revelation.
        Thus I associate myself with the oracle
        And take the side of the murdered king.

        As for the criminal, I pray to God—
        Whether it be a lurking thief, or one of a number—   30
        I pray that that man's life be consumed in evil and wretchedness.
        And as for me, this curse applies no less
        If it should turn out that the culprit is my guest here,
        Sharing my hearth.
                          You have heard the penalty.   35
        I lay it on you now to attend to this
        For my sake, for Apollo's, for the sick
        Sterile city that heaven has abandoned.
        Suppose the oracle had given you no command:

Should this defilement go uncleansed for ever?   40
You should have found the murderer: your king,
A noble king, had been destroyed!
                              Now I,
Having the power that he held before me,
Having his bed, begetting children there
Upon his wife, as he would have, had he lived—   45
Their son would have been my children's brother,
If Laïos had had luck in fatherhood!
(But surely ill luck rushed upon his reign)—
I say I take the son's part, just as though
I were his son, to press the fight for him   50
And see it won! I'll find the hand that brought
Death to Labdakos' and Polydoros' child,
Heir of Kadmos' and Agenor's line.
And as for those who fail me,
May the gods deny them the fruit of the earth,   55
Fruit of the womb, and may they rot utterly!
Let them be wretched as we are wretched, and worse!
For you, for loyal Thebans, and for all
Who find my actions right, I pray the favor
Of justice, and of all the immortal gods.   60

CHORAGOS: Since I am under oath, my lord, I swear
   I did not do the murder, I cannot name
   The murderer. Might not the oracle
   That has ordained the search tell where to find him?
OEDIPUS: An honest question. But no man in the world   65
   Can make the gods do more than the gods will.
CHORAGOS: There is one last expedient—
OEDIPUS: Tell me what it is.
   Though it seem slight, you must not hold it back.
CHORAGOS: A lord clairvoyant to the lord Apollo,
   As we all know, is the skilled Teiresias.   70
   One might learn much about this from him, Oedipus.
OEDIPUS: I am not wasting time:
   Creon spoke of this, and I have sent for him—
   Twice, in fact; it is strange that he is not here.
CHORAGOS: The other matter—that old report—seems useless.   75
OEDIPUS: Tell me. I am interested in all reports.
CHORAGOS: The King was said to have been killed by highwaymen.
OEDIPUS: I know. But we have no witnesses to that.
CHORAGOS: If the killer can feel a particle of dread,
   Your curse will bring him out of hiding!

OEDIPUS: No.   80
    The man who dared that act will fear no curse

[Enter the blind seer TEIRESIAS *led by a* PAGE.*]*

CHORAGOS: But there is one man who may detect the criminal.
        This is Teiresias, this is the holy prophet
        In whom, alone of all men, truth was born.
OEDIPUS: Teiresias: seer: student of mysteries,   85
        Of all that's taught and all that no man tells,
        Secrets of Heaven and secrets of the earth:
        Blind though you are, you know the city lies
        Sick with plague; and from this plague, my lord,
        We find that you alone can guard or save us.   90

        Possibly you did not hear the messengers?
        Apollo, when we sent to him,
        Sent us back word that this great pestilence
        Would lift, but only if we established clearly
        The identity of those who murdered Laïos.   95
        They must be killed or exiled.

                                Can you use
        Bird flight or any art of divination
        To purify yourself, and Thebes, and me
        From this contagion? We are in your hands.
        There is no fairer duty   100
        Than that of helping others in distress.
TEIRESIAS: How dreadful knowledge of the truth can be
        When there's no help in truth! I knew this well,
        But did not act on it: else I should not have come.
OEDIPUS: What is troubling you? Why are your eyes so cold?   105
TEIRESIAS: Let me go home. Bear your own fate, and I'll
        Bear mine. It is better so: trust what I say.
OEDIPUS: What you say is ungracious and unhelpful
        To your native country. Do not refuse to speak.
TEIRESIAS: When it comes to speech, your own is neither temperate   110
        Nor opportune. I wish to be more prudent.
OEDIPUS: In God's name, we all beg you—
TEIRESIAS: You are all ignorant.
        No; I will never tell you what I know.
        Now it is my misery; then, it would be yours.
OEDIPUS: What! You do know something, and will not tell us?   115
        You would betray us all and wreck the State?
TEIRESIAS: I do not intend to torture myself, or you.
        Why persist in asking? You will not persuade me.

OEDIPUS: What a wicked man you are! You'd try a stone's
    Patience! Out with it! Have you no feeling at all?   120

TEIRESIAS: You call me unfeeling. If you could only see
    The nature of your feelings . . .

OEDIPUS: Why,
    Who would not feel as I do? Who could endure
    Your arrogance toward the city?

TEIRESIAS: What does it matter!   125
    Whether I speak or not, it is bound to come.

OEDIPUS: Then, if "it" is bound to come, you are bound
    to tell me.

TEIRESIAS: No, I will not go on. Rage as you please.

OEDIPUS: Rage? Why not!
          And I'll tell you what I think: 130
    You planned it, you had it done, you all but
    Killed him with your own hands: if you had eyes,
    I'd say the crime was yours, and yours alone.

TEIRESIAS: So? I charge you, then,
    Abide by the proclamation you have made.   135
    From this day forth
    Never speak again to these men or to me;
    You yourself are the pollution of this country.

OEDIPUS: You dare say that! Can you possibly think you have
    Some way of going free, after such insolence?   140

TEIRESIAS: I have gone free. It is the truth sustains me.

OEDIPUS: Who taught you shamelessness? It was not your craft.

TEIRESIAS: You did. You made me speak. I did not want to.

OEDIPUS: Speak what? Let me hear it again more clearly.

TEIRESIAS: Was it not clear before? Are you tempting me?   145

OEDIPUS: I did not understand it. Say it again.

TEIRESIAS: I say that you are the murderer whom you seek.

OEDIPUS: Now twice you have spat out infamy. You'll
    pay for it!

TEIRESIAS: Would you care for more? Do you wish to be really angry?   150

OEDIPUS: Say what you will. Whatever you say is worthless.

TEIRESIAS: I say you live in hideous shame with those
    Most dear to you. You cannot see the evil.

Oedipus: It seems you can go on mouthing like this for ever.

Teiresias: I can, if there is power in truth.

Oedipus: There is: 155
    But not for you, not for you,
    You sightless, witless, senseless, mad old man!

Teiresias: You are the madman. There is no one here
　　　Who will not curse you soon, as you curse me.
Oedipus: You child of endless night! You cannot hurt me   160
　　　Or any other man who sees the sun.
Teiresias: True: it is not from me your fate will come.
　　　That lies within Apollo's competence,
　　　As it is his concern.
Oedipus:　　　　　　　Tell me:
　　　Are you speaking for Creon, or for yourself?   165
Teiresias: Creon is no threat. You weave your own doom.
Oedipus: Wealth, power, craft of statesmanship!
　　　Kingly position, everywhere admired!
　　　What savage envy is stored up against these,
　　　If Creon, whom I trusted, Creon my friend,   170
　　　For this great office which the city once
　　　Put in my hands unsought—if for this power
　　　Creon desires in secret to destroy me!

　　　He has brought this decrepit fortune-teller, this
　　　Collector of dirty pennies, this prophet fraud—   175
　　　Why, he is no more clairvoyant than I am!
　　　　　　　　　　　　　　Tell us:
　　　Has your mystic mummery ever approached the truth?
　　　When that hellcat the Sphinx was performing here,
　　　What help were you to these people?
　　　Her magic was not for the first man who came along: 180
　　　It demanded a real exorcist. Your birds—
　　　What good were they? or the gods, for the matter of that?
　　　But I came by,
　　　Oedipus, the simple man, who knows nothing—
　　　I thought it out for myself, no birds helped me!   185
　　　And this is the man you think you can destroy,
　　　That you may be close to Creon when he's king!
　　　Well, you and your friend Creon, it seems to me,
　　　Will suffer most. If you were not an old man,
　　　You would have paid already for your plot.   190
Choragos: We cannot see that his words or yours
　　　Have spoken except in anger, Oedipus,
　　　And of anger we have no need. How can God's will
　　　Be accomplished best? That is what most concerns us.
Teiresias: You are a king. But where argument's concerned   195
　　　I am your man, as much a king as you.
　　　I am not your servant, but Apollo's.

I have no need of Creon to speak for me.

Listen to me. You mock my blindness, do you?
But I say that you, with both your eyes, are blind: 200
You cannot see the wretchedness of your life,
Not in whose house you live, no, nor with whom.
Who are your father and mother? Can you tell me?
You do not even know the blind wrongs
That you have done them, on earth and in the world below.   205
But the double lash of your parents' curse will whip you
Out of this land some day, with only night
Upon your precious eyes.
Your cries then—where will they not be heard?
What fastness of Kithairon will not echo them?   210
And that bridal-descant of yours—you'll know it then,
The song they sang when you came here to Thebes
And found your misguided berthing.
All this, and more, that you cannot guess at now,
Will bring you to yourself among your children.   215
Be angry, then. Curse Creon. Curse my words.
I tell you, no man that walks upon the earth
Shall be rooted out more horribly than you.

OEDIPUS: Am I to bear this from him?—Damnation
Take you! Out of this place! Out of my sight!   220

TEIRESIAS: I would not have come at all if you had not asked me.

OEDIPUS: Could I have told that you'd talk nonsense, that
You'd come here to make a fool of yourself, and of me?

TEIRESIAS: A fool? Your parents thought me sane enough.

OEDIPUS: My parents again!—Wait: who were my parents?   225

TEIRESIAS: This day will give you a father, and break your heart.

OEDIPUS: Your infantile riddles! Your damned abracadabra!

TEIRESIAS: You were a great man once at solving riddles.

OEDIPUS: Mock me with that if you like; you will find it true.

TEIRESIAS: It was true enough. It brought about your ruin.   230

OEDIPUS: But if it saved this town?

TEIRESIAS [*to the* PAGE]:   Boy, give me your hand.

OEDIPUS: Yes, boy; lead him away.
                    —While you are here
We can do nothing. Go; leave us in peace.

TEIRESIAS: I will go when I have said what I have to say.   235
How can you hurt me? And I tell you again:
The man you have been looking for all this time,
The damned man, the murderer of Laïos,
That man is in Thebes. To your mind he is foreignborn,

But it will soon be shown that he is a Theban,   240
A revelation that will fail to please.

                     A blind man,
Who has his eyes now; a penniless man, who is rich now;
And he will go tapping the strange earth with his staff;
To the children with whom he lives now he will be
Brother and father—the very same; to her   245
Who bore him, son and husband—the very same
Who came to his father's bed, wet with his father's blood.

Enough. Go think that over.
If later you find error in what I have said,
You may say that I have no skill in prophecy.   250

[Exit TEIRESIAS, *led by his* PAGE; OEDIPUS *goes into the palace.]*

ODE 1°

Strophe 1

Chorus: The Delphic stone of prophecies
      Remembers ancient regicide
      And a still bloody hand.
      That killer's hour of flight has come.
      He must be stronger than riderless   5
      Coursers of untiring wind,
      For the son of Zeus° armed with his father's thunder
      Leaps in lightning after him;
      And the Furies° follow him, the sad Furies.

Antistrophe 1

      Holy Parnossos' peak of snow   10
      Flashes and blinds that secret man,
      That all shall hunt him down:
      Though he may roam the forest shade
      Like a bull gone wild from pasture
      To rage through glooms of stone.   15
      Doom comes down on him; flight will not avail him;
      For the world's heart calls him desolate,
      And the immortal Furies follow, for ever follow.

Strophe 2

      But now a wilder thing is heard
      From the old man skilled at hearing Fate in the   20

s.d. Ode a poetic song   **7 son of Zeus** Apollo   **9 the Furies** women spirits who punished
those guilty of evil

wingbeat of a bird.
Bewildered as a blown bird, my soul hovers and cannot find
Foothold in this debate, or any reason or rest of mind.
But no man ever brought—none can bring
Proof of strife between Thebes' royal house,   25
Labdakos' line° and the son of Polybos;°
And never until now has any man brought word
Of Laïos' dark death staining Oedipus the King.

Antistrophe 2

Divine Zeus and Apollo hold
Perfect intelligence alone of all tales ever told;   30
And well though this diviner works, he works in his own night;
No man can judge that rough unknown or trust in second sight,
For wisdom changes hands among the wise.
Shall I believe my great lord criminal
At a raging word that a blind old man let fall?   35
I saw him, when the carrion woman faced him of old,
Prove his heroic mind! These evil words are lies.

SCENE 2

CREON: Men of Thebes:
I am told that heavy accusations
Have been brought against me by King Oedipus.
I am not the kind of man to bear this tamely.

If in these present difficulties   5
He holds me accountable for any harm to him
Through anything I have said or done—why, then,
I do not value life in this dishonor.
It is not as though this rumor touched upon
Some private indiscretion. The matter is grave.   10
The fact is that I am being called disloyal
To the State, to my fellow citizens, to my friends.

CHORAGOS: He may have spoken in anger, not from his mind.

CREON: But did you hear him say I was the one
Who seduced the old prophet into lying?   15

CHORAGOS: The thing was said; I do not know how seriously.

CREON: But you were watching him! Were his eyes steady?
Did he look like a man in his right mind?

CHORAGOS: I do not know.

26 Labdakos' line descendants of Labdakos   **Polybos** king of Corinth, foster father of Oedipus

I cannot judge the behavior of great men.
But here is the King himself.

[Enter OEDIPUS.*]*

OEDIPUS: So you dared come back.   20
Why? How brazen of you to come to my house,
You murderer!
                    Do you think I do not know
That you plotted to kill me, plotted to steal my throne?
Tell me, in God's name: am I coward, a fool,
That you should dream you could accomplish this?   25
A fool who could not see your slippery game?
A coward, not to fight back when I saw it?
You are the fool, Creon, are you not? hoping
Without support or friends to get a throne?
Thrones may be won or bought: you could do neither.   30

CREON: Now listen to me. You have talked; let me talk; too.
You cannot judge unless you know the facts.

OEDIPUS: You speak well: there is one fact; but I find it hard
To learn from the deadliest enemy I have.

CREON: That above all I must dispute with you.   35

OEDIPUS: That above all I will not hear you deny.

CREON: If you think there is anything good in being stubborn
Against all reason, then I say you are wrong.

OEDIPUS: If you think a man can sin against his own kind
And not be punished for it, I say you are mad.   40

CREON: I agree. But tell me: what have I done to you?

OEDIPUS: You advised me to send for that wizard, did you not?

CREON: I did. I should do it again.

OEDIPUS: Very well. Now tell me:
How long has it been since Laïos—

CREON: What of Laïos?

OEDIPUS: Since he vanished in that onset by the road?   45

CREON: It was long ago, a long time.

OEDIPUS: And this prophet,
Was he practicing here then?

CREON: He was; and with honor, as now.

OEDIPUS: Did he speak of me at that time?

CREON: He never did;
At least, not when I was present.

OEDIPUS: But . . . the enquiry?
I suppose you held one?

CREON: We did, but we learned nothing.   50

OEDIPUS: Why did the prophet not speak against me then?

Creon: I do not know; and I am the kind of man
    Who holds his tongue when he has no facts to go on.

Oedipus: There's one fact that you know, and you could tell it.

Creon: What fact is that? If I know it, you shall have it.   55

Oedipus: If he were not involved with you, he could not say
    That it was I who murdered Laïos.

Creon: If he says that, you are the one that knows it!—
    But now it is my turn to question you.

Oedipus: Put your questions. I am no murderer.   60

Creon: First, then: You married my sister?

Oedipus: I married your sister.

Creon: And you rule the kingdom equally with her?

Oedipus: Everything that she wants she has from me.

Creon: And I am the third, equal to both of you?

Oedipus: That is why I call you a bad friend.   65

Creon: No. Reason it out, as I have done.
    Think of this first. Would any sane man prefer
    Power, with all a king's anxieties,
    To that same power and the grace of sleep?
    Certainly not I.   70
    I have never longed for the king's power—only his rights.
    Would any wise man differ from me in this?
    As matters stand, I have my way in everything
    With your consent, and no responsibilities.
    If I were king, I should be a slave to policy.   75
    How could I desire a scepter more
    Than what is now mine—untroubled influence?
    No, I have not gone mad; I need no honors,
    Except those with the perquisites I have now.
    I am welcome everywhere; every man salutes me,   80
    And those who want your favor seek my ear,
    Since I know how to manage what they ask.
    Should I exchange this ease for that anxiety?
    Besides, no sober mind is treasonable.
    I hate anarchy   85
    And never would deal with any man who likes it.

    Test what I have said. Go to the priestess
    At Delphi, ask if I quoted her correctly.
    And as for this other thing: if I am found
    Guilty of treason with Teiresias,   90
    Then sentence me to death! You have my word
    It is a sentence I should cast my vote for—

But not without evidence!
You do wrong
When you take good men for bad, bad men for good.
A true friend thrown aside—why, life itself   95
Is not more precious!
In time you will know this well:
For time, and time alone, will show the just man,
Though scoundrels are discovered in a day.

CHORAGOS: This is well said, and a prudent man would ponder it.
Judgments too quickly formed are dangerous.   100

OEDIPUS: But is he not quick in his duplicity?
And shall I not be quick to parry him?
Would you have me stand still, hold my peace, and let
This man win everything, through my inaction?

CREON: And you want—what is it, then? To banish me?   105

OEDIPUS: No, not exile. It is your death I want,
So that all the world may see what treason means.

CREON: You will persist, then? You will not believe me?

OEDIPUS: How can I believe you?

CREON: Then you are a fool.

OEDIPUS: To save myself?

CREON: In justice, think of me.   110

OEDIPUS: You are evil incarnate.

CREON: But suppose that you are wrong?

OEDIPUS: Still I must rule.

CREON: But not if you rule badly.

OEDIPUS: O city, city!

CREON: It is my city, too!

CHORAGOS: Now, my lords, be still. I see the Queen,
Iocastê, coming from her palace chambers;   115
And it is time she came, for the sake of you both.
This dreadful quarrel can be resolved through her.

[Enter IOCASTÊ.*]*

IOCASTÊ: Poor foolish men, what wicked din is this?
With Thebes sick to death, is it not shameful
That you should rake some private quarrel up?   120

[To OEDIPUS.*]*

Come into the house.
—And you, Creon, go now:
Let us have no more of this tumult over nothing.

CREON.   Nothing? No, sister: what your husband plans for me
Is one of two great evils: exile or death.

OEDIPUS: He is right.

Why, woman, I have caught him squarely   125
Plotting against my life.

CREON: No! Let me die
Accurst if ever I have wished you harm!

IOCASTÊ: Ah, believe it, Oedipus!
In the name of the gods, respect this oath of his
For my sake, for the sake of these people here!   130

Strophe 1

CHORAGOS: Open your mind to her, my lord. Be ruled by her, I beg you!

OEDIPUS: What would you have me do?

CHORAGOS: Respect Creon's word. He has never spoken like a fool,
And now he has sworn an oath.

OEDIPUS: You know what you ask?

CHORAGOS: I do.

OEDIPUS: Speak on, then.   135

CHORAGOS: A friend so sworn should not be baited so,
In blind malice, and without final proof.

OEDIPUS: You are aware, I hope, that what you say
Means death for me, or exile at the least.

Strophe 2

CHORAGOS: No, I swear by Helios, first in Heaven!   140
May I die friendless and accurst,
The worst of deaths, if ever I meant that!
    It is the withering fields
        That hurt my sick heart:
    Must we bear all these ills,   145
        And now your bad blood as well?

OEDIPUS: Then let him go. And let me die, if I must,
Or be driven by him in shame from the land of Thebes.
It is your unhappiness, and not his talk,
That touches me.
                    As for him—   150
Wherever he is, I will hate him as long as I live.

CREON: Ugly in yielding, as you were ugly in rage!
Natures like yours chiefly torment themselves.

OEDIPUS: Can you not go? Can you not leave me?

CREON: I can.   155
You do not know me; but the city knows me,
And in its eyes I am just, if not in yours.

[Exit CREON.*]*

Antistrophe 1

CHORAGOS: Lady Iocastê, did you not ask the King
    to go to his chambers?

IOCASTÊ: First tell me what has happened.   160

CHORAGOS: There was suspicion without evidence; yet it rankled
    As even false charges will.

IOCASTÊ: On both sides?

CHORAGOS: On both.

IOCASTÊ: But what was said?

CHORAGOS: Oh let it rest, let it be done with!
    Have we not suffered enough?   165

OEDIPUS: You see to what your decency has brought you:
    You have made difficulties where my heart saw none.

Antistrophe 2

CHORAGOS: Oedipus, it is not once only I have told you—
    You must know I should count myself unwise
    To the point of madness, should I now forsake you—   170
        You, under whose hand,
            In the storm of another time,
        Our dear land sailed out free,
            But now stand fast at the helm!

IOCASTÊ: In God's name, Oedipus, inform your wife as well:
    Why are you so set in this hard anger?

OEDIPUS: I will tell you, for none of these men deserves
    My confidence as you do. It is Creon's work,
    His treachery, his plotting against me.   175

IOCASTÊ: Go on, if you can make this clear to me.

OEDIPUS: He charges me with the murder of Laïos.

IOCASTÊ: Has he some knowledge? Or does he speak from hearsay?

OEDIPUS: He would not commit himself to such a charge,
    But he has brought in that damnable soothsayer   180
    To tell his story.

IOCASTÊ: Set your mind at rest.
    If it is a question of soothsayers, I tell you
    That you will find no man whose craft gives knowledge
    Of the unknowable.

                Here is my proof:

An oracle was reported to Laïos once   185
(I will not say from Phoibos himself, but from
His appointed ministers, at any rate)

That his doom would be death at the hands of his own son—
His son, born of his flesh and of mine!
Now, you remember the story: Laïos was killed   190
By marauding strangers where three highways meet;
But his child had not been three days in this world
Before the King had pierced the baby's ankles
And left him to die on a lonely mountainside.

Thus, Apollo never caused that child   195
To kill his father, and it was not Laïos' fate
To die at the hands of his son, as he had feared.
This is what prophets and prophecies are worth!
Have no dread of them.
                        It is God himself
Who can show us what he wills, in his own way.   200

OEDIPUS: How strange a shadowy memory crossed my mind,
        Just now while you were speaking; it chilled my heart.

IOCASTÊ: What do you mean? What memory do you speak of?

OEDIPUS: If I understand you, Laïos was killed
        At a place where three roads meet.

IOCASTÊ: So it was said;   205
        We have no later story.

OEDIPUS: Where did it happen?

IOCASTÊ: Phokis, it is called: at a place where the Theban Way
        Divides into the roads towards Delphi and Daulia.

OEDIPUS: When?

IOCASTÊ: We had the news not long before you came
        And proved the right to your succession here.   210

OEDIPUS: Ah, what net has God been weaving for me?

IOCASTÊ: Oedipus! Why does this trouble you?

OEDIPUS: Do not ask me yet.
        First, tell me how Laïos looked, and tell me
        How old he was.

IOCASTÊ: He was tall, his hair just touched   215
        With white; his form was not unlike your own.

OEDIPUS: I think that I myself may be accurst
        By my own ignorant edict.

IOCASTÊ: You speak strangely.
        It makes me tremble to look at you, my King.

OEDIPUS: I am not sure that the blind man cannot see.   220
        But I should know better if you were to tell me—

IOCASTÊ: Anything—though I dread to hear you ask it.

OEDIPUS: Was the King lightly escorted, or did he ride
        With a large company, as a ruler should?

IOCASTÊ: There were five men with him in all: one was a herald;   225
  And a single chariot, which he was driving.
OEDIPUS: Alas, that makes it plain enough!
            But who—
  Who told you how it happened?
IOCASTÊ: A household servant,
  The only one to escape.
OEDIPUS: And is he still
  A servant of ours?
IOCASTÊ: No; for when he came back at last   230
  And found you enthroned in the place of the dead king,
  He came to me, touched my hand with his, and begged
  That I would send him away to the frontier district
  Where only the shepherds go—
  As far away from the city as I could send him.   235
  I granted his prayer; for although the man was a slave,
  He had earned more than this favor at my hands.
OEDIPUS: Can he be called back quickly?
IOCASTÊ: Easily.
  But why?
OEDIPUS: I have taken too much upon myself
  Without enquiry; therefore I wish to consult him.   240
IOCASTÊ: Then he shall come.
       But am I not one also
  To whom you might confide these fears of yours?
OEDIPUS: That is your right; it will not be denied you,
  Now least of all; for I have reached a pitch
  Of wild foreboding. Is there anyone   245
  To whom I should sooner speak?
  Polybos of Corinth is my father.
  My mother is a Dorian: Meropê.
  I grew up chief among the men of Corinth
  Until a strange thing happened—   250
  Not worth my passion, it may be, but strange.
  At a feast, a drunken man maundering in his cups
  Cries out that I am not my father's son!
  I contained myself that night, though I felt anger
  And a sinking heart. The next day I visited   255
  My father and mother, and questioned them. They stormed,
  Calling it all the slanderous rant of a fool;
  And this relieved me. Yet the suspicion
  Remained always aching in my mind;
  I knew there was talk; I could not rest;   260

And finally, saying nothing to my parents,
I went to the shrine at Delphi.
The god dismissed my question without reply;
He spoke of other things.

    Some were clear,
Full of wretchedness, dreadful, unbearable: 265
As, that I should lie with my own mother, breed
Children from whom all men would turn their eyes;
And that I should be my father's murderer.

I heard all this, and fled. And from that day
Corinth to me was only in the stars   270
Descending in that quarter of the sky,
As I wandered farther and farther on my way
To a land where I should never see the evil
Sung by the oracle. And I came to this country
Where, so you say, King Laïos was killed.   275
I will tell you all that happened there, my lady.

There were three highways
Coming together at a place I passed;
And there a herald came towards me, and a chariot
Drawn by horses, with a man such as you describe 280
Seated in it. The groom leading the horses
Forced me off the road at his lord's command;
But as this charioteer lurched over towards me
I struck him in my rage. The old man saw me
And brought his double goad down upon my head 285
As I came abreast.

    He was paid back, and more!
Swinging my club in this right hand I knocked him
Out of his car, and he rolled on the ground.

       I killed him.

I killed them all.
Now if that stranger and Laïos were—kin,   290
Where is a man more miserable than I?
More hated by the gods? Citizen and alien alike
Must never shelter me or speak to me—
I must be shunned by all.

    And I myself
Pronounced this malediction upon myself!   295

Think of it: I have touched you with these hands,

These hands that killed your husband. What defilement!

Am I all evil, then? It must be so,
Since I must flee from Thebes, yet never again
See my own countrymen, my own country,   300
For fear of joining my mother in marriage
And killing Polybos, my father.
                                        Ah,
If I was created so, born to this fate,
Who could deny the savagery of God?
O holy majesty of heavenly powers!   305
May I never see that day! Never!
Rather let me vanish from the race of men
Than know the abomination destined me!

CHORAGOS: We too, my lord, have felt dismay at this.
But there is hope: you have yet to hear the shepherd.   310

OEDIPUS: Indeed, I fear no other hope is left me.

IOCASTÊ: What do you hope from him when he comes?

OEDIPUS: This much:
If his account of the murder tallies with yours,
Then I am cleared.

IOCASTÊ: What was it that I said
Of such importance?

OEDIPUS: Why, "marauders," you said,   315
Killed the King, according to this man's story.
If he maintains that still, if there were several,
Clearly the guilt is not mine: I was alone.
But if he says one man, singlehanded, did it,
Then the evidence all points to me.   320

IOCASTÊ: You may be sure that he said there were several;
And can he call back that story now? He cannot.
The whole city heard it as plainly as I.
But suppose he alters some detail of it:
He cannot ever show that Laïos' death   325
Fulfilled the oracle: for Apollo said
My child was doomed to kill him; and my child—
Poor baby!—it was my child that died first.
No. From now on, where oracles are concerned,
I would not waste a second thought on any.   330

OEDIPUS: You may be right.
                        But come: let someone go
For the shepherd at once. This matter must be settled.

IOCASTÊ: I will send for him.

I would not wish to cross you in anything,

And surely not in this.—Let us go in.   335

[Exeunt into the palace.]

ODE II

Strophe 1

CHORUS: Let me be reverent in the ways of right,

Lowly the paths I journey on;

Let all my words and actions keep

The laws of the pure universe

From highest Heaven handed down.   5

For Heaven is their bright nurse,

Those generations of the realms of light;

Ah, never of mortal kind were they begot,

Nor are they slaves of memory, lost in sleep:

Their Father is greater than Time, and ages not.   10

Antistrophe 1

The tyrant is a child of Pride

Who drinks from his great sickening cup

Recklessness and vanity,

Until from his high crest headlong

He plummets to the dust of hope.   15

That strong man is not strong.

But let no fair ambition be denied;

May God protect the wrestler for the State

In government, in comely policy,

Who will fear God, and on His ordinance wait.   20

Strophe 2

Haughtiness and the high hand of disdain

Tempt and outrage God's holy law;

And any mortal who dares hold

No immortal Power in awe

Will be caught up in a net of pain: 25

The price for which his levity is sold.

Let each man take due earnings, then,

And keep his hands from holy things,

And from blasphemy stand apart—

Else the crackling blast of heaven   30

Blows on his head, and on his desperate heart;

Though fools will honor impious men,

In their cities no tragic poet sings.

Antistrophe 2

Shall we lose faith in Delphi's obscurities,
We who have heard the world's core   35
Discredited, and the sacred wood
Of Zeus at Elis praised no more?
The deeds and the strange prophecies
Must make a pattern yet to be understood.
Zeus, if indeed you are lord of all,   40
Throned in light over night and day,
Mirror this in your endless mind:
Our masters call the oracle
Words on the wind, and the Delphic vision blind!
Their hearts no longer know Apollo,   45
And reverence for the gods has died away.

SCENE 3

[Enter IOCASTÊ.*]*

IOCASTÊ: Princes of Thebes, it has occurred to me
To visit the altars of the gods, bearing
These branches as a suppliant, and this incense.
Our King is not himself: his noble soul
Is overwrought with fantasies of dread,   5
Else he would consider
The new prophecies in the light of the old.
He will listen to any voice that speaks disaster,
And my advice goes for nothing.

[She approaches the altar, right.]

To you, then, Apollo,
Lycean lord, since you are nearest, I turn in prayer.   10
Receive these offerings, and grant us deliverance
From defilement. Our hearts are heavy with fear
When we see our leader distracted, as helpless sailors
Are terrified by the confusion of their helmsman.

[Enter MESSENGER.*]*

MESSENGER: Friends, no doubt you can direct me: 15
Where shall I find the house of Oedipus,
Or, better still, where is the King himself?
CHORAGOS: It is this very place, stranger; he is inside.
This is his wife and mother of his children.
MESSENGER: I wish her happiness in a happy house,   20
Blest in all the fulfillment of her marriage.

IOCASTÊ: I wish as much for you: your courtesy
    Deserves a like good fortune. But now, tell me:
    Why have you come? What have you to say to us?

MESSENGER: Good news, my lady, for your house and your husband.   25

IOCASTÊ: What news? Who sent you here?

MESSENGER: I am from Corinth.
    The news I bring ought to mean joy for you,
    Though it may be you will find some grief in it.

IOCASTÊ: What is it? How can it touch us in both ways?

MESSENGER: The people of Corinth, they say,   30
    Intend to call Oedipus to be their king.

IOCASTÊ: But old Polybos—is he not reigning still?

MESSENGER: No. Death holds him in his sepulchre.

IOCASTÊ: What are you saying? Polybos is dead?

MESSENGER: If I am not telling the truth, may I die myself.   35

IOCASTÊ: [*to a* MAIDSERVANT]:   Go in, go quickly; tell this to your master.
    O riddlers of God's will, where are you now!
    This was the man whom Oedipus, long ago,
    Feared so, fled so, in dread of destroying him—
    But it was another fate by which he died.   40

[Enter OEDIPUS, *center.]*

OEDIPUS: Dearest Iocastê, why have you sent for me?

IOCASTÊ: Listen to what this man says, and then tell me
    What has become of the solemn prophecies.

OEDIPUS: Who is this man? What is his news for me?

IOCASTÊ: He has come from Corinth to announce your father's death!   45

OEDIPUS: Is it true, stranger? Tell me in your own words.

MESSENGER: I cannot say it more clearly: the king is dead.

OEDIPUS: Was it by treason? Or by an attack of illness?

MESSENGER: A little thing brings old men to their rest.

OEDIPUS: It was sickness, then?

MESSENGER: Yes, and his many years.   50

OEDIPUS: Ah!
    Why should a man respect the Pythian hearth,° or
    Give heed to the birds that jangle above his head?
    They prophesied that I should kill Polybos,
    Kill my own father; but he is dead and buried,   55
    And I am here—I never touched him, never,
    Unless he died in grief for my departure,

---

52 Pythian hearth an alternate name for Delphi. It came from Python, the dragon that guarded Delphi until Apollo killed it and established his oracle there.

And thus, in a sense, through me. No Polybos
Has packed the oracles off with him underground.
They are empty words.

IOCASTÊ:	Had I not told you so?	60

OEDIPUS: You had; it was my faint heart that betrayed me.

IOCASTÊ: From now on never think of those things again.

OEDIPUS: And yet—must I not fear my mother's bed?

IOCASTÊ: Why should anyone in this world be afraid,
Since Fate rules us and nothing can be foreseen?   65
A man should live only for the present day.
Have no more fear of sleeping with your mother.
How many men, in dreams, have lain with their mothers!
No reasonable man is troubled by such things.

OEDIPUS: That is true; only—   70
If only my mother were not still alive!
But she is alive. I cannot help my dread.

IOCASTÊ: Yet this news of your father's death is wonderful.

OEDIPUS: Wonderful. But I fear the living woman.

MESSENGER: Tell me, who is this woman that you fear?   75

OEDIPUS: It is Meropê, man; the wife of King Polybos.

MESSENGER: Meropê? Why should you be afraid of her?

OEDIPUS: An oracle of the gods, a dreadful saying.

MESSENGER: Can you tell me about it or are you sworn to silence?

OEDIPUS: I can tell you, and I will.   80
Apollo said through his prophet that I was the man
Who should marry his own mother, shed his father's blood
With his own hands. And so, for all these years
I have kept clear of Corinth, and no harm has come—
Though it would have been sweet to see my parents again.   85

MESSENGER: And is this the fear that drove you out of Corinth?

OEDIPUS: Would you have me kill my father?

MESSENGER:	As for that	

You must be reassured by the news I gave you.

OEDIPUS: If you could reassure me, I would reward you.

MESSENGER: I had that in mind, I will confess: I thought   90
I could count on you when you returned to Corinth.

OEDIPUS: No: I will never go near my parents again.

MESSENGER: Ah, son, you still do not know what you are doing—

OEDIPUS: What do you mean? In the name of God tell me!

MESSENGER: —If these are your reasons for not going home.   95

OEDIPUS: I tell you, I fear the oracle may come true.

MESSENGER: And guilt may come upon you through your parents?

OEDIPUS: That is the dread that is always in my heart.

MESSENGER: Can you not see that all your fears are groundless?

OEDIPUS: How can you say that? They are my parents, surely? 100

MESSENGER: Polybos was not your father.

OEDIPUS: Not my father?

MESSENGER: No more your father than the man speaking to you.

OEDIPUS: But you are nothing to me!

MESSENGER: Neither was he.

OEDIPUS: Then why did he call me son?

MESSENGER: I will tell you:

Long ago he had you from my hands, as a gift. 105

OEDIPUS: Then how could he love me so, if I was not his?

MESSENGER: He had no children, and his heart turned to you.

OEDIPUS: What of you? Did you buy me? Did you find me by chance?

MESSENGER: I came upon you in the crooked pass of Kithairon.

OEDIPUS: And what were you doing there?

MESSENGER: Tending my flocks. 110

OEDIPUS: A wandering shepherd?

MESSENGER: But your savior, son, that day.

OEDIPUS: From what did you save me?

MESSENGER: Your ankles should tell you that.

OEDIPUS: Ah, stranger, why do you speak of that childhood pain?

MESSENGER: I cut the bonds that tied your ankles together.

OEDIPUS: I have had the mark as long as I can remember. 115

MESSENGER: That was why you were given the name you bear.°

OEDIPUS: God! Was it my father or my mother who did it?

Tell me!

MESSENGER: I do not know. The man who gave you to me

Can tell you better than I.

OEDIPUS: It was not you that found me, but another?

MESSENGER: It was another shepherd gave you to me.

OEDIPUS: Who was he? Can you tell me who he was?

MESSENGER: I think he was said to be one of Laïos' people.

OEDIPUS: You mean the Laïos who was king here years ago? 125

MESSENGER: Yes; King Laïos; and the man was one of his herdsmen.

OEDIPUS: Is he still alive? Can I see him?

MESSENGER: These men here

Know best about such things.

OEDIPUS: Does anyone here

Know this shepherd that he is talking about?

116 name you bear the name "Oedipus" means "swollen-foot"

Have you seen him in the fields, or in the town?   130
If you have, tell me. It is time things were made plain.
CHORAGOS: I think the man he means is that same shepherd
You have already asked to see. Iocastê perhaps
Could tell you something.
OEDIPUS: Do you know anything
About him, Lady? Is he the man we have summoned?   135
Is that the man this shepherd means?
IOCASTÊ: Why think of him?
Forget this herdsman. Forget it all.
This talk is a waste of time.
OEDIPUS: How can you say that,
When the clues to my true birth are in my hands?
IOCASTÊ: For God's love, let us have no more questioning!   140
Is your life nothing to you?
My own is pain enough for me to bear.
OEDIPUS: You need not worry. Suppose my mother a slave,
And born of slaves: no baseness can touch you.
IOCASTÊ: Listen to me, I beg you: do not do this thing!   145
OEDIPUS: I will not listen; the truth must be made known.
IOCASTÊ: Everything that I say is for your own good!
OEDIPUS: My own good
Snaps my patience, then: I want none of it.
IOCASTÊ: You are fatally wrong! May you never learn who you are!
OEDIPUS: Go, one of you, and bring the shepherd here.   150
Let us leave this woman to brag of her royal name.
IOCASTÊ: Ah, miserable!
That is the only word I have for you now.
That is the only word I can ever have.

[Exit into the palace.]

CHORAGOS: Why has she left us, Oedipus? Why has she gone   155
In such a passion of sorrow? I fear this silence:
Something dreadful may come of it.
OEDIPUS: Let it come!
However base my birth, I must know about it.
The Queen, like a woman, is perhaps ashamed
To think of my low origin. But I   160
Am a child of luck; I cannot be dishonored.
Luck is my mother; the passing months, my brothers,
Have seen me rich and poor.
                              If this is so,
How could I wish that I were someone else?
How could I not be glad to know my birth?   165

ODE III

Strophe

CHORUS: If ever the coming time were known
          To my heart's pondering,
          Kithairon, now by Heaven I see the torches
          At the festival of the next full moon,
          And see the dance, and hear the choir sing   5
          A grace to your gentle shade:
          Mountain where Oedipus was found,
          O mountain guard of a noble race!
          May the god who heals us lend his aid,
          And let that glory come to pass   10
          For our king's cradling-ground.

Antistrophe

          Of the nymphs that flower beyond the years.
          Who bore you, royal child,
          To Pan of the hills or the timberline Apollo,
          Cold in delight where the upland clears,   15
          Or Hermês for whom Kyllenê's heights° are piled?
          Or flushed as evening cloud,
          Great Dionysos,° roamer of mountains,
          He—was it he who found you there,
          And caught you up in his own proud   20
          Arms from the sweet god-ravisher
          Who laughed by the Muses'° fountains?

SCENE 4

OEDIPUS: Sirs: though I do not know the man,
           I think I see him coming, this shepherd we want:
           He is old, like our friend here, and the men
           Bringing him seem to be servants of my house.
           But you can tell, if you have ever seen him   5

[Enter SHEPHERD escorted by servants.]

CHORAGOS: I know him, he was Laïos' man. You can trust him.

OEDIPUS: Tell me first, you from Corinth: is this the shepherd
            We were discussing?

16 Kyllenê's heights a holy mountain, the birthplace of Hermes   **18 Dionysos** god of wine and revelry also called Bacchos   **22 the Muses** sisters who inspire poetry and music, arts and sciences

MESSENGER: This is the very man.

OEDIPUS [*to* SHEPHERD]:   Come here. No, look at me. You must answer

    Everything I ask.—You belonged to Laïos?   10

SHEPHERD: Yes: born his slave, brought up in his house.

OEDIPUS: Tell me: what kind of work did you do for him?

SHEPHERD: I was a shepherd of his, most of my life.

OEDIPUS: Where mainly did you go for pasturage?

SHEPHERD: Sometimes Kithairon, sometimes the hills nearby.   15

OEDIPUS: Do you remember ever seeing this man out there?

SHEPHERD: What would he be doing there? This man?

OEDIPUS: This man standing here. Have you ever seen him before?

SHEPHERD: No. At least, not to my recollection.

MESSENGER: And that is not strange, my lord. But I'll refresh   20

    His memory: he must remember when we two

    Spent three whole seasons together, March to September,

    On Kithairon or thereabouts. He had two flocks;

    I had one. Each autumn I'd drive mine home

    And he would go back with his to Laïos' sheepfold.—   25

    Is this not true, just as I have described it?

SHEPHERD: True, yes; but it was all so long ago.

MESSENGER: Well, then: do you remember, back in those days

    That you gave me a baby boy to bring up as my own?

SHEPHERD: What if I did? What are you trying to say?   30

MESSENGER: King Oedipus was once that little child.

SHEPHERD: Damn you, hold your tongue!

OEDIPUS: No more of that!

    It is your tongue needs watching, not this man's.

SHEPHERD: My King, my Master, what is it I have done wrong?

OEDIPUS: You have not answered his question about the boy.   35

SHEPHERD: He does not know . . . He is only making trouble . . .

OEDIPUS: Come, speak plainly, or it will go hard with you.

SHEPHERD: In God's name, do not torture an old man!

OEDIPUS: Come here, one of you; bind his arms behind him.

SHEPHERD: Unhappy king! What more do you wish to learn?   40

OEDIPUS: Did you give this man the child he speaks of?

SHEPHERD: I did.

    And I would to God I had died that very day.

OEDIPUS: You will die now unless you speak the truth.

SHEPHERD: Yet if I speak the truth, I am worse than dead.

OEDIPUS: Very well; since you insist upon delaying—   45

SHEPHERD: No! I have told you already that I gave him the boy.

OEDIPUS: Where did you get him? From your house? From somewhere else?

    From somewhere else?

SHEPHERD: Not from mine, no. A man gave him to me.

OEDIPUS: Is that man here? Do you know whose slave he was?   50

SHEPHERD: For God's love, my King, do not ask me any more!

OEDIPUS: You are a dead man if I have to ask you again.

SHEPHERD: Then . . . Then the child was from the palace of Laïos.

OEDIPUS: A slave child? or a child of his own line?

SHEPHERD: Ah, I am on the brink of dreadful speech!   55

OEDIPUS: And I of dreadful hearing. Yet I must hear.

SHEPHERD: If you must be told, then . . .

                                      They said it was Laïos' child,

    But it is your wife who can tell you about that.

OEDIPUS: My wife!—Did she give it to you?

SHEPHERD: My lord, she did.

OEDIPUS: Do you know why?

SHEPHERD: I was told to get rid of it.   60

OEDIPUS: An unspeakable mother!

SHEPHERD: There had been prophecies . . .

OEDIPUS: Tell me.

SHEPHERD: It was said that the boy would kill his own father.

OEDIPUS: Then why did you give him over to this old man?

SHEPHERD: I pitied the baby, my King,   65

    And I thought that this man would take him far away

    To his own country.

               He saved him—but for what a fate!

    For if you are what this man says you are,

    No man living is more wretched than Oedipus.

OEDIPUS: Ah God!   70

    It was true!

          All the prophecies!

               —Now,

    O light, may I look on you for the last time!

    I, Oedipus,

    Oedipus, damned in his birth, in his marriage damned,

    Damned in the blood he shed with his own hand!   75

[He rushes into the palace.]

ODE IV

Strophe 1

CHORUS: Alas for the seed of men.

    What measure shall I give these generations

    That breathe on the void and are void

And exist and do not exist?

Who bears more weight of joy   5
Than mass of sunlight shifting in images,
Or who shall make his thought stay on
That down time drifts away?
Your splendor is all fallen.

O naked brow of wrath and tears,   10
O change of Oedipus!
I who saw your days call no man blest—
Your great days like ghosts gone.

Antistrophe 1

That mind was a strong bow.
Deep, how deep you drew it then, hard archer,   15
At a dim fearful range,
And brought dear glory down!

You overcame the stranger—
The virgin with her hooking lion claws—
And though death sang, stood like a tower   20
To make pale Thebes take heart.

Fortress against our sorrow!

Divine king, giver of laws,
Majestic Oedipus!
No prince in Thebes had ever such renown,   25
No prince won such grace of power.

Strophe 2

And now of all men ever known
Most pitiful is this man's story:
His fortunes are most changed, his state
Fallen to a low slave's   30
Ground under bitter fate.

O Oedipus, most royal one!
The great door that expelled you to the light
Gave it night—ah, gave night to your glory:
As to the father, to the fathering son.   35

All understood too late.

How could that queen whom Laïos won,
The garden that he harrowed at his height,
Be silent when that act was done?

Antistrophe 2

But all eyes fail before time's eye. 40
All actions come to justice there.
Though never willed, though far down the deep past,
Your bed, your dread sirings,
Are brought to book at last.
Child by Laïos doomed to die, 45
Then doomed to lose that fortunate little death,
Would God you never took breath in this air
That with my wailing lips I take to cry:

For I weep the world's outcast.

I was blind, and now I can tell why: 50
Asleep, for you had given ease of breath
To Thebes, while the false years went by.

EXODOS

[Enter, from the palace, the SECOND MESSENGER.*]*

SECOND MESSENGER: Elders of Thebes, most honored in this land,
What horrors are yours to see and hear, what weight
Of sorrow to be endured, if, true to your birth,
You venerate the line of Labdakos!
I think neither Istros nor Phasis, those great rivers, 5
Could purify this place of the corruption
It shelters now, or soon must bring to light—
Evil not done unconsciously, but willed.

The greatest griefs are those we cause ourselves.
CHORAGOS: Surely, friend, we have grief enough already; 10
What new sorrow do you mean?
SECOND MESSENGER: The Queen is dead.
CHORAGOS: Iocastê? Dead? But at whose hand?
SECOND MESSENGER: Her own.
The full horror of what happened you cannot know,
For you did not see it; but I, who did, will tell you
As clearly as I can how she met her death. 15

When she had left us,
In passionate silence, passing through the court,
She ran to her apartment in the house,
Her hair clutched by the fingers of both hands.
She closed the doors behind her; then, by that bed 20
Where long ago the fatal son was conceived—
That son who should bring about his father's death—

We heard her call upon Laïos, dead so many years,
And heard her wail for the double fruit of her marriage,
A husband by her husband, children by her child.   25

Exactly how she died I do not know:
For Oedipus burst in moaning and would not let us
Keep vigil to the end: it was by him
As he stormed about the room that our eyes were caught.
From one to another of us he went, begging a sword,   30
Cursing the wife who was not his wife, the mother
Whose womb had carried his own children and himself.
I do not know: it was none of us aided him,
But surely one of the gods was in control!
For with a dreadful cry   35
He hurled his weight, as though wrenched out of himself,
At the twin doors: the bolts gave, and he rushed in.
And there we saw her hanging, her body swaying
From the cruel cord she had noosed about her neck.
A great sob broke from him heartbreaking to hear,   40
As he loosed the rope and lowered her to the ground.

I would blot out from my mind what happened next!
For the King ripped from her gown the golden brooches
That were her ornament, and raised them, and plunged them down
Straight into his own eyeballs, crying, "No more,   45
No more shall you look on the misery about me,
The horrors of my own doing! Too long you have known
The faces of those whom I should never have seen,
Too long been blind to those for whom I was searching!
From this hour, go in darkness!" And as he spoke,   50
He struck at his eyes—not once, but many times;
And the blood spattered his beard,
Bursting from his ruined sockets like red hail.

So from the unhappiness of two this evil has sprung,
A curse on the man and woman alike. The old   55
Happiness of the house of Labdakos
Was happiness enough: where is it today?
It is all wailing and ruin, disgrace, death—all
The misery of mankind that has a name—
And it is wholly and for ever theirs.   60
CHORAGOS: Is he in agony still? Is there no rest for him?
SECOND MESSENGER: He is calling for someone to lead him to the gates
    So that all the children of Kadmos may look upon
    His father's murderer, his mother's—no,

I cannot say it!

>   And then he will leave Thebes,   65
Self-exiled, in order that the curse
Which he himself pronounced may depart from the house.
He is weak, and there is none to lead him,
So terrible is his suffering.

>   But you will see:
Look, the doors are opening; in a moment   70
You will see a thing that would crush a heart of stone.

[The central door is opened; OEDIPUS, *blinded, is led in.]*

CHORAGOS: Dreadful indeed for men to see.
> Never have my own eyes
> Looked on a sight so full of fear.

> Oedipus!   75
> What madness came upon you, what daemon
> Leaped on your life with heavier
> Punishment than a mortal man can bear?
> No: I cannot even
> Look at you, poor ruined one.   80
> And I would speak, question, ponder,
> If I were able. No.
> You make me shudder.

OEDIPUS: God. God.
> Is there a sorrow greater?   85
> Where shall I find harbor in this world?
> My voice is hurled far on a dark wind.
> What has God done to me?

Choragos: Too terrible to think of, or to see.

Strophe 1

Oedipus: O cloud of night,   90
> Never to be turned away: night coming on,
> I cannot tell how: night like a shroud!
> My fair winds brought me here.

>   Oh God. Again
> The pain of the spikes where I had sight,
> The flooding pain   95
> Of memory, never to be gouged out.

Choragos: This is not strange.
> You suffer it all twice over, remorse in pain,
> Pain in remorse.

Antistrophe 1

OEDIPUS: Ah dear friend   100
　　　　Are you faithful even yet, you alone?
　　　　Are you still standing near me, will you stay here,
　　　　Patient, to care for the blind?
　　　　　　　　　　The blind man!
　　　　Yet even blind I know who it is attends me,
　　　　By the voice's tone—   105
　　　　Though my new darkness hide the comforter.
CHORAGOS: Oh fearful act!
　　　　What god was it drove you to rake black
　　　　Night across your eyes?

Strophe 2

OEDIPUS: Apollo. Apollo. Dear   110
　　　　Children, the god was Apollo.
　　　　He brought my sick, sick fate upon me.
　　　　But the blinding hand was my own!
　　　　How could I bear to see
　　　　When all my sight was horror everywhere?   115
CHORAGOS: Everywhere; that is true.
OEDIPUS: And now what is left?
　　　　Images? Love? A greeting even,
　　　　Sweet to the senses? Is there anything?
　　　　Ah, no, friends: lead me away   120
　　　　Lead me away from Thebes.
　　　　　　　　　　Lead the great wreck
　　　　And hell of Oedipus, whom the gods hate.
CHORAGOS: Your fate is clear, you are not blind to that.
　　　　Would God you had never found it out!

Antistrophe 2

OEDIPUS: Death take the man who unbound   125
　　　　My feet on that hillside
　　　　And delivered me from death to life! What life?
　　　　If only I had died,
　　　　This weight of monstrous doom
　　　　Could not have dragged me and my darlings down.   130
CHORAGOS: I would have wished the same.
OEDIPUS: Oh never to have come here
　　　　With my father's blood upon me! Never
　　　　To have been the man they call his mother's husband!
　　　　Oh accurst! O child of evil,   135

To have entered that wretched bed—
the selfsame one!
More primal than sin itself, this fell to me.

CHORAGOS: I do not know how I can answer you.
You were better dead than alive and blind.

OEDIPUS: Do not counsel me any more. This punishment   140
That I have laid upon myself is just.
If I had eyes,
I do not know how I could bear the sight
Of my father, when I came to the house of Death,
Or my mother: for I have sinned against them both   145
So vilely that I could not make my peace
By strangling my own life.
Or do you think my children,
Born as they were born, would be sweet to my eyes?
Ah never, never! Nor this town with its high walls,
Nor the holy images of the gods.
For I,   150
Thrice miserable—Oedipus, noblest of all the line
Of Kadmos, have condemned myself to enjoy
These things no more, by my own malediction
Expelling that man whom the gods declared
To be a defilement in the house of Laïos.   155
After exposing the rankness of my own guilt,
How could I look men frankly in the eyes?
No, I swear it,
If I could have stifled my hearing at its source,
I would have done it and made all this body   160
A tight cell of misery, blank to light and sound:
So I should have been safe in a dark agony
Beyond all recollection.
Ah Kithairon!
Why did you shelter me? When I was cast upon you,
Why did I not die? Then I should never   165
Have shown the world my execrable birth.

Ah Polybos! Corinth, city that I believed
The ancient seat of my ancestors: how fair
I seemed, your child! And all the while this evil
Was cancerous within me!
For I am sick   170
In my daily life, sick in my origin.
O three roads, dark ravine, woodland and way
Where three roads met you, drinking my father's blood,

My own blood, spilled by my own hand: can you remember
The unspeakable things I did there, and the things   175
I went on from there to do?

                     O marriage, marriage!
The act that engendered me, and again the act
Performed by the son in the same bed—
Ah, the net
Of incest, mingling fathers, brothers, sons,
With brides, wives, mothers: the last evil   180
That can be known by men: no tongue can say
How evil!

          No. For the love of God, conceal me
Somewhere far from Thebes; or kill me; or hurl me
Into the sea, away from men's eyes for ever.
Come, lead me. You need not fear to touch me.   185
Of all men, I alone can bear this guilt.

[Enter CREON.*]*

CHORAGOS: We are not the ones to decide; but Creon here
    May fitly judge of what you ask. He only
    Is left to protect the city in your place.
OEDIPUS: Alas, how can I speak to him? What right have I   190
    To beg his courtesy whom I have deeply wronged?
CREON: I have not come to mock you, Oedipus,
    Or to reproach you, either.

[To ATTENDANTS.*]*

                     —You, standing there:
    If you have lost all respect for man's dignity,
    At least respect the flame of Lord Helios: 195
    Do not allow this pollution to show itself
    Openly here, an affront to the earth
    And Heaven's rain and the light of day. No, take him
    Into the house as quickly as you can.
    For it is proper   200
    That only the close kindred see his grief.
OEDIPUS: I pray you in God's name, since your courtesy
    Ignores my dark expectation, visiting
    With mercy this man of all men most execrable:
    Give me what I ask—for your good, not for mine.   205
CREON: And what is it that you would have me do?
OEDIPUS: Drive me out of this country as quickly as may be
    To a place where no human voice can ever greet me.
CREON: I should have done that before now—only,

God's will had not been wholly revealed to me.   210

OEDIPUS: But his command is plain: the parricide
Must be destroyed. I am that evil man.

CREON: That is the sense of it, yes; but as things are,
We had best discover clearly what is to be done.

OEDIPUS: You would learn more about a man like me?   215

CREON: You are ready now to listen to the god.

OEDIPUS: I will listen. But it is to you
That I must turn for help. I beg you, hear me.

The woman in there—
Give her whatever funeral you think proper: 220
She is your sister.
                    —But let me go, Creon!
Let me purge my father's Thebes of the pollution
Of my living here, and go out to the wild hills,
To Kithairon, that has won such fame with me,
The tomb my mother and father appointed for me,   225
And let me die there, as they willed I should.
And yet I know
Death will not ever come to me through sickness
Or in any natural way: I have been preserved
For some unthinkable fate. But let that be.   230
As for my sons, you need not care for them.
They are men, they will find some way to live.
But my poor daughters, who have shared my table,
Who never before have been parted from their father—
Take care of them, Creon; do this for me.   235
And will you let me touch them with my hands
A last time, and let us weep together?
Be kind, my lord,
Great prince, be kind!
                    Could I but touch them,
They would be mine again, as when I had my eyes.   240

[Enter ANTIGONÊ *and* ISMENÊ, *attended.]*

Ah, God!
Is it my dearest children I hear weeping?
Has Creon pitied me and sent my daughters?

CREON: Yes, Oedipus: I knew that they were dear to you
In the old days, and know you must love them still.   245

OEDIPUS: May God bless you for this—and be a friendlier
Guardian to you than he has been to me!

Children, where are you?
Come quickly to my hands: they are your brother's—
Hands that have brought your father's once clear eyes   250
To this way of seeing—
                                        Ah dearest ones,
I had neither sight nor knowledge then, your father
By the woman who was the source of his life!
And I weep for you—having no strength to see you—,
I weep for you when I think of the bitterness   255
That men will visit upon you all your lives.
What homes, what festivals can you attend
Without being forced to depart again in tears?
And when you come to marriageable age,
Where is the man, my daughters, who would dare   260
Risk the bane that lies on all my children?
Is there any evil wanting? Your father killed
His father; sowed the womb of her who bore him;
Engendered you at the fount of his own existence!
That is what they will say of you.
                                        Then, whom   265
Can you ever marry? There are no bridegrooms for you,
And your lives must wither away in sterile dreaming.
O Creon, son of Menoikeus!
You are the only father my daughters have,
Since we, their parents, are both of us gone for ever.   270
They are your own blood: you will not let them
Fall into beggary and loneliness;
You will keep them from the miseries that are mine!
Take pity on them; see, they are only children,
Friendless except for you. Promise me this,   275
Great Prince, and give me your hand in token of it.

[CREON clasps his right hand.]

Children:
I could say much, if you could understand me,
But as it is, I have only this prayer for you:
Live where you can, be as happy as you can—   280
Happier, please God, than God has made your father!
CREON: Enough. You have wept enough. Now go within.
OEDIPUS: I must; but it is hard.
CREON: Time eases all things.
OEDIPUS: But you must promise—
CREON: Say what you desire.

OEDIPUS: Send me from Thebes!

CREON: God grant that I may!   285

OEDIPUS: But since God hates me . . .

CREON: No, he will grant your wish.

OEDIPUS: You promise?

CREON: I cannot speak beyond my knowledge.

OEDIPUS: Then lead me in.

CREON: Come now, and leave your children.

OEDIPUS: No! Do not take them from me!

CREON: Think no longer

That you are in command here, but rather think   290

How, when you were, you served your own destruction.

[Exeunt into the house all but the CHORUS; *the* CHORAGOS *chants directly to the audience.]*

CHORAGOS: Men of Thebes: look upon Oedipus.

This is the king who solved the famous riddle

And towered up, most powerful of men.

No mortal eyes but looked on him with envy,   295

Yet in the end ruin swept over him.

Let every man in mankind's frailty

Consider his last day; and let none

Presume on his good fortune until he find

Life, at his death, a memory without pain.   300

MAKING CONNECTIONS

1. Do you believe Oedipus is to blame for what happens to him? Is his fate inescapable? Explain.
2. What is the primary conflict of the play?
3. Oedipus opens the play by initiating a search for whoever has defiled the honor of Thebes. How does his search change as detail after detail comes to light? How does the attitude of the chorus change? Why do you think Iocastê becomes less aggressive about pursuing the truth?
4. Why is Oedipus so nasty to Creon and Teiresias?
5. How is Oedipus behaving at the end of the play? To what extent does he maintain his nobility despite the horror of his earlier predicament?
6. What do the choragus and the chorus bring to the play? Do the choral odes add anything? If so, what?
7. While violence, like Iocastê's suicide and Oedipus's blinding, is reported by messengers, ancient Greek playwrights did not believe it was appropriate to show violence onstage. Do you think this is a good idea? What difference does it make in this play?

⚑MAKING AN ARGUMENT

1. In the light of Aristotle's definition of a tragic hero on page 92, write a comparison of Oedipus, Antigonê, and Creon. Are they all tragic heroes? What is Creon's role in each play? Cite the text of both plays for support.

LUIS VALDEZ [B. 1940]

Playwright and filmmaker Luis Valdez was born in Delano, California, to farm worker parents. In 1964, after graduating from San Jose State University, where he first began writing and directing plays, Valdez joined the United Farm Workers Union, staging improvisations and short scenes meant to educate union members, who were mostly migrant workers, about labor issues. These experiences resulted in his founding of the El Teatro Campesino,
a theater company devoted to exploring aspects of the Chicano experience. The company, which over the years has earned an enviable reputation in the theater world, has remained Valdez's artistic home throughout his career. In addition to his work in the theater, Valdez has written and directed a number of films, most notably La Bamba *(1987), the story of the Chicano pop musician Ritchie Valens.* Los Vendidos, *one of his first efforts at playwriting, was written in 1967. The title can be translated as "The Sellouts."*

LOS VENDIDOS   [1967]

CHARACTERS
HONEST SANCHO
SECRETARY
FARM WORKER
JOHNNY
REVOLUCIONARIO
MEXICAN-AMERICAN

SCENE: *Honest Sancho's Used Mexican Lot and Mexican Curio Shop. Three models are on display in Honest Sancho's shop: to the right, there is a Revolucionario, complete with sombrero, carrilleras and curabina. At center, on the floor, there is the Farm Worker, under a broad straw sombrero. At stage left is the Pachuco, filero in hand. Honest Sancho is moving among his models, dusting them off and preparing for another day of business.*

SANCHO: *Bueno, bueno, mis monos, vamos a ver a quien vendemos ahora, ¿no?*
               [*to audience*] *¡Quihubo!* I'm Honest Sancho and this is my shop. *Antes fui contratista pero ahora logré tener mi negocito.* All I need now is a customer. [*A bell rings offstage.*] Ay, a customer!
SECRETARY [*entering*]:   Good morning, I'm Miss Jiménez from—

SANCHO: *¡Ah, una chicana!* Welcome, welcome *Señorita* Jiménez.

SECRETARY [*Anglo pronunciation*]:   JIM-enez.

SANCHO: *¿Qué?*

SECRETARY: My name is Miss JIM-enez. Don't you speak English? What's wrong with you?

SANCHO: Oh, nothing, Señorita JIM-enez. I'm here to help you.

SECRETARY: That's better. As I was starting to say, I'm a secretary from Governor Reagan's office, and we're looking for a Mexican type for the administration.

SANCHO: Well, you come to the right place, lady. This is Honest Sancho's Used Mexican Lot, and we got all types here. Any particular type you want?

SECRETARY: Yes, we were looking for somebody suave—

SANCHO: Suave.

SECRETARY: Debonair.

SANCHO: *De buen aire.*

SECRETARY: Dark.

SANCHO: *Prieto.*

SECRETARY: But of course not too dark.

SANCHO: *No muy prieto.*

SECRETARY: Perhaps, beige.

SANCHO: Beige, just the tone. *Así como cafecito con leche, ¿no?*

SECRETARY: One more thing. He must be hardworking.

SANCHO: That could only be one model. Step right over here to the center of the shop, lady. [*They cross to the* FARM WORKER.] This is our standard farm worker model. As you can see, in the words of our beloved Senator George Murphy, he is "built close to the ground." Also take special notice of his four-ply Goodyear *huaraches,* made from the rain tire. This wide-brimmed sombrero is an extra added feature—keeps off the sun, rain, and dust.

SECRETARY: Yes, it does look durable.

SANCHO: And our farm worker model is friendly. *Muy amable.* Watch. [*snaps his fingers*]

FARM WORKER [*lifts up head*]:   *Buenos días, señorita.* [*His head drops.*]

SECRETARY: My, he's friendly.

SANCHO: Didn't I tell you? Loves his *patrones!* But his most attractive feature is that he's hard working. Let me show you. [*Snaps fingers.* FARM WORKER *stands.*]

FARM WORKER: *¡El jale!* [*He begins to work.*]

SANCHO: As you can see, he is cutting grapes.

SECRETARY: Oh, I wouldn't know.

SANCHO: He also picks cotton. [*Snap.* FARM WORKER *begins to pick cotton.*]

SECRETARY: Versatile isn't he?

SANCHO: He also picks melons. [*Snap.* FARM WORKER *picks melons.*] That's his slow speed for late in the season. Here's his fast speed. [*Snap.* FARM WORKER *picks faster.*]

SECRETARY: *¡Chihuahua!* . . . I mean, goodness, he sure is a hard worker.

SANCHO [*pulls the* FARM WORKER *to his feet*]:   And that isn't the half of it. Do you see these little holes on his arms that appear to be pores? During those hot sluggish days in the field, when the vines or the branches get so entangled, it's almost impossible to move; these holes emit a certain grease that allow our model to slip and slide right through the crop with no trouble at all.

SECRETARY: Wonderful. But is he economical?

SANCHO: Economical? *Señorita,* you are looking at the Volkswagen of Mexicans. Pennies a day is all it takes. One plate of beans and tortillas will keep him going all day. That, and chile. Plenty of chile. *Chile jalapeños, chile verde, chile colorado.* But, of course, if you do give him chile [*Snap.* FARM WORKER *turns left face. Snap.* FARM WORKER *bends over.*] then you have to change his oil filter once a week.

SECRETARY: What about storage?

SANCHO: No problem. You know these new farm labor camps our Honorable Governor Reagan has built out by Parlier or Raisin City? They were designed with our model in mind. Five, six, seven, even ten in one of those shacks will give you no trouble at all. You can also put him in old barns, old cars, river banks. You can even leave him out in the field overnight with no worry!

SECRETARY: Remarkable.

SANCHO: And here's an added feature: Every year at the end of the season, this model goes back to Mexico and doesn't return, automatically, until next spring.

SECRETARY: How about that. But tell me: does he speak English?

SANCHO: Another outstanding feature is that last year this model was programmed to go out on STRIKE! [*Snap.*]

FARM WORKER: *¡HUELGA! ¡HUELGA! Hermanos, sálganse de esos files.* [*Snap. He stops.*]

SECRETARY: No! Oh no, we can't strike in the state capitol.

SANCHO: Well, he also scabs. [*Snap.*]

FARM WORKER: *Me vendo barato, ¿y qué?* [*Snap.*]

SECRETARY: That's much better, but you didn't answer my question. Does he speak English?

Sancho: *Bueno . . . no, pero* he has other—

Secretary: No.

Sancho: Other features.

Secretary: NO! He just won't do!

Sancho: Okay, okay *pues.* We have other models.

Secretary: I hope so. What we need is something a little more sophisticated.

Sancho: Sophisti—*¿qué?*

Secretary: An urban model.

Sancho: Ah, from the city! Step right back. Over here in this corner of the shop is exactly what you're looking for. Introducing our new 1969 JOHNNY PACHUCO model! This is our fast-back model. Streamlined. Built for speed, low-riding, city life. Take a look at some of these features. Mag shoes, dual exhausts, green chartreuse paint-job, dark-tint windshield, a little poof on top. Let me just turn him on. [*Snap*. JOHNNY *walks to stage center with a pachuco bounce.*]

SECRETARY: What was that?

SANCHO: That, *señorita,* was the Chicano shuffle.

SECRETARY: Okay, what does he do?

SANCHO: Anything and everything necessary for city life. For instance, survival: He knife fights. [*Snap*. JOHNNY *pulls out switchblade and swings at* SECRETARY.]

*[*SECRETARY *screams.]*

SANCHO: He dances. [*Snap.*]

JOHNNY [*singing*]:   "Angel Baby, my Angel Baby . . . " [*Snap.*]

SANCHO: And here's a feature no city model can be without. He gets arrested, but not without resisting, of course. [*Snap.*]

JOHNNY: ¡En la madre, la placa! I didn't do it! I didn't do it! [JOHNNY *turns and stands up against an imaginary wall, legs spread out, arms behind his back.*]

SECRETARY: Oh no, we can't have arrests! We must maintain law and order.

SANCHO: But he's bilingual!

SECRETARY: Bilingual?

SANCHO: *Simón que yes.* He speaks English! Johnny, give us some English. [*Snap.*]

JOHNNY [*comes downstage*]:   Fuck you!

SECRETARY [*gasps*]:   Oh! I've never been so insulted in my whole life!

SANCHO: Well, he learned it in your school.

SECRETARY: I don't care where he learned it.

SANCHO: But he's economical!

SECRETARY: Economical?

SANCHO: Nickels and dimes. You can keep Johnny running on hamburgers, Taco Bell tacos, Lucky Lager beer, Thunderbird wine, *yesca—*

SECRETARY: *Yesca?*

SANCHO: *Mota.*

SECRETARY: *Mota?*

SANCHO: *Leños . . . Marijuana.* [*Snap;* JOHNNY *inhales on an imaginary joint.*]

SECRETARY: That's against the law!

JOHNNY [*big smile, holding his breath*]:   Yeah.

SANCHO: He also sniffs glue. [*Snap.* JOHNNY *inhales glue, big smile.*]

JOHNNY: That's too much man, *ése.*

SECRETARY: No, Mr. Sancho, I don't think this—

SANCHO: Wait a minute, he has other qualities I know you'll love. For example, an inferiority complex. [*Snap.*]

JOHNNY [*to* SANCHO]:   You think you're better than me, huh *ése?* [*swings switchblade.*]

SANCHO: He can also be beaten and he bruises, cut him and he bleeds; kick him and he—[*He beats, bruises and kicks* PACHUCO.] would you like to try it?

SECRETARY: Oh, I couldn't.

SANCHO: Be my guest. He's a great scapegoat.

SECRETARY: No, really.

SANCHO: Please.

SECRETARY: Well, all right. Just once. [*She kicks* PACHUCO.] Oh, he's so soft.

SANCHO: Wasn't that good? Try again.

SECRETARY [*kicks* PACHUCO]:   Oh, he's so wonderful! [*She kicks him again.*]

SANCHO: Okay, that's enough, lady. You ruin the merchandise. Yes, our Johnny Pachuco model can give you many hours of pleasure. Why, the L.A.P.D. just bought twenty of these to train their rookie cops on. And talk about maintenance. Señorita, you are looking at an entirely self-supporting machine. You're never going to find our Johnny Pachuco model on the relief rolls. No, sir, this model knows how to liberate.

SECRETARY: Liberate?

SANCHO: He steals. [*Snap.* JOHNNY *rushes the* SECRETARY *and steals her purse.*]

JOHNNY: *¡Dame esa bolsa, vieja!* [*He grabs the purse and runs. Snap by* SANCHO *: He stops.*]

[SECRETARY *runs after* JOHNNY *and grabs purse away from him, kicking him as she goes.*]

SECRETARY: No, no, no! We can't have any *more* thieves in the state administration. Put him back.

SANCHO: Okay, we still got other models. Come on, Johnny, we'll sell you to some old lady.

[SANCHO *takes* JOHNNY *back to his place.*]

SECRETARY: Mr. Sancho, I don't think you quite understand what we need. What we need is something that will attract the women voters. Something more traditional, more romantic.

SANCHO: Ah, a lover. [*He smiles meaningfully.*] Step right over here, *señorita.* Introducing our standard Revolucionario and/or Early California Bandit type. As you can see he is well built, sturdy, durable. This is the International Harvester of Mexicans.

SECRETARY: What does he do?

SANCHO: You name it, he does it. He rides horses, stays in the mountains, crosses deserts, plains, rivers, leads revolutions, follows revolutions, kills, can be killed, serves as a martyr, hero, movie star—did I say movie star? Did you ever see *Viva Zapata? Viva Villa? Villa Rides? Pancho Villa Returns? Pancho Villa Goes Back? Pancho Villa Meets Abbott and Costello—*

SECRETARY: I've never seen any of those.

SANCHO: Well, he was in all of them. Listen to this. [*Snap.*]

REVOLUCIONARIO [*scream*]:   *¡VIVA VILLAAAAA!*

SECRETARY: That's awfully loud.

SANCHO: He has a volume control. [*He adjusts volume. Snap.*]

REVOLUCIONARIO [*mousey voice*]:   *¡Viva Villa!*

SECRETARY: That's better.

SANCHO: And even if you didn't see him in the movies, perhaps you saw him on TV. He makes commercials. [*Snap.*]

REVOLUCIONARIO: Is there a Frito Bandito in your house?

SECRETARY: Oh yes, I've seen that one!

SANCHO: Another feature about this one is that he is economical. He runs on raw horsemeat and tequila!

SECRETARY: Isn't that rather savage?

SANCHO: *Al contrario,* it makes him a lover. [*Snap.*]

REVOLUCIONARIO [*to* SECRETARY]:   *¡Ay, mamasota, cochota, ven pa'ca!* [*He grabs* SECRETARY *and folds her back—Latin-lover style.*]

SANCHO [*Snap.* REVOLUCIONARIO *goes back upright.*]:   Now wasn't that nice?

SECRETARY: Well, it was rather nice.

SANCHO: And finally, there is one outstanding feature about this model I KNOW the ladies are going to love: He's a GENUINE antique! He was made in Mexico in 1910!

SECRETARY: Made in Mexico?

SANCHO: That's right. Once in Tijuana, twice in Guadalajara, three times in Cuernavaca.

SECRETARY: Mr. Sancho, I thought he was an American product.

SANCHO: No, but—

SECRETARY: No, I'm sorry. We can't buy anything but American-made products. He just won't do.

SANCHO: But he's an antique!

SECRETARY: I don't care. You still don't understand what we need. It's true we need Mexican models such as these, but it's more important that he be *American.*

SANCHO: American?

SECRETARY: That's right, and judging from what you've shown me, I don't think you have what we want. Well, my lunch hour's almost over, I better—

SANCHO: Wait a minute! Mexican but American?

SECRETARY: That's correct.

SANCHO: Mexican but . . . [*a sudden flash.*] AMERICAN! Yeah, I think we've got exactly what you want. He just came in today! Give me a minute. [*He exits. Talks from backstage.*] Here he is in the shop. Let me just get some papers off. There. Introducing our new 1970 Mexican-American! Ta-ra-ra-ra-ra-ra-RA-RAAA!

[SANCHO *brings out the* MEXICAN-AMERICAN *model, a clean-shaven middle-class type in a business suit, with glasses.*]

SECRETARY [*impressed*]:   Where have you been hiding this one?

SANCHO: He just came in this morning. Ain't he a beauty? Feast your eyes on him! Sturdy US STEEL frame, streamlined, modern. As a matter of fact, he is built exactly like our Anglo models except that he comes in a variety of darker shades: naugahyde, leather, or leatherette.

SECRETARY: Naugahyde.

SANCHO: Well, we'll just write that down. Yes, *señorita,* this model represents the
apex of American engineering! He is bilingual, college educated, ambitious!
Say the word "acculturate" and he accelerates. He is intelligent, well-man-
nered, clean—did I say clean? [*Snap.* MEXICAN-AMERICAN *raises his arm.*] Smell.

SECRETARY [*smells*]:   Old Sobaco, my favorite.

SANCHO [*Snap.* MEXICAN-AMERICAN *turns toward* SANCHO]:   Eric! [*to* SECRETARY] We call
him Eric García. [*to* ERIC] I want you to meet Miss JIM-enez, Eric.

MEXICAN-AMERICAN: Miss JIM-enez, I am delighted to make your acquaintance. [*He
kisses her hand.*]

SECRETARY: Oh, my, how charming!

SANCHO: Did you feel the suction? He has seven especially engineered suction
cups right behind his lips. He's a charmer all right!

SECRETARY: How about boards? Does he function on boards?

SANCHO: You name them, he is on them. Parole boards, draft boards, school boards,
taco quality control boards, surf boards, two-by-fours.

SECRETARY: Does he function in politics?

SANCHO: *Señorita,* you are looking at a political MACHINE. Have you ever heard of
the OEO, EOC, COD, WAR ON POVERTY? That's our model! Not only that, he
makes political speeches.

SECRETARY: May I hear one?

SANCHO: With pleasure. [*Snap.*] Eric, give us a speech.

MEXICAN-AMERICAN: Mr. Congressman, Mr. Chairman, members of the board, honored
guests, ladies and gentlemen. [SANCHO *and* SECRETARY *applaud.*] Please, please.
I come before you as a Mexican-American to tell you about the problems of the
Mexican. The problems of the Mexican stem from one thing and one thing
alone: He's stupid. He's uneducated. He needs to stay in school. He needs to be
ambitious, forward-looking, harder-working. He needs to think American,
American, American, AMERICAN, AMERICAN, AMERICAN. GOD BLESS AMER-
ICA! GOD BLESS AMERICA! GOD BLESS AMERICA!! [*He goes out of control.*]

[SANCHO *snaps frantically and the* MEXICAN-AMERICAN *finally slumps forward, bending at the waist.*]

SECRETARY: Oh my, he's patriotic too!

SANCHO: *Sí, señorita,* he loves his country. Let me just make a little adjustment here.
[*Stands* MEXICAN-AMERICAN *up.*]

SECRETARY: What about upkeep? Is he economical?

SANCHO: Well, no, I won't lie to you. The Mexican-American costs a little bit more,
but you get what you pay for. He's worth every extra cent. You can keep him
running on dry Martinis, Langendorf bread.

SECRETARY: Apple pie?

SANCHO: Only Mom's. Of course, he's also programmed to eat Mexican food on ceremonial functions, but I must warn you an overdose of beans will plug up his
exhaust.

SECRETARY: Fine! There's just one more question: HOW MUCH DO YOU WANT FOR HIM?

SANCHO: Well, I tell you what I'm gonna do. Today and today only, because you've been so sweet, I'm gonna let you steal this model from me! I'm gonna let you drive him off the lot for the simple price of—let's see taxes and license included—$15,000.

SECRETARY: Fifteen thousand DOLLARS? For a MEXICAN!

SANCHO: Mexican? What are you talking, lady? This is a Mexican-AMERICAN! We had to melt down two *pachucos,* a farm worker and three *gabachos* to make this model! You want quality, but you gotta pay for it! This is no cheap run-about. He's got class!

SECRETARY: Okay, I'll take him.

SANCHO: You will?

SECRETARY: Here's your money.

SANCHO: You mind if I count it?

SECRETARY: Go right ahead.

SANCHO: Well, you'll get your pink slip in the mail. Oh, do you want me to wrap him up for you? We have a box in the back.

SECRETARY: No, thank you. The governor is having a luncheon this afternoon, and we need a brown face in the crowd. How do I drive him?

SANCHO: Just snap your fingers. He'll do anything you want.

[SECRETARY snaps. MEXICAN-AMERICAN steps forward.]

MEXICAN-AMERICAN: *RAZA QUERIDA, ¡VAMOS LEVANTANDO ARMAS PARA LIBERANOS DE ESTOS DESGRACIADOS GABACHOS QUE NOS EXPLOTAN¡ VAMOS.*

SECRETARY: What did he say?

SANCHO: Something about lifting arms, killing white people, etc.

SECRETARY: But he's not supposed to say that!

SANCHO: Look, lady, don't blame me for bugs from the factory. He's your Mexican-American; you bought him, now drive him off the lot!

SECRETARY: But he's broken!

SANCHO: Try snapping another finger.

[SECRETARY snaps. MEXICAN-AMERICAN comes to life again.]

MEXICAN-AMERICAN: ¡ESTA GRAN HUMANIDAD HA DICHO BASTA! ¡Y SE HA PUESTO EN MARCHA! ¡BASTA! ¡BASTA! ¡VIVA LA RAZA! ¡VIVA LA CAUSA! ¡VIVA LA HUELGA! ¡VIVAN LOS BROWN BERETS! ¡VIVAN LOS ESTUDIANTES! ¡CHICANO POWER!

[The MEXICAN-AMERICAN turns toward the SECRETARY, who gasps and backs up. He keeps turning toward the PACHUCO, FARM WORKER, and REVOLUCIONARIO, snapping his fingers and turning each of them on, one by one.]

PACHUCO [*Snap. To* SECRETARY]:   I'm going to get you, baby! *¡Viva La Raza!*

FARM WORKER [*Snap. To* SECRETARY]:   *¡Viva la huelga! ¡Viva la Huelga! ¡VIVA LA HUELGA!*

REVOLUCIONARIO [*Snap. To* SECRETARY]:   *¡Viva la revolución! ¡VIVA LA REVOLUCIÓN!*

[*The three models join together and advance toward the* SECRETARY, *who backs up and runs out of the shop screaming.* SANCHO *is at the other end of the shop holding his money in his hand. All freeze. After a few seconds of silence, the Pachuco moves and stretches, shaking his arms and loosening up. The* FARM WORKER *and* REVOLUCIONARIO *do the same.* SANCHO *stays where he is, frozen to his spot.*]

JOHNNY: Man, that was a long one, *ése.* [*Others agree with him.*]

FARM WORKER: How did we do?

JOHNNY: Perty good, look at all that *lana,* man! [*He goes over to* SANCHO *and removes the money from his hand.* SANCHO *stays where he is.*]

REVOLUCIONARIO: *En la madre,* look at all the money.

JOHNNY: We keep this up, we're going to be rich.

FARM WORKER: They think we're machines.

REVOLUCIONARIO: *Burros.*

JOHNNY: Puppets.

MEXICAN-AMERICAN: The only thing I don't like is—how come I always got to play the goddamn Mexican-American?

JOHNNY: That's what you get for finishing high school.

FARM WORKER: How about our wages, *ése?*

JOHNNY: Here it comes right now. Three-thousand dollars for you, three-thousand dollars for you, three-thousand dollars for you, and three-thousand dollars for me. The rest we put back into the business.

MEXICAN-AMERICAN: Too much, man. Heh, where you *vatos* going tonight?

FARM WORKER: I'm going over to Concha's. There's a party.

JOHNNY: Wait a minute, *vatos.* What about our salesman? I think he needs an oil job.

REVOLUCIONARIO: Leave him to me.

[*The* PACHUCO, FARM WORKER, *and* MEXICAN-AMERICAN *exit, talking loudly about their plans for the night. The* REVOLUCIONARIO *goes over to* SANCHO, *removes his derby hat and cigar, lifts him up and throws him over his shoulder.* SANCHO *hangs loose, lifeless.*]

REVOLUCIONARIO [*to audience*]:   He's the best model we got! *¡Ajua!* [*Exit.*]

MAKING CONNECTIONS

1. How would you characterize this play? Is it surrealistic? Political? A parable? Does it have a moral? If so, what is it?

2. What do you think is the significance of the different ways Sancho and the Secretary pronounce "Jimenez"? What do we learn about the Secretary through her pronunciation of her name?

3. How are the Farm Worker, Johnny, and the Revolucionario different? Why does the Secretary reject each?

4. What happens at the end of the play? Why are the four "models" ultimately more real than Sancho?

MAKING AN ARGUMENT

1. Immigrants in our culture are treated differently than the rest of society. Or
   are they? Take a position on this statement and write about the ways that
   this play reveals the problem—or not. Cite the text of the play and other
   sources for support.

◆ ESSAYS ◆

CONNECTING THROUGH COMPARISON: WORK AND IDENTITY

The two pieces that follow address a subtheme of this section: work and identity.
Read and discussed together, they invite comparisons and connections—not only
with each other—but with your own sense of work and your own identity.

RICHARD RODRIGUEZ [B. 1944]

*Richard Rodriguez was born in San Francisco, the son of
Mexican immigrants. He received a Ph.D. in English
Renaissance Literature from the University of California
at Berkeley. His essays have appeared in a variety of pub-
lications, and he has published several books, including*
Hunger of Memory *(1981),* The Ethics of Change *(1992),*
Days of Obligation *(1993), and his latest,* Brown: The Last
Discovery of America *(2003). He is a contributing editor to*

Harper's Magazine *and* U.S. News and World Report, *and a lecturer, freelance
writer, educational consultant, and frequent contributor to the* Lehrer News Hour
on public television. He lives in San Francisco.

WORKERS   [1982]

It was at Stanford, one day near the end of my senior year, that a friend told me about
a summer construction job he knew was available. I was quickly alert. Desire
uncoiled within me. My friend said that he knew I had been looking for summer
employment. He knew I needed some money. Almost apologetically he explained:
It was something I probably wouldn't be interested in, but a friend of his, a contractor, needed someone for the summer to do menial jobs. There would be lots of
shoveling and raking and sweeping. Nothing too hard. But nothing more interesting
either. Still, the pay would be good. Did I want it? Or did I know someone who did?

I did. Yes, I said, surprised to hear myself say it.

In the weeks following, friends cautioned that I had no idea how hard physical
labor really is. ("You only *think* you know what it is like to shovel for eight hours
straight.") Their objections seemed to me challenges. They resolved the issue. I
became happy with my plan. I decided, however, not to tell my parents. I wouldn't

tell my mother because I could guess her worried reaction. I would tell my father only after the summer was over, when I could announce that, after all, I did know what "real work" is like.

The day I met the contractor (a Princeton graduate, it turned out), he asked me whether I had done any physical labor before. "In high school, during the summer," I lied. And although he seemed to regard me with skepticism, he decided to give me a try. Several days later, expectant, I arrived at my first construction site. I would take off my shirt to the sun. And at last grasp desired sensation. No longer afraid. At last become like a *bracero*.[1] "We need those tree stumps out of here by tomorrow," the contractor said. I started to work.

5   I labored with excitement that first morning   and all the days after. The work was harder than I could have expected. But it was never as tedious as my friends had warned me it would be. There was too much physical pleasure in the labor. Especially early in the day, I would be most alert to the sensations of movement and straining. Beginning around seven each morning (when the air was still damp but the scent of weeds and dry earth anticipated the heat of the sun), I would feel my body resist the first thrusts of the shovel. My arms, tightened by sleep, would gradually loosen; after only several minutes, sweat would gather in beads on my forehead and then—a short while later—I would feel my chest silky with sweat in the breeze. I would return to my work. A nervous spark of pain would fly up my arm and settle to burn like an ember in the thick of my shoulder. An hour, two passed. Three. My whole body would assume regular movements; my shoveling would be described by identical, even movements. Even later in the day, my enthusiasm for primitive sensation would survive the heat and the dust and the insects pricking my back. I would strain wildly for sensation as the day came to a close. At three-thirty, quitting time, I would stand upright and slowly let my head fall back, luxuriating in the feeling of tightness relieved.

Some of the men working nearby would watch me and laugh. Two or three of the older men took the trouble to teach me the right way to use a pick, the correct way to shovel. "You're doing it wrong, too fucking hard," one man scolded. Then proceeded to show me—what persons who work with their bodies all their lives quickly learn—the most economical way to use one's body in labor.

"Don't make your back do so much work," he instructed. I stood impatiently listening, half listening, vaguely watching, then noticed his work-thickened fingers clutching the shovel. I was annoyed. I wanted to tell him that I enjoyed shoveling the wrong way. And I didn't want to learn the right way. I wasn't afraid of back pain. I liked the way my body felt sore at the end of the day.

I was about to, but, as it turned out, I didn't say a thing. Rather it was at that moment I realized that I was fooling myself if I expected a few weeks of labor to gain me admission to the world of the laborer. I would not learn in three months what my father had meant by "real work." I was not bound to this job; I could imagine its rapid conclusion. For me the sensations of exertion and fatigue could be savored. For my father or uncle, working at comparable jobs when they were my age, such sensations were to be feared. Fatigue took a different toll on their bodies—and minds.

[1]**bracero** laborer

It was, I know, a simple insight. But it was with this realization that I took my first step that summer toward realizing something even more important about the "worker." In the company of carpenters, electricians, plumbers, and painters at lunch, I would often sit quietly, observant. I was not shy in such company. I felt easy, pleased by the knowledge that I was casually accepted, my presence taken for granted by men (exotics) who worked with their hands. Some days the younger men would talk and talk about sex, and they would howl at women who drove by in cars. Other days the talk at lunchtime was subdued; men gathered in separate groups. It depended on who was around. There were rough, good-natured workers. Others were quiet. The more I remember that summer, the more I realize that there was no single *type* of worker. I am embarrassed to say I had not expected such diversity. I certainly had not expected to meet, for example, a plumber who was an abstract painter in his off hours and admired the work of Mark Rothko. Nor did I expect to meet so many workers with college diplomas. (They were the ones who were not surprised that I intended to enter graduate school in the fall.) I suppose what I really want to say here is painfully obvious, but I must say it nevertheless: The men of that summer were middle-class Americans. They certainly didn't constitute an oppressed society. Carefully completing their work sheets; talking about the fortunes of local football teams; planning Las Vegas vacations; comparing the gas mileage of various makes of campers—they were not *los pobres*[2] my mother had spoken about.

10   On two occasions, the contractor hired a group of Mexican aliens. They were employed to cut down some trees and haul off debris. In all, there were six men of varying age. The youngest in his late twenties; the oldest (his father?) perhaps sixty years old. They came and they left in a single old truck. Anonymous men. They were never introduced to the other men at the site. Immediately upon their arrival, they would follow the contractor's directions, start working—rarely resting—seemingly driven by a fatalistic sense that work which had to be done was best done as quickly as possible.

I watched them sometimes. Perhaps they watched me. The only time I saw them pay me much notice was one day at lunchtime when I was laughing with the other men. The Mexicans sat apart when they ate, just as they worked by themselves. Quiet. I rarely heard them say much to each other. All I could hear were their voices calling out sharply to one another, giving directions. Otherwise, when they stood briefly resting, they talked among themselves in voices too hard to overhear.

The contractor knew enough Spanish, and the Mexicans—or at least the oldest of them, their spokesman—seemed to know enough English to communicate. But because I was around, the contractor decided one day to make me his translator. (He assumed I could speak Spanish.) I did what I was told. Shyly I went over to tell the Mexicans that the *patrón*[3] wanted them to do something else before they left for the day. As I started to speak, I was afraid with my old fear that I would be unable to pronounce the Spanish words. But it was a simple instruction I had to convey. I could say it in phrases.

The dark sweating faces turned toward me as I spoke. They stopped their work to hear me. Each nodded in response. I stood there. I wanted to say something

[2]**los pobres** the poor   [3]**patrón** boss

more. But what could I say in Spanish, even if I could have pronounced the words right? Perhaps I just wanted to engage them in small talk, to be assured of their confidence, our familiarity. I thought for a moment to ask them where in Mexico they were from. Something like that. And maybe I wanted to tell them (a lie, if need be) that my parents were from the same part of Mexico.

I stood there.

15   Their faces watched me. The eyes of the man directly in front of me moved slowly over my shoulder, and I turned to follow his glance toward *el patrón* some distance away. For a moment I felt swept up by that glance into the Mexicans' company. But then I heard one of them returning to work. And then the others went back to work. I left them without saying anything more.

When they had finished, the contractor went over to pay them in cash. (He later told me that he paid them collectively—"for the job," though he wouldn't tell me their wages. He said something quickly about the good rate of exchange "in their own country.") I can still hear the loudly confident voice he used with the Mexicans. It was the sound of the *gringo*[4] I had heard as a very young boy. And I can still hear the quiet, indistinct sounds of the Mexican, the oldest, who replied. At hearing that voice I was sad for the Mexicans. Depressed by their vulnerability. Angry at myself. The adventure of the summer seemed suddenly ludicrous. I would not shorten the distance I felt from *los pobres* with a few weeks of physical labor. I would not become like them. They were different from me. . . .

That summer I worked in the sun may have made me physically indistinguishable from the Mexicans working nearby. (My skin was actually darker because, unlike them, I worked without wearing a shirt. By late August my hands were probably as tough as theirs.) But I was not one of *los pobres*. What made me different from them was an attitude of *mind,* my imagination of myself. . . .

In the end, my father was right—though perhaps he did not know how right or why—to say that I would never know what real work is. I will never know what he felt at his last factory job. If tomorrow I worked at some kind of factory, it would go differently for me. My long education would favor me. I could act as a public person—able to defend my interests, to unionize, to petition, to speak up—to challenge and demand. (I will never know what real work is.) I will never know what the Mexicans knew, gathering their shovels and ladders and saws.

Their silence stays with me now. The wages those Mexicans received for their labor were only a measure of their disadvantaged condition. Their silence is more telling. They lack a public identity. They remain profoundly alien. Persons apart. People lacking a union obviously, people without grounds. They depend upon the relative good will or fairness of their employers each day. For such people, lacking a better alternative, it is not such an unreasonable risk.

20   Their silence stays with me. I have taken these many words to describe its impact. Only: the quiet. Something uncanny about it. Its compliance. Vulnerability. Pathos. As I heard their truck rumbling away, I shuddered, my face mirrored with sweat. I had finally come face to face with *los pobres.*

[4]**gringo** Yankee

MARGE PIERCY [B. 1936]

Born in Detroit, Michigan, to a working-class family, Marge Piercy attended the University of Michigan (B.A., 1957) and Northwestern University (M.A., 1958). Piercy began writing poems as a result of her involvement in the antiwar movement of the 1960s. In 1969, in reaction to what she considered the misogyny of many activists, she changed her focus to the growing women's movement. She has published many volumes of poetry, beginning with Breaking Camp *in 1968, and many novels.* City of Darkness, City of Light: A Novel *appeared in 1996, and her latest novel,* Sex Wars, *was published in 2005. Much of her work is political, and she has expressed a desire for her writing to be "useful." She has written: "To find ourselves spoken for in art gives dignity to our pain, our anger, our lust, our losses. We can hear what we hope for and what we most fear in the small release of cadenced utterance."*

TO BE OF USE   [1973]

The people I love the best
jump into work head first
without dallying in the shallows
and swim off with sure strokes almost out of sight.
They seem to become natives of that element,   5
the black sleek heads of seals
bouncing like half-submerged balls.

I love people who harness themselves, an ox to a heavy cart,
who pull like water buffalo, with massive patience,
who strain in the mud and the muck to move things forward,   10
who do what has to be done, again and again.

I want to be with people who submerge
in the task, who go into the fields to harvest
and work in a row and pass the bags along,
who are not parlor generals and field deserters   15
but move in common rhythm
when the food must come in or the fire be put out.

The work of the world is common as mud,
Botched, it smears the hands, crumbles to dust.
But the thing worth doing well done   20
has a shape that satisfies, clean and evident.
Greek amphoras for wine or oil,
Hopi vases that held corn, are put in museums
but you know they were made to be used.
The pitcher cries for water to carry   25
and a person for work that is real.

MAKING CONNECTIONS

1. What is the tone of the Rodriguez essay? Do you think the narrator sees himself as better than the workers he describes? Explain.
2. What does the writer mean by "Their objections seemed to me challenges"?
3. To what extent have you experienced hard, physical labor? Does your experience of it match the writer's? Could you say, "I liked the way my body felt sore at the end of the day"? Explain.
4. The writer says, "I would not learn in three months what my father had meant by 'real work.'" Explain.
5. With reference to the Mexican workers, the writer says, "What made me different from them was an attitude of *mind*, my imagination of myself . . . ." What does he mean?
6. In what way has the author/narrator "grown" from the experience he describes here? What do you think he wants us to understand from his essay?
7. Do you agree with the premise of Piercy's poem—that it's important "to be of use"? Why?
8. The speaker says that Greek amphoras and Hopi vases "are put in museums / but you know they were made to be used." What does she mean?

MAKING AN ARGUMENT

1. How important is usefulness in our culture? We live in a culture where people often identify themselves by what they do for a living. But how do we get our identities from our work? Both Rodriguez and Piercy address this issue, but seem to approach it from different directions. Write a comparison of "Workers" and "To Be of Use" and how each addresses the issue of identity and work. Cite the text of both for support.

JOAN DIDION [B. 1934]

Joan Didion was born in Sacramento, California, and attended the University of California at Berkeley, graduating in 1956. She began her writing career as a promotional copywriter at Vogue *magazine, eventually becoming an associate feature editor. Following the publication of her first novel,* Run River, *in 1963, she moved to California and earned her living as a freelance reporter. In 1968, she collected her work in* Slouching Towards Bethlehem, *which, with its unsentimental tone and precise prose, became a commercial and critical success. She has since written numerous essays, novels, and screenplays, and her latest book,* The Year of Magical Thinking *(2005), which won the National Book*

Award, is a deeply moving memoir about her husband's death and its impact on her. When asked about her relatively low output as a writer, Didion responded that she constantly revises and hones her writing: "I'm not much interested in spontaneity, what concerns me is total control."

WHY I WRITE   [1976]

Of course I stole the title for this talk, from George Orwell.[1] One reason I stole it was that I like the sound of the words: Why I Write. There you have three short unambiguous words that share a sound, and the sound they share is this:

 I

 I

 I

In many ways writing is the act of saying *I,* of imposing oneself upon other people, of saying *listen to me, see it my way, change your mind.* It's an aggressive, even a hostile act. You can disguise its aggressiveness all you want with veils of subordinate clauses and qualifiers and tentative subjunctives, with ellipses and evasions—with the whole manner of intimating rather than claiming, of alluding rather than stating—but there's no getting around the fact that setting words on paper is the tactic of a secret bully, an invasion, an imposition of the writer's sensibility on the reader's most private space.

I stole the title not only because the words sounded right but because they seemed to sum up, in a no-nonsense way, all I have to tell you. Like many writers I have only this one "subject," this one "area": the act of writing. I can bring you no reports from any other front. I may have other interests: I am "interested," for example, in marine biology, but I don't flatter myself that you would come out to hear me talk about it. I am not a scholar. I am not in the least an intellectual, which is not to say that when I hear the word "intellectual" I reach for my gun, but only to say that I do not think in abstracts. During the years when I was an undergraduate at Berkeley I tried, with a kind of hopeless late-adolescent energy, to buy some temporary visa into the world of ideas, to forge for myself a mind that could deal with the abstract.

In short I tried to think. I failed. My attention veered inexorably back to the specific, to the tangible, to what was generally considered, by everyone I knew then and for that matter have known since, the peripheral. I would try to contemplate the Hegelian dialectic[2] and would find myself concentrating instead on a flowering pear tree outside my window and the particular way the petals fell on my floor. I would try to read linguistic theory and would find myself wondering instead if the lights were on in the bevatron up the hill. When I say that I was wondering if the lights were on in the bevatron you might immediately suspect, if you deal in ideas at all, that I was registering the bevatron as a political symbol, thinking in shorthand about the military-industrial complex and its role in the university community, but you would be wrong. I was only wondering if the lights were on in the bevatron, and how they looked. A physical fact.

---

[1]**George Orwell** (1903–1950) a prominent British writer   [2]**Hegelian dialectic** trying to find the truth by synthesizing an idea with its opposite

5   I had trouble graduating from Berkeley, not because of this inability to deal with ideas—I was majoring in English, and I could locate the house-and-garden imagery in *The Portrait of a Lady*[3] as well as the next person, "imagery" being by definition the kind of specific that got my attention—but simply because I had neglected to take a course in Milton[4]. For reasons which now sound baroque I needed a degree by the end of that summer, and the English department finally agreed, if I would come down from Sacramento every Friday and talk about the cosmology of *Paradise Lost*, to certify me proficient in Milton. I did this. Some Fridays I took the Greyhound bus, other Fridays I caught the Southern Pacific's City of San Francisco on the last leg of its transcontinental trip. I can no longer tell you whether Milton put the sun or the earth at the center of his universe in *Paradise Lost*, the central question of at least one century and a topic about which I wrote 10,000 words that summer, but I can still recall the exact rancidity of the butter in the City of San Francisco's dining car, and the way the tinted windows on the Greyhound bus cast the oil refineries around Carquinez Straits into a grayed and obscurely sinister light. In short my attention was always on the periphery, on what I would see and taste and touch, on the butter, and the Greyhound bus. During those years I was traveling on what I knew to be a very shaky passport, forged papers: I knew that I was no legitimate resident in any world of ideas. I knew I couldn't think. All I knew then was what I couldn't do. All I knew then was what I wasn't, and it took me some years to discover what I was.

Which was a writer.

By which I mean not a "good" writer or a "bad" writer but simply a writer, a person whose most absorbed and passionate hours are spent arranging words on pieces of paper. Had my credentials been in order I would never have become a writer. Had I been blessed with even limited access to my own mind there would have been no reason to write. I write entirely to find out what I'm thinking, what I'm looking at, what I see and what it means. What I want and what I fear. Why did the oil refineries around Carquinez Straits seem sinister to me in the summer of 1956? Why have the night lights in the bevatron burned in my mind for twenty years? *What is going on in these pictures in my mind?*

When I talk about pictures in my mind I am talking, quite specifically, about images that shimmer around the edges. There used to be an illustration in every elementary psychology book showing a cat drawn by a patient in varying stages of schizophrenia. This cat had a shimmer around it. You could see the molecular structure breaking down at the very edges of the cat: the cat became the background and the background the cat, everything interacting, exchanging ions. People on hallucinogens describe the same perception of objects. I'm not a schizophrenic, nor do I take hallucinogens, but certain images do shimmer for me. Look hard enough, and you can't miss the shimmer. It's there. You can't think too much about these pictures that shimmer. You just lie low and let them develop. You stay quiet. You don't talk to many people and you keep your nervous system from shorting out and you try to locate the cat in the shimmer, the grammar in the picture.

---

[3]*The Portrait of a Lady* a late-nineteenth-century novel by Henry James   [4]**Milton** a seventeenth-century English poet

Just as I meant "shimmer" literally I mean "grammar" literally. Grammar is a piano I play by ear, since I seem to have been out of school the year the rules were mentioned. All I know about grammar is its infinite power. To shift the structure of a sentence alters the meaning of that sentence, as definitely and inflexibly as the position of a camera alters the meaning of the object photographed. Many people know about camera angles now, but not so many know about sentences. The arrangement of the words matters, and the arrangement you want can be found in the picture in your mind. The picture dictates the arrangement. The picture dictates whether this will be a sentence with or without clauses, a sentence that ends hard or a dying-fall sentence, long or short, active or passive. The picture tells you how to arrange the words and the arrangement of the words tells you, or tells me, what's going on in the picture. *Nota bene:*[5]

10   It tells you.

You don't tell it.

Let me show you what I mean by pictures in the mind. I began *Play It as It Lays* just as I have begun each of my novels, with no notion of "character" or "plot" or even "incident." I had only two pictures in my mind, more about which later, and a technical intention, which was to write a novel so elliptical and fast that it would be over before you noticed it, a novel so fast that it would scarcely exist on the page at all. About the pictures: the first was of white space. Empty space. This was clearly the picture that dictated the narrative intention of the book—a book in which anything that happened would happen off the page, a "white" book to which the reader would have to bring his or her own bad dreams—and yet this picture told me no "story," suggested no situation. The second picture did. This second picture was of something actually witnessed. A young woman with long hair and a short white halter dress walks through the casino at the Riviera in Las Vegas at one in the morning. She crosses the casino alone and picks up a house telephone. I watch her because I have heard her paged, and recognize her name: she is a minor actress I see around Los Angeles from time to time, in places like Jax and once in a gynecologist's office in the Beverly Hills Clinic, but have never met. I know nothing about her. Who is paging her? Why is she here to be paged? How exactly did she come to this? It was precisely this moment in Las Vegas that made *Play It as It Lays* begin to tell itself to me, but the moment appears in the novel only obliquely, in a chapter which begins:

"Maria made a list of things she would never do. She would never: walk through the Sands or Caesar's alone after midnight. She would never: ball at a party, do S-M unless she wanted to, borrow furs from Abe Lipsey, deal. She would never: carry a Yorkshire in Beverly Hills."

That is the beginning of the chapter and that is also the end of the chapter, which may suggest what I meant by "white space."

15   I recall having a number of pictures in my mind when I began the novel I just finished, *A Book of Common Prayer.* As a matter of fact one of these pictures was of that bevatron I mentioned, although I would be hard put to tell you a story in which nuclear energy figured. Another was a newspaper photograph of a hijacked

[5]*Nota bene* Latin for "note well"

707 burning on the desert in the Middle East. Another was the night view from a room in which I once spent a week with paratyphoid, a hotel room on the Colombian coast. My husband and I seemed to be on the Colombian coast representing the United States of America at a film festival (I recall invoking the name "Jack Valenti"[6] a lot, as if its reiteration could make me well), and it was a bad place to have fever, not only because my indisposition offended our hosts but because every night in this hotel the generator failed. The lights went out. The elevator stopped. My husband would go to the event of the evening and make excuses for me and I would stay alone in this hotel room, in the dark. I remember standing at the window trying to call Bogotá (the telephone seemed to work on the same principle as the generator) and watching the night wind come up and wondering what I was doing eleven degrees off the equator with a fever of 103. The view from that window definitely figures in *A Book of Common Prayer,* as does the burning 707, and yet none of these pictures told me the story I needed.

The picture that did, the picture that shimmered and made these other images coalesce, was the Panama airport at 6 A.M. I was in this airport only once, on a plane to Bogotá that stopped for an hour to refuel, but the way it looked that morning remained superimposed on everything I saw until the day I finished *A Book of Common Prayer.* I lived in that airport for several years. I can still feel the hot air when I step off the plane, can see the heat already rising off the tarmac at 6 A.M. I can feel my skirt damp and wrinkled on my legs. I can feel the asphalt stick to my sandals. I remember the big tail of a Pan American plane floating motionless down at the end of the tarmac. I remember the sound of a slot machine in the waiting room. I could tell you that I remember a particular woman in the airport, an American woman, a *norteamericana,* a thin *norteamericana* about 40 who wore a big square emerald in lieu of a wedding ring, but there was no such woman there.

I put this woman in the airport later. I made this woman up, just as I later made up a country to put the airport in, and a family to run the country. This woman in the airport is neither catching a plane nor meeting one. She is ordering tea in the airport coffee shop. In fact she is not simply "ordering" tea but insisting that the water be boiled, in front of her, for twenty minutes. Why is this woman in this airport? Why is she going nowhere, where has she been? Where did she get that big emerald? What derangement, or disassociation, makes her believe that her will to see the water boiled can possibly prevail?

"She had been going to one airport or another for four months, one could see it, looking at the visas on her passport. All those airports where Charlotte Douglas's passport had been stamped would have looked alike. Sometimes the sign on the tower would say 'Bienvenidos' and sometimes the sign on the tower would say 'Bienvenue,' some places were wet and hot and others dry and hot, but at each of these airports the pastel concrete walls would rust and stain and the swamp off the runway would be littered with the fuselages of cannibalized Fairchild F-227's and the water would need boiling.

"I knew why Charlotte went to the airport even if Victor did not."

20   "I knew about airports."

These lines appear about halfway through *A Book of Common Prayer,* but I wrote them during the second week I worked on the book, long before I had any idea where Charlotte Douglas had been or why she went to airports. Until I wrote these lines I had no character called "Victor" in mind: the necessity for mentioning a name, and the name "Victor," occurred to me as I wrote the sentence. *I knew why Charlotte went to the airport* sounded incomplete. *I knew why Charlotte went to the airport even if Victor did not* carried a little more narrative drive. Most important of all, until I wrote these lines I did not know who "I" was, who was telling the story. I had intended until that moment that the "I" be no more than the voice of the author, a nineteenth-century omniscient narrator. But there it was:

"I knew why Charlotte went to the airport even if Victor did not."

"I knew about airports."

This "I" was the voice of no author in my house. This "I" was someone who not only knew why Charlotte went to the airport but also knew someone called "Victor." Who was Victor? Who was this narrator? Why was this narrator telling me this story? Let me tell you one thing about why writers write: had I known the answer to any of these questions I would never have needed to write a novel.

MAKING CONNECTIONS

1. In your own words, answer the central question of this essay: Why does Joan Didion write?
2. Do any of the revelations made in this essay surprise you? What, for example, do you think of Didion's saying she writes, in part, because she is not an abstract thinker?
3. Do you agree that writing is in itself necessarily a selfish act? Why or why not?

MAKING AN ARGUMENT

1. Didion describes not only "why" she writes but "how." She has said of her process: "I'm not much interested in spontaneity, what concerns me is total control." In the light of her statement about control, describe the structure of this essay and some of the techniques she uses—and write about their effectiveness. Cite the text of the essay for support.

FREDERICK DOUGLASS [1818-1895]

Frederick Douglass was born a slave on a plantation in Maryland. His father was probably a white overseer. After being separated from his mother at the age of eight, Douglass worked first in the household of a wealthy family, and then as a field hand, where he suffered brutal beatings. In 1838, when he was twenty-one, Douglass escaped to the North. Fearful because of his fugitive slave status, Douglass nevertheless attracted public notice after

*delivering a powerful antislavery speech at an abolitionist convention in
Nantucket, and he was subsequently asked to become a full-time speaker on
behalf of the Massachusetts Anti-Slavery Society. In 1845, he published his harrowing and inspiring* Narrative of the Life of Frederick Douglass, an American
Slave, *which he later revised and titled the* Life and Times of Frederick Douglass.
*The book made him famous, and consequently, more at risk. He moved to
England, where he lectured extensively, eventually earning enough money to
buy his freedom and return to the United States. A tireless advocate for the rights
of African-Americans and women, he spent the rest of life in the public eye, holding a number of governmental and political positions and publishing his own
newspaper,* The North Star.

LEARNING TO READ AND WRITE   [1845]

I lived in Master Hugh's family about seven years. During this time, I succeeded in
learning to read and write. In accomplishing this, I was compelled to resort to various stratagems. I had no regular teacher. My mistress, who had kindly commenced to
instruct me, had, in compliance with the advice and direction of her husband, not
only ceased to instruct, but had set her face against my being instructed by any one
else. It is due, however, to my mistress to say of her, that she did not adopt this course
of treatment immediately. She at first lacked the depravity indispensable to shutting
me up in mental darkness. It was at least necessary for her to have some training in
the exercise of irresponsible power, to make her equal to the task of treating me as
though I were a brute.

My mistress was, as I have said, a kind and tender-hearted woman; and in the
simplicity of her soul she commenced, when I first went to live with her, to treat me
as she supposed one human being ought to treat another. In entering upon the
duties of a slaveholder, she did not seem to perceive that I sustained to her the relation of a mere chattel, and that for her to treat me as a human being was not only
wrong, but dangerously so. Slavery proved as injurious to her as it did to me. When
I went there, she was a pious, warm, and tender-hearted woman. There was no
sorrow or suffering for which she had not a tear. She had bread for the hungry,
clothes for the naked, and comfort for every mourner that came within her reach.
Slavery soon proved its ability to divest her of these heavenly qualities. Under its
influence, the tender heart became stone, and the lamblike disposition gave way to
one of tiger-like fierceness. The first step in her downward course was in her ceasing to instruct me. She now commenced to practice her husband's precepts. She
finally became even more violent in her opposition than her husband himself. She
was not satisfied with simply doing as well as he had commanded; she seemed anxious to do better. Nothing seemed to make her more angry than to see me with a
newspaper. She seemed to think that here lay the danger. I have had her rush at me
with a face made all up of fury, and snatch from me a newspaper, in a manner that
fully revealed her apprehension. She was an apt woman; and a little experience soon
demonstrated, to her satisfaction, that education and slavery were incompatible
with each other.

From this time I was most narrowly watched. If I was in a separate room any
considerable length of time, I was sure to be suspected of having a book, and was at

once called to give an account of myself. All this, however, was too late. The first step had been taken. Mistress, in teaching me the alphabet, had given me the *inch,* and no precaution could prevent me from taking the *ell.*

The plan which I adopted, and the one by which I was most successful, was that of making friends of all the little white boys whom I met in the street. As many of these as I could, I converted into teachers. With their kindly aid, obtained at different times and in different places, I finally succeeded in learning to read. When I was sent on errands, I always took my book with me, and by going one part of my errand quickly, I found time to get a lesson before my return. I used also to carry bread with me, enough of which was always in the house, and to which I was always welcome; for I was much better off in this regard than many of the poor white children in our neighborhood. This bread I used to bestow upon the hungry little urchins, who, in return, would give me that more valuable bread of knowledge. I am strongly tempted to give the names of two or three of those little boys, as a testimonial of the gratitude and affection I bear them; but prudence forbids; not that it would injure me, but it might embarrass them; for it is almost an unpardonable offence to teach slaves to read in this Christian country. It is enough to say of the dear little fellows, that they lived on Philpot Street, very near Durgin and Bailey's ship-yard. I used to talk this matter of slavery over with them. I would sometimes say to them, I wished I could be as free as they would be when they got to be men. "You will be free as soon as you are twenty-one, *but I am a slave for life!* Have not I as good a right to be free as you have?" These words used to trouble them; they would express for me the liveliest sympathy, and console me with the hope that something would occur by which I might be free.

5   I was now about twelve years old, and the thought of being *a slave for life* began to bear heavily upon my heart. Just about this time, I got hold of a book entitled "The Columbian Orator." Every opportunity I got, I used to read this book. Among much of other interesting matter, I found in it a dialogue between a master and his slave. The slave was represented as having run away from his master three times. The dialogue represented the conversation which took place between them, when the slave was retaken the third time. In this dialogue, the whole argument in behalf of slavery was brought forward by the master, all of which was disposed of by the slave. The slave was made to say some very smart as well as impressive things in reply to his master—things which had the desired though unexpected effect; for the conversation resulted in the voluntary emancipation of the slave on the part of the master.

In the same book, I met with one of Sheridan's mighty speeches on and in behalf of Catholic emancipation. These were choice documents to me. I read them over and over again with unabated interest. They gave tongue to interesting thoughts of my own soul, which had frequently flashed through my mind, and died away for want of utterance. The moral which I gained from the dialogue was the power of truth over the conscience of even a slaveholder. What I got from Sheridan was a bold denunciation of slavery, and a powerful vindication of human rights. The reading of these documents enabled me to utter my thoughts, and to meet the arguments brought forward to sustain slavery; but while they relieved me of one difficulty, they brought on another even more painful than the one of which I was relieved. The more I read, the more I was led to abhor and detest my enslavers. I could regard them in no other light than a band of successful robbers, who had left their homes, and gone to Africa, and stolen us from our homes, and in a strange land reduced us to slavery. I loathed them as being the meanest as well as the most wicked of men. As I read and contemplated the subject, behold! that very discontentment which Master Hugh had predicted would follow my learning to read had already come, to torment and sting my soul to unutterable anguish. As I writhed under it, I would at times feel that learning to read had been a curse rather than a blessing. It had given me a view of my wretched condition, without the remedy. It opened my eyes to the horrible pit, but to no ladder upon which to get out. In moments of agony, I envied my fellow-slaves for their stupidity. I have often wished myself a beast. I preferred the condition of the meanest reptile to my own. Any thing, no matter what, to get rid of thinking! It was this everlasting thinking of my condition that tormented me. There was no getting rid of it. It was pressed upon me by every object within sight or hearing, animate or inanimate. The silver trump of freedom had roused my soul to eternal wakefulness. Freedom now appeared, to disappear no more forever. It was heard in every sound, and seen in every thing. It was ever present to torment me with a sense of my wretched condition. I saw nothing without seeing it, I heard nothing without hearing it, and felt nothing without feeling it. It looked from every star, it smiled in every calm, breathed in every wind, and moved in every storm.

I often found myself regretting my own existence, and wishing myself dead; and but for the hope of being free, I have no doubt but that I should have killed myself, or done something for which I should have been killed. While in this state of mind, I was eager to hear any one speak of slavery. I was a ready listener. Every little while, I could hear something about the abolitionists. It was some time before I found what the word meant. It was always used in such connections as to make it an interesting word to me. If a slave ran away and succeeded in getting clear, or if a slave killed his master, set fire to a barn, or did any thing very wrong in the mind of a slaveholder, it was spoken of as the fruit of *abolition.* Hearing the word in this connection very often, I set about learning what it meant. The dictionary afforded me little or no help. I found it was "the act of abolishing"; but then I did not know what was to be abolished. Here I was perplexed. I did not dare to ask any one about its meaning, for I was satisfied that it was something they wanted me to know very little about. After a patient waiting, I got one of our city papers, containing an account of the number of petitions from the north, praying for the abolition of slavery in the District of Columbia, and of the slave trade between the States. From this time I understood the words *abolition* and *abolitionist,* and always drew near when that word was spoken, expecting to hear something of importance to myself and fellow-slaves. The light broke in upon me by degrees. I went one day down on the wharf of Mr. Waters; and seeing two Irishmen unloading a scow of stone, I went, unasked, and helped them. When we had finished, one of them came to me and asked me if I were a slave. I told him I was. He asked, "Are ye a slave for life?" I told him that I was. The good Irishman seemed to be deeply affected by the statement. He said to the other that it was a pity so fine a little fellow as myself should be a slave for life. He said it was a shame to hold me. They both advised me to run away to the north; that I should find friends there, and that I should be free. I pretended not to be interested in what they said, and treated them as if I did not understand them; for I feared they might be treacherous. White men have been known to encourage slaves to escape, and then, to get the reward, catch them and return them to their mas ters. I was afraid that these seemingly good men might use me so; but I nevertheless remembered their advice, and from that time I resolved to run away. I looked forward to a time at which it would be safe for me to escape. I was too young to think of doing so immediately; besides, I wished to learn how to write, as I might have occasion to write my own pass. I consoled myself with the hope that I should one day find a good chance. Meanwhile, I would learn to write.

The idea as to how I might learn to write was suggested to me by being in Durgin and Bailey's ship-yard, and frequently seeing the ship carpenters, after hewing, and getting a piece of timber ready to use, write on the timber the name of that part of the ship for which it was intended. When a piece of timber was intended for the larboard side, it would be marked thus—"L." When a piece was for the starboard side, it would be marked thus—"S." A piece for the larboard side forward, would be marked thus—"L. F." When a piece was for starboard side forward, it would be marked thus—"S. F." For larboard aft, it would be marked thus—"L. A." For starboard aft, it would be marked thus—"S. A." I soon learned the names of these letters, and for what they were intended when placed upon a piece of timber in the ship-yard. I immediately commenced copying them, and in a short time was able to make the four letters named. After that, when I met with any boy who I knew could write, I would tell him I could write as well as he. The next word would be, "I don't believe you. Let me see you try it." I would then make the letters which I had been so fortunate as to learn, and ask him to beat that. In this way I got a good many lessons in writing, which it is quite possible I should never have gotten in any other way. During this time, my copy-book was the board fence, brick wall, and pavement; my pen and ink was a lump of chalk. With these, I learned mainly how to write. I then commenced and continued copying the Italics in Webster's Spelling Book, until I could make them all without looking on the book. By this time, my little Master Thomas had gone to school, and learned how to write, and had written over a number of copy-books. These had been brought home, and shown to some of our near neighbors, and then laid aside. My mistress used to go to class meeting at the Wilk Street meetinghouse every Monday afternoon, and leave me to take care of the house. When left thus, I used to spend the time in writing in the spaces left in Master Thomas's copy-book, copying what he had written. I continued to do this until I could write a hand very similar to that of Master Thomas. Thus, after a long, tedious effort for years, I finally succeeded in learning how to write.

MAKING CONNECTIONS

1. Imagine yourself in Frederick Douglass's position as a slave. Would you run away as he did or would you accept your plight? Explain. Imagine yourself as a person who was in a position to help a runaway slave. How would you respond?

2. Why does Master Hugh's wife change her mind about helping Douglass to read and write?

3. What similarities does Douglass find between his own situation and the struggle for Catholic emancipation in Ireland? What does he learn from *The Columbian Orator?*

4. In what way is Douglass's learning to read and write a powerful statement against the evil of slavery?

MAKING AN ARGUMENT

1. Of all the things he could be taught, why is reading and writing the most important skill for Douglass to learn? Write about the importance of reading and writing for him as well as for anyone who wants to be successful in contemporary society. Cite the text of the essay for support.

MARTIN LUTHER KING, JR. [1929-1968]

Martin Luther King, Jr., was born in Atlanta, Georgia. His father was a minister, and his mother, a teacher. He received a B.A. from Morehouse College in 1951, a Ph.D. from Boston University in 1955, and a D.D. from the Chicago Theological Seminary in 1957. King embraced the teachings of Indian leader Mahatma Gandhi, who preached nonviolence as a route to social reform. In 1955 and 1956, applying Gandhi's teaching, King became a national celebrity after organizing a successful boycott of Montgomery, Alabama's, segregated bus system. In the following years, King moved to the forefront of the movement to dismantle all forms of desegregation in the United States, organizing the march on Washington in 1963 and challenging the voting laws in Selma, Alabama, in 1965. In 1964, he became the youngest man ever to win the Nobel Peace Prize. During his lifetime his publications included Stride Toward Freedom: The Montgomery Story *(1958),* Why We Can't Wait *(1964), and his famous open letter in which he defended his nonviolent philosophy,* Letter from Birmingham City Jail *(1963), written while he was imprisoned for organizing protests. King was assassinated on April 4, 1968. "I Have a Dream" was delivered on August 28, 1963, to an audience of over 250,000 who had gathered at the Lincoln Memorial as part of the march on Washington.*

I HAVE A DREAM [1963]

Five score years ago, a great American, in whose symbolic shadow we stand, signed the Emancipation Proclamation. This momentous decree came as a great beacon light of hope to millions of Negro slaves who had been seared in the flames of withering injustice. It came as a joyous daybreak to end the long night of captivity.

But one hundred years later, we must face the tragic fact that the Negro is still not free. One hundred years later, the life of the Negro is still sadly crippled by the manacles of segregation and the chains of discrimination. One hundred years later, the Negro lives on a lonely island of poverty in the midst of a vast ocean of material prosperity. One hundred years later, the Negro is still languishing in the corners of

American society and finds himself an exile in his own land. So we have come here today to dramatize an appalling condition.

In a sense we have come to our nation's Capitol to cash a check. When the architects of our republic wrote the magnificent words of the Constitution and the Declaration of Independence, they were signing a promissory note to which every American was to fall heir. This note was a promise that all men would be guaranteed the unalienable rights of life, liberty, and the pursuit of happiness.

It is obvious today that America has defaulted on this promissory note insofar as her citizens of color are concerned. Instead of honoring this sacred obligation, America has given the Negro people a bad check; a check which has come back marked "insufficient funds." But we refuse to believe that the bank of justice is bankrupt. We refuse to believe that there are insufficient funds in the great vaults of opportunity of this nation. So we have come to cash this check—a check that will give us upon demand the riches of freedom and the security of justice. We have also come to this hallowed spot to remind America of the fierce urgency of *now*. This is no time to engage in the luxury of cooling off or to take the tranquilizing drug of gradualism. *Now* is the time to make real the promises of Democracy. *Now* is the time to rise from the dark and desolate valley of segregation to the sunlit path of racial justice. *Now* is the time to open the doors of opportunity to all of God's children. *Now* is the time to lift our nation from the quicksands of racial injustice to the solid rock of brotherhood.

5   It would be fatal for the nation to overlook the urgency of the moment and to underestimate the determination of the Negro. This sweltering summer of the Negro's legitimate discontent will not pass until there is an invigorating autumn of freedom and equality. 1963 is not an end, but a beginning. Those who hope that the Negro needed to blow off steam and will now be content will have a rude awakening if the nation returns to business as usual. There will be neither rest nor tranquility in America until the Negro is granted his citizenship rights. The whirlwinds of revolt will continue to shake the foundations of our nation until the bright day of justice emerges.

But there is something I must say to my people who stand on the warm threshold which leads into the palace of justice. In the process of gaining our rightful place we must not be guilty of wrongful deeds. Let us not seek to satisfy our thirst for freedom by drinking from the cup of bitterness and hatred. We must forever conduct our struggle on the high plane of dignity and discipline. We must not allow our creative protest to degenerate into physical violence. Again and again we must rise to the majestic heights of meeting physical force with soul force. The marvelous new militancy which has engulfed the Negro community must not lead us to a distrust of all white people, for many of our white brothers, as evidenced by their presence here today, have come to realize that their destiny is tied up with our destiny and their freedom is inextricably bound to our freedom. We cannot walk alone.

And as we walk, we must make the pledge that we shall march ahead. We cannot turn back. There are those who are asking the devotees of civil rights, "When will you be satisfied?" We can never be satisfied as long as the Negro is the victim of the unspeakable horrors of police brutality. We can never be satisfied as long as our bodies, heavy with the fatigue of travel, cannot gain lodging in the motels of the highways and the hotels of the cities. We cannot be satisfied as long as the Negro's basic mobility is from a smaller ghetto to a larger one. We can never be satisfied as long as a Negro in Mississippi cannot vote and a Negro in New York believes he has nothing for which to vote. No, no, we are not satisfied, and we will not be satisfied until justice rolls down like waters and righteousness like a mighty stream.

I am not unmindful that some of you have come here out of great trials and tribulations. Some of you have come fresh from narrow jail cells. Some of you have come from areas where your quest for freedom left you battered by the storms of persecution and staggered by the winds of policy brutality. You have been the veterans of creative suffering. Continue to work with the faith that unearned suffering is redemptive.

Go back to Mississippi, go back to Alabama, go back to South Carolina, go back to Georgia, go back to Louisiana, go back to the slums and ghettoes of our northern cities, knowing that somehow this situation can and will be changed. Let us not wallow in the valley of despair.

10   I say to you today, my friends, that in spite of the difficulties and frustrations of the moment I still have a dream. It is a dream deeply rooted in the American dream.

I have a dream that one day this nation will rise up and live out the true meaning of its creed: "We hold these truths to be self-evident; that all men are created equal."

I have a dream that one day on the red hills of Georgia the sons of former slaves and the sons of former slaveowners will be able to sit down together at the table of brotherhood.

I have a dream that the state of Mississippi, a desert state sweltering with the heat of injustice and oppression, will be transformed into an oasis of freedom and justice.

I have a dream that my four little children will one day live in a nation where they will not be judged by the color of their skin but by the content of their character.

15   I have a dream today.

I have a dream that the state of Alabama, whose governor's lips are presently dripping with the words of interposition and nullification, will be transformed into a situation where little black boys and black girls will be able to join hands with little white boys and white girls and walk together as sisters and brothers.

I have a dream today.

I have a dream that one day every valley shall be exalted, every hill and mountain shall be made low, the rough places will be made plain, and the crooked places will be made straight, and the glory of the Lord shall be revealed, and all flesh shall see it together.

This is our hope. This is the faith with which I return to the South. With this faith we will be able to hew out of the mountain of despair a stone of hope. With this faith we will be able to transform the jangling discords of our nation into a beautiful symphony of brotherhood. With this faith we will be able to work together, to pray together, to struggle together, to go to jail together, to stand up for freedom together, knowing that we will be free one day.

20   This will be the day when all of God's children will be able to sing with new meaning.

> My country, tis of thee
> Sweet land of liberty,
>   Of thee I sing:
> Land where my fathers died,
> Land of the pilgrims' pride,
> From every mountainside
>   Let freedom ring.

And if America is to be a great nation this must become true. So let freedom ring from the prodigious hilltops of New Hampshire. Let freedom ring from the mighty mountains of New York. Let freedom ring from the heightening Alleghenies of Pennsylvania!

Let freedom ring from the snowcapped Rockies of Colorado!

Let freedom ring from the curvaceous peaks of California!

But not only that; let freedom ring from Stone Mountain of Georgia!

25   Let freedom ring from Lookout Mountain of Tennessee!

Let freedom ring from every hill and molehill of Mississippi. From every mountainside, let freedom ring.

When we let freedom ring, when we let it ring from every village and every hamlet, from every state and every city, we will be able to speed up that day when all of God's children, black men and white men, Jews and Gentiles, Protestants and Catholics, will be able to join hands and sing in the words of the old Negro spiritual, "Free at last! Free at last! Thank God almighty, we are free at last!"

MAKING CONNECTIONS

1. What is the dream of Martin Luther King, Jr.?
2. He says his dream is derived from the "American Dream." What is the American Dream?
3. What does he mean by "This will be the day when all of God's children will be able to sing with new meaning 'My country, tis of thee / Sweet land of liberty'"?
4. What is the tone of this essay? Who is the intended audience? What is its objective?

MAKING AN ARGUMENT

1. This is both an inspirational speech and an effective essay. Analyze the style, structure, and use of figurative language—especially the imagery—in the essay and write about its effectiveness. Cite the text of the essay for support.

CHARLES FRUEHLING SPRINGWOOD AND C. RICHARD KING

Charles Fruehling Springwood is an Assistant Professor of Anthropology at Illinois Wesleyan University. C. Richard King is an Assistant Professor of Anthropology at Drake University They are coeditors of Team Spirits: The Native American Mascots Controversy *(2001) and coauthors of* Beyond the Cheers: Race as Spectacle in College Sport *(2001).*

'PLAYING INDIAN': WHY NATIVE AMERICAN MASCOTS MUST END [2001]

American Indian icons have long been controversial, but 80 colleges still use them, according to the National Coalition on Racism in Sports and Media. Recently, the struggles over such mascots have intensified, as fans and foes across the country have become increasingly outspoken.

At the University of Illinois at Urbana-Champaign, for example, more than 800 faculty members have signed a petition against retaining Chief Illiniwek as the university's mascot. Students at Indiana University of Pennsylvania have criticized the athletics teams' name, the Indians. The University of North Dakota has experienced rising hostilities on campus against its Fighting Sioux. Meanwhile, other students, faculty members, and administrators have vehemently defended those mascots.

Why, nearly 30 years after Dartmouth College and Stanford University retired their American Indian mascots, do similar mascots persist at many other institutions? And why do they evoke such passionate allegiance and strident criticism?

American Indian mascots are important as symbols because they are intimately linked to deeply embedded values and world-views. To supporters, they honor indigenous people, embody institutional tradition, foster shared identity, and intensify the pleasures of college athletics. To those who oppose them, however, the mascots give life to racial stereotypes as well as revivify historical patterns of appropriation and oppression. They often foster discomfort, pain, and even terror among many American Indian people.

5　　A 1999 flier, distributed at the University of Illinois at Urbana-Champaign, graphically depicts the multilayered and value laden images that American Indian mascots evoke. Beneath the masthead, a white gunslinger gazes at the viewer knowingly while pointing a drawn pistol at an Indian dancer in full regalia. A caption in large letters spells out the meaning of the scene: "Manifest Destiny: Go! Fight! Win!" Although arguably extreme, this flier, when placed alongside what occurs at college athletic events—fans dressing in paint and feathers, halftime mascot dances, crowds cheering "the Sioux suck"—reminds us that race relations, power, and violence are inescapable aspects of mascots.

We began to study these mascots while we were graduate students in anthropology at the University of Illinois in the early 1990s. American Indian students and their allies were endeavoring to retire Chief Illiniwek back then, as well, and the campus was the scene of intense debates. Witnessing such events inspired us to move beyond the competing arguments and try to understand the social forces and historical conditions that give life to American Indian mascots—as well as to the passionate support of, and opposition to, them. We wanted to understand the origins of mascots; how and why they have changed over time; how arguments about mascots fit into a broader racial context; and what they might tell us about the changing shape of society.

Over the past decade, we have developed case studies on the role that mascots have played at the halftime ceremonies of the University of Illinois, Marquette University, Florida State University, and various other higher-education institutions. Recently, we published an anthology, *Team Spirits: The Native American Mascots Controversy,* in which both American Indian and European American academics explored "Indian-ness," "whiteness," and American Indian activism. They also suggested strategies for change—in a variety of contexts that included Syracuse University and Central Michigan University, the Los Angeles public schools, and the Washington Redskins. Our scholarship and that of others have confirmed our belief that mascots matter, and that higher-education institutions must retire these hurtful symbols.

The tradition of using the signs and symbols of American Indian tribes to identify an athletic team is part of a much broader European American habit of "playing Indian," a metaphor that Philip Joseph Deloria explores in his book of that title (Yale University Press, 1998).

In his historical analysis, Deloria enumerates how white people have appropriated American Indian cultures and symbols in order to continually refashion North American identities. Mimicking the indigenous, colonized "other" through imaginary play—as well as in literature, in television, and throughout other media—has stereotyped American Indian people as bellicose, wild, brave, pristine, and even animalistic.

10　　Educators in particular should realize that such images, by flattening conceptions of American Indians into mythological terms, obscure the complex histories and misrepresent the identities of indigenous people. Moreover, they literally erase from public memory the regnant terror that so clearly marked the encounter between indigenous Americans and the colonists from Europe.

That higher-education institutions continue to support such icons and ensure their presence at athletics games and other campus events—even in the face of protest by the very people who are ostensibly memorialized by them—suggests not only an insensitivity to another race and culture, but also an urge for domination. Power in colonial and postcolonial regimes has often been manifested as the power to name, to appropriate, to represent, and to speak—and to use such powers over others. American Indian mascots are expressive practices of precisely those forms of power.

Consider, for example, the use of dance to feature American Indian mascots. Frequently, the mascot, adorned in feathers and paint, stages a highly caricatured "Indian dance" in the middle of the field or court during halftime. At Urbana-Champaign, Chief Illiniwek sports an Oglala war bonnet to inspire the team; at Florida State University, Chief Osceola rides across the football field, feathered spear held aloft.

Throughout U.S. history, dance has been a controversial form of expression. Puritans considered it sinful; when performed by indigenous people, the federal government feared it as a transgressive, wild, and potentially dangerous form of expression. As a result, for much of the latter half of the 19th century, government agents, with the support of conservative clergy, attempted to outlaw native dance and ritual. In 1883, for example, the Department of the Interior established rules for Courts of Indian Offenses. Henry Teller, the secretary of the department, anticipated the purpose of such tribunals in a letter that he wrote to the Bureau of Indian Affairs stating that they would end the "heathenish practices" that hindered the assimilation of American Indian people. As recently as the 1920s, representatives of the federal government criticized American Indian dance, fearing the "immoral" meanings animated by such performances.

The majority of Indian mascots were invented in the first three decades of the 20th century, on the heels of such formal attempts to proscribe native dance and religion, and in the wake of the massive forced relocation that marked the 19th-century American Indian experience. European Americans so detested and feared native dance and culture that they criminalized those "pagan" practices. Yet at the same time they exhibited a passionate desire for certain Indian practices and characteristics—evidenced in part by the proliferation of American Indian mascots.

15   Although unintentional perhaps, the mascots' overtones of racial stereotype and political oppression have routinely transformed intercollegiate-athletic events into tinderboxes. Some 10 years ago at Urbana-Champaign, several Fighting Illini boosters responded to American Indian students who were protesting Chief Illiniwek by erecting a sign that read "Kill the Indians, Save the Chief." And, in the wake of the North Dakota controversy, faculty members who challenged the Fighting Sioux name have reported to us that supporters of the institution's symbol have repeatedly threatened those who oppose it.

Although many supporters of such mascots have argued that they promote respect and understanding of American Indian people, such symbols and the spectacles associated with them are often used in insensitive and demeaning ways that further shape how many people perceive and engage American Indians. Boosters of teams employing American Indians have enshrined largely romanticized stereotypes—noble warriors—to represent themselves. Meanwhile, those who support competitive teams routinely have invoked images of the frontier, Manifest Destiny, ignoble savages, and buffoonish natives to capture the spirit of impending athletics contests and their participants. In our studies, we find countless instances of such mockery on the covers of athletics programs, as motifs for homecoming floats, in fan cheers, and in press coverage.

For example, in 1999, *The Knoxville News-Sentinel* published a cartoon in a special section commemorating the appearance of the University of Tennessee at the Fiesta Bowl. At the center of the cartoon, a train driven by a team member in a coonskin cap plows into a buffoonish caricature of a generic Indian, representing the team's opponent, the Florida State Seminoles. As he flies through the air, the Seminole exclaims, "Paleface speak with forked tongue! This land is ours as long as grass grows and river flows. Oof!"

The Tennessee player retorts, "I got news, pal. This is a desert. And we're painting it orange!" Below them, parodying the genocide associated with the conquest of North America, Smokey, a canine mascot of the University of Tennessee, and a busty Tennessee fan speed down Interstate 10, dubbed "The New and Improved Trail of Tears." What effect can such a cartoon have on people whose ancestors were victims of the actual Trail of Tears?

The tradition of the Florida State Seminoles bears its share of responsibility for inviting that brand of ostensibly playful, yet clearly demeaning, discourse. For, at FSU, the image of the American Indian as warlike and violent is promoted without hesitation. Indeed, the Seminoles' football coach, Bobby Bowden, is known to scribble "Scalp 'em" underneath his autograph.

20   Such images and performances not only deter cross-cultural understanding and handicap social relations, they also harm individuals because they deform indigenous traditions, question identities, and subject both American Indians and European Americans to threatening experiences. For example, according to a *Tampa Tribune* article, a Florida resident and Kiowa tribe member, Joe Quetone, took his son to a Florida State football game during the mid-1990s. As students ran through the stands carrying tomahawks and sporting war paint, loincloths, and feathers, Quetone and his son overheard a man sitting nearby turn to a little boy and say, "Those are real Indians down there. You'd better be good, or they'll come up and scalp you!"

Environmental historian Richard White has suggested that "[White Americans] are pious toward Indian peoples, but we don't take them seriously; we don't credit them with the capacity to make changes. Whites readily grant certain nonwhites a 'spiritual' or 'traditional' knowledge that is timeless. It is not something gained through work or labor; it is not contingent knowledge in a contingent world." The omnipresence of American Indian mascots serves only to advance the inability to accept American Indians as indeed contingent, complicated, diverse, and genuine Americans.

Ultimately, American Indian mascots cannot be separated from their origins in colonial conditions of exploitation. Because the problem with such mascots is one of context, they can never be anything more than a white man's Indian.

Based on our research and observations, we cannot imagine a middle ground for colleges with Indian mascots to take—one that respects indigenous people, upholds the ideals of higher education, or promotes cross-cultural understanding. For instance, requiring students to take courses focusing on American Indian heritage, as some have suggested, reveals a troubling vision of the fit between curriculum, historic inequities, and social reform. Would we excuse colleges with active women's-studies curriculums if their policies and practices created a hostile environment for women?

Others have argued that colleges with American Indian mascots can actively manage them, promoting positive images and restricting negative uses. Many institutions have already exerted greater control over the symbols through design and licensing agreements. But they can't control the actions of boosters at their institutions or competitors at others. For example, the University of North Dakota would probably not prefer fans at North Dakota State University to make placards and T-shirts proclaiming that the "Sioux suck." Such events across the nation remind us that mascots are useful and meaningful because of their openness and flexibility—the way that they allow individuals without institutional consent or endorsement to make interpretations of self and society.

25   American Indian mascots directly contradict the ideals that most higher-education institutions seek—those of transcending racial and cultural boundaries and encouraging respectful relations among all people who live and work on their campuses. Colleges and universities bear a moral responsibility to relegate the unreal and unseemly parade of "team spirits" to history.

MAKING CONNECTIONS

1. If the ethnic group that you come from were used as a mascot, would that bother you? Explain.
2. Is there a difference between using "The Fighting Irish" as a mascot (as it is done at the University of Notre Dame) or using "The Seminoles" (as it is done at Florida State University)? Explain.

MAKING AN ARGUMENT

1. Disagreeing with the premise of this essay, the Seminole Tribal Council voted unanimously in 2005 to support Florida State University's use of "Seminole" as their team's nickname. Do you think the use of this nickname—or others like it—should be supported? Write an argument for or against the use of Native American nicknames and mascots for sports teams. Cite the text of this essay and other sources for support.

JONATHAN SWIFT [1667-1745]

Jonathan Swift was born to English parents in Ireland and attended Trinity College in Dublin. Forced to flee Ireland during the period of turmoil that followed the abdication of James II, Swift lived ten years in the household of a wealthy relative, where he spent his time reading and where he first discovered his talent as a writer of satire. After many years of indecision, Swift decided on a career in the Church of England, which in turn led to his involvement in politics, where he was an active member of the Tory party. In 1713, he reluctantly returned to Ireland following his appointment as dean of St. Patrick's Cathedral in Dublin, and eventually became a fervent Irish patriot in the struggle for Irish independence. Swift wrote "A Modest Proposal" (1729), widely considered the greatest satire produced in English, in response to his disgust with the heartless policies of the English government toward the poor in Ireland.

A MODEST PROPOSAL   [1729]

For preventing the Children of Poor People in Ireland from Being a Burden to Their Parents or Country, and for Making Them Beneficial to the Public

It is a melancholy object to those who walk through this great town or travel in the country, when they see the streets, the roads and cabindoors crowded with beggars of the female sex, followed by three, four, or six children, all in rags, and importuning every passenger for an alms. These mothers, instead of being able to work for their honest livelihood, are forced to employ all their time in strolling to beg sustenance for their helpless infants: who as they grow up either turn thieves for want of work, or leave their dear native country to fight for the pretender in Spain, or sell themselves to the Barbadoes.

I think it is agreed by all parties that this prodigious number of children in the arms, or on the backs, or at the heels of their mothers, and frequently of their fathers, is in the present deplorable state of the kingdom a very great additional grievance; and, therefore, whoever could find out a fair, cheap, and easy method of making these children sound, and useful members of the commonwealth, would deserve so well of the public as to have his statue set up for a preserver of the nation.

But my intention is very far from being confined to provide only for the children of professed beggars; it is of a much greater extent, and shall take in the whole number of infants at a certain age who are born of parents in effect as little able to support them as those who demand our charity in the streets.

As to my own part, having turned my thoughts for many years upon this important subject, and maturely weighed the several schemes of other projectors,[1] I have always found them grossly mistaken in their computation. It is true a child just dropped from its dam may be supported by her milk for a solar year, with little other nourishment; at most not above the value of 2s,[2] which the mother may certainly get, or the value in scraps, by her lawful occupation of begging; and it is exactly at one year old that I propose to provide for them in such a manner as, instead of being a charge upon their parents or the parish, or wanting food and raiment for the rest of their lives, they shall on the contrary contribute to the feeding, and partly to the clothing of many thousands.

5   There is likewise another great advantage in my scheme, that it will prevent those voluntary abortions, and that horrid practice of women murdering their bastard children, alas! too frequent among us! sacrificing the poor innocent babes I doubt more to avoid the expense than the shame, which would move tears and pity in the most savage and inhuman breast.

The number of souls in this kingdom being usually reckoned one million and a half, of these I calculate there may be about 200,000 couples whose wives are breeders; from which number I subtract 30,000 couples who are able to maintain their own children (although I apprehend there cannot be so many, under the present distresses of the kingdom); but this being granted, there will remain 170,000 breeders. I again subtract 50,000 for those women who miscarry, or whose children die by accident or disease within the year. There only remain 120,000 children of poor parents annually born. The question therefore is, how this number shall be reared and provided for, which, as I have already said, under the present situation of affairs, is utterly impossible by all the methods hitherto proposed. For we can neither employ them in handicraft or agriculture; we neither build houses (I mean in the country) nor cultivate land; they can very seldom pick up a livelihood by stealing, until they arrive at six years old, except where they are of towardly parts; although I confess they learn the rudiments much earlier; during which time they can, however, be properly looked upon only as probationers; as I have been informed by a principal gentleman in the County of Cavan, who protested to me that he never knew above one or two instances under the age of six, even in a part of the kingdom so renowned for the quickest proficiency in that art.

---

[1]**projectors** planners   [2]**2s** two shillings

I am assured by our merchants, that a boy or a girl before twelve years old is no saleable commodity; and even when they come to this age they will not yield above or 3£[3] or 3£. 2s. 6d.[4] at most on the exchange; which cannot turn to account either to the parents or the kingdom, the charge of nutriment and rags having been at least four times that value.

I shall now therefore humbly propose my own thoughts, which I hope will not be liable to the least objection.

I have been assured by a very knowing American of my acquaintance in London, that a young healthy child well nursed is at a year old a most delicious, nourishing, and wholesome food, whether stewed, roasted, baked, or boiled; and I make no doubt that it will equally serve in a fricassee, or a ragout.

10   I do therefore humbly offer it to public consideration that of the 120,000 children already computed, 20,000 may be reserved for breed, whereof only one-fourth part to be males; which is more than we allow to sheep, black-cattle, or swine; and my reason is, that these children are seldom the fruits of marriage, a circumstance not much regarded by our savages; therefore one male will be sufficient to serve four females. That the remaining 100,000 may, at a year old, be offered in sale to the persons of quality and fortune through the kingdom, always advising the mother to let them suck plentifully in the last month, so as to render them plump and fat for a good table. A child will make two dishes at an entertainment for friends; and when the family dines alone, the fore or hind quarter will make a reasonable dish, and seasoned with a little pepper or salt will be very good boiled on the fourth day, especially in winter.

I have reckoned upon a medium that a child just born will weigh 12 pounds, and in a solar year, if tolerably nursed, increaseth to 28 pounds.

I grant this food will be somewhat dear, and therefore very proper for landlords, who, as they have already devoured most of the parents, seem to have the best title to the children.

Infant's flesh will be in season throughout the year, but more plentiful in March, and a little before and after: for we are told by a grave author, an eminent French physician, that fish being a prolific diet, there are more children born in Roman Catholic countries about nine months after Lent than at any other season; therefore, reckoning a year after Lent, the markets will be more glutted than usual, because the number of popish infants is at least three to one in this kingdom: and therefore it will have one other collateral advantage, by lessening the number of papists among us.

I have already computed the charge of nursing a beggar's child (in which list I reckon all cottagers, laborers, and four-fifths of the farmers) to be about 2s per annum, rags included; and I believe no gentleman would repine to give 10s for the carcass of a good fat child, which, as I have said, will make four dishes of excellent nutritive meat, when he hath only some particular friend or his own family to dine with him. Thus the squire will learn to be a good landlord, and grow popular among his tenants; the mother will have 8s net profit, and be fit for work until she produces another child.

---

[3]**3£** three pounds   [4]**6d** six pence

15   Those who are more thrifty (as I must confess the times require) may flay the carcass; the skin of which artificially dressed, will make admirable gloves for ladies, and summer boots for fine gentlemen.

As to our city of Dublin, shambles[5] may be appointed for this purpose in the most convenient parts of it, and butchers we may be assured will not be wanting: although I rather recommend buying the children alive, and dressing them hot from the knife as we do roasting pigs.

A very worthy person, a true lover of his country, and whose virtues I highly esteem, was lately pleased in discoursing on this matter to offer a refinement upon my scheme. He said that many gentlemen of this kingdom, having of late destroyed their deer, he conceived that the want of venison might be well supplied by the bodies of young lads and maidens, not exceeding fourteen years of age nor under twelve; so great a number of both sexes in every county being now ready to starve for want of work and service; and these to be disposed of by their parents, if alive, or otherwise by their nearest relations. But with due deference to so excellent a friend and so deserving a patriot, I cannot be altogether in his sentiments; for as to the males, my American acquaintance assured me from frequent experience that their flesh was generally tough and lean, like that of our schoolboys by continual exercise, and their taste disagreeable; and to fatten them would not answer the charge. Then as to the females, it would, I think with humble submission be a loss to the public, because they soon would become breeders themselves: and besides, it is not improbable that some scrupulous people might be apt to censure such a practice (although indeed very unjustly), as a little bordering upon cruelty; which, I confess, hath always been with me the strongest objection against any project, how well soever intended.

But in order to justify my friend, he confessed that this expedient was put into his head by the famous Psalmanazar,[6] a native of the island Formosa, who came from thence to London above twenty years ago; and in conversation told my friend that in his country when any young person happened to be put to death, the executioner sold the carcass to persons of quality as a prime dainty; and that in his time the body of a plump girl of fifteen, who was crucified for an attempt to poison the emperor, was sold to his imperial majesty's prime minister of state, and other great mandarins of the court, in joints from the gibbet, at 400 crowns. Neither indeed can I deny, that if the same use were made of several plump young girls in this town, who without one single groat to their fortunes cannot stir abroad without a chair, and appear at the playhouse and assemblies in foreign fineries which they never will pay for, the kingdom would not be the worse.

Some persons of a desponding spirit are in great concern about the vast number of poor people, who are aged, diseased, or maimed, and I have been desired to employ my thoughts what course may be taken to ease the nation of so grievous an encumbrance. But I am not in the least pain upon that matter, because it is very well known that they are every day dying and rotting by cold and famine, and filth and

---

[5]**shambles** slaughterhouses   [6]**Psalmanazar** George Psalmanazar (c. 1679–1763), wrote *An Historical and Geographical Description of Formosa* (1704). He had never been to Formosa and his book was quickly discovered to be fraudulent.

vermin, as fast as can be reasonably expected. And as to the younger laborers, they are now in as hopeful a condition: they cannot get work, and consequently pine away from want of nourishment, to a degree that if at any time they are accidentally hired to common labor, they have not strength to perform it; and thus the country and themselves are delivered from the evils to come.

20   I have too long digressed, and therefore shall return to my subject. I think the advantages by the proposal which I have made are obvious and many, as well as of the highest importance.

For first, as I have already observed, it would greatly lessen the number of papists, with whom we are yearly overrun, being the principal breeders of the nation; as well as our most dangerous enemies; and who stay at home on purpose to deliver the kingdom to the Pretender, hoping to take their advantage by the absence of so many good Protestants, who have chosen rather to leave their country than stay at home and pay tithes against their conscience to an Episcopal curate.

Secondly, The poorer tenants will have something valuable of their own, which by law may be made liable to distress and help to pay their landlord's rent, their corn and cattle being already seized, and money a thing unknown.

Thirdly, Whereas the maintenance of 100,000 children from two years old and upwards, cannot be computed at less than 10s. a-piece per annum, the nation's stock will be thereby increased £ 50,000 per annum, besides the profit of a new dish introduced to the tables of all gentlemen of fortune in the kingdom who have any refinement in taste. And the money will circulate among ourselves, the goods being entirely of our own growth and manufacture.

Fourthly, The constant breeders beside the gain of 8s sterling per annum by the sale of their children, will be rid of the charge of maintaining them after the first year.

25   Fifthly, This food would likewise bring great custom to taverns, where the vintners will certainly be so prudent as to procure the best receipts for dressing it to perfection, and consequently have their houses frequented by all the fine gentlemen, who justly value themselves upon their knowledge in good eating; and a skilful cook, who understands how to oblige his guests, will contrive to make it as expensive as they please.

Sixthly, This would be a great inducement to marriage, which all wise nations have either encouraged by rewards or enforced by laws and penalties. It would increase the care and tenderness of mothers towards their children, when they were sure of a settlement for life to the poor babes, provided in some sort by the public, to their annual profit instead of expense. We should soon see an honest emulation among the married women, which of them could bring the fattest child to the market. Men would become as fond of their wives during the time of their pregnancy as they are now of their mares in foal, their cows in calf, or sows when they are ready to farrow; nor offer to beat or kick them (as it is too frequent a practice) for fear of a miscarriage.

Many other advantages might be enumerated. For instance, the addition of some thousand carcasses in our exportation of barreled beef, the propagation of swine's flesh, and improvement in the art of making good bacon, so much wanted among us by the great destruction of pigs, too frequent at our tables, which are no way comparable in taste or magnificence to a well-grown, fat, yearling child, which roasted whole will make a considerable figure at a lord mayor's feast or any other public entertainment. But this and many others I omit, being studios of brevity.

Supposing that 1,000 families in this city would be constant customers for infants' flesh, besides others who might have it at merry-meetings, particularly weddings and christenings, I compute that Dublin would take off annually about 20,000 carcasses; and the rest of the kingdom (where probably they will be sold somewhat cheaper) the remaining 80,000.

I can think of no one objection that will possibly be raised against this proposal, unless it should be urged that the number of people will be thereby much lessened in the kingdom. This I freely own, and it was indeed one principal design in offering it to the world. I desire the reader will observe, that I calculate my remedy for this one individual kingdom of Ireland and for no other that ever was, is, or I think ever can be upon earth. Therefore let no man talk to me of other expedients: of taxing our absentees at 5s. a pound: of using neither clothes, nor household furniture except what is of our own growth and manufacture: of utterly rejecting the materials and instruments that promote foreign luxury: of curing the expensiveness of pride, vanity, idleness, and gaming in our women: of introducing a vein of parsimony, prudence, and temperance: of learning to love our country, in the want of which we differ even from Laplanders and the inhabitants of Topinamboo: of quitting our animosities and factions, nor act any longer like the Jews, who were murdering one another at the very moment their city was taken: of being a little cautious not to sell our country and conscience for nothing: of teaching landlords to have at least one degree of mercy towards their tenants: lastly, of putting a spirit of honesty, industry, and skill into our shopkeepers; who, if a resolution could now be taken to buy only our native goods, would immediately unite to cheat and exact upon us in the price, the measure, and the goodness, nor could ever yet be brought to make one fair proposal of just dealing, though often and earnestly invited to it.

30   Therefore I repeat, let no man talk to me of these and the like expedients, till he hath at least a glimpse of hope that there will ever be some hearty and sincere attempt to put them in practice.

But as to myself, having been wearied out for many years with offering vain, idle, visionary thoughts, and at length utterly despairing of success, I fortunately fell upon this proposal; which, as it is wholly new, so it has something solid and real, of no expense and little trouble, full in our own power, and whereby we can incur no danger in disobliging England. For this kind of commodity will not bear exportation, the flesh being of too tender a consistence to admit a long continuance in salt, although perhaps I could name a country which would be glad to eat up our whole nation without it.

After all, I am not so violently bent upon my own opinion as to reject any offer proposed by wise men, which shall be found equally innocent, cheap, easy, and effectual. But before something of that kind shall be advanced in contradiction to my scheme, and offering a better, I desire the author or authors will be pleased maturely to consider two points. First, as things now stand, how they will be able to find food and raiment for 100,000 useless mouths and backs. And secondly, there being a round million of creatures in human figure throughout this kingdom, whose whole subsistence put into a common stock would leave them in debt 2,000,000£ sterling, adding those who are beggars by profession to the bulk of farmers, cottagers, and laborers with their wives and children who are beggars in effect; I desire those politicians who dislike my overture, and may perhaps be so bold to attempt an answer, that they will first ask the parents of these mortals, whether they would not at this day think it a great happiness to have been sold for food at a year old in the manner I prescribe, and thereby have avoided such a perpetual scene of misfortunes as they have since gone through, by the oppression of landlords, the impossibility of paying rent without money or trade, the want of common sustenance, with neither house nor clothes to cover them from the inclemencies of weather, and the most inevitable prospect of entailing the like or greater miseries upon their breed for ever.

I profess in the sincerity of my heart; that I have not the least personal interest in endeavoring to promote this necessary work, having no other motive than the public good of my country, by advancing our trade, providing for infants, relieving the poor, and giving some pleasure to the rich. I have no children by which I can propose to get a single penny; the youngest being nine years old, and my wife past child-bearing.

MAKING CONNECTIONS

1. This is a work of satire. How do you know? What words or phrases or exaggerations indicate this?
2. According to the narrator, what are the advantages of his proposal?

MAKING AN ARGUMENT

1. If Swift doesn't really mean the exaggerated things he proposes, why do you think he proposes them? Identify the issues that Swift raises and write an essay that translates his exaggerated propositions into the steps toward social justice he implies should be taken. Cite the text of the essay for support.

HENRY DAVID THOREAU [1817-1862]

Henry David Thoreau was born and raised in Concord, Massachusetts, to a hardworking but poor family. As a child, he worked at home in a so-called "family-circle" factory making pencils. Determined to get an education, he worked his way through Harvard, and afterward, held a series of posts as a teacher. Beginning in 1843, while working as a handyman at the house of the poet and philosopher Ralph Waldo Emerson, Thoreau became a part of the Transcendentalist movement—an influential circle of American writers and thinkers who believed that the earth was a microcosm of the entire universe, and that the human soul was the same as that of the "Over-Soul." From 1845 to 1847, on land owned by Emerson, Thoreau lived in a cabin he built on Walden Pond in an effort to "front only the essential facts of life." He later edited the journal he kept during this period—Thoreau kept a journal his entire life—and published it as Walden: or, Life in the Woods *in 1854, which, though it attracted little notice during his lifetime, has become one of the most influential books in American literature. After Thoreau returned to the world, he worked for a time in his family's*

pencil business, and later traveled to Canada, Maine, Minnesota, Cape Cod, and New York. Politically active (as in the excerpt below from his famous tract "Civil Disobedience," an explanation of his refusal to pay a poll tax while at Walden), he spoke publicly on many issues, most notably against the Fugitive Slave Law. He died in 1862 of tuberculosis, following a trip to Minnesota.

FROM *CIVIL DISOBEDIENCE*   [1849]

How can a man be satisfied to entertain an opinion merely, and enjoy *it?* Is there any enjoyment in it, if his opinion is that he is aggrieved? If you are cheated out of a single dollar by your neighbor, you do not rest satisfied with knowing that you are cheated, or with saying that you are cheated, or even with petitioning him to pay you your due; but you take effectual steps at once to obtain the full amount, and see that you are never cheated again. Action from principle, the perception and the performance of right, changes things and relations; it is essentially revolutionary, and does not consist wholly with anything which was. It not only divides states and churches, it divides families; ay, it divides the *individual,* separating the diabolical in him from the divine.

Unjust laws exist: shall we be content to obey them, or shall we endeavor to amend them, and obey them until we have succeeded, or shall we transgress them at once? Men generally, under such a government as this, think that they ought to wait until they have persuaded the majority to alter them. They think that, if they should resist, the remedy would be worse than the evil. But it is the fault of the government itself that the remedy *is* worse than the evil. *It* makes it worse. Why is it not more apt to anticipate and provide for reform? Why does it not cherish its wise minority? Why does it cry and resist before it is hurt? Why does it not encourage its citizens to be on the alert to point out its faults and *do* better than it would have them? Why does it always crucify Christ, and excommunicate Copernicus and Luther, and pronounce Washington and Franklin rebels?

· · · · ·

I meet this American government, or its representative, the state government, directly, and face to face, once a year—no more—in the person of its tax-gatherer; this is the only mode in which a man situated as I am necessarily meets it; and it then says distinctly, Recognize me; and the simplest, most effectual, and, in the present posture of affairs, the indispensablest mode of treating with it on this head, of expressing your little satisfaction with and love for it, is to deny it then. My civil neighbor, the tax-gatherer, is the very man I have to deal with,—for it is, after all, with men and not with parchment that I quarrel,—and he has voluntarily chosen to be an agent of the government. How shall he ever know well what he is and does as an officer of the government, or as a man, until he is obliged to consider whether he shall treat me, his neighbor, for whom he has respect, as a neighbor and well-disposed man, or as a maniac and disturber of the peace, and see if he can get over this obstruction to his neighborliness without a ruder and more impetuous thought or speech corresponding with his action. I know this well, that if one thousand, if one hundred, if ten men whom I could name,—if ten *honest* men only,—ay, if *one* HONEST man, in this State of Massachusetts, *ceasing to hold slaves,* were actually to withdraw from this co-partnership, and be locked up in the county jail therefore, it would be the abolition of slavery in America. For it matters not how small the beginning may seem to be: what is once well done is done forever. But we love better to talk about it: that we say is our mission. Reform keeps many scores of newspapers in its service, but not one man. If my esteemed neighbor, the State's ambassador, who will devote his days to the settlement of the question of human rights in the Council Chamber, instead of being threatened with the prisons of Carolina, were to sit down the prisoner of Massachusetts, that State which is so anxious to foist the sin of slavery upon her sister,—though at present she can discover only an act of inhospitality to be the ground of a quarrel with her,—the Legislature would not wholly waive the subject the following winter.

Under a government which imprisons any unjustly, the true place for a just man is also a prison. The proper place to-day, the only place which Massachusetts has provided for her freer and less desponding spirits, is in her prisons, to be put out and locked out of the State by her own act, as they have already put themselves out by their principles. It is there that the fugitive slave, and the Mexican prisoner on parole, and the Indian come to plead the wrongs of his race should find them; on that separate, but more free and honorable ground, where the State places those who are not *with* her, but *against* her,—the only house in a slave State in which a free man can abide with honor. If any think that their influence would be lost there, and their voices no longer afflict the ear of the State, that they would not be as an enemy within its walls, they do not know by how much truth is stronger than error, nor how much more eloquently and effectively he can combat injustice who has experienced a little in his own person. Cast your whole vote, not a strip of paper merely, but your whole influence. A minority is powerless while it conforms to the majority; it is not even a minority then; but it is irresistible when it clogs by its whole weight. If the alternative is to keep all just men in prison, or give up war and slavery, the State will not hesitate which to choose. If a thousand men were not to pay their tax bills this year, that would not be a violent and bloody measure, as it would be to pay them, and enable the State to commit violence and shed innocent blood. This is, in fact, the definition of a peaceable revolution, if any such is possible. If the tax-gatherer, or any other public officer, asks me, as one has done, "But what shall I do?" my answer is, "If you really wish to do anything, resign your office." When the subject has refused allegiance, and the officer has resigned his office, then the revolution is accomplished. But even suppose blood should flow. Is there not a sort of blood shed when the conscience is wounded? Through this wound a man's real manhood and immortality flow out, and he bleeds to an everlasting death. I see this blood flowing now. . . .

MAKING CONNECTIONS

1. Do you think it's ever permissible to break the law? Explain.
2. How well does Thoreau make his point? What are the major reasons he gives to justify these "disobedient" actions?

MAKING AN ARGUMENT

1. Compare this essay to Sophocles's *Antigonê* on page 104 and/or Plato's "The Allegory of the Cave" (p. 1294). Cite the texts of each for support.

CASE STUDY IN CULTURAL CONTEXT

Writers of the Harlem Renaissance

The purpose of this Case Study is to provide you with historical and cultural material for a self-contained research unit on the writers of the Harlem Renaissance. It contains a small sample of the many works of poetry, fiction, and essays produced during a period of extraordinary creativity. Literature was only one aspect of an artistic explosion that included music, dance, painting, and sculpture.

What forces and circumstances came together to create this artistic and cultural renaissance? Perhaps the most important factor was the great migration of African-Americans to the North following the end of post–Civil War Reconstruction in the South. Oppressive, legal segregation was endorsed by rulings of the U.S. Supreme Court. An official attitude and attendant actions that treated African-Americans as less than human and unprotected before the law—including widespread lynchings—made it impossible for many African-Americans to remain in the South. Though there is not universal agreement about how long this renaissance lasted or even its location in Harlem, New York City and Harlem in the 1920s were essential to its flowering. Chicago, Philadelphia, and Cleveland were among other destinations favored by oppressed southern blacks, but New York, the largest, most sophisticated, and diverse city in the country, was the most popular destination. And the timing was right. Real estate investment and speculation in Harlem created an overabundance of middle-class housing. Facing economic ruin, landlords were willing to break the color barrier and offer fashionable housing to all classes of blacks now migrating to the city, including leading artists, musicians, and writers. Harlem quickly became the strongest magnet for and primary producer of African-American art, culture, and politics in the country.

The essays, poems, and fiction that follow are only a tiny sampling of what was produced by the writers of this period. Though their work is not included, W. E. B. Dubois, James Weldon Johnson, Arthur Schomburg, Jessie Fauset, Marcus Garvey, Nella Larsen, Arna Bontemps, Sterling Brown, Wallace Thurman, Rudolph Fisher, Angela Weld Grimke, Helene Johnson, and others made important contributions to or had a significant influence on the work produced during this period. The work that follows represents a range of what was produced by these writers. It begins with Alain Locke's "The New Negro," a declaration of a new era and a call to break the stereotypes of African-Americans long fostered in this country, and it ends with a retrospective on Zora Neale Hurston by Alice Walker. In between, much of the work represented is by Langston Hughes and Zora Neale Hurston, who are, perhaps, the two most prominent writers of this era. For the sake of comparison, two of Hughes's works written later in his career, the short story "One Friday Morning" and the poem "Theme for English B," are also included.

1102

ALAIN LOCKE [1886–1954]

Alain Locke grew up in Philadelphia and graduated magna cum laude from Harvard University. He was the first African-American to be a Rhodes Scholar and earned a degree from Oxford University in 1911. When he returned to the United States, he taught at Howard University, where he eventually became chair of the philosophy department. In addition to publishing a substantial body of his own work, he was an influential booster of the Harlem Renaissance and mentor for many of its artists, including Langston Hughes, Zora Neale Hurston, and Claude McKay.

THE NEW NEGRO   [1925]

In the last decade something beyond the watch and guard of statistics has happened in the life of the American Negro and the three norns[1] who have traditionally presided over the Negro problem have a changeling in their laps. The Sociologist, the Philanthropist, the Race-leader are not unaware of the New Negro, but they are at a loss to account for him. He simply cannot be swathed in their formulae. For the younger generation is vibrant with a new psychology; the new spirit is awake in the masses, and under the wary eyes of the professional observers is transforming what has been a perennial problem into the progressive phases of contemporary Negro life.

Could such a metamorphosis have taken place as suddenly as it has appeared to? The answer is no; not because the New Negro is not here, but because the Old Negro had long become more of a myth than a man. The Old Negro, we must remember, was a creature of moral debate and historical controversy. His has been a stock figure perpetuated as an historical fiction partly in innocent sentimentalism, partly in deliberate reactionism. The Negro himself has contributed his share to this through a sort of protective social mimicry forced upon him by the adverse circumstances of dependence. So for generations in the mind of America, the Negro has been more of a formula than a human being—a something to be argued about, condemned or defended, to be "kept down," or "in his place," or "helped up," to be worried with or worried over, harassed or patronized, a social bogey or a social burden. The thinking Negro even has been induced to share this same general attitude, to focus his attention on controversial issues, to see himself in the distorted perspective of a social problem. His shadow, so to speak, has been more real to him than his personality. Through having had to appeal from the unjust stereotypes of his oppressors and traducers to those of his liberators, friends and benefactors he has had to subscribe to the traditional positions from which his case has been viewed. Little true social or self-understanding has or could come from such a situation.

But while the minds of most of us, black and white, have thus burrowed in the trenches of the Civil War and Reconstruction, the actual march of development has

---

[1]**three norns** the three fates of Norse mythology

simply flanked these positions, necessitating a sudden reorientation of view. We have not been watching in the right direction; set North and South on a sectional axis, we have not noticed the East till the sun has us blinking.

Recall how suddenly the Negro spirituals revealed themselves; suppressed for generations under the stereotypes of Wesleyan hymn[2] harmony, secretive, half-ashamed, until the courage of being natural brought them out—and behold, there was folk-music. Similarly, the mind of the Negro seems suddenly to have slipped from under the tyranny of social intimidation and to be shaking off the psychology of imitation and implied inferiority. By shedding the old chrysalis of the Negro problem we are achieving something like a spiritual emancipation. Until recently, lacking self-understanding, we have been almost as much of a problem to ourselves as we still are to others. But the decade[3] that found us with a problem has left us with only a task. The multitude perhaps feels as yet only a strange relief and a new vague urge, but the thinking few know that in the reaction the vital inner grip of prejudice has been broken.

5   With this renewed self-respect and self-dependence, the life of the Negro community is bound to enter a new dynamic phase, the buoyancy from within compensating for whatever pressure there may be of conditions from without. The migrant masses, shifting from countryside to city, hurdle several generations of experience at a leap, but more important, the same thing happens spiritually in the life-attitudes and self-expression of the Young Negro, in his poetry, his art, his education and his new outlook, with the additional advantage, of course, of the poise and greater certainty of knowing what it is all about. From this comes the promise and warrant of a new leadership. As one of them[4] has discerningly put it:

> We have tomorrow
> Bright before us
> Like a flame.
>
> Yesterday, a night-gone thing
> A sun-down name.
>
> And dawn today
> Broad arch above the road we came.
> We march!

This is what, even more than any "most creditable record of fifty years of freedom," requires that the Negro of today be seen through other than the dusty spectacles of past controversy. The day of "aunties," "uncles" and "mammies" is equally gone. Uncle Tom and Sambo have passed on, and even the "Colonel" and "George"[5] play barnstorm roles from which they escape with relief when the public spotlight is off. The popular melodrama has about played itself out, and it is time to scrap the fictions, garret the bogeys and settle down to a realistic facing of the facts.

[2]**Wesleyan hymn** after Charles Wesley (1707–1788), English hymnist and brother of John Wesley, founder of Methodism   [3]**decade** the 1920s   [4]**one of them** Langston Hughes (1902–1967). The following lines are from "Youth."   [5]**the "Colonel" and "George"** typical forms of interracial address during slavery and segregation

First we must observe some of the changes which since the traditional lines of opinion were drawn have rendered these quite obsolete. A main change has been, of course, that shifting of the Negro population which has made the Negro problem no longer exclusively or even predominantly Southern. Why should our minds remain sectionalized, when the problem itself no longer is? Then the trend of migration has not only been toward the North and the Central Midwest, but city-ward and to the great centers of industry—the problems of adjustment are new, practical, local and not peculiarly racial. Rather they are an integral part of the large industrial and social problems of our present-day democracy. And finally, with the Negro rapidly in process of class differentiation, if it ever was warrantable to regard and treat the Negro *en masse* it is becoming with every day less possible, more unjust and more ridiculous.

In the very process of being transplanted, the Negro is becoming transformed.

The tide of the Negro migration, northward and city-ward, is not to be fully explained as a blind flood started by the demands of war industry coupled with the shutting off of foreign migration, or by the pressure of poor crops coupled with increased social terrorism in certain sections of the South and Southwest. Neither labor demand, the bollweevil[6] nor the Ku Klux Klan is a basic factor, however contributory any or all of them may have been. The wash and rush of this human tide on the beach line of the northern city centers is to be explained primarily in terms of a new vision of opportunity, of social and economic freedom, of a spirit to seize, even in the face of an extortionate and heavy toll, a chance for the improvement of conditions. With each successive wave of it, the movement of the Negro becomes more and more a mass movement toward the larger and the more democratic chance—in the Negro's case a deliberate flight not only from countryside to city, but from medieval America to modern.

10   Take Harlem as an instance of this. Here in Manhattan is not merely the largest Negro community in the world, but the first concentration in history of so many diverse elements of Negro life. It has attracted the African, the West Indian, the Negro American; has brought together the Negro of the North and the Negro of the South; the man from the city and man from the town and village; the peasant, the student, the business man, the professional man, artist, poet, musician, adventurer and worker, preacher and criminal, exploiter and social outcast. Each group has come with its own separate motives and for its own special ends, but their greatest experience has been the finding of one another. Proscription and prejudice have thrown these dissimilar elements into a common area of contact and interaction. Within this area, race sympathy and unity have determined a further fusing of sentiment and experience. So what began in terms of segregation becomes more and more, as its elements mix and react, the laboratory of a great race-welding. Hitherto, it must be admitted that American Negroes have been race more in name than in fact, or to be exact, more in sentiment than in experience. The chief bond between them has been that of a common condition rather than a common consciousness; a problem in common rather than a life in common. In Harlem, Negro life is seizing upon its

[6]**bollweevil** a snout beetle notorious for destroying cotton crops

first chances for group expression and self-determination. It is—or promises at least to be—a race capital. That is why our comparison is taken with those nascent centers of folk-expression and self-determination which are playing a creative part in the world today. Without pretense to their political significance, Harlem has the same role to play for the New Negro as Dublin has had for the New Ireland or Prague for the New Czechoslovakia.

Harlem, I grant you, isn't typical—but it is significant, it is prophetic. No sane observer, however sympathetic to the new trend, would contend that the great masses are articulate as yet, but they stir, they move, they are more than physically restless. The challenge of the new intellectuals among them is clear enough—the "race radicals" and realists who have broken with the old epoch of philanthropic guidance, sentimental appeal and protest. But are we after all only reading into the stirrings of a sleeping giant the dreams of an agitator? The answer is in the migrating peasant. It is the "man farthest down" who is most active in getting up. One of the most characteristic symptoms of this is the professional man, himself migrating to recapture his constituency after a vain effort to maintain in some Southern corner what for years back seemed an established living and clientele. The clergyman following his errant flock, the physician or lawyer trailing his clients, supply the true clues. In a real sense it is the rank and file who are leading, and the leaders who are following. A transformed and transforming psychology permeates the masses.

When the racial leaders of twenty years ago spoke of developing race-pride and stimulating race-consciousness, and of the desirability of race solidarity, they could not in any accurate degree have anticipated the abrupt feeling that has surged up and now pervades the awakened centers. Some of the recognized Negro leaders and a powerful section of white opinion identified with "race work" of the older order have indeed attempted to discount this feeling as a "passing phase," an attack of "race nerves" so to speak, an "aftermath of the war," and the like. It has not abated, however, if we are to gauge by the present tone and temper of the Negro press, or by the shift in popular support from the officially recognized and orthodox spokesmen to those of the independent, popular, and often radical type who are unmistakable symptoms of a new order. It is a social disservice to blunt the fact that the Negro of the Northern centers has reached a stage where tutelage, even of the most interested and well-intentioned sort, must give place to new relationships, where positive self-direction must be reckoned with in ever increasing measure. The American mind must reckon with a fundamentally changed Negro.

The Negro too, for his part, has idols of the tribe to smash. If on the one hand the white man has erred in making the Negro appear to be that which would excuse or extenuate his treatment of him, the Negro, in turn, has too often unnecessarily excused himself because of the way he has been treated. The intelligent Negro of today is resolved not to make discrimination an extenuation for his shortcomings in performance, individual or collective; he is trying to hold himself at par, neither inflated by sentimental allowances nor depreciated by current social discounts. For this he must know himself and be known for precisely what he is, and for that reason he welcomes the new scientific rather than the old sentimental interest. Sentimental interest in the Negro has ebbed. We used to lament this as the falling off of our friends; now we rejoice and pray to be delivered both from self-pity and condescension. The mind of each radical group has had a bitter weaning, apathy or hatred on one side matching disillusionment or resentment on the other; but they face each other today with the possibility at least of entirely new mutual attitudes.

It does not follow that if the Negro were better known, he would be better liked or better treated. But mutual understanding is basic for any subsequent cooperation and adjustment. The effort toward this will at least have the effect of remedying in large part what has been the most unsatisfactory feature of our present stage of race relationships in America, namely the fact that the more intelligent and representative elements of the two race groups have at so many points got quite out of vital touch with one another.

15   The fiction is that the life of the races is separate, and increasingly so. The fact is that they have touched too closely at the unfavorable and too lightly at the favorable levels.

While inter-racial councils have sprung up in the South, drawing on forward elements of both races, in the Northern cities manual laborers may brush elbows in their everyday work, but the community and business leaders have experienced no such interplay or far too little of it. These segments must achieve contact or the race situation in America becomes desperate. Fortunately this is happening. There is a growing realization that in social effort the cooperative basis must supplant long-distance philanthropy, and that the only safeguard for mass relations in the future must be provided in the carefully maintained contacts of the enlightened minorities of both race groups. In the intellectual realm a renewed and keen curiosity is replacing the recent apathy; the Negro is being carefully studied, not just talked about and discussed. In art and letters, instead of being wholly caricatured, he is being seriously portrayed and painted.

To all of this the New Negro is keenly responsive as an augury of a new democracy in American culture. He is contributing his share to the new social understanding. But the desire to be understood would never in itself have been sufficient to have opened so completely the protectively closed portals of the thinking Negro's mind. There is still too much possibility of being snubbed or patronized for that. It was rather the necessity for fuller, truer self-expression, the realization of the unwisdom of allowing social discrimination to segregate him mentally, and a counter-attitude to cramp and fetter his own living—and so the "spite-wall" that the intellectuals built over the "color-line" has happily been taken down. Much of this reopening of intellectual contacts has centered in New York and has been richly fruitful not merely in the enlarging of personal experience, but in the definite enrichment of American art and letters and in the classifying of our common vision of the social tasks ahead.

The particular significance in the re-establishment of contact between the more advanced and representative classes is that it promises to offset some of the unfavorable reactions of the past, or at least to re-surface race contacts somewhat for the future. Subtly the conditions that are molding a New Negro are molding a new American attitude.

However, this new phase of things is delicate; it will call for less charity but more justice; less help, but infinitely closer understanding. This is indeed a critical stage of race relationships because of the likelihood, if the new temper is not understood, of engendering sharp group antagonism and a second crop of more calculated prejudice. In some quarters, it has already done so. Having weaned the Negro, public opinion cannot continue to paternalize. The Negro today is inevitably moving forward under the control largely of his own objectives. What are these objectives? Those of his outer life are happily already well and finally formulated, for they are none other than the ideals of American institutions and democracy. Those of his inner life are yet in process of formation, for the new psychology at present is more of a consensus of feeling than of opinion, of attitude rather than of program. Still some points seem to have crystallized.

20   Up to the present one may adequately describe the Negro's "inner objectives" as an attempt to repair a damaged group psychology and reshape a warped social perspective. Their realization has required a new mentality for the American Negro. And as it matures we begin to see its effects; at first, negative, iconoclastic, and then positive and constructive. In this new group psychology we note the lapse of sentimental appeal, then the development of a more positive self-respect and self-reliance; the repudiation of social dependence, and then the gradual recovery from hyper-sensitiveness and "touchy" nerves, the repudiation of the double standard of judgment with its special philanthropic allowances and then the sturdier desire for objective and scientific appraisal; and finally the rise from social disillusionment to race pride, from the sense of social debt to the responsibilities of social contribution, and offsetting the necessary working and common-sense acceptance of restricted conditions, the belief in ultimate esteem and recognition. Therefore the Negro today wishes to be known for what he is, even in his faults and shortcomings, and scorns a craven and precarious survival at the price of seeming to be what he is not. He resents being spoken of as a social ward or minor, even by his own, and to being regarded a chronic patient for the sociological clinic, the sick man of American Democracy. For the same reasons, he himself is through with those social nostrums and panaceas, the so-called "solutions" of his "problem," with which he and the country have been so liberally dosed in the past. Religion, freedom, education, money—in turn, he has ardently hoped for and peculiarly trusted these things; he still believes in them, but not in blind trust that they alone will solve his life-problem.

Each generation, however, will have its creed, and that of the present is the belief in the efficacy of collective effort, in race cooperation. This deep feeling of race is at present the mainspring of Negro life. It seems to be the outcome of the reaction to proscription and prejudice; an attempt, fairly successful on the whole, to convert a defensive into an offensive position, a handicap into an incentive. It is radical in tone, but not in purpose and only the most stupid forms of opposition, misunderstanding or persecution could make it otherwise. Of course, the thinking Negro has shifted a little toward the left with the world-trend, and there is an increasing group who affiliate with radical and liberal movements. But fundamentally for the present the Negro is radical on race matters, conservative on others, in other words, a "forced radical," a social protestant rather than a genuine radical. Yet under further pressure and injustice iconoclastic thought and motives will inevitably increase. Harlem's quixotic radicalisms call for their ounce of democracy today lest tomorrow they be beyond cure.

The Negro mind reaches out as yet to nothing but American wants, American ideas. But this forced attempt to build his Americanism on race values is a unique social experiment, and its ultimate success is impossible except through the fullest sharing of American culture and institutions. There should be no delusion about this. American nerves in sections unstrung with race hysteria are often fed the opiate that the trend of Negro advance is wholly separatist, and that the effect of its operation will be to encyst the Negro as a benign foreign body in the body politic. This cannot be—even if it were desirable. The racialism of the Negro is no limitation or reservation with respect to American life; it is only a constructive effort to build the obstructions in the stream of his progress into an efficient dam of social energy and power. Democracy itself is obstructed and stagnated to the extent that any of its channels are closed. Indeed they cannot be selectively closed. So the choice is not between one way for the Negro and another way for the rest, but between American institutions frustrated on the one hand and American ideals progressively fulfilled and realized on the other.

There is, of course, a warrantably comfortable feeling in being on the right side of the country's professed ideals. We realize that we cannot be undone without America's undoing. It is within the gamut of this attitude that the thinking Negro faces America, but with variations of mood that are if anything more significant than the attitude itself. Sometimes we have it taken with the defiant ironic challenge of McKay:[7]

> Mine is the future grinding down to-day
> Like a great landslip moving to the sea,
> Bearing its freight of debris far away
> Where the green hungry waters restlessly
> Heave mammoth pyramids, and break and roar
> Their eerie challenge to the crumbling shore.

Sometimes, perhaps more frequently as yet, it is taken in the fervent and almost filial appeal and counsel of Weldon Johnson's:[8]

> O Southland, dear Southland!
> Then why do you still cling
> To an idle age and a musty page,
> To a dead and useless thing?

But between defiance and appeal, midway almost between cynicism and hope, the prevailing mind stands in the mood of the same author's *To America*,[9] an attitude of sober query and stoical challenge:

> How would you have us, as we are?
>   Or sinking 'neath the load we bear,
> Our eyes fixed forward on a star,
>   Or gazing empty at despair?

---

[7]**McKay** Claude McKay (1889–1948). Harlem Renaissance poet   [8]**Weldon Johnson's** from *O Southland!* (1907)   [9]*To America* published in 1917

> Rising or falling? Men or things?
>> With dragging pace or footsteps fleet?
> Strong, willing sinews in your wings,
>> Or tightening chains about your feet?

More and more, however, an intelligent realization of the great discrepancy between the American social creed and the American social practice forces upon the Negro the taking of the moral advantage that is his. Only the steadying and sobering effect of a truly characteristic gentleness of spirit prevents the rapid rise of a definite cynicism and counter-hate and a defiant superiority feeling. Human as this reaction would be, the majority still deprecate its advent, and would gladly see it forestalled by the speedy amelioration of its causes. We wish our race pride to be a healthier, more positive achievement than a feeling based upon a realization of the shortcomings of others. But all paths toward the attainment of a sound social attitude have been difficult; only a relatively few enlightened minds have been able as the phrase puts it "to rise above" prejudice. The ordinary man has had until recently only a hard choice between the alternatives of supine and humiliating submission and stimulating but hurtful counter-prejudice. Fortunately from some inner, desperate resourcefulness has recently sprung up the simple expedient of fighting prejudice by mental passive resistance, in other words by trying to ignore it. For the few, this manna may perhaps be effective, but the masses cannot thrive upon it.

25   Fortunately there are constructive channels opening out into which the balked social feelings of the American Negro can flow freely.

Without them there would be much more pressure and danger than there is. These compensating interests are racial but in a new and enlarged way. One is the consciousness of acting as the advance-guard of the African peoples in their contact with Twentieth Century civilization; the other, the sense of mission of rehabilitating the race in world esteem from that loss of prestige for which the fate and conditions of slavery have so largely been responsible. Harlem, as we shall see, is the center of both these movements; she is the home of the Negro's "Zionism."[10] The pulse of the Negro world has begun to beat in Harlem. A Negro newspaper carrying news material in English, French and Spanish, gathered from all quarters of America, the West Indies and Africa has maintained itself in Harlem for over five years. Two important magazines,[11] both edited from New York, maintain their news and circulation consistently on a cosmopolitan scale. Under American auspices and backing, three pan-African congresses have been held abroad for the discussion of common interests, colonial questions and the future cooperative development of Africa. In terms of the race question as a world problem, the Negro mind has leapt, so to speak, upon the parapets of prejudice and extended its cramped horizons. In so doing it has linked up with the growing group consciousness of the dark-peoples and is gradually learning their common interests. As one of our writers has recently put it: "It is imperative that we understand the white world in its relations to the non-white world." As with the Jew, persecution is making the Negro international.

---

[10]**"Zionism"** an international movement aimed at securing a homeland for the Jewish people
[11]**magazines** probably *Opportunity* and the *Crisis*

As a world phenomenon this wider race consciousness is a different thing from the much asserted rising tide of color. Its inevitable causes are not of our making. The consequences are not necessarily damaging to the best interests of civilization. Whether it actually brings into being new Armadas[12] of conflict or argosies[13] of cultural exchange and enlightenment can only be decided by the attitude of the dominant races in an era of critical change. With the American Negro, his new internationalism is primarily an effort to recapture contact with the scattered peoples of African derivation. Garveyism[14] may be a transient, if spectacular, phenomenon, but the possible role of the American Negro in the future development of Africa is one of the most constructive and universally helpful missions that any modern people can lay claim to.

Constructive participation in such causes cannot help giving the Negro valuable group incentives, as well as increased prestige at home and abroad. Our greatest rehabilitation may possibly come through such channels, but for the present, more immediate hope rests in the revaluation by white and black alike of the Negro in terms of his artistic endowments and cultural contributions, past and prospective. It must be increasingly recognized that the Negro has already made very substantial contributions, not only in his folk-art, music especially, which has always found appreciation, but in larger, though humbler and less acknowledged ways. For generations the Negro has been the peasant matrix of that section of America which has most undervalued him, and here he has contributed not only materially in labor and in social patience, but spiritually as well. The South has unconsciously absorbed the gift of his folk-temperament. In less than half a generation it will be easier to recognize this, but the fact remains that a leaven of humor, sentiment, imagination and tropic nonchalance has gone into the making of the South from a humble, unacknowledged source. A second crop of the Negro's gifts promises still more largely. He now becomes a conscious contributor and lays aside the status of a beneficiary and ward for that of a collaborator and participant in American civilization. The great social gain in this is the releasing of our talented group from the arid fields of controversy and debate to the productive fields of creative expression. The especially cultural recognition they win should in him prove the key to that revaluation of the Negro which must precede or accompany any considerable further betterment of race relationships. But whatever the general effect, the present generation will have added the motives of self-expression and spiritual development to the old and still unfinished task of making material headway and progress. No one who understandingly faces the situation with its substantial accomplishment or views the new scene with its still more abundant promise can be entirely without hope. And certainly, if in our lifetime the Negro should not be able to celebrate his full initiation into American democracy, he can at least, on the warrant of these things, celebrate the attainment of a significant and satisfying new phase of group development, and with it a spiritual Coming of Age.

[12]**Armadas** fleets of warships   [13]**argosies** merchant ships   [14]**Garveyism** the Back to Africa movement of Marcus Garvey (1887–1940)

Archibald J. Motley, Jr. (American, 1891–1981). *Blues,* 1929. Chicago Historical Society.

LANGSTON HUGHES [1902–1967]

One of the most important figures of the Harlem Renaissance, Langston Hughes was born in Joplin, Missouri, and graduated from Lincoln University in Pennsylvania. As a young man, he traveled the world as a merchant seaman, visiting Africa and living for a time in Paris and Rome. A poet, writer of fiction, playwright, lyricist, editor, critic, and essayist, Hughes published two volumes of autobiography, The Big Sea *(1940) and* I Wonder as I Wander *(1956). Hughes's work, which is filled with the sounds and music of the African-American experience, has influenced generations of American writers.*

FROM THE BIG SEA   [1940]

I was there. I had a swell time while it lasted. But I thought it wouldn't last long. (I remember the vogue for things Russian, the season the Chauve-Souris first came to town.) For how could a large and enthusiastic number of people be crazy about Negroes forever? But some Harlemites thought the millennium had come. They thought the race problem had at last been solved through Art plus Gladys Bently. They were sure the New Negro would lead a new life from then on in green pastures of tolerance created by Countee Cullen, Ethel Waters, Claude McKay, Duke Ellington, Bojangles, and Alain Locke.

I don't know what made any Negroes think that—except that they were mostly intellectuals doing the thinking. The ordinary Negroes hadn't heard of the Negro Renaissance. And if they had, it hadn't raised their wages any. As for all those white folks in the speakeasies and night clubs of Harlem—well, maybe a colored man could find *some* place to have a drink that the tourists hadn't yet discovered.

Then it was that house-rent parties began to flourish—and not always to raise the rent either. But, as often as not, to have a get-together of one's own, where you could do the black-bottom with no stranger behind you trying to do it, too. Non-theatrical, non-intellectual Harlem was an unwilling victim of its own vogue. It didn't like to be stared at by white folks. But perhaps the downtowners never knew this—for the cabaret owners, the entertainers, and the speakeasy proprietors treated them fine—as long as they paid.

The Saturday night rent parties that I attended were often more amusing than any night club, in small apartments where God knows who lived—because the guests seldom did—but where the piano would often be augmented by a guitar, or an odd cornet, or somebody with a pair of drums walking in off the street. And where awful bootleg whiskey and good fried fish or steaming chitterling were sold at very low prices. And the dancing and singing and impromptu entertaining went on until dawn came in at the window.

These parties, often termed whist parties or dances, were usually announced by brightly colored cards stuck in the grille of apartment house elevators. Some of the cards were highly entertaining in themselves:

We got yellow girls, we've got black and tan
Will you have a good time? - YEAH MAN !

𝕬 𝕾𝖔𝖈𝖎𝖆𝖑 𝖂𝖍𝖎𝖘𝖙 𝕻𝖆𝖗𝖙𝖞
—GIVEN BY—
MARY WINSTON

147 West 145th Street   Apt.5

▼▼▼▼▼▼▼▼▼▼▼▼▼▼▼▼▼▼▼▼▼▼▼▼▼▼▼▼

SATURDAY EVE., MARCH 19th, 1932

▲▲▲▲▲▲▲▲▲▲▲▲▲▲▲▲▲▲▲▲▲▲▲▲▲▲▲▲

GOOD MUSIC   REFRESHMENTS

H U R R A Y

COME AND SEE WHAT IS IN STORE FOR YOU AT THE

TEA CUP PARTY

GIVEN BY MRS. VANDERBILT SMITH

at 409 EDGECOMBE AVENUE
NEW YORK CITY
Apartment 10 - A

on Thursday evening, January 23rd, 1930
at 8:30 P. M.

ORIENTAL – GYPSY – SOUTHERN MAMMY – STARLIGHT
and other readers will be present

Music and Talent   —   —   Refreshments Served

Ribbons-Maws and Tretters A Specialty.

Fall in line, and watch your step, For there'll be
Lots of Browns with plenty of Pep At

A Social Whist Party

Given by

Lucille & Minnie

149 West 117th Street, N. Y. Gr. floor, W,

Saturday Evening, Nov. 2nd 1929

Refreshments Just It   Music Won't Quit

If Sweet Mamma is running wild, and you are looking
for a Do-right child, just come around and
linger awhile at a

SOCIAL WHIST PARTY

GIVEN BY

PINKNEY & EPPS

260 West 129th Street   Apartment 10

SATURDAY EVENING, JUNE 9, 1928

GOOD MUSIC   REFRESHMENTS

Railroad Men's Ball

AT CANDY'S PLACE

FRIDAY, SATURDAY & SUNDAY,

April 29-30, May 1, 1927

Black Wax, says change your mind and say they
do and he will give you a hearing, while MEAT
HOUSE SLIM, laying in the bin
killing all good men.

L. A. VAUGH, *President*

OH BOY   OH JOY

The Eleven Brown Skins

of the

Evening Shadow Social Club

are giving their

Second Annual St. Valentine Dance

Saturday evening, Feb. 18th, 1928

At 129 West 136th Street, New York City

Good Music   Refreshments Served

Subscription   25 Cents

---

*Some wear pajamas, some wear pants, what does it matter
just so you can dance, at*

A Social Whist Party

GIVEN BY

MR. & MRS. BROWN

AT 258 W. 115TH STREET, APT. 9

SATURDAY EVE., SEPT. 14, 1929

The music is sweet and everything good to eat!

Almost every Saturday night when I was in Harlem I went to a house—rent party. I wrote lots of poems about house-rent parties, and ate thereat many a fried fish and pig's foot—with liquid refreshments on the side. I met ladies' maids and truck drivers, laundry workers and shoe shine boys, seamstresses and porters. I can still hear their laughter in my ears, hear the soft slow music, and feel the floor shaking as the dancers danced.

THE NEGRO ARTIST AND THE RACIAL MOUNTAIN   [1926]

One of the most promising of the young Negro poets said to me once, "I want to be a poet—not a Negro poet," meaning, I believe, "I want to write like a white poet"; meaning subconsciously, "I would like to be a white poet"; meaning behind that, "I would like to be white." And I was sorry the young man said that, for no great poet has ever been afraid of being himself. And I doubted then that, with his desire to run away spiritually from his race, this boy would ever be a great poet. But this is the mountain standing in the way of any true Negro art in America—this urge within the race toward whiteness, the desire to pour racial individuality into the mold of American standardization, and to be as little Negro and as much American as possible.

But let us look at the immediate background of this young poet. His family is of what I suppose one would call the Negro middle class: people who are by no means rich yet never uncomfortable nor hungry—smug, contented, respectable folk, members of the Baptist church. The father goes to work every morning. He is a chief steward at a large white club. The mother sometimes does fancy sewing or supervises parties for the rich families of the town. The children go to a mixed school. In the home they read white papers and magazines. And the mother often says, "Don't be like niggers" when the children are bad. A frequent phrase from the father is, "Look how well a white man does things." And so the word white comes to be unconsciously a symbol of all virtues. It holds for the children beauty, morality, and money. The whisper of "I want to be white" runs silently through their minds. This young poet's home is, I believe, a fairly typical home of the colored middle class. One sees immediately how difficult it would be for an artist born in such a home to interest himself in interpreting the beauty of his own people. He is never taught to see that beauty. He is taught rather not to see it, or if he does, to be ashamed of it when it is not according to Caucasian patterns.

For racial culture the home of a self-styled "high-class" Negro has nothing better to offer. Instead there will perhaps be more aping of things white than in a less cultured or less wealthy home. The father is perhaps a doctor, lawyer, landowner, or politician. The mother may be a social worker, or a teacher, or she may do nothing and have a maid. Father is often dark but he has usually married the lightest woman he could find. The family attends a fashionable church where few really colored faces are to be found. And they themselves draw a color line. In the North they go to white theaters and white movies. And in the South they have at least two cars and house "like white folks." Nordic manners, Nordic faces, Nordic hair, Nordic art (if any), and an Episcopal heaven. A very high mountain indeed for the would-be racial artist to climb in order to discover himself and his people.

But then there are the low-down folks, the so-called common element, and they are the majority—may the Lord be praised! The people who have their hip of gin on Saturday nights and are not too important to themselves or the community, or too well fed, or too learned to watch the lazy world go round. They live on Seventh Street in Washington or State Street in Chicago and they do not particularly care whether they are like white folks or anybody else. Their joy runs, bang! into ecstasy. Their religion soars to a shout. Work maybe a little today, rest a little tomorrow. Play awhile. Sing awhile. O, let's dance! These common people are not afraid of spirituals, as for a long time their more intellectual brethren were, and jazz is their child. They furnish a wealth of colorful, distinctive material for any artist because they still hold their own individuality in the face of American standardizations. And perhaps these common people will give to the world its truly great Negro artist, the one who is not afraid to be himself. Whereas the better-class Negro would tell the artist what to do, the people at least let him alone when he does appear. And they are not ashamed of him— if they know he exits at all. And they accept what beauty is their own without question.

5   Certainly there is, for the American Negro artists who can escape the restrictions the more advanced among his own group would put upon him, a great field of unused material ready for his art. Without going outside his race, and even among the better classes with their "white" culture and conscious American manners, but still Negro enough to be different, there is sufficient matter to furnish a black artist with a lifetime of creative work. And when he chooses to touch on the relations between Negroes and whites in this country with their innumerable overtones and undertones surely, and especially for literature and the drama, there is an inexhaustible supply of themes at hand. To these the Negro artist can give his racial individuality, his heritage of rhythm and warmth, and his incongruous humor that so often, as in the Blues, becomes ironic laughter mixed with tears. But let us look again at the mountain.

A prominent Negro clubwoman in Philadelphia paid eleven dollars to hear Raquel Meller sing Andalusian[1] popular songs. But she told me a few weeks before she would not think of going to hear "that woman," Clara Smith,[2] a great black artist, sing Negro folksongs. And many an upper-class Negro church, even now, would not dream of employing a spiritual in its services. The drab melodies in white folks' hymnbooks are much to be preferred. "We want to worship the Lord correctly and quietly. We don't believe in 'shouting.' Let's be dull like the Nordics," they say, in effect.

The road for the serious black artist, then, who would produce a racial art is most certainly rocky and the mountain is high. Until recently he received almost no encouragement for his work from either white or colored people. The fine novels of Chesnutt[3] go out of print with neither race noticing their passing. The quaint charm and humor of Dunbar's[4] dialect verse brought to him, in his day, largely the same kind of encouragement one would give a sideshow freak (A colored man writing poetry! How odd!) or a clown (How amusing!).

The present vogue in things Negro, although it may do as much harm as good for the budding colored artist, has at least done this: it has brought him forcibly to the

---

[1] **Andalusian** from a region of Spain   [2] **Clara Smith** major blues singer (1885–1935)   [3] **Chesnutt** Charles Chesnutt (1858–1932), author of three novels, *The House behind the Cedars* (1900), *The Marrow of Tradition* (1901), and *The Colonel's Dream* (1905); a biography of Frederick Douglass; and two short story collections, *The Conjure Woman* (1899) and *The Wife of His Youth and Other Stories of the Color Line* (1899)   [4] **Dunbar's** Paul Laurence Dunbar (1872–1906), poet and author of the novel *Sport of the Gods* (1907)

attention of his own people among whom for so long, unless the other race had noticed him beforehand, he was a prophet with little honor. I understand that Charles Gilpin[5] acted for years in Negro theaters without any special acclaim from his own, but when Broadway gave him eight curtain calls, Negroes, too, began to beat a tin pan in his honor. I know a young colored writer, a manual worker by day, who had been writing well for the colored magazines for some years, but it was not until he recently broke into the white publications and his first book was accepted by a prominent New York publisher that the "best" Negroes in his city took the trouble to discover that he lived there. Then almost immediately they decided to give a grand dinner for him. But the society ladies were careful to whisper to his mother that perhaps she'd better not come. They were not sure she would have an evening gown.[6]

The Negro artist works against an undertow of sharp criticism and misunderstanding from his own group and unintentional bribes from the whites. "Oh, be respectable, write about nice people, show how good we are," say the Negroes. "Be stereotyped, don't go too far, don't shatter our illusions about you, don't amuse us too seriously. We will pay you," say the whites. Both would have told Jean Toomer not to write *Cane*.[7] The colored people did not praise it. The white people did not buy it. Most of the colored people who did read *Cane* hate it. They are afraid of it. Although the critics gave it good reviews the public remained indifferent. Yet (excepting the work of Du Bois[8]) *Cane* contains the finest prose written by a Negro in America. And like the singing of Robeson,[9] it is truly racial.

10   But in spite of the Nordicized Negro intelligentsia and the desires of some white editors we have an honest American Negro literature already with us. Now I await the rise of the Negro theater. Our folk music, having achieved world-wide fame, offers itself to the genius of the great individual American composer who is to come. And within the next decade I expect to see the work of a growing school of colored artists who paint and model the beauty of dark faces and create with new technique the expressions of their own soul-world. And the Negro dancers who will dance like flames and the singers who will continue to carry our songs to all who listen—they will be with us in even greater numbers tomorrow.

Most of my own poems are racial in theme and treatment, derived from the life I know. In many of them I try to grasp and hold some of the meanings and rhythms of jazz. I am as sincere as I know how to be in these poems and yet after every reading I answer questions like these from my own people: Do you think Negroes should always write about Negroes? I wish you wouldn't read some of your poems to white folks. How do you find anything interesting in a place like a cabaret? Why do you write about black people? You aren't black. What makes you do so many jazz poems?

But jazz to me is one of the inherent expressions of Negro life in America; the eternal tom-tom beating in the Negro soul—the tom-tom of revolt against weariness in a white world, a world of subway trains, and work, work, work; the tom-tom of joy

---

[5]**Charles Gilpin** American actor (1878–1930)   [6]This incident, which happened to Hughes himself in 1925, is related in his autobiography *The Big Sea* (1940).   [7]*Cane* a 1923 collection of short stories and poetry about the rural South and the urban North   [8]**Du Bois** W. E. B. Du Bois (1868–1963) helped found the NAACP and edited its journal, *Crisis,* from 1910 to 1934; he is best known for *The Souls of Black Folk* (1903).   [9]**Robeson** Paul Robeson (1898–1976), actor and singer.

and laughter, and pain swallowed in a smile. Yet the Philadelphia clubwoman is ashamed to say that her race created it and she does not like me to write about it. The old subconscious "white is best" runs through her mind. Years of study under white teachers, a lifetime of white books, pictures, and papers, and white manners, morals, and Puritan standards made her dislike the spirituals. And now she turns up her nose at jazz and all its manifestations—likewise almost everything else distinctly racial. She doesn't care for the Winold Reiss[10] portraits of Negroes because they are "too Negro." She does not want a true picture of herself from anybody. She wants the artist to flatter her, to make the white world believe that all Negroes are as smug and as near white in soul as she wants to be. But, to my mind, it is the duty of the younger Negro artist, if he accepts any duties at all from outsiders, to change through the force of his art that old whispering "I want to be white," hidden in the aspirations of his people, to "Why should I want to be white? I am a Negro—and beautiful."

So I am ashamed for the black poet who says, "I want to be a poet, not a Negro poet," as though his own racial world were not as interesting as any other world. I am ashamed, too, for the colored artist who runs from the painting of Negro faces to the painting of sunsets after the manner of the academicians because he fears the strange un-whiteness of his own features. An artist must be free to choose what he does, certainly, but he must also never be afraid to do what he might choose.

Let the blare of Negro jazz bands and the bellowing voice of Bessie Smith singing Blues penetrate the closed ears of the colored near-intellectuals until they listen and perhaps understand. Let Paul Robeson singing "Water Boy," and Rudolph Fisher writing about the streets of Harlem, and Jean Toomer holding the heart of Georgia in his hands, and Aaron Douglas drawing strange black fantasies cause the smug Negro middle class to turn from their white, respectable, ordinary books and papers to catch a glimmer of their own beauty. We younger Negro artists who create now intend to express our individual dark-skinned selves without fear or shame. If white people are pleased we are glad. If they are not, it doesn't matter. We know we are beautiful. And ugly too. The tom-tom cries and the tom-tom laughs. If colored people are pleased we are glad. If they are not, their displeasure doesn't matter either. We build our temples for tomorrow, strong as we know how, and we stand on top of the mountain, free within ourselves.

[10]**Wilnold Reiss** portrait painter (1886–1953)

THE NEGRO SPEAKS OF RIVERS°   [1921]

I've known rivers:
I've known rivers ancient as the world and older than the
    Flow of human blood in human veins.

My soul has grown deep like the rivers.

I bathed in the Euphrates when dawns were young.   5
I built my hut near the Congo and it lulled me to sleep.

For commentary about this poem, see pp. 1140–1141.

I looked upon the Nile and raised the Pyramids above it.
I heard the singing of the Mississippi when Abe Lincoln went down
      To New Orleans, and I've seen its muddy bosom turn all golden
        in the sunset.   10

I've known rivers:
Ancient, dusky rivers.

My soul has grown deep like the rivers.

I, Too   [1925]

I, too, sing America.

I am the darker brother.
They send me to eat in the kitchen
When company comes,
But I laugh,   5
And eat well,
And grow strong.

Tomorrow,
I'll sit at the table
When company comes.   10
Nobody'll dare
Say to me,
"Eat in the kitchen,"
Then.

Besides,   15
They'll see how beautiful I am
And be ashamed—

I, too, am America.

THE WEARY BLUES   [1926]

    Droning a drowsy syncopated tune,
Rocking back and forth to a mellow croon,
    I heard a Negro play.
    Down on Lenox Avenue the other night
    By the pale dull pallor of an old gas light   5
    He did a lazy sway . . . .
    He did a lazy sway . . . .
To the tune o' those Weary Blues.
With his ebony hands on each ivory key
He made that poor piano moan with melody.   10
    O Blues!
Swaying to and fro on his rickety stool
He played that sad raggy tune like a musical fool.
    Sweet Blues!

Coming from a black man's soul.   15
  O Blues!
In a deep song voice with a melancholy tone
I heard that Negro sing, that old piano moan—
"Ain't got nobody in all this world,
    Ain't got nobody but ma self.   20
    I's gwine to quit ma frownin'
    And put ma troubles on the shelf."
Thump, thump, thump, went his foot on the floor.
He played a few chords then he sang some more
    "I got the Weary Blues   25
    And I can't be satisfied.
    Got the Weary Blues
    And can't be satisfied—
    I ain't happy no mo'
    And I wish that I had died."   30
And far into the night he crooned that tune.
The stars went out and so did the moon.
The singer stopped playing and went to bed
While the Weary Blues echoed through his head.
He slept like a rock or a man that's dead.   35

ONE FRIDAY MORNING   [1939]

The thrilling news did not come directly to Nancy Lee, but it came in little indirections that finally added themselves up to one tremendous fact: she had won the prize! But being a calm and quiet young lady, she did not say anything, although the whole high school buzzed with rumors, guesses, reportedly authentic announcements on the part of students who had no right to be making announcements at all—since no student really knew yet who had won this year's art scholarship.

But Nancy Lee's drawing was so good, her lines so sure, her colors so bright and harmonious, that certainly no other student in the senior art class at George Washington High was thought to have very much of a chance. Yet you never could tell. Last year nobody had expected Joe Williams to win the Artist Club scholarship with that funny modernistic water color he had done of the high-level bridge. In fact, it was hard to make out there was a bridge until you had looked at the picture a long time. Still, Joe Williams got the prize, was feted by the community's leading painters, club women, and society folks at a big banquet at the Park-Rose Hotel, and was now an award student at the Art School—the city's only art school.

Nancy Lee Johnson was a colored girl, a few years out of the South. But seldom did her high-school classmates think of her as colored. She was smart, pretty, and brown, and fitted in well with the life of the school. She stood high in scholarship, played a swell game of basketball, had taken part in the senior musical in a soft, velvety voice, and had never seemed to intrude or stand out, except in pleasant ways, so it was seldom even mentioned—her color.

Nancy Lee sometimes forgot she was colored herself. She liked her classmates and her school. Particularly she liked her art teacher, Miss Dietrich, the tall red-haired woman who taught her law and order in doing things; and the beauty of working step by step until a job is done; a picture finished; a design created; or a block print carved out of nothing but an idea and a smooth square of linoleum, inked, proofs made, and finally put down on paper—clean, sharp, beautiful, individual, unlike any other in the world, thus making the paper have a meaning nobody else could give it except Nancy Lee. That was the wonderful thing about true creation. You made something nobody else on earth could make but you.

5   Miss Dietrich was the kind of teacher who brought out the best in her students—but their own best, not anybody else's copied best. For anybody else's best, great though it might be, even Michelangelo's, wasn't enough to please Miss Dietrich, dealing with the creative impulses of young men and women living in an American city in the Middle West, and being American.

Nancy Lee was proud of being American, a Negro American with blood out of Africa a long time ago, too many generations back to count. But her parents had taught her the beauties of Africa, its strength, its songs, its mighty rivers, its early smelting of iron, its building of the pyramids, and its ancient and important civilizations. And Miss Dietrich had discovered for her the sharp and humorous lines of African sculpture, Benin, Congo, Makonde. Nancy Lee's father was a mail carrier, her mother a social worker in a city settlement house. Both parents had been to Negro colleges in the South. And her mother had gotten a further degree in social work from a Northern university. Her parents were, like most Americans, simple, ordinary people who had worked hard and steadily for their education. Now they were trying to make it easier for Nancy Lee to achieve learning than it had been for them. They would be very happy when they heard of the award to their daughter—yet Nancy did not tell them. To surprise them would be better. Besides, there had been a promise.

Casually, one day, Miss Dietrich asked Nancy Lee what color frame she thought would be best on her picture. That had been the first inkling.

"Blue," Nancy Lee said. Although the picture had been entered in the Artist Club contest a month ago, Nancy Lee did not hesitate in her choice of a color for the possible frame, since she could still see her picture clearly in her mind's eye for that picture waiting for the blue frame had come out of her soul, her own life, and had bloomed into miraculous being with Miss Dietrich's help. It was, she knew, the best water color she had painted in her four years as a high-school art student, and she was glad she had made something Miss Dietrich liked well enough to permit her to enter in the contest before she graduated.

It was not a modernistic picture in the sense that you had to look at it a long time to understand what it meant. It was just a simple scene in the city park on a spring day, with the trees still leaflessly lacy against the sky, the new grass fresh and green, a flag on a tall pole in the center, children playing, and an old Negro woman sitting on a bench with her head turned. A lot for one picture, to be sure, but it was not there in heavy and final detail like a calendar. Its charm was that everything was light and airy, happy like spring, with a lot of blue sky, paper-white clouds, and air showing through. You could tell that the old Negro woman was looking at the flag, and that the flag was proud in the spring breeze, and that the breeze helped to make the children's dresses billow as they played.

10   Miss Dietrich had taught Nancy Lee how to paint spring, people, and a breeze on what was only a plain white piece of paper from the supply closet. But Miss Dietrich had not said make it like any other spring-people-breeze ever seen before. She let it remain Nancy Lee's own. That is how the old Negro woman happened to be there looking at the flag—for in her mind the flag, the spring, and the woman formed a kind of triangle holding a dream Nancy Lee wanted to express. White stars on a blue field, spring, children, ever-growing life, and an old woman. Would the judges at the Artist Club like it?

One wet, rainy April afternoon Miss O'Shay, the girls' vice-principal, sent for Nancy Lee to stop by her office as school closed. Pupils without umbrellas or rain-coats were clustered in doorways, hoping to make it home between showers. Outside the skies were gray. Nancy Lee's thoughts were suddenly gray, too.

She did not think she had done anything wrong, yet that tight little knot came in her throat just the same as she approached Miss O'Shay's door. Perhaps she had banged her locker too often and too hard. Perhaps the note in French she had written to Sallie halfway across the study hall just for fun had never gotten to Sallie but into Miss O'Shay's hands instead. Or maybe she was failing in some subject and wouldn't be allowed to graduate. Chemistry! A pang went through the pit of her stomach. She knocked on Miss O'Shay's door. That familiarly solid and competent voice said, "Come in."

Miss O'Shay had a way of making you feel welcome, even if you came to be expelled.

"Sit down, Nancy Lee Johnson," said Miss O'Shay. "I have something to tell you." Nancy Lee sat down. "But I must ask you to promise not to tell anyone yet."

15   "I won't, Miss O'Shay," Nancy Lee said, wondering what on earth the principal had to say to her.

"You are about to graduate," Miss O'Shay said. "And we shall miss you. You have been an excellent student, Nancy, and you will not be without honors on the senior list, as I am sure you know."

At that point there was a light knock on the door. Miss O'Shay called out, "Come in," and Miss Dietrich entered. "May I be a part of this, too?" she asked, tall and smiling.

"Of course," Miss O'Shay said. "I was just telling Nancy Lee what we thought of her. But I hadn't gotten around to giving her the news. Perhaps, Miss Dietrich, you'd like to tell her yourself."

Miss Dietrich was always direct. "Nancy Lee," she said, "your picture has won the Artist Club scholarship."

20   The slender brown girl's eyes widened, her heart thumped, then her throat tightened again. She tried to smile, but instead tears came to her eyes.

"Dear Nancy Lee," Miss O'Shay said, "we are so happy for you." The elderly white woman took her hand and shook it warmly while Miss Dietrich beamed with pride.

Nancy Lee must have danced all the way home. She never remembered quite how she got there through the rain. She hoped she had been dignified. But certainly she hadn't stopped to tell anybody her secret on the way. Raindrops, smiles, and tears mingled on her brown cheeks. She hoped her mother hadn't yet gotten home and that the house was empty. She wanted to have time to calm down and look natural before she had to see anyone. She didn't want to be bursting with excitement—having a secret to contain.

Miss O'Shay's calling her to the office had been in the nature of a preparation and a warning. The kind, elderly vice-principal said she did not believe in catching young ladies unawares, even with honors, so she wished her to know about the coming award. In making acceptance speeches she wanted her to be calm, prepared, not nervous, overcome, and frightened. So Nancy Lee was asked to think what she would say when the scholarship was conferred upon her a few days hence, both at the Friday morning high-school assembly hour, when the announcement would be made, and at the evening banquet of the Artist Club. Nancy Lee promised the vice-principal to think calmly about what she would say.

Miss Dietrich had then asked for some facts about her parents, her background, and her life, since such material would probably be desired for the papers. Nancy Lee had told her how, six years before, they had come up from the Deep South, her father having been successful in achieving a transfer from the one post office to another, a thing he had long sought in order to give Nancy Lee a chance to go to school in the North. Now they lived in a modest Negro neighborhood, went to see the best plays when they came to town, and had been saving to send Nancy Lee to art school, in case she were permitted to enter. But the scholarship would help a great deal, for they were not rich people.

25 "Now Mother can have a new coat next winter," Nancy Lee thought, "because my tuition will all be covered for the first year. And once in art school, there are other scholarships I can win."

Dreams began to dance through her head, plans and ambitions, beauties she would create for herself, her parents, and the Negro people—for Nancy Lee possessed a deep and reverent race pride. She could see the old woman in her picture (really her grandmother in the South) lifting her head to the bright stars on the flag in the distance. A Negro in America! Often hurt, discriminated against, sometimes lynched—but always there were the stars on the blue body of the flag. Was there any other flag in the world that had so many stars? Nancy Lee thought deeply, but she could remember none in all the encyclopedias or geographies she had ever looked into.

"Hitch your wagon to a star," Nancy Lee thought, dancing home in the rain. "Who were our flag-makers?"

Friday morning came, the morning when the world would know—her high-school world, the newspaper world, her mother and dad. Dad could not be there at the assembly to hear the announcement, nor see her prize picture displayed on the stage, nor to listen to Nancy Lee's little speech of acceptance, but Mother would be able to come, although Mother was much puzzled as to why Nancy Lee was so insistent she be at school on that particular Friday morning.

When something is happening, something new and fine, something that will change your very life, it is hard to go to sleep at night for thinking about it, and hard to keep your heart from pounding, or a strange little knot of joy from gathering in your throat. Nancy Lee had taken her bath, brushed her hair until it glowed, and had gone to bed thinking about the next day, the big day, when before three thousand students, she would be the one student honored, her painting the one painting to be acclaimed as the best of the year from all the art classes of the city. Her short speech of gratitude was ready. She went over it in her mind, not word for word (because she didn't want it to sound as if she had learned it by heart), but she let the thoughts flow simply and sincerely through her consciousness many times.

30   When the president of the Artist Club presented her with the medal and scroll of the scholarship award, she would say:

     "Judges and members of the Artist Club, I want to thank you for this award that means so much to me personally and through me to my people, the colored people of this city, who, sometimes, are discouraged and bewildered, thinking that color and poverty are against them. I accept this award with gratitude and pride, not for myself alone, but for my race that believes in American opportunity and American fairness—and the bright stars in our flag. I thank Miss Dietrich and the teachers who made it possible for me to have the knowledge and training that lie behind this honor you have conferred upon my painting. When I came here from the South a few years ago, I was not sure how you would receive me. You received me well. You have given me a chance and helped me along the road I wanted to follow. I suppose the judges know that every week here at assembly the students of this school pledge allegiance to the flag. I shall try to be worthy of that pledge, and of the help and friendship and understanding of my fellow citizens of whatever race or creed, and of our American dream of 'Liberty and justice for all!'"

     That would be her response before the students in the morning. How proud and happy the Negro pupils would be, perhaps almost as proud as they were of the one colored star on the football team. Her mother would probably cry with happiness. Thus Nancy Lee went to sleep dreaming of a wonderful tomorrow.

     The bright sunlight of an April morning woke her. There was breakfast with her parents—their half-amused and puzzled faces across the table, wondering what could be this secret that made her eyes so bright. The swift walk to school; the clock in the tower almost nine; hundreds of pupils streaming into the long, rambling old building that was the city's largest high school; the sudden quiet of the homeroom after the bell rang; then the teacher opening her record book to call the roll. But just before she began, she looked across the room until her eyes located Nancy Lee.

     "Nancy," she said, "Miss O'Shay would like to see you in her office, please."

35   Nancy Lee rose and went out while the names were being called and the word *present* added its period to each name. Perhaps, Nancy Lee thought, the reporters from the papers had already come. Maybe they wanted to take her picture before assembly, which wasn't until ten o'clock. (Last year they had had the photograph of the winner of the award in the morning papers as soon as the announcement had been made.)

     Nancy Lee knocked at Miss O'Shay's door.

     "Come in."

     The vice-principal stood at her desk. There was no one else in the room. It was very quiet.

     "Sit down, Nancy Lee," she said. Miss O'Shay did not smile. There was a long pause. The seconds went by slowly. "I do not know how to tell you what I have to say," the elderly woman began, her eyes on the papers on her desk. "I am indignant and ashamed for myself and for this city." Then she lifted her eyes and looked at Nancy Lee in the near blue dress, sitting there before her. "You are not to receive the scholarship this morning."

40   Outside in the hall the electric bells announcing the first period rang, loud and interminably long. Miss O'Shay remained silent. To the brown girl here in the chair, the room grew suddenly smaller, smaller, smaller, and there was no air. She could not speak.

Miss O'Shay said, "When the committee learned that you were colored, they changed their plans."

Still Nancy Lee said nothing, for there was no air to give breath to her lungs.

"Here is the letter from the committee, Nancy Lee." Miss O'Shay picked it up and read the final paragraph to her.

" 'It seems to us wiser to arbitrarily rotate the award among the various high schools of the city from now on. And especially in this case since the student chosen happens to be colored, a circumstance which unfortunately, had we known, might have prevented this embarrassment. But there have never been any Negro students in the local art school, and the presence of one there might create difficulties for all concerned. We have high regard for the quality of Nancy Lee Johnson's talent, but we do not feel it would be fair to honor it with the Artist Club award.' " Miss O'Shay paused. She put the letter down.

45 "Nancy Lee, I am very sorry to have to give you this message."

"But my speech," Nancy Lee said, "was about . . . ." The words stuck in her throat. " . . . about America . . . ."

Miss O'Shay had risen; she turned her back and stood looking out the window at the spring tulips in the school yard.

"I thought, since the award would be made at assembly right after our oath of allegiance," the words rumbled almost hysterically from Nancy Lee's throat now, "I would put part of the flag salute in my speech. You know, Miss O'Shay, that part about 'liberty and justice for all.' "

"I know," said Miss O'Shay, slowly facing the room again. "But America is only what we who believe in it make it. I am Irish. You may not know, Nancy Lee, but years ago we were called the dirty Irish, and mobs rioted against us in the big cities, and we were invited to go back where we came from. But we didn't go. And we didn't give up, because we believed in the American dream, and in our power to make that dream come true. Difficulties, yes. Mountains to climb, yes. Discouragements to face, yes. Democracy to make, yes. That is it, Nancy Lee! We still have in this world of ours democracy to *make*. You and I, Nancy Lee. But the premise and the base are here, the lines of the Declaration of Independence and the words of Lincoln are here, and the stars in our flag. Those who deny you this scholarship do not know the meaning of those stars, but it's up to us to make them know. As a teacher in the public schools of this city, I myself will go before the school board and ask them to remove from our system the offer of any prizes or awards denied to any student because of race or color."

50 Suddenly Miss O'Shay stopped speaking. Her clear, clear blue eyes looked into those of the girl before her. The woman's eyes were full of strength and courage. "Lift up your head, Nancy Lee, and smile at me."

Miss O'Shay stood against the open window with the green lawn and the tulips beyond, the sunlight tangled in her gray hair, her voice an electric flow of strength to the hurt spirit of Nancy Lee. The Abolitionists who believed in freedom when there was slavery must have been like that. The first white teachers who went into the Deep South to teach the freed slaves must have been like that. All those who stand against ignorance, narrowness, hate, and mud on stars must be like that.

Nancy Lee lifted her head and smiled. The bell for assembly rang. She went through the long hall filled with students, toward the auditorium.

"There will be other awards," Nancy Lee thought. "There are schools in other cities. This won't keep me down. But when I'm a woman, I'll fight to see that these things don't happen to other girls as this has happened to me. And men and women like Miss O'Shay will help me."

She took her seat among the seniors. The doors of the auditorium closed. As the principal came onto the platform, the students rose and turned their eyes to the flag on the stage.

55   One hand went to the heart, the other outstretched toward the flag. Three thousand voices spoke. Among them was the voice of a dark girl whose cheeks were suddenly wet with tears, ". . . one nation indivisible, with liberty and justice for all."

"That is the land we must make," she thought.

THEME FOR ENGLISH B   [1951]

The instructor said,

Go home and write
A page tonight.

And let that page come out of you—
Then, it will be true.   5

I wonder if it's that simple?

I am twenty-two, colored, born in Winston-Salem.
I went to school there, then Durham, then here
To this college on the hill above Harlem.
I am the only colored student in my class.   10
The steps from the hill lead down to Harlem,
Through a park, then I cross St. Nicholas,
Eighth Avenue, Seventh, and I come to the Y,
The Harlem Branch Y, where I take the elevator
Up to my room, sit down, and write this page: 15

It's not easy to know what is true for you or me
At twenty-two, my age. But I guess I'm what
I feel and see and hear. Harlem, I hear you:
Hear you, hear me—we two—you, me talk on this page.
(I hear New York, too.) Me—who?   20

Well, I like to eat, sleep, drink, and be in love.
I like to work, read, learn, and understand life.
I like a pipe for a Christmas present,
Or records—Bessie, bop, or Bach.

I guess being colored doesn't make me not like   25
The same things other folks like who are other races.
So will my page be colored that I write?
Being me, it will not be white.
But it will be

A part of you instructor.   30
You are white—
Yet a part of me, as I am part of you.
That's American.
Sometimes perhaps you don't want to be a part of me.
Nor do I often want to be a part of you.   35
But we are, that's true!
As I learn from you,
I guess you learn from me—
Although you're older—and white—
And somewhat more free.   40

This is my page for English B.

CLAUDE MCKAY   [1889–1948]

*Claude McKay was born to peasant farmers in Sunny Ville,
Jamaica. He won an award for his first volume of poetry,
Songs of Jamaica, published in London in 1912. The award
money allowed McKay to travel to the United States, where
he studied for a time at the Tuskegee Institute and at
Kansas State University before settling in New York City.
Energized by the racism he encountered, McKay continued
to write poetry, much of it political, as he became active in
a number of social causes. McKay became one of the lead-
ing features of the Harlem Renaissance.* Home to Harlem, *his 1928 novel about a
black soldier's return home following World War I, was a tremendous commercial
success. His other works include two novels,* Banjo: A Story Without a Plot *(1929)
and* Banana Bottom *(1933), and an autobiography,* A Long Way from Home
(1937).

AMERICA   [1921]

Although she feeds me bread of bitterness,
And sinks into my throat her tiger's tooth,
Stealing my breath of life, I will confess
I love this cultured hell that tests my youth!
Her vigor flows like tides into my blood,   5
Giving me strength erect against her hate.
Her bigness sweeps my being like a flood.
Yet as a rebel fronts a king in state,
I stand within her walls with not a shred
Of terror, malice, not a word of jeer.   10
Darkly I gaze into the days ahead,
And see her might and granite wonders there,
Beneath the touch of Time's unerring hand,
Like priceless treasures sinking in the sand.

GWENDOLYN B. BENNETT [1902–1981]

*Gwendolyn Bennett was born in Giddings, Texas, studied
Fine Arts at Columbia University and the Pratt Institute,
and taught art at Howard University, in Washington, D.C.
In addition to her poetry, she published illustrations in
the prominent journals* Opportunity *and* Crisis. *Her poetry
(including "Heritage," below) expresses an appreciation of
the beauty of her African descent and a sadness in
response to the ways in which it had been defiled.*

HERITAGE   [1923]

I want to see the slim palm-trees,
Pulling at the clouds
With little pointed fingers. . . .

I want to see lithe Negro girls,
Etched dark against the sky   5
While sunset lingers.

I want to hear the silent sands,
Singing to the moon
Before the Sphinx-still face. . . .

I want to hear the chanting   10
Around a heathen fire
Of a strange black race.

I want to breathe the Lotus flow'r,
Sighing to the stars
With tendrils drinking at the Nile. . . .   15

I want to feel the surging
Of my sad people's soul
Hidden by a minstrel-smile.

JEAN TOOMER [1894–1967]

*One of the important figures of the Harlem Renaissance,
Jean Toomer was born in Washington, D.C. Toomer, who
was of mixed racial heritage, was raised in the house of
his grandfather, who had been governor of Louisiana
during Reconstruction. In 1921, Toomer held a position for
a few months as principal of a technical institute in
Sparta, Georgia, traveling to the Deep South for the first
time in his life. The experience inspired him to write his
great masterpiece,* Cane *(1923), an experimental novel made up of the poems,
songs, and stories he encountered among the African-Americans of the region. The*

*novel established Toomer's reputation, and throughout the twenties his work
appeared in many of the leading African-American and avante-garde journals of
the day. He was largely forgotten until the republication of* Cane *in 1969 reawak-
ened interest in his life and works.*

REAPERS   [1923]

Black reapers with the sound of steel on stones
Are sharpening scythes. I see them place the hones
In their hip-pockets as a thing that's done,
And start their silent swinging, one by one.
Black horses drive a mower through the weeds,   5
And there, a field rat, started squealing bleeds,
His belly close to ground. I see the blade,
Blood-stained, continue cutting weeds and shade.

COUNTEE CULLEN [1903–1946]

*Countee Cullen was adopted by a Methodist minister and
spent his childhood years living in Harlem. He attended
New York University and Harvard. While a college student,
he published his first poetry and soon became identified
with the black writers of the Harlem Renaissance period.
His works of poetry include* Color *(1925),* Copper Sun
(1927), and The Black Christ *(1929), and other works
include a novel,* One Way to Heaven *(1932), and a collec-
tion of poems,* Medea *(1935). On These I Stand, *a collection of his favorite poems,
was published the year after he died. Another of his poems, "Incident," published
in 1925, appears on page 24 of this text.*

YET DO I MARVEL   [1925]

I doubt not God is good, well-meaning, kind,
And did He stoop to quibble could tell why
The little buried mole continues blind,
Why flesh that mirrors Him must some day die,
Make plain the reason tortured Tantalus   5
Is baited by the fickle fruit, declare
If merely brute caprice dooms Sisyphus
To struggle up a never-ending stair.
Inscrutable His ways are, and immune
To catechism by a mind too strewn   10
With petty cares to slightly understand
What awful brain compels His awful hand.
Yet do I marvel at this curious thing:
To make a poet black, and bid him sing!

FROM THE DARK TOWER   [1927]

(To Charles S. Johnson)

We shall not always plant while others reap
The golden increment of bursting fruit,
Not always countenance, abject and mute,
That lesser men should hold their brothers cheap;
Not everlastingly while others sleep   5
Shall we beguile their limbs with mellow flute,
Not always bend to some more subtle brute;
We were not made eternally to weep.

The night whose sable breast relieves the stark,
White stars is no less lovely being dark,   10
And there are buds that cannot bloom at all
In light, but crumple, piteous, and fall;
So in the dark we hide the heart that bleeds,
And wait, and tend our agonizing seeds.

ANNE SPENCER [1882–1975]

*Born Anne Bethel Bannister, Anne Spencer graduated from
the Virginia Seminary in 1899. She was an avid gardener
and taught in a public school in West Virginia. She did not
publish her first poem until 1920, when James Weldon
Johnson, noted editor and writer, encouraged her to
submit it to* Crisis, *an important journal of the time. Most
of her poetry is more concerned with gender than with
race, and fewer than thirty of her poems were published
during her lifetime. After she died, her home and garden in Lynchburg, Virginia,
were given the status of historic landmark.*

LADY, LADY   [1925]

Lady, Lady, I saw your face,
Dark as night withholding a star . . .
The chisel fell, or it might have been
You had borne so long the yoke of men.

Lady, Lady, I saw your hands,   5
Twisted, awry, like crumpled roots,
Bleached poor white in a sudsy tub,
Wrinkled and drawn from your rub-a-dub.

Lady, Lady, I saw your heart,
And altared there in its darksome place   10
Were the tongues of flame the ancients knew,
Where the good God sits to spangle through.

GEORGIA DOUGLAS JOHNSON [1886–1966]

Considered the most popular female poet of the Harlem Renaissance, Georgia Douglas Johnson never actually lived in Harlem. She grew up in Rome, Georgia, and Atlanta. She taught in Marietta, Georgia, and was an assistant school principal in Atlanta. While many of her poems and short stories address the issue of race and race relations, it's clear that her favorite topic was the role of love in the lives of women. The following poem was set to music and became a very popular song of the late 1920s.

I WANT TO DIE WHILE YOU LOVE ME   [1927]

I want to die while you love me,
   While yet you hold me fair,
While laughter lies upon my lips
   And lights are in my hair.

I want to die while you love me,   5
   And bear to that still bed,
Your kisses turbulent, unspent,
   To warm me when I'm dead.

I want to die while you love me,
   Oh, who would care to live   10
Till love has nothing more to ask
   And nothing more to give!

I want to die while you love me
   And never, never see
The glory of this perfect day   15
   Grow dim or cease to be.

ZORA NEALE HURSTON [c. 1891–1960]

Zora Neale Hurston was born and spent her early childhood in Eatonville, Florida. When her mother died in 1912, she spent the rest of her years growing up being moved from one relative to another. In 1925 she moved to New York City and became a prominent member of the Harlem Renaissance. A distinguishing feature of her work is that her characters speak in the black country dialect of her native Florida. Her best-known novel is Their Eyes Were Watching God *(1937).*

SWEAT   [1926]

I

It was eleven o'clock of a Spring night in Florida. It was Sunday. Any other night, Delia Jones would have been in bed for two hours by this time. But she was a washwoman, and Monday morning meant a great deal to her. So she collected the soiled clothes on Saturday when she returned the clean things. Sunday night after church, she sorted and put the white things to soak. It saved her almost a half-day's start. A great hamper in the bedroom held the clothes that she brought home. It was so much neater than a number of bundles lying around.

She squatted on the kitchen floor beside the great pile of clothes, sorting them into small heaps according to color, and humming a song in a mournful key, but wondering through it all where Sykes, her husband, had gone with her horse and buckboard.

Just then something long, round, limp, and black fell upon her shoulders and slithered to the floor beside her. A great terror took hold of her. It softened her knees and dried her mouth so that it was a full minute before she could cry out or move. Then she saw that it was the big bull whip her husband liked to carry when he drove.

She lifted her eyes to the door and saw him standing there bent over with laughter at her fright. She screamed at him.

5   "Sykes, what you throw dat whip on me like dat? You know it would skeer me—looks just like a snake, an' you knows how skeered Ah is of snakes."

"Course Ah knowed it! That's how come Ah done it." He slapped his leg with his hand and almost rolled on the ground in his mirth. "If you such a big fool dat you got to have a fit over a earth worm or a string, Ah don't keer how bad Ah skeer you."

"You ain't got no business doing it. Gawd knows it's a sin. Some day Ah'm goin-tuh drop dead from some of yo' follishness. 'Nother thing, where you been wid mah rig? Ah feeds dat pony. He ain't fuh you to be drivin' wid no bull whip."

"You sho' is one aggravatin' nigger woman!" he declared and stepped into the room. She resumed her work and did not answer him at once. "Ah done tole you time and again to keep them white folks' clothes outa dis house."

He picked up the whip and glared at her. Delia went on with her work. She went out into the yard and returned with a galvanized tub and set it on the washbench. She saw that Sykes had kicked all of the clothes together again, and now stood in her way truculently, his whole manner hoping, *praying*, for an argument. But she walked calmly around him and commenced to re-sort the things.

10   "Next time, Ah'm gointer kick 'em outdoors," he threatened as he struck a match along the leg of his corduroy breeches.

Delia never looked up from her work, and her thin, stooped shoulders sagged further.

"Ah ain't for no fuss t'night, Sykes. Ah just come from taking sacrament at the church house."

He snorted scornfully. "Yeah, you just come from de church house on a Sunday night, but heah you is gone to work on them clothes. You ain't nothing but a hypocrite. One of them amen-corner Christians—sing, whoop, and shout, then come home and wash white folks' clothes on the Sabbath."

He stepped roughly upon the whitest pile of things, kicking them helter-skelter as he crossed the room. His wife gave a little scream of dismay, and quickly gathered them together again.

15   "Sykes, you quit grindin' dirt into these clothes! How can Ah git through by Sat'day if Ah don't start on Sunday?"

"Ah don't keer if you never git through. Anyhow, Ah done promised Gawd and a couple of other men, Ah ain't gointer have it in mah house. Don't gimme no lip neither, else Ah'll throw 'em out and put mah fist up side yo' head to boot."

Delia's habitual meekness seemed to slip from her shoulders like a blown scarf. She was on her feet; her poor little body, her bare knuckly hands bravely defying the strapping hulk before her.

"Looka heah, Sykes, you done gone too fur. Ah been married to you fur fifteen years, and Ah been takin' in washin' fur fifteen years. Sweat, sweat, sweat! Work and sweat, cry and sweat, pray and sweat!"

"What's that got to do with me?" he asked brutally.

20   "What's it got to do with you, Sykes? Mah tub of suds is filled yo' belly with vit-tles more times than yo' hands is filled it. Mah sweat is done paid for this house and Ah reckon Ah kin keep on sweatin' in it."

She seized the iron skillet from the stove and struck a defensive pose, which act surprised him greatly, coming from her. It cowed him and he did not strike her as he usually did.

"Naw you won't," she panted, "that ole snaggle-toothed black woman you runnin' with ain't comin' heah to pile up on *mah* sweat and blood. You ain't paid for nothin' on this place, and Ah'm gointer stay right heah till Ah'm toted out foot fore-most."

"Well, you better quit gittin' me riled up, else they'll be totin' you out sooner than you expect. Ah'm so tired of you Ah don't know whut to do. Gawd! How Ah hates skinny wimmen!"

A little awed by this new Delia, he sidled out of the door and slammed the back gate after him. He did not say where he had gone, but she knew too well. She knew very well that he would not return until nearly daybreak also. Her work over, she went on to bed but not to sleep at once. Things had come to a pretty pass!

25   She lay awake, gazing upon the debris that cluttered their matrimonial trail. Not an image left standing along the way. Anything like flowers had long ago been drowned in the salty stream that had been pressed from her heart. Her tears, her sweat, her blood. She had brought love to the union and he had brought a longing after the flesh. Two months after the wedding, he had given her the first brutal beat-ing. She had the memory of his numerous trips to Orlando with all of his wages when he had returned to her penniless, even before the first year had passed. She was young and soft then, but now she thought of her knotty, muscled limbs, her harsh knuckly hands, and drew herself up into an unhappy little ball in the middle of the big feather bed. Too late now to hope for love, even if it were not Bertha it would be someone else. This case differed from the others only in that she was bolder than the others. Too late for everything except her little home. She had built it for her old days, and planted one by one the trees and flowers there. It was lovely to her, lovely.

Somehow, before sleep came, she found herself saying aloud: "Oh well, whatever goes over the Devil's back, is got to come under his belly. Sometime or ruther, Sykes, like everybody else, is gointer reap his sowing." After that she was able to build a spiritual earthworks against her husband. His shells could no longer reach her. AMEN. She went to sleep and slept until he announced his presence in bed by kick-ing her feet and rudely snatching the covers away.

"Gimme some kivah heah, an' git yo' damn foots over on yo' own side! Ah oughter mash you in yo' mouf fuh drawing dat skillet on me."

Delia went clear to the rail without answering him. A triumphant indifference to all that he was or did.

II

The week was full of work for Delia as all other weeks, and Saturday found her behind her little pony, collecting and delivering clothes.

30   It was a hot, hot day near the end of July. The village men on Joe Clarke's porch even chewed cane listlessly. They did not hurl the cane-knots as usual. They let them dribble over the edge of the porch. Even conversation had collapsed under the heat.

"Heah come Delia Jones," Jim Merchant said, as the shaggy pony came 'round the bend of the road toward them. The rusty buckboard was heaped with baskets of crisp, clean laundry.

"Yep," Joe Lindsay agreed. "Hot or col', rain or shine, jes' ez reg'lar ez de weeks roll roun' Delia carries 'em an' fetches 'em on Sat'day."

"She better if she wanter eat," said Moss. "Syke Jones ain't wuth de shot an' powder hit would tek tuh kill 'em. Not to *huh* he ain't."

"He sho' ain't," Walter Thomas chimed in. "It's too bad, too, cause she wuz a right pretty li'l trick when he got huh. Ah'd uh mah'ied huh mahself if he hadnter beat me to it."

35   Delia nodded briefly at the men as she drove past.

"Too much knockin' will ruin *any* 'oman. He done beat huh 'nough tuh kill three women, let 'lone change they looks," said Elijah Moseley. "How Syke kin stommuck dat big black greasy Mogul he's layin' roun' wid, gits me. Ah swear dat eightrock couldn't kiss a sardine can Ah done thowed out de back do' 'way las' yeah."

"Aw, she's fat, thass how come. He's allus been crazy 'bout fat women," put in Merchant. "He'd a' been tied up wid one long time ago if he could a' found one tuh have him. Did Ah tell yuh 'bout him come sidlin' roun' *mah* wife—bringin' her a basket uh peecans outa his yard fuh a present? Yessir, mah wife! She tol' him tuh take 'em right straight back home, 'cause Delia works so hard ovah dat washtub she reckon everything on de place taste lak sweat an' soapsuds. Ah jus' wisht Ah'd a' caught 'im 'roun' dere! Ah'd a' made his hips ketch on fiah down dat shell road."

"Ah know he done it, too. Ah sees 'im grinnin' at every 'oman dat passes," Walter Thomas said. "But even so, he useter eat some mighty big hunks uh humble pie tuh git dat li'l 'oman he got. She wuz ez pretty ez a speckled pup! Dat wuz fifteen years ago. He useter be so skeered uh losin' huh, she could make him do some parts of a husband's duty. Dey never wuz de same in de mind."

"There oughter be a law about him," said Lindsay. "He ain't fit tuh carry guts tuh a bear."

40   Clarke spoke for the first time. "Tain't no law on earth dat kin make a man be decent if it ain't in 'im. There's plenty men dat takes a wife lak dey do a joint uh sugar-cane. It's round, juicy, an' sweet when dey gits it. But dey squeeze an' grind, squeeze an' grind an' wring tell dey wring every drop uh pleasure dat's in 'em out. When dey's satisfied dat dey is wrung dry, dey treats 'em jes' lak dey do a cane-chew. Dey thows 'em away. Dey knows whut dey is doin' while dey is at it, an' hates

theirselves fuh it but they keeps on hangin' after huh tell she's empty. Den dey hates huh fuh bein' a cane-chew an' in de way."

"We oughter take Syke an' dat stray 'oman uh his'n down in Lake Howell swamp an' lay on de rawhide till they cain't say Lawd a' mussy. He allus wuz uh ovahbearin niggah, but since dat white 'oman from up north done teached 'im how to run a automobile, he done got too beggety to live—an' we oughter kill 'im," Old Man Anderson advised.

A grunt of approval went around the porch. But the heat was melting their civic virtue and Elijah Moseley began to bait Joe Clarke.

"Come on, Joe, git a melon outa dere an' slice it up for yo' customers. We'se all sufferin' wid de heat. De bear's done got *me!*"

"Thass right, Joe, a watermelon is jes' whut Ah needs tuh cure de eppizudicks," Walter Thomas joined forces with Moseley. "Come on dere, Joe. We all is steady customers an' you ain't set us up in a long ime. Ah chooses dat long, bow-legged Floridy favorite."

45   "A god, an' be dough. You all gimme twenty cents and slice away," Clarke retorted. "Ah needs a col' slice m'self. Heah, everybody chip in. Ah'll lend y'all mah meat knife."

The money was all quickly subscribed and the huge melon brought forth. At that moment, Sykes and Bertha arrived. A determined silence fell on the porch and the melon was put away again.

Merchant snapped down the blade of his jacknife and moved toward the store door.

"Come on in, Joe, an' gimme a slab uh sow belly an' uh pound uh coffee—almost fuhgot 'twas Sat'day. Got to git on home." Most of the men left also.

Just then Delia drive past on her way home, as Sykes was ordering magnificently for Bertha. It pleased him for Delia to see.

50   "Git whutsoever yo' heart desires, Honey. Wait a minute, Joe. Give huh two bottles uh strawberry soda-water, uh quart parched ground-peas, an' a block uh chewin' gum."

With all this they left the store, with Sykes reminding Bertha that this was his town and she could have it if she wanted it.

The men returned soon after they left, and held their watermelon feast.

"Where did Syke Jones git da 'oman from nohow?" Lindsay asked.

"Ovah Apopka. Guess dey musta been cleanin' out de town when she lef'. She don't look lak a thing but a hunk uh liver wid hair on it."

55   "Well, she sho' kin squall," Dave Carter contributed. "When she gits ready tuh laff, she jes' opens huh mouf an' latches it back tuh de las' notch. No ole granpa alligator down in Lake Bell ain't go nothin' on huh."

III

Bertha had been in town three months now. Sykes was still paying her room-rent at Della Lewis'—the only house in town that would have taken her in. Sykes took her frequently to Winter Park to "stomps." He still assured her that he was the swellest man in the state.

"Sho' you kin have dat li'l ole house soon's Ah git dat 'oman outa dere. Everything b'longs tuh me an' you sho' kin have it. Ah sho 'bominates uh skinny 'oman. Lawdy, you sho' is got one portly shape on you! You kin git *anything* you wants. Dis is *mah* town an' you sho' kin have it."

Delia's work-worn knees crawled over the earth in Gethsemane[1] and up the rocks of Calvary many, many times during these months. She avoided the villagers and meeting places in her efforts to be blind and deaf. But Bertha nullified this to a degree, by coming to Delia's house to call Sykes out to her at the gate.

Delia and Sykes fought all the time now with no peaceful interludes. They slept and ate in silence. Two or three times Delia had attempted a timid friendliness, but she was repulsed each time. It was plain that the breaches must remain agape.

60   The sun had burned July to August. The heat streamed down like a million hot arrows, smiting all things living upon the earth. Grass withered, leaves browned, snakes went blind in shedding, and men and dogs went mad. Dog days!

Delia came home one day and found Sykes there before her. She wondered, but started to go on into the house without speaking, even though he was standing at the kitchen door and she must either stoop under his arm or ask him to move. He made no room for her. She noticed a soap box beside the steps, but paid no particular attention to it, knowing that he must have brought it there. As she was stooping to pass under his outstretched arm, he suddenly pushed her backward, laughingly.

"Look in de box dere Delia, Ah done brung yuh somethin'!"

She nearly fell upon the box in her stumbling, and when she saw what it held, she all but fainted outright.

"Syke! Syke, mah Gawd! You take dat rattlesnake 'way from heah! You *gottuh*. Oh, Jesus, have mussy!"

65   "Ah ain't got tuh do nuthin' uh de kin'—fact is Ah ain't got tuh do nothin' but die. Tain't no use uh you puttin' on airs makin' out lak you skeered uh dat snake— he's gointer stay right heah tell he die. He wouldn't bite me cause Ah knows how tuh handle 'im. Nohow he wouldn't risk breakin' out his fangs 'gin *yo* skinny laigs."

"Naw, now Syke, don't keep dat thing 'round tryin' tuh skeer me tuh death. You knows Ah'm even feared uh earth worms. Thass de biggest snake Ah evah did se. Kill 'im Syke, please."

"Doan ast me tuh do nothin' fuh yuh. Goin' 'round tryin' tuh be so damn aster-perious. Naw, Ah ain't gonna kill it. Ah think uh damn sight mo' uh him dan you! Dat's a nice snake an' anybody doan lak 'im kin jes' hit de grit."

The village soon heard that Sykes had the snake, and came to see and ask questions.

"How de hen-fire did you ketch dat six-foot rattler, Syke?" Thomas asked.

70   "He's full uh frogs so he cain't hardly move, thass how Ah eased up on 'm. But Ah'm a snake charmer an' knows how to handle 'em. Shux, dat ain't nothin'. Ah could ketch one eve'y day if Ah so wanted tuh."

"What he needs is a heavy hick'ry club leaned real heavy on his head. Dat's de bes' way tuh charm a rattlesnake."

"Naw, Walt, y'all jes' don't understand dese diamon' backs lak Ah do," said Sykes in a superior tone of voice.

The village agreed with Walter, but the snake stayed on. His box remained by the kitchen door with its screen wire covering. Two or three days later it had digested its

[1]**Gethsemane** a reference to the garden where Jesus was betrayed (in the Gospels) before being tried and crucified on Calvary or Golgotha, the "hill of skulls."

meal of frogs and literally came to life. It rattled at every movement in the kitchen or the yard. One day as Delia came down the kitchen steps she saw his chalky-white fangs curved like scimitars hung in the wire meshes. This time she did not run away with averted eyes as usual. She stood for a long time in the doorway in a red fury that grew bloodier for every second that she regarded the creature that was her torment.

That night she broached the subject as soon as Sykes sat down to the table.

75 "Syke, Ah wants you tuh take dat snake 'way fum heah. You done starved me an' Ah put up widcher, you done beat me an Ah took dat, but you don kilt all mah insides bringin' dat varmint heah."

Sykes poured out a saucer full of coffee and drank it deliberately before he answered her.

"A whole lot Ah keer 'bout how you feels inside uh out. Dat snake ain' goin' no damn wheah till Ah gits ready fuh 'im tuh go. So fur as beatin' is concerned, yuh ain't took near all dat you gointer take ef yuh stay 'round *me*."

Delia pushed back her plate and got up from the table. "Ah hates you, Sykes," she said calmly. "Ah hates you tuh de same degree dat Ah useter love yuh. Ah done took an' took till mah belly is full up tuh mah neck. Dat's de reason Ah got mah letter fum de church an' moved mah membership tuh Woodbridge—so Ah don't haftuh take no sacrament wid yuh. Ah don't wantuh see yuh 'round me atall. Lay 'round wid dat 'oman all yuh wants tuh, but gwan 'way from me an' mah house. Ah hates yuh lak uh suck-egg dog."

Sykes almost let the huge wad of corn bread and collard greens he was chewing fall out of his mouth in amazement. He had a hard time whipping himself up to the proper fury to try to answer Delia.

80 "Well, Ah'm glad you does hate me. Ah'm sho' tiahed uh you hangin' ontuh me. Ah don't want yuh. Look at yuh stringey old neck! Yo' rawbony laigs an' arms is enough tuh cut uh man tuh death. You looks jes' lak de devvul's doll-baby tuh *me*. You cain't hate me no worse dan Ah hates you. Ah been hatin' *you* fuh years."

"Yo' ole black hide don't look lak nothin' tuh me, but uh passle uh wrinkled up rubber, wid yo' big ole yeahs flappin' on each side lak uh paih uh buzzard wings. Don't think Ah'm gointuh be run 'way fum mah house neither. Ah'm goin' tuh de white folks 'bout *you*, mah young man, de very nex' time you lay yo' han's on me. Mah cup is done run ovah." Delia said this with no signs of fear and Sykes departed from the house, threatening her, but made not the slightest move to carry out any of them.

That night he did not return at all, and the next day being Sunday, Delia was glad she did not have to quarrel before she hitched up her pony and drove the four miles to Woodbridge.

She stayed to the night service—"love feast"—which was very warm and full of spirit. In the emotional winds her domestic trials were borne far and wide so that she sang as she drove homeward,

> Jurden water, black an' col
> Chills de body, not de soul
> An 'Ah wantah cross Jurden in uh calm time.

She came from the barn to the kitchen door and stopped.

"Whut's de mattah, ol' Satan, you ain't kicken' up yo' racket?" She addressed the snake's box. Complete silence. She went on into the house with a new hope in its birth struggles. Perhaps her threat to go to the white folks had frightened Sykes! Perhaps he was sorry! Fifteen years of misery and suppression had brought Delia to the place where she would hope *anything* that looked towards a way over or through her wall of inhibitions.

85   She felt in the match-safe behind the stove at once for a match. There was only one there.

"Dat niggah wouldn't fetch nothin' heah tuh save his rotten neck, but he kin run thew whut Ah brings quick enough. Now he done toted off nigh on tuh haff un box uh matches. He done had dat 'oman heah in mah house, too."

Nobody but a woman could tell how she knew this even before she struck the match. But she did and it put her into a new fury.

Presently she brought in the tubs to put the white things to soak. This time she decided she need not bring the hamper out of the bedroom; she would go in there and do the sorting. She picked up the pot-bellied lamp and went in. The room was small and the hamper stood hard by the foot of the white iron bed. She could sit and reach through the bedposts—resting as she worked.

"Ah wantah cross Jurden in uh calm time." She was singing again. The mood of the "love feast," had returned. She threw back the lid of the basket almost gaily. Then, moved by both horror and terror, she sprang back toward the door. *There lay the snake in the basket!* He moved sluggishly at first, but even as she turned round and round, jumped up and down in insanity of fear, he began to stir vigorously. She saw him pouring his awful beauty from the basket upon the bed, then she seized the lamp and ran as fast as she could to the kitchen. The wind from the open door blew out the light and the darkness added to her terror. She sped to the darkness of the yard, slamming the door after her before she thought to set down the lamp. She did not feel safe even on the ground, so she climbed up in the hay barn.

90   There for an hour or more she lay sprawled upon the hay a gibbering wreck.

Finally she grew quiet, and after that came coherent thought. With this stalked through her a cold, bloody rage. Hours of this. A period of introspection, a space of retrospection, then a mixture of both. Out of this an awful calm.

"Well, Ah done de bes' Ah could. If things ain't right, Gawd knows tain't mah fault."

She went to sleep—a twitch sleep—and woke up to a faint gray sky. There was a loud hollow sound below. She peered out. Sykes was at the woodpile, demolishing a wire-covered box.

He hurried to the kitchen door, but hung outside there some minutes before he entered, and stood some minutes more inside before he closed it after him.

95   The gray in the sky was spreading. Delia descended without fear now, and crouched beneath the low bedroom window. The drawn shade shut out the dawn, shut in the night. But the thin walls held back no sound.

"Dat ol' scratch is woke up now!" She mused at the tremendous whirr inside, which every woodsman knows, is one of the sound illusions. The rattle is a ventriloquist. His whirr sounds to the right, to the left, straight ahead, behind, close under foot—everywhere but where it is. Woe to him who guesses wrong unless he is prepared to hold up his end of the argument! Sometimes he strikes without rattling at all.

Inside, Sykes heard nothing until he knocked a pot lid off the stove while trying to reach the match-safe in the dark. He had emptied his pockets at Bertha's.

The snake seemed to wake up under the stove and Sykes made a quick leap into the bedroom. In spite of the gin he had had, his head was clearing now.

"Mah Gawd!" he chattered, "ef Ah could on'y strack uh light!"

100   The rattling ceased for a moment as he stood paralyzed. He waited. It seemed that the snake waited also.

"Oh, fuh de light! Ah thought he'd be too sick"—Sykes was muttering to himself when the whirr began again, closer, right underfoot this time. Long before this, Sykes' ability to think had been flattened down to primitive instinct and he leaped— onto the bed.

Outside Delia heard a cry that might have come from a maddened chimpanzee, a stricken gorilla. All the terror, all the horror, all the rage that man possibly could express, without a recognizable human sound.

A tremendous stir inside there, another series of animal screams, the intermittent whirr of the reptile. The shade torn violently down from the window, letting in the red dawn, a huge brown hand seizing the window stick, great dull blows upon the wooden floor punctuating the gibberish of sound long after the rattle of the snake had abruptly subsided. All this Delia could see and hear from her place beneath the window, and it made her ill. She crept over to the four o'clocks and stretched herself on the cool earth to recover.

She lay there. "Delia, Delia!" She could hear Sykes calling in a most despairing tone as one who expected no answer. The sun crept on up, and he called. Delia could not move—her legs had gone flabby. She never moved, he called, and the sun kept rising.

105   "Mah Gawd!" she heard him moan, "Mah Gawd fum Heben!" She heard him stumbling about and got up from her flower-bed. The sun was growing warm. As she approached the door she heard him call out hopefully, "Delia, is dat you Ah hear?"

She saw him on his hands and knees as soon as she reached the door. He crept an inch or two toward her—all that he was able, and she saw his horribly swollen neck and his one open eye shining with hope. A surge of pity too strong to support her bore her away from that eye that must, could not, fail to see the tubs. He would see the lamp. Orlando with its doctors was too far. She could scarcely reach the chinaberry tree, where she waited in the growing heat while inside she knew the cold river was creeping up and up to extinguish that eye which must know by now that she knew.

COMMENTARY ON "THE NEGRO SPEAKS OF RIVERS"

LANGSTON HUGHES   [1940]

The one of my poems that has perhaps been most often reprinted in anthologies, was written on the train during this trip to Mexico when I was feeling very bad. It's called "The Negro Speaks of Rivers" and was written just outside St. Louis, as the train rolled toward Texas.

It came about in this way. All day on the train I had been thinking about my father and his strange dislike of his own people. I don't understand it, because I was a Negro, and I like Negroes very much. One of the happiest jobs I had ever had was during my freshman year in high school, when I worked behind the soda fountain for a Mrs. Kitzmiller, who ran a refreshment parlor on Central Avenue in the heart of the colored neighborhood. People just up from the South used to come in for ice cream and sodas and watermelon. And I never tired of hearing them talk, listening to the thunderclaps of their laughter, to their troubles, to their discussions of the war and the men who had gone to Europe from the Jim Crow South, their complaints over the high rent and the long overtime hours that brought what seemed like big checks, until the weekly bills were paid. They seemed to me like the gayest and the bravest people possible—these Negroes from the southern ghettos—facing tremendous odds, working and laughing and trying to get somewhere in the world.

I had been in to dinner early that afternoon on the train. Now it was just sunset, and we crossed the Mississippi, slowly, over a long bridge. I looked out the window of the Pullman at the great muddy river flowing down toward the heart of the South, and I began to think what that river, the old Mississippi, had meant to Negroes in the past—how to be sold down the river was the worst fate that could overtake a slave in times of bondage. Then I remembered reading how Abraham Lincoln had made a trip down the Mississippi on a raft to New Orleans, and how he had seen slavery at its worst, and had decided within himself that it should be removed from American life. Then I began to think about other rivers in our past—the Congo, and the Niger, and the Nile in Africa—and the thought came to me; "I've known rivers," and I put it down on the back of an envelope I had in my pocket, and within the space of ten or fifteen minutes, as the train gathered speed in the dusk, I had written this poem, which I called "The Negro Speaks of Rivers":

> I've known rivers:
> I've known rivers ancient as the world and older than the
>   flow of human blood in human veins.
>
> My soul has grown deep like the rivers.
>
> I bathed in the Euphrates when dawns were young.
> I built my hut near the Congo and it lulled me to sleep.
> I looked upon the Nile and raised the pyramids above it.
> I heard the singing of the Mississippi when Abe Lincoln
>   went down to New Orleans, and I've seen its muddy
>   bosom turn all golden in the sunset.
>
> I've known rivers:
> Ancient, dusky rivers.
>
> My soul has grown deep like the rivers.

No doubt I changed a few words the next day, or maybe crossed out a line or two. But there are seldom many changes in my poems, once they're down. Generally, the first two or three lines come to me from something I'm thinking about, or looking at, or doing, and the rest of the poem (if there is to be a poem) flows from those first few lines, usually right away. If there is a chance to put the poem down then, I write it down. If not, I try to remember it until I get to a pencil and paper; for poems are like rainbows: they escape you quickly.

JESSIE FAUSET [1926]

Very perfect is the memory of my first literary acquaintance with Langston Hughes. In the unforgettable days when we were publishing *The Brownies' Book* we had already appreciated a charming fragile conceit which read:

> Out of the dust of dreams,
> Fairies weave their garments;
> Out of the purple and rose of old memories,
> They make purple wings.
> No wonder we find them such marvelous things.

Then one day came "The Negro Speaks of Rivers." I took the beautiful dignified creation to Dr. Du Bois and said: "What colored person is there, do you suppose, in the United States who writes like that and yet is unknown to us?" And I wrote and found him to be a Cleveland high school graduate who had just gone to live in Mexico. Already he had begun to assume that remote, so elusive quality which permeates most of his work. Before long we had the pleasure of seeing the work of the boy, whom we had sponsored, copied and recopied in journals far and wide. "The Negro Speaks of Rivers" even appeared in translation in a paper printed in Germany.

ONWUCHEKWA JEMIE [1973]

"The Negro Speaks of Rivers" is perhaps the most profound of these poems of heritage and strength. Composed when Hughes was a mere 17 years old, and dedicated to W. E. B. Du Bois, it is a sonorous evocation of transcendent essences so ancient as to appear timeless, predating human existence, longer than human memory. The rivers are part of God's body, and participate in his immortality. They are the earthly analogues of eternity: deep, continuous, mysterious. They are named in the order of their association with black history. The black man has drunk of their life-giving essences, and thereby borrowed their immortality. He and the rivers have become one. The magical transformation of the Mississippi from mud to gold by the sun's radiance is mirrored in the transformation of slaves into free men by Lincoln's Proclamation (and, in Hughes' poems, the transformation of shabby cabarets into gorgeous palaces, dancing girls into queens and priestesses by the spell of black music). As the rivers deepen with time, so does the black man's soul; as their waters ceaselessly flow, so will the black soul endure. The black man has seen the rise and fall of civilizations from the earliest times, seen the beauty and death-changes of the world over the thousands of years, and will survive even this America. The poem's meaning is related to Zora Neale Hurston's judgment of the mythic High John de Conquer, whom she held as a symbol of the triumphant spirit of black America: that John was of the "Be" class. "*Be* here when the ruthless man comes, and *be* here when he is gone." In a time and place where black life is held cheap and the days of black men appear to be numbered, the poem is a majestic reminder of the strength and fullness of history, of the source of that life which transcends even ceaseless labor and burning crosses.

R. BAXTER MILLER   [1989]

"Rivers" presents the narrator's skill in retracing known civilization back to the source in East Africa. Within thirteen lines and five stanzas, through the suggestion of wisdom by anagoge, we re-project ourselves into aboriginal consciousness. Then the speaker affirms the spirit distilled from human history, ranging from 3000 B.C. through the mid-nineteenth century to the author himself at the brink of the Harlem Renaissance. The powerful repeated "I've known rivers. / Ancient, dusky rivers" closes the human narrative in nearly a circle, for the verse has turned itself subtly from an external focus to a unified and internal one: "My soul has grown deep like the rivers." Except for the physical and spiritual dimensions, the subjective "I" and the "river" read the same.

When the Euphrates flows from eastern Turkey southeast and southwest into the Tigris, it recalls the rise as well as the fall of the Roman Empire. For over two thousand years the water helped delimit that domain. Less so did the Congo, which south of the Sahara demarcates the natural boundaries between white and Black Africa. The latter empties into the Atlantic Ocean; the Nile flows northward from Uganda into the Mediterranean; in the United States the Mississippi River flows southeast from north central Minnesota to the Gulf of Mexico. Whether north or south, east or west, "River" signifies the fertility as well as the dissemination of life in concentric half-circles. The liquid, as the externalized form of the contemplative imagination, has both depth and flow. "The Negro Speaks of Rivers" reclaims the origins in Africa of both physical and spiritual humanity.

ALICE WALKER   [1979]

ZORA NEALE HURSTON: A CAUTIONARY TALE AND A PARTISAN VIEW

During the early and middle years of her career Zora was a cultural revolutionary simply because she was always herself. Her work, so vigorous among the rather pallid productions of many of her contemporaries, comes from the essence of black folk life. During her later life she became frightened of the life she had always dared bravely before. Her work too became reactionary, static, shockingly misguided and timid. (This is especially true of her last novel, *Seraphs on the Sewannee,* which is not even about black people, which is no crime, but *is* about white people for whom it is impossible to care, which is.)

A series of misfortunes battered Zora's spirit and her health. And she was broke. *Being broke made all the difference.*

Without money of one's own in a capitalist society, there is no such thing as independence. This is one of the clearest lessons of Zora's life, and why I consider the telling of her life "a cautionary tale." We must learn from it what we can.

5   Without money, an illness, even a simple one, can undermine the will. Without money, getting into a hospital is problematic and getting out without money to pay for the treatment is nearly impossible. Without money, one becomes dependent on other people, who are likely to be—even in their kindness—erratic in their support

and despotic in their expectations of return. Zora was forced to rely, like Tennessee Williams's Blanche, "on the kindness of strangers." Can anything be more dangerous, if the strangers are forever in control? Zora, who worked so hard, was never able to make a living from her work.

She did not complain about not having money. She was not the type. (Several months ago I received a long letter from one of Zora's nieces, a bright ten-year-old, who explained to me that her aunt was so proud that the only way the family could guess she was ill or without funds was by realizing they had no idea where she was. Therefore, none of the family attended either Zora's sickbed or her funeral.) Those of us who have had "grants and fellowships from 'white folks'" know this aid is extended in precisely the way welfare is extended in Mississippi. One is asked, *curtly,* more often than not: How much do you need *just to survive?* Then one is— if fortunate—given a third of that. What is amazing is that Zora, who became an orphan at nine, a runaway at fourteen, a maid and manicurist (because of necessity and not from love of the work) before she was twenty—with one dress—managed to become Zora Neale Hurston, author and anthropologist, at all.

For me, the most unfortunate thing Zora ever wrote is her autobiography. After the first several chapters, it rings false. One begins to hear the voice of someone whose life required the assistance of too many transitory "friends." A Taoist proverb states that *to act sincerely with the insincere is dangerous.* (A mistake blacks as a group have tended to make in America.) And so we have Zora sincerely offering gratitude and kind words to people one knows she could not have respected. But this unctuousness, so out of character for Zora, is also a result of dependency, a sign of her powerlessness, her inability to pay back her debts with anything but words. They must have been bitter ones for her. In her dependency, it should be remembered, Zora was not alone—because it is quite true that America does not support or honor us as human beings, let alone as blacks, women, and artists. We have taken help where it was offered because we are committed to what we do and to the survival of our work. Zora was committed to the survival of her people's cultural heritage as well.

In my mind, Zora Neale Hurston, Billie Holiday, and Bessie Smith form a sort of unholy trinity. Zora *belongs* in the tradition of black women singers, rather than among "the literati," at least to me. There were the extreme highs and lows of her life, her undaunted pursuit of adventure, passionate emotional and sexual experience, and her love of freedom. Like Billie and Bessie she followed her own road, believed in her own gods, pursued her own dreams, and refused to separate herself from "common" people. It would have been nice if the three of them had had one another to turn to, in times of need. I close my eyes and imagine them: Bessie would be in charge of all the money; Zora would keep Billie's masochistic tendencies in check and prevent her from singing embarrassing anything-for-a-man songs, thereby preventing Billie's heroin addiction. In return, Billie could be, along with Bessie, the family that Zora felt she never had.

We are a people. A people do not throw their geniuses away. And if they are thrown away, it is our duty *as artists and as witnesses for the future* to collect them again for the sake of our children, and, if necessary, bone by bone.

A Sample Student Essay

In the student essay that follows, William Winters compares Countee Cullen's "Incident" (p. 24) with Langston Hughes's poem "Theme for English B" (p. 1127), as they reflect Hughes's beliefs in "The Negro Artist and the Racial Mountain."

William Winters

Dr. Madden

English 102

November 16, 200X

The Racial Mountain

In his essay "The Negro Artist and the Racial Mountain," Langston Hughes insists that the black artist can find "a lifetime of creative work" without going outside his own race (1117). He asserts further that race "relations between Negroes and whites . . . with their innumerable overtones and undertones" provide an "inexhaustible supply of themes" (1117). Two poems about race relations, Countee Cullen's "Incident" and Hughes' own poem "Theme for English B," provide us with examples of Hughes' view. Each has a different theme and both have a strong sense of the "innumerable overtones and undertones" in relations between the races.

When someone passes judgment on someone else based on that person's race or ethnicity we call it racism. Most of us have been fortunate enough not to be the subject of racist remarks. We never thought about what it would be like to have someone direct racist comments at us. Even though we cannot understand how it feels to be a victim of racism unless we experience it in real life, these two poems give us a small taste of it. Though the poems were written twenty-six years apart, and they address different aspects of being black in a white society, each continues to have a strong impact.

Countee Cullen's "Incident" is short, simple, and to the point, and though the young boy has only visited Baltimore for a short time, racism is branded into his mind forever. Here we have an innocent eight-year-old child whose heart and head are "filled with glee" (2) because he is excited about visiting the city of Baltimore. The child sees another boy and smiles at him. The boy then points to him and calls the child a "nigger." When the speaker describes this happening, I could feel the child's heart sink. And my heart sank too. The child must have felt he was not wanted in this new place.

Countee Cullen does an excellent job of letting the reader see the world through the child's eyes.

Racism is not something we are born with. Instead, it is something we learn from others. The child in the poem did not judge the other boy by the color of his skin. When the child smiled at him, the color of the boy's skin did not even cross his young mind. However, the young bigot has now made the child aware that people feel strongly about the color of his skin. That bigoted child was not born a racist. He learned to hate from others. This brief, simple poem is very powerful and says a lot with a few words.

Langston Hughes' "Theme for English B" also deals with the topic of racism. It gets its message across very well, too, but in a slightly different way. Unlike "Incident," it does not put us in the shoes of the main character. It feels more like having a conversation with the speaker in the poem. He seems more like a friend, and as he continues to speak we identify and sympathize with him. The message we get from this poem is that people are generally the same, but the color of their skin can separate them.

The main character is very aware of his ethnicity. He describes himself as "twenty-two, colored, born in Winston-Salem" (7). He also tells us that he is the only "colored" student in his class. This contrasts with the poem "Incident," in which the speaker, who is only eight years old, has not yet learned to see the world in black and white. The speaker says he likes to "eat, sleep, drink, and be in love" (21). He also tells us of other "normal" things that he likes. He does this to show that his interests are the same as white people's. Some people might be surprised by this!

He continues, however, by saying, "So will my page be colored that I write? / Being me, it will not be white" (27-28). Here he is telling us that even though he enjoys many of the same things that white people enjoy, his paper will be different because he is black. For him, this is an excellent segue into another thought: "Sometimes perhaps you don't want to be a part of me. / Nor do I often want to be a part of you" (34-35). Here, too, he indicates that though we share the same humanity, there are things that make us different. Our ethnic backgrounds, where we grew up, our families, our individual personalities make us different. But this difference is good. It is not something negative. It is good for all of us to have pride in our backgrounds. It gives us the opportunity to learn something from each other. As the speaker in the poem says, "That's American" (33). It is the abuse of these differences that separates ethnicity from racism.

We are all different. We come from different races, cultures, classes, and families. These differences, however, are good. They make us unique and give us something to have pride in. Much too often our ethnicity is looked upon as something negative and this results in racism. Unlike our ethnicity, racism is not something we are born with, but something we learn from others and living our lives. Racism is not logical; it is stupid. How can we dislike someone just because of the color of their skin? Yes, there are evil people in all races, yet there are good people too.

In "The Negro Artist and the Racial Mountain," Langston Hughes suggests that race relations are very complex and that there is more than enough material here for black artists to write about. The poems "Incident" and "Theme for English B" are strong reflections of this belief.

[New Page]

Works Cited

Cullen, Countee. "Incident." <u>Exploring Literature</u>. Ed. Frank Madden. 3rd ed. New York: Longman, 2007. 24.

Hughes, Langston. "The Negro Artist and the Racial Mountain." <u>Exploring Literature</u>. Ed. Frank Madden. 3rd ed. New York: Longman, 2007. 1116-1119.

Hughes, Langston. "Theme for English B." <u>Exploring Literature</u>. Ed. Frank Madden. 3rd ed. New York: Longman, 2007. 1127-1128.

EXPLORING THE LITERATURE OF CULTURE AND IDENTITY: OPTIONS FOR MAKING CONNECTIONS AND ARGUMENTS

MAKING CONNECTIONS

1. Consider the ways in which your culture and identity have affected your life. Do any of the stories, poems, plays, or essays in this section remind you of your own experiences or the circumstances in your life? Choose one or more of these works and write a response essay that compares your experience or circumstances with those in the literature.

2. Where we grow up, the society or culture we grow up in, and similar factors can influence how we see the world and our response to literature. Based on these values, we may agree or disagree with what an author says or what characters say or do. So too, the ideas expressed about culture and identity in literature may influence us and the formation of our values. Write an essay about the ways in which one or more works in this section either provoked a moral judgment on your part or helped you learn something.

MAKING AN ARGUMENT

1. In her book *Patterns of Culture,* anthropologist Ruth Benedict wrote, "From the moment of his birth the customs into which [an individual] is born shape his experience and behavior. By the time he can talk, he is the little creature of his culture." Consider this quote, and write an essay about how an author or a character in one or more works in this section is influenced by his or her culture.

2. In his 1859 book *Critique of Political Economy,* political and economic philosopher Karl Marx wrote, "It is not the consciousness of men that determines their existence, but on the contrary it is their social existence that determines their consciousness." Write about this quote as it affects the way a character or an author in one or more works in this section sees the world.

3. Choose a quote (or quotes) from the introduction to this section, Culture and Identity (pp. 940–941), and pair it (or them) with one of the longer pieces in this section that either supports it or argues against it. For example, Thoreau's statement from *Walden* "If a man does not keep pace with his companions, . . . Let him step to the music which he hears, however measured or far away" might be paired with the excerpt from his essay "Civil Disobedience." If you choose Karl Marx's statement about social existence determining consciousness, you might choose Luis Valdez's *Los Vendidos* to support it. Write an essay that compares or contrasts a quote (or quotes) from the introduction with a story, poem, play, or essay that supports or argues against it.

A Research Option

William Faulkner's story "A Rose for Emily," Edwin Arlington Robinson's "Mr. Flood's Party," Luis Valdez's play *Los Vendidos,* and Martin Luther King, Jr.'s "I Have a Dream" all have something important to say about the impact of culture and identity. Each of these works, however, springs from a very different historical, social, or political context.

Expanding our exploration of literature to include the context in which these works were produced can be an enriching and enlightening experience. Choose one or more of these or other works in this section and write a research essay that includes secondary source material about the historical, social, or political background of the literature.

Writing About Connections Across Themes

Most of the literature in the text has been organized into theme sections, but good literature is much too complex to be reduced to a single, broad theme. Many of the works included under Culture and Identity could just as easily fit under other themes—and in many cases works arranged in other themes could fit here as well.

Choose one or more of the following works from earlier chapters or other themes and consider how they can be linked to Culture and Identity—and how this combination of the work with more than one theme provides additional insight into the literature and fresh topics for writing.

From Chapter 1
   "Zimmer in Grade School"—p. 11
   "Not Waving But Drowning"—p. 12
   "Barbie Doll"—p. 14
   "Ballad of Birmingham"—p. 17
From Chapter 2
   "Incident"—p. 24
   "Eleven"—p. 26
   "Mothers"—p. 31
   "Salvation"—p. 32
From Chapter 5
   "Eveline"—p. 190
From Family and Friends
   "Marriage Is a Private Affair"—p. 206
   "Sonny's Blues"—p. 211
   "The Red Convertible"—p. 236
   "The Road"—p. 243
   "Digging"—p. 270
   "For My Father"—p. 278
   "Advice to Youth"—p. 340
From Innocence and Experience
   "Snow"—p. 439
   "The Lesson"—p. 440
   "Battle Royal"—p. 448
   "The Stolen Party"—p. 459
   "Pain for a Daughter"—p. 512
From Women and Men
   "Life"—p. 737
   "Shiloh"—p. 762
   "The Day It Happened"—p. 773
   Anne Sexton's "Cinderella"—p. 804
   Bruno Bettelheim's "Cinderella"—p. 807
   Trifles—p. 824

Collaboration: Writing and Revising with Your Peers

In addition to applying your own values and standards to writing about the literature in this section, you may find it beneficial to share and discuss your work with classmates. Getting feedback from others can help you generate and clarify your ideas and revise and edit your writing more effectively.

Choose a work, topic, or one of the options for writing about culture and identity above, and work with a partner or in a small group. Exchange journal entries or response sheets, generate questions together, do a group semantic map (see pp. 41–42), or simply share and respond to each other's ideas.

After you have written a rough draft of your essay, share it with a partner or your group. Respondents should function primarily as sensitive readers and give honest, constructive responses. They should try to be aware of each writer's purpose, discuss concerns particular to each writer, and comment on the effectiveness of the essay's organization, support, clarity, and voice. (For a comprehensive checklist for revision, see p. 46).

In the final stage of your writing, editing and proofreading might be done in a similar fashion. A partner or group of readers might help you check for correct grammar, spelling, punctuation, and typos. (A comprehensive checklist for editing is on p. 49).

A Writing/Research Portfolio Option

A portfolio is a collection of your work, related materials, and commentary about your work collected over time. Gathering materials in a portfolio will provide you with resources for research and development. You can use your portfolio to collect your writing about the literature in this section, find a topic to write about, revise or add to your work, or keep multiple drafts and monitor the changes you make as you revise.

Among the resources you might include:

- Your responses to the quotes and prompts about culture and identity from the beginning of this section, the questions you had right after you finished reading each piece of literature, or your journal entries.

- What your classmates, instructor, or published critics had to say about the literature and how their comments may have influenced your interpretation.

- Information you have gathered from the library and the Internet about the historical, social, and political context of the work or its author.

Faith & Doubt

Faith and Doubt

A DIALOGUE ACROSS HISTORY

All men know the utility of useful things; but they do not know the utility of futility.
—Chuang-tzu, 369–286 B.C.

The business of the samurai consists in reflecting on his own station in life, in discharging loyal service to his master if he has one, in deepening his fidelity in associations with friends, and with due consideration of his own position, in devoting himself to duty above all.
—Yamaga Soko, c. 1650

Men never do evil so completely and cheerfully as when they do it from religious conviction.
—Blaise Pascal, *Pensees,* 1670

In the Affairs of this World, Men are saved not by Faith but by the want of it.
—Benjamin Franklin, *Poor Richard's Almanac,* 1757

Morality is not properly the doctrine of how we may make ourselves happy, but how we make ourselves worthy of happiness.
—Immanuel Kant, 1788

The only thing necessary for the triumph of evil is for good men to do nothing.
—Edmund Burke, c. 1800

Life can only be understood backwards; but it must be lived forwards.
—Soren Kierkegard, c. 1850

There lives more faith in honest doubt, / Believe me, than in half the creeds.
—Alfred Lord Tennyson, "In Memoriam," 1850

The mass of men lead lives of quiet desperation.
 —Henry David Thoreau, *Walden*, 1854

The essence of religion consists solely in the question, "Why do I live and what is my relation to the infinite universe around me?"
 —Leo Tolstoi, c. 1878

So long as man remains free he strives for nothing so incessantly and so painfully as to find someone to worship.
 —Fedor Dostoevski, *The Brothers Karamazov*, 1879

Like all weak men he laid an exaggerated stress on not changing one's mind.
 —Somerset Maugham, *Of Human Bondage*, 1915

A life without religion is a life without principles, and a life without principles is like a ship without a rudder.
 —Mahatma Gandhi, *Autobiography*, 1924

The certainties of one age are the problems of the next.
 —R. H. Tawney, *Religion and the Rise of Capitalism*, 1926

Truth has no special time of its own. Its hour is now—always.
 —Albert Schweitzer, *Out of My Life and Thought*, 1949

Liberty is the possibility of doubting, the possibility of making a mistake, the possibility of searching and experimenting, the possibility of saying "No" to any authority—literary, artistic, philosophic, religious, social, and even political.
 —Ignazio Silone, essay in *The God That Failed*, 1950

I cannot and will not cut my conscience to fit this year's fashions.
 —Lillian Hellman, letter, 1952

We are born into a world where alienation awaits us.
 —R. D. Laing, *The Politics of Experience*, 1967

We all want to know why. Man is the asking animal. And while the finding, the belief that we have found the Answer, can separate us and make us forget our humanity, it is the seeking that continues to bring us together, that makes and keeps us human.
 —Daniel Boorstin, *The Seekers*, 1998

FAITH AND DOUBT: EXPLORING YOUR OWN VALUES AND BELIEFS

We all want something to believe in—something to give our lives meaning. But we seek and act out our beliefs in many different ways. Many people join communities that share a common religious, ethical, ethnic, or political belief. Others see individual conscience as the most important guide for their beliefs and actions.

In what way do your values and beliefs influence how you see the world? Do religious, ethical, ethnic, or cultural values form the core of those beliefs? If you are deeply religious, that's probably at the heart of almost everything you value. If you are not religious, the nature of your experiences, the values you grew up with, influential people in your life, what you read, or other factors may strongly influence your perspective.

The *certainty* of your beliefs, however, may be challenged by almost everything you experience. What part does *doubt* about religion and other beliefs play in your life? In what way have events in your life or in the world—or the literature you've read—challenged what you believe in? Before you respond to the literature in this section, you may want to think about your own beliefs and/or doubts and how they affect your point of view.

READING AND WRITING ABOUT FAITH AND DOUBT

Exploring your beliefs and values and connecting your experience with what you read is an important first step toward our ultimate goal—an appreciation of literature and the ability to think and write critically about it. Critical analysis will require rereading and reflection, writing and revising, gathering evidence, and constructing a solid argument to support your responses.

At least one aspect of the many stories, poems, plays, and essays in this section is concerned with the conflict of faith and doubt: from young soldiers struggling to stay connected with life back home in the midst of the horror and absurdity of war in Tim O'Brien's story "The Things They Carried," to the seeming randomness of fate in Thomas Hardy's poem "Hap." The brief quotes that open this section also give you some idea of the number of compelling ethical, political, and social arguments that are connected to faith and doubt. Religion, conscience, self-reflection, self-interest, and emotion versus intellect head a long list of concerns. Any of these or other related issues might provide a fine topic for building an argument and writing an essay.

◆ FICTION ◆

RAYMOND CARVER [1938–1988]

Raymond Carver was born in Clatskanie, Oregon, and raised in Yakima, Washington. After working at a series of low-paying jobs, he entered Humboldt State University in 1963, where he first began to write poetry and short stories, and then went on to earn an M.F.A. from the University of Iowa in 1966. Usually set among working-class people, his stories, like "Cathedral," often hinge on moments of sudden insight. His collections include Put

Yourself in My Shoes *(1974),* Will You Please Be Quiet, Please? *(1976),* What We Talk About When We Talk About Love *(1981),* Cathedral *(1983), and* Where I'm Calling from: New and Collected Stories *(1988). His stories inspired* Short Cuts, *the critically acclaimed 1993 film directed by Robert Altman. Carver died of lung cancer in 1988. Unlike many writers who came of age in the 1970s, Carver did not see the writing of fiction as a political act:"It just has to be there for the pleasure we take in doing it, and the different kind of pleasure that's taken in reading something that's durable and made to last, as well as beautiful in and of itself. Something that throws off these sparks—a persistent and steady glow, however dim."*

CATHEDRAL   [1984]

This blind man, an old friend of my wife's, he was on his way to spend the night. His wife had died. So he was visiting the dead wife's relatives in Connecticut. He called my wife from his in-laws'. Arrangements were made. He would come by train, a five-hour trip, and my wife would meet him at the station. She hadn't seen him since she worked for him one summer in Seattle ten years ago. But she and the blind man had kept in touch. They made tapes and mailed them back and forth. I wasn't enthusiastic about his visit. He was no one I knew. And his being blind bothered me. My idea of blindness came from the movies. In the movies, the blind moved slowly and never laughed. Sometimes they were led by seeing-eye dogs. A blind man in my house was not something I looked forward to.

That summer in Seattle she had needed a job. She didn't have any money. The man she was going to marry at the end of the summer was in officers' training school. He didn't have any money, either. But she was in love with the guy, and he was in love with her, etc. She'd seen something in the paper: HELP WANTED—*Reading to Blind Man,* and a telephone number. She phoned and went over, was hired on the spot. She'd worked with this blind man all summer. She read stuff to him, case studies, reports, that sort of thing. She helped him organize his little office in the county social-service department. They'd become good friends, my wife and the blind man. How do I know these things? She told me. And she told me something else. On her last day in the office, the blind man asked if he could touch her face. She agreed to this. She told me he touched his fingers to every part of her face, her nose—even her neck! She never forgot it. She even tried to write a poem about it. She was always trying to write a poem. She wrote a poem or two every year, usually after something really important had happened to her.

When we first started going out together, she showed me the poem. In the poem, she recalled his fingers and the way they had moved around over her face. In the poem, she talked about what she had felt at the time, about what went through her mind when the blind man touched her nose and lips. I can remember I didn't think much of the poem. Of course, I didn't tell her that. Maybe I just don't understand poetry. I admit it's not the first thing I reach for when I pick up something to read.

Anyway, this man who'd first enjoyed her favors, the officer-to-be, he'd been her childhood sweetheart. So okay. I'm saying that at the end of the summer she let the blind man run his hands over her face, said goodbye to him, married her childhood etc., who was now a commissioned officer, and she moved away from Seattle. But they'd kept in touch, she and the blind man. She made the first contact after a year or so. She called him up one night from an Air Force base in Alabama. She wanted to talk. They talked. He asked her to send him a tape and tell him about her life. She did this. She sent the tape. On the tape, she told the blind man about her husband and about their life together in the military. She told the blind man she loved her husband but she didn't like it where they lived and she didn't like it that he was part of the military-industrial thing. She told the blind man she'd written a poem and he was in it. She told him that she was writing a poem about what it was like to be an Air Force officer's wife. The poem wasn't finished yet. She was still writing it. The blind man made a tape. He sent her the tape. She made a tape. This went on for years. My wife's officer was posted to one base and then another. She sent tapes from Moody AFB, McGuire, McConnell, and finally Travis, near Sacramento, where one night she got to feeling lonely and cut off from people she kept losing in that moving-around life. She got to feeling she couldn't go it another step. She went in and swallowed all the pills and capsules in the medicine chest and washed them down with a bottle of gin. Then she got into a hot bath and passed out.

5   But instead of dying, she got sick. She threw up. Her officer—why should he have a name? he was the childhood sweetheart, and what more does he want?—came home from somewhere, found her, and called the ambulance. In time, she put it all on a tape and sent the tape to the blind man. Over the years, she put all kinds of stuff on tapes and sent the tapes off lickety-split. Next to writing a poem every year, I think it was her chief means of recreation. On one tape, she told the blind man she'd decided to live away from her officer for a time. On another tape, she told him about her divorce. She and I began going out, and of course she told her blind man about it. She told him everything, or so it seemed to me. Once she asked me if I'd like to hear the latest tape from the blind man. This was a year ago. I was on the tape, she said. So I said okay, I'd listen to it. I got us drinks and we settled down in the living room. We made ready to listen. First she inserted the tape into the player and adjusted a couple of dials. Then she pushed a lever. The tape squeaked and someone began to talk in this loud voice. She lowered the volume. After a few minutes of harmless chitchat, I heard my own name in the mouth of this stranger, this blind man I didn't even know! And then this: "From all you've said about him, I can only conclude—" But we were interrupted, a knock at the door, something, and we didn't ever get back to the tape. Maybe it was just as well. I'd heard all I wanted to.

Now this same blind man was coming to sleep in my house.

"Maybe I could take him bowling," I said to my wife. She was at the draining board doing scalloped potatoes. She put down the knife she was using and turned around.

"If you love me," she said, "you can do this for me. If you don't love me, okay. But if you had a friend, any friend, and the friend came to visit, I'd make him feel comfortable." She wiped her hands with the dish towel.

"I don't have any blind friends," I said.

10   "You don't have *any* friends," she said. "Period. Besides," she said, "goddamn it, his wife's just died! Don't you understand that? The man's lost his wife!"

I didn't answer. She'd told me a little about the blind man's wife. Her name was Beulah. Beulah! That's a name for a colored woman.

"Was his wife a Negro?" I asked.

"Are you crazy?" my wife said. "Have you just flipped or something?" She picked up a potato. I saw it hit the floor, then roll under the stove. "What's wrong with you?" she said. "Are you drunk?"

"I'm just asking," I said.

15   Right then my wife filled me in with more detail than I cared to know. I made a drink and sat at the kitchen table to listen. Pieces of the story began to fall into place.

Beulah had gone to work for the blind man the summer after my wife had stopped working for him. Pretty soon Beulah and the blind man had themselves a church wedding. It was a little wedding—who'd want to go to such a wedding in the first place?—just the two of them, plus the minister and the minister's wife. But it was a church wedding just the same. It was what Beulah had wanted, he'd said. But even then Beulah must have been carrying the cancer in her glands. After they had been inseparable for eight years—my wife's word, *inseparable*—Beulah's health went into rapid decline. She died in a Seattle hospital room, the blind man sitting beside the bed and holding on to her hand. They'd married, lived and worked together, slept together—had sex, sure—and then the blind man had to bury her. All this without his having ever seen what the goddamned woman looked like. It was beyond my understanding. Hearing this, I felt sorry for the blind man for a little bit. And then I found myself thinking what a pitiful life this woman must have led. Imagine a woman who could never see herself as she was seen in the eyes of her loved one. A woman who could go on day after day and never receive the smallest compliment from her beloved. A woman whose husband could never read the expression on her face, be it misery or something better. Someone who could wear makeup or not—what difference to him? She could, if she wanted, wear green eye-shadow around one eye, a straight pin in her nostril, yellow slacks and purple shoes, no matter. And then to slip off into death, the blind man's hand on her hand, his blind eyes streaming tears—I'm imagining now—her last thought maybe this: that he never even knew what she looked like, and she on an express to the grave. Robert was left with a small insurance policy and half of a twenty-peso Mexican coin. The other half of the coin went into the box with her. Pathetic.

So when the time rolled around, my wife went to the depot to pick him up. With nothing to do but wait—sure, I blamed him for that—I was having a drink and watching the TV when I heard the car pull into the drive. I got up from the sofa with my drink and went to the window to have a look.

I saw my wife laughing as she parked the car. I saw her get out of the car and shut the door. She was still wearing a smile. Just amazing. She went around to the other side of the car to where the blind man was already starting to get out. This blind man, feature this, he was wearing a full beard! A beard on a blind man! Too much, I say. The blind man reached into the back seat and dragged out a suitcase. My wife took his arm, shut the car door, and, talking all the way, moved him down the drive and then up the steps to the front porch. I turned off the TV. I finished my drink, rinsed the glass, dried my hands. Then I went to the door.

My wife said, "I want you to meet Robert. Robert, this is my husband. I've told you all about him." She was beaming. She had this blind man by his coat sleeve.

20   The blind man let go of his suitcase and up came his hand.

I took it. He squeezed hard, held my hand, and then he let it go.

"I feel like we've already met," he boomed.

"Likewise," I said. I didn't know what else to say. Then I said, "Welcome. I've heard a lot about you." We began to move then, a little group, from the porch into the living room, my wife guiding him by the arm. The blind man was carrying his suitcase in his other hand. My wife said things like, "To your left here, Robert. That's right. Now watch it, there's a chair. That's it. Sit down right here. This is the sofa. We just bought this sofa two weeks ago."

I started to say something about the old sofa. I'd liked that old sofa. But I didn't say anything. Then I wanted to say something else, small-talk, about the scenic ride along the Hudson. How going *to* New York, you should sit on the right-hand side of the train, and coming *from* New York, the left-hand side.

25   "Did you have a good train ride?" I said. "Which side of the train did you sit on, by the way?"

"What a question, which side!" my wife said. "What's it matter which side?" she said.

"I just asked," I said.

"Right side," the blind man said. "I hadn't been on a train in nearly forty years. Not since I was a kid. With my folks. That's been a long time. I'd nearly forgotten the sensation. I have winter in my beard now," he said. "So I've been told, anyway. Do I look distinguished, my dear?" the blind man said to my wife.

"You look distinguished, Robert," she said. "Robert," she said. "Robert, it's just so good to see you."

30   My wife finally took her eyes off the blind man and looked at me. I had the feeling she didn't like what she saw. I shrugged.

I've never met, or personally known, anyone who was blind. This blind man was late forties, a heavy-set, balding man with stooped shoulders, as if he carried a great weight there. He wore brown slacks, brown shoes, a light-brown shirt, a tie, a sports coat. Spiffy. He also had this full beard. But he didn't use a cane and he didn't wear dark glasses. I'd always thought dark glasses were a must for the blind. Fact was, I wished he had a pair. At first glance, his eyes looked like anyone else's eyes. But if you looked close, there was something different about them. Too much white in the iris, for one thing, and the pupils seemed to move around in the sockets without his knowing it or being able to stop it. Creepy. As I stared at his face, I saw the left pupil turn in toward his nose while the other made an effort to keep in one place. But it was only an effort, for that eye was on the roam without his knowing it or wanting it to be.

I said, "Let me get you a drink. What's your pleasure? We have a little of everything. It's one of our pastimes."

"Bub. I'm a Scotch man myself," he said fast enough in this big voice.

"Right," I said. Bub! "Sure you are. I knew it."

35   He let his fingers touch his suitcase, which was sitting alongside the sofa. He was taking his bearings. I didn't blame him for that.

"I'll move that up to your room," my wife said.

"No, that's fine," the blind man said loudly. "It can go up when I go up."

"A little water with the Scotch?" I said.

"Very little," he said.

40   "I knew it." I said.

He said, "Just a tad. The Irish actor, Barry Fitzgerald? I'm like that fellow. When I drink water, Fitzgerald said, I drink water. When I drink whiskey, I drink whiskey." My wife laughed. The blind man brought his hand up under his beard. He lifted his beard slowly and let it drop.

I did the drinks, three big glasses of Scotch with a splash of water in each. Then we made ourselves comfortable and talked about Robert's travels. First the long flight from the West Coast to Connecticut, we covered that. Then from Connecticut up here by train. We had another drink concerning that leg of the trip.

I remembered having read somewhere that the blind didn't smoke because, as speculation had it, they couldn't see the smoke they exhaled. I thought I knew that much and that much only about blind people. But this blind man smoked his cigarette down to the nubbin and then lit another one. This blind man filled his ashtray and my wife emptied it.

When we sat down at the table for dinner, we had another drink. My wife heaped Robert's plate with cube steak, scalloped potatoes, green beans. I buttered him up two slices of bread. I said, "Here's bread and butter for you." I swallowed some of my drink. "Now let us pray," I said, and the blind man lowered his head. My wife looked at me, her mouth agape. "Pray the phone won't ring and the food doesn't get cold," I said.

45   We dug in. We ate everything there was to eat on the table. We ate like there was no tomorrow. We didn't talk. We ate. We scarfed. We grazed that table. We were into serious eating. The blind man had right away located his foods, he knew just where everything was on his plate. I watched with admiration as he used his knife and fork on the meat. He'd cut two pieces of meat, fork the meat into his mouth and then go all out for the scalloped potatoes, the beans next, and then he'd tear off a hunk of buttered bread and eat that. He'd follow this up with a big drink of milk. It didn't seem to bother him to use his fingers once in a while, either.

We finished everything, including half a strawberry pie. For a few moments, we sat as if stunned. Sweat beaded on our faces. Finally, we got up from the table and left the dirty plates. We didn't look back. We took ourselves into the living room and sank into our places again. Robert and my wife sat on the sofa. I took the big chair. We had us two or three more drinks while they talked about the major things that had come to pass for them in the past ten years. For the most part, I just listened. Now and then I joined in. I didn't want him to think I'd left the room, and I didn't want her to think I was feeling left out. They talked of things that had happened to them—to them—these past ten years. I waited in vain to hear my name on my wife's sweet lips: "And then my dear husband came into my life"—something like that. But I heard nothing of the sort. More talk of Robert. Robert had done a little of everything, it seemed, a regular blind jack-of-all-trades. But most recently he and his wife had had an Amway distributorship, from which, I gathered, they'd earned their living, such as it was. The blind man was also a ham radio operator. He talked in his loud voice about conversations he'd had with fellow operators in Guam, in the Philippines, in Alaska, and even in Tahiti. He said he'd have a lot of friends there if he ever wanted to go visit those places. From time to time, he'd turn his blind face toward me, put his hand under his beard, ask me something. How long had I been in my present position? (Three years.) Did I like my work? (I didn't.) Was I going to stay with it? (What were the options?) Finally, when I thought he was beginning to run down, I got up and turned on the TV.

My wife looked at me with irritation. She was heading toward a boil. Then she looked at the blind man and said, "Robert, do you have a TV?"

The blind man said, "My dear, I have two TVs. I have a color set and a black-and-white thing, an old relic. It's funny, but if I turn the TV on, and I'm always turning it on, I turn on the color set. It's funny, don't you think?"

I didn't know what to say to that. I had absolutely nothing to say to that. No opinion. So I watched the news program and tried to listen to what the announcer was saying.

50   "This is a color TV," the blind man said. "Don't ask me how, but I can tell."

"We traded up a while ago," I said.

The blind man had another taste of his drink. He lifted his beard, sniffed it, and let it fall. He leaned forward on the sofa. He positioned his ashtray on the coffee table, then put the lighter to his cigarette. He leaned back on the sofa and crossed his legs at the ankles.

My wife covered her mouth, and then she yawned. She stretched. She said. "I think I'll go upstairs and put on my robe. I think I'll change into something else. Robert, you make yourself comfortable," she said.

"I'm comfortable," the blind man said.

55   "I want you to feel comfortable in this house," she said.

"I am comfortable," the blind man said.

After she'd left the room, he and I listened to the weather report and then to the sports roundup. By that time, she'd been gone so long I didn't know if she was going to come back. I thought she might have gone to bed. I wished she'd come back downstairs. I didn't want to be left alone with a blind man. I asked him if he wanted another drink, and he said sure. Then I asked if he wanted to smoke some dope with me. I said I'd just rolled a number. I hadn't, but I planned to do so in about two shakes. "I'll try some with you," he said.

"Damn right," I said. "That's the stuff."

I got our drinks and sat down on the sofa with him. Then I roll us two fat numbers. I lit one and passed it. I brought it to his fingers. He took it and inhaled.

60   "Hold it as long as you can," I said. I could tell he didn't know the first thing.

My wife came back downstairs wearing her pink robe and her pink slippers.

"What do I smell?" she said.

"We thought we'd have us some cannabis," I said.

My wife gave me a savage look. Then she looked at the blind man and said, "Robert, I didn't know you smoked."

65   He said, "I do now, my dear. There's a first time for everything. But I don't feel anything yet."

"This stuff is pretty mellow," I said. "This stuff is mild. It's dope you can reason with," I said. "It doesn't mess you up."

"Not much it doesn't, bub," he said, and laughed.

My wife sat on the sofa between the blind man and me. I passed her the number. She took it and toked and then passed it back to me. "Which way is this going?" she said. Then she said, "I shouldn't be smoking this. I can hardly keep my eyes open as it is. That dinner did me in. I shouldn't have eaten so much."

"It was the strawberry pie," the blind man said. "That's what did it," he said, and he laughed his big laugh. Then he shook his head.

70   "There's more strawberry pie," I said.

"Do you want some more, Robert?" my wife said.

"Maybe in a little while," he said.

We gave our attention to the TV. My wife yawned again. She said, "Your bed is made up when you feel like going to bed, Robert. I know you must have had a long day. When you're ready to go to bed, say so." She pulled his arm. "Robert?"

He came to and said, "I've had a real nice time. This beats tapes, doesn't it?"

75   I said, "Coming at you," and I put the number between his fingers. He inhaled, held the smoke, and then let it go. It was like he'd been doing it since he was nine years old.

"Thanks, bub," he said. "But I think this is all for me. I think I'm beginning to feel it," he said. He held the burning roach out for my wife.

"Same here," she said. "Ditto. Me, too." She took the roach and passed it to me. "I may just sit here for a while between you two guys with my eyes closed. But don't let me bother you, okay? Either one of you. If it bothers you, say so. Otherwise, I may just sit here with my eyes closed until you're ready to go to bed," she said. "Your bed's made up, Robert, when you're ready. It's right next to our room at the top of the stairs. We'll show you up when you're ready. You wake me up now, you guys, if I fall asleep." She said that and then she closed her eyes and went to sleep.

The news program ended. I got up and changed the channel. I sat back down on the sofa. I wished my wife hadn't pooped out. Her head lay across the back of the sofa, her mouth open. She'd turned so that her robe had slipped away from her legs, exposing a juicy thigh. I reached to draw her robe back over her, and it was then that I glanced at the blind man. What the hell! I flipped the robe open again.

"You say when you want some strawberry pie," I said.

80   "I will," he said.

I said, "Are you tired? Do you want me to take you up to your bed? Are you ready to hit the hay?"

"Not yet," he said. "No, I'll stay up with you bub. If that's all right. I'll stay up until you're ready to turn in. We haven't had a chance to talk. Know what I mean? I feel like me and her monopolized the evening." He lifted his beard and he let it fall. He picked up his cigarettes and his lighter.

"That's all right," I said. Then I said, "I'm glad for the company."

And I guess I was. Every night I smoked dope and stayed up as long as I could before I fell asleep. My wife and I hardly ever went to bed at the same time. When I did go to sleep, I had these dreams. Sometimes I'd wake up from one of them, my heart going crazy.

85   Something about the church and the Middle Ages was on the TV. Not your run-of-the-mill TV fare. I wanted to watch something else. I turned to the other channels. But there was nothing on them, either. So I turned back to the first channel and apologized.

"Bub, it's all right," the blind man said. "It's fine with me. Whatever you want to watch is okay. I'm always learning something. Learning never ends. It won't hurt me to learn something tonight. I got ears," he said.

We didn't say anything for a time. He was leaning forward with his head turned at me, his right ear aimed in the direction of the set. Very disconcerting. Now and then his eyelids drooped and then they snapped open again. Now and then he put his fingers into his beard and tugged, like he was thinking about something he was hearing on the television.

On the screen, a group of men wearing cowls was being set upon and tormented by men dressed in skeleton costumes and men dressed as devils. The men dressed as devils wore devil masks, horns, and long tails. This pageant was part of a procession. The Englishman who was narrating the thing said it took place in Spain once a year. I tried to explain to the blind man what was happening.

"Skeletons," he said. "I know about skeletons," he said, and he nodded.

90   The TV showed this one cathedral. Then there was a long, slow look at another one. Finally, the picture switched to the famous one in Paris, with its flying buttresses and its spires reaching up to the clouds. The camera pulled away to show the whole of the cathedral rising above the skyline.

There were times when the Englishman who was telling the thing would shut up, would simply let the camera move around over the cathedrals. Or else the camera would tour the countryside, men in fields walking behind oxen. I waited as long as I could. Then I felt I had to say something. I said, "They're showing the outside of this cathedral now. Gargoyles. Little statues carved to look like monsters. Now I guess they're in Italy. Yeah, they're in Italy. There's paintings on the walls of this one church."

"Are those fresco paintings, bub?" he asked, and he sipped from his drink.

I reached for my glass. But it was empty. I tried to remember what I could remember. "You're asking me are those frescoes?" I said. "That's a good question. I don't know."

The camera moved to a cathedral outside Lisbon. The differences in the Portuguese cathedral compared with the French and Italian were not that great. But they were there. Mostly the interior stuff. Then something occurred to me, and I said, "Something has occurred to me. Do you have any idea what a cathedral is? What they look like, that is? Do you follow me? If somebody says cathedral to you, do you have any notion what they're talking about? Do you know the difference between that and a Baptist church, say?"

95   He let the smoke dribble from his mouth. "I know they took hundreds of workers fifty or a thousand years to build," he said. "I just heard the man say that, of course. I know generations of the same families worked on a cathedral. I heard him say that, too. The men who began their life's work on them, they never lived to see the completion of their work. In that wise, bub, they're no different from the rest of

us, right?" He laughed. Then his eyelids drooped again. His head nodded. He seemed to be snoozing. Maybe he was imagining himself in Portugal. The TV was showing another cathedral now. This one was in Germany. The Englishman's voice droned on. "Cathedrals," the blind man said. He sat up and rolled his head back and forth. "If you want the truth, bub, that's about all I know. What I just said. What I heard him say. But maybe you could describe one to me? I wish you'd do it. I'd like that. If you want to know, I really don't have a good idea."

I stared hard at the shot of the cathedral on the TV. How could I even begin to describe it? But say my life depended on it. Say my life was being threatened by an insane guy who said I had to do it or else.

I stared some more at the cathedral before the picture flipped off into the countryside. There was no use. I turned to the blind man and said, "To begin with, they're very tall." I was looking around the room for clues. "They reach way up. Up and up. Toward the sky. They're so big, some of them, they have to have these supports. To help hold them up, so to speak. These supports are called buttresses. They remind me of viaducts, for some reason. But maybe you don't know viaducts, either? Sometimes the cathedrals have devils and such carved into the front. Sometimes lords and ladies. Don't ask me why this is," I said.

He was nodding. The whole upper part of his body seemed to be moving back and forth.

"I'm not doing so good, am I?" I said.

100   He stopped nodding and leaned forward on the edge of the sofa. As he listened to me, he was running his fingers through his beard. I wasn't getting through to him, I could see that. But he waited for me to go on just the same. He nodded, like he was trying to encourage me. I tried to think what else to say. "They're really big," I said. "They're massive. They're built of stone. Marble, too, sometimes. In those olden days, when they built cathedrals, men wanted to be close to God. In those olden days, God was an important part of everyone's life. You could tell this from their cathedral-building. I'm sorry," I said, "but it looks like that's the best I can do for you. I'm just no good at it."

"That's all right, bub," the blind man said. "Hey, listen. I hope you don't mind my asking you. Can I ask you something? Let me ask you a simple question, yes or no. I'm just curious and there's no offense. You're my host. But let me ask if you are in any way religious? You don't mind my asking?"

I shook my head. He couldn't see that, though. A wink is the same as a nod to a blind man. "I guess I don't believe in it. In anything. Sometimes it's hard. You know what I'm saying?"

"Sure, I do," he said.

"Right," I said.

105   The Englishman was still holding forth. My wife sighed in her sleep. She drew a long breath and went on with her sleeping.

"You'll have to forgive me," I said. "But I can't tell you what a cathedral looks like. It just isn't in me to do it. I can't do any more than I've done."

The blind man sat very still, his head down, as he listened to me.

I said, "The truth is, cathedrals don't mean anything special to me. Nothing. Cathedrals. They're something to look at on late-night TV. That's all they are."

It was then that the blind man cleared his throat. He brought something up. He took a handkerchief from his back pocket. Then he said, "I get it, bub. It's okay. It happens. Don't worry about it," he said. "Hey, listen to me. Will you do me a favor? I got an idea. Why don't you find us some heavy paper? And a pen. We'll do something. We'll draw one together. Get us a pen and some heavy paper. Go on, bub, get the stuff," he said.

110 So I went upstairs. My legs felt like they didn't have any strength in them. They felt like they did after I'd done some running. In my wife's room, I looked around. I found some ballpoints in a little basket on her table. And then I tried to think where to look for the kind of paper he was talking about.

Downstairs, in the kitchen, I found a shopping bag with onion skins in the bottom of the bag. I emptied the bag and shook it. I brought it into the living room and sat down with it near his legs. I moved some things, smoothed the wrinkles from the bag, spread it out on the coffee table.

The blind man got down from the sofa and sat next to me on the carpet.

He ran his fingers over the paper. He went up and down the sides of the paper. The edges, even the edges. He fingered the corners.

"All right," he said. "All right, let's do her."

115 He found my hand, the hand with the pen. He closed his hand over my hand. "Go ahead, bub, draw," he said. "Draw. You'll see. I'll follow along with you. It'll be okay. Just begin now like I'm telling you. You'll see. Draw," the blind man said.

So I began. First I drew a box that looked like a house. It could have been the house I lived in. Then I put a roof on it. At either end of the roof, I drew spires. Crazy.

"Swell," he said. "Terrific. You're doing fine," he said. "Never thought anything like this could happen in your lifetime, did you, bub? Well, it's a strange life, we all know that. Go on now. Keep it up."

I put in windows with arches. I drew flying buttresses. I hung great doors. I couldn't stop. The TV station went off the air. I put down the pen and closed and opened my fingers. The blind man felt around over the paper. He moved the tips of his fingers over the paper, all over what I had drawn, and he nodded.

"Doing fine," the blind man said.

120 I took up the pen again, and he found my hand. I kept at it. I'm no artist. But I kept drawing just the same.

My wife opened up her eyes and gazed at us. She sat up on the sofa, her robe hanging open. She said, "What are you doing? Tell me, I want to know."

I didn't answer her.

The blind man said, "We're drawing a cathedral. Me and him are working on it. Press hard," he said to me. "That's right. That's good," he said. "Sure. You got it, bub, I can tell. You didn't think you could. But you can, can't you? You're cooking with gas now. You know what I'm saying? We're going to really have us something here in a minute. How's the old arm?" he said. "Put some people in there now. What's a cathedral without people?"

My wife said, "What's going on? Robert, what are you doing? What's going on?"

125   "It's all right," he said to her. "Close your eyes now," the blind man said to me.

I did it. I closed them just like he said.

"Are they closed?" he said. "Don't fudge."

"They're closed," I said.

"Keep them that way," he said. "Don't stop now. Draw."

130   So we kept on with it. His fingers rode my fingers as my hand went over the paper. It was like nothing else in my life up to now.

Then he said, "I think that's it. I think you got it," he said. "Take a look. What do you think?"

But I had my eyes closed. I thought I'd keep them that way for a little longer. I thought it was something I ought to do.

"Well?" he said. "Are you looking?"

My eyes were still closed. I was in my house. I knew that. But I didn't feel like I was inside anything.

135   "It's really something," I said.

MAKING CONNECTIONS

1. Why does the narrator consistently refer to Robert as "the blind man"? Why doesn't he use his name?

2. The narrator states, "A blind man in my house was not something I looked forward to." What does the narrator have against blind people? Or do you think he objects to something specific about Robert? If so, what might that be?

3. How does the wife's relationship with her husband differ from her relationship with Robert? It there anything that Robert offers her that her husband doesn't?

4. Are there things you need to see to understand? What do you think contributes more to understanding: seeing or experiencing? Explain.

5. Does Robert learn what a cathedral is in this story? Prior to their drawing together, does the narrator know much more about cathedrals than Robert does? What does the narrator learn to "see"?

MAKING AN ARGUMENT

1. The narrator of this story is not a particularly sympathetic character. Write about the effectiveness of the narration and the narrator's development as he moves toward his—"It's really something"—realization at the end of the story. To what extent would a more sympathetic narrator work just as well—or better? Cite the text of the story for support.

2. Write an essay that compares the marriage in this story with Leroy and Norma's marriage in Bobbie Ann Mason's "Shiloh" on page 762. Cite the text of both stories for support.

NATHANIEL HAWTHORNE [1804–1864]

Nathaniel Hawthorne was born in Salem, Massachusetts, to a once-influential Puritan family. Two of his ancestors had served as judges: one in the persecution of Quakers, the other in the Salem witch trials. His father, a ship's captain, died when Hawthorne was four, and his mother, after moving the family back to her parents' house, became a recluse, emerging from her room only for meals. Following an injury that left him lame, Hawthorne was educated mostly at home. After attending Bowdoin College in Maine, he returned home to live with his sisters and mother, where he began writing and publishing stories. In 1828, he published a little-read novel about his college experiences, Fanshawe. *His next publication,* Twice-Told Tales *(1837)—a collection of stories—fared better. After his marriage in 1842 and the birth of a daughter, Hawthorne wrote less, working as a customs inspector at various times to support his young family. In 1849, following the death of his mother, Hawthorne moved back to Salem, where he wrote his masterpiece,* The Scarlet Letter. *The book was an enormous critical and financial success, as was his next novel,* The House of the Seven Gables *(1851). Hawthorne was then financially able to devote himself fully to his writing. Later in his life, following the election of his college friend Franklin Pierce to the presidency, Hawthorne served as American consul at Liverpool from 1853 to 1857, and then remained in Europe until 1860, where he wrote his final novel,* The Marble Faun *(1860). He died in Concord, Massachusetts, in 1864.*

YOUNG GOODMAN BROWN   [1828]

Young Goodman Brown came forth at sunset into the street at Salem village; but put his head back, after crossing the threshold, to exchange a parting kiss with his young wife. And Faith, as the wife was aptly named, thrust her own pretty head into the street, letting the wind play with the pink ribbons of her cap while she called to Goodman Brown.

"Dearest heart," whispered she, softly and rather sadly, when her lips were close to his ear, "prithee put off your journey until sunrise and sleep in your own bed to-night. A lone woman is troubled with such dreams and such thoughts that she's afeared of herself sometimes. Pray tarry with me this night, dear husband, of all nights in the year."

"My love and my Faith," replied young Goodman Brown, "of all nights in the year, this one night must I tarry away from thee. My journey, as thou callest it, forth and back again, must needs be done 'twixt now and sunrise. What, my sweet, pretty wife, dost thou doubt me already, and we but three months married?"

"Then God bless you!" said Faith, with the pink ribbons; "and may you find all well when you come back."

5   "Amen!" cried Goodman Brown. "Say thy prayers, dear Faith, and go to bed at dusk, and no harm will come to thee."

So they parted; and the young man pursued his way until, being about to turn the corner by the meeting-house, he looked back and saw the head of Faith still peeping after him with a melancholy air, in spite of her pink ribbons.

"Poor little Faith!" thought he, for his heart smote him. "What a wretch am I to leave her on such an errand! She talks of dreams, too. Methought as she spoke there was trouble in her face, as if a dream had warned her what work is to be done to-night. But no, no; 'twould kill her to think it. Well, she's a blessed angel on earth; and after this one night I'll cling to her skirts and follow her to heaven."

With this excellent resolve for the future, Goodman Brown felt himself justified in making more haste on his present evil purpose. He had taken a dreary road, darkened by all the gloomiest trees of the forest, which barely stood aside to let the narrow path creep through, and closed immediately behind. It was all as lonely as could be; and there is this peculiarity in such a solitude, that the traveler knows not who may be concealed by the innumerable trunks and the thick boughs overhead; so that with lonely footsteps he may yet be passing through an unseen multitude.

"There may be a devilish Indian behind every tree," said Goodman Brown to himself; and he glanced fearfully behind him as he added, "What if the devil himself should be at my very elbow!"

10 His head being turned back, he passed a crook of the road, and, looking forward again, beheld the figure of a man, in grave and decent attire, seated at the foot of an old tree. He arose at Goodman Brown's approach and walked onward side by side with him.

"You are late, Goodman Brown," said he. "The clock of the Old South was striking as I came through Boston, and that is full fifteen minutes agone."

"Faith kept me back a while," replied the young man, with a tremor in his voice, caused by the sudden appearance of his companion, though not wholly unexpected.

It was now deep dusk in the forest, and deepest in that part of it where these two were journeying. As nearly as could be discerned, the second traveller was about fifty years old, apparently in the same rank of life as Goodman Brown, and bearing a considerable resemblance to him, though perhaps more in expression than features. Still they might have been taken for father and son. And yet, though the elder person was as simply clad as the younger, and as simple in manner too, he had an indescribable air of one who knew the world, and who would not have felt abashed at the governor's dinner table or in King William's court, were it possible that his affairs should call him thither. But the only thing about him that could be fixed upon as remarkable was his staff, which bore the likeness of a great black snake, so curiously wrought that it might almost be seen to twist and wriggle itself like a living serpent. This, of course, must have been an ocular deception, assisted by the uncertain light.

"Come, Goodman Brown," cried his fellow-traveller, "this is a dull pace for the beginning of a journey. Take my staff, if you are so soon weary."

15 "Friend," said the other, exchanging his slow pace for a full stop, "Having kept covenant by meeting thee here, it is my purpose now to return whence I came. I have scruples touching the matter thou wot'st of."

"Sayest thou so?" replied he of the serpent, smiling apart. "Let us walk on, nevertheless, reasoning as we go; and if I convince thee not thou shalt turn back. We are but a little way in the forest yet."

"Too far! too far!" exclaimed the goodman, unconsciously resuming his walk. "My father never went into the woods on such an errand, nor his father before him. We have been a race of honest men and good Christians since the days of the martyrs; and shall I be the first of the name of Brown that ever took this path and kept"—

"Such company, thou wouldst say," observed the elder person, interpreting his pause. "Well said, Goodman Brown! I have been as well acquainted with your family as with ever a one among the Puritans; and that's no trifle to say. I helped your grandfather, the constable, when he lashed the Quaker woman so smartly through the streets of Salem: and it was I that brought your father a pitch-pine knot, kindled at my own hearth, to set fire to an Indian village, in King Philip's war. They were my good friends, both; and many a pleasant walk have we had along this path, and returned merrily after midnight. I would fain be friends with you for their sake."

"If it be as thou sayest," replied Goodman Brown, "I marvel they never spoke of these matters: or, verily, I marvel not, seeing that the least rumor of the sort would have driven them from New England. We are a people of prayer, and good works to boot, and abide no such wickedness."

20   "Wickedness or not," said the traveller with the twisted staff, "I have a very general acquaintance here in New England. The deacons of many a church have drunk the communion wine with me; the selectmen of divers towns make me their chairman; and a majority of the Great and General Court are firm supporters of my interest. The governor and I, too—But these are state secrets."

"Can this be so?" cried Goodman Brown, with a stare of amazement at his undisturbed companion. "Howbeit, I have nothing to do with the governor and council; they have their own ways, and are no rule for a simple husbandman like me. But, were I to go on with thee, how should I meet the eye of that good old man, our minister, at Salem village? Oh, his voice would make me tremble both Sabbath day and lecture day."

Thus far the elder traveller had listened with due gravity; but now burst into a fit of irrepressible mirth, shaking himself so violently that his snake-like staff actually seemed to wriggle in sympathy.

"Ha! ha! ha!" shouted he again and again; then composing himself, "Well, go on, Goodman Brown, go on; but, prithee, don't kill me with laughing."

"Well, then, to end the matter at once," said Goodman Brown, considerably nettled, "there is my wife, Faith. It would break her dear little heart; and I'd rather break my own."

25   "Nay, if that be the case," answered the other, "e'en go thy ways, Goodman Brown. I would not for twenty old women like the one hobbling before us that Faith should come to any harm."

As he spoke he pointed his staff at a female figure on the path, in whom Goodman Brown recognized a very pious and exemplary dame, who had taught him his catechism in youth, and was still his moral and spiritual adviser, jointly with the minister and Deacon Gookin.

"A marvel, truly, that Goody Cloyse should be so far in the wilderness at nightfall," said he. "But with your leave, friend, I shall take a cut through the woods until we have left this Christian woman behind. Being a stranger to you, she might ask whom I was consorting with and whither I was going."

"Be it so," said his fellow-traveller. "Betake you the woods, and let me keep the path."

Accordingly the young man turned aside, but took care to watch his companion, who advanced softly along the road until he had come within a staff's length of the old dame. She, meanwhile, was making the best of her way, with singular speed for so aged a woman, and mumbling some indistinct words—a prayer, doubtless—as she went. The traveller put forth his staff and touched her withered neck with what seemed the serpent's tail.

30   "The devil!" screamed the pious old lady.

"Then Goody Cloyse knows her old friend?" observed the traveller, confronting her and leaning on his writhing stick.

"Ah, forsooth, and is it your worship indeed?" cried the good dame. "Yea, truly is it, and in the very image of my old gossip, Goodman Brown, the grandfather of the silly fellow that now is. But—would your worship believe it?—my broomstick hath strangely disappeared, stolen, as I suspect, by that unhanged witch, Goody Cory, and that, too, when I was all anointed with the juice of smallage, and cinquefoil, and wolf's bane—"

"Mingled with fine wheat and the fat of a new-born babe," said the shape of old Goodman Brown.

"Ah, your worship knows the recipe," cried the old lady, cackling aloud. "So, as I was saying, being all ready for the meeting, and no horse to ride on, I made up my mind to foot it; for they tell me there is a nice young man to be taken into communion to-night. But now your good worship will lend me your arm, and we shall be there in a twinkling."

35   "That can hardly be," answered her friend. "I may not spare you my arm, Goody Cloyse; but here is my staff, if you will."

So saying, he threw it down at her feet, where, perhaps, it assumed life, being one of the rods which its owner had formerly lent to the Egyptian magi. Of this fact, however, Goodman Brown could not take cognizance. He had cast up his eyes in astonishment, and, looking down again, beheld neither Goody Cloyse nor the serpentine staff, but his fellow-traveller alone, who waited for him as calmly as if nothing had happened.

"That old woman taught me my catechism," said the young man; and there was a world of meaning in this simple comment.

They continued to walk onward, while the elder traveller exhorted his companion to make good speed and persevere in the path, discoursing so aptly that his arguments seemed rather to spring up in the bosom of his auditor than to be suggested by himself. As they went, he plucked a branch of maple to serve for a walking stick, and began to strip it of the twigs and the little boughs, which were wet with evening dew. The moment his fingers touched them they became strangely withered and dried up as with a week's sunshine. Thus the pair proceeded, at a good free pace, until suddenly, in a gloomy hollow of the road, Goodman Brown sat himself down on the stump of a tree and refused to go any farther.

"Friend," said he, stubbornly, "my mind is made up. Not another step will I budge on this errand. What if a wretched old woman do choose to go to the devil when I thought she was going to heaven: is that any reason why I should quit my dear Faith and go after her?"

40   "You will think better of this by and by," said his acquaintance, composedly. "Sit here and rest yourself a while; and when you feel like moving again, there is my staff to help you along."

Without more words, he threw his companion the maple stick, and was as speedily out of sight as if he had vanished into the deepening gloom. The young man sat a few moments by the roadside, applauding himself greatly, and thinking with how clear a conscience he should meet the minister in his morning walk, nor shrink from the eye of good old Deacon Gookin. And what calm sleep would be his that very night, which was to have been spent so wickedly, but so purely and sweetly now, in the arms of Faith! Amidst these pleasant and praiseworthy meditations, Goodman Brown heard the tramp of horses along the road, and deemed it advisable to conceal himself within the verge of the forest, conscious of the guilty purpose that had brought him thither, though now so happily turned from it.

On came the hoof tramps and the voices of the riders, two grave old voices, conversing soberly as they drew near. These mingled sounds appeared to pass along the road, within a few yards of the young man's hiding-place; but, owing doubtless to the depth of the gloom at that particular spot, neither the travellers nor their steeds were visible. Though their figures brushed the small boughs by the wayside, it could not be seen that they intercepted, even for a moment, the faint gleam from the strip of bright sky athwart which they must have passed. Goodman Brown alternately crouched and stood on tiptoe, pulling aside the branches and thrusting forth his head as far as he durst without discerning so much as a shadow. It vexed him the more, because he could have sworn, were such a thing possible, that he recognized the voices of the minister and Deacon Gookin, jogging along quietly, as they were wont to do, when bound to some ordination or ecclesiastical council. While yet within hearing, one of the riders stopped to pluck a switch.

"Of the two, reverend sir," said the voice like the deacon's, "I had rather miss an ordination dinner than to-night's meeting. They tell me that some of our community are to be here from Falmouth and beyond, and others from Connecticut and Rhode Island, besides several of the Indian powwows, who, after their fashion, know almost as much deviltry as the best of us. Moreover, there is a goodly young woman to be taken into communion."

"Mighty well, Deacon Gookin!" replied the solemn old tones of the minister. "Spur up, or we shall be late. Nothing can be done, you know, until I get on the ground."

45   The hoofs clattered again; and the voices, talking so strangely in the empty air, passed on through the forest, where no church had ever been gathered or solitary Christian prayed. Whither, then, could these holy men be journeying so deep into the heathen wilderness? Young Goodman Brown caught hold of a tree for support, being ready to sink down on the ground, faint and overburdened with the heavy sickness of his heart. He looked up to the sky, doubting whether there really was a heaven above him. Yet there was the blue arch, and the stars brightening in it.

"With heaven above and Faith below, I will yet stand firm against the devil!" cried Goodman Brown.

While he still gazed upward into the deep arch of the firmament and had lifted his hands to pray, a cloud, though no wind was stirring, hurried across the zenith and hid the brightening stars. The blue sky was still visible, except directly overhead, where this black mass of cloud was sweeping swiftly northward. Aloft in the air, as if from the depths of the cloud, came a confused and doubtful sound of voices. Once the listener fancied that he could distinguish the accents of townspeople of his own, men and women, both pious and ungodly, many of whom he had met at the communion table, and had seen others rioting at the tavern. The next moment, so indistinct were the sounds, he doubted whether he had heard aught but the murmur of the old forest, whispering without a wind. Then came a stronger swell of those familiar tones, heard daily in the sunshine at Salem village, but never until now from a cloud of night. There was one voice, of a young woman, uttering lamentations, yet with an uncertain sorrow, and entreating for some favor, which, perhaps, it would grieve her to obtain; and all the unseen multitude, both saints and sinners, seemed to encourage her onward.

"Faith!" shouted Goodman Brown, in a voice of agony and desperation; and the echoes of the forest mocked him, crying, "Faith! Faith!" as if bewildered wretches were seeking her all through the wilderness.

The cry of grief, rage, and terror was yet piercing the night, when the unhappy husband held his breath for a response. There was a scream, drowned immediately in a louder murmur of voices, fading into far-off laughter, as the dark cloud swept away, leaving the clear and silent sky above Goodman Brown. But something fluttered lightly down through the air and caught on the branch of a tree. The young man seized it, and beheld a pink ribbon.

50   "My Faith is gone!" cried he, after one stupefied moment. "There is no good on earth; and sin is but a name. Come, devil; for to thee is this world given."

And, maddened with despair, so that he laughed loud and long, did Goodman Brown grasp his staff and set forth again, at such a rate that he seemed to fly along the forest path rather than to walk or run. The road grew wilder and drearier and more faintly traced, and vanished at length, leaving him in the heart of the dark wilderness, still rushing onward with the instinct that guides mortal man to evil. The whole forest was peopled with frightful sounds—the creaking of the trees, the howling of wild beasts, and the yell of Indians; while sometimes the wind tolled like a distant church bell, and sometimes gave a broad roar around the traveller, as if all Nature were laughing him to scorn. But he was himself the chief horror of the scene, and shrank not from its other horrors.

"Ha! ha! ha!" roared Goodman Brown when the wind laughed at him. "Let us hear which will laugh loudest. Think not to frighten me with your deviltry. Come witch, come wizard, come Indian powwow, come devil himself, and here comes Goodman Brown. You may as well fear him as he fear you."

In truth, all through the haunted forest there could be nothing more frightful than the figure of Goodman Brown. On he flew among the black pines, brandishing his staff with frenzied gestures, now giving vent to an inspiration of horrid blasphemy, and now shouting forth such laughter as set all the echoes of the forest laughing like demons around him. The fiend in his own shape is less hideous than when he rages in the breast of man. Thus sped the demoniac on his course, until, quivering among the trees, he saw a red light before him, as when the felled trunks and branches of a clearing have been set on fire, and throw up their lurid blaze against the sky, at the hour of midnight. He paused, in a lull of the tempest that had driven him onward, and heard the swell of what seemed a hymn, rolling solemnly from a distance with the weight of many voices. He knew the tune; it was a familiar one in the choir of the village meeting-house. The verse died heavily away, and was lengthened by a chorus, not of human voices, but of all the sounds of the benighted wilderness pealing in awful harmony together. Goodman Brown cried out, and his cry was lost to his own ear by its unison with the cry of the desert.

In the interval of silence he stole forward until the light glared full upon his eyes. At one extremity of an open space, hemmed in by the dark wall of the forest, arose a rock, bearing some rude, natural resemblance either to an altar or a pulpit, and surrounded by four blazing pines, their tops aflame, their stems untouched, like candles at an evening meeting. The mass of foliage that had overgrown the summit of the rock was all on fire, blazing high into the night and fitfully illuminating the whole field. Each pendent twig and leafy festoon was in a blaze. As the red light arose and fell, a numerous congregation alternately shone forth, then disappeared in shadow, and again grew, as it were, out of the darkness, peopling the heart of the solitary woods at once.

55   "A grave and dark-clad company," quoth Goodman Brown.

In truth they were such. Among them, quivering to and fro between gloom and splendor, appeared faces that would be seen next day at the council board of the province, and others which, Sabbath after Sabbath, looked devoutly heavenward, and benignantly over the crowded pews, from the holiest pulpits in the land. Some affirm that the lady of the governor was there. At least there were high dames well known to her, and wives of honored husbands, and widows, a great multitude, and ancient maidens, all of excellent repute, and fair young girls, who trembled lest their mothers should espy them. Either the sudden gleams of light flashing over the obscure field bedazzled Goodman Brown, or he recognized a score of the church members of Salem village famous for their especial sanctity. Good old Deacon Gookin had arrived, and waited at the skirts of that venerable saint, his revered pastor. But, irreverently consorting with these grave, reputable, and pious people, these elders of the church, these chaste dames and dewy virgins, there were men of dissolute lives and women of spotted fame, wretches given over to all mean and filthy vice, and suspected even of horrid crimes. It was strange to see that the good shrank not from the wicked, nor were the sinners abashed by the saints. Scattered also among their pale-faced enemies were the Indian priests, or powwows, who had often scared their native forest with more hideous incantations than any known to English witchcraft.

"But where is Faith?" thought Goodman Brown; and, as hope came into his heart, he trembled.

Another verse of the hymn arose, a slow and mournful strain, such as the pious love, but joined to words which expressed all that our nature can conceive of sin, and darkly hinted at far more. Unfathomable to mere mortals is the lore of fiends. Verse after verse was sung; and still the chorus of the desert swelled between like the deepest tone of a mighty organ; and with the final peal of that dreadful anthem there came a sound, as if the roaring wind, the rushing streams, the howling beasts, and every other voice of the unconcerted wilderness were mingling and according with the voice of guilty man in homage to the prince of all. The four blazing pines threw up a loftier flame, and obscurely discovered shapes and visages of horror on the smoke wreaths above the impious assembly. At the same moment the fire on the rock shot redly forth and formed a glowing arch above its base, where now appeared a figure. With reverence be it spoken, the figure bore no slight similitude, both in garb and manner, to some grave divine of the New England churches.

"Bring forth the converts!" cried a voice that echoed through the field and rolled into the forest.

60   At the word, Goodman Brown stepped forth from the shadow of the trees and approached the congregation, with whom he felt a loathful brotherhood by the sympathy of all that was wicked in his heart. He could have well-nigh sworn that the shape of his own dead father beckoned him to advance, looking downward from a smoke wreath, while a woman, with dim features of despair, threw out her hand to warn him back. Was it his mother? But he had no power to retreat one step, nor to resist, even in thought, when the minister and good old Deacon Gookin seized his arms and led him to the blazing rock. Thither came also the slender form of a veiled female, led between Goody Cloyse, that pious teacher of the catechism, and Martha Carrier, who had received the devil's promise to be queen of hell. A rampant hag was she. And there stood the proselytes beneath the canopy of fire.

"Welcome, my children," said the dark figure, "to the communion of your race. Ye have found thus young your nature and your destiny. My children, look behind you!"

They turned; and flashing forth, as it were, in a sheet of flame, the fiend worshippers were seen; the smile of welcome gleamed darkly on every visage.

"There," resumed the sable form, "are all whom ye have reverenced from youth. Ye deemed them holier than yourselves and shrank from your own sin, contrasting it with their lives of righteousness and prayerful aspirations heavenward. Yet here are they all in my worshipping assembly. This night it shall be granted you to know their secret deeds: how hoary-bearded elders of the church have whispered wanton words to the young maids of their households; how many a woman, eager for widows' weeds, has given her husband a drink at bedtime and let him sleep his last sleep in her bosom; how beardless youths have made haste to inherit their fathers' wealth; and how fair damsels—blush not, sweet ones—have dug little graves in the garden, and bidden me, the sole guest, to an infant's funeral. By the sympathy of your human hearts for sin ye shall scent out all the places—whether in church, bedchamber, street, field, or forest— where crime has been committed, and shall exult to behold the whole earth one stain of guilt, one mighty blood spot. Far more than this. It shall be yours to penetrate, in every bosom, the deep mystery of sin, the fountain of all wicked arts, and which inexhaustibly supplies more evil impulses than human power—than my power at its utmost—can make manifest in deeds. And now, my children, look upon each other."

They did so; and, by the blaze of the hell-kindled torches, the wretched man beheld his Faith, and the wife her husband, trembling before that unhallowed altar.

65   "Lo, there ye stand, my children," said the figure, in a deep and solemn tone, almost sad with its despairing awfulness, as if his once angelic nature could yet mourn for our miserable race. "Depending upon one another's hearts, ye had still hoped that virtue were not all a dream. Now are ye undeceived. Evil is the nature of mankind. Evil must be your only happiness. Welcome again, my children, to the communion of your race."

"Welcome," repeated the fiend worshippers, in one cry of despair and triumph.

And there they stood, the only pair, as it seemed, who were yet hesitating on the verge of wickedness in this dark world. A basin was hollowed, naturally, in the rock. Did it contain water, reddened by the lurid light? or was it blood? or, perchance, a liquid flame? Herein did the shape of evil dip his hand and prepare to lay the mark of baptism upon their foreheads, that they might be partakers of the mystery of sin, more conscious of the secret guilt of others, both in deed and thought, than they could now be of their own. The husband cast one look at his pale wife, and Faith at him. What polluted wretches would the next glance show them to each other, shuddering alike at what they disclosed and what they saw!

"Faith! Faith!" cried the husband, "look up to heaven, and resist the wicked one."

Whether Faith obeyed he knew not. Hardly had he spoken when he found himself amid calm night and solitude, listening to a roar of the wind which died heavily away through the forest. He staggered against the rock, and felt it chill and damp; while a hanging twig, that had been all on fire, besprinkled his cheek with the coldest dew.

70   The next morning young Goodman Brown came slowly into the street of Salem village, staring around him like a bewildered man. The good old minister was taking a walk along the graveyard to get an appetite for breakfast and meditate his sermon, and bestowed a blessing, as he passed, on Goodman Brown. He shrank from the venerable saint as if to avoid an anathema. Old Deacon Gookin was at domestic worship, and the holy words of his prayer were heard through the open window. "What God doth the wizard pray to?" quoth Goodman Brown. Goody Cloyse, that excellent old Christian, stood in the early sunshine at her own lattice, catechizing a little girl who had brought her a pint of morning's milk. Goodman Brown snatched away the child as from the grasp of the fiend himself. Turning the corner by the meeting-house, he spied the head of Faith, with the pink ribbons, gazing anxiously forth, and bursting into such joy at sight of him that she skipped along the street and almost kissed her husband before the whole village. But Goodman Brown looked sternly and sadly into her face, and passed on without a greeting.

Had Goodman Brown fallen asleep in the forest and only dreamed a wild dream of a witch-meeting?

Be it so if you will; but alas! it was a dream of evil omen for young Goodman Brown. A stern, a sad, a darkly meditative, a distrustful, if not a desperate man did he become from the night of that fearful dream. On the Sabbath day, when the congregation were singing a holy psalm, he could not listen because an anthem of sin rushed loudly upon his ear and drowned all the blessed strain. When the minister spoke from the pulpit with power and fervid eloquence, and, with his hand on the open Bible, of the sacred truths of our religion, and of saint-like lives and triumphant deaths, and of future bliss or misery unutterable, then did Goodman Brown turn pale, dreading lest the roof should thunder down upon the gray blasphemer and his hearers. Often, awaking suddenly at midnight, he shrank from the bosom of Faith; and at morning or eventide, when the family knelt down at prayer, he scowled and muttered to himself, and gazed sternly at his wife, and turned away. And when he had lived long, and was borne to his grave a hoary corpse, followed by Faith, an aged woman, and children and grandchildren, a goodly procession, besides neighbors not a few, they carved no hopeful verse upon his tombstone, for his dying hour was gloom.

MAKING CONNECTIONS

1. What is the significance of the names in this story? For example, is Faith aptly named? Explain.
2. In what way does the setting of this story, Puritan New England, influence your response?
3. Why do you suppose the stranger in the woods looks like Goodman Brown himself?
4. This is a story about good and evil. How are they defined here? In what way is this story about human nature? How would you interpret the story's theme?

MAKING AN ARGUMENT

1. Do you think Brown's experience was real or a dream? Write an argument that supports one or the other position. Be sure to account for all the evidence in the text (not just the evidence that supports your view), and cite the text of the story for support.

PAM HOUSTON [B. 1962]

Pam Houston was born in New Jersey but has spent much of her life in the west, northwest, and elsewhere—sailing, hiking, and hunting. She has a Ph.D. in Creative Writing from the University of Utah, published a collection of short stories, Cowboys Are My Weakness *(1992), (from which the following story is taken) while still in graduate school, and has published articles in such magazines as* Mirabella *and* Mademoiselle. *She edited* Women and Hunting: Essays, Fiction, and Poetry *(1994) and her own collection of essays is entitled* A Little More About Me *(2000). Her latest book is a novel,* Sight Hound *(2005).*

A BLIZZARD UNDER BLUE SKY   [1992]

The doctor said I was clinically depressed. It was February, the month in which depression runs rampant in the inversion-cloaked Salt Lake Valley and the city dwellers escape to Park City, where the snow is fresh and the sun is shining and everybody is happy, except me. In truth, my life was on the verge of more spectacular and satisfying discoveries than I had ever imagined, but of course I couldn't see that far ahead. What I saw was work that wasn't getting done, bills that weren't getting paid, and a man I'd given my heart to weekending in the desert with his ex.

The doctor said, "I can give you drugs."

I said, "No way."

She said, "The machine that drives you is broken. You need something to help you get it fixed."

5   I said, "Winter camping."

She said, "Whatever floats your boat."

One of the things I love the most about the natural world is the way it gives you what's good for you even if you don't know it at the time. I had never been winter camping before, at least not in the high country, and the weekend I chose to try and fix my machine was the same weekend the air mass they called the Alaska Clipper showed up. It was thirty-two degrees below zero in town on the night I spent in my snow cave. I don't know how cold it was out on Beaver Creek. I had listened to the weather forecast, and to the advice of my housemate, Alex, who was an experienced winter camper.

"I don't know what you think you're going to prove by freezing to death," Alex said, "but if you've got to go, take my bivvy sack; it's warmer than anything you have."

"Thanks," I said.

10   "If you mix Kool-Aid with your water it won't freeze up," he said, "and don't forget lighting paste for your stove."

"Okay," I said.

"I hope it turns out to be worth it," he said, "because you are going to freeze your butt."

When everything in your life is uncertain, there's nothing quite like the clarity and precision of fresh snow and blue sky. That was the first thought I had on Saturday morning as I stepped away from the warmth of my truck and let my skis slap the snow in front of me. There was no wind and no clouds that morning, just still air and cold sunshine. The hair in my nostrils froze almost immediately. When I took a deep breath, my lungs only filled up halfway.

I opened the tailgate to excited whines and whimpers. I never go skiing without Jackson and Hailey: my two best friends, my yin and yang of dogs. Some of you might know Jackson. He's the oversized sheepdog-and-something else with the great big nose and the bark that will shatter glass. He gets out and about more than I do. People I've never seen before come by my house daily and call him by name. He's all grace, and he's tireless; he won't go skiing with me unless I let him lead. Hailey is not so graceful, and her body seems in constant indecision when she runs. When we ski she stays behind me, and on the downhills she tries to sneak rides on my skis.

15   The dogs ran circles in the chest-high snow while I inventoried my backpack one more time to make sure I had everything I needed. My sleeping bag, my Thermarest, my stove, Alex's bivvy sack, matches, lighting paste, flashlight, knife. I brought three pairs of long underwear—tops and bottoms—so I could change once before I went to bed, and once again in the morning, so I wouldn't get chilled by my own sweat. I brought paper and pen, and Kool-Aid to mix with my water. I brought Mountain House chicken stew and some freeze-dried green peas, some peanut butter and honey, lots of dried apricots, coffee and Carnation instant breakfast for morning.

Jackson stood very still while I adjusted his backpack. He carries the dog food and enough water for all of us. He takes himself very seriously when he's got his pack on. He won't step off the trail for any reason, not even to chase rabbits, and he gets nervous and angry if I do. That morning he was impatient with me. "Miles to go, Mom," he said over his shoulder. I snapped my boots into my skis and we were off.

There are not too many good things you can say about temperatures that dip past twenty below zero, except this: They turn the landscape into a crystal palace and they turn your vision into Superman's. In the cold thin morning air the trees and mountains, even the twigs and shadows, seemed to leap out of the background like a 3-D movie, only it was better than 3-D because I could feel the sharpness of the air.

I have a friend in Moab who swears that Utah is the center of the fourth dimension, and although I know he has in mind something much different and more complicated than subzero weather, it was there, on that ice-edged morning, that I felt on the verge of seeing something more than depth perception in the brutal clarity of the morning sun.

As I kicked along the first couple of miles, I noticed the sun crawling higher in the sky and yet the day wasn't really warming, and I wondered if I should have brought another vest, another layer to put between me and the cold night ahead.

20   It was utterly quiet out there, and what minimal noise we made intruded on the morning like a brass band: the squeaking of my bindings, the slosh of the water in Jackson's pack, the whoosh of nylon, the jangle of dog tags. It was the bass line and percussion to some primal song, and I kept wanting to sing to it, but I didn't know the words.

Jackson and I crested the top of a hill and stopped to wait for Hailey. The trail stretched out as far as we could see into the meadow below us and beyond, a double track and pole plants carving through softer trails of rabbit and deer.

"Nice place," I said to Jackson, and his tail thumped the snow underneath him without sound.

We stopped for lunch near something that looked like it could be a lake in its other life, or maybe just a womb-shaped meadow. I made peanut butter and honey sandwiches for all of us, and we opened the apricots.

"It's fabulous here," I told the dogs. "But so far it's not working."

25   There had never been anything wrong with my life that a few good days in the wilderness wouldn't cure, but there I sat in the middle of all those crystal-coated trees, all that diamond-studded sunshine, and I didn't feel any better. Apparently clinical depression was not like having a bad day, it wasn't even like having a lot of bad days, it was more like a house of mirrors, it was like being in a room full of one-way glass.

"Come on, Mom," Jackson said. "Ski harder, go faster, climb higher."

Hailey turned her belly to the sun and groaned.

"He's right," I told her. "It's all we can do."

After lunch the sun had moved behind our backs, throwing a whole different light on the path ahead of us. The snow we moved through stopped being simply white and became translucent, hinting at other colors, reflections of blues and purples and grays. I thought of Moby Dick, you know, the whiteness of the whale, when white is really the absence of all color, and whiteness equals truth, and Ahab's search is finally futile, as he finds nothing but his own reflection.

30   "Put your mind where your skis are," Jackson said, and we made considerably better time after that.

The sun was getting quite low in the sky when I asked Jackson if he thought we should stop to build the snow cave, and he said he'd look for the next good bank. About one hundred yards down the trail we found it, a gentle slope with eastern exposure that didn't look like it would cave in under any circumstances. Jackson started to dig first.

Let me make one thing clear. I knew only slightly more about building snow caves than Jackson, having never built one, and all my knowledge coming from disaster tales of winter camping fatalities. I knew several things *not* to do when building a snow cave, but I was having a hard time knowing what exactly to do. But Jackson helped, and Hailey supervised, and before too long we had a little cave built. Just big enough for three. We ate dinner quite pleased with our accomplishment and set the bivvy sack up inside the cave just as the sun slipped away and dusk came over Beaver Creek.

The temperature, which hadn't exactly soared during the day, dropped twenty degrees in as many minutes, and suddenly it didn't seem like such a great idea to change my long underwear. The original plan was to sleep with the dogs inside the bivvy sack but outside the sleeping bag, which was okay with Jackson the super-metabolizer, but not so with Hailey, the couch potato. She whined and wriggled and managed to stuff her entire fat body down inside my mummy bag, and Jackson stretched out full-length on top.

One of the unfortunate things about winter camping is that it has to happen when the days are so short. Fourteen hours is a long time to lie in a snow cave under the most perfect of circumstances. And when it's thirty-two below, or forty, fourteen hours seems like weeks.

35   I wish I could tell you I dropped right off to sleep. In truth, fear crept into my spine with the cold and I never closed my eyes. Cuddled there, amid my dogs and water bottles, I spent half of the night chastising myself for thinking I was Wonder Woman, not only risking my own life but the lives of my dogs, and the other half trying to keep the numbness in my feet from crawling up to my knees. When I did doze off, which was actually more like blacking out than dozing off, I'd come back to my senses wondering if I had frozen to death, but the alternating pain and numbness that started in my extremities and worked its way into my bones convinced me that I must still be alive.

It was a clear night, and every now and again I would poke my head out of its nest of down and nylon to watch the progress of the moon across the sky. There is no doubt that it was the longest and most uncomfortable night of my life.

But then the sky began to get gray, and then it began to get pink, and before too long the sun was on my bivvy sack, not warm, exactly, but holding the promise of warmth later in the day. And I ate apricots and drank Kool-Aid flavored coffee and celebrated the rebirth of my fingers and toes, and the survival of many more important parts of my body. I sang "Rocky Mountain High" and "If I Had a Hammer," and yodeled and whistled, and even danced the two-step with Jackson and let him lick my face. And when Hailey finally emerged from the sleeping bag a full hour after I did, we shared a peanut butter and honey sandwich and she said nothing ever tasted so good.

We broke camp and packed up and kicked in the snow cave with something resembling glee.

I was five miles down the trail before I realized what had happened. Not once in that fourteen-hour night did I think about deadlines, or bills, or the man in the desert. For the first time in many months I was happy to see a day beginning. The morning sunshine was like a present from the gods. What really happened, of course, is that I remembered about joy.

40   I know that one night out at thirty-two below doesn't sound like much to those of you who have climbed Everest or run the Iditarod or kayaked to Antarctica, and I won't try to convince you that my life was like the movies where depression goes away in one weekend, and all of life's problems vanish with a moment's clear sight. The simple truth of the matter is this: On Sunday I had a glimpse outside of the house of mirrors, on Saturday I couldn't have seen my way out of a paper bag. And while I was skiing back toward the truck that morning, a wind came up behind us and swirled the snow around our bodies like a blizzard under blue sky. And I was struck by the simple perfection of the snowflakes, and startled by the hopefulness of sun on frozen trees.

MAKING CONNECTIONS

1. The narrator of the story has been diagnosed with clinical depression. To what extent does the title of the story convey her condition?

2. What is it about her circumstances that makes her not think about "deadlines, or bills, or the man in the desert"? Have you ever found yourself in circumstances like this? Explain.

MAKING AN ARGUMENT

1. Pam Houston, like a number of other writers, seems to suggest that we are most appreciative of being alive when we are confronted with physical danger. Write an essay that compares and contrasts this story with Philip Simmons's essay "Learning to Fall" on page 1300. Account for the different circumstances of the narrators and their similar themes. Cite the text of both works to support your view.

TIM O'BRIEN [B. 1946]

Tim O'Brien was born in Austin, Minnesota. He was drafted immediately after he graduated from Macalester College in 1968, and served in the infantry for two years during the Vietnam War. He has since published four novels and a book of anecdotes, all based on his war experiences. He told an interviewer in Publishers Weekly *that for him, writing "requires a sense of passion, and my passion as a human being and as a writer intersect in Vietnam, not in the physical stuff but in the issue of Vietnam—of courage, rectitude, enlightenment, holiness, trying to do the right thing in the world." The following story is taken from his collection* The Things They Carried *(1990), narrated by a character named "Tim O'Brien." His novel* In the Lake of the Woods *was named by* Time *magazine as the best novel of 1994. His most recent novel is* Tomcat in Love

(1998). He is currently a visiting professor at Southwest Texas State University where he teaches in the Creative Writing Program.

THE THINGS THEY CARRIED

[1990]

First Lieutenant Jimmy Cross carried letters from a girl named Martha, a junior at Mount Sebastian College in New Jersey. They were not love letters, but Lieutenant Cross was hoping, so he kept them folded in plastic at the bottom of his rucksack. In the late afternoon, after a day's march, he would dig his foxhole, wash his hands under a canteen, unwrap the letters, hold them with the tips of his fingers, and spend the last hour of light pretending. He would imagine romantic camping trips into the White Mountains in New Hampshire. He would sometimes taste the envelope flaps, knowing her tongue had been there. More than anything, he wanted Martha to love him as he loved her, but the letters were mostly chatty, elusive on the matter of love. She was a virgin, he was almost sure. She was an English major at Mount Sebastian, and she wrote beautifully about her professors and roommates and midterm exams, about her respect for Chaucer and her great affection for Virginia Woolf. She often quoted lines of poetry; she never mentioned the war, except to say, Jimmy, take care of yourself. The letters weighed ten ounces. They were signed "Love, Martha," but Lieutenant Cross understood that Love was only a way of signing and did not mean what he sometimes pretended it meant. At dusk, he would carefully return the letters to his rucksack. Slowly, a bit distracted, he would get up and move among his men, checking the perimeter, then at full dark he would return to his hold and watch the night and wonder if Martha was a virgin.

The things they carried were largely determined by necessity. Among the necessities or near-necessities were P-38 can openers, pocket knives, heat tabs, wristwatches, dog tags, mosquito repellent, chewing gum, candy, cigarettes, salt tablets, packets of Kool-Aid, lighters, matches, sewing kits, Military Payment Certificates, C rations, and two or three canteens of water. Together, these items weighed between fifteen and twenty pounds, depending upon a man's habits or rate of metabolism. Henry Dobbins, who was a big man, carried extra rations; he was especially fond of canned peaches in heavy syrup over pound cake. Dave Jensen, who practiced field hygiene, carried a toothbrush, dental floss, and several hotel-sized bars of soap he'd stolen on R&R[1] in Sydney, Australia. Ted Lavender, who was scared, carried tranquilizers until he was shot in the head outside the village of Than Khe in mid-April. By necessity, and because it was SOP,[2] they all carried steel helmets that weighed 5 pounds including the liner and camouflage cover. They carried the standard fatigue jackets and trousers. Very few carried underwear. On their feet they carried jungle boots—2.1 pounds—and Dave Jensen carried three pairs of socks and a can of Dr. Scholl's foot powder as a precaution against trench foot. Until he was shot, Ted Lavender carried six or seven ounces of premium dope, which for him was a necessity. Mitchell Sanders, the RTO,[3] carried condoms. Norman Bowker carried a diary.

[1]**R&R** the military abbreviation for "rest and rehabilitation," a brief vacation from active service
[2]**SOP** standard operating procedure   [3]**RTO** Radio and Telephone Operator

Rat Kiley carried comic books. Kiowa, a devout Baptist, carried an illustrated New Testament that had been presented to him by his father, who taught Sunday school in Oklahoma City, Oklahoma. As a hedge against bad times, however, Kiowa also carried his grandmother's distrust of the white man, his grandfather's old hunting hatchet. Necessity dictated. Because the land was mined and booby-trapped, it was SOP for each man to carry a steel-centered, nylon-covered flak jacket, which weighed 6.7 pounds, but which on hot days seemed much heavier. Because you could die so quickly, each man carried at least one large compress bandage, usually in the helmet band for easy access. Because the nights were cold, and because the monsoons were wet, each carried a green plastic poncho that could be used as a raincoat or ground sheet or makeshift tent. With its quilted liner, the poncho weighed almost two pounds, but it was worth every ounce. In April, for instance, when Ted Lavender was shot, they used his poncho to wrap him up, then to carry him across the paddy, then to lift him into the chopper that took him away.

They were called legs or grunts.

To carry something was to "hump" it, as when Lieutenant Jimmy Cross humped his love for Martha up the hills and through the swamps. In its intransitive form, "to hump" meant "to walk," or "to march," but it implied burdens far beyond the intransitive.

5   Almost everyone humped photographs. In his wallet, Lieutenant Cross carried two photographs of Martha. The first was a Kodacolor snapshot signed "Love," though he knew better. She stood against a brick wall. Her eyes were gray and neutral, her lips slightly open as she stared straight-on at the camera. At night, sometimes, Lieutenant Cross wondered who had taken the picture, because he knew she had boyfriends, because he loved her so much, and because he could see the shadow of the picture taker spreading out against the brick wall. The second photograph had been clipped from the 1968 Mount Sebastian yearbook. It was an action shot—women's volleyball—and Martha was bent horizontal to the floor, reaching, the palms of her hands in sharp focus, the tongue taut, the expression frank and competitive. There was no visible sweat. She wore white gym shorts. Her legs, he thought, were almost certainly the legs of a virgin, dry and without hair, the left knee cocked and carrying her entire weight, which was just over one hundred pounds. Lieutenant Cross remembered touching that left knee. A dark theater, he remembered, and the movie was *Bonnie and Clyde,* and Martha wore a tweed skirt, and during the final scene, when he touched her knee, she turned and looked at him in a sad, sober way that made him pull his hand back, but he would always remember the feel of the tweed skirt and the knee beneath it and the sound of the gunfire that killed Bonnie and Clyde, how embarrassing it was, how slow and oppressive. He remember kissing her good night at the dorm door. Right then, he thought, he should've done something brave. He should've carried her up the stairs to her room and tied her to the bed and touched that left knee all night long. He should've risked it. Whenever he looked at the photographs, he thought of new things he should've done.

What they carried was partly a function of rank, partly of field specialty.

As a first lieutenant and platoon leader, Jimmy Cross carried a compass, maps, code books, binoculars, and a .45-caliber pistol that weighted 2.9 pounds fully loaded. He carried a strobe light and the responsibility for the lives of his men.

As an RTO, Mitchell Sanders carried the PRC-25 radio, a killer, 26 pounds with its battery.

As a medic, Rat Kiley carried a canvas satchel filled with morphine and plasma and malaria tablets and surgical tape and comic books and all the things a medic must carry, including M&M's[4] for especially bad wounds, for a total weight of nearly 20 pounds.

10 As a big man, therefore a machine gunner, Henry Dobbins carried the M-60, which weighed 23 pounds unloaded, but which was almost always loaded. In addition, Dobbins carried between 10 and 15 pounds of ammunition draped in belts across his chest and shoulders.

As PFCs or Spec 4s, most of them were common grunts and carried the standard M-16 gas-operated assault rifle. The weapon weighed 7.5 pounds unloaded, 8.2 pounds with its full 20-round magazine. Depending on numerous factors, such as topography and psychology, the riflemen carried anywhere from 12 to 20 magazines, usually in cloth bandoliers, adding on another 8.4 pounds at minimum, 14 pounds as maximum. When it was available, they also carried M-16 maintenance gear—rods and steel brushes and swabs and tubes of LSA oil—all of which weighed about a pound. Among the grunts, some carried the M-79 grenade launcher, 5.9 pounds unloaded, a reasonably light weapon except for the ammunition, which was heavy. A single round weighed 10 ounces. The typical load was 25 rounds. But Ted Lavender, who was scared, carried 34 pounds when he was shot and killed outside Than Khe, and he went down under an exceptional burden, more than 20 pounds of ammunition, plus the flak jacket and helmet and rations and water and toilet paper and tranquilizers and all the rest, plus the unweighed fear. He was dead weight. There was no twitching or flopping. Kiowa, who saw it happen, said it was like watching a rock fall, or a big sandbag or something—just boom, then down—not like the movies where the dead guy rolls around and does fancy spins and goes ass over teakettle—not like that, Kiowa said the poor bastard just flat-fuck fell. Boom. Down. Nothing else. It was a bright morning in mid-April. Lieutenant Cross felt the pain. He blamed himself. They stripped off Lavendar's canteens and ammo, all the heavy things, and Rat Kiley said the obvious, the guy's dead, and Mitchell Sanders used his radio to report one U.S. KIA[5] and to request a chopper. Then they wrapped Lavender in his Poncho. They carried him out to a dry paddy, established security, and sat smoking the dead man's dope until the chopper came. Lieutenant Cross kept to himself. He pictured Martha's smooth young face, thinking he loved her more than anything, more than his men, and now Ted Lavender was dead because he loved her so much and could not stop thinking about her. When the dustoff arrived, they carried Lavender aboard. Afterward they burned Than Khe. They marched until dusk, then dug their holes, and that night Kiowa kept explaining how you had to be there, how fast it was, how the poor guy just dropped like so much concrete. Boom-down, he said. Like cement.

In addition to the three standard weapons—the M-60, M-16, and M-79—they carried whatever presented itself, or whatever seemed appropriate as a means of killing or staying alive. They carried catch-as-catch-can. At various times, in various situa-

---

[4]**M&M's** comic slang for medical supplies   [5]**KIA** killed in action

tions, they carried M-14s and CAR-15s and Swedish Ks and grease guns and captured AK-47s and Chi-Coms and RPGs and Simonov carbines and black market Uzis and .38-caliber Smith & Wesson handguns and 66 mm LAWs and shotguns and silencers and blackjacks and bayonets and C-4 plastic explosives. Lee Strunk carried a sling-shot; a weapon of last resort, he called it. Mitchell Sanders carried brass knuckles. Kiowa carried his grandfather's feathered hatchet. Every third or fourth man carried a Claymore antipersonnel mine—3.5 pounds with its firing device. They all carried fragmentation grenades—14 ounces each. They all carried at least one M-18 colored smoke grenade—24 Ounces. Some carried CS or tear gas grenades. Some carried white phosphorus grenades. They carried all they could bear, and then some, includ-ing a silent awe for the terrible power of the things they carried.

In the first week of April, before Lavendar's died, Lieutenant Jimmy Cross received a good-luck charm from Martha. It was a simple pebble, an ounce at most. Smooth to the touch, it was a milky white color with flecks of orange and violet, oval-shaped, like a miniature egg. In the accompanying letter, Martha wrote that she had found the pebble on the Jersey shoreline, precisely where the land touched water at high tide, where things came together but also separated. It was this sepa-rate-but-together quality, she wrote, that had inspired her to pick up the pebble and to carry it in her breast pocket for several days, where it seemed worthless, and then to send it through the mail, by air, as a token of her truest feeling for him. Lieutenant Cross found this romantic. But he wondered what her truest feelings were, exactly, and what she meant by separate-but-together. He wondered how the tides and waves had come into play on that afternoon along the jersey shoreline when Martha saw the pebble and bent down to rescue it from geology. He imagined bare feet. Martha was a poet, with the poet's sensibilities, and her feet would be brown and bare, the toenails unpainted, the eyes chilly and somber like the ocean in March, and though it was painful, he wondered who had been with her that afternoon. He imagined a pair of shadows moving along the strip of sand where things came together but also separated. It was phantom jealousy, he knew, but he couldn't help himself. He loved her so much. On the march, through the hot days of early April, he carried the pebble in his mouth, turning it with his tongue, tasting sea salt and moisture. His mind wandered. He had difficulty keeping his attention on the war. On occasion he would yell at his men to spread out the column, to keep their eyes open, but then he would slip away into daydreams, just pretending, walking barefoot along the Jersey shore, with Martha, carrying nothing. He would feel himself rising. Sun and waves and gentle winds, all love and lightness.

What they carried varied by mission.

15   When a mission took them to the mountains, they carried mosquito netting, machetes, canvas tarps, and extra bug juice.

If a mission seemed especially hazardous, or if it involved a place they knew to be bad, they carried everything they could. In certain heavily mined AOs,[6] where the land was dense with Toe Poppers and Bouncing Betties, they took turns humping a

[6]**AOs** areas of operation

28-pound mine detector. With its headphones and big sensing plate, the equipment was a stress on the lower back and shoulders, awkward to handle, often useless because of the shrapnel in the earth, but they carried it anyway, partly for safety, partly for the illusion of safety.

On ambush, or other night missions, they carried peculiar little odds and ends. Kiowa always took along his New Testament and a pair of moccasins for silence. Dave Jensen carried night-sight vitamins high in carotene. Lee Strunk carried his slingshot; ammo, he claimed, would never be a problem. Rat Kiley carried brandy and M&M's candy. Until he was shot, Ted Lavender carried the starlight scope, which weighed 6.3 pounds with its aluminum carrying case. Henry Dobbins carried his girl-friend's pantyhose wrapped around his neck as a comforter. They all carried ghosts. When dark came, they would move out single file across the meadows and paddies to their ambush coordinates, where they would quietly set up the Claymores and lie down and spend the night waiting.

Other missions were more complicated and required special equipment. In mid-April, it was their mission to search out and destroy the elaborate tunnel complexes in the Than Khe area south of Chu Lai. To blow the tunnels, they carried one-pound blocks of pentrite high explosives, four blocks to a man, 68 pounds in all. They carried wiring, detonators, and battery-powered clackers. Dave Jensen carried earplugs. Most often, before blowing the tunnels, they were ordered by higher command to search them, which was considered bad news, but by and large they just shrugged and carried out orders. Because he was a big man, Henry Dobbins was excused from tunnel duty. The others would draw numbers. Before Lavender died there were 17 men in the platoon, and whoever drew the number 17 would strip off his gear and crawl in head first with a flashlight and Lieutenant Cross's .45-caliber pistol. The rest of them would fan out as security. They would sit down or kneel, not facing the hole, listening to the ground beneath them, imagining cobwebs and ghosts, whatever was down there—the tunnel walls squeezing in—how the flash-light seemed impossibly heavy in the hand and how it was tunnel vision in the very strictest sense, compression in all ways, even time, and how you had to wiggle in—ass and elbows—a swallowed-up feeling—and how you found yourself worrying about odd things—will your flashlight go dead? Do rats carry rabies? If you screamed, how far would the sound carry? Would your buddies hear it? Would they have the courage to drag you out? In some respects, though not many, the waiting was worse than the tunnel itself. Imagination was a killer.

On April 16, when Lee Strunk drew the number seventeen, he laughed and mut-tered something and went down quickly. The morning was hot and very still. Not good, Kiowa said. He looked at the tunnel opening, then out across a dry paddy toward the village of Than Khe. Nothing moved. No clouds or birds or people. As they waited, the men smoked and drank Kool-Aid, not talking much, feeling sympa-thy for Lee Strunk but also feeling the luck of the draw. You win some, you lose some, said Mitchell Sanders, and sometimes you settle for a rain check. It was a tired line and no one laughed.

20   Henry Dobbins ate a tropical chocolate bar. Ted Lavender popped a tranquilizer and went off to pee.

After five minutes, Lieutenant Jimmy Cross moved to the tunnel, leaned down, and examined the darkness. Trouble, he thought—a cave-in maybe. And then suddenly, without willing it, he was thinking about Martha. The stresses and fractures, the quick collapse, the two of them buried alive under all that weight. Dense, crushing love. Kneeling, watching the hole, he tried to concentrate on Lee Strunk and the war, all the dangers, but his love was too much for him, he felt paralyzed, he wanted to sleep inside her lungs and breathe her blood and be smothered. He wanted her to be a virgin and not a virgin, all at once. He wanted to know her. Intimate secrets— why poetry? Why so sad? Why that grayness in her eyes? Why so alone? Not lonely, just alone—riding her bike across campus or sitting off by herself in the cafeteria. Even dancing, she danced alone—and it was the aloneness that filled him with love. He remembered telling her that one evening. How she nodded and looked away. And how, later, when he kissed her, she received the kiss without returning it, her eyes wide open, not afraid, not a virgin's eyes, just flat and uninvolved.

Lieutenant Cross gazed at the tunnel. But he was not there. He was buried with Martha under the white sand at the Jersey shore. They were pressed together, and the pebble in his mouth was her tongue. He was smiling. Vaguely, he was aware of how quiet the day was, the sullen paddies, yet he could not bring himself to worry about matters of security. He was beyond that. He was just a kid at war, in love. He was twenty-two years old. He couldn't help it.

A few moments later Lee Strunk crawled out of the tunnel. He came up grinning, filthy but alive. Lieutenant Cross nodded and closed his eyes while the others clapped Strunk on the back and made jokes about rising from the dead.

Worms, Rat Kiley said. Right out of the grave. Fuckin' zombie.

25   The men laughed. They all felt great relief.

Spook city, said Mitchell Sanders.

Lee Strunk made a funny ghost sound, a kind of moaning, yet very happy, and right then, when Strunk made that high happy moaning sound, when he went Ahhooooo, right then Ted Lavender was shot in the head on his way back from peeing. He lay with his mouth open. The teeth were broken. There was a swollen black bruise under his left eye. The cheekbone was gone. Oh shit, Rat Kiley said, the guy's dead. The guy's dead, he kept saying, which seemed profound—the guy's dead. I mean really.

The things they carried were determined to some extent by superstition. Lieutenant Cross carried his good-luck pebble. Dave Jensen carried a rabbit's foot. Norman Bowker, otherwise a very gentle person, carried a thumb that had been presented to him as a gift by Mitchell Sanders. The thumb was dark brown, rubbery to the touch, and weighed four ounces at most. It had been cut from a VC corpse, a boy of fifteen or sixteen. They'd found him at the bottom of an irrigation ditch, badly burned, flies in his mouth and eyes. The boy wore black shorts and sandals. At the time of his death he had been carrying a pouch of rice, a rifle, and three magazines of ammunition.

You want my opinion, Mitchell Sanders said, there's a definite moral here.

30   He put his hand on the dead boy's wrist. He was quiet for a time, as if counting a pulse, then he patted the stomach, almost affectionately, and used Kiowa's hunting hatchet to remove the thumb.

Henry Dobbins asked what the moral was.

Moral?

You know. Moral.

Sanders wrapped the thumb in toilet paper and handed it across to Norman Bowker. There was no blood. Smiling, he kicked the boy's head, watched the flies scatter, and said, It's like with that old TV show—Paladin. Have gun, will travel.

35   Henry Dobbins thought about it.

Yeah, well, he finally said. I don't see no moral.

There it is, man.

Fuck off.

They carried USO stationery and pencils and pens. They carried Sterno, safety pins, trip flares, signal flares, spools of wire, razor blades, chewing tobacco, liberated joss sticks and statuettes of the smiling Buddha, candles, grease pencils, *The Stars and Stripes,* fingernail clippers, Psy Ops leaflets, bush hats, bolos, and much more. Twice a week, when the resupply choppers came in, they carried hot chow in green Mermite cans and large canvas bags filled with iced beer and soda pop. They carried plastic water containers, each with a two-gallon capacity. Mitchell Sanders carried a set of starched tiger fatigues for special occasions. Henry Dobbins carried Black Flag insecticide. Dave Jensen carried empty sandbags that could be filled at night for added protection. Lee Strunk carried tanning lotion. Some things they carried in common. Taking turns, they carried the big PRC-77 scrambler radio, which weighed thirty pounds with its battery. They shared the weight of memory. They took up what others could no longer bear. Often, they carried each other, the wounded or weak. They carried infections. They carried chess sets, basketballs, Vietnamese-English dictionaries, insignia of rank, Bronze Stars and Purple Hearts, plastic cards imprinted with the Code of Conduct. They carried diseases, among them malaria and dysentery. They carried lice and ringworm and leeches and paddy algae and various rots and molds. They carried the land itself—Vietnam, the place, the soil—a powdery orange-red dust that covered their boots and fatigues and faces. They carried the sky. The whole atmosphere, they carried it, the humidity, the monsoons, the stink of fungus and decay, all of it, they carried gravity. They moved like mules. By daylight they took sniper fire, at night they were mortared, but it was not battle, it was just the endless march, village to village, without purpose, nothing won or lost. They marched for the sake of the march. They plodded along slowly, dumbly, leaning forward against the heat, unthinking, all blood and bone, simple grunts, soldiering with their legs, toiling up the hills and down into the paddies and across the rivers and up again and down, just humping, one step and then the next and then another, but no volition, no will, because it was automatic, it was anatomy, and the war was entirely a matter of posture and carriage, the hump was everything, a kind of inertia, a kind of emptiness, a dullness of desire and intellect and conscience and hope and human sensibility. Their principles were in their feet. Their calculations were biological. They had no sense of strategy or mission. They searched the villages without knowing what to look for, not caring, kicking over jars of rice, frisking children and old men, blowing tunnels, sometimes setting fires and sometimes not, then forming up and moving on to the next village, then other villages, where it would always be the same. They carried their own lives. The pressures were enor-

mous. In the heat of early afternoon, they would remove their helmets and flak jackets, walking bare, which was dangerous but which helped ease the strain. They
would often discard things along the route of march. Purely for comfort, they would
throw away rations, blow their Claymores and grenades, no matter, because by nightfall the resupply choppers would arrive with more of the same, then a day or two
later still more, fresh watermelons and crates of ammunition and sunglasses and
woolen sweaters—the resources were stunning—sparklers for the Fourth of July, colored eggs for Easter. It was the great American war chest—the fruits of science, the
smokestacks, the canneries, the arsenals at Hartford, the Minnesota forests, the
machine shops, the vast fields of corn and wheat—they carried like freight trains;
they carried it on their backs and shoulders—and for all the ambiguities of Vietnam,
all the mysteries and unknowns, there was at least the single abiding certainty that
they would never be at a loss for things to carry.

40   After the chopper took Lavender away, Lieutenant Jimmy Cross led his men into
the village of Than Khe. They burned everything. They shot chickens and dogs, they
trashed the village well, they called in artillery and watched the wreckage, then they
marched for several hours through the hot afternoon, and then at dusk, while Kiowa
explained how Lavender died, Lieutenant Cross found himself trembling.

He tried not to cry. With his entrenching tool, which weighed five pounds, he
began digging a hole in the earth.

He felt shame. He hated himself. He had loved Martha more than his men, and
as a consequence Lavender was now dead, and this was something he would have
to carry like a stone in his stomach for the rest of the war.

All he could do was dig. He used his entrenching tool like an ax, slashing, feeling both love and hate, and then later, when it was full dark, he sat at the bottom of
his foxhole and wept. It went on for a long while. In part, he was grieving for Ted
Lavender, but mostly it was for Martha, and for himself, because she belonged to
another world, which was not quite real, and because she was a junior at Mount
Sebastian College in New Jersey, a poet and a virgin and uninvolved, and because he
realized she did not love him and never would.

Like cement, Kiowa whispered in the dark. I swear to God—boom-down. Not a
word.

45   I've heard this, said Norman Bowker.

A pisser, you know? Still zipping himself up. Zapped while zipping.

All right, fine. That's enough.

Yeah, but you had to see it, the guy just—

I heard, man. Cement. So why not shut the fuck *up*?

50   Kiowa shook his head sadly and glanced over at the hole where Lieutenant
Jimmy Cross sat watching the night. The air was thick and wet. A warm dense fog
had settled over the paddies and there was the stillness that precedes rain.

After a time Kiowa sighed.

One thing for sure, he said. The lieutenant's in some deep hurt. I mean that
crying jag—the way he was carrying on—it wasn't fake or anything, it was real
heavy-duty hurt. The man cares.

Sure, Norman Bowker said.

Say what you want, the man does care.

55   We all got problems.

Not Lavender.

No, I guess not, Bowker said. Do me a favor, though.

Shut up?

That's a smart Indian. Shut up.

60   Shrugging, Kiowa pulled off his boots. He wanted to say more, just to lighten up his sleep, but instead he opened his New Testament and arranged it beneath his head as a pillow. The fog made things seem hollow and unattached. He tried not to think about Ted Lavender, but then he was thinking how fast it was, no drama, down and dead, and how it was hard to feel anything except surprise. It seemed un-christian. He wished he could find some great sadness, or even anger, but the emotion wasn't there and he couldn't make it happen. Mostly he felt pleased to be alive. He liked the smell of the New Testament under his cheek, the leather and ink and paper and glue, whatever the chemicals were. He liked hearing the sounds of night. Even his fatigue, it felt fine, the stiff muscles and the prickly awareness of his own body, a floating feeling. He enjoyed not being dead. Lying there, Kiowa admired Lieutenant Jimmy Cross's capacity for grief. He wanted to share the man's pain, he wanted to care as Jimmy Cross cared. And yet when he closed his eyes, all he could think was Boom-down, and all he could feel was the pleasure of having his boots off and the fog curling in around him and the damp soil and the Bible smells and the plush comfort of night.

After a moment Norman Bowker sat up in the dark.

What the hell, he said. You want to talk, *talk*. Tell it to me.

Forget it.

No, man, go on. One thing I hate, it's a silent Indian.

65   For the most part they carried themselves with poise, a kind of dignity. Now and then, however, there were times of panic, when they squealed or wanted to squeal but couldn't, when they twitched and made moaning sounds and covered their heads and said Dear Jesus and flopped around on the earth and fired their weapons blindly and cringed and sobbed and begged for the noise to stop and went wild and made stupid promises to themselves and to God and to their mothers and fathers, hoping not to die. In different ways, it happened to all of them. Afterward, when the firing ended, they would blink and peek up. They would touch their bodies, feeling shame, then quickly hiding it. They would force themselves to stand. As if in slow motion, frame by frame, the world would take on the old logic—absolute silence, then the wind, then sunlight, then voices. It was the burden of being alive. Awkwardly, the men would reassemble themselves, first in private, then in groups, becoming soldiers again. They would repair the leaks in their eyes. They would check for casualties, call in dustoffs, light cigarettes, try to smile, clear their throats and spit and begin cleaning their weapons. After a time someone would shake his head and say, No lie, I almost shit my pants, and someone else would laugh, which meant it was bad, yes, but the guy had obviously not shit his pants, it wasn't that bad, and in any case nobody would ever do such a thing and then go ahead and talk about it. They would squint into the dense, oppressive sunlight. For a few moments, perhaps, they would fall silent, lighting a joint and tracking its passage from man to

man, inhaling, holding in the humiliation. Scary stuff, one of them might say. But then someone else would grin or flick his eyebrows and say, Roger-dodger, almost cut me a new asshole, *almost.*

There were numerous such poses. Some carried themselves with a sort of wistful resignation, others with pride or stiff soldierly discipline or good humor or macho zeal. They were afraid of dying but they were even more afraid to show it.

They found jokes to tell.

They used a hard vocabulary to contain the terrible softness. *Greased* they'd say. *Offed, lit up, zapped while zipping.* It wasn't cruelty, just stage presence. They were actors. When someone died, it wasn't quite dying, because in a curious way it seemed scripted, and because they had their lines mostly memorized, irony mixed with tragedy, and because they called it by other names, as if to encyst and destroy the reality of death itself. They kicked corpses. They cut off thumbs. They talked grunt lingo. They told stories about Ted Lavender's supply of tranquilizers, how the poor guy didn't feel a thing, how incredibly tranquil he was.

There's a moral here, said Mitchell Sanders.

70 They were waiting for Lavender's chopper, smoking the dead man's dope.

The moral's pretty obvious, Sanders said, and winked. Stay away from drugs. No joke, they'll ruin your day every time.

Cute, said Henry Dobbins.

Mind blower, get it? Talk about wiggy. Nothing left, just blood and brains.

They made themselves laugh.

75 There it is, they'd say. Over and over—there it is, my friend, there it is—as if the repetition itself were an act of poise, a balance between crazy and almost crazy, knowing without going, there it is, which meant be cool, let it ride, because Oh yeah, man, you can't change what can't be changed, there it is, there it absolutely and positively and fucking well *is.*

They were tough.

They carried all the emotional baggage of men who might die. Grief, terror, love, longing—these were intangibles, but the intangibles had their own mass and specific gravity, they had tangible weight. They carried shameful memories. They carried the common secret of cowardice barely restrained, the instinct to run or freeze or hide, and in many respects this was the heaviest burden of all, for it could never be put down, it required perfect balance and perfect posture. They carried their reputations. They carried the soldier's greatest fear, which was the fear of blushing. Men killed, and died, because they were embarrassed not to. It was what had brought them to the war in the first place, nothing positive, no dreams of glory or honor, just to avoid the blush of dishonor. They died so as not to die of embarrassment. They crawled into tunnels and walked point and advanced under fire. Each morning, despite the unknowns, they made their legs move. They endured. They kept humping. They did not submit to the obvious alternative, which was simply to close the eyes and fall. So easy, really. Go limp and tumble to the ground and let the muscles unwind and not speak and not budge until your buddies picked you up and lifted you into the chopper that would roar and dip its nose and carry you off to the world. A mere matter of falling, yet no one ever fell. It was not courage, exactly; the object was not valor. Rather, they were too frightened to be cowards.

By and large they carried these things inside, maintaining the masks of composure. They sneered at sick call. They spoke bitterly about guys who had found release by shooting off their own toes or fingers. Pussies, they'd say. Candyasses. It was fierce, mocking talk, with only a trace of envy or awe, but even so, the image played itself out behind their eyes.

They imagined the muzzle against flesh. So easy: squeeze the trigger and blow away a toe. They imagined it. They imagined the quick, sweet pain, then the evacuation to Japan, then a hospital with warm beds and cute geisha nurses.

80   And they dreamed of freedom birds.

At night, on guard, staring into the dark, they were carried away by jumbo jets. They felt the rush of takeoff. *Gone!* they yelled. And then velocity—wings and engines—a smiling stewardess—but it was more than a plane, it was a real bird, a big sleek silver bird with feathers and talons and high screeching. They were flying. The weights fell off, there was nothing to bear. They laughed and held on tight, feeling the cold slap of wind and altitude, soaring, thinking *It's over, I'm gone!*—they were naked, they were light and free—it was all lightness, bright and fast and buoyant, light as light, a helium buzz in the brain, a giddy bubbling in the lungs as they were taken up over the clouds and the war, beyond duty, beyond gravity and mortification and global entanglements—*Sin loi!*[7] they yelled, *I'm sorry, mother-fuckers, but I'm out of it, I'm goofed, I'm on a space cruise, I'm gone!*—and it was a restful, unencumbered sensation, just riding the light waves, sailing that big silver freedom bird over the mountains and oceans, over America, over the farms and great sleeping cities and cemeteries and highways and the golden arches of McDonald's. It was flight, a kind of fleeing, a kind of falling, falling higher and higher, spinning off the edge of the earth and beyond the sun and through the vast, silent vacuum where there were no burdens and where everything weighed exactly nothing—*Gone!* They screamed, *I'm sorry but I'm gone!*—and so at night, not quite dreaming, they gave themselves over to lightness, they were carried, so they were purely borne.

On the morning after Ted Lavender died, First Lieutenant Jimmy Cross crouched at the bottom of his foxhole and burned Martha's letters. Then he burned the two photographs. There was a steady rain falling, which made it difficult, but he used heat tabs and Sterno to build a small fire, screening it with his body, holding the photographs over the tight blue flame with the tips of his fingers.

He realized it was only a gesture. Stupid, he thought. Sentimental, too, but mostly just stupid.

Lavender was dead. You couldn't burn the blame.

85   Besides, the letters were in his head. And even now, without photographs, Lieutenant Cross could see Martha playing volleyball in her white gym shorts and yellow T-shirt. He could see her moving in the rain.

When the fire died out, Lieutenant Cross pulled his poncho over his shoulders and ate breakfast from a can.

There was no great mystery, he decided.

---

[7] *Sin loi!* Vietnamese for "sorry"

In those burned letters Martha had never mentioned the war, except to say, Jimmy, take care of yourself. She wasn't involved. She signed the letters Love, but it wasn't love, and all the fine lines and technicalities did not matter. Virginity was no longer an issue. He hated her. Yes, he did. He hated her. Love, too, but it was a hard, hating kind of love.

The morning came up wet and blurry. Everything seemed part of everything else, the fog and Martha and the deepening rain.

90   He was a soldier, after all.

Half smiling, Lieutenant Jimmy Cross took out his maps. He shook his head hard, as if to clear it, then bent forward and began planning the day's march. In ten minutes, or maybe twenty, he would rouse the men and they would pack up and head west, where the maps showed the country to be green and inviting. They would do what they had always done. The rain might add some weight, but otherwise it would be one more day layered upon all the other days.

He was realistic about it. There was that new hardness in his stomach. He loved her but he hated her.

No more fantasies, he told himself.

Henceforth, when he thought about Martha, it would be only to think that she belonged elsewhere. He would shut down the daydreams. This was not Mount Sebastian, it was another world, where there were no pretty poems or midterm exams, a place where men died because of carelessness and gross stupidity. Kiowa was right. Boom-down, and you were dead, never partly dead.

95   Briefly, in the rain, Lieutenant Cross saw Martha's gray eyes gazing back at him. He understood.

It was very sad, he thought. The things men carried inside. The things men did or felt they had to do.

He almost nodded at her, but didn't.

Instead he went back to his maps. He was now determined to perform his duties firmly and without negligence. It wouldn't help Lavender, he knew that, but from this point on he would comport himself as a soldier. He would dispose of his good-luck pebble. Swallow it, maybe, or use Lee Strunk's slingshot, or just drop it along the trail. On the march he would impose strict field discipline. He would be careful to send out flank security, to prevent straggling or bunching up, to keep his troops moving at the proper pace and at the proper interval. He would insist on clean weapons. He would confiscate the remainder of Lavender's dope. Later in the day, perhaps, he would call the men together and speak to them plainly. He would accept the blame for what had happened to Ted Lavender. He would be a man about it. He would look them in the eyes, keeping his chin level, and he would issue the new SOPs in a calm, impersonal tone of voice, a lieutenant's voice, leaving no room for argument or discussion. Commencing immediately, he'd tell them, they would no longer abandon equipment along the route of march. They would police up their acts. They would get their shit together, and keep it together, and maintain it neatly and in good working order.

100   He would not tolerate laxity. He would show strength, distancing himself.

Among the men there would be grumbling, of course, and maybe worse, because their days would seem longer and their loads heavier, but Lieutenant Jimmy Cross reminded himself that his obligation was not to be loved but to lead. He would dispense with love; it was not now a factor. And if anyone quarreled or complained, he would simply tighten his lips and arrange his shoulders in the correct command posture. He might give a curt little nod. Or he might not. He might just shrug and say, Carry on, then they would saddle up and form into a column and move out toward the villages of Than Khe.

MAKING CONNECTIONS

1. Describe Jimmy Cross. What do you know about him? How does he change?
2. How are you affected by the setting? What brings the setting to life?
3. Why is Lavender's death referred to so often in the story? Kiowa believes that Cross is crying over Lavender's death. Do you agree? Is there any other reason he might be crying? Explain.
4. Why does Jimmy Cross burn Martha's letters?
5. Why is the list of what they carried repeated so often in the story?
6. Do you carry things that indicate something important about you—or your current situation? Explain.

MAKING AN ARGUMENT

1. In addition to the physical things they carried, the narrator says, "They carried all the emotional baggage of men who might die." Using this story and poems you've selected from the subtheme Connecting Through Comparison: The Impact of War that begins on page 1240, write an essay about the "emotional baggage" of war. Cite the text of the story and the selected poems to support your view.

Flannery O'Connor [1925–1964]

Flannery O'Connor was born in Savannah, Georgia, and at the age of twelve, moved with her family to nearby Milledgeville. After graduating from Women's College of Georgia, O'Connor attended the University of Iowa, earning an M.F.A. in 1947. Following graduation, she stayed for a short time at Yaddo, a prestigious writer's colony in Saratoga Springs, New York, and then with friends in New York City and Connecticut. In 1950, after she was diagnosed with lupus, an incurable degenerative disease, she returned to Milledgeville, where she spent the rest of her life. O'Connor was a devout Roman Catholic. A profound faith permeates her work, which, with its blend of grotesque characterizations and religious faith, is often characterized as Southern gothic. About her stories she wrote: "My subject in fiction is the action of grace in a territory held largely by the devil."

A Good Man Is Hard to Find [1955]

The grandmother didn't want to go to Florida. She wanted to visit some of her connections in east Tennessee and she was seizing at every chance to change Bailey's mind. Bailey was the son she lived with, her only boy. He was sitting on the edge of his chair at the table, bent over the orange sports section of the *Journal*. "Now look here, Bailey," she said, "see here, read this," and she stood with one hand on her thin hip and the other rattling the newspaper at his bald head. "Here this fellow that calls himself The Misfit is aloose from the Federal Pen and headed toward Florida and you read here what it says he did to these people. Just you read it. I wouldn't take my children in any direction with a criminal like that aloose in it. I couldn't answer to my conscience if I did."

Bailey didn't look up from his reading so she wheeled around then and faced the children's mother, a young woman in slacks, whose face was as broad and innocent as a cabbage and was tied around with a green head-kerchief that had two points on the top like a rabbit's ears. She was sitting on the sofa, feeding the baby his apricots out of a jar. "The children have been to Florida before," the old lady said. "You all ought to take them somewhere else for a change so they would see different parts of the world and be broad. They never have been to east Tennessee."

The children's mother didn't seem to hear her but the eight-year-old boy, John Wesley, a stocky child with glasses, said, "If you don't want to go to Florida, why dontcha stay at home?" He and the little girl, June Star, were reading the funny papers on the floor.

"She wouldn't stay at home to be queen for a day," June Star said without raising her yellow head.

5   "Yes and what would you do if this fellow, The Misfit, caught you?" the grandmother asked.

"I'd smack his face," John Wesley said.

"She wouldn't stay at home for a million bucks," June Star said. "Afraid she'd miss something. She has to go everywhere we go."

"All right, Miss," the grandmother said. "Just remember that the next time you want me to curl your hair."

June Star said her hair was naturally curly.

10   The next morning the grandmother was the first one in the car, ready to go. She had her big black valise that looked like the head of a hippopotamus in one corner, and underneath it she was hiding a basket with Pitty Sing, the cat, in it. She didn't intend for the cat to be left alone in the house for three days because he would miss her too much and she was afraid he might brush against one of the gas burners and accidentally asphyxiate himself. Her son, Bailey, didn't like to arrive at a motel with a cat.

She sat in the middle of the back seat with John Wesley and June Star on either side of her. Bailey and the children's mother and the baby sat in front and they left Atlanta at eight forty-five with the mileage on the car at 55890. The grandmother wrote this down because she thought it would be interesting to say how many miles they had been when they got back. It took them twenty minutes to reach the outskirts of the city.

The old lady settled herself comfortably, removing her white cotton gloves and putting them up with her purse on the shelf in front of the back window. The children's mother still had on slacks and still had her head tied up in a green kerchief, but the grandmother had on a navy blue straw sailor hat with a bunch of white violets on the brim and a navy blue dress with a small white dot in the print. Her collars and cuffs were white organdy trimmed with lace and at her neckline she had pinned a purple spray of cloth violets containing a sachet. In case of an accident, anyone seeing her dead on the highway would know at once that she was a lady.

She said she thought it was going to be a good day for driving, neither too hot nor too cold, and she cautioned Bailey that the speed limit was fifty-five miles an hour and that the patrolmen hid themselves behind billboards and small clumps of trees and sped out after you before you had a chance to slow down. She pointed out interesting details of the scenery: Stone Mountain; the blue granite that in some places came up to both sides of the highway; the brilliant red clay banks slightly streaked with purple; and the various crops that made rows of green lace-work on the ground. The trees were full of silver-white sunlight and the meanest of them sparkled. The children were reading comic magazines and their mother had gone back to sleep.

"Let's go through Georgia fast so we won't have to look at it much," John Wesley said.

15   "If I were a little boy," said the grandmother, "I wouldn't talk about my native state that way. Tennessee has the mountains and Georgia has the hills."

"Tennessee is just a hillbilly dumping ground," John Wesley said, "and Georgia is a lousy state too."

"You said it," June Star said.

"In my time," said the grandmother, folding her thin veined fingers, "children were more respectful of their native states and their parents and everything else. People did right then. Oh look at the cute little pickaninny!" she said and pointed to a Negro child standing in the door of a shack. "Wouldn't that make a picture, now?" she asked and they all turned and looked at the little Negro out of the back window. He waved.

"He didn't have any britches on," June Star said.

20   "He probably didn't have any," the grandmother explained. "Little niggers in the country don't have things like we do. If I could paint, I'd paint that picture," she said.

The children exchanged comic books.

The grandmother offered to hold the baby and the children's mother passed him over the front seat to her. She set him on her knee and bounced him and told him about the things they were passing. She rolled her eyes and screwed up her mouth and stuck her leathery thin face into his smooth bland one. Occasionally he gave her a faraway smile. They passed a large cotton field with five or six graves fenced in the middle of it, like a small island. "Look at the graveyard!" the grandmother said, pointing it out. "That was the old family burying ground. That belonged to the plantation."

"Where's the plantation?" John Wesley asked.

"Gone With the Wind," said the grandmother. "Ha. Ha."

25   When the children finished all the comic books they had brought, they opened the lunch and ate it. The grandmother ate a peanut butter sandwich and an olive and would not let the children throw the box and the paper napkins out the window. When there was nothing else to do they played a game by choosing a cloud and

making the other two guess what shape it suggested. John Wesley took one of the shape of a cow and June Star guessed a cow and John Wesley said, no, an automobile, and June Star said he didn't play fair, and they began to slap each other over the grandmother.

The grandmother said she would tell them a story if they would keep quiet. When she told a story, she rolled her eyes and waved her head and was very dramatic. She said once when she was a maiden lady she had been courted by a Mr. Edgar Atkins Teagarden from Jasper, Georgia. She said he was a very good-looking man and a gentleman and that he brought her a watermelon every Saturday afternoon with his initials cut in it, E. A. T. Well, one Saturday, she said, Mr. Teagarden brought the watermelon and there was nobody at home and he left it on the front porch and returned in his buggy to Jasper, but she never got the watermelon, she said, because a nigger boy ate it when he saw the initials, E. A. T.! This story tickled John Wesley's funny bone and he giggled and giggled but June Star didn't think it was any good. She said she wouldn't marry a man that just brought her a watermelon on Saturday. The grandmother said she would have done well to marry Mr. Teagarden because he was a gentleman and had bought Coca-Cola stock when it first came out and that he had died only a few years ago, a very wealthy man.

They stopped at The Tower for barbecued sandwiches. The Tower was a part stucco and part wood filling station and dance hall set in a clearing outside of Timothy. A fat man named Red Sammy Butts ran it and there were signs stuck here and there on the building and for miles up and down the highway saying, TRY RED SAMMY'S FAMOUS BARBECUE. NONE LIKE FAMOUS RED SAMMY'S! RED SAM! THE FAT BOY WITH THE HAPPY LAUGH! A VETERAN! RED SAMMY'S YOUR MAN!

Red Sammy was lying on the bare ground outside The Tower with his head under a truck while a gray monkey about a foot high, chained to a small chinaberry tree, chattered nearby. The monkey sprang back into the tree and got on the highest limb as soon as he saw the children jump out of the car and run toward him.

Inside, The Tower was a long dark room with a counter at one end and tables at the other and dancing space in the middle. They sat down at a board table next to the nickelodeon and Red Sam's wife, a tall burnt-brown woman with hair and eyes lighter than her skin; came and took their order. The children's mother put a dime in the machine and played "The Tennessee Waltz," and the grandmother said that tune always made her want to dance. She asked Bailey if he would like to dance but he only glared at her. He didn't have a naturally sunny disposition like she did and trips made him nervous. The grandmother's brown eyes were very bright. She swayed her head from side to side and pretended she was dancing in her chair. June Star said play something she could tap to so the children's mother put in another dime and played a fast number and June Star stepped out onto the dance floor and did her tap routine.

30   "Ain't she cute?" Red Sam's wife said, leaning over the counter. "Would you like to come be my little girl?"

"No I certainly wouldn't," June Star said. "I wouldn't live in a broken-down place like this for a million bucks!" and she ran back to the table.

"Ain't she cute?" the woman repeated, stretching her mouth politely.

"Aren't you ashamed?" hissed the grandmother.

Red Sam came in and told his wife to quit lounging on the counter and hurry up with these people's order. His khaki trousers reached just to his hip bones and his stomach hung over them like a sack of meal swaying under his shirt. He came over and sat down at a table nearby and let out a combination sigh and yodel. "You can't win," he said. "You can't win," and he wiped his sweating red face off with a gray handkerchief. "These days you don't know who to trust," he said. "Ain't that the truth?"

35   "People are certainly not nice like they used to be," said the grandmother.

"Two fellers come in here last week," Red Sammy said, "driving a Chrysler. It was a old beat-up car but it was a good one and these boys looked all right to me. Said they worked at the mill and you know I let them fellers charge the gas they bought? Now why did I do that?"

"Because you're a good man!" the grandmother said at once.

"Yes'm, I suppose so," Red Sam said as if he were struck with this answer.

His wife brought the orders, carrying the five plates all at once without a tray, two in each hand and one balanced on her arm. "It isn't a soul in this green world of God's that you can trust," she said. "And I don't count nobody out of that, not nobody," she repeated, looking at Red Sammy.

40   "Did you read about that criminal, The Misfit, that's escaped?" asked the grand-mother.

"I wouldn't be a bit surprised if he didn't attact this place right here," said the woman. "If he hears about it being here, I wouldn't be none surprised to see him. If he hears it's two cent in the cash register, I wouldn't be a tall surprised if he . . . ."

"That'll do," Red Sam said. "Go bring these people their Co'-Colas," and the woman went off to get the rest of the order.

"A good man is hard to find," Red Sammy said. "Everything is getting terrible. I remember the day you could go off and leave your screen door unlatched. Not no more."

He and the grandmother discussed better times. The old lady said that in her opin-ion Europe was entirely to blame for the way things were now. She said the way Europe acted you would think we were made of money and Red Sam said it was no use talking about it, she was exactly right. The children ran outside into the white sunlight and looked at the monkey in the lacy chinaberry tree. He was busy catching fleas on himself and biting each one carefully between his teeth as if it were a delicacy.

45   They drove off again into the hot afternoon. The grandmother took cat naps and woke up every few minutes with her own snoring. Outside of Toombsboro she woke up and recalled an old plantation that she had visited in this neighborhood once when she was a young lady. She said the house had six white columns across the front and that there was an avenue of oaks leading up to it and two little wooden trellis arbors on either side in front where you sat down with your suitor after a stroll in the garden. She recalled exactly which road to turn off to get to it. She knew that Bailey would not be willing to lose any time looking at an old house, but the more she talked about it, the more she wanted to see it once again and find out if the little twin arbors were still standing. "There was a secret panel in this house," she said craftily, not telling the truth

but wishing that she were, "and the story went that all the family silver was hidden in it when Sherman came through but it was never found . . . "

"Hey!" John Wesley said. "Let's go see it! We'll find it! We'll poke all the wood-work and find it! Who lives there? Where do you turn off at? Hey Pop, can't we turn off there?"

"We never have seen a house with a secret panel!" June Star shrieked. "Let's go to the house with the secret panel! Hey Pop, can't we go see the house with the secret panel!"

"It's not far from here, I know," the grandmother said. "It wouldn't take over twenty minutes."

Bailey was looking straight ahead. His jaw was as rigid as a horseshoe. "No," he said.

50   The children began to yell and scream that they wanted to see the house with the secret panel. John Wesley kicked the back of the front seat and June Star hung over her mother's shoulder and whined desperately into her ear that they never had any fun even on their vacation, that they could never do what THEY wanted to do. The baby began to scream and John Wesley kicked the back of the seat so hard that his father could feel the blows in his kidney.

"All right!" he shouted and drew the car to a stop at the side of the road. "Will you all shut up? Will you all just shut up for one second? If you don't shut up, we won't go anywhere."

"It would be very educational for them," the grandmother murmured.

"All right," Bailey said, "but get this: this is the only time we're going to stop for anything like this. This is the one and only time."

"The dirt road that you have to turn down is about a mile back," the grand-mother directed. "I marked it when we passed."

55   "A dirt road," Bailey groaned.

After they had turned around and were headed toward the dirt road, the grand-mother recalled other points about the house, the beautiful glass over the front door-way and the candle-lamp in the hall. John Wesley said that the secret panel was probably in the fireplace.

"You can't go inside this house," Bailey said. "You don't know who lives there."

"While you all talk to the people in front, I'll run around behind and get in a window," John Wesley suggested.

"We'll all stay in the car," his mother said.

60   They turned onto the dirt road and the car raced roughly along in a swirl of pink dust. The grandmother recalled the times when there were no paved roads and thirty miles was a day's journey. The dirt road was hilly and there were sudden washes in it and sharp curves on dangerous embankments. All at once they would be on a hill, looking down over the blue tops of trees for miles around, then the next minute, they would be in a red depression with the dust-coated trees looking down on them.

"This place had better turn up in a minute," Bailey said, "or I'm going to turn around."

The road looked as if no one had traveled on it in months.

"It's not much farther," the grandmother said and just as she said it, a horrible thought came to her. The thought was so embarrassing that she turned red in the face and her eyes dilated and her feet jumped up, upsetting her valise in the corner. The instant the valise moved, the newspaper top she had over the basket under it rose with a snarl and Pitty Sing, the cat, sprang onto Bailey's shoulder.

The children were thrown to the floor and their mother, clutching the baby, was thrown out the door onto the ground; the old lady was thrown into the front seat. The car turned over once and landed right-side-up in a gulch off the side of the road. Bailey remained in the driver's seat with the cat—gray-striped with a broad white face and an orange nose—clinging to his neck like a caterpillar.

65   As soon as the children saw they could move their arms and legs, they scrambled out of the car, shouting, "We've had an ACCIDENT!" The grandmother was curled up under the dashboard, hoping she was injured so that Bailey's wrath would not come down on her all at once. The horrible thought she had had before the accident was that the house she had remembered so vividly was not in Georgia but in Tennessee.

Bailey removed the cat from his neck with both hands and flung it out the window against the side of a pine tree. Then he got out of the car and started looking for the children's mother. She was sitting against the side of the red gutted ditch, holding the screaming baby, but she only had a cut down her face and a broken shoulder. "We've had an ACCIDENT!" the children screamed in a frenzy of delight.

"But nobody's killed," June Star said with disappointment as the grandmother limped out of the car, her hat still pinned to her head but the broken front brim standing up at a jaunty angle and the violet spray hanging off the side. They all sat down in the ditch, except the children, to recover from the shock. They were all shaking.

"Maybe a car will come along," said the children's mother hoarsely.

"I believe I have injured an organ," said the grandmother, pressing her side, but no one answered her. Bailey's teeth were clattering. He had on a yellow sport shirt with bright blue parrots designed in it and his face was as yellow as the shirt. The grandmother decided that she would not mention that the house was in Tennessee.

70   The road was about ten feet above and they could see only the tops of the trees on the other side of it. Behind the ditch they were sitting in there were more woods, tall and dark and deep. In a few minutes they saw a car some distance away on top of a hill, coming slowly as if the occupants were watching them. The grandmother stood up and waved both arms dramatically to attract their attention. The car continued to come on slowly, disappeared around a bend and appeared again, moving even slower, on top of the hill they had gone over. It was a big black battered hearse-like automobile. There were three men in it.

It came to a stop just over them and for some minutes, the driver looked down with a steady expressionless gaze to where they were sitting, and didn't speak. Then he turned his head and muttered something to the other two and they got out. One was a fat boy in black trousers and a red sweat shirt with a silver stallion embossed on the front of it. He moved around on the right side of them and stood staring, his mouth partly open in a kind of loose grin. The other had on khaki pants and a blue striped coat and a gray hat pulled down very low, hiding most of his face. He came around slowly on the left side. Neither spoke.

The driver got out of the car and stood by the side of it, looking down at them. He was an older man than the other two. His hair was just beginning to gray and he wore silver-rimmed spectacles that gave him a scholarly look. He had a long creased face and didn't have on any shirt or undershirt. He had on blue jeans that were too tight for him and was holding a black hat and a gun. The two boys also had guns.

"We've had an ACCIDENT!" the children screamed.

The grandmother had the peculiar feeling that the bespectacled man was someone she knew. His face was as familiar to her as if she had known him all her life but she could not recall who he was. He moved away from the car and began to come down the embankment, placing his feet carefully so that he wouldn't slip. He had on tan and white shoes and no socks, and his ankles were red and thin. "Good afternoon," he said. "I see you all had you a little spill."

75 "We turned over twice!" said the grandmother.

"Oncet," he corrected. "We seen it happen. Try their car and see will it run, Hiram," he said quietly to the boy with the gray hat.

"What you got that gun for?" John Wesley asked. "Whatcha gonna do with that gun?"

"Lady," the man said to the children's mother, "would you mind calling them children to sit down by you? Children make me nervous. I want all you to sit down right together there where you're at."

"What are you telling US what to do for?" June Star asked.

80 Behind them the line of woods gaped like a dark open mouth. "Come here," said their mother.

"Look here now," Bailey began suddenly, "we're in a predicament! We're in . . ."

The grandmother shrieked. She scrambled to her feet and stood staring. "You're The Misfit!" she said. "I recognized you at once!"

"Yes'm," the man said, smiling slightly as if he were pleased in spite of himself to be known, "but it would have been better for all of you, lady, if you hadn't of reckernized me."

Bailey turned his head sharply and said something to his mother that shocked even the children. The old lady began to cry and The Misfit reddened.

85 "Lady," he said, "don't you get upset. Sometimes a man says things he don't mean. I don't reckon he meant to talk to you thataway."

"You wouldn't shoot a lady, would you?" the grandmother said and removed a clean handkerchief from her cuff and began to slap at her eyes with it.

The Misfit pointed the toe of his shoe into the ground and made a little hole and then covered it up again. "I would hate to have to," he said.

"Listen," the grandmother almost screamed, "I know you're a good man. You don't look a bit like you have common blood. I know you must come from nice people!"

"Yes mam," he said, "finest people in the world." When he smiled he showed a row of strong white teeth. "God never made a finer woman than my mother and my daddy's heart was pure gold," he said. The boy with the red sweat shirt had come around behind them and was standing with his gun at his hip. The Misfit squatted down on the ground. "Watch them children, Bobby Lee," he said. "You know they make me nervous."

He looked at the six of them huddled together in front of him and he seemed to be embarrassed as if he couldn't think of anything to say. "Ain't a cloud in the sky," he remarked, looking up at it. "Don't see no sun but don't see no cloud neither."

90   "Yes, it's a beautiful day," said the grandmother. "Listen," she said, "you shouldn't call yourself The Misfit because I know you're a good man at heart. I can just look at you and tell."

"Hush!" Bailey yelled. "Hush! Everybody shut up and let me handle this!" He was squatting in the position of a runner about to sprint forward but he didn't move.

"I pre-chate that, lady," The Misfit said and drew a little circle in the ground with the butt of his gun.

"It'll take a half a hour to fix this here car," Hiram called, looking over the raised hood of it.

"Well, first you and Bobby Lee get him and that little boy to step over yonder with you," The Misfit said, pointing to Bailey and John Wesley. "The boys want to ast you something," he said to Bailey. "Would you mind stepping back in them woods there with them?"

95   "Listen," Bailey began, "we're in a terrible predicament! Nobody realizes what this is," his voice cracked. His eyes were as blue and intense as the parrots in his shirt and he remained perfectly still.

The grandmother reached up to adjust her hat brim as if she were going to the woods with him but it came off in her hand. She stood staring at it and after a second she let it fall on the ground. Hiram pulled Bailey up by the arm as if he were assisting an old man. John Wesley caught hold of his father's hand and Bobby Lee followed. They went off toward the woods and just as they reached the dark edge, Bailey turned and supporting himself against a gray naked pine trunk, he shouted, "I'll be back in a minute, Mamma, wait on me!"

"Come back this instant!" his mother shrilled but they all disappeared into the woods.

"Bailey Boy!" the grandmother called in a tragic voice but she found she was looking at The Misfit squatting on the ground in front of her. "I just know you're a good man," she said desperately. "You're not a bit common!"

"Nome, I ain't a good man," The Misfit said after a second as if he had considered her statement carefully, "but I ain't the worst in the world neither. My daddy said I was a different breed of dog from my brothers and sisters. "You know,' Daddy said, 'it's some that can live their whole life out without asking about it and it's others has to know why it is, and this boy is one of the latters. He's going to be into everything!'" He put on his black hat and looked up suddenly and then away deep into the woods as if he were embarrassed again. "I'm sorry I don't have on a shirt before you ladies," he said, hunching his shoulders slightly. "We buried our clothes that we had on when we escaped and we're just making do until we can get better. We borrowed these from some folks we met," he explained.

100   "That's perfectly all right," the grandmother said. "Maybe Bailey has an extra shirt in his suitcase."

"I'll look and see terrectly," The Misfit said.

"Where are they taking him?" the children's mother screamed.

"Daddy was a card himself," The Misfit said. "You couldn't put anything over on him. He never got in trouble with the Authorities though. Just had the knack of handling them."

"You could be honest too if you'd only try," said the grandmother. "Think how wonderful it would be to settle down and live a comfortable life and not have to think about somebody chasing you all the time."

105   The Misfit kept scratching in the ground with the butt of his gun as if he were thinking about it. "Yes'm, somebody is always after you," he murmured.

The grandmother noticed how thin his shoulder blades were just behind his hat because she was standing up looking down on him. "Do you ever pray?" she asked.

He shook his head. All she saw was the black hat wiggle between his shoulder blades. "Nome," he said.

There was a pistol shot from the woods, followed closely by another. Then silence. The old lady's head jerked around. She could hear the wind move through the tree tops like a long satisfied insuck of breath. "Bailey Boy!" she called.

"I was a gospel singer for a while," The Misfit said. "I been most everything. Been in the arm service, both land and sea, at home and abroad, been twice married, been an undertaker, been with the railroads, plowed Mother Earth, been in a tornado, seen a man burnt alive oncet," and looked up at the children's mother and the little girl who were sitting close together, their faces white and their eyes glassy; "I even seen a woman flogged," he said.

110   "Pray, pray," the grandmother began, "pray, pray . . . "

"I never was a bad boy that I remember of," The Misfit said in an almost dreamy voice, "but somewheres along the line I done something wrong and got sent to the penitentiary. I was buried alive," and he looked up and held her attention to him by a steady stare.

"That's when you should have started to pray," she said. "What did you do to get sent to the penitentiary that first time?"

"Turn to the right, it was a wall," The Misfit said, looking up again at the cloudless sky. "Turn to the left, it was a wall. Look up it was a ceiling, look down it was a floor. I forget what I done, lady. I set there and set there, trying to remember what it was I done and I ain't recalled it to this day. Oncet in a while, I would think it was coming to me, but it never come."

"Maybe they put you in by mistake," the old lady said vaguely.

115   "Nome," he said. "It wasn't no mistake. They had the papers on me."

"You must have stolen something," she said.

The Misfit sneered slightly. "Nobody had nothing I wanted," he said. "It was a head-doctor at the penitentiary said what I had done was kill my daddy but I know that for a lie. My daddy died in nineteen ought nineteen of the epidemic flu and I never had a thing to do with it. He was buried in the Mount Hopewell Baptist churchyard and you can go there and see for yourself."

"If you would pray," the old lady said, "Jesus would help you."

"That's right," The Misfit said.

120   "Well then, why don't you pray?" she asked trembling with delight suddenly.

"I don't want no hep," he said. "I'm doing all right by myself."

Bobby Lee and Hiram came ambling back from the woods. Bobby Lee was dragging a yellow shirt with bright blue parrots in it.

"Throw me that shirt, Bobby Lee," The Misfit said. The shirt came flying at him and landed on his shoulder and he put it on. The grandmother couldn't name what the shirt reminded her of. "No, lady," The Misfit said while he was buttoning it up, "I found out the crime don't matter. You can do one thing or you can do another, kill a man or take a tire off his car, because sooner or later you're going to forget what it was you done and just be punished for it."

The children's mother had begun to make heaving noises as if she couldn't get her breath. "Lady," he asked, "would you and that little girl like to step off yonder with Bobby Lee and Hiram and join your husband?"

125   "Yes, thank you," the mother said faintly. Her left arm dangled helplessly and she was holding the baby, who had gone to sleep, in the other. "Hep that lady up, Hiram," The Misfit said as she struggled to climb out of the ditch, "and Bobby Lee, you hold onto that little girl's hand."

"I don't want to hold hands with him," June Star said. "He reminds me of a pig."

The fat boy blushed and laughed and caught her by the arm and pulled her off into the woods after Hiram and her mother.

Alone with The Misfit, the grandmother found that she had lost her voice. There was not a cloud in the sky nor any sun. There was nothing around her but woods. She wanted to tell him that he must pray. She opened and closed her mouth several times before anything came out. Finally she found herself saying, "Jesus, Jesus," meaning, Jesus will help you, but the way she was saying it, it sounded as if she might be cursing.

"Yes'm," The Misfit said as if he agreed. "Jesus thrown everything off balance. It was the same case with Him as with me except He hadn't committed any crime and they could prove I had committed one because they had the papers on me. Of course," he said, "they never shown me my papers. That's why I sign myself now. I said long ago, you get you a signature and sign everything you do and keep a copy of it. Then you'll know what you done and you can hold up the crime to the punishment and see do they match and in the end you'll have something to prove you ain't been treated right. I call myself The Misfit," he said, "because I can't make what all I done wrong fit what all I gone through in punishment."

130   There was a piercing scream from the woods, followed closely by a pistol report. "Does it seem right to you, lady, that one is punished a heap and another ain't punished at all?"

"Jesus!" the old lady cried. "You've got good blood! I know you wouldn't shoot a lady! I know you come from nice people! Pray! Jesus, you ought not to shoot a lady. I'll give you all the money I've got!"

"Lady," The Misfit said, looking beyond her far into the woods, "there never was a body that give the undertaker a tip."

There were two more pistol reports and the grandmother raised her head like a parched old turkey hen crying for water and called, "Bailey Boy, Bailey Boy!" as if her heart would break.

"Jesus was the only One that ever raised the dead," The Misfit continued, "and He shouldn't have done it. He thrown everything off balance. If He did what He said, then it's nothing for you to do but throw away everything and follow Him, and if He didn't, then it's nothing for you to do but enjoy the few minutes you got left the best way you can—by killing somebody or burning down his house or doing some other meanness to him. No pleasure but meanness," he said and his voice had become almost a snarl.

135   "Maybe He didn't raise the dead," the old lady mumbled, not knowing what she was saying and feeling so dizzy that she sank down in the ditch with her legs twisted under her.

    "I wasn't there so I can't say He didn't," The Misfit said. "I wisht I had of been there," he said, hitting the ground with his fist. "It ain't right I wasn't there because if I had of been there I would of known. Listen lady," he said in a high voice, "if I had of been there I would of known and I wouldn't be like I am now." His voice seemed about to crack and the grandmother's head cleared for an instant. She saw the man's face twisted close to her own as if he were going to cry and she murmured, "Why you're one of my babies. You're one of my own children!" She reached out and touched him on the shoulder. The Misfit sprang back as if a snake had bitten him and shot her three times through the chest. Then he put his gun down on the ground and took off his glasses and began to clean them.

    Hiram and Bobby Lee returned from the woods and stood over the ditch, looking down at the grandmother who half sat and half lay in a puddle of blood with her legs crossed under her like a child's and her face smiling up at the cloudless sky.

    Without his glasses, The Misfit's eyes were red-rimmed and pale and defenseless looking. "Take her off and throw her where you thrown the others," he said, picking up the cat that was rubbing itself against his leg.

    "She was a talker, wasn't she?" Bobby Lee said, sliding down the ditch with a yodel.

140   "She would have been a good woman," The Misfit said, "if it had been somebody there to shoot her every minute of her life."

    "Some fun!" Bobby Lee said.

    "Shut up, Bobby Lee," The Misfit said. "It's no real pleasure in life."

MAKING CONNECTIONS

1. What is the point of the long introductory section, where we are introduced to the grandmother and her family before and during the early stages of the trip? Would the story be better if it began with a brief introduction and then the accident? Explain.

2. The Misfit says of Jesus, " 'He thrown everything off balance.' " Why does he say that, and what do you think he is making reference to? Support your comments with reference to details in the story.

3. This is a nightmarish story filled with sudden violence and cold-blooded killing. But is there a spiritual element to this story? Why do you think The Misfit reacts so violently to the grandmother's comment " 'Why you're one of my babies. You're one of my own children' "?

4. To what extent is the grandmother heroic in the story? What does The Misfit mean when he says, "She would have been a good woman if it had been someone there to shoot her every minute of her life"?

MAKING AN ARGUMENT

1. Flannery O'Connor has written that "Much of my fiction takes its character from a reasonable use of the unreasonable." To what extent is that the case in "A Good Man Is Hard to Find"? Write an essay that shows how this story exemplifies a "reasonable use of the unreasonable." Cite the text of this story (and if appropriate, other O'Connor stories you have read) for support.

LUIGI PIRANDELLO [1867–1936]

Luigi Pirandello was born in Sicily to well-to-do parents. He attended the University of Rome and the University of Bonn, where he first began writing poetry and fiction. In 1896, he married the daughter of his father's business partner. The marriage was a happy one, and Pirandello pursued a career as a writer until the collapse of the family business in 1904 left him impoverished. The stress of these events drove his wife insane, and for the next fif-
teen years Pirandello took care of her, until finally committing her to an institution in 1919. Though he accepted a position as a teacher at a girl's school in order to support his family, Pirandello continued to write and publish novels, stories, and plays. In 1924, he became the director of his own company, the Art Theatre of Rome, which eventually toured throughout the world, influencing a generation of directors, playwrights, and actors. In 1934, he was awarded the Nobel Prize for literature. Questions about the perception of reality, truth, and the self are at the center of much of his work. Nowhere are his concerns more clearly presented than in his most famous work, the play Six Characters in Search of an Author, *which created a sensation when it appeared in 1922.*

WAR   [1939]

The passengers who had left Rome by the night express had had to stop until dawn at the small station of Fabriano in order to continue their journey by the small old-fashioned local joining the main line with Sulmona.

At dawn, in a stuffy and smoky second-class carriage in which five people had already spent the night, a bulky woman in deep mourning was hoisted in—almost like a shapeless bundle. Behind her, puffing and moaning, followed her husband—a tiny man, thin and weakly, his face death-white, his eyes small and bright and looking shy and uneasy.

Having at last taken a seat he politely thanked the passengers who had helped his wife and who had made room for her; then he turned round to the woman trying to pull down the collar of her coat, and politely inquired:

"Are you all right, dear?"

5   The wife, instead of answering, pulled up her collar again to her eyes, so as to hide her face.

"Nasty world," muttered the husband with a sad smile.

And he felt it his duty to explain to his traveling companions that the poor woman was to be pitied, for the war was taking away from her her only son, a boy of twenty to whom both had devoted their entire life, even breaking up their home at Sulmona to follow him to Rome, where he had to go as a student, then allowing him to volunteer for war with an assurance, however, that at least for six months he would not be sent to the front and now, all of a sudden, receiving a wire saying that he was due to leave in three days' time and asking them to go and see him off.

The woman under the big coat was twisting and wriggling, at times growling like a wild animal, feeling certain that all those explanations would not have aroused even a shadow of sympathy from those people who—most likely—were in the same plight as herself. One of them, who had been listening with particular attention, said:

"You should thank God that your son is only leaving now for the front. Mine has been sent there the first day of the war. He has already come back twice wounded and been sent back again to the front."

"What about me? I have two sons and three nephews at the front," said another passenger.

"Maybe, but in our case it is our *only* son," ventured the husband.

"What difference can it make? You may spoil your only son with excessive attentions, but you cannot love him more than you would all your other children if you had any. Paternal love is not like bread that can be broken into pieces and split amongst the children in equal shares. A father gives *all* his love to each one of his children without discrimination, whether it be one or ten, and if I am suffering now for my two sons, I am not suffering half for each of them but double . . . "

"True . . . true . . . " sighed the embarrassed husband, "but suppose (of course we all hope it will never be your case) a father has two sons at the front and he loses one of them, there is still one left to console him . . . while . . . "

"Yes," answered the other, getting cross, "a son left to console him but also a son left for whom he must survive, while in the case of the father of an only son if the son dies the father can die too and put an end to his distress. Which of the two positions is the worse? Don't you see how my case would be worse than yours?"

"Nonsense," interrupted another traveler, a fat, red-faced man with bloodshot eyes of the palest gray.

He was panting. From his bulging eyes seemed to spurt inner violence of an uncontrolled vitality which his weakened body could hardly contain.

"Nonsense," he repeated, trying to cover his mouth with his hand so as to hide the two missing front teeth. "Nonsense. Do we give life to our children for our own benefit?"

The other travelers stared at him in distress. The one who had had his son at the front since the first day of the war sighed: "You are right. Our children do not belong to us. They belong to the Country . . . "

"Bosh," retorted the fat traveler. "Do we think of the Country when we give life to our children? Our sons are born because . . . well, because they must be born and when they come to life they take our own life with them. This is the truth. We belong to them but they never belong to us. And when they reach twenty they are exactly what we were at their age. We too had a father and mother, but there were so many other things as well . . . girls, cigarettes, illusions, new ties . . . and the Country, of course, whose call we would have answered—when we were twenty—

even if father and mother had said no. Now at our age, the love of our Country is still great, of course, but stronger than it is the love for our children. Is there any one of us here who wouldn't gladly take his son's place at the front if he could?"

20   There was a silence all round, everybody nodding as to approve.

"Why then," continued the fat man, "shouldn't we consider the feelings of our children when they are twenty? Isn't it natural that at their age they should consider the love for their Country (I am speaking of decent boys, of course) even greater than the love for us? Isn't it natural that it should be so, as after all they must look upon us as upon old boys who cannot move any more and must stay at home? If Country exists, if Country is a natural necessity, like bread, of which each of us must eat in order not to die of hunger, somebody must go to defend it. And our sons go, when they are twenty, and they don't want tears, because if they die, they die inflamed and happy (I am speaking, of course, of decent boys). Now, if one dies young and happy, without having the ugly sides of life, the boredom of it, the pettiness, the bitterness of disillusion . . . . what more can we ask for him? Everyone should stop crying; everyone should laugh, as I do . . . or at least thank God—as I do—because my son, before dying, sent me a message saying that he was dying satisfied at having ended his life in the best way he could have wished. That is why, as you see, I do not even wear mourning . . . "

He shook his light fawn coat as to show it; his livid lip over his missing teeth was trembling, his eyes were watery and motionless, and soon after he ended with a shrill laugh which might well have been a sob.

"Quite so . . . quite so . . . " agreed the others.

The woman who, bundled in a corner under her coat, had been sitting and listening had—for the last three months—tried to find in the words of her husband and her friends something to console her in her deep sorrow, something that might show her how a mother should resign herself to send her son not even to death but to a probably dangerous life. Yet not a word had she found amongst the many which had been said . . . and her grief had been greater in seeing that nobody—as she thought—could share her feelings.

25   But now the words of the traveler amazed and almost stunned her. She suddenly realized that it wasn't the others who were wrong and could not understand her but herself who could not rise up to the same height of those fathers and mothers willing to resign themselves, without crying, not only to the departure of their sons but even to their death.

She lifted her head, she bent over from her corner trying to listen with great attention to the details which the fat man was giving to his companions about the way his son had fallen as a hero, for his King and his Country, happy and without regrets. It seemed to her that she had stumbled into a world she had never dreamt of, a world so far unknown to her and she was so pleased to hear everyone joining in congratulating that brave father who could so stoically speak of his child's death.

Then suddenly, just as if she had heard nothing of what had been said and almost as if waking up from a dream, she turned to the old man, asking him:

"Then . . . is your son really dead?"

Everybody stared at her. The old man, too, turned to look at her, fixing his great, bulging, horribly watery light gray eyes, deep in her face. For some little time he tried to answer, but words failed him. He looked and looked at her, almost as if only then—at that silly, incongruous question—he had suddenly realized at last that his son was really dead—gone for ever—for ever. His face contracted, became horribly distorted, then he snatched in haste a handkerchief from his pocket and, to the amazement of everyone, broke into harrowing, heartrending, uncontrollable sobs.

MAKING CONNECTIONS

1. How do you think about sacrificing a family member or loved one to war?
2. At one point the red-faced man says, "'I do not even wear mourning.'" How does the narrator's description of him bear this out?
3. What is your reaction to the ending of the story? Why do you think the red-faced man begins to sob when the woman asks him, "'Then . . . is your son really dead?'"
4. The structure of this story is based on a number of shifts from dialogue to description and from one character to another. Is it effective? Explain.
5. Do you think this is a story about war or about parents' love for their children, or something else? Explain.

MAKING AN ARGUMENT

1. Like Amy Lowell's poem "Patterns" on page 1241, this story does not focus on those who die in war but rather on those who are left behind. Using "War" and "Patterns" (and any other works you think appropriate), write an essay about the impact of war on those left behind. Cite the texts of the works for support.

JOHN STEINBECK [1902–1968]

John Steinbeck was born and grew up in Salinas, California, where he worked on farms and ranches and often witnessed the plight of oppressed migrant farm workers. He would later reference these experiences in novels like The Grapes of Wrath *(1939), a story about dispossessed farm workers from the dust bowl of Oklahoma, which won the Pulitzer Prize in 1940. Other best-known novels of his include* Of Mice and Men *(1937), Tortilla Flat (1935), In Dubious Battle (1936), East of Eden (1952), and* The Winter of Our Discontent *(1961). One of America's most popular novelists, Steinbeck received the Nobel Prize for literature in 1962. "The Chrysanthemums" is taken from a collection of short stories,* The Long Valley, *that was published in 1938.*

THE CHRYSANTHEMUMS   [1937]

The high gray-flannel fog of winter closed off the Salinas Valley from the sky and from all the rest of the world. On every side it sat like a lid on the mountains and made of the great valley a closed pot. On the broad, level land floor the gang plows bit deep and left the black earth shining like metal where the shares had cut. On the foothill ranches across the Salinas River, the yellow stubble fields seemed to be bathed in pale cold sunshine, but there was no sunshine in the valley now in December. The thick willow scrub along the river flamed with sharp and positive yellow leaves.

It was a time of quiet and of waiting. The air was cold and tender. A light wind blew up from the southwest so that the farmers were mildly hopeful of a good rain before long; but fog and rain do not go together.

Across the river, on Henry Allen's foothill ranch there was little work to be done, for the hay was cut and stored and the orchards were plowed up to receive the rain deeply when it should come. The cattle on the higher slopes were becoming shaggy and rough-coated.

Elisa Allen, working in her flower garden, looked down across the yard and saw Henry, her husband, talking to two men in business suits. The three of them stood by the tractor shed, each man with one foot on the side of the little Fordson. They smoked cigarettes and studied the machine as they talked.

5   Elisa watched them for a moment and then went back to her work. She was thirty-five. Her face was lean and strong and her eyes were as clear as water. Her figure looked blocked and heavy in her gardening costume, a man's black hat pulled down over her eyes, clod-hopper shoes, a figured print dress almost completely covered by a big corduroy apron with four big pockets to hold the snips, the trowel and scratcher, the seeds and the knife she worked with. She wore heavy leather gloves to protect her hands while she worked.

She was cutting down the old year's chrysanthemum stalks with a pair of short and powerful scissors. She looked down toward the men by the tractor shed now and then. Her face was eager and mature and handsome; even her work with the scissors was over-eager, over-powerful. The chrysanthemum stems seemed too small and easy for her energy.

She brushed a cloud of hair out of her eyes with the back of her glove, and left a smudge of earth on her cheek in doing it. Behind her stood the neat white farm house with red geraniums close-banked around it as high as the windows. It was a hard-swept looking little house with hard-polished windows, and a clean mud-mat on the front steps.

Elisa cast another glance toward the tractor shed. The strangers were getting into their Ford coupe. She took off a glove and put her strong fingers down into the forest of new green chrysanthemum sprouts that were growing around the old roots. She spread the leaves and looked down among the close-growing stems. No aphids were there, no sowbugs or snails or cutworms. Her terrier fingers destroyed such pests before they could get started.

Elisa started at the sound of her husband's voice. He had come near quietly, and he leaned over the wire fence that protected her flower garden from cattle and dogs and chickens.

10   "At it again," he said. "You've got a strong new crop coming."

Elisa straightened her back and pulled on the gardening glove again. "Yes. They'll be strong this coming year." In her tone and on her face there was a little smugness.

"You've got a gift with things," Henry observed. "Some of those yellow chrysanthemums you had this year were ten inches across. I wish you'd work out in the orchard and raise some apples that big."

Her eyes sharpened. "Maybe I could do it, too. I've a gift with things, all right. My mother had it. She could stick anything in the ground and make it grow. She said it was having planters' hands that knew how to do it."

"Well, it sure works with flowers," he said.

15   "Henry, who were those men you were talking to?"

"Why, sure, that's what I came to tell you. They were from the Western Meat Company. I sold those thirty head of three-year-old steers. Got nearly my own price, too."

"Good," she said. "Good for you."

"And I thought," he continued, "I thought how it's Saturday afternoon, and we might go into Salinas for dinner at a restaurant, and then to a picture show—to celebrate, you see."

"Good," she repeated. "Oh, yes. That will be good."

20   Henry put on his joking tone. "There's fights tonight. How'd you like to go to the fights?"

"Oh, no," she said breathlessly. "No, I wouldn't like fights."

"Just fooling, Elisa. We'll go to a movie. Let's see. It's two now. I'm going to take Scotty and bring down those steers from the hill. It'll take us maybe two hours. We'll go in town about five and have dinner at the Cominos Hotel. Like that?"

"Of course I'll like it. It's good to eat away from home."

"All right, then. I'll go get up a couple of horses."

25   She said, "I'll have plenty of time to transplant some of these sets, I guess."

She heard her husband calling Scotty down by the barn. And a little later she saw the two men ride up the pale yellow hillside in search of the steers.

There was a little square sandy bed kept for rooting the chrysanthemums. With her trowel she turned the soil over and over, and smoothed it and patted it firm. Then she dug ten parallel trenches to receive the sets. Back at the chrysanthemum bed she pulled out the little crisp shoots, trimmed off the leaves of each one with her scissors and laid it on a small orderly pile.

A squeak of wheels and plod of hoofs came from the road. Elisa looked up. The country road ran along the dense bank of willows and cottonwoods that bordered the river, and up this road came a curious vehicle, curiously drawn. It was an old spring-wagon, with a round canvas top on it like the cover of a prairie schooner. It was drawn by an old bay horse and a little grey-and-white burro. A big stubble-bearded man sat between the cover flaps and drove the crawling team. Underneath the wagon, between the hind wheels, a lean and rangy mongrel dog walked sedately. Words were painted on the canvas, in clumsy, crooked letters. "Pots, pans, knives, scissors, lawn mores, Fixed." Two rows of articles, and the triumphantly definitive "Fixed" below. The black paint had run down in little sharp points beneath each letter.

Elisa, squatting on the ground, watched to see the crazy, loose-jointed wagon pass by. But it didn't pass. It turned into the farm road in front of her house, crooked old wheels skirling and squeaking. The rangy dog darted from between the wheels and ran ahead. Instantly the two ranch shepherds flew out at him. Then all three stopped, and with stiff and quivering tails, with taut straight legs, with ambassadorial dignity, they slowly circled, sniffing daintily. The caravan pulled up to Elisa's wire fence and stopped. Now the newcomer dog, feeling out-numbered, lowered his tail and retired under the wagon with raised hackles and bared teeth.

30   The man on the wagon seat called out, "That's a bad dog in a fight when he gets started."

Elisa laughed. "I see he is. How soon does he generally get started?"

The man caught up her laughter and echoed it heartily. "Sometimes not for weeks and weeks," he said. He climbed stiffly down, over the wheel. The horse and the donkey drooped like unwatered flowers.

Elisa saw that he was a very big man. Although his hair and beard were greying, he did not look old. His worn black suit was wrinkled and spotted with grease. The laughter had disappeared from his face and eyes the moment his laughing voice ceased. His eyes were dark, and they were full of the brooding that gets in the eyes of teamsters and of sailors. The calloused hands he rested on the wire fence were cracked, and every crack was a black line. He took off his battered hat.

"I'm off my general road, ma'am," he said. "Does this dirt road cut over across the river to the Los Angeles highway?"

35   Elisa stood up and shoved the thick scissors in her apron pocket. "Well, yes, it does, but it winds around and then fords the river. I don't think your team could pull through the sand."

He replied with some asperity. "It might surprise you what them beasts can pull through."

"When they get started?" she asked.

He smiled for a second. "Yes. When they get started."

"Well," said Elisa, "I think you'll save time if you go back to the Salinas road and pick up the highway there."

40   He drew a big finger down the chicken wire and made it sing. "I ain't in any hurry, ma'am. I go from Seattle to San Diego and back every year. Takes all my time. About six months each way. I aim to follow nice weather."

Elisa took off her gloves and stuffed them in the apron pocket with the scissors. She touched the under edge of her man's hat, searching for fugitive hairs. "That sounds like a nice kind of a way to live," she said.

He leaned confidentially over the fence. "Maybe you noticed the writing on my wagon. I mend pots and sharpen knives and scissors. You got any of them things to do?"

"Oh, no," she said quickly. "Nothing like that." Her eyes hardened with resistance.

"Scissors is the worst thing," he explained. "Most people just ruin scissors trying to sharpen 'em, but I know how. I got a special tool. It's a little bobbit kind of thing, and patented. But it sure does the trick."

45   "No. My scissors are all sharp."

"All right, then. Take a pot," he continued earnestly, "a bent pot, or a pot with a hole. I can make it like new so you don't have to buy no new ones. That's a savings for you."

"No," she said shortly. "I tell you I have nothing like that for you to do."

His face fell to an exaggerated sadness. His voice took on a whining undertone. "I ain't had a thing to do today. Maybe I won't have no supper tonight. You see I'm off my regular road. I know folks on the highway clear from Seattle to San Diego. They save their things for me to sharpen up because they know I do it so good and save them money."

"I'm sorry," Elisa said irritably. "I haven't anything for you to do."

50   His eyes left her face and fell to searching the ground. They roamed about until they came to the chrysanthemum bed where she had been working. "What's them plants, ma'am?"

The irritation and resistance melted from Elisa's face. "Oh, those are chrysanthemums, giant whites and yellows. I raise them every year, bigger than anybody around here."

"Kind of a long-stemmed flower? Looks like a quick puff of colored smoke?" he asked.

"That's it. What a nice way to describe them."

"They smell kind of nasty till you get used to them," he said.

55 "It's a good bitter smell," she retorted, "not nasty at all."

He changed his tone quickly. "I like the smell myself."

"I had ten-inch blooms this year," she said.

The man leaned farther over the fence. "Look. I know a lady down the road a piece, has got the nicest garden you ever seen. Got nearly every kind of flower but no chrysanthemums. Last time I was mending a copper-bottom washtub for her (that's a hard job but I do it good), she said to me, 'If you ever run acrost some nice chrysanthemums I wish you'd try to get me a few seeds.' That's what she told me."

Elisa's eyes grew alert and eager. "She couldn't have known much about chrysanthemums. You *can* raise them from seed, but it's much easier to root the little sprouts you see there."

60 "Oh," he said. "I s'pose I can't take none to her, then."

"Why yes you can," Elisa cried. "I can put some in damp sand, and you can carry them right along with you. They'll take root in the pot if you keep them damp. And then she can transplant them."

"She'd sure like to have some, ma'am. You say they're nice ones?"

"Beautiful," she said. "Oh, beautiful." Her eyes shone. She tore off the battered hat and shook out her dark pretty hair. "I'll put them in a flower pot, and you can take them right with you. Come into the yard."

While the man came through the picket gate Elisa ran excitedly along the geranium-bordered path to the back of the house. And she returned carrying a big red flower pot. The gloves were forgotten now. She kneeled on the ground by the starting bed and dug up the sandy soil with her fingers and scooped it into the bright new flower pot. Then she picked up the little pile of shoots she had prepared. With her strong fingers she pressed them in the sand and tamped around them with her knuckles. The man stood over her. "I'll tell you what to do," she said. "You remember so you can tell the lady."

65 "Yes, I'll try to remember."

"Well, look. These will take root in about a month. Then she must set them out, about a foot apart in good rich earth like this, see?" She lifted a handful of dark soil for him to look at. "They'll grow fast and tall. Now remember this: In July tell her to cut them down, about eight inches from the ground."

"Before they bloom?" he asked.

"Yes, before they bloom." Her face was tight with eagerness. "They'll grow right up again. About the last of September the buds will start."

She stopped and seemed perplexed. "It's the budding that takes the most care," she said hesitantly. "I don't know how to tell you." She looked deep into his eyes, searchingly. Her mouth opened a little, and she seemed to be listening. "I'll try to tell you," she said. "Did you ever hear of planting hands?"

70 "Can't say I have, ma'am."

"Well, I can only tell you what it feels like. It's when you're picking off the buds you don't want. Everything goes right down into your fingertips. You watch your fingers work. They do it themselves. You can feel how it is. They pick and pick the buds.

They never make a mistake. They're with the plant. Do you see? Your fingers and the plant. You can feel that, right up your arm. They know. They never make a mistake. You can feel it. When you're like that you can't do anything wrong. Do you see that? Can you understand that?"

She was kneeling on the ground looking up at him. Her breast swelled passionately.

The man's eyes narrowed. He looked away self-consciously. "Maybe I know," he said. "Sometimes in the night in the wagon there—"

Elisa's voice grew husky. She broke in on him, "I've never lived as you do, but I know what you mean. When the night is dark—why, the stars are sharp-pointed, and there's quiet. Why, you rise up and up! Every pointed star gets driven into your body. It's like that. Hot and sharp and—lovely."

75   Kneeling there, her hand went out toward his legs in the greasy black trousers. Her hesitant fingers almost touched the cloth. Then her hand dropped to the ground. She crouched low like a fawning dog.

He said, "It's nice, just like you say. Only when you don't have no dinner, it ain't."

She stood up then, very straight, and her face was ashamed. She held the flower pot out to him and placed it gently in his arms. "Here. Put it in your wagon, on the seat, where you can watch it. Maybe I can find something for you to do."

At the back of the house she dug in the can pile and found two old and battered aluminum saucepans. She carried them back and gave them to him. "Here, maybe you can fix these."

His manner changed. He became professional. "Good as new I can fix them." At the back of his wagon he set a little anvil, and out of an oily tool box dug a small machine hammer. Elisa came through the gate to watch him while he pounded out the dents in the kettles. His mouth grew sure and knowing. At a difficult part of the work he sucked his underlip.

80   "You sleep right in the wagon?" Elisa asked.

"Right in the wagon, ma'am. Rain or shine I'm dry as a cow in there."

"It must be nice," she said. "It must be very nice. I wish women could do such things."

"It ain't the right kind of a life for a woman."

Her upper lip raised a little, showing her teeth. "How do you know? How can you tell?" she said.

85   "I don't know, ma'am," he protested. "Of course I don't know. Now here's your kettles, done. You don't have to buy no new ones."

"How much?"

"Oh, fifty cents'll do. I keep my prices down and my work good. That's why I have all them satisfied customers up and down the highway."

Elisa brought him a fifty-cent piece from the house and dropped it in his hand. "You might be surprised to have a rival some time. I can sharpen scissors, too. And I can beat the dents out of little pots. I could show you what a woman might do."

He put his hammer back in the oily box and shoved the little anvil out of sight. "It would be a lonely life for a woman, ma'am, and a scary life, too, with animals creeping under the wagon all night." He climbed over the singletree, steadying himself with a hand on the burro's white rump. He settled himself in the seat, picked up the lines. "Thank you kindly, ma'am," he said. "I'll do like you told me; I'll go back and catch the Salinas road."

90   "Mind," she called, "if you're long in getting there, keep the sand damp."

"Sand, ma'am? . . . . Sand? Oh, sure. You mean around the chrysanthemums. Sure I will." He clucked his tongue. The beasts leaned luxuriously into their collars. The mongrel dog took his place between the back wheels. The wagon turned and crawled out the entrance road and back the way it had come, along the river.

Elisa stood in front of her wire fence watching the slow progress of the caravan. Her shoulders were straight, her head thrown back, her eyes half-closed, so that the scene came vaguely into them. Her lips moved silently, forming the words "Good-bye—good-bye." Then she whispered, "That's a bright direction. There's a glowing there." The sound of her whisper startled her. She shook herself free and looked about to see whether anyone had been listening. Only the dogs had heard. They lifted their heads toward her from their sleeping in the dust, and then stretched out their chins and settled asleep again. Elisa turned and ran hurriedly into the house.

In the kitchen she reached behind the stove and felt the water tank. It was full of hot water from the noonday cooking. In the bathroom she tore off her soiled clothes and flung them into the corner. And then she scrubbed herself with a little block of pumice, legs and thighs, loins and chest and arms, until her skin was scratched and red. When she had dried herself she stood in front of a mirror in her bedroom and looked at her body. She tightened her stomach and threw out her chest. She turned and looked over her shoulder at her back.

After a while she began to dress, slowly. She put on her newest underclothing and her nicest stockings and the dress which was the symbol of her prettiness. She worked carefully on her hair, penciled her eyebrows and rouged her lips.

95   Before she was finished she heard the little thunder of hoofs and the shouts of Henry and his helper as they drove the red steers into the corral. She heard the gate bang shut and set herself for Henry's arrival.

His step sounded on the porch. He entered the house calling, "Elisa, where are you?"

"In my room, dressing. I'm not ready. There's hot water for your bath. Hurry up. It's getting late."

When she heard him splashing in the tub, Elisa laid his dark suit on the bed, and shirt and socks and tie beside it. She stood his polished shoes on the floor beside the bed. Then she went to the porch and sat primly and stiffly down. She looked toward the river road where the willow-line was still yellow with frosted leaves so that under the high grey fog they seemed a thin band of sunshine. This was the only color in the grey afternoon. She sat unmoving for a long time. Her eyes blinked rarely.

Henry came banging out of the door, shoving his tie inside his vest as he came. Elisa stiffened and her face grew tight. Henry stopped short and looked at her. "Why—why, Elisa. You look so nice!"

100   "Nice? You think I look nice? What do you mean by 'nice'?"

Henry blundered on. "I don't know. I mean you look different, strong and happy."

"I am strong? Yes, strong. What do you mean 'strong'?"

He looked bewildered. "You're playing some kind of a game," he said helplessly. "It's a kind of a play. You look strong enough to break a calf over your knee, happy enough to eat it like a watermelon."

For a second she lost her rigidity. "Henry! Don't talk like that. You didn't know what you said." She grew complete again. "I'm strong," she boasted. "I never knew before how strong."

105   Henry looked down toward the tractor shed, and when he brought his eyes back to her, they were his own again. "I'll get out the car. You can put on your coat while I'm starting."

Elisa went into the house. She heard him drive to the gate and idle down his motor, and then she took a long time to put on her hat. She pulled it here and pressed it there. When Henry turned the motor off she slipped into her coat and went out.

The little roadster bounced along on the dirt road by the river, raising the birds and driving the rabbits into the brush. Two cranes flapped heavily over the willow-line and dropped into the riverbed.

Far ahead on the road Elisa saw a dark speck. She knew.

She tried not to look as they passed it, but her eyes would not obey. She whispered to herself sadly, "He might have thrown them off the road. That wouldn't have been much trouble, not very much. But he kept the pot," she explained. "He had to keep the pot. That's why he couldn't get them off the road."

110   The roadster turned a bend and she saw the caravan ahead. She swung full around toward her husband so she could not see the little covered wagon and the mismatched team as the car passed them.

In a moment it was over. The thing was done. She did not look back.

She said loudly, to be heard above the motor, "It will be good, tonight, a good dinner."

"Now you're changed again," Henry complained. He took one hand from the wheel and patted her knee. "I ought to take you in to dinner oftener. It would be good for both of us. We get so heavy out on the ranch."

"Henry," she asked, "could we have wine at dinner?"

115   "Sure we could. Say! That will be fine."

She was silent for a while; then she said, "Henry, at those prize fights, do the men hurt each other very much?"

"Sometimes a little, not often. Why?"

"Well, I've read how they break noses, and blood runs down their chests. I've read how the fighting gloves get heavy and soggy with blood."

He looked around at her. "What's the matter, Elisa? I didn't know you read things like that." He brought the car to a stop, then turned to the right over the Salinas River bridge.

120   "Do any women ever go to the fights?" she asked.

"Oh, sure, some. What's the matter, Elisa? Do you want to go? I don't think you'd like it, but I'll take you if you really want to go."

She relaxed limply in the seat. "Oh, no. No. I don't want to go. I'm sure I don't." Her face was turned away from him. "It will be enough if we can have wine. It will be plenty." She turned up her coat collar so he could not see that she was crying weakly—like an old woman.

MAKING CONNECTIONS

1. Have you ever been frustrated because you were not getting the attention you deserved? If you were placed in Elisa's position, would you feel the same way that she does? Explain.

2. Describe the setting of "The Chrysanthemums." What effect does the setting have on your response to the story? Which passages are most effective in conveying the setting to you?

3. Discuss the interactions between Elisa and the two men in the story. To what extent do the men try to manipulate her and she them?

4. How can you account for Elisa's sadness at the end of the story? Why do you think she is interested in the prize fights? Why does she ask, "do the men hurt each other very much?"

5. What is the theme of this story? Why do you think it is called "The Chrysanthemums"?

MAKING AN ARGUMENT

1. Describe Elisa. Do we learn about her directly or indirectly? What is her conflict? To what degree is it internal or external? What is the relationship between her character and the conflict? Does she change or develop in the course of the story? Do you think she deserves what happens to her? Should she have known better? Write an essay about the characterization of Elisa. Cite the text of the story for support.

◆ POETRY ◆

CONNECTING THROUGH COMPARISON: SEPTEMBER 11, 2001

The three poems that follow address a subtheme of this section: September 11, 2001. Read and discussed together, they invite comparisons and connections—not only with each other—but with your own experience of the events of that day.

DEBORAH GARRISON   [B. 1965]

Deborah Garrison was born in Ann Arbor, Michigan, and has a degree in Creative Writing from Brown University. She is a senior nonfiction editor at *the* New Yorker, *where she has worked since 1986. In 1998 she published a collection of poems,* A Working Girl Can't Win and Other Poems. *She lives in Montclair, New Jersey, with her husband and daughter.*

I SAW YOU WALKING   [2001]

I saw you walking through Newark Penn Station
in your shoes of white ash. At the corner
of my nervous glance your dazed passage
first forced me away, tracing the crescent

berth you'd give a drunk, a lurcher, nuzzling   5
all comers with ill will and his stench, but
not this one, not today: one shirt arm's sheared
clean from the shoulder, the whole bare limb
wet with muscle and shining dimly pink,
the other full-sheathed in cotton, Brooks Bros.   10
type, the cuff yet buttoned at the wrist, a
parody of careful dress, preparedness—
so you had not rolled up your sleeves yet this
morning when your suit jacket (here are
the pants, dark gray, with subtle stripe, as worn   15
by men like you on ordinary days)
and briefcase (you've none, reverse commuter
come from the pit with nothing to carry
but your life) were torn from you, as your life
was not. Your face itself seemed to be walking,   20
leading your body north, though the age
of the face, blank and ashen, passing forth
and away from me, was unclear, the sandy
crown of hair powdered white like your feet, but
underneath not yet gray-forty-seven?   25
forty-eight? the age of someone's father—
and I trembled for your luck, for your broad,
dusted back, half shirted, walking away;
I should have dropped to my knees to thank God
you were alive, o my God, in whom I don't believe.   30

BRIAN DOYLE [B. 1941]

Brian Doyle is the editor of Portland Magazine *at the University of Portland in Oregon. He is the author of three collections of essays:* Credo (1999), Saints Passionate & Peculiar (2002), *and (with his father, Jim Doyle)* Two Voices (1996). *Doyle's essays have been reprinted in the* Best American Essays *anthologies for 1998 and 1999. The prose poem "Leap" was included in a PBS television special about the impact of September 11 called "Faith and Doubt."*

LEAP   [2002]

A couple leaped from the south tower, hand in hand. They reached for each other and their hands met and they jumped.

Jennifer Brickhouse saw them falling, hand in hand.

Many people jumped. Perhaps hundreds. No one knows. They struck the pavement with such force that there was a pink mist in the air.

The mayor reported the mist.

A kindergarten boy who saw people falling in flames told his teacher that the   5
birds were on fire. She ran with him on her shoulders out of the ashes.

Tiffany Keeling saw fireballs falling that she later realized were people. Jennifer
Griffin saw people falling and wept as she told the story. Niko Winstral saw
people free-falling backwards with their hands out, like they were parachuting.
Joe Duncan on his roof on Duane Street looked up and saw people jumping.
Henry Weintraub saw people "leaping as they flew out." John Carson saw six
people fall, "falling over themselves, falling, they were somersaulting." Steve
Miller saw people jumping from a thousand feet in the air. Kirk Kjeldsen saw
people flailing on the way down, people lining up and jumping, "too many
people falling." Jane Tedder saw people leaping and the sight haunts her at
night. Steve Tamas counted fourteen people jumping and then he stopped
counting. Stuart DeHann saw one woman's dress billowing as she fell, and he
 saw a shirtless man falling end over end, and he too saw the couple leaping
hand in hand.

Several pedestrians were killed by people falling from the sky. A fireman was
killed by a body falling from the sky.

But he reached for her hand and she reached for his hand and they leaped out
the window holding hands.

I try to whisper prayers for the sudden dead and the harrowed families of the
dead and the screaming souls of the murderers but I keep coming back to his
hand and her hand nestled in each other with such extraordinary ordinary succinct ancient naked stunning perfect simple ferocious love.

Their hands reaching and joining are the most powerful prayer I can imagine,   10
the most eloquent, the most graceful. It is everything that we are capable of
against horror and loss and death. It is what makes me believe that we are not
craven fools and charlatans to believe in God, to believe that human beings
have greatness and holiness within them like seeds that open only under great
fires, to believe that some unimaginable essence of who we are persists past the
dissolution of what we were, to believe against such evil hourly evidence that
love is why we are here.

No one knows who they were: husband and wife, lovers, dear friends, colleagues, strangers thrown together at the window there at the lip of hell.
Maybe they didn't even reach for each other consciously, maybe it was instinc-
tive, a reflex, as they both decided at the same time to take two running steps
and jump out the shattered window, but they did reach for each other, and they
held on tight, and leaped, and fell endlessly into the smoking canyon, at two
hundred miles an hour, falling so far and so fast that they would have blacked
out before they hit the pavement near Liberty Street so hard that there was a
pink mist in the air.

Jennifer Brickhouse saw them holding hands, and Stuart DeHann saw them
holding hands, and I hold onto that.

BILLY COLLINS [B. 1941]

(See biography on p. 1017.) This poem was read before Congress at its joint session in New York City on September 6, 2002.

THE NAMES   [2002]

Yesterday, I lay awake in the palm of the night.
A fine rain stole in, unhelped by any breeze,
And when I saw the silver glaze on the windows,
I started with A, with Ackerman, as it happened,
Then Baxter and Calabro,   5
Davis and Eberling, names falling into place
As droplets fell through the dark.

Names printed on the ceiling of the night.
Names slipping around a watery bend.
Twenty-six willows on the banks of a stream.   10

In the morning, I walked out barefoot
Among thousands of flowers
Heavy with dew like the eyes of tears,
And each had a name—
Fiori inscribed on a yellow petal   15
Then Gonzalez and Han, Ishikawa and Jenkins.

Names written in the air
And stitched into the cloth of the day.
A name under a photograph taped to a mailbox.
Monogram on a torn shirt,   20
I see you spelled out on storefront windows
And on the bright unfurled awnings of this city.
I say the syllables as I turn a corner—
Kelly and Lee,
Medina, Nardella, and O'Connor.   25

When I peer into the woods,
I see a thick tangle where letters are hidden
As in a puzzle concocted for children.
Parker and Quigley in the twigs of an ash,
Rizzo, Schubert, Torres, and Upton,   30
Secrets in the boughs of an ancient maple.

Names written in the pale sky.
Names rising in the updraft amid buildings.
Names silent in stone
Or cried out behind a door.   35
Names blown over the earth and out to sea.

In the evening—weakening light, the last swallows.
A boy on a lake lifts his oars.
A woman by a window puts a match to a candle,
And the names are outlined on the rose clouds—   40
Vanacore and Wallace,
(let X stand, if it can, for the ones unfound)
Then Young and Ziminsky, the final jolt of Z.

Names etched on the head of a pin.
One name spanning a bridge, another undergoing a tunnel.   45
A blue name needled into the skin.
Names of citizens, workers, mothers and fathers,
The bright-eyed daughter, the quick son.
Alphabet of names in green rows in a field.
Names in the small tracks of birds.   50
Names lifted from a hat
Or balanced on the tip of the tongue.
Names wheeled into the dim warehouse of memory.
So many names, there is barely room on the walls of the heart.

MAKING CONNECTIONS

1. All three poems are about the horrific events of September 11, 2001, but
   their narrative perspectives are quite different. Compare and contrast each
   speaker's point of view in these poems and how you were affected by each.
2. The speaker in "Leap" is describing one of the most horrible aspects of the
   World Trade Center disaster—people jumping from the buildings. But is the
   tone of this prose poem negative? Explain.
3. These poems are very graphic in their use of imagery. Which images were
   you most affected by? Why?

MAKING AN ARGUMENT

1. Written at different times after September 11, 2001, each of these poems
   seems to have a different purpose in mind. Identify what you believe is the
   purpose of each poem and write an essay that supports your view. Compare
   the poems and cite the text of each poem for support.

MATTHEW ARNOLD [1822–1888]

Poet and critic Matthew Arnold was born in Laleham, a tiny village along the Thames in England. Arnold attended Oxford University, where he spent as much time roaming the countryside and writing poems as he did on his formal studies. After working for a time for a member of Parliament, Arnold secured a post as an inspector of schools in 1851, a position he held for most of his life. In addition, he served as a Professor of Poetry at Oxford for ten years, beginning in 1857. In his old age, Arnold embarked on two lecture tours of the United States (1883 and 1886). He died suddenly in 1888, shortly after returning from his second trip. A famous literary critic as well as a poet, Arnold strongly believed that the primary purpose of literature was a moral one—that it should "animate and ennoble" its readers. His first collection of poetry, The Strayed Reveler and Other Poems, *was published in 1849 and was followed by six others, including* Poems, Second Series *(1855), in which "Dover Beach" first appeared. His works of literary criticism include two volumes of* Essays in Criticism *(1865 and 1888),* Literature and Dogma *(1873), and* The Study of Poetry *(1880), in which he argued that "most of what now passes for religion and philosophy will be replaced by poetry."*

DOVER BEACH   [1867]

The sea is calm tonight.
The tide is full, the moon lies fair
Upon the straits; on the French coast the light
Gleams and is gone; the cliffs of England stand,
Glimm'ering and vast, out in the tranquil bay.   5
Come to the window, sweet is the night-air!
Only, from the long line of spray
Where the sea meets the moon-blanched land,
Listen! you hear the grating roar
Of pebbles which the waves draw back, and fling,   10
At their return, up the high strand,
Begin, and cease, and then again begin,
With tremulous cadence slow, and bring
The eternal note of sadness in.

Sophocles long ago   15
Heard it on the Aegean, and it brought
Into his mind the turbid ebb and flow
Of human misery; we

Find also in the sound a thought,
Hearing it by this distant northern sea.   20

The Sea of Faith
Was once, too, at the full, and round earth's shore
Lay like the folds of a bright girdle furled.
But now I only hear
Its melancholy, long, withdrawing roar,   25
Retreating, to the breath
Of the night-wind, down the vast edges drear
And naked shingles' of the world.

Ah, love, let us be true
To one another! for the world, which seems   30
To lie before us like a land of dreams,
So various, so beautiful, so new,
Hath really neither joy, nor love, nor light,
Nor certitude, nor peace, nor help for pain—,
And we are here as on a darkling plain   35
Swept with confused alarms of struggle and flight,
Where ignorant armies clash by night.

MAKING CONNECTIONS

1. Does this poem seem like a typical love poem to you? If so, how? If not, why not?
2. What is the speaker's attitude toward nature?
3. How do you think the speaker formed his impression of nature? To what extent is an answer suggested in the poem?
4. In the final image of the poem, the speaker says, "we are here as on a darkling plain / Swept with confused alarms of struggle and flight, / Where ignorant armies clash by night." What do you think he means?
5. According to the speaker, what is the importance of love in this world?

MAKING AN ARGUMENT

1. In the Dialogue Across History that opens this theme, Tennyson is quoted: "There lives more faith in honest doubt, / Believe me, than in half the creeds." Arnold's poem seems to express this "honest doubt." Write about the effectiveness of the imagery in the poem in conveying this theme. Cite the text of the poem for support.

ROBERT BRIDGES [1844-1930]

*Robert Bridges was born the son of a prosperous landowner
and took his degree at Corpus Christi College, Oxford, where
he made friends with Gerard Manley Hopkins. He was a
medical student at St. Bartholomew's Hospital, London, and
practiced medicine until 1881 when illness forced his retirement. For the rest of his life he dedicated himself to his writing. In 1913 he was named Poet Laureate of England.*

LONDON SNOW   [1880]

When men were all asleep the snow came flying,
In large white flakes falling on the city brown,
Stealthily and perpetually settling and loosely lying,
    Hushing the latest traffic of the drowsy town;
Deadening, muffling, stifling its murmurs failing;   5
Lazily and incessantly floating down and down;
    Silently sifting and veiling road, roof and railing;
Hiding difference, making unevenness even,
Into angles and crevices softly drifting and sailing.
    All night it fell, and when full inches seven   10
It lay in the depth of its uncompacted lightness,
The clouds blew off from a high and frosty heaven;
    And all woke earlier for the unaccustomed brightness
Of the winter dawning, the strange unheavenly glare:
The eye marvelled—marvelled at the dazzling whiteness;   15
    The ear hearkened to the stillness of the solemn air;
No sound of wheel rumbling nor of foot falling,
And the busy morning cries came thin and spare.
    Then boys I heard, as they went to school, calling;
They gathered up the crystal manna to freeze   20
Their tongues with tasting, their hands with snowballing;
    Or rioted in a drift, plunging up to the knees;
Or peering up from under the white-mossed wonder,
"O look at the trees!" they cried. "O look at the trees!"
    With lessened load, a few carts creak and blunder,   25
Following along the white deserted way,
A country company long dispersed asunder:
    When, now, already the sun, in pale display
Standing by Paul's high dome, spread forth below
His sparkling beams, and awoke the stir of the day.   30
    For now doors open, and war is waged with the snow;
And trains of sombre men, past tale of number,

Tread long brown paths, as toward their toil they go:
   But even for them awhile no cares encumber
Their minds diverted; the daily word is unspoken,   35
The daily thoughts of labour and sorrow slumber
At the sight of the beauty that greets them, for the charm they
   have broken.

 ## MAKING CONNECTIONS

1. To what extent does your own experience of snow affect your response to
   this poem?
2. The speaker says, "For now doors open, and war is waged with the snow."
   Pick out phrases in the poem that describe "the charm they have broken."

MAKING AN ARGUMENT

1. This poem was written well over a century ago, but its images are still very
   much alive. Write about the language and poetic devices in this poem, their
   effect on you, and their effectiveness in re-creating this scene. Cite the text
   of the poem to support your view.

STEPHEN CRANE [1871–1900]

*Stephen Crane was the youngest of fourteen children born
to a Methodist minister in Newark, New Jersey. After briefly
attending LaFayette College and Syracuse University,
Crane moved to New York City to work as a freelance journalist. He lived an often impoverished existence and came
to know life in the slums firsthand. These experiences
inspired his first novel,* Maggie, a Girl of the Streets *(1893),
which he published at his own expense under a pseudo-
nym. The novel impressed members of New York's literary elite and set the stage
for the publication of his second novel,* The Red Badge of Courage *(1895). In
1895, Crane also published a book of short poems,* The Black Riders. *In 1899,*
Other Lines *and another collection of poems,* War Is Kind, *would prove influential
after his death. Crane died of tuberculosis when he was only 28.*

THE WAYFARER   [1895]

The wayfarer,
Perceiving the pathway to truth,
Was struck with astonishment.
It was thickly grown with weeds.
"Ha," he said,   5
"I see that none has passed here
In a long time."
Later he saw that each weed

Was a singular knife.
"Well," he mumbled at last,   10
"Doubtless there are other roads."

A MAN SAID TO THE UNIVERSE   [1899]

A man said to the universe:
"Sir, I exist!"
"However," replied the universe,
"The fact has not created in me
A sense of obligation."   5

MAKING CONNECTIONS

1. In "The Wayfarer," why is the wayfarer struck with astonishment?
2. Why does he change his mind about following the path? Do you find this
   ironic? Explain.
3. In "A Man Said to the Universe," what do you think the man expects from
   the universe?
4. Why does he say, "'I exist!'"? Are you surprised by the universe's response?
   Explain.

MAKING AN ARGUMENT

1. Using either or both of these poems, write a comparison with Matthew
   Arnold's "Dover Beach" on page 1221 or Pam Houston's "A Blizzard Under
   Blue Sky" on page 1176.

JOHN DONNE   [1572–1631]

*John Donne was born into a Roman Catholic family and
attended Oxford and Cambridge. As a young man, in
response to the rabid anti-Catholic sentiments of
Elizabethan England, he abandoned his faith and
determined to make his way in the court of Queen Elizabeth
I using his charm, learning, and poetic abilities. In 1601, he
destroyed his chances for serious advancement by secretly
marrying Ann More, the niece of Sir Thomas Egerton, his
employer. Donne then struggled to make ends meet,
publishing treatises and poetry only occasionally. In 1615, after years of resistance,
he converted to Anglicanism and became a priest. Renowned for his preaching,
Donne was considered one of the greatest preachers of the age. In 1621, he was
appointed Dean of St. Paul's Cathedral, a post he held until his death. His poetry,
most of which was published posthumously, is usually divided into two periods: his
love poetry is said to date from the beginning of his career, while his religious poems
are said to date from his later years. The greatest of the so-called metaphysical school
of poets, Donne's poetry is remarkable for its elaborate conceits (extended
metaphors), unconventional imagery, and highly compressed meanings.*

A VALEDICTION FORBIDDING MOURNING [1633]

As virtuous men pass mildly away,
And whisper to their souls to go,
Whilst some of their sad friends do say,
"The breath goes now," and some say "No:"

So let us melt, and make no noise,   5
No tear-floods, nor sigh-tempests move;
'Twere profanation of our joys
To tell the laity our love.

Moving of th' earth brings harms and fears;
Men reckon what it did and meant;   10
But trepidation of the spheres,
Though greater far, is innocent.

Dull sublunary lovers' love
(Whose soul is sense) cannot admit
Absence, because it doth remove   15
Those things which elemented it.

But we by a love so much refined
That ourselves know not what it is,
Inter-assured of the mind,
Care less, eyes, lips, and hands to miss.   20

Our two souls, therefore, which are one,
Though I must go, endure not yet
A breach, but an expansion,
Like gold to airy thinness beat.

If they be two, they are two so   25
As stiff twin compasses are two:
Thy soul, the fixed foot, makes no show
To move, but doth, if th' other do.

And though it in the center sit,
Yet when the other far doth roam,   30
It leans and harkens after it,
And grows erect as that comes home.

Such wilt thou be to me, who must,
Like th' other foot, obliquely run;
Thy firmness makes my circle just,   35
And makes me end where I begun.

DEATH, BE NOT PROUD [1633]

Death, be not proud, though some have called thee
Mighty and dreadful, for thou art not so;

For those whom thou think'st thou dost overthrow
Die not, poor Death, nor yet canst thou kill me.
From rest and sleep, which but thy pictures be,   5
Much pleasure, then from thee much more must flow,
And soonest our best men with thee do go,
Rest of their bones, and soul's delivery.
Thou art slave to fate, chance, kings, and desperate men,
And dost with poison, war, and sickness dwell,   10
And poppy or charms can make us sleep as well,
And better than thy stroke; why swell'st thou then?
One short sleep past, we wake eternally
And death shall be no more; Death, thou shalt die.

MAKING CONNECTIONS

1. The speaker in "A Valediction Forbidding Mourning" says, "But we by a love so much refined / That ourselves know not what it is." What do you think he means?
2. Do you agree with the speaker's conclusion in this poem?
3. Why do you think the speaker in "Death, Be Not Proud" suggests that Death is proud? Do you agree? Explain.
4. The speaker concludes, "Death, thou shalt die." What is the speaker's reasoning to support this? Do you agree? Explain.
5. Compare this poem to John Keats's "When I Have Fears That I May Cease to Be" on page 1234.

MAKING AN ARGUMENT

1. Both of Donne's poems are about death, but the speaker's intended audience, the structure, the tone, and other factors in the poems differ. Write an essay that compares and contrasts the two poems. Cite the text of both poems for support.

MARK DOTY [B. 1953]

Mark Doty is the author of several collections of poems including Atlantis *(1995);* Turtle, Swan *(1987);* Bethlehem in Broad Daylight *(1991);* and My Alexandria *(1993), which won the National Book Critics Circle Award, the* Los Angeles Times *Book Award, the T. S. Eliot Award, and the National Poetry Series Award, and was a finalist for the National Book Award. Doty has also been the recipient of grants from the National Endowment for the Arts and the Guggenheim Foundation. He lives in Provincetown, Massachusetts.*

BRILLIANCE

[1993]

Maggie's taking care of a man
who's dying; he's attended to everything,
said goodbye to his parents,

paid off his credit card.
She says *Why don't you just*
run it up to the limit?   5

but he wants everything
squared away, no balance owed,
though he misses the pets

he's already found a home for   10
—he can't be around dogs or cats,
too much risk. He says,

I can't have anything.
She says, A *bowl of goldfish?*
He says he doesn't want to start   15

with anything and then describes
the kind he'd maybe like,
how their tails would fan

to a gold flaring. They talk
about hot jewel tones,   20
gold lacquer, say maybe

they'll go pick some out
though he can't go much of anywhere and then
abruptly he says *I can't love*

anything I can't finish.   25
He says it like he's had enough
of the whole scintillant world,

though what he means is
he'll never be satisfied and therefore
has established this discipline,   30

a kind of severe rehearsal.
That's where they leave it,
him looking out the window,

her knitting as she does because
she needs to do something.   35
Later he leaves a message:

Yes to the bowl of goldfish.
Meaning: let me go, if I have to,
in brilliance. In a story I read,

a Zen master who'd perfected
his detachment from the things of the world
remembered, at the moment of dying,   40

a deer he used to feed in the park,
and wondered who might care for it,
and at that instant was reborn   45

in the stunned flesh of a fawn.
So, Maggie's friend—
is he going out

into the last loved object
of his attention?   50
Fanning the veined translucence

of an opulent tail,
undulant in some uncapturable curve,
is he bronze chrysanthemums,

copper leaf, hurried darting,   55
doubloons, icon-colored fins
troubling the water?

MAKING CONNECTIONS

1. Why do you think the dying man wants a bowl of goldfish? What would you want in the same situation?
2. To what extent is "Brilliance" an appropriate title for this poem?

MAKING AN ARGUMENT

1. This poem begins with a man who is dying and ends with an image of goldfish darting through the water. Write about the structure of the poem and its images and how they convey its content. Cite the text of the poem for support.

ROBERT FROST [1874–1963]

(See biography on p. 78.)

FIRE AND ICE   [1923]

Some say the world will end in fire,
Some say in ice.
From what I've tasted of desire
I hold with those who favor fire.
But if I had to perish twice,   5

I think I know enough of hate
To say that for destruction ice
Is also great
And would suffice.

MAKING CONNECTIONS

1. What do you think fire and ice symbolize in this poem?
2. How are you affected by the rhyme scheme? In what way does it serve as a vehicle for the poem's meaning?
3. Discuss the conclusion of the poem. How does the word "suffice" as a rhyme for "ice" affect the meaning of the poem?

MAKING AN ARGUMENT

1. Write a comparison of this poem with other Frost poems in this text—"Out, Out . . . ." on page 505 and "Mending Wall" on page 268. Is there a similar philosophy expressed in all three? If not, how do they differ? Cite the text of all three for support.

TESS GALLAGHER [B. 1943]

Tess Gallagher was born in Port Angeles, Washington. She received B.A. and M.A. degrees from the University of Washington, where she studied Creative Writing, and an M.F.A. from the University of Iowa. She has received fellowships from the Guggenheim Foundation, two National Endowment of the Arts Awards, the Maxine Cushing Gray Foundation Award, and the Elliston Award for "best book of poetry published by a small press" for the collection Instructions to the Double *(1976). Gallagher has taught at St. Lawrence University; Kirkland College; University of Montana, Missoula; University of Arizona, Tucson; Syracuse University; and Willamette University. Her recent collections include* My Black Horse: New and Selected Poems *(1995),* Owl-Spirit Dwelling *(1994), and* Moon Crossing Bridge *(1992).*

THE HUG   [1987]

A woman is reading a poem on the street
and another woman stops to listen. We stop too,
with our arms around each other. The poem
is being read and listened to out here
in the open. Behind us   5
no one is entering or leaving the houses.

Suddenly a hug comes over me and I'm

giving it to you, like a variable star shooting light
off to make itself comfortable, then
subsiding. I finish but keep on holding   10
you. A man walks up to us and we know he hasn't
come out of nowhere, but if he could, he
would have. He looks homeless because of how
he needs. "Can I have one of those?" he asks you,
and I feel you nod. I'm surprised,   15
surprised you don't tell him how
it is—that I'm yours, only
yours, etc., exclusive as a nose to
its face. Love—that's what we're talking about, love
that nabs you with "for me   20
only" and holds on.

So I walk over to him and put my
arms around him and try to
hug him like I mean it. He's got an overcoat on
so thick I can't feel   25
him past it. I'm starting the hug
and thinking, "How big a hug is this supposed to be?
How long should I hold this hug?" Already
we could be eternal, his arms falling over my
shoulders, my hands not   30
meeting behind his back, he is so big!

I put my head into his chest and snuggle
in. I lean into him. I lean my blood and my wishes
into him. He stands for it. This is his
and he's starting to give it back so well I know he's   35
getting it. This hug. So truly, so tenderly
we stop having arms and I don't know if
my lover has walked away or what, or
if the woman is still reading the poem, or the houses—
what about them?—the houses.   40
Clearly, a little permission is a dangerous thing.
But when you hug someone you want it
to be a masterpiece of connection, the way the button
on his coat will leave the imprint of
a planet in my cheek   45
when I walk away, when I try to find some place
to go back to.

MAKING CONNECTIONS

1. Have you ever experienced a hug as intense as this one? In what way is this
   hug "a masterpiece of connection"?

2. What are the implications of the speaker looking for a place "to go back to" at the end of the poem? In how many ways has the button left "an imprint of / a planet"?
3. To what extent is the hug symbolic?

MAKING AN ARGUMENT

1. Both "The Hug" and Robert Frost's "Mending Wall" on page 268 address the issue of human interaction. But they seem to have very different things to say about it. Or do they? Write an essay that compares and contrasts these poems. Cite the text of both poems to support your view.

THOMAS HARDY [1840-1928]

Thomas Hardy was born near Dorchester in southwestern England. Apprenticed to an architect at the age of fifteen, Hardy received very little formal schooling outside of the local schools he attended as a boy, but improved himself by reading in his spare time. Unhappy as an architect, he began writing fiction and poetry and, though his first novel was not a success, the success of his second, Under the Greenwood Tree *(1872), allowed him to devote himself to a literary career. Hardy followed this with a string of eleven remarkable novels set in his native Dorchester (called Wessex in the novels), including* Far from the Madding Crowd *(1874),* The Return of the Native *(1879),* The Mayor of Casterbridge *(1887), and* Tess of the D'Urbervilles *(1891). These often bleak novels share a common theme—that human destiny is controlled not by human will but by forces beyond humankind's control. Disillusioned after the hostile reception to* Jude the Obscure *(1895), considered by many modern critics to be his greatest work, Hardy turned to writing highly original poetry that often explored the same themes as his novels. His* Collected Poems *was published in 1931.*

HAP

[1898]

If but some vengeful god would call to me
From up the sky, and laugh: "Thou suffering thing,
Know that thy sorrow is my ecstasy
That thy love's loss is my hate's profiting!"

Then I would bear it, clench myself and die,   5
Steeled by the sense of ire unmerited;
Half-eased in that a Powerfuller than I
Had willed and meted me the tears I shed.

But not so. How arrives it joy lies slain,
And why unblooms the best hope ever sown?   10

Crass Casualty obstructs the sun and rain,
And dicing Time for gladness casts a moan. . . .
These purblind Doomsters had as readily strown
Blisses about my pilgrimage as pain.

MAKING CONNECTIONS

1. Does it make sense to you that the speaker would prefer to be doomed by
   an evil force rather than by blind chance? Explain.
2. Compare this poem with Stephen Crane's "A Man Said to the Universe" on
   page 1225. Are they saying the same thing? Explain.

MAKING AN ARGUMENT

1. The attitude of the speaker in this poem is very pessimistic. He does not specify a particular event that caused him to feel this way, but we can imagine, have
   heard about, or have experienced the kinds of events that might make him feel
   this way. What is your response to what he says? Write an essay that agrees or
   disagrees with the speaker's conclusion in the poem. Cite the text of the poem
   and your own knowledge and/or experience for support.

A. E. HOUSMAN [1859–1934]

(See biography on p. 508.)

TO AN ATHLETE DYING YOUNG   [1896]

The time you won your town the race
We chaired you through the market-place;
Man and boy stood cheering by,
And home we brought you shoulder-high.

To-day, the road all runners come,   5
Shoulder-high we bring you home,
And set you at your threshold down,
Townsman of a stiller town.

Smart lad, to slip betimes away
From fields where glory does not stay   10
And early though the laurel grows
It withers quicker than the rose.

Eyes the shady night has shut
Cannot see the record cut,
And silence sounds no worse than cheers   15
After earth has stopped the ears:

Now you will not swell the rout

Of lads that wore their honours out,
Runners whom renown outran
And the name died before the man.   20

So set, before its echoes fade,
The fleet foot on the sill of shade,
And hold to the low lintel up
The still-defended challenge-cup.

And round that early-laurelled head   25
Will flock to gaze the strengthless dead
And find unwithered on its curls
The garland briefer than a girl's.

MAKING CONNECTIONS

1. Who is the "you" addressed by the speaker? Both the first and second stanzas make reference to carrying the subject "shoulder-high." What does the
   term mean in each stanza? In what way is it ironic?
2. Dying young is not a pleasant prospect. But what does the speaker mean by
   "Now you will not swell the rout / Of lads that wore their honours out"? Is
   there a positive side to dying young? Explain.

MAKING AN ARGUMENT

1. Write an essay that compares and contrasts this poem with "Mr. Flood's
   Party" on page 1008. Cite the text of both poems for support.

JOHN KEATS [1795–1821]

*John Keats was born in London and abandoned a medical
career for writing when a number of his poems were published. His work is characterized by a passionate concern
with the relationship between beauty and truth and emotion and knowledge. He died of tuberculosis at the age of
twenty-six.*

WHEN I HAVE FEARS THAT I MAY CEASE TO BE   [1818]

When I have fears that I may cease to be
    Before my pen has gleaned my teeming brain,
Before high-piled books, in charact'ry,
    Hold like rich garners the full-ripened grain;
When I behold, upon the night's starred face,   5
    Huge cloudy symbols of a high romance,
And think that I may never live to trace

Their shadows, with the magic hand of chance;
And when I feel, fair creature of an hour,
 That I shall never look upon thee more,   10
Never have relish in the fairy power
 Of unreflecting love—then on the shore
Of the wide world I stand alone, and think
 Till love and fame to nothingness do sink.

MAKING CONNECTIONS

1. Do you ever have fears that you may cease to be? If so, how do those fears affect your response to this poem?
2. Keats was only twenty-three years old when he wrote this poem—and he died at twenty-six—so young death turned out to be a reality for him. What is the speaker especially anxious about? To what extent is this surprising for a poet? If Keats had lived much longer and had been older when he wrote this poem, do you think the speaker's anxieties might have been different? Explain.

MAKING AN ARGUMENT

1. Write a comparison of this poem with John Donne's "Death, Be Not Proud" and/or "A Valediction Forbidding Mourning" on pages 1225-1227. Cite the text of the poems to support your views.

GALWAY KINNELL [B. 1927]

Born and raised in Providence, Rhode Island, Galway Kinnell first became interested in poetry while attending Wilbraham Academy, a prep school in Massachusetts. He attended college at Princeton University (where his room-mate was the poet W. S. Merwin) and later earned an M.A. from the University of Rochester. His first collection of poems, What a Kingdom It Was, *was published in 1960, and* Imperfect Thirst *appeared in 1994. His latest collection is titled* New Selected Poems *(2001). A dedicated teacher as well as a poet, Kinnell has taught at numerous universities and held writing workshops throughout the world. He currently divides his time between Vermont and New York City, where he is a professor at New York University. His intensely personal poetry often explores the darkest aspects of human consciousness. In a 1989 interview with* Contemporary Authors, *Kinnell described the ideal reader: "As far as the person who buys and reads your poems is concerned, every living reader is an ideal reader. Anybody who recognizes the poem and puts something of his or her own experience into it is the ideal reader. The less than ideal reader is the one who reads without engagement: very often the critic."*

SAINT FRANCIS AND THE SOW   [1980]

The bud
stands for all things
even for those things that don't flower,
for everything flowers, from within, of self-blessing;
though sometimes it is necessary   5
to reteach a thing its loveliness,
to put a hand on its brow
of the flower
and retell it in words and in touch
it is lovely   10
until it flowers again from within of self-blessing;
as Saint Francis
put his hand on the creased forehead
of the sow, and told her in words and in touch
blessings of earth on the sow, and the sow   15
began remembering all down her thick length
from the earthen snout all the way
through the fodder and slops to the spiritual curl of the tail,
from the hard spininess spiked out from the spine
down through the great broken heart   20
to the sheer blue milken dreaminess spurting and shuddering
from the fourteen teats into the fourteen mouths sucking and
    blowing beneath them:
the long, perfect loveliness of sow.

MAKING CONNECTIONS

1. What is a sow? Do you think a sow is an appropriate subject for a poem?
   Explain.
2. To what extent is it "necessary / to reteach a thing its loveliness"? Why is it
   "necessary," and how can you do it?
3. What does the speaker mean by "until it flowers again from within of self-
   blessing"?
4. According to the speaker the sow has a "broken heart." Why? What do you
   think he means?

MAKING AN ARGUMENT

1. Write a comparison of this poem with the excerpt from Walt Whitman's
   Song of Myself on page 1239 or other poems in this text where relearning
   "loveliness" is "necessary." Cite the texts of the poems to support your
   views.

WILLIAM STAFFORD [1914-1992]

William Stafford grew up in Kansas, earned a Ph.D. from Iowa State University, and for many years taught at Lewis and Clark College in Portland, Oregon. The rural regions he lived in are central to his poetry; he spent much of his time hunting, camping, and fishing, and he often wrote about the relationship between humans and animals. His collection of poems Traveling Through the Dark, *from which the poem below is taken, received the National Book Award in 1963.*

TRAVELING THROUGH THE DARK   [1960]

Traveling through the dark I found a deer
dead on the edge of the Wilson River road.
It is usually best to roll them into the canyon:
that road is narrow; to swerve might make more dead.

By glow of the taillight I stumbled back of the car   5
and stood by the heap, a doe, a recent killing;
she had stiffened already, almost cold.
I dragged her off; she was large in the belly.

My fingers touching her side brought me the reason—
her side was warm; her fawn lay there waiting,   10
alive, still, never to be born.
Beside that mountain road I hesitated.

The car aimed ahead its lowered parking lights;
under the hood purred the steady engine.
I stood in the glare of the warm exhaust turning red;   15
around our group I could hear the wilderness listen.
I thought hard for us all—my only swerving—
then pushed her over the edge into the river.

MAKING CONNECTIONS

1. Do you think "Traveling Through the Dark" is an appropriate title for this poem? Explain.
2. What does the speaker mean when he says "I thought hard for us all—my only swerving"?
3. Why does he roll the dead deer into the canyon? Does the pregnancy make any difference? Do you think it should? Explain.

MAKING AN ARGUMENT

1. This poem has vivid details of the scene and the speaker's car. Identify the images in the poem and write about the way they create the moment of choice and the burden for the speaker. Cite the text of the poem to support your views.

DYLAN THOMAS [1914–1953]

Dylan Thomas was born in Swansea, Wales, a region of Great Britain with its own linguistic and cultural heritage. Though he began publishing his work when he was only twenty, Thomas struggled throughout his life to make ends meet, first as a reporter in London, and later, when he was better established, by writing screenplays and short stories from his home in Wales. Beginning in the late 1940s, Thomas became internationally famous for his poetry readings both in person and on the radio, making numerous recordings and touring both in England and the United States. In 1953, Thomas, who was well-known for his drinking, died following a drinking binge in New York City. The influence of the Welsh language can be clearly felt throughout his works, particularly in his remarkable radio play Under Milk Wood *(1954), which depicts a day in the life of the inhabitants of a Welsh village.*

DO NOT GO GENTLE INTO THAT GOOD NIGHT   [1952]

Do not go gentle into that good night,
Old age should burn and rave at close of day;
Rage, rage against the dying of the light.

Though wise men at their end know dark is right,
Because their words had forked no lightning they   5
Do not go gentle into that good night.

Good men, the last wave by, crying how bright
Their frail deeds might have danced in a green bay,
Rage, rage against the dying of the light.

Wild men who caught and sang the sun in flight,   10
And learn, too late, they grieved it on its way,
Do not go gentle into that good night.

Grave men, near death, who see with blinding sight
Blind eyes could blaze like meteors and be gay,
Rage, rage against the dying of the light.   15

And you, my father, there on the sad height,
Curse, bless, me now with your fierce tears, I pray.
Do not go gentle into that good night.
Rage, rage against the dying of the light.

MAKING CONNECTIONS

1. Who is the speaker in this poem? To what extent do you think that influences his attitude toward this death?
2. Were you surprised by the advice of this poem? Why?

3. If "wise men . . . know that dark is right," why do you think the speaker wants his father to rage against it?

4. This poem is a villanelle (see p. 1356). How does the form of the poem support its content?

MAKING AN ARGUMENT

1. Dylan Thomas's "Do Not Go Gentle into That Good Night" and John Donne's "Death, Be Not Proud" seem to have different attitudes toward death. Identify the theme of each poem and write an essay that takes a position in favor of one view or the other. Cite the text of both poems for support.

WALT WHITMAN [1819–1892]

(See biography on p. 83.)

SONG OF MYSELF 6   [1855]

A child said *What is the grass?* fetching it to me with full hands;
How could I answer the child? I do not know what it is any more than he.

I guess it must be the flag of my disposition, out of hopeful green stuff woven.

Or I guess it is the handkerchief of the Lord,
A scented gift and remembrancer designedly dropped,   5
Bearing the owner's name someway in the corners, that we may see and remark,
    and say *Whose?*

Or I guess the grass is itself a child, the produced babe of the vegetation.

Or I guess it is a uniform hieroglyphic,
And it means, Sprouting alike in broad zones and narrow zones,   10
Growing among black folks as among white,
Kanuck, Tuckahoe, Congressman, Cuff, I give them the same,
    I receive them the same.

And now it seems to me the beautiful uncut hair of graves.

Tenderly will I use you curling grass,   15
It may be you transpire from the breasts of young men,
It may be if I had known them I would have loved them,
It may be you are from old people, or from offspring taken soon out of their
    mothers' laps,
And here you are the mothers' laps.   20

This grass is very dark to be from the white heads of old mothers,
Darker than the colorless beards of old men,
Dark to come from under the faint red roofs of mouths.
O I perceive after all so many uttering tongues,
And I perceive they do not come from the roots of mouths for nothing.   25

I wish I could translate the hints about the dead young men and women,
And the hints about old men and mothers, and the offspring taken soon out of
  their laps.

What do you think has become of the young and old men?
And what do you think has become of the women and children?   30

They are alive and well somewhere,
The smallest sprout shows there is really no death,
And if ever there was it led forward life, and does not wait at the end to arrest it,
And ceased the moment life appeared.

All goes onward and outward, nothing collapses,   35
And to die is different from what anyone supposed, and luckier.

MAKING CONNECTIONS

1. Who is the speaker in this poem? How does he experience the world? Do
   you experience the world this way? Explain.
2. What do you think he means by "to die is different from what anyone supposed,
   and luckier"? Does the rest of this poem support that statement? Explain.

MAKING AN ARGUMENT

1. Write a comparison of Whitman's view of death with the views expressed
   in "Death, Be Not Proud" on page 1226, "When I Have Fears That I May
   Cease to Be" on page 1234, or "Brilliance" on page 1227. Cite the text of the
   poems to support your view.

CONNECTING THROUGH COMPARISON: THE IMPACT OF WAR

The six poems that follow address a subtheme of this section: the impact of war.
Read and discussed together, they invite comparisons and connections—not only
with each other—but with your own experience of and reactions to this topic.

THOMAS HARDY   [1840–1928]

(See biography on p. 1232.)

THE MAN HE KILLED   [1902]

  Had he and I but met
    By some old ancient inn,
We should have sat us down to wet
    Right many a nipperkin!

But ranged as infantry,
   And staring face to face,
I shot at him as he at me,
   And killed him in his place.

I shot him dead because—
   Because he was my foe.
Just so: my foe of course he was;
   That's clear enough; although

He thought he'd list, perhaps,
   Off-hand like—just as I—
Was out of work—had sold his traps—   15
   No other reason why.

Yes; quaint and curious war is!
   You shoot a fellow down
You'd treat, if met where any bar is,
   Or help to half-a-crown.   20

AMY LOWELL [1874–1925]

*Amy Lowell was born into a distinguished New England
family, where she spent much time browsing through her
father's impressive library. She attended the Brooklyn
Institute of Arts and Sciences, Tufts College, Columbia
University, and Baylor University. A 1902 visit to the theater, where she saw the famed actress Eleanora Duse,
inspired her to become a poet, and she spent the next years
perfecting her art, publishing her first volume of poems,* A
Dome of Many-Coloured Glass, *in 1912. About the same time she met Ada Dwyer
Russell, the woman who would become her lifelong companion and editor.
Greatly influenced by the imagist movement, which rejected sentimentality in
favor of precision in images and language, Lowell traveled to Europe to befriend
the movement's leading practitioners and returned to become its champion in the
United States. Her books of poetry include* Sword Blades and Poppy Seed *(1914),*
Men, Women and Ghosts *(1916), and the posthumously published* What's O'Clock,
which was awarded the Pulitzer Prize in 1926.

PATTERNS   [1915]

I walk down the garden-paths,
And all the daffodils
Are blowing, and the bright blue squills.
I walk down the patterned garden-paths
In my stiff, brocaded gown.   5
With my powdered hair and jewelled fan,
I too am a rare

Pattern. As I wander down
The garden paths.

My dress is richly figured,   10
And the train
Makes a pink and silver stain
On the gravel, and the thrift
Of the borders.
Just a plate of current fashion,   15
Tripping by in high-heeled, ribboned shoes.
Not a softness anywhere about me,
Only whalebone and brocade.
And I sink on a seat in the shade
Of a lime tree. For my passion   20
Wars against the stiff brocade.
The daffodils and squills
Flutter in the breeze
As they please.
And I weep;   25
For the lime-tree is in blossom
And one small flower has dropped upon my bosom.

And the splashing of waterdrops
In the marble fountain
Comes down the garden paths.   30
The dripping never stops.
Underneath my stiffened gown
Is the softness of a woman bathing in a marble basin,
A basin in the midst of hedges grown
So thick, she cannot see her lover hiding,   35
But she guesses he is near,
And the sliding of the water
Seems the stroking of a dear
Hand upon her.
What is Summer in a fine brocaded gown!   40
I should like to see it lying in a heap upon the ground.
All the pink and silver crumpled up on the ground.

I would be the pink and silver as I ran along the paths,
And he would stumble after,
Bewildered by my laughter.   45
I should see the sun flashing from his sword-hilt and the buckles on his shoes.
I would choose
To lead him in a maze along the patterned paths,
A bright and laughing maze for my heavy-booted lover.
Till he caught me in the shade,   50
And the buttons of his waistcoat bruised my body as he clasped me,
Aching, melting, unafraid.

With the shadows of the leaves and the sundrops,
And the plopping of the waterdrops,
All about us in the open afternoon—   55
I am very like to swoon
With the weight of this brocade,
For the sun sifts through the shade.

Underneath the fallen blossom
In my bosom   60
Is a letter I have hid.
It was brought to me this morning by a rider from the Duke.
'Madam, we regret to inform you that Lord Hartwell
Died in action Thursday night.'
As I read it in the white, morning sunlight,   65
The letters squirmed like snakes.
'Any answer, Madam,' said my footman.
'No,' I told him.
'See that the messenger takes some refreshment.
No, no answer.'   70
And I walked into the garden,
Up and down the patterned paths,
In my stiff, correct brocade.
The blue and yellow flowers stood up proudly in the sun,
Each one.   75
I stood upright too,
Held rigid to the pattern
By the stiffness of my gown;
Up and down I walked,
Up and down.   80

In a month he would have been my husband.
In a month, here, underneath this lime,
We would have broke the pattern;
He for me, and I for him,
He as Colonel, I as Lady,   85
On this shady seat.
He had a whim
That sunlight carried blessing.
And I answered, 'It shall be as you have said.'
Now he is dead.   90

In Summer and in Winter I shall walk
Up and down
The patterned garden paths
In my stiff, brocaded gown.
The squills and daffodils   95
Will give place to pillared roses, and to asters, and to snow.
I shall go

Up and down,
In my gown.
Gorgeously arrayed,   100
Boned and stayed.
And the softness of my body will be guarded from embrace
By each button, hook, and lace.
For the man who should loose me is dead,
Fighting with the Duke in Flanders,   105
In a pattern called a war.
Christ! What are patterns for?

WILFRED OWEN [1893–1918]

*Born in the Shropshire region of England, Wilfred Owen
spent two years studying to be a clergyman before becoming disillusioned with the Anglican church. In 1914, World
War I broke out. Owen spent a year debating whether or
not his Christian beliefs allowed him to fight. In 1915, he
decided to enlist. He became a commander, and in 1916
was stationed with the Lancashire Fusiliers in the trenches
in France. In 1917, Owen suffered a nervous breakdown
and was sent to an army hospital in Scotland to recover. He spent fourteen
months at the hospital, where, befriended by the poet Sigfried Sassoon, he turned
to writing poetry. Shipped back to the front, he was killed in action at Sambre
Canal, France, only one week before the end of the war. Only four of Owen's
poems were published during his lifetime. The rest were collected and published by
Sassoon in 1920. Sassoon said of Owen: "My trench sketches were like rockets, set
up to illuminate the darkness. . . . It was Owen who revealed how, out of realistic horror and scorn, poetry might be made." The last two lines (and title) of
"Dulce et Decorum Est" are taken from an ode by Horace, a great Roman poet. It
means: "It is sweet and fitting to die for one's country."*

DULCE ET DECORUM EST   [1918]

Bent double, like old beggars under sacks,
Knock-kneed, coughing like hags, we cursed through sludge,
Till on the haunting flares we turned our backs
And towards our distant rest began to trudge.
Men marched asleep. Many had lost their boots   5
But limped on, blood-shod. All went lame; all blind;
Drunk with fatigue; deaf even to the hoots
Of tired, outstripped Five-Nines that dropped behind.

Gas! gas! Quick, boys!—An ecstasy of fumbling,
Fitting the clumsy helmets just in time;   10
But someone still was yelling out and stumbling
And flound'ring like a man in fire or lime . . .

Dim, through the misty panes and thick green light,
As under a green sea, I saw him drowning.
In all my dreams, before my helpless sight,   15
He plunges at me, guttering, choking, drowning.

If in some smothering dreams you too could pace
Behind the wagon that we flung him in,
And watch the white eyes writhing in his face,
His hanging face, like a devil's sick of sin;   20
If you could hear, at every jolt, the blood
Come gargling from the froth-corrupted lungs,
Obscene as cancer, bitter as the cud
Of vile, incurable sores on innocent tongues,—
My friend, you would not tell with such high zest   25
To children ardent for some desperate glory.
The old Lie: *Dulce et decorum est*
Pro patria mori.

CARL SANDBURG [1878–1967]

Born in Galesburg, Illinois, to Swedish-immigrant parents,
Carl Sandburg quit school at thirteen and worked for a
number of years at a series of low-paying jobs, even spending
time as a hobo riding trains around the Midwest. Following
his service in the army during the Spanish-American War
(1898), Sandburg returned to Galesburg and worked his
way through Lombard (now Knox) College. He left without a
degree but with a sense that he wanted to be a poet, pub-
lishing his first (and largely forgotten) collection of poetry, In Reckless Ecstasy, *in*
1904. For the next four years, Sandburg again worked at a number of odd jobs, until
he married and eventually settled into a job as a reporter for the Chicago Daily News.
In 1916, he published Chicago Poems *and soon became one of the leading members*
of the Chicago Group, which included such famous writers as Theodore Dreiser, Ben
Hecht, and Edgar Lee Masters. Beginning in the 1920s, Sandburg began touring the
country with his guitar and giving readings of his poetry, a practice he continued
until he died. In addition to his numerous volumes of free verse poems, Sandburg
published a monumental six-volume biography of Abraham Lincoln, one of his per-
sonal heroes, that won the Pulitzer Prize for history in 1940.

GRASS   [1918]

Pile the bodies high at Austerlitz and Waterloo.
Shovel them under and let me work—
    I am the grass; I cover all.

And pile them high at Gettysburg
And pile them high at Ypres and Verdun   5

Shovel them under and let me work.
Two years, ten years, and passengers ask the conductor:
    What place is this?
    Where are we now?

    I am the grass.   10
    Let me work.

RANDALL JARRELL [1914–1965]

Randall Jarrell was a native of Nashville, Tennessee, and graduated from Vanderbilt University. His early poetry collections include Blood from a Stranger *(1942) and two books based on his Army Air Corps experiences,* Little Friend, Little Friend *(1945)—from which the poem below is taken—and* Losses *(1948). His reputation as a poet was firmly established by his later collections,* The Woman at the Washington Zoo *(1960), which won the National Book Award, and* The Lost World *(1966). In addition to his creative work, Jarrell was a well-respected literary critic and taught at Kenyon College, the University of Texas, Sarah Lawrence College, and the University of North Carolina.*

THE DEATH OF THE BALL TURRET GUNNER   [1945]

From my mother's sleep I fell into the State,
And I hunched in its belly till my wet fur froze.
Six miles from earth, loosed from its dream of life,
I woke to black flak and the nightmare fighters.
When I died they washed me out of the turret with a hose.   5

YUSEF KOMUNYAKAA [B. 1947]

Yusef Komunyakaa was born in Bogalusa, Louisiana, and served in the Vietnam War. His volumes of poetry include Copacetic *(1984),* I Apologize for the Eyes in My Head *(1986), and* Neon Vernacular, *which won the Pulitzer Prize in 1994."Facing It," a poem about the Vietnam Memorial in Washington, D.C., is taken from* Dien Cai Dau *(1988). He teaches at Indiana University.*

FACING IT   [1988]

My black face fades,
hiding inside the black granite.
I said I wouldn't,
dammit: No tears.
I'm stone. I'm flesh.   5

My clouded reflection eyes me
like a bird of prey, the profile of night
slanted against morning. I turn
this way—the stone lets me go.
I turn that way—I'm inside   10
the Vietnam Veterans Memorial
again, depending on the light
to make a difference.
I go down the 58,022 names,
half-expecting to find   15
my own in letters like smoke.
I touch the name Andrew Johnson;
I see the booby trap's white flash.
Names shimmer on a woman's blouse
but when she walks away   20
the names stay on the wall.
Brushstrokes flash, a red bird's
wings cutting across my stare.
The sky. A plane in the sky.
A white vet's image floats   25
closer to me, then his pale eyes
look through mine. I'm a window.
He's lost his right arm
inside the stone. In the black mirror
a woman's trying to erase names: 30
No, she's brushing a boy's hair.

MAKING CONNECTIONS

1. Who is the speaker in the "The Man He Killed"? What does his diction tell
   you about him?
2. What do you think he concludes? To what extent do you agree?
3. Describe the setting of "Patterns." To what extent is it an appropriate setting
   for the news the speaker receives?
4. After receiving the news of her lover's death, the speaker says, "I stood
   upright too, / Held rigid to the pattern / By the stiffness of my gown." What
   do you think she means?
5. How would you answer the question at the end of the poem "What are patterns for?"
6. Compare this poem to Emily Dickinson's "After Great Pain, a Formal Feeling
   Comes" on page 1310.
7. In *"Dulce et Decorum Est"* when the speaker says at the beginning of the
   last stanza, "If in some smothering dreams you too could pace," "you" seems
   to refer to us—the readers. What does he assume about "us"? What does he
   assume might change our view?
8. Why does he call the Latin saying that is the title of this poem "The old Lie"?

9. In "Grass," what do "Austerlitz," "Waterloo," "Gettysburg," "Ypres," and "Verdun" refer to?

10. Why would the passengers ask the conductor, "What place is this?" Does it matter? Explain.

11. A ball turret was a round, bubble-like chamber that stuck out of the belly of a bomber and was especially vulnerable to gunfire from other planes or the ground. To what extent is "The Death of the Ball Turret Gunner" a metaphor for a mother's womb? Do you think it's an appropriate image? Explain.

12. Who is the speaker in "Facing It"? What is the speaker's point of view?

13. How many different things does he see reflected in the wall? In what way is it fitting that he mistakes the woman's brushing the boy's hair as trying to erase names?

14. Compare any of these poems to Stephen Crane's "War Is Kind" on page 73.

MAKING AN ARGUMENT

1. Except for "*Dulce et Decorum Est*," all of these poems are removed from the "heat" of battle itself. The speakers are remembering or grieving sad news. But all of them, like the speaker in the Owen poem, seem to state explicitly or implicitly some doubt about the wisdom and necessity of war. Do you agree? Write an essay about the theme of "doubt" as exemplified by the poems in this section. Cite the texts of the poems for support.

◆ DRAMA ◆

DAVID MAMET [B. 1947]

David Mamet was born in Chicago and has written over twenty plays. He is best known for plays like American Buffalo *(1975), which won the New York Drama Critics Circle Award, and* Glengarry Glen Ross *(1984) for which he was awarded a Pulitzer Prize. He has also written several successful screenplays including* The Verdict *(1982), which received an Academy Award nomination, and* The Untouchables *(1987). He has both written and directed a number of movies, including* House of Games *(1987),* Homicide *(1991), the film version of* Oleanna *(1994),* The Spanish Prisoner *(1997),* State and Main *(1991), and* Heist *(2001).*

OLEANNA

to be in *Oleanna*
      That's where I would rather be.
      Than be bound in Norway
      And drag the chains of slavery."
                              —folk song

CHARACTERS
CAROL, *a woman of twenty*
JOHN, *a man in his forties*
The play takes place in John's office.

ONE

John is talking on the phone. Carol is seated across the desk from him.

JOHN *(on the phone):*   And what about the land. *(Pause)* The land. And what about the land? *(Pause)* What about it? *(Pause)* No. I don't understand. Well, yes, I'm I'm . . . no, I'm *sure* it's signif . . . I'm sure it's significant. *(Pause)* Because it's significant to mmmmmm . . . did you call Jerry? *(Pause)* Because . . . no, no, no, no, no. What did they say . . . ? Did you speak to the *real* estate . . . where *is* she . . . ? Well, well, all right. Where are her notes? Where are the notes we took with her. *(Pause)* I thought you were? No. No, I'm sorry, I didn't mean that, I just thought that I saw you, when we were there . . . what . . . ? I thought I saw you with a *pencil.* WHY NOW? is what I'm say . . . well, that's why I say "call Jerry." Well, I can't right now, be . . . no, I *didn't* schedule any . . . Grace: I *didn't* . . . I'm well aware . . . Look: Look. Did you call Jerry? Will you call Jerry . . . ? Because I can't now. I'll be there, I'm sure I'll be there in fifteen, in twenty. I intend to. No, we aren't *going* to lose the, we aren't *going* to lose the house. Look: Look, I'm not minimizing it. The "easement." Did she say "easement"? *(Pause)* What did she *say;* is it a "term of art," are we *bound* by it . . . I'm sorry . . . *(Pause)* are: we: yes. *Bound* by . . . Look: *(He checks his watch.)* before the other side *goes home,* all right? "a term of art." Because: that's right *(Pause)* The yard for the boy. Well, that's the whole . . . Look: I'm going to meet you there . . . *(He checks his watch.)* Is the realtor there? All right, tell her to show you the basement again. Look at the *this* because . . . Bec . . . I'm leaving in, I'm leaving in ten or fifteen . . . Yes. No, no, I'll meet you at the new . . . That's a good. If he thinks it's necc . . . you tell Jerry to meet . . . All right? We *aren't* going to lose the deposit. All right? I'm sure it's going to be . . . *(Pause)* I hope so. *(Pause)* I love you, too. *(Pause)* I love you, too. As soon as . . . I will.

   (He hangs up.) (He bends over the desk and makes a note.) (He looks up.) (To Carol:) I'm sorry . . .

CAROL: *(Pause)* What is a "term of art"?

JOHN: *(Pause)* I'm sorry . . . ?

CAROL: *(Pause)* What is a "term of art"?

JOHN: Is that what you want to talk about?

CAROL: . . . to talk about . . . ?

JOHN: Let's take the mysticism out of it, shall we? Carol? *(Pause)* Don't you think? I'll tell you: when you have some "thing." Which must be broached. *(Pause)* Don't you think . . . ? *(Pause)*

CAROL: . . . don't I think . . . ?

JOHN: Mmm?

CAROL: . . . did I . . . ?

JOHN: . . . what?

CAROL: Did . . . did I . . . did I say something wr . . .

VOHN: *(Pause)* No. I'm sorry. No. You're right. I'm very sorry. I'm somewhat rushed. As you see. I'm sorry. You're right. *(Pause)* What is a "term of art"? It seems to mean a *term*, which has come, through its use, to mean something *more specific* than the words would, to someone *not acquainted* with them . . . indicate. That, I believe, is what a "term of art," would mean. *(Pause)*

CAROL: You don't know what it means . . . ?

JOHN: I'm not sure that I know what it means. It's one of those things, perhaps you've had them, that, you look them up, or have someone explain them to you, and you say "aha," and, you immediately *forget* what . . .

CAROL: You don't do that.

VOHN: . . . I . . . ?

CAROL: You don't do . . .

JOHN: . . . I don't, what . . . ?

CAROL: . . . for . . .

JOHN: . . . I don't for . . .

CAROL: . . . no . . .

JOHN: . . . forget things? Everybody does that.

CAROL: No, they don't.

JOHN: They don't . . .

CAROL: No.

JOHN: *(Pause)* No. Everybody does that.

CAROL: Why would they do that . . . ?

JOHN: Because. I don't know. Because it doesn't interest them.

CAROL: No.

JOHN: I think so, though. *(Pause)* I'm sorry that I was distracted.

CAROL: You don't have to say that to me.

JOHN: You paid me the compliment, or the "obeisance"—all right—of coming in here . . . All right. *Carol.* I find that I am at a *standstill.* I find that I . . .

CAROL: . . . what . . .

JOHN: . . . one moment. In regard to your . . . to your . . .

CAROL: Oh, oh. You're buying a new house!

JOHN: No, let's get on with it.

CAROL: "get on"? *(Pause)*

JOHN: I know how . . . *believe* me. I know how . . . potentially *humiliating* these . . . I have no desire to . . . I have no desire other than to help you. But *(He picks up some papers on his desk.)* I won't even say "but." I'll say that as I go back over the . . .

CAROL: I'm just, I'm just trying to . . .

JOHN: . . . no, it will not do.

CAROL: . . . what? What will . . . ?

JOHN: No. I see, I see what you, it . . . (*He gestures to the papers.*) but your work . . .

CAROL: I'm just: I sit in class I . . . (*She holds up her notebook.*) I take notes . . .

JOHN: (*simultaneously with* "notes"): Yes. I understand. What I am trying to *tell* you is that some, some basic . . .

CAROL: . . . I . . .

JOHN: . . . one moment: some basic missed communi . . .

CAROL: I'm doing what I'm told. I bought your book, I read your . . .

JOHN: No, I'm sure you . . .

CAROL: No, no, no. I'm doing what I'm told. It's *difficult* for me. It's *difficult* . . .

JOHN: . . . but . . .

CAROL: I don't . . . lots of the *language* . . .

JOHN: . . . please . . .

CAROL: The *language,* the "things" that you say . . .

JOHN: I'm sorry. No. I don't think that that's true.

CAROL: It *is* true. I . . .

JOHN: I think . . .

CAROL: It *is* true.

JOHN: . . . I . . .

CAROL: Why would I . . . ?

JOHN: I'll tell you why: you're an incredibly bright girl.

CAROL: . . . I . . .

JOHN: You're an incredibly . . . you have no problem with the . . . Who's kidding who?

CAROL: . . . I . . .

JOHN: No. No. I'll tell you why. I'll tell . . . I think you're *angry,* I . . .

CAROL: . . . why would I . . .

JOHN: . . . wait one moment. I . . .

CAROL: It *is* true. I have *problems* . . .

JOHN: . . . every . . .

CAROL: . . . I come from a different *social* . . .

JOHN: . . . ev . . .

CAROL: a different economic . . .

JOHN: . . . Look:

CAROL: No. I: when I *came* to this school:

JOHN: Yes. Quite . . . (*Pause*)

CAROL: . . . does that mean nothing . . . ?

JOHN: . . . but look: look . . .

CAROL: . . . I . . .

JOHN: (*Picks up paper.*) Here: Please: Sit down. (*Pause*) Sit down. (*Reads from her paper.*) "I think that the ideas contained in this work express the author's feelings in a way that he intended, based on his results." What can that mean? Do you see? What . . .

CAROL: I, the best that I . . .

JOHN: I'm saying, that perhaps this course . . .

CAROL: No, no, no, you can't, you can't . . . I have to . . .

JOHN: . . . how . . .

CAROL: . . . I have to pass it . . .

JOHN: Carol, I.

CAROL: I *have* to pass this course, I . . .

JOHN: Well.

CAROL: . . . don't you . . .

JOHN: Either the . . .

CAROL: . . . I . . .

JOHN: . . . either the, I . . . either the *criteria* for judging progress in the class are . . .

CAROL: No, no, no, no, I have to pass it.

JOHN: Now, look: I'm a human being, I . . .

CAROL: I did what you told me. I did, I did everything that, I read your *book,* you told me to buy your book and read it. Everything you *say* I . . . *(She gestures to her notebook.) (The phone rings.)* I do. . . . Ev . . .

JOHN: . . . look:

CAROL: . . . everything I'm told . . .

JOHN: Look. Look. I'm not your *father. (Pause)*

CAROL: What?

JOHN: I'm.

CAROL: Did I say you were my father?

JOHN: . . . no . . .

CAROL: Why did you say that . . . ?

JOHN: I . . .

CAROL: . . . why . . . ?

JOHN: . . . in class I . . . *(He picks up the phone.) (Into phone:)* Hello. I can't talk now. Jerry? Yes? I underst . . . I can't talk now. I know . . . I know . . . Jerry. I can't *talk* now. Yes, I. Call me back in . . . Thank you. *(He hangs up.) (To Carol:)* What do you want me to do? We are two people, all right? Both of whom have subscribed to . . .

CAROL: No, no . . .

JOHN: . . . certain arbitrary . . .

CAROL: No. You have to help me.

JOHN: Certain institutional . . . you tell me what you want me to do. . . . You tell me what you want me to . . .

CAROL: How can I go back and tell them the *grades* that I . . .

JOHN: . . . what can I do . . . ?

CAROL: *Teach* me. *Teach* me,

JOHN: . . . I'm trying to teach you.

CAROL: I read your book. I read it. I don't under . . .

JOHN: . . . you don't understand it.

CAROL: No.

JOHN: Well, perhaps it's not well *written* . . .

CAROL: *(simultaneously with* "written"): No. No. No. I want to *understand* it.

JOHN: What don't you understand? *(Pause)*

CAROL: *Any* of it. What you're trying to say. When you talk about . . .

JOHN: . . . yes . . . ? *(She consults her notes.)*

CAROL: "Virtual warehousing of the young" . . .

JOHN: "Virtual warehousing of the young." If we artificially prolong adolescence . . .

CAROL: . . . and about "The Curse of Modern Education."

JOHN: . . . well . . .

CAROL: I don't . . .

JOHN: Look. It's just a *course,* it's just a *book,* it's just a . . .

CAROL: No. No. There are *people* out there. People who came *here.* To know something they didn't *know.* Who *came* here. To be *helped.* To be *helped.* So someone would *help* them. To *do* something. To *know* something. To get, what do they say? "To get on in the world." How can I do that if I don't, if I fail? But I don't *understand.* I don't *understand.* I don't understand what anything means . . . and I walk around. From morning 'til night: with this one thought in my head. I'm *stupid.*

JOHN: No one thinks you're stupid.

CAROL: No? What am I . . . ?

JOHN: I . . .

CAROL: . . . what am I, then?

JOHN: I think you're angry. Many people are. I have a *telephone* call that I have to make. And an *appointment,* which is rather *pressing;* though I sympathize with your concerns, and though I wish I had the time, this was not a previously scheduled meeting and I . . .

CAROL: . . . you think I'm nothing . . .

JOHN: . . . have an appointment with a *realtor,* and with my wife and . . .

CAROL: You think that I'm stupid.

JOHN: No. I certainly don't.

CAROL: You said it.

JOHN: No. I did not.

CAROL: You did.

JOHN: When?

CAROL: . . . you . . .

JOHN: No. I never did, or never would say that to a student, and . . .

CAROL: You said, "What can that mean?" *(Pause)* "What can that mean?" . . . *(Pause)*

JOHN: . . . and what did that mean to you . . . ?

CAROL: That meant I'm stupid. And I'll never learn. That's what that meant. And you're right.

JOHN: . . . I . . .

CAROL: But then. But then, what am I doing here . . . ?

JOHN: . . . if you thought that I . . .

CAROL: . . . when nobody wants me, and . . .

JOHN: . . . if you interpreted . . .

CAROL: Nobody *tells* me anything. And I *sit* there . . . in the *corner.* In the *back.* And everybody's talking about "this" all the time. And "concepts," and "precepts" and, and, and, and, and, WHAT IN THE WORLD ARE YOU *TALKING* ABOUT? And I read your book. And they said, "Fine, go in that class." Because you talked about responsibility to the young. I DON'T KNOW WHAT IT MEANS AND I'M *FAILING* . . .

JOHN: May . . .

CAROL: No, you're right. "Oh, hell." I failed. Flunk me out of it. It's garbage. Everything I do. "The ideas contained in this work express the author's feelings." That's right. That's right. I know I'm stupid. I know what I am. *(Pause)* I know what I am, Professor. You don't have to tell me. *(Pause)* It's pathetic. Isn't it?

JOHN: . . . Aha . . . *(Pause)* Sit down. Sit down. Please. *(Pause)* Please sit down.

CAROL: Why?

JOHN: I want to talk to you.

CAROL: Why?

JOHN: Just sit down. *(Pause)* Please. Sit down. Will you, please . . . ? *(Pause. She does so,)* Thank you.

CAROL: What?

JOHN: I want to tell you something.

CAROL: *(Pause)* What?

JOHN: Well, I know what you're talking about.

CAROL: No. You don't.

JOHN: I think I do. *(Pause)*

CAROL: How can you?

JOHN: I'll tell you a story about myself. *(Pause)* Do you mind? *(Pause)* I was raised to think myself stupid. That's what I want to tell you. *(Pause)*

CAROL: What do you mean?

JOHN: Just what I said. I was brought up, and my earliest, and most persistent memories are of being told that I was stupid. "You have such *intelligence.* Why must you behave so *stupidly?*" Or, "Can't you *understand?* Can't you *understand?*" And I could *not* understand. I could *not* understand.

CAROL: What?

JOHN: The simplest problem. Was beyond me. It was a mystery.

CAROL: What was a mystery?

JOHN: How people learn. How *I* could learn. Which is what I've been speaking of in class. And of *course* you can't hear it. Carol. Of *course* you can't. *(Pause)* I used to speak of "real people," and wonder what the *real* people did. The *real* people. Who were they? *They* were the people other than myself. The *good* people. The *capable* people. The people who could do the things, *I* could not do: learn, study, retain . . . all that *garbage*—which is what I have been talking of in class, and that's *exactly* what I have been talking of—If you are told . . . Listen to this. If the young child is told he cannot understand. Then he takes it

as a *description* of himself. What am I? I am *that which can not understand*
And I saw you out there, when we were speaking of the concepts of . . .

CAROL: I can't understand any of them.

JOHN: Well, then, that's *my* fault. That's not your fault. And that is not verbiage. That's
what I firmly hold to be the truth. And I am sorry, and I owe you an apology.

CAROL: Why?

JOHN: And I suppose that I have had some *things* on my mind . . . We're buying a
house, and . . .

CAROL: People said that you were stupid . . . ?

JOHN: Yes.

CAROL: When?

JOHN: I'll tell you when. Through my life. In my childhood; and, perhaps, they
stopped. But I heard them continue.

CAROL: And what did they say?

JOHN: They said I was incompetent. Do you see? And when I'm tested the, the, the
feelings of my youth about the *very subject of learning* come up. And I . . . I
become, I feel "unworthy," and "unprepared." . . .

CAROL: . . . yes.

JOHN: . . . eh?

CAROL: . . . yes.

JOHN: And I feel that I must fail. *(Pause)*

CAROL: . . . but then you *do* fail. *(Pause)* You have to. *(Pause)* Don't you?

JOHN: A *pilot.* Flying a plane. The pilot is flying the plane. He thinks: Oh, my *God,*
my mind's been drifting! Oh, my God! What kind of a cursed imbecile am I,
that I, with this so precious cargo of *Life* in my charge, would allow my attention to wander. Why was I born? How deluded are those who put their trust
in me, . . . et cetera, so on, and he crashes the plane.

CAROL: *(Pause)* He could just . . .

JOHN: That's right.

CAROL: He could say:

JOHN: My attention *wandered* for a moment . . .

CAROL: . . . uh huh . . .

JOHN: I had a *thought* I did not like . . . but now:

CAROL: . . . but now it's . . .

JOHN: That's what I'm telling you. It's time to put my attention . . . see: it is not: this is
what I learned. It is Not Magic. Yes. Yes. *You.* You are going to be frightened.
When faced with what may or may not be but which you are going to perceive
as a test. You will become frightened. And you will say: "I am incapable of . . . "
and everything *in* you will think these two things. "I must. But I can't." And you
will think: Why was I born to be the laughing-stock of a world in which everyone is better than I? In which I am entitled to nothing. Where I can not learn.
(Pause)

CAROL: Is that . . . *(Pause)* Is that what I have . . . ?

JOHN: Well. I don't know if I'd put it that way. Listen: I'm talking to you as I'd talk to my son. Because that's what I'd like him to have that I never had. I'm talking to you the way I wish that someone had talked to me. I don't know how to do it, other than to be *personal*, . . . but . . .

CAROL: Why would you want to be personal with me?

JOHN: Well, you see? That's what I'm saying. We can only interpret the behavior of others through the screen we . . . *(The phone rings.)* Through . . . *(To phone:)* Hello . . . ? *(To Carol:)* Through the screen we create. *(To phone:)* Hello. *(To Carol:)* Excuse me a moment. *(To phone:)* Hello? No, I can't talk nnn . . . I know I did. In a few . . . I'm . . . is he coming to the . . . yes. I talked to him. We'll meet you at the No, because I'm with a *student*. It's going to be fff . . . This is important, too. I'm with a *student*, Jerry's going to . . . Listen: the sooner I get off, the sooner I'll be down, all right. I love you. Listen, listen, I said. "I love you," it's going to work *out* with the, because I feel that it is, I'll be right down. All right? Well, then it's going to take as long as it takes. *(He hangs up.)* *(To Carol:)* I'm sorry.

CAROL: What was that?

JOHN: There are some problems, as there usually are, about the final agreements for the new house.

CAROL: You're buying a new house.

JOHN: That's right.

CAROL: Because of your promotion.

JOHN: Well, I suppose that that's right.

CAROL: Why did you stay here with me?

JOHN: Stay here.

CAROL: Yes. When you should have gone.

JOHN: Because I like you.

CAROL: You like me.

JOHN: Yes.

CAROL: Why?

JOHN: Why? Well? Perhaps we're similar. *(Pause)* Yes. *(Pause)*

CAROL: You said "everyone has problems."

JOHN: Everyone has problems.

CAROL: Do they?

JOHN: Certainly.

CAROL: You do?

JOHN: Yes.

CAROL: What are they?

JOHN: Well. *(Pause)* Well, you're perfectly right. *(Pause)* If we're going to take off the Artificial *Stricture,* of "Teacher," and "Student," why should *my* problems be any more a mystery than your own? Of *course* I have problems. As you saw.

CAROL: . . . with what?

JOHN: With my *wife* . . . with *work* . . .

CAROL: With work?

JOHN: Yes. And, and, perhaps my problems are, do you see? *Similar* to yours.

CAROL: Would you tell me?

JOHN: All right. *(Pause)* I came *late* to teaching. And I found it Artificial. The notion of "I know and you do not"; and I saw an *exploitation* in the education process. I told you. I hated school, I hated teachers. I hated everyone who was in the position of a "boss" because I *knew*—I didn't *think,* mind you, I *knew I* was going to fail. Because I was a fuckup. I was just no goddamned good. When I . . . late in life . . . *(Pause)* When I *got out from under* . . . when I worked my way out of the need to fail. When I . . .

CAROL: How do you do that? *(Pause)*

JOHN: You have to look at what you are, and what you feel, and how you act. And, finally, you have to look at how you act. And say: If that's what I *did,* that must be how I think of myself.

CAROL: I don't understand.

JOHN: If I fail all the time, it must be that I think of myself as a failure. If I do not want to think of myself as a failure, perhaps I should begin by *succeeding* now and again. Look. The tests, you see, which you encounter, in school, in college, in life, were designed, in the most part, for idiots. *By* idiots. There is no need to fail at them. They are not a test of your worth. They are a test of your ability to retain and spout back misinformation. Of *course* you fail them. They're *nonsense.* And I . . .

CAROL: . . . no . . .

JOHN: Yes. They're *garbage.* They're a *joke.* Look at me. Look at me. The Tenure Committee. The Tenure Committee. Come to judge me. The Bad Tenure Committee.

The "Test." Do you see? They put me to the test. Why, they had people voting on me I wouldn't employ to wax my car. And yet, I go before the Great Tenure Committee, and I have an urge, to *vomit,* to, to, to puke my *badness* on the table, to show them: "I'm no good. Why would you pick *me?*"

CAROL: They granted you tenure.

JOHN: Oh no, they announced it, but they haven't *signed.* Do you see? "At any moment . . . "

CAROL: . . . mmm . . .

JOHN: "They might not *sign*" . . . I might not . . . the *house* might not go through . . . Eh? Eh? They'll find out my "dark secret." *(Pause)*

CAROL: . . . what is it . . . ?

JOHN: There *isn't* one. But *they* will find an index of my badness . . .

CAROL: Index?

JOHN: A ". . . pointer." A "Pointer." You see? Do you see? I *understand* you. I. Know. That. Feeling. Am I entitled to my job, and my nice *home,* and my *wife,* and my *family,* and so on. This is what I'm saying: That theory of education which, that *theory:*

CAROL: I . . . I . . . *(Pause)*

JOHN: What?

CAROL: I . . .

JOHN: What?

CAROL: I want to know about my grade. *(Long pause)*

JOHN: Of course you do.

CAROL: Is that bad?

JOHN: No.

CAROL: Is it bad that I asked you that?

JOHN: No.

CAROL: Did I upset you?

JOHN: No. And I apologize. Of *course* you want to know about your grade. And, of course, you can't concentrate on anyth . . . *(The telephone starts to ring.)* Wait a moment.

CAROL: I should go.

JOHN: I'll make you a deal.

CAROL: No; you have to . . .

JOHN: Let it ring. I'll make you a deal. You stay here. We'll start the whole course over. I'm going to say it was not you, it was I who was not paying attention. We'll start the whole course over. Your grade is an "A." Your final grade is an "A." *(The phone stops ringing.)*

CAROL: But the class is only half over . . .

JOHN *(simultaneously with "over")*: Your grade for the whole term is an "A." If you will come back and meet with me. A few more times. Your grade's an "A." Forget about the paper. You didn't like it, you didn't like writing it. It's not important. What's important is that I awake your interest, if I can, and that I answer your questions. Let's start over. *(Pause)*

CAROL: Over. With what?

JOHN: Say this is the beginning.

CAROL: The beginning.

JOHN: Yes.

CAROL: Of what?

JOHN: Of the class.

CAROL: But we can't start over.

JOHN: I say we can. *(Pause)* I say we can.

CAROL: But I don't believe it.

JOHN: Yes, I know that. But it's true. What is The Class but you and me? *(Pause)*

CAROL: There are rules.

JOHN: Well. We'll break them.

CAROL: How can we?

JOHN: We won't tell anybody.

CAROL: Is that all right?

JOHN: I say that it's fine.

CAROL: Why would you do this for me?

JOHN: I like you. Is that so difficult for you to . . .

CAROL: Um . . .

JOHN: There's no one here but you and me. *(Pause)*

CAROL: All right. I did not understand. When you referred . . .

JOHN: All right, yes?

CAROL: When you referred to hazing.

JOHN: Hazing.

CAROL: You wrote, in your book. About the comparative . . . the comparative . . . *(She checks her notes.)*

JOHN: Are you checking your notes . . . ?

CAROL: Yes.

JOHN: Tell me in your own . . .

CAROL: I want to make sure that I have it right.

JOHN: No. Of course. You want to be exact.

CAROL: I want to know everything that went on.

JOHN: . . . that's good.

CAROL: . . . so I . . .

JOHN: That's very good. But I was suggesting, many times, that that which we wish to retain is retained oftentimes, I think, *better* with less expenditure of effort.

CAROL: *(Of notes)* Here it is: you wrote of *hazing.*

JOHN: . . . that's correct. Now: I said "hazing." It means ritualized annoyance. We shove this book at you, we say read it. Now, you say you've read it? I think that you're *lying.* I'll *grill* you, and when I find you've lied, you'll be disgraced, and your life will be ruined. It's a sick game. Why do we do it? Does it educate? In no sense. Well, then, what is higher education? It is something-other-than-useful.

CAROL: What is "something-other-than-useful?"

JOHN: It has become a ritual, it has become an article of faith. That all must be subjected to, or to put it differently, that all are entitled to Higher Education. And my point . . .

CAROL: You disagree with that?

JOHN: Well, let's address that. What do you think?

CAROL: I don't know.

JOHN: What do you think, though? *(Pause)*

CAROL: I don't know.

JOHN: I spoke of it in class. Do you remember my example?

CAROL: Justice.

JOHN: Yes. Can you repeat it to me? *(She looks down at her notebook.)* Without your notes? I ask you as a favor to me, so that I can see if my idea was interesting.

CAROL: You said "justice" . . .

JOHN: Yes?

CAROL: . . . that all are entitled . . . *(Pause)* I . . . I . . . I . . .

JOHN.   Yes. To a speedy trial. To a fair trial. But they needn't be given a trial *at all* unless they stand accused. Eh? Justice is their right, should they choose to avail themselves of it, they should have a fair trial. It does not follow, of necessity, a person's life is incomplete without a trial in it. Do you see?

My point is a confusion between equity and *utility* arose. So we confound the *usefulness* of higher education with our, granted, right to equal access to the same. We, in effect, create a *prejudice* toward it, completely independent of . . .

CAROL: . . . that it is prejudice that we should go to school?

JOHN: Exactly. *(Pause)*

CAROL: How can you say that? How . . .

JOHN: Good. Good. *Good.* That's right! Speak up! What is a prejudice? An unreasoned belief. We are all subject to it. None of us is not. When it is threatened, or opposed, we feel anger, and feel, do we not? As you do now. Do you not? Good.

CAROL: . . . but how can you . . .

JOHN: . . . let us examine. Good.

CAROL: How . . .

JOHN: Good. Good. When . . .

CAROL: I'M SPEAKING . . . *(Pause)*

JOHN: I'm sorry.

CAROL: How can you . . .

JOHN: . . . I beg your pardon.

CAROL: That's all right.

JOHN: I beg your pardon.

CAROL: That's all right.

JOHN: I'm sorry I interrupted you.

CAROL: That's all right.

JOHN: You were saying?

CAROL: I was saying . . . I was saying . . . *(She checks her notes.)* How can you say in a class. Say in a college class, that college education is prejudice?

JOHN: I said that our predilection for it . . .

CAROL: Predilection . . .

JOHN: . . . you know what that means.

CAROL: Does it mean "liking"?

JOHN: Yes.

CAROL: But how can you say that? That College . . .

JOHN: . . . that's my *job,* don't you know.

CAROL: What is?

JOHN: To provoke you.

CAROL: No.

JOHN: Oh. Yes, though.

CAROL: To provoke me?

JOHN: That's right.

CAROL: To make me mad?

JOHN: That's right. To force you . . .

CAROL: . . . to make me mad is your job?

JOHN:　To force you to . . . listen: *(Pause)* Ah. *(Pause)* When I was young somebody told me, are you ready, the rich copulate less often than the poor. But when they do, they take more of their clothes off. Years. Years, mind you, I would compare experiences of my own to this dictum, saying, aha, this fits the norm, or ah, this is a variation from it. What did it mean? Nothing. It was some jerk thing, some school kid told me that took up room inside my head. *(Pause)*

Somebody told *you,* and you hold it as an article of faith, that higher education is an unassailable good. This notion is so dear to you that when I question it you become angry. Good. Good, I say. Are not those the very things which we should question? I say college education, since the war, has become so a matter of course, and such a fashionable necessity, for those either of or aspiring *to* to the new vast middle class, that we *espouse* it, as a matter of right, and have ceased to ask, "What is it good for?" *(Pause)*

What might be some reasons for pursuit of higher education?
One: A love of learning.
Two: The wish for mastery of a skill.
Three: For economic betterment.
(Stops. Makes a note.)

CAROL:　I'm keeping you.

JOHN:　One moment. I have to make a note . . .

CAROL:　It's something that I said?

JOHN:　No, we're buying a house.

CAROL:　You're buying the new house.

JOHN:　To go with the tenure. That's right. Nice *house,* close to the *private school* . . . *(He continues making his note.)* . . . We were talking of economic *betterment (Carol writes in her notebook.)* . . . I was thinking of the School Tax. *(He continues writing.) (To himself:)* . . . *where is it written* that I have to send my child to public school. . . . Is it a law that I have to improve the City Schools at the expense of my own interest? And, is this not simply *The White Man's Burden?* Good. And *(Looks up to Carol)* . . . does this interest you?

CAROL:　No. I'm taking notes . . .

JOHN:　You don't have to take notes, you know, you can just listen.

CAROL:　I want to make sure I remember it. *(Pause)*

JOHN:　I'm not lecturing you, I'm just trying to tell you some things I think.

CAROL:　What do you think?

JOHN:　Should all kids go to college? *Why* . . .

CAROL:　*(Pause)* To learn.

JOHN:　But if he does not learn.

CAROL:　If the child does not learn?

JOHN:　Then why is he in college? Because he was told it was his "right"?

CAROL:　Some might find college instructive.

JOHN:　I would hope so.

CAROL: But how do they feel? Being told they are wasting their time?

JOHN: I don't think I'm telling them that.

CAROL: You said that education was "prolonged and systematic hazing."

JOHN: Yes. It can be so.

CAROL: . . . if education is so *bad,* why do you do it?

JOHN: I do it because I love it. *(Pause)* Let's. . . . I suggest you look at the demographics, wage-earning capacity, college- and non-college-educated men and women, 1855 to 1980, and let's see if we can wring some worth from the statistics. Eh? And . . .

CAROL: No.

JOHN: What?

CAROL: I can't understand them.

JOHN: . . . you . . . ?

CAROL: . . . the "charts." The *Concepts,* the . . .

JOHN: "Charts" are simply . . .

CAROL: When I leave here . . .

JOHN: Charts, do you see . . .

CAROL: No, I can't. . . .

JOHN: You can, though.

CAROL: NO, NO—I DON'T UNDERSTAND. DO YOU SEE??? I DON'T *UNDERSTAND* . . .

JOHN: What?

CAROL: *Any* of it. *Any* of it. I'm *smiling* in class, I'm *smiling,* the whole time. What are you *talking* about? What is everyone *talking* about? I don't *understand.* I don't know what it *means.* I don't know what it means to *be* here . . . you tell me I'm intelligent, and then you tell me I should not be *here,* what do you *want* with me? What does it *mean?* Who should I *listen* to . . . I . . .
(He goes over to her and puts his arm around her shoulder.)
NO! *(She walks away from him.)*

JOHN: Sshhhh.

CAROL: No, I don't under . . .

JOHN: Sshhhhh.

CAROL: I don't know what you're *saying* . . .

JOHN: Sshhhhh. It's all right.

CAROL: . . . I have to . . .

JOHN: Sshhhhh. Sshhhhh. Let it go a moment. *(Pause)* Sshhhhh . . . let it go. *(Pause)* Just let it go. *(Pause)* Just let it go. It's all right. *(Pause)* Sshhhhh. *(Pause)* I understand . . . *(Pause)* What do you feel?

CAROL: I feel bad.

JOHN: I know. It's all right.

CAROL: I . . . *(Pause)*

JOHN: What?

CAROL: I . . .

JOHN: What? Tell me.

CAROL: I don't understand you.

JOHN: I know. It's all right.

CAROL: I . . .

JOHN: What? *(Pause)* What? *Tell* me.

CAROL: I can't tell you.

JOHN: No, you must.

CAROL: I can't.

JOHN: No. Tell me. *(Pause)*

CAROL: I'm bad. *(Pause)* Oh, God. *(Pause)*

JOHN: It's all right.

CAROL: I'm . . .

JOHN: It's all right.

CAROL: I can't talk about this.

JOHN: It's all right. Tell me.

CAROL: Why do you want to know this?

JOHN: I don't want to know. I want to know whatever you . . .

CAROL: I always . . .

JOHN: . . . good . . .

CAROL: I always . . . all my life . . . I have never told anyone this . . .

JOHN: Yes. Go on. *(Pause)* Go on.

CAROL: All of my life . . . *(The phone rings.) (Pause. John goes to the phone and picks it up.)*

JOHN: *(into phone):*   I can't talk now. *(Pause)* What? *(Pause)* Hmm. *(Pause)* All right, I . . . I. Can't. Talk. Now. No, no, no, I *Know* I did, but. . . . What? Hello. What? She *what?* She *can't,* she said the agreement is void? How, how is the agreement *void? That's Our House.*

I have the *paper;* when we come down, next week, with the payment, and the paper, that house is . . . wait, wait, wait, wait, wait, wait, wait: Did Jerry . . . is Jerry there? *(Pause)* Is *she* there . . . ? Does she have a *lawyer* . . . ? How the *hell,* how the *Hell.* That is . . . it's a question, you said, of the *easement.* I don't underst . . . it's not the *whole agreement.* It's just the *easement,* why would she? Put, put, put, *Jerry* on. *(Pause)* Jer, *Jerry:* What the *Hell* . . . that's my *house.* That's . . . Well, I'm no, no, no, I'm *not* coming ddd . . . List, *Listen, screw* her. You *tell* her. You, listen: I want you to take *Grace,* you take Grace, and get out of that house. You *leave* her there. Her and her lawyer, and you *tell* them, we'll see them in court next . . . no. No. Leave her there, leave her to *stew* in it: You tell her, we're *getting* that house, and we are going to . . . No. I'm *not* coming down. I'll be damned if I'll sit in the same rrr . . . the next, you tell her the next time I *see* her is in court . . . I . . . *(Pause)* What? *(Pause)* What? I don't understand. *(Pause)* Well, what about the house? *(Pause)* There isn't any problem with the hhh . . . *(Pause)* No, no, no, that's all right. All ri . . . All right . . . *(Pause)* Of course. Tha . . . Thank you. No, I will. Right away. *(He hangs up.) (Pause)*

CAROL: What is it? *(Pause)*

JOHN: It's a surprise party.

CAROL: It is.

JOHN: Yes.

CAROL: A party for you.

JOHN: Yes.

CAROL: Is it your birthday?

JOHN: No.

CAROL: What is it?

JOHN: The tenure announcement.

CAROL: The tenure announcement.

JOHN: They're throwing a party for us in our new house.

CAROL: Your new house.

JOHN: The house that we're buying.

CAROL: You have to go.

JOHN: It seems that I do.

CAROL: *(Pause)* They're proud of you.

JOHN: Well, there are those who would say it's a form of aggression.

CAROL: What is?

JOHN: A surprise.

TWO

John *and* Carol *seated across the desk from each other.*

JOHN: You see, *(pause)* I love to teach. And flatter myself I am *skilled* at it. And I love the, the aspect of *Performance.* I think I must confess that.

When I found I loved to teach I swore that I would not become that cold, rigid automaton of an instructor which I had encountered as a child.

Now, I was not unconscious that it was given me to err upon the other side. And, so, I asked and *ask* myself if I engaged in heterodoxy, I will not say "gratuitously" for I do not care to posit orthodoxy as a given good—but, "to the detriment of, of my students." *(Pause)*

As I said. When the possibility of tenure opened, and, of course, I'd long pursued it, I was, of course *happy,* and *covetous* of it. I asked myself if I was wrong to covet it. And thought about it long, and, I hope, truthfully, and saw in myself several things in, I think, no particular order. *(Pause)*

That I *would* pursue it. That I *desired* it, that I was not pure of longing for security, and that that, perhaps, was not reprehensible in me. That I had duties *beyond* the school, and that my duty to my home, for instance, was, or should be, if it were not, of an equal weight. That tenure, and security, and yes, and *comfort,* were not, of themselves, to be scorned; and were even worthy of honorable pursuit. And that it was given me. Here, in this place, which I enjoy, and in which I find comfort, to assure myself of—as far as it rests in The Material—a continuation of that joy and comfort. In exchange for what? Teaching? Which I love.

What was the price of this security? To obtain *tenure.* Which tenure the committee is in the process of granting me. And on the basis of which I contracted to purchase a house. Now, as you don't have your own family, at this point, you may not know what that means. But to me it is important. A home. A Good Home. To raise my family. Now: The Tenure Committee will meet. This is the process, and a *good* process. Under which the school has functioned for quite a long time. They will meet, and hear your complaint—which you have the right to make; and they will dismiss it. They will *dismiss* your complaint; and, in the intervening period, I will lose my house. I will not be able to close on my house. I will lose my *deposit,* and the home I'd picked out for my wife and son will go by the boards. Now: I see I have angered you. I understand your anger at teachers. I was angry with mine. I felt hurt and humiliated by them. Which is one of the reasons that I went into education.

CAROL: What do you want of me?

JOHN: *(Pause)* I was hurt. When I received the report. Of the tenure committee. I was shocked. And I was hurt. No, I don't mean to subject you to my weak sensibilities. All right. Finally, I didn't understand. Then I thought: is it not always at those points at which we reckon ourselves unassailable that we are most vulnerable and . . . *(Pause)* Yes. All right. You find me pedantic. Yes. I am. By nature, by *birth,* by profession. I don't know . . . I'm always looking for a *paradigm* for . . .

CAROL: I don't know what a paradigm is.

JOHN: It's a model.

CAROL: Then why can't you use that word? *(Pause)*

JOHN: If it is important to you. Yes, all right. I was looking for a model. To continue: I feel that one point.

CAROL: I . . .

JOHN: One second . . . upon which I am unassailable is my unflinching concern for my students' dignity. I asked you here to . . . in the spirit of *investigation,* to ask you . . . to ask . . . *(Pause)* What have I done to you? *(Pause)* And, and, I suppose, how can I make amends. Can we not settle this now? It's pointless, really, and I want to know.

CAROL: What you can do to force me to retract?

JOHN: That is not what I meant at all.

CAROL: To bribe me, to convince me . . .

JOHN: . . . No.

CAROL: To retract . . .

JOHN: That is not what I meant at all. I think that you know it is not.

CAROL: That is not what I know. I *wish* I . . .

JOHN: I do not want to . . . you wish what?

CAROL: No, you said what amends can you make. To force me to retract.

JOHN: That is not what I said.

CAROL: I have my notes.

JOHN: Look. Look. The Stoics say . . .

CAROL: The Stoics?

JOHN: The Stoical Philosophers say if you remove the phrase "I have been injured," you have removed the injury. Now: Think: I know that you're upset. Just tell me. Literally. Literally: what wrong have I done you?

CAROL: Whatever you have done to me—to the extent that you've done it to *me,* do you know, rather than to me as a *student,* and, so, to the student body, is contained in my report. To the tenure committee.

JOHN: Well, all right. *(Pause)* Let's see. *(He reads.)* I find that I am sexist. That I am *elitist.* I'm not sure I know what that means, other than it's a derogatory word, meaning "bad." That I . . . That I insist on wasting time, in nonprescribed, in self-aggrandizing and theatrical *diversions* from the prescribed *text* . . . that these have taken both sexist and pornographic forms . . . here we find listed . . . *(Pause).* Here we find listed . . . instances ". . . closeted with a student" . . . "Told a rambling, sexually explicit story, in which the frequency and attitudes of fornication of the poor and rich are, it would seem, the central point . . . moved to *embrace* said student and . . . all part of a pattern . . . " *(Pause)*

(He reads.) That I used the phrase "The White Man's Burden" . . . that I told you how I'd asked you to my room because I quote like you. *(Pause)*

(He reads.) "He said he 'liked' me. That he 'liked being with me.' He'd let me write my examination paper over, if I could come back oftener to see him in his office." *(Pause) (To Carol:)* It's *ludicrous.* Don't you know that? It's not *necessary.* It's going to *humiliate* you, and it's going to cost me my *house,* and . . .

CAROL: It's "*ludicrous* . . . "?

John picks up the report and reads again.

JOHN: "He told me he had problems with his wife; and that he wanted to take off the artificial stricture of Teacher and Student. He put his arm around me . . . "

CAROL: Do you deny it? Can you deny it . . . ? Do you see? *(Pause)* Don't you see? You don't see, do you?

JOHN: I don't see . . .

CAROL: You think, you think you can deny that these things happened; or, if they *did,* if they *did,* that they meant what you *said* they meant. Don't you see? You drag me in here, you drag us, to listen to you "go on"; and "go on" about this, or that, or we don't "express" ourselves very well. We don't say what we mean. Don't we? Don't we? We *do* say what we mean. And you say that "I don't understand you. . . . " Then *you* . . . *(Points.)*

JOHN: "Consult the Report"?

CAROL: . . . that's right.

JOHN: You see. You see. Can't you. . . . You see what I'm saying? Can't you tell me in your own words?

CAROL: Those are my own words. *(Pause)*

JOHN: *(He reads.)* "He told me that if I would stay alone with him in his office, he would change my grade to an A." *(To Carol:)* What have I done to you? Oh. My God, are you so hurt?

CAROL: What I "feel" is irrelevant. *(Pause)*

JOHN: Do you know that I tried to help you?

CAROL: What I know I have reported.

JOHN: I would like to help you now. I would. Before this escalates.

CAROL *(simultaneously with* "escalates"): You see. I don't think that I need your help. I don't think I need anything you have.

JOHN: I feel . . .

CAROL: I don't *care* what you feel. Do you see? DO YOU SEE? You can't *do* that anymore. You. Do. Not. Have. The. Power. Did you misuse it? *Someone* did. Are you part of that group? *Yes. Yes.* You Are. You've *done* these things. And to say, and to say, "Oh. Let me help you with your problem . . . "

JOHN: Yes. I understand. I understand. You're *hurt*. You're *angry*. Yes. I think your *anger* is *betraying* you. Down a path which helps no one.

CAROL: I don't *care* what you think.

JOHN: You don't? *(Pause)* But you talk of *rights*. Don't you see? *I* have rights too. Do you see? I have a *house* . . . part of the *real* world; and The Tenure Committee, Good Men and True . . .

CAROL: . . . Professor . . .

JOHN: . . . Please: *Also* part of that world: you understand? This is my *life*. I'm not a *bogeyman*. I don't "stand" for something, I . . .

CAROL: . . . Professor . . .

JOHN: . . . I . . .

CAROL: Professor. I came here as a *favor*. At your personal request. Perhaps I should not have done so. But I did. On my behalf, and on behalf of my group. And you speak of the tenure committee, one of whose members is a woman, as you know. And though you might call it Good Fun, or An Historical Phrase, or An Oversight, or, All of the Above, to refer to the committee as Good Men and True, it is a demeaning remark. It is a sexist remark, and to overlook it is to countenance continuation of that method of thought. It's a remark . . .

JOHN: OH COME ON. Come on. . . . Sufficient to deprive a family of . . .

CAROL: Sufficient? Sufficient? Sufficient? Yes. It is a *fact* . . . and that story, which I quote, is *vile* and *classist*, and *manipulative* and *pornographic*. It . . .

JOHN: . . . it's pornographic . . . ?

CAROL: What gives you the *right*. Yes. To speak to a *woman* in your private . . . Yes. Yes. I'm sorry. I'm sorry. You feel yourself empowered . . . you say so yourself. To *strut*. To *posture*. To "perform." To "Call me in here . . . " Eh? You say that higher education is a joke. And treat it as such, you *treat* it as such. And *confess* to a taste to play the *Patriarch* in your class. To grant *this* To deny *that*: To embrace your students.

JOHN: How can you assert. How can you stand there and

CAROL: How can you *deny* it. You did it to me. *Here.* You *did.* . . . You *confess.* You love the Power. To *deviate.* To *invent,* to transgress . . . to *transgress* whatever norms have been established for us. And you think it's charming to "question" in yourself this taste to mock and destroy. But you should question it. Professor. And you pick those things which you feel *advance* you: publication, *tenure,* and the steps to get them you call "harmless rituals." And you perform those steps. Although you say it is hypocrisy. But to the aspirations of your students. Of *hardworking students,* who come here, who *slave* to come here—you have no idea what it cost me to come to this school—you *mock* us. You call education "hazing," and from your so-protected, so-elitist seat you hold our confusion as a *joke,* and our hopes and efforts with it. Then you sit there and say "what have I done?" And ask me to understand that *you* have aspirations too. But I tell you. I tell you. That you are vile. And that you are exploitative. And if you possess one ounce of that inner honesty you describe in your book, you can look in yourself and see those things that I see. And you can find revulsion equal to my own. Good day. *(She prepares to leave the room.)*

JOHN: Wait a second, will you, just one moment. *(Pause)* Nice day today.

CAROL: What?

JOHN: You said "Good day." I think that it is a nice day today.

CAROL: *Is* it?

JOHN: Yes, I think it is.

CAROL: And why is that important?

JOHN: Because it is the essence of all human communication. I say something conventional, you respond, and the information we exchange is not about the "weather," but that we both agree to converse. In effect, we agree that we are both human. *(Pause)*

I'm not a . . . "exploiter," and you're not a . . . "deranged," what? *Revolutionary* . . . that we may, that we may have . . . positions, and that we may have . . . desires, which are in *conflict,* but that we're just human. *(Pause)* That means that sometimes we're *imperfect. (Pause)* Often we're in conflict . . . *(Pause) Much* of what we do, you're right, in the name of "principles" is *self-serving* . . . much of what we do is *conventional. (Pause)* You're right. *(Pause)* You said you came in the class because you wanted to learn about *education.* I don't know that I can teach you about education. But I know that I can tell you what I *think* about education, and then *you* decide. And you don't have to fight with me. *I'm* not the subject. *(Pause)* And where I'm *wrong* . . . perhaps it's not your job to "fix" me. I don't want to fix *you.* I would like to tell you what I *think,* because that *is* my job, conventional as it is, and flawed as I may be. And then, if you can show me some better *form,* then we can proceed from there. But, just like "nice day, isn't it . . . ?" I don't think we can proceed until we accept that each of us is human. *(Pause)* And we still can have difficulties. We *will* have them . . . that's all right too. *(Pause)* Now:

CAROL: . . . wait . . .

JOHN: Yes. I want to hear it.

CAROL: . . . the . . .

JOHN: Yes. Tell me frankly.

CAROL: . . . my position . . .

JOHN: I want to hear it. In your own words. What you want. And what you feel.

CAROL: . . . I . . .

JOHN: . . . yes . . .

CAROL: My Group.

JOHN: Your "Group" . . . ? *(Pause)*

CAROL: The people I've been talking to . . .

JOHN: There's no shame in that. Everybody needs advisers. Everyone needs to expose themselves. To various points of view. It's not wrong. It's essential. Good. Good. Now: You and I . . . *(The phone rings.)*

You and I . . .

(He hesitates for a moment, and then picks it up.) (Into phone) Hello. *(Pause)* Um . . . no, I know they do. *(Pause)* I know she does. Tell her that I . . . can I call you back? . . . Then tell her that I think it's going to be fine. *(Pause)* Tell her just, just hold on, I'll . . . can I get back to you? . . . Well . . . no, no, no, we're *taking* the house . . . we're . . . no, no, nn . . . no, she will nnn, it's not a *question* of refunding the dep . . . no . . . it's not a *question* of the deposit . . . will you call Jerry? Babe, baby, will you just call Jerry? Tell him, nnn . . . tell him they, well, they're to keep the deposit, because the deal, be . . . because the deal is going to go *through* . . . because I know . . . be . . . will you please? Just *trust* me. Be . . . well, I'm dealing with the complaint. Yes. Right *Now.* Which is why I . . . yes, no, no, it's really, I can't *talk* about it now. Call Jerry, and I can't talk now. Ff . . . fine. Gg . . . good-bye. *(Hangs up.) (Pause)* I'm sorry we were interrupted.

CAROL: No . . .

JOHN: I . . . I was saying:

CAROL: You said that we should agree to talk about my complaint.

JOHN: That's correct.

CAROL: But we *are* talking about it.

JOHN: Well, that's correct too. You see? This is the *gist* of education.

CAROL: No, no. I mean, we're talking about it at the Tenure Committee Hearing. *(Pause)*

JOHN: Yes, but I'm saying: we can talk about it *now,* as easily as . . .

CAROL: No. I think that we should stick to the process . . .

JOHN: . . . wait a . . .

CAROL: . . . the "conventional" process. As you said. *(She gets up.)* And you're right, I'm sorry if I was, um, if I was "discourteous" to you. You're right.

JOHN: Wait, wait a . . .

CAROL: I really should go.

JOHN: Now, look, granted. I have an interest. In the status quo. All right? Everyone does. But what I'm saying is that the *committee* . . .

CAROL: Professor, you're right. Just don't impinge on me. We'll take our differences, and . . .

JOHN: You're going to make a . . . look, look, look, you're going to . . .

CAROL: I shouldn't have come here. They told me . . .

JOHN: One moment. No. No. There are *norms,* here, and there's no reason. Look: I'm trying to *save* you . . .

CAROL: No one *asked* you to . . . you're trying to save *me?* Do me the courtesy to . . .

JOHN: I *am* doing you the courtesy. I'm talking *straight* to you. We can settle this *now.* And I want you to sit *down* and . . .

CAROL: You must excuse me . . . *(She starts to leave the room.)*

JOHN: Sit down, it seems we each have a. . . . Wait one moment. Wait one moment . . . just do me the courtesy to . . .

He restrains her from leaving.

CAROL: LET ME GO.

JOHN: I have no desire to *hold* you, I just want to *talk* to you . . .

CAROL: LET ME GO. LET ME GO. WOULD SOMEBODY *HELP* ME? WOULD SOMEBODY *HELP* ME PLEASE . . . ?

THREE

At rise, Carol and John are seated.

JOHN: I have asked you here. *(Pause)* I have asked you here against, against my . . .

CAROL: I was most surprised you asked me.

JOHN: . . . against my better *judgment,* against . . .

CAROL: I was most surprised . . .

JOHN: . . . against the . . . yes. I'm sure.

CAROL: . . . If you would like me to leave, I'll leave. I'll go right now . . .   *(She rises.)*

JOHN: Let us begin *correctly,* may we? I feel . . .

CAROL: That is what I wished to do. That's why I came here, but now . . .

JOHN: . . . I feel . . .

CAROL: But now perhaps you'd like me to leave . . .

JOHN: I don't want you to leave. I asked you to come . . .

CAROL: I didn't have to come here.

JOHN: No. *(Pause)* Thank you.

CAROL: All right. *(Pause) (She sits down.)*

JOHN: Although I feel that it *profits,* it would *profit* you something, to . . .

CAROL: . . . what I . . .

JOHN: If you would hear me out, if you would hear me out.

CAROL: I came here to, the court officers told me not to come.

JOHN: . . . the "court" officers . . . ?

CAROL: I was shocked that you asked.

JOHN: . . . wait . . .

CAROL: Yes. But I did *not* come here to hear what it "profits" me.

JOHN: The "court" officers . . .

CAROL: . . . no, no, perhaps I should leave . . . *(She gets up.)*

JOHN: Wait.

CAROL: No. I shouldn't have . . .

JOHN: . . . wait. Wait. Wait a moment.

CAROL: Yes? What is it you want? *(Pause)* What is it you want?

JOHN: I'd like you to stay.

CAROL: You want me to stay.

JOHN: Yes.

CAROL: You do.

JOHN: Yes. *(Pause)* Yes. I would like to have you hear me out. If you would. *(Pause)* Would you please? If you would do that I would be in your debt. *(Pause)* *(She sits.)* Thank you. *(Pause)*

CAROL: What is it you wish to tell me?

JOHN: All right. I cannot . . . *(Pause)* I cannot help but feel you are owed an apology. *(Pause)* *(Of papers in his hands)* I have read. *(Pause)* And reread these accusations.

CAROL: What "accusations"?

JOHN: The, the tenure comm . . . what other accusations . . . ?

CAROL: The tenure committee . . . ?

JOHN: Yes.

CAROL: Excuse me, but those are not accusations. They have been *proved.* They are facts.

JOHN: . . . I . . .

CAROL: No. Those are not "accusations."

JOHN: . . . those?

CAROL: . . . the committee *(The phone starts to ring.)* the committee has . . .

JOHN: . . . All right . . .

CAROL: . . . those are not accusations. The Tenure Committee.

JOHN: ALL RIGHT. ALL RIGHT. ALL RIGHT. *(He picks up the phone.)* Hello! Yes. No. I'm here. Tell Mister . . . No, I can't talk to him now . . . I'm sure he has, but I'm fff . . . I know . . . No, I have no time t . . . tell Mister . . . tell Mist . . . tell Jerry that I'm *fine* and that I'll call him right aw . . . *(Pause)* My wife . . . Yes. I'm sure she has. Yes, thank you. Yes, I'll call her too. I cannot talk to you now. *(He hangs up.)* *(Pause)* All right. It was good of you to come Thank you. I have studied. I have spent some time studying the indictment.

CAROL: You will have to explain that word to me.

JOHN: An "indictment" . . .

CAROL: Yes.

JOHN: Is a "bill of particulars." A . . .

CAROL: All right. Yes.

JOHN: In which is alleged . . .

CAROL: No. I cannot allow that. I cannot allow that. Nothing is alleged. Everything is proved . . .

JOHN: Please, wait a sec . . .

CAROL: I cannot *come* to allow . . .

JOHN: If I may . . . If I may, from whatever you feel is "established," by . . .

CAROL: The issue here is not what I "feel." It is not my "feelings," but the feelings of women. And men. Your superiors, who've been "polled," do you see? To whom *evidence* has been presented, who have *ruled,* do you see? Who have weighed the testimony and the evidence, and have *ruled,* do you see? That you are *negligent.* That you are *guilty,* that you are found *wanting,* and in *error;* and are *not,* for the reasons so-told, to be given tenure. That you are to be disciplined. For facts. For *facts.* Not "alleged," what is the word? But *proved.* Do you see? *By your own actions.*

That is what the tenure committee has said. That is what my lawyer said. For what you did in class. For what you did *in this office.*

JOHN: They're going to discharge me.

CAROL: As full well they should. You don't understand? You're angry? What has *led* you to this place? Not your sex. Not your race. Not your class. YOUR OWN ACTIONS. And you're *angry.* You *ask* me here. What *do* you want? You want to "charm" me. You want to "convince" me. You want me to recant. I will *not* recant. Why should I . . . ? What I say is right. You tell me, you are going to tell me that you have a wife and child. You are going to say that you have a career and that you've worked for twenty years for this. Do you know what you've *worked* for? *Power.* For *power.* Do you understand? And you sit there, and you tell me *stories.* About your *house,* about all the private *schools,* and about *privilege,* and how you are entitled. To *buy,* to *spend,* to *mock,* to *summon.* All your stories: All your silly weak *guilt,* it's all about *privilege;* and you won't know it. Don't you see? You worked twenty years for the right to *insult* me. And you feel entitled to be *paid* for it. Your Home. Your Wife . . . Your sweet "deposit" on your house . . .

JOHN: Don't you have feelings?

CAROL: That's my point. You see? Don't you have feelings? Your final argument. What is it that has no feelings. *Animals.* I don't take your side, you question if I'm Human.

JOHN: Don't you have feelings?

CAROL: I have a responsibility. I . . .

JOHN: . . . to . . . ?

CAROL: To? This institution. To the *students.* To my *group.*

JOHN: . . . your "group." . . .

CAROL: Because I speak, yes, not for myself. But for the group; for those who suffer what I suffer. On behalf of whom, even if I, were, inclined, to what, forgive? Forget? What? Overlook your . . .

JOHN: . . . my behavior?

CAROL: . . . it would be wrong.

JOHN: Even if you were inclined to "forgive" me.

CAROL: It would be wrong.

JOHN: And what would transpire.

CAROL: Transpire?

JOHN: Yes.

CAROL: "Happen?"

JOHN: Yes.

CAROL: Then *say* it. For Christ's sake. Who the *hell* do you think that you are? You want a post. You want unlimited power. To do and to say what you want. As it pleases you—Testing, Questioning, Flirting . . .

JOHN: I never . . .

CAROL: Excuse me, one moment, will you?

(She reads from her notes.)

> The twelfth: "Have a good day, dear."
>
> The fifteenth: "Now, don't *you* look fetching . . . "
>
> April seventeenth: "If you girls would come over here . . . " I saw you. I saw you, Professor. For two semesters sit there, stand there and exploit our, as you thought, "paternal prerogative," and what is that but rape, I swear to God. You asked me in here to explain something to me, as a child, that I did not understand. But I came to explain something to you. You Are Not God. You ask me why I came? I came here to instruct you.

(She produces his book.)

And your book? You think you're going to show me some "light"? You "*maverick*." Outside of tradition. No, no, *(She reads from the book's liner notes.)* "*of* that fine tradition of *inquiry.* Of Polite *skepticism*" . . . and you say you believe in free intellectual discourse. YOU BELIEVE IN NOTHING. YOU BELIEVE IN NOTHING AT ALL.

JOHN: I believe in freedom of thought.

CAROL: Isn't that fine. *Do* you?

JOHN: Yes. I do.

CAROL: Then why do you question, for one moment, the committee's decision refusing your tenure? Why do you question your suspension? You believe in what *you call* freedom of thought. Then, fine. *You* believe in freedom-of-thought *and* a home, and, *and* prerogatives for your kid, *and* tenure. And I'm going to tell you. You believe *not* in "freedom of thought," but in an elitist in, in a protected hierarchy which rewards you. And for whom you are the clown. And you mock and exploit the system which pays your rent. You're wrong. I'm not wrong. You're wrong. You think that I'm full of hatred. I know what you think I am.

JOHN: Do you?

CAROL: You think I'm a, of course I do. You think I am a frightened, repressed, confused, I don't know, abandoned young thing of some doubtful sexuality, who
wants, power and revenge. *(Pause) Don't* you? *(Pause)*

JOHN: Yes. I do. *(Pause)*

CAROL: Isn't that better? And I feel that that is the first moment which you've
treated me with respect. For you told me the truth. *(Pause)* I did not come
here, as you are assured, to gloat. Why would I want to gloat? I've profited nothing from your, your, as you say, your "misfortune." I came here, as you did me
the honor to *ask* me here, I came here to *tell* you something.
(Pause) That I think . . . that I think you've been wrong. That I think you've
been terribly wrong. Do you hate me now? *(Pause)*

JOHN: Yes.

CAROL: Why do you hate me? Because you think me wrong? No. Because I have, you
think, *power* over you. Listen to me. Listen to me, Professor. *(Pause)* It is the
power that you hate. So deeply that, that any atmosphere of free discussion is
impossible. It's not "unlikely." It's *impossible.* Isn't it?

JOHN: Yes.

CAROL: *Isn't* it . . . ?

JOHN: Yes. I suppose.

CAROL: Now. The thing which you find so cruel is the self-same process of selection
I, and my group, go through *every day of our lives.* In admittance to school.
In our tests, in our class rankings. . . . Is it unfair? I can't tell you. But, if it is fair.
Or even if it is "unfortunate but necessary" for us, then, by God, so must it be
for you. *(Pause)* You write of your "responsibility to the young." Treat us with
respect, and that will *show* you your responsibility. You write that education is
just hazing. *(Pause)* But we worked to get to this school.
(Pause) And some of us. *(Pause)* Overcame prejudices. Economic, sexual,
you cannot begin to imagine. And endured humiliations I *pray* that you and
those you love never will encounter. *(Pause)* To gain admittance here. To
pursue that same dream of security *you* pursue. We, who, who are, at any
moment, in danger of being deprived of it. By . . .

JOHN: . . . by . . . ?

CAROL: By the administration. By the teachers. By *you.* By, say, one low grade, that
keeps us out of graduate school; by one, say, one capricious or inventive
answer on our parts, which, perhaps, you don't find amusing. Now you *know,*
do you see? What it is to be subject to that power. *(Pause)*

JOHN: I don't understand. *(Pause)*

CAROL: My charges are not trivial. You see that in the haste, I think, with which they
were accepted. A *joke* you have told, with a sexist tinge. The language you use,
a verbal or physical caress, yes, yes, I know, you say that it is meaningless. I
understand. I differ from you. To lay a hand on someone's shoulder.

JOHN: It was devoid of sexual content.

CAROL: I say it was not. I SAY IT WAS NOT. Don't you begin to *see* . . . ? Don't you begin to understand? IT'S NOT FOR YOU TO SAY.

JOHN: I take your point, and I see there is much good in what you refer to.

CAROL: . . . do you think so . . . ?

JOHN: . . . but, and this is not to say that I cannot change, in those things in which I am deficient . . . But, the . . .

CAROL: Do you hold yourself harmless from the charges of sexual exploitativeness . . . ? *(Pause)*

JOHN: Well, I . . . I . . . I . . . You know I, as I said, I . . . think I am not too old to *learn,* and I *can* learn, I . . .

CAROL: Do you hold yourself innocent of the charge of . . .

JOHN: . . . wait, wait, wait . . . All right, let's go back to . . .

CAROL: YOU FOOL. Who do you think I am? To come here and be taken in by a *smile.* You little yapping fool. You think I want "revenge." I don't want revenge. I WANT UNDERSTANDING.

JOHN: . . . *do* you?

CAROL: I do. *(Pause)*

JOHN: What's the use. It's over.

CAROL: Is it? What is?

JOHN: My job.

CAROL: Oh. Your job. That's what you want to talk about. *(Pause) (She starts to leave the room. She steps and turns back to him.)* All right. *(Pause)* What if it were possible that my Group withdraws its complaint. *(Pause)*

JOHN: What?

CAROL: That's right. *(Pause)*

JOHN: Why.

CAROL: Well, let's say as an act of friendship.

JOHN: An act of friendship.

CAROL: Yes. *(Pause)*

JOHN: In exchange for what.

CAROL: Yes. But I don't think, "exchange." Not "in exchange." For what do we derive from it? *(Pause)*

JOHN: "Derive."

CAROL: Yes.

JOHN: *(Pause)* Nothing. *(Pause)*

CAROL: That's right. We derive nothing. *(Pause)* Do you see that?

JOHN: Yes.

CAROL: That is a little word, Professor. "Yes." "I see that." But you will.

JOHN: And you might speak to the committee . . . ?

CAROL: To the committee?

JOHN: Yes.

CAROL: Well. Of course. That's on your mind. We might.

JOHN: "If" what?

CAROL: "Given" what. Perhaps. I think that that is more friendly.

JOHN: GIVEN WHAT?

CAROL: And, believe me, I understand your rage. It is not that I don't feel it. But I do not see that it is deserved, so I do not resent it. . . . All right. I have a list.

JOHN: . . . a list.

CAROL: Here is a list of books, which we . . .

JOHN: . . . a list of books . . . ?

CAROL: That's right. Which we find questionable.

JOHN: What?

CAROL: Is this so bizarre . . . ?

JOHN: I can't believe . . .

CAROL: It's not necessary you believe it.

JOHN: Academic freedom . . .

CAROL: Someone chooses the books. If you can choose them, others can. What are you, "God"?

JOHN: . . . no, no, the "dangerous." . . .

CAROL: You have an agenda, we have an agenda. I am not interested in your feelings or your motivation, but your actions. If you would like me to speak to the Tenure Committee, here is my list. You are a Free Person, you decide. *(Pause)*

JOHN: Give me the list. *(She does so. He reads.)*

CAROL: I think you'll find . . .

JOHN: I'm capable of reading it. Thank you.

CAROL: We have a number of *texts* we need re . . .

JOHN: I see that.

CAROL: We're amenable to . . .

JOHN: Aha. Well, let me look over the . . . *(He reads.)*

CAROL: I think that . . .

JOHN: LOOK. I'm reading your demands. All right?! *(He reads) (Pause)* You want to ban my book?

CAROL: We do not . . .

JOHN *(OF LIST):*   It says here . . .

CAROL: . . . We want it removed from inclusion as a representative example of the university.

JOHN: Get out of here.

CAROL: If you put aside the issues of personalities.

JOHN: Get the fuck out of my office.

CAROL: No, I think I would reconsider.

JOHN: . . . you think you can.

CAROL: We can and we *will.* Do you want our support? That is the only quest . . .

JOHN: . . . to ban my *book* . . . ?

CAROL: . . . that is correct . . .

JOHN: . . . this . . . this is a *university* . . . we . . .

CAROL: . . . and we have a statement . . . which we need you to . . . *(She hands him a sheet of paper.)*

JOHN: No, no. It's out of the question. I'm sorry, I don't know what I was thinking of. I want to tell you something. I'm a teacher. I am a teacher. Eh? It's my *name* on the door, and *I* teach the class, and that's what I do. I've got a book with my name on it. And my son will *see* that *book* someday. And I have a respon . . . No, I'm sorry I have a *responsibility* . . . to *myself*, to my *son*, to my *profession*. . . . I haven't been *home* for two days, do you know that? Thinking this out.

CAROL: . . . you haven't?

JOHN: I've been, no. If it's of interest to you. I've been in a *hotel. Thinking. (The phone starts ringing.) Thinking* . . .

CAROL: . . . you haven't been home?

JOHN: . . . *thinking*, do you see?

CAROL: Oh.

JOHN: And, and, I owe you a debt, I see that now. *(Pause)* You're *dangerous*, you're *wrong* and it's my *job* . . . to say no to you. That's my job. You are absolutely right. You want to ban my book? Go to *hell*, and they can do whatever they want to me.

CAROL: . . . you haven't been home in two days . . .

JOHN: I think I told you that.

CAROL: . . . you'd better get that phone. *(Pause)* I think that you should pick up the phone. *(Pause)*

John picks up the phone.

JOHN *(ON PHONE):*   Yes. *(Pause)* Yes. Wh . . . I. I. I had to be away. All ri . . . did they wor . . . did they worry ab . . . No. I'm all right, now, Jerry. I'm f . . . I got a little turned *around*, but I'm *sitting* here and . . . I've got it figured out. I'm fine. I'm fine don't worry about me. I got a little bit mixed up. But I am not sure that it's not a blessing. It cost me my job? Fine. Then the job was not worth having. Tell Grace that I'm coming home and everything is fff . . . *(Pause)* What? *(Pause)* *What? (Pause)* What do you *mean?* WHAT? Jerry . . .
Jerry. They . . . Who, who, what can they do . . . ? *(Pause)* NO. *(Pause)* NO. They can't do th . . . What do you mean? *(Pause)* But how . . . *(Pause)* She's, she's, she's *here* with me. To . . . Jerry. I don't underst . . . *(Pause) (He hangs up.) (To Carol:)* What does this mean?

CAROL: I thought you knew.

JOHN: What. *(Pause)* What does it mean. *(Pause)*

CAROL: You tried to rape me. *(Pause)* According to the law. *(Pause)*

JOHN: . . . what . . . ?

CAROL: You tried to rape me. I was leaving this office, you "pressed" yourself into me. You "pressed" your body into me.

JOHN: . . . I . . .

CAROL: My Group has told your lawyer that we may pursue criminal charges.

JOHN: . . . no . . .

CAROL: . . . under the statute. I am told. It was battery.

JOHN: . . . no . . .

CAROL: Yes. And attempted rape. That's right. *(Pause)*

JOHN: I think that you should go.

CAROL: Of course. I thought you knew.

JOHN: I have to talk to my lawyer.

CAROL: Yes. Perhaps you should. *(The phone rings again.) (Pause)*

JOHN: *(Picks up phone. Into phone:)* Hello? I . . . Hello . . . ? I . . . Yes, he just called. No . . . I. I can't talk to you now, Baby. *(To Carol:)* Get out.

CAROL: . . . your wife . . . ?

JOHN: . . . who it is is no concern of yours. Get out. *(To phone:)* No, no, it's going to be all right. I. I can't talk now, Baby. *(To Carol:)* Get out of here.

CAROL: I'm going.

JOHN: Good.

CAROL *(exiting):*   . . . and don't call your wife "baby."

JOHN: What?

CAROL: Don't call your wife baby. You heard what I said.

Carol starts to leave the room. John grabs her and begins to beat her.

JOHN: You vicious little bitch. You think you can come in here with your political correctness and destroy my life?

He knocks her to the floor.

After how I treated you . . . ? You should be . . . *Rape you* . . . ? Are you kidding me . . . ?

He picks up a chair, raises it above his head, and advances on her.

I wouldn't touch you with a ten-foot pole. You little *cunt* . . .

She cowers on the floor below him. Pause. He looks down at her. He lowers the chair. He moves to his desk, and arranges the papers on it. Pause. He looks over at her.

. . . well . . .

Pause. She looks at him.

CAROL: Yes. That's right.

(She looks away from him, and lowers her head. To herself:) . . . yes. That's right.

End

MAKING CONNECTIONS

1. Describe John and Carol. Did you find yourself favoring one or the other as the play progressed? Explain.

2. The entire play is set in John's office. Why? In what way is this setting important to the play?

3. At the beginning of both Act 2 and Act 3, time has passed, and we are presented with new and important information. Were you surprised or shocked by these revelations? Explain.
4. What is your reaction to the ending of the play? To the charge against John? To his physical attack of Carol?
5. Who do you think is right, John or Carol? Why?
6. What is the central idea or theme of this play? What does it mean?

MAKING AN ARGUMENT

1. Take a position in favor of (or against) John or Carol. Write an essay supporting your position. Cite the text of the play—and any other appropriate sources—to support your view.

JOHN MILLINGTON SYNGE [1871–1909]

Irish dramatist, poet, prose writer, and folklorist, J. M. Synge was a major contributor to the Irish Literary Revival and one of the cofounders of the Abbey Theatre. He is best known for two critically acclaimed plays, Riders to the Sea *(1905), and* The Playboy of the Western World *(1907), which caused riots in Dublin during its opening run at the Abbey Theatre. Although he came from a middle-class Protestant background, Synge's writings focused on the* lives of Catholic peasants on the Aran Islands off the west coast of Ireland—and their experience of a world dominated by a relentless struggle with the sea. Synge wrote four other notable plays during his brief, cancer-shortened, life. In the Shadow of the Glen *and* The Well of the Saints *were produced in 1905. Two other plays* Deirdre of the Sorrows *(1910) and* The Tinker's Wedding *(1912) were produced posthumously.*

RIDERS TO THE SEA

LIST OF CHARACTERS
MAURYA, *an old woman*
BARTLEY, *her son*
CATHLEEN, *her daughter*
NORA, *a younger daughter*
MEN *and* WOMEN

SCENE: *An island off the West of Ireland.*
Cottage kitchen, with nets, oil-skins, spinning-wheel, some new boards standing by the wall, etc. Cathleen, a girl of about twenty, finishes kneading cake, and puts it down in the pot-oven by the fire; then wipes her hands, and begins to spin at the wheel. Nora, a young girl puts her head in at the door.

NORA (*in a low voice*). Where is she?

CATHLEEN. She's lying down, God help her, and may be sleeping, if she's able.

Nora comes in softly, and takes a bundle from under her shawl.

CATHLEEN (*spinning the wheel rapidly*). What is it you have?

NORA. The young priest is after bringing them. It's a shirt and a plain stocking were got off a drowned man in Donegal.

Cathleen stops her wheel with a sudden movement, and leans out to listen.

NORA. We're to find out if it's Michael's they are, some time herself will be down looking by the sea.

CATHLEEN. How would they be Michael's, Nora? How would he go the length of that way to the far north?

NORA. The young priest says he's known the like of it. "If it's Michael's they are," says he, "you can tell herself he's got a clean burial by the grace of God, and if they're not his, let no one say a word about them, for she'll be getting her death," says he, "with crying and lamenting."

The door which Nora half-closed is blown open by a gust of wind.

CATHLEEN (*looking out anxiously*). Did you ask him would he stop Bartley going this day with the horses to the Galway fair?

NORA. "I won't stop him," says he, "but let you not be afraid. Herself does be saying prayers half through the night and the Almighty God won't leave her destitute," says he, "with no son living."

CATHLEEN. Is the sea bad by the white rocks, Nora?

NORA. Middling bad, God help us. There's a great roaring in the west, and it's worse it'll be getting when the tide's turned to the wind. (*She goes over to the table with the bundle.*) Shall I open it now?

CATHLEEN. Maybe she'd wake up on us, and come in before we'd done. (*Coming to the table.*) It's a long time we'll be, and the two of us crying.

NORA. (*goes to the inner door and listens*). She's moving about on the bed. She'll be coming in a minute.

CATHLEEN. Give me the ladder, and I'll put them up in the turf-loft, the way she won't know of them at all, and maybe when the tide turns she'll be going down to see would he be floating from the east.

They put the ladder against the gable of the chimney; Cathleen goes up a few steps and hides the bundle in the turf-loft. Maurya comes from the inner room.

MAURYA (*looking up at Cathleen and speaking querulously*). Isn't it turf enough you have for this day and evening?

CATHLEEN. There's a cake baking at the fire for a short space (*throwing down the turf*) and Bartley will want it when the tide turns if he goes to Connemara.

Nora picks up the turf and puts it round the pot-oven.

MAURYA (*sitting down on a stool at the fire*). He won't go this day with the wind rising from the south and west. He won't go this day, for the young priest will stop him surely.

NORA.   He'll not stop him, mother, and I heard Eamon Simon and Stephen Pheety
    and Colum Shawn saying he would go.

MAURYA.   Where is he itself?

NORA.   He went down to see would there be another boat sailing in the week, and
    I'm thinking it won't be long till he's here now, for the tide's turning at the
    green head, and the hooker's° tacking from the east.

CATHLEEN.   I hear some one passing the big stones.

NORA (*looking out*).   He's coming now, and he in a hurry.

BARTLEY (*comes in and looks round the room. Speaking sadly and quietly*).
    Where is the bit of new rope, Cathleen, was bought in Connemara?

CATHLEEN (*coming down*).   Give it to him, Nora; it's on a nail by the white boards. I
    hung it up this morning, for the pig with the black feet was eating it.

NORA (*giving him a rope*).   Is that it, Bartley?

MAURYA.   You'd do right to leave that rope, Bartley, hanging by the boards. (*Bartley
    takes the rope.*) It will be wanting in this place, I'm telling you, if Michael is
    washed up tomorrow morning, or the next morning, or any morning in the
    week, for it's a deep grave we'll make him by the grace of God.

BARTLEY (*beginning to work with the rope*).   I've no halter the way I can ride down on
    the mare, and I must go now quickly. This is the one boat going for two weeks or
    beyond it, and the fair will be a good fair for horses I heard them saying below.

MAURYA.   It's a hard thing they'll be saying below if the body is washed up and
    there's no man in it to make the coffin, and I after giving a big price for the
    finest white boards you'd find in Connemara.

She looks round at the boards.

BARTLEY.   How would it be washed up, and we after looking each day for nine days,
    and a strong wind blowing a while back from the west and south?

MAURYA.   If it wasn't found itself, that wind is raising the sea, and there was a star up
    against the moon, and it rising in the night. If it was a hundred horses, or a
    thousand horses you had itself, what is the price of a thousand horses against
    a son where there is one son only?

BARTLEY (*working at the halter, to Cathleen*).   Let you go down each day, and see
    the sheep aren't jumping in on the rye, and if the jobber comes you can sell
    the pig with the black feet if there is a good price going.

MAURYA.   How would the like of her get a good price for a pig?

BARTLEY (*to Cathleen*).   If the west wind holds with the last bit of the moon let you
    and Nora get up weed enough for another cock for the kelp:° It's hard set
    we'll be from this day with no one in it but one man to work.

MAURYA.   It's hard set we'll be surely the day you're drownd'd with the rest! What
    way will I live and the girls with me, and I an old woman looking for the grave?

*Bartley lays down the halter, takes off his old coat, and puts on a newer one of the
same flannel.*

hooker a small fishing boat   **kelp** seaweed

BARTLEY (*to Nora*).   Is she coming to the pier?

NORA (*looking out*).   She's passing the green head and letting fall her sails.

BARTLEY (*getting his purse and tobacco*).   I'll have half an hour to go down, and you'll see me coming again in two days, or in three days, or maybe in four days if the wind is bad.

MAURYA (*turning round to the fire, and putting her shawl over her head*).   Isn't it a hard and cruel man won't hear a word from an old woman, and she holding him from the sea?

CATHLEEN.   It's the life of a young man to be going on the sea, and who would listen to an old woman with one thing and she saying it over?

BARTLEY (*taking the halter*).   I must go now quickly. I'll ride down on the red mare, and the gray pony'll run behind me. . . . The blessing of God on you.

He goes out.

MAURYA (*crying out as he is in the door*).   He's gone now, God spare us, and we'll not see him again. He's gone now, and when the black night is falling I'll have no son left me in the world.

CATHLEEN.   Why wouldn't you give him your blessing and he looking round in the door? Isn't it sorrow enough is on every one in this house without your sending him out with an unlucky word behind him, and a hard word in his ear?

Maurya takes up the tongs and begins raking the fire aimlessly without looking round.

NORA (*turning towards her*).   You're taking away the turf from the cake

CATHLEEN (*crying out*).   The Son of God forgive us, Nora, we're after forgetting his bit of bread.

She comes over to the fire.

NORA   And it's destroyed he'll be going till dark night, and he after eating nothing since the sun went up.

CATHLEEN (*turning the cake out of the oven*).   It's destroyed he'll be, surely. There's no sense left on any person in a house where an old woman will be talking for ever.

Maurya sways herself on her stool.

CATHLEEN (*cutting off some of the bread and rolling it in a cloth; to Maurya*).   Let you go down now to the spring well and give him this and he passing. You'll see him then and the dark word will be broken, and you can say "God speed you," the way he'll be easy in his mind.

MAURYA (*taking the bread*).   Will I be in it as soon as himself?

CATHLEEN.   If you go now quickly.

MAURYA (*standing up unsteadily*).   It's hard set I am to walk.

CATHLEEN (*looking at her anxiously*).   Give her the stick, Nora, or maybe she'll slip on the big stones.

NORA.   What stick?

CATHLEEN.   The stick Michael brought from Connemara

MAURYA (*taking a stick Nora gives her*).   In the big world the old people do be leaving things after them for their son and children, but in this place it is the young men do be leaving things behind for them that do be old.

She goes out slowly. Nora goes over to the ladder.

CATHLEEN.   Wait, Nora, maybe she'd turn back quickly. She's that sorry, God help her, you wouldn't know the thing she'd do.

NORA.   Is she gone around by the bush?

CATHLEEN (*looking out*).   She's gone, now! Throw it down quickly, for the Lord knows when she'll be out of it again.

NORA (*getting the bundle from the loft*).   The young priest said he'd be passing tomorrow; and we might go down and speak to him below if it's Michael's they are surely.

CATHLEEN (*taking the bundle*).   Did he say what way they were found?

NORA (*coming down*).   "There were two men" says he, "and they rowing round with poteen° before the cocks crowed and the oar of one of them caught the body, and they passing the black cliffs of the north."

CATHLEEN (*trying to open the bundle*).   Give me a knife, Nora the strings perished with the salt water and there's a black knot on it you wouldn't loosen in a week.

NORA (*giving her a knife*).   I've heard tell it was a long way to Donegal.

CATHLEEN (*cutting the string*).   It is surely. There was a man in here a while ago— the man sold us that knife—and he said if you set off walking from the rock beyond, it would be seven days you'd be in Donegal.

NORA.   And what time would a man take, and he floating?

Cathleen opens the bundle and takes out a bit of a stocking. They look at them eagerly.

CATHLEEN (*in a low voice*).   The Lord spare us, Nora! isn't it a queer hard thing to say if it's his they are surely?

NORA.   I'll get his shirt off the hook the way we can put the one flannel on the other. (*She looks through some clothes hanging in the corner.*) It's not with them, Cathleen, and where will it be?

CATHLEEN.   I'm thinking Bartley put it on him in the morning, for his own shirt was heavy with the salt in it. (*Pointing to the corner.*) There's a bit of a sleeve was of the same stuff. Give me that and it will do.

Nora brings it to her and they compare the flannel.

CATHLEEN.   It's the same stuff, Nora; but if it is itself aren't there great rolls of it in the shops of Galway, and isn't it many another man may have a shirt of it as well as Michael himself?

NORA   (*who has taken up the stocking and counted the stitches, crying out*). It's Michael, Cathleen, it's Michael; God spare his soul, and what will herself say when she hears this story, and Bartley on the sea?

poteen whiskey

CATHLEEN   (*taking the stocking*). It's a plain stocking.

NORA   It's the second one of the third pair I knitted, and I put up three score stitches, and I dropped four of them.

CATHLEEN   (*counts the stitches*). It's that number is in it. (*Crying out.*) Ah, Nora, isn't it a bitter thing to think of him floating that way to the far north, and no one to keen° him but the black hags that do be flying on the sea?

NORA   (*swinging herself round, and throwing out her arms on the clothes*). And isn't it a pitiful thing when there is nothing left of a man who was a great rower and fisher, but a bit of an old shirt and a plain stocking?

CATHLEEN   (*after an instant*). Tell me is herself coming, Nora? I hear a little sound on the path.

NORA   (*looking out*). She is, Cathleen. She's coming up to the door.

CATHLEEN.   Put these things away before she'll come in. Maybe it's easier she'll be after giving her blessing to Bartley, and we won't let on we've heard anything the time he's on the sea.

NORA   (*helping Cathleen to close the bundle*). We'll put them here in the corner.

They put them into a hole in the chimney corner. Cathleen goes back to the spinning-wheel.

NORA.   Will she see it was crying I was?

CATHLEEN.   Keep your back to the door the way the light'll not be on you.

Nora sits down at the chimney corner, with her back to the door. Maurya comes in very slowly, without looking at the girls, and goes over to her stool at the other side of the fire. The cloth with the bread is still in her hand. The girls look at each other, and Nora points to the bundle of bread.

CATHLEEN   (*after spinning for a moment*). You didn't give him his bit of bread?

Maurya begins to keen softly, without turning round.

CATHLEEN.   Did you see him riding down?

Maurya goes on keening.

CATHLEEN   (*a little impatiently*). God forgive you; isn't it a better thing to raise your voice and tell what you seen, than to be making lamentation for a thing that's done? Did you see Bartley, I'm saying to you.

MAURYA   (*with a weak voice*). My heart's broken from this day.

CATHLEEN   (*as before*). Did you see Bartley?

MAURYA   I seen the fearfulest thing.

CATHLEEN   (*leaves her wheel and looks out*). God forgive you; he's riding the mare now over the green head, and the gray pony behind him.

MAURYA   (*starts, so that her shawl falls back from her head and shows her white tossed hair. With a frightened voice*). The gray pony behind him.

CATHLEEN   (*coming to the fire*). What is it ails you, at all?

Keen a mournful weeping and wailing

MAURYA   (*speaking very slowly*). I've seen the fearfulest thing any person has seen, since the day Bride Dara seen the dead man with the child in his arms.

CATHLEEN AND NORA.   Uah.

They crouch down in front of the old woman at the fire.

NORA.   Tell us what it is you seen.

MAURYA.   I went down to the spring well, and I stood there saying a prayer to myself. Then Bartley came along, and he riding on the red mare with the gray pony behind him. (*She puts up her hands, as if to hide something from her eyes.*) The Son of God spare us, Nora!

CATHLEEN.   What is it you seen?

MAURYA.   I seen Michael himself.

CATHLEEN   (*speaking softly*). You did not, mother, it wasn't Michael you seen, for his body is after being found in the far north, and he's got a clean burial by the grace of God.

MAURYA   (*a little defiantly*). I'm after seeing him this day, and he riding and galloping. Bartley came first on the red mare; and I tried to say "God speed you," but something choked the words in my throat. He went by quickly; and "the blessing of God on you," says he, and I could say nothing. I looked up then, and I crying, at the gray pony, and there was Michael upon it—with fine clothes on him, and new shoes on his feet.

CATHLEEN   (*begins to keen*). It's destroyed we are from this day. It's destroyed, surely.

NORA.   Didn't the young priest say the Almighty God wouldn't leave her destitute with no son living?

MAURYA   (*in a low voice, but clearly*). It's little the like of him knows of the sea. . . . Bartley will be lost now, and let you call in Eamon and make me a good coffin out of the white boards, for I won't live after them. I've had a husband, and a husband's father, and six sons in this house—six fine men, though it was a hard birth I had with every one of them and they coming to the world—and some of them were found and some of them were not found, but they're gone now the lot of them. . . . There were Stephen and Shawn were lost in the great wind, and found after in the Bay of Gregory of the Golden Mouth, and carried up the two of them on the one plank, and in by that door.

She pauses for a moment, the girls start as if they heard something through the door that is half open behind them.

NORA   (in a whisper). Did you hear that, Cathleen? Did you hear a noise in the northeast?

CATHLEEN   (*in a whisper*). There's someone after crying out by the seashore.

MAURYA (*continues without hearing anything*).   There was Sheamus and his father, and his own father again, were lost in a dark night, and not a stick or sign was seen of them when the sun went up. There was Patch after was drowned out of a curagh° that turned over. I was sitting here with Bartley, and he a baby, lying on my two knees, and I seen two women, and three women, and four women coming in, and they crossing themselves, and not saying a word. I looked out then, and there were men coming after them, and they holding a thing in the half of a red sail, and water dripping out of it—it was a dry day, Nora—and leaving a track to the door.

She pauses again with her hand stretched out towards the door. It opens softly and old women begin to come in, crossing themselves on the threshold, and kneeling down in front of the stage with red petticoats over their heads.

MAURYA (*half in a dream, to Cathleen*).   Is it Patch, or Michael, or what is it at all?

CATHLEEN.   Michael is after being found in the far north, and when he is found there how could he be here in this place?

MAURYA.   There does be a power of young men floating round in the sea, and what way would they know if it was Michael they had, or another man like him, for when a man is nine days in the sea, and the wind blowing, it's hard set his own mother would be to say what man was in it.

CATHLEEN.   It's Michael, God spare him, for they're after sending us a bit of his clothes from the far north.

She reaches out and hands Maurya the clothes that belonged to Michael. Maurya stands up slowly and takes them in her hand. Nora looks out.

NORA.   They're carrying a thing among them and there's water dripping out of it and leaving a track by the big stones.

CATHLEEN (*in a whisper to the women who have come in*).   Is it Bartley it is?

ONE OF THE WOMEN.   It is surely, God rest his soul.

Two younger women come in and pull out the table. Then men carry in the body of Bartley, laid on a plank, with a bit of sail over it, and lay it on the table.

CATHLEEN (*to the women, as they are doing so*).   What way was he drowned?

ONE OF THE WOMEN.   The gray pony knocked him into the sea, and he was washed out where there is a great surf on the white rocks.

Maurya has gone over and knelt down at the head of the table. The women are keening softly and swaying themselves with a slow movement. Cathleen and Nora kneel at the other end of the table. The men kneel near the door.

MAURYA (*raising her head and speaking as if she did not see the people around her*).   They're all gone now, and there isn't anything more the sea can do to me. . . . I'll have no call now to be up crying and praying when the wind breaks from the south, and you can hear the surf is in the east and the surf is in the west, making a great stir with the two noises, and they hitting one on the other. I'll have no call now to be going down and getting Holy Water in the

curagh a canoe-like canvass-bottomed boat

dark nights after Samhain,° and I won't care what way the sea is when the other women will be keening (*To Nora.*) Give me the Holy Water, Nora, there is a small cup still on the dresser.

Nora gives it to her.

MAURYA (*drops Michael's clothes across Bartley's feet and sprinkles the Holy Water over him*).   It isn't that I haven't prayed for you, Bartley, to the Almighty God. It isn't that I haven't said prayers in the dark night till you wouldn't know what I'ld be saying; but it's a great rest I'll have now, and it's time surely. It's a great rest I'll have now, and great sleeping in the long nights after Samhain, if it's only a bit of wet flour we do have to eat, and maybe a fish that would be stinking.

She kneels down again, crossing herself, and saying prayers under her breath.

CATHLEEN (*to an old man*).   Maybe yourself and Eamon would make a coffin when the sun rises. We have fine white boards herself bought, God help her, thinking Michael would be found, and I have a new cake you can eat while you'll be working.

THE OLD MAN (*looking at the boards*).   Are there nails with them?

CATHLEEN.   There are not, Colum; we didn't think of the nails.

ANOTHER MAN.   It's a great wonder she wouldn't think of the nails, and all the coffins she's seen made already.

CATHLEEN.   It's getting old she is, and broken.

Maurya stands up again very slowly and spreads out the pieces of Michael's clothes beside the body, sprinkling them with the last of the Holy Water.

NORA (*in a whisper to Cathleen*).   She's quiet now and easy but the day Michael was drowned you could hear her crying out from this to the spring well. It's fonder she was of Michael, and would any one have thought that?

CATHLEEN (*slowly and clearly*).   An old woman will be soon tired with anything she will do, and isn't it nine days herself is after crying and keening, and making great sorrow in the house?

MAURYA (*puts the empty cup mouth downwards on the table and lays her hands together on Bartley's feet*).   They're all together this time, and the end is come. May the Almighty God have mercy on Bartley's soul, and on Michael's soul, and on the souls of Sheamus and Patch, and Stephen and Shawn (*bending her head*); and may He have mercy on my soul, Nora, and on the soul of every one is left living in the world.

She pauses, and the keen rises a little more loudly from the women, then sinks away.

MAURYA   (*continuing*). Michael has a clean burial in the far north, by the grace of the Almighty God. Bartley will have a fine coffin out of the white boards, and a deep grave surely. What more can we want than that? No man at all can be living for ever, and we must be satisfied.

She kneels down again and the curtain falls slowly.

Samhain All Saints' Day, November 1st

MAKING CONNECTIONS

1. Discuss the impact of the setting on conflict and characterization in this play.
2. Maurya says, "In the big world the old people be leaving things after them for their sons and children, but in this place it is the young men do be leaving things behind for them that be old." What does she mean? What difference does it make to the culture of these people?
3. Synge wrote the dialogue in this play to conform to the speech patterns of the people of the Aran islands. Do you think it is effective or do you think it would be just as effective to have them speak standard English—and be understood more easily? Explain.
4. Compare and contrast this play with Stephen Crane's poem "A Man Said to the Universe" on page 1225 or Thomas Hardy's "Hap" on page 1232.

MAKING AN ARGUMENT

1. At the end of the play, Maurya comments on the death and "clean" burial of her only remaining sons: "What more can we want than that. No man at all can be living for ever, and we must be satisfied." Do you agree? Write an essay that takes a position for or against her opinion. Cite the text of the play and (if appropriate) other sources to support your view.

◆ ESSAYS ◆

DAN BARRY [B. 1958]

Dan Barry has been writing the "About New York" column for the New York Times *since 2003. He shared a Pulitzer Prize in 1994 for investigative reporting, and was awarded the 2003 American Society of Newspaper Editors Award for deadline reporting, and the 2005 Berger Award from the Columbia University Graduate School of Journalism. He was a major contributor to the newspaper's award-winning coverage of the World Trade Center disaster and its aftermath, and the coverage of New Orleans and the Gulf Coast in the wake of Hurricane Katrina—from which the article below is taken. He has written a memoir,* Pull Me Up, *which was published in 2004.*

HURRICANE KATRINA: THE CORPSE ON UNION STREET   [2005]

NEW ORLEANS, Sept. 7—In the downtown business district here, on a dry stretch of Union Street, past the Omni Bank automated teller machine, across from a parking garage offering "early bird" rates: a corpse. Its feet jut from a damp blue tarp. Its knees rise in rigor mortis.

Six National Guardsmen walked up to it on Tuesday afternoon and two blessed themselves with the sign of the cross. One soldier took a parting snapshot like some visiting conventioneer, and they walked away. New Orleans, September 2005.

Hours passed, the dusk of curfew crept, the body remained. A Louisiana state trooper around the corner knew all about it: murder victim, bludgeoned, one of several in that area. The police marked it with traffic cones maybe four days ago, he said, and then he joked that if you wanted to kill someone here, this was a good time.

Night came, then this morning, then noon, and another sun beat down on a dead son of the Crescent City.

That a corpse lies on Union Street may not shock; in the wake of last week's hurricane, there are surely hundreds, probably thousands. What is remarkable is that on a downtown street in a major American city, a corpse can decompose for days, like carrion, and that is acceptable.

Welcome to New Orleans in the post-apocalypse, half baked and half deluged: pestilent, eerie, unnaturally quiet.

Scraggly residents emerge from waterlogged wood to say strange things, and then return into the rot. Cars drive the wrong way on the interstate and no one cares. Fires burn, dogs scavenge, and old signs from les bons temps have been replaced with hand-scrawled threats that looters will be shot dead.

The incomprehensible has become so routine here that it tends to lull you into acceptance. On Sunday, for example, several soldiers on Jefferson Highway had guns aimed at the heads of several prostrate men suspected of breaking into an electronics store.

A car pulled right up to this tense scene and the driver leaned out his window to ask a soldier a question:

"Hey, how do you get to the interstate?"

Maybe the slow acquiescence to the ghastly here—not in Baghdad, not, in Rwanda, here—is rooted in the intensive news coverage of the hurricane's aftermath: floating bodies and obliterated towns equal old news. Maybe the concerns of the living far outweigh the dignity of a corpse on Union Street. Or maybe the nation is numb with post-traumatic shock.

Wandering New Orleans this week, away from news conferences and search-and-rescue squads, has granted haunting glimpses of the past, present and future, with the rare comfort found in, say, the white sheet that flaps, not in surrender but as a vow, at the corner of Poydras Street and St. Charles Avenue.

"We Shall Survive," it says, as though wishing past the battalions of bulldozers that will one day come to knock down water-corrupted neighborhoods and rearrange the Louisiana mud for the infrastructure of an altogether different New Orleans.

Here, then, the New Orleans of today, where open fire hydrants gush the last thing needed on these streets; where one of the many gag-inducing smells—that of rancid meat—is better than MapQuest in pinpointing the presence of a market; and where images of irony beg to be noticed.

The Mardi Gras beads imbedded in mud by a soldier's boot print. The "takeaway" signs outside restaurants taken away. The corner kiosk shouting the Aug. 28 headline of New Orleans's Times-Picayune: "Katrina Takes Aim."

Rush hour in downtown now means pickups carrying gun-carrying men in sunglasses, S.U.V.'s loaded with out-of-town reporters hungry for action, and the occasional tank. About the only ones commuting by bus are dull-eyed suspects shuffling two-by-two from the bus-and-train terminal, which is now a makeshift jail.

Maybe some of them had helped to kick in the portal to the Williams Super Market in the once-desirable Garden District. And who could blame them if all they wanted was food in those first desperate days? The interlopers took the water, beer, cigarettes and snack food. They did not take the wine or the New Orleans postcards.

On the other side of downtown across Canal Street in the French Quarter, the most raucous and most unreal of American avenues is now little more than an empty alley with balconies.

The absence of sweetly blown jazz, of someone cooing "ma chère," of men sporting convention nametags and emitting forced guffaws—the absence of us— assaults the senses more than any smell.

Past the famous Cafe du Monde, where a slight breeze twirls the over-head fans for no one, past the statue of Joan of Arc gleaming gold, a man emerges from nothing on Royal Street. He is asked, "Where's St. Bernard Avenue?"

"Where's the ice?" he asks in return, eyes narrowed in menace. "Where's the ice? St. Bernard's is that way, but where's the ice?"

In Bywater and the surrounding neighborhoods, the severely damaged streets bear the names of saints who could not protect them. Whatever nature spared, human nature stepped up to provide a kind of democracy in destruction.

At the Whitney National Bank on St. Claude Avenue, diamond-like bits of glass spill from the crushed door, offering a view of the complementary coffee table. A large woman named Phoebe Au—"Pronounced 'Awe,' " she says—materializes to report that men had smashed it in with a truck. She fades into the neighborhood's broken brick, and a thin woman named Toni Miller materializes to correct the record.

"They used sledgehammers," she said.

Farther down St. Claude Avenue, where tanks rumble past a smoldering building, the roads are cluttered with vandalized city buses. The city parked them on the riverbank for the hurricane, after which some hoods took them for fare-free joy rides through lawless streets, and then discarded them.

On Clouet Street, where a days old fire continues to burn where a warehouse once stood, a man on a bicycle wheels up through the smoke to introduce himself as Strangebone. The nights without power or water have been tough, especially since the police took away the gun he was carrying—"They beat me and threatened to kill me," he says—but there are benefits to this new world.

"You're able to see the stars," he says. "It's wonderful."

Today, law enforcement troops began lending muscle to Mayor C. Ray Nagin's vow to evacuate by force any residents too attached to their pieces of the toxic metropolis. They searched the streets for the likes of Strangebone, and that woman who's name sounds like Awe.

Meanwhile, back downtown, the shadows of another evening crept like spilled black water over someone's corpse.

MAKING CONNECTIONS

1. To what extent is the corpse a symbol of the aftermath of the hurricane?
2. This article is not simply reporting the news, it's commenting on it. Beyond the hurricane, what is the purpose of the article? What is it saying?

MAKING AN ARGUMENT

1. Write an essay that compares the impact of a natural disaster like Hurricane Katrina with war or a terrorist attack. Is it any easier to reconcile the loss of life? Is it harder? Cite the text of this article—and/or any other sources—to support your view.

ALBERT CAMUS [1913–1960]

French philosopher, novelist, dramatist, and journalist Albert Camus was born and raised in Algeria. Though his family was not particularly well educated, Camus was an excellent student throughout his youth, graduating with honors from the University of Algiers in 1936. At the outbreak of World War II, he worked as a reporter first in Algeria and then in France. His greatest works, which are often characterized as "absurdist," were written during this period and include the novel The Stranger, *the essay "The Myth of Sisyphus," and the play* Caligula. *During the German occupation of France, Camus, together with his friend the existentialist philosopher Jean-Paul Sartre, became one of the intellectual leaders of the French resistance, working late at night on the newspaper* Combat, *which went on to became one of France's most important post war newspapers. Following the war, the now-famous Camus turned away from journalism, and concentrated on writing novels and plays. Although he was often called a philosopher or existentialist, Camus rejected all labels, defining himself simply as "a man with a passion for the human heart." He was awarded the Nobel Prize for literature in 1957. In 1960, he was killed in a car accident in the south of France.*

THE MYTH OF SISYPHUS

The gods had condemned Sisyphus to ceaselessly rolling a rock to the top of a mountain, whence the stone would fall back of its own weight. They had thought with some reason that there is no more dreadful punishment than futile and hopeless labor.

If one believes Homer, Sisyphus was the wisest and most prudent of mortals. According to another tradition, however, he was disposed to practice the profession of highwayman. I see no contradiction in this. Opinions differ as to the reasons why he became the futile laborer of the underworld. To begin with, he is accused of a certain levity in regard to the gods. He stole their secrets. Aegina, the daughter of Aesopus, was carried off by Jupiter. The father was shocked by that disappearance and complained to Sisyphus. He, who knew of the abduction, offered to tell about it on condition that Aesopus would give water to the citadel of Corinth. To the celestial thunderbolts he preferred the benediction of water. He was punished for this in the underworld. Homer tells us also that Sisyphus had put Death in chains. Pluto could not endure the sight of his deserted, silent empire. He dispatched the god of war, who liberated Death from the hands of her conqueror.

It is said also that Sisyphus, being near to death, rashly wanted to test his wife's love. He ordered her to cast his unburied body into the middle of the public square. Sisyphus woke up in the underworld. And there, annoyed by an obedience so contrary to human love, he obtained from Pluto permission to return to earth in order to chastise his wife. But when he had seen again the face of this world, enjoyed water and sun, warm stones and the sea, he no longer wanted to go back to the infernal darkness. Recalls, signs of anger, warnings were of no avail. Many years more he lived facing the curve of the gulf, the sparkling sea, and the smiles of earth. A decree of the gods was necessary. Mercury came and seized the impudent man by the collar and, snatching him from his joys, led him forcibly back to the underworld, where his rock was ready for him.

You have already grasped that Sisyphus is the absurd hero. He *is,* as much through his passions as through his torture. His scorn of the gods, his hatred of death, and his passion for life won him that unspeakable penalty in which the whole being is exerted toward accomplishing nothing. This is the price that must be paid for the passions of this earth. Nothing is told us about Sisyphus in the underworld. Myths are made for the imagination to breathe life into them. As for this myth, one sees merely the whole effort of a body straining to raise the huge stone, to roll it and push it up a slope a hundred times over; one sees the face screwed up, the cheek tight against the stone, the shoulder bracing the clay-covered mass, the foot wedging it, the fresh start with arms outstretched, the wholly human security of two earth-clotted hands. At the very end of his long effort measured by skyless space and time without depth, the purpose is achieved. Then Sisyphus watches the stone rush down in a few moments toward that lower world whence he will have to push it up again toward the summit. He goes back down to the plain.

5   It is during that return, that pause, that Sisyphus interests me. A face that toils so close to stones is already stone itself! I see that man going back down with a heavy yet measured step toward the torment of which he will never know the end. That hour like a breathing-space which returns as surely as his suffering, that is the hour of consciousness. At each of those moments when he leaves the heights and gradually sinks toward the lairs of the gods, he is superior to his fate. He is stronger than his rock.

If this myth is tragic, that is because its hero is conscious. Where would his torture be, indeed, if at every step the hope of succeeding upheld him? The workman of today works every day in his life at the same tasks, and his fate is no less absurd. But it is tragic only at the rare moments when it becomes conscious. Sisyphus, proletarian of the gods, powerless and rebellious, knows the whole extent of his wretched condition; it is what he thinks of during his descent. The lucidity that was to constitute his torture at the same time crowns his victory. There is no fate that cannot be surmounted by scorn.

If the descent is thus sometimes performed in sorrow, it can also take place in joy. This word is not too much. Again I fancy Sisyphus returning toward his rock, and the sorrow was in the beginning. When the images of earth cling too tightly to memory, when the call of happiness becomes too insistent, it happens that melancholy rises in man's heart: this is the rock's victory, this is the rock itself. The boundless grief is too heavy to bear. These are our nights of Gethsemane. But crushing truths perish from being acknowledged. Thus, Oedipus at the outset obeys fate without knowing it. But from the moment he knows, his tragedy begins. Yet at the same moment, blind and desperate, he realizes that the only bond linking him to the world is the cool hand of a girl. Then a tremendous remark rings out: "Despite so many ordeals, my advanced age and the nobility of my soul make me conclude that all is well." Sophocles' Oedipus, like Dostoevsky's Kirilov, thus gives the recipe for the absurd victory. Ancient wisdom confirms modern heroism.

One does not discover the absurd without being tempted to write a manual of happiness. "What! by such narrow ways—?" There is but one world, however. Happiness and the absurd are two sons of the same earth. They are inseparable. It would be a mistake to say that happiness necessarily springs from the absurd discovery. It happens as well that the feeling of the absurd springs from happiness. "I conclude that all is well," says Oedipus, and that remark is sacred. It echoes in the wild and limited universe of man. It teaches that all is not, has not been, exhausted. It drives out of this world a god who had come into it with dissatisfaction and a preference for futile sufferings. It makes of fate a human matter, which must be settled among men.

All Sisyphus' silent joy is contained therein. His fate belongs to him. His rock is his thing. Likewise, the absurd man, when he contemplates his torment, silences all the idols. In the universe suddenly restored to its silence, the myriad wondering little voices of the earth rise up. Unconscious, secret calls, invitations from all the faces, they are the necessary reverse and price of victory. There is no sun without shadow, and it is essential to know the night. The absurd man says yes and his effort will henceforth be unceasing. If there is a personal fate, there is no higher destiny, or at least there is but one which he concludes is inevitable and despicable. For the rest, he knows himself to be the master of his days. At that subtle moment when man glances backward over his life, Sisyphus returning toward his rock, in that slight pivoting he contemplates that series of unrelated actions which becomes his fate, created by him, combined under his memory's eye and soon sealed by his death. Thus, convinced of the wholly human origin of all that is human, a blind man eager to see who knows that the night has no end, he is still on the go. The rock is still rolling.

10   I leave Sisyphus at the foot of the mountain! One always finds one's burden again. But Sisyphus teaches the higher fidelity that negates the gods and raises rocks. He too concludes that all is well. This universe henceforth without a master seems to him neither sterile nor futile. Each atom of that stone, each mineral flake of that night-filled mountain, in itself forms a world. The struggle itself toward the heights is enough to fill a man's heart. One must imagine Sisyphus happy.

MAKING CONNECTIONS

1. Sisyphus is condemned to roll the rock to the top of the hill, but never complete his task. Why is this such a terrible punishment?
2. Camus says, "The workman of today works every day in his life at the same tasks, and his fate is no less absurd [than that of Sisyphus]." What does he mean? Do you agree? Explain.

MAKING AN ARGUMENT

1. In the opening quotes for this theme, Thoreau is quoted as writing, "The mass of men [and women] lead lives of quiet desperation." How is Camus suggesting we should lead our lives? Is it a solution to the "quiet desperation" that Thoreau suggests we suffer from? Write an essay that interprets what Camus is suggesting and agree or disagree with his premise. Cite the text of the essay for support.

PLATO [427–347 B.C.]

The philosopher Plato was born in Athens and founded a school called the Academy there circa 387 B.C. He presided over this Academy, an institution devoted to research and instruction in philosophy and the sciences, until his death. During this time he wrote approximately thirty dialogues. Though Plato himself is not named as a participant, his own teacher, Socrates, is the "I" in these dialogues and moves the discussion along with a series of well-aimed leading questions. It is through these dialogues that Plato presented his own theories on a variety of subjects. The "Allegory of the Cave" that follows is taken from those dialogues.

THE ALLEGORY OF THE CAVE

And now, I said, let me show in a figure how far our nature is enlightened or unenlightened;—Behold! human beings living in an underground den, which has a mouth open towards the light and reaching all along the den; here they have been from their childhood, and have their legs and necks chained so that they cannot move, and can only see before them, being prevented by the chains from turning round their heads. Above and behind them a fire is blazing at a distance, and between the fire and the prisoners there is a raised way; and you will see, if you look, a low wall built along the way, like the screen which marionette players have in front of them, over which they show the puppets.

I see.

And do you see, I said, men passing along the wall carrying all sorts of vessels, and statues and figures of animals made of wood and stone and various materials, which appear over the wall? Some of them are talking, others silent.

You have shown me a strange image, and they are strange prisoners.

5   Like ourselves, I replied; and they see only their own shadows, or the shadows
of one another, which the fire throws on the opposite wall of the cave?

True, he said; how could they see anything but the shadows if they were never
allowed to move their heads?

And of the objects which are being carried in like manner they would only see
the shadows?

Yes, he said.

And if they were able to converse with one another, would they not suppose
that they were naming what was actually before them?

10   Very true.

And suppose further that the prison had an echo which came from the other
side, would they not be sure to fancy when one of the passers-by spoke that the
voice which they heard came from the passing shadow?

No question, he replied.

To them, I said, the truth would be literally nothing but the shadows of the images.

That is certain.

15   And now look again, and see what will naturally follow if the prisoners are
released and disabused of their error. At first, when any of them is liberated and compelled suddenly to stand up and turn his neck round and walk and look towards the
light, he will suffer sharp pains; the glare will distress him, and he will be unable to
see the realities of which in his former state he had seen the shadows; and then conceive some one saying to him, that what he saw before was an illusion, but that now,
when he is approaching nearer to being and his eye is turned towards more real
existence, he has a clearer vision—what will be his reply? And you may further imagine that his instructor is pointing to the objects as they pass and requiring him to
name them,—will he not be perplexed? Will he not fancy that the shadows which
he formerly saw are truer than the objects which are now shown to him?

Far truer.

And if he is compelled to look straight at the light, will he not have a pain in his
eyes which will make him turn away to take refuge in the objects of vision which he
can see, and which he will conceive to be in reality clearer than the things which are
now being shown to him?

True, he said.

And suppose once more, that he is reluctantly dragged up a steep and rugged
ascent, and held fast until he is forced into the presence of the sun himself, is he not
likely to be pained and irritated? When he approaches the light his eyes will be dazzled, and he will not be able to see anything at all of what are now called realities.

20   Not all in a moment, he said.

He will require to grow accustomed to the sight of the upper world. And first
he will see the shadows best, next the reflections of men and other objects in the
water, and then the objects themselves; then he will gaze upon the light of the
moon and the stars and the spangled heaven; and he will see the sky and the stars
by night better than the sun or the light of the sun by day?

Certainly.

Last of all he will be able to see the sun, and not mere reflections of him in the
water, but he will see him in his own proper place, and not in another; and he will
contemplate him as he is.

Certainly.

25   He will then proceed to argue that this is he who gives the season and the years, and is the guardian of all that is in the visible world, and in a certain way the cause of all things which he and his fellows have been accustomed to behold?

Clearly, he said, he would first see the sun and then reason about him.

And when he remembered his old habitation, and the wisdom of the den and his fellow prisoners, do you not suppose that he would felicitate himself on the change, and pity them?

Certainly, he would.

And if they were in the habit of conferring honors among themselves on those who were quickest to observe the passing shadows and to remark which of them went before, and which followed after, and which were together; and who were therefore best able to draw conclusions as to the future, do you think that he would care for such honors and glories, or envy the possessors of them? Would he not say with Homer,

> Better to be the poor servant of a poor master,

and to endure anything, rather than think as they do and live after their manner?

30   Yes, he said, I think that he would rather suffer anything than entertain these false notions and live in this miserable manner.

Imagine once more, I said, such a one coming suddenly out of the sun to be replaced in his old situation; would he not be certain to have his eyes full of darkness?

To be sure, he said.

And if there were a contest, and he had to compete in measuring the shadows with the prisoners who had never moved out of the den, while his sight was still weak, and before his eyes had become steady (and the time which would be needed to acquire this new habit of sight might be very considerable), would he not be ridiculous? Men would say of him that up he went and down he came without his eyes; and that it was better not even to think of ascending; and if any one tried to loose another and lead him up to the light, let them only catch the offender, and they would put him to death.

No question, he said.

35   This entire allegory, I said, you may now append, dear Glaucon, to the previous argument; the prison house is the world of sight, the light of the fire is the sun, and you will not misapprehend me if you interpret the journey upwards to be the ascent of the soul into the intellectual world according to my poor belief, which, at your desire, I have expressed—whether rightly or wrongly God knows. But, whether true or false, my opinion is that in the world of knowledge the idea of good appears last of all, and is seen only with an effort; and, when seen, is also inferred to be the universal author of all things beautiful and right, parent of light and of the lord of light in this visible world, and the immediate source of reason and truth in the intellectual; and that this is the power upon which he who would act rationally either in public or private life must have his eye fixed.

I agree, he said, as far as I am able to understand you.

Moreover, I said, you must not wonder that those who attain to this beatific vision are unwilling to descend to human affairs; for their souls are ever hastening into the upper world where they desire to dwell; which desire of theirs is very natural, if our allegory may be trusted.

Yes, very natural.

And is there anything surprising in one who passes from divine contemplations to the evil state of man, misbehaving himself in a ridiculous manner, if, while his eyes are blinking and before he has become accustomed to the surrounding darkness, he is compelled to fight in courts of law, or in other places, about the images or the shadows of images of justice, and is endeavoring to meet the conceptions of those who have never yet seen absolute justice?

40   Anything but surprising, he replied.

Anyone who has common sense will remember that the bewilderments of the eyes are two kinds, and arise from two causes, either from coming out of the light or from going into the light, which is true of the mind's eye, quite as much as of the bodily eye; and he who remembers this when he sees anyone whose vision is perplexed and weak, will not be too ready to laugh; he will first ask whether that soul of man has come out of the brighter life, and is unable to see because unaccustomed to the dark, or having turned from darkness to the day is dazzled by excess of light. And he will count the one happy in his condition and state of being, and he will pity the other; or, if he have a mind to laugh at the soul which comes from below into the light, there will be more reason in this than in the laugh which greets him who returns from above out of the light into the den.

That, he said, is a very just distinction.

But then, if I am right, certain professors of education must be wrong when they say that they can put a knowledge into the soul which was not there before, like sight into blind eyes.

They undoubtedly say this, he replied.

45   Whereas, our argument shows that the power and capacity of learning exists in the soul already; and that just as the eye was unable to turn from darkness to light without the whole body, so too the instrument of knowledge can only by the movement of the whole soul be turned from the world of becoming into that of being, and learn by degrees to endure the sight of being, and of the brightest and best of being, or in other words, of the good.

Very true.

And must there not be some art which will effect conversion in the easiest and quickest manner; not implanting the faculty of sight, for that exists already, but has been turned in the wrong direction, and is looking away from the truth?

Yes, he said, such an art may be presumed.

And whereas the other so-called virtues of the soul seem to be akin to bodily qualities, for even when they are not originally innate they can be implanted later by habit and exercise, the virtue of wisdom more than anything else contains a divine element which always remains, and by this conversion is rendered useful and profitable; or, on the other hand, hurtful and useless. Did you never observe the narrow intelligence flashing from the keen eye of a clever rogue—how eager he is, how clearly his paltry soul sees the way to his end; he is the reverse of blind, but his keen eyesight is forced into the service of evil, and he is mischievous in proportion to his cleverness?

50   Very true, he said.

But what if there had been a circumcision of such natures in the days of their youth; and they had been severed from those sensual pleasures, such as eating and drinking, which, like leaden weights, were attached to them at their birth, and which drag them down and turn the vision of their souls upon the things that are below— if, I say, they had been released from these impediments and turned in the opposite direction, the very same faculty in them would have seen the truth as keenly as they see what their eyes are turned to now.

Very likely.

Yes, I said; and there is another thing which is likely, or rather a necessary inference from what has preceded, that neither the uneducated and uninformed of the truth, nor yet those who never make an end of their education, will be able ministers of State; not the former, because they have no single aim of duty which is the rule of all their actions, private as well as public; nor the latter, because they will not act at all except upon compulsion, fancying that they are already dwelling apart in the islands of the blessed.

Very true, he replied.

55   Then, I said, the business of us who are the founders of the State will be to compel the best minds to attain that knowledge which we have already shown to be the greatest of all—they must continue to ascend until they arrive at the good; but when they have ascended and seen enough we must not allow them to do as they do now.

What do you mean?

I mean that they remain in the upper world: but this must not be allowed; they must be made to descend again among the prisoners in the den, and partake of their labors and honors, whether they are worth having or not.

But is not this unjust? he said; ought we to give them a worse life, when they might have a better?

You have again forgotten, my friend, I said, the intention of the legislator, who did not aim at making any one class in the State happy above the rest; the happiness was to be in the whole State, and he held the citizens together by persuasion and necessity, making them benefactors of the State, and therefore benefactors of one another; to this end he created them, not to please themselves, but to be his instruments in binding up the State.

60   True, he said, I had forgotten.

Observe, Glaucon, that there will be no injustice in compelling our philosophers to have a care and providence of others; we shall explain to them that in other States, men of their class are not obliged to share in the toils of politics: and this is reasonable, for they grow up at their own sweet will, and the government would rather not have them. Being self-taught, they cannot be expected to show any gratitude for a culture which they have never received. But we have brought you into the world to be rulers of the hive, kings of yourselves and of the other citizens, and have educated you far better and more perfectly than they have been educated, and you are better able to share in the double duty. Wherefore each of you, when his turn comes, must go down to the general underground abode, and get the habit of seeing in the dark. When you have acquired the habit, you will see ten thousand times better than the inhabitants of the den, and you will know what the several images are, and what they represent, because you have seen the beautiful and just and good in their truth. And thus our State, which is also yours, will be a reality, and not a dream only, and will be administered in a spirit unlike that of other States, in which men fight with one another about shadows only and are distracted in the struggle for power, which in their eyes is a great good. Whereas the truth is that the State in which the rulers are most reluctant to govern is always the best and most quietly governed, and the State in which they are most eager, the worst.

Quite true, he replied.

And will our pupils, when they hear this, refuse to take their turn at the toils of State, when they are allowed to spend the greater part of their time with one another in the heavenly light?

Impossible, he answered; for they are just men, and the commands which we impose upon them are just; there can be no doubt that every one of them will take office as a stern necessity, and not after the fashion of our present rulers of State.

65   Yes, my friend, I said; and there lies the point. You must contrive for your future rulers another and a better life than that of a ruler, and then you may have a well-ordered State; for only in the State which offers this, will they rule who are truly rich, not in silver and gold, but in virtue and wisdom, which are the true blessings of life. Whereas if they go to the administration of public affairs, poor and hungering after their own private advantage, thinking that hence they are to snatch the chief good, order there can never be; for they will be fighting about office, and the civil and domestic broils which thus arise will be the ruin of the rulers themselves and of the whole State.

Most true, he replied.

And the only life which looks down upon the life of political ambition is that of true philosophy. Do you know of any other?

Indeed, I do not, he said.

MAKING CONNECTIONS

1. An allegory is an extended metaphor. What is the cave a metaphor for? What is Plato really describing here?
2. Do you think this metaphor works—that the darkness and light of a cave can be applied so broadly to human knowledge? Explain.
3. According to the narrator, "the State in which the rulers are most reluctant to govern is always the best . . . and the State in which they are most eager, the worst." What does he mean? To what extent do you agree?

MAKING AN ARGUMENT

1. Write an essay that compares and contrasts "The Allegory of the Cave" with the excerpt from Thoreau's "Civil Disobedience" on page 1100. Do Plato and Thoreau agree about the purpose of government? About the rights of the individual? About the nature of knowledge? Cite the text of both pieces for support.

PHILIP SIMMONS   [1958–2002]

In 1993 at the age of thirty-five, Philip Simmons, a Professor of Literature and Creative Writing at Lake Forest College, a literary critic, and a fiction writer, was diagnosed with ALS, or Lou Gehrig's disease. The essay that follows is taken from his collection Learning to Fall, *which was written and published during his illness. After an exceptionally long struggle with ALS, Simmons died in New Hampshire in 2002.*

LEARNING TO FALL   [2000]

Because I've spent the happier parts of my life at the southern edge of New Hampshire's White Mountains, two peaks rule my imagination: Mount Washington for its sheer size, its record winds and killing weather, and Mount Chocorua for its noble profile and for the legend of the defiant Pequawket Indian chief who leaped to his death from its summit, cursing the white men who had pursued him there. I climbed Chocorua many times as a boy, and from the time of our courtship, my wife and I counted a hike to its summits as one of our annual rituals. On one such hike we made the romantic and wildly impractical decision to build a seasonal home here in New Hampshire, the place of my boyhood summers, over a thousand miles away from the Midwestern flatlands where we live and work most of the year. On the same hike, incidentally, I talked a teenage boy out of jumping off of the large angular boulder that perches just a few yards down from the summit on the east side. The boy had climbed atop the rock, about the size of a one-car garage, and then could not quite bring himself to climb down again. As he was on the point of leaping, encouraged by his friends below, I summoned my best classroom voice and said "Don't do that." I then talked him down the way he had come up. In the back of my mind I was thinking that this young man was not cut out for Chief Chocorua's fate.

Barring a miracle, I'll not climb Chocorua again. It's been almost four years since I was diagnosed with Lou Gehrig's disease, a degenerative and ultimately fatal neurological disease with no effective treatment and no cure. In that time, I've managed to finish climbing all 49 of the New Hampshire peaks above 4,000 feet, a task begun at age six with my first ascent of Mount Washington. Now, however, my legs won't go the distance, and I must content myself with the lesser triumphs of getting on my socks in the morning and making it down the stairs. On the day last summer when I began writing this essay, my wife Kathryn and our seven-year-old son Aaron were climbing Mount Washington without me. Unable to join them in body, I did a quick search of the Web and found a live view from a camera mounted in the observatory at the summit. Pointed north, the camera showed the darkly hunched peaks of the northern Presidential Range beneath blue sky. Another click of the mouse gave me the current weather conditions. A near perfect July day: visibility 80 miles, wind at 35 miles per hour, temperature 42 degrees. Satisfied that my wife and son would experience the summit at its best, I then set out to discover, in their honor, what it might be possible to say about climbing, and not climbing. About remaining upright, and learning to fall.

Actors and stunt men learn to fall: as kids we watched them leap from moving trains and stage coaches. I have a dim memory of an eighth grade acting class in which I was taught to fall, but I can't remember the technique. Athletes learn to fall, and most people who have played sports have at some point had a coach tell them how to dive and roll, an art I never mastered. Devotees of the martial arts learn to fall, as do dancers and rock climbers. Mostly, though, we learn to do it badly.

My earliest memory: I'm standing alone at the top of the stairs, looking down, scared. I call for my mother, but she doesn't come. I grip the banister and look down: I have never done this on my own before. It's the first conscious decision of my life. On some level I must know that by doing this I'm becoming something new: I am becoming an "I." The memory ends here: my hand gripping the rail above my head, one foot launched into space.

5   Forty years later, encroaching baldness has made it easier to see the scars I gained from that adventure. Still, I don't regret it. One has to start somewhere. Is not falling, as much as climbing, our birth right? In the Christian theology of the fall, we all suffer the fall from grace, the fall from our primordial connectedness with God. My little tumble down the stairs was my own expulsion from the Garden: ever after I have been falling forward and down into the scarred years of conscious life, falling into the knowledge of pain, grief, and loss.

We have all suffered, and will suffer, our own falls. The fall from youthful ideals, the waning of physical strength, the failure of a cherished hope, the loss of our near and dear, the fall into injury or sickness, and late or soon, the fall to our certain ends. We have no choice but to fall, and little say as to the time or the means.

Perhaps, however, we do have some say in the manner of our falling. That is, perhaps we have a say in matters of *style*. As kids we all played the game of leaping from a diving board or dock, and before hitting the water striking some outrageous or goofy pose: axe-murderer, Washington crossing the Delaware, rabid dog. Maybe it comes to no more than this. But I'd like to think that learning to fall is more than merely a matter of posing, more than an opportunity to play it for laughs. In fact I would have it that in the way of our falling we have the opportunity to express our essential humanity.

There's a well-known Zen parable about the man who was crossing a field when he saw a tiger charging at him. The man ran, but the tiger gained on him, chasing him toward the edge of a cliff. When he reached the edge, the man had no choice but to leap. He had one chance to save himself: a scrubby branch growing out of the side of the cliff about half way down. He grabbed the branch and hung on. Looking down, what did he see on the ground below? Another tiger.

Then the man saw that a few feet off to his left a small plant grew out of the cliff, and from it there hung one ripe strawberry. Letting go with one hand he found that he could stretch his arm out just far enough to pluck the berry with his fingertips and bring it to his lips.

10   How sweet it tasted!

I'm sure we've all found ourselves in this predicament.

I found myself in it summer before last, half way up the rock slide on the north peak of Mount Tripyramid. The north slide of Tripyramid is a mile of slick granite slabs and loose gravel partially grown over with scrubby spruce and birch on a pitch as steep as the roof of your house. I had done this hike as a boy, in canvas sneakers and long pants, but had not remembered how hard it was. Earlier that summer my weakening, wobbly legs had managed to get me up Chocorua with only a little trouble on the upper ledges. But here they had failed me. I had already fallen twice, bruising ribs, gashing knees, mashing one elbow to pulp. Standing there looking out over the valley, my legs shook and each breath brought pain. I had been in tight spots in the mountains before, but this was the closest I had ever felt to the entire wretched business of litters, rescue teams, and emergency vehicles. I looked out at the mountains because they were the only thing I could look at. The view down the slope at my feet was terrifying, the view up at the climb ahead intolerable.

Tigers either way.

In such a situation, one looks for blessings. As I stood there in pain looking neither up nor down but out across the valley to where granite peaks rose against a turbulent sky, I counted among my blessings the fact that it wasn't raining. The steep rock slide, treacherous as it was now, would be deadly when wet. I had other blessings to count, as well. Three years into the course of an illness that kills most people in four or five, I belonged, statistically speaking, in a wheelchair, not on the side of a mountain. I was happy to be standing anywhere, and especially happy, all things considered, to be standing here, in my beloved White Mountains, looking out over miles of forested wilderness.

15   There was, however, that turbulent sky. Fact was, rain had been threatening all day. Those of you who have never stood in a high place and watched a rain storm move toward you across a valley have missed one of the things the words "awesome" and "majestic" were invented to describe. You're never quite sure you're seeing the rain itself: just a gray haze trailing below clouds drifting slow and steady as high sailed ships. Beautiful, yes, but in my present circumstances I felt something more than beauty. Seeing such a storm come at me now across that vast space I felt the astonishment of the sublime, which Edmund Burke defined in the eighteenth century as "not pleasure, but a sort of delightful horror, a sort of tranquility tinged with terror." It was as though I had been privileged with a glimpse of my own death, and found it the most terrible and beautiful thing I had ever seen.

I suppose I could stop here and wrap all this up with a neat moral. I could give out the sort of advice you find in the magazines sold at the grocery store. You know what I mean. I've done my share of grocery shopping, and like all red-blooded American dads I reward myself by reading the women's magazines in the check-out line. Seems I can't get enough of "Three Weeks to Thinner Thighs," and "Ten Successful Men Tell What They Really Want in Bed." And I've always gotten my best parenting advice from *Working Mother* magazine. The articles in *Working Mother* follow a rigid formula: start with a catchy anecdote, then trot out an appropriately credentialed expert on whatever problem the anecdote was meant to illustrate—the whiny child, the fussy eater—then let the expert get down to the business of dishing out nuggets of advice set off in the text with bullet points. The formula is comforting and efficient. You know just what's coming, and if you're in a hurry you can skip the anecdote and credentials and get right to the bullet points.

I could do the same thing with the stories I've told so far. Surely the story of the tigers and my escapade on Mount Tripyramid yield nuggets of advice worthy of a bullet point or two:

- Don't wait for a tragedy to start appreciating the little things in life. We shouldn't have to be chased by tigers or leap off a cliff to savor the sweetness of a single strawberry.

- Stop and smell the honeysuckle. Or at least for goodness' sake stop and watch a rain storm the next time you see one.

- Count your blessings. Appreciate what you have instead of complaining about what you don't.

Now all of this is good advice. But I'm not writing this to give advice. I'm writing, I suppose, to say that life is not a problem to be solved. What do I mean by that? Surely life presents us with problems. When I have a toothache, I try to think rationally about its causes. I consider possible remedies, their costs and consequences. I might consult an expert, in this case a dentist, who is skilled in solving this particular sort of problem. And thus we get through much of life. As a culture we have accomplished a great deal by seeing life as a set of problems to be solved. We have invented new medicines, we have traveled to the moon, developed the computer on which I am writing this essay. We learned our method from the Greeks. From childhood on we are taught to be little Aristotles. We observe the world, we break down what we see into its component parts. We perceive problems and set about solving them, laying out our solutions in ordered sequences like the instructions for assembling a child's bicycle. We have gotten so good at this method that we apply it to everything, and so we have magazine articles telling us the six ways to find a mate, the eight ways to bring greater joy into your life, the ten elements of a successful family, the twelve steps toward spiritual enlightenment. We choose to see life as a technical matter.

And here is where we go wrong. For at its deepest levels life is not a problem, but a mystery. The distinction, which I borrow from the philosopher Gabriel Marcel, is fundamental: problems are to be solved, true mysteries are not. Personally, I wish I could have learned this lesson more easily—without, perhaps, having to give up my tennis game. But each of us finds his or her own way to mystery. At one time or another, each of us confronts an experience so powerful, bewildering, joyous, or terrifying that all our efforts to see it as a "problem" are futile. Each of us is brought to the cliff's edge. At such moments we can either back away in bitterness or confusion, or leap forward into mystery. And what does mystery ask of us? Only that we be in its presence, that we fully, consciously, hand ourselves over. That is all, and that is everything. We can participate in mystery only by letting go of solutions. This letting go is the first lesson of falling, and the hardest.

20   I offer my stories not as illustrations of a problem, but as entrances into the mystery of falling. And now I'll offer not advice, not bullet points, but mystery points, set off in my text not with the familiar round dots but with question marks:

?   If spiritual growth is what you seek, don't ask for more strawberries, ask for more tigers.

?   The threat of the tigers, the leap from the cliff, are what give the strawberry its savor. They cannot be avoided, and the strawberry can't be enjoyed without them. No tigers, no sweetness.

?   In falling we somehow gain what means most. In falling we are given back
our lives even as we lose them.

My balance is not so good these days, and a short time before I began work on
this essay last summer, I fell on the short path that leads through the woods from our
driveway to the compost pile. I had just helped my six-year-old daughter into the car,
and turned to start down the path, when I stumbled and went down hard. I lay
stunned for a few moments, face numb, lip bleeding, chest bruised, my daughter
Amelia standing over me asking quite reasonably, what I was doing down there and
whether I was all right. I wish I could have managed an answer such as "practicing
my yoga" or "listening for hoofbeats." What I was doing was learning to fall. In the
following days I did some thinking about the expression "watch your step," and even
better, "mind your step." I thought about the Buddhist practice of walking meditation
in which one becomes fully mindful of each step placed upon the earth. One of the
blessings of my current stumbling condition is that I must practice this meditation
continually, becoming mindful where I once was heedless. To walk upright upon the
earth—what a blessing! When my wife and son left for their hike up Mount
Washington and I set to work on this essay, I was also thinking about the expression
"to fall on one's face," that perfect metaphor for those failures that cure us of com-
placency and pride.

The next day I learned that within minutes of my finishing a paragraph on
these subjects and calling it quits for the afternoon, Kathryn found herself briefly air-
borne on Mount Washington. She and Aaron had made the summit, drunk in the gorgeous view I had peeped at via computer gimmickry, and then begun their descent
down the treeless rock pile of the summit cone. Still well above treeline, on a steep
slope approaching a precipice, her toe caught a rock and launched her up and out
as though she intended a glider tour of the Great Gulf Wilderness. I can only imagine my son's thoughts as he watched his mother take flight, but surely my wife felt
in those instants the pull toward twin possibilities for transcendence—upward
toward some unearthly ascension and downward toward death—before crashing to
the rocks, my son watching her bounce and roll toward the abyss, wondering if she
would ever stop, Kathryn at last coming to rest, sorely convinced that her escape
from earthy toil would not come so easily, in the meantime suffering the ordinary
and decidedly untranscendent fate of three cracked ribs and a punctured lung.

What to make of all this? I'm a husband, but I'm also a writer, and even while
making the necessary phone calls, dealing with the health insurance, and driving to
the hospital, any writer worth his salt is on some level thinking "this is good material." Writers, like bears, are willing to feed on almost anything.

Think again of falling as a figure of speech. We fall on our faces, we fall for a joke,
we fall for someone, we fall in love. In each of these falls, what do we fall away from?
We fall from ego, we fall from our carefully constructed identities, our reputations,
our precious selves. We fall from ambition, we fall from grasping, we fall, at least temporarily, from reason. And what do we fall into? We fall into passion, into terror, into
unreasoning joy. We fall into humility, into compassion, into emptiness, into oneness
with forces larger than ourselves, into oneness with others whom we realize are likewise falling. We fall, at last, into the presence of the sacred, into godliness, into mystery, into our better, diviner natures.

25   After a few nights in the hospital and two difficult months my wife's ribs have mended. And I did make it to the top of Mount Tripyramid that day, despite the storm that splattered the rocks and sent us scurrying for rain gear. For I was not alone: my wife was there, and two of my brothers, and two young friends who hauled me, bloody and bowed, to the summit.

But this is not a story of triumph over adversity. The man chased by tigers does not win in the end, at least not Hollywood fashion. In Christian theology we fall so that we can rise again later. That's a good story, too, but not the one I'm telling today. I would rather, at least for now, find victory in the falling itself, in learning how to live fully, consciously in the presence of mystery. When we learn to fall we learn to accept the vulnerability that is our human endowment, the cost of walking upright on the earth.

In the northern part of our town there's a stream that comes down out of the mountains, and at one place that we call the Pothole it makes a pool of emerald clear water ten feet deep. Every summer from my boyhood until quite recently I would climb the rocks high above that pool and fling my body into the air. A summer was not complete without the thrill of that rushing descent, the slap of the water, the shock of its icy embrace. I have a photograph, taken two years ago, of what would prove to be my last such jump. In the foreground, seen from the back, my wife stands waist deep in water, shading her eyes with one hand, watching. She has never approved of this ritual, something most grown men leave behind with their teenage years, but there I am, half way down, pale against the dark rocks that I rush past. You can see my wet footprints on the rock over my head that I've just left. My eyes are focused downward on the water rushing toward my feet, and I am happy, terrified, alive.

We are all—all of us—falling. We are all, now, this moment, in the midst of that descent, fallen from heights that may now seem only a dimly remembered dream, falling toward a depth we can only imagine, glimpsed beneath the water's surface shimmer. And so let us pray that if we are falling from grace, dear God let us also fall *with* grace, *to* grace. If we are falling toward pain and weakness, let us also fall toward sweetness and strength. If we are falling toward death, let us also fall toward life.

MAKING CONNECTIONS

1. Have you ever been faced with a debilitating illness or injury? If so, what did you find most frustrating in that experience? What, most illuminating?
2. What does he mean by "When we learn to fall we learn to accept the vulnerability that is our human endowment, the cost of walking upright on the earth?" Do you agree? Explain.

MAKING AN ARGUMENT

1. Both Philip Simmons's "Learning to Fall" and Camus's "The Myth of Sisyphus" on page 1291 seem to be saying that "life is not a problem to be solved." Write an essay that compares and contrast the way that these two pieces address this theme. Cite the text of both essays for support.

CASE STUDY IN CONTEXTUAL CRITICISM

The Poetry of Emily Dickinson

By presenting some insights into the life of Emily Dickinson, a rich sampling of her work, and representative critical commentary, this Case Study provides you with contextual material sufficient for a self-contained research unit.

HER LIFE (1830–1886)

Emily Dickinson was born to a well-to-do, well-known family in Amherst, Massachusetts. Her grandfather was one of the founders of Amherst College, and her father was a state senator, U.S. congressman, and the lawyer and treasurer of Amherst College. At home, her father created and dominated a highly conservative, religious atmosphere in which he read morning prayers and scripture to both family and servants. Dickinson attended Amherst Academy, but after a subsequent unhappy year at the Mount Holyoke Female Seminary (which would become Mount Holyoke College), she returned home and gradually removed herself from outside responsibilities. She traveled rarely and led an almost solitary existence.

In order to protect her from books that might "joggle" her mind, her father forbade the reading of novels—a prohibition that did not stop her from reading and admiring novelists like the Brontë sisters or George Eliot. She read the Bible, classical myths, and Shakespeare—and often made allusions to them in her poems. And she read and admired the poetry of Keats, Robert and Elizabeth Barrett Browning, Tennyson, and the work of American contemporaries like Hawthorne, Emerson, and Thoreau.

Although she submitted a number of poems for publication, only a few were published during her lifetime—and those anonymously. And though it was reported that she dressed only in white, and was known throughout Amherst as an eccentric recluse, she had ongoing relationships with a number of people who provided her with feedback about her poetry. Most notable among these contacts were her sister-in-law, Susan Gilbert Dickinson, with whom she had a close friendship, and Thomas Wentworth Higginson, the editor of the *Atlantic Monthly,* whom she considered her mentor. And there were other men in her life: Benjamin Newton, who worked for her father and with whom she discussed books; Samuel Bowles, a newspaper editor and friend of the family; Charles Wadsworth, a Presbyterian minister; and widower and longtime friend Judge Otis Lord. But though Dickinson wrote powerful poems about the passion and disappointments of love, there is no evidence to indicate with whom she might have been in love—or evidence that she had ever been physically intimate with any man. What little we know of her exterior life, however, her remarkably insightful poems tell us a great deal about her rich, reflective interior life.

HER WORK

Dickinson published only a tiny number of the nearly two thousand exquisitely crafted and startlingly original poems she composed during her lifetime, and she made her sister and brother promise to destroy all her work after her death. Her sister, Lavinia, did destroy her letters, but (fortunately) could not bring herself to destroy the poems—many of which were sewn into booklets or tied in bundles and hidden in bureau draws. After numerous revisions in wording, punctuation, rhyme, and structure were made to Dickinson's poetry to "conform" her work to nineteenth-century sensibilities, nine volumes of her work were published in the 1890s—and in subsequent editions during the first half of the twentieth century. Not until Thomas H. Johnson published his three-volume edition of her work in 1955, however, did Dickinson's verses become available as she originally composed them.

Dickinson's stature continued to grow throughout the twentieth century, and today, along with Walt Whitman, she is considered one of the two great poetic geniuses of the nineteenth century and a cofounder of modern American poetry. But while Dickinson and Whitman both wrote unconventional poetry, and their work is filled with brilliant originality, their poems are quite different. Whitman's poetry is expansive and public; the verse lines are long—and his themes are large and broadly focused. Dickinson's poems are tightly compressed and inward with a focus on intensely felt moments.

Dickinson's poetry is complex yet wonderfully simple. Her vivid, penetrating language offers and suggests complex thought and emotion—intensifying, clarifying, and re-creating experience. Her images, her timing, her sounds and structures, and her indirections are inner-life magical.

THE POEMS

If you are unfamiliar with her unique style, her poetry may provide some difficulty—at least initially. The word combinations in her lines sometimes leave spaces you are expected to fill, and her language anticipates your interpretation. The poems require active engagement—an engagement that will fill in the gaps. Read each poem several times—and out loud. Listen carefully, and give yourself time to sense the images; immerse yourself in them, feel them before you try to figure them out. Once they are felt—"where the meanings are"—you'll be well on your way to understanding them.

SUCCESS IS COUNTED SWEETEST   [C. 1859]

Success is counted sweetest
By those who ne'er succeed.
To comprehend a nectar
Requires sorest need

Not one of all the purple Host   5
Who took the Flag today
Can tell the definition
So clear of Victory

As he defeated—dying—
On whose forbidden ear   10
The distant strains of triumph
Burst agonized and clear!

FAITH IS A FINE INVENTION   [c. 1861]

"Faith" is a fine invention
For gentlemen who *see*—
But *microscopes* are prudent
In an Emergency.

THERE'S A CERTAIN SLANT OF LIGHT   [c. 1861]

There's a certain Slant of light,
Winter Afternoons—
That oppresses, like the Heft
Of Cathedral Tunes—

Heavenly Hurt, it gives us—   5
We can find no scar,
But internal difference,
Where the Meanings, are—

None may teach it—Any—
'Tis the Seal Despair—   10
An imperial affliction
Sent us of the Air—

When it comes, the Landscape listens—
Shadows—hold their breath—
When it goes, 'tis like the Distance   15
On the look of Death—

I LIKE A LOOK OF AGONY   [c. 1861]

I like a look of Agony,
Because I know it's true—
Men do not sham Convulsion,
Nor simulate, a Throe—

The Eyes glaze once—and that is Death—   5
Impossible to feign
The Beads upon the forehead
By homely Anguish strung.

WILD NIGHTS—WILD NIGHTS!

[c. 1861]

Wild nights—Wild Nights!
Were I with thee
Wild Nights should be
Our luxury!

Futile—the Winds—   5
To a heart in port—
Done with the Compass—
Done with the Chart!

Rowing in Eden—
Ah! the Sea!   10
Might I but moor—Tonight—
In Thee!

THE BRAIN—IS WIDER THAN THE SKY—

[c. 1862]

The Brain—is wider than the sky—
For—put them side by side—
The one the other will contain
With ease—and You—beside—

The Brain is deeper than the sea—   5
For—hold them—Blue to Blue—
The one the other will absorb—
As Sponges—buckets—do—

The Brain is just the weight of God—
For—Heft them—Pound for Pound—   10
And they will differ—if they do—
As syllable from Sound—

MUCH MADNESS IS DIVINEST SENSE—

[c. 1862]

Much Madness is divinest Sense—
To a discerning Eye—
Much Sense—the starkest Madness—
'Tis the Majority
In this, as All, prevail—   5
Assent—and you are sane—
Demur—you're straightway dangerous—
And handled with a Chain—

I'VE SEEN A DYING EYE

[c. 1862]

I've seen a Dying Eye
Run round and round a room—
In search of Something—as it seemed—

Then Cloudier become—
And then—obscure with Fog—
And then—be soldered down
Without disclosing what it be
'Twere blessed to have seen—

I HEARD A FLY BUZZ—WHEN I DIED—   [c. 1862]

I heard a fly buzz—when I died—
The Stillness in the Room
Was like the Stillness in the Air—
Between the Heaves of Storm—

The Eyes around—had wrung them dry—   5
And Breaths were gathering firm
For that last Onset—when the King
Be witnessed—in the Room—

I willed my Keepsakes—Signed away
What portion of me be   10
Assignable—and then it was
There interposed a Fly—

With Blue—uncertain stumbling Buzz—
Between the light—and me—
And then the Windows failed—and then   15
I could not see to see—

AFTER GREAT PAIN, A FORMAL FEELING COMES   [c. 1862]

After great pain, a formal feeling comes—
The Nerves sit ceremonious, like Tombs—
The stiff Heart questions was it He, that bore,
And Yesterday, or Centuries before?

The Feet, mechanical, go round—   5
Of Ground, or Air, or Ought—
A Wooden way
Regardless grown,
A Quartz contentment, like a stone—

This is the Hour of Lead—   10
Remembered, if outlived,
As Freezing persons, recollect the Snow—
First—Chill—then Stupor—then the letting go—

SOME KEEP THE SABBATH GOING TO CHURCH   [c. 1862]

Some keep the Sabbath going to Church—
I keep it, staying at Home—
With a Bobolink for a Chorister—

And an Orchard, for a Dome—

Some keep the Sabbath in Surplice—   5
I just wear my Wings—
And instead of tolling the Bell, for Church,
Our little Sexton—sings.

God preaches, a noted Clergyman—
And the sermon is never long,   10
So instead of getting to Heaven, at last—
I'm going, all along.

THIS WORLD IS NOT CONCLUSION—   [C. 1862]

This World is not Conclusion.
A Sequel stands beyond—
Invisible, as Music—
But positive, as Sound—
It beckons, and it baffles—   5
Philosophy—don't know—
And through a Riddle, at the last—
Sagacity, must go—
To guess it, puzzles scholars—
To gain it, Men have borne   10
Contempt of Generations
And Crucifixion, shown—
Faith slips—and laughs, and rallies—
Blushes, if any see—
Plucks at a twig of Evidence—
And asks a Vane, the way—
Much Gesture, from the pulpit—
Strong Hallelujahs roll—
Narcotics cannot still the Tooth
That nibbles at the soul—

THERE IS A PAIN—SO UTTER—   [c. 1862]

There is a pain—so utter—
It swallows substance up—
Then covers the Abyss with Trance—
So memory can step
Around—across—upon it—   5
As one within a Swoon—
Goes safely—where an open eye—
Would drop Him—Bone by Bone.

BECAUSE I COULD NOT STOP FOR DEATH   [c. 1863]

Because I could not stop for Death—
He kindly stopped for me

The Carriage held but just Ourselves—
And Immortality.

We slowly drove—He knew no haste,   5
And I had put away
My labor and my leisure too,
For His Civility—

We passed the School, where Children strove
At Recess—in the Ring—
We passed the Fields of Gazing Grain—
We passed the Setting Sun—

Or rather—He passed Us—
the Dew drew quivering and chill—
For only Gossamer, my Gown—   15
My Tippet° —only Tulle° —

We paused before a House that seemed
A swelling of the Ground—
The Roof was scarcely visible—
The Cornice—in the Ground—

Since then—'tis Centuries—and yet
Feels shorter than the Day
I first surmised the Horses' Heads
Were toward Eternity—   20

Tippet shawl   **Tulle** silk netting

THE BUSTLE IN A HOUSE   [c. 1866]

The Bustle in a House
The Morning after Death
Is solemnest of industries
Enacted upon Earth—

The Sweeping up the Heart   5
And putting love away
We shall not want to use again
Until Eternity.

TELL ALL THE TRUTH BUT TELL IT SLANT—   [c. 1868]

Tell all the Truth but tell it slant—
Success in Circuit lies
Too bright for our Infirm Delight
The Truth's superb surprise

As Lightning to the Children eased   5
With explanations kind
The Truth must dazzle gradually
Or every man be blind—

MAKING CONNECTIONS

1. What similarities in structure, rhythm, and word choice do you notice among Dickinson's poems?
2. The poems above are arranged chronologically. Do you see any evidence that Dickinson's work has evolved over time? Are there noticeable changes or developments in ideas or styles? Explain.
3. To what extent does your reading and understanding of earlier poems in the sequence help you read and understand some of the later ones?

SUCCESS IS COUNTED SWEETEST

1. Do you agree with the title? Explain.
2. To what extent does your own experience influence your response?

FAITH IS A FINE INVENTION

1. What does the speaker mean "For gentleman who see"?
2. In what way do microscopes represent a different way of seeing?

THERE'S A CERTAIN SLANT OF LIGHT

1. What is the setting for this poem? Why does the speaker call it a "Slant of light" rather than a "light"?
2. What does she mean by "None may teach it"? To what extent can this apply to the subjects of her other poems as well?

I LIKE A LOOK OF AGONY

1. Do you find it startling that the speaker likes "a look of agony"? Explain.
2. To what extent is this a poem about other "looks" the speaker has seen?

WILD NIGHTS — WILD NIGHTS!

1. How can we reconcile this poem with Dickinson's reclusive life?
2. What is the central metaphor of the poem? To what extent does it work?

THE BRAIN — IS WIDER THAN THE SKY —

1. How could the brain be "wider than the sky"?
2. To what extent does this poem represent Dickinson's life and writing?

MUCH MADNESS IS DIVINEST SENSE —

1. What do you think the speaker means by "Much Madness"? By "Much Sense"?
2. Who is the "Majority" that prevail? Do you think they should? Explain.

I'VE SEEN A DYING EYE

1. In what way is this poem more about those looking on than it is about the dying person?
2. In what way is the eye running around the room—and why?

I HEARD A FLY BUZZ — WHEN I DIED —

1. Who is the speaker in the poem?
2. Why do you think the poet chose a "fly" and not something more exotic?

AFTER GREAT PAIN, A FORMAL FEELING COMES

1. What kind of "great pain" does the speaker make reference to?
2. To what extent is your response affected by your own experience? How do the images convey the meaning?

SOME KEEP THE SABBATH GOING TO CHURCH

1. Describe how the speaker keeps the Sabbath.
2. What does the speaker mean by "instead of getting to heaven . . . / I'm going all along"?

THIS WORLD IS NOT CONCLUSION

1. What is the "tooth that nibbles at the soul"?
2. Compare this poem to "Faith Is a Fine Invention."

THERE IS A PAIN—SO UTTER—

1. Why do you think the speaker seems unable to finish the first line?
2. Compare this poem with "The Bustle in a House" or "After Great Pain, a Formal Feeling Comes."

BECAUSE I COULD NOT STOP FOR DEATH

1. To what extent is the title and first line of this poem ironic?
2. What concrete images in the poem signify death?

THE BUSTLE IN A HOUSE

1. Why do you think there is such a bustle in the house? Have you ever experienced one like it? Explain.
2. Compare this poem to "There Is a Pain—So Utter—" or "After Great Pain, a Formal Feeling Comes."

TELL ALL THE TRUTH BUT TELL IT SLANT—

1. How does this poem compare with the popular saying "Honesty is the best policy"? Do you think it's right when telling the truth to "tell it slant"? Explain.
2. Consider the words and images in this brief poem. Do you think they convey the message of the poem effectively? How so?

MAKING AN ARGUMENT

1. The sixteen Dickinson poems in this Case Study are connected to the theme of this section—Faith and Doubt—but what other, more specific thematic connections can you find between and among her poems? Identify a consistent theme in her work, and write an essay that supports your view. Cite the text of the poems for support.
2. Both Emily Dickinson and Walt Whitman were innovative geniuses who transcended the poetic conventions of their age—but their work is very different. Write an essay that compares and contrasts the style, structure, and content of Dickinson's poems with Whitman's poems in this anthology: "When I Heard the Learn'd Astronomer" (p. 83), "There Was a Child Went Forth" (p. 514), and "Song of Myself 6" (p. 1239).

3. Given the unusual nature of her images and metaphors, Dickinson's work is often compared with that of John Donne. Write an essay that compares her poetry and her metaphors with those in Donne's poems: "A Valediction Forbidding Mourning" (p. 1226) and "Death, Be Not Proud" (p. 1227).

EMILY DICKINSON—IN HER OWN WORDS

TO SUSAN GILBERT (DICKINSON)

late April 1852

So sweet and still, and Thee, Oh Susie, what need I more, to make my heaven whole?

Sweet Hour, blessed Hour, to carry me to you, and to bring you back to me, long enough to snatch one kiss, and whisper Good bye, again.

I have thought of it all day, Susie, and I fear of but little else, and when I was gone to meeting it filled my mind so full, I could not find a *chink* to put the worthy pastor; when he said "Our Heavenly Father," I said "Oh Darling Sue"; when he read the 100th Psalm, I kept saying your precious letter all over to myself, and Susie, when they sang—it would have made you laugh to hear one little voice, piping to the departed. I made up words and kept singing how I loved you, and you had gone, while all the rest of the choir were singing Hallelujahs. I presume nobody heard me, because I sang *so small,* but it was a kind of a comfort to think I might put them out, singing of you. I a'nt there this afternoon, tho', because I am here, writing a little letter to my dear Sue, and I am very happy. I think of ten weeks—Dear One, and I think of love, and you, and my heart grows full and warm, and my breath stands still. The sun does'nt shine at all, but I can feel a sunshine stealing into my soul and making it all summer, and every thorn, a *rose.* And I pray that such summer's sun shine on my Absent One, and cause her bird to sing!

You have been happy, Susie, and now are sad—and the whole world seems lone; but it wont be so always, "some days *must* be dark and dreary"! You wont cry any more, will you, Susie, for my father will be your father, and my home will be your home, and where you go, I will go, and we will lie side by side in the kirkyard.

5   I have parents on earth, dear Susie, but your's are in the skies, and I have an earthly fireside, but you have one above, and you have a "Father in Heaven," where I have *none*—and *sister* in heaven, and I know they love you dearly, and think of you every day.

Oh I wish I had half so many dear friends as you in heaven—I could'nt spare them now—but to know they had got there safely, and should suffer nevermore—Dear Susie! . . .

Emilie—

TO T. W. HIGGINSON

25 April 1862

Mr Higginson,

Your kindness claimed earlier gratitude—but I was ill—and write today, from my pillow.

Thank you for the surgery—it was not so painful as I supposed. I bring you others—as you ask—though they might not differ—

While my thought is undressed—I can make the distinction, but when I put them in the Gown—they look alike, and numb.

You asked how old I was? I made no verse—but one or two—until this winter—Sir—

5   I had a terror—since September—I could tell to none—and so I sing, as the Boy does by the Burying Ground—because I am afraid—You inquire my Books—For Poets—I have Keats—and Mr and Mrs Browning. For Prose—Mr Ruskin—Sir Thomas Browne—and the Revelations. I went to school—but in your manner of the phrase—had no education. When a little Girl, I had a friend, who taught me Immortality—but venturing too near, himself—he never returned—Soon after, my Tutor, died—and for several years, my Lexicon—was my only companion—Then I found one more—but he was not contented I be his scholar—so he left the Land.

You ask of my Companions Hills—Sir—and the Sundown—and a Dog—large as myself, that my Father bought me—They are better than Beings—because they know—but do not tell—and the noise in the Pool, at Noon—excels my Piano. I have a Brother and Sister—My Mother does not care for thought—and Father, too busy with his Briefs—to notice what we do—He buys me many Books—but begs me not to read them—because he fears they joggle the Mind. They are religious—except me—and address an Eclipse, every morning—whom they call their "Father." But I fear my story fatigues you—I would like to learn—Could you tell me how to grow—or is it unconveyed—like Melody—or Witchcraft?

You speak of Mr Whitman—I never read his Book—but was told that he was disgraceful—

I read Miss Prescott's "Circumstance," but it followed me, in the Dark—so I avoided her—

Two Editors of Journals came to my Father's House, this winter, and asked me for my Mind—and when I asked them "Why," they said I was penurious—and they, would use it for the World—

10   I could not weigh myself—Myself—

My size felt small—to me—I read your Chapters in the Atlantic—and experienced honor for you—I was sure you would not reject a confiding question—

Is this—Sir—what you asked me to tell you?

                                        Your friend,
                                        E—Dickinson.

IN OTHERS' WORDS

THOMAS WENTWORTH HIGGINSON [1823-1911]

ON MEETING DICKINSON FOR THE FIRST TIME   [1870]

A large county lawyer's house, brown brick, with great trees & a garden—I sent up my card. A parlor dark & cool & stiffish, a few books & engravings & an open piano. . . .

A step like a pattering child's in entry & in glided a little plain woman with two smooth bands of reddish hair & a face a little like Belle Dove's; not plainer—with no good feature—in a very plain & exquisitely clean white pique & a blue net worsted shawl. She came to me with two day lilies which she put in a sort of childlike way into my hand & said "These are my introduction" in a soft frightened breathless childlike voice—& added under her breath Forgive me if I am frightened; I never see strangers & hardly know what I say—but she talked soon & thenceforward continuously—& deferentially—sometimes stopping to ask me to talk instead of her—but readily recommencing . . . thoroughly ingenuous & simple . . . & saying many things which you would have thought foolish & I wise—& some things you wd. hv. liked. I add a few over the page. . . .

"Women talk; men are silent; that is why I dread women."

"My father only reads on Sunday—he reads *lonely* & *rigorous* books."

5   "If I read a book [and] it makes my whole body so cold no fire ever can warm me I know *that* is poetry. If I feel physically as if the top of my head were taken off, I know *that* is poetry. These are the only ways I know it. Is there any other way."

"How do most people live without any thoughts. There are many people in the world (you must have noticed them in the street) How do they live. How do they get strength to put on their clothes in the morning"

"When I lost the use of my Eyes it was a comfort to think there were so few real *books* that I could easily find some one to read me all of them"

"Truth is such a *rare* thing it is delightful to tell it."

"I find ecstasy in living—the mere sense of living is joy enough"

10   I asked if she never felt want of employment, never going off the place & never seeing any visitor "I never thought of conceiving that I could ever have the slightest approach to such a want in all future time" (& added) "I feel that I have not expressed myself strongly enough."

From a letter to his wife, August 16, 1870

Mabel Loomis Todd [1856-1932]

The Character of Amherst   [1881]

I must tell you about the *character* of Amherst. It is a lady whom the people call the *Myth*. She is a sister of Mr. Dickinson, & seems to be the climax of all the family oddity. She has not been outside of her own house in fifteen years, except once to see a new church, when she crept out at night, & viewed it by moonlight. No one who calls upon her mother & sister ever see her, but she allows little children once in a great while, & one at a time, to come in, when she gives them cake or candy, or some nicety, for she is very fond of little ones. But more often she lets down the sweetmeat by a string, out of a window, to them. She dresses wholly in white, & her mind is said to be perfectly wonderful. She writes finely, but no one *ever* sees her. Her sister, who was at Mrs. Dickinson's party, invited me to come & sing to her mother sometime   People tell me the *myth* will hear every note—she will be near, but unseen. . . . Isn't that like a book? So interesting.

From a letter to her parents, November 6, 1881

RICHARD WILBUR   [B. 1921]

ON DICKINSON'S SENSE OF PRIVATION   [1960]

What did Emily Dickinson do, as a poet, with her sense of privation? One thing she quite often did was to pose as the laureate and attorney of the empty-handed, and question God about the economy of His creation. Why, she asked, is a fatherly God so sparing of His presence? Why is there never a sign that prayers are heard? Why does Nature tell us no comforting news of its Maker? Why do some receive a whole loaf, while others must starve on a crumb? Where is the benevolence in shipwreck and earthquake? By asking such questions as these, she turned complaint into critique, and used her own sufferings as experiential evidence about the nature of the deity. The God who emerges from these poems is a God who does not answer, an unrevealed God whom one cannot confidently approach through Nature or through doctrine.

But there was another way in which Emily Dickinson dealt with her sentiment of lack—another emotional strategy which was both more frequent and more fruitful. I refer to her repeated assertion of the paradox that privation is more plentiful than plenty; that to renounce is to possess the more; that "The Banquet of abstemiousness/Defaces that of wine." We all know how the poet illustrated this ascetic paradox in her behavior—how in her latter years she chose to live in relative retirement, keeping the world, even in its dearest aspects, at a physical remove. She would write her friends, telling them how she missed them, then flee upstairs when they came to see her; afterward, she might send a note of apology, offering the odd explanation that "We shun because we prize." Any reader of Dickinson biographies can furnish other examples, dramatic or homely, of this prizing and shunning, this yearning and renouncing: in my own mind's eye is a picture of Emily Dickinson watching a gay circus caravan from the distance of her chamber window.

> From "Sumptuous Destitution" in *Emily Dickinson: Three Views,*
> by Richard Wilbur, Louise Bogan, and Archibald MacLeish

SANDRA M. GILBERT   [B. 1936] AND SUSAN GUBAR   [B. 1944]

ON DICKINSON'S WHITE DRESS   [1979]

Today a dress that the Amherst Historical Society assures us is *the* white dress Dickinson wore—or at least one of her "Uniforms of Snow"—hangs in a drycleaner's plastic bag in the closet of the Dickinson homestead. Perfectly preserved, beautifully flounced and tucked, it is larger than most readers would have expected this self-consciously small poet's dress to be, and thus reminds visiting scholars of the enduring enigma of Dickinson's central metaphor, even while it draws gasps from more practical visitors, who reflect with awe upon the difficulties of maintaining such a costume. But what exactly did the literal and figurative whiteness of this costume represent? What rewards did it offer that would cause an intelligent woman to overlook those practical difficulties? Comparing Dickinson's obsession with whiteness to Melville's, William R. Sherwood suggests that "it reflected in her case the Christian mystery and not a Christian enigma . . . a decision to announce . . . the assumption of a worldly death that paradoxically involved regeneration." This, he adds, her gown—"a typically slant demonstration of truth"—should have revealed "to anyone with the wit to catch on."

We might reasonably wonder, however, if Dickinson herself consciously intended her wardrobe to convey any one message. The range of associations her white poems imply suggests, on the contrary, that for her, as for Melville, white is the ultimate symbol of enigma, paradox, and irony, "not so much a color as the visible absence of color, and at the same time the concrete of all colors." Melville's question [in *Moby-Dick*] might, therefore, also be hers: "is it for these reasons that there is such a dumb blankness, full of meaning, in a wide landscape of snows—a colorless, all-color of atheism from which we shrink?" And his concluding speculation might be hers too, his remark "that the mystical cosmetic which produces every one of [Nature's] hues, the great principle of light, for ever remains white or colorless in itself, and if operating without medium upon matter, would touch all objects . . . with its own blank tinge." For white, in Dickinson's poetry, frequently represents both the energy (the white heat) of Romantic creativity, and the loneliness (the polar cold) of the renunciation or tribulation Romantic creativity may demand, both the white radiance of eternity—or Revelation—and the white terror of a shroud.

From *The Madwoman in the Attic: The Woman Writer and the Nineteenth-Century Literary Imagination*

CRITICAL COMMENTARY ON HER POETRY

HELEN MCNEIL

DICKINSON'S METHOD

from Emily Dickinson   [1986]

Many Victorian poems describe unexamined abstractions, as if society agreed about what constituted sorrow or love. These could be personified, and their attributes could be listed and elaborated metaphorically. Dickinson takes on a frightening abstraction and evolves its attributes from experience, not tradition. In poetry and philosophy, the subject—the experiencing person—may wonder about the existence of other minds. Dickinson wrote many poems on this problem. In "Pain—has an Element of Blank," she contemplates the possibility that there may be circumstances in which the perceiving consciousness also does not exist, erased by its own emotion. "The Soul has Bandaged moments—" she begins another poem; the abstract soul is a bandaged body, in a metaphor which denies dualism. Time is also represented physically, bound up by pain. As Dickinson concludes at the end of "The Soul has Bandaged moments—," such recognitions "are not brayed of Tongue—" in the public discourse of her society, or, for that matter, our society either.

Dickinson wrote about feeling, but out of feeling she constructed a theory of knowledge—not *beyond* feeling, or free from it, or in any way separate, but using it as a kind of knowing. In effect—though not in conventional terms—she is an epistemological poet, a poet who advances a theory of knowledge. Dickinson made this concern explicit. After the forms of the verb "to be," "know" is the most frequently used verb in Dickinson's poetry, appearing 230 times, more even than any noun except "day."

Dickinson's constant pressure towards knowing means that she can treat even the most tormented situations with great calm. She can begin by writing "I felt a Funeral, in my Brain," or "Pain—has an Element of Blank—" or "I felt my life with both my hands—" and then proceed to delineate that state with a commanding accuracy. In a manner more resembling the Metaphysical poets than her Victorian contemporaries, male or female, she uses emotionally heightened states as occasions for clarity.

American poetry characteristically embodies acts of process: the Dickinsonian "process" is passionate investigation. Her investigative process often implies narrative by taking speaker and reader through a sequence of rapidly changing images, even when all the action is interior. These investigations structure Dickinson's poetry; I suspect that the flexibility of her investigative movement is the major reason why Dickinson generally was contented with common meter. She may even have enjoyed the way her condensed discoveries press against the limits of a small form.

CYNTHIA GRIFFIN WOLFF [B. 1935]

ON THE MANY VOICES IN DICKINSON'S POETRY   [1986]

There were many "Voices." This fact has sometimes puzzled Dickinson's readers. One poem may be delivered in a child's Voice; another in the Voice of a young woman scrutinizing nature and the society in which she makes her place. Sometimes the Voice is that of a woman self-confidently addressing her lover in a language of passion and sexual desire. At still other times, the Voice of the verse seems so precariously balanced at the edge of hysteria that even its calmest observations grate like the shriek of dementia. There is the Voice of the housewife and the Voice that has recourse to the occasionally agonizing, occasionally regal language of the conversion experience of latter-day New England Puritanism. In some poems the Voice is distinctive principally because it speaks in the aftermath of wounding and can comprehend extremities of pain. Moreover, these Voices are not always entirely distinct from one another: the child's Voice that opens a poem may yield to the Voice of a young woman speaking the idiom of ardent love; in a different poem, the speaker may fall into a mood of almost religious contemplation in an attempt to analyze or define such abstract entities as loneliness or madness or eternity; the diction of the housewife may be conflated with the sovereign language of the New Jerusalem, and taken together, they may render some aspect of the wordsmith's labor. No manageable set of discrete categories suffices to capture the diversity of discourse, and any attempt to simplify Dickinson's methods does violence to the verse.

Yet there is a paradox here. This is, by no stretch of the imagination, a body of poetry that might be construed as a series of lyrics spoken by many different people. Disparate as these many Voices are, somehow they all appear to issue from the same "self.". . . It is the enigmatic "Emily Dickinson" readers suppose themselves to have found in this poetry, even in the extreme case when Dickinson's supposed speaker is male. One explanation for this sense of intrinsic unity in the midst of diversity is the persistence with which Dickinson addresses the same set of problems, using a remarkably durable repertoire of linguistic modes. Evocations of injury and wounding—threats to the coherence of the self—appear in the earliest poems and continue until the end; ways of rendering face-to-face encounters change, but this preoccupation with "interview" is sustained by metaphors of "confrontation" that weave throughout. The summoning of one or another Voice in a given poem, then, is not an unselfconscious emotive reflection of Emily Dickinson's mood at the moment of creation. Rather, each different Voice is a calculated tactic, an attempt to touch her readers and engage them intimately with the poetry. Each Voice had its unique advantages; each its limitations. A poet self-conscious in her craft, she calculated this element as carefully as every other.

From Emily Dickinson

ALLEN TATE

ON "BECAUSE I COULD NOT STOP FOR DEATH"

from "Emily Dickinson," in Collected Essays   [1959]

If the word "great" means anything in poetry, this poem is one of the greatest in the English language. The rhythm charges with movement the pattern of suspended action back of the poem. Every image is precise and, moreover, not merely beautiful, but fused with the central idea. Every image extends and intensifies every other. The third stanza especially shows Miss Dickinson's power to fuse, into a single order of perception, a heterogeneous series: the children, the grain, and the setting sun (time) have the same degree of credibility; the first subtly preparing for the last. The sharp *gazing* before *grain* instills into nature a cold vitality of which the qualitative richness has infinite depth. The content of death in the poem eludes explicit definition. He is a gentleman taking a lady out for a drive. But note the restraint that keeps the poet from carrying this so far that it becomes ludicrous and incredible; and note the subtly interfused erotic motive, which the idea of death has presented to most romantic poets, love being a symbol interchangeable with death. The terror of death is objectified through this figure of the genteel driver, who is made ironically to serve the end of Immortality. This is the heart of the poem: she has presented a typical Christian theme in its final irresolution, without making any final statements about it. There is no solution to the problem; there can be only a presentation of it in the full context of intellect and feeling. A construction of the human will, elaborated with all the abstracting powers of the mind, is put to the concrete test of experience: the idea of immortality is confronted with the fact of physical disintegration. We are not told what to think; we are told to look at the situation.

The framework of the poem is, in fact, the two abstractions, mortality and eternity, which are made to associate in equality with the images: she sees the ideas, and thinks the perceptions. She did, of course, nothing of the sort; but we must use the logical distinctions, even to the extent of paradox, if we are to form any notion of this rare quality of mind. She could not in the proper sense think at all, and unless we prefer the feeble poetry of moral ideas that flourished in New England in the eighties, we must conclude that her intellectual deficiency contributed at least negatively to her great distinction. Miss Dickinson is probably the only Anglo-American poet of her century whose work exhibits the perfect literary situation—in which is possible the fusion of sensibility and thought. Unlike her contemporaries, she never succumbed to her ideas, to easy solutions, to her private desires . . .

Neither the feeling nor the style of Miss Dickinson belongs to the seventeenth century; yet between her and Donne there are remarkable ties. Their religious ideas, their abstractions, are momently toppling from the rational plane to the level of perception. The ideas, in fact, are no longer the impersonal religious symbols created anew in the heat of emotion, that we find in poets like Herbert and Vaughan. They have become, for Donne, the terms of personality; they are mingled with the miscellany of sensation. In Miss Dickinson, as in Donne, we may detect a singularly morbid concern, not for religious truth, but for personal revelation. The modern word is self-exploitation. It is egoism grown irresponsible in religion and decadent in morals. In religion it is blasphemy; in society it means usually that culture is not self-contained and sufficient, that the spiritual community is breaking up. This is, along with some other features that do not concern us here, the perfect literary situation.

PAULA BENNETT [B. 1936]

ON "I HEARD A FLY BUZZ—WHEN I DIED—" [1990]

Dickinson's rage against death, a rage that led her at times to hate both life and death, might have been alleviated, had she been able to gather hard evidence about an afterlife. But, of course, she could not. "The *Bareheaded life*—under the grass—," she wrote to Samuel Bowles in c. 1860, "worries one like a Wasp." If death was the gate to a better life in "the childhood of the kingdom of Heaven," as the sentimentalists—and Christ—claimed, then, perhaps, there was compensation and healing for life's woes. . . . But how do we know? What can we know? In "I heard a Fly buzz—when I died," Dickinson concludes that we do not know much. . . .

Like many people in her period, Dickinson was fascinated by death-bed scenes. How, she asked various correspondents, did this or that person die? In particular, she wanted to know if their deaths revealed any information about the nature of the afterlife. In this poem, however, she imagines her own death-bed scene, and the answer she provides is grim, as grim (and, at the same time, as ironically mocking), as anything she ever wrote.

In the narrowing focus of death, the fly's insignificant buzz, magnified tenfold by the stillness in the room, is all that the speaker hears. This kind of distortion in scale is common. It is one of the "illusions" of perception. But here it is horrifying because it defeats every expectation we have. Death is supposed to be an experience of awe. It is the moment when the soul, departing the body, is taken up by God. Hence the watchers at the bedside wait for the moment when the "King" (whether God or death) "be witnessed" in the room. And hence the speaker assigns away everything but that which she expects God (her soul) or death (her body) to take.

What arrives instead, however, is neither God nor death but a fly, "[w]ith Blue—uncertain—stumbling Buzz," a fly, that is, no more secure, no more sure, than we are. Dickinson had associated flies with death once before in the exquisite lament, "How many times these low feet / staggered." In this poem, they buzz "on the / chamber window," and speckle it with dirt, reminding us that the housewife, who once protected us from such intrusions, will protect us no longer. Their presence is threatening but only in a minor way, "dull" like themselves. They are a background noise we do not have to deal with yet.

5   In "I heard a Fly buzz," on the other hand, there is only one fly and its buzz is not only foregrounded. Before the poem is over, the buzz takes up the entire field of perception, coming between the speaker and the "light" (of day, of life, of knowledge). It is then that the "Windows" (the eyes that are the windows of the soul as well as, metonymically, the light that passes through the panes of glass) "fail" and the speaker is left in darkness—in death, in ignorance. She cannot "see" to "see" (understand).

Given that the only sure thing we know about "life after death" is that flies—in their adult form and more particularly, as maggots—devour us, the poem is at the very least a grim joke. In projecting her death-bed scene, Dickinson confronts her ignorance and gives back the only answer human knowledge can with any certainty give. While we may hope for an afterlife, no one, not even the dying, can prove it exists.

From *Emily Dickinson: Woman Poet*

POEMS ABOUT EMILY DICKINSON

LINDA PASTAN [B. 1932]

EMILY DICKINSON   [1971]

We think of her hidden in a white dress
among the folded linens and sachets
of well-kept cupboards, or just out of sight
sending jellies and notes with no address
to all the wondering Amherst neighbors.   5
Eccentric as New England weather
the stiff wind of her mind, stinging or gentle,
blew two half-imagined lovers off.
Yet legend won't explain the shear sanity   10
of vision, the serious mischief
of language, the economy of pain.

BILLY COLLINS [B. 1941]

TAKING OFF EMILY DICKINSON'S CLOTHES   [1998]

First, her tippet made of tulle,
easily lifted off her shoulders and laid
on the back of a wooden chair.

And her bonnet,
the bow undone with a light forward pull.   5

Then the long white dress, a more
complicated matter with mother-of-pearl
buttons down the back,
so tiny and numerous that it takes forever
before my hands can part the fabric,   10
like a swimmer's dividing water,
and slip inside.

You will want to know
that she was standing
by an open window in an upstairs bedroom,   15
motionless, a little wide-eyed,
looking out at the orchard below,
the white dress puddled at her feet
on the wide-board, hardwood floor.

The complexity of women's undergarments   20
in nineteenth-century America
is not to be waved off,
and I proceeded like a polar explorer
through clips, clasps, and moorings,
catches, straps, and whalebone stays   25
sailing toward the iceberg of her nakedness.

Later, I wrote in a notebook
it was like riding a swan into the night,
but, of course, I cannot tell you everything—
the way she closed her eyes to the orchard,   30
how her hair tumbled free of its pins,
how there were sudden dashes
whenever we spoke.

What I can tell you is
it was terribly quiet in Amherst   35
that Sabbath afternoon,
nothing but a carriage passing the house,
a fly buzzing in a windowpane.

So I could plainly hear her inhale
when I undid the very top   40
hook-and-eye fastener of her corset

and I could hear her sigh when finally it was unloosed,
the way some readers sigh when they realize
that Hope has feathers,
that reason is a plank,   45
that life is a loaded gun
that looks right at you with a yellow eye.

A Student Essay

Sophie Drake

Prof. Madden

Eng 102

September 26, 200X

A Dash of Meaning

It is fortunate that Emily Dickinson's brother and sister did not destroy her poems after her death (as she had requested), or we would be without the work of a great American poet. When we consider the original condition of those poems, it is understandable that for their initial publication they were revised to fit the standards of the 1890's by removing dashes and correcting other forms of punctuation and structure. However, it is also fortunate that in the 1950's Thomas Johnson restored Emily Dickinson's poems to their original form (Madden 1307). Very important among these restorations is the restoration of the dashes. By themselves, the dashes convey very little. But placed strategically before and after Dickinson's unusual images, they convey a great deal. The meaning they convey is in the clarifying pause and personal response they prompt from the reader.

"There's a certain Slant of light" is a poem filled with dashes that encourage us to pause and digest unusual images by personalizing them. The first dash follows a capitalized (emphasized) "Winter Afternoons—"(2) and prompts us to recall our own experience of winter afternoons and the pale light of winter that seems only a "Slant" of light, but a slant of light that weighs on us like "the Heft/Of Cathedral Tunes—" (4). Each of the twelve dashes in this poem follow an image we are prompted to recall from our own experience, and the poem concludes with a haunting but familiar image of the dim light of a winter's day descending into night: "When it goes, 'tis like the Distance/on the look of Death—" (15–16).

Sometimes the dashes simply make us pause to understand a provocative opening statement: "I like a look of Agony, / Because I know it's true—"(1–2). We understand that Dickinson is not referring to everything about the look of agony but only one thing, its authenticity. She then follows with a similar sentiment about the look of death, "Impossible to feign" (6). The dashes invite us to be part of a process of discovery. They seem to pause the poem for our response. It's almost as if we are having a conversation with the poet, a conversation that has us comparing our own internal responses to the world with hers, the dashes telling us when it's our turn. Helen McNeil supports the idea of this "internal" process when she says of Dickinson's poetry that "Her investigative process often [takes] speaker and reader through a sequence of rapidly changing images, even when all the action is interior" (1320).

In "I heard a Fly buzz—when I died—" (1), the dashes surround the key phrase in the poem. There is nothing special about hearing a fly buzz, but hearing a fly buzz at the moment of death, as the last event in our lives, is worthy of notice. It's the dashes before and after "when I died" that let us pause and digest the irony and meaning of the moment. There are fourteen other dashes in this poem that work in a similar way. Many things are being described in this monumental moment, the "Stillness in the Air—" (3) "The Eyes around—" (5). They are the kind of images we would expect to see at such a moment, and we are given time to digest them with help from the dashes. These predictable images put us back in the death scene, until suddenly "—and then it was / There interposed a fly—" (12). The preceding dash transitions us to the fly; the dash following gives us pause to imagine and reflect upon the usually unimportant fly now dominating the last vision of the speaker. As Paula Bennett describes it, the fly's buzz "is not only foregrounded. Before the poem is over, the buzz takes up the entire field of perception, coming between the speaker and the 'light' (of day, of life, of knowledge)" (1323). The dashes in the poem help us to experience that.

Allen Tate describes "Because I could not stop for Death—" as "one of the greatest [poems] in the English language." He says that "Every image intensifies every other," and he praises the poet's power "to fuse, into a single order of perception, a heterogeneous series: the children, the grain, and the setting sun (time)" (1321). The poem's twenty-two strategically placed dashes help us to experience this singular vision and intensity. The poem is a journey toward eternity, and the dashes connect each leg of the journey to the next and connect us (by giving us time to pause and reflect) to each of those legs. Death is a coachman who (because "I could not stop") "kindly stopped for me—" (2). The dash lines (—) seem to extend the miles on our journey and what we see out the coach window as we encounter "the School" (9), "the Fields and Grazing Grain—" (11), "the Setting Sun—" (12) (as both distance and time pass) until we reach the grave, "A swelling of the Ground—" (18), and finally after centuries, the realization that "the Horses' Heads / Were toward Eternity—" (24). That last dash is as much a question mark—prompting our own thoughts on the matter of an afterlife.

It would be foolish to suggest that the dashes in Dickinson's poetry are as important as her words and the striking images that result from those words. What makes her a brilliant poet is her use of words. But the dashes matter. They prompt us to pause and to clarify our own thoughts on the image at hand and the subject of the poem at large. They put us in an interior dialogue with the speaker in the poem. They magnify and extend the poem's images—and our responses. They are a dash of meaning.

[New Page]

Works Cited

Bennett, Paula. "On 'I heard a Fly buzz—when I died—.'" <u>Exploring Literature</u>. Ed. Frank Madden. 3rd ed. New York: Longman, 2007. 1322.

Dickinson, Emily. "Because I could not stop for Death." <u>Exploring Literature</u>. Ed. Frank Madden. 3rd ed. New York: Longman, 2007. 1311-1312.

——— "I heard a Fly buzz—when I died—." <u>Exploring Literature</u>. Ed. Frank Madden. 3rd ed. New York: Longman, 2007. 1310.

——— "I like a look of Agony." <u>Exploring Literature</u>. Ed. Frank Madden. 3rd ed. New York: Longman, 2007. 1308.

——— "There's a certain Slant of light." <u>Exploring Literature</u>. Ed. Frank Madden. 3rd ed. New York: Longman, 2007. 1308.

Madden, Frank. "Emily Dickinson: Poetry and Criticism." <u>Exploring Literature</u>. Ed. Frank Madden. 3rd ed. New York: Longman, 2007. 1306.

McNeil, Helen. "Dickinson's Method." <u>Exploring Literature</u>. Ed. Frank Madden. 3rd ed. New York: Longman, 2007. 1319.

Tate, Allen. "On 'Because I could not stop for Death.'" <u>Exploring Literature</u>. Ed. Frank Madden. 3rd ed. New York: Longman, 2007. 1321.

Exploring the Literature of Faith and Doubt: Options for Making Connections and Arguments

MAKING CONNECTIONS

1. Consider the ways your beliefs and values have affected your life. Do any of the stories, poems, plays, or essays in this section remind you of your own experiences or circumstances in your life? If so, choose one or more of these works and write a response essay that compares your experiences or circumstances with those in the literature.

2. Our own values, beliefs, and/or doubts affect the way we see the world and can strongly influence our response to the literature in this section. We may agree or disagree with what an author says or what characters say or do. So too, this literature may influence us and the formation of our values and beliefs. Write an essay about the ways in which one or more works in this section either provoked a moral judgment on your part or helped you learn something.

MAKING AN ARGUMENT

1. In his 1788 work *Critique of Practical Reason,* Immanuel Kant wrote: "Morality is not properly the doctrine of how we may make ourselves happy, but how we make ourselves worthy of happiness." Do you agree? Consider this quote, and write an essay about how an author or a character in one or more works in this section defines morality or his or her values.

2. In his poem "In Memoriam," Alfred Lord Tennyson expresses his view of faith and doubt in the following lines: "There lives more faith in honest doubt, / Believe me, than in half the creeds." Do you agree? Write about this quote as it affects the way a character or an author in one or more works in this section sees the world.

3. Choose a quote (or quotes) in the introduction to this section on Faith and Doubt (pp. 1153–1154) and pair it (or them) with one of the longer pieces in this section that either supports it or argues against it. For example, Yamaga Soko's comment about the unquestioning loyalty of the samurai warrior might be paired with Wilfred Owen's "*Dulce et Decorum Est,*" which might be seen as an argument against it. If you choose R. D. Laing's comment about alienation, you might choose Matthew Arnold's poem "Dover Beach" to support it. Write an essay that compares or contrasts a quote (or quotes) from the introduction with a story, poem, play, or essay that supports it or argues against it.

A Research Option

Nathaniel Hawthorne's story "Young Goodman Brown" and Wilfred Owen's poem *"Dulce et Decorum Est"* have something important to say about the dilemma of faith and doubt. Each of these works, however, springs from a very different historical, social, or political context.

Expanding our exploration of literature to include the context in which these works were produced can be an enriching and enlightening experience. Choose one or more of these or other works in this section, and write a research essay that includes secondary source material about the historical, social, or political background of the literature.

Writing About Connections Across Themes

Most of the literature in the text has been organized into theme sections, but good literature is much too complex to be reduced to a single, broad theme. Many of the works included under Faith and Doubt could just as easily fit under other themes—and in many cases works appearing in other themes could fit here as well.

Choose one or more of the following works from earlier chapters or other themes and consider how they can be linked to Faith and Doubt—and how this combination of the work with more than one theme provides additional insight into the literature and fresh topics for writing.

Collaboration: Writing and Revising with Your Peers

In addition to applying your own values and standards to writing about the literature in this section, you may find it beneficial to share and discuss your work with classmates. Getting feedback from others can help you generate and clarify your ideas and revise and edit your writing more effectively.

Choose a work, a topic, or one of the options above for writing about faith and doubt, and work with a partner or in a small group. Exchange journal entries or response sheets, generate questions together, do a group semantic map (see pp. 00–00), or simply share and respond to each other's ideas.

After you have written a rough draft of your essay, share it with a partner or your group. Respondents should function primarily as sensitive readers and give honest, constructive responses. They should try to be aware of each writer's purpose, discuss concerns particular to each writer, and comment on the effectiveness of the essay's organization, support, clarity, and voice (for a comprehensive checklist of revision, see p. 46).

In the final stage of your writing, editing and proofreading might be done in a similar fashion. A partner or group readers might help you check for correct grammar, spelling, punctuation, and typos (a comprehensive checklist for editing is on p. 49).

A Writing/Research Portfolio Option

A portfolio is a collection of your work, related materials, and commentary about your work collected over time. Gathering materials in a portfolio will provide you with resources for research and development. You can use your portfolio to collect your writing about the literature in this section, to find a topic to write about, to revise or add to your work, or to keep multiple drafts and monitor the changes you make as you revise.

Among the resources you might include:

• Your responses to the quotes and prompts about faith and doubt at the beginning of this section, the questions you had right after you finished reading each piece of literature, or your journal entries.

• What your classmates, instructor, or published critics had to say about the literature and how their comments may have influenced your interpretation.

• Information you have gathered from the library and Internet about the historical, social, or political context of the work or its author.

Appendix A

Critical Approaches to Literature

Earlier in the text you were introduced to four different perspectives from which to interpret literature: reader-based, text-based, context-based, and author-based approaches. In this section we take a closer look at each of these critical perspectives.

Try to keep in mind that these approaches may easily overlap, and critics will often combine them in their analyses. A reader-based approach, though emphasizing personal response, may call on the text for detailed support or make reference to contextual issues. Text-based approaches, though emphasizing the text, may interpret the elements of the text through contextual knowledge. Context-based approaches may consider the attitudes of the reader and the author, and derive support from the text. Author-based criticism may consider the author's style and structure in the text and the influence of readers and contextual issues on the author.

The difference between one critical approach and another may be more a matter of emphasis than kind, and drawing upon several perspectives can yield a rich interpretation. What distinguishes one approach from another is the answer to a fundamental question: *Where is the meaning?* In the reader? In the text? In the world around the text? In the author? How we answer this question will determine the approach we take.

The explanations below will define each approach. To clarify their differences in practice, let's apply each of them to two works of literature: the modern poem "Those Winter Sundays" (p. 13) and the ancient Greek drama Antigonê (p. 104). As you read these applications, it will be clear that some works of literature yield better results with some approaches than others.

Further Reading: Introduction to Literary Theory

Bressler, Charles. *Literary Criticism: An Introduction to Theory and Practice.* Third Edition. 2002.

Dobie, Ann B. *Theory into Practice. Introduction to Literary Criticism.* 2001.

Eagleton, Terry. *Literary Theory: An Introduction.* 1983.

READER-BASED CRITICISM

The basic premise of **reader-based** or **reader-response** critical theory is that literature does not exist separate from those who read it. The critical approach reflected in this book is reader-based. Readers are encouraged to respond personally to literature, to think about the ways their backgrounds influence their responses, and to support their responses with reference to the literature itself.

Throughout this book, readers have been encouraged to supplement this reader-based approach with other perspectives. Discussions of the elements of literature and close reading and textual analysis in Chapters 3 and 4 rely on text-based practices. So too, suggestions for secondary-source research in Chapter 5 encourage an exploration of literature typical of context-based and author-based approaches.

A reader-response approach to "Those Winter Sundays" might emphasize the reader's identification with the speaker in the poem. The student writer of the response essay at the end of Chapter 2, for example, compares her relationship with her father to that of the father-son relationship in the poem. She cites words and lines that remind her of her own situation and draws ample support from both her own life and the text of the poem to illustrate similarities and differences.

An example of a reader-response approach to *Antigonê* might include identification with or personal reactions to Antigonê, Ismenê, Creon, or Haimon. Readers might pass judgments on Creon or imagine how they would have behaved when faced with Antigonê's predicament. They might address which character is most like them, identify characters that remind them of people they know, and comment on how these personal connections affect their responses.

Further Reading on Reader-Based Criticism

Bleich, David. *Subjective Criticism.* 1978.
Brenner, Gerry. *Performative Criticism: Experiments in Reader Response,* 2004.
Davis, Todd F. and Kenneth Womack. *Formalist Criticism and Reader-Response Theory.* 2002.
Holland, Norman N. *The Dynamics of Literary Response.* 1973, 1989.
Iser, Wolfgang. *The Act of Reading.* 1978.
Rabinowitz, Peter. *Before Reading.* 1987.
Rosenblatt, Louise. *The Reader, the Text, the Poem.* 1978.
Tompkins, Jane O. *Reader-Response Criticism: From Formalism to Post-Structuralism.* 1980.

TEXT-BASED CRITICISM
Formalism

Formalism seeks to *objectify* the text—to examine it in isolation from its reader, its context, and its author. **New Criticism,** the most popular type of formalism, is not new. It was given its name more than half a century ago as a reaction to the older biographical and historical approaches that preceded it. Though its popularity has now declined, it was the most dominant form of literary criticism in the twentieth century. As the designation "formalism" suggests, this approach closely examines elements of form/structure and language such as genre, plot, characterization, narration, tone, irony, diction, imagery, metaphor, and symbol. A formalist critic constructs meaning by focusing exclusively on the elements of the text and the way they work together to form a unified, coherent whole.

Because the background, values, and feelings of the reader and the author cannot be objectively evaluated, formalism sees them as irrelevant or erroneous in the construction of a stable meaning. It classifies reliance on a reader's emotional response as an **affective fallacy** and reliance on knowledge of an author's life or intentions as an **intentional fallacy.**

A formalist response to "Those Winter Sundays," for example, would stick closely to the text of the poem. It might try to establish the meaning of the poem through analysis of the language, the images, symbols, speaker's tone, and how they work together to build and to support the speaker's concluding rhetorical question, "what did I know/of love's austere and lonely offices?" (13).

A similar approach to *Antigonê* might consider how well the play fulfills the definition of tragedy. It might examine the structure of the plot, details of characterization, function of the chorus, and way these elements form an organic unity—how the structure of the play naturally culminates in the final lines of Choragos as he sums up the meaning of the play.

Further Reading on Formalist Criticism

Brooks, Cleanth, and Robert Penn Warren. *Understanding Poetry.* 1938.
Davis, Todd F. and Kenneth Womack. *Formalist Criticism and Reader-Response Theory.* 2002.
Empson, William. *Seven Types of Ambiguity.* 1958.
Ransom, John Crowe. *The New Criticism.* 1941.
Richards, I. A. *Practical Criticism.* 1928.
Wellek, Rene, and Austin Warren. *Theory of Literature.* 1949, 1973.

Deconstruction

Like formalism, **deconstruction** focuses exclusively on the text and requires close reading. Unlike formalism, however, which examines parts and relationships to construct a whole, the intention of deconstruction, as its name suggests, is to break down the whole—to deconstruct its meaning. While formalism emphasizes structure and the stability of interpreting the text in isolation, deconstruction insists on the instability and transitory nature of the text.

An early proponent of deconstruction was Jacques Derrida, who explained it through the French word *differance,* which means both "to differ" and "to defer." First, this view asserts that nothing can be known in isolation. We can only know the meaning of something by how it differs from something else to which it is related. All knowledge is based on difference, and all language is relational. We can only know "dark" in relation to "light," "up" to "down," "good" to "evil." Second, any stable or definitive meaning or interpretation must be deferred or put off perpetually because meaning, like the world, is always changing. What authors intend is different than what they write or what readers read. No text has a definitive meaning. So we cannot say one interpretation is right and another wrong.

Rather than attempting to construct an interpretation of its own, a deconstructionist approach to either "Those Winter Sundays" or *Antigonê* might try to reveal any number of alternative meanings for the poem or the play. It might question the credibility of the speaker in the poem and Choragos in the play and attempt to dismantle other interpretations by demonstrating the instability of their meaning.

Further Reading on Deconstruction

Berman, Art. *From the New Criticism to Deconstruction.* 1988.

Culler, Jonathan. *On Deconstruction: Theory and Criticism after Structuralism.* 1983.

de Man, Paul. *Allegories of Reading.* 1979.

Derrida, Jacques. *Of Grammatology. Trans. Gayatri Spivak.* 1974.

Hartmann, Geoffrey H., et al. *Deconstruction and Criticism.* 1979.

McQuillan, Martin. ed. *Deconstruction: A Reader.* 2001.

Norris, Christopher. *Deconstruction: Theory and Practice.* 1982, 1991.

CONTEXT-BASED CRITICISM

Historical Criticism

The basic premise of **historical criticism** is that literature benefits from being read in its own historical context. Important to this perspective are the political, economic, and psychological influences of the era that produced the literature and its author. The audience for whom it was written and how its meaning and the connotations of its language may have changed over time are among the factors important to this type of interpretation.

A recent development in historical criticism, **New Historicism,** questions the validity of traditional historical criticism and argues that we can only view the past from the "informed" present. It insists that we see the past through our own values and view the "official" history of the ruling classes with skepticism, that the history of those defeated and oppressed must also be revealed.

A historical critic's view of "Those Winter Sundays" might identify the period in which the poem was set and examine the forces at work in that era. For example, the author was an African American born in 1913. Research into the economic conditions and racial attitudes prevalent during the period when the poet was growing up might help the reader understand the nature of the father's work and the cold and sparse setting of the poem.

A similar view of *Antigonê* might focus on the structure of Greek government and the tenets of Greek religion when the play was written. It might consider the burial of Polyneices and compare the audience's expectations of that era with those of a modern audience and explore the significance of those differences.

Further Reading on Historical Criticism

Auerbach, Erich. *Mimesis: The Representation of Reality in Western Literature.* 1953.

Brannigan, John. *New Historicism and Cultural Materialism.* 1998.

Foucault, Michel. *Madness and Civilization. Trans. Richard Howard.* 1965.

Gallagher, Catherine and Stephen Greenblatt. *Practicing New Historicism.* 2001.

Greenblatt, Stephen. *Marvellous Possessions.* 1991.

Hamilton, Paul. *Historicism.* 1996.

Herman, Peter C. ed. *Historicizing Theory,* 2004.

Veser, H. Aram. *The New Historicism.* 1989.

Gender (Feminist, Lesbian, Gay) Criticism

Gender criticism examines how literature reflects sexual identity or orientation. It may address the ways in which an author's gender has influenced his or her work. It may examine the gender-based portrayal of literary characters and their behavior.

It may explore the way in which literature supports or rejects societal norms that foster gender stereotypes. It may emphasize gay and lesbian issues.

Its most popular form is **Feminist Criticism,** which has emerged as a powerful literary force during the last 50 years. Among the issues feminist critics address are literary depictions of women, assumptions about women generated by male writers, the recurring pattern in literature of male dominance, female passivity, and sexism in literature as it reflects the societies that fostered it.

A feminist response to "Those Winter Sundays" might consider the restrained nature of a father-son relationship that seems to suppress the communication of feelings. It might question why there is no mother in this household or why this male speaker took so long to realize his feelings for his father.

A similar approach to *Antigonê* might emphasize the overtly sexist nature of Creon's response to Antigonê and Ismenê—how his sexist words and attitude echoed an assumption about the inequality of the sexes tacitly supported by ancient Greek society. It might scrutinize the causes of Ismenê's passivity and the consequences of Antigonê's assertiveness.

Further Reading on Gender Criticism

Abel, Elizabeth, ed. *Writing and Sexual Difference.* 1982.

Cosslet, Tess, et al. *Feminism and Autobiography.* 2000.

Fetterly, Judith. *The Resisting Reader: A Feminist Approach to American Fiction.* 1978.

Jagose, Annamarie. *Queer Theory: An Introduction.* 1996.

Kent, Kathryn R. *Making Girls into Women: American Women's Writing and the Rise of Lesbian Identity.* 2003.

Malinowski, Sharon and Christa Brelin. *The Gay and Lesbian Literary Companion.* 1995.

Ruthven, K. K. *Feminists Literary Studies: An Introduction.* 1984.

Sedgwick, Eve. *Epistemology of the Closet.* 1991.

Showalter, Elaine. *The New Feminist Criticism.* 1986.

Political-Economic Criticism

Political-economic criticism focuses on the influence and the consequences of the economic social order in literature. Its most popular form is **Marxist Criticism,** which argues that literature reflects the class structure and class struggle that produced it. It emphasizes the social content of literature and scrutinizes the economic circumstances of literature for instances of exploitation. It also analyzes the ways in which text, author, and readers reveal class attitudes.

A Marxist view of "Those Winter Sundays" might emphasize the poor economic situation of this family—how their economic plight and its consequence, the unceasing labor of the father to make ends meet, has created circumstances that made it impossible for the father to have the time for meaningful communication with his son.

A similar view of *Antigonê* might expose the arrogance of Creon as typical of the ruling class—how he exploits and silences the proletariat/laboring class messengers and guards of Polyneices' body—and forces them to go against their own consciences.

Further Reading on Political-Economic Criticism

Eagleton, Terry. *Criticism and Ideology: A Study in Marxist Literary Theory.* 1976.

Howard, Jean E. and Scott Cutler Shershow. *Marxist Shakespeares.* 2001.
Lentricchia, Frank. *Criticism and Social Change.* 1983.
Sartre, Jean-Paul. *What is Literature?* 1949.
Williams, Raymond. *Marxism and Literature.* 1977.

Psychoanalytic Criticism

Derived from the psychological theory of Sigmund Freud, **psychoanalytic criticism** emphasizes the underlying meaning in the narrative, actions, and dialogue of literature. Sexual symbols, dreams, and repressed feelings are central to a psychological analysis of the characters. The creative process and psychological makeup of the author may also be of special interest. An excellent example of psychoanalytic criticism in this text is "Hamlet's Oedipus Complex" by Ernest Jones on page 669.

A psychoanalytic view of "Those Winter Sundays," for example, might focus on the repressed the speaker and question why his feelings of affection for his father has lain dormant for so many years. It might conjecture about the competition between father and son for the affection of the unnamed, unmentioned mother in this family.

Given the incestuous nature of the relationship between Antigonê's parents, Oedipus and Iocastê, a psychoanalytic critic might be overwhelmed with material for exploration here. For example, what psychological burden does Antigonê carry because of the bizarre relationship between her parents? Such a question might yield some very interesting ideas.

Further Reading on Psychoanalytic Criticism

Chodorow, Nancy. *Feminism and Psychoanalytic Theory.* 1990.
Crews, Frederick C., ed. *Psychoanalysis and Literary Process.* 1970.
Ellmann, Maud. *Psychoanalytic Literary Criticism.* 1995.
Frankland, Graham. *Freud's Literary Culture.* 2000.
Hartmann, Geoffrey. *Psychoanalysis and the Question of Text.* 1979.
Kurzweil, Edith, and William Phillips, eds. *Literature and Psychoanalysis.* 1983.
Trilling, Lionel. *Freud and the Crisis of Our Culture.* 1955.
Wright, Elizbeth. *Psychoanalytic Criticism: A Reappraisal.* 1998.

Archetypal Criticism

Derived from the theories of psychologist Carl Jung, this approach assumes that we share a "collective unconscious" that has been shaped by the repeated experiences of our ancestors. It asserts that through this collective unconscious we indirectly share a knowledge of **archetypes**— universal images, patterns, and forms like the seasons, the sun, the moon, the wise old man or woman, fire, night, and blood. Of special interest to an archetypal critic are images, descriptive detail, plot patterns, and types of characters that appear frequently in literature and that seem to evoke nonrational but powerful responses from our unconscious memory.

An archetypal critic, for example, might approach "Those Winter Sundays" by identifying some of the more powerful images and symbols in the poem. Both the speaker's and the reader's response to a father who "makes banked fires blaze," and "who had driven out the cold" as an archetypal image might prompt some rich exploration.

A similar view of *Antigonê* might explore connections between the play and the many haunting and powerful mythological images and references presented in the dialogue and choral odes throughout the play.

Further Reading on Archetypal Criticism

Bodkin, Maud. *Archetypal Patterns in Poetry.* 1958.

Brady, Patrick. *Memory and History as Fiction: An Archetypal Approach to the Historical Novel.* 1993.

Campbell, Joseph. *The Hero with a Thousand Faces.* 1949.

Frye, Northrop. *Anatomy of Criticism.* 1957.

Lentricchia, Frank. *After the New Criticism.* 1980.

Moon, Beverly. *An Encyclopedia of Archetypal Symbolism.* 1997.

Author-Based Criticism

Author-based or **biographical** criticism emphasizes the relationship between authors' lives and their works. Finding out about an author's life, of course, requires reading a **biography** or **autobiography** of the author. An effective literary biography brings the author's work and life together. And literary biographies can be highly controversial.

Of special interest in biographical criticism is the way in which authors' lives have influenced their writing—how details and people in their own lives have entered their work. Exploring these connections may lead to a deeper understanding of a work's meaning.

A biographical critic's response to "Those Winter Sundays," for example, might include research on Robert Hayden's growing up and his relationship with his father. A biographical critic might seek connections between the events in Hayden's life and his psychological or emotional state when he wrote the poem.

A similar view of *Antigonê* might search for whatever details are available about the life and career of its author, Sophocles. With few biographical details available, a biographical critic might look for clues about Sophocles and his opinions in this and other plays and conjecture about his background based on knowledge of his contemporaries.

Further Reading and Examples of Biographical Criticism

Ackroyd, Peter. *Shakespeare.* 2005.

Edel, Leon. *Literary Biography.* 1957.

Ellmann, Richard. *James Joyce.* 1983.

Farr, Judith. *The Passion of Emily Dickinson.* 1992.

Felber, Lynette. *Literary Liaisons: Auto/Biographical Appropriations in Modernist Women's Writing.* 2002.

Greenblatt, Stephen. *Will in the World.* 2004.

Jellinek, Estelle C. *Women's Autobiography: Essays in Criticism.* 1986.

Kaplan, Fred. *The Singular Mark Twain: A Biography.* 2003.

Shapiro, James. *A Year in the Life of William Shakespeare: 1599.*

Appendix B

Writing About Film

From earliest times, people have loved stories. Before books, stories were passed along by word of mouth. Great storytellers, like the Greek bard Homer or the Anglo-Saxon narrator of *Beowulf,* wove their tales in poetry, which was pleasurable to listen to and easy to remember. With the invention of writing, stories could be recorded on parchment or paper. Storytellers became writers, authors whose tales could be read far beyond the reach of their own voices. Today we get our stories from a variety of media, including radio, movies, television, video, and computers. New technologies keep widening the storytelling circle.

WHY WRITE ABOUT FILM?

For more than one hundred years, filmmakers have been part of this tradition. The art of motion pictures, while relatively crude and simple in its infancy, has matured into one of the most powerful and eloquent forms of literature. Although movies vary in purpose and quality, just as printed literature does, many movies are worth close attention. Writing about film is a good way to learn more about this important medium: how it works, why it affects us as it does, and what it means to others. And since the movie screen is a kind of mirror, reflecting our cultural values and individual dreams, writing about film is another way to learn about ourselves.

Like the stories, poems, plays, and essays in this book, films are fitting subjects to help you understand your personal responses, to develop your critical thinking skills, and to explore the world beyond your immediate experience through analysis, argument, and research. In this appendix, you'll learn how to write about film from a number of perspectives: through response essays, film reviews, critical essays, film comparisons, and research papers. You'll see what film and written literature have in common and how they differ. You'll review the tools used by filmmakers to tell their stories, and you'll learn how to prepare to write about their films.

The author of this book thanks William V. Costanzo for contributing this appendix on film. William Costanzo has a Ph.D. from Columbia University and has spoken and published widely on the use of film and technology in English classes. He is the author of four books on this topic: *Double Exposure: Composing Through Writing and Film* (1984), *The Electronic Text* (1989), *Reading the Movies* (1992), and *Great Films and How To Teach Them* (2004).

FILM AS LITERATURE

Fiction films—movies that tell stories, as opposed to documentary films, which are more like essays—depend on the same narrative elements as novels and short stories. They have characters, settings, and plots. They present events from particular points of view. They possess a certain structure, tone, style, and often symbolism. These are the basic elements of storytelling.

Filmmakers use different tools for handling these elements. Whereas a writer is limited to the written word, a director has cameras, actors, sets, lights, editing consoles, sound, and more. The actors represent characters through the repertoire of performance, including gesture, facial expression, intonation, make-up, and costumes. The setting is represented by actual locations or by sets constructed by a team of carpenters and designers. The plot—that chain of related events leading to the story's climax—is played out in a succession of scenes fashioned by scriptwriters, filmed by cinematographers under the director's watchful eye, and rearranged into a final sequence by film editors. While a writer might specify a particular point of view by using "I saw" or "she noticed," the filmmaker might use the camera to control perspective, framing the subject as a close-up or shooting the subject from different angles. To create tone and mood, a writer manipulates the instruments of language—atmospheric adjectives, sentence rhythm, muscular or supple verbs. The filmmaker creates these effects with lighting, color, music, and sound effects.

One big difference between written literature and film regards authorship. A story or a novel has one name on the title page, but who is the author of a movie? Sometimes the director has a strong hand in shaping the film, but often the actors, scriptwriters, cinematographers, or editors make equal or stronger contributions. Try counting all the names that roll by on the closing credits of a major feature film.

Another difference lies in the nature of language and the medium of film. A movie shows the characters, settings, and events as motion pictures and adds the auditory dimension of voice-over narration, music, dialogue, and sound effects. A writer must describe events in words. The reader must interpret those words, picturing a story's people and places in the mind's eye, transforming the written text into a movie directed by his or her own imagination.

PREPARING TO WRITE ABOUT FILMS

Before you launch into an essay or a film review, it helps to be clear about your topic, purpose, audience, format, scope, and slant. You might ask yourself the following questions:

- What film or films have I chosen to write about?
- What approach will I be taking? (For each purpose, there is probably a set of stylistic and structural expectations (a format) that you can follow.)
- Will I be examining my personal reactions (a response essay), summarizing and evaluating the film (film review), relating one film to other films by the same director (comparison essay), or finding out more about how the film was made (research essay)?
- Who is my intended audience? What are my readers likely to know about movies, and what will I need to tell them?

- How far beyond the film itself will my essay range (its scope)?
- What particular theories, opinions, or viewpoints (slant) will I be bringing to this film?

Since movies require some form of projection system, you'll need to be familiar with the technical features of the system you use. Since you can fast forward or rewind your way through scenes, a VCR is good for close analysis as well. VCR's are being replaced by the more popular Digital Video Disc recordings (DVDs), which are more compact and can be displayed either on your television set or computer screen. Of course, if you've chosen to write about a film that hasn't been released yet for home viewing, you'll probably need to make several trips to the theatre. In this case, since you can't control the film, you need to rely on your memory, focused attention, and techniques for taking notes in the dark. However, viewing movies in a theatre setting can give you valuable information about audience response that you can't get when you're home alone. You can see for yourself how people react to different scenes and include these observations in your review.

When you take notes, decide ahead of time what you'll be looking for. Some of this is standard production information, but some helpful questions might include:

- Who are the directors, scriptwriters, cinematographers, editors, art directors, composers, and producers?
- Who are the principal performers, and what roles do they play?
- When was the film originally released, and what studio produced it?

Some information will help you summarize the story. Look for the chief features of the plot: the central conflict, the complications, high points, and final outcome.

- Are there any subplots (secondary stories going on at the same time as the main plot)?
- What are the key scenes? Where do they take place, and how does each scene develop the story or reveal something new about its characters?

Pay particular attention to the opening and closing shots, since these are often carefully constructed to introduce the story's crucial elements or to tie them all together. Notice how the movie's title, cultural allusions, and symbolic details contribute to the story's theme or themes.

Sometimes it's a good idea to read something about a film before watching it. This helps to orient your expectations, to prepare you for the journey, so you can recognize the significance of events when they occur. It's easier to spot telling details like a shadow on the wall or an ominous gathering of birds when you know what you're looking for. After your first or second screening, you may want to do some serious research. Find out more about the director's life and other films. Read about the actors. Find a documentary on the making of the film. If the story relates to some real-life event, look for a factual account of the event.

The strategies that help you write essays about literature can serve you well when writing about film. Try brainstorming, listing, or freewriting to get down first impressions and ideas. Keep a viewing log or double-entry journal (one side for your first run through the film, the other side for reflections and re-screenings) to record your thoughts as they evolve over time. Make an outline or concept map to help organize all the information you have collected.

WRITING RESPONSE ESSAYS

A response essay describes your reactions to a film. It's a good way to explore the personal feelings, memories, and ideas that the film triggered for you—and to clarify them for your readers. Sometimes by explaining your responses to another person, you come to understand them better yourself.

You might begin simply by talking to your friends about the movie that you saw. Start with your general impressions. What words describe your overall response? Then get specific. Tell them what pleased or upset you most. Which characters were really interesting, funny, or weird? Which scenes had you enthralled? When were you aware of the music, photography, or special effects?

Now look for the reasons behind your responses. What explanations can you give for such strong or weak reactions? Did any of the characters or settings remind you of people or places in your life? Did you identify closely with any scenes? What additional associations—with other movies, historical events, or works of literature or art— might help to clarify the thoughts and feelings you experienced during the film?

The final format of a response essay need not be formal. It may be conversational in tone, like a journal, but it should share something important about your film experience. It should both *show* and *tell* about the film as it occurred to you. If you're successful, your readers should be able to see what you saw, hear what you heard, and understand how you felt.

WRITING FILM REVIEWS

A film review introduces a new film to readers who might want to see it. Typically, film reviews include a plot summary, descriptions of the main performances, perhaps some references to interesting film techniques, background information on the production, and an account of the movie's themes. An important purpose of a film review is evaluation. Readers want to know whether this film is for them.

Keep your summary brief. Let your readers know what the movie is about without ruining it for them. Don't give away the ending or spoil any surprises along the way. Try to give them both the gist and flavor of the film. Compare it to other films that they might know. Is it a romantic comedy, a horror film, a film noir, or a quirky independent film? Does Brad Pitt play the usual heartthrob? Is Julia Roberts up to her performance in *Erin Brokovitch* or just another pretty woman? What makes the film special and unique?

Evaluate the movie in specific terms. Describe one or two scenes in detail to convey a sense of the acting. In addition to particular performances, you might comment on the spectacular underwater photography, the musical score that swells unnecessarily behind every romantic moment, the fast-paced editing that propels the action forward, or the annoying use of handheld cameras to create a pseudo-documentary effect.

Nearly every newspaper, as well as many magazines and Web sites, publish film reviews. Sample a few before writing your final draft. Notice that they tend to be somewhat more formal than personal responses but less formal than critical or research essays. They follow the same general format and include the same kinds of information, yet they reflect the particular styles and interests of the author and the intended audience.

WRITING CRITICAL ESSAYS

Critical essays go beyond description. They analyze a film and develop a thesis about it. The focus here is more on the text of the film itself than on your personal responses or evaluation. A formal analysis examines the film's formal aspects, or how it is constructed. This is an opportunity to notice the many technical and artistic decisions about casting, lighting, camera work, set design, editing, and sound that contribute to the film experience.

One way to begin a formal study is to analyze a particular scene shot by shot. Use a VCR or DVD to view the scene repeatedly.

- Number every shot, and jot down what you notice about each shot
- Describe the action (what the characters do) and the setting (where and when the action takes place).
- Describe the camerawork—is it a close-up or long shot? A high angle (seen from above) or low angle (seen from below)? Does the camera pan (pivot horizontally) to the left, track forward (move closer to the subject), zoom in (adjust the lens so that objects seem to get closer)?
- Describe the lighting—is it bright and buoyant? Dark and mysterious? Glamorously illuminated from above?
- Describe the sound (dialogue, narration, music, sound effects).

You might also want to record the length of each shot, since timing is an important feature of editing. A shot-by-shot analysis can help you appreciate a film's creative features, and it can provide you with evidence to support your broad claims about the film.

Any good analysis should have a payoff. There's little point in breaking something down into its component parts unless the process serves a bigger purpose. That's the function of your thesis—to clarify some larger understanding of the film. Your goal might be to show how *The Godfather* uses parallel editing to reveal Michael Corleone's hypocrisy. As support, you might analyze the scene in which Michael (played by Al Pacino) attends his godson's baptism while his henchmen slaughter all his rivals. Or your thesis might concern Stephen Spielberg's use of black and white photography in *Schindler's List*. Here you might analyze the Krakow ghetto scene in which a little girl's red coat contrasts strikingly with the grim documentary tones of the liquidation.

When writing a critical essay, assume that readers are already familiar with the film. There's no need to worry about giving away the plot. Critical essays tend to be more formal than film reviews, introducing the thesis in the opening paragraph and developing it with the tools of argument: clear reasoning and supportive evidence. Your readers should be able to follow every turn of thought to your conclusion. At best, they will agree with you; at worst, they'll understand your point even if they disagree.

WRITING COMPARISON ESSAYS

While watching a film, you may be reminded of something else: a similar film, a work of literature, or maybe a current event. A comparison essay is one way to explore such similarities. There should be a solid basis for comparison. Two films may be by the same director, feature the same actor, take place in the same location, belong to the same genre (science fiction, black comedy, the Western), or focus on the same topic or theme. You might compare sequels to the original, or you might compare the movie and the book.

Comparison essays are usually organized in one of two ways—either they compare A and B separately, using a block format; or they compare A and B side by side, using a point-by-point strategy. For example, a block comparison of the three *Godfather* films would first describe the original *The Godfather* (1972) before moving on to *The Godfather II* (1979) and *The Godfather III* (1990). A point-by-point comparison might contrast the time frames for all three films before comparing their plots, then their characters, and so on. Either way, the final purpose of such comparisons is to learn something that might not be available by studying one film by itself.

Film adaptations are especially good subjects for a literature class. They give you a chance to compare the movie version to the original work. You get to notice what was added and left out. You get to judge the filmmaker's interpretation of characters, settings, and themes against your own visual imagination. Do the actors look and act as you pictured them when you read the book? Do the sets and locations live up to your expectations? Is the movie faithful to the spirit of the written work? How do the experiences of watching and reading differ? Ultimately, which experience is more satisfying for you?

Many of the stories in this book have been adapted for the screen. Anton Chekhov's "The Lady with the Pet Dog," William Faulkner's "A Rose for Emily," and Nathaniel Hawthorne's "Young Goodman Brown" are all short films. Joyce Carol Oates's short story, "Where Are You Going, Where Have You Been?" has been turned into a feature-length production, titled *Smooth Talk* (1985), with Laura Dern as Connie and Treat Williams as Arnold Friend. Since the story itself was based on actual events, you might compare both fictional versions to the newspaper accounts of what reporters called "The Pied Piper of Tucson."

Nearly all of the plays in *Exploring Literature* have been interpreted on film, some more than once. Read the section on *"Desperately Seeking Hamlet: Four Interpretations"* (pages 662–665), which compares four filmed interpretations of *Hamlet*. Since drama is meant to be performed rather than read, comparing a script to a movie of the play is a little like comparing sheet music to a concert. You can learn a lot about the play, the nature of performance, and yourself by comparing what you experience on the page and on the screen.

WRITING RESEARCH ESSAYS

At some point while watching a film you may want to know more than meets the eye. Perhaps you're interested in learning more about an actor, a director, or how the film was made. A film about prohibition in 1920s Chicago or drug trafficking in modern Argentina may arouse your curiosity about those places and events. The purpose of a research essay is to find out about more about some aspect of the film by investigating outside sources. It's an opportunity to look behind the screen.

Lots of leading questions could be asked about the making of a film, such as:

- Where did the idea for this film originate?
- How did the final script come to be written?
- What technical innovations—in camera work, lighting, color, or special effects—were used during production, and how were they achieved?

- Were there special problems in shooting on location or creating the sets? How were they solved?
- What musical decisions were made for the sound track, and how do they contribute to the total film experience?
- What are the director's hallmarks in this and other films? How did the actors behave on and off the set?

You might also have questions about the economic, social, and cultural aspects of the film:

- How much did it cost to make, and how much did it earn?
- How important were the promotions, tie-ins, theatrical releases, and video sales?
- How did the public respond to the final film? What did the critics say?
- Do you see this film as part of a larger trend, perhaps a trend in ritualized violence or a growing fear of natural disasters? If so, what other films does it resemble, and what do these films say collectively about life today?
- How does the film represent different kinds of people: men and women, rich and poor, old and young, or various ethnic groups?
- What cultural beliefs about sexuality, politics, or family are challenged or confirmed by the film?

Such questions lead both inward to a closer look at the film itself and outward to the conditions that produced it. Your role as researcher and writer is to make meaningful connections between these two perspectives—the text and the cultural context. Although the information comes from primary and secondary sources, you're the one who puts it all together. Remember, the final essay represents *your* interpretation in *your* own voice. What makes it worth writing and reading are the insights you arrive at based on your research.

Review the sections on Research in Chapter 5 and Appendix C on Documentation. These pages will guide you to reliable sources and remind you how to cite those sources in the body of your essay as well as on the works cited page. These days, excellent background material can be found on DVD editions of films, including documentaries, interviews, production notes, rehearsal footage, outtakes, production stills, and storyboards. The Internet offers a wealth of useful Web sites, though their quality and dependability varies widely. Don't overlook traditional print sources, either. Often the best information may come from a biography, film journal, or movie review.

As you write your essay, keep in mind all the people who make movies, enjoy them, and write about them. The circle of cinematic storytelling is an ever-widening community. What you write can be a ticket of admission to the circle.

By writing about movies, you also widen the circle of literature to include some of the best stories of our times. You get to apply much of what you've learned about good written literature to a new medium, and you begin to appreciate the differences between the media of print and film. At the same time, you get to sharpen the all-important skills of critical thinking, persuasive writing, and research. And, if you practice reading literature with a filmmaker's eye, you learn to enrich your reading with the powers of your visual imagination.

Appendix C

Documentation

A DIRECTORY OF MLA FORMATTING AND DOCUMENTATION

The Physical Layout of the Research Essay

Citing Sources in the Text of the Essay

Documenting the Works Cited

Books

Periodicals

The Physical Layout of the Research Essay

Individual course requirements may vary from this MLA format, so check with your instructor before writing your essay.

Type of Paper Your research essay should be typed on 8 1/2" x 11" unlined paper.

Margins Top and bottom margins should be one inch from the edge of the paper. Left and right margins should be one inch from the edge of the paper.

Spacing The text of your research essay should be double-spaced. Quotations should be double-spaced. Your works cited page should be double-spaced.

Page Numbers Number all pages in the upper-right-hand corner about 1/2 inch from the top edge of the paper. If possible, type your name before the page number.

Heading and Title Your research essay does not require a separate title page. At the top and left margin of your first page, print the following:

> Your Name
> Your Instructor's Name
> The Title and Number of the Course
> The Date
> Center the Title
> (Do not underline, place in quotations, or capitalize all the letters in your title. Double space between the title and the first line of your writing.)
> The Text
> of Your
> Essay

Works Cited Page The Works Cited page is a separate page at the end of the essay.
1. Works are listed in alphabetical order.
2. Each listing is double-spaced, and there is double-spacing between listings.
3. The first line of each listing begins at the left margin. All other lines are indented five spaces.
4. Only works cited in the text of your essay are included.

Documentation—MLA Style

Because it is the most popular form for those who do literary research, the style we use here for documentation is taken from the *MLA Handbook for Writers of Research Papers*.

Citing Sources in the Text of the Essay

The source from which you have taken the information is cited directly in the essay through parenthetic reference in the following ways:

1. Ideas or information rephrased in your own words.
   The author's last name and the page number in parentheses: (Brown 253)
   Example: The conditions in those schools were reported as terrible (Brown 253).

2. Ideas or information put into your own words but with the author's name mentioned in the text.
   Page number in parentheses: (253)
   Example: Brown reported that the conditions in the schools he visited were terrible (253).

3. Direct quotation—prose
   Direct prose quotations of *four lines or less* are put in quotation marks and integrated into the text of your writing.
   Example: "I could not believe the appalling conditions I saw" (Brown 253).

   or

   Brown said, "I could not believe the appalling conditions I saw" (253).

4. Direct prose quotations of *five or more lines* are double-spaced and separated from the text of your writing by starting the quote on a new line and indenting the left margin an inch.
   Example: It was very clear that Dr. Grantly was taking much longer to die than anyone expected:

   > A month since the physicians had named four weeks as the outside period during which breath could be supported within the body of the dying man. At the end of the month the physicians wondered, and named another fortnight. The old man lived on wine alone, but at the end of the fortnight he still lived; and the tidings of the ministry became more frequent. (Trollope 3)

5. Direct quotation—poetry
   Direct quotations of *three lines or fewer* may be put in quotation marks and integrated into the text of your writing. Use a slash (/) with a space on each side to separate the lines of verse.
   Example: I sense deep regret in Robert Hayden's last lines: "What did I know, what did I know / of love's austere and lonely offices?" (13).

6. Direct quotations of *more than three lines* should be double-spaced and begin on a new line. Indent all quoted lines one inch from the left margin and use no quotation marks.
   Example: I was deeply affected by the scene described in William Stafford's poem:

   > The car aimed ahead its lowered parking lights;
   > under the hood purred the steady engine.
   > I stood in the glare of the warm exhaust turning red;
   > around our group I could hear the wilderness listen. (13-16)

7. Direct quotation—drama
   Quoted dialogue between two or more characters should be separated from the text. Begin each quote with the character's name indented one inch from the

left margin, written in all capital letters, and followed by a period. All additional lines below that first line should be indented three additional spaces. Line-numbered verse plays are cited in parentheses by act, scene, and line numbers; prose plays by page numbers.

Example: In Sophocles' play, Ismene's attempt to talk Antigone out of her defiance is futile:

> ISMENÊ. But no one must hear of this, you must tell no one!
> I will keep it a secret, I promise!
> ANTIGONÊ. Oh, tell it! Tell everyone!
> Think how they'll hate you when it all comes out
> If they learn that you knew about it all the time!
> ISMENÊ. So fiery! You should be cold with fear.
> ANTIGONÊ. Perhaps. But I am doing what I must. (Pro. 68-75)

Works Cited Documentation

The descriptions and examples below account for many of the sources you are likely to use, but this is not an exhaustive list. If the source you are using is not accounted for, the best source of additional information is Joseph Gibaldi's MLA Handbook for Writers of Research Papers, sixth edition, published by the Modern Language Association of America, 2003.

Books

1.   A Book by One Author
   Author's Name (reversed). Title of Book (underlined). City of Publication: Publishing Company, Year of Publication.
   Examples:
   Ellmann, Richard. James Joyce. New York: Oxford University Press, 1959.
   Sledge, Linda Ching. A Map of Paradise. New York: Bantam Books, 1997.

2.   A Book by Two or Three Authors
   Author's Name (reversed) and Second Author's Name. Title of Book (underlined). City of Publication: Publishing Company, Year of Publication.
   Examples:
   Desmond, Adrian and James Moore. Darwin. New York: Warner, 1991.
   Gilbert, Sandra and Susan Gubar. The Madwoman in the Attic: The Woman Writer and the Nineteenth Century Literary Imagination. New Haven: Yale University Press, 1979.

3.   A Work in an Anthology
   Author's Name (reversed). "Name of the Work" (in quotation marks). Title of the Anthology (underlined). Number of edition. Editor's name(s). City of Publication: Publishing Company, Year of Publication, Page Range.
   Examples:
   Chopin, Kate. "The Story of an Hour." Literature for Composition. 6th ed. Ed. Sylvan Barnet, William Burto, and Marcia Stubbs. New York: Longman, 2003. 12-14.
   Valdez, Luis. "Los Vendidos." Exploring Literature. 3rd ed. Ed. Frank Madden. New York: Longman, 2007. 1061-1070.

4.   A Work in a Collection by the Same Author
   Author's Name (reversed). "Title of the Work "(in quotation marks). Title of the

Collection (underlined). City of Publication: Publishing Company, Year of Publication. Page Range.

Examples:

Cheever, John. "The Enormous Radio." The Stories of John Cheever. New York: Knopf, 1978. 33-41.

Sontag, Susan, "The Aesthetics of Silence." Styles of Radical Will. New York: Farrar, 1969. 3-34.

5. An Introduction, Foreword, or Afterword

Author's Name. Introduction. Title of Book (underlined). By (author of book's name). City of Publication: Publishing Company, Year of Publication, Page Range.

Examples:

Costanzo, William V. Introduction. Reading the Movies. By William Costanzo. Urbana, IL: NCTE, 1992.

Orne, Martin T. Foreword. Anne Sexton. By Dianne Wood Middlebrook. Boston: Houghton Mifflin, 1991. xii-xxiii.

6. A Reference Book (Encyclopedia, Dictionary, etc.)

Title of Entry (if a person, reverse the name). Title of Reference Book (underlined). Number and/or Year of Edition.

Examples:

"Symbol." The New Encyclopedia Britannica: Micropaedia. 1974 ed.

"Sheridan, Richard Brinsley." The Oxford Companion to English Literature. 5th ed. 1985.

7. An Author with Two or More Works

Author's Name (reversed, in first entry of author only). Rest of Publication Information.

In subsequent listings, type three hyphens, followed by a period and the title.

Example:

Costanzo, William V. The Electronic Text. Englewood Cliffs, N.J.: Educational Technology Pub., 1989.

---. Reading the Movies. Urbana, Ill.: NCTE, 1992.

8. A Translated Book

Author's Name (reversed). Title of Book (underlined). Translator. City of Publication: Publishing Company, Year of Publication.

Example:

Homer. The Odyssey. Trans. Robert Fagles. New York: Penguin, 1996.

Periodicals

9. An Article in a Magazine

Author's Name (reversed). "Title of Article" (in quotation marks). Title of Magazine (underlined) Date of Publication (date, month, year): Page Range. If monthly or bimonthly, list month(s) as date. If no author's name appears, begin with the title of the article (but not "a" or "the").

Examples:

Korda, Michael. "The Third Man." New Yorker 25 Mar. 1996: 44-51.

Updike, John. "The Literary Life." Civilization Dec. 1996: 56-73.

10. An Article in a Scholarly Journal
    Author's Name (reversed). "Title of Article" (in quotation marks). Title of Journal (underlined) and Volume Number (year of publication, in parentheses): Page Range.
    Examples:
    Kamps, Ivo. "Possible Pasts: Historiography and Legitimation in Henry VIII." College English 58 (1996): 192-215.
    Wilkinson, James. "A Choice of Fictions: Historians, Memory, and Evidence." PMLA 111 (1996): 80-92.

11. An Article in a Newspaper
    Author's Name (reversed). "Title of Article" (in quotation marks). Title of Newspaper (underlined) and Date. Edition: Section Letter and Beginning Page Number.
    Examples:
    Grimes, William. "A Woman of Words That Win Pulitzers." New York Times 4 June 1996: C1.
    Wu, Jim. "Authors Praise New Forms." New York Times 8 March 1987, Sec. 2:1.

12. A Review
    Reviewer's Name (reversed). "Title of Review" (in quotation marks). Rev. of Title of Work Reviewed, by Author of Work Reviewed. Publication (underlined) Publication Date: Inclusive Page Numbers.
    Examples:
    Fraser, Kennedy. "Piper Pipe That Song Again." Rev. of Blake, by Peter Ackroyd. New Yorker 27 May 1996: 127-31.
    Vendler, Helen. Rev. of Essays on Style, ed. Roger Fowler. Essays in Criticism 16 (1966): 457-63.

Internet Sources

While there is not yet universal agreement about citing Internet sources, and relevant information is not always available, it is essential that you give as much information as you can—at least enough information that readers of your work can find the source themselves. To verify the quality and reliability of an online source, see the suggestions in the checklist in Chapter 5, 181–182.

For additional information, the Modern Language Association has its own comprehensive set of guidelines for citing Internet sources that you can access at <http://www.mla.org>.

Citing Online Sources from the Internet (if this information is available)

    Author's Name (reversed).
    Title (in quotations or underlined as appropriate).
    Publication Information.
    Title of Project, Database, Etc. (underlined).
    Volume, Issue, or Identifying Number (if available).
    Date of Electronic Publication.
    Page, Paragraph, or Section Numbers.
    Institution or Organization Sponsoring the Site.

Your Date of Access.

Electronic Address (within angle brackets).

13. An Entire Internet Database or Scholarly Project Site:

Bartleby.com:Great Books Online. Ed. Steven van Leeuwen. 2002. 24 May 2003. <http://www.bartleby.com>.

14. A Document or Online Book within a Scholarly Project or Database

Austen, Jane. Persuasion. 1818. Project Gutenberg. Ed. Sharon Partridge. Feb. 1994. 18 May 2004 <http://wwwgutenberg.net/dirs/etext94/persu11.txt.>.

15. A Personal or Professional Site:

Van Noate, Judith. Theater Connections. J. Murrey Atkins Library, UNC Charlotte. 6 April 2003 <http://libweb.uncc.edu/ref-arts/theater>.

16. An Online Book:

Twain, Mark. The Adventures of Tom Sawyer. Internet Wiretap Online. Carnegie-Mellon University. 22 Feb. 2002. <http:www.cs.cmu.edu/Web/people/rgs/sawyer-table.html>.

17. An Article in an Online Periodical:

Sohmer, Steve. "Opening Day at Shakespeare's Globe." Early Modern Literary Studies 3.1 (1997): 46 pars. 24 May 2003. <http://www.shu.ac.uk/emls/03-1/sohmjuli.html>.

18. An Article in an Encyclopedia on the Internet

"Hawthorne, Nathaniel." Britannica Online. Vers. 98.2. April 1998. Encyclopedia Britannica. 16 October 1998 <http://www.eb/com/:220>.

19. An Article in a Newspaper on the Internet

Markon, Jerry. "Virginia Colleges May Bar Illegal Immigrants." washingtonpost.com 26 Feb. 2004. 6 April 2004. <http://www.washing-tonpost.com/wp-dyn/articles/A6936-2004Feb25.html>.

20. An Article in a Magazine on the Internet

Pitta, Julie. "Un-Wired?" Forbes 20 April 1998. 4 Sept. 2002 <http://www.forbes.com/Forbes/98/0420/6108045a.html.>.

21. An E-mail

Courage, Richard. "Re: Assessment Rubric." E-mail to the author. 10 March 2005.

22. An Online Posting

Lardaro, Barbara. "Reaction to Joyce's Portrait of the Artist as a Young Man." WebCT. ENG 224H_XFM. Online posting. Dec. 5, 2004. 6 Dec. 2004. <http://webct.sunywcc.edu:8900/webct/public/home.pl.>.

Other Electronic Sources

23. A Periodical CD-ROM Database

Author's Name (reversed). "Title" (in quotation marks). Name of Source (electronic journal, conference, database, etc., underlined). Number of Volume or Issue. Year or Date of Publication. Publication Medium (CD-ROM, diskette, tape). Vendor. Date of Electronic Publication.

Barron, James. "After 17 Years, Cicada Emerges for Ritual of Sex and Death." New York Times Ondisc. CD-ROM. UMI-Proquest. 4 June 1996.

24. **A Nonperiodical CD-ROM Publication**

Author's Name (reversed). <u>Title</u> (underlined). Medium of Publication. City of Publication. Publisher. Date of Publication.

Shakespeare, William. <u>All's Well That Ends Well</u>. <u>William Shakespeare: The Complete Works on CD-ROM</u>. CD-ROM. Abingdon, Eng.: Andromeda Interactive, 1994.

Other Sources

25. **A Personal Interview**

Person's Name (reversed). Type of Interview (telephone, mail, on-line, personal, etc.). Date.

Martin, James. Telephone interview. 3 June 2004.

26. **A Lecture**

Speaker's Name (reversed). "Title of the Lecture" (in quotation marks). Nature of the Meeting. Location. Date.

Haynes, Terry. "The Problematic Essay: Right and Responsibility." Conference on College Composition and Communication. Hyatt Regency, Milwaukee. 28 Mar. 1996.

Worley, Demetrice A. "Telling Tales in School: An African American Woman's Voice in Composition." MLA Convention. Sheraton Washington, Washington, D.C. 28 Dec. 1996.

27. **A TV or Radio Program**

"Title of Episode or Segment" (in quotation marks). <u>Title of Program</u> (underlined). Name of the Network. Call Letters of the Local Station. Date of Broadcast.

"The Irish Question." The Story of English. PBS. WNET, New York. 6 Apr. 1985.

<u>Brideshead Revisited</u>, Episode 4. With Anthony Andrews and Jeremy Irons. PBS. WETA, Washington, D.C. 24 July 1984.

28. **A Sound Recording**

Name of Person (composer, conductor, performers—whoever should be emphasized). <u>Title of the Recording</u> (underlined). Manufacturer, Year of Issue. Medium (CD, LP, audiocassette, audiotape).

Mozart, Wolfgang Amadeus. Symphony no. 40 in G minor. Vienna Philharmonic. Cond. Leonard Bernstein. Deutsche Grammophon, 1984. Audiocassette.

Rea, Stephen. <u>James Joyce's Ulysses</u>. BBC Audio, 1993. Audiocassette.

29. **A Film or Video Recording**

<u>Title of Film or Video</u> (underlined). Director. Distributor, Year.

<u>Agamemnon</u>. By Aeschylus. Dir. Peter Hall. The National Theatre of Great Britain, 1983.

<u>Rozencrantz and Guildenstern Are Dead</u>. Dir. Tom Stoppard. Perf. Gary Oldman, Tim Roth, and Richard Dreyfuss. Cinecom Entertainment, 1990.

Sample Works Cited

Works Cited

<u>Agamemnon</u>. By Aeschylus. Dir. Peter Hall. The National Theatre of Great Britain, 1983.

Austen, Jane. <u>Persuasion</u>. 1818. <u>Project Gutenberg</u>. Ed. Sharon Partridge. Feb. 1994. 18 May 2004 <http://wwwgutenberg.net/dirs/etext94/persul1.txt.>.

Barron, James. "After 17 Years, Cicada Emerges for Ritual of Sex and Death." New York Times Ondisc. CD-ROM. UMI-Proquest. 4 June 1996.

Cheever, John. "The Enormous Radio." The Stories of John Cheever. New York: Knopf, 1978. 33-41.

Costanzo, William V. The Electronic Text. Englewood Cliffs N.J.: Educational Technology Pub., 1989.

---. Reading the Movies. Urbana, Ill.: NCTE, 1992.

Courage, Richard. "Re: Assessment Rubric." E-mail to the author. 10 March 2005.

Desmond, Adrian and James Moore. Darwin. New York: Warner, 1991.

Grimes, William. "A Woman of Words That Win Pulitzers." New York Times 4 June 1996: C1.

"Hawthorne, Nathaniel." Britannica Online. Vers. 98.2. April 1998. Encyclopedia Britannica. 16 October 1998 <http://www.eb/com/:220>.

Haynes, Terry. "The Problematic Essay: Right and Responsibility." Conference on College Composition and Communication. Hyatt Regency, Milwaukee. 28 Mar. 1996.

Homer. The Odyssey. Trans. Robert Fagles. New York: Penguin, 1996.

"The Irish Question." The Story of English. PBS. WNET, New York. 6 Apr. 1985.

Kamps, Ivo. "Possible Pasts: Historiography and Legitimation in Henry VIII." College English 58 (1996): 192-215.

Korda, Michael. "The Third Man." New Yorker. 25 Mar. 1996: 44-51.

Lardaro, Barbara. "Reaction to Joyce's Portrait of the Artist as a Young Man." WebCT. ENG 224H_XFM. On-line posting. Dec. 5, 2004. 6 Dec. 2004. <http://webct.sunywcc.edu:8900/webct/public/home.pl.>.

Martin, James. Phone interview. 3 June 2002.

Pitta, Julie. "Un-Wired?" Forbes 20 April 1998. 4 Sept. 2002 <http://www.forbes.com/Forbes/98/0420/6108045a.html.>.

Rea, Stephen. James Joyce's Ulysses. BBC Audio, 1993. Audiocassette.

"Sheridan, Richard Brinsley." The Oxford Companion to English Literature. 5th ed., 1985.

Sledge, Linda Ching. A Map of Paradise. New York: Bantam Books, 1997.

Twain, Mark. The Adventures of Tom Sawyer. Internet Wiretap Online Library. Carnegie-Mellon University. 22 Feb. 1999. <http:www.cs.cs.cmu.edu/Web/people/rgs/sawyr-table.html>.

Valdez, Luis. "Los Vendidos." Exploring Literature. 3rd ed. Ed. Frank Madden. New York: Longman, 2007. 1061-1070.

Van Noate, Judith. Theater Connections. J. Murrey Atkins Library, UNC Charlotte. 6 April 2003 <http://libweb.uncc.edu/ref-arts/theater>.

Voice of the Shuttle English Literature. University of California, Santa Barbara. Rev. 1999. 22 Feb. 1999. <http://www.humanitas.ucsb.edu/shuttle/english.html>.

GLOSSARY OF LITERARY TERMS

abstract language words which represent broad qualities or characteristics (e.g., interesting, good, fine, horrible, lovely)

allegory an extended metaphor

alliteration the repetition of initial consonant sounds in words close together (e.g. "sad Sunday school superintendent stare")

allusion a reference to another literary /artistic/historic, work, author, character, or event (frequently biblical or mythological)

amphitheater a semi-circular large, outdoor theater with seats rising in tiers from a central acting area

anecdote a brief personal story used to illustrate a point

archaic language language no longer in use

arena stage (or Theater in the Round) a theater with seats surrounding the stage

argumentative essay an essay that tries to prove a point by supporting it with evidence

aside a brief comment by an actor, heard by the audience, but not the other characters on stage

antagonist a character who seems to be the major force in opposition to the protagonist or main character

assonance the repetition of internal vowel sounds in words close together (time line, free and easy)

atmosphere the dominant mood or tone of setting

autobiography an account of the author's own life

ballad a narrative poem, usually sung or recited

blank verse unrhymed iambic pentameter

box set a stage set composed of "flats" or connected walls enclosing three sides of the stage, with an invisible "fourth wall" open to the audience

character a person in fiction, drama, or poetry

characterization the development of characters in fiction, drama, or poetry

catastrophe the reversal of the tragic hero's good fortune in Greek Tragedy

catharsis an emotional purging or cleansing experienced by an ancient Greek audience at the end of a tragedy

chorus a group of actors in Greek drama who comment on the action of the play. The role of the chorus came directly from drama as religious ritual and dates from a time when there were no individual actors. What the chorus says about the action reflects the traditional values of ancient Greek culture. Chorus members chanted their lines together and moved as a unit from side to side on the stage.

climax the turning point of plot in fiction or drama

closed form poetry that follows traditional patterns of rhyme, meter, and line groupings

comedy The traditional plot of comedy is the reverse of tragedy. The protagonist, usually an ordinary person, has a problem. The plot of the play is an extrication from the problem and improvement of circumstances. The reversal of fortune is from bad to good; the falling action becomes a rising action with a happy ending.

complication the building of the conflict in plot as part of the rising action

concrete language words which represent specific, particular, graphic qualities and characteristics

conflict the struggle of opposing external or internal forces. External conflict may be physical (characters against nature) or social (characters against each other or against society). Internal conflict is a struggle of opposing forces within a character.

connotation the personal definition or association triggered by a word

consonance repetition of final consonant sounds in words close together (short and sweet, struts and frets)

convention an accepted or traditional feature of a work (e.g., the Greek Chorus, the Shakespearian aside, blank verse)

couplet a pair of rhyming verse lines

crisis the turning point of plot (closely related to "climax" which seems to complete its action)

critical essay an essay that interprets and/or evaluates

denotation the literal, dictionary definition of a word

denouement the resolution of the plot in fiction or drama (an "untying" of the complications at the end of the story line)

dialogue conversation of characters in fiction or drama

didactic teaching a lesson or having a "moral"

documentation accounting for and giving credit to the origin of a source

dramatic monologue In a dramatic monologue, the poet, like an actor in a play, speaks through the voice and personality of another person.

dramatis personae the list of characters in a play

Elizabethan the era beginning with the reign of Elizabeth I, Queen of England from 1558 to 1603 and ending with the Puritan's closing of the theaters in 1642

ellipsis (. . .) indication of an omission of words in a quote

epic a long narrative poem, usually depicting the values of a culture through the adventures of a hero

explication a line by line explanation of a poem or other literary work

exposition the introduction of essential characters, setting, circumstances of a story or play

expository essay an essay which shares, explains, suggests, or explores information, emotion, and ideas

expressionism a movement in drama which emphasizes subjectivity of perception

falling action the action which follows the crisis and climax (*see also* catastrophe, denouement, resolution, catharsis)

figurative language language which expresses more than a literal meaning (e.g., metaphor, simile)

flat character a character not fully developed who seems to represent a "type" more than a real personality (*see also* stock character)

foot a combination of syllables which represent one measure of meter in a verse line

"fourth wall" the invisible wall open to the audience in a box set (*see also* box set)

free verse Poetry without standardized rhyme, meter, or structure. It is not formless, however, but relies on its own words and content to determine its best form.

genre a form or type of literature (e.g., fiction, poetry, drama, the essay)

groundlings members of an Eliza-bethan audience who paid a very low entrance fee and stood in the open area below and around the stage. Because they stood on the ground unprotected from the weather—they were called "groundlings," a term meant to disparage their social standing as much as to describe their location in the theater.

hubris excessive pride which usually leads to the downfall of the tragic hero in Greek drama

hyperbole an exaggeration in figurative language

iambic an unstressed/stressed combination of syllables in a metrical foot

image / imagery descriptive language which helps us see, hear, smell, taste, or feel

inductive/deductive reasoning
    inductive reasoning moves from observation of spe cific circumstances and makes a general conclusion; **deductive** reasoning takes a general truth and applies it to specific circumstances

interpretation an analysis of a work to determine its meaning

irony The two most popular forms of irony are verbal irony and situational irony. **Verbal irony** results from the contrast between what is said by a character and what is meant. **Irony of situation** results from the contrast between what is expected and what actually happens.

limerick a five-line poem. The first, second, and fifth lines rhyme (aaa) and so do the third and fourth (bb). The first, third, and fifth have the same verbal rhythm (meter) and length, and so do the second and fourth.

lyric poetry characterized by the expression of the poet's innermost feelings, thoughts, and imagination

magical realism fiction that blends realistic or ordinary details and events with those that are magical or fantastic. Gabriel Garcia Marquez's "A Very Old Man with Enormous Wings" (p. 988) exemplifies this form.

melodrama plays with elaborate but oversimplified plots, flat characters, excessive sentiment, and happy endings

metafiction fiction that explores the process of its own language and creation as it tells the story

metaphor an implied comparison of two apparently dissimilar things

meter describes rhythm in a poem. It refers to the pattern of stressed and unstressed syllables in a line of verse. The group of syllables making up one metrical unit is called a **foot.** The metrical feet most commonly used are **iambic** (unstressed-stressed), **trochaic** (stressed-unstressed), **anapestic** (two unstressed-one stressed), and **dactylic** (one stressed-two unstressed).
    The number of feet in each line is described as **monometer** (one foot), **dimeter** (two feet), **trimeter** (three feet), **tetrameter** (four feet), **pentameter** (five feet), **hexameter** (six feet), **heptameter** (seven feet), and **octameter** (eight feet). The most common form of meter in poetry written in English is **iambic** (unstressed-stressed) **pentameter** (five feet)

microcosm a smaller version or "little world"

monologue a speech by a single character

mood the atmosphere or tone of a work

narrative essay An essay that tells a story. Most essays of this type spring from an event or experience in the writer's life.

narrative poem a poem that tells a story

narrator the voice of the speaker in a story

Neoclassicism a movement which dominated during the eighteenth century and was notable for its adherence to the "forms" of classical drama

ode a formal lyric poem recited for ceremonial occasions

onomatopoeia a word which sounds like what it represents (e.g., the "buzzing" of a bee)

open form poetry that does not follow traditional patterns of rhyme, meter, and line groupings (*see also* free verse)

orchestra the playing area in an ancient Greek theater

parados the ode chanted by the chorus as they enter in Greek tragedy

paraphrase to record someone else's words in the writer's own words

pentameter five feet of verse line

personal essay an essay which emphasizes a personal, subjective view

personification giving human qualities to things nonhuman

Petrarchan Sonnet The oldest form of the sonnet is the Italian or Petrarchan Sonnet (named for its greatest practitioner—Petrarch). Its rhyme scheme is usually an octave (eight lines) and a sestet (six lines). The octave usually follows a pattern of **abbaabba.** The concluding sestet may be **cdecde** or **cdcdcd** or **cdedce.**

plot the structure of the story; the pattern of twists and turns the story takes

point of view the perspective from which the narrator speaks to us. Generally, the pronoun which dominates the narration will signal which point of view is represented. The terms most commonly used to identify point of view are **first person, third person, omniscient, objective,** and **shifting.**

primary/secondary sources A primary source is the original text or materials. A secondary source is commentary about that original material.

props objects or items used by the actors on the stage

proscenium arch a frame around the stage which separates the actors and the set from the audience

protagonist the main character in a story or drama

quatrain a four-line stanza

Realism a movement in literature to represent life as it really is. It is often characterized by accurate depiction of ordinary people in their natural surroundings.

recognition the point near the end of a classic tragedy when the protagonist recognizes the causes and consequences of his reversal

resolution the final phase of the falling action in plot when things are returned to normal

reversal the change from good to bad fortune in classic tragedy; from bad to good fortune in classic comedy

rhyme when final vowel and consonant sounds in the last syllable of one word match those of another, usually at the end of lines

rhythm the pattern of sound in a poem. The most structured form of rhythm is meter, the pattern of stressed and unstressed syllables.

rising action that point in the plot when conflict and our emotional involvement intensifies

Romanticism a movement that values literature as an expression of unique feelings, attitudes, and experiences

round character a fully developed character with the complexities of real person

satire ridiculing stupidity, vice, folly through exaggeration and humor

scansion analysis of the kind and number of metrical feet in a poem

script the printed text of a drama

sentimentality evoking a predictable emotional response with a clichéd prompt

set structures on the stage which represent the setting of the play

setting the environment in which the work takes place

Shakespearian Sonnet The most popular form in English is the English or Shakespearian Sonnet. It is a fourteen-line poem of three quatrains (four-line units) and a final couplet (a two-line unit) in the rhyme scheme **abab cdcd efef gg.** It presents the content of the poem in predictable ways. The first two quatrains will often present a problem. The third quatrain is often pivotal and will begin a reversal. The final couplet most often suggests a solution.

simile an announced comparison introduced with the words "like" or "as"

soliloquy Delivered by a character alone on the stage, soliloquies are a "thinking out loud" shared with the audience. They are often statements of a philosophical, reflective nature, and they are highlights of Shakespeare's plays.

sonnet a fourteen-line lyric poem usually in iambic pentameter

speaker the narrator of a story or poem

stage directions descriptions (in the text of the play) of the set, the props, voice and movements of the actors, and the lighting

stanza a unit of lines in a poem which usually share a metrical or thematic pattern

stock character a character not fully developed who seems to represent a "type" more than a real personality (*see also* flat character)

style the choice of words and sentence structure which makes each author's writing different

summary the material condensed to its main points

surrealistic drama seeks its truth in the irrationality of the unconscious mind

symbol an object or action that represents more than itself

symbolist drama seeks its truth in symbols, myths, and dreams

syntax the ordering of words in a sentence

theme the overall meaning we derive from the poem, story, play, or essay

thesis the point of the essay

thrust stage a stage that extends into the audience

tone the attitude expressed by the writer toward the subject

tragedy Classic tragedy follows the plight of a noble person who is flawed by a defect and whose actions cause him to break some moral law and suffer downfall and destruction.

tragic flaw the tragic hero's flaw (often excessive pride or hubris) which leads directly to a reversal of his good fortune (**catastrophe**)

tragic hero as defined by Aristotle, a man of noble stature who is admired by society but flawed

tragicomedy a play that combines the elements of tragedy and comedy

unities The unities of time, place, and action as principles of dramatic composition have been hotly debated since Aristotle's *Poetics*. In brief, **unity of time** suggests the action of the play occur in a 24 hour period; **unity of place** suggests the action occur in one place or location; and **unity of action** that all parts of the play should be related in a clear causal pattern.

unreliable narrator a narrator who tells the story from a biased, erroneous perspective

verse a line or the form of poetry

villanelle a nineteen-line poem having only two rhymes and repeating two of the lines in a set pattern. Dylan Thomas' "Do Not Go Gentle into That Good Night" (p. 1238) exemplifies this form.

voice the personality or style of the writer or narrator that seems to come to life in the words

LITERARY AND PHOTO CREDITS

LITERARY CREDITS

Achebe, Chinua, "Marriage Is a Private Affair" from *Girls at War and Other Stories* by Chinua Achebe. © 1972, 1973 by Chinua Achebe. Used by permission of Doubleday, a division of Random House, Inc. and Harold Ober Associates, Inc.

Alexie, Sherman, "On the Amtrak from Boston to New York City" from *First Indian on the Moon.* © 1993 by Sherman Alexie. By permission of Hanging Loose Press.

Alvarez, Julia, "Dusting" and "Snow" from *Homecoming.* © 1984, 1996 by Julia Alvarez. Published by Plume, an imprint of Dutton Signet, a division of Penguin Books USA, Inc.; originally published by Grove Press. Reprinted by permission of Susan Bergholz Literary Services, New York. All rights reserved.

Anderson, Michael, "'A Raisin in the Sun': A Landmark Lesson in Being Black" from *The New York Times,* 3/7/1997. © 1997 by The New York Times Co. Reprinted by permission.

Angelou, Maya, "Phenomenal Woman" from *And Still I Rise.* © 1978 by Maya Angelou. Reprinted by permission of Random House, Inc.

Anzaldúa, Gloria, "To Live in the Borderlands Means You" from *Borderlands/La Frontera: The New Mestiza.* © 1987 by Gloria Anzaldúa. Reprinted by permission of Aunt Lute Books.

Atwood, Margaret, "Siren Song" from *Selected Poems 1966–1984* by Margaret Atwood. © Margaret Atwood 1990. Reprinted by permission of the Oxford University Press Canada. "You Fit Into Me" from *Power Politics.* © 1971 by Margaret Atwood. Reprinted by permission of House of Anansi Press, a division of Stoddart Publishing, 34 Lesmill Rd., North York, Ontario.

Auden, W. H., "Musée des Beaux Arts" and "The Unknown Citizen" from *W. H. Auden: Collected Poems,* Edward Mendelson, ed. © 1940 and renewed 1968 by W. H. Auden. Reprinted by permission of Random House, Inc.

Baldwin, James, "Sonny's Blues," originally published in *Partisan Review.* Collected in *Going To Meet the Man,* © 1965 by James Baldwin. Copyright renewed. Published by Vintage Books. Reprinted by arrangement with the James Baldwin Estate. "Sweet Lorraine" from the Introduction to *To be Young, Gifted, and Black: Lorraine Hansberry in Her Own Words.* Originally published in Esquire (Nov. 1969). Collected in *The Price of the Ticket: Collected Non-Fiction, 1948–1985,* published by St. Martin's, 1985. Reprinted by arrangement with the James Baldwin Estate.

Bambara, Toni Cade, "The Lesson" from *Gorilla, My Love.* © 1972 by Toni Cade Bambara. Reprinted by permission of Random House, Inc.

Barry, Dan, "The Corpse on Union Street" from *The New York Times,* September 8, 2005. © 2005 by The New York Times Co. Reprinted with permission.

Bennett, Gwendolyn B., "Heritage" from *Opportunity Magazine,* 1926.

Bennett, Paula, "On 'I Heard a Fly Buzz—When I Died'" from *Emily Dickinson, Woman Poet,* 1990. Reprinted by permission of Pearson Education Limited.

Bettelheim, Bruno, from "Cinderella" from *The Uses of Enchantment.* © 1975, 1976 by Bruno Bettelheim. Reprinted by permission of Alfred A. Knopf, a division of Random House, Inc.

Bishop, Elizabeth, "In the Waiting Room" from *The Complete Poems 1927–1979* by Elizabeth Bishop. © 1979, 1983 by Alice Helen Methfessel. Reprinted by permission of Farrar, Straus & Giroux, Inc.

Bloom, Claire, "Playing Gertrude on Television" from *Playing Gertrude for the BBC TV,* 1980 from BBC TV *Shakespeare's* Hamlet. Reprinted by permission.

Boyle, T. Coraghessan, "Greasy Lake" from *Greasy Lake and Other Stories* by T. Coraghessan Boyle, copyright © 1979, 1981, 1982, 1983, 1984, 1985 by T. Coraghessan Boyle. Used with permission of Viking Penguin, a division of Penguin Putnam Inc.

Brooks, Gwendolyn, "We Real Cool" from *Blacks.* © 1991 by Gwendolyn Brooks. Published by Gwendolyn Brooks through Third World Press, Chicago, 1991. Reprinted by permission of the author.

Camus, Albert, from *The Myth of Sisyphus* by Albert Camus, translated by Justin O'Brien, copyright © 1955, 1983 by Alfred A. Knopf, a division of Random House, Inc. Used by permission of Alfred A. Knopf, a division of Random House, Inc.

Carter, Steven R., "Hansberry's Artistic Misstep" from *Hansberry's Drama: Commitment Amid Complexity.* Urbana, IL: University of Illinois Press, 1991.

Carver, Raymond, "Cathedral" from *Cathedral.* © 1981 by Raymond Carver. Reprinted by permission of Alfred A. Knopf, a division of Random House, Inc.

Chasin, Helen, "The Word *Plum*" from *Coming Close and Other Poems.* © 1986. Reprinted by permission of the publisher, Yale University Press.

Cheever, John, "Reunion" from *The Stories of John Cheever.* © 1978 by John Cheever. Used by permission of Alfred A. Knopf, a division of Random House, Inc.

Chekhov, Anton, "The Lady with the Pet Dog" from *The Portable Chekhov* by Anton Chekhov, edited by Avrahm Yarmolinsky. © 1947, © 1968 by Viking Penguin, Inc. Renewed © 1975 by Avrahm Yarmolinsky. Used by permission of Viking Penguin, a division of Penguin Putnam Inc. "The Proposal" from pages 981–990 of *The Plays of Anton Chekov* by Paul Schmidt. Copyright © 1997 by Paul Schmidt. Reprinted by permission of HarperCollins Publishers, Inc.

Cheney, Anne, "The African Heritage in *A Raisin in the Sun*" from *Lorraine Hansberry* by Cheney, Anne. Macmillan Reference USA. Reprinted by permission of The Gale Group.

Cisneros, Sandra, "Eleven" from *Woman Hollering Creek.* © 1991 by Sandra Cisneros. Published by Vintage Books, a division of Random House, Inc., and originally in hardcover by Random House, Inc. Reprinted by permission of Susan Bergholz Literary Services, New York. All rights reserved.

Cofer, Judith Ortiz, excerpt from "First Love" reprinted with permission from the publisher of *Year of Our Revolution* by Judith Ortiz Cofer. Houston: Arte Publico Press–University of Houston, © 1998.

1357

Valdez, Luis, "Los Vendidos" reprinted with permission from the publisher of *Luis Valdez—Early Works.* Houston: Arte Publico Press–University of Houston, 1971.

Walker, Alice, "Everyday Use" from *In Love & Trouble: Stories of Black Women.* © 1973 by Alice Walker. Reprinted by permission of Harcourt, Inc. "Zora Neale Hurston: A Cautionary Tale and a Partisan View" by Alice Walker from *Zora Neale Hurston: A Literary Biography.* Copyright 1977 by Board of Trustees of the University of Illinois. Used with permission of the University of Illinois Press.

Welty, Eudora, "A Worn Path" from *A Curtain of Green and Other Stories.* © 1941 and renewed 1969 by Eudora Welty. Reprinted by permission of Harcourt, Inc.

Wilbur, Richard, from "Sumptious Destitution" in *Emily Dickinson: Three Views* by Richard Wilbur, Louise Bogan and Archibald MacLeish, 1960 by Amherst College Press. Reprinted by permission of the author.

Wilkerson, Margaret, excerpt from the Introduction to *Les Blancs: The Collected Last Plays of Lorraine Hansberry,* Robert Nemiroff, ed. New York, Vintage Books Edition, 1994. Introduction © 1994 by Margaret B. Wilkerson. Reprinted by permission of Margaret Wilkerson.

Williams, Tennessee, from *The Glass Menagerie.* © 1945 The University of The South. Reprinted by permission of Georges Borchardt, Inc. or the Tennessee Williams Estate.

Williams, William Carlos, "At the Ball Game" from *Collected Poems: 1909-1939, Volume I.* © 1938 by New Directions Publishing Corp. Reprinted by permission of New Directions Publishing Corp.

Wolff, Cynthia Griffin, from *Emily Dickinson,* copyright © 1986 by Cynthia Griffin Wolff. Used by permission of Alfred A. Knopf, a division of Random House, Inc.

Woolf, Virginia, "If Shakespeare Had a Sister" from *A Room of One's Own.* © 1929 by Harcourt, Inc. and renewed 1957 by Leonard Woolf. Reprinted by permission of Harcourt, Inc.

Yeats, W. B., "The Lake Isle of Innisfree" reprinted with the permission of Simon & Schuster from *The Collected Works of W. B. Yeats, Volume I: The Poems,* revised and edited by Richard J. Finneran. New York: Macmillan, 1989.

Yellen, Samuel, "Nighthawks" First published in *Commentary,* 1951. Reprinted by permission of Marilyn Gaylin for the Estate of Samuel Yellen.

Zimmer, Paul, "Zimmer in Grade School" from *Crossing to Sunlight.* © 1976 by Paul Zimmer. Reprinted by permission of the author.

PHOTO CREDITS

p. 190: Commerce Graphics Ltd. p. 202: Gislain and Marie David de Lossy/Getty Images p. 206: AP Wide World Photos p. 211: Bettmann/CORBIS p. 233: Bettmann/CORBIS p. 236: Nancy Crampton p. 243: Courtesy of Linda Ching Sledge p. 250: Nancy Crampton p. 259: AP Wide World Photos p. 265: Courtesy of Elizabeth Gaffney p. 267: Dorothy Alexander p. 268: Brown Brothers p. 270: Nancy Crampton p. 272: Fay Godwin p. 273: Gavin Geoffrey Dillard p. 276: Dorothy Alexander p. 278: Courtesy Glide Memorial Church p. 280: Nancy Crampton p. 281: Imogen Cunningham p. 282: The photograph of Cathy Song is from SCHOOL FIGURES, by Cathy Song, © 1994. Reprinted by permission of the University of Pittsburgh Press. p. 284: Bettmann/CORBIS p. 335: Eli Reed/Magnum p. 340: Culver Pictures, Inc. p. 344: Bettmann/CORBIS p. 435: Christine Basler/Getty Images p. 440: Vintage Books p. 446: Thomas Bulfinch by Joseph Blackburn, about 1757. 76.2 x 66 cm. Gift of Mr. And Mrs. J. Templeman Coolidge; 45.516. © 2003 Museum of Fine Arts, Boston. p. 448: Nancy Crampton p. 459: Courtesy of The Estate of Layle Silbert. p. 468: Jill Krementz, Inc. p. 490: Bettmann/CORBIS p. 500: Print Collection, Miriam and Ira D. Wallach Division of Arts, Prints and Photographs, The New York Public Library, Astor, Lenox, and Tilden Foundations p. 501: Michael Nicholson/CORBIS p. 504: Sophie Bassouls/CORBIS Sygma p. 508: Hulton Archive/Getty Images p. 509: Bettmann/CORBIS p. 510: Bettmann/CORBIS p. 512: Bettmann/CORBIS p. 514: Library of Congress p. 517: Sortino p. 521: AP/Wide World Photos p. 529: Ralph Orlowski/Getty Images p. 537: National Portrait Gallery, London p. 663: Photofest (2) p. 664: Donald Cooper/Photostage (2) p. 685: see credits for p. 688, 686, 694, 700, 698, 692, 696, 690 p. 686: Pieter Brueghel, the Elder (Dutch, 1525-1569). "Landscape with the Fall of Icraus." Musees Royaux d'Art Ancien, Musees Royaux des Beaux-Arts, Brussels, Belgium. Photo: Scala/Art Resource, NY. p. 688: Jacopo Robusti Tintoretto (Italian, 1518-1594). "Crucifixion." Scuola Grande di San Rocco, Venice, Italy. Photo: Erich Lessing/Art Resource, NY. p. 690: Edward Hopper (American, 1882-1967). "Nighthawks," 1942. Oil on canvas, 84.1 x 152.4 cm. Friends of American Art Collection, 1942.51, © The Art Institute of Chicago. Photo: Robert Hashimoto. p. 692: Vincent van Gogh (Dutch, 1853-1890). "The Starry Night." 1889. Oil on canvas, 73.7 x 92.1 cm. Acquired through the Lillie P. Bliss Request (472.1941). The Museum of Modern Art, New York, NY, U.S.A. Digital Image © The Museum of Modern Art/Licensed by SCALA / Art Resource, NY. p. 694: Henri Matisse(French, 1869-1954) © Copyright. "Dance (first version)." March 1909. Oil on canvas, 8' 6 1/2" x 129' 1/2". Gift of Nelson A. Rockefeller in honor of Alfred H. Barr, Jr. (201.1963). © Succession H. Matisse, Paris / ARS, NY. The Museum of Modern Art, New York, NY, U.S.A. Digital Image © The Museum of Modern Art/Licensed by SCALA / Art Resource, NY. p. 696: Jean-Francois Millet (French, 1814-1875). "The Gleaners." 1857. Oil on canvas, 83.6 x 111 cm. Musee d'Orsay, Paris, France. Inv.: RF 592. Photo: Jean Schormans/Reunion des Musees Nationaux/Art Resource, NY. p. 698: Edwin Romanzo Elmer (American, 1850-1923). "Mourning Picture." 1890. Oil on canvas, 70.9 x 91.4 cm. Smith College Museum of Art, Northampton, Massachusetts. Purchased. p. 700: Jan Vermeer (Dutch, 1632-1675). "The Loveletter," c. 1670. Oil on canvas, 44 x 38.5 cm. © Rijksmuseum Amsterdam p. 709: Digital Vision/Superstock p. 713: Bettmann/CORBIS p. 725: Bettmann/CORBIS p. 737: George Hallett/South Picture Portal p. 745: Bettmann/CORBIS p. 750: Bettmann/CORBIS p. 762: Jerry Bauer p. 773: Linda Haas/Firebrand Books p. 776: Hulton Archive/Getty Images p. 777: Hulton Archive/Getty Images p. 778: Culver Pictures, Inc. p. 780: Nancy Crampton p. 783: Culver Pictures, Inc. p. 784: Hulton Archive/Getty Images p. 786: Nancy Crampton p. 788: © 1994 Jean Weisinger p. 789: Photo by Mark Thompson © 2006 p. 790: AP/Wide World Photos p. 792: Keystone/Getty Images p. 794: Bettmann/CORBIS p. 796: Dorothy Alexander p. 799: Nancy Crampton p. 800: Brown Brothers p. 807: Jerry Bauer p. 824: AP/Wide World Photos p. 852: AP/Wide World Photo p. 856: Hulton-Deutsch Collection/CORBIS p. 939: Seth Joel/Getty Images p. 943: Nancy Crampton p. 951: J.A. Scholtin/Missouri Historical Society, St. Louis p. 955: Leo Bern Keating/Black Star p. 962: Sigrid Estrada p. 964: CORBIS p. 972: AP/Wide World Photo p. 977: Jaishri Abichandani p. 982: AP/Wide World Photos p. 989: Bettmann/CORBIS p. 990: Culver Pictures, Inc. p. 991: By permission of the

INDEX OF AUTHORS, TITLES, AND FIRST LINES OF POEMS

INDEX OF TERMS

citing sources. *See also* documentation
  in text of essay, 1347
clarity, 47, 48
climax, 62, 63, 92, 1354
close reading, 55
closing
  of argument, 164
  of critical essay, 169
clustering, 41–42, 186
collaboration, 7–8, 42, 434, 682,
  1150, 1330
collection, 1349
comedy, 92–93, 1354
commas, inside quotation marks, 49
comparative essay, 155
  about film, 1343
comparing, 29
  with Venn diagram, 29–30
computer spell checkers, 49–50
conflict, 61, 66, 91, 1354
  in analytical essay, 154
connotation, 72, 1354
consonance, 80, 1354
context-based criticism, 1334–1337
contextual essay, 156
contrasting, with Venn diagram, 29–30
crisis, 63, 92, 1354
critical approaches to literature,
  1331–1352
  reader-based criticism,
    1331–1332
  text-based criticism, 1332–1334
critical essay, 148–149, 165–172,
  1354
  about film, 1342
  revising, 169–172
  supporting argument in,
    166–167
critical thinking, personal response
  and, 4
culture, 12–13

deconstruction, 1333–1334
denotation, 72, 1354
denouement (untying), 62, 1354
describing, 25
details, 25–26
diction, 64, 93
didactic, 94, 1354
dimeter, 81
directed freewriting, 39, 186
discussion groups, on Internet, 180
documentation, 48–49, 183, 1354
  MLA style, 1345–1353
double-entry logs, 7
drafting, 36–37, 42–43
drama, 89–94
  periods of, 95–103
  quoting, 49
dramatic monologue, 84, 1354

economic criticism. *See* Political-
  economic criticism
editing, 49
electronic sources, 1350–1352
ellipsis, 184, 1354
essays
  analytical, 153–155
  argumentation in, 156–165
  comparative, 155, 1343
  contextual, 156

critical, 148–149, 1342
  reading and analyzing, 137–138
  research, 174–175, 1343–1344
  response, 21–22
  thematic, 155–156
  types of, 138–139
ethical evaluation, 156
evaluation, 150
  philosophical or ethical, 156
evidence, in arguments, 163
experience, 435
explication, 84, 1354
  in analytical essay, 155
exploration, 55
exposition, 62, 92, 1354
expository essays, 138, 1354
expressionism, 101, 1354
external conflict, 61, 91

falling action, 62, 63, 92, 1354
feasibility, in critical essay, 166
feminist criticism, 1334–1335
fiction, 58
fiction prose, quoting, 49
figurative language, 75–76, 1354
film, 1353
  as literature, 1339
  writing about, 1338–1344
final draft, 36–37
first person, 59
  in essay, 37
flat (stock) characters, 64, 93, 1354
flats, 101
foreword, 1349
form, in analytical essay, 153
formal essays, 139
formalism, 1332–1333
formatting, 48–49
  MLA style, 1345–1353
free (open form) verse, 83, 1354
freewriting, 39, 186

gay criticism, 1334–1335
gender (feminist, lesbian, gay) criticism, 1334–1335
Greek drama, 95

Harlem Renaissance, 1102
heptameter, 81
hero, tragic, 92
hexameter, 81
historical criticism, 1334

iambic pentameter, 81, 1355
ideas, collaboration for, 42
imagery, 74, 1355
imagination, 19
inductive reasoning, 161, 1355
informal essays, 139
informing, in essay, 140–141
innocence, 435
internal conflict, 61, 91
Internet
  citing sources from, 1350–1352
  evaluating sources from, 181
  research sources on, 180–181
interpretation, 83–84, 150, 1355
  in context, 855
interpretive communities, 7–8, 175
interview, 1352
introduction, 1349
irony, 65, 73, 140, 1355

journals, 5–7
  citing articles in, 1350
  double-entry, 7
  first response and, 38
  language, 66
  in analytical essay, 153
  in drama, 93
  in essays, 139–141
  of Greek drama, 96
  of modern drama, 101–102
  in poetry, 72–73
  of Shakespeare, 98–99
  style and, 64–65

lecture, 1352
lesbian criticism, 1334–1335
library, as research source, 177
lighting, theatrical, 101
limerick, 80–81, 1355
limited point of view, third-person,
  59–60
listing, 40
listservs, 180
literary criticism, Aristotle's *Poetics*
  as, 92
literary research, popular areas of,
  176–177
literature
  critical approaches to,
    1331–1337
  film as, 1339
location, 60, 91
logs, 5–7
longer works, citing titles of, 48
lyric poetry, 84, 1355

mapping, 41–42
meaning, of poem, 83–84
metaphor, personification and, 77
meter, 81, 1355
method acting, 101
MLA documentation style,
  1345–1353
modern drama, 49, 100–102
monometer, 81
Montaigne, Michel de, 137
moral, 65, 94

narration, 58–59, 66
  in analytical essay, 153–154
narrative essays, 138, 1355
narrative poetry, 85, 1355
newsgroups, 180–181
newspaper, citing articles in, 1350
nonfiction prose, quoting, 49
note-taking, 182

octameter, 81
omniscient point of view, third-
  person, 60
opening, of argument, 164
organization, 46
Othello (Shakespeare), 98
outline
  after-draft, 47
  of critical essay, 170

painting, 685
  poetry and, 683
parados (choral ode), 95, 1355
paraphrasing, 183, 185, 1355
participation, 19
pentameter, 81, 1355

people, as research sources, 177
periodicals, 1349
periods, inside quotation marks, 49
person
    first, 59
    first or third, 37
personification, 77, 1355
philosophical evaluation, 156
plagiarism, 184, 185
plays. *See also* Drama
    reading of, 90
plot, 62–63, 66, 91–92, 1355
    in analytical essay, 154
Poetics, The (Aristotle), 92
poetry, 86
    painting and, 683
    reading and analyzing, 71–72
    types of, 84–85
point of view, 59, 90, 153, 1355
    shifting, 60
    third-person, 59–60
political-economic criticism,
    1335–1336
portfolio option, 434, 682, 938,
    1150, 1330
preaching, in essays, 140–141
prereading, 55
primary source, 174, 1355
proofreading, 49
    of argumentative essay, 165
    of critical essay, 170
proposition, 160
    in critical essay, 166
proscenium arch, 100, 1355
prose, quoting, 49
protagonist, 64, 93, 1355
psychoanalytic criticism, 1336

quatrains, 80, 1355
questioning, 39–40
    for research essay, 186
quotation marks, periods and
    commas in, 49
quoting, 49, 184, 185

radio program, 1352
reader-based criticism,
    1331–1332
readers, ourselves as, 8
reading
    of essays, 137–138
    first response to, 4–5
    of plays, 90
    types of, 8–9
reading log, 5–7
realism, 100, 1355
reference works, 178–180, 1349
reliability, 59
research, 174–199

research essay, 174–175
    about film, 1343–1344
    physical layout of, 1346
research option, 433, 684, 936,
    1150, 1330
resolution, 62, 63, 92, 1355
response essay, 21–22
    critical essay and, 165–166
    about film, 1341
    voice and, 23
revealing, in essays, 140–141
review, 1350
    film, 1341
revision, 37, 46–49
    of argument, 164–165
rhyme, 80–81, 1355
rhythm, 80–81, 1355
rising action, 62, 63, 92, 1355
round characters, 64, 1355

search engines, 180
secondary sources, 174–175, 1355
semantic mapping (clustering),
    41–42, 186, 701, 703
set and setting, 90–91
setting, 60, 66, 1356
    in analytical essay, 154
Shakespearean drama, 96–100
shifting point of view, 60
shorter works, quoting titles of, 48
simile, 76, 1356
soliloquies, 97, 1356
sonnets, 81–82, 1356
sound, 79–81
sound recording, 1352
sources
    citing in text of essay, 1347
    documenting, 183
    integrating into writing,
        182–183
spell checkers, 49–50
staging
    of Greek drama, 95
    of Shakespearean drama, 97
Stanislavski, Constantin, 101
stock characters, 64
style, 66–67
    in drama, 93
    in essays, 140
    language and, 64–65
    in poetry, 72–73
subject, of essay, 160
substantiation, 161–162
summarizing, 184, 185, 1356
support, 46, 48
surrealism, 101
symbol, 64, 78, 1356
    in drama, 94, 1356

symbolism, 101

tetrameter, 81
text-based criticism,
    1332–1334
theater
    in modern drama, 100
    origins of concept, 95
thematic essay, 155–156
theme, 65, 67, 83, 1356
    in analytical essay, 154–155
    in drama, 94
    of essays, 140
thesis statement, 159–160, 1356
    in critical essay, 166
    support for, 160–164
third-person point of view, 59–60
    in essay, 37
    limited, 59–60
    omniscient, 60
titles, documenting, 48
tone, 72–73, 139, 1356
topics, 38–39
tragedy, 92, 1356
tragic hero, 92, 1356
tragicomedy, 101, 1356
trimeter, 81
truth, fiction and, 58
TV program, 1352

unity, 46, 1356

Venn diagram, 29–30
verse
    blank, 82–83
    free (open form), 83
    sonnets, 81–82
verse drama, quoting, 49
video recording, 1352
voice, 47, 60, 72, 152
    in essays, 139–140
    response to literature and, 23
    writing and, 22–23

warrants, in arguments, 163–164
Web browsers, 180
word choice, in essays, 140
Works Cited, 49, 1346
    documentation for,
        1348–1353
    sample, 1352–1353
writing
    to compare, 29
    to describe, 25
    about film, 1338–1344
    integrating sources into,
        182–183
    to learn about literature, 4
    voice and, 22–23